Envoy to the Promised Land

Envoy to the Promised Land

The Diaries and Papers of
James G. McDonald
1948–1951

EDITED BY

Norman J. W. Goda,
Richard Breitman,
Barbara McDonald Stewart,
and Severin Hochberg

INDIANA UNIVERSITY PRESS

PUBLISHED IN ASSOCIATION WITH THE
UNITED STATES HOLOCAUST MEMORIAL MUSEUM
WASHINGTON, DC

with major support from

The Gilbert and Eleanor Kraus Fund
for the Study of the Fate and Rescue
of Children in the Holocaust

The assertions, arguments, and conclusions contained herein are those
of the author and the volume editors. They do not necessarily reflect
the opinions of the United States Holocaust Memorial Museum. This
work is published with the support of the Jack, Joseph and Morton
Mandel Center for Advanced Holocaust Studies, United States
Holocaust Memorial Museum.

This book is a publication of

Indiana University Press
Office of Scholarly Publishing
Herman B Wells Library 350
1320 East 10th Street
Bloomington, Indiana 47405 USA

iupress.indiana.edu

Manufactured in the United States of America

Cataloging information is available from the Library of Congress.

ISBN 978-0-253-02534-0 (cloth)

1 2 3 4 5   22 21 20 19 18 17

CONTENTS

ACKNOWLEDGMENTS

The editing of McDonald's diaries from his years in Israel has been a very big job; it would have been impossible without the support of the following people. Paul Shapiro, the director of the Jack, Joseph and Morton Mandel Center for Advanced Holocaust Studies at the United States Holocaust Museum, believed in this project from its inception and was encouraging at every step. Benton Arnovitz, the center's director of academic publications, read the finished manuscript with extreme care, saving the editors from embarrassing errors and from inconsistencies with the previous three volumes of McDonald's papers. Stephen Mize, a former archivist and now program manager at the museum, located the McDonald diaries in 2004 and was a critical resource throughout the editing process. Bradley Bauer, the museum's chief archivist, made records available when we needed them. Judith Cohen and Caroline Waddell of the museum's photo archive were patient and helpful as we searched the museum's excellent collection.

Elsewhere, Tom McCutchon of the Rare Book and Manuscript Library at Columbia University was hospitable and helpful. Randy Sowell at the Harry S. Truman Library and Museum was instrumental to our work, as were William Cunliffe and Eric van Slander at the National Archives and Records Administration. The invaluable collection at the University of Florida's Isser and Rae Price Library of Judaica and its director, Rebecca Jefferson, were critical to the preparation of this volume. Professor Tuvia Friling of Ben-Gurion University of the Negev read the entire manuscript with great care. He offered many invaluable comments that improved the manuscript. He also provided key references from David Ben-Gurion's unpublished diary and other records from the Ben-Gurion Archives, as well as from Knesset debates and other Israeli sources. George Chakvetadze of Alliance USA provided excellent maps for the volume. Lyndee Stalter and Gail Naron Chalew provided painstaking and thorough copyediting, and Mikala Guyton was endlessly patient with our last-minute corrections. Finally, those directing Indiana University Press—first Janet Rabinowitch and then after her retirement, Robert Sloan, and after his retirement, Dee Mortensen—believed in this project, were patient with the editors, and brought the final volume to fruition.

We are also profoundly grateful for the financial support of the Jack, Joseph and Morton Mandel Center for Advanced Holocaust Studies at the United States Holocaust Memorial Museum; for the financial support of the Israel Institute in Washington, DC; and for the generosity of Norman and Irma Braman of Miami, Florida. Again, this was a big project. It could not have been completed without their support.

. . . .

Barbara Ann McDonald Stewart—Bobby—the second daughter of James G. McDonald, helped to shepherd McDonald's diaries and papers to the United States Holocaust Memorial Museum more than a decade ago. She was a coeditor on all four published volumes. This fourth volume was special to her and to us, since Bobby, twenty-one years old in July 1948, had accompanied her father on his mission to Israel. With consummate skill she ran the day-to-day business of the US residence, which became a center of diplomatic and social activity in Israel's early years. She also accompanied her father on excursions and to official social gatherings, winning the hearts of Israeli officials and their families.

In helping to edit the final volume, Bobby not only read every line several times for accuracy; based on her sharp memory and her own handwritten diary, she vividly shared her experiences and provided a far better understanding of conditions than would have been available otherwise. She passed away at age 89 on December 31, 2015, as volume four was going through its final edits. After the last editorial meeting she attended on November 12, she enjoyed a glass of wine with her daughter Linda in celebration of the long successful journey in publishing her father's papers. It was a life goal, nearing completion.

Bobby was a fine scholar, a valued colleague, and a good friend. We dedicate this volume to her memory.

Norman J. W. Goda

Richard Breitman

Severin Hochberg

A NOTE ON THE EDITING

James G. McDonald's diaries and papers from his years in Israel are volu-
minous. These diaries and some private correspondence are held by the United
States Holocaust Memorial Museum. The Rare Book and Manuscript Library
at Columbia University also houses a broad range of McDonald's correspondence and papers. In addition, McDonald's official correspondence and related
records are in the published and unpublished records of the United States Department of State, held at the National Archives and Records Administration
in College Park, Maryland, and in the papers of Clark Clifford, David Niles,
and others at the Harry S. Truman Presidential Library and Museum in Independence, Missouri. Related papers are also in the records of the Israeli Foreign Ministry, which has published the series *Documents on the Foreign Policy of
Israel*, and in the published records of the United Nations.

The editors organized this volume around McDonald's extensive dictated
diaries. We removed diary items of a purely personal nature, such as medical
appointments, personal finances, and so forth. We interspersed, in italics, explanatory materials of our own, as well as relevant excerpts from McDonald's
personal letters, from his despatches to the State Department, and from other
documents concerning McDonald. We tried to clarify the complex issues with
which he dealt, from Israel's frontiers to the status of Jerusalem, to refugees, to
truces between Israel and its neighbors, to the Israeli economy, to relations between American Jews and Israeli leaders. In so doing, we sought a work that is
not only useful to scholars but is also logical and readable to anyone interested in
the early days of Israel and the Middle East conflict.

McDonald knew, met, and referred to hundreds of people in the United
States, Europe, and Israel who had an interest in Israel and the shaping of the
Middle East, from diplomats to business leaders to important cultural figures.
We provided brief biographical sketches in the footnotes, with later mentions
referring to the initial biographical sketches. We are unable to cite each biographical source, but material for biographical sketches came from numerous
reference works, including the State Department's *Foreign Service List*, the *Encyclopedia Judaica*, the *Encyclopedia of Zionism and Israel*, *Who's Who in Israel*,
obituaries from the *New York Times* or from the *Bulletin* of the Jewish Tele-

graphic Agency, and online sources such as the website of the Israeli Knesset and the fine online encyclopedia at the Jewish Women's Archive.

McDonald dictated his diary. His typists often misspelled place names and personal names, sometimes providing only initials. We provided names where we could identify individuals. We updated the spellings and transliterations of certain place names that include the Hebrew letter "Bet," changing "Negeb" to "Negev," "Beersheba to Be'er Sheva," and so on. For Hebrew transliterations involving the article "Ha" (the), we adopted the current usage for most words and names—"HaShomer HaTzair," for example—but kept the older form for those proper names in very common usage in the English-speaking world, such as the theater "Habimah" and the newspaper *Haaretz*. We changed the name of the country "Transjordan" to "Jordan" when the name of that country changed from the former to the latter in April 1949. We also changed the names of Israeli personalities when they themselves changed their first or last names to Hebrew, such as Eliahu Epstein, later Eliahu Elath; Moshe Shertok, later Moshe Sharett; and so on. McDonald also referred to "Israel policy," "Israel politicians," whereas one would say "Israeli" today. We made that change to avoid awkward phrasing. We also lowercased official titles such as "president," "prime minister," and "mediator," to conform to current style. In direct quotations of official documents or letters, however, we left capitalizations as we found them.

ABBREVIATIONS

ACPC	American Christian Palestine Committee
AFL	American Federation of Labor
AFSC	American Friends Service Committee
AIOC	Anglo-Iranian Oil Company
AIPAC	American Israel Public Affairs Committee
AJC	American Jewish Committee
ALA	Arab Liberation Army
AMA	American Medical Association
AP	Associated Press
ARAMCO	Arabian American Oil Company
ATA	Arigei Totzeret Artzeinu—Fabrics Manufactured in Our Land
AZEC	American Zionist Emergency Council
BBC	British Broadcasting Corporation
BOAC	British Overseas Airways Corporation
BMEO	British Middle East Office
CARE	Cooperative for Assistance and Relief Everywhere
CCIA	Commission of the Churches on International Affairs, World Council of Churches
CIA	Central Intelligence Agency
CIO	Congress of Industrial Organizations
CRL	Consolidated Refineries, Ltd.
DELASEM	Delegation for the Assistance of Jewish Emigrants (Italy)
DFPI	*Documents on the Foreign Policy of Israel* (published Israeli diplomatic documents)
DP	Displaced Person
ECA	Economic Cooperation Administration
ESM	Economic Survey Mission
FCC	Federal Communications Commission
FBO	Office of Foreign Buildings Operations
FEA	Foreign Economic Administration
FPA	Foreign Policy Association

FRUS	*Foreign Relations of the United States* (published US diplomatic documents series)
GHQ	General Headquarters, Tel Aviv
GTI	Greece, Turkey, and Iran
HMG	His Majesty's Government
ICA	Jewish Colonization Association
ICFTU	International Confederation of Free Trade Unions
ICRC	International Committee of the Red Cross
IDF	Israeli Defense Forces
ILGWU	International Ladies Garment Workers' Union
ILO	International Labor Organization
IMF	International Monetary Fund
INEA	Institute of Near Eastern Affairs
INS	Immigration and Naturalization Service
IPC	Iraq Petroleum Company
IPO	Israel Philharmonic Orchestra
IRO	International Refugee Organization
IT&T	International Telephone and Telegraph
IZL	Irgun Zvai Leumi BeEretz Israel —National Military Organization in the Land of Israel [aka Irgun]
JCR	Jewish Cultural Reconstruction
JDC	American Jewish Joint Distribution Committee
JNF	Jewish National Fund [Keren Kayemet LeIsrael]
JTA	Jewish Telegraphic Agency
JVA	Jordan Valley Authority
Lehi	Lohemei Herut Israel—Fighters for the Freedom of Israel [aka Stern Gang]
LF	Lot File
MAC	Mixed Armistice Commission
Mapai	Mifleget Poalei Eretz Israel—Land of Israel Workers' Party
Mapam	Mifleget HaPoalim HaMeuhedet—United Workers Party
MC	Microcopy
MGM	Metro-Goldwyn-Mayer
MP	Military Police
NAACP	National Association for the Advancement of Colored People
NARA	National Archives and Records Administration, College Park, Maryland
NEA	Office of Near Eastern and African Affairs, Department of State
NEAT	Near East Air Transport
NSC	National Security Council
NYHS	New York Historical Society

OCI	Overseas Consultants, Inc.
OMGUS	Office of Military Government United States
ONA	Overseas News Agency
OSS	Office of Strategic Services
OPA	Office of Price Administration
PCC	Palestine Conciliation Commission
PEC	Palestine Economic Corporation
PICA	Palestine Jewish Colonization Society
PIO	Palestine Information Office
RAF	Royal Air Force
RG	Record Group
SHAEF	Supreme Headquarters Allied Expeditionary Force
SOE	Special Operations Executive
TAPLINE	Trans-Arabian Pipeline
TVA	Tennessee Valley Authority
TWA	Trans World Airlines
UJA	United Jewish Appeal
UK	United Kingdom
UN	United Nations
UNEF	United Nations Emergency Force
UNESCO	United Nations Educational, Scientific and Cultural Organization
UNICEF	United Nations International Children's Emergency Fund
UNRPR	United Nations Relief for Palestinian Refugees
UNRRA	United Nations Relief and Rehabilitation Administration
UNRWA	United Nations Relief and Works Agency
UNSCOP	United Nations Special Committee on Palestine
UNTSO	United Nations Truce Supervision Organization
UP	United Press International
UPA	United Palestine Appeal
USFET	United States Forces European Theater
USIE	United States International Informational and Educational Exchange Program
USIS	United States Information Service
USHMM	United States Holocaust Memorial Museum
USSDCF-PIFA	*Confidential U.S. State Department Central Files. Palestine and Israel Foreign Affairs, 1950–1954* (microfilm publication)
WHO	World Health Organization
WIZO	Women's International Zionist Organization
ZOA	Zionist Organization of America

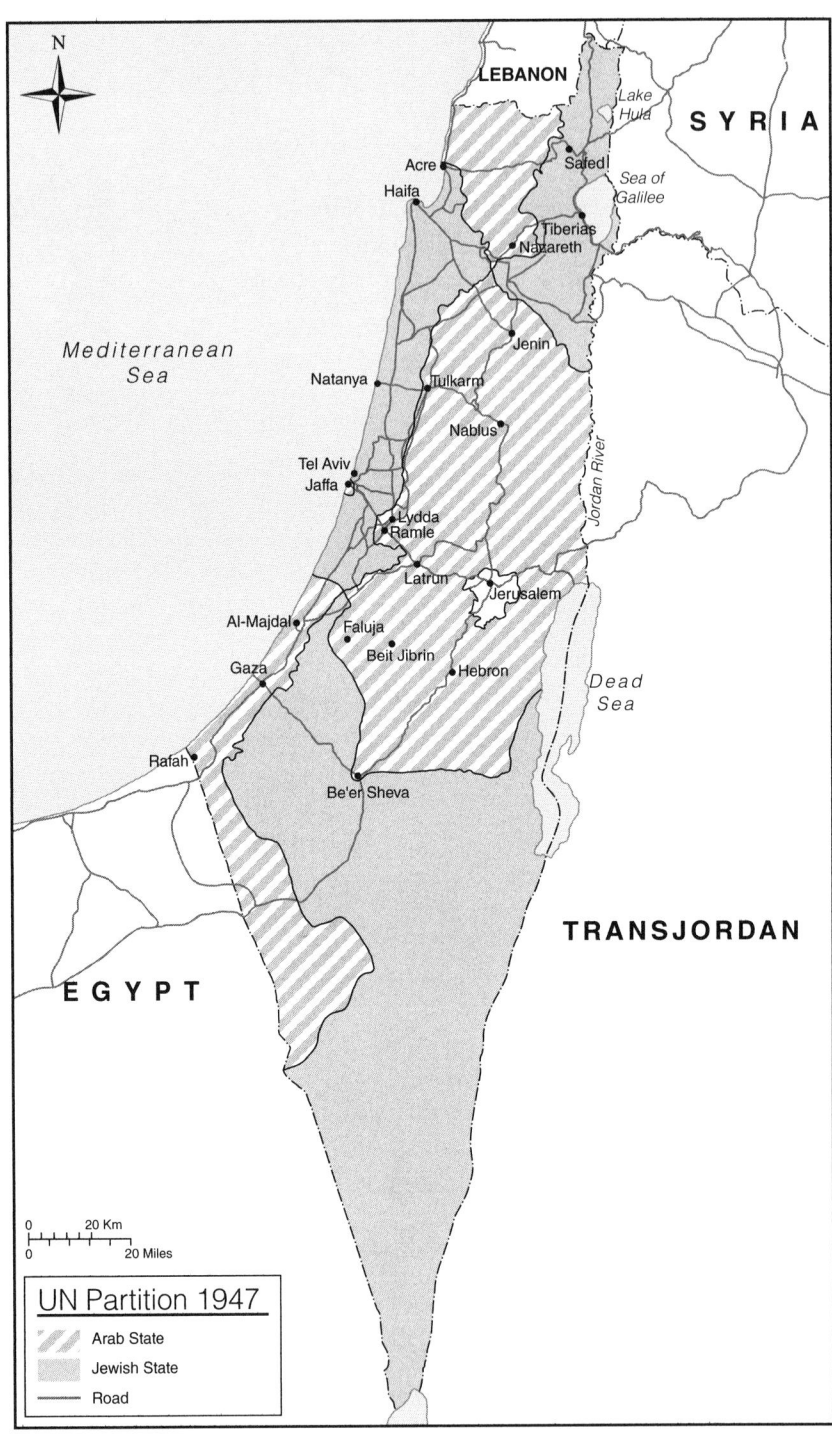

N

LEBANON

SYRIA

Lake Hula

Acre

Safed

Sea of Galilee

Haifa

Tiberias

Nazareth

Mediterranean Sea

Jenin

Natanya

Tulkarm

Nablus

Tel Aviv

Jaffa

Lydda

Ramle

Jordan River

Latrun

Jerusalem

Al-Majdal

Faluja

Beit Jibrin

Hebron

Gaza

Dead Sea

Rafah

Be'er Sheva

TRANSJORDAN

EGYPT

0   20 Km

0   20 Miles

UN Partition 1947

Arab State

Jewish State

Road

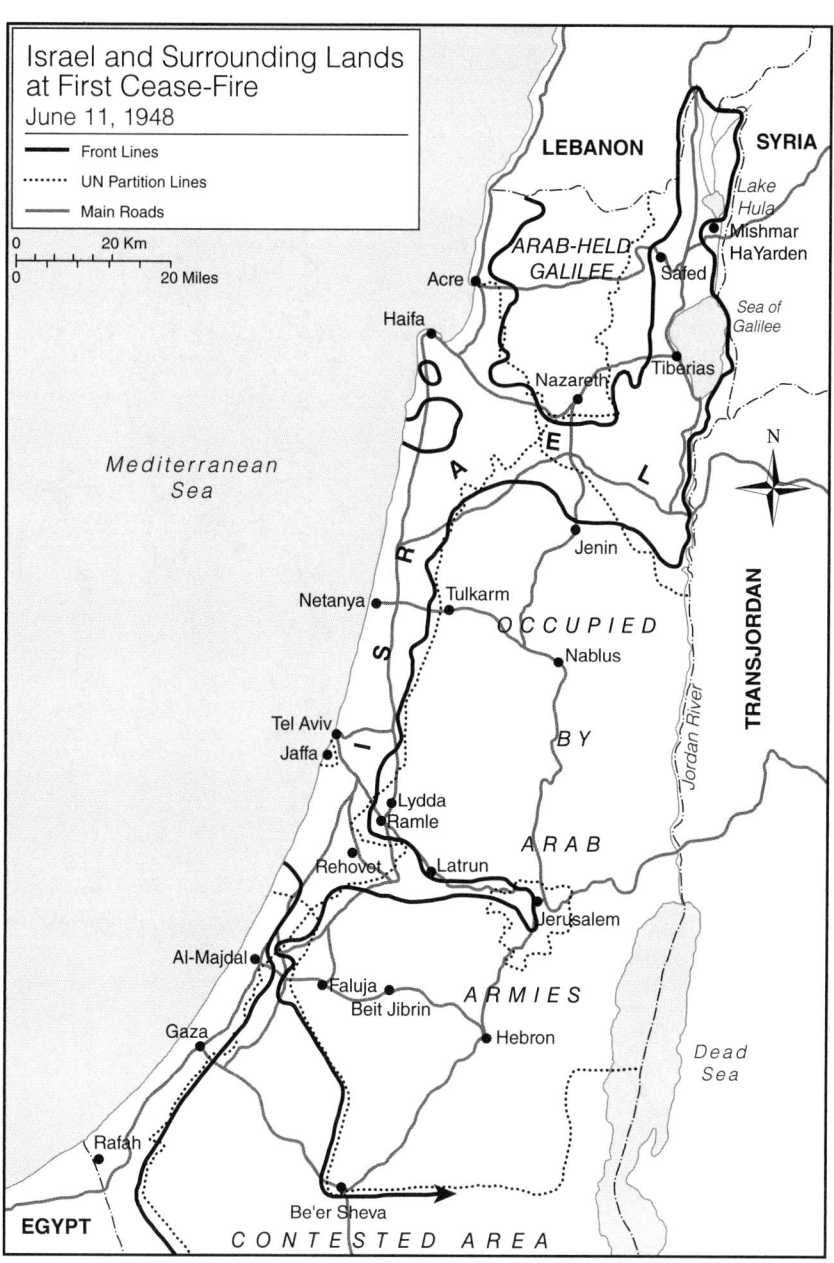

Israel and Surrounding Lands
at First Cease-Fire
June 11, 1948

Front Lines
UN Partition Lines
Main Roads

0   20 Km
0   20 Miles

LEBANON   SYRIA

ARAB-HELD GALILEE

Lake Hula

Mishmar HaYarden

Acre   Safed

Haifa   Sea of Galilee

Nazareth   Tiberias

I S R A E L

Mediterranean Sea

N

Jenin

Netanya   Tulkarm   O C C U P I E D

Nablus

TRANSJORDAN

Jordan River

B Y

Tel Aviv

Jaffa

Lydda
Ramle   A R A B

Rehovot   Latrun

Jerusalem

Al-Majdal   A R M I E S

Faluja   Beit Jibrin

Gaza   Hebron

Dead Sea

Rafah

EGYPT   Be'er Sheva   C O N T E S T E D   A R E A

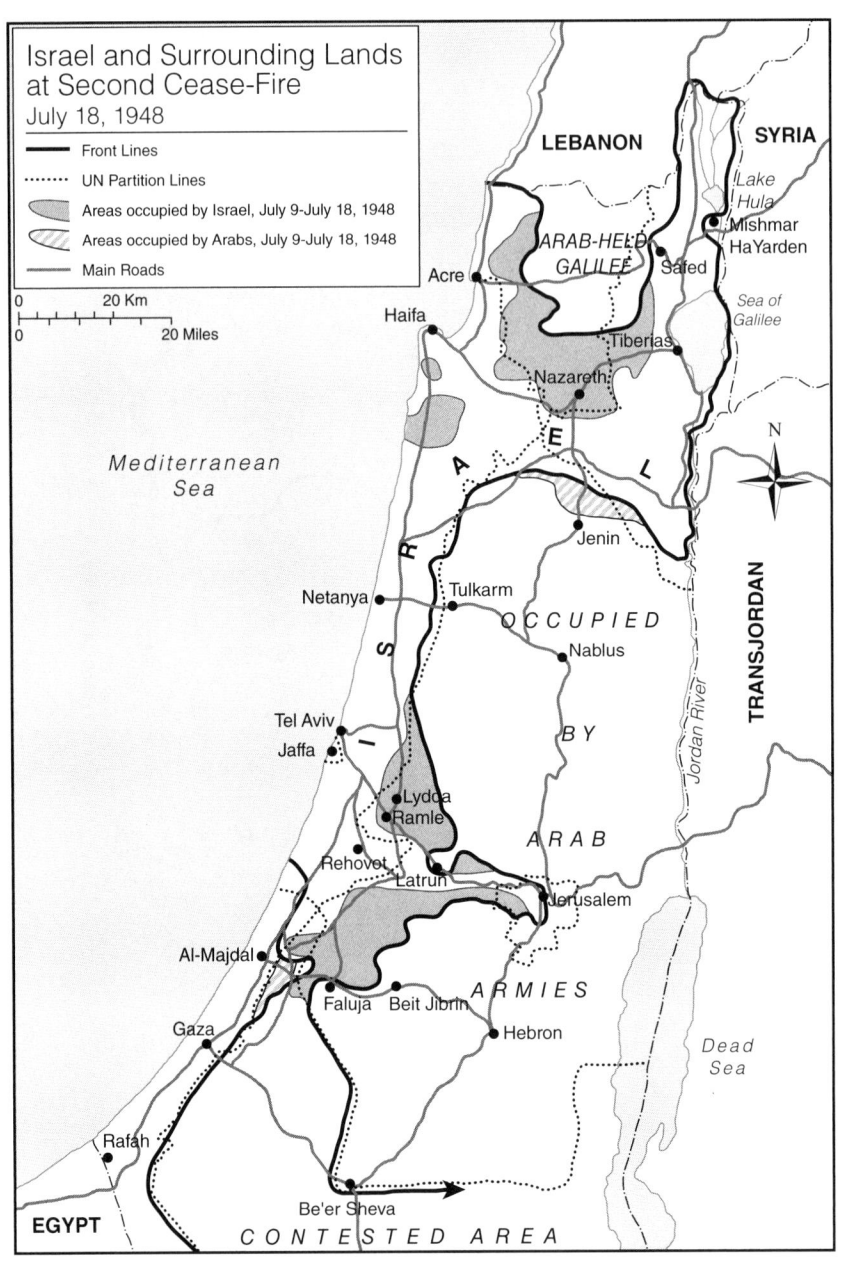

Israel and Surrounding Lands at Second Cease-Fire
July 18, 1948

— Front Lines
······· UN Partition Lines
Areas occupied by Israel, July 9-July 18, 1948
Areas occupied by Arabs, July 9-July 18, 1948
— Main Roads

0   20 Km
0   20 Miles

LEBANON

SYRIA

Lake
Hula

Mishmar
HaYarden

ARAB-HELD
GALILEE

Safed

Acre

Sea of
Galilee

Haifa

Tiberias

Nazareth

Mediterranean
Sea

I S R A E L

Jenin

Netanya

Tulkarm

OCCUPIED

Nablus

Tel Aviv

B Y

Jaffa

Lydda

Ramle

A R A B

Rehovot

Latrun

Jerusalem

Al-Majdal

A R M I E S

Faluja   Beit Jibrin

Gaza

Hebron

Dead
Sea

Rafah

TRANSJORDAN

Jordan River

N

EGYPT

Be'er Sheva

C O N T E S T E D   A R E A

N

LEBANON

Lake Hula

S Y R I A

Acre

Mishmar HaYarden

Safed

Haifa

Sea of Galilee

Nazareth

Mediterranean Sea

Jenin

Tulkarm

Qalqilya

Nablus

Tel Aviv
Jaffa

Lydda

Ramle

Ramallah
Jericho

Jordan River

Amman

Jerusalem

Bethlehem

Hebron

Dead Sea

Gaza

Rafah

ISRAEL

Be'er Sheva

Al-Auja

JORDAN

E G Y P T

0	20 Km
0	20 Miles

Israel and its Neighbors
Armistice Lines 1949

Israel	Demilitarized Zones
Road	//// Territory gained, 1948–49

Eilat

Aqaba

Envoy to the Promised Land

Introduction

Just before modern Israel emerged as a state in May 1948, key US officials hesitated and backtracked. Under Secretary of State Robert Lovett told Moshe Shertok of the Jewish Agency for Palestine that the United States had supported the United Nations decision to partition Palestine in the expectation that there would be a peaceful transition to dual states. Now, on the third anniversary of the end of World War II in Europe, war between Jews and Arabs shook Palestine. A broader regional conflict involving the Arab states loomed if Jewish officials there declared independence. Influenced by intelligence reports that suggested Arab military superiority, Lovett and Secretary of State George C. Marshall, US Army chief of staff during World War II and a military heavyweight without peer, warned that the Arabs might well win. Would it not be better to accept a truce and to delay independence?[1] Apart from geopolitical concerns, Lovett and Marshall might have considered that the domestic political effects—another war accompanied by the mass slaughter of Jews—would roil the United States in a presidential election year.

One group in Israel certainly associated the present with the immediate past. Most troops in the Jewish militia known as the Haganah, renamed the Israel Defense Forces in the wake of Israel's Declaration of Independence, had lost relatives during the Holocaust (a term not yet in common use). They took Arab threats of annihilation seriously, but they hardly saw them as a reason to retreat from statehood.[2] David Ben-Gurion, the chairman of the Jewish Agency Executive, knew that the prospective Jewish state had acquired international legitimacy with unusual difficulty. On November 29, 1947 the UN General Assembly voted to split the British Mandate of Palestine into economically linked Jewish and Arab states. To postpone independence was to put this solution at risk and submit to continued foreign control. On May 14, 1948, as the Mandate officially ended, Israel declared independence and created a provisional government headed by Prime Minister Ben-Gurion. Israel's Arab neighbors, supported by volunteers from as far away as Morocco and Yemen, invaded. Thus, in the midst of a Cold War with the Soviet Union in Europe, the Middle East war that Lovett and Marshall feared had begun.

---

1. Benny Morris, *1948: The First Arab-Israeli War* (New Haven: Yale University Press, 2008), 175.
2. Ibid., 198.

What would the rest of the world do? President Harry S. Truman provided recognition immediately.[3] Hoping to undermine Britain's regional influence, the Soviet Union followed suit three days later. But most states withheld recognition. For the preceding two decades the United Kingdom had openly opposed the reestablishment of a Jewish state. The United Kingdom's strategic position depended on defensive arrangements with Egypt, Transjordan, and Iraq and on its trade and oil interests in Arab states.[4] France and Italy also withheld recognition. Each had colonial interests in North Africa and, like Britain, worried about Muslim reactions. Other countries feared Jewish rule over the Christian Holy Places in Jerusalem and elsewhere in Israel.

If Israel's fate depended primarily on its own military, political, and diplomatic capability, it rested secondarily on its still tenuous and contested tie with the United States. The State Department bureaucracy had bitterly opposed US recognition. Its Office of Near Eastern and African Affairs had warned for years that support for a Jewish state would alienate the entire Arab world, risking US geopolitical and oil interests. Even worse, it meant tension with the United Kingdom during the Berlin crisis—the Soviet blockade of Berlin and the Allied airlift. Secretary of State Marshall said that if speedy recognition of Israel were White House policy, then he would not vote for Truman in the November 1948 election. Historian Robert L. Beisner writes that Truman's long-standing suspicions of the State Department "boiled to a fury . . . when it resisted his decision to recognize Israel."[5]

James G. McDonald's unlikely appointment as US special representative to the new state, and then as the first US ambassador there, emerged from this clash. Then sixty-one years old, McDonald, an Indiana University-trained academic, had been chairman of the Foreign Policy Association, a member of the *New York Times* editorial staff, and an expert who worked to help Jewish refugees through the League of Nations and for both Presidents Franklin D. Roosevelt and Truman. Despite this accomplished career, his hopes of becoming a senior diplomat had eroded. His support for Jewish emigration from Europe to Palestine and the re-creation of a Jewish state had made him deeply unpopular with State Department officials. But the State Department's pro-Arab tilt induced Truman to turn to McDonald.

3. Standard works on Truman's recognition of Israel and State Department opposition to it include Michael J. Cohen, *Truman and Israel* (Berkeley: University of California Press, 1990); Zvi Ganin, *Truman, American Jewry, and Israel* (New York: Holmes & Meier, 1979); Michael T. Benson, *Harry S. Truman and the Founding of Israel* (Westport, CT: Praeger, 1997); Allis Radosh and Ronald Radosh, *A Safe Haven: Harry S. Truman and the Founding of Israel* (New York: Harper Collins, 2009): Frank W. Brecher, *American Diplomacy and the Israeli War of Independence* (Jefferson, NC: McFarland, 2013).

4. British policy is surveyed in Wm. Roger Louis, *The British Empire in the Middle East, 1945–1951: Arab Nationalism, the United States, and Postwar Imperialism* (New York: Oxford University Press, 1984). See also Michael J. Cohen, *Fighting World War Three from the Middle East: Allied Contingency Plans, 1945–1954* (London: Frank Cass, 1997).

5. Robert L. Beisner, *Dean Acheson: A Life in the Cold War* (New York: Oxford University Press, 2006), 112.

Under Secretary Lovett, apparently incredulous, asked the White House if it realized "that McDonald is a known 'fellow traveler'?" This baseless charge, on the eve of a new "red scare" in the United States, carried the antisemitic canard that Jewish causes blended naturally into communism. Lovett later told Secretary of Defense James Forrestal that he "should not tell McDonald anything he is not prepared to have stated to the Jewish Agency."[6] Such attitudes explained why the State Department consistently excluded McDonald from its discussions on the peacemaking process, which it expected would produce a truncated Jewish state that the Arabs might stomach. McDonald, partly aware of his exclusion, developed his own channels of communication with the White House, preventing the State Department from burying his recommendations. Keeping the White House informed, he helped to bring about US diplomatic support of Israel at some critical moments.

Even before arriving in Israel with his daughter Barbara Ann (Bobby), McDonald resumed his practice of dictating a diary, and he did so assiduously during his time there. Eventually, the pages were scattered and for decades were in private hands. They came together at the United States Holocaust Memorial Museum in 2004 and have since undergone editing and publishing. The 1948–1951 diary appears here for the first time.

Using State Department records for the most part, Peter L. Hahn wrote a fine book on US policy in the early years of the Arab-Israeli conflict; that book includes but a dozen or so brief references to McDonald.[7] Elsewhere, Hahn writes that two bureaucracies—the State Department and the Israeli Foreign Ministry—"battled for Truman's blessing."[8] But as McDonald's diary shows, he was a major participant in this battle and was more than occasionally able to tip the balance.

In his own memoir, published in 1951, McDonald gave an overview of his two-and-one-half-year mission.[9] But the controversial events of Israel's birth and expansion were too recent and too complex, and his many personal relationships too important, for him to express himself with complete candor.

Despite the length of the diary, the editors tried to include in this published version all information of historical significance, trimming mostly personal matters or trivia. We also interspersed passages from McDonald's letters to friends and confidants, material from his private papers, and exchanges with the State Department and the White House—they fill out matters alluded to in the diary. All non-diary sources and our own editorial explanations appear in italics, making it easy for readers to distinguish them from the diary.

6. Brecher, *American Diplomacy and the Israeli War of Independence*, 92.

7. Peter L. Hahn, *Caught in the Middle East: U.S. Policy Toward the Arab-Israeli Conflict, 1945–1961* (Chapel Hill: University of North Carolina Press, 2004).

8. Peter L. Hahn, "Alignment by Coincidence: Israel, the United States, and the Partition of Jerusalem, 1949–1953," *International History Review* 21 (September 1999): 689, cited by Beisner, *Acheson*, 216.

9. James G. McDonald, *My Mission in Israel, 1948–1951* (New York: Simon & Schuster, 1951). McDonald gained the title ambassador in early 1949.

Many issues of 1948 still haunt Israel's diplomacy today: the disputed boundaries of the new state, the status of Jerusalem, the questions of peace with Arab states and Israel's quest for security, Israel's fraught relationship with the United Nations, and the problem of Palestinian refugees. On all these matters and others, McDonald talked with Israelis, Americans, and UN officials, both at his residence in Tel Aviv and as he traveled around the country. He met often, both formally and informally, with Israeli president Chaim Weizmann, Prime Minister Ben-Gurion, and Foreign Minister Shertok (later Sharett), as well as future leaders such as Menachem Begin. These conversations offered inside information about Israeli policies and perspectives as presented to a sympathetic American, and they are still of considerable historical importance for the early history of Israel.

McDonald did not always agree with Israeli government officials, and still less with their domestic political opponents, but he tried to understand them all and help Washington to do so. He managed to allay fears in Washington that Israeli democracy was vulnerable to communism, and he certainly helped American officials separate themselves from British misjudgments of Western strategic interests. McDonald's diary explains the origins of the special relationship between the United States and Israel.

Life in Israel, 1948–1950

BARBARA MCDONALD STEWART

When we arrived in August 1948, there was still fighting along the borders, alternating with UN cease-fires. Egyptian planes appeared over the Mediterranean, prompting air-raid warnings in Tel Aviv and Haifa.

As the "gates of Jerusalem" were finally opened, the new country suffered growing pains from immigration. Displaced persons came from camps in Germany, Austria, and Italy as well as from Eastern Europe and the Middle East. Apartments were at a premium, and even diplomats who wanted to set up legations could not find office space or living space for their personnel, even if they were willing to pay "key money." When we arrived in Tel Aviv, we were housed on the second floor of the Gat Rimon, one of two four-story hotels facing the seashore. The Soviets were lodged on the third floor, and our respective flags flew at the front corners of the hotel. It took more than a month before a satisfactory American residence could be found, and the Russians took even longer to organize their compound. There were shortages of everything. No one was starving, but food was of limited variety, and one never knew what would be available. It took weeks to get a new telephone or to get utilities hooked up, and a new refrigerator had to be ordered from the States.

Finally, after much negotiation, an appropriate residence was found in the Tel Binyamin neighborhood of the Tel Aviv suburb of Ramat Gan. The owners had left the basic furniture and equipment, as we had none. We also took over the domestic workers: a cook who spoke Russian and Hebrew; her husband, the gardener, who likewise spoke Russian and Hebrew; and a maid who spoke Hebrew and French. Looking back, I think we should have started afresh, but I was totally untrained in running a house, particularly one with guests for most meals and tea in between. Sarah, the cook, was flexible or at least, I could not understand her complaints. Shalom was our chauffeur, but that job does not describe him. He was more of a major-domo. He did much of the shopping and could find almost anything if it was to be had in Tel Aviv. He had lived in the city for many years and was totally protective of the ambassador. Fortunately, his English was very good.

Protocol was at a minimum, and when there were not enough glasses for all the guests, or in another case not enough napkins, I went next door and borrowed from Mrs. Sharett, the foreign minister's wife. Most meals somehow worked out. My father had a knack for keeping the conversation flowing and bringing out the best in his guests so I could relax once the food was on the table. I do remember one disaster. We were given a live turkey for Thanksgiving. How to bring it to the table? Yossi, the gardener, chased it around the yard with a BB gun and filled it so full of shot that we could not eat it.

We entertained government officials, American staff members, and what my father called "visiting firemen," but we were also invited out for dinner, tea, and cocktails. Whenever a staff member arrived, there was a party to welcome him and another when he departed. Despite shortages we had some wonderful food, and I brought home my favorite recipes for Russian borscht and coulibiac. Entertaining was mostly informal, and little alcohol was served. Sometimes there was wine with dinner, but more often fruit juice or punch. Flowers were abundant, always appreciated and fortunately not expensive.

Prime Minister Ben-Gurion stands out most for his personality and sincerity and the amazing breadth and depth of his mind. Conversation at dinner was not about politics so much as history and literature or whether Jesus spoke Aramaic. Moshe Sharett also had an incredible mind and extraordinary knowledge. Eliezer Kaplan, the finance minister, too was amazing. The elegance and the gracious hospitality of the Weizmanns savored of old world elegance in sharp contrast to the normal casual dining. I clearly remember my terror at discovering that, due to some quirk of circumstance, I was to have dinner alone with Chaim Weizmann in Vevey, Switzerland. After the first few minutes of awkwardness, I had a really good time. The president was charming. Madame Edis de Philippe, the reigning diva and director of Israel's National Opera Company, invited us to each new opera performance. Shoshana Yadin became my friend as well as Hebrew teacher and introduced me to Israeli theater after she married Josef Yadin, one of the founders and leading actors in the Chamber Theater.

We met a steady stream of visitors who came for political, religious, or artistic reasons—or just curiosity about the new country—for example, Henry

Morgenthau Jr., Eddie Cantor, Eddie Jacobson and his wife Bluma, Serge Koussevitzky, and the man whose visits I enjoyed the most, Leonard Bernstein. He came regularly to conduct the Israel Philharmonic Orchestra. His enthusiasm and energy were contagious. I remember particularly, apart from the music, his reclining on the wall around the roof where we took visitors to see the view and enjoy the cooler moments of the evening. He could talk for hours about music or Israel.

We were invited to visit kibbutzim, Orthodox and older Zionist ones; factories to see Israel's progress, a textile factory, a spaghetti plant; and a day care facility, among other places. The visits themselves were interesting, but what impressed me most was not so much Israelis' pride in their work, but more pride that they existed in Israel despite all the problems. Each visit was a reason to celebrate.

It was amazing to travel around the country and see the biblical sites and the familiar biblical names. It was a new country, and yet it was so very old. In spring the wild poppies covered the land with red, white, and lavender. Were they the "lilies of the field"? Jerusalem was as magical as everyone said. At Christmas we went to Bethlehem to the Church of the Nativity and at Easter to Jerusalem to the Church of the Holy Sepulcher. My mother and I joined friends driving to Beirut, Damascus, and Baghdad. We stopped on the way back to see the temples of Baalbek, fabulous despite the rain and sleet.

The embassy residence served uniquely as a gathering place, a workplace, and a place of entertainment. McDonald had an office there and spent more time at the residence than in his office in Tel Aviv. His secretary, Miss Harriet Clark, lived there, initially because of the lack of apartment space in Tel Aviv, and then later because McDonald found it handy to have her so available. There really was very little family privacy. From early morning until after dinner there were visitors: staff, American tourists, Israelis, governmental and diplomatic courtesy calls. Often guests brought flowers. Between these gifts and flowers in the garden, the house looked festive despite its rather utilitarian furnishings and stark modern architecture. The most outstanding feature was the view from the flat roof, particularly in the cool of the evening. You could see an expanse of Tel Aviv and the Mediterranean and perhaps a beautiful sunset.

Daily life had its ups and downs, but underlying all was the sense of living in an historic moment, and that feeling was supported by the mutual respect and trust between the leaders of the Israeli government and McDonald. There was an excitement in the air, a sense of wonder at the very existence of the new state, a determination to make it work. Despite many differences of opinion, there was a common goal, the success of the establishment of Israel.

Our November 1948 trip to the UN General Assembly in Paris for discussions on Arab refugees and the conference on refugees in Istanbul in November 1949 highlighted the central role that Israel played in the new Middle East. It was McDonald's hope that Israel would be an inspiration for democracy and a catalyst for modernization in the whole region.

In 2010 I returned to Israel and had the opportunity to have tea with President Shimon Peres. His young aide de camp had never heard of James G. McDonald, and the president explained that he, McDonald, was the American who had done more than any other to establish the close relationship between Israel and the United States. Peres then went on to explain that in 1948 he had been an aide to Ben-Gurion but had not gone to meetings with McDonald because, at that time, he did not speak English.

The years spent in Israel were demanding and exhausting for my father. He took very seriously his job to be, as he put it, the eyes and ears of his government. His emotions and personal opinions were not part of his reporting. However, in times of crisis, such as the assassination of Count Folke Bernadotte in September 1948, he worked tirelessly to keep either government from doing something precipitously without a full understanding of the situation. These years were also tremendously rewarding for him, helping the new nation establish itself. It was the culmination of a career of educating and helping others, particularly Jews. He continued, after his resignation and until his final illness, making speeches around the U.S.A. and abroad, raising money for Israel Bonds. He realized that political friendship was one thing, but what Israel then needed were funds to bring about economic stability.

Living in Israel during its first years created an emotional bond. Returning sixty years later was like a homecoming, even though I could recognize very little. Peace and understanding seemed even further away than in 1948. Yet I still look forward to the day when Israel can fulfill my father's hope and become a beacon for peace and prosperity in the Middle East.

1. June–July 1948

Furious with US recognition of Israel, the State Department aimed to limit it. The United States recognized the new Provisional Government of Israel as the de facto authority in the state of Israel, rather than providing de jure recognition of Israel. The Department argued that the UN partition resolution of November 29, 1947, made no provision for independence, that Israel's borders were still undetermined, and that Israel had yet to prove its democratic credentials.

Under Secretary of State Robert Lovett[1] initially argued that there was no need to create a US mission in Israel at all, but then decided that a small mission was desirable as a way to maintain the proper de facto relationship.[2] Loy Henderson, head of the Office for Near Eastern and African Affairs since 1945, suggested that Charles F. Knox Jr.—a career foreign service officer who had last served in the US embassy in Caracas—lead the mission in Tel Aviv as acting special representative.[3]

Israel wanted full diplomatic relations as enjoyed by other states. On June 16, 1948, its representative at the UN, Abba Eban,[4] told Judge Samuel Rosenman— who had served as President Harry S. Truman's special counsel after President Franklin Roosevelt's death—that Washington should establish full diplomatic relations to "ensure Presidential control of US Palestine policy."[5] Clark Clifford, current White House counsel and Truman's top adviser, concurred. Henderson's delay in appointing even a special representative, Clifford reasoned, was designed to appease the Arab governments. Clifford also suspected that Henderson wanted "a career man as

1. Robert A. Lovett (1895–1986), Wall Street investment banker; assistant secretary of war for air, 1941–1945, presiding over expansion of the US Army Air Force; head of the Lovett Committee, October–December 1945, providing recommendations to the US government on the expansion of postwar intelligence; returned to private investment banking, December 1945; under secretary of state, July 1947–January 1949; secretary of defense, 1951–1953.
2. Memorandum by Lovett to president, May 26, 1948, United States, Department of State, *Foreign Relations of the United States* [hereafter *FRUS*], *1948: The Near East, South Asia, and Africa*, v. V, pt. 2 (Washington, DC: Government Printing Office, 1976), 1051–1053; memorandum by Lovett to president, May 27, 1948, *FRUS*, 1948, v. V, pt. 2, 1058–1060.
3. Memorandum by Henderson, May 17, 1948; Knox to Wilkins, May 26, 1948; Henderson to Lovett, June 7, 1948, National Archives and Records Administration, College Park, MD [hereafter NARA], Record Group [RG] 59, Entry [E] 1434, Lot File [LF] 54 D 403, box 8.
4. Abba Eban (1915–2002), South African-born, British-educated scholar of Hebrew and Arabic; emigrated to Palestine, 1940; served in British Army as intelligence officer in Palestine during World War II; served as Jewish Agency liaison to the UN Special Committee on Palestine, 1947; Jewish Agency [after 1949 Israeli] representative to the UN, 1947–1959; Israeli ambassador to United States, 1950–1959; Israeli minister of foreign affairs, 1966–1974.
5. Epstein to Shertok, June 3, 1948, Yehoshua Freundlich, ed., *Documents on the Foreign Policy of Israel* [hereafter DFPI], v.1 (Jerusalem: Israel State Archives, 1981), document [d.] 138. Eban to Rosenman, June 16, 1948, *DFPI*, v. 1, d. 192. Also Goldmann to Shertok, June 18, 1948, *DFPI*, v. 1, d. 209.

American Minister to Israel [so that] Mr. Henderson's hand will be strengthened and his hold on the situation will be further entrenched."[6]

It was a critical moment. After the Arab states attacked the new Jewish state, the Israelis successfully defended themselves and secured additional territory beyond the partition lines (see textbox 1.1). British Foreign Secretary Ernest Bevin, who had contested the Zionist enterprise and who had tried repeatedly to convince the United States to oppose the partition plan, now insisted that the United States and Britain had to work together to limit the ramifications of the Jewish state. This meant reducing its territory. Washington and London drafted UN Security Council Resolution 50 of May 29, 1948. It called for a four-week cease-fire and appointed a mediator— Count Folke Bernadotte of the Swedish Red Cross. Known for his negotiations with Heinrich Himmler at the end of World War II on behalf of concentration camp prisoners, Bernadotte was now to supervise the Israeli-Arab truce with the assistance of UN Truce Commission established earlier and also to help create a peace settlement for Palestine.[7] The first UN truce supervisors arrived on June 10, and the initial truce was enacted on June 11, 1948.

Truman supported the cease-fire resolution, and he noted that de jure recognition of Israel would have to wait until peace was established.[8] But he was unwilling to support designs to shrink the size of the Jewish state. He complained about Bevin's intrigues, said that Loy Henderson would be reassigned abroad, and decided to appoint a permanent representative. On June 22 he mentioned Major General John Hilldring, a supporter of Israel, as a possibility. But Hilldring had had recent conflicts with the State Department and was in ill health.[9]

Later the same day, Clifford telephoned McDonald, whom he had known for many years. Truman came to trust McDonald after a decisive meeting in July 1946, when McDonald told the president that the State Department would wreck the White House's desire to send 100,000 Jewish refugees to Palestine. McDonald wrote the president at the time, "If now or later my knowledge of Jewish affairs and my experience over more than a decade with Jewish personalities all over the world . . . can be of use to you, I should be happy."[10]

6. Memorandum by Clifford, June 17, 1948 in *FRUS*, 1948, v. V, pt. 2, 1117–1119.

7. *FRUS*, 1948, v. V, 1064–1072, 1077–1079, 1080–1081. UN Security Council Resolutions are located at www.un.org/en/sc/documents/resolutions.

8. Memorandum by Leonard C. Meeker, June 22, 1948, *FRUS*, 1948, v. V, pt. 2, 1127–1129.

9. Major General (ret.) John H. Hilldring (1895–1974), chief of the US Army's Civil Affairs Division, 1943–1946; US delegate at the Potsdam Conference, 1945; retired from Army, 1946; assistant secretary of state for occupied areas at Truman's nomination, March 1946–August 1947; sympathetic to Jewish DPs' desire to go to Palestine; appointed to US delegation to the UN at the behest of White House adviser David Niles with Truman's approval, September 1947; acted to counteract State Department's maneuvering against the partition plan. In April 1948 the White House tried to insert Hilldring into the State Department to direct US policy toward Palestine. Hilldring got a cool reception, and senior officials informed him that he would be excluded from important discussions. See Cohen, *Truman and Israel*, pp. 91–93, 204–206.

10. Norman J. W. Goda, Barbara McDonald Stewart, Severin Hochberg, and Richard Breitman, eds., *To the Gates of Jerusalem: The Diaries and Papers of James G. McDonald, 1945–1947* (Bloomington: Indiana University Press in association with the United States Holocaust Memorial Museum, 2014), 250.

Was at home alone in the afternoon looking over some old personal files, thinking about planning a book of "Memoirs." It was about four o'clock when the phone rang, Clark Clifford on the other end. We first talked about family for about five minutes or so. Finally, I said, "What's on your mind?" He replied that he wanted to talk to me in the strictest confidence at once. I said all right, I would come to Washington any time he suggested. To this he answered, "I mean now."

His first words then were, "Are you a Democrat?" My reply was easy since I had been born a Democrat and had not bothered to change and had continued to be so enrolled.[11] Could I, he wanted to know, go to Israel as the government's first representative? He wanted me to know that he was not canvassing a list—that I was the one person he was to inquire about. I was somewhat equivocal in my response, pleading desire to rest, absence of wife, etc. He seemed not to consider these factors important, saying that things might move very quickly, but if nothing happened, I was to regard the conversation as completely confidential. I agreed.

Within the hour Clifford called back again saying in substance: I have seen the president, he is delighted, wants to make the announcement at six o'clock. I said all right. We then discussed conditions. Clifford assured me that the mission was to be of the highest rank of any abroad with comparable compensation. There was to be an adequate staff, mine was to be a recess appointment subject to senatorial confirmation.[12] I was to hear from him very soon about seeing the president and begin[ning] my study [briefings] at the Department of State.

At 4:25 pm on June 22, after speaking to McDonald, Clifford told Under Secretary Lovett by telephone that Truman had selected McDonald for the post of special representative of the United States to Israel. The president, he added, "wanted the announcement made this afternoon." Clifford purported not to know McDonald, noting only that he had been on the Anglo-American Committee of Inquiry in 1946. Lovett vociferously objected. He asked whether the president had "considered the fact that Mr. McDonald is a confirmed Zionist" and "whether the President had considered the possible . . . untold consequences." Clifford said that he knew none of the background, but that "the President was positive, had made up his mind, and that there was obviously no room for argument. . . . The decision had already been made."[13] The

---

11. According to his family, McDonald had voted for Franklin D. Roosevelt in every presidential election except 1940.

12. The US Senate confirmed McDonald in March 1949, after Truman appointed him as ambassador following the de jure recognition of Israel. See Chapter 9.

13. On the discussion, see memorandum by Lovett, June 22, 1948, *FRUS*, 1948, v. V, pt. 2, 1131–1132; Diaries of Robert Lovett, Under Secretary of State, 1947–1948, [hereafter Lovett Diary], entry of June 22, 1948, Brown Brothers Harriman Collection, New York Historical Society Library [hereafter NYHS] box 112, folder 2. See Brecher, *American Diplomacy and the Israeli War of Independence*, 54.

announcement was made the same night. Eliahu Epstein, Israel's representative in Washington, immediately conveyed his country's approval.[14]

Since Ruth [McDonald's wife] was out in Indiana and Janet [McDonald's eldest daughter] had gone to the hospital for a few days and Halsey [Barrett, McDonald's son-in-law] was not at home, I was left alone with my thoughts to get ready for dinner at Mrs. Frieda Warburg's.[15] At seven I heard the announcement on the air. The dinner at Frieda's was a sort of celebration. Besides the hostess and myself and her oldest daughter [Carola], there were present the Sam Lewisohns[16] and Mrs. Max Warburg [Frieda's sister-in-law].

Wednesday, June 23
Talked with Arthur Baer on the telephone.[17] Arthur Lourie[18] telephoned me, heard news of Mrs. Harmer's arrest in Cairo.[19] Talked with Miss Schulkind,[20] later with Dr. Robert Nathan.[21] Clifford called to announce dates

14. Eliahu Epstein [later Elath] (1903–1990), Ukrainian-born diplomat and trained Arabist; settled in Palestine, 1924; director, Jewish Agency Middle East Department, 1934–1945; headed Jewish Agency's political office in Washington, 1945–1948; appointed special representative of the Provisional Government of Israel to Washington, May 1948, and ambassador with de jure recognition in March 1949. His approval of McDonald is in memorandum of telephone conversation between Epstein and Satterthwaite, June 22, 1948, NARA, RG 59, State Department Central Files, Palestine, Microcopy [MC] 1390, reel 15, frame 944.

15. Frieda Warburg (1876–1958), wife of the late Felix M. Warburg (1871–1937) and the daughter of Jacob Schiff; her philanthropic activities extended to various Jewish charities including the United Jewish Appeal, the Hebrew University, and the Hadassah Hospital in Jerusalem. The Warburgs knew McDonald well owing to Felix's leadership in the American Jewish Joint Distribution Committee and their mutual work on behalf of Jewish refugees.

16. Samuel A. Lewisohn (1884–1951), New York financier and philanthropist who served on the board of several New York art galleries.

17. Arthur B. Baer (1895–1970), president of Stix, Baer and Fuller (SBF) department stores in St. Louis; helped arrange McDonald's meeting with Truman in June 1947 through Treasury Secretary John Snyder. See Goda et al., eds., *To the Gates of Jerusalem*, 248–249, for this meeting.

18. Arthur Lourie (1903–1978), South African-born Jewish Agency and Israeli diplomat; political secretary, Jewish Agency, London, 1933–1948; in United States for most of World War II representing Weizmann; member, Jewish Agency delegation to San Francisco UN conference, 1945; director, Jewish Agency UN Office 1946–1948; Israeli consul general in New York and deputy representative to UN, 1948–1952; raised to rank of minister 1951; assistant director general, Ministry of Foreign Affairs, 1954–1957; ambassador on special mission to emperor of Ethiopia 1955; member, Israeli delegation to UN General Assembly 1949–1953; ambassador to Canada 1957–1959; ambassador to Great Britain, 1960–1965.

19. Yolande Harmer [Hebrew Har-Mor] (1913–1959), Egyptian-Jewish journalist; recruited as intelligence agent by Yishuv operative Reuven Zaslansky [later Shiloah], 1944, and later by Moshe Shertok, 1945–1946; had access to leading Egyptian officials in King Farouk's court in Cairo and provided important intelligence in the 1948 war; arrested in Cairo for espionage, June 1948; released in September after intervention by South African legation (she was married to a South African) on condition that she leave the country; went to Paris and worked for Israeli Foreign Ministry by cultivating Egyptian contacts. See Stanton Griffis to McDonald, September 29, 1948, McDonald Papers, Columbia University, box 12, folder 5; Ian Black and Benny Morris, *Israel's Secret Wars: A History of Israel's Intelligence Services* (New York: Grove Press, 1991), 61–70.

20. Helen S. Schulkind (1899–1960), communal Jewish leader in New York and secretary at United Jewish Appeal.

21. Robert R. Nathan (1908–2001), prominent US economist who aided with US wartime mobilization; studied economic capacity and immigration potential of Palestine for the American Palestine Institute; testified to the Anglo-American Committee for Palestine in January 1946. See Goda et al., eds., *To the Gates of Jerusalem*, 31–32.

Textbox 1.1.
Israel's War of Independence
MAY-JUNE 1948

On November 29, 1947, the United Nations General Assembly passed Resolution 181 calling for the partition of the British Mandate of Palestine into predominantly Jewish and Arab states linked by a customs union. Jerusalem was to be a separate political entity—a demilitarized *corpus separatum* under UN trusteeship. Neither the British mandatory authority nor the UN was prepared to enforce partition, and Arab anti-Jewish riots erupted in Jerusalem days after the UN vote. The grand mufti of Jerusalem, Haj Amin al-Husseini, who had lived in exile since 1937 and in Cairo since 1946, assumed leadership of the Arab Higher Executive, which claimed to represent Palestine's Arabs. He long had called for the physical destruction of Palestine's Jewish community. His loyalists in Palestine formed irregular militias, which attacked Jewish settlements and the roads leading to them.

The Haganah, the Jewish militia in Palestine, led the defense of the Jewish-assigned areas as well as of Jewish settlements in the Arab-assigned region. In April 1948, with the arrival of weapons from Czechoslovakia, Jewish fighters turned to offensive operations, partly to secure Jewish populations and partly to prepare for an expected invasion by the Arab states. They opened a narrow corridor to supply western Jerusalem, the New City, where 100,000 Jews lived. They conquered Arab villages that served as enemy bases. They also captured cities with mixed populations in the Jewish-assigned region; those municipalities included Tiberias, Haifa, and Jaffa. As the Mandate ended, they pressed into the Western Galilee to protect Haifa from the north.

Ordinary Arabs were caught in the middle. The Arab militias had stifled moderates, quashed local peace initiatives, requisitioned money and property, and carried out reprisals against enemies. As a result, thousands of Arabs fled their homes in rural villages, the coastal cities, and western Jerusalem for Arab towns and villages in eastern Palestine and to neighboring states. Arab flight accelerated after April 9, 1948, when Jewish irregulars from the Irgun Zvai Leumi (National Military Organization—IZL) and Lohemei Herut Israel (Fighters for the Freedom of Israel—Lehi) killed between 80 and 120 Arab civilians—the number is still disputed—in the village of Deir Yassin, west of Jerusalem. Jewish authorities condemned the killings. But Arab panic spread, and Haganah advances spurred additional flight, punctuated by Haganah units' destruction of some Arab villages based on local security assessments. By the end of the British Mandate, more than 300,000 Arabs had fled Jewish-controlled territory. The Jewish Agency had had no overarching plan to drive them out, but leaders such as David Ben-Gurion, the Jewish Agency Executive's chairman, viewed their departure as beneficial to the new state, which could now more easily accommodate Jewish refugees from Europe.

On May 14, 1948, as the British Mandate came to an end, the Jewish leadership proclaimed the independence of the State of Israel. The declaration did not define Israel's boundaries. A coalition provisional government was created under Ben-Gurion, and the Haganah was renamed the Israeli Defense Forces (IDF). As the British pulled out once and for all, the Arab states neighboring Israel, along with Iraq, attacked the new state amidst great popular enthusiasm in their capitals. Four thousand volunteer fighters known as the Arab Liberation Army (ALA; headquartered in Damascus and commanded by the Arab League) already had infiltrated through northern Palestine.

Aimed at rescuing Arab Palestine, the invasion simultaneously devolved into a land grab. The Egyptians pressed north through Gaza to within twenty-four miles of Tel Aviv, which they bombed, and through Be'er Sheva and Hebron toward Bethlehem. The Syrians attacked in the northeast, pressing along the southern edge of the Sea of Galilee. Lebanon provided logistical support to the ALA in the Galilee region itself. Secret meetings between King Abdullah of Transjordan and Jewish Agency officials had raised Israeli hopes that Transjordan would simply occupy and annex the Arab-assigned territories of Palestine west of the Jordan River and accept the Jewish state in return. But Abdullah could not withstand Arab opinion. Worried that Jewish forces would seize the Old City of Jerusalem with its Muslim holy places, he entered the war. His British-trained army, known as the Arab Legion, together with Iraqi forces, secured much of the hilly region of Samaria and Judea. Meanwhile, a bitter fight unfolded in Jerusalem between Israeli and Arab Legion forces.

The UN called for a general arms embargo for Palestine, which the United States, Britain, and France strictly observed. The Arab states were unprepared for the arms cutoff. Iraq and Transjordan had renewed their defense agreements with Britain, but they lacked equipment and ammunition for a long struggle. Egypt and Britain were in the midst of negotiating a new mutual assistance pact, but negotiations were tense, and the Egyptians had not restocked their arsenal. Only the Arab Legion was properly trained and battle tested. Egypt and Syria, meanwhile, entered the war as much to counter Abdullah's expansion as to destroy the Jewish state. The Jewish leadership, in contrast, had expected the war. With financial aid from Jewish groups in the United States, it secretly purchased additional weapons, including surplus aircraft from sources in Europe and in the United States, and it used to advantage its interior supply lines.

Israel could not relieve the Jewish Quarter of Jerusalem's Old City, defend the Jewish settlements between Gaza and Tel Aviv, or stop the Egyptians from cutting the road to the Jewish settlements in the northern Negev. But the new state could defend itself and even expand. The IDF halted Egyptian progress northward and pushed most Syrian forces out. It expanded its hold on the Western Galilee, quickly taking the coastal city of Acre. It also maintained and widened the approaches to the corridor from the Israeli coastal plain to western Jerusalem, establishing protection for the Jewish population there.

with the president, Lovett, and himself for the following Thursday. Talked on the phone with Ben Katz.[22] Got Emanuel Neumann's reaction about Washington possibilities.[23] Spoke to the Foreign Policy Association staff.

On June 23, Clifford called Lovett again. Lovett recorded that "the President wants McDonald to come here [the State Department] on Friday [June 25] . . . and wants McDonald to see whoever he should talk with in the State [Department]."[24]

Thursday, June 24

Many calls in the office from people expressing their good wishes. Mrs. Hanna Colt[25] asked to give a party before we left. *Times* photographer came over. Lunch with Arthur Lourie and [a] representative of [the] Haganah [now Israeli Defense Forces].[26] Arthur seems somewhat fearful of disunity, while the Haganah representative explained the psychology of [the] underground groups and their difficulty in adjusting themselves to normal relationships.[27] Talked with Judge Joseph Proskauer[28] on telephone about my conferences of the next day with Lovett and others. Also talked with Jacob Blaustein[29] about the same subject.

The battle over McDonald's appointment continued. On June 24 Israeli president Weizmann, who knew McDonald well, telegraphed Truman: "Allow me to express to you my heartfelt thanks for the appointment of James Grover MacDonald

22. Benjamin S. Katz (1892–1969), president, Gruen Watch Company, 1935–1953; donor to Jewish charities.
23. Emanuel Neumann (1893–1980), Latvian-born American Zionist leader; co-founder of United Palestine Appeal [UPA], 1921–1925; chairman, executive committee of the UPA, 1925–1928; president, Jewish National Fund [JNF], 1929–1930; member, Jewish Agency, 1931–1941; vice chairman (under Abba Hillel Silver), American Zionist Emergency Council [AZEC], 1943–1949; president, Zionist Organization of America [ZOA], 1947–1949. Neumann's testimony to the Anglo-American Committee is in Goda et al., eds., *To the Gates of Jerusalem*, 32.
24. Lovett Diary, entry of June 23, 1948, NYHS, box 112, folder 2.
25. Mrs. Hannah Colt, graduate of Smith College; active in Democratic politics; friend of McDonald from Bronxville.
26. Possibly Reuven Dafni (1913–2005), member of the Haganah delegation to the United States, 1946–1947, and IDF representative at the Israeli consulate in New York after 1948, or Teddy Kollek, head of the Haganah delegation in the United States, 1947–1948.
27. Refers to Irgun Zvai Leumi BeEretz Israel (National Military Organization in the Land of Israel [aka Irgun, aka IZL]), the Revisionist Zionist movement's military wing under Menachem Begin, and Lohemei Herut Israel (Fighters for the Freedom of Israel [aka Lehi aka Stern Gang]).
28. Joseph M. Proskauer (1877–1971), New York State Supreme Court judge, 1923–1930; president of American Jewish Committee (AJC), 1943–1949, remaining as honorary president thereafter. The AJC abandoned its opposition to a Jewish state in May 1947 when it officially advocated partition.
29. Jacob Blaustein (1882–1970) Baltimore-born co-founder, with his father, of the American Oil Company, 1910; active in numerous Jewish organizations, US government boards, and advisory committees; served Roosevelt and Truman on mobilization questions as well as human rights and displaced persons issues; executive secretary, American Jewish Committee, 1948; executive chairman after 1949.

[sic] as special representative to Israel. I am certain that this appointment will give deep satisfaction to the community of Israel and to Jewry generally."[30]

On the same day, Lovett spoke again with Clifford. "*I told Clifford that the Secretary [of State George Marshall] had been very much concerned at the procedures followed in the appointment made on June 22, particularly the precipitate action and failure to give the Department of State an opportunity to put the President in possession of any pertinent facts which might be at its disposal.*" Lovett added, "*The Secretary's concern had been such that he had written a long-hand letter from Walter Reed Hospital to the President yesterday.*"[31] Lovett persuaded Marshall not to send the letter, but noted that "*[the] Secretary was pretty hot about it.*"[32]

Eliahu Epstein learned that Truman, in considering the State Department's objections, privately replied, "*I am not expected to appoint to Israel an anti-Zionist.*"[33]

Friday, June 25—Washington

Call from Cleveland. Rabbi [Abba Hillel] Silver[34] said he was delighted and urged—stressing that only [King] Abdullah [of Transjordan] is fighting, [the] British, therefore, alone [are] responsible—that US can call [their] bluff.[35] He asked that I tell the president that he and his colleagues are the president's friends and are not working against him.[36] Promised to attend ZOA [Zionist Organization of America][37] convention [in Pittsburgh July 2–6] if president approved.[38] Jacob Blaustein called from Baltimore. Invited me to come to see him to talk. Promised to try to arrange it.

Long conference with Clifford at the White House. He told me in the strictest confidence [the] inside story of UN partition, of rumors of many months previous of NEA [Office of Near Eastern and African Affairs] sabotage,

30. Weizmann to Truman, June 24, 1948, McDonald Papers, USHMM, box 7, folder 1.

31. Memorandum of telephone conversation between Lovett and Clifford, June 24, 1948, NARA, RG 59, MC 1390, reel 15, frame, 953.

32. Lovett Diary, entry of June 24, 1948, NYHS, box 112, folder 2; memorandum by Lovett, *FRUS*, 1948, v. V, pt. 2, 1140.

33. Epstein to Shertok, June 24, 1948, *DFPI*, v. 1, d. 225.

34. Abba Hillel Silver (1893–1963), Lithuanian-born American Reform rabbi based in Cleveland and vocal leader of American Zionist movement; president, United Palestine Appeal, 1938–1943; co-chairman, United Jewish Appeal, 1938–1944; president, ZOA, 1945–1946; chairman, AZEC, 1933–1934, 1945–1949, which coordinated Zionist activity in the United States; chairman, the Jewish Agency for Palestine, American Section 1946–1948. See essays in Mark A. Raider, Jonathan D. Sarna, Ronald W. Zweig, eds., *Abba Hillel Silver and American Zionism* (New York: Frank Cass, 1977); and Ofer Schiff, *The Downfall of Abba Hillel Silver and the Foundation of Israel* (Syracuse, NY: Syracuse University Press, 2014).

35. Silver mistakenly assumed that King Abdullah did not favor a cease-fire. The Arab Legion had taken the area of Samaria and Judea and controlled most of Jerusalem, but its forces and supplies were exhausted. Silver was correct that Abdullah was dependent on British military supplies. See David Tal, *War in Palestine 1948: Strategy and Diplomacy* (London: Routledge, 2003), 269–272.

36. Refers to Silver's earlier critique of Truman in March 1948. See note 40.

37. Most important Zionist organization in the United States.

38. McDonald did not attend, but General Hilldring did, commenting that Israel's achievements since November 1947 were "nothing short of amazing" and "a near miracle." JTA *Bulletin*, July 7, 1948.

of Truman's unwillingness to believe them, and of Warren Austin's[39] statement, which was issued without the president's knowledge. General Marshall approved it, thinking that [the] general understanding earlier with [the] president that under certain circumstances [a] new program might be necessary was authorization for this departure. [The] statement was [a] blow to Truman and followed by [a] terrific row.[40] [The] president is determined to have his own way. On recognition, [the] Department was still dragging feet. Decision taken with approval of General Marshall and telephone knowledge of Joseph C. Satterthwaite.[41] Department [is] given to tendentious leaks. This and other factors led to president's decision to name [his] own man. Department acquiesced. Then General Hilldring's letter about health gave [the] opposition [an] excuse for General Marshall to release Hilldring.

My job is to keep the president and Clifford informed, the former not to be dependent upon Marshall and Lovett and, through them, upon NEA. I am to keep those unsympathetic from "gumming up" the new state of Israel. The president, whom I saw at 1:00, was very cordial. In answer to my quip that had he been my friend he would have sent me to South Africa, he replied, "I thought I was your friend," expressed personal confidence in me, and told of his anxiety for independent reports direct to him when necessary. I emphasized that he sat in the driver's seat and could drive if he would. I pointed out the unique role of Abdullah, wholly dependent on the British. He was amused by my story of Abdullah's colored favorite wife and of many stories about King Farouk. He assented to my appearance at the ZOA convention, listened without comment to the message from Neumann and Silver, ok'd my brief non-committal paragraph statement, and urged me to meet Stanton Griffis.[42]

39. Warren Austin (1877–1962), US ambassador to the United Nations, 1947–1953.

40. McDonald refers to the State Department's attempt to sabotage the November 29, 1947, partition resolution, culminating in Austin's March 19, 1948, proposal to the UN Security Council that partition be suspended since it could not be implemented peacefully and that the General Assembly subsequently consider a temporary UN trusteeship over Palestine. Austin's speech was not cleared in advance with the White House, and Truman came under attack by Zionist leaders, Democratic Party leaders, and the national press for backtracking on partition. Eleanor Roosevelt even threatened to resign from the US delegation to the UN. After a tense meeting at the White House with State Department officials (Marshall and Lovett were both out of town), Truman held a press conference on March 25 to give assurances that the White House had not abandoned partition. Truman never forgave the State Department for the embarrassment; the State Department continued to resent the White House's Palestine policy as politically motivated and injurious to US interests in the Middle East. Cohen, *Truman and Israel*, 188–198; Brecher, *American Diplomacy and the Israeli War of Independence*, 5–32.

41. Joseph C. Satterthwaite (1900–1990), career foreign service officer; first secretary of the legation and consul in Damascus, 1944–1945; assistant chief, Division of Near Eastern Affairs, 1945–1946; special assistant to the director, Office of Near Eastern and African Affairs, 1946–1947; deputy director, Office of Near Eastern and African Affairs, 1947–1948; director, Office of Near Eastern and African Affairs, 1948–1949.

42. Stanton Griffis (1887–1974), US ambassador extraordinary and plenipotentiary to Egypt, 1948–1949.

Since I had not heard of [Earl] Warren's nomination,[43] I asked the president what they had done at Philadelphia.[44] He told me and then commented rather ruefully that Warren did not belong on the Dewey ticket, that Warren had criticized Congress as severely as he himself had done. Then he added, "California and New York are two big states!"

On [my] second talk with Clifford, he emphasized earlier suspicions of [the] NEA and reliance on me to prevent "gumming up" of the new state. [The] White House wants to see it succeed on basis of [the General] Assembly decision [for partition]. In the president's anteroom met Justice Robert H. Jackson[45] and Judge Rosenman and chatted with them briefly. Later telephoned to Felix Frankfurter.

Afternoon conference with Lovett was participated in by Joseph Satterthwaite, Gordon Mattison,[46] and, [Robert McClintock].[47] In [the] course of general discussion I denounced the Austin statement and noted Mattison's extreme confusion. Lovett agreed that it was bad logic and thus tended to confirm Clifford's earlier statement that Lovett was ignorant of it. Together we agreed that Charles F. Knox[48] and Curtis W. Barnes[49] should go ahead, that the staff should consist of three secretaries and [a] full set of service attachés. Lovett favored the attaché idea in part in order to bring in a number of armed guards.

As to compensation, NEA had planned the Mission to be Class C, salary $15,000. I protested, quoting Clifford's promise that it should be of the highest grade. Lovett suggested the same as Egypt. It was finally settled at $20,000 with allowances for rent, service, etc., which were fixed later. Lovett stressed the importance of adequate independent American reporting. In this connection [he] cited the anticipated value of Griffis in Egypt.

McDonald gave his frank views of George Wadsworth and Pinkney Tuck, US diplomats in the Middle East whom McDonald had criticized in 1946 as being overtly pro-Arab. Lovett countered by praising Griffis in Egypt, saying, "It was a relief to have a man in such a post who was not either pro-Arab or pro-Zion or pro-anything, but just plain pro-American." Lovett noted afterward in his memorandum, "Mr. McDonald seemed to be not unresponsive to this observation, since he

43. Earl Warren (1891–1974), governor of California; 1943–1953; running mate of Thomas Dewey in 1948 presidential election; 14th chief justice of the Supreme Court, 1953–1969.

44. The Republican Party convention occurred in Philadelphia from June 21–25, 1948.

45. Justice Robert H. Jackson (1892–1954), Supreme Court justice and US chief of counsel at the Trial of the Major War Criminals at Nuremberg.

46. Gordon H. Mattison (1915–1999), assistant chief, Division of Near Eastern Affairs.

47. Robert M. McClintock (1909–1976), Office of United Nations Affairs, later ambassador to Lebanon, Argentina.

48. Charles F. Knox (1906–1982), commercial attaché in the US Embassy in Caracas, 1945–1948; McDonald's counselor of embassy in Tel Aviv, 1948–1949. On June 1948, Lovett had suggested him for the position of "acting representative to Israel" on the assumption that the truce might not hold and that he needed a man "who could be ordered in and ordered out quickly." Brecher, *American Diplomacy and the Israeli War of Independence*, 54.

49. Curtis W. Barnes became McDonald's chief administrative officer. He had been the senior economic analyst in the US Embassy in Caracas since 1943.

reverted to it and said he wondered how my Foreign Service advisers would take such a crack. My Foreign Service advisers said that they knew perfectly what I had in mind."[50]

Lovett denied that there was any connection between Pinkney Tuck's resignation and [the US] recognition [of Israel]. This impression [is] the result of Jewish propaganda. Tuck had had to decide about the Suez post before recognition was announced.[51]

Lovett praised Eliahu Epstein and other leaders, but charged some Jews and Arabs with distortion and subversive activities. Said he was fearful of Irgun and the Sternists, that they might threaten the state.[52] Throughout, I sensed no criticism whatever by Lovett of Britain. On the contrary, he seemed to assume that it was an objective mediator. As to my leaving time, Lovett said there was no hurry. Later, I was to realize that I was fortunate that I was to have just about a month of preparation, which is the time usually provided. I told Lovett that I had not asked the president when he wanted me to go for fear he would make it earlier, before I could really be ready.

McDonald did not leave for Tel Aviv until July 23. He explained to Sumner Welles, the under secretary of state during President Roosevelt's administration, "Never before did I realize how enslaving a briefing program can be. It was not so much the Department's briefing as it was that I had so many things to do—preparing my staff in Tel Aviv, reading the 'top secret' files, getting acquainted with the men who will process my reports, and struggling to clear up my private affairs [in New York]."[53]

The State Department continued work on a peace plan consistent with Britain's desire to placate the Arab states. Though McDonald was the president's appointee, the Department excluded him from these discussions. As late as July 1, a memorandum from the American delegation at the UN warned again that McDonald was "a professional Zionist."[54]

Saturday, June 26 [New York]

Golf in the morning. Wedding in the afternoon. At the Siwanoy [Country Club] reception [in Bronxville] I had interesting and helpful chat with Jack

50. *FRUS*, 1948, v. V, pt. 1, 1151–1152. For McDonald and Wadsworth, see references in Goda et al., eds., *To the Gates of Jerusalem.*

51. Somerville Pinkney Tuck (1891–1967), career foreign service officer; interim US representative to Vichy France, 1942, where he intervened on behalf of Jewish children; envoy extraordinary and then ambassador to Egypt, 1944–1948; participated in initiative to rescue Hungarian Jewish children, 1944; remained opposed to creation of Jewish state owing to US interests in Arab world; resigned and left government service, May 30, 1948; afterwards served on the board of directors of the Suez Canal Company.

52. See note 27 above.

53. McDonald to Welles, August 2, 1948, McDonald Papers, Columbia University, box 5, folder 10.

54. McClintock to Rusk, July 1, 1948, *FRUS*, 1948, v. V, pt. 2, 1171–1179.

Ewing.[55] He is suspicious of the loyalty of Lovett [and] is ready to do whatever he can with Truman. Said the latter could not be brought to see the real attitude of Lovett. He regards General Marshall as able, favors General Hilldring, and warned me that accusations of being pro-Jewish would be used to my injury.

Sunday, June 27

Delightful luncheon at Sam Lewisohn's discussing possible assistant. Margaret Lewisohn[56] suggested young Henry Morgenthau III.[57] I called his father, who was pleased at the suggestion and gave me his son's address.[58] I called the latter and we made a date for the next day.

Monday, June 28

Busy day at the office. Conference with Henry Morgenthau III about being my assistant. It left me less enthusiastic than I had been. Brief visit with Eddie Cantor at the Waldorf before he went off to the theatre.[59] Eddie bade me goodbye rather tearfully. Dinner conference with Ben Abrams.[60] He is rather cold about personal organization [and is] more enthusiastic about university basis.[61] He is undoubtedly sincere, but so busy that one wonders if he could be effective. Night train to Washington.

Tuesday, June 29—Washington

Breakfast with Eliahu Epstein at Mayflower. Covered a lot of ground in a preliminary way and prepared for [a] later conference. One will be able to work with him advantageously for the advancement of the president's policy. The rest of the Washington day spent at the office with documents and other preparations.

55. Oscar R. "Jack" Ewing" (1889–1980), head of Federal Security Agency, 1947–1953; vice chairman, Democratic National Committee, 1942–1947; organizer of an unofficial policy group under Truman, 1947–1952. McDonald knew Ewing as a classmate from Indiana University and maintained contact, explaining later that Ewing "is authoritatively said to be one of [Truman's] closest political associates and to have been decisively helpful in the critical days of May '48 when it was a very close question as to whether or not the US would recognize the new State [of Israel]." McDonald to Halsey and Janet Barrett, January 3, 1950, McDonald Papers, Columbia University, box 14, folder 15.

56. Margaret Seligman Lewisohn (1895–1954), wife of Samuel Lewisohn, advocate for education and active in Democratic politics.

57. Henry Morgenthau III (1917–), eventually became a producer for public television.

58. Henry Morgenthau Jr. (1891–1967), secretary of the Treasury, 1934–1945; helped establish War Refugee Board in January 1944, which rescued Jews late in the war; general chairman, United Jewish Appeal, 1947–1950.

59. Eddie Cantor (1892–1964), New York-born entertainer; heavily involved in Jewish causes. His relationship with McDonald, including his efforts to help secure McDonald a diplomatic post in 1945, is covered in Goda et al., eds., *To the Gates of Jerusalem*, 18–20.

60. Benjamin Abrams (1893–1967), Romanian-born businessman and close friend of McDonald; emigrated to the United States with his family, 1907; since 1922 president of the Emerson Radio and Phonograph Corporation; leading Jewish philanthropist and co-treasurer of the American Jewish Joint Distribution Committee [JDC] after the war; closely involved through numerous associated charities with Jewish refugee issues.

61. May refer to McDonald's idea from 1946 for a think tank on antisemitism and refugees. See Goda et al., eds., *To the Gates of Jerusalem*, 264–265.

Arrived at the Louis B. Mayer–United Jewish Appeal dinner at the Astor a little after eight.[62] Had time to greet Abraham J. Balaban,[63] the mayor,[64] Eric Johnston,[65] and Will Hays,[66] and others and to have a bite before the speaking began. The chairman [Henry Morgenthau Jr.] and [Harry P.] Fierst[67] wanted to hold me until the end, but I told them that I was so exhausted that either I spoke very near the beginning or not at all. We compromised and I spoke third, following two brief talks by the Balabans. During the course of the dinner Balaban told me of his enthusiasm about Griffis.

My problem in speaking was to avoid any diplomatic indiscretions. I tied Mayer up to the United Jewish Appeal and for the rest spoke about the four pictures hung on the walls, those of Weizmann, [Moshe] Shertok, Golda Meyerson, and Ben-Gurion. When I finished there was a good response, with Mayer shaking my hands warmly and bearing in his eyes—if such ever appeared there—signs of tears. The next day Fierst called me to say that mine had been the major event of the evening.

Sessions with Satterthwaite about staff and status. Said they had been able to fix the mission at a "B" rating—$20,000. Also discussed Miss [Harriet] Clark's status[68] and that of my outside assistant. Decision to send Knox ahead with Barnes. Brief conference with George Warren, bearing only indirectly on my mission.[69] Herbert Fierst[70] warned re[garding] Loy Henderson. David Niles[71] approved Pittsburgh [ZOA] date and thought $20,000 rating for mission fair.

62. McDonald gave a speech at the United Jewish Appeal testimonial dinner for Mayer (1884–1967), the head of MGM and past chairman of the UJA. He predicted that Israel would emerge stronger for its present trials. "Jewish Policemen in New York Pledge $10,000 for United Jewish Appeal Campaign," JTA *Bulletin*, July 1, 1948.

63. Abraham J. Balaban (1889–1962), builder of luxurious theaters and cinemas; manager of the Roxy Theater near Times Square, June 1948.

64. William O'Dwyer (1890–1964), mayor of New York City, 1946–1950.

65. Eric A. Johnston (1896–1963), president, Motion Picture Association of America, 1946–1963.

66. William Harrison Hays (1879–1954), former Republican politician and US postmaster general, 1921; president, Motion Picture Producers and Distributors of America, the film industry's censorship body, 1921–1945.

67. Harry P. Fierst (1883–1959), Kovno-born New York clothing manufacturer; founder of the American Zionist Youth Council; active with Chabad and United Palestine Appeal, and held leadership positions in the ZOA. His wife Miriam (1891–1974) was a national officer of Hadassah and JNF.

68. McDonald's personal secretary, whom he wanted to work at the mission in Tel Aviv.

69. George L. Warren (1890–1981), adviser to US delegation, Evian Conference, 1938; President's Advisory Committee on Political Refugees, 1938–1944; member of US delegation to UNRRA, 1944–1946; adviser on Refugees and Displaced Persons, Department of State, 1944–1968; US representative to UN Special Committee on Refugees and Displaced Persons, 1946; US representative to preparatory commission, International Refugee Organization, 1947–1948; US representative to General Council and Executive Committee, IRO, 1948–1952; adviser to US delegation to UN, 1948–1950.

70. Herbert A. Fierst (1915–2005), Washington attorney; special assistant to John Hilldring when Hilldring served as assistant secretary of state for occupied areas, 1946–1947; worked specifically with Jewish displaced persons in occupied Germany and Austria.

71. David Niles (1888–1952), White House adviser to Roosevelt and Truman, 1942–1951; son of Russian Jewish immigrants and sympathetic to Zionism.

All day at the office. Time filled with multiplicity of details incident to Washington and the trip. Tentative decision to sail on *Nieuw Amsterdam* on July 23. Griffis called, and we promised to get acquainted in Washington.

Thursday, July 1—Washington
Got acquainted at breakfast with Herbert J. Cummings.[72] I liked his directness and informality.

McDonald's diary has no entries between July 1 and July 19. But the repercussions of his appointment continued. In a telephone conversation with Clifford, Lovett complained that the Department had "gotten some very unpleasant messages about timing of McDonald appointment." He also worried about the White House's decision to transfer Loy Henderson from his post as head of the Office of Near Eastern and African Affairs to head the US Embassy in India. Lovett warned, "We are right on the razor's edge now of trying to get an agreement to an extension of the truce. To have any change here which would give Arabs added feeling that we have gotten rid of [a] fellow they must regard as their friend would be [a] pretty awkward situation."[73]

Just as the UN truce was expiring on July 8 (textbox 1.2), Charles Knox and Curtis Barnes arrived in Tel Aviv. They found a capital city at war, subject to daily Egyptian bombing. Knox immediately wrote his sister that "one sees many older people and lots of children—the young men and women are at the front." "I am disturbed," he continued, "because I can't get on with the business of setting up the mission. More than half the day I am sitting in air raid shelters . . . waiting for the all clear."[74]

Even after the second truce began on July 18, conditions were difficult. "Not only is Tel Aviv a normally crowded city," Knox reported to Washington, "but there are several tens of thousands of persons living here temporarily who have come here from areas seriously affected by the war, or down from Jerusalem. I believe that statistics show that average occupancy is something over four persons to a room. There is a great deal of residential building going on, and people are ready to move into such structures before the plaster is dry on the walls." The Israel Defense Forces (IDF) also requisitioned new buildings, Knox said, "as fast as they are finished."

Knox hoped to find embassy office space with eighteen rooms, but had to settle for a three-month lease for a well-located space with five rooms. The IDF requisitioned

72. Herbert J. Cummings (1915–2000), political adviser to Allied Expeditionary Force, 1944; economic adviser to Allen Dulles in US Embassy in Bern; involved after 1944 with location of Nazi assets in neutral countries (Operation Safehaven) as the assistant chief of the Bureau of Foreign Activity Correlation in the State Department; joined McDonald's team in 1948 as an economic attaché but also had intelligence responsibilities. Truman personally arranged the assignment. McDonald, *My Mission in Israel*, 14–15.

73. Lovett Diary, entry of July 2, 1948, NYHS, box 12, folder 3.

74. Knox to Jessica Knox, July 8, 1948, July 17, 1948, Harry S. Truman Library and Museum [hereafter Truman Library], Papers of Charles F. Knox, box 1, folder Correspondence 1948–1949.

Textbox 1.2.
The "Ten Days"
JULY 8–JULY 18, 1948

On July 8 the four-week truce ended with an Egyptian attack on Israel in the northern Negev. But the Israelis benefited from renewed warfare. In the center, Israeli forces broadened the approaches to Jerusalem and occupied the Arab towns of Lydda (now Lod) and Ramle, whose location within Arab salients had threatened Tel Aviv. In the north, the IDF attacked the Arab Liberation Army and occupied parts of the Lower Galilee, including the mixed Muslim/Christian Arab town of Nazareth. Israeli B-17s, meanwhile, flew numerous sorties over Cairo and Damascus.

UN Security Council Resolution 54 of July 15, 1948, introduced by the United States, ordered a new indefinite cease-fire that was supposed to last until the establishment of peace between Israel and its neighbors. Violations of the UN truce were to trigger machinery leading to UN sanctions. This truce was implemented on July 18. But now Israel held the upper hand: The IDF numbered more than 63,000 soldiers, and the Arab armies lacked everything from reserves to ammunition. And although the Arabs effectively held 85 square kilometers of the territory assigned to the Jews in the 1947 partition, the IDF had captured more than 1,000 square kilometers of territory initially assigned to the Arabs. The so-called ten days of fighting between the truces generated an additional 100,000 Arab refugees through mass flight and, particularly in the cases of Lydda and Ramle, expulsions.[1]

In the last week of July, Israel officially challenged the truce, which called for Jerusalem's demilitarization. The Provisional Government declared that the New City, with its 100,000 Jews, was now Israeli-occupied territory, soon to receive military administration and an Israeli military governor.

---

1. Benny Morris, *The Birth of the Palestinian Refugee Problem Revisited* (New York: Cambridge University Press, 2004), 197–209, 216, 236.

forty rooms on the same floor. "I personally think," reported Knox, "that the only solution to this situation is for the [US] Government to either buy a building or build one." In the meantime, the US mission had neither coding facilities nor a secure mail route from Tel Aviv. Knox's first letters went by courier via Jerusalem and Cairo, arriving three weeks later in Washington.

McDonald did not know Knox, who noted to the Division of Near Eastern Affairs that "I am under orders from McDonald not to report anything in re [the] local political situation until he arrives." Knox immediately developed a liking for the new state and respect for its citizens. "Israel," he reported, "is a vital, living country already. Irrespective of any other factors, the people here have now sealed their compact with destiny by a river of spilled blood and they won't turn back."[75]

Monday, July 19—New York

Met Ben Abrams and went to his office. On the way down [I] told him of my decision following conferences a few days earlier with Jimmy Rosenberg.[76] I summed up also my impressions of the NEA and the Washington situation generally. At his office I telephoned Washington. I spoke first to Fraser Wilkins,[77] who assured me all the papers would be in order on Wednesday. I spoke also to Satterthwaite [Henderson's successor at NEA]. In order to defeat Satterthwaite's plan not to have me see Lovett again, I telephoned the latter's office, gave the secretary a list of my Wednesday engagements, and added that I wanted to see the Under Secretary in order to get my final sailing orders.

After making some other calls, I talked with Ben Abrams, telling him that if he wanted, I would be glad if he would have a few people for luncheon on Thursday. This he was pleased to arrange. Conference with Emanuel Neumann [at] my office. He wanted to talk mostly about a possible substitute for Hilldring in the position of special assistant. He did not, however, have any suggestions that seemed to me suitable. Charles Fahy[78] did not seem to me to be eligible in view of his firm's recent relations with the [Jewish] Agency and its relations to the Israeli representative in Washington. His other suggestion, James Roosevelt,[79] seemed to me even less likely to be acceptable. He would, I think, have liked for me to tell him more about the situation in Washington, but I felt

75. Knox to Satterthwaite, July 26, 1948, NARA, RG 59, E 1434, LF 54 D 403, box 8; Knox to Fraser Wilkins, July 27, 1948, Truman Library, Charles F. Knox, Jr. Papers, box 1, Correspondence 1948–1949.
76. James Naumburg Rosenberg (1874–1970), New York attorney and close friend of McDonald; founding member of the JDC and member of its executive board; member of executive board of American Jewish Committee; worked to rescue Jews in 1939 and later to settle them in the Dominican Republic. Mentioned extensively in Richard Breitman, Barbara McDonald Stewart, and Severin Hochberg, eds., *Advocate for the Doomed: The Diaries and Papers of James G. McDonald, 1932–1935* (Bloomington: Indiana University press, in association with the United States Holocaust Memorial Museum, 2007). Also Allen Wells, *Tropical Zion: General Trujillo, FDR, and the Jews of Sosúa* (Durham, NC: Duke University Press, 2009), 45–47, 85–87, 103–104.
77. Fraser Wilkins (1909–1989), career foreign service officer; vice consul in US missions in Baghdad and Tangier during World War II; served in the Division of Near Eastern Affairs, Department of State, 1946–1950. His Truman Library Oral History is at www.trumanlibrary.org /oralhist/wilkins.htm.
78. Charles Fahy (1892–1979), solicitor-general under Roosevelt, 1941–1945; director of the legal division of the US delegation to the Allied Control Council in Germany, 1945–1946; legal adviser, Department of State, 1946–1947. Argued in a memorandum to Lovett on May 4, 1948, that the United States should recognize the partition of Palestine as a fait accompli because the Haganah had made partition a reality on the ground, and gave the memorandum to the Jewish Agency, which sent it to the White House. See Zvi Ganin, *Truman, American Jewry, and Israel, 1945–1948*, 182–183.
79. James Roosevelt (1907–1991), eldest son of Franklin and Eleanor Roosevelt; businessman, Marine Corps officer, and White House aide during his father's administration; chairman of California Democratic Committee, 1946–1948; opposed Truman's candidacy in 1948 and tried to convince Dwight D. Eisenhower to run as the Democratic candidate; US representative from California's 26th district, 1955–1965.

that I could not. I merely explained why I had delayed my leaving and under-lined the necessity of becoming acquainted with the documents, completing my staff and building my rear guard defenses.

At the luncheon at the *Times* besides Arthur Hays Sulzberger[80] and my-self were present: Anne O'Hare McCormick,[81] who had come in for it though Monday is her day off, Charles Merz,[82] Tolischus,[83] Duffus,[84] and Callender.[85] I talked very frankly about the internal situation of the State Department, of the extent to which one had to anticipate overt and indirect opposition, giving illustrations of what had taken place in the past and mak-ing clear the difficulties I faced. Some of my listeners were obviously shocked, but Anne O'Hare McCormick, despite her friendliness towards me, remained obdurate.

We talked also for a time about South Africa.[86] I was a little embarrassed not to be able to say to them that I had met their correspondent or knew of his work. I could hardly hide my conviction that Arnold T. Steele of the *[New York Herald] Tribune* was doing a better job. I explained why I thought there were exaggerations in the current misgivings about the Jewish position in South Africa and about the relationship of the Union and the British Em-pire.[87] At some stage in this discussion somebody said that when I came back from Palestine I should take an assignment to do a series of articles from South Africa.

There was the usual discussion about how long my assignment would last, about possible confirmation, and the attitude of Dewey. I explained to them that these questions were the least of my worries. As Arthur and I walked out to-gether (it was then nearly twenty minutes of three), something was said about the influence of the Jewish fighting record on the attitude of non-Jews towards the Jews. To make it easier for Arthur, I commented that it is very difficult to know

80. Arthur Hays Sulzberger (1891–1968), publisher, *New York Times*, 1935–1961; strongly anti-Zionist; supported the anti-Zionist American Council for Judaism; deemphasized news of the Holocaust during the war out of concern regarding Jewish claims of unique victimhood; blamed Zionism for Jewish deaths. See Laurel Leff, *Buried by the Times: The Holocaust and America's Most Important Newspaper* (New York: Cambridge University Press, 2005).

81. Anne O'Hare McCormick (1880–1954), foreign news correspondent, *New York Times*; had obtained interviews with Mussolini, Hitler, and Stalin in 1930s; Pulitzer Prize, 1937.

82. Charles Merz (1893–1977), editor, *New York Times*, 1938–1961.

83. Otto D. Tolischus (1890–1967), German-born *New York Times* correspondent, Berlin, 1933–1940; expelled from Germany, 1940; later an editor with *New York Times*.

84. Robert L. Duffus (1888–1972), writer, *New York Times*, 1937–1971.

85. Harold Callender (1912–1979), Paris bureau chief, *New York Times*, 1944–1957; author of *A Preface to Peace* (New York: Alfred A. Knopf, 1944).

86. McDonald was in South Africa for six weeks in April and May 1948 on a speaking and fundraising tour for the Zionist Federation of Great Britain and Ireland on behalf of dis-placed persons. He had long talks with Prime Minister Jan Smuts (1939–June 1948) and with friends of Smuts's successor Daniel F. Malan, whose government (June 1948–1954) went on to es-tablish the apartheid system. McDonald to Niles, May 31, 1948, McDonald Papers, Columbia University, box 16, folder 7.

87. Despite Smuts's pro-Zionist policies, South Africa had antisemitic elements among its Afrikaner population. The National Party, which opposed Smuts, pressed for anti-Jewish policies. See Milton Shain, *The Roots of Antisemitism* (Charlottesville: University Press of Virginia, 1994).

in advance what the influence of any major development will be. He assented reluctantly when I added that from many sides I was receiving testimony that non-Jews were favorably impressed by the military record in Palestine. I could see that Arthur's anti-Zionism was wearing thin.

Tuesday, July 20

To the office for a hectic hour and a half before having to take the train to meet the family to drive to Hyde Park. We were a little late in arriving at Mrs. Roosevelt's house, because we mistakenly thought her cottage would be near the main house.[88] When we finally arrived, as might have been anticipated, we found her busy serving the last stages of an outdoor picnic to fifteen or twenty people. These included nine of her grandchildren, her two sons, Jimmy and Elliot, her secretary Malvina Thompson, a man and his wife from the State Department, and a few others. There was no opportunity to talk until after the crowd had dispersed, when Mrs. Roosevelt joined us for a quiet half an hour or so.

She was amusing in her comments on one of her grandchildren, the son of the DuPont wife, who had been brought up by a governess and was sensitive to all drafts, etc.[89] Mrs. Roosevelt thought that a couple of weeks in the rough and tumble of the Roosevelt clan would do him a lot of good. Mrs. Roosevelt was critical of Lewis Douglas[90] on the ground that he, and in particular his wife, were socially ambitious and had been taken into camp by British society. She felt that Paul Felix Warburg[91] had an unfortunate influence on the ambassador by accentuating his snobbery and by leaning over backwards on Jewish matters. Illustrative of Warburg's unfortunate influence, she cited a party given for her by the ambassador in connection with the unveiling of the monument to FDR. She had hoped to meet there a number of working members of the embassy staff and other Americans. But, thanks to Warburg's influence, there were hardly any Americans present, few of the members of the staff. The great majority were British aristocracy in whom Eleanor said she was not interested.

Mrs. Roosevelt was sympathetic towards Truman but also tended to be sympathetic towards Jimmy's criticisms. The latter told with gusto of Truman's

---

88. Truman appointed Eleanor Roosevelt (1884–1962) to the first US delegation to the UN General Assembly in December 1946. She served on Committee Three (Committee on Humanitarian, Social, and Cultural Concerns) and served as the chair of the UN's Commission on Human Rights, 1947–1951. In 1948 she was primarily occupied with the drafting of the Universal Declaration of Human Rights, which was presented to the General Assembly for adoption in December. See Mary Ann Glendon, *A World Made New: Eleanor Roosevelt and the Universal Declaration of Human Rights* (New York: Random House, 2001).

89. Refers to Franklin Delano Roosevelt III (1938–), son of Franklin Delano Roosevelt Jr. and Ethel du Pont.

90. Lewis William Douglas (1894–1974), Arizona businessman and Democratic politician; deputy head of the War Shipping Administration, 1941–1944; US ambassador to United Kingdom, 1947–1950.

91. Paul Felix Warburg (1904–1965), son of Felix and Frieda Warburg; embassy attaché and special assistant to Lewis Douglas.

undignified actions at the convention. Both the Roosevelts deplored the inclusion of the call for a special session in the acceptance speech.[92] Mrs. Roosevelt thought that the Russian bogey was being overplayed in Palestine and that it was essential for peace there, and in the world, that we work with Russia and give evidence of our willingness to assume that they wanted peace. She was so inclined to stress the Russian problem that it was a little difficult to keep Palestine in the forefront. Had I not had to return for an appointment at the *Herald Tribune*, it would have been interesting to listen to her and Jimmy comment on other aspects of the Democratic political scene. As I was leaving, she said that if I had anything to say at any time to her personally I should send it on, indicating if there was anything she was free to publish.[93]

At the *Tribune* conference were present: Mrs. Reid,[94] Mr. Parsons,[95] the managing editor [Eric Hawkins][96] and one of the other staff members. Mrs. Reid was most cordial. They all listened with keen interest to my tale of the situation in NEA. She asked questions, however, which showed that she was not well informed on Palestine, for she seemed to think that [Count] Bernadotte's scheme had some merit. Parsons was more realistic. I had to leave the conference early to catch my plane, but short as it was, it was worthwhile. Arriving in Washington at 9:30, I tried to get in touch with Rosenman and learned that he was not due until midnight.

> *On June 27, 1948, Count Bernadotte had proposed the outlines of a peace arrangement that, when revised and completed in September, became known as the "Bernadotte Plan." It initially featured a union between Transjordan and Palestine under King Abdullah. The union would contain Arab and Jewish autonomous zones with linked economies, services, and developmental projects, as well as coordinated foreign, defense, and even immigration policies. Israel would keep all or part of the Western Galilee, but the Negev, most of which had been assigned to the Jews by the UN partition resolution in 1947, would go to the Arab state. Jerusalem would also be within Transjordan's borders with special protections for the Holy Places and municipal autonomy for the Jewish community there. The status of Jaffa would be reconsidered; Haifa, which had been assigned to the Jews in 1947, would become a free port; and Lydda, then still in Arab possession, a free airport. All Arab refugees, then counted at 300,000, would be allowed to return to their homes.[97] The Israelis rejected Bernadotte's initial outlines. As Foreign Minister Moshe Shertok had told Bernadotte in mid-June, "There could be no going back on what had been achieved." Eban added*

92. Truman promised to call a special session of the Republican-led Congress in July to address inflation and the housing shortage, issues that were in the Republican platform.
93. In her "My Day" newspaper column, which ran from 1936 to 1962.
94. Helen Rogers Reid (1882–1970), president, *New York Herald Tribune*, 1947–1953.
95. Geoffrey Parsons Jr. (1908–1981), editor, *New York Herald Tribune*, 1944–1950.
96. Eric Hawkins (1888–1969), managing editor, *New York Herald Tribune*, after managing the Paris edition until 1940; published materials relating to the Nazi Final Solution.
97. Bernadotte to Shertok, June 27, 1948, *DFPI*, v. 1, d. 239 and appendix.

that Bernadotte's proposals were "unacceptable."[98] *The Arabs also rejected Bernadotte's suggestions, partly because the terms favored Transjordan at the expense of Egypt and Syria, but mostly because the Arab League continued to call for a unitary Palestine under Arab rule.*[99]

Wednesday, July 21—Washington

Breakfast with Cummings and [Herbert] Fierst. Checked on memorandum and letter. Discussed other last minute precautions. Conference with General Omar Bradley, chief of staff, at the Pentagon.[100] Rather general talk except about weakness of Arabs militarily and Russian nonpenetration. Emphasized importance of able and loyal attachés. Found Bradley friendly and helpful. Next, to James Forrestal, who, though obviously under heavy pressure, gave me sufficient time and immediately paved the way for me to see his three chief colleagues.[101] Intentionally I did not talk policy except in the most general terms, for I did not wish him to think that I was propagandizing him.

Kenneth Royall, secretary of the Army,[102] impressed me most unfavorably; a rather fat and wordy southern type. He seemed more concerned to make points of no consequence than to listen to my brief statement of my point of view about the attaché. Nonetheless, my visit to him may not have been without some value. Stuart Symington,[103] on the other hand, seemed much more simple and direct. He at once told one of his associates to handle the matter of the attaché in the way in which I suggested. As I left, we chatted pleasantly about some of his friends in St. Louis. If he should speak to the president about my visit, it would be, I think, in a favorable way.

McDonald to Satterthwaite, July 9, 1948: "In reference to the military, naval, and air attachés who may be assigned to the Mission at Tel Aviv, I assume that I shall be given an opportunity to acquaint myself with the men's records before any final decision is made by the departments directly involved. I should be grateful if you would confirm this."[104]

---

98. Meetings between Bernadotte and Shertok, June 17, 18, 1948, *DFPI*, v. 1, d. 205; Jessup to secretary of state, no. 845, July 6, 1948, *FRUS*, 1948, v. V, pt. 2, 1191–1192.

99. Relevant documents in *DFPI*, v. 1, d. 239, 266, 306; *FRUS*, 1948, v. V, pt. 2, 1156–1157.

100. McDonald visited Bradley (Army chief of staff, 1948–1949) and his subordinates to ensure that he would receive highly qualified military attachés in Tel Aviv.

101. James Forrestal (1892–1949), secretary of defense, 1947–1948; pro-Arab in sympathies; like Marshall, opposed US recognition of Israel for fear of its repercussions in the Arab world; later said that his misgivings concerning Israel had dissipated. Allen Lesser, *Israel's Impact, 1950–51: A Personal Record* (Lanham, MD: University Press of America, 1984), 280.

102. Kenneth C. Royall (1894–1971), under secretary of war, 1945–1947; first secretary of the US Army after the abolition of the War Department and the creation of the Department of Defense, 1947–1949; forced into retirement for his resistance to the racial integration of the Army.

103. Stuart Symington (1901–1988), first secretary of the Air Force, 1947–1950; later senator from Missouri, 1953–1976.

104. McDonald to Satterthwaite, July 9, 1948, McDonald Papers, USHMM, box 9, July 1948.

Hurried back to the new State Department building for my session with General George Marshall. He received me cordially for more than ¾ of an hour. During that time he received three or four notes from his secretary, but had no telephone calls. I began by telling him that I interpreted my obligation as being that of a reporter, to be, to the best of my ability, eyes and ears for him, the Department, and the president. I did not disguise, indeed I rather emphasized, my background of close Jewish associations from the time I was high commissioner through my chairmanship of FDR's Advisory Committee on Political Refugees, my association with [Myron] Taylor at Evian[105] and the Anglo-American Committee of Inquiry, and subsequent work for the United Jewish Appeal.[106] Nor did I claim impartiality or lack of prejudice. Similarly, I spoke frankly about what I regarded as the lack of impartiality and prejudice of most of the men in the field and of many in NEA. I reiterated, however, that despite my background I intended to be as objective in my reporting as could be humanly possible.

Satterthwaite briefed Marshall for his meeting with McDonald. US policy on Palestine, he said, was based on previous UN actions. By now this also meant support of the Bernadotte Plan's principles, if not all of its details. Harold Beeley, Bevin's top Near Eastern adviser, argued that Arab control of the Negev, which the Jews were assigned in 1947 but which Israel did not yet hold, was essential so that Britain could maintain a land linkage between Egypt and Transjordan. Haifa, meanwhile, had to be a free port.[107] "[The] conviction is growing on all levels [of the Foreign Office]," reported US Ambassador Lewis Douglas from London, "that [the] early establishment [of a] small compact Jewish state would be in [the] best interest [of the] Arabs."[108] Eban wryly noted, "Bevin's intentions toward Israel, are intentions no longer of murder, but only of amputation."[109]

London believed that the UN could impose such a territorial solution as it had the truce. The State Department also discussed what it called a "sensible territorial solution for the Palestine problem" that included Jewish population transfers to a smaller Israel.[110] A July 1 memo from the US delegation at the UN noted, "The basic

105. Refers to international conference at Évian-les-Bains in July 1938, which was held on the initiative of President Roosevelt in an effort to find solutions to the issue of Jewish refugees. Myron Taylor headed the US delegation. See Breitman et al.., *Refugees and Rescue*, 121–146.

106. See Goda et al., eds., *To the Gates of Jerusalem*, for McDonald's role in these bodies.

107. Harold Beeley (1909–2001), Near Eastern expert in Foreign Office. For his role with the Anglo-American Committee of Inquiry in 1946, see Goda et al., eds., *To the Gates of Jerusalem*. Ambassador Douglas noted on Beeley: "I do not think it is an exaggeration to say that about two thirds of the British ideas [regarding] Palestine during the past few years have originated in Harold's mind." Douglas to Satterthwaite, Joe #1, July 28, 1948, NARA, RG 59, MC 1390, reel 16, frames 252–253.

108. Douglas to secretary of state, no. 2712, June 19, 1948, *FRUS*, 1948, v. V, pt. 2, 1124–1125; also documents in *FRUS*, 1948, v. V, pt. 2, 1019–1020, 1099–1100, 1122–1124, 1143–1145.

109. Eban to Shertok, June 22, 1948, *DFPI*, v. 1, d. 218.

110. Memorandum by McClintock, June 23, 148, *FRUS*, 1948, v. V, pt. 2, 1134–1137; Jessup to secretary of state, no. 831, June 30, 1948, *FRUS*, 1948, v. V, pt. 2, 1161–1171.

factors influencing UK policy towards Palestine are similar if not wholly identical with ours."[111] *McDonald was not part of these discussions.*

The secretary, on his part, talked much more freely than I anticipated, urged me not to fall into the common practice of substituting long despatches for brief substantial ones. He referred to a current "communist rat hunt," highlighted by the previous day's testimony by Robert C. Alexander from the [State Department's] Visa Division that the UN is a funnel for the admission of many subversive agents,[112] the difficulties of securing independent reporting, and finally my own appointment. By the time he came to this point, we had become so friendly that he told me frankly that he had opposed my nomination (not, he added, because he objected to me, for he found in my record nothing to which exception could be taken), but because he resented having my appointment announced to him without any previous opportunity for consultation or comment. I left with the feeling that he is a square-shooter, but much more alert and vigorous than I had thought he would be.

Following this conference, I began to question the advisability of leaving with the president the memorandum which I had prepared so laboriously on NEA and the necessity for the naming by the president of a special assistant to the secretary on Palestine. Later my decision was definite, and I destroyed all copies of the memorandum, except one for my own files. As I left the secretary's office, I found Dean Rusk of the UN section and a group of reporters waiting for him.[113]

McDonald's memorandum for the president, which he destroyed save for a single copy, is dated July 21, 1948.

PERSONAL AND CONFIDENTIAL

To: The President
From: James G. McDonald

On the eve of my departure for Israel—I leave day after tomorrow—I feel impelled by my overriding loyalty to the President to submit this frank memorandum.

From my personal observations in recent weeks of the attitudes—acknowledged and subconscious—of the men in the Office of Near Eastern and African Affairs (NEA) with whom I have been working closely I am convinced

111. Jessup to secretary of state, no. 837, July 1, 1948, *FRUS*, 1948, v. V, pt. 2, 1180–1186.
112. Marshall refers to testimony before the Senate Judiciary Committee to the effect that hundreds of foreign agents came into the United States under UN diplomatic protection.
113. Dean Rusk (1909–1994), protégé of General Marshall during World War II; served in War Department, 1945–1946; joined Department of State permanently when Marshall became secretary as the director of the State Department's Office of United Nations Affairs; protested the recognition of Israel; advocated UN-sponsored legal solutions to the Palestine conflict in 1940s and 1950s. See Thomas W. Zeiler, *Dean Rusk: Defending the American Mission Abroad* (Wilmington, DE: Scholarly Resources, 2000), 19–22.

that the success of my mission to Israel and of the policy of the United States
Government on Palestine will depend largely upon new and direct supervi-
sion of NEA.

The transfer of Mr. Loy Henderson will in itself solve none of the diffi-
culties with NEA. On the contrary the Department's prompt naming of
Mr. Henderson's deputy Joseph C. Satterthwaite as Director foreshadows a
continuation of the Henderson tradition and practices in the NEA. This would
be fatal to the President's hopes.

I suggest that to assure the carrying out of the President's Palestine policy
it is necessary that [there] be appointed a Special Assistant to the Secretary of
State, under the Secretary, to have over-all policy power on all matters relat-
ing to Palestine and to have direct access to the Secretary.

This change will be vitally important during the next months.[114]

To the White House, where I showed Samuel I. Rosenman the draft of the
letter and the memorandum. He liked the letter and strengthened my feeling
that the memorandum should not be given to the president. Just before going
into the president's office, I told Clifford that I hoped he would call Charles
Sawyer[115] about Cummings since David Niles had failed to move Sawyer. Rather
to my surprise, Clifford begged off, suggesting that I speak to the president
about it, saying that if the latter gave him explicit instructions, he would call
Sawyer.

McDonald, like many US officials during the Cold War, was concerned about
social and economic factors in Israel that could either make the country vulnerable to a
communist takeover or create suspicion that the new state would become communist.
He was particularly interested in the Histadrut (the General Federation of Laborers)
and the Mapam Party, which was not communist but was friendly toward the
USSR. His interest in Cummings, who had served as the assistant chief of the State
Department's Bureau of Foreign Activity Correlation, probably reflected these con-
cerns. Cummings served McDonald as an economic attaché and also undertook some
intelligence work in Israel.

The president was extremely cordial but anticipated, I think, only a brief
and formal farewell call. I disillusioned him about this by talking as frankly as
I could on the subject matter of my memorandum. Indeed, at least three times
during our twenty minutes or so together, I explained the imperative necessity
from his point of view as well as mine that the Department be strengthened
on Palestine. In the course of this discussion, I told him that he could, if he
would, help me greatly in two ways, one of which would be relatively easy and

114. McDonald to the president, July 21, 1948, McDonald Papers, Columbia University,
box 5, folder 2.
115. Charles W. Sawyer (1887–1979), Roosevelt's ambassador to Belgium and minister to
Luxembourg, 1944–1946; Truman's secretary of commerce, 1948–1953.

the other he might consider undesirable. The first was to urge Charles Sawyer to release Cummings. His response was immediate. He asked for the name, called Sawyer on the phone and, though the latter gave him an argument, firmly but kindly insisted, and Cummings was released. The whole conversation was on the plane: Charles, I am asking you a personal favor. I know your problems, I know the difficulties, but this is a special situation, dangerous and important, etc.

As to the letter, he was equally prompt. Reading it through carefully, he said, "There is nothing here that I can't sign" and seemed about to sign my copy. I suggested he put it on his own stationary and asked him if he could have it before I left Clifford's office in about twenty minutes. He called his secretary and I had the letter in time.

> July 21, 1948
> Dear Mr. McDonald,
>
> In wishing you Godspeed in your important mission I am well aware of the difficulties in making effective our policy aimed at a peaceful settlement of differences among the nations of the Near East and co-operation among them.
>
> Success of your efforts will depend largely on teamwork and alertness of all persons concerned with this problem both here and abroad and upon hearty collaboration with you. In addition to your regular reports to the Department of State, I shall expect you to keep me personally informed on such matters as relate to the arms embargo, the appropriate time for full recognition, and types of assistance as may be required by and can properly be granted to the new State.
>
> Let me assure you that you have my fullest confidence and support.
>
> With all good wishes,
> Sincerely yours,
> Harry Truman

One example of ways in which White House and Department of State matters get mixed up; I showed him a copy of Weizmann's very cordial telegram to me about my appointment.[116] The president at once said, "Well, I answered that." When I showed him a copy of the actual reply which had gone out prepared by John Waldo, substitute on the Palestine desk,[117] and signed as a matter of routine by Lovett, the president recognized that this was a stupid way to have handled the matter, and he seemed somewhat annoyed that the Weizmann telegram took ten or twelve days to get to the State Department, but I did not urge him to take any remedial action.

---

116. Aaron Kleinman, ed., *The Letters and Papers of Chaim Weizmann* [hereafter *Weizmann Papers*], Series A, v. 23 (New York: Rutgers University Press, 1980), d. 195.
117. John A. Waldo Jr. (b. 1904), US Department of State, Division of Near Eastern Affairs.

Before and after the interview, I chatted with Senator James Howard McGrath, chairman of the Democratic National Committee, briefly about the substance of my memorandum.[118] He told me that Jacob Blaustein had tried to speak to him about it and related subjects, but he had told him to act through me. This interpretation was not the same as Blaustein's interpretation.

Clifford was delighted with the president's action on Cummings and heartily approved of the letter, which came into his office while I was still there. He expressed gratitude for my frequent calls to his mother, about which, he said, she always wrote him.[119]

Hurried over to the State Department official luncheon at Blair Lee House for Epstein and some of his colleagues, and for me and NEA officials, including Ernest A. Gross of the Legal Department of the Department of State.[120] Most of my talk during the luncheon was with Gross about the Department's interpretation of recognition and the reported differences between the White House and the State Department's lawyers on this subject. Judge Rosenman had previously referred to this. According to Gross, there had been de jure recognition of the state of Israel but only de facto recognition of the Provisional Government of Israel. To his mind the next step, de jure recognition of the government, could and should be taken without waiting for any change. Indeed, he emphasized that he saw very little practical difference between the two types of recognition. This attitude of his took on added importance in the light of my subsequent conversation with Lovett.

The State Department's initial insistence on de facto rather than de jure recognition of Israel in May 1948 aimed to limit anger in London and in the Arab world. In the White House, Samuel Rosenman noted to Clark Clifford that de facto recognition was indeed something less than full recognition. Clifford wanted the problem rectified. The Israelis viewed it as a snub, the Soviets had followed the US step with full de jure recognition, and Clifford worried that the Republicans could exploit the issue in the November presidential election. Gross's opinion was based on Truman's statement of May 14: "The United States recognizes the provisional government as the de facto authority of the State of Israel." To Gross, the mention of the "State of Israel" assumed de jure recognition.[121]

118. James Howard McGrath (1903–1966), governor of Rhode Island, 1941–1945; solicitor general of the United States, 1945–1946; US senator from Rhode Island, 1947–1949; chairman, Democratic National Committee, 1946–1949, and managed Truman's election campaign in 1948; US attorney general, 1949–1952.

119. Georgia McAdams Clifford held a children's story hour in Chautauqua in the 1930s. McDonald's daughter Barbara attended it.

120. Ernest A. Gross (1906–1999), joined State Department as a legal adviser, 1931; served in other government agencies, 1933–1945; rejoined State Department as primary legal adviser and as assistant secretary of state for occupied areas under John Hilldring.

121. See Austin to secretary of state, no. 653, May 15, 1948. *FRUS*, 1948, v. V, pt. 2, 997–998; Memorandum by Loy Henderson, May 16, 1948, *FRUS*, 1948, v. V, pt. 2, 1001–1002; Memorandum by Lovett, May 26, 1948, *FRUS*, 1948, v. V, pt. 2, 1051–1053; Rosenman to

There were no speeches, Satterthwaite speaking briefly and well, Epstein replied in few words, and I similarly. Satterthwaite and some of the other NEA boys and I drove over to the Department together, where Fraser Wilkins and I went in to see Lovett. This interview, which proved to be very important, I had arranged myself despite Satterthwaite's opinion, expressed a few days earlier, that it was unnecessary for me to see the under secretary again. This conference, like that with the secretary, was much more satisfactory than I dared hope because both Lovett and I were frank.

Most of the talk was about recognition. From it I saw clearly the difference between the White House's position and that of Lovett, and, perhaps I should add, of the Department. Clifford explained that he hoped I would understand that the White House was anxious for action by September; that I should find out whether or not the government of Israel regarded such action as important; and if so, they [White House] urged that they [Israel] facilitate it by changes, which would make it easier. Lovett, in contrast, kept urging the necessity of concrete changes in Israel such as a constituent assembly or elections. The government must prove that it is not a junta. He stressed that the Irgun and Sternists still continued to be recalcitrant, to make their own proclamations, and in other ways to indicate potential or active hostility to Tel Aviv. Lovett belittled the idea that there were technical differences between the White House and the lawyers of the Department of State on the issue. He said it was not a question [of] technicalities or law, but of politics. He implied that the Department of State could have no part in this, that it had to consider, on the contrary, not taking action which would be embarrassing in other parts of the world, Kashmir, Nepal, et al. Clearly, he is inclined to delay, I would say, as long as possible, in contrast with the White House's desire to act as soon as practicable. I showed Lovett the letter from the president. He read it carefully, made no comment but was, I think, impressed, as certainly was Wilkins.

I underlined with Lovett, as I had with the secretary, my desire to do an objective job of reporting. I was frank about my background and my differences with NEA and many of the men in the field. Despite these avowals, or perhaps because of them, Lovett's reaction was such as to encourage me in the belief that he is friendlier. My general impression of him is that he is very conservative, even perhaps more than that, very sympathetic with Britain, and has been convinced by [Ambassador Lewis] Douglas of Bevin's good faith, and that while perhaps not being pro-Arab, he is certainly not pro-Jewish. Despite all of these elements, I think he is doing what he believes to be to the best interests of the country. Anyhow, we parted on friendly terms.

Lovett noted, "I told Mr. McDonald that I had no specific instructions to give him at this time with regard to American policy in Palestine but that we would inform

Clifford, July 29, 1948, Truman Library, Papers of Clark M. Clifford, Subject File, 1945–1954, box 12, folder Palestine, Misc. Correspondence, 1 of 3. Also Peter L. Hahn, *Caught in the Middle East*, 50–51.

him of developments as they took place in the future."[122] *McDonald later informed Arthur Lourie of the meeting with Lovett. McDonald, Lourie wrote, "described Mr. Lovett as not basically anti-Semitic or hostile, but as conservative, pro-British and still troubled by ideas of Red infiltration into Israel."*[123]

Wilkins brought in my passports and tickets, and together we cleared up such matters as had to be attended to before I left Washington. John L. Sullivan, secretary of the Navy, was friendly enough but seemingly almost a little suspicious of what I wanted.[124] Unlike Symington, who gave instructions that we should have the best planes available and suitable for the Tel Aviv field, he said that he was so opposed to naval vessels being in Palestinian waters [that] one could not be kept at Tel Aviv, but that there would always be some within easy reach. He also indicated his opposition to any continued commitment on any sort of patrol of the coast. I told him I thought this was very wise. I left feeling that we had gotten acquainted, but not sure that the gain was greater than that.

My final conference of a long day was with Lewis L. Strauss of the Atomic Energy Commission.[125] Even though Forrestal had called Strauss about seeing me, I was surprised at the latter's warmth. We then talked about South Africa and the community there and my new job. Strauss said he was sure that of all the ambassadors and ministers now in service I was the one who would most certainly be renamed by the new president. He seemed to have no doubt that there would be a change in administration. Despite his traditional anti-Zionism and his knowledge of my position, he gave the impression that he thought my choice was a perfect one. He asked me to stay over for dinner, saying he would cancel his engagement, but I was by that time so tired that I insisted on leaving on schedule, taking the 7:45 plane. He did one favor by promising to call one of his old colleagues in the Navy to give added assurance about the type of attaché I would have.

Thursday, July 22

Cleaned up odds and ends at the office. Luncheon at the Waldorf, Ben Abrams host. [Guests included Samuel Leidersdorf,[126] Lester Udell,[127] Morris

---

122. Memorandum by Lovett, July 21, 1948, *FRUS*, 1948, v. V, pt. 2, 1232–1233.
123. Memorandum by Lourie, July 23, 1948, *DFPI*, v. 1, d. 366.
124. John L. Sullivan (1899–1982), assistant secretary of the US Navy, 1946–1947; first secretary of the Navy following organization of the Department of Defense, 1947–1949.
125. Lewis Lichtenstein Strauss (1896–1974), Jewish philanthropist and government official; involved with JDC after World War I; executive board, American Jewish Committee; served in Naval Intelligence during World War II; appointed as a commissioner of the new Atomic Energy Commission by Truman in 1947; skeptical of Zionism.
126. Samuel David Leidersdorf (1881–1968), New York-born founder of one of the world's largest accounting firms; active in American Jewish Committee, longtime treasurer and fundraiser for New York branch of United Jewish Appeal; also did McDonald's income taxes.
127. Lester Udell (1894–1965), clothier who sent winter coats to DPs in Europe; chairman, Board of Directors of Beth Midrash Gavoha, a Haredi (ultra-Orthodox) yeshiva founded in 1943.

Haft[128] and James Rosenberg]. There were no speeches. I talked informally about the problem of personal defense and reparations. I told something of the story of my appointment. Nevertheless, the central problem was quite clear in everybody's mind. They all were deeply friendly in their attitudes. I left with the feeling that each would welcome a chance to be useful in any way. Before lunch I spoke with Mrs. [Georgia] Clifford on the phone. She evidently was touched by my doing so. She sent her warmest love to Bobby. In the late afternoon someone called me at home about the possibility of seeing Fahy, whom I had met a couple of weeks earlier in Washington, in New York Thursday. I pleaded my inability to meet anyone unless at the boat. Mrs. Colt's party, an out-of-doors buffet supper, was wholly delightful. About twenty-five friends were there. I had an opportunity to talk with Congressman Gwinn, who may later cooperate in Washington.[129]

Emanuel Neumann called to speak about personalities. Suggested Fahy and one or two other names, none of which seemed to me suitable. We talked about Washington, but I was uncommunicative except in the most general way. I found my earlier impression strengthened that he would act only when his own personal or immediate organizational interest was involved. Talked on the telephone also with Arthur Lourie; made date for the next day.

Friday, July 23

The packing and trip to the boat [with Bobby, Herbert Cummings and Harriet Clark] was without incident except for Morris Waldman's[130] stupidly losing Lourie's car, resulting in an extra hour of anxiety and delay. Lourie and I discussed a number of problems, but most of the time I did the talking. I asked him to make clear to Tel Aviv two points: One, what may have seemed my dilatoriness in leaving was not, as had been said, the result of my desire to see my grandchild, but because of the following necessities: a) building my staff and fighting through with the Department the problem of adequate personnel and financing; b) briefing and reading the files in the Department; c) protecting "my rear."[131]

The other subject was of de jure recognition. I asked him to explain to Tel Aviv that from the Department's point of view there would have to be some change in the situation in Israel such as [convening a] constituent assembly or [holding] elections, or something else indicating popular support. At the

128. Morris W. Haft (1886–1968), major clothing manufacturer (Haft Bros.); president, Brooklyn Federation of Jewish Charities; co-founder of the United Jewish Appeal.
129. Ralph Waldo Gwinn (1884–1962), Indiana-born Republican congressman from New York, 1945–1959; earned his law degree from Columbia University.
130. Morris D. Waldman (1879–1963), Hungarian-born social worker and director of numerous charities; executive secretary, American Jewish Committee, 1928–1945; tried afterward to reconcile his skepticism toward Zionism with the state of Israel, which he supported.
131. McDonald also noted that he wanted to be able to visit Ernest Bevin in London, Chaim Weizmann in Switzerland, and Pope Pius XII. See the Israeli reports in *DFPI*, v. 1, d. 366, 418.

White House the attitude was less technical; there the desire was to move just as soon as possible. Moreover, the lawyers there gave sanction to such an attitude. My emphasis to Lourie was that if the Israeli authorities considered a change very desirable, they should seriously study the possibilities of facilitating it. Incidentally, there was some reference to the work of Eliahu Epstein in Washington. I underlined the importance of the fine relationships he had established with our people and asked that this be passed on. There was no time for Lourie to tell me his impressions of Palestine, from where he has just returned, because of the confusion incident to Mr. Waldman's mistake.[132] The usual photographers and press people, the latter vainly trying to get me to be foolishly indiscreet.

Dave Niles called. I told him of the Wednesday conferences. He was delighted that the president had acted on Cummings and with the action on the letter. As to the memorandum, he thought perhaps it was wise not to have left it with the president but suggested that I leave a copy with him, which he would keep in his safe for use in an emergency. Later, I decided not to do this either.

One July 29, the day before his ship landed at Southampton, McDonald wrote the following to David Niles:

> *Here is a copy of the [Truman] letter. I hope you think it is about right. Certainly I thought the Chief wonderful to give it to me so quickly.*
>
> *I am not, however, enclosing [my] memorandum, partly because I do not have it with me and partly because I am a little doubtful about the wisdom of sending it even though I am confident that you would handle it with the utmost discretion. Let's talk about it on the telephone when I have reached Switzerland.[133] By that time, I will have talked to both Bevin and Weizmann. Moreover, by then I may have some more useful suggestions than I had earlier about an organic change at home. I will cable you from Switzerland suggesting a time when it might be convenient for you and possible for me to take your call.*
>
> *My final conferences at the Department, particularly those with the Under Secretary and the Secretary, were more satisfactory than I dared to hope for. The Secretary, for example, could not have been franker.*
>
> *I want to thank you for everything you have done for me during the past difficult months and to tell you that the knowledge that you are at your desk will be much needed assurance to me.*
>
> *Please also tell your Chief that I am personally and deeply grateful for his indications of confidence and that with this as my first line of defense at home, I hope to be able to do something to advance his policy.[134]*

132. Lourie's account of this meeting is in *DFPI*, v. 1, d. 366. He reported McDonald's comment that Truman was looking for an excuse to accord de jure recognition.

133. Editorial note, entry of August 3, 1948.

134. McDonald to David Niles, July 29, 1948, McDonald Papers, Columbia University, box 16, folder 7.

A similar letter was sent to Clifford on the same day, in which McDonald added that he did not trust the security of the telephone lines in London, and that it would be best to talk by telephone after he reached Switzerland.[135]

My impressions after a month of study and work in Washington with the men in the Department of State and at the White House leaves me with a much fuller picture than I could have had previously of the difficulties of my mission. It is true that the recent military developments preceding the latest truce show clearly the Jewish military superiority—a superiority underlined by the top-secret documents that I have been reading, in which the British repeatedly warn the Arabs that they are beaten, and Abdullah that his Legion has but four days more of ammunition. On the other hand, the coming of the truce before a clear decision was reached about Jerusalem, the Negev, and some of the other areas leaves the Israeli government at a disadvantage with the dissident groups [the Irgun and Lehi], who can argue with a measure of reason that, had the fighting gone on for another fortnight, the Jewish position would have been very much stronger. They will tend to blame Tel Aviv for weakness in yielding to US and UN pressure.[136]

It is clear from what Lovett and others in the NEA have said, or [have] left unsaid, that they regard continued open or threatened opposition [from the dissident groups] as justification for no de jure recognition. And such opposition tends to make more difficult and to postpone such steps as a constituent assembly and a general election, which NEA holds to be essential to such recognition. The top-secret documents indicate too the bias of the NEA in favor of the Arab position, at least to the extent of accepting the thesis that Arab friendship is essential to avoid Russian penetration into the Arab world to the detriment, if not the destruction, of our strategic and oil position there. Tendentious circular inquiry by Loy Henderson asking in effect for reports from the American representatives in the Arab states that "excessive humiliation" of those states would lead to revolution since only one or two of the governments is firmly grounded. Such revolt would lead to invitations by one or the other party to Russia.

Revealing, too, in the documents is the enthusiastic support by Lewis Douglas in London of the British position. Repeatedly he becomes almost poetic in his appeal for "unity" with the British.[137] He seems not to realize at all that Bevin is anything other than objective on both sides and anxious only to

135. McDonald to Clifford, July 29, 1948, McDonald Papers, Columbia University, box 9, folder 16. See also entry for August 3, 1948.

136. Israeli agreement to UN Security Council Resolution 54 of July 15, 1948, for an immediate cease-fire came after a heated cabinet discussion in which Ben-Gurion argued for continued fighting to relieve isolated Jewish settlements. Yet the IDF also needed a respite. See Gabriel Sheffer, *Moshe Sharett: Biography of a Political Moderate* (New York: Oxford University Press, 1996), pp. 343–345.

137. Douglas's most important reports from May to July 1948 and after are printed in *FRUS*, 1948, v. V, pt. 2.

get a fair settlement. Perhaps, however, the most disquieting element in the situation, which my month of briefing disclosed, is the attitude of the men in NEA [who will] have to process my despatches and be my channel with the government. Loy Henderson's "love letter" to me[138] and the cordialness of his successor, Satterthwaite, and the men under him, do not disguise the fact that I am regarded as an outsider, as a presidential appointment "put over" on the Department. Whether the men will go so far as to distort my despatches, as I have been warned repeatedly they will, I of course do not know. But it would be fatuous to assume that they have changed their fundamental preconceptions. Satterthwaite is less strong and will be less dominant than Loy Henderson and will, I think, not intend to be other than correct in his relations with me. The same, I think, will apply to Mattison and Wilkins. But they would be less than human if they did not welcome opportunities to prove they had been correct in their judgments, [while] those, including the president, Clifford, and others, whose views I represent, had been mistaken.

The cloak and dagger details of intrigue, distortion, espionage, etc. which have been repeated to me many times by men whose judgment commands respect and whose friendship for me I cannot doubt, give me a bizarre background to my mission as I leave. Nonetheless, I am still inclined to be skeptical about the charges that there will be constant efforts by some of those whose duty it would be to work with me to betray me. Encouraging at the end were the attitudes of the president and of the secretary; the latter's frankness and the former's letter. Encouraging, too, was the attitude of Lovett, though on this I have to have some reservations. Whether the scheme for the special assistant to the secretary will in fact be carried out, I doubt. With Hilldring's elimination, the difficulties of finding someone who would be enthusiastically welcomed by the secretary are very great. Nonetheless, the need for this change is so vital that I intend to continue to strive to bring it about.

VOYAGE

Saw a good deal of Mr. Sidney L. Herold and his family; we became, I thought, good friends.[139] Others whom I met and chatted with more or less casually included Dr. Mr. [Harry] Greenstein, on his way to Germany and perhaps to Palestine in connection with work of the adviser to [US military governor in Germany] General Lucius Clay.[140]

138. Not found.

139. Sidney L. Herold (1880–1950), successful Shreveport, Louisiana, attorney, scholar of international law, and executive director of the ZOA, Southwestern Region.

140. Harry Greenstein (1896–1971), Baltimore attorney and social welfare leader; executive director, Associated Jewish Charities in Baltimore, 1928–1965; director, UNRRA welfare mission to Greece, Albania, and Yugoslavia, 1943–1945; visited Vatican at the request of Rabbi Yitzhak Herzog in Palestine to gain support for a Jewish state, autumn 1945; special consultant to the adviser on Jewish Affairs to Commander of US Forces in Europe, July 1948–February 1949; adviser on Jewish Affairs to Commander of US Forces in Europe, February–October 1949. See entries of April 6, 1949, and October 22, 1949.

The news [received the fourth day at sea] about Janet and her baby [the infant did not survive] was more unnerving than I believed anything could be. But, supporting one another, Bobby and I did the best we could.

Friday, July 30

Landing at Southampton and arrival in London were simplified by the cooperation of the consul general [George Tait] and his colleagues and by that of Mr. Lewis Jones[141] and the embassy car at Waterloo. Bobby and I went directly to the Dorchester and Miss Clark and Cummings to Claridges.

In my first talk with Jones, I emphasized the importance of my seeing Bevin and my desire to do this as early in the week as possible in order to get on to Switzerland, Rome, and Tel Aviv. To the embassy at four, for my conference with the ambassador. We were met by Paul Felix Warburg [US attaché] with whom we chatted indifferently until the ambassador was ready. Warburg's attitude confirmed what I had heard earlier. Lewis Douglas lived up to his reputation for friendliness, seemed to be frank, and gave repeated manifestations of weariness whenever the subject of the Berlin crisis arose. Early in our talk I showed him the president's letter and told him of my desire to see Bevin and his colleagues. He replied that it had been tentatively arranged and would let me know Tuesday more about the time. He thought that I would be able to go on from Bevin to Hector McNeil[142] and then to Michael Wright.[143]

As to the British position, he said he was confident that His Majesty's Government had accepted the inevitability of the Jewish state and was delaying recognition only in order to maintain its influence with the Arab states and to avoid unnecessary conflict. Bevin's personal attitude he thought was this, too. As to the latter's position towards a whole people, Douglas hesitated to give a categorically affirmative reply from which hesitation I took my own conclusions.[144] Douglas thought that the British military had been surprised by the Arab weakness. I could not but wonder whether on this point the [General Headquarters] had been quite frank with Douglas. On the vital question of His Majesty's Government's attitude towards [Israel's] frontiers, Douglas indicated no appreciation of the vital significance of the Negev to Israel. Typical of an objective observer was Bobby's comment, as she heard my dictating the above, to the effect that she got the impression that Douglas accepted all the views of His Majesty's Government.

---

141. George Lewis Jones (1907–1971), US vice consul, Cairo, 1941–1942; assistant chief, Division of Near Eastern Affairs, 1945–1946; counselor of embassy, London, 1946–1949; considered the US embassy's expert on the Middle East; director, Division of Near Eastern Affairs, 1950–1952.

142. Hector McNeil (1907–1955), parliamentary under secretary for foreign affairs, 1945; minister of state, Foreign Office after 1946; and de facto deputy to the foreign secretary.

143. Michael Wright (1901–1976), superintending under-secretary of state, North American Department, British Foreign Office after 1948.

144. The inference being that Bevin was antisemitic.

In answer to my question about Bernadotte, the ambassador had no comment, not being well acquainted with Bernadotte. Douglas thought that [Arthur] Creech-Jones[145] was not figuring largely in the Palestine problem. At any rate, Douglas had not ever discussed it with Creech-Jones. In general, I got the impression that the ambassador had recently been so absorbed in the Berlin crisis that his knowledge of other developments had become rather vague. At the end he assured me that he was confident that if only we, presumably our government, were patient, we and the British could work along together in harmony and achieve a solution. Patience, he added, was the watchword.

I wish I could have shared this optimism. The weakness of the ambassador's position seemed to me to be a lack of comprehension of the real attitude of either Jews or Arabs: the determination of the former not to yield anything of the November 29 settlement, and of the latter not to acquiesce in the Jewish state. Moreover, the assumption of complete good faith or of objectivity in the attitude of other parties was, it seemed to me, rather naïve. Similarly might be characterized the assumption that the necessity of Anglo-American cooperation required acquiescence on our part. I left with the understanding that Douglas would let me know Tuesday what time that day I should see Bevin. Made tentative arrangements to have a long talk with Lewis Jones.

Long session with Ivor Joseph Linton, the acting representative of Israel here.[146] He told me of the refusal of His Majesty's Government to concede any official status to the Israeli delegation or to any individual. He said he had about reached the point where he could no longer continue to be merely tolerated as an unrecognized "agent." He told me that Weizmann was anxious to see me at Vevey.[147] Linton developed elaborately his thesis that His Majesty's Government has not really accepted as final a viable Israeli state.[148] He questioned their acceptance of an internationalized Jerusalem or of Jewish control of the Negev and Aqaba. On the former point he cited the sudden reversal of Alexander Cadogan and other British representatives at Lake Success on the US trusteeship resolution of this year. This, he felt, foreshadowed the British purpose to pave the way for Abdullah's seizure of Jerusalem.[149] He was not surprised,

145. Arthur Creech-Jones (1891–1964), secretary of state for the colonies, 1946–1950; deferred to Bevin on Middle Eastern Affairs.
146. Ivor Joseph Linton (1900–1982), Russian-born English Zionist; Jewish Agency representative to London. Because the UK had yet to recognize Israel, he had no official status at this point beyond his position as political secretary of the Jewish Agency Office in London.
147. In Switzerland on Lake Geneva. Owing to the aftereffects of his eye treatments, Weizmann had yet to travel to Israel since Israel's declaration of independence.
148. Israel military intelligence had drawn the same conclusion. See Zahava Ostfeld, *Tsava nolad: shelavim ʿikariyim b-veniyat ha-tsava be-hanhagato shel David Ben-Gurion* [*An Army Is Born: Main Stages in the Buildup of the Army Under the Leadership of David Ben-Gurion*], 2 vols. (Tel Aviv: Ministry of Defense, 1994), vol. 1, 363.
149. Alexander Cadogan (1884–1968), permanent under secretary, Foreign Office, 1938–1946; British representative to the United Nations, 1946–1950. The British refused to support or reject the US trusteeship proposal of March 19, 1948, which would have delayed the end of the Mandate. They did, however, back the US-backed Security Council Resolution 48 of April 23, 1948, which called for a truce in Palestine and established the UN Truce Commission in Jerusalem.

therefore, when that attempt was actually made by the Legion. Of the several personalities involved here, he thought that [Harold] Beeley was now more understanding than Wright or the chief. He was sorry I would not have a chance to see my young friend.[150] He thought that my visit here might be of very substantial importance. I urged him to explain to his colleagues in Tel Aviv my reasons for not going there more directly and immediately. He said he would. We agreed to meet again before I left.

Saturday, July 31

Dined at Sir Simon Marks's.[151] The food was, as always, perfect. The discussion would have been more satisfactory had not Miriam[152] and Rebecca,[153] as usual, continued to interrupt any talk of more than a sentence in length. Simon and Israel Sieff[154] and I had a few minutes of serious conversation before we joined the ladies after dinner. It centered on the problem of the relationship between the Diaspora Zionist groups and the Yishuv on the Government of Israel. Both men were intensely interested in my prospective conferences here, and I promised to talk with them before I left. Simon and Sieff were both touchingly appreciative of my appointment and can, I am sure, be counted on to aid in any way possible. I checked with them about the meeting at New Court with Lionel and Anthony de Rothschild in January 1934. They confirmed my recollection that I had come there with Harry Sacher,[155] Weizmann, Sieff, and Simon Marks.[156] Home after arranging to be with them for part of the day on Monday.

Martin Jones, *Failure in Palestine: British and United States Policy After the Second World War* (New York: Mansell, 1986), 314–316.

150. Probably David Herbert Samuel, grandson of Herbert Samuel. See entry of November 2, 1949.

151. Sir Simon Marks (1888–1964), Manchester-born British businessman, philanthropist, and Zionist; with Israel Sieff built Marks and Spencer, a penny bazaar chain, into a major business; part of Chaim Weizmann's Manchester group before World War I; helped press for Balfour Declaration; knighted in 1944 for work on the wartime Scientific Coordination Committee.

152. Simon Marks's wife, Israel Sieff's sister.

153. Israel Sieff's wife, Simon Marks's sister.

154. Israel Moses Sieff (1889–1972), Manchester-born British businessman, philanthropist, and Zionist; also part of Weizmann's Manchester group; business associate and brother-in-law to Simon Marks. On the death of his son Daniel Sieff in 1933 at age 18, he established, along with Marks, the Daniel Sieff Research Institute in Rehovot in 1934, which later became the Weizmann Institute of Science.

155. Harry Sacher (1881–1971), London-born Zionist, journalist [*Manchester Guardian*], author of books on Palestine and Israel, and lawyer; aided Weizmann in securing the Balfour Declaration; moved to Palestine in 1920 and returned to London in 1930; law firm Sacher, Horowitz & Klebanoff had offices in London, Haifa, and Jerusalem in the 1920s; married Simon Marks's sister Miriam (1892–1975) in 1915 and became a Marks & Spencer director in 1930.

156. McDonald refers to his February 5, 1934, fundraising meeting attended by these figures. See Breitman et al., eds., *Advocate for the Doomed*.

2. August 1948

Bobby and I started off to the Wallace collection only to find it and the National Galleries closed in the morning, and so on to St. Paul's, where we arrived in time for the morning service. I was very glad to go, because I had not been in this marvelous example of Christopher Wren's genius in many years. Later, we walked across the Thames and admired the dome, which rivals in perfection and size that of St. Peter's. Had lunch with Eli Karlin and his uncle, Arnold Karlinski, his wife, and Peter.[1]

Dinner with the "family" and Mr. and Mrs. Lewis Jones. Jones and I had a long and, for me, valuable talk during and following the meal. Replying to my question, he asserted, as had the ambassador, that the British government has accepted in good faith the existence of Israel and delays recognition only in order to maintain its influence with the Arabs and in order to persuade them to "acquiesce" in the new state of affairs. To secure full acquiescence, His Majesty's Government is trying, in addition, to use pressure to win some concessions, which would enable the Arabs to face more successfully their peoples. He seemed to feel that there were now no essential differences among the British leaders and that Creech-Jones had withdrawn from the issue.

His Majesty's Government's attitude towards Jerusalem, Aqaba, and the Negev were all directed by the above considerations. From this I got that the Bernadotte proposal of a few weeks ago was essentially that of His Majesty's Government.[2] Jones had no very convincing reply to my question as to how giving Jerusalem to Abdullah would satisfy more than one Arab state. About Haifa and the oil refinery, Jones was very clear and informative. The shutting

---

1. The Karlinskis, good friends of McDonald, came to England from Ukraine during the Russian Revolution. They lived in various places thereafter, engaged in various businesses, including the manufacture of construction materials. Arnold's sister Sonia lived in Israel. She changed the surnames of her children, Noah and Eli, to Karlin. Eli Karlin (1926–1966) was born in Haifa, earned a Ph.D. in English from Yale University in 1947, and held dual British-Israeli citizenship. He lived in London from 1948 to 1949, and then in Israel from 1949 to 1950. He and his older brother Noah helped McDonald with various information-gathering tasks in Israel. Sonia was part of McDonald's social circle there.

2. See editorial note in entry of July 20, 1948. Similarities existed between British aims and those of Bernadotte, and planning became more coordinated in August after Israel rejected Bernadotte's original plan. Bernadotte needed British and US backing, and each government hoped to have Bernadotte, as UN mediator, endorse the idea of the smaller Jewish state that each envisioned. In-person consultation on the details between the United States, Britain, and Bernadotte came in mid-September 1948. See Louis, *The British Empire in the Middle East*, 540–542; Cohen, *Fighting World War III from the Middle East*, 106–107.

off by Iraq of the flow of oil had been the first step in the closing of the refinery. Later came the withdrawal of Arab workers and the British attempt to negotiate with Iraq for reopening of the line; the subsequent Jewish operation of the refinery utilizing the existing crude, and thus, securing approximately a fortnight's supply of gasoline had, in the opinion of His Majesty's Government and also of Lewis Jones, served to delay accord with Iraq.[3] Jones did not dissent very sharply, however, from my comment that it was always possible to find an excuse for failure. When I showed Jones the president's letter, he seemed impressed. Later, he told me with seeming conviction that he thought my appointment was a brilliant move on the part of the government. He explained this by saying that with my record for friendliness, I should be able to exercise substantial influence for moderation in Israel and to discourage swings leftward and rightward. I did not accept this optimistic view.

We then went on to discuss the contrasting or at least varying views as between the White House and the State Department. I used the question of de jure recognition as an illustration.[4] I urged that he and the ambassador should keep in mind that the White House's future program is fairly clear and that the possibility of future unilateral action should not be ignored. I stressed that I too believed in Anglo-American cooperation but that we ought to be more markedly in the driver's seat.

The day previous, Saturday morning, Jones had called me up to say that in the course of his talk with the ambassador, there had been expressed some concern lest there be publicity in connection with my requested session with Ernest Bevin. I assured him that, so far as I was concerned, there would be no leak, and I understood the reasons for the desired non-publicity. Instead of being surprised by this request, I was rather surprised that the ambassador had not made it earlier, because it is obvious that the interview, if misinterpreted, could be embarrassing to Douglas. On the whole, I like Jones almost as much as I did not like the madame.

Speaking of Dr. Weizmann and the delay in his return to Palestine, Jones said that he understood that this was because the Israeli authorities estimated that it would require from four to eight hundred men to guarantee Weizmann's safety. This I had heard previously but with a basic difference. My understanding was that the defense was against danger from Arab attack on Rehovot should Weizmann live there, as he naturally would. Jones put it, however, in a quite different way. The defense would be necessary against the danger of

3. With the end of the Mandate the Iraqi government halted the flow of crude oil from Kirkuk to the refinery at Haifa, the third largest in the Middle East, which was owned by Consolidated Refineries, Inc., a British-run company. Work at the refinery stopped. The Provisional Government, after failing to convince the British to restart operations, assumed control and refined the small supply of crude oil—40,000 tons—left in the tanks. Israel negotiated with Romania afterward for supplies of crude. Uri Bialer, *Oil and the Arab-Israeli Conflict, 1948–1963* (New York: St. Martin's, 1999), 21–58; Hahn, *Caught in the Middle East*, 124; Natan Aridan, *Britain, Israel and Anglo-Jewry, 1949–57* (London: Routledge, 2004), 36–37.

4. See entry of July 21, 1948.

assassination [by Israeli extremists]. The importance of this rumor is the manner in which it can be used to discredit the Israeli government and to help justify delaying recognition, for if the regime cannot protect its own president from assassination except by excessive precautions, it does not deserve recognition. After dinner, completed travel arrangements to Geneva, Rome and on to Athens.

Monday, August 2

After a couple of hours work, off to the country with the [Simon] Markses.

Tuesday, August 3

Met Jones and chatted with him for a few minutes before we joined the ambassador and drove over to the Foreign Office. En route the talk was nonconsequential except that the ambassador said that, after we had seen Bevin for five minutes or so, Jones would take me in to Bernard Burrows, the head of what corresponds to the Near Eastern Division,[5] in lieu of conferences with McNeil, who is out of town, and Wright, who is leaving.

Douglas reported to Marshall in a telegram that Bevin now thought in terms of the following settlement, which incorporated parts of the Bernadotte Plan. Israel had to be recognized as a reality, not linked with Transjordan. But it would include the Western Galilee and not the Negev, the status of which would be left to the Arabs to determine. This would allow Britain to maintain a land bridge from Egypt to Transjordan. Jerusalem would be under an international administration of some sort. Haifa would become either a free port or be placed under international administration. Jaffa's status would be determined later. Bevin hoped that Washington would work with London and the UN to bring about such a settlement. As it was, Bevin said, the plan would be hard to sell to the Arabs.

Neither this telegram nor future State Department correspondence concerning peace conditions for Palestine was shared with McDonald while he was in London.[6] He had to find out Bevin's views on his own.

We were shown into Bevin's office promptly. He was sitting [in] back of his desk glowering. He is larger than I remembered him, with a good color, obviously in a deliberately unpleasant mood. As an opening conciliatory move, I said that I had never assumed that his statement made to us at the luncheon given to the Anglo-American Committee of Inquiry in January 1946 had been

5. Bernard Burrows (1910–2002), career British diplomat; served in Cairo, 1938–1945; head of the Eastern Department in the Foreign Office, 1945–1950. See Sir Bernard Burrows, *Diplomat in a Changing World* (London: Memoir Club, 2001).
6. Douglas to secretary of state, no. 3484, August 2, 1948, *FRUS*, 1948, v. V, pt. 2, 1266–1271.

as unqualified as [Bartley] Crum had written.[7] Immediately, in a tone of arrogance, which bordered on insolence, he replied: "On the contrary, I gave an unequivocal pledge that I would accept the report if it were unanimous. Moreover, I kept my pledge. There were ten points in your program. I accepted all ten. President Truman accepted only one."[8]

I was so aghast at the effrontery of this distortion that I waited to see if Douglas would make some comment, but he remained silent and then seized the first opportunity to introduce me. Bevin went on to emphasize his charge that the sole responsibility for the non-acceptance of our report and, hence, for the subsequent developments in Palestine was at Truman's door. Bevin then launched into an attack on the Jews, charging that they were not grateful for all Britain had done for them in Palestine, that they had deliberately shot British police and soldiers, hanged sergeants, and now were alienating British opinion by their attitude towards the Arab refugees.[9] He said that many of these refugees had been driven out of areas in which there had been no fighting and were now in dire conditions.

I timidly ventured to say that it would be helpful to me if I could look forward to having a British colleague. He flushed and said, "That is something which I can't discuss." I mildly replied that I had not meant to put a leading question, but merely to state a fact. Douglas said something about the general situation, to which Bevin replied in effect that it was too bad that he and his colleagues had to be bothered at this time of [the Berlin] crisis by Palestine. One got from the very brief conference the following impressions:

1) Bevin is bitterly resentful that he has not been able to make good his boast that he would stake his reputation on success in Palestine;[10]
2) He has worked himself apparently into the conviction that Truman, if not wholly, is at least primarily responsible for this failure, and he is bitterly angry at the president;[11]
3) Not unnaturally, he finds another scapegoat in what the Israeli government does or does not do;

7. Bartley C. Crum (1900–1959), corporate and celebrity attorney; member of the Anglo-American Committee, 1946. His account of Bevin's comment is in his memoir of the Committee, *Behind the Silken Curtain: A Personal Account of Anglo-American Diplomacy in Palestine and the Middle East* (New York: Simon & Schuster, 1947), 61.

8. Bevin's critical promise of July 28, 1946, to accept the recommendations of the Anglo-American Committee if they were unanimous is covered in Goda et al., eds., *To the Gates of Jerusalem*, 58–59, 232–233.

9. The IZL had kidnapped and hanged two British sergeants on June 30, 1947, in retaliation for the British hanging of two members of the IZL on June 29. It acted despite calls from Yishuv representatives to spare the British sergeants. Michael J. Cohen, *Britain's Moment in Palestine: Retrospect and Perspectives, 1917–1948* (New York: Routledge, 2014), 476–478.

10. On announcing the formation of the Anglo-American Committee for Palestine in the House of Commons in November 1945, Bevin proclaimed, "I will stake my political future on solving the problem." Alan Bullock, *Ernest Bevin: Foreign Secretary, 1945–1951* (London: Heineman, 1983), 179.

11. Discussed in Goda et al., eds., *To the Gates of Jerusalem*, 224–268.

4) And perhaps this is most important: he has developed the technique to the point of a fine art of arrogantly taking the offensive in order to put at a disadvantage the person with whom he is dealing. In other words, he is the bully who is carrying over into the Foreign Office the worst of his traits as a trade union leader. I had the feeling as I left that the proper way to negotiate with him would be to call his bluff and let him know that the act, which he put on, is regarded as a sign of weakness, rather than of strength. I did not get the impression, however, that Mr. Douglas would share this view.

After the meeting, Joseph Linton, the Israeli representative in London, reported McDonald's comment that "in the face of Mr. Bevin's outburst, he [McDonald] had not been able to make any of the points that he had prepared. He thought, however, that the interview had been useful, because it had given him an insight into the atmosphere of the Foreign Office."[12]

Went on with Jones to see Bernard Burrows, whom I found to be the usual cultured, soft-spoken British Foreign Office official. To him I said most of the things I would have said to Bevin, had I had a mission to do so and had the latter shown less of a dictator mentality. Parenthetically, I might add that neither in my two talks with Mussolini nor my one with Hitler did I get a stronger sense of ruthlessness than I did from Bevin.[13]

I talked about the political situation at home, and I said that there would always be an election on hand or in the course of preparation, and that the next months were not unique. I told of Dewey's statement to me at a dinner some months ago that were he in the White House, there would be the closest possible integration between his office and the Department of State. We discussed possible recognition by the British, and Burrows was, as I expected, wholly noncommittal.[14] In answer to my question as to whether there was anyone there with whom I could talk, he replied only a man acting as consul at Haifa[15] and another who from time to time comes down from Jerusalem.

It was in this connection that Jones volunteered the "startling" opinion that once the Arabs recognized Israel, the British would also do so. My reply was that by that time the British recognition would be of no value, that in my personal opinion the way for the British to win Arab acquiescence would be to

---

12. *DFPI*, v. 1, d. 418.

13. For Hitler and Mussolini, see Breitman et al., eds., *Advocate for the Doomed*, entries of April 8, 1933, May 15, 1934. McDonald's first meeting with Mussolini was in 1928.

14. In 1948 the Labour government based its policy of withholding recognition on these factors: the partition resolution's language, Britain's suspicion of communism in Israel, lack of clarity concerning the new state's borders (especially given Britain's designs on the Negev), and British appeasement of the Arab states. On nonrecognition from May 1948 to January 1949, see Aridan, *Britain, Israel, and Anglo-Jewry*, 1–28.

15. Cyril Marriott (1897–1977), British consul general in Haifa, cared little for Jews, insisted that the state of Israel did not exist, threatened the mayor of Haifa with British attacks on the city, and protested on behalf of the British government and oil interests against the Israeli use of refinery facilities there. Aridan, *Britain, Israel, and Anglo-Jewry*, 1–28.

present them with a *fait accompli*. Perhaps the most interesting part of the talk with Burrows was his account of "screwing out of the Treasury" the night previous the assent to the proposed 100,000 pound contribution to the program of alleviation of the plight of the Arab refugees. His account supplemented that of [Sir Alexander] Cadogan at Lake Success without adding anything substantially new.[16] Jones said he had heard nothing from Washington as to our reaction to the British proposal. I said that personally I now felt that if my opinion were asked, I would urge our government to participate with the British in such a program of relief. Burrows said he would like to see me on the way back after I had personal experience of responsibility in the area. I left my greetings for Beeley and parted.

One other point about the Bevin interview. Douglas seemed to be pleased at my behavior, which, as I think back on it, was rather that of a poltroon, though less in my connection than in Douglas's. It seemed to me obvious that Douglas is prepared to play down the Palestine issue in order to—as I should think mistakenly—hope to win support on what he regards as major issues. In any case, his guarded statement to me the previous Friday in answer to my question about Bevin's attitude towards the Jews, that perhaps the latter was "slightly unsympathetic," was a model of understatement. It was also perhaps something of a measure of Douglas's own feelings.[17]

On August 4, 1948, McDonald wrote to Douglas, "I was shocked by the arrogance and distortion which we met. In more than thirty years of association with public men in all parts of the world, I have never personally heard from a high official so gross a misstatement of the elements of a problem or so direct a charge of bad faith against the head of a great state. Thinking it over, I can only wonder at our restraint."[18]

In a telephone call the next day from Chaim Weizmann's home in Switzerland, McDonald told Clark Clifford that Bevin placed the entire blame for Britain's failures in Palestine on Truman. "His feeling toward the President is something that is difficult to describe," said McDonald. "I haven't met anyone since Hitler who seems to me to have such a mental complex as he has. . . . He's arrogant—opinionated—and he would put the whole responsibility on your Chief. It is almost a psychosis with him. . . . He hates your Chief and he would like to ruin him."[19]

16. On August 2, 1948 Cadogan announced to the Security Council that Britain would make a contribution to a UN fund [$400,000] for Arab refugees from Palestine, whom he numbered between 250,000 and 550,000 persons. He added that the Security Council should impress on the mediator the urgency of the refugee issue, that the International Committee of the Red Cross should be involved in alleviating the refugees' plight, that Jewish displaced persons in Europe were aggravating the Palestine problem, and that they should be repatriated in Europe through UN agencies. JTA *Bulletin*, August 3, 1948.

17. McDonald's entry of August 3, 1948, on the meeting with Bevin was typed on personal stationary and sent to his wife Ruth separately.

18. McDonald to Douglas, August 4, 1948, McDonald Papers, USHMM, box 7, folder 5.

19. Telephone conversation between Clifford and McDonald, August 5, 1949, Truman Library, David K. Niles Papers, box 30, folder 1948 August–December.

On August 16 (from Tel Aviv) McDonald added, "In any case, it is clear that the British official statement that they will recognize Israel when the Arabs do is tantamount to long or indefinite postponement."[20]

Wednesday, August 4

Last-minute shopping, then Bobby and I went for a quick visit to the Wallace Collection, where, as always, I was impressed by the beauty of the pictures and the other art objects. Lunch with Sir Simon [Marks] and [Israel] Sieff in the former's office. It was in the nature of a farewell party. I showed them the president's letter; they told me of Marcus Sieff's work with Ben-Gurion and urged me to see Marcus in Israel.[21]

The flight from London to Geneva by Swissair DC-3 was uneventful. Met and chatted at the station for a little while with Dr. Menachem Kahany, Israel's unofficial representative in Geneva.[22] In Vevey, and to bed before midnight.

Thursday and Friday, August 5–6

In Vevey with Dr. Weizmann. He seemed quite well, but deeply worried by Mrs. [Vera] Weizmann's continued weakness. She had but one meal with us. In our series of long talks, during the course of which I gave Weizmann the inside story of recent weeks, I made the following chief points:

1) Bevin is unreconstructed and cannot be changed. Weizmann attributed Bevin's attitude primarily to frustration. He had set up the Anglo-American Committee of Inquiry on Palestine, and it had failed him. He had referred the matter to the UN, and it had failed him. Weizmann says now danger is that Bevin would seek to use the mediator [Bernadotte] to achieve what neither we nor the UN had helped him to do. The British, Weizmann said, had deliberately left the country in chaos.

2) Churchill, in a letter to a friend of Weizmann, expressed warm personal friendship for the latter, but declined to intervene in the Palestine situation on the grounds that having only limited energy, he could not. He spoke, however, of the "terrific mess," which he implied was largely due to Bevin and Co.[23]

20. McDonald to Clifford, August 16, 1948, McDonald Papers, USHMM, box 7, folder 5.

21. Colonel Marcus Sieff (1913–2001), son of Israel Sieff and an officer in the British army; at Ben-Gurion's request became adviser for transportation and supplies to the Israeli Ministry of Defense; helped with the logistical preparations for the War of Independence; also corresponded with Winston Churchill, aiding Churchill's criticism of the Labour government's refusal to recognize Israel. Martin Gilbert, *Churchill and the Jews: A Lifelong Friendship* (New York: Henry Holt, 2007), 273.

22. Shertok sent Kahany, the Jewish Agency's wartime representative to the League of Nations, to Geneva to represent the Provisional Government to the UN offices there and to try to secure recognition by Switzerland. *DFPI*, v. 1, p. 47.

23. Churchill's opinions of Bevin's handling of Palestine are covered in Gilbert, *Churchill and the Jews*, 268–279 and idem., *Winston S. Churchill*, v. VIII: *'Never Despair' 1945–1965* (Boston: Houghton Mifflin, 1988), 454–458.

3) Weizmann outlined his hopes for two or three new universities or professional or technical schools within Israel, either as independent units or as branches of the Hebrew University. The latter, he said, being located as it was in the new part of Jerusalem, which is essentially, despite its newness, international, could never be wholly Jewish. Moreover, he argued that, as compared with Switzerland, there would be need, within the next years in Israel, for his proposed additional technical and advanced facilities. He spoke of the necessity of developing an adequate counter-influence to the military one in Israel. He had long been concerned lest the latter influence, though essential for defense, in which service it had performed so brilliantly, might overshadow Israel's true problems. This he envisaged as so developing the sciences, the new techniques, and the arts, [so] that the small country would become as Athens had been, an influence for enlightenment and progress out of proportion to its size. As to the financial problem, he thought there would be increasing response from private sources and that the state could, through national funds, make up the difference.

4) As an example of far-ranging Israeli potential influence, Weizmann spoke of the approach to him by Nehru's sister [Vijaya Lakshmi Nehru Pandit][24] and by a spokesman of Burma. These Hindus anticipated fruitful cooperation with the Jews of Israel and, ultimately, a kind of defensive working together. They spoke of the Jews as a Western influence they need not fear, which could help them. Such cooperation would not be anti-Moslem but would be cultural and defensive.

5) As to recognition, he saw no hope from Britain. From France he was not optimistic. Robert Schuman[25] had promised to act when Georges Bidault[26] should be out, but was not doing so.[27] Weizmann's talks with Léon Blum and others had not been encouraging.[28] The French continued to argue about the danger from their Moslems (20,000,000?)

6) Was optimistic about progress in Palestine. On British tendentious pretentions of massacre of Jews by Arabs had been proved phantoms; on the contrary, the Arabs had fled en masse, many of them with arms in their hands. In some cases flight was so precipitous that coins were left on the tables. It was another case of David and Goliath.

24. Vijaya Lakshmi Nehru Pandit (1900–1990), Indian diplomat; ambassador to the USSR, 1947–1949; sister to Jawaharlal Nehru, who was prime minister of India from 1947–1964.
25. Robert Schuman (1886–1963), premier of France, November 24, 1947–July 26, 1948, and September 5–11, 1948.
26. Georges Bidault (1899–1983), French foreign minister, January 1947–July 1948.
27. Schuman became foreign minister on July 26, 1948. The French government did not recognize Israel until May 21, 1949. See Frédérique Schillo, *La France et la création de l'État d'Israël: 18 février 1947–11 mai 1949* (Paris: Artcom', 1997).
28. Léon Blum (1872–1950), first Jewish premier of France, 1936–1937, 1938, 1946–1947; vice premier July 28–September 5, 1948.

7) The Arab Legion had been used deliberately in a campaign of destruction of the Holy City.[29] This treatment should be contrasted with the Jews' treatment of Nazareth, where no fighting was permitted, and where, following its surrender, no Jewish troops or arms were permitted to enter. Catholic authorities had thanked the Jewish commander [Moshe Carmel] for his consideration.[30] In contrast, Weizmann regarded the Arab members of the Legion as being in effect hired assassins.

8) Danger point during September would be the UN [General] Assembly and possible use of mediator to modify UN decision by excluding the Negev. This will never be accepted by the Jews. To achieve it every Jew would have to be carried out bodily. By September there will be a Jewish Army there of 10,000 men. Weizmann cannot see why the British want the Negev. He is sure the Egyptians do not want it. As to Britain's purposes, he spoke of earlier diggings and excavations, all of which were quickly covered up. He cited a remark of Bevin in which the latter had said in effect, "What do you Jews mean by sticking your nose in the Negev?"[31] Weizmann apparently suspects that there are secret reasons for the British interest.

9) In answer to my question whether he planned to go to Rome, Weizmann said that he saw no point to his trying to see the pope. He, however, gave me the strongest possible assurances that the Israelis would respectfully and effectively [protect] the rights of the Church and of the Holy Places as defined in the memo of the Catholic Near East Welfare Association, a copy of which was given to me at Cardinal Francis Spellman's luncheon [on June 5, 1948].

Francis Joseph Cardinal Spellman (1889–1967), the archbishop of New York, was the most important Catholic official in the United States, a longtime confidant of

29. Regular and irregular Israeli forces' skirmishes with Transjordan's Arab Legion for control of Jerusalem's Old City were fierce. After its capture by the Arab Legion on May 28, 1948, Arab soldiers blew up the Rav Yehuda HaHasid Synagogue (known as the Hurva synagogue), Jerusalem's largest synagogue, which had been built in 1864 by immigrant Jews from Lithuania. It had sheltered civilians during the fighting while also serving as a fortress. The combat and subsequent demolition destroyed twenty-seven other synagogues and thirty schools, and brought wholesale desecration of the world's oldest Jewish cemetery at Jerusalem's Mount of Olives. See Michael R. Fischbach, *Jewish Property Claims Against Arab Countries* (New York: Columbia University Press, 2008), 86.

30. Nazareth in the Lower Galilee housed the Arab Liberation Army's central command headquarters. When the IDF took the city without a fight on July 16, 1948, Ben-Gurion prohibited the robbing or looting of any sacred Christian sites and ordered that the city's residents, most of whom were Arab Christians, were not to be expelled. Weizmann is incorrect that no Jewish troops entered the city. See Benny Morris, *The Road to Jerusalem: Glubb Pasha, Palestine and the Jews* (London: I. B. Tauris, 2003), 155–171; idem., *The Birth of the Palestinian Refugee Problem Revisited* (New York: Cambridge University Press, 2004), 417–420; Mustafa Abbasi, "Nazareth in the War for Palestine: The Arab City that Survived the Nakba," *Holy Land Studies* 9. no. 2 (2010): 185–207; Tal, *War in Palestine*, 209–214, 336–339; Uri Bialer, *Cross on the Star of David: The Christian World in Israel's Foreign Policy, 1948–1957* (Bloomington: Indiana University Press, 2005), 8.

31. Weizmann may be referring here to his disappointing meetings with Bevin in 1945. See Joseph Gorny, *The British Labour Movement and Zionism, 1917–1948* (London: Frank Cass, 1983), 205.

Pope Pius XII, and the president of the Catholic Near East Welfare Association. Spellman's immediate subordinate in that organization was Monsignor Thomas Mc-Mahon (1909–1956), the secretary of the Catholic Near East Welfare Association and the chairman of the Catholic Church's mission in Beirut.

The memorandum, dated June 5, 1947, called for a system of legal guarantees for the Catholic community and Catholic Holy Places in Palestine. Local Catholic prelates in Palestine during the war had published exaggerated claims of Israeli damages to Catholic sites. By August, McMahon petitioned the UN secretary-general to establish a commission of inquiry on Israel's treatment of its Christian minority.[32]

Weizmann had favored the internationalization of Jerusalem to appease the Christian world. However, the Provisional Government rejected internationalization owing to the UN's inability to protect Jerusalem's Jewish inhabitants when war erupted.[33] Still the Israelis did not want the Vatican as an enemy; the pope influenced policies in Western Europe and Latin America. Ben-Gurion was sensitive to Catholic accusations. When the Israelis captured Nazareth in mid-July, he ordered that any soldiers who looted or desecrated Christian Holy Places in the city were to be shot.[34]

After his meeting with Weizmann, McDonald wrote McMahon: "Dr. Weizmann . . . told me categorically and without any reservations that his Government would give and make effective guarantees on all the points raised in your memorandum. He assured me, too, that he was confident that the authorities here in Israel would give similarly unqualified guarantees." Regardless, Spellman and McMahon relentlessly pressed US and UN officials for the internationalization of Jerusalem as called for in General Assembly Resolution 181.[35]

10) In very emotional language, Weizmann asked me to intimate to Eliezer Kaplan,[36] Moshe Shertok, and Ben-Gurion his feeling about their so long silence during so critical a period. Deplored unnecessary worry during recent months. Pointed out that no provision made for establishment or finances for head of state. Also, Weizmann wondered how he was to get to Israel. Would prefer to go by the *SS Kedma*.[37] He could not, he thought, go on any [ship] which touched an Egyptian port, or did not fit into the dignity

32. The memorandum is printed in Constantine Rackauskas, *The Internationalization of Jerusalem* (Washington, DC: Catholic Association for International Peace, 1957), 73–78. Catholic reports from 1948 in Adriano Ercole Ciani, "The Vatican, American Catholics, and the Struggle for Palestine, 1917–1958: A Study of Cold War Roman Catholic Transnationalism," Ph.D. diss., University of Western Ontario, 2011, 226–231; also Bialer, *Cross on the Star of David*, 10.
33. Weizmann to Shertok, June 26, 1948, *DFPI*, v. 1. d. 235.
34. *FRUS*, 1948, v. V, pt. 2, 1141–1142; 1154–1155; note 30.
35. McDonald to McMahon, August 18, 1948, McDonald Papers, USHMM, box 7, folder 5; Shlomo Slonim, *Jerusalem in America's Foreign Policy, 1947–1997* (The Hague: Kluwer Law International, 1998), 124, 126, 140, 142.
36. Eliezer Kaplan (1891–1952), Belorussian-born engineer and labor Zionist; member of Mapai and Jewish Agency; signatory, declaration of independence, 1948; minister of finance, 1948–1952; minister of trade and industry, 1948–1950.
37. Weizmann could not fly due to his health. The SS *Kedma* [Eastward] was the first ship purchased by ZIM, Israel's state-owned shipping company. Bought and refurbished in 1947, it eventually transported thousands of Jewish refugees to Israel.

of the head of the state. Delightful dinner up on the hill overlooking Vevey, Montreux, and the Lake.

Saturday, August 7

Goodbye to Weizmann. By train to Geneva, where we arrived on time at 12:48 to be met by some Swiss from the consulate with our tickets and other papers. We were two hours late taking off KLM on a DC-3. The trip was at times a little rough, going down the Rhône Valley and over the Alps, but was comparatively smooth from the beginning of the Mediterranean to Rome. We had lovely views of the Riviera coast. Were met at the airport at 8:20 Rome time by Mr. Joseph N. Greene of the embassy and Mr. Franklin C. Gowen of Mr. Myron Taylor's office.[38] They could not have been more helpful. At the Excelsior, Greene and I talked a little about plans for Monday. Then Gowen got hold of Count Enrico Galeazzi, who fortunately was free for dinner.[39]

At dinner Count Galeazzi and I talked about the Vatican and Israel. When he had confirmed his earlier impression that I was an official government representative to Israel, he, with restrained feeling, pointed out that even now the Vatican state was not recognized by our Government and that Mr. Taylor's status was that of a personal representative of the president.[40] He emphasized that, of course, the Vatican was making no complaint. I was careful in my talk with Count Galeazzi, because I felt that what I said would be reported to His Holiness, whom Count Galeazzi would probably see on Monday, since he saw him regularly every day. Throughout, Count Galeazzi showed the same friendliness as in our previous talks.

Monday, August 9

To the embassy to check on the transportation to Athens and onward. Brief conference with the chargé, Mr. Homer Byington, in which it was decided that he would go along with me to the [Count Carlo] Sforza[41] appointment, which Greene would arrange. In the afternoon with Bobby and Miss Clark to see the wonderful Moses by Michelangelo in St. Peter's in Chains Cathedral and then to St. Paul's Basilica outside the walls. Its perfect proportions, excellent taste, and vastness impressed me more than ever.

---

38. Myron Taylor (1874–1959), president's personal representative to the Vatican, 1939–1950; in Washington during McDonald's visit; Gowen was the special assistant to Taylor. Greene was second secretary and vice consul in the US Embassy in Rome.

39. Count Enrico P. Galeazzi (1896–1986), Roman-born architect; designed Vatican buildings in Rome; friend and adviser to Pope Pius XII since the latter's years as secretary of state Eugenio Pacelli (Pius XII's given name). As high commissioner and in 1938 after the Evian conference, McDonald had dealt with him as a conduit to Pacelli. See Breitman et al., eds., *Advocate for the Doomed*, 89, 605–608, 799–800; idem, *Refugees and Rescue*, 140.

40. The United States did not recognize the Vatican as a sovereign entity with ambassadorial representation until 1969.

41. Count Carlo Sforza (1872–1952), Italian antifascist aristocrat and diplomat; forced into exile by Mussolini in 1926; returned in 1943; Italian foreign minister, 1947–1951; McDonald knew Sforza during his exile. McDonald, *My Mission in Israel*, 31.

At dinner on the Berenino roof,[42] met Mr. Gowen's guest, Professor Thomas Whittemore, curator of the Byzantine coins at the Fogg Museum, who has been for years [since 1931] at work on the frescoes of St. Sophia.[43] He told me that he had started preliminary studies of the job of repairing some of the frescoes in the Dome of the Rock when political and military difficulties called a halt. He admitted that the Moslem religious leaders had been difficult but thought that he could have gone ahead.

Met with the Jewish leaders and the head of the International Refugee Organization [William Hallam Tuck] and his chief colleagues at the Zionist offices.[44] It was wholly informal. Aryeh Stern made a few friendly remarks.[45] Mr. Raffaele Cantoni was eloquently generous.[46] Then there was fruit and cake and champagne. I spoke briefly. Was back in the hotel by 10:45.

Tuesday, August 10

Early start to Castel Gandolfo with Mr. Gowen, Bobby, and Miss Clark. The town shows cruel signs of bombing but is for the most part intact. The papal palace is huge but perfectly proportioned, with lovely views over the lake and to the Alban Hills to the west and to the neighboring valley. The pope received Mr. Gowen and me promptly a few minutes after nine. He was, as always, extremely gracious. He was non-committal as I talked about the need for the internationalization of Jerusalem and the danger of the Bernadotte proposal [that Jerusalem be in Arab territory with municipal autonomy for local communities and special arrangements for the Holy Places], simply repeating his emphasis on the holy nature of the city.

McDonald wrote President Truman on August 16, 1948, that the pope "expressed deep concern" regarding "the internationalization of Jerusalem and the potential menace to Christianity from inflamed Moslem nationalism."[47]

---

42. Hotel Bernini in Rome, known for its terrace view.

43. Thomas Whittemore (1871–1950), US academic and archaeologist; founded the Byzantine Institute in 1930.

44. William Hallam Tuck (1890–1966), US businessman whose career included leadership positions in relief work under his friend Herbert Hoover during and after World War II. The International Refugee Organization [IRO] was officially founded in 1946 by the UN to assume the duties of the UNRRA, which it did from 1948 until its functions were assumed by the Office of the United Nations High Commissioner for Refugees in 1952. Tuck was IRO director-general from 1947 until July 1949.

45. Aryeh Stern, Haganah and then IDF representative in Italy; recruited from DP camps for the nascent Israeli forces.

46. Raffaele Cantoni (1896–1971), Italian Jewish socialist at the forefront of rescue efforts in Italy during the war through his chairmanship of DELASEM (Delegation for the Assistance of Jewish Emigrants). In 1946 he became the president of the Union of Jewish Communities in Italy and worked to reintegrate Italian Jews into Italian society. See Mario Toscano, "The Abrogation of Racial Laws and the Reintegration of Jews in Italian Society (1943–1948)," in *The Jews Are Coming Back: The Return of Jews to their Countries of Origin after WWII*, ed. David Bankier (Jerusalem: Yad Vashem, 2009), 148–168. McDonald had met Cantoni in 1946 while on the Anglo-American Committee for Palestine. See Goda et al., eds., *To the Gates of Jerusalem*, 111–112.

47. McDonald to Truman, August 16, 1948, McDonald Papers, USHMM, box 7, folder 5.

In response to my report of what Weizmann had said about the guarantees which the Jews would give, he said "Would these guarantees be effective?" Clearly, he meant to imply that verbal guarantees would not be sufficient.

It was only after he read and reread my letter from the president that he spoke. When he confirmed from the letter that I was the official representative of the government to Israel, he commented on the contrast with the type of relationship with the Vatican state. Time and again he underlined that he was making no complaint, but was merely taking account of an incontestable fact: "Your government can, of course, do what it will. We express no dissatisfaction. We simply see and note the fact."[48] Had he put the matter less considerately, the situation might have been a little embarrassing for Gowen and me. With only half seriousness, I suggested that the governmental recognition of Israel might be a precedent for other recognition. Towards the end of the audience, His Holiness expressed his heartfelt hope for the success of my mission. It was at this point that I asked if I might present Bobby and Miss Clark. He received them with his characteristic gentleness. Before we left he gave us very simply, but impressively, the papal benediction.

Before we left the grounds, Gowen did us the great favor of driving through the papal gardens where the pope goes to walk two or three miles every day in the late afternoon. This was a special privilege, because the garden is never open to the public and because it was so beautiful with its formal flower arrangements, its lovely avenues of trees, and its long vistas. As we travelled back to town, this time over the old Appian Way with its tombs, we were unanimous that our colleague, Herbert J. Cummings, had missed a wonderful morning.

My plans to go with Bobby and Miss Clark to the Sistine Chapel were upset by the necessity of following up on our transportation and by the early appointment with [Count] Sforza. The chargé and I were at the Foreign Office promptly at twelve and were immediately received. After some personal and family greetings, during the course of which Sforza asked to be remembered to Janet and the family, I explained to him that what I had to say was purely personal and that, of course, if the president or the Department had any message for him, they would send it through the embassy.

On recognition he was quite frank. Italy would not move until the [Italian] colony question had been settled. He was personally very friendly to the Zionists [and] was, he felt, close to Weizmann, but Italy could not take the risk of minor disturbances in the colonies, which could later be charged with having been in any part responsible for an adverse colonial decision.[49] About the transit

48. McDonald reported to Truman that the pope "clearly implied [US] discrimination against the Vatican State as opposed to Israel." McDonald to Truman, August 16, 1948, McDonald Papers, USHMM, box 7, folder 5.

49. The Italians hoped until 1949 to gain British support for a partial reacquisition of its former colony of Libya, which Italy had officially renounced under Allied pressure in 1947. See Fritz Liebreich, *Britain's Naval and Political Reaction to the Illegal Immigration of Jews to Palestine,*

visas for the 500 Jewish children, about which I had spoken to him in April, he said that the short transit permissions were all ready, but that they could not grant the longer stays of three to six months now. On this point he agreed with the minister of the interior [Mario Scelba] and others, who held that to do so would be to invite the permanent stay of some of the children. There was neither room nor food for them, since Italy had unemployment and was increasing its population at the rate of 100,000 a year.[50] On the matter of Italian alleviation of strictness in granting individual transit visas from North Africa to Palestine, Sforza made no comment, saying it was not his business. We closed with some personal gossip about Sforza's role in America as lecturer and teacher, his relations with Smuts, of whom he is very fond, etc.[51]

At the hotel I found Aryeh Stern and Cantoni waiting for me. I gave them a brief factual account of the conference with Sforza and brief references to the visit at Castel Gandolfo. They seemed not surprised that the results with Sforza were not more encouraging. They were movingly friendly as we said goodbye.

Wednesday, August 11

Up early and to the airport by 6:15. There I was not greatly surprised to find a score of Zionist friends and acquaintances from New York who had just arrived on a chartered plane from Paris. Among them were Rabbi Israel Goldstein,[52] Judge and Mrs. Morris Rothenberg[53] and the irreplaceable Mendel Fisher.[54]

One of the engines of our Viking needed a slight overhaul, and there was a delay of an hour in our takeoff. During that hour another group of Zionist friends and acquaintances landed from England to change planes to Pan African Line to Israel. The earlier group was going on in their converted Bristol bomber. Among the new arrivals was Rebecca Sieff, who looked well and characteristically began to make what sounded like a speech.[55] Her son Marcus,

1945–1948 (London: Routledge, 2005), 55–74; Wm. Roger Louis, *Ends of British Imperialism: The Scramble for Empire, Suez and Decolonization* (London: I. B. Tauris, 2006), 505–511.

50. Italy was the primary staging area for illegal Jewish immigration to Palestine from 1945 to 1947 despite British pressure on the Italian government. Changes occurred in spring 1947 when UNRRA suspended its activity in Italy, which placed the financial responsibility for Jewish refugees on the Italian government. McDonald spoke to Sforza about the transit visas on his return trip from South Africa to New York. McDonald, *My Mission in Israel*, 31–32.

51. Both Sforza and Smuts addressed the Council on Foreign Relations shortly after its establishment in the 1920s. See Michael Wala, *The Council on Foreign Relations and American Foreign Policy in the Early Cold War* (Providence, RI: Berghahn, 1994), 24.

52. Israel Goldstein (1896–1986), Philadelphia-born rabbi; president, Zionist Organization of America [ZOA], 1943–1945; treasurer of Jewish Agency Executive, 1948–1949. See Israel Goldstein, *My World as a Jew: The Memoirs of Israel Goldstein* (Cranbury, NJ: Cornwall Books, 1984).

53. Judge Morris Rothenberg (1885–1950), delegate to several Zionist conferences from United States and close to Weizmann; president, ZOA, 1932–1936; president, Jewish National Fund [JNF], 1943–1949; member, International Board of Directors, Palestine Foundation Fund.

54. Mendel N. Fisher (1899–1975), Russian-born journalist, social worker, and fundraiser; member, ZOA Executive Board; executive director, Jewish National Fund of America, 1934–1961.

55. Rebecca Sieff (1890–1966), sister of Sir Simon Marks; wife of Israel Sieff; leading English Zionist and one of the first women, along with Vera Weizmann, elected to the Council of the

who had reached Rome the day before from Israel, came out to meet her. He and I had a brief but interesting talk during which I stressed some of the points his father had raised to me in London. I hope to see him on his return to Israel.

Flight to Athens was uneventful, the views were beautiful and quite unclouded, except that Naples itself was blacked out, though Vesuvius showed clearly through the clouds. Received at the airport by Colonel Robert W. van der Velde, who is to be my military attaché,[56] and a few minutes later by Mr. Karl L. Rankin, the chargé in Athens.[57] On arrival at the Hotel King George, we learned that Miss Clark and Cummings were still, so far as we knew, in Rome.

After welcome baths, Bobby and I had a pleasant lunch with Rankin and the colonel. [Rankin's] attitude is shown by his evident annoyance that a Mr. Yohanan Cohen was impertinent enough to be issuing visas for Israel from a room in the hotel.[58] In answer to my question as to whether the Greek government acquiesced in this, he said, "Yes," but added with feeling, "This man is not recognized." Here again, as with Jason Paige in Rome,[59] who came so quickly to the defense of Loy Henderson when I ventured to make only the mildest suggestion that the latter had not always operated by White House policy, I seemed to see evidence of the foreign service officer line. Earlier in Rome, Greene had spoken with a sense of pride of the strictness with which he and his colleagues were interpreting State Department instructions about clearing chartered planes from the States to Israel. When I had asked Greene if he had specific instructions to be so strict, he replied that the Department latterly had been vague and that despite the embassy's efforts to have the Department be more explicit, more specific instructions had not come. It was at this point that I said to Greene and Paige that if I were in their positions, I would not make myself the goat, that unless the Department were specific, I would interpret my instructions to act on the recognized desires of the president.

After a nap Bobby and I had a wonderful visit under the guidance of Miss Alison Franz, cultural attaché of the embassy, to the Acropolis and earlier diggings in the marketplace. On the way, we had tea with some of the archeological staff, including the retired chief, Mr. Steiner. The sunset from the Acropolis was startlingly beautiful.

English Zionist Federation; president, Women's International Zionist Organization [WIZO], 1920–1966; emigrated to Israel in 1948, residing in Tel Mond while her husband remained in London. WIZO aided with the arrival of Jewish refugees.

56. Colonel Robert Whitsett van der Velde (1912–1996), military attaché to US mission in Tel Aviv, appointed September 1948.

57. Karl L. Rankin (1898–1991), career foreign service officer; served in Cairo in 1944; counselor of embassy in Athens, 1947–1949.

58. Yohanan Cohen (1917–2013), Lodz-born Zionist; emigrated to Palestine, 1937; joined Haganah, 1938; part of the Bricha, the underground organization facilitating illegal Jewish immigration to Palestine, after the war; later Knesset member and diplomat.

59. Jason Paige Jr., attaché, US Embassy in Rome since March 1947.

Back to the hotel to be relieved to learn, first, that the military attaché's plane would be available for flight the next day at eight a.m. Securing the use of the Army plane was a minor triumph. The embassy had asked Washington for the usual required special permission to take the plane out of Greece. The reply was delayed. I became nervous about getting away Thursday morning, so I urged the colonel to show a photostatic copy of the president's letter to the attaché and say to him that he knew the president would want this collaboration.

Thursday, August 12

Up moderately early. Off in our VIP DC-3 at 8:25. As a special favor, the pilot circled Rhodes. The arrival and the takeoff half an hour later from Cyprus gave a clear bird's eye view of the island. There was no time for a visit to the camps since the pilot had to be back in Greece in the early evening.[60]

The arrival at Haifa was auspicious, a perfect landing, greeted by a smart guard of honor, by Mr. Charles Knox; the American consul at Haifa, Mr. Aubrey E. Lippincott,[61] a representative of the [Israeli] Foreign Office, and by a dozen or so of other officials. After the photographs at the plane, there was a bountiful tea, a brief press interview, and a police-escorted trip down the coast to Tel Aviv.

The ride down was almost as quick as it would have been in normal times, notable chiefly for the absence of Arabs, of whom we saw only a few, the complete absence of British military equipment, which had so congested the roads the year previous, and by the signs of manifold Jewish activity everywhere. One of the roads into Tel Aviv had been cleared of traffic so that we drove up to the [Gat Rimon] hotel without delay. There we were thrilled by hundreds of men, women, and children, all in a festive and friendly mood. Again there were seemingly endless photographs with the demand, so usual in America, for a return because some moving camera people had not gotten satisfactory shots. Before going upstairs there was another brief press interview.

In Tel Aviv, Charles Knox had rented rooms in the Hotel Gat Rimon—one of the few functioning hotels there—as McDonald's initial residence. "The reception outside the hotel," McDonald wrote, "where hundreds of men, women and children

---

60. McDonald refers to the British-controlled camps in Cyprus, where the British detained illegal Jewish immigrants. More than 51,000 Jews were sent to Cyprus beginning in August 1946. From November 1946 until May 1948 the British allowed about 26,000 to enter Palestine against the monthly quota of 1,500 certificates. Between May and September 1948 another 13,000 traveled to Israel, and the remaining 11,000 emigrated between January and February 1949. See Dalia Ofer, "Holocaust Survivors as Immigrants: The Case of Israel and the Cyprus Detainees," *Modern Judaism* 16, no. 1 (Feb. 1996): 1–23.

61. Aubrey E. Lippincott, (1905–1984) US consul in Haifa; reported to Washington on the mass Arab evacuation from the city and later pressed the Israeli authorities for the return of Arab property. The United States had opened a consulate at Haifa in January 1948 on Loy Henderson's urging because of the importance of the port, the oil refinery there, and the presence of American construction workers. Memorandum by Henderson, December 22, 1947, NARA, RG 59, E 1434, LF 54 D 403, box 8.

Textbox 2.1.
Haifa

The entry point to Israel in August 1948 was the port city of Haifa, the gateway to Tel Aviv. Before the partition resolution, Haifa had been a mixed Arab-Jewish city, with 65,000 Arab Muslims and Christians and 70,000 Jews. Fighting began days after the UN partition resolution, as irregulars loyal to Amin al-Husseini launched sniper attacks and ambushes, countered by more effective Haganah reprisals. Lack of confidence in the Arab leadership, together with growing food shortages, led as many as 30,000 middle- and upper-class Arabs, especially Christians, to flee for Syria and Lebanon by the end of March 1948. Arab irregulars who robbed and intimidated Arab civilians contributed to this flow. By March 1948 whole Arab districts were empty, plundered by Arab irregulars.

The Haganah launched a final assault in Haifa on April 21. Uncoordinated Arab resistance ended the next day. The speed of victory surprised the Haganah itself and triggered an additional exodus of some 15,000 Arabs, beginning with Arab commanders. The Jewish leadership offered reasonable terms and tried to persuade the Arabs to stay, but local Arab notables loyal to the mufti ordered Haifa's remaining Arabs, some 30,000 to 40,000, to leave the city rather than live under what they characterized as murderous Jewish rule. This, combined with subsequent rough Haganah martial law in Arab neighborhoods, resulted in the departure of all but 4,000 Arabs by mid-May. The mufti promised refugees a victorious return in the future.

The British, who had hoped to end the fighting, mainly protected the port area so as to secure their own exit. They completely evacuated the city by July 1. Haifa thereafter became a Jewish city, with the Arab population concentrated in two downtown neighborhoods for reasons of security during the subsequent war with the Arab states. Other damaged Arab neighborhoods were demolished and rebuilt to accommodate Jewish immigrants.[1]

---

1. Accounts in Morris, *The Birth of the Palestinian Refugee Problem Revisited*, 99–109, 173, 187–211; Efraim Karsh, "Nakbat Haifa: Collapse and Dispersion of a Major Palestinian Community," *Middle Eastern Studies*, 37, no. 4 (2001): 25–70.

had been waiting for hours, was, it seemed to me, a moving demonstration of welcome and friendship."[62]

"Tel Aviv is terribly crowded because of the war and the truce," McDonald wrote to his family. "The latter has brought with it many UN observers who fill one of the

62. McDonald to Weizmann, August 23, 1948, McDonald Papers, USHMM, Box 7, folder 5.

hotels. Our hotel is especially crowded because in addition to our delegation it contains members of the Russian delegation. Immediately above me is the Russian Minister."[63]

The Soviet legation staff, which had arrived earlier, were also received with an honor guard at Haifa. The Soviet minister, Pavel Ivanovich Ershov, was a humorless Soviet bureaucrat, typical of the type preferred by the Soviet foreign minister, V. I. Molotov. None of the Soviet delegates seems to have had any previous connection with Jews or Zionism in the USSR.[64]

The first sight of the rooms was a shock. While mine looked out upon the sea just across the road, it was tiny, there was no lavatory, and open to friendly eyes or otherwise from three sides and no telephone in the room. Bobby and Miss Clark's room was a small dormitory, one looking out on the apartments about eighteen feet away. Fortunately, they, too, had a balcony and, of course, were free to use mine. At the dinner, which we took downstairs in the main dining room, we were treated like royalty, but with indifferent food. By then we were to discover the most serious defect of the Gat Rimon, the indefatigable orchestra, which played loudly Palestinian songs and jazz and Viennese music until midnight each night.

Friday, August 13

After a series of conferences with Mr. Knox, and a brief inspection of our offices at 52 Nachlat Binyamin Street, Mr. Knox and I made our first call on Mr. [Moshe] Shertok. This had been arranged by the chief of protocol [Michael Simon]. I think that Mr. Knox was pleased to have me insist that he go along. I was pleasantly surprised to find the Foreign Office, which is in a residence in Sarona,[65] pleasantly cool indoors and on the balcony overlooking a little garden. Miss Esther Herlitz[66] and the chief of protocol chatted with us during the few minutes we waited to see Mr. Shertok.

The latter was warmly cordial to me and appeared to have become good friends with Mr. Knox. In our conversation we covered in general terms a wide range but did not deal specifically or in any way to deserve [a] detailed report on any topic. Mr. Shertok showed a keen interest in Truman's letter,[67] was

63. McDonald to Family, August 27, 1948, McDonald Papers, USHMM, box 7, folder 5.

64. Yehoshua Freundlich, "A Soviet Outpost in Tel Aviv: The Soviet Legation in Israel, 1948–1953," *Journal of Israeli History* 22, no. 1 (Spring 2003): 37–55. In general Yaacov Ro'i, *Soviet Decision Making in Practice: The USSR and Israel, 1947–1954* (New Brunswick, NJ: Transaction Books, 1980).

65. Sarona, a German colony formed in the 1870s and taken over by the British during World War II. Located in the center of Tel Aviv, its buildings formed the government precinct [Kiryat HaMemshala or HaKirya] in the first years of statehood.

66. Esther Herlitz (b. 1921), German-born Israeli diplomat; emigrated to Palestine, 1933; acting director of the US Section of the Israeli Foreign Ministry, 1948.

67. Shertok had noted earlier in government circles that "[McDonald's] appointment was plainly made under White House directive, contrary to the State Department." See Ya'akov and Rina Sharett, eds., *Davar davur: Devarim shebe-'al-peh be-zirot penim ve-huts [Speaking Out: Israeli Foreign Minister's Speeches, May–December 1948]* (Tel Aviv: Moshe Sharett Heritage Society, 2013), 298–299. The editors are grateful to Tuvia Friling for this reference.

concerned about Weizmann's feelings, and said he has written a long letter, that the SS *Kedma* would be sent to bring Weizmann back. He mentioned, too, the possibility of elections for a constituent assembly late in September and the constitutional regime to follow promptly after the constituent assembly had completed its work. After we had finished, there were again the news and motion picture cameras for which Shertok and I sat in his garden for as much as five or eight minutes, thus having the opportunity for the extension of our talk.

From Shertok, Knox and I went on to Walter Eytan,[68] who, with Miss Herlitz and the chief of protocol, talked informally about a number of matters, including the exigencies of the Israeli representation in Lake Success and in Washington, and the problem of houses. I had previously told Shertok that I thought [Lazar] Braudo's price of $10,000 a year for three years [for rental of his house as the ambassadorial residence] was profiteering, and in any case it was completely out of our range. Eytan spoke about requisitioning and seemed confident that the whole business could be worked out satisfactorily.

Tel Aviv had few private homes for rent, and those available were expensive. Owners evaded government price controls on rents by demanding additional "key money" in advance.[69] McDonald was reluctant to request that the Israeli government requisition a residence. He eventually rented a house in the Tel Aviv suburb of Tel Binyamin from Lazar Braudo (1880–1956), a Lithuanian-born South African Zionist who had been president of the South African Zionist Federation before he moved to Palestine in 1933 and who served until 1947 as the chairman of the board of directors of the Anglo-Palestine Bank.

After numerous heated arguments, McDonald accepted Braudo's terms—which amounted to $30,000 for three years. This far exceeded the State Department allowance of $6,000 per year. As McDonald explained to Nathaniel Goldstein, the attorney general of New York, "it [the residence] will cost me much more than my Government allowance. But is it essential to do one's job as it should be done."[70]

McDonald described the house as "a beautiful and spacious residence in the most attractive suburb of the city." It was good for entertaining and for hosting important guests—no small detail in light of Tel Aviv's noise and housing crunch. McDonald did most of his work in the residence as well. The house's main advantage, however, was that it was next door to the home of Foreign Minister Moshe Shertok, and diagonally across that of Leo Kohn, the Foreign Ministry's political adviser.[71] McDonald

68. Walter Eytan (1910–2001), Munich-born, Oxford-educated medievalist; worked in the British code-breaking section at Bletchley Park during World War II; moved to Jerusalem in 1946 and became Shertok's chief assistant and spokesman in the latter's role as director of the Jewish Agency's political department; first director-general of the Israeli Foreign Ministry; designed the ministry's administration after the British model. Gabriel Sheffer, *Sharett*, 281–282.

69. Explained in Knox to Satterthwaite, July 26, 1948, NARA, RG 59, E 1434, LF 54 D 403, box 8.

70. McDonald to Goldstein, October 1, 1948, McDonald Papers. Columbia University, box 11 folder 12.

71. Entry of October 11, 1948.

moved into the residence in September. Until then, he remained at the Gat Rimon Hotel.

In the afternoon Mr. Reuven Shiloah[72] came to call on Mr. Knox and me. Being the right hand man of Ben-Gurion, he talked authoritatively about a good many matters. He expressed complete confidence about the military situation. He was not sure registration, etc., could be completed in time for elections by the end of November but said that the plans were being pushed rapidly. Apparently one element of delay is the failure to agree up to now on the form of registration. The draft of a constitution is ready or has been submitted to a preliminary committee. Shiloah promised to let us know when I should make my first call on Ben-Gurion. Incidentally, he made a generous offer that the Provisional Government would lend a car if we were seriously short.

Mrs. Hadassah Samuel[73] and her son Dan[74] came to call. I invited them to have dinner, but they would only have coffee. Dan was just back from Oxford and already in the Israeli Army uniform of a lieutenant. He joked about the contrast between his rank and pay with the British Army in Egypt, where he was a major with the daily compensation twice that of his monthly Israeli pay. His regiment is composed about half of other [non-Israeli] troops. For a little while he and I talked upstairs. I explained what was concerning me a little. He said he would see what talk he could hear.

Saturday, August 14

Our first Sabbath from our window had all the appearances of a gala holiday with milling throngs along the sea front and on the beach. Luncheon with Mr. Julius Simon of the Palestine Economic Corporation and his associate

---

72. Reuven Shiloah [formerly Zaslansky] (1909–1959), worked with OSS station in Cairo during World War II; belonged, along with Teddy Kollek, Ehud Avriel, and others, to a parallel advisory group to Ben-Gurion on security and intelligence matters that operated alongside the Jewish Agency Executive and cabinet in the pre-state and early statehood years; close personal aide and adviser to Ben-Gurion regarding security and intelligence; liaison between the Israeli Ministries of Defense and Foreign Affairs; first director of the Mossad after 1949; garnered key intelligence concerning Arab invasion plans, British intentions, and UN observers; became a key interlocutor for McDonald. See Haggai Eshed, *Reuven Shiloah—The Man Behind the Mossad: Secret Diplomacy in the Creation of Israel* (Abingdon, UK: Frank Cass, 1997), 101–113; Tuvia Friling, "Organizing Jewish Resistance: The Decision-Making and Executive Array in the Yishuv Rescue Operations During the Holocaust," in *Jewish Resistance Against the Nazis*, ed. Patrick Henry (Washington, DC: Catholic University of America Press, 2014), 245–278.

73. Hadassah Samuel [née Goor] (1897–1986), Jaffa-born activist; wife of Edwin Samuel, who was the son of Herbert Samuel, first British high commissioner of Palestine; headed WIZO after 1929 and, after 1936, the Council of Working Women, which recruited Jewish women in Palestine for the British army during World War II. See Anat Granit-Hacohen, "Female or Feminist Initiative: Hadassah Samuel and Yishuv Women Recruit to the British Forces in WW2," http://www.aisisraelstudies.org/papers/granit-hacohen2008.pdf.

74. Dan Judah Samuel (1925–2014), Jerusalem-born second son of Edwin and Hadassah Samuel; fought in British Army during World War II; traveled from Oxford to Haifa and joined IDF in May 1948.

Mr. [Lee] Harris.[75] Simon kindly volunteered to have his secretary take our mail back with her, leaving by air that afternoon. We all welcomed the chance to get off confidential and personal letters.

Long conferences with Golda Meyerson, first with her alone and later with the staff. She looked well, walked without a limp, but said it still pained her to walk.[76] After talking about the States and her mission to Moscow (incidentally, she said she knew no Russian) and the story of my appointment, we discussed among other questions the following:

1) Chaim Weizmann's attitude and future position. She insisted that his real grievance, or at any rate his most substantial one, was the refusal of his former colleagues who now constitute the Provisional Government to accept his idea of the presidency. He would have the president have powers more nearly comparable to those of the American presidency, but here the plan is to have more nearly the French or British system.[77] As to the rumor that the delay in his return was due to fear for his safety and inability to guarantee it, she denied that there was anything in the report, that instead everyone should have known that he could not stand the heat and would not in case consider returning before September 15. As to his disappointment at not hearing more often from here, she said that he should realize that when Kaplan had not written, it must have been because of the overwhelming burdens they all have been and are carrying.

2) Cummings pressed her on the issue of possible communist orientation or even seizure here. She quietly but firmly pointed out that on the basis of her quarter century of work with (she might have said leadership in) the labor movement [Histadrut], which had given her an intimacy of knowledge of labor people, probably unrivaled, that there was no such possibility in the foreseeable future.

3) I was interested that her daughter is going with her on her mission to Moscow towards the end of the month but is being married meanwhile. We also

75. The Palestine Economic Corporation [PEC] came into existence in 1921 to undertake the development of the Jewish national home through the procurement of credit for borrowers in Palestine. Julius Simon was its president from 1931 to 1951. By 1948 it had $5 million invested, and Simon hoped to attract imports from the United States, particularly industrial equipment. See JTA *Bulletin*, February 19, 1948. Simon had also dealt with McDonald in 1934 when it was hoped that more Jewish refugees could go to Palestine. See Breitman et al., eds., *Advocate for the Doomed*, 390.

76. Golda Meyerson [later Meir] (1898–1978), labor Zionist, senior officer in Histadrut since 1934, and in 1948 the Provisional Government's first ambassador to Moscow. Her arrival was postponed owing to a sprained ankle, the Israeli government apologizing to Moscow for the delay. Shertok to Epstein, July 22, 1948, Eytan Bentsur and Boris Kolokolov, eds., *Documents on Israeli-Soviet Relations, 1941–1953*, v. 1: *1941–May 1949* (London: Frank Cass, 2000), d. 140.

77. Weizmann explained these views to Shertok on June 26, 1948. *Weizmann Papers*, ser. A, v. 23, d. 201.

talked about housing, and she promised to get in touch with Ernest David Bergmann at the Weizmann Institute.[78]

Sunday, August 15

Out to Rebecca Sieff's at Tel Mond with Bobby and Eugene Francis Mc-Mahon.[79] The [forty-mile] drive was uneventful, and after we reached the side road at Tel Mond, lined with trees, was restful. The gate to the Sieff place was opened. Rebecca was not down yet, so we had a restful hour or two before lunch. The place is not on a scale or elegance comparable to Weizmann's at Rehovot, but is very comfortable and sufficiently spacious. It shows some signs of not having been completed because of the war, and its garden neglected because of [a] shortage of help. Though the place is only comparatively few feet above the sea, the prevailing westward wind was so strong that it was cool and refreshing.

Our lunch, made up of some of Rebecca's food and our 5-in-1 rations, tasted excellent.[80] After a nap and tea, we drove back to town fairly early, because McMahon did not like the stories of the sounds of shooting during the nights previous or the sounds of shooting that afternoon in the near distance. Our driver insisted that these sounds were from [IDF] practice, but McMahon was not satisfied. Just before we left, the woman in charge of the place reported that the Iraqis were only four miles away. Later, Lieutenant Colonel Albert L. Perry, [senior UN truce observer with the United Nations Truce Supervision Organization],[81] told me that this was absurd, that they were across the main road, a distance of six or eight miles. So we left with the feeling that Tel Mond was out of bounds except for short daytime excursions. This was the harder, because Rebecca Sieff had been extremely generous in offering to make it available to me at any time and for any period. Home, refreshed by even a few hours away from the Gat Rimon.

Monday, August 16

For the first time in my own office. It is quite ample though not quite ready. Telephone arrangements still uncompleted. Having been unable to sleep the night before, I spent most of my half-conscious hours dictating a number of important communications home. In the office, I was able to give Miss Clark all of them, including letters to the president, Clifford, Marshall, Niles, and a telegram to the Department.

78. Ernst David Bergmann (1903–1975), German-born chemist; worked in the Sieff Institute since 1934; close relationship with Weizmann and Ben-Gurion; became chief of the IDF's scientific department in August 1948.

79. Eugene Francis McMahon, US security attaché in Tel Aviv, also possibly a Central Intelligence Agency employee, assigned July 28, 1948.

80. 5-in-1 US Army rations were developed in 1942 to feed five men for one day with no cooking utensils.

81. Explained in entry of August 16, 1948.

After a very short nap, over with Mr. Knox to Ben-Gurion's house. Mr. Shiloah the previous day had come to say that the prime minister wanted to meet me informally. I thought it desirable to take Mr. Knox along, particularly for the latter's morale. In my personal file is a copy of a despatch written by Mr. Knox on our visit, which is an accurate summary. I should add that I was delighted with Mrs. Paula Ben-Gurion, whom somehow I had never met before. She is an old-fashioned, motherly person, quite unawed by her husband, with a good sense of humor. Her grandchildren are beautiful. The air raid warning was my first experience of the sort (probably, however, not my last).[82]

One of McDonald's major tasks concerned the UN Security Council resolutions regarding Palestine, which touched on several pressing issues.

The first was the international status of Jerusalem as called for in the 1947 partition resolution. Security Council Resolution 49 of May 22, 1948, called for a cease-fire in Palestine.[83] Particularly in Jerusalem, the cease-fire was to be supervised by a Truce Commission.[84] The Truce Commission was made up of the Security Council members with consular representatives in Jerusalem (the United States, France, and Belgium), was to report to the secretary-general, and was to receive sufficient UN personnel to carry out its task. With Security Council Resolution 50 of May 29, 1948, the Security Council assigned not only a mediator [Bernadotte] but also a group of military observers, known as the United Nations Truce Supervision Organization (UNTSO). Officers and troops came from the three states on the Truce Commission. By August, 115 US military personnel were in Israel/Palestine as UN observers.[85]

Bitter fighting in Jerusalem made the truce there tenuous. The Arab Legion, on Abdullah's orders, had attacked in the eastern part of the city on May 19, 1948, just as the Haganah had created a corridor between the Jewish New City in the west and the Jewish Quarter of the Old City. The king was determined to protect the Arab Holy Places on the Temple Mount. During the fighting, the Legion captured the Old City's Jewish Quarter, expelling its residents. For the rest, the Legion tried to maintain the north-south axis that would protect the Old City and Arab East Jerusalem.[86] The Israeli government assumed that the Legion aimed to take the entire city.

The Security Council tried to bolster Bernadotte's authority in its Resolution 54 of July 15, 1948, which called again for an unconditional cease-fire in Jerusalem,

---

82. Ben-Gurion wrote in his diary: "McDonald met with me in the afternoon with his aide Knox. They delivered the president's letter, in which he asks about full recognition, revoking the embargo, and financial assistance to the state. In fact, McDonald spoke most of the time." Ben-Gurion Diary, entry of August 16, 1948, Ben-Gurion Archives, Midreshet Ben-Gurion, Israel [hereafter Ben-Gurion Diary]. The editors are grateful to Tuvia Friling for this reference.
83. See www.un.org/en/ga/search/view_doc.asp?symbol=S/RES/49%281948%29, accessed December 2015.
84. The Truce Commission was officially established in April 1948 by Security Council Resolution 48. Ibid.
85. In general see Neil Caplan, *Futile Diplomacy: The United Nations, the Great Powers, and Middle East Peacemaking, 1948–1954* (London: Frank Cass, 1997); Hahn, *Caught in the Middle East*, 51.
86. Benny Morris, *The Road to Jerusalem*, 155–67.

with the Truce Commission and mediator now to ensure the city's demilitarization and to report breaches of the truce.[87] Since demilitarization would have weakened Israel's hold on the New City, the Israelis rejected it, insisting that the UN could not protect Jerusalem's 100,000 Jews. In accordance with a July 25 cabinet decision, Ben-Gurion on August 2 issued a proclamation (retroactive to May 15) that Israeli forces were responsible for public safety in the occupied parts of Jerusalem and its approaches. He appointed a military governor for Israeli-occupied Jerusalem, Dov Joseph,[88] who proclaimed that Israeli law applied in the occupied area.[89] Bernadotte warned Shertok on August 10 that Israeli "stock was dropping" with the UN.[90] But as Golda Meyerson told the US consul general in Jerusalem, John MacDonald, the next day, Israel would never let Jerusalem come under international control. The city would either become Jewish, or it would be partitioned, with Transjordan receiving the eastern environs and the Old City becoming a museum of sorts under UN supervision.[91]

Events quickly vindicated Meyerson's assessment. The Ras al-'Ain water pumping station in Arab Legion-controlled Latrun supplied the New City with fresh water. Under the truce, the pumping station was supposed to keep operating, but Israeli authorities complained repeatedly to the UN that the Arab Legion had halted the flow of water. On August 12, 1948, Arab Legion personnel blew up the station.[92]

Bernadotte and the Truce Commission, meanwhile, insisted that Israeli forces in Jerusalem refrain from responding to Arab snipers, arguing that their restraint would lead to an end to the sniping and eventual demilitarization. In Jerusalem, Joseph, as military governor, pointed to the dubious nature of such hopes and had no intention of surrendering Israel's military advantage. He frequently argued with Bernadotte and his representatives. Bernadotte believed that demilitarization was necessary and that the Israelis were at fault for blocking it.[93]

Conferences lasting until nearly nine. The first was with Colonel Albert L. Perry, the senior UN observer [with the UNTSO]. He told us the detailed story of the blowing [up] of the pumps at Latrun. According to him, the UN guards had driven two of the Legionnaires and some Arabs in ordinary clothes

87. See www.un.org/en/ga/search/view_doc.asp?symbol=S/RES/54%281948%29, accessed December 2015.

88. Dov Joseph (1899–1980), Canadian-born attorney; emigrated to Palestine, 1918; member of Mapai since 1933; Ben-Gurion's military governor of Israeli-occupied Jerusalem, 1948–1949; minister of rationing and supply in first elected government, 1949–1950.

89. Announcement in Meron Medzini, ed., *Israel's Foreign Relations: Selected Documents, 1947–1974* (Jerusalem: Ministry of Foreign Affairs, 1976), 219–220. Also Knox to secretary of state, no. 37, August 3, 1948, NARA, RG 59, MC 1390, reel 16, frame 449.

90. Bernadotte-Shertok discussion, August 10, 1948, *DFPI*, v. 1, d. 441.

91. MacDonald to secretary of state, no. 1190, August 12, 1949, *FRUS*, 1948, v. V, pt. 2, 1307.

92. On the Latrun station, see *DFPI*, v. 1, d. 229, 281, 422, 441, 451.

93. *DFPI*, v. 1, d. 424, 452, 476; *FRUS*, 1948, v. V, pt. 2, 1257–1258, 1276–1279, 1301–1302. Also Dov Joseph, *The Faithful City: The Siege of Jerusalem, 1948* (New York: Simon and Schuster, 1960), 261–289; and Ruth Lapidoth and Moshe Hirsch, eds., *The Jerusalem Question and its Resolution: Selected Documents* (Dortrecht: Martinus Nijhoff, 1994), 22–26, 53–54.

away from the pumps with their truck a little after ten. The guards had then withdrawn, since they were unarmed, to the monastery a few yards away. A few hours later they heard the explosion. Examination showed that the explosives had been scientifically placed both within the cylinders and so underneath the pumps that they were completely wrecked. There was no chance that it could have been accidental or an amateur's job. Perry was outraged by the action, but insisted that there was nothing he or his guards could have done since they were unarmed and thus [he] could not take responsibility for leaving them [the guards] in no-man's-land during the night. The responsibility went back directly, he said, to the failure of the UN to supply armed guards [for the pumping station], even after the most urgent requests.

Later that evening, McDonald reported, in his first despatch from Tel Aviv to the State Department: "Mediator's optimism reported from Stockholm about present truce finds no supporting evidence here. . . . Personally convinced truce in reality not increasing chances [of] peace but rather contrary. Hence conditions appear to call for concentration [of] efforts [to] secure real peace negotiations. I realize this point [of] view parallels that recently expressed by [Provisional Government] but that does not invalidate soundness [of] point [of] view."[94] In a private letter to David Niles at the White House, McDonald hinted further at Bernadotte's lack of realism.[95]

The British consul in Haifa, Cyril Marriott, reported to London that the Latrun "demolition was carried out with such skill that strong suspicion exists at UN office that Jews may have been responsible." Ambassador Douglas forwarded this theory to Washington.[96] McDonald later reported, "Marriott's insinuating [that the] Jews may have been responsible [for the] destruction [of the] Latrun pumping station is dangerous and mischievous conjecture completely unwarranted by circumstantial evidence as personally told [to] me by USA Colonel Perry who was in control of [the] station for [the] UN at [the] time. . . . Station was wholly within Arab territory and Jews had no access thereto. I am sure [that the Department] will ignore such tendentiously misleading conjectures."[97]

After a late dinner, I foolishly continued my conferences with Knox until nearly midnight with the result that I was so alert that sleep was difficult. Next day made Bobby promise thereafter to see that I did not work after dinner.

Tuesday, August 17
At the office during the morning. At lunch ran into American Zionists, this time Rabbi Israel Goldstein and Rabbi Abba Hillel Silver. Tentatively

94. McDonald to secretary of state, no. 55, August 16, 1948, *FRUS*, 1948, v. V, pt. 2, 1315–1316.
95. McDonald to Niles, August 16, 1948, McDonald Papers, USHMM box 7, folder 5.
96. Douglas to secretary of state, no. 3576, August 18, 1948, NARA, RG 59, 501.BB Palestine, box 2120, folder 4.
97. McDonald to secretary of state, no. 83, August 31, 1948, NARA, RG 59, MC 1390, reel 16, frame 689.

decided on a party for the [Zionist] Actions Committee at Braudo's house to serve, among other purposes, that of a reconciliation gesture to Braudo.[98] Tea with the [Harry] Davidowitzes, through whose kindness we have our car.[99] Mrs. [Ida] Davidowitz,[100] who came late because of a delay on the Burma Road,[101] will I think be as good as her word to help out with whatever furnishings may be needed [for the party].

At 7:30 Dr. Aryeh Altman, Revisionist leader, came.[102] Our conversation was partly general, and it was necessary for me to see Colonel Perry again at eight before Mr. Altman had time to give me the "lowdown" on the local scene. I was just as well pleased, for I was tired and preferred to have that story later. Perry was in a rather too voluble mood to carry conviction as he talked on about the military situation here. Nonetheless, he was persuasive on the point that John MacDonald's chauffeur had had imperative orders which made him race away from the scene of the killing of the Jewish liaison officer who had gotten out of the car to open the barrier for John MacDonald's party and that, therefore, no fault could be attributed to the latter. It was at this point that Knox spoke up and said that if under similar circumstances he or any other members

98. The Zionist Actions Committee (or Zionist General Council) was the international Zionist governing body that acted between sessions of the World Zionist Organization. One hundred fifty delegates met in Jerusalem and then Tel Aviv for a ten-day session in August 1948. The pending question concerned the relationship between the Zionist Organization and the state of Israel. American and British Zionist leaders called for separation of the two and for the resignation from the Zionist Organization of Israeli government members. They were concerned about the perceptions of dual loyalties and the possible perception that the Zionist Organization was an Israeli "Comintern." The Zionist Organization, they proposed, would continue to be responsible for the welfare of Jews in the Diaspora. Ben-Gurion rejected the separation proposal because of Israel's precarious position. The connection, he said, had to continue. Ben-Gurion did, however, resign his position as chairman of the Jewish Agency. See Zvi Ganin, *An Uneasy Relationship: American Jewish Leadership and Israel, 1948–1957* (Syracuse, NY: Syracuse University Press, 2005), 18–21; and Ariel L. Feldestein, *Ben-Gurion, Zionism and American Jewry, 1948–1963* (London: Routledge, 2006), 15–18.

99. Harry S. Davidowitz (1887–1973), Belorussian-born US rabbi; wounded as US military chaplain in World War I; rabbi at the Conservative Park Synagogue, Cleveland, 1929–1934; emigrated to Palestine with his family, 1934; thereafter Hebrew scholar, translated works of Shakespeare into Hebrew.

100. Ida B. Davidowitz (1938–1963), wife of Harry Davidowitz; emigrated from the United States to Israel in 1934; assistant to Henrietta Szold in Youth Aliyah; later the first theater critic for the *Jerusalem Post*.

101. After mid-May 1948 the Arab Legion occupied the Sha'ar HaGai [Gate of the Valley], the key section of the main access route to Jerusalem where the road begins its ascent though a gorge. Named for the famous Allied supply route to China during World War II, the "Burma Road" was an improvised bypass that circumvented the Arab Legion's position and provided Israeli access to Jerusalem.

102. Aryeh Altman (1902–1982), Ukrainian-born, US-educated Revisionist Zionist politician; emigrated to Palestine, 1925, and joined the political wing of Ze'ev Jabotinsky's Union of Revisionist Zionists, known as HaTzionim HaRevisionistim (the Revisionist Zionists [acronym HaTzohar]); became head of HaTzohar after Jabotinsky's death in 1940. Initially HaTzohar was Israel's largest right-wing political party, with three of its members on the Provisional State Council. These included Altman, the head of the executive committee of what was now called the Zionist Revisionist Organization of Israel. HaTzohar opposed the military wing of the Revisionist movement, the IZL, led by Menachem Begin. Altman predicted that Arab aggression would trigger an all-out Jewish fight for Palestine.

of the staff had been shot and I were in the car, the chauffeur would be absolutely bound to do what John MacDonald's chauffeur had done.

On August 16 an Arab sniper killed an IDF liaison officer named Ze'ev Herzog, who was escorting US Consul General John MacDonald—a member of the Security Council's Truce Commission—to northern Jerusalem's Mandelbaum Gate. MacDonald's driver sped away, leaving Herzog to die in the road.

Wednesday, August 18

During morning had my first two callers at the office. Rabbi Jacob Herzog, son of the chief [Ashkenazic] rabbi [Yitzhak Herzog] and employed in the Ministry of Religion Department of Christian Communities,[103] first explained the scope of his office, insisted that it could not possibly be used to restrict freedom of religion or teaching or pilgrimage or the Christian control of the Holy Places, but that rather it was intended to ensure such freedom and such Christian control. His real purpose, however, in coming was to solicit my cooperation in gaining [an] audience in Rome for men from his department with men on a comparable level among the Franciscans and those in charge of Catholic interests here.[104]

His people wish to talk about such practical questions as what the Vatican wanted done about the Holy Places, how it thought the Provisional Government could help. The other problem was to find out how the Vatican wanted several Roman and Uniate churches dealt with. After nearly an hour's discussion, I suggested that Mr. Herzog write me a letter, but instead of mailing it, that he bring it over, and we could together decide whether it was in the most appropriate form. I was then to determine whether or not I could, in my personal capacity, write to our friend Gowen and solicit his informal and personal introduction of the men from here to the appropriate Church authorities.[105]

Dr. [Paul] Mohn,[106] one of the political advisers to Count Bernadotte, who had asked yesterday for an interview, came a little after twelve and stayed for what was a very long hour. He is part of the Swedish group that Count Bernadotte has brought in to play a much larger role than seemingly was envisioned by the Security Council. Mohn's story was a long and sometimes tedious

103. Jacob [Ya'akov] Herzog (1921–1972), Dublin-born son of Rabbi Yitzhak Herzog and brother of Chaim Herzog; served in Israeli Ministry of Religious Affairs and advised the Israeli Foreign Ministry on the issue of Jerusalem and relations with the Vatican, 1948–1954; headed the US division of the Foreign Ministry while advising Ben-Gurion, 1954–1957; then served in the Israeli Embassy in Washington, 1957–1960. Rabbi Yitzhak HaLevi Herzog (1888–1959) was the Polish-born chief Ashkenazic rabbi of Palestine and then Israel, 1936–1959.
104. The Franciscan *Custodia* in Jerusalem, which maintained Catholic Holy Places there, had become extremely hostile to Israel since the war began. Herzog hoped to go around them and work directly with the Vatican. See Uri Bialer, *Cross on the Star of David*, 10–12.
105. See entry of October 27, 1948.
106. Paul Mohn (1898–1957), geographer and diplomat; Swedish delegate to UNSCOP in 1947; instrumental in drawing the partition map accepted by the UNSCOP majority; on Bernadotte's staff as political adviser to the UNTSO, 1948. See Benny Morris, *1948*, 47.

but always clear account of Jewish sins of omission and commission under the terms of the truce. Among the complaints was the unwillingness of the Provisional Government to accept the count's dictum on the limitation of men of military age. In his mind Count Bernadotte has fixed a quota of 500 a month. This has already been substantially exceeded, hence, the issue was up to Count Bernadotte whether he would issue an order.

Count Bernadotte had announced on June 8 that he would limit the immigration of Jewish men of military age into Israel, with immigrants to be inspected at embarkation points in Europe.[107] *He based the order on UN Security Council Resolution 50 of May 29, 1948, which said that Israel and the Arab states "will not introduce fighting personnel into Palestine." Shertok objected that "we . . . cannot accept hydra-headed inspection of [the] entire world" and that Israel "could not under any circumstances agree to international control of Jewish immigration into its territory." Mohn countered on July 6 that the case of Palestine was unique.*[108]

The British halted the immigration to Israel of able-bodied military-aged Jews— about 11,000 of them—who were then living in detention camps in Cyprus. London insisted that this step was critical in winning Arab support for the truce. Secretary of State Marshall on August 3 quietly ordered US Army authorities in Germany and Austria to cooperate with Bernadotte's clearance procedures to ban the immigration of "fighting personnel."[109] *To coordinate with Bernadotte, Marshall worked through the UN in New York and Lippincott in Haifa rather than McDonald in Tel Aviv, who was not even informed of the policy until more than a week after his own inquiry on September 7 and a follow-up request of September 16.*[110]

Another complaint was that allegedly Arab villages were being blown up or destroyed by bulldozers, in some cases the populations being forced out at bayonet point. He cited three villages on the Haifa–Tel Aviv Road, which had been leveled as a part of "police operations." In Upper Galilee it was charged that the men of the village[s] had been rounded up and forcibly deported. In other cases there have been charges of abductions. Before the [UNTSO], made up of General Aage Lundström[111] and the ranking French, American and Belgian officers, two decisions had come down, both against the Jews.

107. Bernadotte to Shertok, June 8, 1948, *DFPI*, v. 1, d. 156.

108. Shertok to Eban, June 15, 1948, *DFPI*, v. 1, d. 185; also d. 281.

109. On immigration restrictions, see *FRUS*, 1948, v. V, pt. 2, 1082–1083, 1091–1093, 1099–1100, 1104, 1348–1349; Shertok meeting with Bernadotte, July 6, 1948, *DFPI*, v. 1, d. 281.

110. See Carmel Offie to secretary of state, no. 439, July 1, 1948, NARA, RG 59, MC 1390, reel 16, frames 000–022; Marshall to US delegation to UN, no. 517, August 9, 1948; Marshall to Lippincott, no. 327, August 26, 1948, NARA, RG 59, 501.BB Palestine, Box 2120, folder 3; Marshall to McDonald, no. 98, September 16, 1948, NARA, RG 59, 501.BB Palestine, Box 2120, folder 5.

111. Aage Lundström (1890–1975), Swedish air force general who served as chief of staff of the UNTSO, August–September 1948.

Arab refugees had fled Palestine, some before the partition resolution in 1947, more during the ensuing fighting, and more still after the Arab states invaded Israel. In areas where there were security concerns, Israeli units also expelled Arab inhabitants. Bernadotte called repeatedly for the return of some 300,000 Arab refugees, which was the best estimate of the total in the summer of 1948.

The Israeli government determined that, for the most part, Arabs who had fled or were expelled would not be permitted to return. It repeatedly argued that Arab returnees would not have fled had Israel not been attacked, that they represented a security risk so long as the war continued, that the solution to their plight was mass relocation in the other Arab states, and that their fate should be part of a permanent peace settlement for the region.

Mohn referred specifically to the villages of Jaba, Ijzim, and 'Ein Ghazal, twenty kilometers south of Haifa, overlooking the coastal road toward Tel Aviv. Arab snipers there had routinely shot at Israeli vehicles. The IDF captured the area on July 26. Inhabitants who had not already fled were expelled. The Arab League complained to Bernadotte that the IDF had committed atrocities, including burning civilians alive, a claim rejected by UN investigators. The UN did conclude that the Israeli assault on the villages was an unjustified truce violation. Bernadotte condemned the villages' subsequent destruction and insisted that the Arab inhabitants be allowed to return.

The IDF also captured a number of Arab villages in Western Galilee during Operation Dekel, *launched against the Arab Liberation Army [ALA] between July 8 and July 18. Most of the Druze and Christian population remained, but most of the Muslim population fled. Five villages were completely emptied of Muslim inhabitants and leveled.[112] Four of these had strongly supported the ALA and had a long history, going back to 1936, of anti-Jewish activity.*

In all, some 350 Arab villages in Israeli territory were demolished in 1948 and 1949. Members of kibbutzim harvested the maturing Arab wheat and barley crops. Jewish pioneers and some 110,000 arriving immigrants moved onto formerly Arab-owned lands, especially in the Jerusalem corridor, in the Galilee, and in former Arab districts of the cities, including Jerusalem.[113]

Among petty [Israeli] interferences with the UN work, Mohn cited the requirement, at one stage, of 24 hours clearance notices for UN planes to leave the ground. This would, as he pointed out, make response in an emergency impossible. The time had subsequently been reduced, he added, to, I think, an hour. Rather whiningly, he spoke about other difficulties "willfully" being made by the Jewish authorities.[114] He insisted that there was no advantage to the Jews in moving into a state of war, that there was a tendency to [ignore] the moderates and to cooperate with the extremists. As a possible indication that

---

112. Saffuriya, Al Mujeidil, Málul, Ar Ruweis, and Ad Damun.
113. In general see Morris, *Palestinian Refugee Problem Reconsidered*, 309–413; on the Haifa-Tel Aviv road, 438–441; on the Galilee villages, 415–423.
114. The Israeli government worried that foreign aircraft, especially those flown by British pilots, were performing reconnaissance for the Egyptian Army and the Arab Legion.

there are plans for "aggression" in Jerusalem is the seeming cooperation of Irgun with the government authorities. Towards the end, as I kept wondering what Mohn really wanted from me, he asked me: "What does the US want?" My answer could be easily imagined. I told him that as far as my own role was concerned, I assumed that the US would let the mediator know its views through the Security Council. It was interesting to have him tell me that the UN had just named John Reedman of South Africa as a representative to the Provisional Government.[115] I couldn't tell, however, from Mohn's account just what this involved.

I tried during the course of all this to refrain from any criticism of the count [Bernadotte]. It was difficult not to interrupt Mohn's long indictment. This was the more so because he seemed to regard the Arab violations, even when on a scale such as that of Latrun, as being more or less incidental, while those of the Jews were interpreted as deliberate parts of a general plan of sabotage of the mediator's efforts.[116] Perhaps the most significant part of Mohn's talk was his confession that there had been divided counsel among those advising Count Bernadotte on the Jerusalem recommendation. Mohn had opposed it; Ralph Bunche had been among those who favored it. The latter's argument was that it would be a bit of sticky flypaper to catch the Arab support. When asked whether the US would approve it, he said that our country had no interest in details but was concerned only with peace. I could hardly believe that this is a wholly accurate account of Bunche's attitude since it is so inconsistent with his reputation for intelligence.[117]

Chatted with Emanuel Neumann and Selig Brodetsky[118] for a minute before lunch. Dinner with Dr. David W. Senator of the [Hebrew] University.[119]

115. John N. Reedman, British-born South African economist; served on UNSCOP, 1947; appointed to Bernadotte's staff, 1948, his official title in Palestine was special representative of the UN secretary-general.

116. Major Arab violations of the truce also included Egypt's refusal to allow Israeli supply convoys to cross Egyptian lines to reach Jewish settlements in the Negev. The Israelis tried in late July and early August to run armed convoys through Egyptian lines, but generally could not break through. Settlements in the Negev ran dangerously short of food, some calling for evacuation. The IDF turned to airlifts. Tal, *War in Palestine*, 355–356.

117. Ralph J. Bunche (1903–1971), Harvard-trained political scientist who studied French colonialism and who taught at Howard University while working on African American causes in 1930s and afterward; member of OSS as an analyst in colonial affairs, 1941–1944; part of US delegations at Dumbarton Oaks meetings (1944) and the San Francisco conference (1945) for planning the UN and writing the UN Charter; headed UN's Trusteeship Division, which was to move League of Nations mandates to UN trusteeship and then independence, 1945–1947; special assistant to the representative of the secretary-general, UNSCOP, but was pessimistic concerning the partition plan, 1947; principal secretary to the five-member UN Palestine Commission, which was to supervise the transitional period between the partition resolution and the end of the Mandate, 1947–1948. After Bernadotte's appointment as mediator in May 1948, Bunche was made chief representative of the secretary-general in Palestine, in which position he worked closely with Bernadotte. On Bunche's role in negotiations, see Elad Ben-Dror, *Ralph Bunche and the Arab–Israeli Conflict: Mediation and the UN, 1947–1949* (London: Routledge, 2016).

118. Selig Brodetsky (1888–1954), Ukrainian-born English mathematician; president, Board of Deputies of British Jews, 1940–1949; president of Hebrew University, 1949–1952.

119. David Werner Senator (1896–1953), German-born scholar of Jewish settlement; settled in Jerusalem, 1924; secretary of the Joint Distribution Committee's European Office, Berlin,

He told me: the tragic and heroic story of the attempt to keep the university and the Hadassah institutions [on Mount Scopus] open; the death of Chaim Yassky and others in the ambush of the convoy on their way up to Mount Scopus; the fighting in Jerusalem; the preparation of the Jewish population for street defense; the rigors of water and food shortages; the heroism of old as well as young and the present nearly hopeless situation.[120]

Demilitarization he regards as completely impractical and undesirable. It would be, he said, an open invitation for terrorists on both sides to take over the city. The only possible alternative—and it may be too late for this—is a form of internationalization or partition. But the essential condition of success for either plan [must] be an announcement of a policy of international enforcement that would have to have teeth in it. Otherwise, it would be regarded as only one more futile UN gesture. The mediator's Jerusalem proposal had been [linked] to his and the UN's prestige and to the prospects of peace in Jerusalem.

At the concert Bobby and I found ourselves next to Miss Herlitz and Mr. Simon, both of the office of protocol. We were delighted with the young pianist Abraham Sternklar,[121] whose program was a formidable one, including a Schubert Sonata in A, Brahms's Sonata in F, and two substantial pieces by the artist and also a piece each by Dukas and Albeniz. It was a relief to hear something other than the Gat Rimon's orchestra.

McDonald often attended the performances of the Israel Philharmonic Orchestra, which attracted world-class Jewish and non-Jewish conductors and musicians, as well as plays at Habimah, Israel's main theater. Aside from enjoying the performances, he aimed to make the US presence known. He marveled to his friend Manny Goldman, a clothier in New York: "Another example of 'normalcy' is the continuation of the regular series of symphony concerts and of the performances of the Habimah and other theaters in Tel Aviv and elsewhere. Nothing seems to daunt these people or even deter them from carrying on as if there could be no question whatever about the future. One can have only the highest admiration for this sort of courageous confidence."[122]

1925–1929; Jewish Agency Executive, 1930–1935; helped German Jewish émigrés through Reich Representation of German Jews, 1933–1939; registrar, Hebrew University, 1937–1949; executive vice president, Hebrew University, 1949–1953.

120. As the end of the Mandate approached, Arab forces in the Old City blockaded the Hadassah Hospital and the Hebrew University on Mt. Scopus, which the Haganah also used as a base. Spotty access to Mt. Scopus was maintained via a narrow passage through the Arab neighborhood of Sheikh Jarrah, but sniper fire kept convoys to a minimum. As supplies dwindled in the hospital, a convoy went through Sheikh Jarrah on April 13, 1948. The lead vehicle hit a mine, and the remainder of the convoy was halted and sprayed with gunfire. Seventy-nine members of the convoy were killed, including Chaim Yassky, the hospital's director and twenty-nine women. The ambush was represented as a response to the IZL-Lehi killings of Arab civilians at Deir Yassin. Supplies could not reach the hospital thereafter, and it was closed in May 1948. See Benny Morris, *1948*, 128–129.

121. Abraham Sternklar (1930–), Trieste-born Israeli pianist, one of the first performers with the Israel Philharmonic; came to the United States for further study at McDonald's urging and studied at Julliard for five years.

122. McDonald to Emanuel Goldman, October 18, 1949, McDonald Papers, box 11, folder 17.

Lunch with Brodetsky. Talk about situation in Britain and the US's suggestion of possible Provisional Government special emissary [from Great Britain]. In late afternoon walked along beach at Herzliya. The air was cool but the sun still hot. It was the first real exercise I have had.

Friday, August 20

Preparations in the morning for the formal presentation at the prime minister's official residence. In contrast with the Russians [whose presentation ceremony was August 17] we were in completely informal dress. There were no bands. I was sorry only that through lack of preparation Bobby and Miss Clark were not present. My speech to Ben-Gurion was a brief two or three sentences, which had been carefully prepared. His reply was similar.[123]

We then at once began to talk for nearly forty minutes. We canvassed some of the issues most vital. He appreciated, I think, my friendly frankness, and my emphasis on the two dangerous illusions.

McDonald told Ben-Gurion that the Provisional Government could not disregard the mid-August warning by the US deputy delegate to the UN Security Council, Phillip Jessup. Jessup had warned both Israel and the Arab states that the truce was not to be considered an interlude and that only the Security Council could terminate it.[124] McDonald also warned that, should the UN impose sanctions against Israel, the United States would participate, albeit reluctantly. He noted, however, that the current disputes over Arab refugees, Israel's borders, and the status of Jerusalem would not provoke sanctions by themselves.[125]

Toward the end he [Ben-Gurion] raised the question of [a] possible special role of one of two men. Later, I learned that the one I knew [was] better had been chosen.[126] Ben-Gurion was convincing, as had been Shertok, in the declaration that there could be no yielding on matters concerning independence or security.[127]

123. For texts see McDonald Papers, USHMM, box 7, folder 5.
124. See *FRUS*, 1948, v. V, pt. 2, 1321.
125. McDonald, *My Mission in Israel*, 48–50.
126. Could refer to Reuven Shiloah's role as an intermediary between Ben-Gurion and McDonald.
127. Ben-Gurion stated that the indefinite truce only aided the "Arabs aggressors," because Israel could not remain on an war footing indefinitely owing to the economic needs of arriving refugees. For McDonald's report see McDonald to secretary of state, no. 63, August 20, 1948, *FRUS*, 1948, v. V, pt. 2, 1334; McDonald, *My Mission in Israel*, 49. Ben-Gurion's notes included the following: "[McDonald] expressed his concern that some decisions that will be taken by the State Department, that would be considered as wise and just by them, will be accepted in Israel as the opposite, such as [repatriating] the refugees. . . . As long as a foreign army is present, we cannot resettle enemies of the state, even if we were sanctioned [by the UN]. McDonald said he received a long [telegram] . . . and has yet to decode it fully. He will tell us when he knows. . . . [H]e does not work for the [State] Department, and wishes to ensure [good] relations between the two countries. . . . [He] advised speaking with the president soon." Ben-Gurion Diary, entry of August 20, 1948. The editors are grateful to Tuvia Friling for this reference.

Fig. 2.1. US special representative James McDonald, in the private meeting with Israeli prime minister David Ben-Gurion, after presenting his credentials, August 20, 1948, United States Holocaust Memorial Museum.

Back to the office. Shertok came to the office at about twenty past twelve, having gone to the hotel by mistake. Knox and I first discussed with him the inquiry about Jerusalem demilitarization.[128] He asked for time to reply, and the date was fixed for Sunday noon. We then went on to discuss the same subject as with Ben-Gurion and got the same reply.[129]

In the late afternoon Bobby and I went out to Rehovot, where we had a delightful evening as Miss Frieda Goldschmidt's guests in the attractive small apartment at the Club.[130] Dr. Benjamin Bloch,[131] Ernst David Bergmann, and Miss Goldschmidt showed us around, and we had a wonderful view from the top of the new Science Building off the Judean hills. After dinner the roof was

128. The Department of State was concerned because of reports from John MacDonald that the Israelis might risk UN sanctions in order to capture the remainder of Jerusalem. John MacDonald to secretary of state, no. 1210, August 19, 1948, *FRUS*, 1948, v. V, pt. 2, 1327–1328.

129. McDonald reported that it "was evident that Ben-Gurion had told Shertok [of] my previous conversation." McDonald to secretary of state, no. 64, NARA, MC 1390, reel 16, frame 595.

130. Dr. Frieda Goldschmidt (1899–1971), former chemist at University of Berlin; looked after Weizmann's interests in his absence.

131. Dr. Benjamin Bloch (1900–1959), Galician-born physicist invited by Weizmann in 1934 to help establish the Daniel Sieff Research Institute; essentially directed the institute after 1936.

exquisitely quiet and the stars reassuring with the moon bright in utter perfection.

John MacDonald's reports from the US consulate general in Jerusalem to Washington reporting Israeli truce violations were copied to the US Missions in Damascus, Baghdad, and Cairo, but not to McDonald in Tel Aviv. Nor did McDonald receive exchanges between the State Department and its UN delegation concerning possible peace negotiations. Nor were exchanges between Secretary Marshall and Ambassador Douglas in London concerning Bevin's and Bernadotte's proposals regarding the fate of Jerusalem, the Galilee, the Negev, Haifa, and Jaffa shared with McDonald.

These State Department discussions concerned Israeli "aggression" in Jerusalem in violation of the truce, ideas for an Israeli state smaller than envisioned in the partition resolution, an international Jerusalem, and the return of Arab refugees as called for by Bernadotte.[132] On August 16, Marshall had personally notified Truman of "the apparent tendency of the Provisional Government of Israel to assume a more aggressive attitude in Palestine," particularly regarding its stance toward Bernadotte, Jerusalem, and the refugee issue. The Israelis, Marshall added, seemed intent on breaking the truce, and the trend was especially worrisome to London. He suggested stern American warnings to Eliahu Epstein in Washington.[133] Two days later he warned John MacDonald in Jerusalem that "the Jews are seemingly lifting their sights and are campaigning to attain [a] new objective; namely control [of] Jerusalem itself."[134]

On Marshall's inquiry McDonald reported from Tel Aviv on August 19, that the New York Times *had overblown the meaning of a recent speech by Ben-Gurion that "we cannot allow an indefinite truce to continue as long as it is able to kill the population of Jerusalem by means of thirst;" that Israel could not agree to an indefinite truce, "for it means control over the Jewish state and immigration;" and that "unless the UN is able or willing to insure peace within the very near future, we shall have to bring this about by our own efforts."[135]*

Saturday, August 21

Morning visit to Weizmann house and gardens. The latter are suffering from lack of adequate upkeep. The house was rather gruesome with its elaborate camouflage. Bobby was able to get some picture of its potential beauty inside. As we sat in the shade of the mulberry tree eating our fresh oranges, one could sense the potential peace and charm of that neighborhood. Before the walk I worked for a couple of hours on drafts for Washington. Afterwards dictated to Bobby. After a nap and tea in which we were joined by Mrs. Bernstein

132. See especially Marshall's lengthy top-secret despatch to Douglas, nos. 3187 and 3208, August 12, 1948 and August 13, 1949 respectively, in *FRUS*, 1948, v. V, pt. 2, 1303–1306, 1308–1310.

133. Memorandum by Marshall, August 16, 1948, *FRUS*, 1948, v. V, pt. 2, 1313–1315.

134. Marshall to MacDonald, no. 838, August 18, 1948, *FRUS*, 1948, v. V, pt. 2, 1321.

135. McDonald to secretary of state, no. 62, August 19, 1948 [received August 22, 1948], NARA, RG 59, 501.BB Palestine, box 2120, folder 4.

(whose husband, [Peretz] a chemist, decided to stay in Rehovot instead of Chicago), we drove back to town.

The opera *Thaïs*, where we were the guests of the management and the prima donna, was not in its performance a competitor of the Met but was of special interest to us because, as the US representative, I was greeted by an enthusiastic and friendly crowd outside and inside. There was a mix-up about the failure of the orchestra to play the Russian anthem when it played ours and the Jewish one [*Hatikvah*]. It was not serious, and since we were in no way responsible, it was amusing to us.[136]

A very un-Sabbathlike day—prolonged conferences among ourselves and by Knox and me with Shertok, and the despatches and telegrams to Washington which grew out of these sessions. Filled morning and afternoon kept me from getting off to Rehovot until late. The alarming reports from Haifa via Washington to the effect that mass action could be expected within hours or days in Jerusalem and north of Tel Aviv were checked in our Office of Communications. The report there was negative. As to checking this on [the] highest level, it was agreed that if we heard nothing further, opinion was unanimous.

Report about demilitarization in Jerusalem was negative for reasons indicated in telegram of August 22. I had anticipated this report and did not need to change text of my telegram to Truman and Marshall on this point. Knox was naturally delighted that we were able to get off so promptly replies to the Department's questions. Shertok promised to send somebody with Jerusalem map to make clear to me existing lines. Incidentally, he gave me his views about current controversy regarding the Government House–Red Cross area.

On August 20 the US consulate at Haifa under Aubrey Lippincott, without informing McDonald, warned the State Department that "responsible neutral elements here are unanimous in [the] conviction that [the] Jews are about to make [a] determined attempt to take all [of] Jerusalem and that by [the] end of [the] week they may possibly succeed."[137] The next day Marshall ordered McDonald to "telegraph immediately your estimate of [the] situation" and to "call immediately on Ben-Gurion and Shertok and impress upon them the risks [the Provisional Government] will run in [the Security Council] of being found the aggressor, with consequent sanctions, etc. Furthermore you should point out the continued determination of this government to do [the] utmost to preserve [the] truce and through it peace in Palestine."[138]

---

136. The orchestra did not play the anthem of the Soviet Union because the Soviet minister, Pavel Ershov, was not present. The four members of the Soviet delegation, in McDonald's words, "left the theater reportedly in high dudgeon to the consternation of the Israeli Chef de Protocol and to that of the impresario of the opera." McDonald to Ruth McDonald, April 21, 1948, McDonald Papers, Box 7, August 7.

137. Lippincott to secretary of state, no. 334, August 20, 1948, NARA, RG 59, 501.BB Palestine, box 2120, folder 4.

138. Marshall to American mission in Tel Aviv, no. 59, August 21, 1948, *FRUS*, 1948, v. V, pt. 2, 1334–1335.

On August 22 McDonald advised Shertok of the "grave Washington concern." Shertok replied that "any reports [that the Provisional Government was] about to take general action [in] Jerusalem or northern Galilee in violation of truce were 'fantastic,'" though he rejected an indefinite truce. "My estimate," McDonald reported to the secretary and to the president both, "is that [the Provisional Government] will not now take deliberate overt action, but if increasingly tense situation is to be relieved there must be evidence [in the] near future through [the] UN or otherwise of measurable progress toward peace."[139] McDonald added that Israel had rejected the earlier Arab proposal of August 7 for demilitarizing Jerusalem because the Arabs could take the whole city too easily once Israeli forces had withdrawn. The UN, McDonald added, would not have the stomach to defend the city's Jews.

A "crisis," McDonald reported to Truman and Marshall, "is in the making." Washington demanded maintenance of the truce, the demilitarization of Jerusalem, and the return of the Arab refugees. The Israelis, he explained, wanted negotiations toward a lasting, permanent peace. "Striving to see the whole problem objectively, I have reached [the] conclusion that the Jewish emphasis on peace negotiations now is sounder than the present UN and US emphasis on truce and demilitarization." Israel would not sacrifice its security needs. "I cannot too strongly emphasize my conviction that, rather than submit to what would be regarded as infringement [on] independence and weakening of security, they would fight both the US and the UN. . . . My urgent plea . . . is that our government guard zealously against permitting its good intentions and love of peace [to] betray it into supporting a UN policy which would mean armed conflict with Israel."[140]

Great relief to get out of town to Rehovot in time for dinner. I should note also that we were delayed in getting to the Foreign Office through a check which was being made in the streets of all persons of military age.

Monday, August 23
Most of the morning spent getting material ready for the pouch. Long conference with Mr. Randolph Roberts [vice consul] of the consulate at Haifa. It is not quite clear to me why he came down, but we both took advantage of his presence to talk around a good many subjects. I told him the story of my appointment and my relations to the president and the Department. I asked some naïve questions about relations of consulates to the chief of mission. He rather apologetically explained that their last week's political despatch [of August 20] had been an exception and that they would do their utmost to keep us informed of their communications. I did not specifically tell him that

139. McDonald to secretary of state, [personal attention president and secretary], no. 66, August 22, 1948, *FRUS*, 1948, v. V, pt. 2, 1336–1337.
140. McDonald to secretary of state [personal attention president and secretary], no. 70, August 24, 1948, *FRUS*, 1948, v. V, pt. 2, 1337–1339.

all political reporting was to be done from here, but I think he got the correct impression.[141]

Tuesday, August 24

Lovely breakfast, after a cool night, which included yogurt, fresh fruit, boiled eggs, and ripe figs. Miss Goldschmidt came in time to say goodbye and to urge us to come as often as we could. She was pleased that I had passed on her messages to Weizmann. As to our visiting with members of the staff there, this is left for later this week.

In the office at nine and over to our formal call on the Russian minister in his "office" on the floor above us at the Gat Rimon. Knox and I, after passing the guard at the door, found A. S. Semioshkin [attaché of the Soviet Legation] and his interpreter sitting formally at a little table. We shook hands, and I began to talk about our mutual discomforts at the hotel and about our housing problems. [Russian Minister Pavel Ivanovich Ershov] wanted to know what progress we had made, and I told him frankly. In answer to my question, he said they had made no progress. I said I hoped he would come and have tea with me on the roof of "our" house even before we had taken full possession. He said he would like to but could not until he had a house in which to receive me in turn. At any rate, this exchange saved me from waiting downstairs indefinitely for him to pay me a purely formal call. We chatted a little about Moscow and Leningrad after I had spoken of my visits there.[142] I told him then that I had spoken to [Andrei] Gromyko about him, and he confirmed that they knew one another but not well.[143] The minister seems rather frail. I am sure that his self-imposed confinement at the Gat Rimon has done nothing to make him sturdier. I think he would be likeable and friendly if he felt that he dared. Back to the office to check and sign [an] important letter to Clark Clifford for the pouch, if and when the courier arrives. After a nap and tea, out to Rehovot for the night. Bobby and her supplementary [Hebrew] teachers, Aviva and Naomi, made a pretty picture as the youngsters kept Bobby repeating Hebrew sounds, particularly the gutturals, until they were satisfied.

Wednesday, August 25

The delay in the arrival of the courier caused me to send my important personal letter to Clark Clifford by Dr. Bergmann to Switzerland, to be mailed there.

---

141. The US consulate in Haifa continued to submit political reports without informing Tel Aviv. See for example Lippincott to secretary of state, no. 48, October 28, 1949, NARA, RG 59, 501.BB Palestine, box 2121, folder 2.

142. McDonald visited in 1929 as president of the Foreign Policy Association and again from August 28–September 3, 1935, to explore the possibility of settling Jewish refugees in Birobidzhan. See Breitman et al., eds., *Refugees and Rescue*, 14–19.

143. Andrei Gromyko (1909–1989), famously grim Soviet diplomat; entered Soviet Ministry of Foreign Affairs in 1939; Soviet ambassador to US, 1943–1945; Soviet ambassador to the UN, 1945–1952; Soviet foreign minister, 1957–1985.

On August 24, 1948 McDonald wrote Clark Clifford:

> *To you I want to explain more fully why, from the point of view of the [Provisional Government], the seeming continued concentration of the US and the UN on the indefinite prolongation of the truce is a) tantamount to taking sides with the Arabs against the Jews, and b) may finally force the [Provisional Government] to resume the war despite the possibility of US and UN sanctions.*

> 1) *So long as the Arabs refuse peace negotiations either directly with the Jews or through the UN or other auspices, it should be perfectly clear that Israel cannot demobilize. Until through such negotiations the Arab states recognize the existence of an independent Israel, the Jewish authorities will know that the Arabs are continuing to prepare to destroy the Jewish state. Hence, an indefinite truce is from Israel's point of view equivalent to a death sentence to be executed at the convenience of the Arabs.*

> 2) *Economically, a prolonged truce is unbearable for Israel because by precluding demilitarization it keeps perhaps as many as 70 or 80 thousand men and women under arms. To argue that Israel does not need such a disproportionately large section of its population in the Army falls on deaf ears here because the [governmental] authorities are determined to rely on their own strength to defend their independence and security; and naturally, they will insist on being the judge of what such strength ought to be. The danger is that the time may come when [the Provisional Government] will consider resumption of war as a lesser burden than the continuation of armed truce.*

> *My own conclusion is that since the President and the Department want peace, they should concentrate on getting peace negotiations started. To reply that this is difficult or that the Arabs won't accept is to confess that the Arabs can indefinitely call the tune.*

> *On this issue, I do not think that the US should be overly influenced by the views of either the Mediator [Bernadotte] or the British. The former, so far as I can judge, is almost completely discredited not only among the Jews, but among the Arabs. His inability to enforce his 'decisions' and his loquacious pronouncements have left him neither substantial moral authority nor dignity.*

> *As to the British, it cannot be too strongly emphasized that: a) their record here in recent years has shown that they can be completely unrealistic in their estimate of existing forces; b) they are not, and in the nature of the case cannot be, impartial as between Jews and Arabs. Unless and until this is always kept in mind by Washington, there will be unnecessary misunderstandings about the elements in the problem here.*

*My telegram to the President and General Marshall of August 22 and
this letter to you are motivated by concern lest the US get itself needlessly involved and lest the President be needlessly and gravely embarrassed.*[144]

*That McDonald wrote directly to Clifford over the head of the secretary of state
and even the president was a violation of protocol that McDonald realized afterward. But as he later put it in his memoirs, "at that critical moment I felt—my colleagues Knox and Cummings supporting me—that courtesy and protocol must yield
to truth-telling, as I saw the truth."*[145]

After nap invited Chaim Izak for a long talk.[146] Gist of his points of view
follow[s]: 1) Situation in Jerusalem during fighting was more difficult than one
can imagine. Shortage of water, food, and nearly incessant firing. Physical destruction already large. 2) Despite widespread restlessness, sense of oppressive
economic burden, and assurance of military supremacy, anticipates that Provisional Government plans to maintain truce. 3) In answer to my question: how
could Provisional Government envisage gains sufficient to satisfy public opinion, Izak replied that this might be done through admission to UN and through
international pressure on Arab states. 4) Izak does not regard dissidents as serious potential threat to Provisional Government now.

After dinner, conference upstairs with Abraham Feinberg of Mount Ver-
non [New York], who has just finished fortnight or so tour of Israel visiting
settlements and army units.[147] He was emphatic about restlessness and confidence and doubted ability of the Provisional Government indefinitely to restrain military. Feinberg [is] oppressed by [the] toll being taken of country's
resources by truce—a truce of "attrition." We talked about situation at home.
He wanted some message from me, but I felt I must limit myself to general
terms about need for understanding there of A-B-Cs of the problem here.

Thursday, August 26

*The State Department did not finance the mission in Tel Aviv adequately. Mat-
ters became more urgent after August 16, when Israel replaced the British Palestine
pound with the Israeli pound. In effect, the the pound rose from about .25 to about .33
against the dollar, so that all debts and expenses by the mission and its personnel were*

144. McDonald to Clifford, August 24, 1948, McDonald Papers, USHMM, box 7, folder 5.
145. McDonald, *My Mission in Israel*, 50.
146. Chaim Izak, news editor of *Davar*; later its managing editor. See also n. 170.
147. Abraham Feinberg (1908–1998), wealthy New York garment manufacturer and Zionist advocate; helped finance Americans for the Haganah in 1947 and was involved in arms procurement; also an important Democratic Party fundraiser who had known Truman since 1944
and a key supporter during the 1948 presidential campaign who helped organize the president's
whistle-stop tour; accompanied Weizmann during his visit to Truman earlier in the month. Mc-
Donald later said that Feinberg "is a new personality on the Jewish scene but already a very important one. He is rated among the two or three Jews most influential with the President. . . . He
is a splendid fellow and a good friend." McDonald to Janet and Halsey, July 13, 1949, McDonald
Papers, Columbia University, box 14, folder 13.

increased.[148] *In the meantime, the mission still lacked basic equipment and personnel. On August 22, 1948 Charles Knox complained to Satterthwaite that "the Department, through its negligence . . . has compromised the operation of this post." Mission personnel including McDonald, Knox said, were spending their own money awaiting reimbursement. "All," Knox said, "are out of funds."*[149]

Lunch with Judith Epstein.[150] She is oppressed by deterioration of the physical side of the country, perhaps more than others by her sorrow at the destruction wrought on Mount Scopus. This was her prevailing opinion despite the fact she recognized, as does everyone, the near miraculous achievements of the Provisional Government during three short months following the chaotic situation left by British. Discussing the situation here and at home, I felt I could not go further than emphasize need there for A-B-C [basic] education. This I urged as much more important than any intra-Jewish issues. She says she was most grateful.

Out to Rehovot. Dr. Benjamin Bloch and Miss Goldschmidt joined us at dinner. Both urged us to come whenever we chose. Again the night was exquisitely beautiful.

Friday, August 27

On the way in, noticed again convoy forming. Just after we turned off the main road about nine o'clock there were eight trucks. The previous mornings there had been eleven, twelve, and sixteen. None of them was what we would call large trucks; instead, they were all medium or small size and of great diversity of condition. As I said to Bobby, half jokingly, the whole load of this morning's convoy could have been carried by a single AP truck.[151]

At the office sent off my first invitations to visiting firemen, Senators Scott Lucas [D-IL] and William Fulbright [D-AR], and Congressman Andrew Somers [D-NY], despite Curtis Barnes warning of what would be involved in their entertainment.

Lunch with Abba Hillel Silver. He emphasized importance of de jure recognition, loan, and lifting [arms] embargo.[152] Later, however, he concentrated

148. Michael Michaely, *Israel's Foreign Exchange Rate System* (Jerusalem: Maurice Falk Institute for Economic Research in Israel, 1971).

149. Knox to Satterthwaite, August 22, 1948, Truman Library, Knox Papers, Box 1, Folder Correspondence 1948–1949.

150. Judith G. Epstein (1895–1988), Massachusetts-born Zionist leader; president of Hadassah, 1937–1939, 1943–1947; advocate for improved health care in Palestine and chair of the building fund for the Hadassah Hospital on Mount Scopus in 1934.

151. AP refers to British Automotive Products, which refurbished former British military trucks.

152. From May 1948, despite Israeli requests for weapons, Marshall had convinced Truman to maintain the US arms embargo on all sides as the best way to ensure a settlement and avoid incidents that might draw the United States into the war. On August 16 Marshall told Truman that despite Israeli requests, the United States should withhold de jure recognition, oppose Israeli UN membership, and reject the Israeli request for a $100 million loan from the Export-Import Bank because of Israel's continued defiance of Bernadotte. See Hahn, *Caught in the Middle East*, 54.

on need to approach the head of the one state [Transjordan], which might be expected to be amenable [to Israel's existence]. This he thought should be done at once.

Rather slowly and perhaps a little reluctantly, he took my emphasis on the fundamentals [McDonald and Silver then discussed the movement toward parliamentary democracy in Israel and the need to explain the process to key members of the US Congress]. I argued that unless these saw necessity for changed approach, it was unlikely those directly in charge on the highest level would take affirmative line. Silver assented and said he would become teacher. Nonetheless, I left with a sense of [Silver's] inadequacy.

Late afternoon, Foreign Office reception at Shertok's office in the gardens. There must have been well over 125 persons there, including all the top officials except Ben-Gurion and the members of the Actions Committee. My opportunities for talks were: Goldie [Meyerson], who said she was leaving for Moscow Sunday; with Mr. and Mrs. Eliezer Hoofien—the former seemed much older;[153] Mr. [Avraham] Granovsky;[154] David Horowitz, with whom it was agreed that I should talk later;[155] Gershon Agronsky,[156] who said he was going up to London in a few weeks; Mrs. Abe Tulin;[157] the chief rabbis Meir Bar-Ilan,[158] Wolf Gold,[159] et al., Silver, Neumann, Brodetsky, Judge and Mrs. Rothenberg,

153. Eliezer Siegfried Hoofien (1881–1957) Dutch-born economist; emigrated to Palestine, 1912; deputy manager, Anglo-Palestine Bank 1912–1924, and general manager, 1924–1948; chairman of Bank Leumi (National Bank of Israel), 1948–1954; architect of new Israeli currency. Testified before Anglo-American Committee of Inquiry in 1946. See Goda et al., eds., *To the Gates of Jerusalem*, 138.
154. Avraham Granovsky [later Granot] (1890–1962), Bessarabian-born, Swiss-educated jurist; emigrated to Palestine, 1924; signatory, declaration of independence, 1948; began his work with JNF in 1920; director-general of JNF since 1940; chairman of JNF board of directors, 1960–1962; author of three books on land use in Palestine.
155. David Horowitz (1899–1979), Galician-born economist; emigrated to Palestine, 1920; director, Jewish Agency Economic Department; member, Jewish Agency delegation to the UN in 1947; director, Ministry of Finance, 1948–1952; helped found Bank of Israel in 1954 and director until 1971. Testimony before Anglo-American Committee of Inquiry in Goda et al., eds., *To the Gates of Jerusalem*, 145.
156. Gershon Agronsky [later Agron] (1894–1959), Ukrainian-born journalist; worked for the press office of the Zionist Commission, 1920–1921; editor, Jewish Telegraphic Agency *Bulletin*, 1921–1924; founded *The Palestine Post* in 1932, renamed *The Jerusalem Post* in 1950; head of Israel's official information service within the Foreign Ministry, 1949–1951; mayor of Jerusalem, 1955–1959.
157. Abraham Tulin (1879–1973), Ukrainian-born American attorney and Zionist; member, ZOA Executive Committee 1919–1920, 1929–1933; member, American Zionist Emergency Council [AZEC], 1940–1947; afterwards director, Society for the Advancement of the Hebrew Institute for Technology in Haifa; co-author of *Basic Equities of the Palestine Problem* (1947); annotator and editor of *Book of Documents* submitted to UN General Assembly on behalf of the Jewish Agency for Palestine, 1947.
158. Meir Bar-Ilan [formerly Berlin] (1880–1949), Lithuanian-born Orthodox rabbi; developer and head of religious Zionist movement [Mizrahi] in United States and Palestine after being invited into the movement by Rabbi Wolf Gold (see note 159); tried to get US government to conduct rescue efforts during World War II; inspired the founding of Bar-Ilan University in Ramat Gan in 1950.
159. Wolf [Ze'ev] Gold (1889–1956), Stettin-born Orthodox rabbi; helped found Mizrahi in United States with Meier Berlin; emigrated to Palestine in 1935; took part in rescue activities during the Holocaust and the 1943 "Rabbis' March" in Washington; signatory, declaration of independence, 1948, and served on Provisional State Council as member of Mizrahi.

Fig. 2.2. Group portrait of guests at a reception for diplomats and ambassadors held at the Foreign Ministry office in Tel Aviv, August 27, 1948. Pictured are Golda Meyerson, Barbara McDonald, James McDonald, Esther Herlitz, and Moshe Shertok. Israeli Government Press Office.

Mendel Fisher, several members of the government who are still only names to me but whom I am to meet soon.

Took advantage of my meeting with General Lundström, General William Riley,[160] Reedman, and some other UN officials to bring the two generals and the aide-de-corps to Lundström together with the Hadassah gals to discuss: the possibility of repairs being made on the Scopus [hospital] building; possible opportunity for them to visit Scopus. An incidental purpose was to get Lundström to see that the buildings were something more than stone and mortar. Lundström promptly said that visit could be arranged through regular UN plane and then under UN auspices from [Qalandia] airfield to Scopus. He then brought in his aide, and I brought over Riley. For a time, it looked as though the thing could be done without bothering about papers from the other side. Subsequently, doubts were raised when it was learned the plane would come down at Gaza on its way to Jerusalem. Nonetheless, there was some value in

160. Brigadier General William E. Riley (1897–1970), US Marine Corps; decorated staff officer during World Wars I and II; appointed the first chief of staff for the UNTSO after resignation of Lundström, September 1948; remained in that position until his retirement in 1953; helped shape the armistice regime between Israel and its neighbors.

the talk. I liked Lundström, thought him rather remote from harsh realities. Reedman seems an intelligent person. During the course of the above discussion brought in Shertok to check on exit permit. He assented at once.

Tea with Mendel Fisher, joined by Cummings and Silver. Late session with Rose Halprin regarding Mount Scopus and home situation.[161] As to the latter, she admitted inadequacy of the present company and wanted to have specific suggestions about higher talent. Suggested Pinhas Rosen.[162] But we both recognized that these ideas were weakened by time element. To bed late and, as usual in Tel Aviv, inadequate sleep.

Saturday, August 28

Breakfast at the ungodly hour of seven with General Riley. He admitted that the truce is uneasy, that it bears with disproportionate heaviness on Jerusalem, and that it may not last. He spoke highly of John MacDonald as a quiet, efficient official. He was unemotional about Lundström and his Swedish advisers. As to Bunche, he had the prevailing high opinion. As to the Scopus plans, he was very pessimistic, particularly if the plane had to land at Gaza. He thought a special plane essential. He agreed that our communications here were vulnerable and should be supplemented at once. In answer to my question about the relative allocation of UN observers to Israel and Arab territories, he admitted present disproportion, but said plans were to more nearly equalize numbers.

As Miss Clark and I were working on a memo for Halsey [Barrett—McDonald's son-in-law], Daniel De Luce and Carter L. Davidson of the Associated Press called, and I invited them up. The former was just back from Amman,[163] and the latter from Jerusalem.[164] He [Davidson] is the much sounder of the two, and the more silent. De Luce had an easy formula of agreeing always with the British. He also attributed the Truman policy in Palestine solely to instructions of David Niles. He was interesting, however, in his estimates of the weakness of the Arab Legion, which he said had no ammunition, and his references to Abdullah's willingness. I gave them no news and no answers which could be quoted to their various half questions about American policy and the

---

161. Rose Luria Halprin (1896–1978), New York-born American Zionist leader; president of Hadassah, 1932–1934, 1947–1952; lived in Jerusalem from 1934 to 1939 to oversee the construction of Hadassah Hospital on Mount Scopus; treasurer, AZEC, 1942–1945; vice-chair, AZEC, 1945–1947; Jewish Agency Executive, 1946–1966; led effort to set up alternate medical facilities in Jerusalem after Hadassah Hospital was cut off in 1947; helped found the Hebrew-University Hadassah Medical School in 1949 and new Hadassah Hospital in Ein Kerem in 1952.

162. Pinhas Rosen [formerly Felix Rosenblüth] (1887–1978), Berlin-born jurist and Zionist; emigrated to Palestine, 1926; founder and head of New Aliyah Party, 1942, which became the Progressive Party in 1949; signatory of declaration of independence, 1948; minister of justice, 1948–1951; 1952–1956, 1958–1961; close associate of Ben-Gurion in 1940s and early 1950s.

163. Daniel De Luce (1912–2002), war correspondent; won Pulitzer Prize in 1943; roving correspondent covering the Arab Legion, 1948.

164. Carter Davidson (1916–1968), war correspondent in London and Paris during World War II; Associated Press bureau chief in Jerusalem when War of Independence broke out; covered the Israeli fighting in Jerusalem; later a television reporter.

sources thereof, or of the relations between the Department and the White House.

Out to the Mendes Sacks farm just off of the main road to Haifa and just south of the road turning off to Tel Mond.[165] It was a delightful tea party. The Sackses are 100% solid and would bear much cultivation. They cordially invited us out again any time and Bobby and Miss Clark anytime if I could not come. Back regretfully to the noise of the Gat Rimon.

Sunday, August 29

Though it was Sunday, Bobby and I worked at the office on my Halsey memorandum. Though we were interrupted repeatedly we managed to get it typed as far as I had sketched it.

McDonald periodically sent private reports to his daughter Janet and his son-in-law Halsey Barrett. These reports were then forwarded to Clark Clifford at the White House with no risk of being seen by anyone else. In his letter dated August 30, McDonald described what he called the A-B-Cs of the problem in Palestine, assessments that were at odds with UN, British, and even US policies.

The purpose of US policy, he said, was "peace in Palestine, the fullest protection of all Christian interests in Palestine including the Holy Places, and friendship with all of the countries of the Middle East." But central to all of these principles, he argued, was "the restoration of peace at the earliest possible moment in all of Palestine." McDonald noted, "The Provisional Government of Israel has recently reiterated its desire for peace negotiations directly with the Arab states or under UN or other auspices. The [Provisional Government], moreover, has informally indicated to me that it would welcome pressure on Israel and the Arab states, or on Israel and the one Arab state now most likely to be willing to begin peace negotiations. In contrast the Arab states, with one exception, have repeatedly and almost contemptuously rejected all proposals for such peace negotiations."

McDonald wrote that the UN's concentration on "extension indefinitely of the truce is misleading and dangerous," partly because it obscured the real issue of peace, partly because truce was a form of war by other means that would lead again to open warfare, and partly because "it invites Arab continued intransigent resistance to peace negotiations." He continued, "So long as the UN or the Mediator does not demand that the parties discuss peace terms, the Arabs can maintain that there is no Israel with which they are willing to deal. From this attitude the [Provisional Government] can conclude only that the Arab authorities are using the truce as an opportunity to prepare for the eventual destruction of the Jewish State. To expect the [Provisional Government] to accept this situation indefinitely is to misread completely Israeli opinion." Even US and UN sanctions would not deter Israeli defense initiatives.

---

165. Mendes H. Sacks, Baltimore-born horticulturalist; emigrated to Palestine, 1932; leading citrus grower and exporter in Palestine/Israel who led in the marketing success of Jaffa oranges; head of Pardess Citrus Growers' Syndicate (founded in 1902); later general manager of the Citrus Marketing Board of Israel; exponent of private industry in Israel. McDonald spent a great deal of time at the Sacks complex.

"Suicidal though such resistance may seem," McDonald wrote, "I am convinced that the [Provisional Government] would fight and that it would have the unanimous support of its people. Ancient Jewish history offers many examples of comparable 'suicidal' resistance to overwhelming force." Uncritical US support of the UN, he said, "is dangerous because it may involve the United States—despite or even because of American good intentions and American humanitarianism—in an open conflict with a desperate and embattled Israel."

McDonald's private assessment of Bernadotte was caustic: "Count Bernadotte has repeatedly shown and continues to show a serious lack of understanding of Jewish history and of the public opinion of the people of Israel. . . . Had he known of the Jewish millennial prayers for their return to Jerusalem he could not have put forward his proposal that Jerusalem might become the capital of Abdullah's enlarged Trans-Jordania. Two or three months ago the Jews would have accepted the internationalization or the partition of Jerusalem, but the Mediator's suggestion that it might become Moslem was such an unforgivable affront that the [Provisional Government] would now find it much more difficult to accept the earlier compromise solutions."

After reiterating his concerns regarding the objectivity of the British government, McDonald commented on Arab refugees:

> *The plight of the approximately three hundred thousand Arab refugees is a tragedy that continues to grow in intensity and scope. But it is wholly unrealistic to think that the [Provisional Government], except for what Shertok has called "compassionate cases," will permit the return of the mass of refugees as long as the Iraqi, Trans-Jordanian, and Egyptian armies are in the field against their state. Shertok's contention that the problem of the refugees must be taken up at the peace table as a part of a general settlement is difficult to answer. No Israeli government could take any other line. The sooner, therefore, that peace is established the sooner that those among the refugees who desire to do so may have a chance to return to their homes.*

McDonald continued that Soviet influence in Israel would remain limited unless the United States and Israel developed an antagonistic relationship. As for religious sites, McDonald predicted that "the fullest protection of Christian interests in the Holy Places and elsewhere in Palestine can be assured only when the peace is being made." The Holy Places would most likely be placed under the traditional guardianship of their religious authorities.[166]

This [diary] item goes back to Saturday dinner with Major Nicholas Andronovich,[167] Knox, and Cummings. Andronovich was very interesting about the actual situation in Jerusalem, for example, the incidents involving George

---

166. McDonald to Halsey and Janet Barrett, August 30, 1948, McDonald Papers, USHMM, box 7, folder 5.
167. Nicholas Andronovich (1907–1993), ethnic Russian émigré; US Army intelligence agent in Jerusalem during World War II; established close relationships with Jewish and Arab leaders as well as British officials for his reports on Palestine; after 1947 became the CIA representative in the US Consulate General in Jerusalem; later CIA chief of station in Amman.

Paro[168] and, earlier, Thomas Wasson.[169] He, too, spoke highly of John J. MacDonald. On broader policy, he leaned towards prolonged negotiations and a direct method with the most modern of the group. This, however, would require the utilization of high out-of-line talent to carry necessary prestige. On all matters in the special field, Andronovich was enlightening. It was following some of this talk that I gave my warning to Rose [Halprin].

Among the interruptions Sunday morning were those from our friend up the hill [Andronovich], who amplified his views. He also gave me the clearest picture I have had of the lines in Jerusalem. Beyond that he suggested what [political and diplomatic] adjustments there might be. He assumed the inevitability of [Jerusalem's] partition, but under a general international authority leaving to the two sections municipal autonomy. If the international area were widened along the lines of the Lundström demilitarization proposal, there would have to be several municipal autonomous unions. He stressed the necessity of saving face if the war were not to be continued indefinitely. Yet he indicated no doubt of the present disproportion of military strength.

Earlier, Andronovich had talked at some length of Dov Joseph and the brittleness of the latter. It was difficult, he said, to tell where natural brusqueness ended and tactical brusqueness began. Similarly, it was hard to discern up to what point the Irgun and Sternists are used as pressure. In any case, it is clear, he said, that the broad strategy is too narrow in that area, the field left open for foreign operations. As to my sergeant chauffeur friend, he thought, the latter would be useful and that the only question was his background, since this, according to general thinking, might make him a source of penetration. Nonetheless, [Andronovich] agreed that through his friends he would follow up. As he was leaving, I expressed the hope that he was returning soon and gave him cordial greetings for my namesake [John MacDonald].

Another interruption was that of Consul General [Aubrey] Lippincott, with whom I later lunched. He said that the basis of cooperation outlined in Knox's letter would be followed strictly by him. He then told me of his troubles growing out of the Department's cuts on alien help. On this point I volunteered to be any help I could with Washington. My contribution to the conversation was to give him the inside story of my appointment and of intra-organizational relations. I also showed him Truman's letter. He was appreciative of my frankness and will, I think, be loyal and cooperative. On the problem of oil here, he promised to send me an earlier analysis he had made. As to the immediate situation, he thought it difficult but had few, if any, figures.

---

168. George Paro (1909–1990), cipher clerk in the US Consulate General in Jerusalem; kidnapped on August 21, 1948, and held for seventeen hours by Jewish irregulars as a British spy before being rescued by Israeli authorities.

169. Thomas C. Wasson (1896–1948), US consul general in Jerusalem, April–May 1948; member of UN Truce Commission; tried to halt the Arab Legion shelling of Mount Scopus; shot on May 22, 1948, while returning to US consulate from French consulate and died the next day. It was never determined whether the assailant was Arab or Jewish.

McDonald's party for the Actions Committee at the future ambassadorial resi-
dence in Tel Binyamin followed that evening. Lazar Braudo and his wife still occu-
pied the house and co-hosted the event.

Mr. and Mrs. Braudo and Bobby and I received. Either the Braudos or I knew a large proportion of those who came. These included most of the members of the Actions Committee and some of the high governmental officials, Shertok, Kaplan, and others. Among the other more important guests, besides the American ZOA and Hadassah groups, were the editor of the *Davar* [Zalman Shazar], a labor paper and the most important one in Israel.[170] He and I had a nice visit, which is to be followed up.[171] With the other guests there was, in the nature of the case, hardly any time to talk at all.

In order that we might have the maximum number around seven o'clock, I shunted those who started to leave earlier up to the magnificent roof. As a result, almost the whole group was present a little after seven when I read my little talk, which was translated by Mrs. Agronsky. In reply, Rabbi Berlin [Bar-Ilan] made a brief statement in Hebrew. The talk seemed to meet warm approval. After nearly all the guests had left, some of the Hadassah gals and the Braudos and our group sat on the balcony or visited the roof. The Americans were obviously impressed that here was an adequate and proper home for the American Special Representative. Bobby and the staff agree.

Following a very light supper, Bobby and I sat on our balcony at the hotel overlooking the sea and tried to make ourselves heard to one another above the roar of the dance orchestra as we talked about plans for Ruth [McDonald's wife] coming at the earliest moment after Janet no longer needs her. We had to conclude, however, that this probably would not be before the end of September or the first of October when she starts on her mission as the mistress of the American Mission to Israel.

Monday, August 30

Lunch with John Reedman, South African member of the UN, and until recently holding the dual position now merged—UN representative accredited to [the] Provisional Government in matters of truce and one of the political advisers of the count. He has a reputation for being very closed-mouthed. Deliberately, therefore, I talked for most of the lunch about South Africa, and only towards the end did we approach UN and truce questions. There was time for me to hear him say that the truce in itself could not lead to peace but rather lead to war, and that, therefore, it was imperative that moves towards peace negotiations be inaugurated promptly. I think it would be useful for me to see Reedman again.

---

170. *Davar* was the news organ of Mapai and the Histadrut. *Haaretz* was also notable at this time. See also entry of June 10, 1950.
171. See also entry of May 5, 1950.

Awakening from my nap, Bobby brought the not too cheerful news that Congressman Somers was downstairs.[172] I hastily dressed and we had—Bobby and I—tea, and he something more potent, on the balcony. My mind working with unwanted agility, I persuaded Somers to go out to Rehovot with me for the night. This gave us a perfect opportunity to get acquainted. It pleased him. He saw something of the country. Later, Miss Goldschmidt and Mrs. Weizmann joined us at dinner. Meantime, I took Somers for a walk, and we climbed to the roof of the new building, which gave us a splendid view of the sunset and of the afterglow on the Judean hills. The scene could hardly have been more beautiful. After dinner we talked for half an hour or so on the roof and were ready for bed early.

The following [were] the main points.

1) Somers outlined at length for more than an hour his early and continued close relations with Peter Bergson and his part in the organization and support of the latter's several groups.[173] He showed wholehearted sympathy with Bergson's point of view, even on the ship *Altalena*. As to this last, he said that he saw no reason that there should have been the killing of the individuals, or that the ship could not have been handled as had others previously.[174] He recognizes, however, that in addition, conditions have changed and that his chance to be helpful either in consolidating lines here or otherwise depends upon winning confidence of Ben-Gurion. Knox and I will do what we can to arrange for him to see the officials. I urged him, meanwhile, to either stay out of the press or limit his remarks to the most

172. Andrew Lawrence Somers (1895–1949), Irish-born Democratic representative for New York's 6th district (Brooklyn), 1925–1949; opponent of British imperialism; supported the Revisionist Zionist Bergson Group in the United States during World War II.

173. Hillel Kook [aka Peter Bergson] (1915–2001), Lithuanian-born Revisionist Zionist leader who emigrated to Palestine in 1924 and who led Revisionist efforts in the United States during World War II under the pseudonym Peter Bergson. The Bergson Group's attention-getting activities concerning the issue of rescue during the Holocaust alienated other American Jewish leaders. Supported anti-British IZL activities in Palestine after the war, establishing the Hebrew Committee for National Liberation and the American League for a Free Palestine, and was involved in smuggling immigrants and weapons. On support of the Bergson Group and the IZL by Somers, see Judith Tydor Baumel, *The "Bergson Boys" and the Origins of Contemporary Zionist Militancy* (Syracuse, NY: Syracuse University Press, 2005).

174. The *Altalena* was a ship bought by the IZL in 1947. It sailed from France and arrived in Israel on June 20, 1948, with nearly 1,000 IZL fighters, as well as weapons and ammunition earmarked for the IZL. To assert governmental authority and to demonstrate that Israel adhered to the truce—the British had publicized the arrival of the *Altalena*—the Provisional Government, after failed negotiations with IZL leaders, moved to seize the ship. The confrontation between the IDF and IZL in Tel Aviv on June 22 resulted in the sinking of the *Altalena* and the deaths of sixteen IZL fighters and three IDF soldiers. Bergson was one of the five IZL leaders arrested and detained after the incident. On June 1, 1948 the IZL, in an agreement with the IDF, had officially disbanded, but its members had two distinct IZL battalions under IDF command, and the IZL maintained its own forces in Jerusalem. After the *Altalena* affair, fighters in the IZL battalions were dispersed among different IDF units. The IZL units in Jerusalem remained independent for the time being. See Baumel, *Bergson Boys*, 241–243; Morris, *1948*, 271.

innocent and general terms.[175] I think he agreed. His knowledge of things here is extraordinarily uneven, and it would be, naturally, considering the sources of his information. One of his greatest mistakes is to exaggerate largely the role of religion and religious tradition here.

Tuesday, August 31

Despite the beautiful quietness of the night, Somers said he slept not at all, and his looks tended to confirm that. He is not a well man. He has lost a large part of his stomach in an operation, and is overstrained and has come to rely, apparently, more than he should, upon stimulants. On the way out last evening we stopped at the office of the president of the [Provisional State] Council[176] at Rishon and planned to visit the Rishon wine cellars this morning on the way in to Tel Aviv. I realized, however, that it would be impossible for me to wait there, so I left Somers at the municipal office at Rishon with the understanding that he would be delivered at our office after he finished his tour of the winery.

Back to the office I got in touch with Jewish National Fund, [which] arranged to take Somers up to the country today. Somers, not showing up in my office, [so] Knox and I stopped at his hotel to inquire. He explained that he had gotten back late from Rishon and was exhausted and had gone straight to the hotel. I told him of our disappointment since the JNF car had been waiting since noon. We then agreed that he and Fowler Harper[177] should use the car the next day at nine, returning in time for them to go to Jerusalem. It was clear, however, that Somers's and Harper's chief interest was not to see the country but rather to pull off a political coup.

This was then disclosed, and a more harebrained, screwballed scheme I have never known. Here it is: Somers wants to persuade the Provisional Government to designate his friend [probably Bergson] as a special envoy to the US for the purpose of making special purchases. Both Somers and Harper assured us that ships and trucks and other supplies not otherwise available would thus be secured. But the wildest part of the scheme was that disappointment would unify Israel and American Jewry.

In response, I dared not say what I thought and limited myself to the suggestion that there was only one man to whom such a proposal could be presented to—Ben-Gurion—and that we would do our best to arrange for an interview for Somers personally and the loan. His schedule made Friday and Sunday the only days. He said we would work on that basis. Categorically, I

175. Ben-Gurion saw Bergson's actions as separatist, even during World War II, and distrusted him all the more after the *Altalena* affair. See Tuvia Friling, *Arrows in the Dark: David Ben-Gurion, the Yishuv Leadership, and Rescue Attempts During the Holocaust*, 2 vols. (Madison, WI: University of Wisconsin Press, 2005), v. 1, 112–115.

176. The Provisional State Council served as the parliamentary body before the first Israeli elections in 1949. The council's president was officially Chaim Weizmann.

177. Fowler Vincent Harper (1867–1965), Ohio-born attorney; appointed general counsel to the Federal Security Agency in 1939; became public activist in 1940s, regularly appearing on radio program "What America Thinks;" supporter of Bergson.

warned Somers against walking under any circumstances from the YMCA [building][178] to the American consulate in Jerusalem. I explained that it was there that Wasson had been killed and most of the other Americans more or less seriously injured. Somers seemed too unwell or groggy to be much impressed, but Harper promised that he would take the necessary precautions.

Eleven o'clock, interview with Pinhas Rosen, Minister of Justice, at his office in Sarona. He introduced me to half a dozen members or more of his staff, including Ya'akov Shimson Shapira, the attorney general.[179] Stimulated by fruit juice, we had a general talk about the organization of his department, the courts, and, what interested me most, the progress being made by the department in land registration. They are now using the American, and I think he said, the Australian, rather than the British system. It was a pleasant visit but primarily formal.

My next call was on Rabbi Yitzhak-Meir Levin, minister of welfare, at his residence and office, the large, but from the point of view of style, abominable building, Gesundheit House, in the center of town.[180] The whole atmosphere of the rabbi's house and staff was Agudat. We had a pleasant chat, he at first using Hebrew, which was excellently translated by one of his young assistants. Later he used German, and we got on faster. His wife, a typical rabbi's frau, served refreshments, which I had to take, though I was already late for my next appointment. I suggested that the rabbi later tell me at length about the problem of reestablishing religion as a vital factor in the lives of the young people in Israel. He was pleased at this suggestion.

Back to Sarona, and therefore late, for my interview with Bechor-Shalom Sheetrit, minister of police and minority affairs.[181] Here, too, there were refreshments and meeting with members of Sheetrit's staff. The talk was general and on the light side but useful because of the necessary contact with the police here. My impression that Sheetrit is a man of exceptional ability was not changed. The last of the four appointments was with Dr. Fritz [Peretz] Bernstein, Minister of Trade and Industry, also in Sarona.[182] Here there were no associates,

178. On the status of the YMCA building, see entry of December 28, 1948.
179. Ya'akov Shimson Shapira (1902–1993), Ukrainian-born labor activist; emigrated to Palestine, 1924; studied law at Hebrew University; represented Palestine Jewish activists before British authorities; attorney-general, 1948–1950; minister of justice, 1966–1972, 1972–1973.
180. Yitzhak-Meir Levin (1893–1971), Polish-born rabbi; helped found Agudat Israel, the Orthodox Jewish party, 1924; represented Agudat Israel in Polish Sejm, 1937–1939; aided refugees in Warsaw after German invasion; migrated to Palestine, 1940; headed Agudat branch there; signatory, declaration of independence, 1948; sole Agudat Israel member of provisional government as minister of welfare; remained in successive two cabinets in that office as member of the United Religious Front.
181. Bechor-Shalom Sheetrit (1895–1967), Palestine-born lawyer who organized local police units in the late Ottoman and Mandate periods; served as district judge after 1935; leader of the Sephardic and Oriental Communities Party; signatory, declaration of independence, 1948; joined Provisional Government as minister of police and minority affairs; minority affairs section of his office was closed in 1949, and he remained minister of police until his death in 1967.
182. Peretz [formerly Shlomo Fritz] Bernstein (1890–1971), German-born Zionist who left Germany for Netherlands before World War I; emigrated to Palestine, 1936; editor, General Zionist newspaper *HaBoker*, 1936–1946; director, Jewish Agency economics department, 1946–1948;

and we talked more seriously about current anti-American, tendentious press comments and especially about the oil situation. On the latter, he told me that the British were now suggesting the possibility of [shipping] crude [oil] from Kuwait on the Persian Gulf by the way of the Suez [Canal] to Haifa.[183] He was very interesting about the possibilities of Venezuela and elsewhere and about the price which an Eastern European country might require. He confirmed that Britishers were hanging around Haifa and Cyprus in the expectation of the reopening of the Haifa refinery. Left that Cummings would make a date to see him and then some of his technicians in view to get data for [a] report on oil.

signatory, declaration of independence, 1948; minister of trade and industry as only General Zionist member of cabinet, 1948–1949; served in same position, 1952–1955.

183. When the Iraqi oil supply ceased with the creation of Israel, the British looked for other sources of crude, to be moved by tanker, in order to restart refining operations at their refinery in Haifa. Bialer, *Oil and the Arab-Israeli Conflict, 1948–1963*, 39–84.

3. September 1948

Early breakfast appointment with Nahum Goldmann, although actually I had eaten and been at work some time before he came at 8:15.[1] Our talk was in general terms about the crisis reached in the Actions Committee on the issue of participation by the members of the [Israeli] government. Although [Selig] Brodetsky and Hadassah were favoring a compromise, the ZOA [Zionist Organization of America] is insisting on exclusion.

The creation of Israel in 1948 exacerbated the problem of who spoke for Zionism and the world's Jews—the traditional Diaspora bodies such as the World Jewish Congress, Hadassah, and the Jewish Agency or the new government of Israel. Worried about charges of dual loyalty, American Jewish leaders argued that members of the Israeli government had to separate themselves from the Diaspora bodies. Some, particularly Rabbi Silver and Emanuel Neumann of the ZOA, hoped to retain a leading voice in the global Zionist movement. Ben-Gurion accepted the principle of separation, but he would not accept influence by Silver and Neumann over Israeli state policy.[2]

As to Goldmann's own plans, he was vague, talked about rest and temporary retirement, confessing finally that at present he really had nothing to do. This, plus the probability that he is waiting on a formal appointment once Ben-Gurion gives any form of recognition, explains his unwanted reticence.

Talked with [Eliezer] Kaplan and [David] Horowitz in the former's office. I was surprised at Kaplan's emphasis on the importance of Israel's admission to the Assembly [UN]. He seemed not optimistic about the loan or about other aspects of Israeli-US relations, possibly reflecting Epstein's report.

We covered much ground, each speaking with much frankness. I was surprised, too, at his underlining the importance from Israel's point of view of the

---

1. Nahum Goldmann (1895–1982), Belorussian-born German Jew, stripped of citizenship in 1935; represented Jewish Agency in the United States after 1935; president, World Jewish Congress from its formation in 1936 until 1977; advocated partition of Palestine after World War II through quiet diplomacy; in September 1948 head of American section of Jewish Agency. See essays in Mark A. Raider, ed., *Nahum Goldmann: Statesman Without a State* (Albany, NY: SUNY Press, 2009).

2. See Schiff, *The Downfall of Abba Hillel Silver*, 121–143; also the essays in Mark A. Raider, Jonathan D. Sarna, and Ronald W. Zweig, eds., *Abba Hillel Silver and American Zionism* (London: Frank Cass, 1977).

reported recent American protest in Prague against alleged excessive Czech armament supplies to Israel.[3]

Eliahu Epstein came early for luncheon, and our talk lasted until about 3:15, ending with an engagement to meet for dinner at 8:30 on the following Monday before he is scheduled to return to the States. We talked about the following:

1) The visit of Somers, his relations with Peter Bergson, his desire to see Ben-Gurion, and his program for using his friends as a unifying influence in Israel and as a special purchasing agent in US. Epstein's reaction was what I anticipated.[4]
2) Epstein's long talk with Lovett at the Department before I left.[5] It lasted nearly an hour and a half and included the following chief subjects: a) Peace and truce; b) loan; c) refugees; d) admission to UN.

On a) the talk reportedly was general and not the main purpose of Lovett. b) was more to the center of Lovett's thinking. The Department had no objection in principle, but there were practical objections of the Export-Import Bank to overcome. For example, stability of the Provisional Government, its peaceful intentions, the specific projects, etc. On this latest, the most significant comment was that Lovett hoped the projects "could be concentrated near Tel Aviv." Earlier Kaplan and Horowitz had referred to this suggestion as having extraordinary political significance. On the whole, he [Epstein] was discouraged rather than the reverse about this problem. As to c), Lovett expressed his concern, but did not make it a major issue. As to d), it was skirted around rather than discussed.

The Israeli government had asked in May 1948 for a loan of $100 million from the US Export–Import Bank for developmental purposes. Delays from the State Department, which controlled the bank, frustrated Israeli diplomats. Eliahu Epstein wrote Clark Clifford on August 3, "I do not believe that the President can know how repeatedly we have been put off in this matter, from week to week and from month to month."[6] Lovett said the delay owed to the political nature of the loan.[7] Israeli negotiators in Washington who met with officials from the State Department's Division of Near Eastern Affairs confirmed to Epstein on August 31, 1948, that "there is absolutely no prospect receiving loan from Export–Import Bank at this time."[8]

3. Truman expressed concern regarding the supply of weapons from Czechoslovakia to Israel. Shertok later told Epstein to respond to the State Department that Israel would prefer to purchase weapons from the United States, but that "we will have to get arms wherever possible because [it is a] matter of life and death." Shertok to Epstein, September 17, 1948, *DFPI*, v. 1, d. 516.

4. See entry of August 30, 1948.

5. See Memorandum by Lovett, August 26, 1948, *FRUS*, 1948, v. V, pt. 2, 1345–1348.

6. Truman Library, Clifford Papers, Subject File, 1945–54, box 13, folder Palestine Misc., 1 of 3.

7. Memorandum by Lovett, August 26, 1948, *FRUS*, 1948, v. V, pt. 2, 1345–1348.

8. *DFPI*, v. 1, d. 490.

In response to my question, he, unlike Kaplan, thought that a special envoy to Abdullah would be useful, though the latter would not be free to act.[9] The move would nonetheless indicate to him important support should he move towards peace. Kaplan had been of the opinion that this move would distract attention from more important matters, for example, admission to the UN.

He repeated conviction of [the] futility, and worse, of continued concentration merely on [the] truce. All-important was to give the Arab world unmistakable proof of finality of Israel's status. This could be done through reemphasis to states concerned that the US unalterably is committed to peace purposes and resistance to aggression. Also vital that no room be left for hope that US would waver as previously.[10] Only through such clear proof of consistency could [the] Arab states be persuaded to accept Israel as a permanent independent state. Epstein regarded de jure recognition alone and admission as all of great importance, but as in a certain sense [means], rather than [ends].

He said that he was going up to Jerusalem [on] Thursday, spending Friday with a group on the UN, and that he thought that we could advantageously compare notes before he returned to the States next week. I agreed and when he invited me to the Kaete Dan[11] for dinner on Monday, I replied by insisting that he come to us. Tea with the officers of the staff. Then long conference with Knox and Cummings about possible comprehensive restatement to Truman and Marshall. Although they stayed to dinner and we talked afterwards, their reaction to the outline I gave was not helpful, but rather, they seemed to concentrate on the difficulties.

Thursday, September 2

To the office with Bobby and Miss Clark for a few minutes before beginning a series of appointments. Knox showed me despatch from [the US mission in] Baghdad, which gave an extraordinarily interesting summation of an Arab interpretation of the present situation. The main points were: 1) despite military debacle, internal situations did not permit change in [the] form of recognition of Israel. 2) Acquiescence most that could be expected for a year. This goes also for Amman. "Only weapon left is non-recognition." Popular illusions still prevalent; illustrated by Iraqi government's political victory on platform of intransigence towards Israel. 3) Domestic danger would in many places be great if came sudden realization of defeat through, for example, British recognition. 4) No general settlement possible before twelve months, but would be practical to have local frontier agreements under international auspices. 5) Complained

9. The Israeli government at this time communicated to Abdullah through the Belgian consul general in Jerusalem, Jean Nieuwenhuys, who also served as chairman of the UN consular Truce Commission.
10. Refers to the trusteeship proposal from the State Department to the UN Security Council in March 1948.
11. The Kaete Dan was the main hotel on the coast in Tel Aviv.

of ineptness of Arab publicity on refugees, for they had been unable to secure any pictures to date. Urged action by American private agencies through whose relief activities Abdullah's low popular status might be improved. Refugees constitute material, inflammable resentment but are [an] insoluble problem because a) most cannot return, and b) most are unwilling to return.

At ten o'clock to the WIZO baby clinic with Mrs. Braudo and enjoyed almost an hour with the infants, all shades of complexions and personalities ranging from Yemenite darkness to European blondness, and to an infant that strongly suggested Mongol blood. One could not imagine a more spotless institution or one better run. I was much impressed by the doctor and the nurse who were in charge.

Eleven o'clock appointment with Mr. David Remez, the minister of transport and communications at Sarona.[12] There I met his colleagues in charge respectively of post, telegraph, telephone and radio; ports and harbors and shipping; roads and railways; and perhaps some others. Most of the talk was with the minister of posts, etc. about local telephone and overseas communications. He promised to see what could be done about improving our services at Ramat Gan, and of hopes for scrambled overseas telephone and erection soon of 50-watt medium-wave length station and the 50-watt shortwave station.

Neither the line at McDonald's residence nor the telephone lines at the US offices at Ramat Gan were secure. As he wrote to Ben Abrams as late as January 1949 after a telephone call, "The reason for my reticence I hope you understood. It was the fact that our conversation was being listened to by perhaps hundreds of people who with ordinary short wave sets could hear what each of us said as clearly as we could hear one another. . . . Soon the [Israeli] Government promises that trans–Atlantic voices will be scrambled but even they can, [and] undoubtedly will be, unscrambled by interested Russian, British, and other official monitors."[13]

The former would cover the Middle East, and the latter would be intended particularly to reach Jewish communities throughout the world. The minister spoke of his desire to have released the two Constellations purchased for civilian aviation and to establish a non-stop Paris-Lydda route.

Eleven-thirty—a session with Moshe Shapira, minister of immigration and [minister of] health.[14] Here the talk was more general with special emphasis only on the problem of the US interpretation of the military age clause.

12. David Remez (1886–1951), Belorussian-born Labor Zionist; founding member of Mapai, senior member of Histadrut; signatory, declaration of independence, 1948; minister of transport, 1948–1950.

13. McDonald to Benjamin Abrams, January 11, 1949, McDonald Papers, Columbia University, box 6, folder 2.

14. Moshe Shapira (1902–1970), Belorussian-born Mizrahi organizer, educator, and politician; director of Jewish Agency's Aliyah department from 1936–1948; signatory, declaration of independence, 1948; minister of health and minister of immigration, 1948–1951; elected to Knesset as member of United Religious Front, 1949.

They showed me the text of what was said to be the order by the military authorities in Germany prohibiting exit for Palestine [Israel] of: a) youth in military formations or armed and; b) men between the ages of 18 and 55. It was this last which was so controversial.[15]

Brief talk at the office with Lippincott from Haifa. Later, decision to reconsider proposed regular Thursday conferences here. Speaking of communication, they all [Knox and the others] stressed the invaluableness of his facilities [at Haifa], which, for example, kept them closely in touch with Jerusalem. Talk with Mrs. [Judith] Epstein about joining the staff. She will stop here on her way back from Haifa to Jerusalem for a definite answer.

Friday, September 3

At the office completed, with the approval of Knox and Cummings, an important despatch on recognition.[16] Later, I was to learn that it could not be sent because of the arrival of a long and closely related despatch from the Department.

In this despatch Marshall firmly told McDonald that the "integral problem" was the Israeli government's "professing its desire for immediate peace negotiations but maintaining its disinclination to carry out certain essential preliminary steps which you cite as 'partial measures' including maintenance of truce, demilitarization of Jerusalem, and alleviation of Arab refugee problem." Marshall noted that "I do not concur in your conclusion" that "'Jewish emphasis on peace negotiations now is sounder than present US and UN emphasis on truce and demilitarization and refugees.'" He continued, "For your own info, the US feels that the new State of Israel should have boundaries which will make it more homogenous and well-integrated than the hourglass frontiers drawn on the map of the November 29 Resolution. . . . Specifically it would appear to us that Israel might expand into the rich area of Galilee which it now holds in military occupation, in return for relinquishing a large part of the Negev to Transjordan." Jerusalem, the secretary continued, "should form [an] international enclave" though another solution acceptable to all sides with guarantees for the Holy Places would also be acceptable.

Marshall instructed that McDonald should discuss these suggestions with Ben-Gurion and Shertok, making it clear that the suggestions were tentative and that they would be "trying [them] on for size." He concluded, however, that the United States

---

15. The State Department's most recent announcement, conveyed to Bernadotte on August 26, 1948, prohibited the emigration of all "fighting personnel" as per Security Council Resolution 50. The prohibition did not exclude all men of military age, but Israeli authorities had to attain clearance for each male immigrant between 18 and 45 years old from Bernadotte and provide that clearance to the US military authorities. The clearance was to show that prospective immigrants were not "fighting personnel." Marshall to Lippincott, August 26, 1948, *FRUS*, 1948, v. V, pt. 2, 1348–1349; also the US-Israeli exchange of notes of August 26 and September 3, 1948, *Department of State Bulletin*, v. XIX, no. 481, September 19, 1948, 386–387.

16. McDonald's despatch on de jure recognition was eventually sent to Truman and dated September 12, 1948. See *FRUS*, 1948, v. V, pt. 2, 1392–1393.

"will be zealous in advocating that [the Security Council] apply measures, if neces-sary, under Chapter VII of [the UN] Charter" and that sanctions "would have im-mediate consequences in such a state as Israel." He concluded, "We believe that [the] leaders of Israel stand at [a] moment of greatest opportunity for showing true states-manship and thus establish their republic on impregnable moral basis which will lead to sound political and economic development. US stands ready to give Israel its assis-tance to this end."[17] *Truman, perhaps without considering its implications, approved Marshall's memorandum.*[18]

Marshall shared his despatch to McDonald with the British government. "You perceive from this instruction to McDonald," he told Ambassador Douglas, "that our views on possible territorial settlement in Palestine are practically identical with those suggested [by the British]. . . . On [the] question of Security Council power to lay down a permanent frontier and to regard failure to respect this line as [a] breach of truce which would call for sanctions under Chapter VII, we desire to study constitu-tional aspects. . . . As for tactics we agree with Bevin that it is improbable that Jews and Arabs can be brought into face to face negotiations."[19]

Eleven o'clock conference with Minister Mordechai Bentov, minister of labor and development at Sarona.[20] Not until I had been there a little while did I come to take in the fact that he is the author of the bi-nationalism book, which [Judge Joseph] Hutcheson had made required reading for us in 1946.[21] Our talk was more political than any of those with the other ministers had been. Bentov explained to me the fusion of the HaShomer HaTzair with the left wing of the Mapai to form the Mapam. He said that two of the most im-portant members of the group were [Yitzhak] Tabenkin,[22] who does not speak English, and [Yitzhak] Ben-Aharon,[23] who speaks English. He showed intense interest in the attitude of the US as I explained it, and seemed sympathetic to my complaints that much of the tendentious writing recently in the *Palestine Post* and elsewhere could only do harm at home. My story of Forrestal and of

17. Marshall to McDonald, no. 72, September 1, 1948, *FRUS*, 1948, v. V, pt. 2, 1366–1369.
18. Memorandum for the president, August 31, 1948, *FRUS*, 1948, v. V, pt. 2, 1363.
19. Marshall to Douglas, no. 3468, September 1, 1948, NARA, RG 59, 501.BB Palestine, box 2120, folder 5.
20. Mordechai Bentov (1901–1985), Polish-born pioneer; emigrated to Palestine, 1920; founding member of HaShomer HaTzair; founding member of Mapam in January 1948 as a Marxist alternative to Mapai; signatory, declaration of independence, 1948; minister of labor and construction, 1948–1949; elected to Knesset as member of Mapam, 1949.
21. Bentov authored *The Case for a Bi-National Palestine: Memorandum Prepared by the Hashomer Hatzair Workers' Party of Palestine* (1946), a solution that Joseph Hutcheson, the US chair of the Anglo-American Committee of Inquiry on Palestine in 1946, preferred. See Goda et al., eds., *To the Gates of Jerusalem*, passim.
22. Yitzhak Tabenkin (1888–1971), Belorussian-born left-wing Labor Zionist; emigrated to Palestine, 1912; a founder of the kibbutz movement; a founder of the Poalei Zion and of Mapai; left Mapai to help form 'Ahdut HaAvodah , 1944; helped to form Mapam, 1948; rejoined 'Ahdut HaAvodah, 1954.
23. Yitzhak Ben-Aharon (1906–2006), Romanian-born left-wing Labor Zionist; emigrated to Palestine, 1928; British Army 1941–1945; left Mapai to help form 'Ahdut HaAvodah, 1944; helped form Mapam, 1948; rejoined 'Ahdut HaAvodah, 1954.

my appointment he followed with closest attention. He is a man with whom one could profitably talk at length.

Twelve o'clock, conference with Minister Aharon Zisling, minister of agriculture, at Sarona.[24] Since he spoke neither English nor German but only Hebrew, most of the conversation was from his colleague in charge of water resources. His account of the underground volume [of water], which had the earmarks of authenticity, was very encouraging. He saw as many as a half a million people in the Negev and ultimately eight million west of the Jordan. They offered to show me about the country, but I declined for the present.

I was a little late for my 12:30 appointment with Joseph Sprinzak at his office as ad-interim president of the state council.[25] There I found a Mizrachi rabbi, the head of the Jewish National Fund, Mr. Avraham Granovsky,[26] and some other members of the council. The talk was pleasant but not particularly worthy of record. It was left that he and I would talk later about the Histadrut, of which he [Sprinzak] is the head. Back to the office, where I found Knox much concerned about the recent telegram, the full import of which we were able only to guess at because of the uncompleted decoding. Out of the way to pick up forgotten Bobby and home to lunch.

After a brief nap, tea with the Hadassah gals, including Tamar de Sola Pool,[27] Rose Halprin, Mrs. Rebecca Schulman[28] and Mrs. Bertha School-man[29] and Mrs. Ida Davidowitz.[30] It was rather a depressing party since what I had to tell them in clouded metaphors was not encouraging. Tamara tried vainly with her ever-effervescent hope to cheer us up. The meeting may have been useful because it gave them a more realistic appraisal.

Saturday, September 4

After a restless night, I did an hour or so work before breakfast. Before, during and after lunch, discussed with Knox and Cummings the full text of the Department's communication. Agreed that as complete, the document was more

---

24. Aharon Zisling (1901–1964), Belorussian-born leftist Labor Zionist; emigrated to Palestine, 1904; member of Haganah command; founding member of Mapam; minister of agriculture, 1948–1949; opposed settlements on formerly Arab-owned lands.

25. Joseph Sprinzak (1887–1959), Moscow-born Labor Zionist; emigrated to Palestine, 1910; founding member of Histadrut, 1920; general-secretary of Histadrut, 1945–1949; founding member of Mapai, 1930; headed Provisional State Council, 1948–1949; speaker of the Knesset from 1949 to his death.

26. Entry of August 27, 1948.

27. Tamar de Sola Pool (née Hirschenson) (1890–1981), born into Jerusalem rabbinical family; active in Jewish Agency's Youth Aliyah after 1934; president of Hadassah, 1939–1943; helped establish Hadassah Hospital.

28. Rebecca Beiner Schulman (1897–1997), Vienna-born American Zionist activist; trained nurse who started nursing training program for Hadassah after joining organization in 1929; her home in Connecticut became a center of Zionist discussion that included Weizmann and Ben-Gurion during the period 1945–1948; president of Hadassah, 1953–1956.

29. Bertha Singer Schoolman (1897–1974), New York-born Zionist; leading figure in Hadassah; co-chair of Jewish Agency's Youth Aliyah Committee, 1947–1953; established Neve Hadassah Youth Village at Kibbutz Tel Yitzhak in 1949; active in relief work with DPs in Cyprus.

30. See entry of August 17, 1948.

manageable than was at first anticipated from initial glimpses. But agreed to sleep on the problem and face it again Sunday and Monday.[31]

Reception from five until nearly seven for full staff. It went off well. Judith Epstein came out, and I told her of somewhat brighter horizons but of continued necessity for elementary education.[32] In the evening to the opera, *The Barber of Seville*. As always, it was amusing. The music and the ensemble singing were excellent. During the intermissions, chatted with the Kaplans, whom we agreed to call on Friday at five, with the Hadassah gals, and with Madame [Edis] de Philippe, who sat next to me.[33]

Sunday, September 5

To the office early to work on the major weekend job. 11:00 a.m. conference with Minister Yitzhak Gruenbaum, minister of interior.[34] After presenting his several colleagues, we discussed the role of his ministry, which in its control over municipal and regional communities, and, with its power to license the press, is so very different from our department of the same name. Having a little time before my next appointment, I stopped in at the Kaete Dan to inquire about the health of Andrew Somers. Finding him on the terrace alone with a glass of beer, I invited him out to lunch. He seemed pleased to accept.

[At] 12:30, forty-minute conference with Mayor Israel Rokach.[35] Talk ranged from general conditions in the US and city problems there to the future development of Tel Aviv. As I was leaving, he asked me if I would say a few words at the evening function in memory of Fiorello LaGuardia.[36] The ride out with Andrew Somers and the subsequent talk at lunch gave revealing insights into the personality of this rather crude, but not so dumb, congressman. Evidently he has learned much in his few days here, sees the part of his old friend [Bergson] in truer perspective and is at this point concerned only to be able to say when he got home that he has met Ben-Gurion. He was wholly frank in the political use which he intended to make of such an interview and of his other experiences here. Seeing that he no longer wanted to urge upon Ben-Gurion the earlier scatterbrained scheme, I urged Knox that he get in touch with Shiloah to have it arranged if it possibly could be. I was the more anxious

31. Refers to Marshall's no. 72 of September 1, 1948, discussed earlier.

32. McDonald's phrase for explaining the situation in Israel to US policy makers.

33. Edis de Philippe (neé Defilipov) (1912–1979), New York-born, internationally known opera and concert singer, stage director, and ardent Zionist who founded Israel's National Opera Company in 1947 and directed it until her death in 1979.

34. Yitzhak Gruenbaum (1879–1970), Warsaw-born Zionist politician and journalist; tried in Poland to form effective national minorities bloc in Sejm; emigrated to Palestine, 1933; member of Jewish Agency Executive; chair, Jewish Agency Rescue Committee, which tried to rescue Jews in Europe after 1942; signatory, declaration of independence, 1948; minister of interior, 1948–1949.

35. Israel Rokach (1886–1959), Palestine-born, Swiss-educated engineer; General Zionist mayor of Tel Aviv, 1936–1953, oversaw trebling of Tel Aviv in size.

36. Fiorello LaGuardia (1882–1947), mayor of New York, 1934–1946; director-general for UNRRA, 1946.

to see this done in view of the almost certainty that Andrew Somers would give the president a full and perhaps exaggerated picture.

At seven, Bobby and I were at the municipal council reception in the Town Hall for the One World Committee here to secure the naming of a street for Fiorello LaGuardia.[37]

The One World Award Committee had asked for and received from the Tel Aviv Municipal Council the naming of a street after New York mayor Fiorello LaGuardia, who died in September 1947.

I persuaded the group with Rabbi [Israel] Goldstein to come out to the house for evening tea. They seemed delighted with the house and thrilled with the view from the roof. While we were upstairs, Bobby and Shalom [Harazi, McDonald's Israeli chauffeur] managed to get together a presentable high tea, around which we sat and talked until nearly ten. The role[s] of the administration, of the State Department, and of Dewey, John Foster Dulles, and Hoyt Vandenberg were discussed by my fellow Americans, often it seemed to me, with more heat than light. My comments on the local situation had to be, of necessity, very general. Nonetheless, they seemed to be informing and to satisfy them.

Monday, September 6

At the office for intensive effort to complete statement to be presented to Shertok. Conference at eleven o'clock with Rabbi Yehuda Fishman, minister of religion.[38] Young [Jacob] Herzog acted as interpreter. We covered a good deal of ground, including the scope of the ministry, but with particular reference to the question of religious freedom under the new state. I returned to the points raised by Cardinal Spellman and his colleagues in their memorandum and by His Holiness.[39] The answers were satisfactory, but when I suggested that they be put in writing, the minister said he would prefer to have the questions written out first. It was left, therefore, that Herzog would come to the house on Wednesday at six, bringing with him the Spellman memorandum, and that together at that time we would work out the questions, and he would see that I had the answers before he leaves next week for his visit to Rome.

Back to the office for final agreement on the text referred to in first paragraph above. From 3:30 until nearly 4:30, Knox and I were with Shertok. I read carefully our *aide mémoire* and slowly enough for Shertok to take full, if not verbatim, notes.

37. McDonald describes the ceremony in the mayor's office.
38. Yehuda Leib Fishman [later Maimon] (1875–1962), Bessarabian-born rabbi; helped found Mizrahi, 1902; led Mizrahi in Palestine after 1913; minister of religions and war victims, 1948–1951; elected to Knesset as member of United Religious Front, 1949.
39. See entry of August 5–6, 1948.

On September 3 Marshall ordered McDonald to present the United States' basic views to the Provisional Government of Israel: The United States hoped that Israel would be a constructive force in the Middle East, and offered assistance. But the United States also supported the current truce and would support Security Council sanctions against the aggressor if a violation occurred.

In terms of peace negotiations, the US government suggested (1) the exchange of "a large portion of the desert land of the Negev for that portion of fertile Western Galilee which Israel now occupies militarily;" (2) the internationalization of Jerusalem or another settlement acceptable to Israel and the Arab states that also provided safety and access to Holy Places; and (3) "some constructive measures for the alleviation of Arab refugee distress." The United States offered "to commend the above program" to Bernadotte and to the British government so that each might help in securing agreement from Israel's neighbors. The United States discouraged Israeli demands beyond these terms.[40]

[Shertok] expressed appreciation of the interest indicated and desire to aid. He noted with pleasure that the suggestion about Jerusalem left room for flexibility. On the other issues, opinion was reserved until [a] subsequent conference. In answer to the question about Paris negotiations, he gave a detailed, and I have to assume, factual account of the past two months.[41] In Paris, [Eliahu] Sasson[42] and others, spokesmen for Syria, Lebanon, and Transjordan, talked but without results. The more interesting news was what followed from the informal and almost incidental intervention of the Belgian consul general in Jerusalem[43] through his letter of congratulations to Abdullah on the occasion of the Fast of Ramadan, a little more than four weeks ago. Abdullah had at once shown interest and proposed talks in Cyprus and later agreed to them in Paris, but nothing to date had happened, presumably, according to Shertok, because of British influence.[44] Shertok gave a brilliant resumé of his interpretation

40. McDonald's memorandum, which he read to Shertok, as well as his report on Shertok's reaction, is in McDonald to secretary of state, no. 58, September 12, 1948, *FRUS*, 1948, v. V, pt. 2, 1375–1378. See also *DFPI*, v. 1, d. 493.

41. The UN General Assembly opened its third session in Paris on September 21, 1948. Shertok preferred direct approaches to Arab state representatives in Paris in the expectation that the Arab states could be separated from one another. His peace initiatives began after the second truce in August 1948. Negotiations with Transjordan were the most promising, because Israel could offer recognition of Abdullah's annexation of territory in the West Bank. See Sheffer, *Sharett*, 382–384.

42. Eliahu Sasson (1902–1978), Damascus-born Zionist and journalist; emigrated to Palestine, 1927; headed the Arab section of the Jewish Agency's Political Department, 1933–1948; director of Middle East Department in Israeli Foreign Ministry, 1948–1951; later ambassador to Turkey, Italy, and Switzerland.

43. Jean Nieuwenhuys (1906–1961), also the chairman of the UN Truce Commission in Jerusalem. See also n. 9 in this chapter.

44. On September 9, 1948, Shertok reported to Sasson in Paris that Abdullah had spoken to the Belgian consul, relaying the message that he would have a delegation in Paris, ostensibly as observers for the Assembly meeting, whose members would be willing to speak with Sasson "with [a] view toward working out a peace settlement." The king added that he would move independently of the Arab League and that he was taking measures to subdue pro-mufti forces. Shertok to Sasson, September 9, 1948, *DFPI*, v. 1, d. 499.

of British policy during the recent years.[45] The central program was based on persistent and mule-headed wishful thinking, for example,

1) During World War II it was the British consensus of opinion that after the fighting there would be no Palestine problem because Jews would not flock there in numbers; instead, there would be [a] large exodus from Palestine.
2) Later, repression was used as a means to check going to Palestine, but this failed.
3) 1945—Bevin was convinced by Near Eastern experts that any impartial body would find in favor of [its 1939] White Paper policy. Hence, Anglo-American Committee of Inquiry, which unanimously found against 1939.[46]
4) Following King David Hotel explosion [July 22, 1946], the arrest of Agency officials and imprisonment in Latrun had just the opposite effect from that intended. It strengthened the Jewish position and the personal position of Shertok.
5) London Conference threats failed.[47]
6) UN [Special] Commission [on Palestine ; UNSCOP] gave report contrary to what Bevin expected.
7) Refusal of Britain to take any part in UN discussion did not result, as was hoped, in Britain being asked to remain.
8) British non-implementation of UN program [the partition plan] did not, as was intended, prevent its being a basis for Israel.
9) Next British stage was to declare that Israel would get only what it would fight for and could hold.
10) Present policy essentially [the] same device, only a new version of old principle. Example, Sheringham, British consul in Jerusalem, said recently to a Jewish opposite number: "You will have to get down on your knees and ask for mercy." He said this despite the fact that he had said the same thing months before and had been disproved.[48]

Shertok's conclusion was that British policy is rigid, inveterate, and immutable. The direct application of this idea was that one cannot count on British support of Abdullah's peace tendency, but rather the reverse. On the major issues

45. McDonald did not include Shertok's comments on the British government in his September 7 report to the State Department.
46. On the Anglo-American Committee of Inquiry, see Goda et al., eds., *To the Gates of Jerusalem.*
47. Reference to conference in October 1946, initially to include British, Arab, and Zionist representatives to discuss the Morrison-Grady plan for provincial autonomy within mandatory Palestine. Neither the Arab states nor the Arab Higher Committee nor the Jewish Agency Executive accepted the British proposals. Shertok at the time was detained by British authorities in Latrun. Cohen, *Palestine and the Great Powers*, 135–177.
48. John Guy Tempest Sheringham (1913–1995), British vice consul in Jerusalem; told Israeli representatives on June 17, 1948, that it was in their interests that the truce last, that the Jews should drop their demand for access to the Old City's Holy Places, and that the Jews were fortunate that British officers commanded the Arab Legion, thus making it more humane and sparing thousands of lives in Jerusalem. *DFPI*, v. 1, d. 203.

of Jerusalem and Transjordan, it was agreed that these would be discussed with Ben-Gurion after the latter had had time to confer with his colleagues here and from Washington and Lake Success. I urged, however, that I hoped for an early reply.

James M. Long of the Associated Press came into the house at five and stayed until nearly a quarter of eight. At the end, Bobby's pint of dry martinis had disappeared. Among the points which Long made were the following:

1) British settling point—Negev to Egypt, the latter thereby securing prestige but nothing more, because it would do nothing with the territory.
2) Britain, on the other hand, would gain access to Gaza, a potentially deep water harbor, could develop substantial air fields, have important lines of communication to Transjordan, and in general use Negev as a major base. On this point I did not raise with Long the obvious question—why could not all these advantages accrue to Britain and with greater security if the Negev went to Abdullah?
3) Iraq and Syria are finished unless [there is a] new rallying cry. They are hoping for it in Jerusalem, but this is unlikely even though Jerusalem is not wholly won by Israel.
4) Although the Sternists, and to a lesser extent the Irgun, are bitterly critical of the US—some of their spokesmen going so far as to say that US had replaced Britain as number one enemy—there is no present danger of even mild demonstrations, much less anything more serious, because there is no public opinion which would support such action.

Natan Yellin-Mor[49] frankly characterizes the US as enemy on grounds it has replaced Britain in its efforts to curb Israel. Cites UN flag as replacing Union Jack; truce a form of economic oppression and exhaustion; other forms of pressure on Israel. In answer to my question whether Yellin-Mor could believe all this, Long was not sure, but what there was included a considerable measure of old fashioned demagoguery.

5) The Irgun leader [Menachem Begin], Long thinks, is much less effective as a public orator because in looks and mannerism he suggests a man who was and still is after his death the most hated by all Jews.[50]
6) Somers's friend [Peter Bergson] is at present insignificant here.

49. Natan Yellin-Mor (1913–1980), Belorussian-born Revisionist Zionist (Betar) activist in Poland in 1930s; left Poland shortly after outbreak of World War II; arrived illegally in Palestine, 1941, where he met with Avraham Stern and joined Lehi. After Stern was shot and killed by the British in 1942, Yellin-Mor helped lead Lehi. See Zev Golan, *Stern: The Man and His Gang* (Tel Aviv: Yair, 2011).

50. Some of Begin's gestures reminded center and leftist Yishuv leaders of a fascist comportment. Ben-Gurion called Begin a Nazi on several occasions and often compared him to Adolf Hitler.

7) On the issue of my inadequacy with the press, Long said that I had left the men without any understanding of what our government is aiming at, and that this lessens their efficiency both for their agencies and papers and as patriotic Americans. I did not take exception to this but pointed out that I could tell him privately what I could not have said at the press conference, that literally I was then unable to give information because the Department had not outlined the points. And what Truman and Clifford had said to me could not be divulged even in any off-the-record conversation. I expressed the hope that the situation might change and that I could be more helpful in a few weeks.

Long advised me to see [Kenneth] Bilby of the *Tribune*,[51] the French head of the French agency,[52] and [David] Courtney[53]—the latter preferably with one or two other people, so that he would not feel [as if] he [was] being indoctrinated. I agreed that I would do so. I asked Long why we should be blamed for taciturnity when the Russians said nothing and were not criticized. He answered, "Nobody expects anything from the Russians. They are busy carrying on the work which is natural for them." Long spoke of the current criticisms in the Jewish press of the US, tinged with suspicion on several points: a) oil, b) ports, c) bases, d) counter-Russian, e) commercial, f) pro-English. He had no concrete suggestions, however, in answer to my question of what could or should be done to correct these obvious misconceptions and distortions.

To the ballet with Bobby and Miss Clark. Except in the native numbers, most of the performance was rather on the amateur side but on the whole enjoyable. I had a pleasant visit with Mrs. Kaplan while Bobby visited with her daughter.

Tuesday, September 7

Ok'd Knox's draft of first report on yesterday afternoon's talk. Lawrence Lader, a freelance writer of the *New Republic* and the *New Yorker*, came in to chat.[54] He seemed to me a trustworthy and intelligent freelance. He was interested the most apparently in current anti-American charges in the press, [regarding] men of military age, protest to Czechoslovakia, and failures to move more rapidly on [the] loan and de jure recognition. Knox came out to lunch, and we continued our discussion of pending issues.

51. Kenneth W. Bilby (1918–1997), covered the War of Independence and its aftermath for the *New York Herald Tribune*. His book from the time is *New Star in the Near East* (New York: Doubleday, 1950).
52. Roger Lioret (1903–1999), chief correspondent and manager for Palestine, *Agence France Presse*.
53. See entry of September 29, 1948.
54. Lawrence P. Lader (1919–2006), Harvard-educated war journalist, who wrote for the aforementioned publications and others.

After nap, I finished [Jorge García] Granados's book,[55] skimming the chapters which contained little or nothing new and reading those which gave more details of the UNSCOP investigations and especially the last weeks of debate in the Assembly session leading up to November 29 and the final days of the special session preceding May 15. The book has many marks of Gerold Frank's workmanship and is not without its dramatic sections, but it lacks the central thread of melodrama which gave to Bartley Crum's book its driving power and wide appeal.

The evening, the sunset and the next hour or so [were] beautiful on the roof, the sky glorious and the air pleasantly cool. Dinner at the Davidowitzes.[56] Present besides our hosts were Judge and Mrs. Levinthal,[57] their daughter, and later the Shertoks. After dinner came Rose Halprin, the Davidowitz's son-in-law, and Mrs. Schoolman, who has a daughter here. As we were leaving, Shertok suggested that we see him and Ben-Gurion next morning at eleven. When I said that I had a date at twelve with our Russian friend [Major Nicholas Andronovich], he said it would be well to postpone that in order not to be hurried.

Wednesday, September 8

Knox and I met Shertok and Ben-Gurion at the former's office a few minutes before eleven; our talk continued until 12:15 or 12:20.[58] Present also was Epstein, though he took no part at all until the very end and then spoke briefly. Ben-Gurion did nearly all the talking, speaking for the most part with deep feeling and at times showing hardly repressed emotion. He was visibly tired, seeming to me to be more overstrained than at any one of our previous meetings. Perhaps this was an aftermath of his recent slight indisposition, and, of course, of the double burden which he continues to carry during this very anxious time.

Ben-Gurion began by expressing pleasure, which he subsequently reiterated and reemphasized, at [the] US's initiation of what he hoped would be mediation by the US between the Provisional Government and the Arabs—not, as he again and again said, between the Provisional Government and the mediator [Bernadotte]. Indeed, the heart of Ben-Gurion's statement was that there are only two alternatives: 1) Mediation by the US directly between the parties or 2) war. There is, he added, no third alternative.[59] Then, following rather closely our own outline, he discussed:

55. Jorge García Granados, *The Birth of Israel: The Drama as I Saw It* (New York: Knopf, 1948). Granados (1900–1961) was Guatemala's ambassador to the UN; served on the UNSCOP; one of the few Latin American statesmen who had favored partition; helped organize a bloc of Latin American states to vote for the partition resolution.

56. Entry of August 17, 1948.

57. Judge Louis E. Levinthal (1892–1976), Philadelphia-born jurist; president of ZOA, 1940–1943; adviser on Jewish affairs to Office of US Military Government in Germany, 1947–1948; judge on the Philadelphia court of common pleas, 1937–1959.

58. McDonald's report on this meeting is in his no. 98 to secretary of state, September 9, 1948, *FRUS*, 1948, v. V, pt. 2, 1384–1386.

59. Ben-Gurion's diary entry for September 8, 1948 states, "I expressed contentment with the American hope that Israel would become a constructive force, and promised that . . . the US

1) The truce and its related meaning and significance
   a. What does the truce mean? Now and for the future? Now, it means to sanction the continuance on Israel's territory of the invading Arab armies. It sanctions aggression with the tacit approval of UN and the Security Council. The most serious violation of the truce, that at Latrun, did not invoke any action by [the] mediator, UN, or US. Yet that violation threatened the deaths of a hundred to a hundred and ten thousand Jews, because water is life. No signs that [the] mediator, UN, or US have done anything to check arrival Arab reinforcements during truce period.[60]
   b. Future Meaning of Truce. It involves foreign supervision for an indefinite period. We resent this very deeply. We will accept it if it leads to peace but not if it does the contrary. Immigration is a vital issue. It is the very reason for the existence of our state and our presence here. We are at home here. International control is indefensible. It is equivalent to the reestablishment here and outside of the White Paper, not now by Britain, but by the UN and US. It is not an empty phrase when we say "we will fight for freedom of immigration, for the right to return to our country."
2) Regarding suggestion number one [of US memorandum]: His remarks were addressed directly to the phrases "large portion of desert" in exchange for "fertile land militarily occupied." What is the reason for this? Hasn't Transjordan enough desert? After long discussion and with US support, a large portion of the Negev was taken away [from the proposed Jewish state] before November 29.[61] All this land has special meaning for us. It was unoccupied, is potentially usable to us but to no one else. Just as we were the first to work the Dead Sea, why are we asked to surrender [a] "large part?" US's use of "large" terrifies us. You have such a different idea of "large" than Jews here. Why the suggestion? What has happened since November 29 to give Arabs claim to more desert?
3) Regarding suggestion about Jerusalem. Here is something constructive. Glad to note respect for November 29, but does it include corridor? After the last nine months, when UN and world powers did nothing to check Arab invasion or Arab destruction of Latrun, it is a matter of life and death to Jews in Jerusalem that there be "direct access." The vitalness of this cannot be exaggerated. Ready to discuss.

---

government will not be disappointed. I welcome the US initiative to advance peace, and its willingness—if it remains consistent—has the potential, more than anything else, to bring peace. But it is precisely due to this reverence for US government that we must speak openly." We are grateful to Tuvia Friling for this reference.

60. Shertok wrote to Eliahu Sasson in Paris on September 9, 1948, "We have authentic reports 50% increase Arab armies in Palestine during truce." *DFPI*, v. 1, d. 499.

61. The State Department did not support partition during UN deliberations in November 1947 and, once partition seemed inevitable, supported border adjustments to the benefit of the Arabs, including the assignment of the Negev to the Arabs before eventually withdrawing this proposal. As a compromise the Arabs were given the strip of the Western Negev that the Egyptians held in 1948. Cohen, *Palestine and the Great Powers*, 288–290.

4) Is the US ready to mediate? Only two alternatives: US mediation directly between parties or war. Must welcome US first attempt in direction of mediation, but not mediation between Israel and [the] mediator; instead, directly between Israel and Arabs. Otherwise, the most powerful means in the world will have been used for nothing. Again, as he closed, he expressed welcome for US initiative.

5) Shertok added some additional ideas on the exchange idea. He said that under UNSCOP, two and a half million dunams had been subtracted from [the] Jewish Negev. Israel fought in UN for more. That was given in Galilee. Eastern Galilee slightly enlarged as result. No inherent violation on November 29 in Provisional Government's demand for Western Galilee. Instead, some of the assumptions which had been used against the Jews were found now by experience to be invalid. For example: a. limitation of Jewish claims leads to peace; b. that UN would keep peace. Because of these failures, Provisional Government through own efforts had succeeded, but "not yet wholly." In other ways, Provisional Government case strengthened by experience. US idea of enlarged Transjordan does away with earlier US argument that Arab people needs reserve land in Western Galilee. Now problem must be studied against quite different background of ample land reserves in Transjordan. Hence, whole of Galilee should be Jewish and not by way of exchange. As to Jerusalem, Shertok returned to his earlier idea that the US suggestion had flexibility.

Ben-Gurion intervened to remind me of our talk in Paris more than two years ago when he indicated [the] danger of Jews putting down in black and white their minimum demands.[62] These dangers were that such demands became in subsequent negotiations the Jewish maximum and, equally important, the other party would not be the one which could make a binding agreement. Ben-Gurion emphasized that it was his personal view that Israel deserved the whole of western Palestine, but would yield much to reach agreement with Arabs. Jerusalem is more to Jews than Paris to French, or London to British. Deserves whole of city to Dead Sea, but with Arab agreement, would accept much less. Personally would be willing to consider some form of partition. Shertok spoke of internationalization of the Old City.

6) On the problem of refugees, Shertok and Ben-Gurion were clearly not of one mind and evidently had not thought the problem through to a concerted conclusion. Both emphasized that what they had to say was tentative and that the government had reached no decision, except on the general proposition already announced that a comprehensive solution must wait on peace negotiations and on real peace. Pressed by me as to what measures of alleviation might be considered, Shertok replied:

62. See Goda et al., eds., *To the Gates of Jerusalem*, entry of February 7, 1946.

a. Immediate relief through international action and the Arab governments. The latter bear the responsibility because of their aggression and because of their encouragement to the people to flee.
b. Then Shertok turned to what he called ultimate solution through settlement in neighboring countries. Israel would aid through making research and experience in administration available wherever possible.
c. Those that might return he thought would be small proportion. That in the meantime a very limited number of compassionate cases might be received.

Ben-Gurion, seemingly sensing the inadequacy of this reply, stressed that one could not know what would be the solution until there was genuine peace and Arabs could return as friends and neighbors, and not as direct or indirect enemy agents.[63] Either or both Shertok and Ben-Gurion expressed satisfaction with the session.

Late afternoon Mr. Jacob Herzog and Mr. Chaim Vardi of the Department of Religion came in to talk about their trip to Rome and guarantees which could properly be required in order to assure effective religious freedom. As the two young men talked, I got a new realization of the complexity of the subject here in Palestine and of the inadequacy of the statement handed to me [by Francis Cardinal Spellman] in New York, which, on closer examination, obviously did not cover a number of very important points. For example, ecclesiastical jurisdiction—this and other items not mentioned in the New York statement would, according to my young friends, be adequately safeguarded.

One of the immediate problems concerning the young men is the demand of France that its traditional rights, which go back to the Capitulations under the Turks and which were reaffirmed by the Treaty of Mytilene signed in Greece in 1901, be recognized by [the] Israelis.[64] Among these "rights" is that of [the] unlimited privilege of establishing schools in the French language and with curricula not subject to Israeli control. They wanted my advice, which I

63. Shertok, understanding that the refugee issue harmed Israel politically, was willing to allow partial return in conjunction with resettlement schemes undertaken by the Arab states. In backchannel negotiations with King Abdullah, Shertok suggested that the "King start thinking seriously about resettlement in Transjordan bulk [of the] refugees now there, for which we might prevail upon US to give him loan." He added that, owing to Israeli intelligence reports of a 50% increase in Arab forces in Palestine during the truce, the IDF could not spare forces for the mass repatriation of Arab refugees and the security problems it would entail. Ben-Gurion was more noncommittal. His diary for September 8, 1948, reads: "Knox and McDonald asked whether the door was shut on refugee [repatriation]. I replied that I did not believe so—if we negotiate an applicative and stable peace agreement. With such agreement anything is up for discussion." See Sheffer, *Sharett*, 378–379; Shertok to Sasson, September 9, 1948, *DFPI*, v. 1, d. 499; Ben-Gurion diary, entry of September 8, 1948. The editors are grateful to Tuvia Friling for this reference.

64. French protection of Latin Christian interests and custodial authorities in the Levant dates to the sixteenth century and was affirmed in a series of Capitulations by the Ottoman Empire to France through the nineteenth century. The Mytilene Agreement listed educational, charitable, and religious institutions under French protection. The Turks abolished French rights on entering World War I. The French tried to restore their protectorate in Palestine after the war but failed to do so. Catherine Nicault, "The End of the French Religious Protectorate in Jerusalem (1918–1924)," *Bulletin du Centre de recherche française à Jérusalem* 4 (Spring 1999), 77–92. See also entry of January 20, 1949.

was in no position to give, as to what recommendations they should make to their government. I was prepared to agree, however, with their primary assumption that they could better afford to be generous in their attitude towards the Vatican than towards the French government. It was decided that we would talk again after they had returned from Rome from which, if they saw there the proper people, they would bring back enlightening information. Meantime, I promised them a letter to Count Galeazzi.

After half an hour or so, we walked on the roof with Bobby during the time of unusual beauty to forget immediate problems. Eliahu Epstein arrived for dinner. The meal itself was good, and he seemed to brighten under the influence of the company and the food. Afterward, we sat out on the front veranda for an hour and a half or so talking informally and wholly "off the record." These were among the points discussed: 1) He expressed marked satisfaction about the morning conference and at our government's beginning of a new initiative, which he attributed to influence from our office. I did not comment; 2) He expressed much the same concern as that which I felt during the morning at Shertok's inept and, if taken too literally, rather frightening informal statements about refugees. He hoped that we in our report to the Department would not unduly exaggerate Shertok's words; 3) He complained of the difficulty he was having in persuading Kaplan to allocate adequate funds to the Washington office. I told him I could sympathize with him; 4) He said that Kaplan could and should be willing to cooperate with us by giving Braudo [McDonald's landlord] an honorary mission to South Africa and that I should urge it; 5) Talking of persons who might advantageously be persuaded to visit here, he named Bernard Baruch,[65] in whom Ben-Gurion is interested; Arthur Sulzberger, who has expressed a desire to come this winter or spring; Murray Gurfein, one of the most intelligent of [Governor Thomas] Dewey's close advisers;[66] and Roger Straus.[67] I agreed and said that I would see whether I could properly write to one or more of them; 6) He was enthusiastic about Charles Knox, saying that both Ben-Gurion and Shertok were delighted with his friendliness and his evident determination to learn. I, of course, agreed with this appraisal, but expressed concern lest Charles Knox's health be insufficient to stand a long strain here; 7) As we walked out to his car, he movingly urged that the two of us who were in exceptional positions to help should spare no effort to "win the peace."

---

65. Bernard Baruch (1870–1965), American Jewish financier and philanthropist; former adviser to Presidents Wilson and Roosevelt; Truman's representative to the UN Atomic Energy Commission, 1946–1947.
    66. Murray Gurfein (1907–1979), New York-born lawyer; served in the OSS in Europe during World War II; assistant to Robert Jackson during the Trial of the Major War Criminals, 1945–1946; after 1946 a lawyer in private practice.
    67. Roger William Straus (1891–1957), heir to R. H. Macy family fortune and chairman of American Smelting and Refining, a mining conglomerate owned by his wife Gladys Guggenheim; active in numerous charities, especially those associated with the Reform Jewish movement; founder of the National Conference of Christians and Jews; active in New York State Republican politics and close to Thomas E. Dewey.

The big event of the day was our luncheon for Count Bernadotte and the six top men of his staff: Generals Lundström and Riley, Drs. Bunche and Mohn, and Sir Raphael Cilento[68] and Mr. Reedman. Not until I met one of the count's secretaries at the Kaete Dan did I learn that he was bringing so many. But a scant two-hour's notice was sufficient for Bobby and the household. The luncheon was good and promptly served. In addition to the nine of us, Knox and I and the count's party at the first table, nine others had to be fed—Miss Clark, Bobby, Cummings, the three servants, and Shalom and the two guards. No wonder that later Bobby rather ruefully surveyed the inroads which the luncheon had worked on her scanty budget.

After the usual amenities of conversation, it became quite clear from what the count and his colleagues, particularly Dr. Bunche, said, that they had accepted our invitation in order to persuade us to urge the US vigorously to change the policy expressed to Bunche a little over a fortnight ago.

Bunche had spoken with virtually all of the men in the State Department except for Marshall, Dean Rusk, and Phillip C. Jessup. His conversations indicated that the US view, and the British view too, was that the UN should not take up the Palestine question in the forthcoming General Assembly meeting.[69]

I pressed Bunche to report to us the reasons given for such a policy. He replied that it seemed to be based on the theory that it would be better to "coast along" with the truce rather than risk failure of a peace effort. He had discerned, he said, nothing more subtle in the argument than this.

Once the group had disclosed their purpose, all the members, particularly General Lundström and the count, joined in underlining their conviction that the truce must fall of its own weight and be followed by war within a few weeks unless vigorous peace efforts were pushed. Lundström said categorically, "If peace is not under way before Christmas, there will be war before then." I remained rather non-committal, except to say that we, too, for several weeks had felt that exclusive concentration on the truce must be fatal, and that I had said this to Washington. Of course, I disclosed nothing of the current exchanges between ourselves and Washington and with the Provisional Government.

Although the count and his staff seemed willing to talk very frankly about the need for peace effort at the United Nations Assembly in Paris, not one of

68. Sir Rafael Cilento (1893–1985), Australian-born physician and public health official; first Allied physician to enter Bergen-Belsen in April 1945; director, UN Disaster Relief Program, 1948–1950, which monitored the Palestinian Arab refugee problem; eventually determined in December 1948 that the Israelis would not take back most refugees and that the refugees would have to be settled in the Arab countries. See entry of October 16, 1948.

69. Marshall noted privately to Ambassador Douglas in London on September 1 that the Department "is not at all anxious to have Palestine issue ventilated at Paris session of [the General Assembly] and our view is identical with that of UK." Marshall to US Embassy London, no. 3468, September 1, 1948, *FRUS*, 1948, v. V, pt. 2, 1369.

them would disclose even by a hint the substance of the peace plan which the count was to present, not formally as a plan but as the logical deduction from his report of his work and on the situation in this area. We could not even guess from what was said whether Bunche's ideas about Jerusalem were essentially unchanged.[70] I was tempted to make a frontal attack on the earlier Jerusalem proposal in order to draw somebody out, but my feeling of being the host restrained me from what might have been a useful maneuver.

After lunch we compared notes on our views about our guests. It was the consensus of opinion that Bernadotte, though very well mannered, is no intellectual giant; that Bunche is extremely able; Lundström somewhat past his prime; Riley, a typical competent professional soldier; Reedman, able; and Mohn, a professor. Sir Raphael said so little that it is hard to judge him. Later at Kaplan's, Kaplan and Herzog were in complete agreement that Mohn is the ablest of the lot and that he deliberately hides his exceptional ability. My only comment is that he certainly hid it from me.

Friday, September 10

Bartley Crum[71] and Gerold Frank[72] came in about 12:50 with their inevitable photographer, who at once proceeded to take motion and still pictures of Bart and me in conference in front of the map of Palestine. As Gerold left a few minutes later, Bart called to him to say, "Don't forget the photographer in connection with our next meeting," which was [with] Shertok. What a glutton for publicity, though charity requires one to say that now, as a publisher, there is more justification for it.

Here in summation is what Bart had to say: In the most friendly manner he told me that the president was delighted with my appointment and the reactions thereto; that the president was anxious to take further positive steps, but that he was being bombarded with negative material from the neighboring missions and felt [the] need for more positive statements from me. Presumably this referred to possibility of de jure recognition, admission, the UN, and the loan. As to [the last], the president is thinking in terms of comprehensive aid

---

70. These were incorporated in Bernadotte's initial suggestions for a peace settlement and included the assignment of Jerusalem to Transjordan's rule, local autonomy for the Jewish population, and UN supervision of the Holy Places.

71. See entry of August 3, 1948. Crum purchased *PM*, a liberal New York newspaper from Marshall Field in 1948, renaming it the *New York Star*. The paper was a strong advocate for Israel, but closed in January 1949. Crum was close to Truman adviser David Niles and might have had designs on the ambassadorship in Tel Aviv. During his trip to Geneva, Paris, Tel Aviv, and Jerusalem in September and October 1948 he kept in touch with Clifford via telegram, warning, among other things, that Marshall backed the Bernadotte Plan and that Truman should provide de jure recognition to Israel. He also suggested that McDonald's help in the negotiations between Israel and Transjordan might bring positive results. See especially Crum to Clifford, October 20, 1948, Truman Library, Clifford Papers, Subject File 1945–54, box 13, folder Palestine Misc. 1 of 3.

72. Gerold Frank (1907–1998), reporter for Overseas News Agency; covered Jewish life in Eastern Europe before World War II; reported on the Anglo-American Committee on Palestine and later events in Israel; also served on B'nai B'rith editorial board, 1950. See Goda et al., eds., *To the Gates of Jerusalem*, 71, entries of March 16, 17, 19, 21, 1946; April 5, 1946.

for whole area, of which Israel would be a part. Bart is convinced, or at least emphatically said he was, that given [a] sufficient affirmative policy, the president can be returned [re-elected]. Bart outlined how in his opinion this could be done through winning of New York, Illinois, California, and Massachusetts. I was not convinced. Bart said that Clark was most helpful, that he, Bart, is cabling openly to Clifford every day and that he, Bart, will show me his next despatch, but it is not to be shown to my staff. Bart said in the beginning that he had told the president what a wonderful appointment mine was. Later, when I reported this to Miss Clark and Bobby, their comment was, "You should have replied that you had failed to note any such ideas in the [New York] *Star*'s editorials.

Bart is here for a very short time, leaving next Wednesday. He goes to Jerusalem Saturday and plans to return that night. I urged him [to] wait until Sunday morning, which would give him ample time to return with Gerold for lunch with us at 1:30. I warned him also about death alley near the American consulate. As to the *Star*, he said he had gone into it because he was convinced of the need for a liberal newspaper. In answer to my question about funds, he said that Marshal Field's $200,000,000 is [in] back of them; that losses at present were $15,000 a week. He recognizes need for more vigorous editorial policy and seemed convinced that there was a fighting chance of success.

McDonald wrote his family the same day: "I am not quite sure what Bart is up to in this trip to Israel in addition to his present role as the publisher of the [New York] Star. *He saw the President before he left and he tells me he is cabling Clark Clifford every day."*[73]

When Miss Clark, Knox, Cummings, and I reached the house a few minutes before 1:30, we saw Bobby and our three guests, Judges Leventhal, [Judge Leon] Powers,[74] and Congressman [Abraham J.] Multer, on the roof.[75] The lunch was pleasant. There was much talk about American politics, with the congressman and Judge Powers disagreeing completely about the president's chances. Powers argued that Truman would be the worst defeated candidate in our history. We talked also about the difficulties of setting up and administering a mission in the light of current administrative and financial regulations of the Department. Multer offered to do something about it when he got home, but I rather discouraged him because I did not know what would be the effect of such intervention, and urged him that he at least talk to Knox before he decided on anything.

73. McDonald to his family, September 11, 1948, McDonald Papers, Columbia University, box 14, folder 13. See entry of December 28, 1948.

74. Judge Leon W. Powers (1888–1959), one of three US judges in the Nuremberg Ministries Case; dissented from the judgment, arguing that only a few German people participated in the persecution of the Jews and that the evidence did not support the German Foreign Ministry's knowledge of extermination policies.

75. Abraham Jacob Multer (1900–1986), Jewish member of US House of Representatives (D-NY) 14th congressional district, 1947–1953; toured Israel, September 3–24, 1948.

The only general talk about the situation here was centered about my emphasis on the need for peace negotiations now. The guests were much interested in this and my report on the feelings of the count and his staff. Multer is to return and talk to me before he leaves.

Friday, September 10

Bobby and I had tea at the Kaplans', at their in-laws' apartment in town. Present besides Mr. and Mrs. Kaplan and Atara were Horowitz, her nephew who had been injured in the war, and Mr. and Mrs. Michael Comay.[76] I should put down what Kaplan said as we were discussing Count Bernadotte's visit to us the day before. I had, or someone else said, the usual thing that the count's proposal to turn the city over to Abdullah had been fatal to Bernadotte's status and also to the Israelis' willingness to accept what they would have accepted previously. Kaplan's cryptic comment was: "Bernadotte did us an excellent turn." The more I have thought of this subsequently, the more significant it seems coming from one so moderate in his views as Kaplan.

Saturday, September 11

At work all morning at home and at the office on a long de jure analysis.[77] Saturday, late morning, John J. MacDonald came down from Jerusalem. He, Knox, and I talked from 11:30 or so until after two. Though Bobby had issued an ultimatum that there were to be no guests on Shabbat while the servants were on leave, she and Miss Clark uncomplainingly produced an excellent lunch with the cooperation of the 5-in-1 [rations]. In addition to my reports to MacDonald on happiness here and on the background of my appointment, which I need not set down, the following were among more interesting things that were said:

1) MacDonald's account of the sniping along Wauchope Street put the direct responsibility on firing from the Old City wall but indirect responsibility on the Jews for continuing to hold the annex to the King David Hotel. He said that there was one comparatively safe entrance, by car, to the American consulate and that it was this road they used regularly.
2) MacDonald said that the Belgian consul general [Jean Nieuwenhuys] made weekly trips to Amman and down to Jerusalem, presumably as part of his [intermediary] activities.
3) Of him MacDonald spoke highly as of the French consul general.[78]

76. Michael S. Comay (1908–1987), South African-born jurist and diplomat; served in South African units in North Africa during World War II; emigrated to Palestine, 1945; worked for the Jewish Agency's Political Department; director, British Commonwealth Division, Israeli Foreign Ministry in 1948; ambassador to Canada, 1953–1957, and Great Britain, 1970–1973.
77. See McDonald to secretary of state [personal attention president and secretary], September 12, 1948. *FRUS*, 1948, v. V, pt. 2, 1392–1394.
78. René Neuville (1899–1952), French diplomat and archaeologist; consul general in Jerusalem, 1946–1952.

4) MacDonald's account of the killing of the Jewish liaison boy did not differ in substance from that in the press. It did, however, disprove the statements of some of those who presume to know what would have happened in such a case. The young man, according to MacDonald, should not have gotten out of the car, because the Jewish soldiers at the check-post would not come out of their refuge because bullets were ricocheting all over the street. The young man was shot in the forehead even before he reached the barrier. One of the men with MacDonald in the car, I think it was one of the other officials, started to get out to carry the wounded boy to safety. MacDonald said to him, "You will certainly be killed." And he ordered the driver to back up and to drive to the Jewish Agency building, from where he hoped an ambulance could be sent at once. Though the distance was only about five minutes, no ambulance would go, and the boy was not carried away until an armored car was available about an hour and a half later.

5) On the question of re-routing the courier, MacDonald argued with Knox that it would not be fair to put Jerusalem on the end of the line from Athens, Haifa, Tel Aviv, that we should concentrate on getting ourselves put on the Athens-Cairo route.

6) MacDonald agreed that an indefinite truce would inevitably be fatal and seemed surprised and shocked to learn that the Department had been, according to Bernadotte's report, holding out against any action at the UN General Assembly Meeting.

7) MacDonald said he regretted that Bernadotte was so little in Jerusalem and that he thought he ought to return there before the UN General Assembly meeting. He added that Bernadotte had said earlier that Jerusalem did not offer the facilities which he needed and which were available in Rhodes.

8) MacDonald spoke of the extension of the truce arrangements for the Red Cross area from Government House as at least one achievement of the Truce Commission. He confirmed the earlier report about General Riley's unjustifiable optimism about an easy settlement.

9) As to Mount Scopus, MacDonald said that Abdullah al-Tel, Jerusalem commander of the [Arab] Legion,[79] had agreed that there should be sufficient supplies sent up to permit the making of the necessary repairs to the Hadassah Hospital, and I presume, the Hebrew University. When I asked if the Truce Commission did not include the right of the Jewish guards to be exchanged from time to time and that the Arab Legion refused to permit this, he answered yes.

79. Lieutenant Colonel Abdullah al-Tel (1918–1973), Transjordanian-born, British-trained army officer; commanded Arab Legion's 6th Regiment in Jerusalem, 1948; days before the start of the war in May 1948, his unit conquered Kibbutz Kfar Etzion, after which irregulars massacred the defenders and destroyed the settlement; later in May 1948, he halted the Haganah's advance toward the Old City in Jerusalem and afterward became Old City's military governor; entered into negotiations with Israeli commander Moshe Dayan for a cease-fire in Jerusalem, November 1948.

10) Illustrative of the attitude of the Stern Gang towards Americans, Mac-Donald told of the recent incident when he and three of his clerks were in a Jerusalem café. Three Stern Gang men, armed, came up to the table and said in effect, "We don't like your government's policy, which in effect replaces that of the British, and we intend to deal with you as we deal with the British."[80]

11) In general, MacDonald said that relations between the Truce Commission and the Jewish authorities, including Dr. Joseph, were becoming more difficult, and more and more the latter and his associates were putting obstacles in the way of the Truce Commission's work—this was a repetition of the version of such relationships given by Major Andronovich a week or so earlier.

12) Asked about the probability of Glubb Pasha's return, MacDonald said that he understood he would do so.[81] As to Abdullah al-Tel's publicly proclaimed optimism of a favorable military decision should there be open hostilities, he said he assumed Abdullah al-Tel really believed it.

13) According to [MacDonald], Wells Stabler,[82] the acting American consul in Amman, is very friendly with Abdullah, being in his palace regularly. I did not get the impression, however, from MacDonald that he thought Stabler's would be a logical promotion in the event that the Department wanted to establish more formal relations with Transjordan.

14) MacDonald's general impressions about the purposes of the Jews in Jerusalem did not differ, it seemed to me, very materially from those we had gathered from Jerusalem officials and others in previous conferences.

---

80. Shertok cabled Epstein on September 17, 1948, as follows: "Consul-General Jerusalem probably warning State Department danger threatening him on part Lehi. We don't minimize Lehi peril, trying to watch situation, but they should know [that the] Consul-General . . . patronizes [a] saloon [,] which is [a] Lehi hangout, [and] apparently gets involved in arguments with them." *DFPI*, v. 1, d. 516.

81. John Bagot Glubb (1897–1986), British officer; served in Iraq in intelligence capacities, 1920–1930; moved to Transjordan, 1930; became second-in-command of the British-subsidized Arab Legion, 1930–1939; commander of Arab Legion, 1939–1956. Under Glubb, who was simultaneously a British subject and under the command of Abdullah, the Legion was transformed from a gendarmerie to a small, mechanized army. Having fought pro-German forces in Iraq and pro-Vichy forces in Syria, it was the only battle-tested Arab force and the only force that attained victories in 1948, partly thanks to Glubb's reorganization in 1948, his expansion of the Legion to more than 10,000 men (including British officers and NCOs from the departing British army), and the arrival of trucks and artillery from the Suez Canal zone. In terms of Palestine partition, Glubb had called for Transjordan to receive the Samaria-Judea region as well as the Negev. Fluent in Arabic, Glubb was a major British voice concerning the Middle East, and the Legion became the main support of the Hashemite monarchy. The Legion's inability—born of ammunition shortages—to protect Lydda and Ramle from Israeli capture in July 1948 wrecked Glubb's popular reputation in Palestine and Transjordan. In the second half of August, Glubb took a month's leave in London, carrying a personal message to Bevin from the king asking for additional weapons (London provided certain items in violation of the arms embargo). Glubb's assessment was that the Arab states would not defeat Israel, no matter how many weapons they received; returned to Amman, September 18, and began to restore the Arab Legion with aid of generous British subsidies. See Benny Morris, *The Road to Jerusalem*.

82. Wells Stabler (1919–2009), US vice consul in Jerusalem since July 1944; later the US chargé d'affaires in Amman.

15) As to MacDonald himself, I got the impression of a straightforward courageous official who was doing his duty and who could not fairly be charged with partisanship.

Sunday, September 12

To the office and spent the first two hours giving a final check with Knox and Cummings on the telegram about de jure recognition. Their suggestions, though they involved no substantive changes, definitely improved the draft. Extended conference with Major Andronovich and Knox and Cummings about communications, both interpretative and affirmative and receptive.

In McDonald's top-secret telegram of September 12, sent directly to the president and Secretary Marshall, he recalled that, on July 21, the president had instructed McDonald to advise him on "the appropriate time for full recognition." He stated, "That time has, I believe, now come."

McDonald further stated that an "indefinite truce cannot lead to peace without positive action to clarify the situation" and that full recognition would accomplish four objectives: (1) It would strengthen Israeli moderates who wished to avoid renewal of war. (2) It would give Arab moderates, particularly King Abdullah, additional impetus to move toward a settlement. (3) It would remove obstacles to peace by showing Arab intransigents "that Israel's existence cannot longer be denied or ignored." (4) It would encourage the British to relax their own policy of nonrecognition. The United States, McDonald said, could not wait for London: "There can be no fruitful peace negotiations until [the] Arab states see that Israel is definitely established."[83]

Marshall responded after speaking with the president. The secretary rejected McDonald's arguments, stating, "We consider premature de jure recognition would inflame Arab world and would make it difficult for Arab states to make those concessions for which Bernadotte has been striving in his efforts to obtain equitable solution of Palestine question. We might expect, in addition, that Moslem states in UN would be strongly affected by premature step favoring Israel and that US and other Western powers would thereby have additional and increased difficulties with other important problems before UN."[84]

Major Andronovich and his wife came out to the house early. From her we learned a good deal about the human side of the difficulties of living under fire [in] Jerusalem. In answer to my statement that I understood that she was John J. MacDonald's hostess, she replied that that title implied a much more leisurely life than she led at the consulate.

She and her husband drive there each morning and return each evening to their home in the former German colony, now Jewish and subject to intermittent

---

83. McDonald to secretary of state [personal attention president and secretary], no. 104, September 12, 1948, *FRUS*, 1948, v. V, pt. 2, 1392–1393.
84. Marshall to McDonald, no. 100, September 17, 1948, *FRUS*, 1948, v. V. pt. 2, 1408–1409.

sniping and shelling. During the day, among her other duties, [is] carrying up water by the bucketful from downstairs to the bathrooms upstairs. An example of an emergency task was caring for a wounded member of the staff on the second floor, for whom she had to make frequent trips down to the fridge to get the cold compresses. Her bathing of a patient under these circumstances was no easy job. Evidently, her life and that of her fellows was life under siege. In the light of her account I could understand better her annoyance with Bartley Crum's easy dogmatism about conditions in Jerusalem.

[Crum and Gerold Frank arrived at McDonald's residence from Jerusalem in the midst of these discussions]. [Crum] was very tired after his hurried trip up and down the Burma Road the day previous, and his intense determination to impress us all with the imminence of a Jerusalem offensive utilizing unprecedentedly destructive weapons made him an unconvincing advocate. Time and again he repeated that unless the Arabs, all of them, got out of Palestine (he was referring of course to the armed forces), they would be "utterly destroyed." And, he added, not only they but their capitals and many of their people as well. He either could not or would not give particulars. We inclined to think it was the former rather than reticence. He and Mrs. Andronovich tangled a number of times about Jerusalem and what should be done with it. He was insistent that it was too late for any solution except a wholly Jewish one. You would have thought from the discussion that it was she who had been there for only part of a day and Bartley Crum for years, so dogmatic was he.

Time and again Bartley Crum recurred to the theme that there was still a unique opportunity for peace through direct American mediation, and that I was the person to conduct it, at least from the point of view of this side. He was emphatic about the enthusiasm of the people and the leaders here about my coming and the need for prompt utilization of this present good will. In connection with some talk about our mission needs here, Bart told me privately that he was going to see to it that government funds were available to relieve me of my prospective magnificent deficit. I don't know quite how it can be done, and I am not sure that he will at home be as keen on it as now. I specifically asked him and Gerold Frank to say nothing about our communications problem. It was nearly five before he and Gerold Frank left.

The US Embassy in London learned from a British report from Jerusalem dated September 15 that "Bartley C. Crum is now in Tel Aviv informing all and sundry that he is [the] personal envoy of President Truman to whom he claims to send personal telegrams daily."[85]

---

85. Bliss to secretary of state, no. 4240, September 22, 1948, NARA, RG 59, MC 1390, reel 16, frame 841.

While they were still at the house, I called Kaplan and Major Andronovich into the study to discuss my idea about a written statement to our friends on the problem raised by some of the things John J. MacDonald had said. After listening, however, to Kaplan and Major Andronovitch, and their argument that to write might be ill-advised because of the danger of leak and misuse, I agreed that if we did anything it would be informal and verbal.

To the Habimah[86] with Bobby and Miss Clark and six of the boys to hear Madame de Philippe in a short but excellent song program. After the intermission we called to pay our respects in her dressing room, she added a song, a Scotch one, and announced that she was singing it in [my] honor.

Monday, September 13

The morning was spent in catching up with back correspondence and in redrafting and stiffening Knox's draft of a telegram on communications. I put it on the personal ground that I could not take the responsibility of permitting ourselves to face the possibility in an emergency of being left voiceless and deaf, and that I protested against the delay and urged the quickest action to give us at least facilities comparable with Haifa and Jerusalem.

Tuesday, September 14

Captain Ya'akov Lifshitz (Rabbi Jacob Gill), one of the leaders of the Unity of the Nation (Ahdut HaUmah), came in to explain the program of his organization and to invite my cooperation.[87] His group, numbering now some 14,000, is made up of men and women, presumably for the most part, of the propertied classes, who feel the necessity of stressing private enterprise and individual initiative as over against what Lifshitz called the predominant leftward groups, the Mapai and Mapam. These, he asserted, have also a Russian orientation in varying degrees, whereas his group is definitely westward or [toward] the United States. He also contrasted his group with [Lehi] or the [IZL under] Menachem Begin. The latter, according to Lifshitz, does not understand the issue, having been here only four years with most of that time spent in the underground. Among the persons Lifshitz mentioned as being leaders in his group were Juda M. Tocatly, the insurance man,[88] the mayor of Tiberias,[89] and the mayor of Petah Tikvah.[90]

---

86. "The Stage" in central Tel Aviv.

87. Ya'akov Lifshitz (Jacob Gill) [1908–1990]), born in Tiberias; founded Ahdut HaUmah, which later merged with the General Zionists; published the newspaper *HaYessod*; served in the Jewish Brigade during World War II; involved in assistance to European Jewry, 1945–1946.

88. Juda M. Tocatly, founder of Aryeh Insurance Company, Ltd. in 1948.

89. Shimon Dahan (1895–1950), Tiberias-born Sephardi who served as mayor, 1938–1950.

90. Yosef Sapir (1902–1972), born in Jaffa; served as mayor of Petah Tikvah, 1940–1951. Petah Tikvah [Beginning of Hope] in 1878 was the first agricultural colony in Palestine and later developed into an urban center.

As Lifshitz talked, I kept wondering what he could expect from me—evidently two things. First, he asked me to give my endorsement to a country-wide council meeting of their organization in Tel Aviv on the 28th. I quickly and categorically explained that this was quite out of the question, that as the representative of the US, I could not become a partisan or give any support to any particular party. To illustrate, I said that for me to do what he asked would be the same as if Epstein in Washington came out in support of Henry A. Wallace, a move which would make him *persona non grata*, just as my comparable support here would render me unacceptable.

The second suggestion of Lifshitz was more interesting. He prefaced it by giving [a] large estimate (on what authority was not quite clear) of expenditures by another foreign power here to advance its point of view through a local party, and through cells in each of the settlements and local communities. He estimated such current expenditure of one power to be at the rate of half a million dollars a year. He asked whether there could not be an educational program in support of a Western point of view, not necessarily a governmental program, but one which would have the support of the West in tangible form, perhaps from private sources. He added that there were a number of able men prepared to cooperate here. He spoke of publications, articles, cinema, etc.

On this second suggestion I was non-committal. I did suggest, however, that if he had tangible data on the "educational" activities such as he indicated above, I should be glad to have some memorandum from him for my personal information. He said he would supply it.

Home early, because Shalom was going to Jerusalem. Knox and Cummings came out for tea. We thus had an opportunity for leisurely and fruitful discussion of: 1) Lifshitz's suggestions and the possibility of a public relations officer being added to the staff. It was decided that a recommendation should ask for the transferal here of Mrs. Mildred Allport, who is holding that position in Bern;[91] 2) The [Arthur] Koestler articles,[92] particularly the third, and the best way of calling it to the attention of Clark Clifford. Decided that this could best be done through a personal letter sent through Multer, with whom we are dining on next Shabbat; 3) General discussion of the present situation, the rather disquieting quiet, the prevailing conciliatory tone. We could not make up our minds. Cummings thought it might be related to the Iraqi rumors; another suggestion was that it was preliminary to the meeting of the

91. Mildred B. Allport (1897–1990), attaché, US legation Bern.
92. Arthur Koestler (1905–1983), prolific Hungarian-born British journalist and writer; one-time communist and Zionist; in Israel as a foreign correspondent, June–October 1948; disillusioned by his time in Israel, as reflected in his articles for the *Manchester Guardian* and his book, *Promise and Fulfillment: Palestine 1917–1949* (New York: Macmillan, 1949), which expressed skepticism toward the Zionist enterprise. McDonald may refer to Koestler's arguments that Israel would never move toward the Soviet bloc and Koestler's sympathy for the IZL and right-wing parties. See David Cesarani, *Arthur Koestler: The Homeless Mind* (London: Heinemann, 1998), 298–330.

General Assembly. We decided not to spend too much time speculating, for we thought that the session tomorrow at the Foreign Office would give us the lead.

Up to the roof for our usual beautiful evening parade. At teatime sent Bobby over to our nearest neighbor [Shertok] to say that I would like to come over for a few minutes at his convenience. Later Chaim [Shertok's son] came to say 9:30, if that were not too late. I had first talked in very general terms about my hope of improvement of American-Israeli relations and my concern lest an unanticipated incident might worsen seriously that prospect. Then I went on to report the recent indications of public resentment by one group [Lehi] and their threats of direct action. I recounted my namesake's [MacDonald's] experience with the three who openly threatened the US, and who said that we would not be allowed to replace Britain and that soon this would be made unmistakable. My friend was deeply interested, told me of [a] plan to end such possibility, of differences of opinion, of the plea for delay, and of the possibility of the matter going to the largest group. I got the impression that he would find valuable what he had learned. In any case, he said he was most grateful. As I was leaving, I learned the subject of this morning's talk, which was not a surprise.

The small extremist group Lohamei Herut Israel [Fighters for the Freedom of Israel], known by its acronym Lehi and called the Stern Gang by the British after its founder Avraham Stern, had fought the British during World War II despite Britain's war against Nazi Germany. It robbed banks to fund its operations, and in 1944 its members assassinated Lord Moyne (Walter Guinness, 1880–1944), the British minister resident in the Middle East. Along with members of the IZL, Lehi members were also responsible for the April 1948 killings of Arab civilians at Deir Yassin. The Israeli government formally disbanded Lehi in May 1948, but its members continued to operate in Jerusalem.[93]

In his 1951 memoir, McDonald recounted Shertok's response to threats from Lehi: "[Shertok] told me in strictest confidence of the Cabinet's decision taken the previous Sunday to dissolve the terrorist organizations. However, a difference of opinion within the Cabinet and a plea for delay had postponed formal action until the following Sunday. . . . I learned today, too, that some members of the Cabinet, including some of the rabbis, had asked [for] the delay in the hope of persuading the terrorists to dissolve peacefully and thus avoid the use of force and consequent bloodshed."[94]

During Tuesday morning at the office, McMahon brought in a friend whose name suggests a great mosque in the southwest [Mecca]. We talked about the Sternists, and he offered every assurance. He said that he was perfectly informed and would know in advance of any action. He offered to make

93. Overview in Bruce Hoffman, *Anonymous Soldiers: The Struggle for Israel, 1917–1947* (New York: Knopf, 2015).
94. McDonald, *My Mission in Israel*, 68–69.

available individuals at the house. He also gave us the private number for emergency use, and the name of the son of my old friend.[95]

Wednesday, September 15

Knox and I spent nearly an hour at the Foreign Office. Before seeing Shertok, we visited with Miss Herlitz, who gave me the Kaplans' private numbers, and who made a note of my need for maps and promised to supply them. The long session with Shertok was a detailed, logical and, I must add, convincing presentation of [the] Provisional Government's case against the Department's action in ordering the refusal of exit permits to men of military age from the occupied areas of Germany and Austria.[96] Shertok's case in essence is:

1) The Security Council resolution of May 29th does not specifically exclude such immigrants, but on the contrary specifically indicates that men of military age who come in are not to be mobilized or trained.
2) This language is the more significant because it is that of the French amendment [to the resolution], which was explained by the French spokesman as being intended to prevent the military use of such immigrants.
3) Since the truce is basically intended to be so enforced that it will not alter the balance of military strength, and since there can be in the nature of the case no control on the utilization by the neighboring states of men of military age, and since immigration does not count with them for military purpose[s], it is obviously a discrimination against Israel, for whom immigration is a normal and natural procedure.
4) Since many of the men excluded by the Department order are husbands and or fathers, their exclusion means the exclusion of their women and children. Such exclusion could never have been intended by the truce.
5) The mediator has flirted with various possible bases for some sort of mathematical or percentage limitation of men of military age, but he has never publicly or in private to the Provisional Government stated a figure of what would be reasonable. Even in his first talk with Shertok the morning before he lunched with us he had not mentioned the problem of such immigrants.[97]
6) Provisional Government had specifically declared in connection with the second truce that it would not and did not accept the principle that the mediator had any power to interfere with the "normal" immigration so long as men of military age were not mobilized.

95. Perhaps refers to Amos Ben-Gurion (1920–2008); served with British Army in World War II; deputy police commissioner, September 1948.
96. See entry of August 18, 1948.
97. Bernadotte's first talk with Shertok was June 17, 1948, at 3 p.m. (*DFPI*, v. 1, d. 205); there was no meeting on the morning of September 9 before he and his staff lunched with McDonald.

7) Limitation, such as the placing of men in camps, which was accepted under the first truce, but which was more and more irksome and intolerable as the truce was prolonged, is wholly unacceptable in an "indefinite" truce.

8) Moreover, while it was possible to urge patience upon those in camps during a limited truce, it is quite impossible to do so during an "indefinite" truce.

9) In answer to my question whether Shertok would make a distinction between the exclusion of men with families and those without, he replied "no"; that while the hardship and injustice might be greater on the men with families, the principle was the same as with unmarried men, and the Provisional Government could not and would not accept the principle that the mediator had any right to interfere with the limitation of either.

10) Shertok spoke with something akin to bitterness, because the US had from his point of view gratuitously gone beyond even the mediator itself in its German ruling. At the end, Shertok said that while the Provisional Government had to be firm, he wanted Washington to understand that he did not approve of some of the language used when this issue was publicly broached by the high representative in Washington [Epstein]. He wished us to present the matter fully to our government and to indicate the firmness of the Provisional Government position and his desire for an amicable issue through quiet exchange of views.

In his report to Washington on this meeting, which was written the following day, McDonald commented that "[the effect] here of [the] Department restriction is deplorable because [it] gives plausible support [to] those critics who charge [that the] US [is] marching step by step with [the] British non-cooperation policy. Thus it delights [the] pro-Russians."[98]

Mr. Barth, manager of the Anglo-Palestine Bank, came in to pay his respects. We discussed a number of matters, including the present very large amount of currency in circulation, the tendency of the Jews as well as the Arabs to keep currency rather than put it in the bank, and the need for early peace as a basis for the prevention of inflation. In answer to my question he spoke deprecatingly, and I think probably justifiably so, of Captain Lifshitz and his individualistic free enterprise bloc. He thought they counted for little and would, following the election, count for less.

At teatime Bartley Crum and I talked for nearly an hour and a half. He was much more restrained than on Sunday and said little about the mysterious weapon, but what little he did say sounded more convincing. Most of his talk was about his meeting with the new leader of the Stern Gang. He is a man

---

98. McDonald to secretary of state, no. 114, September 16, 1948, NARA, 501.BB Palestine, box 2120, folder 5.

in his thirties, a seeming combination of mystic and fanatic, completely insensitive to reason, convinced that the US is replacing Britain, and that only through direct action can the US and the world be convinced that this will not be tolerated.[99]

In response to Bart's argument that this would outrage world opinion, he was completely unconvinced and replied that it was they [the Stern Gang] who had convinced the British that they could be driven out by direct action. Bart referred to the tragedy of Lord Moyne and the unfortunate effects outside, since Moyne was friendly, but the leader replied that the demonstration was all the more telling because Moyne had been a friend. Although he did say that they would not move within the territory of Israel unless making Jerusalem a free zone, Bart thought that there should be special precautions even here. He had been able, he said, to make absolutely no impression and thought that sooner, if not later, the Provisional Government should act.

In an editorial appearing tomorrow in the *Star*, Bart is urging that I be made mediator with full powers. He is also going to urge, he said, on the president, that the post be at once made an embassy, that it is fantastic that the USSR should outrank us, and that the announcement of the change should be made here. This, he argued, would give it special value to the Provisional Government. Bart said he would see the president as soon as he got back, that he would press his points with the utmost vigor, and emphasize the unique opportunity which my presence here gave the president. I told him he could tell the president that we were in a tough spot. . . . we needed the fullest support, and that when I sent him a communication it was because I considered the matter of vital importance and that I hoped he would so regard it.

Late in the evening we enjoyed the unusual experience of observing the party at Shertok's house from the vantage point of my bedroom balcony. Shertok and Ershov seemed in deep conversation as other members of the party chatted together.

Thursday, September 16

First thing at the office, work with Knox on important telegrams, one having to do with current military rumors and the other summing Shertok's presentation of the day previous.

McDonald and Knox also worked on a telegram concerning Shertok's September 16 press conference, in which the foreign minister pointed out that the UN had 118 observers in Israel and only 55 in all of the countries at war with Israel, including 6 in Iraq and 14 in Syria. "While I have no opinion as to effectiveness or procedures of UN supervision, the peculiar and apparently one-sided distribution of UN observers

---

99. Lehi had three leaders: Natan Yellin-Mor, Yitzhak Shamir, and Israel Eldad. All were in their thirties in 1948, but Crum probably refers to Eldad, who was Lehi's chief ideologue.

is undoubtedly what [the] Prime Minister referred to when he confidentially remarked to me that UN observers 'swarm' over Israel."[100]

At ten o'clock the two young engineers in charge of the studies being made for the deep-water harbor in Tel Aviv came in. They were E. Per Sorensen and Daniel J. Houlihan of the Knappen Tippetts Abbett Engineering Co. of New York. It was interesting to have them say that the large plans for Tel Aviv have been substantially reduced after the apparently unexpected successful occupation of Haifa. At present, no plan has been decided upon, and by spring, the project should be ready for consideration by the government. As at present estimated, the plans to build a breakwater about two miles from the shore forming a half moon curve would provide for shipping space larger than Haifa at a cost of approximately 40 to 60 million dollars. Three locations are being considered: one near the present barge basin, the other at Jaffa, and the third north of the Yarkon [River].

With [security attaché Francis] McMahon over to the gala performance of the Russian film *The Village Teacher.*[101] As I entered, there were evident excellent security arrangements. The Russian minister [Ershov] came in exactly on time at 11:20 when the movie was supposed to begin. First, there was a presentation of an uninteresting, rather poor Disney short. Then came *The Village Teacher.* Though obviously propaganda, the film had its good points. The photography was excellent, the acting of the main character varied and convincing, while the children and the peasants played or danced their roles wonderfully. To a predominantly Russian, if not Communist, audience, the film seemed most effective in its most propaganda portions. As I watched its effect here in a foreign land, the center of competing concepts of the world organization and of life, I sensed, as I would not have done at home, the power of the Russian propaganda. I should have recorded that before the films began there were very bad renditions of the Russian national anthem and the *Hatikvah.* The *Star Spangled Banner* was not played, but it would have been silly for me to have made an issue of it, as had the Russians with less excuse at the opening night at the opera.[102]

When the film was over, we all stood up, and it looked for a moment as if it might be embarrassing to see whether Ershov would or would not leave first. He evidently was going to hold an informal reception. I leaned across his box [next to ours] and extended my hand, which he grasped and gave a hearty shake. This evoked cheers from the audience. McMahon and I then slipped

---

100. McDonald to secretary of state, no. 124, September 20, 1948, NARA, 501.BB Palestine, box 2120, folder 5.
101. *The Village Teacher* (1947) won the 1948 Stalin Prize for best film. On the Soviet use of films in diplomacy, Frederick K. Barghoorn, *The Soviet Cultural Offensive: The Role of Cultural Diplomacy in Soviet Foreign Policy* (Princeton, NJ: Princeton University Press, 1960).
102. See entry of August 21–22, 1948.

out, and with the police directing the traffic, Shalom was able to get the car away quickly.

At the Shertok's dinner party, besides the hosts and Bobby and me, were the Hoofiens, the Horowitzes; Yehezkel Sachar, chief inspector of police,[103] and his wife; Miss Syrkin, an American writer;[104] and Mr. Knox. The dinner was informal and pleasant with light and friendly talk. Shortly before the party broke up, I talked at some length to Sachar, repeating much of the warning about possible direct action by the Stern Gang which I had given the Monday night previous to Shertok at his house. Sachar listened attentively but gave no indication that he felt there was any cause for alarm or for emergency action, not even when I repeated what MacDonald and Cummings had said, and stressed how much could be undone by a single blow of the Stern Gang. He commented that when the latter talked most, they were least dangerous.

Friday, September 17

Mr. Levontin of the Anglo-Palestine Bank[105] came in on a courtesy call. Later, Ershov came to return my call. We had a pleasant chat about housing, in which he and his colleagues seem to be making no progress, or at any rate, they said they were not.[106] I tried to sound him out on the report that Bernadotte is considering moving his headquarters from Rhodes to Jerusalem. His reply in effect was that he had not heard of it. The rest of the time we talked about the movie. I was interested to note his surprise when I told him that there were many Russian movies shown at home and that there were even theatres which specialized or had nothing but such films.

The reception for Bobby and me at the Council Building at Ramat Gan by the mayor, Mr. Avraham Krinitzi, Naomi's grandfather,[107] was rather pro-longed but pleasant, including chats about the history of Ramat Gan, the school system, methods of taxation, the new income tax law, etc. When we left, we were greeted by scores of friendly children, and I felt that any reasonable request which we might make of the community would be gladly honored.

At seven, Bobby and I were met a block or two from the Bilu School [an Orthodox institution] by one of the authorities and taken to the vesper services. It was a beautiful and a moving occasion. The room was artistic and simply

---

103. Yehezkel Sachar [formerly Sacharov] (1907–1988); inspector-general of police, 1948–1958; immediate superior of Amos Ben-Gurion.

104. Marie Syrkin (1899–1989), Swiss-born US writer and Zionist advocate; daughter of Nachman Syrkin (1868–1928), Russian-born writer, theorist, and a founder of Socialist Zionism; editor of the *Jewish Frontier*, 1948–1971; published *Blessed Is the Match: The Story of Jewish Resistance* (Philadelphia: Jewish Publication Society of America, 1947), one of the initial accounts of the Warsaw Ghetto uprising, based on interviews with ghetto fighters in Israel.

105. Elie Levontin (1890–1966), executive of Anglo-Palestine Bank (later Bank Leumi); son of its founder, Zalman David Levontin (1856–1940), who had initially aided Theodor Herzl with efforts to purchase land in Palestine.

106. The Soviet delegation was still at the Gat Rimon.

107. Avraham Krinitzi (1886–1969), Belorussian-born mayor of Ramat Gan, 1926–1969. Naomi was Barbara McDonald's Hebrew tutor.

designed, but it was the service which will long stand out in my memory. It was wholly in [the] charge of the children, boys from eight to fourteen. When we entered Bobby was, of course, taken to the women's gallery, where there was, according to her later report, a nearly oppressive crowd of women and girls. I was ushered to the seat of honor at one side of the place where the scroll of the law is kept. As did all the men, I wore my hat.

The service was being led at that point by a small boy who may have been twelve or thirteen but looked much younger. Facing towards [the] ark, he was chanting the prayers in a clear soprano voice with every evidence of understanding and feeling. His eyes from time to time followed the Hebrew text in front of him, but this was more for reassurance than because he needed to do so. The responses were sung fervently and in excellent harmony by the congregation of some two hundred children. Occasionally, the central group of older boys of twelve or fourteen sang alone. Hardly one of them bothered to follow a text. They sang as confidently and as enthusiastically as if they were the members of a kibbutz singing one of Israel's fighting songs. I have never heard either in other synagogues or in church prayers more effectively intoned.

As I sat during the service facing the 200 children and perhaps twice as many of their elders in the back of the synagogue and crowded in the aisles and standing in the outer halls, not to speak of the hundreds of women and girls jammed into a side section, I was struck anew by the variety and "non-Jewishness" of the faces of the boys. Had I not known where I was, I would have sworn that a large portion of the children were Irish or the ordinary mixture of types which one would find in a Midwestern school. I do not recall noting a single "Jewish" physiognomy. What a demonstration this was of the absurdity of attributing any distinctive racial types to this generation of Israeli Jews.

Another notable feature of the boys was that though they are obviously all children of Orthodox and pious parents, none of them showed any mark of the overly studious child. There was not one who looked as if he had been kept at his studies to the detriment of his health. On the contrary, all of them were tanned, and with one or two exceptions, husky specimens. And though they sang enthusiastically and devotedly, they were just like other children during the intervals when they were not singing. Though well behaved as a group, here and there one could note a restless or mischievous child. It was interesting, too, to note the more Eastern and more traditional Jews among the elders. They could be distinguished by their tendency to sway back and forth as they chanted silently or aloud the prayers. Ten minutes or so were set aside during the service for three brief statements in Hebrew by officials of the school and a two-or-three minute statement by me. In this latter I stressed the encouraging feature of the religious enthusiasm of the children and my hope that in the young was Israel's best prospect of ultimate spiritual and cultural triumph.

When the service was over, there were a few minutes when it looked as if some children would be hurt in the crush of hundreds of them to shake my hand and to say "Shalom." Finally, I was led out through one of the side aisles, shaking hands with eager children all the way. There was one face of an older boy, perhaps sixteen or seventeen, which almost startled me. It was that of a Hasidic Polish youth, very blond, with a beautiful face lit up by eyes from which shone deep mysticism and the fire of religious enthusiasm bordering, if not reaching, the point of fanaticism. It was the kind of face which painters have so often depicted when striving to represent Jesus. Outside the synagogue the crush of the crowd, still mostly children, was as great or greater than inside. Since the car was 100 yards or so from the building, I managed to press my way forward through the accompanying crowds of children with their hearty and genuine "Shaloms" and their cheers ringing in my ears even as we drove away. Bobby and I have agreed that it was a rare, almost a unique, stirring, and heartening experience.

What a land of contrasts! We reached home about 8:15, had just dismissed Shalom with the instruction that he need not come back until time to go for Mr. [Harry] Viteles[108] and Mr. Goldsmith,[109] when on entering the house Miss Clark almost breathlessly whispered that Shertok had called a few minutes earlier to say that the mediator had been killed, assassinated "by Jewish irregulars in the Jewish part of Jerusalem." Killed at the same time with him was Colonel [André] Sérot of the French UN observers. At once we realized how great, perhaps overwhelming, this tragedy would prove.

I called Knox and Barnes, who had just finished their supper, and asked them to come over at once. As we talked together, we speculated on the course of events during the course of the next hours and days. Soon, it seemed to me that I should call on Shertok at once in order to get his version of the happenings as a basis for our first report to the government.[110]

On September 16, 1948, Count Bernadotte had asked UN Secretary-General Trygve Lie to present his peace proposal to the General Assembly during its meeting in Paris. Earlier elements remained as follows: 1) acknowledgment of the Jewish state's existence with frontier adjustments. The Negev would become Arab territory; the western frontier of Arab territory would run from Faluja to Ramle and Lydda, then north as per the November 29, 1947 partition line (thus eliminating Israel's corridor to Jerusalem); Israel would receive the entire Galilee region; Haifa would become a free port and Lydda a free airport. 2) The internationalization of Jerusalem under UN auspices with unimpeded access to the city, autonomy for the Arab and Jewish populations, and protection for Holy Places. 3) The right of return or material com-

---

108. Harry Viteles (1894–1971), US-born Tel Aviv representative of the American Jewish Joint Distribution Committee [JDC]; member of the JDC's advisory committee for the Middle East; monitored developments for Jews in Arab countries.

109. Probably Horace Goldsmith (1894–1980), American stockbroker and philanthropist; benefactor of Shaare Zedek Hospital in Jerusalem and Haifa Technion.

110. Knox wrote, "McDonald was so depressed by the event, as we all were, that the meeting was pretty glum." Knox to family, September 28, 1948, Truman Library, Knox Papers, box 1, folder Correspondence 1948–1949.

pensation of all Arab refugees to Jewish territory, which Bernadotte put at 330,000.[111]
Bevin immediately proposed that the United States and United Kingdom back Ber-
nadotte's proposals as a "fair and equitable basis for settlement," before the opening of
the General Assembly meeting in Paris.[112]

On September 17, Bernadotte began the transfer of his headquarters from Rhodes
to Jerusalem, where he thought he could have a greater impact. Dov Joseph's caution
to Bernadotte that Haifa would be safer did not dissuade the mediator. Bernadotte
visited the old British Government House, now in a designated neutral zone and
used by the Red Cross, which he planned to make the new UN headquarters. He
then returned to the YMCA building, which the Red Cross was using as a relief
station.[113]

When Bernadotte's motorcade passed through the Rehavia quarter, Bernadotte
was shot and killed along with UN observer Colonel André Sérot of the French Air
Force.[114] *The assassins came from Lehi and had posed as regular IDF soldiers at a*
checkpoint. Ralph Bunche then assumed the role of acting mediator. He immediately
blamed the Provisional Government for not adequately protecting Bernadotte and for
making what Bunche called "unwarranted and prejudicial statements concerning the
truce supervision," which, Bunche said, "are not the kind of statements which would
be calculated to discourage reprehensible acts of this kind."[115]

McDonald understood, as he wrote to Frieda Warburg, that "the fact that the
deed was committed by Jews in the Jewish part of Jerusalem obviously made the mat-
ter worse. We at once realized that at one blow much of what we had been striving to
accomplish had been undone."[116] *Shertok was shaken. He had already telegraphed Lie*
in Paris: "Outraged by abominable assassination of United Nations Mediator and
Observer Colonel Sérot by desperadoes and outlaws who are execrated by entire people
of Israel and Jewish community of Jerusalem." He conveyed official condolences to
Bunche, but rejected Bunche's argument that his government's criticism of the UN
caused the murders.

Since Lehi also regarded the United States as an enemy, McDonald's residence in
Tel Aviv received additional protection from the US marines previously stationed in
Jerusalem and from the Israeli government. "At once," he wrote to Frieda Warburg, "I
was 'confined' to the house."[117] *McClintock, meanwhile, wrote from Paris, "Berna-*
dotte's death will give maximum weight to the recommendations in his report."[118]

111. United Nations, *Official Records of the General Assembly, Third Session, Part I, Plenary Meetings, Annexes to the Summary Records of Meetings, 1948,* 152.
112. Douglas to Marshall and Lovett, no. 4153, September 17, 1948, *FRUS,* 1948, v. V, pt. 2, 1409–1412; Marshall to Douglas, no. 3690, September 18, 1948, *FRUS,* 1948, v. V, pt. 2, 1413.
113. On the International Committee of the Red Cross, see especially the entries of October 16, 1948, and November 9, 1948. On the YMCA building see entry of December 28, 1948.
114. Accounts of the assassination in Heller, *The Stern Gang,* 239–255; Kati Martin, *A Death in Jerusalem* (New York: Pantheon Books, 1994); and Amitzur Ilan, *Bernadotte in Palestine, 1948: A Study in Contemporary Knight-Errantry* (London: Macmillan, 1989).
115. Ben-Dror, *Ralph Bunche and the Arab-Israeli Conflict,* 97.
116. McDonald to Frieda Warburg, September 22, 1948, McDonald Papers, Columbia University, box 5, folder 8.
117. Ibid.
118. See *FRUS,* 1948, v. V, pt. 2, 1413, n. 1.

Presently McMahon the security attaché and more of his men arrived, bringing with them their sub-machine guns and extra supplies of munitions; the Provisional Government sent a group of men to form a cordon around the house while we sent our note over to Shertok. He replied shortly thereafter, fixing a time for eleven o'clock. After McMahon had established appropriate liaison between our guards and those of the government in charge at Shertok's, Knox, and I were carefully escorted the short distance of not more than one hundred yards from our door to Shertok's. This he opened himself. He, Shiloah, Knox, and I then talked for forty-five minutes. After expressing his government's and his personal horror and deep regret at the assassination, Shertok proceeded: 1) to outline the course of events as the government reports had given them and, 2) to summarize the steps which the Provisional Government had taken or was going to take.

Shertok's historical account did not differ in any essential particular from that received the next day from Jerusalem. The count's party in three or more cars on the way back from Government House was blocked at a narrow place in the road in Rehavia by a jeep from which two or three men rushed back firing at the first cars as they passed until one of them reached the count's car. There he succeeded in firing at point blank range, killing Colonel Sérot instantly and the count a few minutes later.[119] Shertok's review of steps taken and those projected included immediate orders for the arrest of all Sternists, those who resisted to be shot; the closing of all their places of known resort; the most rigid search for the assassins and their accomplices together with the speediest execution of justice once the guilt of the accused should be ascertained. Shertok further explained that special police had been immediately dispatched to Jerusalem and that additional troops were on their way. These reinforcements were the more necessary because there has been some weakening of Jerusalem forces to meet an Arab threat in the north. Already (this was then approximately six hours after the assassination which had taken place a few minutes after five), arrests had begun. The full force of the government's actions would not be felt, however, for several hours.

When Shertok had finished—rather I think to his surprise, and at first perhaps to his consternation—I expressed in soberest tones dissatisfaction with the proposals. I said that they smacked too much of putting the tender arms of the law protectively about those who were guilty. Amplifying, I said that the Provisional Government bore a special responsibility for its tolerance, and that in the eyes of the world the usual judicial procedure would not seem ample. Shertok rather sharply asked what I expected and specifically wanted to know if a certain procedure was in my opinion in order. I replied that it was not for me to give an answer. I was speaking, I said, merely as a friend seeking to help the Provisional Government to see its situation and responsibility as I felt most

119. Bernadotte was shot at the same time as Sérot and died a few minutes later en route to Hadassah Hospital on Mount Scopus.

of the world and certainly my own country would see it. We finally parted on a somewhat lighter note when I said that I had made my protestation partly in order that I might not be proved by subsequent events to have been too much of a "liar" in my earlier telegrams, which had given assurances about the Provisional Government's power and intentions.[120]

McDonald's residence remained under guard. "[We] could not tell," said Knox ten days later, "and still cannot, whether the fanatics had a general plan to assassinate several people, and we are taking no chances." Knox and Barnes spent several nights in McDonald's house for their own safety.[121]

Saturday, September 18

The previous night after Knox's and my return from Shertok's remained rather hectic until Knox and I had completed the drafts of two telegrams and he had taken them off to the MacKay [encoding] office. Earlier, we had flirted with the UN communications service, but both their systems were out of order. The two men, Lieutenant Colonel Trauernicht and Colonel Pooley, who had come out to talk to us, proved to be of no use. Waking and breakfast time showed on many faces the results of a few hours or no sleep. Thanks, however, to Sarah [the mission cook], breakfast was ready in due course for sixteen or eighteen people.

Our first decision was to send off another telegram reemphasizing to the Department the imperative need of an independent communications system. We made our case by pointing out that we just missed being, as I had warned we might be, voiceless and deaf in an emergency. There were many rumors and counter-rumors during the morning, but none added very much to our exact knowledge. An hour or so before lunch, we were delighted to welcome Lieutenant Robertson of the US Navy,[122] who had come down from Jerusalem to help us in a vital technical job. This hardened but seemingly very competent young man gave us the details of what had happened the previous afternoon. There were no marked differences from Shertok's account, that of Robertson being more circumstantial and detailed. For example, he told of the Jewish liaison person going forward to inquire about the hold up in the road, of the gangster shooting of the tires of the first car and of Colonel Frank Begley's efforts from his position as driver of the count's car to block the killer, and of his powder-smudged face which also showed cuts as those made by a razor carelessly handled in shaving.[123] Robertson's further account of the post-assassination events and of the confusion, the improvised guard of honor, the half-care of the

120. Far more basic summary in McDonald to secretary of state, nos. 117, 118, September 17–18, 1948, NARA, RG 59, 501.BB Palestine, box 2120, folder 2.
121. Knox to family, September 28, 1948, Truman Library, Knox Papers, box 1, folder Correspondence 1948–1949.
122. One of the UN observers in Jerusalem.
123. Colonel Frank Begley (US) (d. 1985), UN observer and Bernadotte's security chief. Ilan, *Bernadotte in Palestine*, 82–83.

bodies, the next morning's convoy to Haifa by the way of Lydda, all of this made rather gruesome listening.[124] At lunch fortunately we were regaled by the lieutenant's naïve but not immodest accounts of his technical achievements and his implied conquests among the ladies. His accounts of the first score made me envious that we do not have him on our staff to improvise for us communication facilities such as he had for the consulate and the UN. But we shall settle if he succeeds in his special mission for us today.

After tea and during it, we visited with Mr. Viteles and Mr. Goldsmith of Chicago. Viteles's chief suggestion was that I talk with Chief Rabbi [Yitzhak] Herzog and also with Rabbis Fishman and Berlin [Bar-Ilan] about the same subject I had spoken to Shertok about the previous night. It was at this moment that the telephone rang. It was Shiloah saying that Ben-Gurion would like to see me and would come over here or send the car for me. I naturally accepted the latter alternative and asked if I might bring Knox. Shiloah replied, "As you like." When the car arrived with two policemen, there was a moment of rather amusing concern when someone asked whether it might not be that the car was not from Ben-Gurion at all. Fortunately, some of our guards recognized the policemen, and Knox and I were quickly off to the GHQ [Army General Headquarters, where Ben-Gurion had his office as minister of defense]. It was exhilarating to be out of the house for a few minutes.

Ben-Gurion, sitting in a sparsely furnished room with the walls lined with maps, seemed more refreshed than when Knox and I had been with him and Shertok last Monday. Apparently he thrives on action. Ben-Gurion outlined more fully than had Shertok the government's proposals. With the text before him of the emergency ordinance, which he was presenting to the cabinet a few hours later, he explained its chief provisions. These would outlaw any organization which had assassination as one of its political or other aims, or anyone of whose members had committed such a crime or boasted of having done so. It prescribes heavy penalties for membership in such a body or for financially aiding it or giving shelter to its members. As soon as it is passed, more strenuous measures are to be taken against the Stern Gang. Ben-Gurion also filled out the picture Shertok had given us of the emergency transfer of forces and of the instructions sent to Dov Joseph [Israeli military governor in Jerusalem] the previous evening ordering the promptest and the most thorough action against the dissidents involved in the murder. Almost incidentally, he indicated that while the other group [the IZL] has not, as far as can now be ascertained, been involved, and though they have through several channels disavowed their association with it, he intended that the Provisional Government should make the latter group choose between unqualified loyalty and elimination. GHQ is

124. The bodies were kept in the YMCA building in Jerusalem under UN guard. Trygve Lie insisted that the bodies be moved to Paris for the General Assembly meeting's opening ceremony on September 21. The bodies were thus sent to Haifa and then to Rhodes, Rome, Geneva, and Paris. Ilan, *Bernadotte in Palestine*, 221.

located on the highest hill in Ramat Gan, which at sunset time gave a truly magnificent view. I longed for freedom to enjoy it.

McDonald's midnight report to Washington of September 18, 1948 added the detail that "Ben-Gurion said he was determined [to] end terrorists or illegal groups once and for all."[125] *The government cracked down on the Sternists. The organization was disarmed, and the government arrested some 200 members.*[126]

It remained impossible to prove that Lehi engineered the assassination, and no public admission of the fact occurred until 1977.[127] *Lehi leader Natan Yellin-Mor was arrested and put on trial, but was found guilty, on January 25, 1949, only of leading a terrorist organization. He was sentenced to eight years' imprisonment on February 10. He was elected to the Knesset in Israel's first elections on the day he was sentenced and was released by the government in March so that he could take up his seat on behalf of the Fighters' List, which included a number of ex-Lehi members.*[128]

Sunday, September 19

Up early and read and had tea nearly an hour before breakfast. During the afternoon Congressman Multer came out again, reporting that he was receiving special airplane service to Athens, either Army or UN, he assumed through our telegram intercession to the Department. As he was waiting, I hurriedly dictated a letter to the president, which [Multer] promised to deliver to him personally, even if he were in the West on tour.

McDonald feared that the president might be persuaded to recall him temporarily owing to Bernadotte's murder. He assured the president that the Israeli government was taking strong measures to destroy Lehi. "The more difficult the time," he said, "the more essential our presence."[129] *McDonald also enlisted his other contacts in the United States. He wrote Frieda Warburg three days later that "I hope that my friends at home will under no circumstances permit anything that may happen here stampede them into a feeling that we should turn tail and run. If, as I sincerely trust will not be the case, conditions should worsen, we shall then be more necessary here even than we now are."*[130]

Multer met the president in Oklahoma City immediately on his return. Truman needed little prompting. He wrote McDonald on October 4: "I heartily approve of the course you have pursued and shall, as you recommend, discourage any move to weaken

125. McDonald to secretary of state, no. 122, September 18, 1948, NARA, RG 59, MC 1390, reel 16, frames 819–820.

126. *DFPI*, v. 1, d. 518, 519, 520.

127. Cary David Stanger, "A Haunting Legacy: The Assassination of Count Bernadotte," *Middle East Journal* 42, no. 2 (Spring 1988): 260–72.

128. Heller, *The Stern Gang*, 256–265.

129. McDonald to Truman, September 19, 1948, McDonald Papers, USHMM, box 7, folder 6.

130. McDonald to Frieda Warburg, September 22, 1948, McDonald Papers, Columbia University, box 5, folder 8.

the Mission or withdraw its head as a form of sanctions."[131] *Multer also intervened with Truman with regard to delays on the Export-Import Bank loan to Israel: "Situation in Israel is economically and politically stronger than France, Greece, or China. . . . I earnestly urge you to direct [the] bank to make [the] loan forthwith."*[132]

Multer also wrote Marshall and Trygve Lie personally to protest the Bernadotte Plan and the prospect of taking the Negev from Israel.[133] *To David Niles in the White House he gave a lengthy account of his trip, wherein he said of the Bernadotte Plan, "It is of the utmost importance that one dastardly crime [Bernadotte's murder] should not be made the excuse for the perpetration of another. . . . No one can offer a single valid reason at this time for taking the Negev from the State of Israel."*[134]

Monday, September 20

Still confined to quarters. A refreshing 45 minutes before breakfast with my tea and several chapters of *Josephus*.[135] First two hours after were spent in dictation, including a personal letter to Clifford and in the reading of a mass of documents, which Mr. Knox had brought from the office.

McDonald wrote Clifford as follows: "We should guard . . . against any emotional reaction, which could only make matters worse. In particular I hope the President will, no matter what happens, continue to take the long view. Only by so doing can he avoid playing into the hands of the enemies of Israel and of his policy of peace and cooperation throughout the area."

On a more fundamental point McDonald warned Clifford:

> *To strive constantly as the Department seemingly does for cooperation with Britain on questions affecting this area is a sound procedure only if this desire for parallel action does not paralyze US initiative. To delay doing what desperately needs to be done in the hope that Britain can eventually be persuaded to 'go along' or though fear that the US, acting alone, would weaken the truce is to invite a worsening of conditions as may destroy all prospects of a peaceful solution. Events will not wait on counsels of timidity or procrastination. Those who in the British manner urge delay or non-cooperation with Israel seem to be expecting time to increase the chances of peace; delay is more likely to destroy those chances.*[136]

After lunch and a brief nap, Knox and I went to the Foreign Office to deliver the substance of a circular telegram [from the State Department] addressed to the Provisional Government and the neighboring Arab states, expressing in gen-

---

131. Truman to McDonald, October 4, 1948, in McDonald, *My Mission in Israel*, 82.

132. Press Release from Offices of Abraham J. Multer, October 11, 1948, Truman Library, Papers of David K. Niles, Israel File, box 30, folder August–December 1948.

133. Multer to Marshall, October 5, 1948, and Multer to Lie, October 5, 1948, NARA, RG 59, 501.BB Palestine, box 2121, folder 3.

134. Report on the Middle East by Abraham J. Multer, Truman Library, Papers of David K. Niles, Israel File, box 30, folder August–December 1948.

135. Lion Feuchtwanger's trilogy, *Josephus* (1932).

136. McDonald to Clifford, September 20, 1948, McDonald Papers, USHMM, Box 7, folder 6.

eral terms the US's concern about the maintenance of the truce and its confidence that there would be no repetition of violence.[137] Shertok was seemingly pleasantly surprised at the mildness of the communication. He was quick to give categorical assurance on both counts. Then, in answer to our questions, he elaborated on the subject of the government's strenuous efforts to round up the Sternists.[138] He promised us the text of the new decree within a few hours.

More startling was his statement that the Provisional Government had issued an ultimatum to the Irgun, and that the expiration date was tomorrow at noon. The terms were complete and unconditional absorption in the Israeli Army of the members eligible for that service and the dissolution of the old organization. Its leaders have been holding out for two conditions: 1) The right to have their forces remain in Jerusalem, and; 2) The right to set themselves up again as a separate unit in the event the Provisional Government should compromise on the issue of Jerusalem. Shertok expressed confidence, but not certainty, that the government's terms would be accepted. If not, force would be used to compel acceptance. The only condition which might prevent such use would be an Arab attack militarily.[139]

From 5:15 to 7:15 Arthur Koestler and his attractive young English wife [Mamaine Paget][140] were here for tea and sherry. It was a delightful and civilized two hours. Among the interesting observations by Koestler were the following:

1) The Sternists are liquidated and cannot hope to revive unless the Provisional Government [was] forced to accept a humiliating peace.
2) Like Lehi, the Irgun is also on the way out. Its leaders are genuinely anxious to make a strong showing in the election and they think they will do so (it was evident that Koestler had no knowledge of the present time limit or if he had, he assumed that the Provisional Government's terms would be accepted). When I asked him guardedly about this, he replied that certainly Begin would want to do so, but that there might be some question about some of his associates who were more qualifiedly fanatical. Koestler continued by saying that once out of the underground it would be difficult to return, and this difficulty becomes the greater in proportion as the public as a whole are unsympathetic to underground activities. In general then, Koestler was convinced that short of some disaster to the state, the underground is finished. Whether this process would be completed without friction depended, he thought, on the extent to which Ben-Gurion sought to speed the pace for domestic political purposes.

137. Paraphrased in *FRUS*, 1948, v. V, pt. 2, 1415, n. 2.
138. See Heller, *The Stern Gang*, 256–258.
139. Reported in McDonald to secretary of state, no. 128, September 20, 1948, NARA, RG 59, 501.BB Palestine, box 2120 folder 4. Additional background information is reported in this folder. The IZL's last remaining units that were independent of the IDF were in Jerusalem.
140. Not married until April 1950.

3) As to Loy Henderson, Koestler confessed himself quite confused.

4) Koestler said that his chief interest now in this country is its intellectual future. He sees three possibilities: a) Levantism; b) Clericalism; c) Westernization. By [Levantinism], he means the kind of superficial culture such as is prevalent among the intellectuals of the Arab states with a shallow but non-understanding knowledge of the West. Under [clericalism], he would lump the various possibilities arising from undue rabbinic influence and the vacuum left by nearly 2,000 years of non-creative intellectualism. [Westernization] is self-explanatory, but he doubted that this would be the kind of development.

As Koestler talked and spoke about the sabras—the native-born Palestinian Jews, with their limited provincial outlook, their lack of interest in Western Europe and with their almost complete lack of knowledge of the West, I could see that he felt here the lack of the kind of Western cosmopolitanism with which he had been so familiar in Hungary, Paris, London, and elsewhere. When I said that one had to think of Palestine as a pioneer country in which it was natural that for a generation or two or three, the emphasis would be on material development and perhaps rather crude nationalism rather than on culture, he seemed inclined to agree. He was interested [also] in my references to pioneer America and pioneer South Africa. He did not disagree either when I suggested that one can't extrapolate about a whole people because so many unanticipated elements might enter into the chemical compound. Towards the end of our talk, I said that I had only one fundamental principle about this country, to wit, that it is *sui generis*, in other words, that all comparisons with other countries and people, or rather all analogies with other situations are much more apt to be false than enlightening. It was refreshing to note how Koestler's young wife didn't hesitate to interject her views and how considerate he seemed to be of them and of her.

As we were finishing dinner Major Amos Ben-Gurion [son of David Ben-Gurion] and his police colleague came in. After I had more or less entertained them for a while with my stories of my earlier experiences here, and had mentioned the fact of Koestler's visit, young Ben-Gurion expressed his general distrust and dislike of the intellectual. He implied that if Koestler settled down and did a job of hard work here (not writing books), he would learn something about the country.[141]

On September 21, 1948 the third regular session of the UN General Assembly opened in Paris. The US delegation, appointed by the president, included Secretary

---

141. Koestler's difficult September 13 meeting with David Ben-Gurion, in which Ben-Gurion challenged Koestler's Jewishness and harshly criticized his most recent book *Thieves in the Night* (1946), which itself was a critique of Zionist pioneers in the 1930s, is described in Cesarani, *Arthur Koestler*, 321–325.

Marshall as its chairman, as well as John Foster Dulles,[142] Eleanor Roosevelt,[143] Philip C. Jessup, and Benjamin V. Cohen.[144] A large advisory staff from the State Department—McDonald later referred to them as "technicians"—accompanied the delegation. Led by Dean Rusk in his capacity as the State Department's Director of United Nations Affairs, it also included representatives of the State Department's various divisions, including the Division of Near Eastern Affairs.[145]

Secretary-General Trygve Lie began the session by eulogizing Bernadotte and Sérot and praising Bernadotte's plan as "a just settlement of the Palestine problem."[146] The British and the US foreign policy establishments had accepted it as a just settlement to be imposed in its fundamentals by the UN. Marshall thus announced in the General Assembly that Bernadotte's recommendations "offer a generally fair basis for settlement of the Palestine question."[147] As previously agreed, Bevin quickly stated in the House of Commons that the British government considered Bernadotte's proposals "a single integrated plan," to which it gave "wholehearted and unqualified support."[148] Meanwhile, the State Department had ordered McDonald to inform the Israeli government that "my Government considers that the task of [the] UN so effectively begun by Bernadotte be vigorously continued."[149]

In Paris, Abba Eban privately expressed his "astonishment" to the Americans that Washington supported Bernadotte's report "in its entirety." But he suggested a "cautious reaction, leaving [the Arabs] with [the] task [of a] hostile reaction"[150] Indeed, Syrian Foreign Minister Mushin Barazi complained that the plan confirmed the "Zionist rape of Palestine." The head of the Saudi delegation said that he spoke for all Arabs in noting that "as long as the State of Israel existed the Palestine problem would never be solved." Similar statements came from Azzam Pasha, the secretary-general of the Arab League.[151]

142. John Foster Dulles (1888–1959), successful international lawyer and career diplomat since the Wilson administration; close associate and foreign policy adviser to Governor Thomas Dewey; widely assumed to be the next secretary of state after Dewey's expected November 1948 victory.

143. US representative to the General Assembly's Third (Social and Humanitarian) Committee; primarily busy in Paris with the drafting of the UN Declaration of Human Rights during the Third Session.

144. Benjamin V. Cohen (1893–1983), Indiana-born jurist who held positions in the Roosevelt and Truman administrations; helped write much of the legislation associated with Roosevelt's New Deal as well as the Lend-Lease Act (1941) and the Dumbarton Oaks agreement (1944) that led to the establishment of the UN; part of the US delegation at the Potsdam conference (1945); knew McDonald from McDonald's work with refugees in the 1930s.

145. The delegation with all advisers is listed in *FRUS*, 1948, v. I, 10–15.

146. Andrew W. Cordier and Wilder Foote, eds., *Public Papers of the Secretaries-General of the United Nations*, v. 1: *Trygve Lie, 1946–1953* (New York: Columbia University Press, 1969), 163–165.

147. Marshall statement of September 21, 1948, *FRUS*, 1948, v. V, pt. 2, 1415–1416.

148. Hansard, *Parliamentary Debates, House of Commons*, Series 5, v. 456, 898–899; for the planned order of speeches, see memorandum for the files, September 30, 1948, RG 59, 501.BB Palestine, box 2120, folder 5.

149. Shertok to Epstein, September 20, 1948, *DFPI*, v. 1, d. 525.

150. Eban to Shertok, September 20, 1948, September 22, 1948, *DFPI*, v. 1, d. 523, 532; Epstein to Shertok, September 27/28, 1948, *DFPI*, v. 1, d. 548.

151. Hahn, *Caught in the Middle East*, 56; Conversation with Amir Faisal, head of Saudi delegation, September 22, 1948, *FRUS*, 1948, v. V, pt. 2, 1416; Griffis to Lovett, September 25, 1948, *FRUS*, 1948, v. V, pt. 2, 1422–1423.

On September 23 the Israeli government clearly specified: "We prefer the boundaries of Israel to be finally fixed by formal agreement between the contending parties. Pending that, we regard the territorial settlement of November 29, 1947 as valid, but standing in need of certain improvements in light of events since then." The statement continued that "we see no justification whatever for the exclusion from the Jewish State of the large area of the Negev, comprising over two thirds of Israel's territory. . . . This proposal we shall oppose. . . . Haifa, with its port and oil refineries, is and must remain part of Israel. . . . We consider ourselves entitled to claim Jerusalem as part of Israel subject always to due safeguards for the inviolability and free access to all Holy Places and Shrines. The imperative need for a territorial link between Jerusalem and Israel's coastal plain has already been stressed." As for Arab refugees, the statement noted that "we cannot forget that the initial attack on the Jews after the November 29th resolution was launched by Palestinian Arabs and that neighboring Arab States justified their campaign of aggression against the State of Israel by the call for help that reached them from Arabs within its territory."[152] The Israelis missed few chances in Paris thereafter to express their rejection of the Bernadotte Plan, discovering that the US delegation was divided on the plan's merits.[153]

Israeli representatives tried to reach Truman directly through the president's advisers David Niles and Clark Clifford, and even Truman's personal Kansas City friend Eddie Jacobson. In light of the impending presidential election, all urged him to denounce the Bernadotte Plan.[154]

Tuesday, September 21

Continued before breakfast the study I began late last night of the text of the Provisional Government's emergency decree outlawing terrorist organizations. Then, as Knox worked on his summary of the decree, I began [the] first draft of a despatch regarding possible broader implications of Bernadotte's death. Knox was, I think, rather shocked by the boldness of the draft but did not object in principle. He and later Cummings suggested that it would be desirable to delay the final form until [an] opportunity for continuation of conference with the friend of the previous evening.[155] I agreed and asked Cummings to arrange [a] meeting.

In the meantime McDonald pointed out to the State Department that the death of Bernadotte left two Americans, Bunche and Riley, atop the UN machinery, with the US consul in Jerusalem, John MacDonald, as the current head of the UN Truce

152. Statement in *DFPI*, v. 1, d. 536.

153. Statements from October 1948 in *DFPI*, v. 2; also Shertok to Elath, October 10, 1948, *DFPI*, v. 2, d. 19.

154. *DFPI*, v. I, d. 541, 542, 543; *Weizmann Papers*, Ser. A, v. XXIII, n. 254, 259; *DFPI*, v. 2, n. 16. Also Hahn *Caught in the Middle East*, 57–58.

155. McDonald to secretary of state [personal attention president and acting secretary], no. 133, September 22, 1948, NARA, RG 59, MC 1390, reel 16, frames 843–844, described in the next entry.

Commission. "These men are excellent," he reported, "but it occurs to me, as it probably already has to the Department, that this all-American direction may give ground [to] unwarranted charges of US dominance [of] international machinery."[156]

Anxiously awaited news of reception by the Irgun of Provisional Government ultimatum. Apparently it was accepted. After lunch with Knox and Cummings and brief nap, went out with McMahon and two of the guards for walk on the beach at Herzliya. The beach seemed a place of freedom compared to the house, which I had not left since Friday night, except for visit once to the Foreign Office and another time to GHQ. Back a little after six in time to begin tea with Knox and his young friends, Captain Williams, and the latter's friend from Jerusalem. Both were from the UN, and Williams had had very disturbing experience with [the] Bernadotte tragedy involving care of the body. This and his personal regard for Bernadotte had left him disillusioned, cynical, and bitter, not only towards the Jews but towards the UN also.

Our friend of the night before[157] and Cummings joined us, and after some general talk the three of us adjourned to the porch where we talked until eight o'clock, in spite the fact that our visitor had guests for dinner waiting. He was extremely helpful in suggesting the psychological background and the framework into which my idea might fit.[158] His ideas too about labor, press, and special attaché were valuable, in the realm of theory about interrelations and possible explanations of the recent incident were also extremely suggestive.

The arguments in favor of limited knowledge among the larger groups was strengthened by the obvious source of information on the top level. The fact that there may have been a broader feel of imminence may have been the result not of knowledge, but of the climate of the group created by the imminent effort. In reply to my question as to how many individuals would be essential for action, he said five plus five plus five plus five. He and Cummings were in general agreement about the figures and personnel both showing large and intimate knowledge of liberal La[bor] and Le[hi] personalities. The up-to-date nature and detail of this knowledge, plus the intimacy of his acquaintance with events of last week at our neighbor's [Shertok's] house, made me begin to wonder just what his position is. But in any case he seemed to be able and willing to be of distinct service.

After a light supper with Bobby and Miss Clark, they left for a party in Petah Tikvah. I spent most of the next three hours working on a drastic revision of my morning production. It was an excellent occupation to make one forget the lateness of Bobby and Miss Clark's return. About midnight, McMahon and I, in the freshness and darkness of the front porch discussed the probabilities

156. McDonald to secretary of state, no. 132, September 22, 1948, NARA, RG 59, 501.BB Palestine, box 2120, folder 5.
157. Probably Amos Ben-Gurion.
158. McDonald's supposition that the Soviets might have been behind Bernadotte's murder.

and possibilities of the combinations and permutations. He gave me an extraordinary confirmation from a wholly independent source of our other friend's five times four formula and support for the smaller theory. Indeed it might be that already this was confirmed. The rumor of a dual, unexpected, and hurried visit northward, if it could be confirmed, would be strong support for the pattern outlined in my despatch. McMahon pledged me to complete secrecy, saying that I might not even tell Knox or Williams, for in that event there would be a breach of what he could not afford.

Bobby and Miss Clark arrived about 12:30 to be greeted at the street level by four Israeli police and then in the driveway by Shalom, McMahon and one of our guards and at the door and in the stairway by other guards and by me. Instead of being penitent, they seemed to enjoy the unusual reception committee.

Wednesday, September 22

Despite lateness to bed, up early to give one more examination of my draft, which Miss Clark typed before breakfast. After breakfast, Knox and Cummings approved the draft with minor verbal changes and Cummings's very valuable additions on personnel in the labor and special fields. We decided that this despatch should take precedence over the shorter one replying to the Department's expression of concern about our safety. Knox and Cummings's discussion with me about our friend tended to give credence to the theory of a Washington relationship.

McDonald and his staff worried that Count Bernadotte's assassination would discredit Israel in the eyes of the democratic world and open the door for communist influence there. They even considered the possibility that the Soviets had been behind the assassination toward this end. In a personal despatch of September 22 McDonald urged the president and the State Department to take preventive action by adding key members to the US mission staff. He called for a "special officer of [the] highest capacity with power [to] organize [an] efficient service and understand totalitarian technique, as well [as] Russian, Hebrew, German, Yiddish." He added that he believed "Sam Klaus [to be] ideally fitted" and asked, "Could he possibly be spared now?"[159] McDonald also urged the creation of a "labor attaché to contact immediately labor groups and advise on unofficial American educational program. Suggest [it] may be advisable [to] consult Klaus regarding person." A press officer, he said, was also desirable. Finally, McDonald insisted that the Tel Aviv mission be properly equipped with "adequate communications facilities comparable [to those in] Jerusalem and Haifa . . . . Given

---

159. Samuel Klaus (1904–1963), Treasury Department official, 1944; helped found and then operate the Foreign Economic Administration (FEA), which searched for hidden Nazi assets in neutral countries (Operation Safehaven); knew Herbert J. Cummings who, as a State Department official in 1944, helped set up and run the FEA.

adequate staff and full facilities, including communications, we can, I am confident, hold our own and gradually improve US position here."[160]

McDonald wrote in the context of the early Cold War and in view of the upcoming Israeli elections. Communist parties in Western Europe were popular after World War II. The French Communist Party won a plurality in the October 1945 elections and participated in governing coalitions until their May 1947 ouster over labor and colonial disputes. In Czechoslovakia in February 1948, the Communist Party, which led all other parties with 38 percent of the vote in the 1946 election, took full control of the government from its coalition partners. In the Italian elections of April 1948, US influence had been critical in preventing the Italian Communist Party from winning a mandate to lead a governing coalition.

In Israel, Ben-Gurion's Mapai, which dominated the Provisional Government, was labor oriented but friendly toward the West. The State Department was more concerned with Mapam, formed in January 1948 from left-wing labor elements, which held two cabinet posts in the Provisional Government. Marxist-Zionist in its outlook, Mapam was positively disposed toward Moscow and skeptical of the United States, because it was an ally of Britain. John MacDonald, the consul general in Jerusalem, had sounded the alarm about Mapam in mid-September. James McDonald too, was concerned about Mapam's naiveté concerning the Soviets.[161]

Robert Lovett told the president that it was "possible Count Bernadotte was assassinated by agents of a foreign power although evidence to this effect is not now available. . . . Prior to the receipt of Mr. McDonald's message we had already been working on some of the immediate measures which he urges and are now checking on his new suggestions. We expect to communicate with him shortly."[162] *The State Department decided to send Samuel Klaus to Israel. He arrived at the US Mission in Tel Aviv in mid-November 1948 with instructions to assess the strength of communist penetration in Israel and the possibility of Israeli governmental orientation toward the USSR.*[163]

It was disturbing to learn that the US and Great Britain had come out strongly for the Bernadotte proposals as a whole. Bevin's sanctimonious approval of them, as Bobby and I heard his speech quoted on the radio today, made me a little nauseous. Listening late that night to Bevin's speech, or a considerable portion of it in the House of Commons, Bobby and I realized anew how

160. McDonald to secretary of state [personal attention president and acting secretary], no. 133, September 22, 1948, NARA, RG 59, MC1390, reel 16, frames 843–844. The mission received a permanent labor attaché and a press officer in 1949.

161. MacDonald to secretary of state, no. 1290, September 15, 1948, NARA, RG 59, MC 1390, frame 811.

162. Memorandum for the president, September 25, 1948, NARA, RG 59, 501.BB Palestine, box 2120, folder 5.

163. Some sources from 1948 have Klaus as a CIA employee and others have him sent by Truman himself. Since he ultimately reported to Satterthwaite in the State Department, he probably was sent by that agency. See Uri Bialer, *Between East and West*, 208–209; Joseph Heller, *The Birth of Israel, 1945–1949: Ben-Gurion and His Critics* (Gainesville: University Press of Florida, 2003), 45; Ephaim Karsch, "Israel," in *The Cold War and the Middle East*, eds. Yezid Sayigh and Avi Schlaim (Oxford: Oxford University Press, 1997), 156–185.

difficult the future here may still be.[164] His attitude is not surprising, but one wonders how our people could conceive that the Provisional Government or the people here would trade off the Negev for Galilee, particularly since the former was for the most part allocated to Israel by November 29, and the latter in large part [is] occupied by Israeli forces.

[Aryeh] Altman, the Revisionist leader, came out at six and stayed until nearly eight.[165] Although at the end I had not changed my earlier view that he is dumb and unimaginative, I did learn some things including the following:

1) Negotiations between the [Revisionists Zionists—HaTzohar] and Begin's new Freedom [Herut] Party bogged down after elaborate negotiations. Altman said that had Begin accepted the former's program of four months ago, the combined Right parties could have won possibly as much as 40% of the seats at the next election. This seemed to me a very optimistic estimate.[166]

2) Altman spoke of Begin, as had a number of other people, as a man who, having been here only four years and much of that time underground, could not know the country.

3) As a member of the Law Committee of the State Council, Altman had been in session for six hours with the other members discussing the latest emergency decree. He was critical of its unusual provisions but had no very convincing answer to my question as to how else terrorists could be controlled. It seemed to me another case of idealism inviting its own destruction.

4) Altman expressed concern lest the neighbor to the north [Soviet Union] profit from the negative or neutral attitude of US and Britain. He argued that since Mapam did not differ in any essentials from Mapai, the [latter] was ready to listen to the siren voice.

5) On the subject of our long telegram of the day before, I could evoke no revealing comments from Altman. Either he did not know anything or was not willing to disclose what he knew. He spoke of Lehi as having had, despite its small size, the best of intelligence service and that, therefore, it was not necessarily unnatural to suppose that they could have on their own have known of the count's change of plans.

The news in the late afternoon that three Arab [Legion] soldiers had held up the Jerusalem-bound [UN-led unarmed] Jewish convoy and killed the commander and also three civilians, including an American railroad engineer, John

---

164. In Hansard, *Parliamentary Debates*, Series 5, v. 456, 898–899.
165. Entry of August 17, 1948.
166. On June 15, 1948 Begin created a new political party "Herut" (Freedom). Created from IZL elements, it was separate and distinct from the older political wing of the Revisionist Zionist movement (HaTzohar). See Yonathan Shapiro, *The Road to Power: Herut Party in Israel* (Albany, NY: SUNY Press, 1991); Yechiam Weitz, "The Road to the 'Upheaval': A Capsule History of the Herut Movement, 1948–1977," *Israel Studies* 10, no. 3 (Fall 2005): 54–86; Yaacov Shavit, *Jabotinsky and the Revisionist Movement 1925–1948* (London: Frank Cass, 1988); and Sasson Sofer, *Begin: An Anatomy of Leadership* (Oxford: Basil Blackwell, 1988).

Locke Lewis[167] and Mrs. Simcha Van Vriesland—Mr. [Eliezer] Hoofein's sister-in-law—by shooting them as they crouched in a ditch raised anew the question of a possible crisis in the next few days.

Thursday, September 23

Conference with Knox, who is perhaps even more disturbed than I by the lineup on the Bernadotte proposal. Knox expressed regret that in our telegram about Israel's response to the "try-on for size" proposal, we did not state our own views that the whole suggestion was fantastic.[168] I still think that, in view of the Department's attitude towards me, it was preferable that we merely reported at that time. Now, if and when we have gotten Israel's official reaction to Bernadotte's proposals, we shall from here be in a position to express our views with less chance that they be regarded as mere propaganda.

Visit from Mr. Friedland and his colleague. He is being called back to the States, because four young writers and producers, all Americans, who were to have come out here, suddenly changed their mind and refused to come after the Bernadotte assassination. This is one more reflection of how that tragedy is interpreted at home. Friedland thinks that Mrs. Karlin will come out soon because of the necessity to get her Academy of Fine Arts under way, and in order that Noah may make a beginning on his plan to be helpful to Israel during this early stage.

Cummings came and talked for a couple of hours and talked about his exploratory operation[169] and stayed for supper. Just as we were about ready for bed, Knox and Barnes came in with their night things. It was explained that there had been a "tip" which made it advisable not to spend the night at their house. It was all very vague, but following our fixed practice of taking no unnecessary chances, I was glad that they had come over.

Friday, September 24

Knox and McMahon slept until after 9 o'clock. This was well because both seemed exhausted. They awoke refreshed and were able to carry through a very strenuous day.

A Mr. ["Sammy"] Zerlin of New York and Los Angeles, a client of Robert Szold, about to return to the States by air, agreed to act as messenger for my personal letter to Clark Clifford, sent under cover to Halsey. Zerlin agreed to mail it by air from Paris or London should he be delayed there. This sort of individual messenger involves a certain risk, but the pouch is so slow, and the

---

167. Of Knappen, Tippetts, Abbett, & McCarthy Engineers, which worked on civil engineering projects, including ports development, in Greece, Israel, South America, Caribbean.

168. Refers perhaps to McDonald's report on his September 6 meeting with Shertok, *FRUS*, 1948, v. V, pt. 2, 1375–1378.

169. Cummings tried to penetrate the Stern Gang by taking a Sternist girlfriend. See later entries.

Department code so unsuitable for letters such as this, that I considered it a well-calculated risk.

In his September 24 letter to Clark Clifford, McDonald reiterated his concerns that the Soviets might have been behind Bernadotte's murder. Primarily, however, McDonald argued against the current US alignment with Britain in its support for the Bernadotte Plan: "It cannot be too often repeated that almost no one here trusts Britain's motives or Bevin's protestations of impartiality." McDonald further emphasized "the necessity of recognizing that the Jewish fanatical determination to keep the Negev allotted to it by the UN General Assembly November 29th recommendation is based on the profound conviction that desert though it is today, it can be transformed and made to support many hundreds of thousands of Jews. The suggestion that the Negev be exchanged for Galilee—most of which the Jews now hold—is bitterly unacceptable. The [Provisional Government] will be more able to compromise on Jerusalem than on the Negev."[170]

After lunch and a nap I went over a number of despatches which Knox had prepared for the Department, including a detailed account of events from Friday noon until today, and a critical analysis of the emergency ordinance. I asked that he append to the latter a brief note by me to the effect that I regarded the legislation as essential if progress were to be made in achieving the end which the government was committed to. I could not do otherwise consistent with my talk with our neighbor on the previous Friday night.

Renewed talk of general threats to American officials. I was concerned about Haifa on that count and also because of reports of unsympathetic talk by consular staff. I sent a strong verbal message by McMahon to Lippincott. After supper, at which Barnes and Knox joined us, we had our first session of bridge. It seemed a little strange to break away from public affairs, and I confess that I did not succeed wholly in concentrating on the cards. McMahon had come home when we went to bed.

Saturday, September 25

After a sultry and not too restful night, I enjoyed my tea and half an hour or so of elementary Jewish history. Also before breakfast, Knox, Cummings, Barnes and I listened to McMahon's report. There had been a vague inclusive warning to American officials that they are unwelcome and that they might be endangered. Apparently the roundups of the last days have not been more than ¼ successful—a not too good record. We agreed that Lippincott's talk of possible Marines at Haifa was unwise, and that instead we should from here break down the unwillingness of the Haifa police to give more adequate coverage.

As to Cummings, it was agreed that the latest suggestion of a possible rendezvous at my former taking-off place should not only be discouraged, but

170. McDonald to Clifford, September 24, 1948, McDonald Papers, USHMM, box 7, folder 6.

should be categorically forbidden, for it could not be carried out except by putting our friend in an equivocal and highly dangerous position. He could not move without the knowledge of those with whom we have been cooperating, who would certainly maintain their attention, which on the other side could make Cummings seem to be what he certainly is not. Moreover in the event of a direct clash, he would be in between. On the other hand, it was agreed that for the present McMahon's view about the open liaison should prevail, provided our cooperators understood the situation clearly and provided the other side knew the degree of official attention. Knox was not quite convinced, but McMahon, having the responsibility and feeling that there was value and no offsetting risk, was, it was decided, to call the tune for the present, particularly since Cummings was so anxious to carry on.

At teatime, Major Andronovich came out for a couple of hours before he returned up the hill. As to the Bernadotte tragedy, he had little that was new to add. It had taken place on the road that he travelled twice a day. There was no other [road] from [the] Government House now in use. The decision to go up there was made after lunch. It would have been possible for the count's car to have been observed on the way up, and the observer would then have known that it would have to return the same way. The men approaching the cars from the jeep walked past the first two and only when they reached the third and saw their man did they indicate their hostile intent. The shots later at the other cars were simply to distract attention.

On the point of my major interest, he at first said that there was no ground for suspicion.[171] Later, however, in answer to specific questions, he admitted points which gave circumstantial support. It was as if he had not thought the possibilities through. Moreover, it was he who passed on the report that the Czech consul had granted 24 visas that day. He indicated complete approval of our proposed enlargement of staff. As he was leaving, he said that he would come down any time that I urged him to do so. After he had gone, McMahon and I, walking on the roof, discussed our impressions. He said what surprised me, that he had positive orders not to have any official or other relations with our friend. He did not indicate why.

Sunday, September 26

Reading during the morning. At teatime were joined by Knox and Cummings. We talked mostly about Knox's possible leave, Cummings and I urging him strongly to go.[172] Bilby of the *Tribune* and his wife and a Mr. White of *Time*, came out for tea. She is as beautiful as she was reported to be. The talk covered a wide range, but nothing was said which added much to my knowledge.

---

171. Likely refers to McDonald's suspicion that the Soviets might have had a hand in the assassination.
172. By this time Knox had a variety of health problems brought on by exhaustion.

Off the record, I gave Bilby some of my impressions. Later, we walked on the roof and talked in confidence.

McDonald's "off-the-record" comments were sent to Ogden Reid, the editor of the New York Herald Tribune, *along with an invitation for Reid to visit. The memorandum contained twenty statements concerning the prospects for peace. They included the statement that the Bernadotte Plan would not win acceptance by both Jews and Arabs; that Israel and Transjordan might work out some sort of settlement, but the other members of the Arab League would oppose it; that the Israelis would not give up the Negev; that Bernadotte's initial proposal for Jerusalem to be given to Transjordan had strengthened the demand for a Jewish Jerusalem or at least access to the New City via a corridor from the sea; that progress on the Arab refugee issue was dependent on a peace settlement and that the grand mufti opposed the return of refugees in any case because it would be a tacit recognition of the existence of Israel; and that communism was insignificant in Israel.*[173]

About 8:30 Mr. and Mrs. Shertok came in for a social call, which before the end turned into an official conference. Shertok was obviously tired, since he had gone to Jerusalem on Friday, had had a full day there including on Saturday or the night previous a three-hour speech and questions to and from the whole body of officers of the army, a visit with [Dov] Joseph and a lunch at his own house for John J. MacDonald. Saturday night, he and Mrs. Shertok had flown over the Egyptian lines of the Negev to visit their son [Ya'akov], returning early Sunday morning. That day he had to prepare for his appearance before the state council at a private session on Monday.

The general talk was interesting, but when the women left on a sightseeing tour of the house led by Bobby, Knox, Shertok and I talked shop. Shertok reported that for the first time in many months His Majesty's Government had, through [Hector] McNeil, asked Eban to see them. Shertok said that McNeil explained the British position and "unofficially and personally" his belief that following the Provisional Government's acceptance or acquiescence in the mediator's [Bernadotte's] scheme there would be de jure recognition. Eban had pointed out that the Provisional Government had three serious reservations about the Negev proposed settlement; 1) the colonies [twenty-two settlements] in the northwest; 2) outlet to the Dead Sea; and, 3) that to the Gulf of Aqaba. To this McNeil replied that only one of these evoked his sympathy, that of the colonies.[174] After Shertok left, Knox wrote out, and I suggested, some slight changes to a telegram to the Department summarizing Shertok's comments.[175]

173. McDonald to Reid, September 28, 1948, McDonald Papers, USHMM, box 7, folder 6.
174. On this meeting, Eban to Shertok, September 22, 1948, *DFPI*, v. 1, d. 533.
175. McDonald to secretary of state, no. 148, September 28, 1948, *FRUS*, 1948, v. V, pt. 2 1428–1429. McDonald noted that Shertok was going to Paris that evening to discuss the Bernadotte proposals, but that the government would not budge on the issues of the Negev and Jerusalem. McDonald raised the possibility of a bilateral arrangement between Israel and Transjordan

Earlier in the evening I had suggested that we could perhaps save Shertok's time by taking up with him then the matter which we have asked to present at a formal interview. Shertok begged off, saying that he would rather have this at the office, where he had some material he wished to show us.

Monday, September 27

The day notable for the first letters from home in three weeks, including a glowing one from Janet and by our first telephone call from Israel to home. The connection was excellent, Bobby and I could hear Ruth's voice perfectly, even though it seemed she could not hear quite so well. We were not surprised to have her say that our friends had been alarmed the previous weekend by the confusion in the press between the two McDonalds [referring also to John J. MacDonald] and the reported warnings given to them. I think she felt reassured after our talk.

Meyer Weisgal came for tea and stayed about an hour and a half.[176] Our talk, which was friendly and at times even intimate, was confirmatory rather than revealing of new facts or points of view. He urged that I play the role of mediator between one of my oldest friends [Weizmann] and some others here. Bobby and I had gone to bed, but I was not yet really asleep when Knox and McMahon came in and rather excitedly reported a rumor, passed on to them by someone at the Gat Rimon, to the effect that the Beirut radio had announced the assassination of Shertok. Barnes was asked to come and spend the night, and efforts were made to check the accuracy of the report. It proved to have been groundless. Perhaps it was based upon an earlier rumor that day that Ben-Gurion had been attacked, or was to have been had he not discovered in time that a reported emergency call to the Foreign Office did not come from that source at all. He is supposed to have been out of his house waiting for his car when another car passed at high speed. Suspicious, he went back and telephoned the Foreign Office to be told that they had not called him.

Tuesday, September 28

Very busy all morning preparing a lengthy memorandum which went off to Arthur Hays Sulzberger, Mrs. Helen Rogers Reid, and Eugene Meyer.[177] Other mail connected with Ruth's prospective visit was sent off by hand.

From about 4:15 to 5:35, Knox and I were with Walter Eytan, acting Foreign Minister [Shertok was *en route* to Paris]. I read to him the paraphrase of the Department's expression of its earnest hope that the Provisional Government would accept or at least acquiesce in a settlement based on the mediator's

based on the November 29, 1947, partition lines with small adjustments and economic and security pacts between the two states.

176. Meyer Wolfe Weisgal (1894–1977), Polish-born US journalist; headed Zionist Organization of America, 1921–1930; acted as Chaim Weizmann's informal representative in the United States after 1940; helped expand and then direct the Weizmann Institute of Science after 1949. See Meyer Weisgal, . . . *So Far: An Autobiography* (New York: Transaction, 1971).

177. Eugene Meyer (1875–1959), chairman, Washington Post Company, 1946–1959.

proposals. Since the same subject had previously been discussed in Washington at the Department with Epstein, neither Knox nor I thought it necessary to cover the whole field again. This we felt the more strongly because Shertok on Sunday night had indirectly given the Provisional Government's attitude in his report of Eban's answer to McNeil in Paris.

In reply to my question as to what concessions the Provisional Government could make in reference to the Negev, Eytan said quite definitely that on that subject he was not allowed to speak. Instead, he developed the thesis that the mediator's proposals amounted to reducing Israel's area from 14 million dunams to 5 million, a reduction by nine million or nearly by two-thirds. He also argued that Galilee was not an adequate quid pro quo, among other reasons because it has even now a substantial Arab population. He showed us on the map the large pocket in the north still held by the Arabs where, he said, there were approximately 60,000 people. Continuing, he emphasized that unless the Jews had the Negev for expansion, there would be built up a dangerous population within the constricted area of the reduced Israel.

We also discussed Jerusalem. From what Eytan said, and from what he did not say, it was obvious that the Provisional Government now is strongly set against any form of demilitarization or internationalization except for the Old City. His arguments were only a repetition of what we had heard earlier. As to the Old City, he drew a rough sketch map, the idea for which he attributed to a well-known authority on the city. The latter's scheme would provide for separate entrances for Christians, Jews and Moslems to their respective sections of the city. One obvious hitch was that the Arab entrance would have to cross the Christian route. Another difficulty was the lack of provision for a route outside the Old City connecting Jewish New Jerusalem with Scopus and the Mount of Olives.

In his urgent despatch later that evening to Marshall, McDonald reported that Shertok was en route to Paris to present the Israeli cabinet's response to the Bernadotte Plan. He warned that the Negev proposal was unacceptable for reasons concerning existing settlements, prospective population growth, and strategy (the Israelis suspected that the British wanted an air base there); that the Israelis would not accept Jerusalem's internationalization, but would accept its partition with international protections for the Holy Places; and that an Israeli settlement with Transjordan was possible, "improbable as it may seem at the moment."[178]

The White House also assailed the Bernadotte Plan. It had ordered that it wanted to review any US statement for the UN in advance, but because of the presidential campaign it did not respond to the advance text of Marshall's September 21 endorsement of the plan. Clifford wondered how to counter Dewey's expected condemnation

---

178. McDonald to secretary of state, no. 151, September 28, 1949, *FRUS*, 1948, v. V, pt. 2, 1428–1429; also *DFPI*, v. 1, d. 550; On British air bases in the Negev, see Holmes to secretary of state, no. 4357, October 4, 1948, NARA, RG 59, 501.BB Palestine, box 2121, folder 4.

of the Bernadotte Plan.[179] *On September 29, he called Lovett from a freight-train yard in Tulsa, noting that "the President was deeply concerned by an apparent over-emphasis by the Secretary on the necessity for accepting the Bernadotte Plan in its entirety [emphasis in original]." Truman, Clifford said, had instructed him to send a telegram to Marshall in Paris. Lovett countered—and his subordinates in the UN and Near Eastern staffs agreed—that "the consequences of a telegram indicating a reversal of the President's clear approval of a program discussed with him by the Secretary on September 1 and signed by him on that date would put the Secretary in an intolerable position. . . . The consequences could be absolutely disastrous to us in the United Nations and elsewhere." What Lovett called a "prolonged argument" followed. Later that evening, the president himself called. He suggested, and Lovett accepted, a presidential statement to Rabbi Stephen Wise that would soften any White House commitment: "It seems to me," Truman's statement was to read, "that the Bernadotte Plan offers a basis for continuing efforts to secure a just settlement."*[180]

The following day the State Department drafted an order from Lovett for Mc-Donald. McDonald was to see Ben-Gurion and tell him the following: "The US [Government], which as events have shown, has proved a sincere friend of [the Provisional Government], desires in [the] spirit of friendly counsel to urge that [the Provisional Government] accept or acquiesce in [the] conclusions of [the] Bernadotte Plan in its entirety," including the surrender of the Negev for the Western Galilee, the internationalization of Jerusalem, and the surrender of the corridor to the city in lieu of access by air. In return, Israel's borders would be inviolate. Corresponding despatches were to go to the Arab states. They were never sent. Instead, it was agreed to wait until the president returned to Washington.[181]

Leonard Bernstein and Miss [Helen] Coates, his secretary, came to the house about 6:30 while Knox and Cummings were still here.[182] We had a pleasant hour or so before dinner, a civilized talk at dinner and afterwards. Lenny was quite the life of the party, showing off to excellent advantage without any of the traits which one associates with a prima donna conductor. Bernstein showed an intense interest in everything here, wanted to know all about my

---

179. See Clifford's handwritten notes, undated, in Truman Library, Clifford Papers, Subject File 1945–54, box 13, folder Palestine Misc. Memos, 2 of 3.

180. Memorandum by Lovett, September 29, 1948, *FRUS*, 1948, v. V, pt. 2, 1430–1431. See also Memorandum for the files, September 30, 1948, RG 59, 501.BB Palestine, box 2120, folder 5.

181. Draft in NARA, RG 59, 501.BB Palestine, box 2120, folder 5. See also Memorandum for the files, September 30, 1948, RG 59, 501.BB Palestine, box 2120, folder 5.

182. Leonard Bernstein (1918–1990), Massachusetts-born conductor, composer, and pianist; longtime association with New York Philharmonic after 1943 as conductor and director; devotee of Jewish national home; conducted the Palestine Orchestra in Tel Aviv for first time in April 1947; arrived in Israel in September 1948 and became guest conductor of renamed Israel Philharmonic Orchestra [IPO], performing forty concerts in fifty days, including performances for wounded troops and a symphony in November for 5,000 IDF soldiers in Be'er Sheva, then in an active war zone; remained as the IPO's musical adviser, taking the IPO on a guest tour of the United States in 1950. Allen Shawn, *Leonard Bernstein: An American Musician* (New Haven, CT: Yale University Press, 2014), 88–89.

appointment, about developments since I had arrived, and the prospect for a comprehensive settlement. I spoke to him as frankly as I felt I possibly could. He, on his part, could not have been friendlier. He was particularly amusing in his talk about some personalities and the reaction of many of the ladies to Serge Koussevitsky's marriage.[183]

Wednesday, September 29

Daniel De Luce of the Associated Press came out to tell me that he was filing a story to the effect that the Russian minister [Pavel Ershov] had said to Shertok that his government would view with concern any yielding by the Provisional Government in the Negev which would make way for the development or the retention there of British bases to be used against Russia. The implication evidently was clear or perhaps even underlined that such yielding by the Provisional Government would result in a change by Russia of its friendly attitude towards Israel. I had no comment to make on the story, except that it was interesting and that we had heard nothing whatever to that effect. I asked De Luce if he anticipated any difficulty with the censor in getting the story out, and he said he would let me know if he did have.[184]

Mr. Roy Elston (aka David Courtney) came and spent an hour or so.[185] It was, I thought, a worthwhile session. He traced his transformation from an intelligence officer of His Majesty's Government, first working with Richard Crossman[186] in Western Europe and later in 1945 being assigned to Jerusalem,

183. Serge Koussevitzky (1874–1951), Russian-born composer and conductor; mentor to Bernstein in the United States after 1941; married in 1947 Olga Naumova, who was his secretary for many years as well as the niece of his second wife, who died in 1942. Naumova was also a friend of Bernstein.

184. The Soviet UN delegation in Paris rejected the Bernadotte Plan as inspired by US and British imperialism and called for a return to the borders envisioned by the November 29, 1947, partition plan. Mapam's political secretary Leib Levite, who frequently dealt with the Soviet legation, told Ershov on September 23, 1948, that Mapam rejected the surrender of the Negev because it would stifle Jewish immigration and the Negev would thereafter become a British base. On September 27, 1948, Ershov met Shertok, who informed him that both Britain and the United States were pressuring Israel to accept the Bernadotte Plan, holding out de jure recognition and financial loans as possible rewards for doing so. Israel, however, would resist the surrender of the Negev, Shertok adding that "we do not want bases of any foreign state to be established in the Negev." Ershov, however, said nothing on the Negev issue to Shertok, who might have leaked on his own the story of Soviet pressure to De Luce. See Bentsur and Kolokolov, eds., *Documents on Israeli-Soviet Relations*, v. I, d. 172, 174.

185. Roy Elston (1900–1971), non-Jewish British journalist; expelled before World War II from Germany for critiquing Hitler's treatment of German Jews; became a British operative in Palestine in 1943, working with émigré Jews to send propaganda into the Balkans; lost sympathy for British Palestine policy by the end of World War II; became friends with Gershon Agronsky; refused London's orders to leave Palestine; took a new name for his own protection (David Courtney); and began writing a well-respected column for the *Palestine Post* called "Column One." See Robert St. John, *Shalom Means Peace* (New York: Doubleday, 1949), 94–100; and Walter Laqueur, *Dying for Jerusalem: The Past, Present and Future of the Holiest City* (Naperville, IL: Sourcebooks, 2005), 322–324.

186. Richard Crossman (1907–1974), Labour politician; headed German section of the Political Warfare Executive and then was assistant chief of SHAEF's [Supreme Headquarters Allied Expeditionary Force] Psychological Warfare Division, 1939–1945; served with McDonald on the Anglo-American Committee of Inquiry in 1946. See Goda et al., eds., *To the Gates of Jerusalem* for his interactions with McDonald.

to his role as columnist on the *Palestine Post*. He explained this as a result primarily of his sense of outrage at the anti-Semitism he found among British officials. He was the more shocked because he had expected nothing of the sort. He had come to see it the more clearly because on his staff were a large number of Eastern European Jews who had been gotten for the purpose of aiding British intelligence in following and possibly influencing opinion in Eastern Europe. Nonetheless, these Jews were, in Courtney's opinion, treated most unfairly by the British.

We then analyzed, in what I thought was a revealing manner, the possible reasons for the British change of policy, as illustrated in Bevin's pronouncement in favor of the whole Bernadotte scheme, despite the fact that it obviously pleased only one Arab state, Transjordan. Courtney's explanation was about as follows:

1) Both His Majesty's Government and the US Government had been unhappy about US and Russian agreement [concerning the recognition of Israel]. The British felt, and perhaps the State Department did not need much convincing, argued Courtney, that no good could come from any agreement between Washington and Moscow.
2) The collapse of the Arab League as a political force and as a political organization—perhaps this synchronized with the resignation of Colonel Iltyd Clayton, the head of British Military Intelligence in the Middle East and the promoter and guardian of the League,[187] [meant] that the British had almost no choice except to plumb for a Transjordan solution.
3) The chance for Britain to demonstrate unity with the US in itself is an important factor; perhaps increasingly important because this unity might develop—as indeed is perhaps apparent in De Luce's report above—against a position which the Russians would support, as in this case Israel's retention of the whole of the Negev.
4) In general, it was the result of the obvious collapse of Bevin's tenaciously-held prejudice about Arab strength and Jewish weakness.

We had hardly time to begin a discussion of the broader field of American-Russian relations when I was told that Benn Feller of the International News Service[188] was here to see me. I did, however, tell Courtney that only in this

187. Colonel Iltyd Nicholl Clayton (1886–1955), served with British Military Intelligence in Cairo, 1940–1943; adviser on Arab Affairs to British minister of state in Cairo, 1943–1945; attached to British Embassy in Cairo as special adviser on Middle Eastern affairs and liaison to the Arab League, 1947–1948; warned London before the Israeli War of Independence that the Arabs were unprepared and divided; argued, against the Bernadotte Plan, that it was preferable to divide Palestine's Arab parts between the Arab states rather than have a Palestinian entity within Transjordan. Ben-Gurion and his intelligence personnel believed that Clayton had operated covertly under Bevin's instructions to prevent the partition plan from being realized. Yoav Gelber, *Palestine 1948: War, Escape, and the Emergence of the Palestinian Refugee Problem*, 2nd ed. (Portland, OR: Sussex Academic Press, 2006), 189.
188. Later merged with United Press to become United Press International, 1958.

area did I question some of his conclusions in his column, and that I coveted an opportunity to thrash the whole subject out to him when we [c]ould without the interruptions of the barber and other engagements.[189] He said that he was going off to Jerusalem but that he would be back in a week or so, and we shall arrange to meet then again.

My talk with Feller was long and seemed longer. He had nothing significant to say, was inclined to complain about our lack of press-mindedness, and finally asked what I thought of a visit by the US Fleet to Israel, and were there any plans to this effect. I answered that I knew nothing. When he asked further if I saw any objection to his writing about the desirability of such a visit, I told him I had no opinion. From Feller I learned that Julian Lewis Meltzer, the *New York Times* man in Jerusalem, also has a tie-in with INS [Immigration and Naturalization Service]. This made me wonder why the *Times* is not more adequately represented here regularly.

Thursday, September 30

From eleven until after twelve, Eli Eliachar of Jerusalem, the Sephardic leader who has recently returned from visits to Rome, Paris, London and New York on a mission on behalf of the Jews in Moslem countries, told me of his problem.[190] He estimates that there are between 800 and 900 thousand Jews involved, most of whom are potentially or actually in danger. One of the chief difficulties now is the nearly complete lack of communications between these Jews and the outside world. Eliachar in Washington had seen Loy Henderson and Satterthwaite, got the impression that the latter was somewhat more sympathetic than the former, who had replied that there was very little that the US could do beyond making inquiries. At the moment, Eliachar seemed most concerned about the fate of a rich Iraqi Jew from Baghdad, Stanley Shashoua, who in anticipation of arrest and the confiscation of his large fortune by the Iraqi authorities, had fled to Tehran.[191] There he was fearful of extradition proceed-

189. David Courtney, "Column One," *Palestine Post*, August 25, 1948, criticized Bevin's policy of favoring corrupt Arab governments that played to extreme anti-Zionist sentiment for fear of communism in the Middle East. Argued that "Western policy towards the Middle East has changed from one of imperial arrogance to humiliating appeasement. This background must be realized in working out the prospect of an effective peace between Israel and the Arabs." Argued further that the Israeli desire to negotiate directly with the Arab states was genuine and that UN policy hindered this development, because elements in the Arab governments wished to negotiate. "[The] West must surely know by now that it is backing the wrong horse, not as between Arab and Jew, but as between Arab and Arab, or Moslem and Moslem."

190. Eliahu Eliachar (1898–1981), native Palestinian Jewish writer from an old Jerusalem family; leading spokesman for Sephardic Jews in Palestine and Israel; sent to study and report on the state of Jews in Islamic countries, February 1948; later head of the Council of the Sephardic Community in Israel; argued against the exclusion of Sephardic Jews from leadership positions in Israel.

191. There were 130,000 Jews in Iraq in 1948. In addition to the general persecution of Iraqi Jews, the government tried several wealthy Iraqi Jews in 1948 on charges of smuggling or spying for Israel. The Iraqi government collected some $80 million in fines and impounded property, never returning it. Iraq's Jewish community prepared a memorandum for Bernadotte, which

ings. Eliachar wondered if I could do anything to lessen the chances of such extradition. I said I would do it if I could.

Eliachar and I talked about conditions in the Arab states, and he promised to supply me with some of the books which would be most directly helpful in making me *au courant*. After a brief nap and without tea, Knox and I went off to the 4 o'clock meeting of the state council, where Weizmann was scheduled to make his first formal appearance at five.[192] I received a cordial greeting from the crowd waiting outside the door when we arrived a few minutes before four. While waiting for the proceedings to begin, I chatted for a few minutes with Mrs. [Paula] Ben-Gurion, some of the rabbis, and members of the council. Just at four Ershov arrived and was seated but one seat removed from us. I arose and we shook hands, I must confess, rather reluctantly.

The setting in the hall was in no sense inspiring. It is a smallish room, one of the exhibit halls of the museum, fitted out in rather a drab style for the sessions of the state council. At one end of the room were two raised platforms, one somewhat higher than the other. On the lower, seated at a horseshoe table were the members of the cabinet, with Ben-Gurion, who arrived about 4:30, in the center. On the higher desk sat in the center the president of the state council, Joseph Sprinzak. He was flanked on either side by heads of national organizations, including Avraham Granovsky. In back of the seats of the cabinet members who sat on the two sides of the lower table, there was room, with crowding, for only one row of chairs reserved this day for dignitaries such as the wives of Ben-Gurion, Weizmann, et al.

At the end of the hall near the chairman sat the members of the council at improvised desks, as in a primitive school. Along the wall on each side facing the members were two rows of seats. Knox and I and the Russians sat in the first row at one of these. In about half of the remaining portion of the hall were benches and seats for the press. Behind them were seats for perhaps 75 or 100 of the public. Crowding the steps leading down from the entrance hall to the hall proper were perhaps as many as 50 or 75 press officials, police, et al. The session began promptly with a word or two from the chairman followed by the reading of the agenda by the clerk. David Remez, the minister of communications, opened the discussion on some aspects of education. There was a brief animated debate, which was closed, however, on the motion to the effect that there was no time at this session for an adequate debate of such an important subject. Then Pinhas Rosen, minister of justice, read a statement about patent and trademark regulations, which seemingly interested no one. He was followed by Eliezer

did not reach him before his death. Itamar Levin, *Locked Doors: The Seizure of Jewish Property in Arab Countries* (Westport, CT: Greenwood, 2001), 1–16.

192. After a long delay owing to health problems, Chaim and Vera Weizmann traveled to Israel by special aircraft on September 30, taking up Israeli citizenship and giving up their British citizenship. Weizmann's speech to the Provisional State Council was delivered the same day. See Munya M. Mardor, *Strictly Illegal* (London: Robert Hale, 1964), 228–229, on the flight.

Kaplan, who began a discussion of the budget. Kaplan was the best of the cabinet speakers, but his presentation suffered from the fact that everyone was anxiously waiting for five o'clock and the appearance of Chaim Weizmann.

As we waited, I studied the personalities of the state council and the cabinet. It was noteworthy that none of them is young, nearly all of them being well over fifty, and many well over sixty. They are the leaders of the older generation. But one woman was present as a member. Everything taken together made me think that this meeting was perhaps not unlike one of the first sessions of the American Congress under the Articles of Confederation. On all sides there was great earnestness, and written clearly in the faces of most of the actors were the marks of a long struggle. And likewise, one sensed improvisation as the inevitable accompaniment of the new state still in the process of being carried through its first stages of babyhood.

Weizmann arrived a few minutes after five on the arm of Michael Simon of the protocol office and accompanied by Meyer Weisgal. As he rather hesitatingly made his way forward, he shook hands with some of his oldest colleagues in and out of the government. But even as he mounted the steps, there was neither from the officials nor from the public the kind of spontaneous and vociferous welcome, which, as an American, I rather expected. This, however, does not necessarily mean that there was lacking either enthusiasm or cordiality. When Weizmann was seated, it was evident that his longer vision had been enormously improved since I had been with him at Vevey, for he recognized and waved to a number of us individually who were distant from him 12 or 15 feet. In Vevey he had not been able to see much more than to distinguish light from darkness. His reading vision, on the other hand, judging by the struggle he made to follow his two pages of the prepared address, had changed but little for the better.

Sprinzak gave a short but evidently heartfelt address of welcome. In the same spirit spoke Ben-Gurion also briefly. Weizmann, in his turn, spoke and read so hesitatingly that I am sure that many of the audience were so worried, that we were greatly relieved when he finally finished with it. He would have been more at ease had he spoken extemporaneously. I was glad to note that, in the course of his statement, he showed enthusiasm not only for what had been done, but singled out Ben-Gurion, Kaplan, and Shertok for special praise.

When he finished, the chairman called upon Kaplan to resume his statement but in vain, for the meeting was in no mood to continue at once the routine proceedings. Hence, the recess was declared. During this time there was an informal reception, a number of us going up to speak to Weizmann. Vera looked much better and was as cordial as always, as was he also. I asked her about Rosh Hashanah, I thought to the embarrassment of Simon, who was standing by. A few minutes later she confirmed it, saying she had spoken with Weizmann and that we were to come out early. The Russians having left immediately after the recess was announced, I declined the invitation of one of the photographers to pose with Weizmann, for it would have been undiplomatic for me to have been featured with the president under those circumstances. As we left, the crowd outside, [which] by that time [had] become quite large, greeted me with cheers. Those watching the proceedings from the mission office across the street said that the cheers for the American chief were second only to those given to Ben-Gurion and Weizmann.

4. October 1948

Long conference with staff first about where we should place our new [communications] equipment. It was decided to leave the final decision until the arrival of those who will be responsible for its use. The other subject is unmentionable even here [the evacuation of US citizens in an emergency].[1] Analyzing it following Knox's initial statement based on his last year's experience, we were all forced to recognize that we must have as many possible answers as can be devised and prepared. The obvious and preferred one [evacuation by air] might become practicable with the arrival of one of our new staff members. Second [evacuation by automobiles] could be prepared, but might not be a solution. The third, developed out of Barnes' idea [evacuation by sea], intrigued me most and is the one which I am personally following up. It was agreed by all that this discussion and what might follow from it should be on the highest classification.

Saturday, October 2

Mr. and Mrs. [Emanuel] Celler came out.[2] The congressman and I talked for a half hour or so. His knowledge of the situation here is sketchy and inaccurate. He was more interesting about conditions at home. As to the election, there is no chance whatever, he said, of a Truman victory. On the contrary, Dewey is certain to carry New York and California and will have a sweeping success. Part of the overwhelming trend he attributes to the president's unwillingness to break with his overall military strategy board and take now any prompt and definite action such as *de jure* recognition all alone. Celler illustrated Truman's hesitancy by the latter's refusal to receive a delegation of New York Democratic congressmen who wanted to talk to him about the desperate condition in their constituencies. Celler said that reports to the Department

1. Discussed in McDonald, *My Mission in Israel*, 94.
2. Emanuel Celler (1888–1981), Brooklyn-born Democratic congressman from New York's 10th District (Brooklyn, Queens), 1923–1945; then the redistricted 15th and 11th districts, 1945–1963; opposed congressional passage of the Johnson-Reed Act of 1924, which had developed the immigration quotas that excluded Jews; called for relaxation of quotas before World War II; instrumental in passage of Displaced Persons' Act of 1948, which allowed roughly 400,000 refugees to enter the United States; strong supporter of Jewish statehood, attending UN debates on the partition of Palestine, and opposing postwar loans to Britain based on London's Palestine policy.

from Damascus were being used to counter-balance what I sent from here.[3] Mine made an excellent impression on the president, but he was over-persuaded by the necessity urged upon him of keeping in step with Great Britain in the maintenance of a common front against the USSR.

From 5:00 until nearly 7:00, I had an interesting talk with Nathan Gurdus of *Haaretz*[4] and Roger Lioret, Chief Correspondent and Manager for Palestine, *Agence France-Presse*. After we had had general talk about the press, my guests developed a number of interesting points:

1) The possibility that Russia might change sides and, as Nathan Gurdus put it, be the first great power to recognize Gaza.

The Arab League and the Egyptian government suspected that Transjordan wanted to annex Gaza, and in mid-September 1948 they created an "All-Palestine Government" with a cabinet of ministers and a Palestine National Council. Its seat was in Gaza. On September 28 Haj Amin al-Husseini arrived from Cairo and became the president of the council, which on October 1 ratified a declaration of independence for all of Palestine with Jerusalem as its capital. The Soviets never recognized the All-Palestine Government, nor did the UN.[5]

2) Lioret thought that in the event of war between the West and the USSR, the latter would strike southward at the very beginning in two quick thrusts at the Israeli airfields to seize them by airborne troops and simultaneously at the US airplane carriers in the eastern Mediterranean in order to counter the efforts which the US fighting planes would be making to defeat the attempted seizure of the fields.
3) Gurdus reported that a day or two previous the Moscow radio termed the Negev a British airplane carrier and denounced Weizmann as a British stooge.

---

3. James Hugh Keeley (1895–1985), US minister to Damascus; reports to the State Department emphasized the difficulty of convincing the Syrian government to accept the Bernadotte Plan owing to its fear of "announced Zionist pretentions." See *FRUS*, 1948, v. V, pt. 2, 1421–1422. Keeley's antisemitic tendencies in Hahn, *Caught in the Middle East*, 55–56.
4. Nathan Gurdus (1910–1973), Polish-born, Danish-educated journalist and novelist; *Daily Express* correspondent, Warsaw and Moscow, 1934–1939; escaped from Poland to Palestine via Bucharest, 1939; father died in Warsaw Ghetto, mother in Treblinka; became one of Israel's leading journalists, primarily associated with *Haaretz* and later Agence France-Presse.
5. The All-Palestine Government was recognized by Egypt, Syria, Lebanon, Iraq, Saudi Arabia, and Yemen. King Abdullah of Transjordan countered it in October by calling a "Palestine Arab Congress" in Amman, consisting of Palestinian Arab notables who rejected Amin al-Husseini. Subsequent meetings followed, and in December, the delegates declared their support for the king's protection over the Samaria-Judea region. The Arab Legion also suppressed armed supporters of Amin al-Husseini in Jordanian-occupied territory. Gamal Abd al-Nasser closed the All-Palestine Government's offices in 1959. See Avi Schlaim, "The Rise and Fall of the All-Palestine Government in Gaza," *Journal of Palestine Studies* 20, no. 1 (Autumn 1990): 37–53.

4) Gurdus is convinced that the USSR will be sorely disappointed in Israel, because it will soon learn that the basic orientation here is westward, an orientation which the Russians will be unable to modify.[6]

5) The Sternists are mistaken, said Gurdus, when they think of themselves as allies of the USSR;[7] the latter instead look on the small communist party here as their only reliable ally.[8]

6) In answer to my question about the best way to follow Arab opinion, Gurdus suggested that it was through the monitoring of the Arab radio stations; this work is being done by a number of persons here now, one of whom could doubtless be persuaded to turn over daily his summary of such broadcasts. Perhaps the best of these listeners is Mr. Amnon Kopeliouk of *Davar*.[9] (Owing to the holidays we were unable to get in touch with him immediately.) Another suggestion was Isaac Ben-Ovadia, who does monitoring for the Public Information Office, and is also a journalist.[10]

7) As to the Gaza government, Gurdus thought it was a sham and would come to nothing. As the two men left, Gurdus being carried out in his small wheel chair because [of] his paralyzed legs, seemingly of less use to him than were FDR's, he offered, and I think with all sincerity, to do whatever he possibly could to help me.

Having finished up during the morning a batch of mail, we left it at the Park Hotel for Mrs. Schoolman, who was leaving the next morning. We arrived at the opening concert of the Israel Philharmonic Orchestra just after the Russians had arrived. Our seats, three of them in the right section of the front row of the balcony and two immediately behind, are excellent. Despite the elaborate security arrangements, or perhaps because of them in part, the concert was thrilling. Leonard Bernstein was in good form and carried the orchestra with him throughout the evening. The program consisted of the Third Leonore Overture, and two other Beethoven pieces, the Seventh Symphony and the First Piano Concerto, with Bernstein as soloist. Despite Serge Koussevitsky's strictures against this dual role, Bernstein manages them admirably. We visited him during the intermission in order to avoid the after concert crowd. I thought he would play some encores on the piano as he did in Jerusalem last year and, therefore, suggested to Bobby that she might come home with Mrs. Shertok, but Bernstein disappointed.

6. In general Yaacov Ro'i, *Soviet Decision Making*; Yehoshua Freundlich, "A Soviet Outpost in Tel Aviv;" Laurent Rucker, *Staline, Israël et les Juifs* (Paris: Presses universitaires de France, 2001).

7. Lehi's hopes concerning Moscow as a revolutionary anti-imperialist and geopolitical enemy to the United Kingdom and United States are discussed in Joseph Heller, *The Stern Gang*; Hoffman, *Anonymous Soldiers.*

8. In general see Sondra Miller Rubenstein, *The Communist Movement in Palestine and Israel, 1919–1984* (Boulder, CO: Westview Press, 1985); and Dunia Habib Nahas, *The Israeli Communist Party* (New York: St. Martin's Press, 1976).

9. Amnon Kopeliouk (1930–2009), Jerusalem-born journalist and scholar; son of Arabic scholar Menachem Kopeliouk; wrote for numerous left-wing Israeli newspapers over his career, covering the Arab world. *Davar* was Mapai's newspaper.

10. On Ben-Ovadia, see Dan Kurzman, *Genesis: The First Arab-Israeli War*, 38.

Before the concert and during the intermission, we visited with a number of friends, including the Levinthals. The judge offered to take mail and said that he could be reached at the Davidovitzes Wednesday morning before ten.

Sunday, October 3

From 11:30 until about one, I concentrated though conferences on the problem of the Gaza government. My first visitors were Mr. Ezra Danin,[11] a farmer, with large Arabic experience from Hadera, and Mr. Ya'akov Shimoni,[12] sub-head of the Arabic section of the Foreign Office. My second conference was with Isaac Ben-Ovadia, referred to above. I summarize as if it had been one conference as follows:

1) The Gaza government is a pretense and a paper regime;
2) It is being pushed only half-heartedly even by its foremost proponents, Egypt and Syria;
3) It is being treated as something that might be readily withdrawn if circumstances require;
4) The several announcements about it whether by [Abd al-Rahman] Azzam [Pasha][13] or the political committee of the Arab League or by Egypt have all had the earmarks of tentativeness;
5) On the other hand, the reactions of Abdullah have been sharp and positive. His official spokesman, the Ramallah radio, and the congress of notables called by him in Amman, all have categorically denounced the Gaza government;
6) The tentative list of members of the Gaza cabinet, including friends of Abdullah, was never confirmed;
7) The proponents of the Gaza government, or what they call the Government of All Palestine, would much prefer to have secured in advance Abdullah's acquiescence, but failing that they sought to present him with a *fait accompli*;
8) The proponents know that they risk destroying the Arab League if they insist on their scheme without having won Abdullah's acquiescence. Hence, the many comings and goings to and from Amman by Arab politicians, seeking as mediators or representatives to cajole Abdullah into moderating his intransigent opposition. To date they have been wholly unsuccessful;

11. Ezra Danin (1903–1985), head of the Arab section of Shai (Haganah intelligence branch); member of "Syrian Platoon" that infiltrated into Syria and Lebanon in 1940–1941; accompanied Golda Meyerson to secret meetings with King Abdullah, 1947–1948.

12. Ya'akov Shimoni (1915–1996), Berlin-born deputy director of Arab Division of Jewish Agency; deputy head of Middle East Division of the Foreign Ministry in 1948.

13. Abd al-Rahman Azzam Pasha (1893–1976), London- and Cairo-educated Egyptian politician, diplomat, and writer; adopted pan-Arab and pan-Islamic ideas before World War I; aided resistance in Libya against Italian rule, 1915–1923; Egyptian minister to Iraq, Iran, and Saudi Arabia in the 1930s; secretary-general, Arab League, 1945–1952.

9) One purpose of the Gaza government would be to use it as a front to counter the activities of the Israel representatives at the Assembly of the UN;

10) The personal and family ambitions of the mufti and the Husseinis are a major factor, but by the same token they constitute a major weakness, because the mufti has lost substantially his following among Palestinian Arabs because: a) His nepotism in advancing his relatives and neglecting to keep his promises to others of his followers; b) His failure to be more effective in the war as contrasted with the role of the Arab Legion; c) His part in stimulating the Arab flight from Israeli-held territory. Even among the religious leaders his prestige has declined;

11) Probably the Gaza government will be allowed quietly to die with the explanation that it was premature and must wait for the re-conquest of the whole of Palestine;

12) There can be no doubt, however, [that] a Gaza government maneuver has already gravely weakened the Arab League by disclosing the basic cleavage between Abdullah and most of the other states;

13) The role of Iraq, despite the dynastic tie with Abdullah, is equivocal;

14) Only strong British pressure on Abdullah could bring him to accept the Gaza government, and such pressure is unlikely because of Great Britain's present attitude towards the mediator's proposals. (Soon I was to learn, the next day, that the US was strongly opposing the Gaza government. From this, I assume that the policy of His Majesty's Government was similar.)[14]

William C. Burdett of the consulate in Jerusalem came down with the pouch and stayed for lunch. He did not add much that was new about conditions on the hill [Jerusalem], but he seemed franker and more open than our recent visitors from there. He stressed the friction between the military governor [Dov Joseph] and the Truce Commission, denied that Joseph had offered the mediator protection, said that MacDonald and his colleagues used to find the former military commander more cooperative than the present military governor, who according to Burdett, has the actual commander, his son-in-law, in his pocket.[15] Burdett's chief item of news was that MacDonald has been called back to Washington for conference and was leaving on Wednesday, expecting to arrive in Washington on Friday, and to be gone for an over-all period of about two weeks.

14. Abdullah's delegates to the Arab League meeting voted for the Egyptian initiative on the Gaza government because they had to preserve Arab unity, but the Gaza government threatened Abdullah's desires for parts of Palestine. The resumption of the Israeli offensive against Egypt in mid-October chased the government from Gaza back to Egypt. Uri Bar-Joseph, *The Best of Enemies: Israel and Transjordan in the War of 1948* (London: Frank Cass, 1987), 131–132.

15. Colonel David Shaltiel (1903–1969), commanded Jewish defenses in Jerusalem until August 4, 1948; replaced by Lieutenant Colonel Moshe Dayan on Ben-Gurion's insistence. Neither was Joseph's son-in-law, but Joseph had been critical of Shaltiel.

William C. Burdett (1918–1995) was a career foreign service officer who became a consul in the US consulate general in Jerusalem in 1948. He served as the acting US consul general in Jerusalem after the shooting death of Thomas Wasson and then again after the reassignment of John MacDonald, remaining in this position until early 1950. He was, even as a junior officer, a member of the UN Security Council Truce Commission. He remembered in 1988 that shortly before the British withdrawal from Palestine, the State Department established a naval communications unit across the alley from the US consulate general. "We could receive messages almost instantaneously from Washington." This was far better that the communications system in Tel Aviv, and Burdett thus had an easier time in communicating his views to the State Department than did McDonald. Burdett became increasingly impatient with the Israeli authorities for their supply of weapons and food to Jewish Jerusalem via the Burma Road, which he regarded as a violation of the truce.[16]

From about 5:30 until about 7:30, we had a tea party for the Cellers. Later, we were joined by Dan and David Samuel. The talk covered a wide range. Particularly interesting was my talk on the roof with Dr. [Harris J.] Levine about deep-sea fishing.[17] He made some pertinent suggestions about what was possible and what impossible and promised to make further inquiries. I think he can be counted on. Another suggestion which came from the discussion was that Ben-Gurion be persuaded to receive the American delegation and that he and I and some spokesman of the group make brief statements about the work.

David and Dan we invited for dinner, and when they explained that they thought they ought to be with their mother on the eve of Rosh Hashanah, we sent over for her, and they all three stayed for dinner. It was a pleasant evening, but I must confess that at the end I felt quite exhausted because it had been a day of almost continuous conferences. I should perhaps add that our American guests had been, like previous ones, very much impressed by our house.

Celler visited Jerusalem on October 7 and 8 and told Vice Consul William Burdett that he had been, in his own words, "completely sold on the Jewish state." Celler complained about the "generally hostile attitude found in consulates throughout the Middle East towards [the] Jewish state. Consuls appeared to regard Jews as 'slave people,' just as [the] Nazis did." Celler complained especially of the reports from Burdett himself, "which he stated he had seen and considered anti-Jewish." Israel, he said,

16. Interview of Ambassador William T. Burdett, Association for Diplomatic Studies and Training, Oral History Project, December 16, 1988, www.adst.org/OH%20TOCs/Burdett,%20William%20C.toc.pdf, accessed September 2014.

17. Harris (Harry) J. Levine (1901–1976), chairman, B'nai Zion Israel Committee; longtime fundraiser for Jewish National Fund and chair, JNF, 1950–1960; vice-president of the Zionist Organization of America [ZOA] in the late 1950s. The fishing reference is a euphemism for a settlement between American Zionist leaders and the Israeli government over finance control issues.

was furthermore a bulwark against communism in the Middle East. He continued that he would report his impressions on his return to the United States.[18]

Monday, October 4

First day of Rosh Hashanah. Bobby's and my visit to the Weizmanns' at Rehovot was delayed in order to have time for a quick glance at the incoming telegrams. At luncheon the talk was general and entertaining. Dr. Weizmann seemed tired when he came home from his four hours at the synagogue, but brightened later. He told the story of one of his last gifts to his mother was to stay in the synagogue for the whole of Yom Kippur from earliest morning until late at night. I was surprised to hear him say that he never liked Jerusalem and that most of Israel's troubles had come from there. He does not at present expect to visit Jerusalem. He was not, however, in a mood to talk politics, nor did I desire to press him. He seemed strikingly more pleased with the Provisional Government and his former colleagues than he had been in anticipation. What had been done and the new spirit of the people he found overwhelming. He spoke of the absence of the Arabs as a sort of miracle.

Mrs. Weizmann seemed surprisingly well, was most gracious, and gave the interesting news that Ershov was to be their guest tomorrow. She was very friendly to Bobby as well as [was] her husband. Her house was again a miracle of beauty and good taste. [Afterwards] important session with Cummings on a despatch to the president and acting secretary.

McDonald's despatch relayed confidential statements to Knox by a senior Israeli official that the United States had a "firm friend" in Israel; that the Arab states were "weak, vacillating, and of dubious friendship towards the West and the US;" and that the Arabs would never forgive US support for the initial UN partition scheme. US backing of British designs to award the Negev to Transjordan would win no friends in the Arab world and would create a truncated Israeli state that would be "embittered toward the US." Worse, London's adherence to Bernadotte's Negev proposals damaged direct Israeli negotiations with King Abdullah. McDonald noted here that "we do not know exactly what special reasons motivate US policy and in any event [we] must firmly support that policy whatever it may be. . . . However, our own confidential opinion is that, although adoption of the Negev Bernadotte proposal might serve British strategic interests, it would disproportionately entangle this situation and sow dangerous seeds of bitterness."[19]

18. Burdett to secretary of state no. 1381, October 9, 1948, NARA, RG 59, 501.BB Palestine, box 2121, folder 3.
19. McDonald to secretary of state, [personal for president and acting secretary], no. 161, October 4, 1948, *FRUS*, v. V, pt. 2, 1450–1451.

Mr. [Joshua G.] Marash, the local representative of TWA, came to talk following a worldwide conference of TWA officials in Rome.[20] Marash began by expressing the hope that I could be helpful in persuading the State Department to permit two high TWA officials to visit Israel. This sounded phony, for I doubted that such officials would be dissuaded by any technical Department objection. A few minutes later, Marash indicated that these officials might not like to have Israel visas in their passports, lest this be used as an excuse by Egypt to prohibit their visiting that country. Marash spoke about the need for Israel to put one of its large fields in order so that TWA could resume [flights], but on being questioned, he admitted that the real stumbling block to such resumption was the TWA fear that Egypt would make good its threat to prohibit landings in Cairo if TWA came back to Israel. In other words, as I put it to Marash, I did not see that there was anything for me to do vis-à-vis the State Department or the Provisional Government until TWA made up its mind to challenge Egypt's threat. Marash expressed the personal view that the Cairo authorities would in fact not carry out their threat, but until TWA acts on this assumption, I do not see that I have any role to play. Judging from what Marash said about present flights out of here, the only regular lines are the Czech and Air France or a substitute of the latter. He assured me, however, that if I wanted to fly to Paris or New York, he would always be able to get a seat out of Athens.[21]

Wednesday, October 6

Decided to ask Judge Levinthal to take some family letters and one to Captain [Donald] Frothingham.[22] In order to give him (the judge) a personal message, I went down to Davidowitz's and later found him at the taxi terminal. He did not hesitate about the letters. As to the other message, he listened attentively [and] said that he agreed that [going to the UN General Assembly in] Paris was more important than [going to] Washington and that he would go to see David Niles and explain my point of view.[23]

A little after four Shiloah came. There followed a long and, for me, valuable restatement of the local deeply felt views about the Negev. The substance of the argument was later summarized in a draft telegram for the Department,

20. Joshua Gabriel Marash, (1923–1986), born in Jerusalem; served with TWA, 1945–1948; Israeli Air Force, 1948–1949; KLM, 1950–1951, and later El Al.
21. As part of its Middle Eastern network, TWA was the sole US carrier to Palestine before Israeli independence. Flights were interrupted until July 1949, when preliminary ad hoc agreements were reached with the Israeli government. A bilateral air agreement was reached in June 1950. See entries of July 2, 1949, and June 13, 1950.
22. Captain Donald Frothingham, naval attaché, US mission in Tel Aviv, assigned September 1948. The letter concerned McDonald's wife Ruth, who was sailing on the same ship.
23. McDonald wanted to travel to Paris for the US General Assembly in order to advise the US delegation there concerning Israel.

a copy of which, under date of October 7, is in my personal file.[24] In addition to this large subject, we also talked about the return to Washington of my Jerusalem colleague [MacDonald] and of other possibilities. Casually, but not without purpose, we also spoke about the reconstruction [noise] across the street. Shiloah could be helpful if he were requested. I did not realize until Shiloah had gone that his presence here had been so upsetting to one of my colleagues.

Mr. Maurice Bisgyer[25] and Justice Frumkin,[26] the latter Naomi's grandfather, were here for tea. Bisgyer, on behalf of B'nai B'rith, told of the need for, and his organization's plan to, supply collapsible wheelchairs and other essential equipment for the amputees in the military hospitals here. Later, he told me in private about the visit during the next few days of twenty Democratic congressmen from New York to the president to persuade him to act quickly. Bisgyer thought there was a chance that he would. There is still optimism, or at least hope, in the White House about November 2.

Mr. and Mrs. Granovsky visited for an hour or so. The latter is on her way to the States tomorrow on a speaking tour for Hadassah. They told us of the strain of life in Jerusalem during the past six months, of the miracle of the Burma Road and of the water line developing day by day beside it, of the courage of the people, old and young, and of the extraordinary endurance developed by most of the population.

Of the members of the Truce Commission, both the Granovskys thought the Frenchman [René Neuville] was strongest intellectually and culturally and the most impressive personality, but he had become almost a nervous wreck because his home is almost continuously under fire or the threat of it. MacDonald, they thought, was too young and too lacking in personality. As Mr. Granovsky and I sat in the study, he told of the absolute necessity of Israel's receiving at least the northern Negev with its approximately three to four million dunams.

Thursday, October 7

Rabbi Yitzhak-Meir Levin of the Ministry of Social Welfare was, with his interpreter, at the house for an hour. In eloquent German he talked about the hopes of the rabbis that by a fusion of their forces—Agudat Israel, Mizrahi, and other serious-minded Jews—they would have a 30 to 35% representation in the Constituent Assembly and thus be in a position to wield substantial influence

24. Not found. In Washington, Epstein made it clear to David Niles that "there is not the slightest chance of our being satisfied with any statement by the President in which the Bernadotte Plan will be substituted for the November 29 decision." He reported a difference of opinion on the Bernadotte Plan between Marshall and the president's advisers. Epstein to Abba Hillel Silver, October 8, 1948, *DFPI*, v. 2, d. 16.

25. Maurice Bisgyer (1898–1973), executive secretary, B'nai B'rith, 1937–1964. See his *Challenge and Encounter: Behind the Scenes in the Struggle for Jewish Survival* (New York: Crown, 1967).

26. Gad Frumkin (1887–1960), Turkish correspondent for American and Palestinian newspapers, 1910–1914; chief magistrate in Jerusalem, 1918–1920, judge of Court of Appeal and sole Jewish member of the Supreme Court of Palestine after 1925.

in securing due regard for Jewish religious traditions and the rabbinic law. He was hopeful about increasing religious influence among the youth. Towards the end he asked me about what I thought of the prospects in Paris.

Before and during and for a time after dinner, we talked with Mr. and Mrs. William Haber, who are to be our guests during their stay in Israel. They promise to be easy houseguests. My other first impression was that they knew so surprisingly little about Israel. This particularly applied to Mrs. Haber.[27]

He [Haber] and I discussed a number of subjects, some of them at length:

1) The State Department's instructions to the military commanders not to permit the exit of men of military age was in Haber's view dictated primarily by strategic considerations in the Middle Eastern area and was drafted not in the State Department but in the operations division of the War Department. He based this on what a Mr. Fisher, the opposite number of George Warren[28] and Fierst in the military branch, had said to him. My own impressions were not inconsistent with this interpretation. Despite the prohibition, Haber estimates that more than a thousand men of military age have been leaving the occupied areas and securing without much difficulty French visas in Marseille or on the boats. He estimated that the exits from Germany for Israel during recent months have averaged about 4,000. As he put it, at this rate a real dent would be made in the camps by next spring. Haber said that he thought [US Military Governor in Germany Lucius] Clay was becoming more nearly as sympathetic as [former US Governor Joseph] McNarney had been; [US Political Adviser in Germany Robert] Murphy too seemed more friendly. On the other hand, Haber thought that [Charles] Saltzman[29] was merely correct. George Warren he regarded as friendly and desiring to be helpful, but as not being able to exercise any substantial influence on policy. Haber confirmed that nothing had been done about the system of lists proposed by the mediator.[30] Haber thought that the only probable means through which the flow from Germany could be likely to be slowed up would be through shortage of shipping in the event that the movement directly from Poland and Romania were allowed to get under way.

2) The decision of the IRO [International Refugee Organization] made last spring by the Director [William Hallam] Tuck on his own responsibility should, Haber explained, be reversed.[31] As he gave me the details of the

27. William Haber (1899–1989), Romanian-born professor of economics at the University of Michigan, 1936–1988; member, American Jewish Committee; directed the National Refugee Service during World War II; adviser on Jewish Affairs to Commander of US Forces in Europe, January 1948–January 1949.

28. Entry of June 29, 1948.

29. Charles E. Saltzman (1903–1994), assistant secretary of state for occupied areas, 1947–1949.

30. Whereby lists of proposed immigrants to Israel had to be submitted to Bernadotte's team for approval based on their capability of serving in the IDF. Entry of September 2, 1948

31. The IRO was to finance the emigration of refugees to Israel because, with the establishment of the state, immigration was legal after May 15, 1948. Tuck—based on a decision of

Tuck decision and from what I knew about the IRO, it seemed to me that now was an opportune time for me to raise with the Department and the president the question of reversing Tuck's policy. Haber promised to draft for me a memorandum, which might be made the basis of my telegram.

About 8:30 Mr. and Mrs. Gruson arrived.[32] The three of us visited on the roof for almost two hours. He anticipates remaining here for the *Times* for about two months.

Friday, October 8

Marcus Sieff, who is just back a couple of days from London, told me of his mission there since I saw him on the airfield in Rome. He has seen in some fifty interviews leading members of all the parties except Churchill and Bevin, leaders of the press, and of public opinion. In all these talks, he has stressed the lack of communist influence here and the impossibility that this country should turn towards the USSR unless driven to it by unwise policies of the West. He was surprised to see how prominent, even in well-informed circles such as Anthony Eden represents, was the misunderstanding to the effect that Israel either was now or would soon be communist. He also stressed the possibility of Britain recovering much of its ground here in popular esteem if it moved promptly and affirmatively. He felt that he had removed some misunderstandings and had been somewhat instrumental in improving relations; but he was convinced that the major improvement in His Majesty's Government's attitude was the result of a new awareness of the strategic importance of a strong Israel. Sieff agreed that one of the sticking points in the British mind was their fear lest they could not trust such an Israel.

Among the interesting or significant points that I recall in Marcus Sieff's long account were the following: 1) Ibn Saud's statement to Eden that he did not mind a Jewish state in itself but was fearful of what it might become;[33] 2) Harold Beeley's insistence that he accepted the fact of a Jewish state but with evident serious reservations; 3) McNeil's definite promise of recognition if the Provisional Government accepted a settlement, which need not be literally the mediator's proposal; 4) proof that Beeley had lied when he said that the Foreign

---

May 1947—decided not to finance transports, ostensibly owing to the state of war. Dalia Ofer, "Defining Relationships: The Joint Distribution Committee and Israel, 1948–1950," in *Israel: The First Decade of Independence*, eds. S. Ilan Troen and Noah Lucas (Albany: SUNY Press, 1995), 713–733.

32. Sydney Gruson (1916–1998) and Flora Lewis (1918–2002), correspondents for the *New York Times* and other publications.

33. Churchill and Eden had met with King Ibn Saud on February 17, 1945, in Egypt en route from Yalta to London. Churchill was unsuccessful in convincing the king to accept any scheme whereby more Jews would go to Palestine. The records of the meeting were released only in 2006. See Michael Makovsky, *Churchill's Promised Land: Zionism and Statecraft* (New Haven, CT: Yale University Press, 2007), 219–223; and Martin Gilbert, *Churchill and the Jews: A Lifelong Friendship* (New York: Henry Holt, 2007), 234–238.

Office had not used pressure to discourage Western recognition of the Provisional Government, and that they had not discouraged the Shell Company from supplying the Provisional Government with refined products. Incidentally, Sieff added that an agreement had now been reached and was now in effect between the Shell [Company] and the Provisional Government on this point;[34] 5) British Federation of Industries was ready to send a delegation to Israel, but Sieff pointed out to them and to His Majesty's Government the imperative need for the resumption of normal commercial and political relations; 6) Eden's promise to speak to Bevin; 7) Sir Stafford Cripps's sympathetic interest and his promise to speak to Bevin;[35] 8) Crossman and other Labour men's testimony that Bevin's position had changed; 9) our agreement on [the effectiveness of] Nahum Goldmann; 10) importance of strategic considerations; 11) moderation of reaction on Bernadotte; 12) increasing moderation of press.

The Habers, back from a busy day, had many things to report, most notable of which were his reactions to: 1) The custom dues exacted from incoming refugees, even on the tools for their trades or professions. He thinks it shocking and is going to speak to Kaplan about it;[36] 2) the necessity of being a member of a party if a resident or citizen here is to secure work or have the advantage of other municipal or governmental services. (One and two were reported to Haber by a former JDC worker in Berlin who, with his wife, came here filled with enthusiasm, which has after a few months sorely waned; 3) the difficulty of housing for most people and the exceptionally attractive cooperative apartments for ex-soldiers;[37] 4) the depressing slums of the Yemenites.[38]

---

34. Shell pressed the British government, which had embargoed crude oil shipments to Israel, to send petroleum to Israel lest they lose their distribution rights in the country altogether to the Romanians. In October 1948 Israel reached agreement with Shell and Socony Vacuum to supply Israel on a quarterly basis. Uri Bialer, *Oil and the Arab-Israeli Conflict, 1948–63* (New York: St. Martin's, 1999), 53–57, 61–62.

35. Sir Stafford Cripps (1889–1952), socialist-minded British Labour MP since 1930; ambassador to USSR, 1940–1942; minister of aircraft production, 1942–1945; president, board of trade, 1945–1947; minister for economic affairs, 1947; chancellor of the exchequer, 1947–1950.

36. One of many taxes imposed to pay the costs of absorption of Jewish immigrants; the need for housing, vocational training, education, and the like. See Yitzhak Greenberg, "The Contribution of the Labor Economy to Immigrant Absorption and Population Dispersal During Israel's First Decade," in Troen and Lucas, eds., *Israel: The First Decade of Independence*, 279–296.

37. Overview of the housing issue and the National Housing Authority in Ruth Kark, "Planning, Housing, and Land Policy, 1948–1952," in ibid., 461–494.

38. Yemenite Jews had just begun to arrive and lived in ramshackle slums around Tel Aviv and elsewhere. On their living conditions, see Gideon N. Giladi, *Discord in Zion: Conflict Between Ashkenazi and Sephardi Jews in Israel* (London: Scorpion, 1990), 67–156; Michael A. Weingarten, *Changing Health and Changing Culture: The Yemenite Jews in Israel* (Westport, CT: Praeger, 1992); Joseph Massad, "Zionism's Internal Others: Israel and the Oriental Jews," *Journal of Palestine Studies* 25, no. 4 (Summer 1996): 53–68; and Norman Berdichevski, "The Persistence of the Yemeni Quarter in an Israeli Town," *Studies in Israeli Society*, v. 1: *Migration, Ethnicity, and Community*, ed. Ernest Krausz (New Brunswick, NJ: Transaction, 1980), 73–95.

Haber's report on his talk with Dr. Mohn of the mediator's staff was especially significant. According to Mohn, the mediator had never given any instructions or asked any government to limit the number of "men of military age" coming into Israel. It is true that the mediator had in mind a tentative monthly figure which he thought would be reasonable, but he had never announced it nor asked any government to restrict [the] coming of such personnel. Asked point blank about State Department instructions to the military commanders to prohibit such exits, Mohn said that this must have been determined by considerations of specifically American policy, and he intimated that it was probably the outgrowth of our government's sensitivity to Arab opinion as a factor in Middle East strategy. Haber, in reporting this, expressed himself as having been flabbergasted by Mohn's statement. Haber and I then discussed whether this should be used in an appeal to the Department for a modification of its policy, and we were of the general opinion that it might be better to let sleeping dogs lie. This for two reasons: Mohn's emphatic advice that it would be a serious mistake to have the issue raised by any government with the mediator's office, and two, despite the prohibition, upwards to a thousand men are leaving Germany monthly.

In a memorandum prepared for McDonald, Haber reported that 73,000 Jews had entered Israel between January 1 and October 17, 1948. Since the second truce went into effect on July 18, 27,800 immigrants had arrived, mostly through Haifa. Sixty-five percent came directly from DP camps in Europe, the rest from British detention in Cyprus and also from North Africa. Haber had learned from Moshe Shapira, the minister of immigration, that the Provisional Government wanted to maintain the current rate of 10,000 immigrants per month. He noted further that Mohn and Riley, who in September had wanted to limit sharply the immigration of men of military age, had shifted their position. They had told Haber that 20 percent of recent arrivals in Haifa were men of military age, which was acceptable to the UN. Israeli authorities, Mohn and Riley added, settled arriving men of military age on agricultural settlements, excluding them from military training for the time being.

Haber concluded, "The restrictions imposed on the issuance of visas in the US Zone [of] Germany [and] Austria were the result of action taken by our own government and not imposed by the Mediator." He further argued,

> *In my judgment the restrictions which we have imposed should be removed since the Mediator had established a procedure which provides for the exclusion of men of military age from training . . . and since the Mediator and his staff appear to be of the opinion that this procedure is working satisfactorily. . . . Except for the British, who are preventing the immigration into Israel of some 12,000 persons interned in Cyprus, the United States is the only Western nation which imposed such restrictions against immigration to Israel. Our policy in fact makes it necessary for women and children and the old people to leave our camps unaccompanied by the heads of these families.[39]*

39. Haber's memorandum, "The United Nations Truce and Immigration to Israel," McDonald Papers, USHMM, box 7, folder 7.

An hour and a half conference with Mr. Amnon Kopeliouk, Arabic expert of *Davar* and a colleague who interpreted for us. Kopeliouk seems very well informed, and perhaps just because of that, his conclusions were not as sharp and dogmatic as some of those expressed by others possibly less well informed. Most of our talk was about the Gaza government.

1) According to Kopeliouk, it is almost exclusively a creation of Egypt and the mufti. Azzam is influenced by his Egyptian loyalty and by his Pan-Arabist ideology. When in conflict, the former may prove the stronger.
2) Iraq's attitude is divided, the court being pro-Abdullah and the government pro-Gaza. It was announced this morning on the Baghdad radio that the Iraqi prime minister was going to Amman.[40]
3) A speech yesterday by one of the Gaza cabinet members in Cairo pleaded that Gaza be regarded as a holy war.
4) Mufti has lost popularity because: a) failure of war; b) advice to refugees to leave; c) advancement of relatives and henchmen.
5) [Palestine Arab] Congress called by Abdullah in Amman was measurably representative of Palestinian Arabs, but like all Arab congresses, was to a certain extent packed.[41]
6) Russians would naturally oppose Gaza because: a) violation of November 29; and b) would give Abdullah [the] Negev.
7) None of Arab governments has yet formally recognized Gaza, fearing apparently breakup of League.
8) Very difficult to foresee result of Gaza.
9) Personnel of Gaza cabinet shows predominant mufti influence.
10) Through refusing a post in the cabinet, the mufti, according to a recent Arab broadcast, is to have the power of veto over the government. Kopeliouk promised to give me a memorandum in a few days on the cabinet.

Lunch with Weisgal at the Gat Rimon. Besides Bobby, Miss Clark, and myself were Mr. and Mrs. Michael Simon. In the midst of much talk, some of it amusing by our host, the following points worthy of record emerged.

1) Revolt in ranks of ZOA [Zionist Organization of America] against Silver's and Neumann's alleged attempt to use United Jewish Appeal funds for political purposes in Israel. Henry Montor's resignation [in September from the United Jewish Appeal and United Palestine Appeal] and his leadership

40. Muzahim Amin al-Pachachi (1890–1982), Iraqi jurist and nationalist politician; prime minister of Iraq, June 1946–January 1949. His cabinet sent 18,000 troops to fight the independence of Israel, halted the flow of oil to Haifa, backed the All-Palestine government in Gaza, and opposed the 1949 armistice agreements with Israel.
41. See note 5.

of a group of very wealthy contributors had resulted in an "ultimatum" by Silver to Kaplan, the one member of the Provisional Government who is on the Executive of the Agency.[42]

2) Simon's admission that mail is taken away from passengers at the Haifa airport though "it always reaches its destination," even if belatedly.

3) Weisgal talked loosely about my appearing with Washington's consent at some affair he is planning in the States.

Sunday, October 10

Rapid, excited progress with George Antonius's *The Arab Awakening*.[43] At eleven Mr. [Zvi] Friedland came in. He was leaving the next day. Though I explained to him the hurdles, he agreed to take a personal letter to Clifford and some memoranda to the family. A delightful, and I think useful, dinner built around our guest Marcus Sieff. Others were Knox, Barnes, and Colonel van der Velde and Mr. McMahon. After the meal the two military men remained in a huddle until after four o'clock. In the evening Dr. Levine came out and we talked further about the fishing project. I am to talk to Friedman tomorrow or, rather, Tuesday. Dr. Levine said that they would be glad to send parcels out from time to time on their chartered plane.

McDonald complained to Clifford about communications between Tel Aviv and Washington. Telegrams, he noted, by necessity left certain matters unsaid. Letters, he added, "are almost of no use" because "our courier is appallingly irregular," and letters that McDonald sent through private contacts, he had learned, "are likely to be seized at the Haifa airport, censored, or delayed four to six weeks." He noted that his calls to the Department of State for regular air courier services had not been fulfilled and that "we must have regular and reliable courier service." He also complained that the Department called John MacDonald, the US consul general in Jerusalem for consultations, noting that MacDonald did not speak for the mission in Tel Aviv. "One McDonald can only speak for himself."[44]

42. Henry Montor (1905–1981), US business executive (Consumer Finance Corporation); most important US fundraiser for Jewish causes; one of the founders of the United Jewish Appeal [UJA]; executive vice president of United Palestine Appeal [UPA], 1948; resigned from UJA and UPA, accusing Silver and Neumann of trying to use US-raised funds to alter Israel's social trajectory; formed, with anti-Silverites in the ZOA (Louis Lipsky, Stephen S. Wise, and others) the Committee for Progressive Zionism that accused Silver of interfering in Israeli politics and backing Revisionist Zionists in Israel; began organization of alternate fundraising structures in the United States; later established Israel bond campaign, 1951–1955; well known to McDonald.

43. McDonald had begun to read books on the Arab world to understand it better. He referred to Antonius as "the foremost Arab apologist." Letter to Helen, Leland, Lucius and Sally, October 16, 1948, McDonald Papers, Columbia University, box 7, folder 7.

44. McDonald to Clifford, October 10, 1948, McDonald Papers, USHMM, box 7, folder 7.

Morning conference with Eytan and Miss Herlitz:

1) After they had read the paraphrase of the Department's instructions about foreign consulates in the military zone of Germany, Eytan said that they accepted it in every particular and would write me to that effect.
2) Mrs. [Eleanor] Roosevelt, whom I told them I had invited personally to visit us, may be invited formally by the Provisional Government. They will let us know their decision. In the course of the talk, I made clear that she is not now a representative of either the administration or the opposition.
3) We chatted about Henry Morgenthau, Jr.'s arrival, but neither had anything new to add to my knowledge. Miss Herlitz thought he was arriving the end of the week or the first of the next.[45]
4) As to the mail censorship at Haifa, Eytan told me of the difficulty his office had had in sending off a letter to Shertok and of the row he had raised about it. (A few minutes later I was to have a somewhat different interpretation of this incident from Shiloah, who explained that the hitch had been because the Foreign Office had not put any seal on the envelope to indicate its authenticity.) Eytan said that he was sure we could receive relief, and he would indicate specifically the method later. (As will be noted below, Shiloah was more confident and quicker, in definiteness of offer. This difference indicates, I think, the relative importance of the two men.)
5) Speaking rather incidentally about Jerusalem, MacDonald, and about the possible reasons for his "recall for consultation," Eytan ventured the opinion that the explanation might lie in the Department's knowledge or lack of it about MacDonald's "personal life." I pressed Eytan to tell me what he meant, and this is the story: During recent weeks following the death of the Jewish liaison officer Herzog, when the latter left the consul general's car to lift the barrier between the Jewish and Arab lines and was shot and left lying where he fell while on MacDonald's order the car backed up and returned to the Jewish Agency to call for an ambulance, the consul general has taken to drinking in excess. On a number of occasions in public places, when MacDonald has had too much, he in a voice heard by those at nearby tables would exclaim: "It is not true that I killed Herzog" or "I am not really responsible for the death of Herzog," and so on. His friends would try to hush him and take him home, but not until these seeming disclosures of a subconscious sense of responsibility. Eytan, in answer to my question, said he did not know whether these reports had been brought to the attention of the Department. They had been passed on to Epstein for his own information,

45. Henry Morgenthau Jr. (1891–1967), secretary of the treasury, 1934–1945; general chairman of the United Jewish Appeal, 1948; arrived in Israel on October 20, 1948.

but Eytan said that the Foreign Office does not know whether Epstein told anyone in our government.

6) We chatted for a little while about Paris, and I deduced that the Marshall-Shertok interview has been overplayed in the press. Eytan said that it had been brief, sandwiched in between two other appointments, and was interrupted before it was concluded. Another indication that it was not of great importance was that apparently the discussion was all about Galilee and not about either of the vital subjects, Jerusalem or the Negev.

Shertok emphasized the Israeli stance on the Negev. Marshall asked about the Galilee, which Shertok said Israel also claimed, despite the region's partial exclusion from the November 29 partition resolution.[46] On October 13, 1948, Lovett informed McDonald that Marshall was holding to the Bernadotte Plan in principle, despite Israeli objections regarding the surrender of the Negev.[47]

On October 11 Bunche told David Horowitz, the director-general of the Finance Ministry, that Bernadotte's death had unfortunately made the count's recommendations, which were intended as a basis for negotiation, more rigid. Bunche did not think that the Arab states would formally agree to any solution that brought Jewish agreement. Arab acquiescence would have to suffice. Bunche also noted that, though the right of individual refugees to return to their homes had to be asserted in the UN, he doubted that "the bulk of the refugees will ever return."[48]

7) [Eytan added] that in a talk with Eban in Paris, [Dean] Rusk of the Department had made a unique and interesting suggestion about Jerusalem. This was to the effect that Jewish Jerusalem might become a Jewish trusteeship and Arab Jerusalem a Transjordanian trusteeship, for which annual reports would be made to the Truce [Commission]. Rusk is said to have added that, while this would not be very different from incorporation in the respective states, it would make acceptance by the US easier.[49]

I met Shiloah as I was going into Eytan's office and told the former that I would like to see him for a moment later. When I had concluded the first talk, Shiloah was still working on Shertok's balcony, but joined me immediately in the latter's anteroom. Not particularly to my surprise, our informal conference turned out to be more important than that with Eytan and Herlitz. It included:

---

46. Shertok's assessment of October 11, 1948 is in *DFPI*, v. 2, d. 21.
47. Lovett to McDonald, no. 149, October 13, 1948, *FRUS*, 1948, v. V, pt. 2, 1472–1473.
48. Memorandum of meeting between Bunche and Horowitz, October 11, 1948, *DFPI*, v. 2, n. 23.
49. Raised owing to lack of enthusiasm in US military to send peacekeeping forces to Jerusalem. Israel would administer Jewish parts of Jerusalem, and Transjordan would administer Arab parts in trusteeship; the trusteeship agreements would include international guarantees for free access to Holy Places. See Slonim, *Jerusalem in America's Foreign Policy, 1947–1997*, 116–117.

1) Shiloah's announcement that Colonel van der Velde would be taken in charge by [Chaim] Herzog of military intelligence.[50] The latter's particular function has to do with the military strength of the enemy rather than with other forms of intelligence.

2) Commenting on my statement that the naval and naval air attaché [Frothingham] was due early in November and that I had heard somewhere that there might also be a military air attaché, Shiloah became serious and asked as if there were some feeling back of his question, "Wouldn't that be too much?" We then discussed the matter in its several ramifications, including the necessity of equality of treatment as among the major missions here.

3) Shiloah told me that Lippincott [US consul, Haifa] had called yesterday to say that 49 Marines were arriving for Jerusalem as consulate guards and having nothing to do with the UN.[51] Shiloah went on to raise the question whether it was really very considerate of our government to simply serve notice twenty-four hours in advance that X number of Marines were arriving. Permission had at once been given for their clearance, but he wondered whether it would not have been more appropriate had the matter been cleared earlier on a higher level. My comment was that I personally guessed that the lack of notice was the result of confusion between the Department and the Navy. In support of this supposition, I cited confusion between these two agencies in a smaller matter affecting our emergency food supplies from Greece. Sensing that Shiloah felt rather strongly about both points 2 and 3, I asked him whether the Provisional Government would make a formal inquiry about them, adding that it would be easier for us to raise the questions with the Department if the Provisional Government asked us to. He said he would discuss it with the Foreign Office, and we would hear about it.

4) Shiloah spoke of Major Andronovich and the Provisional Government's dissatisfaction at Andronovich's "roaming about" from Amman to Jerusalem, and now by Andronovich's seeming efforts to find a way to get to Gaza. Shiloah stressed that he had no complaint about Andronovich personally, but that he did not regard Andronovich as a "first-rate" operator because he, Shiloah, had himself been able to elicit from Andronovich information about the Arabs' [military strength]. Shiloah argued from this, that probably a clever Arab would elicit from Andronovich information (without Andronovich's intending to give it) about the Jews' [strength]. In any case, the

50. Chaim "Vivian" Herzog (1918–1997), Belfast-born Israeli jurist, military officer, and politician; son of Rabbi Yitzhak Herzog and brother of Jacob Herzog; emigrated to Palestine, 1935; Haganah, 1936–1939; British Army and Army Intelligence Corps, 1939–1945; chief IDF intelligence, 1948–1950, 1959–1962; president of Israel, 1983–1993; father of Isaac Herzog, head of the Zionist Union in Israel (December 2014–).

51. The Pentagon sent US officers to serve as truce observers, but despite Bernadotte's requests in July and August, the United States refused to send combat troops to guard the UN mission in Jerusalem. The Pentagon worried that a US military presence would anger both sides, that attacks by the Irgun or Lehi could draw the United States into the war, and that the presence of US troops could even trigger a Soviet response. Hahn, *Caught in the Middle East*, 53.

Provisional Government did not now permit, in this time of war, journalists to wander back and forth across the lines, and he clearly intimated that the time might soon come, if indeed it has not already arrived, when Andronovich will be requested, directly or indirectly, to choose one post and stick to it.[52] Though, of course, I gave no indication of my feeling, I must confess that it was difficult not to understand and possibly even sympathize with Shiloah's position. Indeed, Andronovich had himself in some of our talks at the house indicated his surprise at the continued tolerance of the Provisional Government of his diverse activities.

5) As to our mail problems, Shiloah was much more categorical and satisfactory than was Eytan. Shiloah made three proposals, saying that any one or all three of them were at my disposition: a) have any particular envelope sent to the Foreign Office, where it would be sealed and stamped, following which it would not be opened at Haifa no matter who carried it, or taken away; b) supply us with a dozen or so authorizations made out in blank without dates indicating that the bearer was carrying letters which were not to be opened or taken up by the censor at Haifa; c) since the Provisional Government is sending two or three times a week messengers with special envelopes to Paris, any particular letter I might wish to send by such messenger could be sealed and entrusted to the Provisional Government man with certainty that it would not be tampered with *en route* and would be mailed promptly in Paris. What more could one ask? And what a contrast between Shiloah's definiteness and Eytan's feeling that he had to check and double check.

At four Knox, van der Velde, and Cummings [arrived and] were here until after six. They listened with close attention to my report of the session with Shiloah. The following actions were decided upon:

1) not surprised at the report about MacDonald, who they thought had "cracked"; they imagined that Major Andronovich had been the source of the Department's information. We were not, however, called upon to take any action;

2) as to Andronovich and the Provisional Government's attitude towards him, feeling was that he had probably outlived his usefulness; it was decided that we should report the statement about him to the Department;[53]

52. Shiloah had maintained working ties with Andronovich since World War II and was well informed concerning his activities and his ties to Arab interlocutors.

53. McDonald reported Shiloah's complaints, suggesting that Shiloah spoke for Ben-Gurion and that the "Department [should] consider this matter very carefully." Lovett forwarded these concerns to the consulate general in Jerusalem without comment, but noted to McDonald that "for your info [Department] has full confidence [in] ability and discretion [of] Andronovich." McDonald to secretary of state, no. 172, October 11, 1948, NARA, RG 59, MC 1390, reel 17, frame 102; Lovett to McDonald, no. 152, October 14, 1948, NARA, RG 59, MC 1390, reel 17, frame 112.

3) in answer to my report on the service attachés, there was unanimous opinion that if there could be but two, it would be preferable to have an air attaché with a plane. Hence we wired the Department to this effect;
4) everybody was impressed but not surprised at this demonstration of Shiloah's authority.

While I was in conference with the staff on the problems indicated above, Leo Kohn of the Foreign Office[54] came to keep an appointment that I had forgotten. [Owing to a tea at the residence] Kohn and I had no time to talk about his draft constitution. Kohn told interestingly of a memorandum he had prepared for Shertok on Churchill's defense of the policy of maintaining working relations with the provisional government of Ireland at a period when it was under heaviest attack by the Republicans and when there were assassinations and civil war in Ireland. The argument of the colonial secretary, which Kohn thought applicable here today, was that the provisional regime was the only regime with which one could deal. Kohn pointed with satisfaction to the fact that Churchill had been vindicated by events. As Kohn left, he gave me a copy of the draft constitution, and I said that I hoped we would have a chance to discuss it later.

Tuesday, October 12

Disturbing news in the morning that the Stern Gang girl, whom Cummings had been seeing on instructions, was picked up last night, or rather early this morning, when walking from the Gat [Rimon] with our colleague.

Reception at Ben-Gurion's office for Celler and the American members of the Committee of the American Magen David Adom.[55] Present besides the Americans and Knox, van der Velde, Bobby, and I, were leading members of the military staff, some members of the cabinet, including Kaplan, and other notables such as Mrs. Ben-Gurion. Before the speaking, I chatted for a moment with Shiloah and suggested that it would not be necessary to consider making formal inquiries on the points he had raised yesterday. As we were talking, or rather as Ben-Gurion and I were talking later, I called Shiloah over. I took that occasion to tell Ben-Gurion how intelligent and helpful I regarded Shiloah.

Asked Kaplan where Henry Morgenthau, Jr. stood in the internecine UJA row. Kaplan replied that technically Morgenthau was neutral, but that morally he was giving full support to the dissidents. I stressed my desire to stay out of the battle.

---

54. Leo (Yehuda Pinhas) Kohn (1894–1961), Frankfurt-born jurist and diplomat; emigrated to Palestine, 1921; political secretary, Jewish Agency, 1934–1948; Ministry of Foreign Affairs political adviser and liaison officer to UN, 1948–1952.

55. Founded in 1940 in the United States under the auspices of B'nai Zion as "American Red Mogen David" to assist the Palestinian Jewish equivalent of the Red Cross with money, ambulances, and medical staff.

The bitter argument within the United Jewish Appeal [UJA], the largest Jewish fundraising agency in the United States, ostensibly concerned the use of UJA funds, part of which were turned over each year to the United Palestine Appeal [UPA]. One faction in the UJA, led by Abba Hillel Silver and Emanuel Neumann, wanted greater control of these funds in order to secure a stronger American Zionist voice in Israel and in world Zionism more generally. Morgenthau, Henry Montor, and Louis Lipsky—the "dissidents" mentioned by McDonald—formed the opposing faction. They favored the turnover of UJA funds earmarked for Israel to the Israeli government to spend as they saw fit.[56]

Told Ben-Gurion I was glad that he had invited Eleanor Roosevelt, and that I thought it at least probable that she would accept. Speaking to Mrs. Ben-Gurion, I suggested that she and her husband come to dinner, and that if he could not come, that she come alone. She replied, "Of course, he can come. I'll arrange it." Later Ben-Gurion said he thought it would be possible. Miss Herlitz, of whom I inquired, turned me over to Mr. Sternberg, who said that he would get for me the film of the Ben-Gurion picture in which he and I are having so serious a discussion.

The speeches were short and that of Celler perfect. Ben-Gurion spoke briefly, I similarly, then the congressman, and finally Dr. Levontin. I should also record the delightful remark by Mrs. Ben-Gurion to me: "I think Ben-Gurion is a really great man and perfectly suited to his present responsibilities." I was especially interested, too, in her account of how during the *Altalena* fighting, she had, on her husband's instructions, told all her neighbors to abandon their houses but had herself refused to leave. When her husband tried to reach her on the telephone, she did not answer, lest he be disturbed by her remaining. Another illustration of her quality was her statement that because she did not feel that she should "exploit," she kept no servants and had only a charwoman come in. She spoke of the burden of the labor involved but with no tinge of complaint. I forgot to mention above that our guests the Habers were also at the reception.

My nap was interrupted almost before it began by Miss Clark's announcement that Cummings and McMahon were on their way out and had asked Knox to come too. When we were assembled, there was a full dress discussion of the incident of the early morning and its possible "angles." Our only fear was lest the Stern Gang, or some member thereof, might think that Cummings had been in touch with the other side. I urged him to stay with us, but he insisted, and the others rather supported him, that it would be better to act as if nothing had happened and stay at the hotel. It was agreed that the matter would be reported to the Department in such a way as to protect Cummings's record. For once, I felt a little bit more of a diplomat than Knox because, though I had shared his opposition to the continuance of Cummings's contacts with the Stern Gang

56. See Ganin, *An Uneasy Relationship*, 54–60.

after it had been outlawed, I did not, as did Knox, say in effect "I told you so."[57] But, of course, Knox put it in such a gentle way that nobody could be offended. Knox reported that at lunch with van der Velde and Shiloah, the latter had brought up again the questions of the three service attachés and of Major Andronovich. It was agreed that Cummings would draft a despatch urging the arrival of Samuel Klaus by the 23rd so that the two might have a chance to confer.[58]

David Croll of Toronto came in for a brief tea.[59] We chatted about the Histadrut meeting in his hometown, where he had presided and I had been one of the speakers. He told me also of his concern about the attitude of the Provisional Government towards the Arab refugee problem and of the difficulty which this would create for Jews in Canada and the US. I could not seriously disagree with him. While Bobby and Shoshana[60] went off to the Yom Kippur service Miss Clark and I walked in the sunset. Bobby came back in time to enjoy, as did I, Miss Clark's improved version of the 5-in-1.

Having finished Antonius's *Arab Awakening*, which deserves its reputation of being an almost perfect book of its kind, I began General Édouard Brémond, *Le Hedjaz dans la guerre mondiale*, which has been strongly recommended as an antidote to T.E. Lawrence's *The Seven Pillars of Wisdom*.[61] My earlier reading, in addition to the documents and the current press since I came to Tel Aviv, has included Sholem Asch, *Salvation*; Feuchtwanger's *Josephus*; Sarah Gertrude Millan's *Rhodes*; and now I am in the midst of the mediator's final report.

Wednesday, October 13

As the girls were finishing breakfast, Knox, van der Velde, and Cummings came out with drafts of telegrams on Major Andronovich and on the service attachés.[62] I suggested also drafting one on the Jerusalem situation and, before he left, Knox prepared it for my fuller study.

---

57. Knox wryly wrote to Cummings on December 15, 1948, "No word about your girlfriend and I guess she is still a [government] guest." Truman Library, Knox Papers, box 1, folder Correspondence 1948–1949.
58. Entry of September 22, 1948.
59. David Arnold Croll (1900–1991), Moscow-born Canadian Liberal politician; Canada's first Jewish provincial cabinet minister (Ontario), 1934–1937; elected to Canadian House of Commons, 1945, 1949, 1953; appointed to Canadian Senate as first Jewish senator, 1955–1991.
60. Shoshana Kasselman Roberts, one of Barbara McDonald's Hebrew-language tutors; hired by the mission in October 1948 to serve as a badly needed translator.
61. Édouard Brémond (1868–1948), French army general who served in Morocco and wrote *Le Hedjaz dans la guerre mondiale* in 1931. T. E. Lawrence, *The Seven Pillars of Wisdom* (1922), is Lawrence's autobiographical and idealistic account of the Arab revolt of 1916–1918.
62. McDonald on October 13 reported that, when van der Velde was presented to Shiloah as the US military attaché to Israel, Shiloah mentioned Andronovich's "peculiar status" now that the embassy had an accredited military attaché. Andronovich, Shiloah said, was initially accredited to the British mandatory government with jurisdiction in Palestine and Transjordan, but the first of these no longer existed, and the latter was now enemy territory. McDonald reported that Shiloah "again looked askance at Andronovich's frequently crossing Arab-Jewish lines" and noted that "I feel Andronovich's status [is] ambiguous and should be clarified [at] soonest." Lovett countered that "since Jerusalem [is] not part of Israel [Department] cannot agree with Shiloah that there is [a]

Chaim Shertok came over while I was with the staff, and Bobby entertained him. Later, he and I had an hour and a half together. His views are, I judged, not those of his father but rather representative of the young people of his age, 15. For example, he thinks war will have to be resumed and that after the taking of Gaza, Latrun, and all of Jerusalem, Abdullah will be willing to shake hands. Chaim's account of [Moshe] Sneh was unusually interesting; Sneh had been very important in the Haganah and in the General Zionists, but now in the Mapam he was not a leader.[63] He was suffering from two misjudgments: 1) that the Jewish state could not be set up as it was; and 2) that there could be a war between the US and Russia in which the latter would be the victor. Chaim's own plans are to become an aviator or an aviation engineer. His sister, aged 18, is in the Palmach, and his older brother is in one of the Negev settlements. It is a typical Israeli family.

Spoke to Gurdus on the telephone, who reported that the Soviet press of the High Command in Berlin a day or two ago had said that the Gaza government was a reflection of the will of the Palestinian people for self-rule, but that the cabinet was made up of Gestapo agents and Nazi bandits. Gurdus had not heard that Iraq as well as Egypt had recognized Gaza. He thought the Gaza government might now be used as a means of breaching the truce without bringing UN sanctions against the real culprits, Egypt or Iraq.

Gurdus suggested [Isaac] Shamosh, formerly an associate editor of the Arabic paper of Histadrut, as perhaps the best man to follow Arabic opinion for me.[64] Gudrus said he would ask Shamosh to call. Later, Gurdus called to say that he had just heard the announcement on the radio that the US had made public its opposition to the Gaza government. It was Lovett's statement that Gaza did not possess the qualifications requisite for recognition. And thus ended a very quiet Yom Kippur.

Thursday, October 14

A restful forty-five minutes with tea and Brémond. Wrote personal notes to Eisenhower, commenting on his speech of last night,[65] to Forrestal about

connection between between assignment van [der] Velde and status [of] Andronovich." McDonald to secretary of state, no. 175, October 13, 1948, NARA, RG 59, MC 1390, reel 17, frame 118; Lovett to McDonald, no. 161, October 15, 1948, NARA, RG 59, MC 1390, reel 17, frame, 116.

63. Moshe Sneh (1909–1972), Polish-born Zionist journalist; escaped from Poland to Palestine, 1940; chief of staff, Haganah, 1941–1946; adopted a more activist anti-British stance than Ben-Gurion, helping plan IZL bombing of the King David Hotel in July 1946, and was subsequently removed as chief of staff; broke with Ben-Gurion afterward, voting against the partition of Palestine in the Zionist Executive in 1947; moved steadily leftward politically, from the Soviet-friendly Mapam, which he helped found in 1948, to the communist Maki party in 1954. On his politics see Sasson Sofer, *Zionism and the Foundations of Israeli Diplomacy* (New York: Cambridge University Press, 1998).

64. Isaac Shamosh (1912–1971), Syrian-born lawyer and journalist; editor of Arab section of *Al-HaMishmar*, the organ of Mapam; member of various societies that worked for advancement of Sephardic culture; involved in transfer of Aleppo Codex to Israel.

65. Dwight D. Eisenhower's inaugural address as president of Columbia University, October 12, 1948, in which he discussed the communist threat to free institutions and the responsibilities of democratic citizenship.

his address of Air Force Day, to John Foster Dulles about his attitude towards Russia, to Mrs. Roosevelt urging her again to come out, and to Dave Niles inviting him.

The invitation to Niles was similar to others: "You could be assured of a hearty welcome from everybody in the Government and from the people. And Bobby and I would love to put you up at our house and save you the noise and confusion of the downtown hotels."[66]

Later sent these over with Bobby to the Foreign Office, where Miss Herlitz said she would give them to Zvi Friedberg, who is leaving tomorrow morning for the States. As postmaster general, he ought to get them through.[67] It was a relief to have Mrs. Schoolman's cable confirming the arrival of letters. I was glad, too, to hear that Ben Abrams had accepted [the office of co-treasurer] of JDC.

Dr. Mohn came at twelve, and we walked for an hour on the roof discussing:

1) Arab refugee problem and possibility of more American aid. He is convinced total aid will be inadequate and late and that many thousands will die [over the winter]. He said that, of course, the major responsibility rests upon the Arab states, which rejected the November 29 settlement and attacked the Jews. He did not, however, give the Jews a clean bill of health, for he attributed the mass evacuation not merely to mass panic, auto-inspired, but said that the Jewish massacre at Deir Yassin by the Sternists and the utilization later by other Jewish groups of terror engendered by that cry, had been factors in the disastrous exodus. He admitted, however, that there was no evidence whatever that the Jews had anticipated this event. On the contrary, they had strongly urged the Arabs to remain, for example, in Haifa, thinking that they would be needed. It was only later that the discovery was made that work could be carried on without them.[68] Mohn charged that in Jaffa, Acre, and even in Nazareth, where the Jews claim that inter-relations are excellent, there is deliberate or tolerated discrimination in distribution of food and opportunities for work. Mohn said that the UN machinery was very thin and that there were almost no funds for administration of relief. This was the more deplorable because the Arab countries, where most of the refugees are, have had so little experience and have so little competence in this kind of work. He deplored the probable grave lack of supplies not only

66. McDonald to Niles, October 14, 1948, McDonald Papers, Columbia University, box 16, folder 7. Also McDonald to Dulles, October 14, 1948, McDonald Papers, Columbia University, box 2, folder 14.
67. Zvi Friedberg [later Prihar] (1903–1969), director of postal services, Israeli ministry of communications.
68. Fully explained in Benny Morris, *The Birth of the Palestinian Refugee Problem Revisited.*

because of the suffering this would entail, but also because the Arab authorities would be deprived of useful social experience in administering adequate relief.

2) Mohn's view about the Gaza government is very similar to ours. He thought it primarily a Mufti and Egyptian creation. He commented that Egypt was the most difficult country for the UN to deal with.[69] As to Azzam, he thought him a moderate and primarily devoted to the Arab League. Azzam had told Mohn that he had much more important things in mind for the League than Palestine; but as Mohn added, Azzam had been forced to use the Zionists as the one cause on which he could unite all the members of the League.

3) On the moot question of the mediator's first proposal to include Jerusalem in the Arab State, Mohn said this had been purely a practical decision by Bernadotte on the ground that it was surrounded by Arab territory. Mohn said he had fought against it, explaining that while Zionism was only fifty-some years old, Jerusalem had thousands of years of Jewish association.

4) The Negev, despite the sentiment attached to it, would in Mohn's opinion, always remain a land limited to the pioneers.

5) Bunche, according to Mohn, was not in a position, as I had thought, to outline the mediator's plan when the former was in Washington a fortnight or so before Bernadotte's lunch with us on the 10th of September, because at the beginning of the month, the mediator and his staff had not made up their minds definitely on their recommendations. I must check and note the date that the Department asked us to present the series of questions to the Provisional Government, because at that time the Department, and presumably the British, had agreed on the elements of a scheme, for example, the Galilee-Negev deal.

6) Mohn was interested in my report about Rusk's trusteeship-for-Jerusalem scheme.[70] He himself had had an idea for Jewish and Arab autonomous areas within the internationalized larger unit with the old city and international center within the wider international unit. Mount Scopus and its Jewish institutions were to be a sort of a Jewish trust. He had given up this scheme, however, when the count decided to return to the November 29th idea.

7) At lunch Knox raised a number of difficulties about American aid, chiefly that it would require specific congressional action. Nonetheless, I hope to be able to make a strong plea to the Department as soon as Mohn supplies me with the factual data of what has been promised and what [has been] done.

69. Ambassador Griffis reported on October 13, 1948, that Egypt opposed the Bernadotte Plan because of its suspicions that Britain and Transjordan were colluding to create an expanded Transjordan by including Arab Palestine within Transjordan's borders. Griffis to Lovett, no. 1485, October 13, 1948, *FRUS*, 1948, v. V, pt. 2, 1471–1472.
70. Entry of October 11, 1948.

While Mohn was still with us came the word from Haifa about the Provisional Government's concern lest the consignment of shotguns and shells on the S. S. *Excalibur* destined for Beirut [were] to be used by the Arabs. Through Lippincott's intervention, the UN representative secured a pledge from the captain that the consignment would not be off-loaded at Beirut [but would be returned to the US]; later, when Shiloah urged an additional guarantee, Knox instructed Lippincott to secure an additional pledge from the captain. Thus was a potentially annoying incident avoided. Knox was particularly interested, because this was the first arrival of the new ships whose arrangements here had been worked out verbally by Knox and the Provisional Government.[71]

Miss [Judith] Epstein came for tea and stayed through dinner. She is doing a good job with the Hebrew press.

Friday, October 15

Knox and I went through a number of papers. He is still worried lest the Lebanese government, despite the UN and Lippincott's instructions to the captain (the latter instructions were given specifically on Knox's orders approved by me), to forcibly take off the glycerine, shot guns, and shells, to which the Provisional Government had raised such serious objections, when the *Excalibur* was in port at Haifa. I assured Knox that I would stand by him 100%.

Peter Bergson came a little after eleven and stayed until well after twelve. Before his arrival Knox had guessed that Bergson would solicit our support for his application for an American visa. He did nothing of the sort. Instead, he referred so confidently to his trip to the States within a week or two that one would assume that his papers were all in order; I should not be surprised if they were, for he has in the past managed many more difficult tasks than getting a visitor's visa.

Nearly the whole time was taken with Bergson's exposition of his fundamental thesis that there should be a sharp and clear line of demarcation between Jews who are citizens or who wish to become citizens of Israel—and who would be called Israelis or Hebrews—and the others who wish to remain citizens of the countries where they now reside.[72] These latter would be Jews but with no political or nationalist tie with Israel. They would be Americans or British or Frenchmen of Jewish ancestry and, if they were religious, of the Jewish persuasion. This distinction, Bergson regarded, would have these advantages: 1) It would be recognition of a fundamental fact; 2) It would remove many

---

71. The *Excalibur*'s voyage included New York, Marseille, Naples, Alexandria, Tel Aviv, Haifa, and Beirut before returning roughly along the same route. The Israelis detained the ship at Haifa because of its weapons cache, which included shotguns, 600 cases of shotgun shells, and 21 drums of glycerin consigned to the Syrian defense ministry. Riley also insisted on their return. Lippincott to secretary of state, no. 452, October 15, 1948, NARA, RG 59, 510.BB Palestine, box 2121, folder 5; Lovett to US legation Beirut, US consulate Haifa, no. 510, November 17, 1948, NARA, RG 59, 501.BB Palestine, box 2122, folder 4.

72. On Bergson's "Canaanite" approach to citizenship and national identity, see also Goda et al., eds., *To the Gates of Jerusalem*, 40–41.

elements of confusion and would eliminate all questions of dual loyalty on the part of those who did not opt for Israeli citizenship; 3) It would make Israel in all respects a state like other states.

Very interesting was Bergson's account (how accurate I can't judge) of his near-conversion of Arthur Sulzberger at a luncheon at the *Times*. Bergson reported that Sulzberger had said that this conception exactly matched his own. But within a few minutes thereafter, Senator Guy Gillette, following up Bergson's exposition, made a "traditional" Zionist argument, including the point that through the establishment of a Jewish state, Jews outside of Israel would find it easier to dig their roots deeper into the soil of their "adopted" country.[73] At this, Sulzberger is reported to have exploded and to have said in substance: I don't know, Senator Gillette, how long your family has been in America; mine has been here since 1640 and we do not need a Jewish state to make us good Americans. Thereafter, Sulzberger, according to Bergson, regarded the latter's earlier and plausible arguments as merely a trap. For this assumed devious maneuver, Sulzberger felt bitter hostility towards Bergson.

Incidentally, Bergson spoke of the desirability of ceasing to refer to the "State of Israel;" instead, it should be called the "Republic of Israel." His argument was two-fold: 1) "State" is confusing; 2) "State" in Europe has come to connote a Fascist regime. This second point seems to me to have little validity. In the course of the discussion I brought up the name of Ze'ev Jabotinsky. Bergson was much amused by my account of Jabotinsky's retort to Norman Bentwich back in 1934 when he and I were lunching with Jabotinsky in Moscow.[74] As he was leaving, Bergson reiterated that his purpose in the States was to liquidate one or more of his organizations and to make himself completely, as he is now "partially" a private citizen.[75]

Professor [Reuben] Wallenrod of Brooklyn College, here on a Guggenheim fellowship for the study of modern Hebrew literature, came to ask me for my cooperation in securing assistance from the Provisional Government in his seeing the country. I promised to write him a letter to the Jewish National Fund. He also suggested that it might be useful to me to have him arrange for me to meet some of the modern Hebrew writers. I agreed.[76]

Lunch for the Habers with the Davidowitzes and Mrs. Shertok. It went off beautifully, Bobby and Sarah having done their parts perfectly. Naturally, this being a social occasion, there was no confidential political talk. Dr. [Harry]

73. Guy M. Gillette (1897–1973), former Democratic congressman (1933–1936) and senator (1936–1945) from Iowa; president of Bergson's American League for a Free Palestine and political adviser to Bergson's Hebrew Committee of National Liberation. JTA *Bulletin*, August 2, 1945.
74. Breitman et al., eds., *Advocate for the Doomed*, entry of April 18, 1934. The meeting was in Warsaw.
75. On Bergson's visit, see also Knox to secretary of state, no. 81, October 17, 1948, NARA, RG 59, MC 1390, reel 17, frames 181–182.
76. Reuben Wallenrod (1901–1966), professor of Hebrew at Brooklyn College; major figure in Hebrew-language and literature studies in the United States; wrote about American Jewish immigrant life.

Davidowitz was unusually interesting, his extraordinary knowledge of languages and history showing to excellent advantage.[77] As to the prevailing language in Palestine in Jesus's day, he said it was [Hebrew] from which Aramaic grew in the first century. He was of the opinion that Jesus knew Hebrew also. The Habers left immediately after lunch with warmest expressions of appreciation. They were delightful guests.

Saturday, October 16

This day was notable for two long conferences together lasting over three hours with Jacques de Reynier, chief of the Palestine Delegation of the ICRC [International Committee of the Red Cross]. He came with a note of introduction from Max Wolf, adviser to that Committee.[78] Our talks covered a wide range but in detail concentrated on four general subjects: 1) Arab refugees; 2) war prisoners; 3) current personalities; and 4) work of the Red Cross Committee.

Jacques de Reynier, a former Swiss army officer, arrived in Jerusalem in January 1948 as the ICRC's delegate to the city. He worked on both the Arab and Jewish sides to limit the impending conflict, to establish safe zones in Jerusalem, and, once war erupted, to ensure proper treatment of prisoners of war under the Geneva Conventions. By the fall, de Reynier was also concerned with Red Cross aid to Palestinian Arab refugees, who languished in makeshift camps in the Arab countries around Israel, including in areas of Arab Palestine such as Ramallah, Hebron, and Gaza. Most initial aid for Arab refugees came from the West, from organizations that already had an infrastructure in Palestine, such as the ICRC and the American Friends Service Committee. The British too provided tents and some funds.[79]

In late August, Bernadotte had called on national Red Cross societies, UN member states, UNICEF, and numerous other aid societies to provide help for the refugees. He convinced seventeen nations to contribute to an emergency relief operation to run from September to December 1948.[80] Secretary-General Trygve Lie, meanwhile, set up in Beirut a UN Disaster Relief Program, later called the Refugee Relief Project,

---

77. Entry of August 17, 1948.

78. Max Wolf (1899–1962), Swiss German who as a reporter based in Berlin was among the first to report on Nazi policies; escaped Berlin with Gestapo at his heels, 1936; diplomatic correspondent for the *Manchester Guardian* and radio broadcaster from England until 1947; special adviser to Paul Ruegger, president of ICRC in Geneva, 1948–1955; intermediary between the ICRC and the Israeli Foreign Ministry after early 1948; married to Anita Warburg of the Hamburg banking family.

79. See Jacques de Reynier, *1948 à Jérusalem* (Lausanne: Éditions de la Baconnière, 2002). In general, see Dominique-D. Junod, *The Imperiled Red Cross and the Palestine-Eretz-Israel Conflict, 1945–1952: The Influence of Institutional Concerns on a Humanitarian Operation* (London: Routledge, 1996); Asaf Romirowsky and Alexander H. Joffe, *Religion, Politics, and the Origins of Palestine Refugee Relief* (New York: Palgrave, 2013); and Nancy Gallagher, *Quakers in the Israeli-Palestinian Conflict: The Dilemmas of NGO Humanitarian Activism* (New York: American University in Cairo Press, 2007).

80. See Progress Report of the United Nations Mediator on Palestine, September 16, 1948, http://unispal.un.org/UNISPAL.NSF/0/AB14D4AAFC4E1BB985256204004F55FA.

under Raphael Cilento (1893–1985), an Australian public health expert and senior UN health official. The aim was to coordinate all aid, from the Red Cross, the Quakers, and the UN member states.[81]

1) Arab Refugees. Everything de Reynier had to say confirmed and filled out the picture, which Mohn had hinted at, of a UN incidental and inadequate administration of refugees. Cilento's leadership in Beirut is supported merely by one or two men in the several capitals, but without any representation on the spot to control [the] final distribution of goods. Moreover, the Security Council apparently is highly bureaucratic, if one is to judge from the following examples: a) Cilento's insistence that every tent before it leaves Beirut must have "UNO" on it, even if, as has proved to be the case, [this causes] a delay from one to several weeks; b) his rather preemptory statement to [US] Red Cross representative William L. Gower, who had come to Egypt as a substitute for O'Connor,[82] whom [Ambassador Stanford] Griffis had invited to make a personal survey, that Griffis had no status or business in Beirut;[83] c) Griffis's similar statement to [Cilento], to which the latter had replied that he was not dependent upon Griffis's authorization. [The] UN set-up permits it to deal only with governments, and hence makes it impossible for UN representatives to be much more than figureheads. Besides, the idea which the mediator had expressed in Stockholm, that the resources made available for refugees would be a means of influencing Arab governments, is fantastically unrealistic, even more unrealistic than Mohn's statement the other day that the experience the Arabs would get in administering relief would be educational to them, but at the expense of the refugees. According to de Reynier, the waste resulting from the present administration and distribution would be as high as 90%. Translated into human terms, this would mean tens of thousands of lives needlessly lost. De Reynier explained that the International Red Cross could take over quickly and naturally without loss of time and with vastly increased efficiency. From their point of view, relief has not been administered until it has reached the individual sufferer. The transfer from UN to Red Cross could be made the more naturally because the mediator's authority in this realm was parenthetical rather than a major part of his functions. The question of which particular Red Cross organization would take over was, according to de Reynier, merely incidental.

2) The primary task of the ICRC was the supervision of the Geneva Convention regulating the treatment of prisoners of war. At the beginning of the conflict here, none of the governments seemed to know or be interested in

81. On Cilento, see entry of September 9, 1948; in general, see Morris, *1948*, 309–310.
82. Basil O'Connor (1892–1972), president, American Red Cross, 1947–1949.
83. Griffis was observing in his capacity as US ambassador to Egypt and was horrified by what he saw. "The United States," he said publicly, "has been grossly negligent in this humanitarian problem."

the convention. Hence, they expected all sorts of extraneous functions from the Red Cross workers. These were performed while the Red Cross authorities were slowly educating the governments. Now, the work goes smoothly. There are approximately 4,000 Arab prisoners and 2,000 Jewish [prisoners]. The problem of exchange is complicated by the fact that perhaps the majority of the Arab prisoners, at least those that are Palestinian, are not much desired by the Arab states, which therefore lack the full incentive for an exchange arrangement. Perhaps the only way to do this would be to make the exchange en bloc.

3) Personalities. [John] Glubb is the military man personified who has won the confidence of his Arab colleagues. He is disinterested in politics. He always remains the Britisher abroad who on the highest level is the representative of British interests and policies. Abdullah, despite his sophistication and Westernized education, is essentially the desert leader who wants only to get out of his desert a little ways. He is very active, attempts too much, but despite all this is energetic and well considering his age. Abdullah al-Tel seems an excellent gentleman and a capable general whose word de Reynier has found trustworthy. [King] Farouk is essentially the playboy and not interested much in Palestine. He is often at the Swiss Club in Alexandria, where he loves to take part in the shooting exercises. His prime minister[84] is a reasonable and trustworthy person, but the minister of war[85] is extremely difficult. The mufti: According to de Reynier, he is all that we have been told he is. Jamal al-Husseini is only a shadow of the mufti. Bernadotte: A man of wide and genuine human sympathies and of willingness to devote himself to humanity. His intelligence was not as large as his sympathy. Perhaps one proof of this is that he never understood that, as mediator, he had ceased to be the Red Cross leader. It is even possible that this confusion helped to keep him from taking, or permitting to be taken, the elementary security precautions which might have saved his life. He was very ambitious. The height of his hopes was the Nobel Peace Prize. An incidental point made by de Reynier was that the assassination took place in a Sternist area where [Dov] Joseph's writ did not run. This may help to explain both Joseph's failure to give protection and his inability later to give an adequate explanation of that failure.

4) Work of Red Cross people is constantly hazardous. De Reynier and his colleagues are sniped at nearly every day they are in the field, and some days many times. They learn to distinguish between warning shots and those

84. Mahmoud an-Nokrashi Pasha (1888–1948) served as the king's prime minister from 1946 until December 28, 1948, when a member of the Muslim Brotherhood assassinated him.

85. Field Marshal Mohammed Haidar Pasha (1895–1957), held several cabinet posts before being named Egyptian minister of war in 1948, when he assured Prime Minister Nokrashi Pasha that "there will be no war with the Jews. It will be a parade without any risk whatsoever, the army . . . will be in Tel Aviv in two weeks." Named chief of staff by King Farouk after the Wafd Party swept to power in 1950; resigned after an arms scandal and reinstated in 1952; arrested after General Mohammed Naguib's military coup in 1952.

meant to kill, but they never know when they will be under fire, despite the non-political nature of their work. One of de Reynier's colleagues at present was at the airfield of Gaza a few weeks ago when the French UN observers were killed.[86] It seems clear that the French pilot not only failed to notify Gaza of his arrival time, but also ignored all the local regulations about bringing his plane in. The initial gunfire after the plane landed was harmless. It was not until the occupants, on getting out of the plane, instead of remaining standing or walking towards the Arabs, began to run towards the Jewish lines that the fatal firing began. They were killed about 200 meters from the plane in the direction of the Jewish positions. The robbery of the bodies and of the plane which followed, de Reynier dismissed, as what you would expect from Arab soldiers, a small proportion of which were probably regulars.

To Bernstein's second concert with Bobby and Miss Clark. Again Lenny was the stellar attraction as conductor, soloist in Gershwin's *Rhapsody in Blue* and playing his own *Fancy Free*. His Brahms Fourth was a stirring performance. Pleasant visit with Mrs. Ben-Gurion during the intermission and before the concert. Her husband had intended to come but was not permitted because of the blackout.

McDonald wrote his family on October 16 that

> the men at the top of the Government are themselves directly involved in the activities along the front lines because so many of them have their sons and daughters in exposed positions. For example, the daughter of Shertok, the Foreign Minister, is a member of the Palmach, one of the shock troops, and is stationed near Latrun where there has been some of the bitterest fighting . . . [and] one of Shertok's sons is in a beleaguered agricultural settlement in the Negev. . . . Another example is Dr. Bernard Joseph, whose favorite daughter was killed by [an] Egyptian aerial bomb in the Negev ten days or so ago. In Israel to be a high executive does not exempt a son or daughter from the most hazardous post.[87]

Sunday, October 17

Nathan Gurdus called to tell me that fighting was heavy in the south [see textbox 4.1]. Conference with Knox, Cummings, and Colonel van der Velde. All of them approved the long telegram, which I had worked on Saturday. It was sent off during the day. Copy of this in my personal file, perhaps better than diary account, reveals the heart of my talk with de Reynier.

86. Two French UN observers, Lieutenant Colonel Joseph Queru and Captain Pierre Jeannel, were killed at the airfield in Gaza on August 28 as they disembarked from their aircraft. The killers were Saudi irregulars under Egyptian command. The bodies were stripped of their clothes before they could be removed from the airfield. United Nations, Department of Public Information, Press Release PAL/277, September 7, 1948.
87. McDonald to his family, October 16, 1948, McDonald Papers, Columbia University, box 14, folder 13.

Textbox 4.1.
Operation Yoav
OCTOBER 15–22, 1948

On October 14, 1948, McDonald called attention to rising tensions in the Negev. Israeli intelligence reports, he told Washington, showed Egyptian troops moving toward Israeli positions. "Israeli public and Army," McDonald stated, "will never allow Egypt forces [to] get in position [to] annihilate agricultural settlements." He connected Egyptian activity to its support of the Gaza government and predicted to Lovett that King Abdullah would likely stand aside "and let [the] Israel Army maul Egyptian forces in order [to] eliminate both Gaza Government and potential Egyptian menace [to] his territory."[1]

Egypt controlled the road from al-Majdal to Beit Jibrin, cutting off the twenty-five Israeli settlements in the northern Negev. In violation of the truce terms, the Egyptians had fired on Israeli supply convoys for the settlements.[2] On October 6, the Israeli cabinet decided to launch Operation Yoav, a military undertaking aimed at permanently removing Egyptian forces from the Negev by using superior maneuverability and shorter supply lines to isolate and expel them. In Gaza and the Negev Egypt deployed eleven regular army battalions, plus assorted auxiliary formations of Saudis, Sudanese, Muslim Brothers, and Palestinian Arabs. The British had encouraged the Egyptians to consolidate their forces, but they remained unprepared for an Israeli assault.

On October 15, after the Israelis sent a convoy south to provoke an attack and thus provide a pretext for engagement, Operation Yoav began.[3] Israeli aircraft attacked Egyptian airfields and artillery positions. IDF infantry pressed south toward Gaza, relieving pressure on Tel Aviv, while cutting through the Majdal-to-Beit Jibrin road. In the process they isolated and trapped 4,000 Egyptian troops in a pocket around Faluja, a village initially assigned to the Arab state in the 1947 partition plan. More important, the IDF linked the Israeli state with its settlement enclave in the Negev. Leaving their cut-off troops isolated in Faluja, the main body of Egyptian forces pulled back to defensive positions in the Gaza Strip, while the Egyptian government called on Transjordan and Iraq for help. Both refused.

Though Ben-Gurion called the decision to wage the Yoav operation the most important since the decision for independence, he expected the UN Security Council to intervene within four to seven days. On October 19, at the urging of acting mediator Ralph Bunche, the Security Council discussed a text of a resolution calling for an

1. McDonald to Lovett, no. 179, October 14, 1948, *FRUS*, 1948, v. V, pt. 2, 1476–1477.
2. Eban complained about this violation to Trygve Lie on October 8. See *DFPI*, v. 2, d. 15.
3. On the convoy, Shiloah to Shertock, October 14, 1948, *DFPI*, v. 2, d. 25.

immediate cease-fire between Israeli and Egyptian forces in the Negev, for mutual withdrawal to the previous lines of October 14, and for guaranteed Israeli convoys to the Jewish Negev settlements.[4] On the same day IDF forces launched a last-minute offensive to capture Be'er Sheva, taking the city on October 21 and consolidating the Israeli claim to the entire region. Both sides accepted a cease-fire to take effect at noon GMT on October 22, but the Israelis, having achieved their objectives, refused to pull back to the October 14 lines. The offensive created more than 130,000 Arab refugees, many of whom were expelled, and most of whom ended up in the Egyptian-controlled and crowded Gaza Strip.[5]

---

4. See *DFPI*, v. 2, p. 72. The resolution was formalized as Security Council Resolution 61 of November 4, 1948.

5. Morris, *The Birth of the Palestinian Refugee Problem Revisited*, 462–473; Tal, *War in Palestine*, 373–390.

The same day that McDonald met de Reynier, he wrote to personal friends, "Today . . . I have concentrated on the tragic problem of the Arab refugees. (Sometimes I think that I am fated always to be connected directly or indirectly with refugees.) For weeks I have been trying to think of something I could suggest which might be a contribution toward the easing of this terrifying situation. Finally, I think I have an idea which would effect a fundamental improvement."[88]

On October 17, McDonald sent a despatch on the Arab refugee problem directly to Truman and to Lovett as acting secretary of state.[89] *The "Arab refugee tragedy," he said, "is rapidly reaching catastrophic proportions and should be treated as a disaster. UN administrative machine is both inappropriate and inadequate and result[s] in gross inefficiency and wastefulness (All adjectives used above are realistically descriptive and are written out of fifteen years of personal contact with refugee problems.)"*

Of roughly 400,000 refugees, he said, the winter cold and rains would kill approximately "100,000 old men, women and children who are shelterless and have little or no food." He called for immediate shifting of the problem from the UN's machinery, which, he judged, was "completely unsuited [to] energetic and competent handling [of] emergency relief and resettlement problem." The UN could deal only with governments, a process too remote from the human level. The International Red Cross, McDonald suggested, was uniquely "geared to do essential work in all phases," and it already had the personnel working in Arab Palestine and the neighboring states.

88. McDonald to Helen, Leland, Lucius and Sally, October 16, 1948, McDonald Papers, USHMM, box 7, folder 7.

89. McDonald to secretary of state [attention president and acting secretary], no. 188, October 17, 1948, *FRUS*, 1948, v. V, pt. 2, 1486–1487. See also McDonald, *My Mission in Israel*, 98, 100.

Moreover, the removal of refugee work from the acting mediator's purview would free him to pursue mediation itself.

McDonald also wrote Herbert Hoover: "Unless leadership such as you have given in the past can now be conscripted to direct, not merely at the top but all the way down to the individual recipient, the efforts on behalf of these hundreds of thousands of destitute and homeless Arabs, there will be many tens of thousands of needless deaths . . . . I hope you will have the time to examine the situation critically and then will make whatever radical suggestions of change circumstances call for. No one else can do this as can you."[90]

[Colonel Trauernicht, the US United Nations observer, visited McDonald to discuss office space for the UN in Tel Aviv]. More interesting than the above were the colonel's comments on the strained relations between the Egyptian officers and their men in the south and his report that [the] Egyptian air force was manned mostly by Britishers.[91] Revealing of what might be called UN psychology was the colonel's "correction" when I referred to the Egyptian beginning of the bombing. "It was the Jews," he said, "who began it." He seemed to ignore the fact that the Egyptians had refused persistently to fulfill the UN order to allow the Jews to pass their convoys south six hours a day. Also revealing was the colonel's comment that Transjordan would be glad to see the Egyptians put in their place.

Conference with Knox and Cummings about five or six telegrams from the Department. Fortunately, none of them required immediate action. I was very sorry that illness in the Samuel Klaus family has postponed indefinitely his coming and will probably advance Cummings's leaving.[92]

Tea with Marcus Sieff and [Knox and Cummings], and Bobby and Miss Clark. Marcus was optimistic about military and political developments. The administration he found tightened both in the military and in civil life. Marked progress had also been made in the economic sphere. To illustrate, he cited the case of a textile mill, which in the very midst of war and only three miles from the fighting front, had installed modern looms, with the result that it is more efficient than any mill he knows at home. Though he would not be specific about gas stocks, he left the impression that these were not a source of worry. He himself seems to have been instrumental in the recently-announced Shell contract.[93] Later, as we walked together on the roof, we talked about Israel's

90. McDonald to Hoover, October 19, 1948, McDonald Papers, USHMM, box 7, folder 7.
91. From its founding by treaty in 1936, the Royal Egyptian Air Force received pilot training and aircraft from the Royal Air Force and operated from many of the same air bases in the Suez Canal Zone, the Western Desert, and al-Arish air force base. In 1948 it used British Spitfires, Hurricanes, C-47s, and surplus ammunition from World War II.
92. McDonald noted to his family that Cummings had been recalled by the Commerce Department. "Our regret is softened a little by the knowledge that he will be able to do a number of things at home that we should like to have done." McDonald to Janet, Halsey, and Ruth, October 31, 1948, McDonald Papers, USHMM, box 7, folder 7.
93. Entry of October 8, 1948.

representation in London and British representation here. We agreed about Nahum Goldmann and about Cyril Marriott [British consul in Haifa]. As we parted, it was agreed that he would call me and come out to the house before he left to see whether I had any final messages.

I should have noted the visit just before lunch of Mr. Lippincott. He was apparently a little concerned lest his letter to the captain of the *Excalibur*, which Knox and I had instructed him to write, might bring a UN protest on the ground that General Riley's letter to the captain should have been sufficient. Apparently, the ship authorities had been annoyed chiefly by the fact that the vessel was delayed 12 hours, the Jewish protest not having been made during the Day of Atonement. Lippincott's statement about Marriott, the latter's open contempt for "those dirty Jews," and his refusal to come to parties where Jews were to be present, was a confirmation of what Marcus told me later about Marriott's phobia on this subject. According to Marcus, Marriott had even said that South Africa was controlled by Jews, whose ancestors had gone there from Spain after their forced conversion to Catholicism.

Monday, October 18
First day of Sukkot

[In] the late morning Francis Ofner of the *Christian Science Monitor* came,[94] apparently to ask me to give a special interview to the new paper which is to start within a week or ten days under the sponsorship of Mapai and with Ben-Gurion's personal blessing.[95] I said I would let him know within two or three days. Ofner also took the occasion to say that he thought there was need for more cultural and press relationships if the mission were to function with full efficiency. He praised Cummings and said that he would be missed, and that the necessity will be all the greater. I could not very well tell him our plans, but merely indicated that we were conscious of the need and hoped to meet it.

Early in our talk I happened to mention the visit of Gurdus of the French Press Agency. At once, Ofner seemed to be concerned and warned me that Gurdus's background had been such as to raise the question of his possibly being too close to our northern friends [the Soviet Union]. He did not pretend to have definite proof, but thought the evidence pointed towards this special relationship. I had little to say. In the afternoon a pleasant visit from Shoshana at

94. Francis-Amir Ofner (1913–2011), Serbian-born journalist; Betar representative in Yugoslavia who aided with illegal emigration via the Danube to Palestine; captured by Hungarian forces during the invasion of Yugoslavia in April 1941; escaped to Istanbul where he worked for the US Office of War Information and formed an intelligence network, 1942–1945; settled in Tel Aviv, 1945, and became a correspondent for the *Christian Science Monitor*, the *London Observer*, and other outlets. On his wartime activities see Tuvia Friling, "Istanbul 1942–1945: The Kollek-Avriel and Berman-Ofner Networks," in *Secret Intelligence and the Holocaust*, ed. David Bankier (New York: Enigma Books and Yad Vashem), 105–156.

95. The newspaper was *Hador*, opened in 1948 by the Mapai secretariat because it could not fully express party positions in *Davar*, which also served the Histadrut. The newspaper closed in 1955.

teatime. The rest of the day and evening spent quietly finishing Brémond's *Hedjaz*.

Tuesday, October 19

Despite the columns of "news" in the *Palestine Post* about the fighting in the south, there was, it seemed to me, evidence that possibly this flurry had about blown itself out and that the Jewish demonstration of strength had served its purpose—whatever that purpose might have been.[96] Possibly it was to impress Paris, and possibly, too, to demonstrate the shallowness of the Gaza government and, at the same time, indicate Abdullah's seeming willingness to let the Egyptians stew.

The item in the paper about the UN plan to discuss Sir Raphael Cilento's report soon made me very anxious to see the text at the earliest moment. In response to my inquiry at Mohn's office, I was told that the report would be available as of late today or early tomorrow morning.[97] Mohn was in bed with [a] cold but had left word with one of the girls that I was to see it as soon as it was ready.

Wednesday, October 20

Long conference with Alexander Peli and Mr. Boorstein of the *Encyclopaedia Hebraica*.[98] They said they wanted me to do a three-hundred-word article on refugees and [wanted] my suggestions about ways they could improve their American contacts. I agreed to do the piece since I am to have a year or two leeway. More interesting to me was the discussion that followed about cultural relationships between our two peoples. We agreed that this would be an excellent project for American classics. Moreover, they shared my view that the libraries here should be supplied with the standard American books in English. At present there is very little [of] either of these or of the standard reference works, and of these few, many are at present unavailable because of the war and particularly because the Hebrew University and the Rockefeller Museum are out of bounds. This general project requires a group of interested persons in both countries. It is something I should like to work at.

Marcus Sieff came in on his way to Haifa and Paris and London. He was full of the fighting in the south [Operation Yoav] which he interpreted as brilliantly successful. Among the points he stressed were: 1) the severity of the fighting, Egyptians performing better than previously; 2) the disproportion in

96. "Only Cairo Is Optimistic," *Palestine Post*, October 19, 1948.
97. The *Palestine Post* reported that Cilento would complete his report on the Palestinian refugee situation within a few days and that the British planned to bring the problem of 360,000 Arab refugees to the UN Security Council, the UN Political Committee, and the UN Social Committee once the report was submitted. "Refugee Question to Social Committee," *Palestine Post*, October 19, 1948.
98. The encyclopedia, founded by Alexander Peli, was conceived in 1944, and the first volume appeared in 1948. It was completed in 1980.

weapons, Egyptians having approximately ten guns to one; 3) estimated Egyptian strength 20,000; 4) losses heavy, presumably on both sides, though he spoke only of the Egyptian losses; 5) despite Egyptian stout resistance there were indications of bitter feeling within their ranks. For example, some of the soldiers taken prisoners asked to be allowed to go back into the battle and fight against the Egyptian side; they were permitted and fought well; 6) Israeli morale illustrated by return to battle of a score of men all seriously wounded, one of them with [his] ear blown off; 7) Action well-planned and-executed, resulting in three cut-throughs of the Egyptian lines and opening of road to colonies; another 48 hours would, in Marcus's opinion, enable Israelis to cut off and annihilate two or three Egyptian points now perilously held. But the question was, would the forty-eight hours be given; 8) Egyptians had appealed to other Arab states, and there has been no response. This Shertok regarded as particularly significant; 9) one of [the] remaining problems was the Security Council demand for the return to the positions of [the] previous Thursday [October 14]. This, Sieff said, Israel would never grant; 10) finally, Sieff spoke of the current rumor [that] His Majesty's Government had concessions for the oil of the Negev and that three experimental wells had proved rich and were now tapped. On the other hand, the US, it is said, has arranged with Egypt for concessions in the event the Negev goes to Cairo. I expressed the view quite sincerely that I thought these reports were quite unfounded.

Marcus agreed to take our mail and to telephone either himself or ask his father or Simon Marks to telephone the States. It was suggested that the message might be to David Niles or Felix Frankfurter. It was to do with a visit to Paris and settlement of Negev.

Ofner of the *Christian Science Monitor* called, and I begged off from doing the article for the new Mapai paper [*Hador*].

Young Curtis Dall Boettiger called, and he is to come out for lunch tomorrow.[99] His comments on his grandmother's [Eleanor Roosevelt's] plans were to the effect that she probably could not come during the General Assembly, and that it would last so long—adjournment is anticipated on December 7 and may be postponed until the next week—that she could not come afterwards because she is determined to get home for Christmas with her seventeen grandchildren. In reply to my question whether he was with Henry Morgenthau, Jr., he said, "no," that he is going about the country on his own in order to see the things that his grandmother had specifically asked him to look into.

Thursday, October 21

At 2:52 AM, I was wakened from a dreamful sleep by what seemed to me three clearly marked heavy explosions, not very far away. I in turn woke

99. Curtis Roosevelt (1930–2016), eldest grandson of Franklin and Eleanor Roosevelt, and in Palestine on a fact-finding mission at his grandmother's behest; nicknamed "Buzzy," and until 1949 used the last names of his mother Anna Roosevelt's first husband Curtis Dall (his father) and her second husband Clarence Boettiger.

Bobby—this required some effort—and she in a manner so typical of her said very calmly, "I want to get my glasses first." When we were ensconced in the basement, she at once began on her knitting. Her calmness is not inherited. We waited downstairs for more than an hour; then when nothing happened, we grew impatient and without waiting for the all-clear, we went back to bed. At the time of this dictation, 10:49, we have not yet had any news about the bombing, but only about the fighting in the south.

At lunch Curtis Dall (Buzzy) Boettiger was our guest together with Knox and Shoshana. We were all delighted with the young man, who seems surprisingly mature and unspoiled. He is to go about on his own seeing the things his grandmother asked him to see. His account of the front lines in the Negev was graphic. As to his grandmother's possible visit, he thought that she might come early in the year after she had returned home for Christmas. After some short trips over this weekend, he is going up north to Nazareth and Upper Galilee, and Bobby may be invited to hitchhike.

With a heavy police escort we—Bobby and I—reached Weizmann's at about twenty minutes of five. Leonard Bernstein and Miss Coates had just arrived. Weisgal was also present at tea. The talk ranged over a wide field, centering finally, when Dr. Weizmann had come in, on a subject which seemed rather strange almost within sound of the Negev guns. This subject was: Should Dr. [Serge] Koussevitzky be refused an invitation to visit Israel to conduct the orchestra because in his youth at 15 or 16 he had been converted? Lenny, Mrs. Weizmann, Meyer Weisgal, and I were in favor of the invitation on grounds which will be obvious—his distinction as a conductor, his anxiety to show his interest in Israel, and his renascent Judaism. Dr. Weizmann, though expressing no final judgment, argued differently: at the time Koussevitzky had been converted, doubtless in order to free himself from restrictions which would have precluded his continuing his career in Moscow or Petrograd, millions of other Jews had remained faithful. It was not a question of being religious or otherwise, but of forsaking one's own to take the easy way. Mrs. Weizmann thought she had a conclusive retort when she reminded her husband that he had favored as president of his institute a Dr. Fritz Haber who, like Koussevitzky, had been converted as a young man. Dr. Weizmann's answer was that Haber would have, had he accepted, returned to Judaism. The argument, as most arguments, was left inconclusive.[100] The above discussion was the more revealing because Dr. Weizmann is commonly considered an unreligious Jew.

On October 22, 1948 McDonald wrote his accountant and New York UJA treasurer Samuel Leidesdorf a letter summarizing the last forty-eight hours.

---

100. Weizmann offered Haber (1868–1934) the directorship of the Sieff Institute. Haber, a Nobel Prize-winning chemist, began the move to Palestine in 1934, but died of heart failure en route. He had converted to Lutheranism to further his academic career in Imperial Germany. See Daniel Charles, *Master Mind: The Rise and Fall of Fritz Haber, the Nobel Laureate Who Launched the Age of Chemical Warfare* (New York: Harper Collins, 2005).

Perhaps the most significant aspect of these [military] operations and those which followed during the last two days—the cease-fire order is expected at three this afternoon—was the failure of the Egyptians to receive any substantial aid either directly or indirectly from their "allies"—the Iraqis or Abdullah's Arab Legion. The current interpretation here among the Israeli people is that the heads of the other Arab states do not grieve at Egypt's discomfiture. The events of the next days may confirm or weaken this theory. I prefer not to give away my own interpretation. . . .

The prompt action of the Security Council in ordering a cease-fire and the return of the troops of both sides to the positions they held before the operations began is resented publicly on the ground that the Security Council, during the truce, did nothing to force the Egyptians to carry out the Mediator's order to permit Jewish convoys to pass southward to the Negev colonies. That the Security Council acted only after the Israeli forces had taken the matter successfully into their own hands is regarded by the man in the streets here as proof that the UN either cannot or will not force truce observance by the Arab states, but that the Security Council is instead quick to act when the Israeli forces have gained or are about to gain an advantage, even if this is, as in the Negev, to rectify, according to Tel Aviv, a truce violation by the Egyptians. Hence, the universal popular support of the government's decision to settle this issue by their own strength. . . .

After supper at the club of the [Sieff] Institute, the Weizmanns, their guests, and we all arrived at the concert promptly at 8:30. Leonard was in fine form. . . . As the first movement [of the Beethoven concerto] was nearing its end, police and army officials were visibly in action and Weizmann's aide-de-camp came to whisper in his ear that an air raid was on and to ask him if he would go to the shelter. His answer was "no." And, naturally, ours . . . was also "no." As the first movement ended there was a pause during which an announcement from the stage explained the situation and offered an opportunity for anyone to leave who wished to do so. Only a few people left; personally, I saw only two go.

Leonard came back to the stage, was cheered and began the second movement [of Beethoven's Piano Concerto No. 1]. What an eerie feeling to sit there listening to the indescribable beauty of this slow movement . . . conscious that there is a chance (admittedly only a very slight one, but still a chance) that suddenly the roof might cave in. . . . Never do I expect to hear Beethoven or any other music sound so heavenly, contrasting as it did with the frightfulness of war, which the air raid brought so near to us.

Friday, October 22

Bobby and I reached the Kaplans' at 1:15 for lunch. Others there included, besides our host, the Ben-Gurions, Horowitz, Weisgal, Meyer Steinglass,[101]

---

101. Meyer F. Steinglass (1907–1997), journalist, editor of the *Brooklyn Examiner, New Palestine, Toronto Jewish Examiner*; pioneer in public relations, particularly in the use of full-page advertising; helped found United Jewish Appeal; publicity director of Israel Bonds (1951–1978).

and Henry Morgenthau. Ben-Gurion and I had a brief private talk. He asked me what I had been hearing from Washington, to which I truthfully replied "nothing of consequence and nothing at all about the recent events in Paris or the Negev." As to these, he emphasized that the Security Council resolution did not require but merely recommended—among other actions—the return to the Thursday positions following the cease-fire. The other two were keeping the crossroad open and consideration of refugees. I took advantage of our time together to give him a little of what I said to our government about the Arab refugee problem. I stressed with him that non-progress on this issue must have an unfortunate effect on Israel. Though he seemed rather non-committal, I think there was an advantage in having let him know what I had done.

The discussion during the first part of the luncheon was desultory, starting one subject and dropping it and getting nowhere in particular. One reason perhaps was that no one wished or thought it proper to discuss there seriously any of the subjects that were uppermost in our minds, for example, the Negev, the UJA row, etc. Meyer Weisgal, as usual, talked volubly but to no particular point. Morgenthau seemed to me very quiet and almost dull. Mr. and Mrs. Kaplan were quiet. It was not until the question of [Joseph Ernest] Renan's famous aphorism "The desert is the father of monotheism" [was brought up] that the discussion took some form and life. Ben-Gurion showed an extraordinary knowledge of Renan[102] and of many other writers. He waxed enthusiastic about a current Jewish writer on Jewish history who in his first seven volumes has developed what Ben-Gurion characterized as a most interesting new theory, which denies that Judaism is debtor, as it is commonly said, to any of the other ancient religions for its monotheism or other fundamental concept.[103] Thus, the table talk ended on a civilized note. Though we were breaking up almost exactly at three o'clock, Ben-Gurion showed no tendency to look at his watch as the deadline for the cease-fire order came nearer. In answer to my question how he managed to read so much, he replied that he slept very little and read at night.

During the remaining time at the house, I had a nice visit with Mrs. Ben-Gurion, who urged me to change dates so that we could lunch with them on Monday. Comparing housekeeping problems with Bobby, she said she hoped sometime to have a maid regularly and one who would not say, as does her present part-time worker, when she is asked to work on a holiday, "You should be the last to exploit a worker."

We took Henry Morgenthau home to the house, and after we had both had a nap, we talked at some length. He was visibly refreshed by his rest. First, he gave me a clear and, I think, objective picture of the three-sided conflict in the UJA: the Neumann-Silver-ZOA combination; the large city federations, and Henry Montor's group of some thirty large contributors. They are meeting

102. Joseph Ernest Renan (1823–1892), French scholar of early Judaism, Christianity, and of the origins of nations.
103. Ben-Gurion probably refers to Salo W. Baron, *A Social and Religious History of the Jews*, which eventually reached nineteen volumes.

this week in Pittsburgh, where Morgenthau hopes there may be a compromise solution. Montor, Morgenthau reports, is willing to replace his long "ten year record" letter of resignation by a simple two-line one to Rabbi Israel Goldstein if there is a peaceful adjustment to power. In answer to my question as to where Kaplan and his colleagues here stand, Morgenthau replied they are trying to stay out of the matter. Earlier at lunch, Weisgal charged that the Provisional Government had made [an] almost fatal blunder by yielding to Silver and Neumann in their demand for the withdrawal of the Provisional Government's members from the Jewish Agency. Ben-Gurion's reply had been, "One war at a time is enough."

Morgenthau's talk and mine then turned to our role here and the attitude of Washington and Tel Aviv on a number of issues. We had hardly time, however, to do more than begin these exchanges when he had to leave. It was agreed that we would have a long talk the following Monday after we had both lunched with the Ben-Gurions. I should have noted above that Ben-Gurion's most important comment about the Negev fighting was that the victory was being won by about one-fourth of the Israel armies, and his confirmation of what I said earlier, that the Egyptians had appealed for aid and Abdullah had refused it (a cable or communication of some sort had been intercepted).[104]

A pleasant hour with Mr. Moses Bailey of the American Friends Service Committee, who is here to spy out the land preliminary to sending a team of five or six persons to work among the refugees. In typical Quaker style, their project will be small and carried out in an area where they hope to be able to make a contribution towards better Arab-Jewish relations. His people, he said, have no ambition to make "little Christians."[105]

All during the day, when I had time to think about Ruth's letter, which came that morning, I had become increasingly annoyed at the implications in it, in her report of Ben Abrams's statement to her at dinner at his house the evening before she wrote her letter of September 30. My feelings, which were shared by Bobby, were in part put in a letter of this date to Ruth to be shown to Ben Abrams.

---

104. The Arab Legion still suffered from ammunition shortages. On October 12, three days before Operation Yoav, Glubb warned Legion officers in Jerusalem not to fire on Jews there lest the Israelis attack and the Legion be defeated. The Israelis had orders not to open fire in Jerusalem during the operations in the south. Glubb accepted the Israeli occupation of Be'er Sheva and hoped that Transjordan could still possess, aside from Samaria and Judea, the southern Negev (which Israel still did not control) and the Gaza Strip. Bar-Joseph, *The Best of Enemies*, 132–133; Morris, *The Road to Jerusalem*, 194–196.

105. Moses Bailey (1893–1994), one of the first Quakers to arrive in Palestine in the summer of 1948. In late September, when Bailey asked if the American Friends Service Committee could work in Israel, Arthur Lourie expressed skepticism, pointing to the Quakers' earlier connection with Khalil Totah, an anti-Jewish propagandist in the United States. Yet, as Lourie informed Eytan, it would be politically difficult to reject Quaker overtures. Eytan concurred, and in late September 1948, the Israeli government allowed a small Quaker team led by Bailey to function in Israel. See Nancy Gallagher, *Quakers in the Israeli-Palestinian Conflict*, 47–48. On Totah, see Goda et al., eds., *To the Gates of Jerusalem*, 37.

On September 4, 1948, McDonald conveyed to his friend Ben Abrams a series of worries regarding the State Department's insufficient budget for the new mission, and the potential effect on McDonald's own finances. "The cost of living here," he told Abrams, "is fantastic; an egg costs 32¢; a third-rate hotel in which we stayed three weeks was as expensive as the Waldorf. . . . My present rough estimate—it cannot yet be accurate—is that I shall have to spend from $2,000 to $4,000 a month above my total Government income. This is substantially more than I planned for and I hope it will not ruin us."

McDonald continued, "My official duties are intensely interesting but onerous. They occupy seven days a week. Saturday cannot be treated as a holiday for us and Sunday is the busiest day of the week for the [Israeli] Government and, therefore, for us. . . . Moreover, the pressure of important business has been and—as far as I can judge—will continue to be so demanding that none of us shall have any New York luxurious weekends. . . . My solace is that the task is thrillingly absorbing. Indeed it is too much so because it occupied many of my night hours when I am in bed and should be asleep. I shan't mind, however, if I can be useful."[106]

McDonald was also disappointed in the State Department's support of the Bernadotte Plan, as well as the Department's propensity to exclude him from discussions on Israel's future. Truman, meanwhile, seemed unwilling to repudiate the Bernadotte Plan before the presidential elections. Right-wing terror was also a nagging threat following Bernadotte's murder.[107]

Ruth had suggested that McDonald resign. McDonald told her that he wanted to stay. "As the United States representative I can properly be influenced in this matter of staying only by: 1) The feelings of my own Government, and, 2) My personal judgment about my usefulness." Whether the State Department listened to him regarding its support for the Bernadotte Plan "can only be known to a few top people in Washington." As for the Israeli government's attitude toward him, McDonald said, "I am quite satisfied." He continued that he regarded the personal dangers as "slight," and that in terms of personal expenditures, "no one but myself can properly decide whether or not I 'cannot afford' financially to stay. I must be the sole judge whether the probable financial loss is too heavy for me to bear. And I intend to make that decision irrespective of anyone else's judgment—even yours—my dear."[108]

. . . .

After Operation Yoav, the State Department allowed for possible concessions to the Israelis in the northern Negev, "at least," as Lovett said on October 23, "to the extent of a salient into Negev as far as [the] Beersheba-Gaza Road." Marshall agreed, though he refrained from saying so publicly, lest the Israelis demand the entire Negev and the whole peace process fall apart. "The Negev," Marshall told Lovett, "[is a] very

106. McDonald to Abrams, September 4, 1948, McDonald Papers, Columbia University, box 6, folder 2.
107. McDonald to Abrams, October 19, 1948, McDonald Papers, Columbia University, box 6, folder 2.
108. McDonald to Ruth, October 23, 1948, McDonald Papers, USHMM, box 7, folder 7.

*sore point with [the] Arabs. . . . To inform them [at] this juncture [that] we favor giv-
ing northern Negev to Israel would cause incalculable harm [to] our relations [with]
Egypt and other Arab states."*[109] *But Israel's offensive in the Negev had changed the
discussion in Paris.*

*Truman was loath to break with Marshall openly on the eve of the presidential
election and in light of the Berlin crisis. But he slowly distanced himself from the State
Department on Israel. The Democratic Party Platform of July 1948 called for full US
recognition of Israel, Israel's admission to the UN, loans to Israel, recognition of Israel's borders as allotted to the Jewish state in November 1947, and for any changes in
these borders to occur only with Israel's consent. In response to a statement by Republican presidential candidate Thomas Dewey on October 22, Truman on the 24th—
eight days before the election—publicly endorsed the platform. He also ordered that all
official US statements at the UN be cleared with the White House.*[110]

*Bevin protested that Israel had violated the arms embargo by importing weapons
from Czechoslovakia. He warned that if Israeli forces should attack King Abdullah's
Arab Legion next, Britain would invoke its defense treaty with Transjordan. From
London, Ambassador Douglas warned that US support for Israeli expansion into the
Negev would condone aggression, further alienate the Arabs, leave the Middle East
unstable, and play into the hands of the Soviets. "My understanding with Bevin,"
Douglas reported, "clearly implies that if the US takes a pro-Israeli step Britain shall
feel free to take [a] pro-Arab step."*[111]

Shabbat, October 23

Long conference with Knox and Colonel van der Velde about many subjects, including the possibility of my going to Paris. Knox drafted a telegram of
inquiry to the Department [for McDonald].

*Knox's draft reads: "In connection with Arab refugee discussions in Paris I would
be willing if [Department] desires to go [to] Paris for short time and contribute
such knowledge as I have gained from 15 years' association [with] relief and refugee
problems."*[112]

109. On this problem see Lovett to Truman, October 19, 1948, *FRUS*, 1948, v. V, pt. 2,
1494–1495; Lovett to US Delegation, Paris, no. 241, October 19, 1948, *FRUS*, 1948, v. V, pt.2,
1496–1497; Lovett to US Delegation, Paris, no. 286, October 23, 1948, *FRUS*, 1948, v. V, pt. 2,
1508–1509. Marshall to Lovett, no. 476, October 25, 1948, *FRUS*, 1948, v. V, pt. 2, 1514–1515.
110. Epstein to Eytan, October 14, 1948, *DFPI*, v. 2, d. 26; Epstein to Shertok, October 20, 1948, *DFPI*, v. 2, d. 38; Epstein to Eytan, October 21, 1948, *DFPI*, v. 2, d. 48; Epstein to
Shertok, October 25–26, 1948, *DFPI*, d. 60; John Acacia, *Clark Clifford: The Wise Man of Washington* (Lexington: University Press of Kentucky, 2009), pp. 114, 117–118; Hahn, *Caught in the
Middle East*, 57–58.
111. Douglas to acting secretary of state, no. 4621, October 26, 1948, *FRUS*, 1948, v. V, pt.
2, 1516–1518; Marshall to acting secretary of state, no. 90, October 27, 1948, *FRUS*, 1948, v. V,
pt. 2, 1520–1521; Douglas to acting secretary of state, no. 4683, October 29, 1948, *FRUS*, 1948,
v. V, pt. 2, 1530–1533.
112. McDonald Papers, USHMM, box 7, folder 7.

Knox reported on his and van der Velde's long talk with Shiloah about many subjects, including Marine guards in Jerusalem,[113] the usefulness there of Dr. Avraham Bergman, Dr. Joseph's associate;[114] the acceptance of our naval attaché, etc. Shiloah said that there were no active negotiations at the moment between Israel and Transjordan. Shiloah was interested in Pinkerton's mission, which Knox opined might be about refugees.[115] Shiloah also asked about the Troutbeck and McClintock visit to Rhodes. In answer, Knox gave the suggested reply of refugees.[116]

One of Knox's worries at the moment is what should be the action on the pending application of Peter Bergson, Shmuel Merlin,[117] and Menachem Begin for visas to the States. After a considerable discussion, we were of the opinion that if our views were asked, we should favor granting them on the ground that not to do so would be to discriminate among different party members here. Knox also reported that Greenberg of the Foreign Office had conversationally raised a number of questions with him, such as why had we not sent New Year's [Rosh Hashanah] greetings to the government when the Russians had done so. To Knox's relief, I reminded him of my talk with Miss Herlitz and the announcement in the paper that we had sent such greetings at the time I visited Dr. Weizmann at Rehovot the week following his return here.

Early afternoon: Knox and van der Velde at my request came out to hear my theory that Joseph's warning—about increasing tenseness in Jerusalem resulting from non-fulfillment of the Arabs' promise to abide by the mediator's decision that the road to Mount Scopus should be opened for limited purposes—might presage the Israeli army's taking the matter into their own hands as they had in the Negev. I felt like an amateur strategist as I illustrated

113. Twenty Marines were first posted to guard the US consulate after the killing of Thomas Wasson in May 1948, and they were reinforced by twenty-nine more in October. Two were wounded thereafter in protests. Leo J. Daugherty III, *The Marine Corps and the State Department: Enduring Partners in United States Foreign Policy, 1798–2007* (Jefferson, NC: McFarland & Co, 2008), 87.

114. Avraham Bergman [later Biran] (1909–2008), noted archaeologist; chief assistant to the military government in Jerusalem (Dov Joseph); after February 1949, district commissioner for Jerusalem (under the Ministry of the Interior).

115. Lowell C. Pinkerton (1894–1959), US consul general to Jerusalem, 1941–1945 (and OSS representative there after 1942); US minister plenipotentiary to Beirut, 1946–1951. Arab refugees from Haifa and Jaffa living in Beirut appealed to Pinkerton for aid in returning, and Pinkerton reported extensively on them to Washington.

116. Sir John Troutbeck (1894–1971), head of the British Middle East Office in Cairo, and Robert McClintock of the Department of State's Near East Division, had met secretly in Rhodes with Bernadotte in mid-September. Israeli intelligence suggested that Troutbeck had insisted that the Bernadotte Plan exclude the entire Negev from Israeli control. Bernadotte, who initially placed Israel's southern boundary at the 31st parallel, ultimately agreed with Troutbeck. McClintock first suggested an Israeli salient reaching to Be'er Sheva, but later recommended that the State Department endorse the Bernadotte Plan in its entirety. See the meeting of the Israeli delegation to the UN, October 11, 1948, *DFPI*, v. 2, d. 21; Michael J. Cohen, *Fighting World War III in the Middle East* (London: Frank Cass, 1997), 107.

117. Shmuel Merlin (1910–1994), Bessarabian-born Revisionist Zionist leader; arrived in Israel on the *Altalena*; helped found Herut with Begin; served as the party's general secretary.

my points on the detailed map of the Jerusalem area. A telegram was drafted to the department.

> *The Mount Scopus agreement of July 7, 1948, signed by local Israeli and Arab Legion commanders through the UN Truce Commission, dealt with the isolated Israeli enclave of Mount Scopus in eastern Jerusalem, which housed Hadassah Hospital and Hebrew University. Mount Scopus was to be demilitarized, with the UN assuming responsibility for its security. It was to receive food and water in biweekly Israeli convoys through the Arab-controlled areas with Arab Legion and UN escort. The agreement deteriorated during the second truce, as the Arab Legion halted repairs to water pipes and slowed food convoys. The Israelis had pressed for open access to Mount Scopus since the destruction of the Latrun pumping station in August 1948.[118]*
>
> *McDonald emphasized Joseph's statements concerning, in Joseph's words, the "serious and critical position of Israeli police and maintenance staffs on Mt. Scopus" and the inability of the Truce Commission to enforce its terms. The Provisional Government, he said, "might be preparing to decide, as in [the] case of [the] Negev, that if [the] Arabs won't open [the] supply road to Mt. Scopus in conformity [with the] UN decision [the] Israeli Army will do so by force. Such action would relieve Mt. Scopus and also complete Israeli tactical domination [of the] New and Old City of Jerusalem."[119]*

A little earlier, Gurdus had called and told me of Joseph's emphasis, which Bobby and I had heard of the previous night on the Jerusalem radio. He also spoke of the Moscow broadcast in several languages, including Yiddish, attacking savagely the Gaza government and the United States' support of the decision in the Political Committee of the UN General Assembly to delay action on the Palestine problem.[120] He indicated that he would like to know "off the record" what my reaction was: I had none.

Sunday, October 24

Worked as usual in the morning. In the afternoon, Moses Bailey came in and reported that he had had a completely satisfactory conference with Miss Herlitz, who offered all facilities and put him in touch with the appropriate authority. Tentatively, he has decided that the Friends project should be in

118. See Progress Report of the United Nations Mediator on Palestine, September 16, 1948, http://unispal.un.org/UNISPAL.NSF/0/AB14D4AAFC4E1BB985256204004F55FA.
119. McDonald to secretary of state, no. 204, October 24, 1946, NARA, RG 59, 501.BB Palestine, box 2121, folder 2.
120. On October 23, the UN General Assembly's Political Committee narrowly voted to delay the Palestine debate for one week. The US delegation had pressed, on Truman's insistence, for delay until after the presidential election. Marshall reasoned that an additional delay would not be necessary, since the first week of debate would concern procedural matters. See *General Assembly, 3rd Session, Part I, First Committee, Summary Reports, 1948*, 243; Lovett to secretary of state, no. 72, October 18, 1948, *FRUS, 1948*, v. V, pt. 2, 1489–1490; Marshall to acting secretary of state, no. 462, October 23, 1948, *FRUS, 1948*, v. V, pt. 2, 1511.

Nazareth, where there would be an excellent opportunity not only to succor Arab refugees but also to contribute, he hoped, towards Arab-Jewish cooperation.[121] It was a relief to talk with someone whose plans were not discouragingly beyond his means.

Monday, October 25

Luncheon at Ben-Gurion's house. Present besides the prime minister and Madame Morgenthau was the guest of honor, Henry Morgenthau; and Bobby and Knox and I completed the party. It was much more successful than the luncheon a few days earlier for Morgenthau at Kaplan's. This time Ben-Gurion talked very readily, entertaining Bobby with his account of his self-teaching of Turkish and later speaking frankly about his concern for the fate of Manara.[122] Morgenthau said that he thought Truman might carry only three states but disavowed any knowledge of what might be expected from the new president or from John Foster Dulles.[123] Our Israeli friends naturally showed intense interest in these American subjects.

After lunch we went upstairs to Ben-Gurion's extraordinary library, which covers all the walls to the ceilings of two rooms. His greatest pride is his Greek philosophy collection, all in the original language. He told us, too, of his joy in securing recently a very rare edition of a set of volumes in Eastern religion. His books on Palestine and the neighboring states made me envious. He said that his real desire was to be able to hide himself in his library. Before luncheon, Ben-Gurion, in a light mood, chafed Pinhas Rosen on the new Progressive Party and Peretz Bernstein on the General Zionist Party.[124] The progressives are a liberal, conservative party seeking to strengthen private initiative and individual enterprise and to counteract the alleged class bias of the Mapai and the Mapam.

Parenthetically, I let Ben-Gurion know that I was seeing Begin and that he and his colleagues were seeking visas to go to the US Ben-Gurion lifted his eyebrows and asked what they were going to do in the States. Morgenthau hoped that they would not go, because he had trouble enough at home. I indicated that if the Provisional Government did not want them to leave, the obvious answer was to refuse exit visas. I implied that it was not for us to decide whether or not it was suitable of them to go to the States.

Mrs. Ben-Gurion throughout was a friendly, homey, and a little-anxious hostess. But again, I saw nothing in her manner or actions to justify the criticism current among Tel Aviv women. Their attitude is not very different from that of many people at home towards Eleanor and later Mrs. Truman. Morgenthau

---

121. To demonstrate their aim of reconciliation, the AFSC wanted to aid Jewish children and Palestinian Arabs in the Nazareth region. See Gallagher, *Quakers in the Israeli-Palestinian Conflict*, 46–47.
122. See entry of October 28, 1948; also Morris, *1948*, 338–340.
123. Dewey publicly rejected the Bernadotte Plan on October 22, 1948.
124. Entry of August 27, 1948.

begged off from keeping his appointment that afternoon on the ground that Ben-Gurion had asked him to stay there. He is coming to me on Wednesday at five.

Miss Clark and Barnes returned from Haifa in time for tea but without Guy Hope, who was delayed in Paris.[125] Mr. Knox, who came late for supper, brought Bobby her first birthday gift, some lovely roses. After dinner, Knox and I worked for an hour or so. He seemed to me to be needlessly concerned about the top-secret [telegram draft to Washington], which I had read with him at the office earlier. It did not seem to me to imply any intention by the Department to leave us out on the end of a limb in connection with our transmittal of the "trying on for size" suggestion.[126]

Tuesday, October 26

Early morning spent [dictating] important letters to Hoover, Dulles et al.

In light of the expected victory by Thomas Dewey on November 2 and his expected naming of Dulles as secretary of state, McDonald wrote Dulles that "the Russian Mission is substantially larger than ours and is apparently, unlike ourselves, not embarrassed by rigid financial restrictions. Evidently the Kremlin intends to miss no opportunity to make its influence felt here and from here throughout the whole area." McDonald cautiously added that Marshall, Lovett, and the Department were alert to the mission's needs and that the US staff would be expanded in a few weeks with officials who could speak Hebrew, Yiddish, and Russian. McDonald added his concerns regarding Arab refugees and the need for stronger UN programs, noting, "This problem of Arab refugees is more than a human one. It also has its significant and far-reaching political implications. . . . Perhaps sometime we shall have a chance to talk about them."[127]

[In the afternoon], I arrived at the office too late to see Knox, but there I had an opportunity to read two important telegrams, the one reversing the instructions of a day or two earlier regarding the south and the other giving the text of the General Assembly resolution on Arab refugees.

UN General Assembly Resolution 212, eventually published on November 19, 1948 and entitled "Assistance to Palestinian Refugees," noted the refugee problem's "immediate urgency," called for nearly $30 million to aid 500,000 refugees over the next nine months, and invited agencies such as the Red Cross and International Refugee Organization to help in the effort.

125. Ashley Guy Hope (1914–1982), foreign service officer in the mission in Tel Aviv beginning October 15, 1948. See Ashley Guy Hope, *Journal of a Journey: Adventures in Life, 1914–1974* (self-published, 1976).
126. Entry of September 2, 1948.
127. McDonald to Dulles, October 28, 1948, McDonald Papers, USHMM, box 7, folder 7.

The late afternoon before Miss Clark's tea-birthday party and afterwards, discussed with Knox a number of matters, including that of Arab refugees.

Wednesday, October 27

Dr. Jacob Herzog and Dr. Chaim Vardi of the Ministry for Religious Affairs, Department of Christian Communities, during more than an hour and a quarter, gave me an intensely interesting account of their mission to the Vatican.

McDonald had failed to warm Pope Pius XII toward Israel during his July visit. The Israelis learned after McDonald's meeting with the pope that "[the] Vatican likely [will] be [the] last state to recognize Israel. . . . High-level Israeli diplomatic visit discouraged, Pope stating categorically [that he] would not receive Weizmann."[128] *In September Pius XII explained to Myron Taylor—the president's personal representative to the Vatican—that "unwarranted attacks on Catholic institutions and members of our religious orders by irresponsible Jewish elements have caused a painful impression" and that "Arabs have not attacked or molested Catholics, and have generally shown consideration and tolerance."*[129]

The secret and "unofficial" mission of Herzog and Vardi from September 22 to October 7, 1948, which McDonald had facilitated, primarily concerned the religious rights of Catholic communities in Israel. Herzog told Vatican officials that reports concerning Jewish attacks on Christians and Holy Places were greatly exaggerated, if not completely false. He also explained that communists had no influence in Israel. In return, Vatican officials stated that instructions had been sent to Catholic presses to refrain from defamatory attacks on Israel; that regular relations would be established between Israeli authorities and papal delegates in Israel; that the Vatican would stay neutral on the Israeli-Arab war and on the issue of refugees; and that a compromise on the status of Jerusalem might be possible.[130] *On October 24, 1948 in the encyclical* In Multiplicibus Curis *Pope Pius XII bemoaned damages to the Holy Places in Palestine and called for the internationalization of Jerusalem and its outskirts as well as international guarantees for Holy Places elsewhere in Palestine.*

[Herzog and Vardi] said that my letters of introduction to Mr. Gowen and Count Galeazzi had been invaluable to them, that Mr. Gowen had exerted himself throughout the whole of their stay of nearly three weeks to open doors for them and to instruct them in the ways of Vatican diplomacy. In particular at the beginning, he warned the young men against being discouraged by what might seem to them the coolness of the atmosphere when they were first received.

128. *DFPI*, v. I, d. 466.
129. Quoted in Ciani, "The Vatican, American Catholics, and the Struggle for Palestine," 226–227.
130. See Bialer, *Cross on the Star of David*, 12–13; documents in McDonald Papers, USHMM, box 7, folder 8.

The first conference, following the introductory one with Gowen, was with Count Galeazzi in his office at the Vatican. The latter, as special delegate of the Pontifical Commission of the State of the Vatican City, as personal adviser to His Holiness and as consulting architect, was naturally in a position to be of the greatest assistance. He explained the Vatican setup and was instrumental in speeding up the visitors' first interview with Monsignor Pietro Sigismondi, one of the two assistants or under secretaries of state. A few days later they had an interview with His Excellency, Archbishop Valerio Valeri (former nuncio to France) of the Oriental Congregation. It was here, in what one might call the Near Eastern Division of the Vatican Foreign Office, that they hoped to get beyond the stage of general principles reached in the discussion with Sigismondi, but again the talk was on the broader level in an atmosphere, which at first was chilly to cold, but became warmer towards the end.

The second interview with Count Galeazzi was even more cordial than the first, he assuring them that they had made an excellent beginning. The second conference with Sigismondi was not attended by the American Monsignor McGurl, who had been present at the first. This time Sigismondi was from the beginning cordial, urging that since the beginning of a basis of understanding in principle had been obtained, the job now was for the young men to have their government work out the special situations on the spot with the Apostolic Delegate Testa in Bethlehem.[131] They explained that it would be impossible to get in touch with the delegate because, for reason of safety, he felt he could not cross the lines into Jewish Jerusalem, and it was wholly impossible for the Jewish representatives to cross the Arab lines. It was agreed, therefore, that another representative chosen by the apostolic delegate, perhaps Monsignor Vergani, the vicar for the whole of Galilee, might be the man.[132]

In the final conference with Gowen, where Galeazzi dropped in, the young men were again assured that they had made a substantial beginning. Their estimate and that of Gowen is embodied in very restrained language in a letter written by Herzog to Gowen and approved by the latter. The Jewish representatives felt that they had convinced the Vatican authorities of the government's good will, that this conviction had been made known to His Holiness, that there was an understanding now in the Vatican that the abuses, desecrations, etc., had been the work of refugees whom there had been no time to train, and that these excesses were deeply deplored by the Provisional Government authorities. Beyond these, they thought that there was implicit in one of the statements made to them and repeated to the effect that the Vatican stood on

131. Gustavo Testa (1886–1969), apostolic delegate to Palestine until the late 1950s; unsympathetic to Israel, partly because the IDF confiscated his archive during the fighting in 1948 for intelligence purposes; mentioned as a contact in Herzog's meeting with Sigismondi of September 30, 1948. *DFPI*, v. 1, d. 554.

132. Antonio Vergani (1905–1960), general vicar of the Latin Patriarch of Jerusalem for the Galilee; made several visits to Christian Holy Places in the north and reported to the Vatican on his findings, summer 1948. See *DFPI*, v. 1, d. 554, n. 4.

the ground laid by His Holiness two years ago in his statement to a group of representatives from the Arab States to the effect that he supported traditional and acquired rights, thus indicating, as the Jews thought, a recognition of their special status. Moreover, they were of the opinion that the Vatican, according to the authorities there studying the Palestine situation continuously and closely, was now convinced that a strong Israel could be an important factor in the balance of forces between the East and the West. A revealing and an amusing quotation was given from one of the Vatican spokesmen in answer to a Jewish statement, that the former [Arab states] had sometimes put forward untrue pronouncements. The comment was: "No, not untrue, it is merely that their oriental imaginations cause them to lose sight of the truth. Because we have made agreements with them and some of them are represented at the Vatican, they now regard us as allies who have betrayed them."

At the end of our conference I felt no regret at having them in my notes of introduction, rather the contrary. I wondered, however, and on this point they could not enlighten me much, to what extent the substance of these discussions was transmitted to the heads of the hierarchy overseas. The only indication they gave was that Monsignor Angelo Roncalli, papal nuncio in Paris, who with Father Riley in Istanbul, had been directly responsible for saving the lives of thousands of Jews, had in Paris received Herzog with warm affection. This might just have been a continuation of their close relationship in the Turkish days, but Monsignor Roncalli went on to give indication that he had reason to feel that progress had been made in Rome.[133]

As they were leaving, Herzog told me such interesting bits about Ira Hirschmann in Turkey that I am anxious to know more, and am suggesting that Herzog go through a volume of Hirschmann's, which I will give him, marking the doubtful passages.[134] He credited Hirschmann with having saved thousands of Jewish lives by his strenuous and imperious manner towards the diplomatic representatives of the Balkan states during the last stages of the war. But Herzog also said that Hirschmann's indiscretions were incredible, illustrating it

133. Angelo Roncalli (1881—1963), future Pope John XXIII (1958–1963); papal nuncio in Istanbul, 1934–1944, then to liberated France, 1944–1953; informed the Vatican of the Nazi genocide of the Jews; met with Jewish Agency representatives as well as Rabbi Yitzhak Herzog to discuss rescue operations; undertook interventions and rescue work ranging from Slovakia to Hungary to Bulgaria to Transnistria. Yitzhak Herzog met Roncalli in Paris in 1946 to ask for his help in ensuring that the Jewish orphans hidden in Catholic convents would be returned to the Jewish community, a policy for which Roncalli encountered Vatican resistance. See Friling, *Arrows in the Dark*, v. 1, 218–219, 253–256, v. 2, 5; Peter Hoffmann, "Roncalli in the Second World War: Peace Initiatives, the Greek Famine, and the Persecution of the Jews," *Journal of Ecclesiastical History* 40, no. 1 (1989): 74–99; Bialer, *Cross on the Star of David*, 194.

134. Ira A. Hirschmann (1901–1989), Baltimore-born Jewish American businessman and adviser to Mayor Fiorello LaGuardia of New York; War Refugee Board representative in Istanbul, 1944–1945; helped some 6,500 Jews fleeing through Romania reach Palestine through Turkey by negotiating with Romanian and Turkish authorities and by procuring ships. Herzog refers to Hirschmann's memoirs, *Life Line to a Promised Land* (New York: Vanguard Press, 1946), which tended to overstate Hirshmann's own role at the expense of other US representatives. See Friling, *Arrows in the Dark*, v. 2, passim.

with the latter's announcement in a loud voice in the hotel lobby, where there were many Nazi agents, that a highly secret guarantee by the United States of two million pounds on a Turkish ship to carry refugees had been granted. Not necessarily because of this indiscretion, the ship never sailed. I accepted Herzog's invitation, extended on behalf of the minister of religion, to visit for luncheon a nearby and very orthodox community—Agudat—next Tuesday.

Mr. Knox brought me Mr. Lovett's cordial and very long telegram about my refugee suggestions.[135]

Lovett wrote McDonald that he concurred "fully [with] your views [regarding the] disastrous character [of the] Arab refugee problem," that McDonald's ideas had been forwarded to the UN delegation and to US missions in Arab capitals, and that they were also "under consideration at [the] highest levels" including the White House. The American Red Cross, meanwhile, had became more active in organizing distribution of American supplies to Arab refugees—including food and clothing—both for the short-term emergency for 1948 and what was expected to be a long-term problem.[136]

We drafted a reply supporting the draft resolution with its proposed amendment and urging the designation of a director at the top, of [Herbert] Hoover's caliber in Belgium.[137] There was amusement and satisfaction in knowing that my earlier memorandum had been an important element in the drastic moves during the last few days to enlarge and tighten up the efforts on behalf of the Arab refugees.

Mr. Morgenthau came in at 6:30. In the midst of talk about the political situation, I showed him something I had been working on. He was shocked that I thought there was any possibility of the situation I envisaged. Evidently, he had been learning very rapidly during his few days here, so rapidly that he could not understand how any authority, much less that to which I spoke, could be as ununderstanding as the attitude under consideration would have indicated.

Dinner at the Butsam Café of Dizengoff Circle given by the Tel Aviv Municipal Council for Morgenthau, Curtis Dall Boettiger, Nathan Straus, and Steinglass. About thirty people were present besides members of the council, several members of the cabinet, Kaplan, Rosen, et al. Following an elaborate

---

135. McDonald refers to his despatch to secretary of state, no. 188, October 17, 1948, [attention president and acing secretary], *FRUS*, 1948, v. V, pt. 2, 1486–1487.

136. Lovett to McDonald, no. 173, October 22, 1948, McDonald Papers, USHMM, box 7, folder 7; McDonald to secretary of state, no. 212, October 27, 1948, NARA, RG 59, 501.BB Palestine, box 2121, folder 1. See also news reports of October 26 and 28, 1948, in McDonald Papers, USHMM, box 7, folder 7.

137. McDonald refers to Hoover's work heading the Commission for Relief in Belgium during World War I and, more immediately, to the eventual General Assembly Resolution 212 of November 19, 1948. It was based on a US-proposed draft, approved by a delegation from the General Assembly on October 20. See *FRUS*, 1948, v. V. pt. 2, 1497–1498.

five-course dinner during which I chatted most of the time with Nathan Straus, Mayor Rokach spoke for about fifteen minutes. His address was mostly a tribute to Morgenthau and the latter's father, to the father of Straus and some pleasant words about myself.

Conference of forty-five minutes or so with Knox, joined by Colonel van der Velde and Cummings on the balcony of the Gat. I made my argument of the telegram which I had drafted, but Knox had the opposite opinion, that is, that the United States government was moving towards a fuller acceptance of the Provisional Government position on the Negev. I was not persuaded, but agreed that we'd leave the matter until the next morning, asking them meanwhile to study it further.

Thursday, October 28

A session with Knox and Colonel van der Velde and Cummings before going to the Foreign Office reception for Morgenthau. We shelved the proposed draft of last night and turned instead to consideration of the acting secretary's [Lovett's] cordial and very long telegram on the refugee situation and the proposed resolution amendment. We indicated our sense of encouragement and hoped that the new structure would be completed by leadership comparable to that which Hoover had given in World War I in Belgium.[138]

The Foreign Office reception was large and pleasantly informal. I chatted with many people, among them Ben-Gurion and his wife, the latter asking when we were going to invite them; Dr. and Mrs. Weizmann, to whom I introduced van der Velde, General Riley, and Captain Munsey, the last two of whom the Weizmanns said they would plan to invite out to Rehovot. With Mrs. Weizmann and Mrs. Ben-Gurion, I had an amusing conversation about housekeeping, order of arranging guests at the table and protocol; Mrs. Weizmann was telling about her Russian dinner to which, at the insistence of the protocol office she included one or two German-speaking members of the cabinet; to this Mrs. Ben-Gurion's reply was "I wouldn't have invited them." The two ladies, who I judge have not been really friends in the past, seemed to enjoy visiting one another. With Kaplan, I exchanged some words about his possible visit to the States. With one of the Agudat rabbis, I promised to visit one of the Agudat settlements.

Morgenthau and young Boettiger with Colonel Efraim Ben-Artzi[139] were at the house for tea. After this, Boettiger and I walked on the roof for an hour and a quarter. I was much impressed by the young man's discerning comprehension,

138. McDonald to secretary of state, October 27, 1948, McDonald Papers, USHMM, box 7, folder 7. McDonald indeed suggested that the UN name Herbert Hoover as the director of its efforts for Arab refugees.

139. Efraim Ben-Artzi (1910–2001), Polish-born officer; emigrated to Palestine, 1924; joined Haganah during 1929 Arab rebellion; served in British Army during World War II, reaching the rank of lieutenant colonel; helped found the intelligence branch of the IDF and served as IDF attaché to US and Canada, 1948–1950; IDF quartermaster general, 1950–1952; managing director of El Al Airlines, 1952–1960.

his breadth of knowledge and his confident, but not cocky attitude. His questions were to the point and his own observations and conclusions suggestive. His one concern was lest the military situation burst wide open and the Provisional Government subject itself to UN sanctions. In the north he reported that he had observed such substantial Israeli troop movements as might mean a major operation up there [see textbox 4.2].[140] He was emphatic in his criticism of any UN attempt to enforce a readjustment in the Negev, but he wondered how it would be possible for the Provisional Government much longer to restrain the army from a general offensive which he felt would be widely popular. But the young man not only talked, he listened with avid interest and will, I think, report accurately to his grandmother my views on refugees, sanctions, and personnel of the mission here. I predict for him a bright future.

Homey dinner with Morgenthau as the only guest. He was much more charming than I had found him earlier. Later, we spent an hour or so on the roof. He told me that up to then the Provisional Government had not been able to make up its mind on the United Jewish Appeal imbroglio; that Kaplan had not yet been invited by the United Palestine Appeal and did not intend to go unless the invitation came from both sides; he showed great concern about the political situation and sympathy with the Provisional Government's need for a quick solution. The way he spoke of this, rather than what he said, tended to support Boettiger's report that Morgenthau had been advising the Provisional Government in not exactly the same direction that I had been.

Friday, October 29

Hearing the news on the radio at eight of the British-Chinese [draft UN] resolution proposing consideration of sanctions unless there was a "withdrawal" to the lines of October 14 in the Negev, I asked Miss Clark to tell Knox and Colonel van der Velde to come out immediately after breakfast. They agreed that my fears of the night before last had been verified. We got off a strong telegram.

The British-Chinese resolution of October 28, 1948, called for the Security Council to endorse Acting Mediator Bunche's order to the Israeli and Egyptian governments to withdraw to the October 14 lines or face possible sanctions under Article 41 of the UN Charter.[141] Shertok informed Marshall that this would reward the Egyptians for invading Israeli territory and cutting off the Negev settlements, while allowing them to reinforce earlier lines in the Negev. Withdrawal to the October 14 line, he said, "would amount to an act of suicide . . . which the State of Israel in sheer self-preservation will be unable to commit."[142]

McDonald wrote to Washington that the resolution, if approved, would create "a tragic dilemma for Israel and US," because the Provisional Government would resist

140. Boettiger in fact predicted military action within a few days. McDonald to Janet, Halsey and Ruth, October 31, 1948, McDonald Papers, USHMM, box 7, folder 7.
141. See *Security Council, 3rd Year, No. 122*, 12.
142. Shertok to Marshall, October 29, 1948, *FRUS*, 1948, v. V, pt. 2, 1526–1527.

Textbox 4.2.
Operation Hiram

The UN Partition Resolution of November 29, 1947, had assigned the Eastern Galilee to the Jews, and the remainder of the Galilee to the Arabs. In the fighting from May to July 1948, the Israelis pressed into Western and Lower Galilee, leaving the Upper Galilee under Arab control. Operation Hiram, planned in September 1948, aimed to clear the remainder of the Galilee and destroy enemy forces there.

On October 22, units of the Arab Liberation Army (ALA) under the command of the Lebanese general Fawzi al-Qawuqji violated the cease-fire and captured an Israeli-held position overlooking Kibbutz Manara. ALA snipers placed Manara under siege. The Israelis demanded through UN observers that al-Qawuqji withdraw. Despite ammunition shortages for his three thousand troops, he refused, even when the regular Lebanese army ordered him to do so.

With the Egyptians defeated in the south, Ben-Gurion approved the start of operations in the Galilee. On October 28 four Israeli brigades, supported by aircraft, attacked. They surrounded ALA forces and their Syrian reinforcements in several key villages; other ALA forces simply fled. By October 31 the operation was complete, and a new UN cease-fire was in place. Israel now controlled the entire Galilee. It had been a key area in the first- and second-century Jewish revolts against the Romans and had been allocated to the Jews in the partition plan approved by the Royal Commission in 1937. With Ben-Gurion's approval, Israeli forces also occupied several villages within Lebanon—the first time the IDF crossed into sovereign Arab territory—perhaps intending to use Lebanese territory as a bargaining chip in subsequent negotiations.

Israel's northern offensive brought little international criticism. The Bernadotte Plan envisioned the Israelis receiving the Galilee in any event. The crippling of the ALA (its remnant disbanded in May 1949) pleased the Lebanese government. The British, who had no alliance with Lebanon or Syria, were more interested in the Negev. McDonald wrote privately, "The Jewish blow has been an answer to the advances of Fawzi al-Qawuqji, which had endangered and killed some of the defenders of my favorite colony, Manara, high in Galilee just across from the Lebanon frontier."[1]

Ben-Gurion had rejected the UN-imposed ceasefires as a legitimation of the Arab invasions and as detrimental to Israel. But he immediately confirmed Israel's commitment to international order. "The weakness of the UN has not gone unnoticed by us," he told the Provisional State Council on October 28. "But we believe taking advantage of it would be shortsighted. We believe it is in our interest as Jews and

---

1. McDonald to Janet, Halsey, and Ruth, October 31, 1948, McDonald Papers, USHMM, box 7, folder 7.

human beings to reinforce the authority and ability of the UN. A day in which the UN collapses—would be the darkest day in human history, and perhaps one of the most tragic in the history of our nation. We wish for world peace just as much, and perhaps more, than all nations of the world."[2]

The northern offensive had a dark side. Israeli units haphazardly killed some two hundred prisoners and civilians during and after the operation in a dozen or so villages. And though the Provisional Government gave no expulsion order, the offensive, while leaving 30,000 Arab residents of the Galilee in place, also triggered the expulsion and flight of some 30,000 Arabs from the Galilee into Lebanon. They were not allowed to return.

---

2. Minutes of the Provisional State Council, October 28, 1948, Ben-Gurion Archives. We are grateful to Tuvia Friling for this reference.

---

sanctions rather than yield. He reiterated that the Egyptians violated the truce by blockading the Negev settlements; that in the Israeli view, the Egyptian army had no right to be in the Negev owing to the UN's own 1947 partition plan; and that the Israeli offensive clarified the situation, opening the door for separate Israeli peace negotiations with Egypt. The UN threat of sanctions would only muddy the situation while stiffening Israeli resolve and giving the Soviets the chance to pose as Israel's sole friend on the Security Council.[143]

Truman understood the dangers of a split between the United States and Israel. On October 29 he personally informed Marshall that "I am deeply concerned over reports here of action taken in Security Council on Palestine Question. I hope that before this nation takes any position or any statement is made by our Delegation that I be advised of such contemplated action and the implications thereof."[144]

Just before [Bobby] left[145] came a telephone message from Knox that Washington had "relieved" me [said no] of my suggested journey [to Paris] and thus Bobby could go off on hers without fear of missing anything.

At four, Begin and a Mr. [Shmuel] Katz came and stayed until 6:15.[146] Before and after tea we talked on the porch. Deliberately, I spent a good deal of time

---

143. McDonald to acting secretary of state, no. 217, October 29, 1948, *FRUS*, 1948, v. V, pt. 2, 1525–1526.

144. Truman to Marshall, October 29, 1948, Truman Library, Clifford Papers, Subject File 1945–54, box 13, folder Palestine Correspondence Miscellaneous, 1 of 3; Lovett to Marshall, October 28, 1948, no. 119, *FRUS*, 1948, v. V, pt. 2, 1527.

145. For a tour of Haifa, Nazareth, and Tiberias with Harry Beilin, the Jewish Agency liaison to the British Army during World War II and then the Israeli Foreign Ministry's representative in Haifa.

146. Shmuel Katz (1914–2008), South African-born writer, historian; Revisionist Zionist associate of Ze'ev Jabotinsky; senior IZL member; member of first Knesset as member of Herut;

chatting about my earlier relations with Hitler; Jabotinsky, who is revered by Begin and his colleagues and Jewish leaders elsewhere; and also about American politics, etc. In answer to my questions about Israel, Begin talked dispassionately about his Freedom [Herut] Party, its relations to the Revisionists, its prospects in the forthcoming election, etc. He thought that internal politics might be embittered for a time but would become gradually more mutually conciliatory.

Towards the end, Begin spoke of his plans to go to the States, said that they had their exit visas, and wondered about the American ones. I replied that I understood their applications had been sent to Washington and that my own personal view about visas in general was a liberal one; that I was anxious to avoid being mixed up in internal Israeli politics, but that I was sure he would not expect me to indicate what recommendation we might have made or would make if we were asked. He seemed satisfied that my attitude would be friendly. After some last-minute informal references to the Anglo-American Committee's report, its rejection of the White Paper, of the idea of a Jewish or an Arab State, and Bevin's present policy, we said good-bye.

At the beginning of our talk, Begin was obviously reserved and perhaps a little tense, but as time went on he relaxed and even on two or three occasions laughed out loud. One of these was in response to my story about Gladstone, the fifth ace and Disraeli; another was in response to the one about Bentwich and Jabotinsky in Moscow. Begin had been much impressed in my favor by the attack of Lady Astor [in the joint press conference in spring 1947].[147] I really should thank her ladyship. Begin seemed fully aware that the American representative in Israel should not be other than what he is meant to be officially, at the risk of losing his usefulness. I think that if Begin goes to the States, he will in this respect at least emphasize some of the facts of Israeli life. I got the impression that in his speeches in the States, if he goes, there will be much vigorous criticism of Ben-Gurion, Mapai, and the Provisional Government, together with a defense of IZL and his leadership as preparation for support in the States for the [Herut] Party.

In response to my question about the probable makeup of the Constituent Assembly, Begin estimated that Mapai would have the largest number of seats, that second place would be contested for by his group and Mapam, with the other coalitions such as the Orthodox, running poor—fourth or worse. As he talked, I got the impression that there will be much less temptation for any Jewish group to go underground against a Jewish regime. As he put it, that regime may be good or bad, but at any rate it is ours, and against or for it we can work in the open. Begin seemed genuinely interested but not very well informed on American politics. He was interested and amused by my frank, and I hope racy,

adviser to Menachem Begin, 1977; author of numerous books including a two-volume biography of Jabotinsky (1993).

147. See Goda et al., eds., *To the Gates of Jerusalem*, 258–259.

account of some of our traditions and practices. Perhaps he was even a little shocked. I should be glad to see more of him.

Owing to US immigration restrictions Begin and his fellow IZL members were ineligible for visas because of their former terrorist activities. The State Department argued against granting the visa, because it would anger London. McDonald argued that the "Mission recognizes that Begin's presence in US might embarrass Jewish organizations there, but [the] Mission [is] still of [the] mind that refusal might embarrassingly involve us in Israeli politics."[148] On Truman's order, the Department of Justice overruled the State Department. Begin arrived in the United States during the last week of November 1948 on a visitor's visa to raise money for Herut.[149] Robert Lovett refused to receive him. Later the Department of Justice ruled that membership in or sympathy with the IZL was not in itself grounds for exclusion from the United States.[150]

It is worth recording what Weizmann said to me a few days ago about the beauty of Palestine, which fortunately, according to him, had been hidden by desert, swamp, and desolate hills in order that it might be preserved until these ugly layers could be removed by the Jews and the hidden treasures enjoyed by them.

Saturday, October 30

The usual workday, despite Shabbat for the Jews. In the afternoon, Cummings came for his farewell talk, which lasted for more than two hours. He expressed concern about the short-handedness of the staff of the secretarial level and his consequent inability to turn out the reports he had gathered the information for, and the very heavy burden on Knox. I agreed and said that I had at all times been willing to make the strongest possible representations that Knox would approve to the Department.

Cummings spoke at some length about the dissatisfaction of a large part of the business community with "the bureaucratic statism" of the Provisional Government. In particular, in addition to complaints about heavy taxation, he reported strong objections to the encroachments of state-supported enterprises with the strong backing of the Histadrut. He thought that Hope should follow up on the business leads he had made.

Cummings is convinced that the relations between many higher-ups and top leaders of the state were closer than was generally known, and that this accounted for the gentle handling of many who might otherwise have proved too loquacious. He spoke of Sachar and his interesting relations with the mayor of Rishon

---

148. Comments in Lovett to Clifford, no. 29, November 12, 1948 Truman Library, Clifford Papers, Subject File, 1945–54, box 14, folder Palestine Telegrams and Cables 1 of 2.

149. On the visit see Avi Shilon, *Menachem Begin: A Life* (New Haven, CT: Yale University Press, 2012), 141–142; and Robert D. Kumamoto, *International Terrorism and American Foreign Relations, 1945–1976* (Hanover, NH: Northeastern University Press, 1999), 65–68.

150. McDonald, *My Mission to Israel*, 145–146; Brecher, *American Diplomacy and the Israeli War of Independence*, 160.

[LeZion][151] and the large industrialists in Netanya. All of this seemed to make some sense in connection with the suggestion, thrown out one evening by someone in the Provisional Government, that Sachar might go to London when a mission was sent there. Cummings underlined that there were many more interrelations here than one would suspect, and that one had to watch the angles.

We then discussed some of the ways in which he might most usefully help us at home: 1) to find out as soon as possible the way the wind was blowing after the 19th of January [the presidential inauguration]. He should have ways of doing this; 2) to talk like a Dutch uncle to Satterthwaite about Knox and the unfairness of understaffing here; 3) to explain to Gurfein the elements in our problem and to see a number of other people. The next day I gave Cummings letters to be mailed to Hoover, Allen Dulles, Felix Frankfurter, Eugene Meyer, Samuel Leidesdorf, and Gurfein, to all of whom I urged the importance of their talking with Cummings. As we concluded our talk, I felt it had been very wasteful not to have given Knox stenographic help, which would enable [Cummings] to make more out of his extraordinary interesting contacts while here. There was solace, however, in the thought that he would be extraordinarily helpful at home.

On the way to the concert, picked up Madame de Philippe at Habimah, where she was rehearsing her new opera. The concert, at which Leonard Bernstein played the Third Copland Symphony, a Mozart concerto and the Ravel *Valse*, was in the first half a little heavy to most of the listeners to whom Copland was new.

Sunday, October 31

Wonderful start of the day with reading in bed with my tea for an hour and a half and the continuing of it until my appointments began to arrive. First were Knox and the colonel, then before they left, Mr. [Akiva] Persitz, of Mr. [Joseph] Jacobson's office in the ministry of defense.[152] As Persitz was leaving, Mr. and Mrs. Beryl Locker arrived for dinner.[153] Locker was most interesting in his reminiscences of his relations with Bevin and other British authorities. His stories confirmed the general impression of Bevin's arrogance and vanity, the latter utilized so effectively by the permanent officials of the Foreign Office for their own purposes. From time to time Mrs. Locker would join in with an

151. Elyakum Ostashinski (1909–1983), Palestine-born agriculturalist with doctorate in agronomy; mayor of Rishon LeZion, 1946–1951.
152. Joseph Jacobson (b. 1907), Jerusalem-born citrus-grower; member of Haganah staff; after 1948 assistant minister of defense, responsible for purchasing. Akiva Persitz was in charge of requisitioning. His visit concerned details of McDonald's leasing of the Braudo house and the need for new furnishings.
153. Beryl (also Berl) Locker (1887–1972), Galician-born labor Zionist and attorney; secretary, Poalei Zion World Union, 1920–1928; secretary, Poalei Zion in the United States, 1928–1931; member, Jewish Agency Executive, London, 1931–1935; political adviser, Jewish Agency Executive, London, 1935–1945; member, London executive of the Jewish Agency, 1945–1948; chairman, Jerusalem Executive, 1948–1956; author of several books on Jewish history, the Jewish labor movement, and Palestine.

apposite story or illustration. Locker and some other members of the Executive of the Agency are going to the States to try to bring the two United Jewish Appeal factions together. As Locker explained the position of his group objectively and concerned only to point out the needless tragedy which would follow from continued divisions, I felt that he was stronger than I had thought him, and that his mission might be successful.

What a delight to have Bobby back, and with her, Arthur Rosenthal at tea time.[154] My first long talk with Arthur explained why I had sent for him. [He] is so thrilled by what he has seen that any excuse for coming would be sufficient. I think he will learn and will be discreetly useful. Bobby's account of her trip reflected her joy in seeing more of this extraordinarily interesting and beautiful country. We were joined at teatime by Cummings and McMahon on their way to Haifa. This gave me the opportunity to hand to Cummings the several letters I had dictated that morning. After nearly tearful farewells, they left about a quarter of six.

154. Arthur J. Rosenthal (1920–2013), legendary New York-born publisher; served as General Douglas McArthur's publications chief during World War II, and later assisted McDonald's writing efforts. Founded Basic Books in 1952.

5. November 1948

Abba Schwartz of the IRO [International Refugee Organization] spent an hour with me on the roof, during which we talked of many things, including the general situation here, the danger of the US's involvement in sanctions, etc.[1] He told me of the interesting possibility that a large fund [was] handed over to the ICRC [International Committee of the Red Cross] by the Japanese empress just before V-J Day [and] that all or a portion of this might be advantageously earmarked for Arab refugees. I was quick to telegraph my support to the Department of this idea.[2]

Schwartz also outlined a strong argumentation against William Hallam Tuck's adverse decision in the IRO on the issue of paying transportation costs of refugees to Israel. I wired the Department also on this issue.

The IRO had budgeted funds for the movement of Jewish DPs in Europe to Palestine, but stopped payments after Israel declared its independence. Tuck wanted to shift these costs to Israel. McDonald described this policy as "completely untenable." The financial burden on the American Jewish Joint Distribution Committee [JDC], which had paid transport costs for Jewish refugees, would be relieved if the IRO simply used the funds it had already budgeted. McDonald also learned that IRO policy was "developed principally by Tuck's deputy Sir Arthur Rucker, in accordance with [the] desires of [the] British Foreign Office and after consultation with Sir Herbert Emerson." Tuck, he claimed, would change the policy if the United States desired.[3]

Schwartz disavowed any close contacts with or knowledge of the plans of Thomas Dewey and his cohorts, but I suspect that he will be in touch with some of them [in] Paris. At any rate, he promised to write me confidentially from there. He may come to see me again if he is delayed here.

---

1. Abba Phillip Schwartz (1916–1989), Baltimore-born lawyer; member of US Merchant Marine during World War II; reparations director for the IRO, 1947–1949; counsel to the Intergovernmental Committee for European Migration, 1949–1962.
2. Refers to ten million Swiss francs donated to the ICRC in the name of Empress Nagako in the closing days of World War II. The sum was claimed afterward by the US and British occupation authorities on behalf of their prisoners in Japanese captivity, but Swiss authorities blocked the transfer. The State Department determined in 1949 that the funds were subject to Swiss law. McDonald to secretary of state, November 1, 1948, McDonald Papers, USHMM, box 7, folder 8.
3. McDonald memorandum draft, November 1, 1948, McDonald Papers, USHMM, box 7, folder 8.

Colonel van der Velde came before lunch and brought me up to date about the situation in the Negev, where he had been much impressed by the planning and the execution of the Jewish operation and by the heroism of the young people in the settlements, which had literally been under fire for months. Their life under ground was, in his opinion, the strongest possible proof of their endurance. He was struck, too, by the Israeli handling of 150 or so Arab residents of Be'er Sheva, who two or three days after the surrender asked to go to Gaza. They were taken there in trucks by the [Israeli] Army, which thus gave an irrefutable demonstration of humanity, which must have deeply impressed the enemy in Gaza.[4]

[Concerns expressed about Knox's workload and health]. Knox came at lunch during which he discussed a number of problems, including his unfinished political report. Unhappily, I could not be enthusiastic about it because of his central thesis of Jewish "frustration and fear," which I thought was the wrong emphasis and would lead to misunderstanding. I agreed with him about the desirability of more long political reports for background purposes, but argued that we ought not worry about them so long as we were so shorthanded. As to this question, he had written a long airgram detailing our plight and agreed that I might supplement it with a strong telegram in a few days.

After lunch Knox and Colonel van der Velde approved my three telegrams about: 1) the need to guard against a too hasty suggestion of possible action regarding [the] head of mission. This was addressed to Clark Clifford in the form of references to [the] letter of September 19 to the president and his reply of October 4; 2) Japanese aid [and] Arab refugees; 3) IRO, Tuck and passage money, Jewish refugees.

McDonald wrote to Clifford, "I cannot overemphasize that my judgment now is identical with mine [on] September 19," and that it was vital to "avoid possibility of [a] hasty decision [to] withdraw [the] head of mission as a preliminary sanction."[5]

Tuesday, November 2

Colonel van der Velde suggested that there might be a general Arab offensive when the Security Council ended its work unless, of course, in the meantime the Security Council had penalized Israel.

Just before twelve we met Rabbi [Yehuda Leib Maimon] Fishman, head of the ministry of religion and Rabbi [Yitzhak] Herzog of that ministry and with them went to our state visit to Bnei Brak.[6] This all-Orthodox community is

---

4. Many of the Arab inhabitants of Be'er Sheva had left for Hebron during the start of the Yoav offensive. About 350 were expelled to Gaza. Morris, *Birth of Palestinian Refugee Problem Revisited*, 467.

5. McDonald to secretary of state [personal attention Clifford], no. 222, November 1, 1948, *FRUS*, 1948, v. V, pt. 2, 1536.

6. Bnei Brak, agricultural settlement east of Tel Aviv; founded by Polish Hasidim, 1924; attained city status, 1950; now the center of Orthodox Judaism in Israel.

only a few minutes from Ramat Gan, between here [Tel Aviv] and Petah Tik-vah. Just twenty-[four] years old, it is largely the creation of [Rabbi] Yitzhak Gerstenkorn, who bought the land originally and has been from the beginning president of the local council. Under his guidance, Bobby and I visited successively the following institutions:

1) Neveh-Hillel, sanatorium on top of the Shalom-Hill;—the Kupat Holim, the Sick Fund of the Histadrut which embraces about 150,000 members with about 300,000 to its benefits;[7]
2) the secondary school of the Mizrahi Foundation. Here the young children, boys and girls, were lined up before us while a small chorus of girls sang. There was a short talk by one of the girls giving welcome and a brief translation by another. The children were all sturdy looking;
3) the Talmud-Torah school had arranged for its children, all boys, to line one of the streets on both sides and to greet us as cordially as we marched down and back in the middle of the road as if they were a guard of honor and we were inspecting them. Again, we were struck by their uniform healthfulness and their cordiality;
4) the great Talmudic college [Yeshiva] Ponevezh on the Zikhron Meir hill,[8] where we met the famous Rabbi Yosef Kahaneman. His story is amazing; a famous Talmudic scholar in Lithuania, he alone of a large family escaped death at the hands of the Nazis. Arriving in Palestine with only the proceeds from the sale of a single house, he bought a considerable tract of land in or near Bnei Brak. Reserving a small portion of it for his college, he, with the cooperation of a South African Jew of São Paulo, Brazil, managed to subdivide the rest of the property and sell it so profitably that he could begin to build his college.[9] Since then he has shown, for a rabbi, incredible business acumen, using the profits of his ventures always to extend his religious activities. His formal greetings to us were read in Hebrew after which he let himself go in Yiddish, stirring his audience to enthusiasm. I wish I could feel that I was worthy of his praise;
5) the Tel Ra'anan [Children's Home] for fugitive children: maintained by the Mizrachi Women of America.[10] Here were fifty-nine children, boys and girls from 3 and 4 to twelve, all orphans or refugees and all looking as if they were the children of the rich. Their house was originally the center of

7. On health care in 1948 see Shifra Shvarts, *Health and Zionism: The Israeli Health Care System, 1948–1960* (Rochester, NY: University of Rochester Press, 2008).
8. Ponevezh Yeshiva, world renowned, located in Lithuania before World War II.
9. Rabbi Yosef Shlomo Kahaneman (1886–1969), Lithuanian-born rabbi; built three yeshivas there including Ponevezh, all destroyed in the war; emigrated to Palestine, 1940 (he was abroad on a mission at the time); worked unsuccessfully to rescue Lithuanian Jews; built orphanage for refugee children, 1943; built what became one of the world's largest yeshivas in Bnei Brak (Kiryat Ponevezh), 1944, which educated orphans from the Holocaust.
10. Tel Ra'anan was established in 1945 in Tel Litwinsky near Ramat Gan.

the settlement and a combined defense post and outlook. It is beautifully situated but the children were the chief attraction for me;

6) the series of factories at all of which Bobby received presents: Dubek cigarette factory; [Osem pasta] factory; Argaman textile dye factory. While the first two were interesting being quite modern, the last was more so. Incidentally, it was there that Bobby received beautiful cloth suitable for a dress or suit. The director of the factory, as we were walking out, told us of the death of his son in the Negev four months ago. I promised him that I would bring Ruth over to see his plant and to meet him.

The inspection tour was an interesting, and at times exhilarating experience, leaving one wearier than anticipated. My chief impressions, however, were of the extraordinary devotion of the people of this community to their several institutions, and of the variety and superior quality of these. A superficial glance at Bnei Brak would give the impression that it was an unattractive and unprogressive village, whereas in fact it is extraordinarily progressive and creative. Another impression was that the very variety of religious interests there, though all are Orthodox, made each member of the community feel that some part of it was his very own. I include a translation from the Hebrew of the address of welcome at the luncheon given us by the local council.

Among other comments, the speaker said to McDonald, "It is hard to be a diplomat, but even harder to be a friend of Israel. You [have shown] your sympathy and devotion to Israel's cause."[11]

Even after a nap, still semi-exhausted. The arrival of our radio gave me hope of hearing the [US] election returns tomorrow morning. Thinking over the afternoon trip, I was impressed anew with the pride of the people here in everything they have built or are building and their complete absence of any tendency to apologize for what has of necessity been undone. This attitude is delightfully refreshing. Before going to bed made arrangements with the UP to get election returns by phone.

Wednesday, November 3

Up before six and called the UP to hear the startling news that Truman was leading. From then on during the day until a quarter of six in the evening when Dewey threw in the sponge, I followed with a curious sense of unreality the unfolding drama of the president's victory. It seemed incredible and unreal, for it violated every principle of the "science" of political forecasting. Incidentally, too, it showed how wasteful had been our household speculations about ways in which a change of administration would affect our fates.

11. In McDonald Papers, USHMM, box 7, folder 8.

As the result became definite, a number of people called to "congratulate" me. During the day I felt sometimes as if I were living in two worlds simultaneously, the one which we had come to expect, and the one which was to be. Gradually, however, as the truth percolated through the clouds of illusion, I prepared first drafts of important communications to the president and [to] Clifford. During the morning, after an hour or so at the office, I had my first experience in a bookstore, where the prices were discouraging. But I bought a copy of Albert H. Hourani's *Syria and Lebanon*.[12]

Thursday, November 4

Rewrote my telegram to the president and a letter to Clifford.

McDonald wrote the president that Israeli government members were extremely pleased with the election results, which they regarded as a "triumph resulting from your instinctive understanding of and your daring initiative on behalf of the common man. Officials here also recognize that your prestige now exceeds that of any other Western leader." McDonald stated that Shertok was especially pleased, having phoned to say that the election was, in Shertok's words, a "heartening demonstration of a great people's will. And wisdom and of their independent judgment." McDonald added, "Personally, I hope that the British Foreign Minister is as understanding as Shertok."[13]

McDonald wrote Clifford that "we on the firing line" hoped that Clifford would remain in his White House position. Truman had handled recent developments in the UN regarding Israel "with consummate skill." He summarized,

> *The basic problem here is how to transmute the months' old truce, worn thin by violations on both sides, into an enduring peace. I am convinced that our Government can help most by keeping in the forefront of its thinking three central facts: 1) Israel is fighting a defensive war against invading armies of the six surrounding Arab states; 2) The Government and people of Israel will, despite threats or even the use of sanctions, continue their struggle for viable and independent statehood; 3) Israel is—except for Turkey—potentially the strongest bulwark of Western democratic influence in the whole of the Middle East. The danger I fear the most is that in its understandable desire to keep in step with Britain—despite His Majesty's Government's record of a decade of mistakes and humiliations in this area and the British Foreign Minister's malevolence toward President Truman—the [State] Department may yield to Bevin's intransigency. To do that would delay peace, weaken the US's influence, and gratuitously enlarge the influence of the USSR in this strategic area.[14]*

12. Albert Habib Hourani, *Syria and Lebanon: A Political Essay* (Oxford: Oxford University Press, 1946). McDonald met Hourani in Jerusalem in March 1946 when the latter, speaking for the Arab Office, testified before the Anglo-American Committee of Inquiry. See Goda et al., *To the Gates of Jerusalem*, 184–185.

13. McDonald for personal attention president, November 4, 1948, McDonald Papers, USHMM, box 7, folder 8.

14. McDonald to Clifford, November 4, 1948, McDonald Papers, USHMM, box 7, folder 8.

On November 5, McDonald added a few personal lines to David Niles: "If [the] President could read today's Israel press, he would sense extraordinary interest in his triumph and new hope for de jure recognition and loan."[15] *The widely circulated Israeli daily* Yediot Ahronot *reported that Truman would replace Marshall, Lovett, and Forrestal and would then instruct the American UN delegation to vote against sanctions.*

Brief visit to the office, and later a conference at the hotel with Knox on questions to be asked [of] Moshe Shertok. McKelvey and I discussed also the Begin application for a visa.

Pleasant tea with Knox and Mr. Hope. I was delightfully relieved to find the latter not a striped trouser type, but a matter of fact and, I imagine, highly efficient individual. Knox seemed relieved to have him. The Ben-Gurions accept for luncheon on Wednesday, the 10th. We shall probably ask Hope, the colonel, and Arthur B. Rosenthal.

Friday, November 5

Knox called in considerable excitement regarding news of passage of the Sino-Anglo [draft] resolution with the American amendment reiterating the demand for the withdrawal in the Negev to the October 14 lines "within whatever time limit the acting Mediator may think desirable to fix;" the same committee of the [Security] Council "to study as a matter of urgency and to report to the Security Council on further measures appropriate to take under Chapter VII of the Charter."

On November 2 Britain submitted its draft resolution calling for a Security Council committee to advise on sanctions appropriate under Chapter VII, Article 41 of the UN charter [economic and diplomatic sanctions], if either Israel or Egypt failed to return to the October 14 truce lines in the Negev. Lovett supported it partly to avoid an open breach with the British. The Israelis feared that State Department officials in Paris, in defiance of Truman, had aligned with the "most extreme British position," which aimed "to secure the detachment from Israel of the greater part of its territory without its consent."[16]

From Washington, Eliahu Epstein reported that, during a "tense" conversation at the State Department, Satterthwaite and McClintock threatened "serious consequences if we disobey [Security] Council's resolution and Bunche's request."[17] *Epstein wrote that he "worried that no leading Jews had access to Truman." Samuel Rosenman had quarreled with the president, Joseph Proskauer had backed Dewey, and Abba Hillel Silver was persona non grata. It was important, Epstein reported, that McDonald*

---

15. McDonald to Niles, November 5, 1948, McDonald Papers, USHMM, box 7, folder 8.
16. Eban to Shertok, November 4, 1948, *DFPI*, v. 2, d. 98; Eban to Marshall, November 4, 1948, *DFPI*, v. 2, d. 100.
17. Epstein to Eban, November 6, 1948, *DFPI*, v. 2, d. 112.

"immediately send [a] report [to] Truman emphasizing detrimental effects [of the Security] Council's resolution."[18]

Within the US delegation in Paris, Eleanor Roosevelt weighed in.[19] In early October, she had publicly supported the Bernadotte Plan.[20] Her grandson Curtis Boettiger's visit to Israel later that month, and particularly the Negev, helped change her mind.[21] On November 3 she wrote to Marshall,

> Our weight will have to be thrown back of Israel if we really mean to sustain partition as it was envisioned in the original majority plan last year. We have been keeping away from making this definite gesture in the hopes of being able to satisfy Great Britain's fears where the Arabs are concerned, and yet I sometimes wonder if we had been a little firmer with the Arabs from the start and with Great Britain, we might not have solved this question without so much bloodshed a long while ago. . . .
>
> As I look into the picture, I realize that Israel without the Negev cannot possibly be independent and self-supporting in that part of the world. They will undoubtedly fight for it, it means constant fighting in the future. . . . If our decision is that they should have it under the decision taken last year in the General Assembly, we should make our backing of their claim clear and not permit the situation to become confused by the temporary truce decisions we support in the Security Council. The whole hope of success in the partitioning negotiations lies in the knowledge on the part of Great Britain and the Arabs that Israel has our backing. It is one of those decisions in which one cannot remain neutral though one can be fair.
>
> We accepted the majority report on partition because nothing better had ever been suggested and because it was the only thing that seemed to give the State of Israel a substantial basis. Since then we have recognized Israel as a State and have given her to understand that we are ready to give her formal recognition and support her entry into the United Nations and to help her with a loan. This all seems to me very unrealistic if we are not going to give her the support in the negotiations which will make it possible for her to exist at all.[22]

McDonald reinforced Eleanor Roosevelt's position from Tel Aviv. On November 6, he wrote her that "sanctions will be worse than futile because:

1) The threat will not frighten anyone; instead it will only antagonize Israeli public opinion and make the USSR to appear the only sympathetic power;

2) The threat may, however, be sufficient (as Buzz [Curtis Dall Boettiger] will be able to explain more fully)[23] to persuade the Israeli leaders that they had better let the army act at once to clear the whole of Palestine west of the Jordan before sanctions become a reality.

18. Epstein to Eban, November 5, 1948, *DFPI*, v. 2, d. 110.

19. Marshall to acting secretary of state, no. 559, November 1, 1948, *FRUS*, 1948, v. V, pt. 2, 1538–1539; Lovett memorandum to Truman, November 2, 1948, *FRUS*, 1948, v. V, pt. 2, 1539–1540; Lovett to Marshall [eyes only], no. 130, November 2, 1948, *FRUS*, 1948, v. V, pt. 2, 1540–1541; Eban to Elath, November 7, 1948, *DFPI*, v. 2, d. 113.

20. "Despite Objections from Home, I like Bernadotte's Plan," *My Day*, October 6, 1948.

21. See entries of October 20, 21, 27, 1948.

22. Eleanor Roosevelt to Marshall, November 3, 1948, NARA, RG 59, 501.BB Palestine, box 2122, folder 1.

23. Entries of October 20, 21, 27, 1948.

3) To impose sanctions would be to enter upon a course, the end of which, if we persisted in, would be war—an ignoble and mean war—against Israel. Moreover it would be a struggle in which the Jews would be prepared to repeat the heroic resistance of their ancestors nearly nineteen hundred years ago, resistance which was broken by the Romans only after the last Jewish fighting unit had been destroyed and the country rendered desolate and almost empty."[24]

On November 8, Robert Lovett told Clifford, who was in Key West with President Truman, that Eleanor Roosevelt had expressed disapproval of imposing sanctions on Israel. She openly wondered, Lovett said, whether anyone had explained the situation impartially to the president. Lovett sent her letter to Key West.[25]

Under Marshall's leadership the US delegation in Paris had already softened the language of the British draft. The final version noted that the October 14 lines would become provisional truce lines. The acting mediator, Bunche, would determine the timing of the withdrawal and recommend measures to the Security Council in case of noncompliance. The US delegation believed that this change allowed greater flexibility.[26] *The Security Council, with the Soviets abstaining, adopted the US amendments as Resolution 61 of November 4, 1948.*[27] *The British, however, still favored sanctions unless Israel complied. Hector McNeil of the Foreign Office warned that if sanctions were vetoed, London was "firmly committed [to] assist [the] Arabs."*[28]

About ten Knox, Colonel van der Velde, and Mr. Hope came out, and we worked until a quarter past twelve on a long and urgent telegram to the president and the acting secretary [Lovett]. We pointed to the lack of clarity in the Security Council action; to the increasing tension here; to the possibility that unless the Provisional Government had assurance that sanctions would be vetoed by the USSR, that it might authorize the army to take the offensive against the Iraqis, who were, even according to Dr. Bunche, giving substantial provocation.[29] We emphasized that the threat of sanctions would not deter or coerce

24. To Benjamin Cohen, McDonald added, "How blind are men who permit their hatreds and their frustrations to close their minds to realities. And, how tragic that other men should accept such men as dispassionate, disinterested and trustworthy guides." McDonald to Eleanor Roosevelt, November 6, 1948, McDonald to Cohen, November 6, 1948, McDonald Papers, USHMM, box 7, folder 8. These letters are not on official stationary and may have been delivered by Israel's courier service. See entry of October 11, 1948.
25. Lovett Diary, entry of November 8, 1948, NYHS, box 112, folder 4.
26. Rusk to Lovett [eyes only], November 3, 1948, no. 591, *FRUS*, 1948, v. V, pt. 2, 1543–1544.
27. Text in *FRUS*, 1948, v. V, pt. 2, 1546–1547.
28. McClintock memorandum to acting secretary of state, November 5, 1948, *FRUS*, 1948, v. V, pt. 2, 1551–1553; Marshall to acting secretary of state, no. 661, November 9, 1948, *FRUS*, 1948, v. V, pt. 2, 1559–1560.
29. Iraqi forces in Palestine amounted to an armored battalion and four infantry brigades occupying the strategic triangle in Samaria between Nablus, Jenin, and Tulkarm. They held Jenin against an Israeli attack in June 1948 and then guarded the northern flank of the Arab Legion. In theory they could strike toward Haifa, splitting the narrow corridor along the Israeli coastal plain. Kenneth M. Pollack, *Arabs at War: Military Effectiveness, 1948–1991* (Lincoln: University of Nebraska Press, 2002), 150–155.

Israel to return to the October 14 lines, that not even the use of sanctions including force would achieve Israel's surrender; that, therefore, unless [the] powers were prepared to carry through to the end, [the] threat of invocation of sanctions would only play the USSR's game and make Israel turn to Moscow for aid even if the price asked were usurious. In conclusion, we quoted from my letter of yesterday to Clark Clifford modifying only the words "malevolence of Bevin" [for the phrase] "who personally blamed the president for HMG's failures in Palestine since the Anglo-American Committee Report."[30] After the telegram was drafted, I decided to put in a call for Clark Clifford at the White House for today.

Following all this, there was just time to drive out with Bobby to the Weizmanns' for lunch. The only others present besides our hosts were Mrs. Weizmann's brother-in-law and the president's aide. Conversation before, during, and after lunch was sometimes light and at other times very serious. Mrs. Weizmann and her husband for a time before the meal both talked to me at once, she in a gossipy vein and he very soberly: she not hearing him, and he paying no attention to her. As a result, I was somewhat put to it to answer both with any appearance of continuity. She was commenting on the Russians' formalism and ceremony and dress and suggested that unless I found a coat with tails and a white tie, my appearance at next Sunday's party [at the Soviet legation] would be considered an affront. I replied that I would hide behind Bobby's red dress. She wondered how, if the Russians kept themselves as aloof as they are reported to do, they ever found out anything; anyhow, she didn't understand these Russians.

The chief points made by Dr. Weizmann were:

1) his admiration for President Truman, his faith in the latter's sincerity and the confidence he and Mrs. Weizmann had had before November 2 that Truman would be reelected;
2) doubt that sanctions would really be applied;
3) conviction that Negev would never be surrendered until the last Jew there had been killed or carried away forcibly;
4) the threat of sanctions would be futile, and their use would end in bloodshed; if force were used, Jews would resist as they had against the Romans until the last fighting man;
5) faced with sanctions exercised by the powers, Israel would of necessity and with deep regret turn to Russia for aid. He, Dr. Weizmann, would regret this more than he could say, for he knew that in the end this aid would be destructive to Israel's freedom;

---

30. Colonel van der Velde, McDonald added, thought that Israel would defeat the Iraqi forces. Though the mission staff intended it, the telegram did not include the usual directive that it was for the president's personal attention. McDonald to secretary of state, no. 237, November 5, 1948, *FRUS*, 1948, v. V, pt. 2, 1553–1554.

6) throughout his life, a moderate and often indicted for his conciliatory attitude, Dr. Weizmann would have to conclude, if sanctions were invoked, that moderation was an illusion and a futility. He, therefore, would support, in the event of sanctions, quick moves by Israeli forces to seize the whole of Palestine west of the Jordan. If Israeli conciliation were met by sanctions, no reason would remain for not utilizing Israel's force to the utmost and while there was yet time;

7) how inexplicable is the British current habit of tying His Majesty's Government to a cadaver. In this area, too, weak and unreliable Arab states, and in the Far East to a demoralized China;

8) Dr. Weizmann was so contemptuous of Arab weakness that he said the Israeli forces could take Damascus in one hour if they chose, and that not even Glubb Pasha could stop them. How stupid, he said, was Abdullah, who had been secure in Transjordan, assured of funds from Britain and additional funds from the Jews. But he was lured by the desire to sit on the throne of David and, as so many others before him, he has found Jerusalem an uneasy seat.[31] As I was leaving, I reminded the Weizmanns of the suggestion that they would invite General Riley and Colonel van der Velde. Dr. Weizmann urged me to come to see him again if I were recalled to Washington for conference.

Back to the house by 3:30, where I waited until 4:04 for the call to Washington. When it finally came, the connection was clear. In answer to Clark Clifford's salutation "Jim," I warned him that ours was a "party" line; he replied that he understood. I asked him about his mother, who he said is well; he added that she had asked him to let her know when he talked to me or heard from me. His elder daughter is continuing her singing. We laughed about the bandwagon-climbing since last Tuesday. In answer to his question about the reception of the news here, I told him it was regarded as a personal triumph for the president and a vindication of democracy. He said he so regarded it also. I told him that I had sent two telegrams, one yesterday and one today, which I hoped the president would read despite the flood of post-victory congratulations.[32] Clifford asked how they were sent; I replied through the Department. He then said that he would call there at once and ask that they be watched for and sent over to the White House immediately.

31. In his congratulatory letter to Truman, Weizmann was more diplomatic. He conveyed the hope that the president would support Israel in the Security Council in its quest for a lasting peace. He mentioned in particular British efforts to deprive Israel of the Negev through Security Council Resolution 60. "Sheer necessity," he told Truman, "compels us to cling to the Negev." Weizmann to Truman, November 5, 1948, *DFPI*, v. 2, d. 108.

32. McDonald for personal attention of the president, November 4, 1948, McDonald Papers, USHMM, box 7, folder 8, described in entry of November 4, 1948; and particularly McDonald to secretary of state, no. 237, November 5, 1948, *FRUS*, 1948, v. V, pt. 2, 1553–1554, described in entry of November 5, 1948.

Clifford added that he was glad I had called, because "we," presumably the presidential party including Clifford, "are leaving for vacation next Sunday for two weeks."[33] I commented that the president might enjoy his vacation better if he had my second telegram before him before he left. As we were finishing, Clifford said that he was delighted that I had called [and] that I should keep closely in touch with the White House and that they (presumably the White House group) were following closely day-by-day developments here. He could not have been more friendly.

Saturday, November 6

Still gravely concerned lest Truman should leave Washington on his holiday before having taken strong action against sanctions in Paris. Decided to put in another call for Clifford, hoping that before it came through, our telegram of Friday would have reached the White House.

To Shertok's house at 12:00 o'clock. He looked as if he had had a serious cold, the effects of which were still evident. I told him briefly of my interpretation of the current developments and of my hopes. Shertok's rather long statement to me (I was with him until after 1:00) covered the following points:

In September 1948, under Shertok's guidance, Israeli diplomats had begun direct negotiations with representatives from Transjordan and Egypt in Paris. By early November, talks with Egyptian representatives seemed somewhat promising. The Israeli delegation in Paris argued that Security Council threats of sanctions were disrupting these negotiations with Egypt.[34]

1) No progress had been made during the past six weeks on the very tentative and exploratory peace feelers between Israel and Transjordan. The Provisional Government through its unofficial representative, Elias Sasson in Paris, was ready to resume the informal talks at any time. I got the impression that the Provisional Government would utilize any other available intermediary which Transjordan might prefer;

2) Exploratory talks with Egypt, on the other hand, had reached almost the point of informal negotiations. The beginning was through Sasson, who for months had been writing from Paris to a long list of these friends in the neighboring Arab states. One response was from the chamberlain of King Farouk's court. Following upon further exchanges of letters, a representative of the court was sent to Paris to talk with Sasson. The Egyptians contended that Gaza must remain in their country's hands and that Israel should acquiesce in a corridor between the new Palestinian state and Haifa. To these proposals the Provisional Government had answered with a categorical "no" about the corridor but was indefinite as to Gaza. Sasson

33. The president and his staff were in Key West from November 8 to December 9, 1948.
34. *DFPI*, v. 2, d. 91, 92, 97, 100, 101, 110.

stressed that it would be preferable if a desert continued to separate the occupied portions of Egypt and Israel; otherwise with Gaza Egyptian territory and open to Egypt's "teaming missions," Israel's program of colonizing the Negev might be jeopardized. My general impression was that Shertok is hopeful of direct negotiations with Cairo.

3) Speaking of the British, Shertok said it was clear that His Majesty's Government did not mind the Egyptian defeat in the Negev, though London had prodded Cairo on the rash adventure, and that now the British wished to profit from Egypt's military disaster by using the UN to force Israeli troops to withdraw and leave a vacuum into which Britain's "stooge" Abdullah could pour his troops. Shertok reported that McNeil, in a recent talk with Eban, despite the friendliness of the exchange, showed His Majesty's Government's determination to keep control of the Negev [by assigning it to a friendly power].[35] It was in this connection that Shertok spoke of Eban's talk a day or two ago with [Fraser] Wilkins, Ross, and Rusk. At first, these three seemed somewhat shaken by Eban's report of his talk with McNeil but, by their actions later, these men did not indicate that their support of the British position had weakened.[36]

4) Shertok said that he was telephoning Epstein apropos of the projected trip to Paris, which we had mentioned earlier.[37]

Arthur Rosenthal came out for lunch, reported on his travels through the center of the country, and we gossiped about the election.

My call to Clark Clifford was at first delayed while he was in conference, but the connection was made at five o'clock our and ten o'clock their time. We could hear each other perfectly. I was much disappointed, however, to have him tell me that he had not yet received the telegram [of November 5] for the president. Without that before him, my case for the visit to Paris was more difficult to make.

Only the president might authorize McDonald to go to Paris and make his arguments directly to American officials attending the UN session. McDonald believed this step critical.

35. Eban met McNeil on November 3, explaining to him Israel's popular resentment of Great Britain. McNeil was friendly but repeated that Israeli withdrawal from the Negev was essential to a peaceful outcome and that London was under increasing pressure to fulfill its treaty obligations to the Arab states. *DFPI*, v. 2, d. 93.

36. Eban reported on November 3 that, in discussing the pending Security Council resolution, Rusk and Wilkins "indicated little chance concluding paragraph [regarding] sanctions being carried, but [they] put up [a] strong defense [of the] operative parts of the resolution, without, however, indicating commitment" and argued that an Israeli withdrawal would not prejudice the final disposition of the Negev. *DFPI*, v. 2, d. 95.

37. McDonald's attempts to participate in UN General Assembly discussions concerning Israel are in entries of October 6, 20, 23, 29, 1948.

He did, however, say that he would put it before his chief even though it was not the sort of matter in which Truman preferred to enter personally. I stressed again the importance of the telegram.

McDonald discovered that the November 5 telegram to the president, filed that afternoon, was delayed because of the omission of the heading that it was meant for the president's personal attention.

Later, Saturday, we learned through a telegram from the Department that the message finally reached the White House about 4:30 [pm] Saturday. Whether this was before or after the president and Clifford had left, I had no way of ascertaining.

Sunday, November 7

I suggested to Knox that we send the Department a brief telegram explaining that the oversight in our code room had occasioned my anxious telephone inquiries at the White House. The "first rain" came down in sheets, flooding whole sections of Tel Aviv streets. It was our first visible sign of what we might expect during the winter. Only the "latter rains," those of the spring, are expected to be gentle. Because of the flooded conditions of the streets, we were nearly an hour late getting off to our visit to the Poale Agudat Israel kibbutzim.[38] We were accompanied, in addition to Rabbi Binyamin Mintz,[39] by two young women, the one soon to be assigned to the Israeli legation in Prague, and the other a worker in a chocolate factory who gives her spare time to work among Agudat girls.

First, we went to visit a home for working girls, where comfortable quarters and food are supplied for about 15 pounds a month. The Agudat has some fifty of these in the country. From the girls' home we drove south through Rehovot past Givat Brenner to Gedera to Kibbutz Hafetz Haim.[40] Four years old, this community of about 270 persons including 100 children, forty of them refugees, cultivates three thousand dunams and specializes in a large dairy of nearly seventy beautiful Dutch cows. Following the usual pattern of such visits, we went first to the school of the older children and finally ending that part of the tour in the nursery; the cattle barn was a model of cleanliness, and the animals such as these would give pride to any connoisseur. As we were leaving the

38. Poalei Agudat Israel (Orthodox Workers of Israel), founded in Lodz in 1933 as Agudat Israel's trade union branch; safeguarded needs of Orthodox workers, who, among other practices, could not work on Shabbat. In Israel, Poalei Agudat Israel had its own settlements and political party, but was also a branch of the Histadrut.
39. Binyamin Mintz (1903–1961), Lodz-born religious Zionist, emigrated to Palestine, 1925; joined Poale Agudat Israel, 1933, quickly establishing the movement in Israel; member, Provisional State Council, 1948; elected to Knesset as part of United Religious Front, 1949; minister of postal services, 1960–1961. See also entry of May 20, 1949.
40. Hafetz Haim, religious kibbutz initially established in 1937; then reestablished with Orthodox Jews from Germany in 1942.

barn, a group of men maneuvering a heavy modern piece of machinery asked to have our pictures taken with them. On the way back to the dining room we were shown the ground plan of the completed kibbutz with an ambitious and beautiful park, which was to be the center of the group of buildings. A small stretch of lawn and a tiny plot of seemingly rather discouraged flowers were the only visible signs of what the group confidently hopes will be. The dining hall and all the buildings except the stables are more or less makeshift improvisations.

We joined the body of the kibbutz for their two o'clock meal. It was an all-vegetable menu, well cooked and generously ample. Particularly noteworthy and welcome for us were the large pitchers of fresh milk and the generous portions of rich cream. At the end of the meal there was a brief talk of welcome, to which I replied briefly. Following the closing benediction, we visited for a moment the section of the dining hall which, after meals, becomes the library. Then in the midst of warm farewell greetings, we set off.

We were interested to notice that the heavy rains in Tel Aviv had not reached to Hafetz Haim, probably less than twenty miles to the south. From Hafetz Haim to Akir, only a few miles away, we had to pass through the very large military airfield of Akir, which at the height of the war had living accommodations, we were told, for twenty thousand men. I am no judge of the capacity of barracks, and though some of the buildings were near the stage of ruin, I would be willing to credit the 20,000 capacity. Just beyond the airfield, we came to another Agudat kibbutz just in the process of being established as a permanent settlement of the Burma Road. Yesodot, [which] was established near Magdiel in 1948, will have, it is estimated, a hundred men and women and 30 refugee children on 3,500 dunams.[41]

It was particularly interesting to see a kibbutz literally being dug out of the soil. The few buildings were extremely primitive, while tents housed most of the small group. The thick sticky mud, into which the dust had been transformed by a light shower, clung to our shoes and fully justified the heavy boots of the boys and girls. The water tower, always the center of security of a new settlement, was at this stage only a ramshackle platform on which the tanks were just being unloaded. Water itself was still being brought by tank truck from the nearby airfield taps. A tiny corrugated iron synagogue was also the library with its few books. The first aid station was a small pup tent.

Within four or six miles was Latrun and even nearer the Burma Road. Here, as at Hafetz Haim, were the beginning of trenches and dugouts. At Hafetz Haim, however, these defensive constructions had reached the point where the whole of the nearly three hundred settlers could be securely sheltered underground. Later, I hope that we shall be able to see some of the settlements a little further south in the Negev, which had endured Arab gunfire in their underground shelters for months. The only ceremony at Yesodot was the serv-

41. Yesodot was established in July 1948 as a religious kibbutz at the control point of the Burma Road in the Jerusalem corridor.

ing of a native wine and cakes in the dining tent, followed by a few words of welcome, to which I responded. The bakery, a gas oven in a corrugated iron shed, had just produced a couple of dozen loaves of brown bread, one of which was given us by the young baker, a boy of perhaps eighteen. It proved [a] substantial improvement on the Tel Aviv commercial bread.

On the way back we had an interesting talk, particularly with our young Agudat friend, Miss Rothenberg. Arrived home in time for a nap before the Russian October Revolution party. But before I describe the party, I must make reference to an extraordinary young couple we met at Hafetz Haim, the mother twenty-six, the father thirty, with six children, all husky. And what perhaps was most extraordinary, the mother looked less than her age. When I commented on this, one of the Agudat said calmly, "But you see, we need a large population and, moreover, she does not have to care for the children herself; most of that is done for her."

The Soviet diplomatic mission had complained to the Israeli government that the house designated for the Soviet legation, on Rothschild Boulevard in Tel Aviv, had still not been vacated and that the renovation work was proceeding too slowly. The work was quickly completed thereafter, not least because the Israelis needed Soviet support with immigration from Eastern Europe, weaponry, and the UN Security Council. A gala function on November 7 commemorated the anniversary of the Bolshevik Revolution of 1917, known in the USSR as the October Revolution.[42]

The question of proper dress for the Russian party had been the subject of animated discussion throughout all Tel Aviv, particularly since the edict had gone out to anyone who had inquired, that the dress was to be white ties. Bobby's flaming red dress failed to materialize because of sickness of the cutter. She fortunately was offered a beautiful Paris model, black, for a reasonable price, and as a result easily outshone all the other ladies. Her costume was completed with a borrowed cape from Miss Clark, and a purse from Shoshana. I, having no white tie, compromised, and with me, my colleagues Knox and McKelvey put on black ties, the colonel of course appearing with all of his ribbons.

Outside the legation had gathered a crowd of several hundred to eye and welcome the arriving celebrities. But thanks to excellent police arrangement, there was no delay. Members of the legation staff were at the door and each landing on the stairway and scattered throughout the already dense and nearly overpowering crowd. The Russians, of course, were all in their dress uniforms, except for the plainclothes men, who were numerous. During the first half an hour or so, we met and chatted with Madame de Philippe, Mr. and Mrs. Rokach, Dr. Mohn, and a number of other officials. Vainly, however, I looked for Ben-Gurion or Dr. Weizmann, and finally asked our host where they

42. Bentsur and Kolokov, eds., *Documents on Israeli–Soviet Relations*, v. 1, d. 169.

were. He said straight ahead to the right and to the left. We followed his directions only to end up in a hall. Only one other door, guarded by a huge female dragon in black, was visible. Finally, going to one of the windows and sticking my head out, I saw that there was another room in which the celebrities had been shepherded and who were sitting down to tables to eat in a more or less civilized fashion.

Regardless of the fact that we obviously had not been invited, Bobby and I pushed past the black dragon and joined the celebrities. In the room were most of the members of the heads of the army and top Russian officials. It was a little embarrassing, however, because not a single seat was unoccupied at any of the four or five tables. Bobby and I went up to that at which the Weizmanns and Ben-Gurions were sitting and were there made at ease by Ben-Gurion, sharing his chair with Bobby and the wife of one of the officials sharing hers with me. Anyone knowing Ben-Gurion's broad beam will appreciate how little of his chair Bobby got. Anyhow, the arrangement made it easy for Ben-Gurion and me to have a serious talk. He had heard of my conference with Shertok, and as a result of General Riley's statement in Paris and perhaps because of other factors, he was in fine fettle.[43] He was particularly enthusiastic about the president's election, saying repeatedly in different ways that it was a most encouraging demonstration of one man and a vindication of the workings of democracy.

Later, I moved over and sat next to Dr. Weizmann, who said much the same thing about the president and the election. Weizmann repeated what he had said to me the previous Friday: that he had been confident of Truman's victory and [was] delighted with it. He thought Harry Truman more suitable as a president than FDR had been because, though less brilliant, he was closer to the people. Had a good talk also with Kaplan, who again said he was not going to the States just now. He had heard of my talks with Washington and seemed more optimistic than he had ever been about the international situation.

Only after I had chatted a little while with a tall good-looking middle-aged man and his somewhat less attractive wife, and he had made some reference to the Braudos, did I wake up to the fact that he was [Akiva] Persitz, [Joseph] Jacobson's man at the ministry of defense and in charge of requisitioning.[44] He said that [Lazar] Braudo had seemed completely amiable following the

---

43. On November 3, Riley reported to Bunche in Paris that UN truce supervision "has lost whatever authority and moral force it may have had. . . . It now operates almost solely to report violations of the truce, which grow more numerous and open each day, and which reports have less and less significance. . . . Enforcement of the truce at the present is limited almost entirely to issuing threats and requests to Arab forces to refrain from various courses of action that would give the Jews a pretext for taking offensive action, as in the Negev and Galilee." Riley's assessment of the military balance was as follows: "If the Jews so desire, they could undoubtedly clear all of Palestine of Arab forces in a relatively short time." McDonald noted privately that the Israeli press was pleased with Riley's statement, and that "when it comes to telling an unpleasant truth, a professional soldier can be refreshingly downright." See Paris to secretary of state, no. 660, November 9, 1948, NARA, RG 59, 501.BB Palestine, box 2122, folder 2; McDonald to Janet, Halsey, and Ruth, November 8, 1948, McDonald Papers, USHMM, box 7, folder 8.

44. Entry of October 31, 1948.

government's talk with him. I replied I feared this amiability did not extend beyond the period of consciousness of possible governmental action. He was sure that he could keep the matter well in hand. Bobby and I must have the Persitzes over for tea.

Lazar Braudo's excessive rent for McDonald's residence was common knowledge in the Israeli government, which surely did not want to lose McDonald as the US special representative. In November the Ministry of Defense quietly threatened to requisition Braudo's house in order to help ensure a rental price of $500 per month, the limit of McDonald's State Department allowance for housing. The Braudos were privately furious at what they called "improper pressure."[45] *McDonald had chronic problems thereafter concerning the costs of basic repairs, his continued use of the furniture in the home—the US government had not as yet provided him with any—and other routine matters.*

A near diplomatic "incident" was occasioned by my kissing Mrs. Weizmann when we met. Mrs. Ben-Gurion, looking on, exclaimed in effect "what about me?" So I naturally kissed her, too. Paula [Ben-Gurion] has no intention of letting Vera [Weizmann] be more than officially the first lady. She also said to me, "We are very glad to be coming over to you and Bobby's on Wednesday." Chatted briefly during the evening with Joseph Sprinzak, head of Histadrut and chairman of the State Council, [and] with the Israeli chief of staff [*sic*], General Moshe Dayan, and his wife, a pleasantly attractive woman.[46]

Shortly after nine, the party then having been on for two hours, the grave question of protocol, the leaving of the ranking person, Dr. Weizmann, came to the fore. Mr. and Mrs. Ben-Gurion left a moment or two before the Weizmanns, but no one else ventured to do so. Bobby and I and our staff followed immediately after the Weizmanns but waited a few minutes on the stoop in order to let the president and his wife receive without any distraction whatever the plaudits of the crowd. Shalom, as usual, had our car immediately next to the entrance and, in the midst of friendly greetings from the crowd, we all piled into the Packard and went off to the Gat Rimon for a cold drink and a brief post mortem. Personally, [Mr. Knox] deplored the fact that his friend Miss Herlitz was one of the three members of the Foreign Office (all of them working with Western Europe or the United States) who had not been invited to the party.

Arriving home shortly after ten, Bobby and I walked for a little while on the roof and sat for a few minutes admiring the stars. She was very sweet when

45. McDonald to Eddie Jacobson, May 20, 1949, McDonald Papers, Columbia University, box 13, folder 10.
46. Moshe Dayan (1915–1981), born in Degania Alef, Palestine's first kibbutz, to Ukrainian parents; joined Haganah at age 14 and in 1938 became involved in Orde Wingate's Special Night Squads; in 1941 part of Australian-led operation in Vichy-controlled Lebanon, during which he lost an eye; in July 1948 named commander of Israeli forces in Jewish Jerusalem, subsequently helped negotiate armistice agreement with Transjordan in 1949; IDF chief of staff (1953–1958), minister of defense (1967–1974), foreign minister (1977–1979), played key role in Israeli victories in the Suez War (1956) and Six Day War (1967).

we came down to say that she was delighted that I had liked her new dress. But with her usual modesty she added, "after all however, I was the only person there younger than thirty-five." To which I replied: "This is true." But she bore well her responsibilities and position as the "fourth" lady of the land, ranking only after Madame Weizmann, Mrs. Ben-Gurion, and Mrs. Shertok.

Monday, November 8

Stopped at the office for an hour or so to check with Knox and Barnes. We got off a telegram to the Department inquiring "innocently" why it chose to protest directly to Czechoslovakia about its alleged illegal arms supplying to Israel rather than making such protest through the UN.

The Department replied that it had received several reports of US aircraft moving arms from Czechoslovakia to Israel in violation of Security Council truce resolutions and US policies on arms shipments. The planes ignored US Air Force orders to land when flying over Austria, and rather than ordering the Air Force to shoot them down, the United States made representations in Prague.[47]

Bobby and I lunched with the [Norman] Jacobs of Manchester at the Gat.[48] It was pleasant to see these generous-minded friends again who had been so kind to Ruth and me eighteen months before and in whose car we had become snowbound. Had a farewell brief conference with Arthur Rosenthal, who kindly agreed to take home some letters and a verbal message. Home for a nap and for a quiet evening during the curfew occasioned by Israel's first complete census.

On November 8, the British delegation at the UN, led by Harold Beeley and Hector McNeil, argued for sanctions against Israel if the Israelis refused to withdraw from the Negev. Britain threatened to help the Arabs otherwise. On November 10 in Washington, Lovett made his position clear to Eliahu Epstein. He was skeptical of the direct Israeli-Arab negotiations that the Israelis preferred, stated that the British would help the Arabs if matters came to all-out war, and said that the United States, if forced to choose, would back the UN over Israel. He suggested that "if Israel desired to retain the Negev she would have to give up Western Galilee," and that "I would hate to see the matter come to sanctions, but . . . the United Nations could not continue to be disregarded."[49]

47. Lovett to McDonald, no. 216, November 13, 1948, NARA, RG 59, 501.BB Palestine, box 2122, folder 3.
48. Norman M. Jacobs (1902–1977), longtime head of the Zionist Council of Manchester and Salford; worked to help Jewish refugees in the 1930s; settled in Israel, 1951. See Bill Williams, *Jews and Other Foreigners: Manchester and the Rescue of the Victims of European Fascism, 1933–40* (Manchester: Manchester University Press, 2011).
49. Marshall to acting secretary of state, no. 661, November 9, *FRUS*, 1948, v. V, pt. 2, 1559–1560; Memorandum by Lovett, November 10, 1948, *FRUS*, 1948, v. V, pt. 2, 1562–1564; Memorandum by Comay, November 11, 1948, *DFPI*, v. 2, d. 130.

To the office for a number of odd errands. While there, redrafted Knox's telegram on the attitude of public opinion towards possibility of sanctions.

The telegram went out over McDonald's signature:

> [Department] is aware that mission telegrams appraising situation since Negev battle . . . substantiate [General] Riley's reported estimate [of the] military possibilities. . . . Press, public, army and official sentiment here indicate complete solidarity that any UN action to restore Egypt's position [in the] Negev, or to sponsor occupation of [the] Negev by [the] Arab Legion, would be [a] gross injustice. All elements see UN being used deliberately by Great Britain as instrument to force Israel's surrender of [the] Negev to Transjordan as part of [a] British and not UN plan in Middle East and Israel will resist such maneuvers politically, and if driven to desperation, militarily. Israel has sacrificed too much to surrender area to defeated Arab invaders. All are seriously concerned and confused over US policy. Nonetheless there is evident here [a] new animation of hope that peace can be negotiated somehow and that [the] time is ripe for settlement.[50]

From a few minutes after eleven until one o'clock, Dr. Mohn, political adviser of the acting mediator, and I talked. We canvassed nearly every aspect of the Palestine situation, and that in Paris, together with the possibilities and probabilities of Security Council action or inaction. Dr. Mohn's points of view can be generally summarized as follows:

1) Dr. Bunche hopes that the Security Council may decide in favor of the policy of conciliation and support the General Assembly in setting up a conciliation commission.[51] Dr. Bunche would consider work with such a body as holding out a prospect of peace, which his mediatory efforts no longer do;
2) Mohn implied that Bunche was fearful of being made again the form of escape by the Security Council, while the latter would save itself from a clear and firm decision;
3) Mohn thinks that the British are determined [to] hold on to the Negev and will continue to make difficulties for any conciliation program. He doubts, however, that Dr. Bunche was intimidated by the presentations made to him by [Harold] Beeley and the other British representatives yesterday;
4) A proposed extension of the Negev resolution to include northern Galilee would be, according to Mohn, a waste of time and, moreover, be less justified

50. McDonald to secretary of state, no. 245, November 9, 1948, NARA, RG 59, MC 1390, reel 17, frame 417.
51. A General Assembly draft for a conciliation commission which would replace the United Nations Mediator on Palestine emerged from the State Department on October 16, 1948. See *FRUS*, 1948, v. V, pt. 2, 1481–1483. By October 26, Bunche hoped that the General Assembly might simply affirm the existence of the Jewish State, the termination of hostilities, and the right of Arab refugees to return to their homes, while leaving frontier issues to the proposed conciliation commission. The General Assembly in Resolution 194 of December 11 officially established the Palestine Conciliation Commission and its tasks.

than the original resolution, since it is clear that the Arabs under Fawzi Qawukji began the fighting around Manara;

5) Reestablishment of the exchange of guards system on Mount Scopus[52] is, according to Mohn, a triumph for the mediator. He wonders, however, why the Arabs have assented to the continuance of some sixty armed Jewish police in the Hadassah [Hospital] and [Hebrew] University buildings. The UN observers, he says, are of the opinion, quite different from the opinion expressed by Shertok to me last Saturday evening, that these guards, armed with light automatic weapons and perhaps heavier ones, could hold out until the Jewish forces reach them. If this judgment is correct, it changes fundamentally the conclusion one is to draw from Shertok's statement. There is being presented to the mediator a new scheme proposed by the observers under which all armed guards, Jewish and Arab, would be removed from Scopus and replaced by UN personnel. But as Mohn points out, these men, unless armed, might be the easy victims of the Arabs;

6) Mohn expressed the hope that Riley's frank speaking will have dissipated some of the clouds of wishful thinking and great powers' intrigue in Paris. In general, my talk with Mohn left the impression of a man discouraged in his work and disillusioned by the lack of consistent support received from [the] UN. It was as if he shared the views, which he attributed to his chief, that the truce had failed and that conciliation was the only solution.

Conference on the roof with Dr. Max Wolf, legal adviser of the ICRC and a relative of Lola Hahn's husband.[53] He is in Israel on a mission from the ICRC not related to Arab refugees. Seemingly, he is investigating the relations between the Committee's top representatives here, including perhaps de Reynier and the Israeli and other Near Eastern authorities. I asked him about the Empress of Japan fund. He replied that in the middle of August, following interviews with the president and Mr. Lovett, the head of the ICRC received the impression that the transfer to the Committee was about to be authorized by the United States. Nothing since has been reported to the ICRC. Wolf thought that perhaps the matter had bogged down in the Far Eastern Commission. When I heard this, I was uncharitable enough to think that if General McCoy were involved, this explanation would be logical enough.[54]

Wolf, too, as had Dr. Mohn earlier in the day, possibly from the same source, reported that Paris was considering referring the whole business of Arab refugees to the League of International Red Cross Societies. Wolf made no specific criticism of the UN refugee setup. He did, however, indicate that

52. See entry of October 23, 1948.
53. Lola Hahn-Warburg (1901–1989), oldest daughter of Max Moritz Warburg and Alice Warburg; helped organize the *Kindertransport*; husband was Rudolf Hahn (1867–1964), German Jewish industrialist who fled to Britain in 1938.
54. Major General (ret.) Frank McCoy (1874–1954), chairman of the Far Eastern Commission, an international body charged with determining the postwar fate of Japan.

the ICRC would take over if it were asked, but only on condition that the UN guaranteed the financing of the operation. As Wolf left he suggested that we meet later in the week. I told him I would be delighted to see him again. I also urged him to get in touch with our mutual friends in London.

Then followed nearly an hour's conference, also on the roof, with Dr. Pierre Descoeudres, chief of mission to the Middle East of the UN International Children's [Emergency] Fund [UNICEF], with his main office in Beirut. He is a relatively young Genovese.[55] He, too, spoke of the possibility of [the] Red Cross taking over Arab refugee administration. He made no direct criticism of Cilento's efforts, but recognized that the UN was only incidentally interested in refugees whereas the Red Cross Societies were specialists. His own work, limited to children and nursing or pregnant mothers, is being carried on in Israel, Lebanon, Syria, Arab Palestine, and Transjordan. Half of the $12,000,000 recently received from the UNRRA residue funds, having recently been voted in Paris for work in this area, is the basis of present operations.[56] $2,000,000 is to be spent this winter. The administration is through key representatives in the capitals with professional or volunteer representatives in the camps. Little or no relief is distributed in homes. He thinks that there is a relatively slight loss.

As to the larger problem, he estimates that there are now nearly 500,000 Arab refugees: 100,000 in Lebanon, perhaps 250,000 in the Palestine triangle [Tulkarm-Jenin-Nablus][57] and in Jericho, a relatively few in Syria, none in Iraq, and the rest in southern Palestine and Egypt [Gaza]. He stressed the need for a large number of administrators if the Red Cross Societies undertook to take over and obligated themselves to supervise the distribution at the refugee level.[58]

He commented on the way in which the flood of first about 70,000, and within the last days another 30,000 Arab refugees into Lebanon complicated that country's Christian-Moslem problem. This influx threatened to unsettle the balance against the Christians, with the result that the Lebanese Government was openly hostile to the refugees and was treating them with special severity in order to encourage their exit to Syria. He asked me what I had heard about flirtations between Israel and Lebanon to establish closer relations. I replied nothing; I gave a similar reply to this query somewhat like that of Colonel

55. Pierre Descoeudres, part of the Red Cross delegation to Berlin in 1940 that studied conditions for Jews there, visited Buchenwald, and witnessed early deportations of Jews to Lublin district of the General Government; helped keep the ICRC in Geneva informed of these developments; UNICEF's chief of mission in the Middle East, November 1948. Jean-Claude Favez, *The Red Cross and the Holocaust* (New York: Cambridge University Press, 1999), 33–34, 52.

56. The United Nations Relief and Rehabilitation Administration in Europe [UNRRA] had gone out of existence in July 1946, and remaining funds were reallocated to UNICEF, which came into existence in December 1946.

57. The area between Tulkarm, Nablus, and Jenin in northern Samaria became known as the triangle of terror during the Arab revolt of 1936–1939 because of the strength of resistance there. It was occupied by Iraqi troops in 1948–1949.

58. Descoeudres reported that in Gaza, the Egyptian military was not distributing rice and flour received from the UN. Its hands were full with the military campaign. He learned that ten children died of starvation each day in the camps. Gallagher, *Quakers in the Israeli-Palestinian Conflict*, 63–64.

van der Velde's this morning about the Litani and Israel's northern frontier.[59] He promised to get in touch with me if and when he came back to Tel Aviv.

In his telegram to the attention of Truman and Lovett, dated November 10, McDonald recounted his talks with Mohn, Wolf, and Descoeudres. He reiterated that Bunche's "political role weakens his refugee work" and that the Red Cross must take control of the Arab refugee crisis from the UN to prevent a "stark mass tragedy." He added, "I am completely skeptical [of the] UN blanket financial appeal to member states whose responses would be slow and inadequate." He urged that a presidential appeal be made for funds in cooperation with the American Red Cross.

McDonald repeated an earlier suggestion from October 23, rejected on October 29, that he go to the UN General Assembly meeting in Paris. "Without sensitiveness if again disapproved, I repeat [my] earlier suggestion that in [the] role of 'refugee expert' I be asked to testify publicly before third committee on urgency [of] governmental and public response comparable to catastrophic need.[60]* Such appearance of [the] American special representative [to] Israel would help answer Arab criticism that US is disproportionately interested [in] Jewish welfare and [the US] would not be open to [the] charge of political propaganda." He further suggested, in light of the importance of the refugee problem, that the US chiefs of mission in the Middle East meet on neutral ground under Griffis's chairmanship "to exchange views and analyze what can be done with benefit to whole area."*[61]

On November 9 in Washington, Eliahu Epstein and Michael Comay met with a small group of American officials, which included Oscar "Jack" Ewing and David Niles. Niles confirmed that the president opposed sanctions and the separation of the Negev from Israel. (Several Israeli sources confirmed later that, on November 13, Truman told Lovett that he would not accept sanctions.) Yet the president, more than anything else, Niles said, wanted peace in the region. Niles promised, Epstein reported, "to deal [with the] matter [of] McDonald's invitation to Paris, but expressed his doubts [about the] practicability [of the] journey."[62]

Wednesday, November 10

Worked during the morning with staff at home. The Ben-Gurions came promptly at 1:15 for lunch. We were eight altogether, including Knox, Hope,

59. During Operation Hiram, the IDF crossed the Lebanese border and halted at the Litani River.

60. The Third Committee of the General Assembly dealt with social and humanitarian issues.

61. McDonald to secretary of state [personal attention of president and acting secretary], no. 247, November 10, 1948, *FRUS*, 1948, v. V, pt. 2, 1567–1568. Lovett, based on McDonald's despatch, ordered Griffis "to proceed immediately by air with brief stopover at Paris for consultation with [the secretary of state]. Upon your arrival here we should wish to go over Arab refugee problem with you in consultation with the President and would expect upon your return to Near East if feasible to hold a meeting of US Chiefs of Mission in that area at some neutral spot, possibly Rhodes." Lovett to Griffis, no. 1557, November 12, 1948, NARA, RG 58, 501.BB Palestine, Box 2122, folder 2.

62. Epstein to Shertok, *DFPI*, v. 2, d. 117. On sanctions, see Note by Comay, November 15, 1948, *DFPI*, v. 2, d. 142.

and Colonel van der Velde. Before we sat down, I had a brief opportunity to tell Ben-Gurion of my interest in the refugee problem, but I got no clear response from him. Perhaps there was not time for this, but I think it was rather that he had nothing definite that he wanted to say.

During the meal, which was excellent, the talk ranged from subject to subject but without ever settling down on any really serious topic. Both the prime minister and Paula were in good spirits and laughed heartily at two or three of my standard stories. (There is a great advantage in a new audience.) At one point Ben-Gurion asked about the histories of the [American] Civil War, implying that he intended to read up on the subject. This [was] but another indication of the versatility of his mind.[63]

After lunch I took him up to the roof to show him the view. He said that the government had contemplated taking over all the buildings on this hill. Earlier, he had commented that $500 a month [for the special representative's residence] was a very large rental.[64] The chief point he made as we talked on the roof was about the UN. "I cannot," he said, "make head or tail out of what is going on or what they are planning to do." He implied that he was in the same state of mystification about the policy of the US. And, as I later telegraphed the Department, "I was in no position to enlighten him."[65]

At about a quarter of three Paula said they must go. I walked out with them to the street where his khaki-colored and allegedly bullet-proof Packard awaited him. It was preceded by an open jeep with four military police, and it was followed by a small truck with other police. The proof that the party was a major affair was that we used our front door for the first time since the Bernadotte murder. Bobby was congratulated by everyone. In reply to my congratulations, she sweetly said, "It is easy to be a successful hostess when you are at the other end of the table."

Very pleasant dinner, the three of us, with Eddie Cantor's friend Fred Zinnemann at the Armon [Hotel]. Zinnemann, the producer of *The Search* (1948), the MGM Zurich-made film which we all enjoyed so much on the boat, is here to try to find in the lives of the people a story that will make a film.[66] Zinnemann is almost shy and poetic in his manner and so unlike one's common preconception of Hollywood that casually one would not think him a producer at all. He was very grateful for some suggestions I made, and it was agreed that we would talk again after we had gone about the country more. One of my suggestions was that he send for a print of *The Search*, and that if he wished, I would invite a group of people to see a showing of it at our house.

---

63. Ben-Gurion's interest might also have been spurred by his concerns regarding civil strife in the embryonic state, as epitomized by the *Altalena* incident and its aftermath.

64. See entry of August 13, 1948, November 7, 1948.

65. McDonald to secretary of state, no. 252, November 11, 1948, NARA, RG 59, MC 1390, reel 17, frame 432.

66. Fred Zinnemann (1907–1997), Austrian-born filmmaker; moved to the United States, 1934; both parents were murdered by the Nazis. *The Search* was filmed in postwar Germany and concerned a boy and his mother, Czech Jews, who searched for one another after the war in the DP camp system. Zinnemann later directed classics including *From Here to Eternity* (1953).

Later on November 10, Lovett reported to Marshall a November 6 discussion in Key West between the president, himself, and Ambassador Douglas aimed at determining US policy in the wake of Security Council Resolution 61 of November 4. Douglas told Truman that, while the British were serious about rearming Egypt and Transjordan if the war continued, and while London insisted that Transjordan have a port on the Mediterranean, Bevin was also now willing to concede to Israel the northern portion of the Negev, where the Israelis had established settlements. Truman continued to endorse the November 29, 1947, partition plan, which had awarded Israel most of the Negev, while hoping to preserve UN authority and concord with the British.

"In plain language," Lovett reported, "the President's position is that if Israel wishes to retain that part of the Negev granted it under [the] Nov[ember] 29 resolution, it will have to take the rest of [the] Nov[ember] 29 settlement, which means giving up western Galilee and Jaffa. We feel that there is room for a mutually advantageous arrangement—Israel to retain western Galilee and Jaffa in return for relinquishing part of the Negev to the Arab States, presumably Transjordan and Egypt." Lovett added in strict confidence, however, that should Israel trade western Galilee and Jaffa, it would retain part of the Negev along a southeasterly line running from Gaza through Be'er Sheva to the Dead Sea, or possibly, a larger part of the Negev still. Clifford on the president's behalf approved Lovett's report to Marshall. It was not shared with US missions in the Middle East until November 24. Douglas later complained that "when seen on the map, [Lovett's proposed line] goes far beyond the idea of 'adjustments' in the Negev. . . . I do not believe that the UK will buy this one."[67]

Withdrawal of Israeli forces to the October 14 line and the creation of demilitarized zones as stipulated in the resolution would have endangered Israeli settlements in the Negev. In Paris, Shertok told Marshall on November 13 that Tel Aviv preferred a simple armistice in place, with negotiations to proceed from that point. He also expressed dismay that Israel still lacked UN membership and could neither vote in the General Assembly nor negotiate as an equal with the Arab states in a proposed conciliation commission. He warned that, though Israel's sympathies lay with the United States, the Israeli people increasingly saw the USSR as friendlier. Marshall warned Shertok, "Don't overplay your hand."[68]

Thursday, November 11

No holiday for our office on Armistice Day. Worked out with Knox and Hope another telegram to the Department, in which was included a second suggestion about Paris. Mr. Yitzhak Katz, secretary of the chamber of commerce

---

67. Lovett to Marshall [eyes only], no. 148, November 10, 1948, *FRUS*, 1948, v. V, pt. 2, 1565–1567. Also Douglas to Lovett [eyes only], no. 4849, November 12, 1948, *FRUS*, 1948, v. V, pt. 2, 1570–1572; Douglas to Lovett [eyes only], no. 4851, November 12, 1948, *FRUS*, 1948, v. V, pt. 2, 1573–1574; Marshall to acting secretary of state, no. 717, November 12, 1948, *FRUS*, 1948, v. V, pt. 2, 1574–1575.
68. Memorandum by Marshall, November 13, 1948, *FRUS*, 1948, v. V, pt. 2, 1577–1579.

of Tel Aviv and Jaffa, came to pay a courtesy call.[69] He brought with him four or five of his fellows. Much of our talk was about the American election, during which I took an almost mean pleasure in pointing out the extent to which American businessmen had brought the result upon themselves by their failures to support any Republican action to meet the problems of housing, high cost of living, etc. My guests were quick to reply that the situations here and at home were not comparable. They went on to propagandize me against the Kaplan income tax program. They were inclined to blame Horowitz, whom they recognize as a man of affairs [i.e., a businessman].

Friday, November 12

I should have indicated under Thursday morning that an hour or two was spent with Knox and Hope, during which they completed [cutting] the "purple passages" from my draft of my talk.[70] Later, I was convinced that they were correct in cutting out any reference to Russia and the political bosses. On the other hand, I think I was sound in insisting that I keep my point about refusing to appeal for any specific type of policy here—in other words, to leave the text as I had it, closing with my hope for an Israel free to be itself. My only concession was to insert after the words "not a copy of either the West or the East" the word "free" before Israel. The morning busy on last minute revision of text.

The evening meeting under the auspices of the Journalists' Association of Tel Aviv was about what might have been expected. Madame de Philippe and Miss Herlitz went along with us as our guests. The hall was filled, and in addition, perhaps two or three hundred people were standing. The chairman, the editor of *HaBoker*, Joseph Heftmann,[71] was witty, though perhaps a little long in the intervals between the speeches. Joseph Gravitzky, head of the PIO [Palestine Information Office], showed himself a tub-thumping artist.[72] Reuben Rubinstein, a well-known editor of a Yiddish Lithuanian newspaper, was dull in his talk about the refugee camps.[73] When he had finished, nearly two hours of Hebrew talk had passed before I was called upon. My talk went as well as I

69. Yitzhak Katz (1901–1991), Ukrainian-born playwright and government clerk; emigrated to Palestine, 1923; secretary of Jaffa (and Tel Aviv) Chamber of Commerce, 1925–1952.

70. McDonald's first public speech in Israel, which he privately described as "properly colorless." McDonald to Janet, Halsey, and Ruth, November 12, 1948, McDonald Papers, USHMM box 7, folder November 1948.

71. Joseph Heftmann (1888–1955), Polish-born General Zionist; served on the Warsaw Jewish Community Council in 1920s; first secretary-general of Va'ad Leumi, 1921; second editor-in-chief of *HaBoker*, the General Zionist organ in Palestine, founded in 1935.

72. Joseph Gravitzky [later Regev] (1901–1955), Polish-born journalist; reported for *Haint*, the largest Yiddish daily in Warsaw; emigrated to Palestine, 1932; headed press bureau of Jewish Agency; headed Palestine Information Office and then press division of State of Israel's information services.

73. Reuben Rubenstein (1890–1967), Lithuanian-born journalist, edited *Di Yiddishe Stimme* in Kovno for twenty years; headed Jewish faction in the Lithuanian parliament before World War II; arrested by NKVD in 1940 and moved to forced labor camp; migrated to Munich and then Palestine after the war; became a Yiddish-language commentator on state-run radio, Kol Israel.

could have expected. I had the feeling that perhaps somewhat more than half the audience was able to follow it fairly well.

Saturday, November 13

Was busy with this and that, despite it being Sabbath, and had just received Mr. and Mrs. P.L.O. Guy[74] when Knox and Hope arrived with the look on their faces of someone who is about to give the news of a birthday party. They brought the telegram from the Department in which Lovett said that Key West had been consulted and that I was authorized to go to Paris, and that it was hoped I would not be more than ten days absent from my post.[75] It was decided to suggest [a press] release from Washington and put on [the explanatory] ground of technical refugee consultation.

Learned that Mr. Guy, whom, with his wife I had met in Beirut in the spring of '46 at the time I was holding the hand of my young friend Yehuda Hellman, is now in the staff of the Israeli Department of Antiquities.[76] His office is in Jerusalem, but at the moment he is working in Jaffa. He told me of two or three modest "digs" now in operation. By the time my colleagues had left, it was nearly late enough for the Guys to have to leave for lunch. Nonetheless, he did emphasize that, though a Britisher, he regarded his government's policy as terribly mistaken, because only the Jews would or could make anything of the Negev. He quoted T. E. Lawrence from the latter's book on the desert of Zin.[77] On the other hand, if the Jews do not get the Negev, it will, according to Guy, be used and abused for tank training and other military operations, which will there, as they did in North Africa, so dislocate the soil, such as it is, as to increase terribly the sand erosion.

In the evening Bobby and I attended another of Leonard Bernstein's concerts. The program was unusually interesting and the second half most satisfying. Bartok's Symphony for Strings and Ravel's Piano Concerto, which Leonard played, were followed by Schumann's Second Symphony. Though this is not the work with which I am very familiar, I deeply enjoyed it, especially the slow movement.

On November 14, Paul Mohn transmitted to the Israeli Foreign Ministry a communication from Bunche informing Israel of the UN-defined cease-fire lines in the Negev. The IDF was to pull back roughly to the October 14 line, save for forces

---

74. Philip Langstaffe Ord Guy (1885–1952), British archaeologist; chief inspector for the Palestine Department of Antiquities, 1922–1927; director of British School for Archaeology in Jerusalem, 1935–1939; remained in Israel after 1948 and received permission from Israeli authorities to excavate in Jaffa.

75. On November 12, Truman discussed with Lovett the matter of McDonald going to Paris. McDonald's instructions were to go to Paris for consultations with Marshall and Griffis.

76. The story of Hellman's arrest in Beirut as a Zionist agent while working for the *Palestine Post* is in Goda et al., eds., *To the Gates of Jerusalem*, 173–178.

77. C. Leonard Woolley and T. E. Lawrence, *The Wilderness of Zin* (London: Harrison and Sons, 1914).

maintained in the Israeli Negev settlements. Arab forces were to remain at the Gaza—al-Majdal road in the west and the line roughly from Nahalin to the Dead Sea. The areas in between were to be a neutral zone. Be'er Sheva was to be demilitarized. An Egyptian civil administrator was to govern it as an Arab town.[78] The deadline for compliance was November 19. Worried about an impasse, Shertok called for a new resolution that would simply call for an armistice-in-place.[79] On the same day, Lovett reported to Marshall that he had spoken with Clifford, who was with the president in Key West. "As a matter of practice within [the] realm of possibility," Lovett reported, "sanctions as applied by [Security Council] in instant case are out of the question."[80]

Sunday, November 14

Conference with Knox and Colonel van der Velde on Paris plans. The telegram from the Department accepting the idea of a [press] release "if any were necessary," to be played down on the "expert" line, left us in a state of mild confusion. Hope thought we should send another telegram urging the need for some [press] release, but I demurred, pointing out that at the airport I would have to answer a question put by reporters [and] that I would have to say that any statement must come from Washington. Colonel van der Velde was very disappointed that the answer to his request was negative.

The State Department preferred that such a trip not become a news story at all. It released a statement only on November 15 announcing that McDonald would go to Paris to confer on Arab refugees.[81]

On the morning of November 14, McDonald had Ben-Gurion informed that Washington had directed him to go to the UN General Assembly meeting in Paris. "I shall leave on the first plane," he said. "Before I go, however, I am most anxious [to] confer with you. My plans until Washington makes the announcement are 'top secret.'"[82]

Brief conference with Eytan, who stopped here at the house in his way "up to the hill." He told me that Ben-Gurion wanted me for lunch at 1:30. In my drive up to the hill with Shalom, I was preceded by an open jeep with four military police. We were just in time, because I met Ben-Gurion near the restaurant. We lunched alone at what was the most complete meal I have had outside of one or two private homes in Israel. Gefilte fish, chicken livers on toast, delicious soup, mixed grill, portion of chicken and a chop with vegetables, lettuce salad, stewed fruit, and finally, fresh fruit and coffee.

78. *DFPI*, v. 2, d. 137.

79. Shertok to Marshall, November 14, 1948, *FRUS*, 1948, v. V, pt. 2, 1581–1582; Shertok to Eytan, November 15, 1948, *DFPI*, v. 2, d. 143.

80. Lovett to US embassy Paris, no. 476, November 14, 1948, NARA, RG 59, 501.BB Palestine, box 2122, folder 3.

81. Lovett to Tel Aviv, no. 211 to Tel Aviv, November 10, 1948, NARA, 501.BB Palestine, Box 2122, folder 4.

82. McDonald to Ben-Gurion, November 14, 1948, McDonald Papers, USHMM, box 7, folder 8.

The most important portions of our conversation I have recorded in two telegrams to the Department under date of the 15th. The one outlined Ben-Gurion's admiration of the American two-party system, so brilliantly strengthened by Truman's victory.[83] The other subject was Ben-Gurion's confusion and resentment at the Bunche Negev proposal. The suggestion [of a] civil governor for Be'er Sheva seemed to him particularly outrageous. His forces would not, he said, withdraw from their gains. He could not understand why Israel should be penalized for trying to occupy the territory assigned to it by the November 29 General Assembly Resolution, while Egypt should be rewarded for having contemptuously disregarded that resolution and [for] invading the Negev.

I was interested at his significant question, when I told him that I would be going to Paris, whether the idea was the Department's or the president's. He said that Shiloah was coming back tomorrow and that Yigael Yadin, a director of operations in the field, had gone to Paris.[84] He added that if there were anything new before I left, he would have Eytan get in touch with me. Rest of the day spent in telephone conversations with the office and with planning to get ready to leave.

McDonald informed Truman and Lovett of Ben-Gurion's statements regarding the Negev. He commented," I am convinced [that the Provisional Government] would have unanimous support [of the Israeli] people in risking imposition [of] UN sanctions rather than yield in [the] Negev. . . . When in confidence [I] told [the prime minister of] my plans [to] visit this week Paris as refugee 'expert' he expressed pleasure and added, 'It is encouraging that [the] US special representative in Israel should show sympathy [with] all peoples [in the] Middle East.'"[85]

Monday, November 15

Pleasant lunch with the Hoofiens and Hope. Mr. Hoofien was interesting in his economic and political discussion and amusing in his comments on Ronald Storrs whom he characterized as delightful and a dilettante in the strict sense of the word—a man who enjoys the good things of life and has a keen

---

83. McDonald to secretary of state [personal attention Clifford], no. 257, December 15, 1948, NARA, RG 59, MC 1390, reel 17, frame 465. Ben-Gurion had asked about the reduction in the number of splinter parties and the movement to a two-party system, and was especially impressed with the elimination of the impact of Henry Wallace's splinter Progressive Party. He said, "I am afraid we cannot work Mr. Truman's miracle here in the forthcoming elections to the Constituent Assembly. But I shall strive to follow his example."

84. Yigael Yadin (1917–1984), Jerusalem-born son of archaeologist Eliezer Sukenik and himself an accomplished archaeologist; Haganah member from age 15 in 1933; head of IDF operations, May 1948–November 1949; retired from IDF at age 35 due to disagreements with Ben-Gurion over Israel's approach to defense and the scope of the IDF budget; returned to archaeology.

85. McDonald to secretary of state [personal attention president and acting secretary], no. 256, November 17, 1948, Truman Library, Clifford Papers, Subject File, 1945–54, box 14, folder Palestine Telegrams and Cables 2 of 2.

appreciation of beauty in many manifestations, music, art, etc.—but without complete conviction or real principle.[86]

Our tea for Colonel Efraim Ben-Artzi and his wife, Major Victoria Ben-Artzi, who are sailing in a day or two for the States, where he is accredited as the Israeli military attaché, was interrupted by the tempest in a teapot arising from the [movers'] argument about the crates containing our beds to the upper level. Before our guests left, I gave them letters of introduction to Janet Wiecking and the Maucks[87] and a letter to the captain of the Marine Corps soliciting his good offices to discourage any annoyance to them when the ship put in at Alexandria.

Several telephone calls from people inquiring about my Paris trip. The interest in it shows how mistaken the Department was in its suggestion that there might be no need for publicity at all. Merely securing the UN plane seats and the necessary visas was sufficient to give away the whole secret, after which not to have made at least a brief statement would have been to have given an unwarranted air of mystery and therefore of importance to the trip. Hence, after prayerful conference this morning with Hope and Knox, both of whom have had long experience in interpreting Department language, we decided that the Department's publicity telegram left us no alternative except to say as we did in answer to all inquiries: "Mr. McDonald had been called to Paris for consultation with the Secretary." This and no more.

Haaretz *and other Hebrew newspapers reported on November 16 that Israeli leaders hoped that McDonald's trip to Paris would bring a UN retreat from its recent statements concerning the Negev. In Washington, Lovett was nonplussed. "Department's press statement that purpose [of McDonald's trip to Paris] is [the] Arab refugee problem [is] generally disbelieved in [the] Hebrew language press[,] where optimistic speculations range from assertion he is summoned [to] mediate between Egypt and Israel to [the] 'conviction' [that] he is going to argue [the] Israel case before the [Security Council]. These guesses [are] linked with press reports attributed [to] Paris and London that sensational developments in favor [of] Israel [are] expected."[88]*

Tuesday, November 16

Dr. Weizmann and I met in his office at the institute, a modest room with a chemist's desk, on which were two photographs of distinguished chemists. Weizmann was in a serious mood and outlined to me the message which he hoped I would send to the president. In substance it was, as I subsequently put it in a telegram: You know that I am a moderate man who has always avoided

---

86. Sir Ronald Storrs (1881–1955), British imperial official in the Middle East during and after World War I; served in Cairo, 1904 to 1917, where he helped, with T. E. Lawrence, to foment the Arab revolt against Ottoman rule. After the British entry into Jerusalem in 1917, he became the city's military governor, remaining as civil governor until 1926.

87. Janet Wieking, daughter of McDonald's favorite history professor at Indiana University. Wilfred and Billie Mauck, friends living in Washington, DC, area.

88. Lovett to secretary of state, no. 267 [to be passed to McDonald], McDonald Papers, USHMM, box 7, folder 8.

extremes. Nor am I a person given to threats. The situation, however, is so serious that I feel I must warn that the Jews will never surrender the Negev; everyone there will die first. British policy since President Truman made his suggestion in 1945 of a large scale immigration to Palestine of Jewish refugees has been consistently based on fundamental misjudgments: first, that the Jews could not finance the war; second, that the Arabs would drive the Jews into the sea; and, third, currently that the Jews are in the hands of the Russians. This last, like the two previous charges, is false. Israel welcomes Russian support in the UN, but dreads Russian embrace. Not only is Israel Western in its orientation, but the people are democratic and realize that only through the cooperation and support of the US can they become strong and remain free. Only the West, through UN and US-supported humiliation and desertion of Israel, can force the country into the embrace of Russia. Please pass on this appeal to Mr. Truman, whose prestige is incomparably higher among us than that of any other statesman. I fear, he concluded, that UN sanctions against Israel might be a prelude to a new world war.

Our lunch was delayed by an air raid warning. The meal was pleasant, only the Weizmanns and I present. Mrs. Weizmann read a moving letter from an ornithologist friend, Richard Meinertzhagen.[89] They said goodbye to me with much emotion. Their words were that my mission had proved to be of the highest importance, especially if I went on to Washington. Stopped at the office and at the consulate and home, harassed and tired but completely refreshed after a nap.

McDonald emphasized in his report to the president: "Weizmann's consistent reputation for moderation lends special significance to above views."[90]

Long conference with Leo Kohn developed some extraordinarily interesting ideas on both the immediate situation and the longer-range problem. As to the first, he saw acute danger if Israel were humiliated in the Negev, inviting extremism, weakening the moderates at the critical moment when the election is just a few weeks off. On the other side, he recognized the danger to Israel being out in the position of the aggressor if it made no concession to the American and other countries' feelings that the UN must have its authority vindicated. Hence, the necessity for a short-range formula.

On the longer issue, he pointed out the unlikelihood of UN success, the unreality of UN machinery, the use being made by Britain of the Arab weakness to offer to rearm them for the price of being reaccepted as their defender, the possibility that Russia might, seeing this result, be tempted to change its pro-Israel policy, and in any case, Russia would certainly utilize the betrayal of Israel

89. Colonel Richard Henry Meinertzhagen (1878–1967), British adventurer and agent, friend of Israel, and ornithologist; later discovered to have fabricated much of his life story. See Brian Garfield, *The Meinertzhagen Mystery: The Life and Legend of a Colossal Fraud* (Dulles, VA: Potomac Books, 2007).
90. McDonald to secretary of state [personal attention president and acting secretary], no. 260, November 17, 1948, *FRUS*, 1948, v. V, pt. 2, 1606–1607.

as an example of Western imperialism. From all of these and other considerations, he arrived at the desirability of the injection of a wholly new element into
the situation. This he formulated on a wholly personal basis and a most tentative
way. He envisaged a request for mediation by the president. We both agreed
that this could follow only after a shorter problem had been faced and solved.

He stressed the danger of British re-armament of Iraq, Transjordan and
Egypt, [and] the use of these arms including tanks and planes manned by Britishers against Israeli forces.[91] Moreover, this could be only a beginning and
might lead to Israel's destruction. If Israel were indicted as the aggressor, then
Britain could continue the re-armament openly and increase its chances of rebuilding its situation with the Arabs. He saw the thing in its broadest aspects
and urged that I fill out his general outline with the fuller data, which Eban
would give me. He suggested that Shiloah might be available to talk with me in
the morning if he had returned from Paris, and I suggested that the latter
might ride up with me to Haifa.

A jolly dinner with Knox, Hope, and Barnes, and the preparation of the
Washington telegram to the Department and the president [on Weizmann's
statements] and some final items about housekeeping and this dictation concluded the day.

*On November 16 the UN Security Council issued Resolution 62. It reaffirmed
previous resolutions, including the most recent one of November 4, which called for
Israeli–Egyptian pullback to the October 14 truce lines in the Negev. It called for all
sides in the conflict to negotiate either directly or through the acting mediator with a
view toward a general cease-fire with permanent cease-fire lines.[92]*

Wednesday, November 17

Up early final packing and instructions and on the way by 7:30. The trip to
Haifa was uneventful despite Shalom seemingly striving for a record. Reached
Riley's office before 9:00 but, since he was late, chatted with his aide who de-
veloped the thesis that even if Britain were rearming the Arabs, this would be
only about a 50-50 proposition since the Jews on their part were being rearmed.
Riley arrived late so that we had only a few minutes together. He stressed that
there were three steps: first, the acceptance of withdrawal orders of the UN of
November 4th and of November 14th; second, the fixing by the UN of tentative

---

91. Shertok told Marshall in Paris on November 13 that Israel had evidence that the British
were now supplying the Arabs with men and armaments. Marshall said that such reports were
false. The Egyptians had moved additional artillery and tanks to the front during the second
truce, but their own commanders knew that the additional weaponry was inadequate even for
defense. After Operation Yoav Egyptian forces were still unable to break through Israeli lines to
the troops caught in the Faluja pocket. Meanwhile the British were holding to the embargo.
Memorandum by Marshall, *FRUS*, 1948, v. V, pt. 2, 1577–1580. Also Pollack, *Arabs at War*,
18–22.
92. See www.un.org/en/ga/search/view_doc.asp?symbol=S/RES/62 (1948), accessed
December 2015.

boundary lines; third, the final fixation of lines through a boundary commission. The first two steps must be insisted upon now by the UN. As to lines in the south, Riley was indefinite, not caring particularly whether the 31st parallel were chosen or some line north or south of that. I was amazed and a little shocked at Riley's incidental confession that he had not understood that the November 29th resolution had given the whole of the Negev except the Gaza coastal strip to the Jews. In particular, he had not realized that the Jewish area reached down to the Gulf of Aqaba. Indeed, he at first argued with me that this could not have been the case.

At the airfield we were able to observe a small group of refugees who were waiting to be cleared through the customs. The elders and the children all looked well fed and in good health, but with pitifully meager effects. I greeted the children, but their return *shaloms* were tentative and uncertain. Typical of the petty retaliatory actions of the Arab states was a practice disclosed when the Israel customs official asked me if I objected to having my exit stamp in my passport. I said no. The explanation of the question is that the Arab states have a practice of refusing visas or admissions to persons whose passports show previous residence in Israel.

With our permission the transport took off promptly at 10:00. Our UN DC-3 plane was a service job with bucket seats and no toilet facilities. We didn't mind, however, for the trip was smooth. Our stop in Rhodes was so brief (we dropped off the paymaster) that we reached Athens by 2:30. En route we had had another view of Cyprus. Rhodes, from what we could see of it, seemed beautiful.

In Athens were met by Mr. Beyer[93] of the embassy and were delighted to be told that we had seats on the 6:00 pm TWA flight Rome, Geneva, Paris. We had only time enough for lunch and a brief rest and ticket arrangements. I paid with my personal check for Bobby's ticket and by a travel order or voucher for my own. There was no payment for either of us on the UN mail run. The climate was bracing and the sky beautiful so that we could get an impression of how lovely Greece in the winter could be.

Again, without any personal word from Ambassador [Henry F.] Grady, we took off at 6:25.[94] Despite the TWA statement to the embassy that they had had to throw off two passengers to make room for us, there were several vacant seats in the beautiful plush platinum-plate Constellation. It was a delightful contrast with the bare aluminum DC-3 of the morning. Without incident we reached Rome about 10:00 and took off again forty-five minutes later. Just before

93. Roland C. Beyer, second secretary and vice consul.
94. Henry F. Grady (1882–1957), Columbia-trained Ph.D. in economics; US Commerce Department official, 1921–1928; appointed to Allied supervisory commission in Greece, 1945; ambassador to India, 1947–1948; ambassador to Greece, 1948–1950; ambassador to Iran 1950–1951. His history with McDonald began in 1946 when the Morrison-Grady Plan attempted to counteract the recommendations for Palestine that McDonald helped write as part of the Anglo-American Committee of Inquiry. McDonald was instrumental in convincing Truman to reject the Morrison-Grady Plan. See Goda et al., eds., *To the Gates of Jerusalem*, 239–252.

we reached Geneva at 12:00, and when we had begun to calculate our arrival in Paris two hours later, the steward announced that the Paris airport was closed by fog and that we would spend the night in Geneva. Fortunately there were beds for all of us at the [Hotel] Metropole, where Bobby and I turned in at 2:00, feeling that we had done pretty well for the day.

Debate in the General Assembly's First Committee on the Arab-Israeli conflict resumed on November 18. A British draft for a new General Assembly resolution called for the full endorsement of Bernadotte's territorial recommendations, including those regarding the Negev, Jerusalem, Haifa, and Lydda, and the return of Arab refugees. A new Palestine Conciliation Commission [PCC], suggested earlier by Bunche, was also to take over the duties of the acting mediator in implementing the peace.[95]

Three days earlier, Attlee and Bevin had sternly warned that Israeli misbehavior might rupture relations between Great Britain and the United States and also ruin UN authority. If "the Jews" failed to comply with Security Council resolutions, Britain would send a garrison to Aqaba to defend the southern Negev. If Israel attacked the Arab Legion in Palestine, London would provide armed assistance to Transjordan and Egypt, starting with RAF reinforcements to its base at Amman. Foreign Office officials drew a parallel with the 1938 Munich agreement with Nazi Germany. London, they said, would not "sell Abdullah down the river for the sake of a spurious peace." They further insisted that the Arab governments, which had all earlier rejected the Bernadotte Plan, were now ready to accept it. If Israel "behaved appropriately," London would extend the new state de jure recognition.[96]

Shertok and the Israeli delegation in Paris urged the United States to recognize the realities created since November 1947, including the present battle lines, as a basis for negotiations over frontiers. A new US resolution might also internationalize Jerusalem's Old City instead of the entirety of Jerusalem, and begin a permanent solution to the Arab refugee problem "in consultation with all interested Governments, specialized agencies and voluntary organizations." Shertok also made it clear that Israel "will be unable to cooperate [with the] Conciliation Commission unless equalized with Arab states as regards [UN] membership." On November 17, Shertok announced to the First Committee that Israel intended to keep the entire Galilee region, that it would not relinquish the Negev, and that "modern Jerusalem," would become part of Israel.

The Israelis made some conciliatory gestures. On November 19, in order to avoid a full break with the UN, they agreed to a withdrawal of "surplus troops" in the Negev that had entered since October 14, albeit while retaining defensive forces in the Negev and while keeping some 4,000 Egyptian troops trapped in a pocket around

95. British draft of November 18, 1948 in *DFPI*, v. 2, 625–628.
96. Marshall to Lovett [eyes only], no. 134, November 15, 1948, *FRUS*, 1948, v. V, pt. 2, 1585–1589; Memorandum by Douglas for Marshall [in Paris], November 15, 1948, *FRUS*, 1948, v. V, pt. 2, 1590–1591; Douglas to secretary of state, no. 887, November 17, 1948, *FRUS*, 1948, v. V, pt. 2, 1602–1603.

Faluja pending armistice negotiations.[97] *Between November 20 and November 30 they agreed to a cease-fire with Transjordan in Jerusalem that allowed the resumption of convoys to Mount Scopus.*[98]

State Department advisers in Paris, led by Dean Rusk,[99] *supported the British and tried to get the delegation as a whole to "hold our present policy to the lines of the Bernadotte Report." The president's delegates, including John Foster Dulles, Eleanor Roosevelt, and Benjamin Cohen, rejected the Bernadotte Plan.*[100] *McDonald officially went to Paris to give expert advice on the Arab refugee crisis, but he also involved himself with the negotiations over political issues concerning Israel. He lobbied members of the US delegation and kept in constant touch with the White House. His daughter Bobby and Noah Karlin attended UN committee debates and relayed information to him.*[101]

Thursday November 18

We took off at about 11:30 and were due in Paris at 1:00. The panorama view of the Alps was magnificent as we flew above the clouds in brilliant sunlight. Again, the flight was without incident until we reached the Paris neighborhood, where the continued fog required us to circle for fifteen minutes or so before we could land. It was nearly 3:00 before we reached the [Hotel] Crillon. Lunch and an interrupted and futile attempt to make contacts with the delegation were somewhat wearying. But the transfer from our small room to a deluxe suite and the prospect of a full day free of travel difficulties on Friday sent us to bed in [a] cheerful mood. Telephone calls from Hyman Schulson of the Emergency Council[102] at home and of Eliahu Ben-Horin[103] just as I was dropping off to sleep were not the best bedtime stories.

97. Shertok to Marshall, November 14, 1948, *FRUS*, 1948, v. V, pt. 2, 1581–1582; Shertok to Epstein, November 18, 1948, *DFPI*, v. 2, d. 158; Comay to Ross, November 19, 1948, *DFPI*, v. 2, d. 161; Shiloah to Shertok, November 24, 1948, *DFPI*, v. 2, d. 179; Memorandum by McClintock to acting secretary of state, November 17, 1948, *FRUS*, 1948, v. V, pt. 2, pp. 1598–1599; Marshall to acting secretary of state, no. 848, November 19, 1948, *FRUS*, 1948, v. V, pt. 2, 1616; Dulles to secretary of state, no. 946, November 26, 1948, *FRUS*, 1948, v. V, pt. 2, 1630–1631. On Faluja see *DFPI*, v. 2, d. 192, 195; and Pollack, *Arabs at War*, 22–28.

98. Shiloah to Shertok, November 20, 1948, *DFPI*, v. 2, d. 168; Shiloah to Shertok, November 30, 1948, *DFPI*, v. 2, d. 209.

99. Dean Rusk, now director, Office of United Nations Affairs, Department of State, and the ranking career US diplomat at the General Assembly.

100. See Rusk to secretary of state, October 1, 1948, which included his statements to John Foster Dulles, NARA, RG 59, MC 1390, reel 17, frames 005–006; Rusk to Lovett [eyes only], no. 803, November 17, 1948, *FRUS*, 1948, v. V, pt. 2, 1607–1608.

101. Noah Karlin (1926–1964), Jerusalem-born son of Sonia Karlin; part of the Karlinski clan that fled Ukraine during the Russian Revolution and lived in Western Europe, Israel, and the United States. McDonald was a friend of Sonia, who lived in Tel Aviv, and her brother Serge Karlinski, who lived in London. Sonia's sons Noah and Eli unofficially helped McDonald with various tasks. Noah came to the Paris Assembly meeting from London to act as McDonald's personal assistant. Barbara Ann McDonald to Georgia Clifford, December 26, 1948, McDonald Papers, Columbia University, box 9, folder 19.

102. Hyman Schulson (1912–1997), attorney representing the American Zionist Emergency Council [AZEC] in Washington in 1948; in Paris to observe and report on General Assembly meetings as AZEC's special representative.

103. Eliahu Ben-Horin (1902–1966), Ukrainian-born author, journalist, and editor; lived in Palestine, 1921–1941, where he broke with Labor Zionism and became a Revisionist; moved to the United States and became an adviser on Middle Eastern affairs for AZEC.

We were delighted to have Noah Karlin come to tea and at the prospect that he would be around and willing to be helpful during our stay here. Shertok and Eban came in on their way to the French representative's party. I reported briefly on conditions in Tel Aviv, and they told me of developments here. Shertok was touched to have the personal letter and flowers from his wife.

While taking our walk in Geneva, Bobby and I were both impressed anew by the orderliness, the luxury, and cleanliness of the shops and by the dress of people one met in the streets. All of this was in sharp contrast with the nondescript shops and military garb of Tel Aviv, but we were both of the opinion that Israel is now much more interesting than Switzerland.

Friday November 19

Early to the [Hotel] d'Iéna, where the American delegation has its offices. In the car going over, chatted with Fraser Wilkins and some others. The former was suavely cordial, but I was not deceived into thinking that he was delighted I was there. Going in to the building I was extremely fortunate in running into General Marshall at the elevator. He asked me when I had arrived, how I had come, and whether I had seen General Riley. The fact that the answer to the last question was yes did not do harm. General Marshall was hurrying on his way to the morning staff meeting, and nothing was said about an appointment.

During the next hour or so, managed to find a place to hang my hat, a desk and a room, which I shall probably use very little. Misses Walsh and Black in the secretary of the delegation, Winslow's, office,[104] offered to supply me with everything needful and to take and deliver my messages. Brief meeting with Kopper but sufficient to show his strong Arab position.[105] I told him, in effect, that I thought that support of British or Bernadotte proposal would invite repudiation from Washington. Brief words with Ross,[106] Rusk, Corrigan,[107] Jessup,[108] and Dulles.[109] Then up to see Ben Cohen,[110] where fortunately Miss Winslow was able to find me with the message that the secretary wanted to see me.

On November 19, 1949, the General Assembly passed Resolution 212. On the basis of the acting mediator's recommendation, the resolution called for $29.5 million

---

104. Richard S. Winslow, secretary-general in US delegation.

105. Samuel K. C. Kopper (1915–1957), Division of Near Eastern Affairs; afterwards worked for ARAMCO.

106. John C. Ross, deputy to the US representative [ambassador] to the UN [Warren R. Austin], US mission to the United Nations. Austin was in the United States due to illness, leaving Ross as acting representative.

107. Francis Patrick Corrigan (1881–1968), career foreign service officer; adviser to the US mission to the United Nations.

108. Philip C. Jessup (1897–1986), known to McDonald from Foreign Policy Association; assistant secretary-general of UNRRA conference in 1943; now deputy US Representative in the UN Security Council.

109. John Foster Dulles, US delegation to UN, assigned to General Assembly First Committee (Policy and Security).

110. Benjamin V. Cohen, alternate representative, assigned to General Assembly First Committee.

to provide aid for 500,000 Palestine refugees from the period from December 1, 1948, to August 31, 1949. The money was to come from contributions from member and non-member states. The secretary-general was to establish administrative organs to deliver the aid and invite the help of appropriate government agencies, UNICEF, the ICRC, and other voluntary societies. He was also to appoint a director of United Nations Relief for Palestine Refugees.[111]

In the secretary's outer office, I waited for fifteen or twenty minutes while a frantic search was being made for Mr. Durward Sandifer, deputy director of the Office of UN Affairs.[112] The secretary, seemingly having become impatient waiting, asked me to go in. We had hardly started our talk, however, before Sandifer arrived breathless. The following is a précis of the ensuing conversation:

1) General Marshall began by asking about the possible directors of relief. I had previously stressed the great importance of speed. The names, which seemed to meet with General Marshall's approval, were Rooks[113] and Griffis. Sandifer brought up the name of Bayard Dodge, formerly of the [American University] in Beirut.[114] I urged a more vigorous man, while General Marshall seemed to think that Dodge's academic background unfitted him for such an arduous position. Sandifer argued that the Arabs wanted Dodge. It was left in such a way as I got the impression that General Marshall was firm in his support of Rooks or Griffis.

2) General Marshall then asked me about the refugee situation and the attitude of the Israeli authorities. I again urged the need of haste and ample funds. I told of my colleagues' fear lest my interest in Arab refugees jeopardize my position with the Provisional Government, and that I was happy to be able to say that these fears were not justified, but instead Ben-Gurion had given this interest his blessing. As to General Marshall's specific question about [the] Jewish attitude, I explained that I thought the matter had not been thought through, and that I was prepared to urge the authorities to consider more seriously what contribution they could make prior to the peace discussions. I explained that the bulk of Jewish refugees were to be sent to the relatively unoccupied portions of the country and that the Jewish demand for and need of the Negev tied directly into this program. I explained

111. See http://daccess-dds-ny.un.org/doc/RESOLUTION/GEN/NR0/043/83/IMG/NR004383.pdf?OpenElement, accessed December 2015.

112. Durward V. Sandifer (1901–1981), deputy director of State Department Office of United Nations Affairs, Department of State; advised Eleanor Roosevelt on General Assembly's Third Committee (Social, Humanitarian and Cultural).

113. Major General (ret.) Lowell W. Rooks (1893–1973), director-general of UNRRA until it discontinued its work in 1947.

114. Bayard Dodge (1888–1972), specialist in study of Islam; president, American University in Beirut, 1923–1948; retired to Princeton, New Jersey, in 1948, where he published articles arguing that Zionism was a disaster for US policy and US missionary work in the Middle East and that it would augment the Soviet position in the Arab world. See Robert D. Kaplan, *The Arabists: The Romance of an American Elite* (New York: Free Press, 1993), 78–81.

briefly some of the factors which led to the Arab flight, emphasizing the early and nearly uniform desertion by the Arab leaders and the natural though panicky following after by the masses. I told also that the mufti's campaign to prevent return on the triple ground that this would involve acknowledgement of the Provisional Government, would risk destruction of returnees, or, if they got on well, would disprove Arab thesis of [Israel's] incapability.

3) From the refugee discussion, General Marshall gave me an opening, which permitted me to present a much longer and more detailed exposition of my views about Israel than I had dared to hope for. I stressed the creativeness of the regime; the hard-working and careful preparation characteristic of leaders and masses in contrast with the verbalism and slackness of the Arabs; I illustrated this point by telling of the contrast between [Fawzi] al-Qawuqji's unprepared attack on Manara and his shelling of the main road below, and the Jews' quiet but thorough preparation, which, after a few hours of fighting, led to al-Qawuqji's flight and that of most of the Arabs in northern Galilee; of the enthusiasm of my colleagues, diplomatic and military, for Israel's achievements, and the need for me, thought to be "pro-Jewish and pro-Zionist," to restrain their despatches; of the Jewish scientific developments and of one example, that of the sinking of the Egyptian flagship *Farouk* by a radar-controlled missile, which together with the explosives it contained, was all Israeli-made;[115] of my conviction that the communist bogie was without substance, that the people as well as their leaders knew that the USSR embrace was that of death, that the tiny communist party could not hope to grow unless the West left the USSR as Israel's sole friend. In conclusion, I sketched my vision of Israel of five or ten years from now, a country much larger in population than at present, educated and highly trained, capable and willing to be a bulwark not of the West against the East but of its own freedom, which would amount to the same thing. When I finished, I more or less apologized for having made such a long speech.

I was surprised by General Marshall's willingness to listen so long and by his evident great interest and his failure to take exception to anything I said. I could but feel that the conference had been for me a major triumph, and I was glad that I had gone ahead full speed in my affirmative statement regardless of the presence of Sandifer.

McDonald wrote to Halsey and Janet Barrett as follows: "General Marshall clearly favored Ambassador Griffis rather than Dodge . . . who was the candidate of the Arabs and who indeed, without authority, had been invited by the Lebanese

---

115. The *Emir Farouk* was a British-built Egyptian cruiser sunk off the coast of Gaza by the Israeli Navy on October 22, 1948, hours after the imposition of the cease-fire following Operation Yoav. It was sunk by a small boat laden with explosives.

Christian representative to the UN, [Charles] Malik[116] (you will recall that he was the man with whom I once debated Palestine on the air) to come to Paris to receive the appointment." After recounting the lengthy and unexpected chance to brief Marshall on Israel fully, McDonald stated, "I do not recall having ever talked to a seemingly more interested audience."[117]

Back to Ben Cohen's office, who talked about the British stupidity in bringing the Egyptians into the Negev. He would have gone on more at length, but I wanted to get off to the Chaillot.[118] He did, nonetheless, stress the difficulty of keeping the technicians in line. He said he would be available any time I wanted to see him.

Walked to the Chaillot with Mr. Corrigan. Listened there to Andrei Vyshinsky,[119] and afterwards Bobby, Noah Karlin, and I lunched with Corrigan. General talk, until towards the end, when I launched in a full-scale exposition of conditions in Israel and the futility and danger of the British policy and our technicians' tendency to be subservient to it. Corrigan listened interestedly, said he was glad to hear, and left me with the impression that it was not wholly wasted.

Before dinner Ben Cohen showed me the draft of a letter he was proposing to send to Rusk, suggesting gently, but nonetheless clearly, that henceforth no statement should be forwarded to Washington for the president's approval without having been previously approved by the members of the delegation.[120] We took the letter to Mrs. Roosevelt's room, where she enthusiastically approved it. If firmly applied, this new regulation would eliminate many chances for misunderstanding, if not worse.

Saturday November 20

Early conference with a group of Quakers, two of whom were en route to Israel. The chief question they wished to discuss was whether or not in my opinion they should take a large role, many times larger than they originally planned, in the relief administration. When they told me that they were prepared

---

116. Charles Habib Malik (1906–1987), Lebanese Orthodox Christian theologian and philosopher educated at American University of Beirut and at Harvard; spoke for many in the Islamic world and received sympathetic hearings in the State Department; Lebanon's minister/ambassador to the United States, 1945–1955; representative to the San Francisco Conference and ambassador to UN, 1945–1955; UN Commission of Human Rights, 1947–1948; chair, UN Economic and Social Council, 1948; Lebanon's foreign minister, 1956–1958; after 1950 a noted academic with appointments to numerous US universities.

117. McDonald to Halsey and Janet Barrett, November 29, 1948, McDonald Papers, USHMM, box 7, folder 8.

118. The UN meetings took place at the Palais Chaillot (Trocadéro).

119. Andrei Vyshinsky (1883–1954), Soviet jurist and diplomat; chief prosecutor in Soviet purge trials, 1935–1939; member of Soviet delegation at Yalta and Potsdam Conferences, 1945; organized Soviet case in the Trial of the Major War Criminals, 1945–1946; deputy minister of foreign affairs, 1940–1949; minister of foreign affairs, 1949–1953.

120. Cohen to Rusk, November 20, 1948, NARA, RG 59, box 2122, folder 4.

to send as many as sixty persons into the field, I urged them to take the larger responsibility.

While waiting for my telephone call to Washington, Noah telephoned to say that the American statement was being read and I was thereby saved from the mistake of criticizing to Washington a statement which I hadn't read and which, on examination, proved to be much better than I had thought.

On November 20 Philip Jessup gave a preliminary statement of US policy, and two days later he proposed specific amendments to the British resolution draft of November 18. He suggested language more consistent with Truman's intentions. There must be a formal peace or at least a lasting armistice in Palestine; Israel's boundaries should be determined by mutual agreement of the parties aided by the Palestine Conciliation Commission, which would replace the mediator's office; Israel was entitled to the boundaries set forth in the November 29, 1947 partition resolution; modification of these boundaries could be made only if acceptable to Israel; if Israel hoped for additional territory beyond the partition borders it must offer an appropriate exchange; Palestinian refugees should be allowed to return to their homes with compensation given for those who chose not to return; and Jerusalem should receive additional study concerning an international regime, to be presented at the next General Assembly.[121]

Bevin warned Marshall that, unless the United States changed its stance, "there will inevitably be open disagreement between the two delegations in the Assembly." He continued to argue that the "general substance of [the] Bernadotte Report should be approved" regardless of Israel's view.[122]

The Israeli delegation welcomed Jessup's statement, but regretted that the United States, instead of proposing a new resolution, simply amended the earlier British draft. Thus the US changes still called for a compromise between the partition resolution and the Bernadotte Plan regarding frontiers, and did not mention Israel's membership in the UN.[123] Lovett summed up US policy as follows. The Jessup statement "will show [Israel] that attitude of US is favorable to them, but that this [government] is publicly on record as feeling that Bernadotte Plan is a basis for negotiating a settlement. . . . On the other hand we feel that British position is unduly rigid and in fact somewhat unreal. Conditions which prevailed last [September] and which prompted Secretary's statement of [September 21] in support of Bernadotte Plan have materially changed as result of military operations." Lovett summarized: "Israelis want negotiations and no Bernadotte Plan, British want Bernadotte Plan and no negotiations. US position is to bridge gap between these two extremes."[124]

121. Jessup statement in Department of State *Bulletin*, v. XIX, no. 491, 657–660; ibid., v. XIX, no. 492, 686–692. On Truman's approval, see Epstein to Eytan, November 25, 1948, *DFPI*, v. 2, d. 183.

122. Marshall to US embassy in United Kingdom, no. 4422, November 24, 1948, *FRUS*, 1948, v. V, pt. 2 1624–1625.

123. *DFPI*, v. 2, Appendix D, 628–629.

124. Shertok to Namir, November 26, 1948, *DFPI*, v. 2, d. 191; Dulles to acting secretary of state, no. 885, November 22, 1948, *FRUS*, 1948, v. V, pt. 2, 1619–1620; Lovett to Delegation

Dinner and to see *Hamlet* with Bobby and Noah. Jean-Louis Barrault's production was extremely interesting in its staging and lighting but was so filled with action that it gave one hardly any of the impression that is received from a performance in the West.[125] Ran into Count Coudenhove-Kalergi and his wife, who is as silly as ever judging from her remarks about Israel.[126] He, too, was in character, for he handed me one of his propaganda pamphlets.

Sunday November 21

Two-hour conference with Schulson and Ben-Horin. Schulson was full of ideas including liaison, separate US report, clearance of all texts by delegates, and curbing of initiative of technicians. Cited Rusk's alleged statement at the press conference about Jessup's statement that the differences between the British and ourselves were more apparent than real. Schulson also told of an alleged remark by Rusk to Jessup on November 4th, when Pearson of Canada[127] was trying to get a day's delay: "Refuse postponement because another day would enable them to get to Washington." I made no commitments. Rest of the morning spent at the Louvre. A new grand hall has been hung with many of the great pictures.

Secretary Marshall left Paris on November 21, and he met with the president the next day. He had long planned to retire in the winter of 1948. John Foster Dulles served as the acting head of the US delegation for the remainder of the session. McDonald said in a note to Dulles, "Though as you know I am here on the Arab refugee problem, I am at your disposal if you have time and care to ask me any questions about my impressions of the situation in Israel or the attitude of the Israeli authorities on pending political and territorial issues. I had a long, and from my point of view, helpful conference with the Secretary yesterday. . . . I am free almost any time."[128]

To Clifford, McDonald wrote, "I am grateful that the President when consulted by the Department approved my special Paris mission. Secretary Marshall, though he was leaving Paris within a day or two, asked to see me the morning of my arrival. After we had concluded our talk about the most desirable director for the relief of Arab refugees, the Secretary listened with flattering attention to my talk for half an hour

in Paris, no. 551, November 22, 1948, *FRUS*, 1948, v. V, pt. 2, 1621–1622. See also *DFPI*, v. 2, d. 186.

125. Jean-Louis Barrault (1910–1994), French actor and director; created a non-romantic Hamlet. See Louis Verdun Marsh, "Jean-Louis Barrault's *Hamlet*," *Quarterly Journal of Speech* 36, no. 3: 360–364.

126. Richard Nikolaus von Coudenhove-Kalergi (1884–1972), conservative Austrian politician; prewar and postwar advocate of European integration; helped Otto von Habsburg found the Pan-European Union, 1922.

127. Lester Pearson (1897–1972), Canadian diplomat, helped in founding of UN, 1945; Canadian foreign minister, 1948–1957; head of the Canadian UN delegation in 1948; won Nobel Peace Prize for organizing the UN emergency force to help resolve the Suez Canal crisis, 1957; prime minister of Canada, 1963–1968.

128. McDonald to Dulles, November 20, 1948, McDonald Papers, Columbia University, box 2, folder 14.

about Israel and its potential role in the Middle East. Dulles and all his colleagues whom I saw from time to time told me that they considered my presence helpful."[129]

McDonald was less pleased with the career State Department officials. As he wrote Halsey and Janet Barrett,

> *During the ten days which have elapsed since that first interview [with Marshall] I have talked with all the delegates several times but have not had the 'privilege' of any real conference with the Department technicians. Their attitude toward me is correct but it smacks a good deal of that which one would have towards poison ivy. . . . Of course they and I speak pleasantly enough as we pass one another in the corridors or committee room, but that is as far as it goes.*
>
> *There was a suggestion made a week or so ago both within and outside the delegation that I be asked to step outside my technical role in refugees and become a kind of liaison through whom all Palestine material from the technicians would clear en route to the delegates. I was not enthusiastic about this, partly because I knew it would be difficult to arrange, and second, more important, I felt that my proper role was dealing with the members of the delegation and with the White House. In fact it has worked out much better this way than it seems to me it could have conceivably have done otherwise.*[130]

Brief talk in the hall with Dulles about the director of relief, in the course of which I pointed out the danger of Dodge's appointment, and asked Dulles if he would speak to Trygve Lie; Dulles said he would speak to Sandifer.[131] Passed Mrs. Roosevelt in the hall, who invited me for lunch, but I couldn't accept because the [Ben] Gerigs had already come. During the meal, Ben was so ready to agree with me on every point and to criticize his colleagues that I began to doubt his good faith.[132] Anyhow it didn't matter much. Towards the end of our lunch I went over and had a long chat with Mrs. Roosevelt. She showed complete understanding of the problem of keeping the technicians in line and a firm determination to do her part. I do not remember to have seen her more

129. McDonald to Clifford, December 26, 1948, McDonald Papers, Columbia University, box 9, folder 16.

130. McDonald to Halsey and Janet Barrett, November 29, 1948, McDonald Papers, USHMM, box 7, folder 8.

131. Trygve Lie had invited Dodge to Paris. On November 23, Lovett ordered Rusk personally to intervene and press for Lie to appoint Stanford Griffis. "It is my personal belief that Griffis, because of his business experience, Red Cross connections, and intimate knowledge [of the] refugee situation, would be [the] best choice." Lovett to US embassy Paris [eyes only Rusk], no. 562, November 23, 1948, NARA, RG 59, 501.BB Palestine, box 2122, folder 5.

132. Benjamin Gerig (1894–1976), Mennonite peace activist who served in League of Nations, 1930–1940; knew McDonald from McDonald's days as high commissioner for refugees; served in State Department capacities concerning UN and international trusteeships of former colonies and mandates, 1942–1961; helped draft UN charter and served as adviser to early US delegations to UN. Gerlof D. Homan, "Orie Benjamin Gerig: Mennonite Rebel, Peace Activist, International Civil Servant, and American Diplomat 1894–1976," *Mennonite Quarterly Review* 73, no. 4 (October 1999): 751–782.

vigilantly alert. In passing, she quoted General Marshall apropos of a report that one of the staff had made an unjustifiable interpretation of the press conference, that this "didn't matter because anyhow the press was Jewish."

Schulson came in, and during our discussion I became more fearful of the results of the possible Dodge appointment. Immediately called Sandifer on the phone and in the course of the perhaps too earnest presentation of the arguments, hurt his feelings and later apologized.[133] Talked with Ben Cohen about Dodge. More important, I asked his advice about the Wainhouse suggestion.[134] He questioned its desirability from [Washington]'s point of view. I retorted by saying that he, Ben Cohen, must learn to be stiff, that only so could he make effective the procedure he had outlined in his letter to the staff.

Walking down the hall, I met Mr. and Mrs. Jessup, who most cordially invited me into their apartment. I was there for more than an hour. After some brief reference to Dodge, Jessup let me go on with a lecture about Israel, covering most of the points I had discussed with General Marshall. Towards the end, Jessup asked me how I felt the [Israeli] elections would come out. He also made some other inquiries. He could not have been more friendly, but I can't truthfully record that he disclosed anything significant or new about US policy.

Monday November 22

Breakfast with Goldie Meyerson and Gideon Rafael.[135] The talk was about her experiences in Russia, particularly on the domestic side and the restrictions on travel. I also gossiped with her about conditions in Israel.

In the 3rd Committee, chatted with Mrs. Roosevelt, who said that Sandifer had checked the political potentialities of Dodge with Marshall. [John] Reedman took me in to Bunche, who was sitting at the committee table. The latter was very cordial, remembering his lunch with Bobby and me.[136] He agreed that Dodge would be a mistake and suggested that I speak to Trygve Lie. I said

133. McDonald wrote Sandifer on November 20, 1948: "I am terribly sorry that in my anxiety to make my point—that the naming of Dr. Dodge might have unfortunate political repercussions—I seem to [have been] discourteous during our telephone conversation a few minutes ago. I did not intend to suggest that in your handling of the matter you were motivated by anything other than the highest purposes." McDonald Papers, USHMM, box 7, folder 8.
134. David W. Wainhouse (1900–1976), Office of United Nations Affairs, Division of International Security Affairs, Department of State; served as a technical assistant to the US delegation, specifically as an assistant to John Foster Dulles in the First Committee. Suggestion might have concerned wording in the resolution then under discussion regarding a possible Israeli trade of the "Negev," rather than the "southern Negev" for Western Galilee and Jaffa. Marshall to acting secretary of state, no. 862, November 20, 1948, *FRUS*, 1948, v. V, pt. 2, 1618–1619.
135. Gideon Rafael [formerly Ruffer] (1913–1999), German-born Zionist; emigrated to Palestine, 1934; member of Haganah, 1936–1945; traveled to Rhodes to engage in rescue of German Jews, 1940; served in British Army in Syria and Lebanon, 1941–1943, and part of intelligence cooperation between the Yishuv and British intelligence; worked with Jewish Agency and Bricha in smuggling Jews to Western Europe, 1945–1947; Jewish Agency delegation to UN, 1947–1948; helped found Israeli Foreign Ministry, 1948; counselor to Israeli delegation to the UN, 1948–1953; later served in other diplomatic and intelligence posts.
136. Entry of September 9, 1948.

it was out of my bailiwick and suggested that he do the speaking. Brief words with Harold Beeley.

McDonald telegraphed Lovett and Clifford: "After long conference [with] Secretary Marshall and study here [I] am convinced [that] Arab refugee administration will be effective if either Rooks or Griffis is director. Choice of Dodge would create unnecessary difficulties because his leadership [of] anti-Israel forces [in the] US. Hope non-partisan support in Congress will speed essential appropriations because cold winter rains already begun [in the] Judean Hills will be fatal [to] tens of thousands [of] unsheltered starving children and old people."[137]

Delightful dinner with Herbert May[138] as host and his guests, who included my old friend Mrs. Clarence Streit.[139] The telephone call to Ruth was postponed and came through at 4:30 Tuesday morning. She doesn't expect to sail until Thanksgiving or the day after and is booked to Athens, since the Department informed her that I didn't want her to go to Beirut. I insisted that she cable the date of sailing.

Tuesday November 23, 1948

After an early breakfast Schulson came in with an elaborate program for Wainhouse, Dulles et al. Then to Committee One. Brief talk with Eban. Lunch with Shertok and Nahum Goldmann at the former's residence. Shertok said that Trygve Lie had told him that he had to name Dodge. We then went on and talked about the possibility of Israel's admission. They thought there was just a chance of getting the requisite seven votes if the US would actively use its influence with Canada, Columbia, and France.[140]

McDonald had actually solved the problem of the Dodge appointment through his comments to Marshall and his correspondence with Clifford. From Washington, Marshall cabled on November 25 that "we are strongly supporting appointment Griffis as Refugee Administrator and are pressing [the Secretary-General] to nominate

---

137. Sent through Caffery to secretary of state [personal attention Lovett and Clifford], no. 5985, November 22, 1948, Truman Library, Clifford Papers, Subject File, 1945–54, box 14, folder Palestine Telegrams and Cables 2 of 2.

138. Herbert L. May (1877—1966), lawyer who retired at age 45 and devoted himself to humanitarian causes; board member of the Foreign Policy Association, 1932–1952.

139. Clarence K. Streit (1896–1986), journalist who covered the League of Nations and who published *Union Now* (1938), as well as an updated postwar edition; book called for a federation of Western European democracies with the English-speaking nations of the world.

140. Applications for UN membership needed a plurality recommendation from the Security Council to receive a vote in the General Assembly. The Israeli delegation believed that, in the Security Council, Britain, China, and Syria would vote against admission; the United States, USSR, Ukraine, Argentina, and Colombia would vote for admission; Belgium was doubtful; and Canada and France could vote either way. Shertok submitted Israel's request for admission to Trygve Lie on November 29, 1948. See *DFPI*, v. 2, d. 204.

him, although we understand that [the Secretary-General] favors Dodge and has invited him to Paris for consultation."[141]

Conference at four with Dulles. After some joking reference about my miscalculation about the age of Dodge, whom I had called an old man, though he entered Princeton later than I did Indiana, Dulles developed with extraordinary frankness an amazingly encouraging series of propositions:

1) the November 29th partition settlement was in the nature of the case, a gamble, because it could not then be known whether the Arab threats of driving the Jews into the sea or the latter's assurance that they could take the whole of Palestine would be proved correct;
2) he had always the feeling that the creation of a new state is dependent upon the willingness of the people to sacrifice life if need be in battle;
3) the past year has clearly disclosed where the balance of power lies. The Arabs' weakness and the Jews' strength leave no doubt;
4) we must take account of this demonstration in our decisions at this assembly;
5) Britain has been a very unreliable guide because its forecasts have been so frequently proved wrong;
6) while we still should strive to maintain Anglo-American unity, the US should be the senior partner;
7) "This morning at 10:00 at a staff conference I underlined," said Dulles, "these fundamentals to the staff."[142]

In response to Dulles's statement, I enthusiastically expressed my complete assent. I added that all that was needed now was that the technicians be kept in line. Then I went on to develop my thesis about Israel's role in becoming a strong center of modern democracy. As I was leaving, I said that I understood some persons around had a new idea of my possible usefulness to the delegation, but that I was determined not to suggest or accept anything which did not meet with his whole-hearted approval. On this note ended a most satisfactory conference.

McDonald later wrote Halsey Barrett, who knew Dulles, that "you will be glad to know that your friend [John Foster Dulles] has been very cordial and just as helpful. He personally asked the Department for the extension of my ten days' leave.

141. Marshall to McDonald, no. 4524, November 25, 1948, McDonald Papers, USHMM, box 7, folder 8.
142. Dulles also entered negotiations with the British delegation over a new draft of the impending General Assembly resolution that would further discount the Bernadotte Plan. Meeting of Israeli Delegation to United Nations, December 1, 1948, *DFPI*, v. 2, d. 214.

Moreover, shortly after we arrived he took me into his confidence and told me just how he felt about our problem."[143]

Conferences with Comay, Eban, and Rafael. The latter two, while pleased with the American amendments cutting out the operative clauses of the British resolution, found many points of omission and commission to criticize in the US draft.[144] Delayed going out to dinner with the Gestettners until nearly 9:15, waiting on the call to Clifford. It finally came through while we were at the restaurant. The connection was not too good. These were the points covered: 1) family; 2) excellent report according to Clifford on my work in Paris (from whom this could have come I can't imagine); 3) my favorable comment on Dulles and the delegation excepting the technicians; 4) the greater suitability of the Australian than the amended British resolution;[145] 6) importance of US steam behind Israel admission plea; 7) my staying on should be matter of direct request to Lovett. If not, assented to get in touch with Clifford again; 8) "You are doing fine work Jim. Keep it up." Home after 12:00, too tired to make any pretense even of telling Bobby about the telephone conversation.

On November 25 Epstein reported to Tel Aviv that Bevin was pressuring Marshall through the "unfriendly Ambassador Douglas" to move closer to London's resolution draft, but that, according to David Niles, the "President yesterday assured Eddie Jacobson [of] his determination to see [his] pre-election Palestine pledges fully fulfilled [in] both letter and spirit. Same [has] been told me by Clifford and other closest friends [of the] President, who assured that neither [the] British nor [the] Conciliation Commission [will] be able to sabotage President['s] determination [to] support us."[146]

Wednesday November 24
Awake early. Up a little after 6:00. Bath and shaved and at work stoically without tea by 6:45. Then tea, [and] wrote notes to DC[147] and [David Wainhouse]. Delivered them by hand. Read yesterday's documents and prepared some introductory paragraphs. At 8:00 David Popper came to breakfast.[148] After some illuminating details from him about the special and tendentious

143. McDonald to Halsey and Janet Barrett, November 29, 1948, McDonald Papers, USHMM, box 7, folder 8.
144. Comay's criticism in Comay to Ross, November 24, 1948, *DFPI*, v. 2, d. 177.
145. There were several alternative resolution drafts in the First Committee. While the Americans tried to amend the British resolution to prevent a break with London, Israel tried to build support for the Australian draft resolution, which reaffirmed the existence of Israel, called for its admission to the UN, and mentioned the Bernadotte Plan only as one proposal among others to be considered together with the authoritative November 29 resolution. The Australian draft also included a Conciliation Commission, but one without administrative authority. With regard to refugees, it raised the possibility of repatriation or resettlement in other countries. Sharett to Namir, *DFPI*, v. 2, d. 191.
146. Epstein to Eytan, November 25, 1948, *DFPI*, v. 2, d. 183.
147. Unknown.
148. David Popper (1912–2008), assistant chief of the State Department's Division of United Nations Political Affairs.

handling of Palestine by the technicians, we were joined by BW.[149] The latter said that the question of my extension in Paris was easy and that he wanted more than that: my utilization as the "coordinator of all preparatory action on Palestine." I replied that I thought this would probably involve a major battle. Coming back to the question of extension, he suggested that I ask Dean Rusk about it as a routine matter. That this would be preferable to going to Dulles about it, who in turn would ask Rusk.

Down to Ben Cohen's room. He shared BW's general views. The editor of "Day" [*Der Tog*], [the] leading New York Yiddish newspaper, came in for a talk wholly off the record.[150] At 10:00 Charles Fahy, who is here acting as counsel for the Israel delegation, came in. After a brief discussion on the US amendments he, Bobby, Noah, and I all drove to Committee 1. Made a date with Dean Rusk and met him in the hall. I asked him quite casually if as a matter of routine he would ask the Department to extend my absence from Tel Aviv. He said he would send off the request. I then casually told him of my telephone call last night to Clifford and [about] the latter's mother's report about the attorney-generalship.

Mrs. [Yolande] Harmer,[151] Noah, and I to lunch at the Hotel California with Noah's friend, Yadin, manufacturer of storage batteries, who is soon going to Israel. It was a pleasant luncheon with much talk between Harmer and Noah about Egypt.

After a sorely needed nap I worked until Monsignor [Thomas] McMahon of 52nd Street came for tea.[152] Presently we were joined by Buzz Boettiger. I told McMahon about Israel and the Vatican. He told me about the organizational refugee setup at home and the difficulty of bringing the Jews into it and of the solutions to the inclusion of the B'nai B'rith. I then talked about Israel and the refugees.

Rafael came in and showed me an analysis of the US amendments. Again, he emphasized the importance of admission. Dr. Gottman called during the afternoon and gave me the titles of two books, the first which I had inquired about; August Müller, *Der Islam im Morgan- und Abendland*, two vols. (Berlin, 1887); 2) [Carl] Brockelman, *Geschichte der arabischen Literatur* (Berlin, 1909). Delightful dinner with Ben-Horin at Le Savoyard, Rue des Quatres Vents.

Thursday November 25

To [First Committee] and listened with carefully concealed disgust to McNeil's sweetly reasonable speech in which he exaggerated the British concessions, the Jews' unreasonableness, and forgot to say anything about Great Britain's

149. Unknown.
150. Mordechai Danzis (1885–1952), Ukrainian-born editor of *Der Tog* (1947–1952); Revisionist sympathizer.
151. Entry of June 23, 1948.
152. On McMahon, see entry of August 5–6, 1948. 52nd Street is a reference to the Office of the [Catholic] Archdiocese in New York.

record of mistakes or of its real policy. Nonetheless, it was an effective speech, so much so that it filled me with a feeling of disgust at British democracy.[153]

An intellectual tea with Widor Bagge, Swedish Minister to Cairo, Mrs. Harmer, Noah, Bobby in our sitting room. I tried to draw out Bagge, but succeeded only in invoking eloquent and suggestive expositions from Harmer and Noah. I was to see Bagge later privately. After waiting futilely in the room for telephone call from Clifford, I had a long conference with Wainhouse and decided to telegraph Clifford instead.

Friday November 26

Up before 7:00 working on drafts for Clifford and Dulles. Dr. Eli Davis of the Hadassah[154] [Hospital] came in for breakfast at 8:00. Excusing myself, I went down to confer with Wainhouse. Davis's account of the Hadassah pledge of half a million a year for five years to complete the building fund was encouraging news despite the added news that the Friends of the Hebrew University under Dr. Israel Wechsler were so disturbed that Hadassah might withdraw.[155] Davis said that the medical school might open with a class of students who had completed their pre-clinical work abroad. Interestingly, he told me that Rabbi Herzog had officially given the medical authorities the right to perform anatomical dissection on human bodies provided only that 1) the individual had given his consent and; 2) the parts dissected be returned to the body before burial. Davis added that dissection was becoming less and less important with the development of slides, x-rays, charts etc., and that some medical schools had cut down sharply on the time given to dissection.

Brief conferences with Cohen and Wainhouse on the communications to be sent. Finally telegraphed Clifford a general statement eliminating specific reference to technicians (because of the necessity of having to use the Department code), and suggested that Truman call Dulles expressing his appreciation

153. Hector McNeil defended the British draft resolution (with the US amendments), first against the criticism that it did not allow for direct negotiations between Israel and the Arab states, granting instead executive power to the proposed Conciliation Commission. He argued that a strong Conciliation Commission was necessary because, "if direct negotiations were to take place, the Arabs would find themselves in a position of considerable inferiority as a result of Jewish military success. It was much more likely that the proposed negotiations would never begin." He defended against a second criticism that the draft resolution gave too much weight to the terms in the Bernadotte Plan when setting the Conciliation Commission's terms of reference. Here he argued, "The Assembly would be putting too heavy a burden on the commission if it failed to give it very clear general objectives." He further noted the mediator's reasonable insistence that the Jewish and Arab territories be geographically self-contained, and that he hoped that "Israel would not take the strange view that the Arab territory of Palestine was a cake to the slices of which it had equal title with the adjacent Arab states." United Nations, *Official Records of the Third Session of the General* Assembly, Part I, *First Committee, 28 September–8 December 1948*, 759–762.

154. Eli Davis (1908–1997), director-general emeritus of Hadassah Hospital on Mt. Scopus, 1948–1951; led Hadassah rebuilding and maintenance efforts after the Arab attack on hospital personnel in May 1948.

155. Israel S. Wechsler (1886–1962), American neurologist and Jewish leader; helped found American Jewish Physicians Committee in 1921; president of American Friends of Hebrew University (founded 1929), 1947–1951; later known as the father of the Hebrew University movement in the United States.

and urging more of the same good work and calling for enthusiastic support of Israel's admission.

> *November 26, 1948–2 pm*
> *For White House Only*
> *Personal Attention Clifford*
>
> *Despite absolute loyalty and able leadership [of] Dulles and [the] other delegates, I am convinced Bevin still hopes [to] undo [the General] Assembly resolution [of] last November 29 and to secure [his aims] from this UN resolution which Israel would have to reject and thus place itself in position of "flouting" authority [of] UN. President would thus be checkmated and Britain would then be freed—even if sanctions were not imposed—to rearm the [the] Arab states and enable and encourage them [to] continue war against Israel.*
>
> *Unless and until [the] British show [the] Arabs that [the] UK acknowledges Israel to be an inescapable and enduring fact: and until Bevin permits Abdullah to make peace with Israel, British protestations of peaceful intent are mere words to trap the unwary.*
>
> *Would be most helpful if President would personally telephone Dulles assuring latter of full confidence and appreciation [and] urging him to:*
>
> *1) resist firmly any further whittling down [of] US program, and*
> *2) press vigorously [the] President's suggestion that Israel be admitted to UN this session. Such admission depends on enthusiastic American support. (President might forestall [the] threatening crisis and help secure Assembly support [for] essentials [of] his program.)*
>
> *Should you wish supporting data above analysis I could supply it if you would telephone me. . . .*
>
> *Your advice Wednesday when I telephoned you [regarding] remaining [in] Paris was sound. At request [of] Dulles [Department] has granted extension time.*
>
> *James G. McDonald*[156]

. . . .

Rusk was furious. An hour later, at 3 pm on November 26, he telegrammed Lovett:

---

156. McDonald deleted a line from the initial draft stating that the "persistent inclination [of the] Department technicians to make unnecessary concessions to Bevin's anti-Israel policy threatens [the] President's Israel program." McDonald to secretary of state [for White House only, personal attention Clifford], no. 6044, November 26, 1948, McDonald Papers, USHMM, box 7, folder 8. Final version in Truman Library, Clifford Papers, Subject File, 1945–54, box 14, folder Palestine Telegrams and Cables 2 of 2.

Now understand that McDonald has sent [a] message direct to [the] President through State Department channels without [the] knowledge of Dulles which comments adversely upon delegation attitude [regarding] Palestine. Since [the] delegation is acting strictly under instructions and no principal delegate is objecting to our line of action, this may create [an] intolerable situation. Apparently one point of concern is question of UN membership for Israel. Israel has not even applied for membership. . . .

One possibility would be to ask McDonald to hasten back to Tel Aviv with personal message from [the] President to Ben-Gurion stating, among other things: (a) US believes now is time to move definitively to final solution [on] Palestine and we are doing everything possible to bring other parties to attitude of negotiation and settlement; (b) we are anxious to accomplish Israel membership in UN at this session; we believe prospects are fair but know that attitude[s] of other members [of the Security Council] turn on assurance that Israel has no more military objectives in mind and will cooperate with [the Security Council] in maintaining peace; (c) we believe application to [the Security Council] by Israel for UN membership in conjunction with conciliatory attitude toward [Security Council's] effort to establish armistice would be appropriate step; (d) et cetera, et cetera.

Perhaps no trouble will develop [on] this end, but if we begin to get sudden telephone calls which cut across our instructions, reserve a wing at St. Elizabeth's.[157]

Into [First Committee] for a little while and listened to the second day of procedural debate, with the British getting the worst of it; and their resolution [is] becoming less and less the center.[158]

Lunch downstairs with Noah and Bobby. Dean Rusk, who sat down to lunch with us, shocked the three of us by his bland statement that the Assembly might be able to constitute the new Conciliation Commission of the three states now constituting the Truce Commission [France, Belgium, United States] despite Russian opposition because "we've got the votes."

Farewell visit with Ben-Horin at teatime, to whom we gave letters for Knox and Miss Clark, and a message for Samuel Klaus.[159] Bobby, Noah, and I

157. Rusk to secretary of state [eyes only Lovett], no. 6047, November 26, 1948, *FRUS, 1948*, v. V, pt. 2, 1629–1630. St. Elizabeth's was a mental hospital in Washington, DC.

158. See, for example, the Czech statement, which blamed the British and the United States for the failure of the partition, argued that the Bernadotte Plan violated Israeli sovereignty, and stated that both the Arabs and Jews had to agree on territorial exchanges. United Nations, *Official Records of the Third Session of the General Assembly, Part I, First Committee, 28 September–8 December 1948*, 777–778.

159. Entry of September 22, 1948. Klaus left the United States on November 15 and arrived in Israel while McDonald was in Paris. He had a personal meeting with Ben-Gurion and Shiloah on November 22. Ben-Gurion promised to make all published materials and relevant personnel available for Klaus's investigation. Knox to secretary of state, no. 275, November 24, 1948, RG 59, MC 1390, reel 17, frames 497–498.

went to the George Cinq for dinner with Simon Marks, Harry Sacher, and Marcus Sieff. It was an excellent meal, with two and a half hours of talk mostly by me in a lighter vein about Israel.

Saturday November 27

Worked in the hotel most of the morning. Lunch with Widor Bagge, but was rather disappointed not to learn more from him about Egypt's possible policy toward Israel.[160] Bagge was interesting about the king, the latter's habits, his relations to the Wafd and to the British.[161] Bagge was intriguing too in his inquiries about the Bernadotte assassination and by his covert implication that the fear that Bernadotte might fix his headquarters in Jerusalem and thereby increase the international character of the city was a factor in his death. I denied this as strongly as I could.

During the morning sent off telegrams to [David] Dubinsky,[162] [Abba Hillel] Silver and [Emanuel] Neumann, Eddie Cantor, Ben Abrams, [Joseph] Proskauer, and Abe Feinberg[163] asking them to call me tonight or tomorrow night.

The telegrams asked for the recipients to call McDonald. McDonald hoped that they would press the White House to abandon the Bernadotte Plan and to favor Israel's admission to the UN during the current session of the General Assembly. McDonald also discussed the need for Israel's supporters to visit and see the country firsthand.[164]

In a letter to Halsey and Janet Barrett, McDonald recounted, "This is not the place to give the details of my work on this level. Suffice it to say that it has seemed to please [John Foster Dulles] and his colleagues and the people most concerned in Washington. And throughout the whole time I have had something to do with the rather torturous task of setting up the UN new scheme for Palestine."[165]

Hearing that Griffis had been invited to be relief director but that he was hesitating because he would have to take a leave of absence from Cairo, I wired him urgent appeal to accept.[166]

160. On November 30 through Bunche, Egypt made an armistice offer that featured Egypt's keeping the Negev south of the Majdal-Beit Jibrin-Dead Sea line. Shertock to Eytan, November 30, 1948, *DFPI*, v. 2, d. 207.

161. "Wafd" refers to Wafd "Delegation," an Egyptian political party founded by Saad Zaghlul in 1919 as a liberal nationalist constitutionalist party and led by Mustafa al-Nahhas Pasha from 1927 to 1952. The party called for a constitutional monarchy and an elected president. It was dissolved after the 1952 revolution.

162. Entry of November 29, 1948.

163. Entry of August 25, 1948. Feinberg already had contacted Clifford on November 23, 1948, warning about the "State Department doublecross" concerning the British resolution. See Michael J. Cohen, *Truman and Israel* (Berkeley, CA: University of California Press, 1990), 70–76, 102, 261; Truman Library, Clifford Papers, Subject File, 1945–54, box 14, folder Palestine Telegrams and Cables 2 of 2.

164. See, for example, entries of November 29, 1948; November 30, 1948; December 2, 1949.

165. McDonald to Halsey and Janet Barrett, November 29, 1949, McDonald Papers, USHMM, box 7, folder 8.

166. McDonald to Griffis, November 27, 1949, McDonald Papers, USHMM, box 7, folder 8.

Towards 11:00 at night Schulson came in to outline the situation as he saw it. The order of discussion in [the First Committee], with the subject of the withdrawal of foreign troops first fixed by the informal committee controlled by the Russian bloc, promised days of debate with no vote in sight.[167] He thinks that there can be no majority for anything resembling the British resolution or for the American ideas unless we swing toward the Australian concept. In the light of all this, Schulson thinks that admission is the most important issue, but that only US influence on France can do the trick. Schulson did me the honor of asking me what he ought to [bring] up to Silver. I told him enthusiastic support of the president and an appeal to Truman to support his delegates in carrying out to the fullest degree the pre-election pledges, and of course to urge strong admission support.

Sunday November 28

Up early and worked on brief letter to Dulles about his radio speech this evening. Later, he was to tell me that he hoped that he had, in effect, pleased me. Immediately after receiving my note, he telephoned me to say that he would be seriously embarrassed unless Griffis were willing to take a leave of absence and thus make himself available for the refugee directorship. Dulles had brought "strong pressure" on Trygve Lie to have him switch from Dodge to Griffis. The Department technicians had assured Dulles that there would be no difficulty about the leave of absence. I volunteered to reach the White House on the matter since Dulles said that he had to deal directly with the Department. I sent off a strong cable to Clifford.

McDonald to Clifford and Lovett, November 28, 1948: "In light [of the] strong pressure exerted by [the US Delegation] to secure appointment [of] Griffis instead of Dodge as director relief, [US delegation] would be sorely embarrassed if Griffis now declined to make [him]self eligible by refusing to leave embassy post for period [of] refugee work. On my own responsibility and without knowledge [of the US delegation] I beg that President be urged to make personal appeal Griffis who better than anyone else could meet refugee crisis. If compromise [is] necessary Griffis might take leave for three months time required to organize relief distribution."[168]

167. The Soviets on November 25 submitted a draft resolution for the withdrawal of all foreign troops and personnel from Palestine. "Their presence on the territories of the Arab and Jewish States created by the Assembly's Resolution 181 (II) of [29] November was illegal and unjustified and maintained a tense situation which might lead to further military action." Discussion in the First Committee on November 26 suggested that a subcommittee produce a single working paper with all points of agreement and disagreement on the various peace resolution drafts to use as a guide. The Soviets argued that the appointment of such a subcommittee was premature. *Official Records of the Third Session of the General Assembly*, Part I, *First Committee, 28 September–8 December 1948*, November 25, 755; November 26, 786–789.

168. McDonald to Clifford through Caffery, no. 6071, November 28, 1948, McDonald Papers, USHMM, box 7, folder 8; Truman Library, Clifford Papers, Subject File, 1945–54, box 14, folder Palestine Telegrams and Cables 2 of 2.

Griffis accepted the assignment when Trygve Lie offered him the position.[169] *He wrote McDonald, November 29, 1948: "Greatly appreciate your kind words. Have agreed [to] take job."*[170] *The appointment became official on December 4, 1948.*[171]

Immediately after breakfast went out of doors and was thrilled by the heavy hoar frost and the thick winter mist, the like of which we shall not expect to see in Tel Aviv. Rather to my consternation I began to feel wobbly as Bobby and I were visiting the museum of the impressionist French painters. I was in no mood to enjoy them. Nonetheless, it was pleasant to meet there Simon, Marcus, and Harry Sacher, and Noah's two young cousins Edie and Nanna.

Truman replied to Weizmann on November 29:[172]

> *I remember well our conversation about the Negev, to which you referred in your letter. I agree fully with your estimate of the importance of that area to Israel, and I deplore any attempt to take it away from Israel. I had thought that my position would have been clear to all the world, particularly in light of the specific wording of the Democratic Party Platform. . . .*[173]
>
> *Since your letter was written, we have announced in the General Assembly our firm intention to oppose any territorial changes in the November 29th Resolution which are not acceptable to the State of Israel. I am confident that the General Assembly will support us in this basic position. . . .*
>
> *In closing, I want to tell you how happy and impressed I have been at the remarkable progress made by the new State of Israel. What you have received at the hands of the world has been far less than was your due. But you have made more than the most of what you have received, and I admire you for it. I trust that the present uncertainty, with its terribly burdensome consequences, will soon be eliminated. We will do all we can to help by encouraging direct negotiations between the parties looking toward a prompt peace settlement.*[174]

Monday November 29

Chief work during the morning on telegram to White House on [Israeli] admission [to the UN].[175] Sent it off after checking with Wainhouse. It was a

169. Lovett to Clifford, November 28, 1948, Truman Library, Clifford Papers, Subject Files, box 14, folder Palestine Telegrams and Cables 1 of 2.
170. Marshall to McDonald, no. 4569, November 30, 1948, McDonald Papers, USHMM, box 7, folder 8.
171. Dulles to secretary of state, December 4, 1948, NARA, RG 59, 501.BB Palestine, box 2123, folder 13.
172. Ironically, Weizmann did not receive the letter until January 6 the following year because it was mailed with a 5-cent stamp from Washington. See entry of January 6, 1949; Shertok to McDonald, January 5, 1949, McDonald Papers, USHMM, box 7, folder 10.
173. See entry of October 22, 1948.
174. Truman to Weizmann, November 29, 1948, *FRUS*, 1948, v. V, pt. 2, 1633–1634.
175. Draft not found.

strong plea on the merits and as fulfillment of Truman's policy with specific recommendations as to action.[176]

Routine lunch with [Joel] Wolfson of the AJC [American Jewish Committee].[177] The only new point was his question to me about the desirability of an AJC office in Israel. My judgment was affirmative, provided the office was modest and limited to one brilliant and unambitious representative, i.e., unambitious for himself and not inclined to play Jewish politics.

Telephone talk with David Dubinsky.[178] I asked him about a visit to Israel.[179] He replied that his vice-president Charles Zimmerman was already there, had been in Paris the previous Saturday, and that [Dubinsky's] daughter Jean was arriving tomorrow at the [Hotel] Baltimore [in Paris].[180] I urged to Dubinsky to have Zimmerman stay long enough for me to have talks with him and that I hoped for the same with Sam Klaus. I asked him to get in touch with Clifford about the admission [to UN] problem.

McDonald wrote to Dubinsky and other labor leaders whom he knew in the US as follows:

> *The future economic and political development of Israel will depend primarily upon developments in the labor movement. What happens in Israel will affect political developments in the whole of the Middle East. That Israel will be a "pilot plant" setting an example for its tens of millions of Arab neighbors has already been understood and acted upon by some of the largest American manufacturers who have indicated their willingness to advance substantial credits to the Government here.*

176. Dulles also reported on the issue to Marshall on November 29, noting the strong objections of the Arab states and the possible negative effects of Israel's admission for a peaceful settlement. Dulles also noted Rusk's feeling that the United States must support Israeli membership and that the Department could express its interest in the Arab world's welfare on other matters. Dulles to Marshall, November 29, 1948, *FRUS*, 1948, v. V, pt. 2, pp. 1635–1636.

177. Joel David Wolfson (1900–1961) journalist and lawyer with the National Power Commission; head of American Jewish Committee's European Division, 1946–1948; assistant secretary of the interior, 1948–1953.

178. David Isaac Dubinsky (1892–1982), Belorussian-born labor advocate; president, International Ladies Garment Workers' Union [ILGWU], the most powerful union in the American Federation of Labor, 1932–1966; non-Zionist but supported mass Jewish migration to Israel in 1946; through ILGWU helped finance Israel's War of Independence in 1948 via a loan requested by Golda Meyerson; in same year and thereafter made large gifts to Histadrut and United Jewish Appeal. Robert D. Parmet, *The Master of Seventh Avenue: David Dubinsky and the American Labor Movement* (New York: New York University Press, 2005), 220–225, 239–242.

179. McDonald had written Dubinsky several weeks earlier on this subject. Dubinsky to McDonald, November 12, 1948, McDonald Papers, Columbia University, box 2, folder 12.

180. Charles S. Zimmerman (1896–1983), Ukrainian-born vice-president of ILGWU; expelled from the American Communist Party, 1929, and became an enemy of Soviet communism thereafter; emerged as a New Deal liberal after World War II. Dubinsky described him as "the best man for the purpose" of a preliminary study visit to Israel. Zimmerman arrived there on November 28. Dubinsky had also spoken with Samuel Klaus before Klaus left for Israel on November 15, as well as with Herbert Cummings. In his meeting with Klaus on November 22, Ben-Gurion said that a visit by Dubinsky would be a benefit. Dubinsky to McDonald, November 12, 1948, McDonald Papers, Columbia University, box 2, folder 12; Parmet, *Master of Seventh Avenue*, 241.

American labor in my personal opinion has an even larger stake in Israel's future than has American capital. The country has thus far developed essentially as a workers' economy. As you of course know, the Histadrut holds the balance of economic power. The struggle for the soul of Israel is going to be fought out within the trade unions, in the factories, the kibbutzim and among the white collar workers.

McDonald did not think Israel would vote for a communist government, but worried that "Communist penetration will make headway among well-meaning but romantically minded leaders and workers whose opinions of the practices in the USSR and in the satellite states [have] only the scantiest relation to reality."[181]

Telephone talk with [Rabbi] Silver. First I explained the Arab refugee situation, the change from Dodge to Griffis, the need of supporting the latter, the excellent work of the delegation here, and the importance of strong activity on the admission front. He promised to act and was audibly pleased to have been called.

Tuesday November 30
Carefully phrased but strong telegram [regarding] admission to Clifford. Chatted in the lobby with the representative of the Arab press bureau, who among other things stressed that Abdullah would not dare make a separate peace. Incidentally, speaking of Arab lack of unity, he said it wasn't even certain that they were united fully against the Jews.

In the evening two telephone calls. The talk with Eddie Cantor was about his possibly coming to Israel in May and the need to praise Griffis for his refugee responsibility.

181. McDonald to Jacob Potofsky, January 31, 1949, McDonald Papers, Columbia University, box 3, folder 35. This language was repeated in many of McDonald's letters of these months.

6. December 1948

Busy all morning in the hotel. Lunch with Nahum Goldmann, whose information was only supplementary. Chatted for a moment with Jean Dubinsky, who promised me that she would telephone her father regarding [Israel's UN] admission.

Clifford's call came through at five. I spelled out the meaning of my day-before telegram [on admission], explaining that, by the President's support, I was suggesting that he call in the ambassadors concerned and let them know his personal and earnest interest in admission at this session. As usual, Clifford was cautious but promised to lay the matter before Truman.

On December 1 Epstein reported from Washington that Truman, according to Epstein's sources, instructed the US delegation to seek French, Canadian, Argentine, and Colombian support for Israel's admission to the UN. There was especially heavy pressure on the French government.[1]

Tea for a number of guests, including Cy Sulzberger,[2] and Mrs. [Yolande] Harmer. Sulzberger and I alone in the bedroom had a long talk about the revised British resolution and admission. As to the first, I was frank in my emphasis on its complexity, overlapping, and vagueness, and ventured the opinion that many states would hesitate to vote for so omnibus a measure. As to the other topic, I urged in a private message, which Sulzberger said he would send to Abba Hillel Silver, that strong endorsement of prompt action now was the key to the whole problem. Incidentally, I told Sulzberger something of the Lebanese proposal and of the goings-on between Paris and Amman and of the relation between the latter negotiations and the recently adopted cease-fire in Jerusalem. He promised solemnly that nothing of this would be used in the news unless he got it from another source.

After a hurried but pleasant dinner with Noah [Karlin] and Yolande, three of us, not including Yolande went to the Opera Comique to hear *Le portrait de Manon*. It was rather a slapdash performance, but much of the beauty of the

---

1. *DFPI*, v. 2, d. 212, 213.
2. Cyrus Leo Sulzberger II (1912–1993), nephew of Arthur Hays Sulzberger; leading *New York Times* foreign correspondent and columnist, 1939–1978.

music shone through. Skipping the last act and home at 11:00. I met Wainhouse in the hall, and we talked until Bobby came back.

Thursday, December 2

[Gideon] Rafael met me a little after 1:00, explained his point of view about the amended resolution and the admission situation.

On November 30 the British submitted an amended resolution in the General Assembly's First Committee. The draft, influenced by Dulles, called for a conciliation commission that would "enter into consultations" with the governments concerned in order to set the frontiers in Palestine, noting that "certain modifications" to the partition resolution "should be considered [,] taking into account" the progress report of the UN mediator on Palestine. The Bernadotte Plan was eroding.[3]

At 5:00 Governor [Herbert] Lehman's call came through.[4] Fortunately, the connection was good, and I was able to explain simply and clearly the need for presidential, personal intervention. After I made clear that Dulles could not ask the White House and that Lehman could base his call on the Jessup speech, which would be published in the New York afternoon papers within an hour, the governor said that he would telephone Clifford.[5]

Suggestion to Yolande Harmer that she might go to New York on a UJA tour and that I would help her. This seemed to give her a new hope in life. Bobby and I to dinner with Noah and two of his uncles, one of them Serge [Karlinski], and the other [Arnold Karlinski]. The latter was amusing but Serge's monopoly of the conversation reduced his brother's opportunities. Most important part of Serge's talk was that concerning the project for a large modern cement plant in Israel. The foundations have been made, some of the buildings built, and all the equipment is in storage in London. The hitch is twofold: the pressure from the British government and from stockholders to use the equipment elsewhere, and the fact that the present site east of Latrun is just within (two or three kilometers) [of] the present Arab line.[6] My off-the-cuff suggestion of a local frontier rectification was naturally approved. As we left, it was touching to

3. See *DFPI*, v. 2, d. 217; *FRUS*, 1948, v. V, pt. 2, 1636–1638.
4. Herbert H. Lehman (1878–1963), Reform Jewish New York businessman, investment banker (Lehman Brothers), and Democratic politician; lieutenant governor of New York under FDR, 1929–1932; governor of New York, 1933–1942; director of UNRRA, 1943–1946; US Senator from New York, 1949–1957.
5. Jessup's speech to the General Assembly of December 2, 1948, urged immediate admission of Israel to the United Nations.
6. Discussion refers to the cement plant in Hartuv, located near substantial limestone deposits. Planning began in 1934, but the 1936–1939 Arab revolt interrupted the first stages and the outbreak of World War II halted the project entirely. Planning resumed in 1945, but before the equipment had been assembled, the UN adopted the partition plan, and Arab Jewish conflict forced the Jewish inhabitants of the area to flee. Arabs broke into the plant and destroyed the equipment. This meeting between McDonald and the Karlinskis aimed at resuming the plant's development, which required procuring equipment in England and receiving permits to import it into Israel. The editors are grateful to Tuvia Friling for this information.

have both the brothers speak of the "great honor" which had been theirs at dinner. They seemed to know a good deal about my past in reference to the Jews. They both seemed willing, too, that Noah should go to Israel.

Friday, December 3

David Wainhouse dropped in for breakfast. After reading my personal telegrams to Halsey and Roger Straus of yesterday, and learning from the second visitor that the president had yesterday called in the ambassadors from Canada, France, Belgium, and China on the admissions issue, Wainhouse opined that I ought to postpone my return from Sunday until the middle of next week. He promised to suggest some help on this from Dulles.

On November 29, 1948, Israel formally applied to join the UN. Truman favored Israel's immediate admission. Seven votes were needed in the Security Council to forward the application to the General Assembly. On December 17, 1948, five states, including the United States and the USSR, voted for Israel's admission; five states (Great Britain, France, Belgium, Canada, and China) abstained despite Truman's pressure; and Syria voted against.[7]

On December 2 and 3, meanwhile, the General Assembly's First Committee discussed Britain's November 30 draft resolution. The Soviet Union and the Eastern Bloc countries voted against the passages related to the Bernadotte Plan, as did Australia, the Latin American states, and most of the Arab states, the latter objecting to Israel's existence altogether.[8] As McDonald put it, the British draft was "emaciated." "What a success for the strange opportunistic bedfellowship—Russia, the Arab States, and Israel!"[9] The British chastised the Arab states, then told US diplomats that they would now simply watch developments unfold.[10]

On December 3, as debate in the First Committee concluded, McDonald received the following note from David Wainhouse: "Foster [Dulles] said you should feel free to go whenever you think it wise. Your presence here, he says, has been helpful and with the Palestine Committee work coming to a close, he cannot foresee that there will be any necessity for you remaining here."[11]

Tea with Jean Dubinsky, who told me the life history of Sam Klaus. Of very poor parents, he had had a brilliant educational career through law school, became intimately acquainted with the labor movement including communism,

7. Marte Heian-Engdal, Jørgen Jensehaugan, and Hilde Henriksen, "Finishing the Enterprise: Israel's Admission to the United Nations," *International History Review* 35, no. 3 (2013): 465–485.

8. United Nations, *Official Records of the Third Session of the General Assembly*, Part I, *First Committee, 28 September–8 December 1948*, December 2, 3, 1948, 877–914.

9. McDonald, *My Mission in Israel*, 103, 108.

10. Douglas to Lovett, no. 5137, November 7, 1948, *FRUS*, 1948, v. V, pt. 2, 1650; Lewis Jones to Satterthwaite, no. 8, December 8, 1948, *FRUS*, 1948, v. V, pt. 2, 1650–1651.

11. Wainhouse to McDonald, December 3, 1948, McDonald to Fraser Wilkins et al., December 2, 1948, McDonald Papers, USHMM, box 7, folder 9.

[and] is completely incorruptible. He is a cousin of David Dubinsky. Jean also told me a good deal about Charles Zimmerman, her father's vice-president, now in Tel Aviv.

Saturday, December 4

Dulles called on the phone and raised the question of the attitude of the Israel delegation toward the [First Committee] resolution, seeming to imply that it might be useful if I postponed our flight beyond Sunday night.[12] But since this was said rather casually and since he had technically called to inquire about my health, I was not sure of his position, particularly in the light of the very cool good-bye letter of the day before. Hence, I called Wainhouse to ask him for an interpretation. He promised to check, but his later call was negatively helpful. As a result the decision to stay or not was technically determined at the TWA office by the flip of a coin. Later in the day, when I discovered a recurrent temperature, the visit of the doctor confirmed that it would have been a mistake to have tried to travel then.

Our tea party began with a long visit by David Wainhouse, followed by [Harding] Bancroft,[13] Dorothy Fosdick,[14] and at the end, the four musketeers [technicians]—[Fraser] Wilkins, [William] Cargo,[15] [Samuel] Kopper, [and] Ross. The talk with the [technicians] was the most interesting. They were a little shamefaced, it seemed to me, but at the drubbing which they and the British had received in Committee I and possibly also by their failure to have asked the slightest bit of help from me during the previous sixteen days. They were not even inclined to be defensive on behalf of the Arabs. As to the vote in the General Assembly, only Ross was moderately optimistic. They recognized that they were dependent upon Israel's influence with the Russians to win support for sufficient amendments to get the two-thirds required. All of it reflected a sad disillusionment.

McDonald later wrote Halsey and Janet Barrett, "The long talk with four of the State Department technicians was friendly and revealing. These young men, who had not found it necessary to ask my opinion on anything previously, did not even attempt to argue when I pointed out some of the more egregious of their mistakes of tactics. They made no serious defense of their blind following of their principle that almost at any cost the united front [with Britain] must be maintained."[16]

12. Shertok was not fully pleased with the resolution's language concerning Jerusalem and the Arab refugees. *DFPI*, v. 2, d. 224 and entry of December 10, 1948.
13. Harding F. Bancroft (1911–1992), chief, Division of United National Political Affairs, Department of State; after 1956 an executive with the *New York Times*.
14. Dorothy Fosdick (1913–1997), Ph.D. Columbia University; assistant to the director, Office of European Affairs, Department of State; daughter of Harry Emerson Fosdick (1878–1969) of Riverside Church, noted anti-Zionist.
15. William I. Cargo (1917–2005), acting assistant chief, Office of Dependent Area Affairs, Department of State.
16. McDonald to Halsey and Janet Barrett, December 5, 1948, McDonald Papers, USHMM, box 7, folder 8.

Dulles wrote McDonald in April 1949, "I often think of our talks in Paris and of the action taken there, much of it informally, which did a good deal, I think, to break the back of the problem."[17]

Kopper came to life in tones of outraged indignation when he learned of Lebanon's refusal to give up a transit visa [for a direct flight from Paris]. He asked for my passport in order that he might show it to [Charles] Malik. As someone put it later, Kopper was like a fond mother who had carefully groomed her child for a party only to have the youngster spit in the eye of the aunt from whom an inheritance was expected.

McDonald later wrote Lowell Pinkerton, the US minister in Beirut, "In Paris a fortnight ago the Lebanese authorities three times refused my daughter and me transit visas; at the fourth request [they] granted them but then immediately annulled them. I made no issue of this discourtesy because the visas were not absolutely necessary since we did not have to use the UN plane via Beirut to get from Athens to Tel Aviv. Malik told Kopper that he was very grateful for my restraint."[18]

Sunday, December 5, 1948

Lunch with Serge Karlinski, Noah, and Mr. M.[19] The latter talked very interestingly about Egypt, economic conditions there, and the king, to whom he attributes decisive power. M, as I had been warned, was possibly overly optimistic about potential liberal movements in Egypt. He was sure that the present leader of the Wafd would never compromise with the king but that the second in command might. I should like to have listened to M. much longer but was still weary and to bed at 3:00.

During tea-time had a series of visitors. The first of these was Wainhouse, who came with an elaborate program of ways in which the Committee I delegation could help to win the two-thirds vote for the resolution. I promised to make the argument and also to pass on the word that Dulles would be glad to see Moshe Shertok.

Gideon Rafael came in and gave me a full account of developments, explaining that there was a difference of opinion on the desirability of accepting the resolution or of seeking more. He was of the three-quarters of a loaf group, whereas his chief [Shertok] inclined in the direction of perfection. We discussed back and forth the dangers of no resolution and the need of one if there were to be any hope for admission. We tried vainly to get hold of Wainhouse.

17. Dulles to McDonald, April 6, 1949, McDonald Papers, Columbia University, box 2, folder 14.
18. McDonald to Pinkerton, December 16, 1948, McDonald Papers, Columbia University, box 16, folder 11.
19. Possibly Egyptian diplomat Abd al-Mun'im Mustafa. See entries of June 6, 1949, and October 31, 1949.

After dinner alone, Wainhouse came in. Later, when I was exhausted and ready for bed, Ben Cohen came and stayed for nearly an hour. Again we went over the resolution, concentrating for the most part on the problem of Jerusalem. Cohen argued that the resolution was much more favorable than the Israelis seemed to realize. I could only wish that Cohen had had the advantage of knowing Palestine on the ground.

Monday, December 6

Few visitors during the day and still kept indoors, felt neglected and ill at ease with the world. Worked on a letter to Clifford about Dulles, Justice Douglas, and Jack Ewing as contrasted with Ambassadors Douglas and Harriman. Also improved my telegram to Jack Ewing by transforming it into a more intimate letter.

McDonald wrote Clifford, "motivated by my deep desire that the President's second term in the field of foreign policy may be as successful and, if possible, more so than his first." He suggested as the next secretary of state John Foster Dulles, Supreme Court Justice William O. Douglas, or "my old friend" Oscar R. (Jack) Ewing, then the head of the Social Security Administration. "Jack, too, has superb ability, deep interest in and wide knowledge of foreign affairs, and loyalty to the President exceeded by none." Lewis Douglas and Averell Harriman, McDonald said, lacked "independence of excessive influence from 10 Downing Street."[20]

In a subsequent letter to Ewing, McDonald analyzed the UN session in Paris:

> *As a lifelong student of international relations and [an] ardent advocate of an effective world organization, I am more and more convinced that the judgments of the [Security] Council and the [General Assembly] of the UN are sometimes so unrealistic that they diminish rather than increase the chances of peaceful solutions. Watching closely what happened in Paris and assessing it against the background of my knowledge of conditions here [in Israel] and in the neighboring countries, I was frequently frightened at the obvious possibility that the vast and cumbersome UN machinery might do more harm than good. That this was not the result was in my opinion primarily due to Dulles's leadership. He never posed as an expert in this part of the world, but from the beginning he had a grasp of realities which made most of the experts look like amateurs. . . . I hope . . . that all those who have [something] to do with shaping national policies will regard UN decisions, e.g., that for the internationalization of Jerusalem, as general guides rather than as binding obligations which cannot be adjusted to subsequent fundamental changes.[21]*

20. McDonald to Clifford, December 7, 1948, McDonald Papers, USHMM, box 7, folder 9, December 1948.
21. McDonald to Ewing, February 24, 1949, McDonald Papers, Columbia University, box 11, folder 21. A similar letter went to Felix Frankfurter.

The following about Ambassador Griffis belongs above, because he came in to see me at about 7:00 and stayed until past 8:00. He explained that he had wanted to stay in the States to finish an assignment of lobbying in favor of the congressional appropriation for the Arab refugees, and that he might even have to return for this.

On December 6 the White House announced that the president would recommend to Congress that the United States provide 50 percent of the nearly $30 million called for in the UN General Assembly Resolution 212 of November 19, 1948, to provide relief for 500,000 refugees for the next nine months.

He had found the UN a madhouse but had gotten a start. Dodge, "a nice old gentleman" not capable of doing the whole job, had gone off to the northeast and would be useful there. His own headquarters will be in Geneva, because his job will be concerned primarily with securing funds and directing the international cooperation.

In the field, the Quakers are to work in the southern sector, the League of Red Cross Societies in the north or the center, and the Committee of the International Red Cross in the remaining sector. Griffis was skeptical of the ability of the Arab organizations to be of much value. He cited the case of the Egyptian Red Cross, which had declared that 5,000 tents, which had been made available to it, had reached the refugees. Though Griffis was unable to get any one directly to the front, his man did go far enough north to find the tents resting quietly on a siding, still within Egyptian territory and miles from the suffering refugees.

It soon became evident, as we talked, that while Griffis will devote himself unstintingly to his refugee assignment, his heart is in a political situation and in what he spoke of to the president as the "Griffis Plan" for the ending of the war. He said that he had urged it upon the president, General Marshall, and Satterthwaite. All had expressed interest, but none had, so far as he indicated, committed themselves to its support. He had also previously in November talked to Dulles and Jessup about it. He is now prepared, if it is desired, to go unofficially to Cairo to press the matter if the United States were prepared to go through with it. Meantime, he is wholly skeptical of any worthwhile action by the Assembly, he doubts that any resolution will pass, and that if it does, a conciliation commission could have any real influence. Everything, he says, depends upon Egypt being enabled to make peace, which in turn means the king.

His plan, in brief, calls for an American subsidy, perhaps as much as $10,000,000 to be paid to Egypt in the form of irrigation and other engineering schemes. This is to be combined with a form of arrangement which could be interpreted by the Egyptians as a kind of American-Egyptian alliance. The whole would, of course, require a complete Anglo-American understanding.

Territorially, Egypt should receive some token gains in the Negev. Griffis did not think Gaza important. He has in mind also some sort of a corridor across southern Negev for Transjordan, which might thus enable the enlarged Transjordan to be a viable state. He stressed, however, that personally he didn't care if the whole of Palestine west of the Jordan went to Israel. It will be interesting to see whether anything comes of this project, which on the surface, seems to be wholly personal to Griffis.

To the d'Iena, dictation of letters to Clifford and regarding Yolande Harmer.[22] Brief conferences with Wilkins, Rusk, and one or two others regarding Griffis's scheme. None of them seemed to know about it. Brief visit to Committee I, and sat [in] back of Dulles while he was finishing his speech on Korea.[23] Short talk with Comay and Eban regarding Griffis's scheme. They seemed to be quite *au courant*, characterizing it as "Farouk's scheme." Their general attitude was that it was just one more maneuver, not to be taken seriously, at least not here and now. Rode home with Rusk and got the impression of a harassed man.

Wednesday, December 8

The embassy called to say that they had had final word from the Lebanese here that nothing could be done about our transit visas, because there were positive orders from Beirut not to [grant a] visa any passport with Israel visas in it.

Mrs. Roosevelt's visit [in the afternoon] was rather too short for full exposition of the geography of Israel, but I did the best I could with my maps. She would like to come out in the spring, but fears she will be tied up with the Human Rights UN assignment. After Bobby and Yolande left me at dinner [for the theater], I had a pleasant chat with Buzz, who came over to join me. He explained that his uncle, Franklin,[24] had been so delayed en route to Israel that he decided to postpone his visit until spring.

Thursday, December 9

Breakfast with David Wainhouse, who knows nothing about the Griffis plan, and who had been so involved in Korea that he was not informed about the Beeley maneuver in the sub-committee of the Security Council or of Ross's tentative agreement to go along.[25] Talk with Ben Cohen, who knows about [the] Griffis plan, but doesn't seem to think that it is more significant than any

22. To attain a US visitor's visa for her, McDonald to Cecil Gray, consul general in Paris, December 7, 1948, McDonald Papers, USHMM, box 7, folder 9.
23. The debate on Korea concerned a resolution (issued December 12, 1948) regarding the withdrawal of occupying troops, the recognition of the government in Seoul as the legitimate Korean government, and the creation of a new commission to aid with the unification of Korea.
24. Franklin Delano Roosevelt Jr. (1914–1988), fifth of Roosevelt's children, naval officer in World War II; served on the President's Committee on Civil Rights, 1946; congressman from New York's 20th District, 1949–1955.
25. Involving another attempt to have the Israelis withdraw to the battle lines of October 14 or face sanctions.

one of several other ideas. He, like Wainhouse, was most warmly appreciative in his expression of gratitude for my efforts.

Yesterday Nahum Goldmann called and suggested that Max Wolf would be an excellent member of Griffis's staff. I promised to pass along the word. Similarly, yesterday Griffis, in calling to ask me what I had done about his plan—I replied that I had spoken about it to several of the Delegation but that only he personally could "sell" it—said that he would like to have Yolande Harmer as a member of his staff. I was a little surprised because he had seen her and spoken to her for not more than two and a half minutes by the clock. He added that he was impressed by her and that perhaps she would like to be in the publicity section. I promised to pass on the message. This I did.

After vain book shopping trip with Bobby, brief lunch, [and] nap, we held our last tea party. Following pleasant visit with Noah and Yolande, Shertok and Rafael arrived. Going into the next room these two and I spent more than a half an hour analyzing the present situation. Shertok, in his usual logical fashion, outlined it under three headings: first, the political resolution. This had been or would be (since the action must be taken by the Assembly itself) amended to secure the necessary two-thirds votes. The last mention of the Bernadotte Plan to be eliminated; similar action in reference to the provision for the Conciliation Commission to be named by the [Security] Council, this now to be left to the Assembly itself; the one mention of Israel or November 29th to be eliminated. Left would be the undesirable provisions about Jerusalem and demilitarization there, as well as the few undesired words about refugees. This last point, I stressed, could surely not be important. Shertok clearly favors passage because it is essential to consideration of admission and because the alternative is automatic return to [the] May 14th resolution. Shertok is not so sure about the reception of the resolution in Israel. Obviously, he would like to have me use my good offices on my return to explain why more could not have been done.

Shertok's second point was on admission: This he thinks is still possible after the political resolution passes. The following are pledged: US, USSR, Ukraine, Colombia, Argentina, Canada (the latter if the political resolution has passed and if a seventh can be found.) The seventh might be found from France or Belgium. Shertok thinks that admission would compensate for all weaknesses in the political resolution.

Shertok's third point was the Negev and the Security Council's possible action. He was delighted that Tel Aviv had agreed to release the Egyptians from the Faluja pocket[26] and to make another concession. He hoped that the British continuing efforts to use the November 4th resolution as a club could be

26. Shertok's statement on Faluja was inaccurate. Ben-Gurion objected to releasing any Egyptians from the Faluja pocket without peace agreements in place. On December 1, it was agreed that, under UN supervision, an Egyptian convoy with provisions would travel to Faluja from Gaza. After Israel discovered arms in the convoy, it refused to allow further convoys into the pocket. Ralph Bunche ordered an investigation into the UN's approval of a convoy carrying arms. See *DFPI*, v. 2, d. 187, 191, 192, 194, 195.

countered. We then chatted for a while about possible changes in the US Cabinet and presently joined the ladies.

Friday, December 10, 1948

Final telegram to the White House and to Tel Aviv.

Personal attention Clifford. Before returning [to] Tel Aviv tonight [I] feel impelled [to] repeat my previous high praise [for the] efforts made by our delegates to advance [the] President's Palestine policy but also my earlier warnings lest [the] US unintentionally through technical moves become involved in [a] threat of sanctions against Israel. Despite optimistic report [regarding] prospects [for] peace negotiations made by Bunche, [who is] just back from Middle East, [the] British demanded [on] December 8th [an] emergency [Security Council] meeting to force Israel withdrawals to [the] October fourteenth line [in the] Negev. This was [a] dangerous maneuver to embarrass [the] US and other countries urging favorable action [on] Israel admission UN [during] this Assembly. US response made in [Security Council]-sub-committee by Ross without opportunity [for] consultation [by] Dulles or Jessup gave partial US moral support [to] British latest maneuver to indict Israel as [the] aggressor. US technical cooperation with such UK tactics could destroy [the] President's peace hopes [for the] Middle East. If [the] UK were told unequivocally that [the] US will not repeat not be party [to] sanctions or moves [in] that direction I believe [the] UK might finally accept in good faith [a] viable Israel as [a] reality and encourage instead of discourage Abdullah, Farouk, and [the] others [to] make peace. Central fact remains [that the] UK must desire peace with Israel and convince [the] Arab states of such desire before any peace becomes possible.[27]

Dulles called to say good-bye and to tell me about the political resolution and the prospects of its passage. He praised Shertok highly for his clear-headedness, succinctness, and reasonableness. He termed him an unusually capable representative.[28] I told Dulles that Shertok had been with me the night before and that he was urging support of the political resolution, and that I rather thought

27. McDonald to secretary of state [for White House only; personal attention Clifford], no. 6246, December 10, 1948, NARA, RG 59, 501.BB Palestine, box 2123, folder 1.

28. Dulles had met Shertok that morning. See memorandum of conversation, December 10, 1948, NARA, RG 59, 501.BB Palestine, box 2123, folder 1. On January 12, 1949, Shertok gave a lengthy assessment to the Mapai Executive Committee that included not only Israel's desired transition from war to peace and a round condemnation of Great Britain but also the following: "We have not stated that every command and announcement of the UN will be 'implemented and abided by' . . . regardless of its justification or intention in our eyes—but we have also avoided . . . outright and direct objection . . . and [we] have always been sure to preserve, as much as possible, a general framework of sound relations between us and United Nations institutions." The UN, Shertok said, was "a barrier, albeit slight and meager, but nevertheless a barrier between humanity, between human life, and utter destruction." See Louise Fischer, ed., *Moshe Sharett: The Second Prime Minister, Selected Documents (1894–1965)* (Jerusalem: Israel State Archives, 2009), 374–381. The editors are grateful to Tuvia Friling for this reference.

he hoped I would explain in Tel Aviv why more could not have been done. Dulles was generous in his statement that he was glad I had been here.

This is the last of the Paris diary, to which Bobby assents. Yolande, Bobby, and I over to the [Musée du] Petit Palais to see the Munich pictures.[29] The most gorgeous of all were the Rubens. At a little after three, Noah joined us and we all went off to the Invalides station to check in for the plane. A little before five we said goodbye. The flight of about two hours from Paris to Geneva was uneventful. After forty-five minutes or so on the ground, we took off for Rome via the Rhône Valley. We reached Rome in just about three hours and to our surprise met Yolande's friend, Mr. Bagge waiting at the field to go on to Cairo. There was just time for tea when we were called back to the plane. The flight to Athens was another approximately three hours. The arrival in Athens was approximately seven o'clock Athens time, December 11.

On December 11, 1948, the General Assembly issued Resolution 194 formally establishing the Palestine Conciliation Commission [PCC]. Headquartered in Jerusalem, it was to consist of representatives from three states. The PCC was to "take steps to assist the Governments and authorities concerned to achieve a final settlement of all questions outstanding between them," including the final territorial settlement. On Jerusalem, the PCC was to provide "detailed proposals for a permanent international regime [under UN control] for the territory of Jerusalem," defined as the city and its environs. The city was also to be demilitarized "at the earliest possible date." The resolution further stipulated that "refugees wishing to return to their homes and live at peace with their neighbors should be permitted to do so at the earliest practicable date," with compensation paid to those not returning. The PCC was to "facilitate the repatriation, resettlement, and economic and social rehabilitation of the refugees" while closely cooperating with the director of United Nations Relief for Palestinian Refugees.[30]

The secretary-general asked Turkey, France, and the United States to serve on the PCC. Shertok, who had told Dulles on December 10 that the three PCC members should be neutral, that France had "too many Muslim involvements," and that Norway, Australia, and Colombia would form a good commission, was displeased.[31] McDonald suggested candidates for the US delegation to the president and State Department: "Generals Hilldring, [Albert] Wedemeyer,[32] [Joseph Lawton] Collins,[33] or [Joseph] McNarney, if [a] military man [is] under consideration. As regards non-military man[,]

29. Reference to paintings from the Alte Pinakothek in Munich on display in Paris in late 1948.

30. See http://daccess-dds-ny.un.org/doc/RESOLUTION/GEN/NR0/043/65/IMG/NR 004365.pdf?OpenElement.

31. Memorandum of conversation, December 10, 1948, NARA, RG 59, 501.BB Palestine, box 2123, folder 1.

32. Lieutenant General Albert Coady Wedemeyer (1897–1989), served on Marshall's staff in London, 1942; chief of staff to Lord Louis Mountbatten in the South East Asia Command, 1942–1944; commanded US forces in China, 1944–1945; completed study on China and Korea at Truman's request, 1947.

33. Major General Joseph Lawton Collins (1896–1987), commanded VII Corps at Normandy, 1944; Army chief of staff, 1949–1953.

Mark Ethridge,[34] Paul Porter,[35] Paul McNutt[36] or Jack Ewing. As to administrative chief of Commission, [I] suggest that appointment of anyone formerly associated with Mediator's staff be avoided on grounds that completely fresh mind and outlook be brought to [the] problem and to avoid disadvantage of accumulated Arab-Jewish prejudices."[37]

Saturday, December 11

Arrangements were made for us to stay at the King George [in Athens]. After breakfast Mr. Beyer from the embassy came to see us.[38] I went with him to the embassy only to learn that not only was there no transportation available, but that Colonel Bergquist was adamant about [not] taking us [to Israel] without a specific order from Washington.[39] And, I am afraid I could not blame him. Immediately I got off an urgent appeal telegram to Satterthwaite, in the hope that it could be acted upon that morning. Meanwhile, Bergquist kindly set up the flight for Sunday morning at nine in the expectation that the authorization would arrive in time—and to my amazement it did. After four hours or so of sleep, Bobby and I had the first of two teas and saw something of Athens.

Sunday, December 12

At seven-thirty, Bobby called me with the thrice-welcome news that the authorization had come during the night, the embassy car would call for us at eight and we would be off at nine. After a huge breakfast, we were at the airport a little after nine. Major Haney was ready to take off at a quarter of ten.[40] The weather continuing fair, the flight was without incident, and we landed at Haifa at 1:45. It was good to be back, and to find that the reports of rain and cold were so exaggerated. But after the trip down [to Tel Aviv] with Miss Clark and Mr. Reeves in the Packard and noting the flooded conditions and the wrecks along the road, we entered our ice-cold damp house prepared to believe the worst. Hot tea and friendly welcome of friends made things look brighter.

34. See entry of January 16, 1949.
35. Paul A. Porter (1904–1979), lawyer and senior Democratic Party leader; headed Democratic Party campaign, 1944; chairman, Federal Communications Commission, 1944–1946; headed US Economic Mission to Greece with rank of ambassador, 1946–1947. See entry of July 19, 1949.
36. Paul V. McNutt (1891–1955), Indiana Democrat; governor of Indiana, 1933–1937; High Commissioner of the Philippines, 1937–1939, 1945–1946; US ambassador to the Philippines, 1946–1947. Helped persuade State Department to allow about 1,200 Jewish refugees into the Philippines, 1937–1941.
37. McDonald to secretary of state, no. 301, December 13, 1948, NARA, RG 59, MC 1390, reel 17, frame 661.
38. Roland K. Beyer (1913–1974), vice consul, US Embassy, Athens.
39. Colonel Kenneth P. Bergquist (1912–1993), air attaché.
40. Major George W. Haney (1913–1999), assistant air attaché.

McDonald wrote to Clifford, "Our Paris mission has strengthened me in Israel. Of course, the Hebrew press exaggerated the importance of my working there but the net effect here has been good."[41]

Monday, December 13

The day was given over to a series of staff meetings, except for luncheon at the GHQ. Early in the morning I had called Miss Herlitz to say I would like to see Ben-Gurion if he cared to hear about Paris. The answer was a date for lunch alone at his house, with Paula as cook. The Ben-Gurion house was cold as a barn. In the little sitting room was an old-fashioned portable oil "heater," the worse for seeming decades of wear, with a non-boiling tea kettle on top. Paula bustled in and out in her rather worn but well-filled slacks, completing the meal and getting ready for her husband. She was thrilled by Bobby's scarf present, saying she was glad it was not perfume of which she has more than she can use. In a reply to my answer to her question about the Shertoks' [travel] plans, she commented that the Riviera must be very expensive. She clung to this even when I explained that the Shertoks were going to stay with friends.

When Ben-Gurion came a little after 1:30, we went into the dining room, which was icy cold. Complaining of this, Ben-Gurion was greeted by the reply that she would bring in the heater. Its presence, or more likely the ample food which Paula had provided, soon made us feel warmer. At once, Ben-Gurion and I plunged into a discussion of Paris. He was obviously pleased to be told of the fine impression made by Shertok, Eban, et al., and particularly by the words of praise from Dulles. He asked when Shertok was coming back, to which I replied that he was desperately tired and would either have to have a little rest or risk becoming ill. Ben-Gurion listened, but I am not sure he was convinced. The only point that was very new in Ben-Gurion's comment was the suggestion that progress was being made on the loan [from the US Export-Import Bank]. He said that at least Kaplan was optimistic and that he would ask Kaplan to talk with me and to hear about Paris.

Tuesday, December 14

Again a day occupied for the most part with conferences, and the afternoon given over to the labor leaders' reception. But first I must go back to Sunday evening. I was lucky to get hold of Charles Zimmerman and have him come out for dinner. This gave us a chance to get acquainted and for him to tell me in some detail of what he had done since his arrival and as to [David] Dubinsky's attitude.[42] It was evident that he had already learned a great deal,

41. McDonald to Clifford, December 26, 1948, McDonald Papers, Columbia University, box 9, folder 16.
42. See entry of November 29, 1948. McDonald to secretary of state, January 16, 1949, Truman Library, Clifford Papers, Subject File, 1945–54, box 14, folder Palestine—Telegrams and Cables, 1 of 2.

and would be in a position to enlighten his chief. Now back to Monday, tea and dinner with Charles Zimmerman and Sam Klaus.[43] The discussion centered on a possible program for work here, to be sold to the [American Federation of Labor] leaders at home; and, second, the question of the next secretary of state. There was general agreement as to what should be undertaken here. But Zimmerman could not see quite clearly what the sponsoring and financing agency should be at home. On the second topic, Klaus had warned me that the trade unionists are very sympathetic to Averell Harriman [a candidate for secretary of state]. Zimmerman confirmed this. Before our discussion finished he recognized that Justice [William O.] Douglas[44] or Paul Porter might have very strong claims.

Conferences Tuesday morning. Five to seven the reception of [Israeli] labor leaders for Zimmerman. Among the guests were representatives of all the labor groups except the Revisionists, whom the others would not agree to meet with. I talked to a number of the men and women, including Mapam as well as Mapai representatives. Towards the end of the evening Ben-Gurion came in and made the occasion a complete success. Informal supper with the family.

Wednesday, December 15

Lunch with the Weizmanns. Just before I went up to Weizmann's office, I met Leo Kohn, who had been with him. After a brief chat in Weizmann's office, we went to the house and joined Vera. For me, however, the lunch was a depressing affair, because Weizmann was in a bitter humor, full of venom vindictively expressed towards some of his colleagues, particularly his favorite victim [Ben-Gurion]. I did the best I could to maintain a balance, but left rather disheartened. It was agreed, however, that Sam Klaus and Bobby and I should come out on the following Saturday for lunch.

Supper and discussion afterwards with [Eliahu] Ben-Horin and young Dr. Freymann, who had come down from Jerusalem with Bobby. Dr. Freymann was just completing a visit of the Arab refugee camps for his chief, Lowell Pinkerton [US minister in Beirut]. Previously, as health attaché in Jerusalem, he had been closely associated with Wasson and MacDonald and later Burdett.[45] Completely of the Arab point of view, Dr. Freymann and Ben-Horin had an ardent debate. Ben-Horin argued with restraint and skill and wide knowledge.

43. Klaus had arrived in the third week of November 1948. See entries of October 12 and November 26–29, 1948.
44. Entry of July 18, 1949.
45. John Gordon Freymann (1922–); studied Palestinian refugee problem for US Public Health Service; author of "John Gordon Freymann: Correspondence Relating to Service in Palestine and Israel, 1948–1989" [unpublished].

Persuaded Dr. Freymann to spend the day and continue with me his illuminating reports on conditions in the refugee camps. Visit to Sam Sacks's textile factory, a model and 100% modern plant, perhaps the most modern in the whole of the Middle East.[46] It is the one about which Herbert J. Cummings was so enthusiastic.

An hour in the afternoon with Eytan and Miss Herlitz. Aside from my reports on Paris, which I made as graphic and interesting as I could, Eytan was revealing and frank. He gave an explanation of the ill humor of Weizmann. It arises from Ben-Gurion's delay in giving a favorable decision to Weizmann's question about the cabinet minutes. Dr. Eytan also was frank in admitting the progress of the exchanges between Tel Aviv and Amman.[47] From something else that Dr. Eytan said, I rather got the impression that the brilliant answer from Tel Aviv on the Negev during the assembly had been worked out in his office. Dr. Eytan also confirmed Ben-Gurion's suggestion on Monday that the [Export-Import Bank] loan negotiations in Washington had advanced considerably. The technical discussion with the American Export bank had ended satisfactorily, and the problem was now with the political people in the Department. He wondered whether he could give it a push.

Interesting tea with Monsignors McMahon and Vergani, Mr. Knox, Sam Klaus, and Dr. Freymann.

Monsignor Thomas McMahon, director of the Catholic Near East Welfare Association in the United States, was now the Vatican's unofficial emissary in the Middle East. In December he toured the Catholic Holy Places with Antonio Vergani, the vicar-general of the Latin Patriarchate of Jerusalem. They were accompanied by Eliahu Ben-Horin, adviser on Middle East affairs to the American Zionist Emergency Council.

The concrete ideas which Monsignor Vergani had related to the importance of the Provisional Government indicating its good faith by evacuating

---

46. Sam Sacks, owner and director of the Meshi-Sacks textile factory in Ramat Gan, established in 1932 by his father Isaac Sacks, originally of Paterson, New Jersey. Sam Sacks invested heavily in the plant in order to provide good wages and modern conditions. McDonald visited Sacks often. See Joseph B. Glass, "American Olim and the Transfer of Innovation to Palestine, 1917–1939," in *America and Zion: Essays and Papers in Memory of Moshe Davis*, eds. Eli Lederhendler and Jonathan D. Sarna (Detroit: Wayne State University Press, 2002), 201–232.

47. On November 30, 1948, Israel and Transjordan agreed on a permanent cease-fire in Jerusalem. On December 10, Sasson sent a note to King Abdullah suggesting general peace negotiations. Abdullah worried about the reaction of the other Arab states and included parts of the Bernadotte Plan in his initial terms. Israel wanted the removal of Iraqi troops from Palestine and the Arab Legion to pull back from Israel's border. Abdullah soon quickly understood that an arrangement with Israel could ensure Transjordan's annexation of Samaria and Judea. See Bar-Joseph, *The Best of Enemies*, 134–142.

the Carmel convent[48] and the Tabgha Farm near Capernaum.[49] I said that I would inquire about both of these when I had next an opportunity with the higher officials and preferably with Ben-Gurion. I liked Monsignor Vergani and hope to see more of him, for he will have much to tell. Both he and Monsignor McMahon expressed concern about the Russian program in Jerusalem and elsewhere and the evident intention of the Kremlin to use controlled [Greek Orthodox] ecclesiastics for state purposes.[50] After the monsignors left, Knox and Klaus and I worked on despatches.

Reporting on the various meetings he had since his return from Paris with Weizmann, Eytan, and Herlitz, McDonald noted that peace exchanges with Transjordan "are reaching negotiations stage with Abdullah, with Sasson making frequent trips [to] Jerusalem and Eytan considering urging Shertok, despite [the] latter's need for rest, [to] return promptly Tel Aviv." For the rest, McDonald reported that the Provisional Government was "on balance pleased with results [in] Paris and [the] attitude [of the] US delegates."[51]

Friday, December 17

Said goodbye to the young doctor [Freymann] after his promising he would send off to Griffis his recommendations. Work with Knox all morning on accumulated despatches. Together we made a negative decision about one of our colleagues. We drafted a tentative telegram on the loan[52] and sent off the one on refugees.[53] I should record that the day previous I sent off a strong personal message to Satterthwaite about Ruth's being allowed to land at Beirut.[54] Today through the doctor, I sent as appealing a personal letter as I could to Pinkerton in Beirut for his cooperation.

---

48. Refers to the Monastery of Our Lady of Mount Carmel in Haifa, built in the 1830s by the Carmelite monastic order, which was established in the twelfth century. The monastery is the center of the Carmelite world. It was occupied by the IDF in 1948 partly for use as a naval headquarters, and in 1953 it was leased by the Israel government to the Society for the Holy Places. Doron Bar, "Wars and Sacred Space: The Influence of the 1948 War on Sacred Space in the State of Israel," in *Holy Places in the Israeli-Palestinian Conflict: Confrontation and Co-Existence*, eds. Marshal J. Bregger et al. (London: Routledge, 2010), 67–91.

49. Tabgha on the Sea of Galilee has Christian sites dating to the fourth century. Vergani refers to the Church of the Multiplication of Loaves and Fishes, initially built in the fourth century on the site where Jesus is said to have fed five thousand people. In 1892 the German Catholic Mission to Palestine, associated with the archdiocese of Cologne, purchased the site, partly to protect the Byzantine mosaics there. In 1948 the IDF occupied Tabgha because it sat astride the Tiberias–Rosh Pina road overlooking the Syrian border and was needed for combat operations against Syrian forces. Agreement was reached in 1953 whereby the archbishop of Cologne could use the church, but the Israeli government used most of the surrounding lands in return for an annual payment. Bialer, *Cross on the Star of David*, 145, 172–177.

50. In general on Russian ecclesiastical assets, see Bialer, *Cross on the Star of David*, 144–165.

51. McDonald to secretary of state, no. 316, December 17, 1948, Truman Library, Clifford Papers, Subject Files, box 14, folder Palestine—Telegrams and Cables 1 of 2.

52. Described in entry of December 18, 1948.

53. Not found.

54. Entry of December 4, 1948.

Tea with Mrs. Davidowitz, whom I promised that I would cooperate in the opening of the [new] Youth Aliyah Center on January 9.[55] She also secured my promise to do a four-minute recording to be broadcast by WMCA.[56] Later, when I thought of the fact that the reception was half an hour north of Haifa, I was not so sure I should have accepted.

Hearing that Mrs. Anne O'Hare McCormick and her husband had come down with Shalom from Haifa, I sent over and had them come out to the house.[57] For the first nearly an hour, she asked me questions and I talked about conditions here, my appointment, etc. She later showed intense feeling about the Arab refugees in some of the camps she had visited, and thought the tragedy would embitter Jewish-Arab relations for decades. She has a general theory that the transfer of populations is fundamentally bad. She thinks that the present disturbance in Greece goes back to the refugees from Smyrna,[58] and she cited the unhappiness of the Sudeten Germans in Bavaria and their unpopularity there.[59] She and her husband stayed for supper during which we had a pleasant chat about many things. Meanwhile, I called Rehovot and arranged for them, too, to go out with Klaus and me for lunch tomorrow.

Saturday, December 18

To the office in the late morning to work with Knox, Hope, and Klaus on [Klaus's] long telegram arguing for more specific action or action pointing in the direction of de jure recognition and the loan.

In his own telegram McDonald noted that Mapai, which was expected to lead a coalition government after the first elections in 1949, was pro-Western. Mapam, he said, was more leftist, more suspicious of the United States because of its support for the British, and more friendly toward the USSR because of Moscow's support in the UN and the hope that Moscow would allow Soviet Jews to come to Israel with no quid pro quo. The mission expected Mapai to win up to 35 percent of the votes, and Mapam to win 20 percent, but it could not guarantee that Mapam would remain without a voice. In view of this, McDonald said, "Mission [is] of [the] opinion that [a] firm declaration by [the] Department on [the] loan to Israel would accomplish much. De jure recognition statement would show [the] US not lagging behind [the] USSR and not tied to British policies. Mission recommends any announcement

---

55. See entry of February 10, 1949.
56. New York news and talk radio station.
57. McCormick was in the Middle East on assignment from the *New York Times*. See entry of January 23, 1949.
58. Following the Convention Concerning the Exchange of Greek and Turkish Populations, signed in Lausanne in January 1923. The convention resulted in the removal of 1.6 million Greeks from Asia Minor.
59. The Czech government expelled some 2.4 million ethnic Germans from the Sudetenland after World War II.

*simultaneously [in] Washington and Tel Aviv to obtain maximum effect. Depart-
ment requested to keep Mission continuously informed, for its comment.*"[60]

*Two days later McDonald suggested that this despatch be sent to the White House
"in view of my instructions from the President."*[61]

Then Bobby and I, with Klaus, picked up Mr. McCormick on our way out
to Weizmann's for lunch. Anne O'Hare joined us there a few minutes late,
coming from her visit to Negba.[62]

When we met the Weizmanns, Mrs. Weizmann, with unwonted enthusiasm, told me, with her husband's permission, of Weisgal's having secured the
consent of President Truman to attend the dinner for the [Weizmann] Institute [of Science] and to send the Sacred Cow for Dr. Weizmann.[63] It seemed
to me a brilliant coup, and I said so. I suggested, however, that it might be
easier if Mr. and Mrs. Weizmann flew to Paris and took one of the Queens
from there.[64] They agreed. During lunch the talk was general with no references to any of the subjects which Dr. Weizmann had so violently discussed
three days earlier. Instead, the subjects were those which would naturally be
brought forward when foreign journalists were present. After the meal was finished, I suggested that Dr. Weizmann and Klaus talk while I took Mrs. Mc-
Cormick to see the house. She was thrilled as her husband had been at the
magnificence and beauty of the scene from the roof.

*McDonald reported that Weizmann discussed the recruitment of economic ex-
perts in the United States and that he "believes [that the] greatest emphasis should be
placed here [on the] role of science rather than handicraft in future economic development and is devoting his institute [to] this purpose." Weizmann was also "worried
regarding [the] character [of the] immigration from DP camps as dependence psychology [and that it was] insufficiently pioneer in spirit."*[65]

60. McDonald to secretary of state [also to Clifford], no. 323, December 20, 1948, Truman
Library, Clifford Papers, Subject File, 1945–54, box 14, folder Palestine—Telegrams and Cables
1 of 2.
61. McDonald to secretary of state, no. 325, December 21, 1948, NARA, RG 59, MC
1390, reel 17, frame 762.
62. Kibbutz in northern Negev, founded in 1939 by HaShomer HaTzair as the southernmost settlement in mandatory Palestine. In 1948 it was strategically located astride the Majdal–
Beit Jibrin Road. The Egyptians attacked in June and July 1948, but the settlement held and
served as a forward launching point for Operation Yoav in September.
63. The Sacred Cow was a Douglas C-54 Skymaster, a military version of the DC-4, which
became the first presidential aircraft to be called "Air Force One." See also entry of January 20,
1949.
64. Reference to one of the Cunard liners *Queen Mary* or *Queen Elizabeth*.
65. McDonald to secretary of state, no. 334, December 23, 1948, NARA, MC 1390, reel
17, frame 807. Weizmann's comments should be taken in the broader context of Israeli attitudes.
See Idith Zertal, *From Catastrophe to Power: Holocaust Survivors and the Emergence of Israel*
(Berkeley: University of California Press, 1998).

Rabbi Israel Goldstein came in for tea. We talked about Yolande Harmer, concerning whom he promised to write favorably to Harry Shapiro, the newly elected head of the UPA.[66] Though there was little time, Goldstein indicated two complaints, one, that the lobbying at the UN in Paris had not been as good as it had been at Lake Success the year previous, and, two, that the Israeli authorities have not taken an unequivocal line against Henry Montor and the dissenters [in the United Jewish Appeal]. Goldstein indicated that there was some feeling of resentment at home on this latter score. My only comment throughout all of this discussion was to the effect that Israel was more important than any internal differences. To this, of course, Goldstein gave at least verbal assent. As he was leaving, it was agreed that he and his wife would come to see us.

Sunday, December 19

I met and chatted with Colonel Archibald [the new air attaché] and his co-pilot, Captain Cashin, who with two sergeants had come in a few hours earlier with their DC-3, which was parked in the Tel Aviv airport.

Manon with Madame de Philippe in the title role, particularly as compared with the performance which Bobby and I had heard at the Opera Comique a few weeks earlier, was brilliant. Afterwards there was a homey sort of a reception attended by the cast and some of the audience including Mr. and Mrs. Ben-Gurion, the Russians, and ourselves. During the intermissions we had pleasant visits with the Ben-Gurions the Kaplans, the Rokachs, and friendly greetings with the Russians. I was a little surprised to have Kaplan say that the Agudat were making capital of my visit to their kibbutz and to my reported sympathy for Orthodoxy.[67] The only other noteworthy comment of the evening was that of Paula, turning to Bobby, exclaiming, "When is Mama coming?" Home well after midnight to be greeted with the amazing and thrilling news the Ruth was due at the Tel Aviv airport by UN plane Monday morning at 8:30. It seemed incredibly good.

Monday, December 20

Up and to the airport, where Ruth arrived, promptly at nine. The morning spent getting reacquainted, and lunch the same. Tea was a very pleasant party, with all of the officers of the mission except Captain Frothingham present to greet Ruth. The only business transacted was to plan the holiday schedule of social obligations. Before the men left, Knox and I ok'd some telegrams, and he emphasized the warning in his memo about not acting on the suggestion of the monsignors.[68] I listened and read carefully but was not wholly convinced.

66. Harry L. Shapiro (d. 1979), executive director of American Zionist Emergency Council, 1947–1948; elected executive director of United Palestine Appeal in November 1948; supporter of Abba Hillel Silver.

67. Entry of November 7, 1948.

68. Entry of December 16, 1948.

McDonald reported to Washington:

"In [a] confidential and strictly informal talk [by] Shiloah with Knox, [the] former stated [that] Egyptian and Iraqi refusals [to] talk armistice [are] causing increasing concern [in the Provisional Government]." Current Egyptian delays, Shiloah said, were viewed as subterfuges so that the Egyptian army could reform and rearm.

"It is not known [to] what extent Shiloah's remarks reflect official thinking but there is some sentiment in military circles supported in part by [the] press reflecting public disappointment over failure [to] achieve UN membership, that UN may not arrive at any satisfactory solution owing [to] Arab intransigence and that a further indefinite and difficult truce may drag [the] victor into what might be tantamount [to] partial defeat owing [to] economic and financial strain. . . . Israel [is] fully able [to] defeat either Egyptian forces [in the] Negev or Iraqi [forces] in [the Tulkarm-Jenin-Nablus] triangle alternately while holding on other Arab fronts.

"Mission has no reason [to] believe that [Provisional Government] is not fully disposed [to] give Conciliation Commission chance to relieve [the] situation but it is important [that the] Commission get underway without delay. . . . Shertok arrives on 23rd and [the] expectation is [that] he will actively push direct negotiations with Arabs."[69]

In the late afternoon David Courtney came for a long talk. After a general discussion of the developments at Paris, he asked about the loan and de jure recognition. I explained that we had no intimation whatever from Washington on either point, and that we could only have an idea on the basis of general impressions and on our knowledge of what we thought were the president's desires. In answer to his direct question as to what I thought was the betting odds, I replied that I would give something like 51 to 49 on one or both of these actions before the [Israeli] elections. As we talked about Paris, I got the impression that Courtney had become more friendly towards the United States, or at any rate more willing to take account of the American point of view. And, as always with him, I felt that I was talking to a man of exceptional knowledge and breadth of view.

Wednesday, December 22

In the afternoon, a long session with Ben-Horin at teatime. Knox and Hope joined us at tea, later told me of their concern lest the article in *Davar* of today indicated that there had been a breach in our code. I then explained to them of my talk with Courtney the day before and of the connection, which he explained to me between *Davar* and the *Palestine Post*, and of my conclusion from this that the *Davar* piece was by Courtney.[70] They were relieved by this

---

69. McDonald to secretary of state, no. 324, December 21, 1948, NARA, RG 59, MC 1390, reel 17, frames 770–771.

70. "Loan and De Jure Recognition: Truman Has Decided to Take These Steps Even Before Elections in Israel," *Davar*, December 22, 1948; "Even Chance for Loan from US," *Palestine Post*, December 22, 1948.

possibility and were then inclined to share my hope that the *Davar* piece would not be picked up by the foreign press.

On December 22, McDonald telegraphed the State Department and Clifford personally:

> *President's timely action loan and de jure recognition could checkmate Russian attempts [to] weaken predominant moderate pro-Western forces during [the] present electoral campaign. . . .*
>
> *Mission will soon be functioning at full efficiency. Now working out basis through Klaus and Dubinsky's representative Zimmerman, [of] fruitful unofficial cooperation here of large democratic unions [with] AF of L and CIO. Struggle for [the] soul of Israel will be decided in and by [the] labor movement.*
>
> *Meanwhile, if [the] President will give within fortnight clear indication loan and de jure recognition, US friends here should win decisive victory [in the] Constituent Assembly and thus give us time to convince labor here [that] its freedom from totalitarianism depends [on] friendship [with] West. American labor's strong support of President greatly strengthens his position here.*[71]

Thursday, December 23

Klaus's long despatch on the domestic situation here and the possibly decisive importance of action by the US on the loan and *de jure* recognition was finally ready after elaborate revisions which had been carried through the previous two days.

Friday, December 24

Mr. Knox's buffet luncheon.

Saturday, December 25

Christmas dinner buffet with Knox, Frothingham, van der Velde, Archibald, Cashman, Hope, Ruth, Bobby, and me. Miss Clark had gone to Bethlehem the previous day. It was a meal reminiscent of home, and the men seemed to be very appreciative. From five to nearly seven, tea for all the members of the staff. It went well with Hope and Bobby leading the singing.

Sunday, December 26

Worked most of the day. Evening subscription concert at the Philharmonic with [Nicolai] Malko conducting.[72] The program included the Weber *Oberon* overture; the Brahms Piano Concerto, and the Shostakovich First

71. McDonald to secretary of state [personal attention Clifford], no. 333, December 22, 1948, Truman Library, Clifford Papers, Subject File, 1945–54, box 14, folder Palestine—Telegrams and Cables 1 of 2.
72. Nicolai Malko (1883–1961), conductor Leningrad Philharmonic, 1926–1928; left Soviet Union in 1929; settled in United States in 1940.

Symphony. The young soloist struggled valiantly with an indifferent piano. Pleasant visit with the conductor's wife in the intermission.

McDonald recounted the UN General Assembly meetings for Clark Clifford. He also noted:

> *The Department's complete faith in Sam Klaus's penetrating intelligence and sound judgment I have come to share—about de jure recognition and the loan before the Israel Constituent Assembly election. Sam's arguments [contained in McDonald's telegram of December 22] would, I felt, have an exceptional appeal to the President, who, better than anyone else, would grasp the importance of US action in time to strengthen the moderate and pro-Western labor parties before the voting on January 25. My colleagues and I, after having weighed carefully all the technical and other arguments against de jure recognition and loan action prior to the Israel elections, are unanimous that these bases for delay are more than counter-balanced by the practical advantages of action before January 25. My military attaché [van der Velde] is as strongly of this opinion as is Klaus.*
>
> *At last life in Tel Aviv has become what it should be—my wife arrived last Monday, well in time for Christmas. She would have liked to have gone to Bethlehem for Christmas Midnight Mass but the Arabs and Mr. Knox said, "No McDonald is crossing the fighting lines." And, of course, I agreed. Perhaps another year when this land has become in fact one of peace and good will, we shall be allowed to worship at the birth shrine of the Prince of Peace.[73]*

Monday, December 27

In the afternoon at teatime Captain [Bob] Maguire and his colleague Morris of the Alaska Airlines[74] came in to explain the difficulty of fulfilling their contract with the JDC [American Joint Distribution Committee] to transport the approximately 2,000 Yemenites from Aden to Israel. It was clear from what they said of the difficulties made by the Shell and by the British officials in Aden and by similar officials in Nicosia that the British government had decided to yield to Arab pressure and discontinue the transfer of the Yemenites. None of the excuses for inability to supply fuel made sense. I asked the men to give me a detailed statement in order that I might use it as a basis for a report to Washington.

Golda Meyerson called me and made two points:

73. McDonald to Clifford, December 26, 1948, McDonald Papers, Columbia University, box 9, folder 16.
74. Robert F. Maguire (1911–2005), Oregon pilot with management experience; sent to the Middle East on orders of Alaska Airlines president James Wooten as part of Operation Magic Carpet.

Textbox 6.1.
Operation Magic Carpet

The Jews of Yemen, mistreated throughout their history under Turkish and Sharia law, were overwhelmingly poor. The first Yemeni immigrants to Palestine arrived in the 1860s, and worked as laborers. The issuance of the Balfour Declaration and the heightened mistreatment of Jews in Yemen spurred additional Yemeni Jewish emigration in the 1920s. Some traveled by foot to the British protectorate of Aden to the south as a way station for the journey to Palestine. Most, in poor health already, lacked the required funds needed to obtain immigration certificates, and the British authorities closed Aden to additional Yemeni Jewish refugees. The grand mufti also pressed the Yemeni authorities to prevent Jewish emigration. The Jewish Agency, moreover, favored issuing immigration certificates to European Zionists rather than Yemeni Jews in the 1930s. However, when European Jews were trapped, Yemeni Jews received immigration certificates in 1943–1944, and 4,267 immigrated to Palestine.

Despite efforts by the British and Yemeni authorities, 4,000 Yemeni Jews were living in Aden in 1945, many in a primitive refugee camp at Hashed. The UN decision to partition Palestine in November 1947 led to anti-Jewish riots in Aden's cities. A civil war in Yemen that began in February 1948 brought anarchy and renewed anti-Jewish atrocities there. The American Jewish Joint Distribution Committee [JDC] as well as other Jewish organizations had been working to help Yemeni Jews and Jewish refugees in Aden since the 1920s. Now, hoping to move Jewish refugees from Aden to Palestine, the JDC contracted with Alaska Airlines to create an airlift for the refugees.

The British relented, allowing 2,000 refugees to leave in December on conditions that included a total news blackout.[1] The first airplane with Yemeni refugees arrived in Lydda on December 17; it carried orphaned children. Flights arrived thereafter, but the operation was suspended by the end of December, well short of delivering the agreed 2,000 refugees. At McDonald's request Robert Maguire of Alaska Airlines wrote a full explanation for the suspension. Shell Oil in Aden would not supply fuel unless it could be guaranteed its replacement by Shell in Cairo, which the latter refused to do. The RAF in Aden refused to sell fuel to Alaska Airlines or even provide housing for its personnel. BOAC provided fuel for two flights, but then discontinued supplies. The Israelis themselves lacked fuel. UN authorities would not permit high-octane fuel imports for fear that Alaska Airlines was acting as a cover for the Israeli Air Force. Maguire also worried about the six-hour flying time over Egypt in the midst of hostilities.[2]

---

1. Tudor Parfitt, *The Road to Redemption: The Jews of Yemen, 1900–1950* (Leiden: Brill, 1996), 165–187; Esther Meir-Glitzenstein, "Operation Magic Carpet: Constructing the Myth of the Magical Immigration of Yemenite Jews to Israel," *Israel Studies* 16, no. 3 (Fall 2011): 149–173.

2. Robert Maguire to McDonald, December 26, 1948, McDonald Papers, USHMM, box 7, folder 9.

Fig. 6.1. Magic Carpet airlift of Yemeni Jews to Israel, December 1948. Israeli Government Press Office. Photograph by Eldan David.

1) She had checked and there was no basis for the report that the Provisional Government was considering unilateral action towards incorporating Jewish Jerusalem in Israel;

2) She had spoken to the Foreign Office, where Eytan expressed consternation at the thought that Bartley Crum might succeed in his intrigue.

With the aid of the Israeli government, McDonald discovered the reason for Bartley Crum's visit in September 1948. Crum had plotted to supplant McDonald, and his effort was continuing. On December 26, McDonald informed his friend Ben Abrams, "I should not mind so much going home—though I should like to stay until the new state is at peace—but I am determined to do everything I can not to be supplanted by 'my friend' . . . in addition, I am convinced—and so are the heads of the Government here—that my 'friend's' designation as U.S. Representative would soon prove to be a disaster to Israel and an embarrassment to the President."[75]

75. McDonald to Benjamin Abrams, December 26, 1948, McDonald Papers, Columbia University, box 6, folder 2; also McDonald to Halsey and Janet Barrett, December 23, 1948, McDonald Papers, Columbia University, box 14, folder 13.

Word was sent to Eliahu Epstein in Washington to inquire and do everything possible to disappoint my friend. She doubted that the matter could be serious, for otherwise Epstein would have reported it earlier.

Tuesday, December 28

With the family and Curtis Barnes over to the Krinizi factory to confer on furniture. Krinizi said that provided we could get four or five of men released from the army for a period of two months, they could build furniture for the whole house.[76] Incidentally, he offered to supply bedroom furniture for one room as a loan, if needed.

Eban was to come in during the morning but got tied up, and his coming was postponed until Thursday at 10:30. Mr. Knox came out with a number of despatches for my ok, bringing with him Lippincott, who was down from Haifa, on some administrative matters. Knox strongly deprecated my making any statement or giving anything in writing to the Alaska Airways men for fear we would become involved should any controversy arise between the JDC and the company.

During lunch, the Alaska [Airlines] men came out and left with me a statement of fact addressed to me in the form of a letter. Captain Maguire agreed to change a paragraph in which reference was made to our attitude. Meantime, I had arranged for their telephone call to go through this afternoon. They thought it possible that their two planes and crews would be transferred to the Munich-Lydda refugee service. They promised to keep me informed.

[Norman] Bentwich was with us at lunch.[77] The plans of his small group for refugee work among the Arabs seem to be making slow, if any, progress. He is enthusiastic about the Friends. It is sad to note how completely he is out of things here in Israel while he waits for the [Hebrew] University to reopen.

At teatime began a rather hectic series of conferences. First, Mr. Curt Kramarski, editor of *Life in Palestine*, now *Life in Israel*, came to talk about a special edition on American-Israeli friendship. Seemingly, he wants the kind of introduction which would help to make the issue saleable throughout the States and elsewhere.[78] He was so long in his presentation that we had not gotten to the point when word came that Ben-Gurion had telephoned to ask if I could come up immediately. (Earlier in the day I had asked Miss Herlitz to arrange

76. Avraham Krinizi (1886–1969), Belorussian-born mayor of Ramat Gan, 1926–1969.
77. Norman de Mattos Bentwich (1883–1971), Cambridge-educated Zionist and attorney-general in mandatory government in Palestine, where he tried to foster Jewish immigration, 1920–1931; director of League of Nations High Commission for Refugees (McDonald's deputy), 1933–1935; chairman, National Peace Council, 1944–1946; professor of international relations, Hebrew University of Jerusalem, 1932–1951; worked in various capacities concerning restitution in Germany, 1948–1951; author of numerous books attempting to find modus vivendi with Palestinian Arabs. Treated extensively in Breitman et al., eds., *Advocate for the Doomed*.
78. Curt Kramarski, Berlin-born writer and editor in Tel Aviv; also edited the 1939 pamphlet *Beautiful Palestine (Das schöne Palästina)*.

for a five-minute conference and had not told her the reason.) I got a taxi and went to GHQ.

Getting up to Ben-Gurion's office at the GHQ during the blackout is something of an adventure. One is stopped at the foot of the hill, then escorted by military police in a jeep, at the top again stopped at a barrier, and then led to a parking space, where one alighted. From there, led by MPs with dimmed flashlights to Ben-Gurion's anteroom, where the several attending MPs saluted, and then into the secretary's office and finally into the office of the chief. He seemed in good humor, greeted me with the words, "What's the trouble?" To which I replied, "there was no trouble." With a relieved expression, he said, "Good, then I'll tell you about what Ershov said to me yesterday." I indicated my interest. "During the course of a talk," continued Ben-Gurion, "Ershov said emphatically 'there is going to be peace between the Soviet Union and the US'" Ben-Gurion then asked what I thought was the explanation of Ershov's definiteness, adding that he wondered how the Russian representative in Israel could be so intimately informed. My reply was that we had no information, but that I would guess that the Russian optimism was based on the president's reelection and his plan, which he had not been allowed to carry out, to send Chief Justice Vinson to Moscow for a personal session with Stalin.[79] Ben-Gurion indicated that he knew all of this but was still not satisfied that it explained Ershov's pronouncement.

Wishing to see Ben-Gurion in as good a humor as possible, I then showed him the enlarged picture of himself and myself at his HaKirya office[80] taken on the day of my formal presentation. Seemingly, he had not seen it before and was delighted with it. Praising my picture, he pretended not to like his own, but I noted that he sent for his secretary, to whom he gave instructions to order one or more. He said something about how severe he looked, and I explained to him that this is because I had just been warning him that it would be hazardous of the Provisional Government to ignore the possibility that the United States might, if Israel became patently the aggressor, be involved in sanctions against his country. Ben-Gurion's only comment was that there were too many glasses in the picture. He then autographed my copy: To J. McDonald in friendship, D. Ben-Gurion.[81]

The way now having been prepared, I rather apologetically told him that my mission was a housekeeping one, that we had futilely tried to get the Army

79. In October 1948, during the Berlin blockade and the presidential election, Truman asked Supreme Court Chief Justice Fred Vinson to travel to Moscow and meet Stalin personally in an effort to solve the Berlin crisis. Marshall and Lovett considered the idea a foreign policy blunder that would ruin their efforts through the UN, which were based on having the Soviets lift the blockade. The mission was thereby abandoned. Moscow interpreted the affair as reflective of Truman's dissatisfaction with Marshall's policies. Daniel F. Harrington, *Berlin on the Brink: The Blockade, the Airlift, and the Early Cold War* (Lexington: University Press of Kentucky, 2012).
80. HaKirya refers to the government district formed in the center of Tel Aviv during the first years of statehood.
81. Photograph in entry of August 20, 1948.

to release some additional space in the Benin building, where all our offices except my personal one and the consulate are, in order to make room for the service attachés. He was at once interested, started to make notes, and I interrupted to hand him a memorandum, which gave the details. He called in his secretary, to whom he gave instructions to follow through. Word to this effect was repeated to the secretary later when I was leaving.

Since he seemed in no hurry, I decided to check further the report that Klaus had brought from Jerusalem a few days earlier and which he had passed on to the Department. This, based on a statement to Klaus by Avraham Bergman, the assistant to Dr. Joseph, the military governor of Jerusalem, was to the effect that the Provisional Government was contemplating unilateral action to annex Jewish Jerusalem to Israel.[82] Prefacing my question by the statement that one of our jobs at the mission was to let our government know wherever possible "what was going to happen before it happened," I put the blunt question: "Is the Provisional Government planning to declare the New City annexed to Israel before the elections on January 25th?"

Without hesitation and with every indication of sincerity, Ben-Gurion replied in effect, "What Bergman said to Klaus represented Joseph's views and desires, but they did not represent mine. Perhaps we should have done this some time ago, but we have no intention of doing it now. As to the political advantage of such action before the election, I will never play politics with an issue of foreign policy." Then Ben-Gurion immediately, after disavowing any willingness to seek political advantage from the Jerusalem issue, added more than half seriously: "But I haven't any objection to your playing politics. You have done it elsewhere in Italy and in France." I laughed. It was evident that Ben-Gurion knew more about American activities in Italy last early spring than did many of us at home.[83] As I was leaving, I reminded him of our New Year's party and expressed the hope that he would come. He said something about HaKirya on that day, but since I thought I might be supposed to know and could in any event find out later, I refrained from asking him for particulars. On the way out, I told the secretary I hoped that this time we would get action on the rooms.

Back to the house, where tea was continued. There, I listened to [James] Sutton[84] of the Jerusalem YMCA explain a project of the Jerusalem group, interdenominational and international, to raise a fund of $2,000,000 for

---

82. Reported in Burdett to secretary of state, no. 1556, NARA, RG 59, MC 1390, reel 17, frame 822. See also entry of January 6, 1949, n. 40.

83. In May 1947, on the eve of the Marshall Plan, the United States worked with the Christian Democratic-led Italian cabinet to oust Communist Party members from the cabinet. Subsequent anticommunist measures before the April 1948 general election included US propaganda and financial pressures. See James E. Miller, "Taking off the Gloves: The United States and the Italian Elections of 1948," *Diplomatic History* 7, no. 1 (January 1983): 35–56.

84. James Sutton, part of the American colony in Jerusalem and a Quaker associated with the YMCA there.

the enlargement of the interracial hospital for crippled children to be called the Roosevelt Memorial.[85] I suggested that he send me a memorandum about the project, which I could then discuss with my colleagues. I could not be enthusiastic about Mr. Sutton as a possible successor to Mr. [Alva] Miller at the Y.[86]

Dr. [Chaim] Vardi came presently, and as soon as I could persuade Sutton to leave, Vardi and I went into a huddle, which, as is usually the case with talks with him or his colleague young Herzog, was profitable. The following points should be noted:

1) Monsignor McMahon is, according to Monsignor Vergani, here as the representative of the Vatican. This Vardi regards as a very clever move, because had anyone come from Rome, the Arabs would already have protested;

2) the Church properties about which Vergani had been so concerned, the Carmel Convent, is French, and the Tabgha farm, is German;[87]

3) Vardi is convinced that both these properties will soon be returned as was promised. He had spoken to Shiloah recently, telling him that he thought it was time that the delay be ended. Shiloah had asked him for a written statement;

4) since Vardi regarded McMahon's visit as the Vatican's reply to their [Jacob Herzog and Chaim Vardi's] visit [to Rome, September 22 to October 7] he felt encouraged.[88] Moreover, he argued that between the Vatican and Israel there were common interests, such as the need to face common foes in current neo-paganism, communism, etc. He felt that the Vatican was alert to these dangers and to the possibility of Israel being a defensive factor;

5) he felt that Israel would have to yield to France, even if the latter insisted on what was, in effect, extra-territorial rights. In answer to my question as to what this would involve, he replied, complete freedom for the French in all matters connected with their educational and religious institutions, particularly the former.[89] He deeply deplored the fact that the French did not realize that victory for them on this issue would be self-defeating because:

85. The YMCA mission in Jerusalem was completed in 1933 as a step toward religious and international unity. It had nearly 2,000 members by 1944, two-thirds of whom were Christians of various denominations. In 1948 with the outbreak of fighting in Jerusalem, the YMCA building was handed over to the Red Cross, and it became a relief station for wounded and displaced Arabs and Jews with the aid of funds from the YMCA International Committee, the American Friends Service Committee, and the Brethren Service Committee. See the YMCA collection in the Kautz Family YMCA Archives, Elmer L. Anderson Library, University of Minnesota, http://special.lib.umn.edu/findaid/html/ymca/yusa0009x2x2.phtml.

86. Alvah Leslie Miller (1884–1966), Iowa-born general secretary of the YMCA in Jerusalem, 1935–1950.

87. Entry of December 16, 1948.

88. Entry of October 27, 1948.

89. In general see Schillo, *La France et la création de l'État d'Israël*, part 2, chapter 3.

a) it would undermine the local appeal of their institutions and make them much less effective and; b) it would clear the way for similar [ecclesiastical property] claims by the Russians. Victory by the Russians would more than counterbalance France's gain.

Shortly after eight went to the Museum, where the State Council Hall had been reset for Sam Klaus's lecture. Joked with Miss Herlitz about her having inveigled me to the meeting by her statement to me that morning that, since the minister of justice was going, she wondered if I was not also to be there and then [Pinhas] Rosen had begged off on the ground of a cold. Klaus was informal, comprehensive, and interesting. He held closely the interest of his audience, which was composed, I would estimate, of 75 to 100 officials and lawyers.

Earlier in the day we had heard with intense interest of the assassination of the Egyptian Prime Minister Nukrashi Pasha, reportedly by a young student member of the Moslem Brotherhood. We are actively speculating about the effect of the tragedy on the position of Egypt in the war.[90]

Wednesday, December 29

To the office for an hour or so. The attachés, Archibald and Frothingham, were interested and intrigued as was Knox by my rather racy account of my interview with Ben-Gurion the night before. Knox was emphatic that the point about Ben-Gurion's not objecting to our "playing politics" was a topmost secret. . . . Got Knox's approval for two telegrams, the one arguing against acceptance of the proposed Security Council ceasefire and withdrawal resolution introduced by Beeley the day before, and the other reporting Ben-Gurion's categorical denial of the Jerusalem coup rumor.[91]

Just before lunch we were again "entertained" by bombs dropping in triplets near enough to be clearly heard, and the first of them well in advance of any warning siren.

Young Morris, whom I had met in England a year ago last spring in one of the HaShomer [HaTzair] training centers, who with his group had been in Israel a year in training, came to invite me to the foundation day of their new kibbutz, just east of Acre. I would have liked to have gone, but because their site is just beyond the territory assigned to Israel under the partition scheme, I had to decline on the ground that my presence there would be misunderstood. Morris understood; as he was leaving he said, semi-apologetically, "We from

---

90. Mahmoud Fahmi al-Nukrashi Pasha (1888–1948), liberal monarchist prime minister of Egypt, 1945–1946, 1946–1948; outlawed Muslim Brotherhood in December 1948; assassinated by member of Muslim Brotherhood, December 28, 1948. The killing led to the counter-assassination of Hassan al-Banna, who had founded the Brotherhood, on February 12, 1949.

91. See textbox 6.2. McDonald to secretary of state, no. 347, December 29, 1948, NARA, RG 59, MC 1390, reel 17, frame 846.

Textbox 6.2.
Operation Horev

The Israeli and Egyptian governments had formally accepted the UN Security Council's cease-fire resolutions of November 4 and 16, 1948, concerning the Negev. But the Israelis refused the UN order to pull back to the lines of October 14, and the Egyptians, hoping to exit the war but perhaps expecting UN sanctions to be imposed on Israel, insisted on keeping the Negev south of the al-Majdal-Beit Jibrin-Dead Sea line. Ben-Gurion and Shertok refused to consider an Egyptian presence anywhere in the Negev, even the portion assigned to the Arabs in November 1947. Israel's general staff was sure that Israeli forces could drive battered Egyptian forces out of the Negev entirely.

On December 22, the day after Shiloah complained to McDonald regarding Egyptian intransigence, the IDF launched Operation Horev, feinting toward Gaza and trying to crush the Faluja pocket, but focusing on and sweeping the remaining Egyptian positions in the western Negev.[1] By December 28, the IDF had captured the border town of al-Auja (now Nitzana), which had been assigned to the Arabs in the 1947 partition. The Egyptians had used the town as their primary military base against Israel. The town also controlled the only paved road across the Sinai Peninsula and toward Cairo. At Egypt's request, the UN Security Council on December 28 considered two reports by Bunche, which blamed Israel both for the deadlock in the Negev and the resumption of hostilities there.

On the same day, IDF forces pressed across the international boundary into the Sinai Peninsula. They advanced to al-Arish, which controlled the railway running across the northern Sinai and stretching into Israeli territory. Israeli forces aimed to cut off all Egyptian troops in Palestine, including those in Gaza.[2] Already under heavy criticism in the Arab world and particularly in Egypt, Britain reacted strongly. On December 29, Harold Beeley made a speech in the Security Council blaming Israel for the resumption of hostilities and proposing a resolution calling once again for reestablishment of the October 14 truce lines.

From Tel Aviv, McDonald warned that "acceptance by [the Security Council] of [the] Beeley resolution would, we believe, postpone peace in Negev by encouraging Egypt's continued refusal [to] negotiate [an] armistice. Moreover, [the Provisional Government] cannot surrender military gains in Negev, especially since Egypt [has]

---

1. McDonald reported on the opening of hostilities that night, but did not have operational details. McDonald to secretary of state, no. 338, December 23, 1948, NARA, RG 59, MC 1390, reel 17, frame 808.

2. Planning and operational details in Tal, *War in Palestine*, 429–448; Morris, *1948*, 350–374.

3. McDonald to secretary of state, no. 349, December 29, 1948, NARA RG 59, 501.BB Palestine, box 2123, folder 3.

shown no willingness [to] recognize Israel's existence."[3] The Security Council issued Resolution 66 on December 29, calling for a cease-fire and, once again, for the immediate implementation of its Resolution 61, which called for withdrawal to the October 14 lines. Both the United States and the USSR abstained.

McDonald later explained the operation to Supreme Court Justice Felix Frankfurter:

> The military operation undertaken in the south beginning December 23 was decided upon, I believe, only after the most careful weighing of political as well as military factors. From the Israeli point of view the situation . . . was this: The several orders of the UN Security Council and of the UN observers prevented this Government using its military strength to end the war through military victory; and those same international agencies did nothing to force Israel's enemies to make peace. Thus this new state was being bled white by the necessity of keeping an eighth of its population under arms. . . . Faced with the prospect of an indefinite continuation of that bleeding process, civilian leadership and opinion here gave wholehearted approval.[4]

To Ben Abrams he added the following analysis:

> I am hopeful . . . that this period of hostilities will be the last and will be followed by real peace negotiations. . . . In my personal and very confidential opinion, these first steps still wait on Great Britain. Not until Bevin recognizes that his hope of blocking Israel's development as an independent and viable state has finally failed will he permit Abdullah and the other leaders to make peace. . . . When this basic fact is generally understood, action will, I trust, be taken to break this jam by convincing the British that Israel is here to stay and that if permitted to become strong, it will be a powerful force for peace and stability in the Middle East . . . and incidentally an asset to the [British] Empire.[5]

---

4. McDonald to Felix Frankfurter, January 15, 1949, McDonald Papers, Columbia University, box 2, folder 24.
5. McDonald to Benjamin Abrams, December 26, 1948, McDonald Papers, Columbia University, box 6, folder 2.

the kibbutz are not much on etiquette, but we would like you to know that we felt that your designation made you in an especial way our representative." I told him that I hoped to visit them next year.[92]

---

92. McDonald may be referring to Kibbutz Sasa, which was not "just" east of Acre but one mile from the Lebanese border. It was founded in May 1948 by HaShomer HaTzair.

Miss [Judith] Epstein came out to tea, told me of her desire to visit the States, and I promised to give her a letter which could be used with the authorities in connection with her exit visa and also a general letter of recommendation. She thought too that she might like to work with the new cultural and press attaché.

Thursday, December 30

Eban came out for a long talk. He was interested primarily in Israel's admission to the UN. He said that American continued leadership towards this would, between now and the election, be an even more distinctive move than de jure recognition, which was more or less pledged to follow the election or the loan, which has now reached the technical stage of discussion. We talked about Weizmann's projected trip to the States. Eban thought that it would be not only desirable, but necessary that Leo Kohn should go along. Eban was, of course, also well informed on the difficulties incident to Weizmann's occasional infelicities but had, in general, my view about the relative innocuousness of these.

McDonald wrote Ben Abrams on December 31, "Since [Eban] will soon be back in New York, I asked him to call you up and give you an intimate and confidential picture of the situation here and especially the role of the American Mission. . . . He is one of the most brilliant men I have ever met and would, I know, give you a better picture than you could get in any other way of the part which I try to play here and of the relations of the Mission to the [Israeli] Government. . . ."[93]

Friday, December 31

Just before lunch began, a series of events, which were to make this New Year's memorable. Knox called to say that he had to see me immediately about a most important matter, to which I replied, come ahead. It was nearly an hour, however, before he arrived bringing with him Sam Klaus. As soon as I read the top-secret telegram from the Department in the name of the president, I realized the gravity of the situation. This telegram was written in a sharp tone with such phrases as "grave consequences," "review of our attitude towards Israel," "no desire to act drastically if," etc. As Ben-Gurion said about it later, or rather about the paraphrase of it, which was certainly not stronger than the original, it might have been penned by Bevin. Its essential argument was:

1) Provisional Government is demonstrating aggressive and warlike intent;
2) it has invaded Egyptian territory, not accidentally but deliberately; and hence Great Britain might be called on to act under its treaty of 1936 with

93. Abrams spoke with Eban and planned to have him meet other important private citizens. In February 1949, McDonald followed up by noting to Abrams that Eban, "may one of these days be the Foreign Minister of his country." McDonald to Benjamin Abrams, December 31, 1948, February 28, 1949, McDonald Papers, Columbia University, box 6, folder 2.

Egypt in defense of the latter. But the UK added that it would not take action if the Israeli forces withdrew and carried out the Security Council resolution;

3) the US indicated that it regarded immediate withdrawal as a minimum requirement;

4) a long discussion of US friendship, and sponsorship of Provisional Government's UN application and possible need of reconsideration;

5) withholding of press comment until reply received from here;

7) full answers to be sought immediately from Shertok, Ben-Gurion and [at] my "discretion" from Weizmann.

On December 30, British aircraft began aerial patrols in the Sinai to aid the Egyptians, and the same day London informed the White House that if Israel did not withdraw from Egypt, Britain would "take steps to fulfill their obligations under their treaty of 1936 with Egypt."[94] The State Department immediately cabled Mc-Donald with an order from Truman himself. McDonald was to inform Israel's leaders that their "ill-advised action . . . may not only jeopardize [the] peace of Middle East but would also cause [a] reconsideration of [Israel's] application for membership in [the] UN and if necessity a reconsideration by [the US] of its relations with Israel. . . . Immediate withdrawal of Israeli forces from Egyptian territory appears to be [the] minimum requirement giving proof of peaceful intent of [the Provisional Government]." Additional reports that Israel had broken off talks with Transjordan caused additional consternation that "if confirmed, would cause a reevaluation of US-Israeli relations."[95]

My analysis of the document did not give me as tragic an interpretation as that which Knox and Klaus got from it. My reason for moderate optimism was the US insistence on only one specific condition. During the long conference which followed, in which we were joined by Captain Frothingham and Colonel Archibald, which followed Shertok's visit to the house, we decided to send a short interim despatch. But first a brief report on Shertok's visit. As soon as I had read the despatch, I asked Bobby to go next door to tell Shertok, if he were there, that we must see him at once, and if he were not at home his wife was to get in touch with him and give him the message. He was at lunch and replied that he would be over in a few minutes. By the time he came [2:00 pm] Knox and Klaus had completed the paraphrase, which I read to him slowly while he took it down verbatim.[96]

After he thought it over, he said in effect: I realize the gravity of the communication. Because, however, I have been back only twenty-four hours

94. British *note verbale* in *FRUS*, 1948, v. V, pt. 2, 1703; Truman's personal concerns in Heyd to Shertok, December 30, 1948, *DFPI*, v. 2, d. 280.

95. Lovett to McDonald, no. 281, December 30, 1948, *FRUS*, 1948, v. V, pt. 2, 1704.

96. For this paraphrase see *DFPI*, v. 2, d. 283.

and am probably not fully informed on all the points, I shall be able to comment on only two of them. The first was the operations in the Egyptian area. He admitted the presence of Israel troops south and west of the line, but argued that these were not the result of pre-arrangement but were merely tactical moves, which followed inevitably when the military situation reached a point where its own logic took command. This was not very convincing.[97]

On the second point, the negotiations with Transjordan, Shertok was better informed and much more detailed. He insisted that the several exchanges, the last of which had been the night previous in the Old City attended by Dayan, [Reuven Shiloah], [and] a secretary on the Israeli side, and by the Arab commander [Abdullah al-Tel] on the other, had been in the friendliest spirit and that no one had threatened war. It is true that the Jews were insisting that the negotiations extend beyond the existing cease-fire to an armistice looking towards peace. The report as sent to Washington by the US representative was, Shertok insisted, false.

When I insisted with Shertok that I must see Ben-Gurion at the earliest possible moment, he called the latter but, as he feared, Ben-Gurion had already started for Tiberias, where he was going to undergo bath treatments for a threatened thrombosis of the leg. I replied that if it were not possible for him to return, I would go there. Shertok said that he would like to talk to Shiloah first and get his judgment. It was at this point that I wrote a line and handed it to Knox: "Let's keep Shiloah out of this." By this, I meant that we could not be satisfied by any second-hand account of Ben-Gurion's reactions. Knox agreed.

After Shertok had gone, Knox, Klaus, Colonel Archibald, Captain Frothingham, and I went into a huddle. We finally agreed that we could send off an interim message summing up what Shertok had said. After hearing Captain Archibald's detailed exposition of the tactical situation near al-Arish and to the east, we decided that it would be a mistake to include in this first telegram any comment on the military situation or any promise to send a detailed one later.[98] The Department and the War Department should already have received Colonel Archibald's analysis of a few days previous. Nothing new could have been added to that. None of the others was as insistent as I of the necessity of going to Tiberias if Ben-Gurion could not come here, but all agreed that it was desirable.

---

97. The Israeli Foreign Ministry issued a statement the afternoon of December 31 cataloging Egypt's truce violations, its refusal to enter into armistice negotiations, and the UN's inability to move matters along. "For such a final and lasting peace settlement the Government of Israel is ever ready, in the firm conviction that the sooner it is achieved, the better it will be for all concerned." McDonald to secretary of state [attention president and acting secretary], no. 3, January 2, 1949, *FRUS*, 1949, v. VI, 597–598. Shertok's full official response to the communiqué of December 31 is included in McDonald to secretary of state [attention president and acting secretary], January 3, 1949, *FRUS*, 1949, v. VI, 605–606.

98. On the meeting with Shertok see also McDonald to acting secretary of state, December 31, 1948, *FRUS*, 1948, v. V, pt. 2, 1705–1706. See also the account in McDonald, *My Mission in Israel*, 117–118.

Ruth and I prepared to go to the Kaplans' for tea. There I gave Kaplan a slight intimation of what was in the wind and chatted with a number of persons including Mrs. [Edwin] Samuel, the Comays and Mrs. Locker. Waiting anxiously for a telephone call from Knox about Ben-Gurion, I was glad to have Atara [Kaplan's daughter] tell me it came through. Knox was with Shiloah, who had given him a rather full set of comments and who was inclined to discourage our trying to see Ben-Gurion before the latter's return Sunday night. Knox seemed willing to accept this view, but readily agreed to tell Shiloah emphatically that that would not do, and that if Ben-Gurion could not come down, we would go to him. And so it was arranged.

Kaplan expressed something akin to consternation that we considered the situation such as to necessitate a night trip to Tiberias and back. As we were leaving, Shertok came in. I got him in a corner, told him that we were going to Tiberias. He seemed surprised but made no clear comment. After an early supper, in which Knox joined us, the two of us, with McMahon and Shalom, were ready when Shiloah came a little after eight.

Shiloah told McDonald that secret preliminary armistice meetings with Trans-jordan over all outstanding border issues had begun on December 25.[99] *Shiloah and Dayan represented the Israelis, and Abdullah al-Tel represented Transjordan. The meetings, Shiloah said, were conducted in secrecy to prevent embarrassment to King Abdullah in the Arab world and to keep the British from interfering.*[100] *"Shiloah," McDonald reported, "promised [to] keep mission secretly informed." Shiloah added that armistice feelers with Lebanon were promising, and that Israel had sent a message to Egypt's new prime minister offering to negotiate, but that he was unsure whether the intermediary "has the courage to present [the] offer to [the] Prime Minister."*

We were on our way at 8:20, Shiloah and Knox and their driver preceding us, who were in the Packard. The trip up was uneventful and much shorter than I thought it would be; I had not realized that on the open road we would use our full lights. It was a little spooky as we cut across from Hadera to [Mishmar] HaEmek; and definitely mountainous as we climbed up to Nazareth and then on north and east to Tiberias. To my amazement, we did the hundred miles in just two hours and twenty minutes.

99. McDonald to secretary of state, no. 4, January 2, 1949, NARA, RG 59, MC 1390, reel 13, frames 003–004; McDonald to secretary of state, January 2, 1949, *FRUS*, 1949, v. VI, 598–599.

100. The US Embassy in London later reported that the British Foreign Office had encouraged King Abdullah to cooperate more with Egypt and to hold out for the Negev south of the Gaza–Be'er Sheva road, as well as for Haifa and Lydda as free ports. See Holmes to secretary of state, no. 20, January 4, 1949, *FRUS*, 1949, v. VI, 607–609; Bar-Joseph, *The Best of Enemies*, 142–145, and n. 24.

Despite our talk of making the visit inconspicuous, Shiloah led us directly to the lobby, which still contained a score or so of people, up a short flight of steps to an alcove room, separated from the main lobby by curtains, where Ben-Gurion and Paula were waiting for us. Our reception could not have been more cordial. Ben-Gurion seemed to be genuinely grateful that we had come, and amazed that we were going back that night. Before we settled down to business, I asked if we could have tea and if we could have an escort for the return trip. The first came promptly, and the latter was promised.

Ben-Gurion, though he had heard over the telephone the text of our paraphrase, took time to read a paper Shiloah gave to him, which apparently were Shertok's verbatim notes. Knox and I refrained from starting the discussion until Ben-Gurion was obviously ready. Then I read slowly, the same paraphrase I had read to Shertok during the afternoon, Ben-Gurion following his own text carefully. When the reading was finished, during which no one made any interpolations, Ben-Gurion began his counter-exposition and was not interrupted during it. Such discussion as we had, followed later.

Ben-Gurion's general attitude was one of amazed injury that the US could take so stern and "pro-British" a line. My notes show the following main points as made by Ben-Gurion:

1) The Israeli troops are not invaders of Egypt; some forces have crossed the line as part of tactical operations but have already received orders to return.
2) The report of the US representative to his government that Israel had, in effect, given an ultimatum to Transjordan is astonishing. The facts are that "we are on the best of terms with the representative of the government of King Abdullah; we are in the act of negotiating an armistice looking to peace. Nobody has issued threats. We had assumed that in seeking an armistice as a step towards peace we were carrying out an admirable purpose." Talks are still preliminary; detailed reports can be made available from Shiloah or Dayan.
3) Seizing on the British intimation that it might take direct action under the treaty of 1936 if Israel did not abide by the Security Council resolutions, Ben-Gurion said, "We are in friendly touch with the Security Council and not in conflict with it. British cannot be judge of Provisional Government violation of Security Council recommendations. Only Security Council can do that."
4) Israel values highly friendship of the United States, not only on such issues as recognition and admission to the UN, but going back beyond any of these. This makes it more difficult to understand the big club being used by a great and friendly power against a tiny one.
5) Israel is engaged only in self-defense; it is being attacked. "We are," said Ben-Gurion, "the last people in the world to break the peace in the Middle East. We can't imagine our existence without peace. We are a very small country but must reserve the right of self-defense, even if we go down fighting."

Then followed reemphasis upon certain points especially on the alleged untruthfulness of the report from Transjordan. At first, Ben-Gurion was particularly disturbed, because he misread our paraphrase to mean that someone in the Transjordan government had been quoted. But even after that, he continued bitterly resentful of the seeming failure of the UN representative to check and double-check before passing on what Ben-Gurion assumed was [the] British tendentious report. In conclusion, Ben-Gurion summed up his view of the US's presentation by saying that it was in tone and substance as if written by Bevin.

When Ben-Gurion had finished, nearly an hour had passed, and we were ready to go home, but since our promised escort did not arrive for another hour, we marked time by telling stories or discussing issues not on the agenda. It was during this informal talk that Ben-Gurion reverted once more to his favorite American theme, the epic nature of Truman's victory in the elections and its vast significance for democracy. As it got later and later, and Ben-Gurion and Paula were visibly exhausted, I tried to get them to leave us to wait alone for the escort, but they staunchly refused and said goodbye to us as we left. The trip back was as uneventful as the one up.[101] We arrived at the house about 3:30 am. Knox at once began to draft a despatch. Together we finished it at about 4:30. Unhappily, Knox had still to go to the office, type it and leave it for early coding and filing around eight o'clock.[102] Up at a little after eleven and brought my diary up to date before the imminent mass arrivals for our New Year's party.

101. McDonald's memoir adds that Egyptian ships off the coast of Tel Aviv were firing salvos, though out of range. McDonald, *My Mission in Israel*, 122.
102. This despatch is McDonald to secretary of state [attention president and acting secretary], no. 1, January 1, 1949, *FRUS*, 1949, v. VI, 594–595.

7. January 1949

Saturday, January 1, 1949

Though not to bed until nearly five,[1] I felt rested when I got up at eleven. Rest of the morning spent in getting ready for the [New Year's] party. The Gat Rimon staff with their usual efficiency had everything in perfect order well before the five o'clock time set. This was just as well because, as seems to be the fashion in Israel, guests began to arrive as much as a half an hour early. The first of these was Ya'akov Shapira, the attorney general. During the first hour and a quarter, we kept in obedience to Knox's order of a formal reception line consisting, besides Ruth and myself, of the McKelveys and the attachés. Knox was the master greeter. According to actual count, there were 280 guests. By the test of unwillingness to leave, the party was a complete success.

The most important talk, of course, was that with Chaim Weizmann. When he arrived shortly after seven, I took him to the study while the rest of his party mingled with the other guests. He at once broached the subject of the US's representations on its own behalf and that of the UK.[2] He had heard the substance of the communication, and had already decided to make his own reply to it in a personal letter to the president to be delivered by Eban, who is leaving the first of next week. Apparently, he is going to stress the essential defensive nature of Israel's operations and plead with the president to take an over-all and independent view. He is going to stress the offensive nature of the Egyptian invasion and attacks on Israel, mentioning specifically the recent destruction of the water system at Rehovot [Sieff] Institute and the repeated bombings within bomb sound of the mission residence. His decision to write in this way saved me the possible embarrassment of having to have a formal interview and give a formal report.

McDonald nonetheless reported later in the day:

> *At [the] New Year's Day reception in our residence, President Weizmann stated to [the] mission staff that the representations I made yesterday and last night had had profound effect on [the Provisional Government]. Apparently [the] attitude [of] Washington, which I faithfully presented . . . is interpreted here as indicating [a] reversal of attitude of Washington to [the] old British line. In this small country, despite every attempt to*

---

1. Preparation of the telegram to Washington on McDonald's discussion with Ben-Gurion at Tiberias took until this time.
2. Entry of December 31, 1948.

keep secrecy, my representations apparently [are] already widely known in governmen-
tal circles and there is much resentment. . . . Weizmann stated "Why this terrific
pressure against Israel over El Arish when [the] fact is Egyptian armies attacked Israel
with purpose [to] destroy Israel?" El Arish is [an] Egyptian forward base for air attacks
on Israel and attest Israel objectives were to neutralize but not to hold that base. . . .

In obedience [to] pressure [by the] USA so threatening[ly] expressed . . . [Provisional
Government] has ordered withdrawal [of] all forces [from] Egyptian territory.
Mission [is] uncertain as to [the] military effect [of] this withdrawal but USA has
now most certainly incurred serious responsibility if such withdrawal again jeopar-
dizes Israel forces in [the] Negev and encourages Egypt [to] continue attacks on Israel
territory.[3]

I was delighted to note how Dr. Weizmann and Ruth got on together; it was as if they had been most intimate friends. Vera Weizmann was also very friendly. Chatting with the Crossmans,[4] we arranged that they should come for supper on Sunday night the ninth. Had a moment with Shertok, with a bare chance to tell him about the conference in Tiberias and to learn from him that the Provisional Government's reply in written form would be transmitted to us probably Monday. There was also only a brief opportunity to have a word with Eban. We talked about the letter which he would take from Weizmann, and of the possibility of including in it references to the bombing in our vicinity of Ramat Gan. A moment also with Eytan, who suggested that it would not be necessary to have formal discussion of US representations with Weizmann.

The Sam Sackses invited Bobby and Ruth and me for the next weekend to the new hotel in Herzliya. We accepted to go up for dinner Shabbat eve and return in time for supper Sunday. Nice visit with Mr. and Mrs. Mendes Sacks, who urged us to come and see them.

Short chats with several of the American press, including the [Kenneth] Bilbys and the Millers [United Press International].[5] Also with [Michael] Curtiz[6] who has just been doing a movie in Rome and is here looking into the possibility of a short semi-documentary, the theme of which would be the development of one individual. He thought that after the war there would be less interest, hence the desirability of getting something out quickly. Pleasant few words with the Kaplans, with passing reference to the Tiberias junket.

Zvi Friedberg of post, radio and telephone department [in Ministry of Communications] just back from the States, enthusiastic about his trip. Had lunch with David Sarnoff, who invited him a second time and who was helpful

---

3. McDonald to secretary of state [attention president and acting secretary], no. 2, January 1, 1949, NARA, RG 59, 501.BB Palestine, box 2123, folder 1.
4. Entry of September 29, 1948.
5. Robert C. Miller (1915–2004) New Jersey-born legendary war correspondent with United Press and United Press International, 1938–1983; covered US Pacific and European theaters during World War II; later covered Greece, India, Middle East, Korea, and Vietnam.
6. Michael Curtiz (1886–1962), prolific Hungarian-born film director; emigrated to the United States, 1926; family members were murdered at Auschwitz; made iconic films such as *Casablanca* (1942); contributed to funds to bring Jewish refugees in the arts to the United States after World War II.

in the plan for the modernization of communications here.[7] Some cordial words with Sprinzak and Remez and Rabbi Levin. Got pleasantly acquainted with the Colonel Chaim [Vivian] Herzogs, and with several of the other liaison military people. A number of Bobby's old friends, Mrs. [Marian] Greenberg,[8] Mrs. Davidowitz and others—seemed as if we had known them always.

By eight o'clock most of the guests had left. The Weizmanns remained, however, until 8:25 because they were going directly to the symphony concert. Their remaining so long gave an opportunity for the attachés to meet Weizmann, and for nearly all the other members of the staff to meet him and Vera.

Sunday, January 2

[Berl] Locker came out to inquire about the real mission of Sam Klaus. I explained, but my talk about labor did not quite satisfy Locker because he wanted to know why Klaus was so persistent in his inquiries about the Provisional Government's methods of screening prospective immigrants from the satellite [communist] countries. He seemed [satisfied] when I gave the explanation. He insisted, however, that there could be no real system and certainly no uniformity of practices in the several [communist bloc] states. It should be obvious, he added, that we dare not be clearly discriminatory either there or here. There is not, he insisted, any danger from communist penetration, first, because few of the Jews who will come are communists, and second, many who think they are will not remain such here.

We chatted also about conditions at home from where he had just returned. As to the UPA row, he said responsibility was divided.[9] Henry Morgenthau should not have written what he did when he did, and the Silver group should not have capitalized [on] it so strongly. Even now, with formal peace, there is no mutual confidence. As to the potential leadership, Locker had no clear ideas. Neumann may, he thinks, come to settle in Israel [as] the head of a private business organization and thus ultimately be available for [a] high political post. He doubts that Silver will ever seriously attempt to transplant himself.

Just as I was about to go to bed after having waited up for Bobby's return from the theatre, the guard called me to the telephone at 11:10. Shertok was on the line. This is the substance of what he said, which I transmitted within an hour or two to Washington: "At 7:40 this evening an enemy plane, presumably Egyptian, flying from the southwest, dropped three bombs in Jewish Jerusalem, injuring five persons near the exit to the Tel Aviv road. This is the first

7. David Sarnoff (1891–1971), Belorussian-born businessman; emigrated to the United States with his mother and siblings, 1900; spent his entire career in communications, particularly radio; president of RCA after 1930.

8. Marian G. Greenberg (1897–1987), Philadelphia-born Zionist; close associate of Hadassah founder, Henrietta Szold; national board member of Hadassah after 1927; national vice president of Hadassah, 1931–1952; Hadassah's chair of Youth Aliyah, 1936–1941.

9. See entries of October 9, 10, 12, 22, 1949.

bombing of Jerusalem. We expect the US to make promptly strong protests to Egypt." After checking his words, I promised to get the message off.[10]

Tried to get Knox on the phone, vainly, called Hope at the Gat, who said he would come out for the telegram and in the meantime would alert John Carlson.[11] After the excitement was over, I said to Bobby: "Surely the Arabs are the Jews' best friends." It was clear that this attack on Jerusalem would take much of the sting out of the British indictment of the Jews' activities in Egypt.

Monday, January 3

At the office for a staff conference about what should be sent to Washington along with the Provisional Government's formal statement and also on Knox's help. Decided to meet in the afternoon after the Israeli text is available and to draft then a communication to the White House.

Brief visits with Howard Brown of the *Chicago Sun*, with Monsignor Mc-Mahon at the Gat, and Knox at his house. Beginning at teatime and carrying through until about seven, Knox, Klaus, Colonel Archibald, Hope, and I labored on a commentary for the Department on the Provisional Government's January 3 reply to the Department's [telegram of December 30]. The Provisional Government's counterargument was cogently, even eloquently, put.[12] It hit out bluntly at the UK's hostile attitude; it expressed hope that the US, having transmitted without comment the UK's threat to act unilaterally if the Provisional Government did not live up to the Security Council resolutions and under the Treaty of 1936 with Egypt, did not associate itself with the UK arbitrary disregard of the fact that the Security Council decisions could be implemented only by Security Council authorization; it reaffirmed the withdrawal from Egypt; it emphasized the falseness of [the] US representative's report from Transjordan about the pending negotiations;[13] it expressed highest appreciation of the friendship of the US and concluded with the sincere hope that such friendship would never conflict with Israel's vital interest, the right of self-defense. After an hour or so of discussion of points to be included in our commentary and of methods of presenting them, Knox was assigned the task of drafting. Then followed further discussions resulting in a draft for consideration the next morning.[14]

---

10. Reported in McDonald to secretary of state, no. 6, January 2, 1949, and Burdett to secretary of state, no. 1, January 2, 1949, NARA, RG 59, MC 1390, reel 18, frames 009–010. Jean Nieuwenhuys, the head of the UN Truce Commission in Jerusalem, reported Israeli protests concerning this incident on January 10, along with his own comment on behalf of the Truce Commission that Jerusalem's demilitarization would eliminate the pretext for such attacks. Nieuwenhuys to Trygve Lie, January 11, 1949. See http://unispal.un.org/UNISPAL.NSF/0/F4F0674 39105356585256EAC006BA29F.

11. John Carlson, US mission's cypher clerk.

12. Refers to Shertok to McDonald, January 3, 1949, *DFPI*, v. 2, d. 286.

13. Refers to Wells Stabler to Lovett, December 29, 1948, *FRUS*, 1948, v. V, pt. 2, 1699–1700.

14. The Israeli reply was reported in McDonald to secretary of state [attention president and acting secretary], no. 7, January 3, 1949, Truman Library, Clifford Papers, Subject Files, box 14, folder Palestine—Telegrams and Cables 2 of 2.

At breakfast, Miss Clark and I were joined by Monsignor Thomas F. McMahon. Afterwards he and I withdrew to the roof, where the morning sun was delightful.[15] At first, McMahon spoke casually of his impressions of Jerusalem and Amman personalities. He had found Abdullah charming and sincere; Abdullah al-Tel, the Arab commander in Jerusalem, delightful; Major and Mrs. Andronovich exceptionally intelligent and well informed; William Burdett[16] pleasant but not as strong as Major Andronovich. The king, McMahon thought, was genuinely friendly to Catholics.

Following my brief account of Knox's reaction, negative and definite, to Monsignor Vergani's suggestion that I let the Provisional Government officials know of my interest in the return of the Carmel Convent and the Tabgha Farm, McMahon agreed with Knox. He said [that] my making a brief inquiry, informal and impersonal, to Dr. [Chaim] Vardi about what was happening or might happen was as far as one could properly go. McMahon expressed no opinion when I indicated that Samuel Cavert of the Federal Council [of Churches] had asked me to interest myself in the Scots Memorial.[17] He seemed not to know much about it.

Then, coming to the heart of matters, much more important from McMahon's point of view, he developed the following points[18]:

1) Freedom of access to the Holy Places is important but less so than the maintenance of the status quo;
2) The several shrines should be inviolate but he would prefer that all of them had better be destroyed rather than that Christian population be eliminated;
3) He estimated that 75% of the Arab Christians in Israeli-occupied territory were now in exile.
4) The return of these Christian exiles is basic to an Israel-Church rapprochement;
5) The Church could not, however, approve of permission being granted merely for the return of the Christians, for this would obviously jeopardize the Christian position throughout the Arab world. Hence, whatever

15. See entry of December 16, 1948. This two-hour meeting with McDonald is also covered in McDonald's summary, undated, in McDonald Papers, USHMM, box 7, folder 10.

16. McMahon met with Burdett on January 1 to emphasize the Church's desire for the internationalization not only of greater Jerusalem but also of Nazareth. Burdett reported that McMahon "felt Jews would make [a] great mistake if [they] insisted on [the] annexation [of] new Jerusalem since [this] would tend to fan growing anti-Semitism in [the] United States." Burdett to secretary of state, n. 6, January 4, 1949, NARA, RG 59, MC 1390, reel 18, frame 019.

17. Samuel M. Cavert (1888–1976), prominent American Presbyterian; general secretary of the Federal Council of Churches in America; former member of the President's Advisory Committee on Political Refugees, 1938–1945. Reference to St. Andrew's Church in Jerusalem, a memorial to Scottish soldiers killed during the fighting over Jerusalem in 1917.

18. Text on following points borrowed when necessary for clarity from McDonald's separate summary, undated, in McDonald Papers, USHMM, box 7, folder 10.

arrangements are ultimately made for more or less extensive repatriation must be on a non-sectarian basis;

6) The foreign minister and the prime minister, whom McMahon saw together last evening, were not ready to give any general assurances on repatriation. The prime minister seemed less yielding than the foreign minister. Neither had previously seen clearly the relationship between the Church and this problem;

7) Monsignor McMahon had noted with some surprise that neither the prime minister nor the foreign minister had understood clearly that all local matters would have to be worked out with the ecclesiastical local representatives in Israel, Monsignor Vergani in the North and Father Terrence Kuhn in the South. Both are subject to Archbishop Testa in ecclesiastical matters, but the latter as papal nuncio[19] is not directly concerned in Church-State affairs;

8) The Provisional Government authorities should recognize that a considerable non-Jewish minority, or minorities, would be a safeguard against excessive rabbinical control or any tendency towards a theocracy. McMahon cited the beneficent effect of such minorities elsewhere in the world. He foresaw serious Israeli internal clashes between the rabbis and the liberal elements if there were no minorities to whom the rabbinical regulations could not be expected to apply;

9) McMahon thought that an indication to Israelis of interest on my part [concerning] these related problems of Christian exiles, the mass of Arab exiles, the forces of liberalism in the State and its relations to the Church, would be helpful;

10) Having finished the substantive parts of our discussion, I brought up the rumors about Bartley Crum. Though McMahon had never met Bart, he knew a great deal about him. He expressed resentment felt by the hierarchy at Bart's capitalizing on his Catholicism for personal or political effect. McMahon asked me if I had ever heard the phrase "Crum Catholic." I had to confess I had not, but learning of its currency, I at once was convinced that it alone would be enough to defeat Bart's ambitions in this area;

11) From everything McMahon said, though he would, of course, not acquiesce, I got the impression that though his immediate superior is Cardinal Spellman from whom he receives his direct orders, he is in fact so close to the Vatican in his work here that, in effect, if not form, he is a papal representative. His long association with the Catholic Near East Welfare Association has given him an intimacy of knowledge conditions here possessed by few outside the country. This and his genuine friendship for the Jews and for Israel (he insists that it would be most unwise for the Church to

19. Archbishop Gustavo Testa (1909–1962), apostolic delegate to Egypt, Arabia, Eritrea, Abyssinia, and Palestine, 1934–1948; apostolic delegate to Jerusalem, Palestine, Transjordan, and Cyprus, 1948–1953.

take an antagonistic attitude towards Israel) make him an ideal Church representative.[20]

Returning for a moment to Bartley Crum, I made no suggestion to Mc-Mahon about action, except to suggest that, if he heard anything, I should be glad to know of it. I should be surprised, however, if McMahon did not pass on to 52nd Street the rumor about Crum's ambitions. And I should be equally surprised if the authorities in New York neglected to indicate in appropriate circles what they think of Bart.

To the office, for two hours more of conference, redrafting and polishing our despatch to the Department. In this conference, the first where I have had occasion to watch Captain Frothingham in action, I found him more cautious than Colonel Archibald. The despatch, as finally drafted, was a substantial improvement over last evening's effort. One point, which was added, was to take full account of the soon-to-be expected Palestine Conciliation Commission [PCC]. My own personal telegram to Clifford was approved enthusiastically though I am not sure that any one of my colleagues in my position would have written or signed it. (This latter was finally not sent.)

Receipt of Department's note expressing surprise at reaction to the December 30 representation and asserting US friendly purposes.

On January 3, 1949 Lovett ordered McDonald to tell the Israeli leaders that the US message of December 30 was meant "to stop a move with most serious implications which [the British] were contemplating. Another purpose was to avoid if possible [British] rearming of [the] Arabs, which [Britain is] apparently determined to carry out if all Israeli forces [are] not promptly withdrawn from Egypt. . . . You should in fact state that we are making strong representations to [the] Egyptians. . . . Have also requested [that the British] make similar representations."[21]

Over to Shertok's for transmission of communication. Shertok was evidently pleased. He then gave me the schedule of [the] Israeli withdrawal, [the] first order having been issued Friday afternoon; the commanding officer in the field asked for twenty-four hours' delay, withdrawal began Saturday afternoon, and Sunday morning [January 2], "not an Israeli hoof remained in Egypt."

20. McMahon's functions also reported to Washington in McDonald to secretary of state, no. 13, January 11, 1949, NARA, RG 59, MC 1390, reel 18, frame 135.
21. This telegram was cleared through Clark Clifford at the White House. Lovett to McDonald, no. 3, January 3, 1949, *FRUS*, 1949, v. VI, 601–602. Lovett's statement to the king of Egypt, urging his government to undertake armistice negotiations, was issued on January 3, 1949. Lovett to embassy in Cairo, no. 2, January 3, 1949, *FRUS*, 1949, v. VI, 602–603; McDonald to Shertok, January 4, 1949, *DFPI*, v. 2, d. 290.

Chat with [Gershon] Agronsky and the two wives of Agronsky and Shertok before I left.[22] Agronsky is going to the States under the sponsorship of the American Histadrut organization.

On January 4, the Egyptian government informed Acting Mediator Ralph Bunche that it was ready to enter armistice talks with the Israelis under UN auspices, provided Israel agreed to the UN Security Council cease-fire resolution by 2:00 p.m. on January 5.[23] Washington hoped that a peace settlement was near. Consequently, the State Department distanced itself from the British Foreign Office's aims of controlling the Negev.[24]

On January 5 Lovett told the British ambassador, Sir Oliver Franks, that the United States could not exert pressure on Israel to withdraw to the October 14 cease-fire lines in the Negev, as Bevin wished. Lovett said that the United States preferred to work through the Security Council, that direct pressure on states should be used sparingly, and that the United States had to be mindful of its place on the three-member Palestine Conciliation Commission. The Israelis, he said, were already suspicious of the other two members, Turkey and France.

Franks noted that the British were sending reinforcements to Aqaba in accordance with the Anglo-Transjordanian Treaty of March 1948. The forces landed in Aqaba (just east of the Israeli border on the Gulf of Aqaba) on January 5, 1949. "As a matter of friendly comment," Lovett responded, "we wished to raise a little red flag and point out that if the troops came to Transjordan from outside the Near Eastern area, their arrival would be construed in many quarters as a violation of the Security Council truce resolution of May 29, which explicitly forbade the movement of military personnel into Palestine or the neighboring countries."[25]

Eliahu Epstein reported from Washington to Ben-Gurion and Shertok that the British might be preparing "to seize [the] Negev or at least secure an Arab portion if [the] Security Council rejects their proposals."[26] The IDF drew up contingency plans for a Jordanian-British attack.[27] On January 4 Linton reminded Hector McNeil of the Foreign Office that Israel still wished to establish formal relations with Great Britain." Twenty-one countries including Canada, Linton said, now recognized the new state. McNeil replied that even "de facto recognition was going to be very difficult." McNeil then asked why Israel "thought it necessary to start the show again in the Negev against the Egyptians just now?"[28]

---

22. Entry of August 27, 1948.

23. Security Council Resolution no. 66 of December 29, 1948, called for cease-fire and referred back to the provision of the November 4 resolution that called for a return to the lines of October 14, 1948. See www.un.org/en/ga/search/view_doc.asp?symbol=S/RES/66%281948%29.

24. Ross to secretary of state, no. 3, January 4, 1949, *FRUS*, 1949, v. VI, 609–610; Lovett to McDonald, no. 8, January 5, 1949, *FRUS*, 1949, v. VI, 616–617.

25. Memorandum of conversation by Lovett, January 5, 1949, *FRUS*, 1949, v. VI, 611–613.

26. Epstein note of January 3, 1949, *DFPI*, v. 2, d. 289.

27. On the British landing at Aqaba and its meanings see Tal, *War in Palestine*, 458–460.

28. *DFPI*, v. 2, d. 292.

The next day, Epstein reported that the mood in Washington, "and particularly [the] President's continued uneasy and sensitive state of mind, urgently requires [a] plain statement from Tel Aviv that Israel [is] prepared [for a] cease-fire [on the] southern front and [to] undertake immediate peace negotiations [with] Egypt." On January 6 he warned that Truman could come to see Israel as a "trouble-maker, endangering peace by flouting [the] UN." The cease-fire, he said, must be strictly observed.[29]

Wednesday, January 5

Final revision of our major note to the Department. This revision was in the light of the Department's "apology."[30] It made, I think, a strong document. It was in connection with this conference that we decided to hold up my personal one to Clifford.[31] The general impression of the group was, I think, that these final discussions went better because of the absence of one of our group [Klaus] who had recently displayed such intense feeling as to weaken the effectiveness of his judgment. It was this day, though we did not know it at the time, that the Egyptian government accepted the UN Mediator's proposal for cease-fire on the basis of the November 4 and 16th resolutions. The offer, however, reached the Jews too late for their acceptance before the deadline fixed.

In the afternoon a security lecture by [Eugene] McMahon, which included [the] following points: 1) Klaus's disturbance because of my opening the safe in the presence of Golda Meyerson and disclosing where I kept the key, and also reading without paraphrase a portion of a classified document; 2) report of the guards of three or four cases of classified documents left on the desk; 3) my allegedly casual talk, for example about Knox being the real boss, which is credited by Paula. Then followed discussion of these several points, but the whole of it leaving me weak and depressed by the over-emphasis on security and especially by Klaus's exaggeration (only the next day was I to learn from Knox what had really troubled Klaus most).

Gene Currivan of the *Times* and Miller of the UP came out with blood in their eyes because of what they charged was, in effect, deception by me yesterday when I refused to comment on their questions about the reported American representations. In fact, their questions on the telephone Tuesday had been: "Did you deliver a note to the Israeli government today?" Their natural curiosity having been piqued by the release from the Foreign Office in London and

29. Epstein to Shertok, January 5, 1949, *DFPI*, v. 2, d. 293; Epstein to Shertok, January 6, 1949, *DFPI*, v. 2, d. 296.

30. McDonald refers to Lovett to McDonald, January 3, 1949, *FRUS*, 1949, v. VI, 601–602. See entry of January 4, 1949.

31. McDonald to secretary of state [attention president and acting secretary], no. 9, January 5, 1949, *FRUS*, 1949, v. VI, 614–615. McDonald warned that in Israeli eyes the US intervention, however well intentioned, would be interpreted as US support for British policies, especially should Egyptian attacks continue. McDonald again suggested de jure recognition and the approval of the impending US loan to reassure the Israeli public. This telegram was already overtaken by events.

inquiries from their home offices. Under the circumstances, and particularly since I knew that the US was preparing a release, I had no alternative except to say, "no comment." To have answered "yes" would have been to tell an untruth as to Tuesday, and to have answered no would have been to deceive.

I took both of them up sharply, denying that they had any ground for complaint whatever. I then added that if they wanted to be better prepared they should come to see me in advance of a crisis when we could talk freely. I added that, moreover, even in such a situation as Tuesday, the telephone was the very worst form of communication, particularly when one was reached in the midst of a conference with his colleagues, each of whom might have a different idea of what under the circumstances would be correct procedure. After a half an hour or so they left at least seemingly mollified.

The visit of Ruth, Bobby and I to the Russian propaganda film, the opening of which was sponsored by Ershov, was a complete demonstration of security in reverse. The theatre was a madhouse of people in the lobby and on the long circular stairway [on] which one had to climb scores of steps. There were no signs of police, and only towards the very top did we begin to meet the Russian legation officials and, finally, Ershov. Our box was over to the extreme right, the auditorium cold and dismal. *The Young Guard* was three full hours of Soviet war propaganda picturing the heroic sabotage of the youth.[32] There was no mitigation of its grimness.

At the end after waving goodnight to Ershov, the three of us together with Mrs. Weizmann and Major David Arnon[33] and Shalom, struggled to work our way through the crowd, which had been allowed to fill to subway density the score of steps leading down to the main entrance. Bobby led the way, I following, holding onto her and Ruth's hands, then came the major supporting Mrs. Weizmann, and finally Shalom guarding the rear. From a security point of view it was a fantastic position to be in. For several minutes I was not sure we could possibly get through. Fortunately, nearly everyone seemed to recognize us, were friendly, and facilitated Bobby's path-breaking function. When we finally reached the street without casualty and had said goodbye to Mrs. Weizmann and her escort we felt like freed prisoners as we drove along home to a very belated supper.

Thursday, January 6

The mystery of some communication from President Truman to Dr. Weizmann was cleared up by the arrival of a note from Shertok enclosing a copy of the text of a long personal and confidential but extremely important letter from the president to Dr. Weizmann. It was dated November 29, but having been

---

32. 1949 Soviet film directed by Sergei Gerasimov, based on the novel by Alexander Fadeyev.
33. Major David Arnon (1912–1968) was a fixture at the Weizmann house because his wife Ruth ran the household for the Weizmanns. See George Weidenfeld, *Remembering My Good Friends: An Autobiography* (London: Harper Collins, 1995), 215.

mailed with only five-cent postage, it had taken the slow surface route and had just that morning reached Rehovot. Just before I was leaving for the office, Dr. Weizmann got me on the phone to tell me about the letter and to ask if I would cable at once to explain his delay in replying and his failure to have acknowledged the November 29 communication when he had written a few days ago. The nature of the letter was such as to have strengthened substantially Dr. Weizmann's position in the Provisional Government.[34] At the office I sent off a personal telegram to Clifford covering the Dr. Weizmann letter episode and reporting on Ben-Gurion's philosophizing about the president's victory and his vindication of democracy.

McDonald reported to Clifford that, during their discussion in Tiberias, Ben-Gurion "reverted to his favorite American thesis—President Truman's reelection . . . as of epic significance because [of] vindicating democracy in these critical days. [The] Prime Minister concluded that 'irrespective of President's policy toward Israel, he has justified faith in ordinary man and woman.'"[35]

To the Gat to see Colonel van der Velde, who looked a little peaked. He suggested that Knox go home with him and that the two of them see the president in addition to their visits to their own departments. I said I thought this would be helpful, but it would all depend on whether Knox could and wanted to synchronize his plans with those of the colonel.

After lunch and more or less in the midst of my nap came word that Knox was arriving with important and good news. This was the Egyptian acceptance, referred to in yesterday's report above. Getting quickly in touch with Shertok, Knox and I went to the Foreign Office, where we had an hour or so with Shertok, Shiloah and Leo Kohn. Shertok explained that they had accepted the previous evening the mediator's proposal, but that the time lapse had prevented an agreement on a cease-fire hour.[36] Then followed a long discussion about ways to assure [the] utmost speed of agreement. At first, Knox thought that this would be advanced by our possible actions here through Jerusalem. On closer scrutiny, this appeared impractical, and it was decided that we would restrict ourselves to a factual communication to the Department.

Back to the office, where we got off a telegram to this effect enclosing the text of Israel's acceptance.

On January 6 McDonald informed the State Department that Israel would accept a cease-fire provided that Egypt did so simultaneously and provided that the Egyptian government "will thereupon enter into negotiations with the representatives of Israel." Shertok hoped that the cease-fire could go into effect by January 7 or 8.

34. See entry of November 28, 1948.
35. McDonald to Clifford, January 6, 1949, McDonald Papers, USHMM, box 7, folder 10.
36. See also Lourie to Shertok, January 6, 1949, *DFPI*, v. 2, d. 295.

McDonald further reported that Israeli cease-fire talks with Transjordan were going well.[37] *Dean Rusk forwarded McDonald's telegram to Clark Clifford, stating that it "indicates that our representations in Israel and Egypt have borne fruit. I realize that we must keep our fingers crossed on this whole subject; nevertheless, it is better to get a little good news than bad news."*[38]

Later, I noted that the Israeli acceptance made reference to the Security Council resolution of December 29, whereas the Egyptian acceptance spoke of Security Council resolutions November 4 and 16. While at Shertok's office, I read and left with him a copy of the Department's note to the Provisional Government, calling attention to Egypt's acceptance and urging that of Israel.[39] It also pleaded for negotiations that would be conclusive and again underlined America's friendly interest and nonpartisanship. I also explained that a similar note had gone to Egypt.

Knox came out to the house with me from the office. [They discussed Knox's health, his need for a leave, Knox's reluctance to fly to the United States, and his agreement to take two weeks at Tiberias.] We then had a long talk about Klaus. First, Knox explained that Klaus's major upset about me and security was my use of Avraham Bergman's name in my talk with Ben-Gurion about the possibility of the Provisional Government's annexation of the New City.[40] Klaus felt that this involved a breach of confidence and would make his relations with Bergman impossible in the future, because the latter probably would have in the meantime been severely reprimanded if not demoted, by Ben-Gurion. Neither Knox nor I thought this likely; but even if it did occur, the major purpose had been achieved, that is to get from Ben-Gurion a complete and unequivocal denial.[41] This seemed to both of us much more important than any consideration of Klaus's relations to Bergman. As to Klaus's worry about Golda Meyerson, the key and the reading, Knox thought this relatively minor. He indicated surprise that Klaus, who had such a high reputation for intellectuality and objectivity, should have shown himself to be so emotional during our recent political discussions. Knox attributed this to Klaus's intense absorption in his work during the past weeks and his almost continuous association with the people here. Moreover, Knox said that political analysis was not his immediate forte. Knox thought that Klaus had no direct or official relations with a third organization, the nameless one [CIA], but that doubtless his reports will go there also. Knox then told [of] Shiloah's comment when Klaus

37. McDonald to secretary of state, no. 14, January 6, 1949, Truman Library, Clifford Papers, Subject File, 1945–54, box 14, folder Palestine—Telegrams and Cables 2 of 2.

38. Rusk to Clifford, January 6, 1949, Truman Library, Clifford Papers, Subject File, 1945–54, box 14, folder Palestine—Telegrams and Cables 2 of 2.

39. See Lovett to McDonald, no. 8, January 5, 1949, *FRUS*, 1949, v. VI, 616–617.

40. Avraham Bergman [later Biran] (1909–2008), noted archaeologist; chief assistant to the Military Government of Jerusalem (Dov Joseph); and after February 1949 district commissioner for Jerusalem (under the Ministry of the Interior).

41. See entry of December 28, 1948.

had said or had quoted from some book that in Russia there are two systems of reporting from the field, one by the regular diplomatic officers, and the second by officials responsible to a separate organization. Shiloah had then said that "but is this so very different from your system?" Apparently he was thinking of our [Army] major friend in the city on the hill [Andronovich] and Mr. C[arlson] in H[aifa].

To dinner at the Persitz's. We arrived late, 8:15, but dinner was much later. [Guests included Shapira, the attorney general.] The food was excellent and the talk interesting but a little depressing, because it verged on the cynical side. Perhaps the most interesting topic discussed was the probable results of the elections. There was common agreement that Begin's [Herut] party would be third or fourth; first, Mapai with from 35 to 45%, Mapam, 15 to 20%, the Orthodox slate [United Religious Front], 10, 15, to 20%, the General Zionists and the Progressives, each from 5 to 7%, [and] the balance would be divided among the other parties. I suggested half jokingly that sometime before the election a group of us might get together and make up a pool and each to turn in his own exact estimates. The one who was nearest would take the pool.

On January 6 Acting Mediator Ralph Bunche officially informed the Security Council that the Egyptian and Israeli governments had agreed to a cease-fire, to be followed by direct negotiations under UN chairmanship, based on the Security Council resolutions of November 4 and November 16, 1948. The cease-fire would go into effect on January 7 at 2:00 p.m. GMT. The armistice talks were to be held in Rhodes, since this location offered the best possible atmosphere.[42]

Friday, January 7

Breakfast with Eliahu Ben-Horin. I told him in strictest confidence something of the schedule of the previous week, both for his own information, and in order that when he reached home he would be able to show Silver and Neumann that he had been in my confidence. After breakfast, I dictated letters for Ben-Horin to [mail to] Tom Murray,[43] Ben Abrams, Judge Proskauer, Halsey, Mr. Gowen in Rome, Frank Buxton,[44] and gave him a message to Mrs. Harmer and to Shapira. I hesitated about giving him any notes for people in Washington, and finally decided against it.

After lunch while Miss Clark and I were working, Knox called up to say that there had been new and dangerous developments. This was the news of the British reconnaissance flight and the follow-up flight over the battle area in the south and the shooting down of five of the RAF craft by the Israeli forces.

42. Overview of the Rhodes talks in Caplan, *Futile Diplomacy*, v. 3, 34–56; Ben-Dror, *Ralph Bunche and the Arab-Israeli Conflict*, 155–184.
43. Thomas E. Murray Jr. (1891–1961), engineer and member of the Atomic Energy Commission, 1950–1957; influential Catholic layman in New York and close to Cardinal Spellman.
44. Frank Buxton (1877–1977), career journalist, Pulitzer Prize winner, and editor for the *Boston Herald*; served with McDonald on Anglo-American Committee of Inquiry in 1946.

On January 7, 1949, two British formations comprising four Spitfires, four Tempests, and one Mosquito flew over the road from the Sinai into the Gaza Strip, where the IDF was making a final effort to cut off Egyptian forces. IDF fighters intercepted the British aircraft and shot down five of them, two within the boundary of the Jewish state as delineated in 1947.[45] On January 8, the British government issued an official statement that their aircraft had been under strict orders not to cross the frontier and to avoid combat, and that "in view of these unprovoked attacks, our aircraft have now been instructed to regard as hostile any Jewish aircraft encountered over Egyptian territory."[46]

Knox, Colonel Archibald and Sam Klaus, came out with such information as they had gotten from the Israeli authorities. We worked until 7:30 preparing as technical and as informing a telegram to the Department as our inadequate information permitted. Naturally, we were deeply concerned about the possible and probable international repercussions. Our information had come from Shiloah, who arrived at the house at 6:00 to tell us of the first and second reconnaissance and the British losses. Shiloah's emphasis was naturally that the planes were in the battle area, and he was inclined then to think that they were Egyptian pilots, though of course English planes.[47] Only the next day did we get the details.

[McDonald and his family had been invited to spend the weekend at the Sharon, a new luxury hotel in Herzliya, built by Samuel Sacks]. I reached the Sharon in time for dinner. The hotel itself, quite a wonder for Tel Aviv, modern in architecture and tastefully decorated, the rooms were well furnished, had steam heat with hot water. As we were to see the next day and as we had imagined from our view from the beach, the hotel has a commanding site.

Saturday, January 8
Morning spent in the sun and in a long walk north on the beach as far as the so-called Babylon ruins, seemingly a medieval, perhaps Crusader structure.[48] It must have been the site of a much older edifice, however, because embedded in the masonry of what appeared to be remains of a vast breakwater was a

---

45. In general see Zeev Tzahor, "The 1949 Air Clash Between the Israeli Air Force and the RAF," *Journal of Contemporary History* 28, no. 1 (January 1993): 75–101.

46. *DFPI*, v. 2, p. 348, d. 298.

47. Shiloah told McDonald initially on January 7 that the British planes had strafed Israeli troops, that the British actions were unprovoked, and that Israeli pilots had been ordered not to engage the British aircraft. On January 8 he told McDonald that the desert west of al-Auja was not clearly marked in terms of boundaries, but that UN observers had left Tel Aviv for the Negev the previous day and could examine all positions. McDonald to secretary of state, no. 20, January 7, 1949, *FRUS*, 1949, v. VI, 627; McDonald to secretary of state, no. 13, January 8, 1949, *FRUS*, 1949, v. VI, 629–630.

48. The name refers to Tel Arshaf (Arabic Arsuf), one kilometer northeast of Herzliya, which contains the ruins of an ancient port city. The ruins span from the Canaanites to the Crusades and include the Greek city of Apollonia, by which name the site also is known.

Roman or Greek column. During the walk, Klaus and I had a long talk. Among the points discussed were:

1) Knox's future. Klaus thought he should return to the Department and become, if not the successor to Satterthwaite, then the assistant to Satterthwaite's successor in charge of Palestine. Klaus thought, and I was inclined to agree with him, that this would be a better post in the sense of being more strategic than the one I envisioned for Knox as my successor. Klaus added that to carry out the plan would probably require my intervention.

2) Klaus was displeased with Satterthwaite's instructions, particularly the refusal to have him go to Teheran or to have the man from Prague come to meet him in Paris. Klaus interpreted this as Satterthwaite's desire to keep him out of the discussions of the labor attaché for our mission.

3) As to his leaving time, Klaus thought that he might as well go soon, for his work was done, except for an analysis of the election returns. This latter, however, would not justify his "hanging around" during the intervening weeks.

> On December 29 Klaus had written to Satterthwaite: "My work here is nearly finished. . . . My tentative conclusion in general [is that there is] no unusual Soviet penetration question now. Internal situation must be appraised after January 25 elections and then closely observed by persons [with] special qualifications and requires careful nurturing [of] American ties while offering facts on Soviet implications [of] such orientation in terms [of] Zionist ideals."[49]

4) In connection with something else, I took occasion to emphasize that it should now be obvious that Bergman had not suffered through my mentioning him as my source to Ben-Gurion ten days or so ago on the possibility of Israel declaring unilaterally the annexation of the New City. Klaus admitted that Bergman's designation as acting governor during Joseph's sudden mission to the States was proof that Bergman had not lost status with the Provisional Government.

5) In connection with his work on his return to Washington, Klaus thought it would be desirable to have help from me in order to have his recommendation called to the attention of those on the highest level, including the president. I promised that I would write to Clifford and to Ewing.

6) Nothing was said about security, but I received the impression that Klaus had had second thoughts about my alleged violations.

49. Klaus to secretary of state, no. 438, December 29, 1949, NARA, RG 59, MC 1390, reel 17, frame 844.

We got back just in time for the mid-day meal to which the Sackses had kindly invited all three of my Shabbat visitors, Klaus, Knox, and McMahon. Just as we were going, in came a telephone call to Knox from John Carlson that two telegrams had arrived which required immediate action. It required all my powers of persuasion to keep Knox from rushing off without his food. Immediately after the meal he and I, together with Klaus, went into the office. There we found from Washington:

1) A British charge that reconnaissance planes had discovered Jewish troops on Egyptian territory after the time when all were supposed to have withdrawn. A tank trap on a road several miles to the west of al-Auja with anti-tank guns in place was cited as evidence.
2) An Egyptian protest against alleged Jewish troop movements across the line after the cease-fire of two o'clock the previous day. The Egyptians warned that they would not be responsible for negotiations if the Jewish troops were not immediately withdrawn.

We decided to go to van der Velde's room where, in conference with the other attachés, we laid the basis for our reply. In this we urged that the to-be-expected charges and counter-charges of cease-fire violations should be left to investigation by UN observers on the spot.

Driven back to the Sharon by McMahon in time for a late tea. After a rest came a pleasant dinner. During the course of the evening we heard the ten o'clock broadcast in English of Kol Israel with the announcement, which we had had heard earlier, that the planes shot down on Friday were British. That afternoon we had received from our air attaché [Colonel Archibald] the details of the Friday events, including a description of one of the planes shot down. But in none of this discussion with the military people did I receive any satisfactory explanation of the five-to-nothing score in plane losses. This was the more inexplicable in the light of the seemingly proven statement that the British planes carried live ammunition in their guns and some of them bombs. My own guess was that the British pilots did not expect to be attacked and were, therefore, taken unprepared. In listening to the broadcast, I seemed to sense the feeling of pride that the British had suffered so severely in the encounter with the Jewish pilots.

Sunday, January 9

Our hosts left during the middle of the morning while we remained to enjoy the sun and the beach. Had just finished an extremely light lunch and was ready for my nap when Knox called to say he was coming out at once with matters which had to be attended to without delay. Fortunately, I went ahead and had a brief rest before he arrived at 2:30. One communication was from the Department, expressing the hope that there had been no violations of the cease-fire and that there had been no return of Israeli troops to Egypt.[50] The other was a report of UK reaction to the reconnaissance battle with demands for compensation and additional terms, which were threats or near threats. After studying the communications I suggested that we, instead of going to the office, go to van der Velde's room. There with the other attachés we spent a couple of hours. But this time, unlike Saturday, we did not find the Israeli liaison men downstairs at the Gat (on Saturday Herzog and Shiloah were finishing a late lunch with Colonel Archibald and Captain Frothingham when Knox and I arrived). One important question remained unanswered when I left the conference about six.

Back to the house in time for dinner. The Crossmans, having found another excuse for not coming, the Shertoks were our only guests other than Klaus and Knox, who came in very late.[51] The dinner was delightful with no business talk. Shertok and Klaus seemed almost to be fellow landsmen as they exchanged Hebrew reminiscences and classic and biblical allusions. The arrival of Knox after nine enlivened the party. He brought with him the completed text of the telegram, which I ok'd and we sent off that night to the Department.

The telegram described the meeting earlier that day between McDonald and Shertok. Shertok said that Israel was determined to maintain the cease-fire and negotiate with Egypt. After McDonald inquired, Shertok added that some Israeli troops might have remained on Egyptian territory after the cease-fire, owing to the abruptness of the withdrawal order and ongoing operations around Rafah in the Gaza Strip. But all units had been ordered to withdraw from the Egyptian side of the frontier and were doing so. Shertok denied Egyptian claims that Israel had violated the cease-fire and that Israeli planes had attacked a refugee camp. The Israeli government was concerned about the British presence at Aqaba; because there was no Israeli threat to Transjordan, the British troops could only be there to threaten Israel's position in the Negev.[52] Lovett sent the relevant passages to the embassy in Cairo to be shared with the Egyptian government, which was not "to disturb [the] present tense situation."[53]

50. See Lovett to McDonald, no. 13, January 8, 1949, *FRUS*, 1949, v. VI, 629.

51. McDonald thought little of Crossman's work on the Anglo-American Committee of Inquiry in April 1946, and had sharply critiqued Crossman personally for a January 1947 article in *The New Statesman and Nation* in which he blamed American Jews and their financial power for the impasse over Palestine. McDonald wrote his daughter Janet after this dinner incident: "I never did care for Crossman. . . . Now [I am] able to see through him and his shallow skin a little more." See Goda et al., eds., *To the Gates of Jerusalem*, 197–199; McDonald to Crossman, January 7, 1947, McDonald Papers, Columbia University, box 9, folder 23; McDonald to Halsey and Janet Barrett, January 14, 1949, McDonald Papers, USHMM, box 10, folder 7.

52. McDonald to secretary of state, no. 24, January 9, 1949, *FRUS*, 1949, v. VI, 632–633.

53. Lovett to US embassy Cairo, no. 33, January 10, 1949, NARA, RG 59, 501.BB Palestine, box 2123, folder 5.

Conference at the office with the postmaster general [Zvi] Friedberg, during which he told Hope and me about his negotiations for new equipment in the States. He found everywhere a readiness to help the Provisional Government modernize its communication system. It has been agreed, he said, that his work is to be allocated $5,000,000 of the projected US [Export-Import Bank] loan. International Telephone and Telegraph was very cooperative and offered to advance credits for new telephonic equipment. Friedberg also told us about the helpfulness of the Department of Communications head through whose support, and that of the Russians, the Provisional Government was admitted to the International Radio Conference in Mexico City. After I left the conference, Hope continued the talk to make a technical report to the Department.

Both Knox and I were obviously unsympathetic to Sam Klaus's suggestion that he stop off in Geneva on his return trip in order to see [Joseph] Keenan,[54] and to learn from the latter about his instructions from the Department and the president. Our objections, I thought, should have been obvious; Keenan's possible refusal to divulge information; his possible, even probable resentment; the necessity he would be under [pressure] to report Klaus's visit; and finally, the probable futility of the stop and the likely embarrassment all around. Nonetheless, Klaus remained insistent. Later, Knox and I decided definitely that he should be told that he could not do it.

Lunch with Colonel Archibald, van der Velde, Knox and the Axelrods.[55] These latter, recent comers to Israel, are wholly delightful. He and our air officers have established an excellent relationship, and she is very popular with everyone. During the lunch, Knox went over to get Captain Frothingham's reaction to the telegram to the president and the acting secretary [Lovett] which I had drafted that morning and which had been approved in the office. In it, I sought to draw the moral from the weekend developments and to emphasize that the heart of the problem lay in the attitude of Britain and that, hence, the only chance of US carrying through to success its December 30 intervention would be to put the pressure on the UK to work in good faith for peace, and to give up its persistent opposition to Israel's hopes in the Negev.

54. After the UN's creation of the Palestine Conciliation Committee [PCC], President Truman chose Joseph B. Keenan (1888–1954) to head the US delegation. In December 1948, Keenan had just completed his task as US Chief of Counsel for the International Military Tribunal for the Far East. The PCC was to meet in Geneva before taking up its headquarters in Jerusalem. On December 31, 1948, as Israeli troops pushed into the Sinai, Keenan and Truman met in the White House. Keenan remembered Truman's strong concern that the Palestine conflict could become a more general conflagration. The president also told Keenan that no state should be able to flaunt the UN or the Security Council. State Department discussion with Keenan, January 3, 1949, *FRUS*, 1949, v. VI, 599.

55. Harry Axelrod, New York-born aviation expert; chief technical officer at the Ramat David airfield as a foreign volunteer with the IDF; credited with keeping Israeli aircraft operational, 1948–1949.

McDonald's cable read as follows: "British policy is bitterly resented by [the Provisional Government] and [those] people who regard it as [a] direct continuation of persistent UK efforts [to] sabotage establishment of [an] independent and viable Israel." He concluded, "US actions since December 30 and call for armistice negotiations have enhanced US prestige here and, if firmly pursued [in] London and interested capitals in [the Middle East], hold promise of peace."[56]

While waiting [at the RCA building to telephone Ben Abrams], I listened to Arthur Holzman telephone his script to WMCA.[57] I thought it indifferent in style, but what I particularly objected to was his quotation from "certain circles here" to the effect that the US was covertly working with Britain to get an anti-Israel settlement of the Negev outside the UN. When he had finished, I told him that this was not true and implied that it was not even representative of Israel public opinion. His answer was: "Since neither you nor the Provisional Government tell us anything, we have to guess." Though I did not argue this very strongly, I did not think it convincing. I said to him, as I had to Currivan and Miller a few days earlier, that I would always be glad to see them to talk over background which might enable them better to interpret a particular crisis.

Dr. Weizmann called me in the afternoon and urged that I come out to see him as soon as possible. I drove to Rehovot immediately. Though Shalom had instructions to drive carefully and did so, the trip was something of an adventure because of the blackout. Found Weizmann with Leo Kohn and Vera. Weizmann expressed his great concern about the British moves, particularly the reconnaissance flights and that at Aqaba.

On January 24 McDonald reported, "Weizmann's closest colleague, Leo [Kohn], told me that my personal and informal talk with President Weizmann at his request on January 10 resulted in [the Provisional Government's] release of [the] captured British airmen."[58]

He stressed the danger of Russian complications, and Ershov's special friendliness on the previous day [at a reception in Weizmann's house on January 9] appeared to indicate that Israel had at least one Great Power friend. In this connection Kohn was rather inclined to urge Weizmann to play down the Russian angle. Then followed a long discussion of possible British motivation. Weizmann came to the conclusion that it could only be to prevent successful Israeli negotiations with Transjordan and Egypt. He urged me to stress this

---

56. McDonald to secretary of state [attention president and acting secretary], no. 27, January 10, 1949, *FRUS*, 1949, v. VI, 639–640.

57. Arthur Holzman (1914–1991), correspondent for WMCA, a radio station in New York City; reported regularly from Tel Aviv.

58. McDonald to secretary of state, no. 51 [personal attention president], January 24, 1949, NARA, RG 59, MC 1390, reel 18, frame 295.

point with the president and the Department. Weizmann then spoke of the rich mineral resources of the Negev. Iron ore, possibly two million tons, chrome, potash, oil in unknown quantities and possibly uranium. The Israeli government was anxious to have the US participate in the exploitation of these resources.[59]

Weizmann spoke about his plans for the States. I promised that we would fly him and his party to Athens, and said that I was sure the American embassy representatives there would see to it that he was not made uncomfortable by the customs regulations, which have been so annoyingly applied to Israel transit passengers. Weizmann showed me the long letter, which had been written for him to Truman in reply to the latter's communication of November 29 received in Rehovot January 5. It was a good letter, but would have been better, I think, if it had been much shorter. I stayed for dinner and left immediately thereafter.

Weizmann's letter to Truman emphasized that Israel no intention of destroying Egypt, but rather to expel Egyptian invaders from Israeli territory while eliminating further threats through "hot pursuit": "I should reiterate that the Provisional Government of Israel is ready, at any time, to enter into negotiations toward the speediest possible attainment of peace."[60] Truman replied that his representations of December 30 through McDonald concerning the Israeli incursion were "made in the most friendly interest . . . because I was convinced that a situation had developed which threatened to extend the scope of the conflict." The president was pleased that Israeli forces had been withdrawn from Egypt and was encouraged by recent developments toward an armistice.[61]

Tuesday, January 11

Delightful couple of hours of work on the roof in the sun.

McDonald dictated in a note to Benjamin Abrams: "Today, as I dictate this note, we are hopeful that the worst has passed. . . . Hence, my restrained optimism as of today."[62]

After what had been an unusually quiet day, Knox came out at six with a full account of Shiloah's fears about [a] possible Iraqi-Arab Legion-Egyptian

---

59. McDonald's report on Weizmann's comments are in McDonald to secretary of state, no 29, January 11, 1949, NARA, RG 59, MC 1390, frames, 131–132. After discussing Ershov, Weizmann noted, according to McDonald, that "communism 'is almost non-existent in Israel' and could not become an important factor unless people felt deserted or betrayed by all western great power friends."

60. *DFPI*, v. 2, d. 287. McDonald, in reporting on the Egyptian attacks off the coast of Tel Aviv, noted Weizmann's and Moshe Shapira's comments that Israel's attack on al-Arish brought far greater international consternation than Egyptian attacks on Israeli territory. McDonald to secretary of state [attention president and acting secretary], no. 2, January 1, 1949, *FRUS*, 1949, v. VI, 595–596.

61. Truman to Weizmann, January 17, 1949, *FRUS*, 1949, v. VI, 670–671.

62. McDonald to Benjamin Abrams, January 11, 1949, McDonald Papers, Columbia University, box 6, folder 2.

combined offensive. Later, with the assistance of the two colonels, we drafted a telegram to the Department and for the attention of Army and Air Force. We were concerned chiefly lest it could be plausibly, if not reasonably, argued that such an offensive, if it came, had been made possible on the Egyptian side by the US's "intervention" of December 31.

Wednesday, January 12

Another pleasant work morning on the roof. Before eleven Anne O'Hare McCormick and her husband came out. I gave her a frank recapitulation of the last twelve days. She seemed more sympathetic than she had been previously. Her views about the new Secretary of State [Dean Acheson] were interesting. She regards him as extremely able but possibly dangerously ambitious. She also is worried as are some of us about who in the new setup will be the effective undersecretary, for it seems obvious that James Webb, though probably a brilliant man, cannot possibly be the technical head of the Department.[63] She hoped, as do we all, that new personnel will not mean that the president expects to be his own secretary of state.

Dean Acheson, the new secretary of state, had opposed the recognition of Israel while deploring the effect that Israel would have on the West's relationships in the Middle East.[64] He worried about Truman's propensity to look at Israel uncritically, which widened the gap between the president and the State Department. But unlike Marshall, who had been willing to follow the British lead in the Middle East, Acheson understood that the United States and the UN had to assume more prominent influence. He was ultimately successful in moving the president closer to what Acheson saw as a more independent US policy.[65]

. . . .

On January 10 Eban brought a formal complaint against the British to the UN Security Council. He argued that recent British actions, including reconnaissance flights over Israeli territory and the landing of British forces in Aqaba, were detrimental to peace efforts.[66] Truman too was losing patience with London. On January 11, during a meeting with Benjamin Cohen, Truman blamed Bevin for the aircraft incident. The United States, he said, was putting strong pressure on London to end the war of nerves with Israel.[67] The British, meanwhile, advised the Egyptians to go

---

63. James E. Webb (1906–1992); Democrat, attorney, and Marine Corps officer; in 1930s served home-state North Carolina politicians including Truman ally, Governor Oliver Max Gardner; federal treasury and budget official, 1945–1949; undersecretary of state, January 28, 1949–February 29, 1952.
64. Dean Acheson (1893–1971), architect of Truman's containment policy; undersecretary of state, 1945–1947; secretary of state, January 21, 1949–January 20, 1953.
65. Consideration of Acheson's Middle East policy in Robert L. Beisner, *Dean Acheson: A Life in the Cold War* (Oxford: Oxford University Press, 2009), 213–216; Hahn, *Caught in the Middle East*, 67–98.
66. Eban's letter to the secretary-general is in *DFPI*, v. 2, d. 308.
67. Epstein to Shertok, January 11, 1949, *DFPI*, v. 2, d. 310.

slow in Rhodes and not to enter into any firm commitments, regardless of diplomatic pressures by the Israelis.[68]

On January 13, Ambassador Franks, on Bevin's near-frantic orders, pressed Lovett for US support "with respect to the strategic land line of communications [between] Egypt and [the] other Arab States, specifically [the] road from Gaza, Beersheba, and Jericho, to Transjordan." It was "vitally necessary," Franks said, that Israel's southern boundary not extend past this line. Lovett countered that London was mentioning this issue "very late in the day." The real strategic question, Lovett continued, lay in Israel holding a Western, rather than a pro-Soviet, outlook. Placing Israel in a strait-jacket, he said, could force it to turn toward Moscow. The United States adhered to its earlier policy of a peace based on the November 1947 UN resolution. Recent British actions had not been helpful, especially because the Israelis and Egyptians were sitting down, and Israel, Lebanon, and Transjordan were also talking.[69]

Acting Mediator Ralph Bunche presided over the negotiations in Rhodes. The Egyptian delegation was headed by Colonel Mohammed Ibrahim Seif al-Din, reflecting Cairo's insistence on purely military talks. The Israeli governmental delegation, showing Tel Aviv's desire for a comprehensive peace, was led by Walter Eytan, the Foreign Ministry's director general. It included Reuven Shiloah acting as Ben-Gurion's personal representative as well as a military delegation headed by Yigael Yadin (see figure 7.1).[70] *Bunche chaired the first joint meeting on January 13.*[71] *He noted that the talks aimed to implement the cease-fire called for in the Security Council's resolutions of November 4 and 16, 1948, and he urged both sides to avoid military incidents.*[72]

Eban, meanwhile, reported to Shertok that, after many conversations with State Department officials, "Our relations with Washington [are] unprecedentedly cordial. Important [that] official London opinion realize [the] impossibility of securing Anglo-American unity on [an] anti-Israel policy."[73] *On January 21, Epstein added, "Recent reports from McDonald, which [are] apparently being read by [the] President, [are] also extremely helpful. . . . President [is] now convinced [that] his personal support [of] Israel [is] fully vindicated from [the] viewpoint [of] long-range American interests and [is] reported [to be] deeply relieved [that] Israel did not press [its] advantage so far as to threaten [the] broader basic British-American alliance."*[74]

A new settlement in Jerusalem also seemed possible. Moshe Dayan proposed a complicated partition scheme in which Transjordan would receive the Arab parts of

---

68. See for example the telephone conversation between Bromley of the British Embassy in Washington and McClintock of the State Department, January 13, 1949, *FRUS*, 1949, v. VI, 651–653.

69. Lovett to Douglas, no. 149, January 13, 1949, *FRUS*, 1949, v. VI, 658–661.

70. On the delegations and expectations, see Caplan, *Futile Diplomacy*, v. 3, 39–41.

71. On Bunche's critical role in the Rhodes armistice talks, see Shabtai Rosenne, "Bunche at Rhodes: Diplomatic Negotiator," in *Ralph Bunche: The Man and His Times*, ed. Benjamin Rivlin (New York: Holmes & Meier, 1990), 177–185; Ben-Dror *Ralph Bunche and the Arab-Israeli Conflict*, 155–184.

72. Cablegram from acting mediator, January 13, 1949, *FRUS*, 1949, v. VI, 654–656.

73. Eban to Shertok, January 14, 1949, *DFPI*, v. 2, d. 331.

74. Epstein to Shertok, January 21, 1949, *DFPI*, v. 2, d. 346.

Fig. 7.1. Israeli delegation before taking off for Rhodes, Yigael Yadin and Reuven Shiloah pictured, January 12, 1949. Israeli Government Press Office. Photo by Hugo Mendelson.

Jerusalem, including the Old City, and Israel would receive the Jewish sections in the west, with access to Jewish sites in the Old City, including the Western Wall, as well as Hadassah Hospital and Hebrew University on Mount Scopus. The British, however, insisted that Abdullah's gains include Gaza, Lydda, and possibly even Western Galilee.[75]

Thursday, January 13

Long conference on the roof with [James] Wooten [of] Alaska Airlines, who told me of the latest difficulties in fulfilling their JDC contract for the evacuation of the more than 3,000 Yemenite Jews from the camp in Aden.[76] He is very bitter about the British interference not only in Aden, but in Asmara and Cyprus. The latest decision in Cyprus to deny any further fuel supplies and a similar attitude in the other two centers would seem to make his work completely impossible. Tentatively, he is planning [to] go to London to make a row there; if satisfaction is not obtained, he will next appeal to Acheson with the threat of going to the Hill and make there an open and sensational attack on the whole British policy of discriminating against American air interests

75. Burdett to secretary of state, no. 35, January 13, 1949, *FRUS*, 1949, v. VI, 661–663; Burdett to secretary of state, no. 42, January 15, 1949, *FRUS*, 1949, v. VI, 669–670.

76. See entry of December 27, 1948.

even in those areas where American money built the fields. He plans an attack on the $60,000,000 [in] US aid to care for the deficit for that amount of the BOAC [British Overseas Airways Corporation].[77] I found it a little difficult to assess Wooten personally or his influence at home. He promised to let me know the latest developments before he left Israel. I was interested in his talk about Alaska and in his enthusiastic appraisal of my friend Governor Ernest Gruening.[78]

Selig Brodetsky came at twelve. He was chiefly concerned to make up his mind how he could most effectively talk about British policy on his return home. He wanted my ideas on ways in which I thought the latest British moves could be interpreted as detrimental to British interests. I found no difficulty in answering. There was, however, not much time, because I had to hurry off for a 12:30 meeting at the Foreign Office.

Early in the morning Knox had brought out two telegrams from the Department of the previous evening: the one reported Egyptian unwillingness to send high-level officials to Rhodes unless the Israel forces "withdrew from [sic] the line of January 7;" the other expressed the Department's hope that the UK-Israeli air incident should not be allowed to "exacerbate" the Middle Eastern situation.

On January 13, McDonald, on Lovett's orders, informed Shertok that the US government had told all Arab states that the British-Israeli air incident should not lead to further conflict. McDonald further catalogued for Shertok US efforts to encourage the Egyptians to engage in serious talks in Rhodes. The Egyptians, however, had told Washington that they would not appoint a senior official to head their delegation if the Israelis did not pull their troops back to the line of January 7.[79]

Following my reading to Shertok of the paraphrase of [Lovett's] despatches, he explained that Israeli forces could not withdraw to the January 7 line without advancing, since all Israeli troops for several days had been out of Egypt, and well north and east of the January 7 position. As to the level of officials at Rhodes, the Provisional Government had deliberately chosen to send Walter Eytan, the second-highest foreign officer, even though it was anticipated that Egypt would not do the same. The Provisional Government's purpose was to indicate its desire to extend the negotiations beyond armistice to peace terms. They intend to keep Eytan there until it should become clear that the Egyptians do not intend to match his rank. Shertok noted the US expression of hope that the reconnaissance incident should not be permitted to worsen

---

77. BOAC's deficit in 1948–1949 was more than a half-million pounds. Robin Higham, *Speedbird: The Complete History of BOAC* (London: I. B. Tauris, 2013), 107.

78. Ernest H. Gruening (1887–1974), New York-born reporter; entered Democratic politics, 1930s; governor of the Alaska territory, 1939–1953; US senator from Alaska, 1959–1969.

79. McDonald to Shertok, January 13, 1949, *DFPI*, v. 2, d. 322; Lovett to McDonald, no. 20, January 11, 1949, *FRUS*, 1949, v. VI, 643. Egyptian reference to January 7 evidently concerned the line around Rafah, the final IDF objective of Operation Horev.

conditions and replied that on his part he hoped that the same word had been sent to Great Britain.

Shertok then went on to give me three items of definite information and a fourth less definite:

1) Nuri al-Said Pasha[80] had indicated definite interest in the strength of the Israeli forces northeast of Be'er Sheva; 2) The Legion forces had been alerted; 3) One unit of the Legion forces had been ordered forward (less definite); 4) The Egyptian commander in Hebron had been ordered not to permit Legion troops to pass through the city southward; if they asked, he was to say the road was mined and to proceed to mine it; if they insisted, he was to resist by force. When I indicated that this last was hardly consistent with the three previous points, Shertok said that it might be that Egypt was determined not to yield any portion of the Negev to Transjordan's control.

In answer to my question, Shertok said that Ershov had called the previous Friday at Shertok's request in order to hear: 1) Shertok's account of his talk with Andrei Vyshinsky in Paris about emigration from the [Soviet Union's] satellite countries; 2) Shertok's "sympathetic and friendly" account of US actions [from] December 30 forward; Ershov had asked nothing and made no comment. Subsequently Shmuel Friedman of the Foreign Office had called the Russian counselor to deny any Provisional Government part in the press report that Russia had offered, and Provisional Government had refused, the former's offer of aid.[81] Shertok emphasized to me that neither in Moscow nor here had Russia even hinted at aid, nor had it even expressed interest in recent developments.[82]

Guests at luncheon at the house, Commodore Cooper, in charge of the task force at Haifa (three destroyers), and Captain Frothingham, and Knox.[83] A pleasant discussion, quasi-confirmation that one of the Egyptian ships engaged New Year's Eve in the "bombardment" of Tel Aviv was a minesweeper. The commodore invited us to visit him any time before he left Haifa on the 22nd. Late afternoon to Knox's pleasant party of farewell for Klaus and van der Velde.

Friday, January 14

Hour and a half visit in the morning from Mr. Harry Viteles, who had just returned from his missions to Aden and Iran. His story of the situation of the

---

80. Nuri al-Said Pasha (1888–1958), Iraqi politician; prime minister several times including January 6, 1949–December 10, 1949; worked to maintain balance between Iraqi independence and strategic relations with Great Britain; unpopular because he signed a new treaty with Great Britain in January 1948; later instrumental in driving Jews out of Iraq.

81. Shmuel Friedman [later Eliashiv] (1899–1955), director, East European Division, Israeli Foreign Ministry; Israeli representative to Czechoslovakia, Hungary, and the USSR, 1951–1955.

82. Meeting reported in McDonald to secretary of state, no. 34, January 13, 1949, NARA, RG 59, 501.BB Palestine, box 2123, folder 5.

83. The US dispatched three destroyers on June 24, 1948, to Haifa to aid Bernadotte in monitoring the truce. They were to monitor movements on the coast.

Jews in Aden and in the Yemen was intensely interesting.[84] His opinion of Sir Reginald Champion, the governor, formerly a district officer in Palestine, was less than complimentary. He spoke of him as weak and unwilling to adopt and stick to a policy. Perhaps illustrative was a picture of the mufti prominently placed in the dining room.[85] The chief of police [A. E. Sigrist] is also non-cooperative. Viteles is uncertain whether the remaining two or three thousand in the [refugee] camps [in Aden] can be evacuated. The situation of the 40,000 or so Jews in Yemen continues to be dubious.

In Teheran and elsewhere in Iran, Viteles's mission was to investigate conditions of native and refugee Jews, and also from Iran to learn about the conditions of Jews in Iraq. Except for a relatively few rich Jews in Iran, the mass of them, some tens of thousands, live in wretchedness on the verge or below the limit of minimum subsistence. There is no persecution, but conditions are very difficult in Iran. As to Iraq, Viteles's information from Jews who had come to Iran and from the Iraqi press confirmed the seriousness of the plight of leading Iraqi Jews and the possibility that the government might at some stage sacrifice the Jews in whole or in part to the public resentment at the administration's financial failure and the failure in Palestine. Viteles is going to send me the pertinent reports of his investigation. Viteles indicated much interest in the UPA row at home, and I promised him to send the material on it that I received from Miss Schulkind.

In 1947 there were 118,000 Jews in Iraq, comprising 2.6 percent of the population. Most lived in Baghdad (98,000), Basra (10,537), and Mosul (10,345). There was a small upper stratum involved in banking and large-scale trade. Many, however, were middle-class businessmen who rejected Zionism as a threat to their interests and who aimed to integrate with Arab society.

In the 1930s, pan-Arabism, anti-Zionism, and Nazi propaganda compromised the position of Iraqi Jews. In June 1941 in Baghdad a pogrom known as the Farhud *followed a failed pro-German coup by Rashid Ali al-Gailani. It resulted in 180 Jewish deaths, the destruction of hundreds of thousands of dollars in property, and synagogue desecrations. The Hashemite regency restored stability for the rest of the war, but the UN partition resolution of November 1947 triggered nationalist anti-Jewish demonstrations.*

In 1948 the regency moved against Iraq's Jews, restricting their movements and forcing them to make financial contributions to the war against Israel. Jews were accused and detained each day. The army's show trial and September 1948 hanging of

84. See entry of December 27, 1948. Viteles had first visited Aden on behalf of Jewish refugees there in December 1943. His mission this time was from October 8–22, 1948.

85. Sir Reginald Champion (1895–1982), British governor of Aden, 1945–1950; earlier district commissioner of the Galilee; blamed local Jews for December 1947 anti-Jewish riots in Aden; repeatedly tried to send fleeing Yemeni Jewish refugees back to Yemen; worried aloud to Viteles in October 1948 that JDC efforts to remove Jews from Aden would result in more Yemeni Jews fleeing there. See Parfitt, *The Road to Redemption*, 147, 166–183.

*the prominent Jewish industrialist Shafiq Ades—who was strongly anti-Zionist—
for allegedly shipping war material to Israel alarmed the entire Jewish population,
especially since the execution triggered a wave of further anti-Jewish violence in
Basra.*

*In November 1948, some Iraqi Jews escaped through Iran, and by March 1949 a
refugee camp was set up in a Teheran Jewish cemetery, where conditions deteriorated.
The British Foreign Office downplayed the mistreatment of Iraq's Jews; this made
independent accounts coming through Viteles and others all the more important.*[86]

In the afternoon young [Don] Peretz of the Friends Service Committee
came for a visit.[87] He is working in and out from Acre.[88] Up to now, they have
been distributing some twelve or fifteen tons of clothing. He remarked that one of
the difficulties in the personal distribution of this is the necessity of struggling
with the crowds of Arab women who fight to get their portion. He also quoted
the colleague who had recently been in Cairo to the effect that the Egyptian
war minister had said, "For the first time we are glad to have the British here,
or otherwise the Jews would soon be in Cairo."

Long tea conference with Colonel van der Velde and Captain Brady.[89] From
the telegram of inquiry from the colonel's superiors asking specifically about
the degree of foreign penetration, I could understand why, in what Washington
still seems to regard as a crisis, the Army was unwilling to approve van der
Velde's home leave. As we talked, I could see that the military were worried
lest the British directly or indirectly intervene to forestall Jewish penetration
into the southern Negev. How they could do this without inviting open conflict
with the Jews, none of us could picture clearly. Both men, however, are still
unwilling to be optimistic about Britain's intentions. I asked them what they

86. In general, Moshe Gat, *The Jewish Exodus from Iraq, 1948–1951* (London: Frank Cass,
1997), 1–46; and Orit Bashkin, *New Babylonians: A History of Jews in Modern Iraq* (Stanford, CA:
Stanford University Press, 2012), 100–140, 183–228.

87. Don Peretz (b. 1922), Japanese-language interpreter with US Army in Okinawa, 1945;
foreign correspondent, 1945–1948, including in Jerusalem; American Jewish volunteer in Acre
and its environs with the AFSC on behalf of UN Relief for Palestine Refugees; attracted to Judah
Magnes's idea of binationalism in Palestine; later a political scientist specializing in the Israeli-
Palestinian conflict.

88. Acre, a town of 15,000, was part of the Arab state as drawn in the UN partition resolution. Arab refugees from Haifa fled there in the spring of 1948, causing general chaos, as well as
disease, because the Haganah had already cut off the town's water and electricity. In addition,
well-to-do Arabs had fled Acre, and the town was under the control of Arab militias. The British
kept Acre from falling into Israeli hands until they withdrew from the area in May. By the time
the Haganah had taken control of the town on May 18, most of the Arab population had fled to
Lebanon. Five thousand Arabs, most of them refugees from elsewhere, remained, and the IDF
moved them into the walled Old City. Jewish immigrants began settling in the newer parts of
Acre in October 1948; 4,200 were there by April 1950. The AFSC received permission from the
Israeli government in January 1949 to distribute UN relief supplies in Acre and its environs. It
also attempted to create Jewish-Arab ties in Acre. Morris, *The Birth of the Palestinian Refugee
Problem Revisited*, 228–232, 253, 390; and Nancy Gallagher, *Quakers in the Israeli Palestinian
Conflict*, 119–122; 133–135.

89. Captain Lawrence W. Brady (1911–2000), assistant US military attaché in Greece since
September 1947; soon to be reassigned to Tel Aviv.

would think of an inquiry from us to Washington on the nature of the British ambassador's talk with the president yesterday.[90] It was decided to wait and check with Knox tomorrow morning.

I sent Bobby next door with a very tentative suggestion of a talk and our neighbor [Shertok] is to call in the morning about a date. According to his answer to Bobby, he had not heard anything definite about the subject I was most interested in, but had had a meaty report on a related matter—Eban, Epstein and Lovett.[91]

Three telephone calls from Weizmann about our cooperation to get the Crossmans back to London for the Tuesday opening of Parliament. I agreed to support Weizmann's plea with the UN for a place on their plane to Rhodes Sunday morning and to ask our Army plane meeting the UN in Rhodes to take the Crossmans with them. Good for evil!

Saturday, January 15

Beautiful morning for work on the roof. Just before lunch as Sam Klaus was arriving, word came from my neighbor asking me to come to see him. He gave me a report of Eban and Epstein's long and friendly conference with Lovett earlier this week.[92] Indeed, I think it was the day before Franks saw the president. Apparently the discussion centered about the points which the Department had been instructing us to impress upon the Provisional Government: 1) the US's friendly purposes; 2) its desire to forestall the reconnaissance incident and the landing at Aqaba being further irritants; 3) the importance of speedy armistice and peace negotiations; 4) its high hopes for the Rhodes conference and more along this line. I don't recall that Shertok reported anything about recognition or loan.[93] His representatives did get, however, the impression that the US is acting to restrain Britain and to press for affirmative results in the near future. Shertok promised me that he would let me know if he had any definite news about the Franks-Truman talk. It is ironic that we here should be dependent on the Provisional Government for our information about what our own government has to say to the British.

Long conference with Klaus, which left me with the impression that he had happily forgotten his worries about my security "breaches." His procedure

90. Sir Oliver Franks's meeting with Truman, arranged at Prime Minister Attlee's personal request, was a last-ditch effort by Bevin to win Washington over to London's perspective. Truman stressed Anglo-American friendship, but noted that, on Israel, the United States and the United Kingdom were simply not in agreement. He was critical of recent British actions, including the dispatch of troops to Aqaba, which the United States had warned against. On January 16, McDonald learned more about this meeting. Holmes to secretary of state, no. 214, January 18, 1949, *FRUS*, 1949, v. VI, 677–679; Epstein to Shertok, January 14, 1949, *DFPI*, v. 2, d. 329.

91. See entry of January 15, 1949.

92. The three had met in Washington on January 12, 1949. See memorandum by Lovett, January 12, 1949, *FRUS*, 1949, v. VI, 645–647.

93. At the end of the meeting Epstein said that the Export-Import Bank had approved the loan to Israel and that the matter was now before the National Advisory Council. He asked Lovett to put in a good word, and Lovett said he would do so.

from here on in is to be as follows: Following a long staff conference this afternoon and a long final top-secret [despatch] by him to the Department, he will immediately on his return dictate his report. This will be perhaps as much as forty or fifty pages. This report goes to Satterthwaite, and upon him depends its use and Klaus's further activities in making known his views. Klaus hoped that there would be opportunities for him to talk directly with Acheson, Clifford, and others. I, therefore, gave him letters not only to these two but to many others including [James] Forrestal, [Jack] Ewing, [David] Niles, [Justice Felix] Frankfurter, [Matthew] Connelly,[94] [Alben] Barkley,[95] [David] Sarnoff, [Benjamin] Abrams, [Arthur] Sulzberger, [Raymond] Fosdick,[96] [Helen Rogers] Reid, [David] Dubinsky, Dr. [Abba Hillel] Silver, Dr. [Emanuel] Neumann, Eugene Meyer, [Arthur] Vandenberg, [John Foster] Dulles, Abe Feinberg, [Herbert] Lehman, and [Samuel] Rosenman. He was particularly pleased with my suggestions about Forrestal and Acheson. He should be extremely useful at home.

Additional point was given to Klaus's mission in Washington by the draft top-secret [despatch], which Knox presented to the full staff conference at the house at teatime. The military attaché and the air attaché were especially concerned, because telegraphic inquiries which they have had in recent days seemed to indicate that some Washington circles were seriously disturbed by the current propaganda about communist penetration here. Only the day previous, we had sent off a long and detailed analysis answering the several specific questions which had been raised, making emphatically clear the lack of foundation for the current rumors largely instigated by the UK.[97]

At our staff conference Knox opened with a "speech" outlining not only these rumors but also his fears; if the Rhodes talks should fail, and if the military situation worsen, and the election went badly for the Mapai, there might be a contest between extreme right and left endangering public security and requiring or leading to [the] military taking over. Once or twice several men wished to interrupt, but I urged that they let Knox finish. When he had done so, I asked someone to read Knox's draft of a top-secret report, setting out very strongly the steps we had taken to check all possibilities of communist penetration, and our conclusion that there was no ground for current fears. Then followed a critical discussion of the language of the report, which resulted in strengthening and simplifying it. It ended on the note that if there still remained grave doubts in Washington, we urged the sending of special investigators to check our findings.

94. Matthew J. Connelly (1907–1976), appointments secretary to the president, 1945–1953.
95. Alben W. Barkley (1877–1976), vice president of the United States, 1949–1953.
96. Raymond B. Fosdick (1883–1972), friend of Woodrow Wilson; advocate of League of Nations after World War I; president of the Rockefeller Foundation, 1936–1948.
97. McDonald's report of January 10 said that British press reports to the effect that Israel's efforts in the Negev were Soviet inspired had no basis. McDonald to secretary of state [attention president and acting secretary], no. 27, January 10, 1949, *FRUS*, 1949, v. VI, 639.

On January 16 McDonald sent two telegrams. The first was for the president's eyes. It noted that, according to the mission's attachés, there was widespread suspicion in Washington that the Israeli government "is Communist or Soviet dominated," stemming from Moscow's support of Israel in the Security Council, arms traffic from Czechoslovakia, immigration of Jews from Eastern Europe, the rude impact of Jewish social democracy on the Arab world, and British propaganda. "Mission finds no evidence supporting Arab and British newspaper allegations regarding (1) air links with Moscow; (2) Russian military mission in Israel; (3) Communist government administrators, etc." McDonald recounted that "we asked and received [the] visit of [Samuel] Klaus who is Department's expert [on] such matters and [Charles] Zimmerman of [the] AFL to search every aspect of [the] labor movement. . . . Combined efforts [of the] mission and [the] experts fail [to] find any significant Communist or Soviet activity or influence."[98]

The second telegram summarized Klaus's top-secret findings and focused on immigrants from Eastern Europe.[99] The Soviet bloc, it said, was Israel's "chief population source."[100] But Israel was determined to maintain control of immigration and not allow communist agents into the country. Foreign Office officials and Shiloah oversaw the details, and Israeli officials screened prospective immigrants carefully. "In general," McDonald reported, "[the] Soviets [are] not actively working [in] Israel at this time not having yet even established [an] open military attaché or other usual agencies. Responsible and trustworthy [Israeli] officials vehemently deny presence [of] any Soviet mission other than diplomatic and point out smallness [of] country and ease with which presence any such mission could be discovered."

After the meeting broke up, Hope made a suggestion I did not feel I could accept, that I ask the president to intervene to secure Colonel van der Velde's home leave and to strengthen his status with his superiors. I declined on the ground that the latter was not on the level which would justify presidential intervention, and if we sought to secure this, the probabilities were that our efforts would hurt van der Velde rather than help him.

98. McDonald to secretary of state [attention president and acting secretary], no. 40, January 16, 1949, Truman Library, Clifford Papers, Subject File, 1945–54, box 14, folder Palestine—Telegrams and Cables 1 of 2.

99. McDonald to secretary of state, January 16, 1949, no. 41, Truman Library, Clifford Papers, Subject File, 1945–54, box 14, folder Palestine—Telegrams and Cables 1 of 2.

100. In May 1948, there were roughly 2.5 million Jews in the Soviet bloc, 80 percent of whom lived in the USSR. Roughly 80,000 Jews emigrated to Palestine illegally from Romania, Hungary, Bulgaria, Poland, and Czechoslovakia between the end of World War II and Israeli independence, and immigration from these states continued unevenly over the following years. Virtually no Jews were allowed to leave the Soviet Union for Israel during this period. Shertok's meeting on December 12, 1948, in Paris with Andrei Vyshinsky, the Soviet deputy foreign minister, was the highest Israeli-Soviet contact to date. Shertok pressed for "massive aliyah," which would guarantee Israel's survival against its enemies. He also made the case for control of the Negev, which Israel intended to populate. The Soviets were willing to weaken the British, but they remained skeptical of Soviet Jewish emigration owing to their suspicion of Zionism within the USSR. See Bialer, *Between East and West*, 57–90.

Back to the house with Klaus preparatory to sending him up to Haifa. During our brief supper, however, Colonel Lerette[101] and a colleague arrived from Haifa to explain the complication about Crossman and Rhodes. Riley and Bunche had become fearful that Crossman would stop in Rhodes and confuse the press situation there. Hence, they had given positive orders that while Crossman could be flown straight to Athens, he was not to be allowed to land in Rhodes.[102] Klaus left with warmest indications of appreciation and will, I think, be a friendly emissary at home.

McDonald later wrote Ben Abrams: "We are counting on Klaus to [do] a good job in giving the folks at home a sense of proportion about the so-called Communist danger here—a danger which is not any more real than was indicated by the scant 4% of the vote polled by the Communists in the [January 29] Constituent Assembly election here."[103]

Sunday, January 16

While we were preparing to have a bite of supper before going off to the concert, Leo Kohn came. His purpose was to report on the Franks-Truman conference the previous Thursday. According to the word received from Washington, Franks made the following points to the president: 1) American and British interests will be gravely menaced if the differences between the two countries about Palestine are allowed to widen the gap between them; 2) British interests throughout the whole of Asia will be at stake if the aggressiveness of the Jews, which corresponds to the aggressiveness of the Russians, is not checked; 3) Arab states must be guided by US and Britain in order a) to secure sound peace and b) to give Arab leaders excuse for making peace; 4) Talk about UK terms was too general to indicate what would be acceptable; 5) Final emphasis on the vital nature of Anglo-American conflict of interest with Russians in Middle East.

In reply, the president is reported to have made a very strong and firm statement to this effect: 1) Criticism of the reconnaissance flight, of the troop landing at Aqaba, and of the general British handling; 2) Referring almost as if it were Weizmann's recent message to the White House, Truman interpreted Israel's prompt withdrawal and acceptance of cease-fire and negotiations as proof of moderation and conciliation; 3) Agreed on the necessity of Anglo-American consultation but insisted on American advice being asked and taken or at least seriously considered; 4) Asked for British support of Arab-Jewish negotiations even if these were held without Anglo-American direction. The

---

101. Colonel Earl L. Lerette (1913–1993), combat officer during US invasion of Europe; UN observer in Israel charged with monitoring the safe withdrawal of Egyptian troops, early 1949.

102. Crossman's observations from his trip, which were highly critical of Bevin's recent policies, were published in his "How It Looks in Palestine," *New Statesman* 37, January 15, 1949.

103. McDonald to Benjamin Abrams, February 28, 1949, McDonald Papers, Columbia University, box 6, folder 2.

substance of the Weizmann statement to the president the previous Wednesday had been: 1) Weizmann deeply disturbed by British interference between Egypt and Israel; 2) In deference to the US, the Provisional Government had given up strategic position and had withdrawn without insisting on Egyptian withdrawal from Israeli territory; 3) Weizmann urges US good offices [to] prevent British intrigue with Arabs to forestall peaceful settlement.

Kohn and I then talked about the possible successor to Keenan [on the Palestine Conciliation Commission]. Kohn had heard various reports of the cause for [Joseph] Keenan's resignation. He had also heard [Frank] Buxton mentioned as a possible successor. He did not comment on my question about the possibility of Riley.

Keenan resigned suddenly from the PCC for personal reasons. On January 22 Truman replaced him with Mark F. Ethridge (1896–1981), a professional journalist who had served as a State Department observer in Bulgaria and Romania from 1945 to 1947. Ethridge had been one of Truman's personal choices for the Anglo-American Committee on Inquiry on Palestine in late 1945 and was one of McDonald's initial suggestions to Truman to head the US delegation to the PCC.[104]

Monday, January 17
[McDonald and his staff discussed the various problems of communications ranging from ineffective arrangements with the diplomatic pouch to insufficient radio equipment.]

Tuesday, January 18
Again into the office where, with the two colonels and Hope, we drafted a last minute plea for inclusion in the [president's] inaugural message of a statement about de jure recognition or/and the loan.[105]

At the ten o'clock news heard the extraordinary announcement of Bevin's release of the [Jewish] internees from Cyprus[106] and the delayed debate in the

104. In his meeting with Truman on January 28, 1949, Ethridge tried to sidestep the assignment, stating that he had never agreed with the partition map of Israel. Truman replied, "If you're so damned smart, why don't you go over there and recommend a settlement?" McDonald privately wrote on January 26, 1949, that "we are all delighted that Mark Ethridge is the American member." See Truman's list dated November 27, 1945, Truman Library, Papers of Harry S. Truman, PSF Subject File 1940–1953, box 161, folder 9. Oral History interview with Mark F. Ethridge, June 4, 1974, Truman Library, www.trumanlibrary.org/oralhist/ethridge.htm#transcript, accessed November 2013; McDonald to Frieda Warburg, January 26, 1949, McDonald Papers, USHMM, box 7, folder 10.

105. McDonald to secretary of state [personal attention president], no. 43, January 18, 1949, Truman Library, Clifford Papers, Subject File, 1945–54, box 14, folder Palestine—Telegrams and Cables 1 of 2. On January 20 Truman's inaugural address emphasized the threat of communism and his support of democracy, but did not mention Israel specifically.

106. The British intercepted and detained 51,530 illegal Jewish immigrants to Palestine after August 1946. Beginning in November 1946, they slowly allowed the detainees into Palestine, beginning with the elderly and pregnant women. In January 1949, 11,000 detainees remained; they were released by the end of February 1949. See Ofer, "Holocaust Survivors as Immigrants," 1–23.

House of Commons.[107] This and Bevin's conciliatory announcement seemed to me to presage more rapid progress in the peacemaking.

In an aide mémoire *handed to Lovett on January 18, Bevin offered British de facto recognition of Israel if the United States would provide de facto recognition of Transjordan. The US Embassy in London reported the same day that "Bevin has now made his final attempt to sell [the] US on [the] UK Palestine policy" and that London's policy toward Israel would "quietly unbend."*[108]

The Department asked McDonald for his assessment. He replied a few days later that London was to blame for the poor state of Israeli–British relations. The low point, McDonald said, came in January when the British had threatened to invoke the alliance with Egypt, had flown over Israeli territory, and had stationed troops in Aqaba. Still, he noted, the depth of the current schism "will largely be determined by future British actions. . . . The sudden release of the Cyprus detainees . . . may help considerably in restoring a less hateful atmosphere."[109]

. . . .

On January 19, the US Export-Import Bank approved the long-awaited loan of $100 million to Israel. The bank granted $35 million in credit for the purchase of agricultural equipment in the United States and $65 million in additional credits for a variety of Israeli development projects ranging from communication to manufacturing to housing.[110]

Wednesday, January 19

To the recording studio at ten to make the Hadassah record for Arthur Holzman and WMCA. At the end he asked me if I would do a live broadcast the next day in connection with the president's inaugural. After conference with the staff at the office, I begged off. It would have been difficult to do without risking complications.

Conference at the office, where I found that most, if not all, of the irritations of the past few days had been smoothed out. Carlson was back, two code clerks were on the way, staff conferences and regular routing of material were being arranged, and in other ways Mr. Hope was sensing that his desired reorganization was under way.

107. Bevin's statements of January 18, 1949, in Holmes to secretary of state, no. A-116, January 25, 1949, NARA, RG 59, MC 1390, reel 18, frames 287–288.

108. British *aide mémoire* in *FRUS*, 1949, v. VI, 675–676; also Holmes to secretary of state, no. 214, January 18, 1949, *FRUS*, 1949, v. VI, 677–679

109. McDonald to secretary of state, A-25, January 25, 1949, NARA, RG 84, E 2774, box 3, folder 360.

110. Board of Directors, Export-Import Bank Meeting of January 19, 1949, https://fraser.stlouisfed.org/docs/historical/martin/11_01_19490119.pdf.

We sent off a telegram complaining mildly about the failure to notify me about Colonel Burton Andrus in advance and to inquire about his background.[111] We agreed on a regular staff conference for Thursdays, beginning tomorrow at four o'clock at the house.

Thursday, January 20

Sam Sacks came over, and for a time he and Rabbi [Jacob] Herzog, who came a little later, discussed general problems. The two had met in Cairo sometime ago. The three of us discussed the loan. Sacks thought it excellent that there were to be two portions. He thought that the way had now been opened for major economic reconstruction projects. Particularly interesting was his utilization of the phrase, "Israel as a pilot plant for the Middle East." This fit perfectly into what the postmaster general had said to me earlier about the International Telephone & Telegraph interest in the credits it was willing to extend to Israel, because what was successfully done here in communications would sooner or later be copied in the neighboring Arab states. Sacks thought that these basic projects would also increase the chances of credits for private industry.

Herzog and I then had more than an hour together. Our talk divided itself into three parts.

1) His story of big business and the Underground; 2) Monsignor Thomas McMahon, the Catholic Church, and the Provisional Government; 3) the French claims and recognition of the Provisional Government.

1) Herzog's story of the relations between Rokach and other representative business interests, including the mayor of Petah Tikvah, and in the background Sacks, with the underground forces during the later years and months of the mandatory, was like a thriller. An informal staff, unknown to the British, on which the businessmen, the Haganah, the [Jewish] Agency, and the underground forces were represented, existed.[112] Also prominent in this were the religious forces. According to Herzog, Rokach and other conservative businessmen working with the religious group were responsible for the "left," what we now know of as the Mapam and Mapai, not crushing the IZL and the Sternists. Whether they could have been crushed without costly and possible civil war Herzog was uncertain.

---

111. Colonel Burton C. Andrus (1892–1977), career officer with background in armor, military prisons, and intelligence; commandant at US Army prisons for high-ranking German criminals at Mondorf-les-Bains in Luxembourg (codenamed "Ashcan") and at Nuremberg during the Trial of the Major War Criminals; military attaché, US mission in Tel Aviv, assigned January 27, 1949.

112. Reference either to the pre-state National Command (Mifkada Artzit), established in 1931, or Committee X, a supervisory committee for the Haganah, IZL, and Lehi formed in 1945. See Eliot A. Cohen, *Supreme Command: Soldiers, Statesmen, and Leadership in Wartime* (New York: Free Press, 2002), 144–145; Avi Shilon, *Menachem Begin*, 85–90.

Herzog told with seeming objectivity of the great difficulty, indeed of the impossibility, of arguing any question through to a logical conclusion with Begin and his people, not to speak of the Sternists. Nearly always a point would be reached in the discussion—sometimes such a discussion would last all night—when the extremists, having been pinned logically into an inescapable corner, would burst out with the remark that they were, in reality, instruments of God and therefore not subject to logical consideration. His dramatic account of the efforts to get Dov Gruner to sign an appeal for clemency, the latter's refusal to do so unless ordered to do so by Begin, Begin's refusal to give the order on the ground that Dov Gruner was like a commando unit and not subject to orders from the center, the mistaken code, which for a time, induced Dov Gruner to sign, all this made me anxious to have an opportunity to talk with Herzog at length about that dramatic and tragic period.[113]

2) Herzog's account of McMahon's present position was doubly interesting because of the comparison I could draw with what the monsignor himself said to me.[114] According to Herzog, McMahon's concern was with five points discussed below in order of their importance from McMahon's point of view:

   a. Refugees. Herzog's report on this was in essential agreement with what McMahon had told me and which I recorded some weeks ago;

   b. Jerusalem. According to Herzog, McMahon maintains his stand on the November 29th resolution. He urges that full account should be taken of the Church's friendly attitude during the crucial months when, prior to November 29, 1947 when the UN was making its decision and during the subsequent months, when recognition was being considered and acted upon by many states, the Church could, had it chosen to do so, have discouraged favorable action by a number of states, including the Argentine and others in Latin America, and possibly also the US. These adverse efforts had not been made because of underlying friendliness and because of the assumption that the November 29 Jerusalem solution would be adhered to. Now, McMahon argued, it would be gravely unfortunate if the Provisional Government took any unilateral action about the New City, because Abdullah on his part would declare the Old City his capital, thus destroying altogether the idea of internationalization. McMahon, therefore, felt very strongly about any Provisional Government move which would precipitate such a situation;

---

113. Dov Gruner (1912–1947), Hungarian-born member of the Revisionist Betar youth group; emigrated to Palestine illegally, 1940; part of IZL group that attacked the British police station in Ramat Gan, March 1947; captured, tried, sentenced to death, and hanged by the British authorities with three other Irgun members, April 1947. The IZL preferred that Irgun activists die as martyrs. A memorial was built to Gruner in 1954 in Ramat Gan across from the police building he attacked. Udi Lebel, *Politics of Memory: The Israeli Underground's Struggle for Inclusion in the National Pantheon and Military Commemorialization* (London: Routledge, 2013), 117, 247.
114. See entries of December 16, 1948, and December 28, 1948.

c. Russian Church property.[115] McMahon deplored any possible return of this property, valued at approximately 22 million pounds, to the patriarch now in Jerusalem[116] on the ground that this would be to turn it in effect over to the USSR. To this, the Provisional Government had replied that it would be very difficult to resist indefinitely the Russian insistence, being made repeatedly through Ershov, that such return was just and necessary. When I pressed Herzog for an answer as to what the government intended to do, he replied that he thought they had not made up their mind and that certainly they had not yet transferred the title deeds;

d. Relief. McMahon was anxious that the priests and Catholic organizations in the areas, where they were in a position to do so, be invited to participate by the several international organizations in the relief efforts. The Provisional Government's answer to this was that they were quite willing so far as they were concerned;

e. Labor Exchanges. McMahon had complained that the alleged communist control of the Nazareth labor exchange [resulted in] what he claimed was a discrimination against Catholic workers. He also charged that such communist control was used to propagandize for communism. [Herzog] explained that he had told McMahon that the situation complained of in Nazareth and elsewhere was the result, not of encouragement from the center, but had grown out of the communists' initiative in building up its organization among the workers.[117] According to Herzog, [Monsignor Antonio] Vergani[118] and the priests under him had not grasped the importance of the labor exchanges or of the danger from communist propaganda among the workers. Now, however, he said that a vigorous effort was being made under Vergani's leadership to correct this earlier oversight.

In general, Herzog felt that McMahon was genuinely friendly to Israel and sincere in his desire to contribute towards a solution of the issues between

115. "Russian property" comprised some thirty-five, mostly religious properties acquired in the nineteenth century; most were owned by the Russian Orthodox Ecclesiastical Mission, an administrative body of clerics overseen by a synod in Russia. With the Russian Revolution, the USSR claimed ownership of the properties, and the ecclesiastical mission, backed by Russian émigrés, resisted. Israel inherited this problem and leaned toward the Soviets. Moscow had recognized Israel and held the key to future Jewish immigration, while the antisemitic Russian heads of the ecclesiastical mission had fled to Transjordan. Soviet authorities seemed to be preparing for the transfer of properties in late 1948. Shertok meanwhile, wondered about the effect such a transfer might have on Vatican opinion. See Bialer, *Cross on the Star of David*, 144–153.
116. Refers to Archimandrite Leonid, pro-Moscow bishop then residing in Russian Orthodox Ecclesiastical Mission properties.
117. Even before Israeli independence, local labor exchanges provided jobs, which in turn were allocated based on prospective workers' membership in specific labor organizations and the strength of each party on specific labor exchanges. In 1948–1949 this meant that Mapai and Histadrut, not the Israeli communists, controlled the labor exchanges. See Peter Y. Medding, *The Founding of Israeli Democracy, 1948–1967* (New York: Oxford University Press, 1990), 152–155.
118. See entry of October 27, 1948.

the Church and the Provisional Government. He had no doubt that McMahon, despite his disclaimer, was in effect if not in name, the representative of the Vatican.

As to our mutual friend, [Eliahu] Ben-Horin, Herzog had been embarrassed by McMahon's unwillingness to be with him. For example, McMahon had told Herzog definitely that he wanted to go alone to see Shertok and Ben-Gurion, but wanted Herzog or the Provisional Government to make this clear to Ben-Horin. There seemed to be a similar misunderstanding about McMahon's desire to have Ben-Horin go to Rome. According to Herzog, McMahon had said clearly that it would be undesirable for Ben-Horin to see His Holiness. When I heard this, I was a little surprised and embarrassed, because I had taken Ben-Horin at his word when he said that McMahon had arranged for him to see the pope. It was on the basis of this that I had given him my letter to Gowen. When I thought the matter over, however, I was less worried, because I am sure that Gowen would have checked with the Vatican before he took any initiative on behalf of Ben-Horin. Nonetheless, it really was not quite cricket of Ben-Horin to give me the wrong impression. [Herzog] was emphatic, however, that McMahon was really fond of Ben-Horin and wanted to remain friendly with him and hence disliked hurting his feelings.[119]

After we had finished this long talk about the monsignor and his present position, Herzog brought up the question which I think was the real occasion for his visit. This was the problem raised by the French demands in connection with the recognition of [the] Provisional Government. According to Herzog, Paris desires that the Mytilene "treaty" (an exchange of correspondence of 1901), which was subsequently confirmed in 1913 by the Turkish [sic] government [in the Treaty of Constantinople], should be recognized as still operative. In other words, the French were claiming, according to Herzog, practically unlimited right to extend their educational institutions and to operate them without Provisional Government supervision. French spokesmen were insisting that they had no intention of abusing such a right, and that they desired it primarily as a matter of principle. In support of their contention, they were invoking the terms of the Mandate, which provided that any rights which were relinquished by the mandatory should revert to the previous holder and that this should be so even if such rights had not been fully recognized by the mandatory. Another basis for the French claim is found in the terms of the November 29 resolution.[120] These terms, I was subsequently to learn from Dr. Mohn, had been

119. Eliahu Ben-Horin accompanied McMahon and Vergani on their tour of Christian Holy Places in December 1948. He did not meet the pope, but on January 17, 1949, he did meet with Cardinal Eugene Tisserant, cardinal secretary for the Oriental Congregation, who was receiving reports from McMahon. The two agreed that, when Arab repatriation took place in Israel, more Christian Arabs than Muslim Arabs would return. Tisserant also noted that Vergani "started out as a believer in the Arab cause, but he has now changed his views." See the Ben-Horin-Tisserant meeting in *DFPI*, v. 2, d. 338.

120. Since the sixteenth century, France had been the guardian of Catholic interests in the Holy Land. This protection, secured through a series of capitulations, allowed French and other

drafted primarily by the French and by the actual French member of the [Palestine] Conciliation Commission, Claude de Boisanger.[121]

Herzog argued that it would be difficult for [the] Provisional Government to grant such rights to the French, and to refuse them subsequently to other powers, for example, the Russians. He expressed doubt that the Vatican was truly behind the French claim. In Rome, one could get the impression that it was, and the French claim this to be true, but McMahon denies it, saying that this might have been a fact earlier but that it was no longer so. Then finally Herzog came to the point: he wanted me to find out "on a wholly unofficial and informal basis" what the US thought should be [the] Provisional Government's attitude towards the French demands. I replied that I was not certain that I could make the inquiry and that I would check with Mr. Knox, but that in any case I should like to have the pertinent documents. It was left that he would give them to me the first of the week.

At a few minutes before four, the members of the staff began to arrive, and promptly on the hour nearly all were present when we began our tea discussion. Despite Hope's rather peremptory attitude, it was a useful session, during which everyone was brought up to date on current matters and the following decisions taken: 1) As to space, we would continue to work to get all we needed in our present quarters, and only after that was done would we raise the question with the government of finding a building; 2) Eugene McMahon explained the communication situation, and it was agreed that there should be no pressing of the request for the ham set license, that we should welcome the arrival of the new apparatus, that efforts should be pressed to complete the penthouse, and that we should reserve further action until the new equipment and personnel had arrived; 3) the service attachés were to make all of their material available to me and to Hope; 4) The file of everything except top-secret material to be available in the file room and should be read every day or so by all members of the staff; 5) No decision was reached on the follow-up to the action by the US and the UK, but I asked everybody to think of ways in which

Catholic institutions, from monasteries to schools to hospitals, to operate without interference by Ottoman or local Muslim authorities. The Mytilene Agreements with the Ottoman Empire formalized these arrangements. The Ottomans abolished the agreements on entering World War I, but France retained its claims. In 1947 the Jewish Agency promised to maintain French privileges in return for French support in the UN, which France provided only after the partition plan included the internationalization of Jerusalem.

In December 1948 the French government insisted on a formal agreement with Israel similar to the Mytilene Agreements, and concurrently demanded control over a long list of specific institutions ranging from convents to seminaries in Jerusalem and elsewhere. To secure French recognition of Israel, Shertok was willing to agree to reasonable requests. But he would not accept a regime based on capitulations. The French, meanwhile, believed that the Palestine Conciliation Commission would secure the internationalization of Jerusalem as provided in the partition resolution. See Schillo, *La France et la création de l'État d'Israël*, 181–199.

121. Claude Bréart de Boisanger (1899–1999), French diplomat; served in San Francisco (1941) and Indochina (1941–1945) before his appointment to the Palestine Conciliation Commission; insisted in mid-January 1949 that the PCC have its seat in Jerusalem to head off Israel's claims to the city as its capital. Troutman to secretary of state, no. 36, January 18, 1949, NARA, RG 59 501.BB Palestine, box 2123, folder 4.

we could most effectively advise the president and the Department to follow through.

After a light supper, Ruth and Bobby and I went to the Sam Sackses'. There we met twenty-five or thirty people, bankers and their wives. Most interesting discussion came late in the evening when our host got into a very warm argument with the bankers and some of the government representatives about the inadequacy of credit arrangements and more particularly the red tape and serious embarrassment of the export license arrangements. Sacks argued that unless manufacturers were enabled to buy raw material, they would have to close up shop. To this the answer was that the shortage of foreign exchange, the inevitable result of the war and the need of purchasing large amounts of food and other consumer goods, made the existing limitations unavoidable.

Friday, January 21

Work on the diary on the roof in the beautiful sun. An hour or more with Dr. Mohn, who this time had not very much to tell me. He did, however, confirm the reports from other directions that the British had been conducting aerial reconnaissance flights over the Jewish lines for months previous to January 6. For example, he said that the British regularly gave reports based on their observations to Count Bernadotte with the request that he use them as proof of Provisional Government violations of the peace terms. He, Mohn, had been requested by his chief to make representations to the Foreign Office of the Provisional Government on the basis of these reports, and always felt embarrassed in doing so because he could not disclose the source. Speaking of the British policy, Mohn rather casually said that this was, of course, the heart of the matter. He explained the British position by saying that it had become accustomed to controlling in the Middle East through the Arab states which it knew how to handle, and was naturally therefore worried by the emergence of a new power, the Jewish state. Its experience under the Mandate helped to make it less certain that it could work with the Jews.

I was rather surprised to have Dr. Mohn say that for the Conciliation Commission to take over the truce supervision would require further specific action by the Security Council. He deplored that provision in the Assembly's resolution, which made the military authority in control of a given territory responsible for the safety of the Conciliation Commission. He was fearful that this might be used as a means by the Provisional Government to circumscribe and to "control" the activities of the Conciliation Commission.

The French member [Boisanger], Dr. Mohn thought, would be cautious, but well-informed. He had previously acted as a French expert on various technical assignments for his government affecting this area. The chief secretary of the Commission, Pablo de Azcárate, an old international civil servant having been with the League, was competent but would be on the cautious side also.[122] Fraser Wilkins, Dr. Mohn thought, would be rather an amateur.[123] As to Bunche possibly being the American member, Dr. Mohn doubted that Dr. Bunche would want the job, particularly since he as acting mediator "had been carrying on so successfully."

Later de Reynier of the International Red Cross Society came for lunch.[124] I asked him about the displacement of [Pierre] Depage, the Belgian doctor who had done such an outstanding job in the Jericho camp, by all odds the most brilliant work that had been done on behalf of the refugees.[125] De Reynier's somewhat embarrassed reply was to the effect that since the International Committee was to have the responsibility in the area including Jericho, it should have its own personnel, and that Depage was going to be associated in a medical capacity with the League of Red Cross Societies. De Reynier also implied that the International Committee had been partly responsible for the success of Depage's efforts. All of this left me with a sense of bureaucracy gone to seed. At lunch de Reynier, though he talked freely enough, did not add notably to our enlightenment. Rather, he gave the impression of a cold, calculating professional relief worker to whom the job was more important than the victims he was paid to serve.

On the way home, stopped at Knox's apartment and checked with him some current administrative problems at the office. We discussed: Richard Ford, the new counselor-of-mission, due on February 10; the possibility of Knox replacing Satterthwaite—this Knox emphatically repudiated, saying that he would not go into the Department; my hope that he [Knox] might come back here and eventually be my successor. This last would, I think, please Knox, as it certainly would the people here.

Saturday, January 22

Work on the roof during the morning. In the afternoon, out to Weizmann's for tea. Found him weaker than he had been any time since Vevey. He explained that he had suffered an acute attack of "neuralgia with excruciating pains from the top of his head to the sole of his left foot." Subsequently, he had

122. Pablo de Azcárate y Flores (1890–1971), Spanish jurist and diplomat; Spanish delegation to League of Nations, 1922–1931; head of League of Nations Department for the Protection of Ethnic Minorities, 1931–1933; adjutant to secretary-general, League of Nations 1933–1936; Spanish republican government ambassador to London during the Spanish Civil War, 1936–1939; driven into Swiss exile by Francisco Franco's victory in Spain; UN diplomat after 1946; UN Palestine Commission (charged with supervising the transitional period to partition), 1947–1948; UN Truce Commission, Jerusalem, 1948–1952; secretary-general of Palestine Conciliation Commission, 1948–1952. See Pablo de Azcárate, *Mission in Palestine, 1948–1952* (Washington, DC: Middle East Institute, 1966).

123. Fraser Wilkins of the Department of State's Division of Near Eastern and African Affairs was appointed political adviser to American member Mark Ethridge.

124. See entry of October 16, 1948.

125. Pierre Depage (1894–1971), president, Belgian Red Cross. The Jericho district in the Jordan Valley had some 30,000 refugees, and the UN concurred that Depage had done superior work in organizing the camp there. Food issues had been solved, there were educational structures, and sports programs had commenced.

had severe headaches each morning. Dr. Zondek was more than dubious about the American trip now.[126] Weizmann seemed relieved when I suggested possible postponement of the New York dinner until April.

Weizmann paid his respects in most vigorous terms to Rabbi Silver, whom he characterized as an "unscrupulous and arrogant bully"; but Weizmann's choicest terms were reserved for Emanuel Neumann who was, he said, a replica of "Goebbels" with "club foot and crooked mind, the more dangerous of the two." (That is, more dangerous than Silver). With such people "there is no possibility of agreement."[127]

In answer to my inquiry about the results of the scientific expedition which he had told me of the week before into the Negev, he replied, "In strictest confidence and not to be transmitted," that the first examination had disclosed radioactive rock, but not certain whether uranium or thorium; the amount not known but the known deposit seems the result of washings from the neighboring hills where a second expedition will explore further within a few days. Also discovered was what seemed to be the platform of an oil well, with parts of the equipment round about. The platform had not been lifted, however, and the well was in any case of less interest than the other discovery. Weizmann promised to keep me informed of any new developments in the South.[128]

On the way home, stopped at the Gat, where I asked Knox if the confidential data given me by Weizmann could properly be passed on to Truman. Knox's judgment, reaffirmed the next day, was that I could not properly fail to inform my chief. This was on the theory that no head of a state tells to the chief of mission of another state anything of interest to the latter's chief unless it be understood that it will be made available.

Then, a talk with Knox and Hope, who were both disturbed by the fact Colonel Archibald with Captain Frothingham were going off to the south of the Dead Sea, paced by an Israeli plane. The concern was lest an enemy plane might consider that the American was out of bounds and precipitate an incident. Meeting Frothingham, I told him of my doubts, which he said he would pass on. After eleven, though I was not in bed, Colonel Archibald called and said that he had not thought that any question could arise about the route, that they would be very cautious, and that he was confident there would be no incident. I said, ok, particularly if not to go through with it would embarrass [Archibald] with [Harry] Axelrod, the Israeli air liaison.

126. Dr. Hermann Zondek (1887–1979), German-born personal physician to several Israeli leaders; his brother Bernhard (1891–1966) was a renowned gynecologist, and Samuel (1894–1970) was an internist; all three fled Germany in 1933.Weizmann facilitated their emigration to Palestine, arguing that they would further establish the medical profession there.

127. See entry of October 12, 1948.

128. Israel's search for uranium in the Negev began in 1948, and isotope research began at the Weizmann Institute of Science in 1949. Low-grade uranium deposits were found near Be'er Sheva and Sidon in 1950. Generally speaking, the Israelis kept their nuclear program secret from the United States until the latter discovered it in 1958. See Warner D. Farr (USAF Counterproliferation Center), "The Third Temple's Holy of Holies: Israel's Nuclear Weapons," (Maxwell AFB, AL: Air War College, 1999), www.au.af.mil/au/awc/awcgate/cpc-pubs/farr.htm.

Delightful lunch and midday "vacation" with the family and the McCor-
micks at the Sharon Hotel. The food and the weather were perfect. Anne
O'Hare [McCormick] was particularly interesting in her accounts of her visits
with Abdullah and Glubb Pasha. The former she thought a charming old man,
and the latter, a quiet and modest gentleman. From both of them she had gotten
a categorical declaration that had there not been the fateful violation of the truce
in Jerusalem the Legion would not have attacked; Transjordan has no intention
of resuming the war; the Old City will never be given up by Abdullah, though
he has no intention of making it his capital; Abdullah was extremely critical of
Egypt, claiming that it had insisted on Transjordan's coming in, and then had
been the first to agree to negotiations; Gaza, Abdullah said, must be a part of
his enlarged kingdom; Egypt had no conceivable claim to it; Glubb said there
was no alternative to the Arab part of Palestine being joined to Transjordan.

Anne spoke about her articles written since her return, many of which
were carried on the first page. I was struck by the extent to which she had
changed her attitude since she was here only a few weeks ago.[129]

*McDonald wrote Arthur Sulzberger on January 28, 1949, "We were delighted
that you asked Mrs. McCormick to come back to Israel. Her ten pieces have, we understand, made a splendid impression at home. They have been appreciated here, too."*[130]

We reached the Czech consul general's residence, Dr. Victor Grünwald,
about seven, and stayed there until eight.[131] Met a number of the government
people but had a noteworthy talk only with Miss Herlitz and with Simon. The
latter warned me quite seriously that they would expect the presentation of
credentials as minister [upon de jure recognition by the United States] to be
carried through with due form, including formal clothes and appropriate ceremonies. I was inclined to not take him seriously, but he stood his ground and
finally persuaded me that he was serious.

With Miss Herlitz, the talk was on two subjects: 1) The French demands,
which Rabbi [Jacob] Herzog had outlined to me earlier, and the possibility of
French recognition. As to Herzog's suggestion that I find out what the US
thought of the French terms, I told Miss Herlitz that such an informal inquiry
could in my opinion be much more advantageously made verbally by Epstein in
Washington; 2) The other subject was the possible line that Bevin would take
on Tuesday or Wednesday, and in particular, the chances that he might seek to

129. See entry of December 17, 1948.
130. McDonald to Sulzberger, January 28, 1949, McDonald Papers, USHMM, box 7,
folder 10; on McCormick's articles and their tone, see Kathleen Christison, *Perceptions of Palestine: Their Influence on U.S. Middle East Policy* (Berkeley: University of California Press, 1999),
82–84.
131. Dr. Victor Grünwald, born 1897 in Vienna, honorary consul general, Czechoslovakia,
1948–1949.

win support on the ground that he had reestablished an Anglo-American accord. But nothing very new was learned.

To the Gat before the concert. There, Knox and Hope approved the top-secret communication to the president on the Weizmann conference.[132] They also approved a general memorandum to the staff regarding the requirement of permission before leaving town. The concert of the orchestra under the resident leader, [George] Singer,[133] made me feel that there was no need, except for box office purposes, of guest conductors, so well did Singer handle the men. The program was unusually entertaining because of its variety and the ingratiating character of the last number. Mendelssohn's *Ruy Blas*, which I thought I understood better because of my knowledge of the play, was followed by Khachaturian's piano concerto with Pnina Salzman as the able but somewhat mannered soloist.[134] Finally a brilliant performance of Dvorak's Fourth Symphony.

On January 24, 1949, the French government extended de facto recognition to Israel. The Israelis promised to evacuate French religious institutions that the IDF had occupied, to indemnify the institutions for damages, and to hold continued discussions concerning the ultimate legal status of these institutions on the understanding that French status would not be inferior to that of any other country. Israeli accepted in principle the internationalization of Jerusalem's Old City, which held many Christian Holy Places. But Israel insisted on annexation of the New City together with the corridor connecting it to the coastal plain. For their own part, the French insisted that recognition of Israel would not prejudice the final delimitation of Israel's borders by the UN.[135]

Monday, January 24

Mr. M. Z. Frank came out to lunch.[136] Our talk covered many subjects. The only two which deserve recording are: 1) His admiration, larger than he had thought it would be, for the progress under the Provisional Government; 2) his admission that Silver and Neumann might be riding for a fall. He did not say this directly but intimated as much. Silver's avowed purpose to head the American effort in Palestine, and in particular his program of strengthening the central party, Frank thought dangerous, as do I. He added that Neumann was the more inclined to this program because of his old association here with Rokach and other conservatives who were avowedly fearful of the left tenden-

132. McDonald to secretary of state, no. 51, [personal attention president], January 24, 1949, NARA, RG 59, MC 1390, reel 18, frame 295.
133. George Singer (1908–1980), Czech-born composer and conductor; fled Prague in 1939; one of the first conductors with the Palestine Orchestra/Israel Philharmonic.
134. Pnina Salzman (1922–2006), Israeli classical pianist; later became first Israeli pianist to perform in the Soviet Union (1963), and the People's Republic of China (1994).
135. *DFPI*, v. 2, p. 395, d. 354; Schillo, *La France et la création de l'État d'Israël*, 211–222.
136. M. Z. Frank (1897–1975), Russian-born member, American Jewish Committee; director of publicity, Haifa municipality; later covered the fight between Silver and Ben-Gurion. See M. Z. Frank, "American Jewish Community and Israel," *American Jewish Yearbook* 53 (1952): 178–186, www.ajcarchives.org/main.php?GroupingId=10086.

cies of the labor parties. Because of the necessity of agreeing with Hope on the reply to be given to the Griffis message that he was arriving in Jerusalem at one with the Conciliation Commission, I did not encourage Frank to stay long after lunch but invited him most cordially to come back soon again, and this time with Madame Sorani, the very interesting Italian Jewess whom I had met in Rome a year or two ago.[137]

Hope and I decided to send a simple telegram to Griffis, that I could not come to Jerusalem, and inviting him here. Shortly thereafter he telephoned me saying that he had not known that I was not coming to Jerusalem, and that, after he had spent a week or so visiting the camps to the east, he would come down and be our guest.

Tuesday, January 25

Israel's first election day. Tel Aviv was strikingly quiet, though everyone seemed in a holiday mood. There were, however, no more braying loud speakers, massed crowds in the squares or the feverish distribution of campaign leaflets. Everybody settled down to enjoy what was declared a national holiday and to vote.

Nearly an hour at eleven o'clock tea with the Czech consul general Mr. Grünwald and his colleague from Jerusalem, František Nečas,[138] together with a third Czech. Our talk was mostly about the election and about the geography of Czechoslovakia. All of us refrained from anything approaching controversial Russo-American topics.

Conference with Knox and Hope at the hotel regarding my possible visits to Jerusalem. We decided to make a strong suggestion to the Department, rather than timidly to ask their advice.

Miss Herlitz came in at teatime. She gave to Knox, Hope, and me a detailed account of the progress [of Egyptian-Israeli armistice talks] at Rhodes. In substance she said: Nearly all the negotiations had been indirect, that is to say, one side would meet with Bunche and then the other would meet with him. The friendly atmosphere had resulted in the prompt agreement on the preamble. Other points, too, seemed to be becoming less difficult until the 22nd or the 23rd, when new hurdles became apparent. She did not know whether the stiffening of the Egyptian attitude had any relation to British influence. As to the moot question, the evacuation of the Faluja pocket, it had all along been understood that this was to be an integral part of the general settlement. On the eve of the return of two members from each delegation to their respective governments, there had been signed by both sides a two-fold agreement: 1) "A sincere cease-fire;" and, 2) For the evacuation of some wounded

---

137. Possibly the wife of Settimo Sorani, wartime director of the Rome office of DELASEM rescue organization in Italy.
138. František Nečas, Czechoslovak consul, Jerusalem, 1948–1952.

personnel from Faluja and the admission of [a] food convoy to be under the supervision of the UN observers.

The Egyptians initially wanted an armistice line corresponding to the lines of November 13, 1948, plus the maintenance of Egyptian forces in Be'er Sheva, al-Auja, and Bir 'Asluj, pending a final territorial settlement.[139] The Israelis intended to keep their current positions in the Negev, which meant no active Egyptian forces there. Bunche, who had scheduled the Egyptian evacuation from the Faluja pocket to begin on the morning of January 25, blamed Israel for the impasse. He hoped that the Security Council could pressure the two governments.[140]

On January 24, both sides agreed on an extended cease-fire in place, and the agreement was announced the next day. Also on January 24, the Israelis agreed to allow Egyptian convoys with food and medical supplies to enter Faluja for the trapped Egyptian garrison and Arab civilians there, pending agreement on the Egyptian military withdrawal. UN observers were to monitor these agreements.[141]

Aaron Wright and I had a frank talk about developments here and on his views about Arab refugees.[142] He was emphatic that the bulk of these could never return, that their leaving had been almost miraculous, eliminating difficult if not insuperable problems for the new state, but he personally favored a generous financial contribution by the Jews for the settlement of the refugees in the neighboring Arab countries.

Samuel Halprin's[143] visit was interrupted by Knox's and my date with Shertok at 9 o'clock. The latter received us with Shiloah, who had come back a few hours earlier from Rhodes. After we read a paraphrase of the Department's expression of anxious hope that the Provisional Government would be generous in its interpretation of its problems about Faluja's evacuation—this the Department, on the basis of information available to it, assumed was not contingent and was unqualified—and that neither side do anything to make a peaceful solution more difficult,[144] Shertok replied substantially as follows: The misunderstanding about Faluja arose apparently from Bunche's over-optimism in fixing the date January 24 for the beginning of the evacuation. It had been clear

139. Al-Auja and Bir 'Asluj (now Be'er Mash'abim) were strategic points in the Negev along the road from the Sinai to Be'er Sheva used by the Egyptians in the 1948 fighting. Al-Auja was initially assigned to the Arab state and Bir Asluj to the Jewish state in the partition of 1947. The Israelis captured both in Operation Horev in December 1948.

140. More details from Bunche in Henry Grady to secretary of state, no. 152, January 23, 1949, and Austin to secretary of state, no. 85, January 23, 1949, *FRUS*, 1949, v. VI, 689–691, and n. 1.

141. Documents in *FRUS*, 1949, v. VI, 698–700.

142. Aaron Wright, British Zionist and longtime head of the Jewish National Fund in Great Britain; in Israel for consultations with JNF director Avraham Granovsky concerning development and fundraising.

143. Samuel W. Halprin (b. 1892), New York-born businessman; left clothing business and began exporting medical equipment to Palestine before the end of the Mandate; husband of Rose Halprin, president of Hadassah, 1932–1934, 1947–1952.

144. Acheson to McDonald, no. 42, January 24, 1949, *FRUS*, 1949, v. VI, 694–695.

throughout, and Bunche could not have misunderstood, though the Egyptians may have misunderstood from what Bunche said to them, that the evacuation was to be an integral part of a general settlement and was definitely contingent on all the armistice terms having been agreed to or "about to be agreed to." The writing in of the date, January 24, had been agreed to on Bunche's insistence. But he could not have misunderstood that its effectiveness was contingent upon more progress than was subsequently made by that time. (To both Knox and me, however, while we did not doubt Shertok's statement, the Provisional Government's representatives at Rhodes appeared to have been guilty of maladroit negotiations.) Shertok added that his delegates had written a strong letter to Bunche, with a copy for the Egyptians, clarifying the Faluja position.

On the other points, Shertok said: The sticking point appeared to be the Egyptian insistence on their return to al-Auja. Since the Egyptians had been defeated, the Provisional Government could not accept their return as victors. The Gaza-Rafah strip seemed to cause less difficulty. The Provisional Government was prepared to accept any one of several solutions, as, for example, the retention by the Egyptians of political control following the withdrawal to Egypt of armed forces. Shertok would not accept the retention of enemy military control there. Shertok then repeated what Miss Herlitz had told us about the agreement on wounded evacuation, and a new food convoy to Faluja. He assumed that the negotiations would be resumed on Thursday and was moderately optimistic about a final agreement. I should record that, earlier, Miss Herlitz reported that the Egyptian press, in telling of the conference, did not mention the presence in Rhodes of the Israeli representatives and instead left the impression with the reader that the Egyptians were negotiating solely with Bunche.[145]

My talk with Halprin was shorter than I could have wished. He feels very strongly about the Silver-Neumann attitude at home and believes that they are gravely endangered in their leadership. He is most optimistic about business possibilities here, thinks that [the] Provisional Government has performed almost miraculously, and that the future holds the highest promise. He had had an acknowledgement from his wife of the receipt of his letter, giving her the background of the B[artley] C[rum] propaganda. He again said, as he had the first time, that he was delighted to have had this clarified. He could not have been more cordial. He also agreed to act as our messenger.

One other item, the wager between Chaim Shertok and myself about the relative strength of Mapai would show. Our two estimates were placed by him in a sealed envelope.

The war delayed Israel's first elections, promised for October 1, 1948. Voting for the 120-seat Constituent Assembly took place on January 25, 1949. Few could predict the outcome with precision, since the last vote in the Yishuv, for the Assembly

---

145. See McDonald's report on this meeting to the secretary of state, no. 57, January 26, 1949, *FRUS*, 1949, v. VI, 700–702.

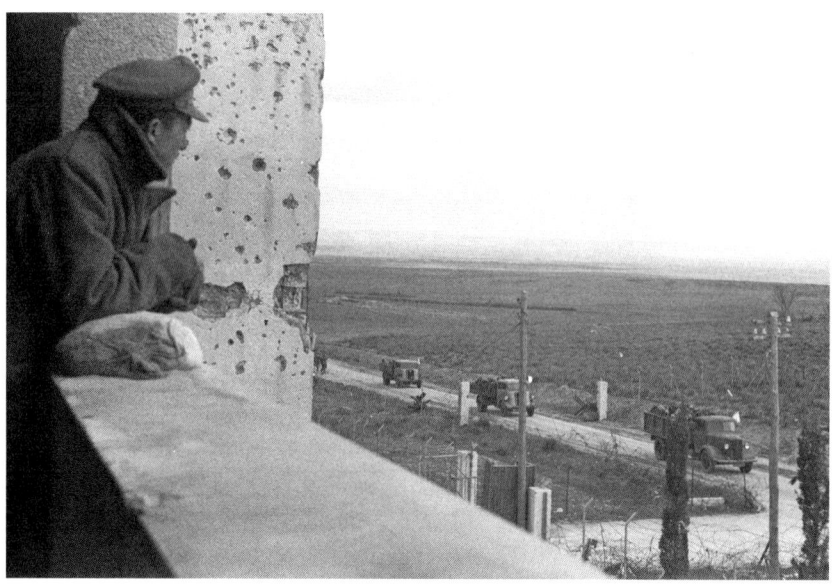

Fig. 7.2. Israeli officer watches the Egyptian evacuation of Faluja, February 27, 1949. Israeli Government Press Office. Photo by Eldan David.

of Representatives, had been in August 1944. Public excitement helped ensure that roughly 440,000, about 87 percent of Israeli voters, turned out.

Ben-Gurion's Mapai won 36 percent of the votes (46 seats), and the more leftist, pro-Soviet Mapam won 15 percent (19 seats). The United Religious Front, a collection of Orthodox groups including Agudat Israel, won 12 percent (16 seats); Menachem Begin's Herut won 11 percent (14 seats); the General Zionists won 5 percent (7 seats); and the Progressive Party 4 percent (5 seats). The remaining thirteen seats were divided between the Sephardic and Oriental Communities (3.5%), Maki [the Israeli communists] (3.5%), and the Democratic List of Nazareth (1.7%). Nine additional parties, including the Workers' Bloc, Ultra Orthodox List, and the Popular Arab Bloc, failed to gain a seat.

McDonald wrote to numerous interlocutors that "Mapai won about as many seats as was expected and will doubtless be the center, under Ben-Gurion, around which will be built the Government coalition during the Constituent Assembly.... None of the extremist parties have gained as they boldly proclaimed they would. Herut, instead of being the second party, as [Begin] hoped, will be fourth. The Communists at the other extreme [made] a poor showing.... This should be a conclusive answer to the widespread alarmist stories about Communist penetration in Israel."[146]

146. McDonald to Arthur H. Sulzberger, January 28, 1949, McDonald Papers, Columbia University, box 4, folder 20.

Rabbi Jacob Herzog came at four. He brought me a copy of the French memorandum "Re œuvres françaises en Terre-Sainte" presented to the United Nations.[147] This I am to return to him. He presented to me also with a generous autograph, a copy in Hebrew and in English of his Mishnah. Through the reading of this, I hope finally to get some understanding of the Talmud.

First we talked at some length about the election results. Herzog was evidently pleased with the showing made by the Orthodox slate and with the relatively poor showing (as compared with Begin's hopes) of the Freedom [Herut] Party. On the question of Mapai alignment, Herzog thought that Ben-Gurion would be more apt to turn to the progressives and the Orthodox and Sephardic, rather than to Mapam. He agreed with my suggestion that, since this election had been for the Constituent Assembly which would decide on the fundamental law of the land, the religious forces had won a larger victory than they could be expected to win in subsequent elections, when the issues would be more economic.

He was enthusiastic in praise of Ben-Gurion, whom he regards as one of those rare leaders who stand out in history because they are "in tune" with the underlying movements of their times. He compared Ben-Gurion with Churchill and regards him much more highly as an effective leader and as understanding much more clearly the needs of his people today than does Weizmann. The latter he considers more brilliant intellectually, but inclined to be querulous and to show at times pettiness, which is remote from Ben-Gurion.

As to the demands of the French and Herzog's suggestion that I find out for him what our government thinks should be the attitude of the Provisional Government, I explained that this inquiry could much better be [pursued] in Washington verbally by Epstein in a talk with Satterthwaite. We agreed that we should meet again soon.

Thursday, January 27

In the morning worked at home. For early tea, I was joined by Leo Kohn, whom I had telephoned to that morning. His forecast of Ben-Gurion's probable program was helpful. He thought the prime minister would seek to have the best of both worlds, that is, to include both Mapam and Mizrahi in his cabinet.[148] Not to do this would be to risk a union in opposition of the extremes, Communist and Mapam on the Left and Herut on the right. Such opposition would make extremely difficult the carrying forward of Ben-Gurion's moderate foreign policy. Moreover, if he chose to build a solid labor bloc by including

147. Refers to 1947 document written by French archaeologist and consul-general in Jerusalem, René Neuville, "Mémorandum relatif aux œuvres françaises en Terre-Sainte présenté à la Commission spéciale des Nations Unies pour la Palestine" (Jerusalem, 1947), which listed French claims to religious institutions in Palestine. For the list see Schillo, *La France et la création de l'État d'Israël*, 192–193.
148. Mizrahi, which melded religion and Zionism, was part of the United Orthodox Front.

Mapam but excluding Mizrahi, he would risk a deep cleavage within the state. This would be particularly true because what takes place in the Constituent Assembly is, from the point of view of the religious, a matter of life and death.

Kohn's reasons for this forecast root in his conviction that Ben-Gurion is one of today's great leaders,"a man in tune with history." He finds nothing petty in Ben-Gurion, but rather an intuitive understanding of the moving forces of his day. He is more the natural leader than Weizmann, whose brilliant intellect and sharp tongue frequently betray him into alienating essential support. As to the procedure following the election, Kohn explained that within seventeen days the Constituent Assembly would be called. He denied that Jerusalem had been determined upon as the place for the opening session, but I think this was merely a diplomatic denial. Weizmann would call the assembly to order and make the inaugural address. Then a speaker would be elected and the organization of the assembly completed. Following that, one of two courses would be adopted: a) the election of the president, almost certainly Weizmann. Within a day or two he would call Ben-Gurion and entrust the latter with the responsibility of organizing a cabinet. This would then be presented and if it received a majority vote would constitute the government; b) the other possibility would be that the assembly would proceed directly to name a prime minister who would choose his cabinet and present it for endorsement. The election of the president would then be held or postponed. Kohn admitted, however, that the first procedure indicated would be simpler and probably preferable.

Turning then to Bevin's speech, Kohn emphasized its lack of generosity and expressed fear lest the statement that if there were renewed hostilities "Britain would find it difficult to stand aside and remain inactive,"[149] was a covert invitation to the Arabs to resume hostilities. He feared too that it might encourage Egyptian intransigence at Rhodes. He reported that Shertok was inclined to share these fears. Kohn noted also that while both Eden and Churchill criticized Bevin and the reconnaissance flights, neither Conservative leader criticized the sending of troops to Aqaba or urged their recall. I reminded Kohn that, on the contrary, Churchill had in the debate a week earlier declared that he hoped the foreign secretary would not "scuttle" at Aqaba.

In the House of Commons debate on January 26 Bevin declared that British planes had a right to fly over Egypt, "where the Jewish forces had no right to be." Mc-Donald reported, "High authority in [Israeli] Foreign Office informs me that Weizmann and Foreign Minister are disturbed over Bevin's speech. . . . This, in opinion of above officials, can be directly interpreted . . . as an open invitation to Arabs that if they resume conflict, Britain will participate therein. Israel intelligence sources also reveal that Mufti's forces serving with Iraq [are] circulating [the] story that Britain will support Arab renewal of hostilities. . . . I . . . would appreciate urgent advice of Department [regarding] its interpretation of Bevin's statement and a clarification if

149. JTA *Bulletin*, January 27, 1949.

possible." Acheson responded: "Department does not believe Bevin intended encourage Arabs renew hostilities."[150]

Kohn told me that he is leaving for two weeks to confer about [the] constitution with William Rappard in Switzerland and to learn in Paris more about the exact functions of the French president.[151] The Israeli presidency is to be modeled on that of the French. Kohn expressed concern that Weizmann might not be willing to spend the time necessary to establish the proper tradition of presidential participation. This would require at least three hours a morning four or five days a week and on many days additional time. Kohn did not see how this could be arranged if Weizmann insisted on continuing his work at the Institute. There were also complications about Weizmann going to the States, for he could not open the Assembly and reach the States for the 19th of February dinner. Moreover, it would be according to Kohn "unseemly" for the president to rush off immediately after the new government had been set up.

From five to nearly seven full staff conference at tea. This was also an occasion for meeting our new colleague, Richard Tetlie, who is to set up our public information service.[152] The conference covered many topics.

1) Tetlie outlined briefly the scope of his work: a reading room with seventy magazines, the receipt and distribution of ten thousand words daily of the USIS [United States Information Service], and related activities.[153] We all expressed the hope that he was going to be supplied with an adequate staff.
2) General talk about the election, and the report which we would make on it. Knox read his draft telegram and I mine, and later we sent off what in substance was mine.[154] I reported on Kohn's fears.

McDonald primarily reassured the State Department concerning the possibility of extremism. The tallies garnered by Mapam and by Herut were smaller than expected, and the "Communist small vote was expected by all competent observers." He reported that many expected a labor coalition to be formed, but that "sharp differences of personality and Mapam's vocal romantic attitude toward USSR may prove

150. McDonald to secretary of state, no. 62, January 27, 1949, and Acheson to McDonald, no. 53, January 31, 1949, NARA, RG 84, E 2775, box 3, folder 320.
151. William E. Rappard (1883–1958), US-born professor of economic history and public finance; co-founder and director of Graduate Institute of International Studies, University of Geneva; former member of the League of Nations Permanent Mandates Commission who had supported Zionist interpretations of the Mandate; close friend of Weizmann.
152. Richard Norman Tetlie (1921–1999), assistant attaché, assigned in November 1948. McDonald had called for such an officer on September 22, 1948.
153. United States Information Service, established in 1948; under State Department supervision, it set up American libraries abroad to enhance understanding of the United States. The State Department insisted, over Pentagon and CIA objections, that the USIS remain a moderate agency that advertised material advantages of the American way of life. See Lori Lyn Bogle, *The Pentagon's Battle for the American Mind: The Early Cold War* (College Station: Texas A&M University Press, 2004), 89–90.
154. See entry of January 25, 1949.

insurmountable obstacles to effective working with Mapai even though the two labor groups are on essential domestic matters in agreement." As for Herut, McDonald said that the "poor showing demonstrates Department's wisdom in allowing Begin to visit US rather than martyrize him by refusal."[155]

3) I reported on Kohn's's outline of [the] probable procedure at the Constituent Assembly.
4) There was general consensus that it would be useful for me to see Weizmann frequently. Later the service attachés gave me additional advice, which may be difficult for me to follow.

On January 27, Secretary of State Acheson sent a memorandum to the president reminding him of his public comment of October 24, 1948, that the United States would extend de jure recognition to Israel when Israel elected a permanent government. Now that the elections had taken place, Acheson suggested that the United States extend full recognition to Israel and also Transjordan. "Subject to your approval," Acheson also wrote, "it is suggested that our Mission in Tel Aviv become an Embassy and that Mr. James G. McDonald, who is your Special Representative, be named Ambassador to Israel." Truman immediately agreed.[156]

Friday, January 28

Mr. Leon Feldun of MGM,[157] as we promenaded on the roof, made the generous offer of private showing here of any of their films of which they had 16 mm copies. We finally decided that we would postpone showing *The Search* until nearer the time of Zinnemann's projected return[158] and show instead to a few sophisticated friends *State of the Union*.[159] I told Feldun that we would fix the day to suit Ben-Gurion's convenience and invite only those government people who would understand. Feldun was enthusiastic about the possibility of showings on the roof as soon as the weather invited.

Mr. and Mrs. David Wahl,[160] friends of Bart Crum and Abe Feinberg, visited us for nearly an hour. Wahl reported that Bart was trying to "extricate"

---

155. McDonald to secretary of state, no. 61, January 28, 1949, Truman Library, Clifford Papers, Subject File, 1945–54, box 14, folder Palestine—Telegrams and Cables 1 of 2.

156. Acheson to Truman, January 27, 1949, *FRUS*, 1949, v. VI, 702–703.

157. Leon Feldun (1908–2002), motion picture executive and overseas agent with United Artists and Metro Goldwyn Mayer; head of MGM/Israel, 1948–1949.

158. Entry of November 11, 1948.

159. *State of the Union* (1948) directed by Frank Capra for MGM; concerned the attempted manipulation of a presidential election.

160. David R. Wahl (1909–), Library of Congress; 1937–1942; Board of Economic Warfare, 1942–1943; Office of Strategic Services, 1943–1945; secretary, American Jewish Conference, 1946; executive director, Americans for the Haganah (financed by Abe Feinberg), 1947; traveled to Israel, met major figures, and proclaimed Begin was a fascist and a threat to Israeli democracy, 1948–1949. Wahl, as was learned in 2007, had been a Soviet agent since the mid-1930s and in 1948–1949 was handled by the KGB under the cryptonym "Pink." John Earl Haynes, Harvey Klehr, and Alexander Vassiliev, *Spies: The Rise and Fall of the KGB in America* (New Haven: Yale University Press, 2009), 207–212, 328.

himself from the *Star* and was about to set up his own law firm in New York. The future of the *Star* was more than dubious. Wahl said that Feinberg had been instrumental in breaking an initial deadlock on the financing of the Truman campaign, and that, throughout and particularly in the closing weeks when pessimism was nearly universal, he fought valiantly and insisted to the president that, come what may, the latter would have the undying gratitude of the great masses of the American people. Feinberg and Truman were close, the former seeing the latter almost once a week.

According to Wahl, other Jews close to Truman are Governor Herbert L. Lehman, David Dubinsky, and our friend Jacob Potofsky.[161] Others in the intimate circle are Jack Ewing, Sam Rayburn,[162] Scott Lucas,[163] [Alben] Barkley, Anne O'Hare McCormick and, of course, [Matthew] Connolly and [Charles] Ross.[164]

To Abe Feinberg, I sent in substance the following message: 1) the president's policy of independence from Britain had been brilliantly successful and if adhered to would bring peace; 2) the importance of Truman seeing Knox on his return and, if possible, also Klaus and van der Velde; 3) my desire to go to Jerusalem from time to time; 4) the importance of following through on the work begun by Sam Klaus.

Gurdus called with the interesting information that there had been no announcement on the Moscow or satellite radios of the Israel election or its result. Miss Herlitz called to say that the final election results would not be announced until next week. She added that there was no news from Washington except that the de jure papers had been signed; there was no explanation for the delay in the announcement. She added that the news from Rhodes was not encouraging.

The Israelis and Egyptians had deadlocked in the Rhodes talks. The Israeli government asked the US government for its good offices with the Egyptians.[165]

Thinking about this last point, I called Knox and asked whether he thought we might make any suggestions to the Department. I shared his feeling that we had not sufficient data and that he should come out. We decided to send a note next door of inquiry. The answer from Shertok was that he knew nothing and

---

161. Jacob Potofsky, (1894–1979), Ukrainian-born trade unionist; president, Amalgamated Clothing Workers of America, 1946–1972.

162. Samuel Rayburn (1882–1961), Texas Democrat; speaker of the House of Representatives, 1940–1947, 1949–1952, 1955–1961.

163. Scott W. Lucas (1892–1968), Democratic US senator from Illinois, 1939–1951; part of US delegation to Bermuda Conference, April 1943; became majority whip with Truman's support, 1946; provided critical support to Truman in 1948 election; Senate majority leader, 1949–1951.

164. Charles Griffith Ross (1885–1950), Independence, Missouri-born journalist with the *St. Louis Post-Dispatch* 1918–1945; White House press secretary, 1945–1950.

165. Egypt insisted on control of al-Auja, and Israel would not release the Egyptian troops in the Faluja pocket until a satisfactory solution over al-Auja was reached. Acheson to US embassy in Cairo, no. 107, January 28, 1948, *FRUS*, 1949, v. VI, 705–706.

had had no word in twenty-four hours; [he] had sent a "snorter" to his colleagues, and would pass on to us any news.

Tetlie joined us for amusing tea at which Knox was the chief entertainer. Further talk with Tetlie about his work and the possibility of his using Shoshana.[166] Telephoned Chaim Weizmann, who said he would be delighted to see me at tea Shabbat at 4:30. During dinner, [Kenneth] Bilby called to ask if [the] Provisional Government had asked us to suggest that Washington use its good offices to save the Rhodes conference. My answer quite truthfully was, no.

Saturday, January 29

Up disgracefully late after eight. Knox called, but since neither of us had any news except that of the BBC about the Western Union[167] agreeing on recognition—this will apply to Holland, Belgium, Luxembourg and Great Britain,[168] France already having recognized, and the news of Australia's and New Zealand's recognition [both on January 29, 1949]—we decided to say nothing to Washington now about Rhodes.

Out to Weizmann's for tea from approximately a quarter of five to ten minutes of seven. He was in fine form, as was Vera. The following are the chief points discussed:

1) The dinner in New York to be postponed to April 23 because of: a) Weizmann's health; and b) the necessity that he be present at and following the convening of the Constituent Assembly.
2) The elections had at first disappointed Weizmann because of the vote given to Herut, but on later consideration, Weizmann had come to regard it as an epoch-marking proof of the soundness of the Zionist ideal. The quietness of the operation, the large participation, all had contributed to this impression.
3) Ben-Gurion was for the first time spoken of by Weizmann with warmth and enthusiasm. Weizmann said that he recognized the value of the extremely difficult work that the prime minister had done.
4) Weizmann's opening address at the Constituent Assembly was then discussed at length. I urged Lincoln's inaugurals and the final address of Moses as models in their brevity, their elevation of thought, their appeal to the best in their hearers. Weizmann said he knew the latter well, and could I find copies of the former for him. Reluctantly, I had to suggest that he ask his office to secure them. Weizmann will, I think, make the most of his opportunity. It will not be a political address, but rather a conception of what Israel can be, of its role as an intellectual and creative force in the world, as something new and distinctive, the realization of a dream delayed in its fulfillment thousands of years. He spoke of the creation of Israel as possibly

166. See entry of October 12, 1948.
167. Based on the March 1948 Treaty of Brussels, which created common institutions aimed at collective security.
168. These recognitions did not begin until May 1949.

the great event in our century. Despite its smallness, it can, he believes, be made a blessing. Here, however, standards are higher than those expected or observed elsewhere, and must be the rule, for in this tiny state will be centered the microscopes of the world. Israel's re-creation is a proof of its uniqueness. Weizmann then went on to develop again his thesis about the need for Israel to become the Switzerland of the Middle East, with a university or technical school for each 500,000 people.

5) Weizmann was much interested in what His Holiness had said to me about the US's relations to Israel as compared with those to the Vatican.[169] He spoke of the family relationship between Israel and the Church.

As I was leaving Weizmann said that we had had a real schmooze.

Sunday, January 30

Lunch with the Viteleses at the Kaete Dan. Were joined there by Frank Kingdon and his new actress wife.[170] The latter was a young and friendly, attractive person. Seeing Dr. Mohn come in alone, I joined him for a little while at his table. As usual I learned something by my talk: 1) The Turkish member of the Conciliation Commission [Hussein C. Yalçin][171] favors changing the site of the commission to somewhere outside of Palestine, but Wilkins stands for remaining in Jerusalem. 2) The Turk appears to favor the Commission limiting itself to conciliation and leaving to the acting mediator's organization [the] truce and related matters.

The Kingdons came out to tea. While the women gossiped about the Kingdons' romance, Kingdon and I talked about developments here and in the States. He contributed the following items: 1) Bart Crum's casual taking of *PM* with no knowledge of balance sheet or of the paper. In Kingdon's opinion, Bart was brought in on a salary. Now Bart is getting out. 2) Perhaps closest of all at the moment to Truman is Clifford, because it was the latter who called the tune about the electoral campaign. Others close are the same as before including Rosenman, Lehman, Dubinsky, Potofsky, the several leaders in the House and Senate, and Jack Ewing and Dave Niles. The latter probably not as close as the others.

169. Entry of August 10, 1948.
170. Frank Kingdon (1894–1972), London-born Methodist minister and educator in New Jersey; fought antisemitism and advocated open doors in Palestine and the United States for Jewish refugees before and during World War II; served for twelve years on executive committee of the National Conference of Christians and Jews; editorial columnist for *New York Post*; suspected of communist sympathies owing to his liberal politics.
171. Hussein Cahit Yalçin (1875–1957), Turkish political scientist, diplomat, and representative to the PCC. Turkey had opposed Palestine's partition and was now cautious toward Israel. By March 1949 Yalçin reported to Ankara that Israel would likely not become communist. On March 28, 1949, because of the US support of Israel, Turkey became the first Muslim state to recognize Israel.

To Ben Gurion's house at 10:30 with Ruth. Paula opened the door for us and told me to go upstairs to see her husband. I found him in bed covered with three or four doubled over blankets engaged in signing a whole stack of some sort of official Hebrew documents. Our talk was rather general, but it disclosed his intentions to have as broad a cabinet as is consistent with collective responsibility. He would not have Mapam in the government unless its leaders would agree to support cabinet policies in the assembly. He hopes to include also the Orthodox, or at least sections of it. He intimated that he thought the Orthodox bloc might split. He was emphatic that the principle of equality for women and men must be accepted. I told him of my talk Saturday with Weizmann and of the latter's cordial praise of Ben-Gurion's accomplishments. I think he was glad to have the news but seemed to take it with a grain of salt. I urged him to come on Thursday night to see *State of the Union*. When I described it to him, he said that the test of democracy is the permission for criticism. For an hour, Ruth and I were at Dr. Bernard Zondek's. If he is as competent as he was thorough, he will be helpful. Incidentally, he said that despite the very heavy strain under which Ben-Gurion had been working, he was on the whole well.[172]

On January 31, 1949 at 4:00 pm, President Truman signed the following:

"On October 24, 1948, the President stated that when a permanent government was elected in Israel, it would promptly be given de jure recognition. Elections for such a government were held on January 25. The votes have now been counted and this government has been officially informed of the results. The United States Government is therefore pleased to extend de jure recognition to the Government of Israel as of this date."[173]

Several days earlier McDonald had written Frieda Warburg: "If this [progress] continues at the present rate, it is not unreasonable to expect that in another six months or so we shall be able to look upon Israel as having passed out of its adolescence into . . . young manhood. Of course, after that, there will be many problems still unsolved. I am convinced, however, that on the record none of these tasks will be insurmountable."[174]

172. McDonald reported the meeting with Weizmann on January 29 and the meeting with Ben-Gurion on January 31 in no. 71 [attention Clifford and secretary], February 1, 1949, NARA, RG 59, MC 1390, reel 18, frames 398–399.

173. Epstein to Shertok, January 31, 1949, *DFPI* v. 2, d. 360.

174. McDonald to Frieda Warburg, January 26, 1949, McDonald Papers, USHMM, box 7, folder 10.

8. February 1949

An hour and a quarter session with Shertok at the Foreign Office. I presented the Department's formal note of full recognition, after which there were mutual congratulations.[1] Then Shertok settled down to a lengthy discussion of a number of points.

1) The prime minister's speech the night previous. Each of the four principles had been aimed in specific directions. The first and the second about cabinet responsibility [of all coalition partners for government policies] and [friendship toward the US and] Russia were directed at Mapam; the one on labor controls was addressed to the right; and that on women's equality [regardless of religion], at the Orthodox. He then cited examples of women's inequality in the rabbinic law in courts, divorce, inheritance, etc.[2]

2) The new cabinet would probably include five or six Mapai; two Mapam, though they might [hold] out for three; in any case everything would be settled as nearly as possible on the proportional principle. Possibly there might be added ministries, which would not be included in the cabinet, to help satisfy certain groups. In any event, there would be a new cabinet post, minister of education.

3) At Rhodes, al-Auja continued to be the sticking point, but a formula seemed possible.[3] A hopeful sign was the direct statement to Shiloah by an Arab that he thought there would be agreement. As to Bunche's invitation to conduct other armistice negotiations at Rhodes, the Provisional Government was accepting but with two conditions; a) that no definite time be fixed until the Egyptian negotiations be concluded; and b) that the other negotiations be not pooled.[4]

4) Negotiations continuing with Transjordan (of this more later).

---

1. Discussed more extensively in McDonald to secretary of state, no. 76, February 1, 1949; McDonald to secretary of state, no. 81, February 1, 1949, NARA, RG 59, MC 1390, reel 18, frames 400–401, 402–405.
2. Given over state radio. "Ben Gurion Outlines Mapai's Conditions for Coalition," *Palestine Post*, February 1, 1949.
3. See entry of January 25, 1949.
4. McDonald reported on this exchange between Bunche and the Israeli government in McDonald to secretary of state, no. 79, February 1, 1949, *FRUS*, 1949, v. VI, 715.

5) As to the Palestine Conciliation Commission [PCC], no one seemed to know quite what it would do or how or when. Azcárate's idea was to have the PCC exercise its good offices with no thought of an elaborate report.[5]

6) The military government of Jerusalem is to be dismantled immediately and the city assimilated in its administration with the rest of Israel. The new representative there will be a kind of district commissioner, perhaps Avraham Bergman, Joseph's assistant. Joseph may go into the cabinet, certainly Goldie Meyerson will. The change of Jerusalem's status "does not necessarily imply a unilateral move towards annexation." It was at this point that I spoke of the implications of the American representative's attendance at the ceremonial opening of the Constituent Assembly in Jerusalem [on February 14]. Shertok said that such attendance would not imply recognition of Jerusalem as part of the state of Israel.

7) With special emphasis on secrecy, Shertok told of Sasson's negotiations with Abdullah, January 31.

McDonald reported Shertok's news that on January 31, Israeli representatives went to Transjordan at the king's invitation. The main points were Abdullah's statement that "he desired peace and that [the] war was not really war but more like an unpleasant incident between friends;" that the British had no objections to the meeting and "gave [the] King [a] free hand except on certain undisclosed points;" and that if Bunche invited Transjordan to negotiate at Rhodes, the king would send an envoy. Shertok said he was baffled at the undisclosed points.[6]

8) I asked Shertok whether anything had been settled about the rank of the American and Provisional Government representatives. He replied that there had been no time to think about it. As to whether Epstein would remain, the reply was that he would if Shertok had the decision, but it was not solely his.

Tea at the Tolkowskys',[7] which made me want to return to visit his library more at leisure. UN wire from Griffis about his planned arrival at Haifa early February 4, to which I replied, urging him to stop at Tel Aviv.

On the evening of February 1, the Israeli government announced the end of military government in Jewish Jerusalem and the inauguration of municipal rule as in other Israeli cities. McDonald quickly reported, "In order to avoid misunderstanding, [the Foreign Minister] explained [that] this action was administrative and not repeat not [an]

5. The PCC had had its first meeting in Geneva on January 17, 1949, and had moved its seat to Jerusalem on the insistence of the French representative, de Boisanger, on January 24.

6. McDonald to secretary of state, no. 80, February 1, 1949, NARA, RG 59, MC 1390, reel 18, frame 393.

7. Shmuel Tolkowsky, (1886–1965), served under Weizmann as member of London Zionist Political Committee, 1916–1918; secretary, Zionist delegation at Paris Peace Conference, 1919; Israeli consul general and then ambassador to Switzerland, 1949–1956; father of Dan Tolkowsky, later commander of the Israeli Air Force.

annexation of Jerusalem. Reason [for the] change is that [the] present setup with [the]
Military Governor and Mayor is confusing and duplicating. New arrangement will ap-
point [a] District Commissioner [the] same as in Haifa and each [Government] Ministry
will hold itself responsible for respective functions in Jerusalem."[8]

Acheson quickly responded to Israel's invitation to the diplomatic corps to attend
the February 14, 1949 ceremonial opening of the Constituent Assembly in Jerusalem:
"[The Department] has serious doubts . . . concerning advisability of any American
*reps [in] Palestine [*sic*] attending [the] opening assembly.*"[9]

Wednesday, February 2

Received wire from Griffis that he would skip Haifa and land in Tel Aviv about nine on Friday.

From twelve until a quarter past one, Eliahu Sasson, [the] Provisional Government's chief Arab negotiator, and Miss Herlitz were at the house. Sasson reported on [the] "frank and friendly" secret conference he had with Abdullah in [king's palace at Shuneh on January 30] as follows[10]:

1) Abdullah anxious for speedy peace negotiations, which should follow immediately after arrangement [of the] armistice, which in his opinion should involve slight difficulty. Favors public peace negotiations in Jerusalem between Transjordan and Israel, initial meeting preferably in Amman. Has notified all Arab governments of his plan and has received assent from Yemen, Saudi Arabia, and Iraq. Egypt and Syria not pleased, but "must follow since I (Abdullah) have decided." Has been assured by two Iraqi high officials, and expects soon to receive similar from Regent [Iraqi Crown Prince Abd al-Ilah] that Transjordan's difficulties with Iraq will disappear.

2) Abdullah attributes his hurry to fear that delay will involve loss. Britain, he says, is using delay in Israel-Transjordan negotiations to gain concessions from other Arab states, notably Syria. King quoted this alleged British argument: "If Abdullah is blocked, what will Syria pay?"

3) Abdullah declined [to] indicate reservations which Britain had imposed on his negotiations with Israel. Will reveal them only after armistice and during peace talks. Inferentially, he permitted [the] conclusion that Aqaba and southern Negev were involved. Transjordan, he said, is not interested in

---

8. McDonald to secretary of state, No. 78, February 1, 1949, NARA, RG 84, E 2774, box 3, folder 350.

9. Burdett to secretary of state, no. 94, February 1, 1949; Acheson to Jerusalem [for Ethridge], no. 62, February 2, 1949, *FRUS*, 1949, v. VI, 717–718.

10. After more than a month of feelers between Shiloah and Dayan on the Israeli side and al-Tel on the Transjordanian side, more formal but still secret negotiations between the two sides began on January 3, 1949. Eliahu Sasson, chief of the Middle East Department in the Israeli Foreign Ministry, who had been acquainted with King Abdullah since 1947 and was a proponent of direct negotiations, was one of Israel's chief negotiators. The primary issues were the division of Jerusalem, the status of the southern Negev plus possible Jordanian corridors to Gaza, and the border between Israel and Samaria/Judea, expected to be annexed by Transjordan. The delegations and their complicated dynamics are covered in Bar-Joseph, *The Best of Enemies*, 150–195.

Negev, "has enough desert land." Gaza, however, as outlet to sea, now that Haifa has been lost, is vital to Transjordan.

4) Abdullah is opposed to the internationalization of whole or part [of] Jerusalem; favors partition, with Old and portion of New City assigned to Transjordan and rest to Israel, both portions remaining under some form of UN supervision. No details [of] such partition were discussed.

5) Arab refugees, Abdullah said, were now no important problem, and after peace [the issue] will solve itself.

6) Had accepted Bunche's invitation [to] armistice negotiations at Rhodes, because all other Arab states had agreed. He is opposed, however, to pooled discussions and reiterated preference [for] direct negotiations with Israel.

7) Abdullah thinks PCC will waste time and delay settlement. Says peace should be possible before Commission has opportunity [to] acquaint itself with problem and before it could report [to] Assembly in September.

8) Israel's elections had pleased Abdullah because they disclosed such slight communist strength. Transjordan, he said, doesn't need elections. He rules, and parliament carries out his will.

9) Interrupting his report of Abdullah's views, Sasson emphasized that from the Provisional Government's viewpoint, armistices would suffice for many months with all the Arab states except Transjordan. With the latter, peace is necessary because the partition of Palestine is involved, and [there are] many questions other than purely military ones that must be settled by formal treaty.

10) In answer [to] my questions, Sasson insisted that the only "ultimatum" to Transjordan which might have been referred to in the report to the Department from Transjordan at the end of December was his open telegram from Paris [in] November to Transjordan's prime minister [Tewfik Abu al-Huda] asking that the convoy be allowed, as previously agreed, to go to Mount Scopus in order "to avoid incidents."[11] Reply within twenty-four hours was friendly, and Amman issued orders to Jerusalem to permit convoy. Subsequent exchanges all friendly.

11) According [to] Sasson, Abdullah denied categorically knowing in advance or having been asked about sending British troops to Aqaba [in] early January. After their arrival, he was presented with paper asking for troops for his signature.

12) King told Sasson he is deeply appreciative of recognition as sign [of] US friendship, adding that he hoped the American government would increasingly interest itself in Transjordan-Israeli relations, and intimated desire [to] lessen [the] degree [of] British tutelage.[12]

11. On the mistaken ultimatum, see entry of December 31, 1948.
12. Summary report in McDonald to secretary of state, no. 88, February 3, 1949, *FRUS*, 1949, v. VI, 721–722.

Knox came at five, just as I was finishing the above summary. After his corrections, the telegram was ready for dispatch tomorrow. At tea, Ruth gave Knox his instructions, which he "carried out most expeditiously," because before he left came the telegram from Washington asking us to inquire of the Provisional Government if they would accept to exchange ambassadors. Knox and I talked of a number of other matters including

1) The need to clarify the right of Crosby[13] in Haifa to do independent political reporting;
2) I approved Knox's comprehensive and strict memorandum against the bringing in by any members of the staff of goods for resale, or of purchasing in Cyprus or elsewhere articles for any non-American members of the staff, or for anyone outside the staff. This rule did not preclude small inexpensive occasional gifts. There have been no violations to date, but the memorandum is intended to preclude such;
3) Knox and I agreed on a letter to Mark Ethridge about my coming up [to Jerusalem] to see him. We sent it up by Mr. English,[14] who stopped at the house while here to get the Jerusalem pouch.

> *Dear Mr. Ethridge,*
>
> *The Department has approved my going to Jerusalem in order that I might have the benefit of one or two long talks with you. I suggest that I arrive there Sunday [February 6]—here in Israel we unfortunately have gotten out of the habit of regarding Sunday as a day of rest. . . .*
>
> *As Mr. Burdett will explain to you, the most secure way to communicate with me is by wire from the Consulate. You can, or course, telephone [,] but the [telephone] wire is open to the public.*
>
> *If your wife has come with you,[15] tell her that I am confident she will find Israel even more stimulating for her literary gift than was Greece.[16]*

4) We were delighted to learn from English that Mr. Ford,[17] whom he knows well, is an excellent man, solid, able, and livable.

About ten o'clock Knox unexpectedly arrived. Having heard on the radio that the UK was about to designate its representative to the Provisional

13. Richard Crosby, vice consul, US consulate general in Jerusalem.
14. Possibly Clifton P. English, the US vice consul in Basra.
15. Willie Snow Ethridge (1902–1982), journalist and writer of some fifteen books including the travelogues. *It's Greek to Me* (1948) and *Going to Jerusalem* (1950).
16. McDonald to Ethridge, February 2, 1949, McDonald papers, Columbia University, box 11, folder 20.
17. Richard Ford, who would replace Knox as McDonald's counselor of embassy, and who was formally assigned on February 4.

Government, Knox thought that we should rush to get the latter's answer to the Department's query about the raised status of the mission here. I telephoned our neighbor [Shertok] who was having a dinner party, and he said he would let us know as soon as he was free. A little after eleven, Knox and I went over. Walter Elliot and some of the other guests had just left.[18] Shiloah was present as we then talked. Both men [Shertok and Shiloah] were obviously pleased by the American invitation, but Shertok promptly began to suggest possible disadvantages, including higher costs and greater difficulty finding suitable personnel. Interestingly, he asked whether, if the US had the first ambassador, our representative would continue then to be the dean of the diplomatic corps even after the USSR had raised the status of its mission. Knox's answer was yes. Shiloah mentioned the status of Cairo and Iraq and of the recent elevation of the mission in Saudi Arabia.[19] Knox and I left with the impression that the Provisional Government's answer would be affirmative.

On February 1, the British government announced that it would extend de facto recognition of Israel.[20]

Thursday, February 3

Before breakfast, I dictated and sent by hand to Shertok a note, in which I made the following personal and unofficial suggestion.

> *Israel in the nature of things is and must remain primarily a symbol of a dream fulfilled and of a larger promise held out. Hence, whatever adds dignity and prestige strengthens the State, not only among Jews here and everywhere but also among its neighbors who more than most other peoples equate prestige with strength. Hence, I conclude that the additional expense incident to the higher status would be more than balanced by the enhanced prestige of Israel—an enhancement which might help to hasten the establishment of peace.[21]*

A few hours later, Shertok telephoned me at the office saying that the answer was "yes" with profound gratitude. There was, however, no indication from any source about the name of the first ambassador to Israel.

---

18. Walter Elliot (1888–1958), Scottish unionist politician who served in Neville Chamberlain's cabinet and who also served on the League of Nations Sixth Committee (Legal Affairs) in 1937, advocating the partition of Palestine.
19. The US legation in Jiddah was officially raised to embassy status on March 18, 1949. J. Rives Childs (1893–1987), previously the US minister, presented his credentials as ambassador.
20. Meeting between Linton and Bevin, February 1, 1949, *DFPI*, v. 2, d. 367.
21. McDonald to Shertok, February 3, 1949, McDonald Papers, USHMM, box 7, folder 11.

Epstein reported to Tel Aviv on February 1 that "Niles informed me confidentially [that the] President, although pressed by many friends applying for Tel Aviv post, [has] decided [to] reappoint McDonald."[22]

Our first movie party seemed a great success.[23] [Guests included government officials including the Ben-Gurions and Shiloah, private businessmen including Sam Sacks; Hadassah figures including Ida Davidowicz, and visiting Americans including Frank Kingdon]. The movie, *State of the Union*, was both from the point of view of sight and sound on a par with the one of the theater. Everyone, including the Ben-Gurions, were pleased.

Particularly happy were the Kingdons, for Frank was given an opportunity to talk with Ben-Gurion, thus escaping having to leave Israel without having seen the prime minister. The latter appeared to be very tired, so much so that Knox wished the next day to send a telegram about it. Although Ben-Gurion and some others were in the study for half an hour or so after the movie during refreshments, there was no political talk to be recorded. Except that I should perhaps add that Ben-Gurion solicitously inquired if I had been designated for the new post. I gave him an autographed copy of the picture taken at our formal reception, which obviously pleased him.

On February 3, the PCC held its first formal meeting in Jerusalem and prepared to embark on a "pre-negotiation" tour of Tel Aviv and the Arab capitals.[24] *The PCC represented a separate UN diplomatic track than the direct armistice negotiations at Rhodes, which were aimed strictly at cease-fires and armistice lines.*[25]

In establishing the PCC in its December 11, 1948, resolution, the UN General Assembly had called for the return of Palestinian Arab refugees to their homes or for compensation if they could not return and had charged the PCC with creating recommendations. The US government supported the resolution, Truman adding his backing in a public statement of January 14, 1949. On February 3, Acheson asked McDonald to formulate his views on the refugee question "within framework [of] final peaceful settlement [of the] Pal[estine] problem. Without approaching [the] Israeli Gov[ernment], what is your estimate [regarding] its intentions [to] permit repatriation and [its] ability reabsorb refugees?"[26]

Friday, February 4

Up at the crack of dawn to meet Griffis and his party at the Tel Aviv airport. Miss Herlitz and Mr. Simon arrived just after I did. Taking advantage of

22. Epstein to Shertok, February 1, 1949, *DFPI*, v. 2, d. 366.
23. McDonald found that movies were an inexpensive way to entertain given the mission's limited budget. See McDonald to Halsey and Janet Barrett, February 18, 1949, McDonald Papers, USHMM, box 7, folder 11.
24. Caplan, *Futile Diplomacy*, v. 3, 59–62
25. Overview of the PCC in ibid., 57–76.
26. Acheson to McDonald, no. 64, February 3, 1949, *FRUS*, 1949, v. VI, 722–723.

our chance for a private talk, I suggested to Miss Herlitz that a communication to Epstein in Washington might be helpful, particularly if Abe Feinberg would emphasize the importance with Clark Clifford or Truman of the avoidance of misinterpretation at the historic [first Knesset] meeting [in Jerusalem] on the 14th. Later, Miss Herlitz told me she thought Epstein would remain at his post, and that certainly, Nahum Goldmann would not go to London, and she gave me the name of the man who would.[27]

Included in Griffis's party, besides his secretary and valet, was Dr. Jack Dinham Cottrell of the World Health Organization.[28] Griffis could not have been more cordial. After very brief delay, he and I drove in one car, and the others followed in the Israeli car to our house. Griffis was properly impressed with the bustling, energetic Tel Aviv in such contrast to the lackadaisical atmosphere of most of the Middle East. He was impressed too by our house and by the views from the roof. Almost immediately, Griffis and Miss Herlitz and I drove to Ben-Gurion's house.

The prime minister was up and looking very much more rested than last night. He and Griffis seemed to hit it off. Certainly, the latter expressed the highest opinion of the former as a learned person and one of driving energy. After explaining to the prime minister at the latter's request the general nature of the organization and its work, Griffis asked the prime minister that the Provisional Government make a contribution in kind in oranges and perhaps in rough textiles for the Arab refugees. The oranges could be delivered by truck to the lines near Gaza and in Jerusalem, where UN trucks would take over. Ben-Gurion, after asking what other countries were doing, said categorically that Israel would aid. A formal request is expected soon.

Though Griffis disavowed his right to discuss any political matters, he dropped from time to time into a discussion of the chances of peace. He was optimistic. Earlier, he told me that he understood that the Egyptians and the Jews had about reached agreement at Rhodes. Griffis repeatedly contrasted the backwardness of the Arabs with the progressiveness of the Jews. He foresaw Israel as a stimulating force throughout the area. He spoke of the high percentage of disease among the Egyptians, but must not have studied the problem much because the word Bilharzia meant nothing to him.[29] He spoke, too, almost contemptuously of the masses of the Arab refugees.

On the question of refugees' resettlement, Griffis did not take exception to Ben-Gurion's emphatic statement that their return could only be discussed for

27. Ivor Joseph Linton remained Israel's representative in London until April 1949, when Mordechai Eliash became the Israeli representative. See entry of February 15, 1949.
28. Jack Dinham Cottrell (1903–1989), London-born doctor; served in New Zealand Army Medical Corps during World War II; headed infectious disease hospital in Egypt, 1940; director of health with UNRRA mission in Austria, 1946–1947; served in World Health Organization in Europe, East Mediterranean, and the Far East, 1947–1964; chief of health section for Arab refugees for United Nations Relief and Works Agency for Palestine Refugees, 1949.
29. Schistosomiasis, a parasitic infection common to countries lacking proper clean water and sanitation facilities.

any considerable number of them as part of a peace settlement, or when peace had been established. Griffis said that the problem would tend to solve itself, provided the refugees were not induced to remain uprooted by being fed in large camps. As to the number of refugees, Griffis was very vague, saying that the estimates range from 900,000 to less than 400,000. He thought it impossible to do more than make a guess, since interested parties tended to exaggerate the figures and because there could be no accurate system of registration, since individuals moved from place to place, sold their food cards, and in other ways made close control impractical.

Griffis asked me to do three things:

1) Discourage Sol Bloom's[30] threat to make the 16 million dollar appropriation conditioned on or limited to comparable amounts raised outside the US.[31] So serious was he about this, that he said, should the US fail to carry out the president's suggestion, the whole relief program would fail, and he would be so discredited that he would leave the Middle East after dark and be unable to return even to his post in Cairo;
2) Telegraph the Department of his visit, of Ben-Gurion's pledge, and suggest publicity about this latter.
3) Use my influence in Switzerland to have de Reynier recalled. As to this, I said I would consider whether I could appeal to Rappard.

On the whole, my impression of Griffis was that he was a hard-hitting, direct businessman with no interest in details or understanding of general principles or theories, but that nonetheless, by conducting his buying and delivery operation on a rigidly practical basis, and by keeping supplies strictly out of the hands of governments, he was much better for the job than [Bayard] Dodge would have been.[32] The latter, Griffis said, was being useful.

Telegram from [Mark] Ethridge to the effect that in the light of conditions [in Jerusalem], and the possibility that my visit would be misunderstood, and since he had been planning to come to Tel Aviv, he would come to see me Sunday morning and return that afternoon. I wired that I would be delighted to see him and urged him to spend the night.

Knox improved my telegram to the Department about the [Constituent Assembly] meeting of February 14th by suggesting that formal acceptance might be coupled with the reservation about November 29. Our argument, in effect, was that [our] absence would be resented, and in the event that our

30. Sol Bloom (1870–1949), Democratic US representative from New York's 19th congressional district, 1922–1949; one of three US representatives to the Bermuda Conference, 1943; chair, House Foreign Affairs Committee, 1939–1947, 1949.

31. Refers to Truman's desire to cover half of the $29.5 million called for by UN General Assembly Resolution of November 19, 1948, to care for 479,000 Palestinian refugees until August 31, 1949. See entries of November 18, 1948, and December 7, 1948. The House and Senate passed the aid package with only minor amendments, and Truman signed it on March 24, 1949.

32. See entries of November 19, 21–23, and 28–29, 1948.

northern friends [the Soviets] were present, might jeopardize our interests here. A secondary argument was that our presence would not mean assent to absorption, and that the historical nature of the occasion would increase the popular and governmental hurt feeling at [our] abstention.

Ruth and Bobby and I were sitting in the living room about eleven at night when a troop of the staff, Knox, Hope, Barnes, Colonel Archibald, Captain Cashman, John Carlson, and Tetlie, rushed in with the message from the Department that "Department pleased inform you President has approved your designation Ambassador to Israel. Department will proceed request agreement if designation agreeable to you." To this I replied, "For Acheson. I accept with great pleasure honor of being designated Ambassador to Israel. Please express to President my deep appreciation his and Department's confidence." It was heartening to feel that one's colleagues—not to speak of one's family—were so genuinely thrilled.

Saturday, February 5

Most of the morning on the roof reading despite the increasing evidences of a new storm. Then over to Mrs. Hadassah Samuel's where the three of us had a pleasant visit with David and Dan and their mother. The talk covered a wide range of Israeli domestic and foreign politics.

Sunday, February 6

Knox came in during my breakfast. For an hour and a half, he and I checked over and disposed of a large accumulation of reports and other material. I was chiefly interested in the intimations from Damascus of increased strain with Amman; the several reports from Prague about Israeli purchases there and alleged training of military personnel;[33] Damascus reports that legation and intelligence officers of three Western powers had identical information that area communist activities were concentrated in Haifa, where "tolerant attitude of Government increased possibility success;" Damascus report that [the] present head of the military [Husni al-Za'im][34] was suspected by president [Shukri al-Quwatli] of flirtations with Abdullah; Damascus report that Fawzi al-Qawuqji had deliberately failed in recent northern operation in cooperation [with] Abdullah; a number of tendentious clippings sent by several missions.

Cyril H. A. Marriott, British consul at Haifa and ad interim representative to Israel, visited for about an hour.[35] His purpose evidently was to learn whether or not we were accepting the Provisional Government's invitation for

---

33. Substantial Israeli arms purchases continued in Czechoslovakia after the War of Independence until early 1951. See Bialer, *Between East and West*, 175–180; Uri Bialer, "Israel's Global Foreign Policy, 1948–1956," in *New Perspectives on Israeli History: The Early Years of the State*, ed. Laurence J. Silberstein (New York: New York University Press, 1991), 232–234.

34. See editorial note in entry of April 6, 1949.

35. See entries of August 3, 1948, and October 17, 1948.

the 14th. I said that we had asked for instructions. He continued that he had verbally accepted before knowing that the place was to be Jerusalem and subsequently had secured tacit assent of the Foreign Office for attendance at Jerusalem. Was going to check about Russian plans and would inform me. Marriott commented critically on Eban's "bad manners" and "ugly looks." His comments were more favorable about Shertok. He expects the British mission to number about 25.

Just after he left, Mark Ethridge and Fraser Wilkins arrived. They had been delayed by road conditions and by an accident. Unable to spend the night, they planned to be on the way back at 3:15 in order [to] reach Jerusalem before dark. In answer to my question, Ethridge said that it was planned that Bunche's organization should continue with its armistice efforts while PCC concentrated on peace treaties. Who would control the truce supervision was not clear. Wilkins said the force would be radically reduced. Ethridge agreed with my idea that the PCC would be well advised to eschew the truce responsibilities if possible, for these could bring only embarrassment and possible interference with the peace efforts. [The] PCC is holding [a] meeting tomorrow morning at ten, and tomorrow night [is] to have conference with Shertok in latter's Jerusalem residence. This to be followed the next day by conference with foreign minister of Transjordan[36] in Jericho. Thereafter, PCC going [to] Cairo, Jidda, Damascus, Baghdad, Beirut, Amman, returning [to] Tel Aviv in a fortnight.

(Before dinner we sent Bobby over to Shertok's house to ascertain whether we could come over to see him for a few minutes.) The answer was regret that other engagements made this impossible. In the light of what Ethridge told me following the meal, I could understand better his and Wilkins's concern linked with something akin to amazement when I read to them the president's letter of November 29 to Weizmann.[37] The portion about the Negev particularly brought starts from both of the visitors. Later, Ethridge expressed the tentative opinion that Truman had probably changed his mind, in part because of the communist success in China. Now Truman was urging the Provisional Government to be generous in the use of its victory. I couldn't but observe mentally that this was a sound premise only if the Arabs did not take advantage of it to become more intransigent. Truman seemed to feel, according to Ethridge, that because the US had taken such an active part in securing November 29 and its subsequent actions, it could reasonably ask cooperation from the Provisional Government.

After Ethridge left, I had the feeling that he would concentrate on practical solutions rather than seeking to fit stubborn facts into preconceived formulae. As he was leaving, I urged him to talk with Monsignor McMahon on the moot question of the extent to which France is, in matters affecting Jerusalem

36. Tawfiq Abu al-Huda (1894–1956), twelve-time prime minister, including December 1947–May 1949, and acting foreign minister; not as interested as King Abdullah in making a formal peace with Israel.

37. Described in entry of November 28, 1948, concerning Israel keeping the Negev.

or Church claims in Israel, representative of the Vatican. I told him that I doubted that Paris was speaking for Rome. He had heard somewhere that the Vatican was supporting Italy's claim to be "the protector of the Holy City." That, too, I told him I very much doubted.

In Rhodes, the Israeli and Egyptian delegations remained at an impasse concerning the Negev. On January 31, 1949, Bunche proposed the withdrawal of Israeli forces from the Negev to the north and the pullback of Egyptian forces from the Palestine region entirely. Exceptions would be Israeli defensive forces in the Negev settlements and Egyptian defensive forces in the Gaza Strip. The Israelis insisted on maintaining forces in Be'er Sheva, Bir 'Asluj, and the strategic crossroads of al-Auja. The Egyptians, who had initially called for a return to the battle lines of October 14, 1948 as per the Security Council's resolution of November 4, 1948, insisted that nothing would be left of that resolution should the Israelis have their way. The Israelis responded that they could not be expected to surrender hard-won gains, thus putting the Negev at renewed risk.

Bunche threatened to refer the matter to the Security Council and to blame Israel for the deadlock. Truman worried that the talks would break down. On February 5 Acheson told Epstein that "the President believed that this was the psychological moment when an armistice could be brought about without injury to the vital interests of any of the parties, if the Israeli Government would approach these discussions in the spirit of broad statesmanship and make concessions which were wholly in accord with the moral position of Israel."[38]

Acheson ordered McDonald to approach the Israeli government with the same request, making it clear that Truman had taken a personal interest.[39] McDonald presented to Shertok a brief memorandum stating that "the United States Government now desires to state its earnest hope that the Government of Israel will be able to make a special effort at accommodation in order to accept the draft of the Acting Mediator as a possible basis for agreement."[40]

Immediately after Ethridge and Wilkins left, Knox and I went over to Shertok's office. There we delivered verbally a paraphrase of the telegram received a few hours earlier from the Department, appealing to the Provisional Government to accept the acting mediator's compromise proposal of a few days earlier, which the Department had been informed from Cairo had been accepted "in principle [subject to only minor modifications]."

Before Knox gave the verbal paraphrase, I told Shertok of Ethridge's concern about the rumors in Jerusalem of a municipal election and a declaration of

38. Patterson to secretary of state, no. 131, February 2, 1949, *FRUS*, 1949, v. VI, 718–719; Memorandum by McClintock to secretary of state, February 4, 1949, *FRUS*, 1949, v. VI, 723–724; Memorandum by Acheson, February 5, 1949, *FRUS*, 1949, v. VI, 725–727; and especially Memorandum by Acheson, February 5, 1949, *FRUS*, 1949, v. VI, 727–729.

39. Acheson to McDonald, no. 75, February 5, 1949, *FRUS*, 1949, v. VI, 730–731.

40. Memorandum dated February 6, 1949, NARA, RG 84, entry 2774, box 2, folder 321.9.

annexation, and also of Ethridge's desire at the request of the PCC to remain at Shertok's after the PCC met on Monday evening. To the last Shertok assented cordially, but as to the first two, he was categorical that:

1) The government and the party of which he is a member and which "exercises some influence" has no present intention of initiating either of the rumored moves. He could not, of course, promise that Begin or some other extremist might not have made such a proposal. Personally, he considered that raising these possibilities, even informally, might have the unfortunate effect of putting ideas in people's heads. On this last point, I gently demurred.

2) As to the Rhodes impasse, which centers now on the exact extent of the Provisional Government's withdrawal from al-Auja, Shertok was inclined to blame Bunche's recent compromise proposal, which the Foreign Ministry said had had the effect of stiffening the Egyptian position. The Provisional Government had yielded as much as it could by agreeing to withdraw from al-Auja itself into the nearby neighborhood and by agreeing that the site of the seat of the armistice commission should be this side of Egyptian territory. There was not much time for a full discussion since Shertok had to hurry off to a cabinet meeting at four, and I had to be at the RCA at 4:15. Knox stayed behind to talk over details with Shiloah.[41]

I had to wait only a few minutes for my call from Abe Feinberg. The connection was good, but because he had not had the word from Washington, which I hoped would have reached him about the complication of my attendance on February 14, I had difficulty making him understand. Finally, however, he got the point and said that he would act. He agreed also to follow up on the 16 million dollar grant with a view to removing the Sol Bloom objection that [the grant] should be conditional on comparable grants on this side. I repeated to Feinberg what Griffis had said, adding that I shared this opinion. Feinberg asked me if I had heard any good news to which I answered in the affirmative. I asked if there would be difficulty on the Hill. He said he did not think so.

Ethridge [had earlier] expressed concern at rumors in Jerusalem and at the implications in the statement by Moshe Dayan and other Israel officials that municipal elections in New City might be decreed and that there might be even a declaration of annexation by the Constituent Assembly.[42] Knox and I

41. Shertok insisted that the Israeli army maintain a defensive presence in the al-Auja area, if not in the town itself, but that Egypt could station defensive units facing al-Auja on its side of the frontier. Shertok also noted that Israel, after insisting on a full Egyptian pullout from the Gaza Strip, was willing to concede the presence of light Egyptian forces there. He reminded McDonald that, because Egypt was the invader, Israel should not be the country that had to retreat. McDonald theorized that the Israelis feared a reconstituted Egyptian force. McDonald to secretary of state, no. 101, February 6, 1949, *FRUS*, 1949, v. VI, 731–732.

42. There was no such declaration, but in March 1949 the Israeli government appointed a new municipal council for Jerusalem, which in turn pressed for annexation.

said that we had no information to this effect and were not inclined to credit the Provisional Government with the intention of such unilateral action. Ethridge said that were such moves made, the PCC might be compelled report back to United Nations a failure, placing responsibility on [the] Provisional Government, and asking for new instructions.

Our lunch was a recess from serious discussion. Ethridge was a delightful guest, with interesting and amusing anecdotes about his experiences in Greece and about his wife, whose plans to join him are not yet settled. At the close of the meal, Ethridge signaled to Wilkins to remain with the family, Knox, and Hope, while he and I went into the study for more confidential talk. Ethridge gave a rather full statement on the attitude of the president. Acheson had said that the Palestine policy was primarily that of Truman. At the White House conference [on January 28] besides the president were the secretary, Ethridge, and Clark Clifford.

The president did most of the talking during the forty-minute period. He stressed:

1) Internationalization of Jerusalem. In interpreting this later, Ethridge seemed to regard as acceptable a nominal internationalization, so long as this maintained the theory of UN supervision;
2) November 29 recommendations still binding so that Provisional Government should be willing to make concessions elsewhere if it insisted upon maintaining gains outside of the partition areas;
3) Couldn't see what anyone would want with the Negev. There was on this point an implied support of the British claim to the southern portion of that area for Transjordan;
4) Corridor from Jerusalem to sea was suggested as another possible concession. But Ethridge was quick to add that this was impossible for the Provisional Government to consider;
5) Galilee should not be held if whole of Negev were kept. Ethridge raised the question of possible cash compensation being paid for Galilee. I said that this was not impossible.

Proceeding beyond these specific points, the president spoke of the large interests of the US in the Middle East; the danger of Russian penetration, particularly in Azerbaijan in northern Persia, or in Iraq or in Syria. Hence, the necessity of [a] prompt peace. Truman spoke of "cards" in his hands to influence [the] Provisional Government. These include: US and his personal, recognized friendship; the financial dependence on the US; possibility of withdrawing US friendship and of using prominent Zionists to appeal to the Provisional Government (this last shows how little the spirit here is understood at home). Ethridge said that the president had suggested that he talk to me and that he was going to [rely] heavily on my help. In turn, I said that I was completely at his [disposal]. Then I developed briefly the following points:

1) The political impossibility of the Provisional Government yielding substantially in the Negev; the possibility of some special arrangement to give the British transit privileges and possibly other rights in the South; the complication of Abdullah's insistence on Gaza or [at] the very least of a corridor leading to that exit to the sea, conflicting with Egypt's insistence on Gaza.

2) The impracticality of a genuine internationalization of Jerusalem, because now both Abdullah and the Jews were unyieldingly opposed. The fantastic proposal of Bernadotte that it might be Abdullah's capital had destroyed all hope of possible Jewish acquiescence. This, coupled with the loss of life and other hardships incident to the defense of the city, solidified Jewish opposition.

3) After outlining the defeat of Fawzi in northern Galilee, I stressed that, in my view, the Provisional Government had been restrained in the use of its military victories and that it might be expected to [so] continue.

I [had] asked Abe Feinberg if the opposition to Ethridge in the Foreign Relations Committee was serious. He said it was not. The talk lasted just six minutes. Returning to the Foreign Office, Miss Herlitz also passed on [to Mc-Donald] some wireless reports to the effect that Clifford was leaving the White House for private practice. (This would be a heavy disadvantage.)

I was agreed with Knox that he would draft a telegram about Rhodes and check with me later. Just to illustrate how crowded a Sunday can be, I should perhaps add that following Knox's morning visit and the arrival of Marriott, Colonel van der Velde and Major Brady came in for a cup of tea and to offer their congratulations. We then discussed some of the problems incident to the colonel's leaving.

Monday, February 7

Worked at home during the morning. Early afternoon to Shertok's office to present Department's appeal for extra efforts to save Rhodes. There was very little time, since he was going to a cabinet meeting in a quarter of an hour. Nonetheless, we paraphrased the Department's telegram and a half-hour or so later left the text of the paraphrase, which was in the hands of the prime minister an hour later.[43]

Before evening, Shiloah gave Knox a long and detailed account of the Rhodes situation and at the end said: "Here, take this file of documents including Bunche's proposal, our comments and other data, so that, after analysis by your military associates, you will be able to make up your own mind as to the soundness of our position and the reasonableness of our contention that we cannot make further concessions without weakening our claim to the Negev and without weakening our military position in the event of the resumption of

43. Memorandum of February 6, 1949, NARA, RG 84, entry 2774, box 2, folder 321.9. Given verbally on that day. See entry of February 6, 1949.

hostilities." Shiloah implied that, but for the American intervention [on] December 31 and Israel's acquiescence, the latter's position vis-à-vis Egypt would today be much better. Knox's comment was that this might "conceivably not have been true if the British had come in."

The tea period at home was confused by the visit of Knox, van der Velde, and Brady while Mrs. Marian Greenberg was here. Three of us decided that we would not accept Shiloah's offer of the documents. Instead, we edited Knox's draft of his conversation with Shiloah and sent it off with our comments.

Shiloah complained that the Egyptians were insisting on full Israeli evacuation from the southern Negev, while still maintaining significant forces in the Gaza Strip. Bunche, he added, seemed to take the Egyptian side. Israel could accept the tone of Bunche's drafts (which blamed Israel for the resumption of hostilities) if this would help Cairo save face. But, Shiloah added, "Israel cannot admit that treatment of Negev area is different than any other area of Israel" and "Israel will not agree to any terms which jeopardize her security . . . or which attempt to create a new military balance, thus setting precedent which will make negotiations with Transjordan and Syria even more difficult." McDonald reported to Washington that he did not accept the documents offered by Shiloah. Acceptance, he said, would have given the impression that the Israelis could bypass the UN and the PCC.[44]

Talk with Mrs. Greenberg of Hadassah was in part about the situation here and in part about the UJA-Silver-Montor-et al. She attributed responsibility almost equally to both sides.

Ruth, Bobby and I went at about eight to the reception for the new conductor, Jascha Horenstein,[45] and Frances Magnes, the violin soloist.[46] I chatted with the conductor first about musical matters and later with Mrs. Magnes about her mother-in-law and Frieda Warburg. Chatted also with the French [chargé d'affaires] [Albert Vanthier], who said that he did not yet have any instructions about going to Jerusalem.[47]

Tuesday, February 8

Chaim Hoffmann,[48] the Provisional Government consul in Munich, gave me a very interesting hour:

44. McDonald to secretary of state, no. 109, February 8, 1949, *FRUS*, 1949, v. VI, 734–735.
45. Jascha Horenstein (1898–1973), Kiev-born Jewish conductor; family emigrated to Germany, 1906, and to Austria, 1911; conducted Berlin Philharmonic and Vienna Symphony Orchestras during the 1920s; conductor and director, Düsseldorf Opera, 1928–1933; fled to the United States in 1940.
46. Frances Magnes (1919–2010), violin soloist and daughter-in-law of Judah Leon Magnes and Beatrice Lowenstein Magnes.
47. Felix Albert Vanthier (1911–1953), French chargé d'affaires in Tel Aviv; presented credentials, February 9, 1949.
48. Chaim Yahil [formerly Hoffmann] (1905–1974), Austrian-born labor Zionist, scholar, and diplomat; emigrated to Palestine, 1929; aided in displaced persons affairs and with illegal

1) He is interested that in the American Zone in [Germany], there could be a squaring of theory with fact. There is no real obstacle to the leaving of men of military age, since the American authorities [approve visas to] whole lists of emigrants without any examination. Nonetheless, there is always the possibility that some new military commander will decide to revert to the letter of State Department orders, hence the desirability of formal change.

2) After a discussion of existing practices of screening prospective emigrants from the satellite countries, Hoffmann promised that he would give me a brief factual memorandum on the present procedures in the several states.

3) In connection with our talk about communist penetration through control of emigration, Hoffmann said that he would give me a brief memorandum on the recent voting in some of those settlements where the voters were newcomers. In those places, the communist vote had been very slight. I told him this data would be valuable to me.

4) Provisional Government is, or hopes soon to be, able to send a consul to Berlin. This waits upon an agreement by the four powers, which Hoffmann anticipates relatively soon. My impression of Hoffmann is that of an able man who had done a difficult job well.

Miss Herlitz called to say that, in an article in *Haaretz*, I was credited with having urged Shertok to make further concessions at Rhodes on the ground that to ask the Egyptians to yield further would be to invite domestic trouble in Egypt. Miss Herlitz added that Shertok was issuing a denial. As a matter of fact, nothing of the sort was said by me in the talk with Shertok.

At teatime Mr. and Mrs. Clarence Pickett spent an hour or an hour and a half with us.[49] He had come up from Egypt by way of Beirut to spend this week here and in Jerusalem before his return to the States. He has been in general charge of the forty-or-so Quaker workers (all of them volunteers on a subsistence basis) who are directing the relief operations in the Gaza-Rafah Strip. His chief points were:

1) There are about 210,000 refugees in that area. This is more than an estimate since a complete census is nearly finished.

2) At present, everyone lives under cover either in former British camps or in tents and are receiving minimum food needs.

3) There is little or no possibility [of] the kind of seepage back into Israeli territory, which was recently reported to us, because the borders are strictly guarded. There is no possibility whatever of refugees "escaping" to Egypt

immigration to Palestine after World War II; first Israeli consul in Munich; later director general of Israeli Foreign Ministry, 1960–1964.

49. Clarence Pickett (1884–1964), Quaker humanitarian, peace activist, and general secretary of the American Friends Service Committee, 1929–1950. See Lawrence McK. Miller, *Witness for Humanity: The Biography of Clarence E. Pickett* (Wallingford, PA: Pendle Hill, 1999). See also entries for October 22, 1948; November 20, 1948; December 20, 28, 1948; and January 14, 1949.

because the frontier there is covered by barbed wire entanglements to a depth of several yards.

4) One example of local complications was the practice of refugees to dig up for fuel the stunted shrubs of which held the sand in place for the native farmers. The latter resent this practice and were inclined to cut off water. The Quakers then sought to supply charcoal for the refugees' fuel and were succeeding when the Egyptian authorities took over supplies of charcoal and imposed a prohibitive tax.

5) He regards Griffis as the ideal choice. He is tough, practical, energetic and shrewd, and able to carry a heavy load. In contrast, Dodge is "too old" and would not have been comparably efficient.

6) Pickett stressed the vital importance of repatriation, without which there could be no hope of a solution.

7) Very desirous to see Weizmann, Ben-Gurion and Shertok, to impress upon them the human side of the problem and the necessity of the return of substantial numbers of the refugees. I explained how difficult the time was for the men he desired to see, just on the eve of the inauguration of the Constituent Assembly, added onto all the other duties pressing upon them; but I said I would do what I could. I tried vainly later with both Weizmann and Ben-Gurion, and reported to Pickett the next day that I was not optimistic about anything this week. I told him that I thought he could save his time by going to Jerusalem, as he desired to do, and return here later. Since, however, he was insistent on returning to the States via Beirut this weekend, the case seemed hopeless.

8) Pickett was interesting in his report on the political situation in Egypt. The king, he thinks, is in strong opposition to the government; the former, spoiled and irritable because of the failure of his plans for Palestine, has become intensely anti-American; the late assassinated prime minister [Mahmoud an-Nukrashi Pasha] had opposed the war but had been forced into it by the king.[50]

When Pickett and his wife left, we both expressed a desire to have a long talk, but his decision to leave on Thursday made this impossible.

In the evening, Ruth, Bobby, Noah, and I went to the concert. We all liked Horenstein and the soloist, Frances Magnes. Her playing of the Mendelssohn concerto was vigorous and full of feeling. The Mahler First Symphony was very pleasant to hear after so long a time. After the concert one of the men connected with the management told me that it had been definitely decided that Serge Koussevitsky would come over for a series of concerts in February 1950.

50. Entry of December 28, 1948.

Long and very successful party at van der Velde's house given by him for colonel and Mrs. Burton C. Andrus and Major and Mrs. Lawrence Brady. It lasted from six until nearly 9:30. I liked the new people and think they will fit in well. The colonel is a wholly different type from van der Velde but should, judging from his record, and maturity, be excellent on the job. That the Pentagon decided to send such a senior officer seems to indicate that they regard this mission as of special importance.[51] The colonel may prove to be a little rigid, but his wife is certain to be a social asset, as will be Mrs. Brady.

On February 18, McDonald wrote to Halsey and Janet Barrett,"With the arrival a few days ago of Colonel and Mrs. Andrus, our staff of military attachés and other personnel is nearly complete. We now lack only a labor attaché and some additional clerical personnel. Soon, therefore, we shall number about fifty persons, including the native employees."[52]

McDonald remained apprehensive about van der Velde's reassignment to US Army Intelligence at Fort Meade. The assignment was not a demotion, but van der Velde never received an explanation for the move, and he met with skepticism during his briefings on Israel. Van der Velde wrote McDonald in March 1949,

> *I have been slightly more than somewhat disillusioned by the apparent fact that many of the persons here that one would think would be 'up' on the situation are not at all. . . . I spoke for over two hours to a high-powered group at [the] CIA which included State and other agency representatives and felt that they were an especially doubting audience when I started . . . by the time I had ended, I felt that all had at least put down their armor and were willing to listen. . . . The joint chiefs work-dogs who listened to me the other day also showed some signs of admitting the possibility that I was not completely brainless. . . . You know the reputation you have here as to leanings. Although still fairly strong, there are a few indications that some may be beginning to believe that you can see more than one side. I have done what I could to strengthen these fledgling ideas.*

McDonald replied in April 1949, "Thanks for reminding me of the reputation I have for 'impartiality.' I never forget this but at the same time I long ago decided not to worry about it but to hew as closely as possible to the line in the hope that eventually actions would do more than earlier reputation. I am grateful for whatever you have [done] or can do in this direction."[53]

No real business was done at the party except that after Mr. Knox was assured by Miss Herlitz that Poland, Czechoslovakia, and Holland were going to the party [opening of Constituent Assembly in Jerusalem on] February 14, he and I got off a telegram to the Department reporting this, and urging again the

---

51. See entry of January 19, 1949.
52. McDonald to Halsey and Janet Barrett, February 18, 1949, McDonald Papers, USHMM, box 7, folder 11.
53. The exchanges are in McDonald Papers, Columbia University, box 20, folder 11.

importance of my being present, particularly since it seemed likely that the Russians might be.[54]

Thursday, February 10

Nearly the whole day spent in connection with the inauguration of the Henrietta Szold Reception Center, sponsored by Hadassah for Youth Aliyah, in Galilee.[55] The weather was not propitious, threatening to continue its nearly fortnight of cold rain, but happily during the out-of-door visits and ceremony, the sun shone. It helped to give us a fuller sense of the beauty of the location in the Lower Galilee hills, ten miles or so east of Haifa.

From the watchtower, which here, as in all of the colonies, is combined with the water tower, one had magnificent views; to the east the lower mountain in which Nazareth nestles; to the north, the higher mountains of Upper Galilee; to the northwest, Haifa and the Acre coastal plain; to the west the nearby Mount Carmel, standing out boldly as if reaching into the sea; to the southwest, Carmel dropping off to the lower range of hills through which the historic passes from the Sharon plain to the Esdraelon Valley wind their ways; to the south and southwest spread the vast (for Israel) and richly fertile valley of the Esdraelon. Within sight, too, of the watchtower, were many Jewish settlements of various types. Thus from this single spot one could glimpse examples of nearly all the forms of Jewish farming activities.

The historically minded observer (and what young Jew of today in Israel is not historically minded) can from the watchtower reconstruct in his imagination some of the historic scenes of the ancient Jewish pageant. Nearby Deborah inspired Barak and the tribes whom she had enlisted to their epic triumph over Sisera; the strategic clash of arms century after century at Meggido, standing astride the main route from the south to the north and the northeast; the triumph of Elijah and the Jewish God [sic] over the priests of Baal and their god on Mount Carmel; not far distant the scene of the final and fatal battle of Saul with the Philistines. Thus, from the watchtower, one could understand better why Henrietta Szold had chosen this spot as the one on which the boys and girls of Youth Aliyah should have their first opportunity to forget the terror of their past and begin their adjustment to their new life in Israel.

The buildings for their accommodation are excellently designed. They are simple, economical, but substantial in construction, and make available the maximum facilities. Already the center cares for 150 boys and girls from the ages of eight to twelve or fourteen. Soon there will be 250, the full capacity.

---

54. Soviet ambassador Pavel Ershov attended the opening of the Constituent Assembly.

55. Henrietta Szold (1860–1945), founder of Hadassah; on request of Chaim Weizmann and Arthur Ruppin in 1933, began to develop and manage Youth Aliyah (founded in 1932) under Hadassah auspices. It brought some 5,000 children to Palestine before the war and another 15,000 in the years immediately afterward. The Szold Reception Center in the Jezreel Valley was dedicated to commemorate the fifteenth anniversary of Youth Aliyah. See Simmons, *Hadassah and the Zionist Project*, chs. 5, 6.

Even though the turnover is completed every six weeks or two months, this and the other reception centers will be quite inadequate to care for the refugee children as they are now pouring into the country. Most of the children, therefore, will have to make their essential adjustments under much less ideal circumstances.

The children themselves, even more than the magnificence of the site and the adequacy of the equipment, thrilled me. There they were dark and brown-eyed boys and girls from the Sephardic communities of Morocco and Turkey and the Ashkenazi communities of Bulgaria, Poland and Hungary, many of these latter, blue-eyed and blond. As yet, few of them know Hebrew. They were still speaking a babel of tongues, including Spanish, Arabic, Turkish, Bulgarian, Yiddish, and Hungarian. They all looked sturdy and happy. The weather was far from warm, but they were comfortable in their heavy American woolen clothes and shoes.

After the luncheon in the main dining hall, where hundreds of guests from Jerusalem, Tel Aviv and elsewhere were served by the children, there followed the inevitable, and as usual, too long program of speeches including those from the chief rabbi [Yitzhak Herzog], the Hadassah representatives, and others including myself. The really bright moment came at the very end when a group of girls sang in unison Hebrew songs and a group of boys and girls danced some of the simpler of the current folk dances. Thus the youngsters gave us concrete evidence of their progress in being at home in Israel.

During the lunch, I was edified by Rabbi Herzog's answers to my questions about the Old Testament. He would have been very friendly in any case but was more so because of my close association with and admiration for his favorite son, Jacob, who is doing such a splendid job in the Ministry of Religion and whom I had been able to help in his contacts with the Vatican in Rome some months ago. I was rather surprised that the chief rabbi asked me whether I thought communism was inconsistent with religion. My answer had to be the empiric one that, until now, modern Russian communism had been bitterly hostile to organized religion. The rabbi wondered whether this need be so.

When the long program was finally over, and Ruth, Mrs. [Ida] Davidowitz, and I were starting for our car, Mrs. Shertok asked if she might go back with us. We were, of course, delighted. Returning we came by way of Haifa, thus circumventing Carmel. This, together with my study of the map later, gave me a clearer picture of that whole northwestern historic and strategic area. Later this spring, I plan to do an extended series of tours to historic sites, as well as to the colonies. Passing through Haifa, I saw more of the war destruction along the main street and the waterfront than on my previous visits. The trip home was delayed by nearly torrential rains. We were back by a quarter of seven.

Home and aware of the unfortunate impression which Shertok had made on Ethridge during the nearly five-hour session he had had with the members of the PCC,[56] I decided that I ought to see Shertok almost immediately. Knox had called me on the phone to explain that apparently London, Paris and Washington were in a huddle to agree on whether or not to go to Jerusalem [for the Assembly opening]. It was evident to me that this might be in part a reflection of reports on Shertok's latest statement to the PCC. Shertok was away from home, but Mrs. Shertok promised to have him call me the first thing in the morning.

Friday, February 11

Mr. Knox came to breakfast, during which we discussed the probable action of the powers and my suggested visit to Shertok. Later we were joined by Tetlie, who explained a little more about Ethridge's reaction to Shertok's presentation. Knox thought that there was danger that the US might be driven to sacrifice Israel if the latter should be guilty of openly flaunting the UN, which had become the center of American foreign policy. Though I did not agree with all of Knox's reasoning, I recognized that his point of view was a good starting point for my personal statement to Shertok.

Presently Shertok called. First, he offered his congratulations on the president's designation of me as ambassador (he had just had the formal inquiry from Epstein about the agreement).[57] He was most cordial in his expression of pleasure at this event. He then asked me to inquire from Washington whether they would accept Epstein [now Eliahu Elath].[58] He then made a date for three o'clock.

Mr. Asher Goren of the Middle East Division of the Foreign Office[59] came to talk to me about Arab refugees. I discovered that he has nothing to do with Israeli policy in this area, but is simply keeping track as well as he can from Arab newspapers and other sources about the numbers and condition of the refugees. He estimated that these totaled between 581,000 and 600,000, divided as follows: the south 150,000; Lebanon 85,000 to 90,000; Syria a similar number; Iraq 5,000; Transjordan 80,000 to 90,000; the [Tulkarm-Jenin-Nablus]

---

56. The PCC met Shertok in Jerusalem on February 7, 1949, before its tour of Arab capitals. Ethridge's immediate concern was recent Israeli steps taken in Jerusalem as they related to past UN resolutions regarding internationalization. Shertok said that Israel would not make Jerusalem its capital, but that it could not leave the safety of its Jews to the UN. Israeli Jerusalem, he said, was for all intents and purposes part of Israel. The opening of the Constituent Assembly there recognized Jerusalem's place at the center of Jewish history. To Boisanger's questions on refugees, Shertok repeated that the exodus was triggered by Arab aggression, that the solution to the issue had to be part of a general peace settlement, and that the main part involved resettlement in the Arab states. Ethridge reported that Shertok appeared "unyielding" and that his views regarding the refugees "offended [the] Commission." See Ethridge to secretary of state [through Burdett], no. 123, February 8, 1949, *FRUS*, 1949, v. VI, 735–738, and 738, n. 1. Also Shertok to Eban, February 9–10, 1949, *DFPI*, v. 2, d. 379.
57. Shertok's letter to this effect, dated February 11, 1949, is in McDonald Papers, USHMM, box 7, folder 11.
58. Epstein took the Hebrew surname Elath after officially assuming the ambassadorial post in Washington.
59. Asher Goren (1919–2014), Foreign Ministry official and scholar; later wrote on the Arab League and translated Arab poetry into Hebrew.

triangle; 170,000; Egypt 11,000 (6,000 of these are in a camp at Kantara [Egyptian port town near Suez], the others scattered in Egypt but without permits to work). Lebanon's policy he summarized as "get rid" of them because of inability to continue contributing towards their help and the danger of increasing the Moslem population; in Syria and Transjordan the cry is "no funds;" there is land to spare but settlement money essential; Iraq needs men for defense and development, there it is a matter of bargaining. As to governments' management, Egypt close control, Syria poor order, and the same in Lebanon, with widespread changes of graft in both countries; in Transjordan also stories of speculators taking advantage of refugees.

As to Israel's policy, Goren could only say that there could be no large-scale resettlement because of public opinion and because the places of most of the Arabs had been or were soon to be occupied [by] Jews, newcomers or others. The government might, however, offer compensation. An inter-departmental committee made up of Ezra Danin of the Foreign Office,[60] Yosef Weitz of the Keren Kayemet,[61] and a representative of the treasury, were studying financial and other aspects of the problem.

At three I was at Shertok's, explaining that my visit was wholly personal and unofficial. I said I was worried about the possible reactions to the rumors and fears [including in the PCC] of Israeli unilateral action affecting Jerusalem. I intimated, too, that Ethridge's reaction to Shertok's presentation had been unfavorable. Shertok, as he himself then said, could scarcely wait until I had finished. He launched into a summary of his statement to the PCC and of his reiterated assurances that the present government and those who would control the next had no intention of taking unilateral [action] affecting the status of the city, but hoped to be able to work out with the UN a mutually satisfactory arrangement. He denied that holding the Assembly's inaugural session in Jerusalem was more than an inevitable historical act required by Jewish tradition. He said that there was nothing tendentious about Jerusalem in Weizmann's speech[62] and that so far as he and his colleagues could control the situation, and he felt they could have their way, none of the actions feared would be taken. Indeed, no one had proposed them.[63]

60. Ezra Danin (1903–1984), Jaffa-born specialist in Arab affairs in the Haganah during the Arab Revolt (1936–1939) and World War II, and then in the Israeli Foreign Ministry; traveled with Golda Meyerson to persuade King Abdullah not to enter the war against Israel, May 1948.

61. Yosef Weitz (1890–1972), Volhynian-born agricultural pioneer in Palestine; director of Jewish National Fund's Forestry Department; advocate of population transfer in the 1940s.

62. Weizmann's speech opening the Assembly quickly reviewed the history of the Zionist movement, but did not make claims to Jerusalem. See *Weizmann Papers*, Ser. B, v. 2, d. 100.

63. Meeting reported in McDonald to secretary of state, no. 120, February 12, 1949, NARA, RG 59, 501.BB, box 2123, folder 8. McDonald added his comment to Shertok that "such action in violation [of] both [the] UN decision and reiterated [in] US policy would create [a] gravely unfortunate reaction [in the] UN and US. I underlined [the] central position [of the] UN in all US foreign policy and [the] probability [that the] US would strongly support any UN action."

As to our attendance at the opening session, he expressed the hope that we would go even if our acceptance were coupled with the caveat which I had suggested to the Department, to the effect that such acceptance did not involve any weakening of the US's well-known stand about internationalization.

On January 31, 1948, McDonald reported to Washington that the Constituent Assembly would open in Jewish Jerusalem on February 14. "All Diplomatic and Consular Corps [are] invited and invitations [are] being issued to myself and Knox. It is obviously essential that [the] Special Representative attend this historic occasion. Request Department's concurrence urgently."[64]

Satterthwaite reported to Acheson on February 9 that in McDonald's view "non-attendance would wound Jewish sensibilities and create an awkward situation for the United States in Israel if the Russian Minister in Tel Aviv [Ershov] should attend. Mr. McDonald advocates that he accompany his acceptance of the Israeli invitation with a formal statement that his attendance at the opening of the Assembly does not imply any change in the United States position on the status of Jerusalem."

Acheson sought a middle path between practical diplomacy and the UN's principle of international control, the latter backed by religious interests including the Vatican. But he agreed with Satterthwaite that McDonald's presence would contradict US policy. On February 10, he secured the president's agreement that McDonald should not attend.[65]

I was scarcely home and ready for my nap when Knox came in with the telegram from the Department instructing us that no one from here or from Jerusalem could be authorized [to] "attend meeting Constituent Assembly if held Jerusalem," declination to be accompanied by "appropriate expression regret," and prospect of pleasure in attending first session in Tel Aviv. The Department's argument was, as expected, that the US in no way should indicate approval of holding the Assembly in Jerusalem. The UN General Assembly had decided that Jerusalem should have special treatment under effective UN control. [The] UN General Assembly had charged the PCC with recommendations for a permanent international regime. The telegram continued,

> Although we believe there is considerable flexibility in what might constitute an appropriate international regime, we believe [that the] Conciliation Commission should have [a] full opportunity to work this out. Under [the] circumstances [the] Israeli decision [to] hold [the] Con-

64. McDonald to secretary of state, no. 68, January 31, 1949, NARA, RG 84, E 2774, box 3, folder 350.
65. *FRUS*, 1949, v. V, 739–741. US policy on Jerusalem summarized in Hahn, *Caught in the Middle East*, 112–117.

stituent Assembly in Jerusalem, attended by known territorial claims of Israel to Jerusalem, would be viewed with serious misgivings by UN members, many of whom are deeply interested in [the] internationalization of Jerusalem. Decision might possibly have [an] adverse effect when [the] Israeli membership application [is] again considered by UN. In [the] Department's opinion [the] decision will also prejudice [the] work of [the] Conciliation Commission, not only in connection with its recommendations for [a] future international Jerusalem regime, but in its attempts to bring [the] parties to agreement, since such apparent manifestation [of the] desire [to] extend Israeli sovereignty to [an] area designated by the UN as international in [the] heart of [the] territory allotted to [the] Arabs by November 29 resolution might have adverse effect on Arab-Israeli negotiations.[66]

Knox came back for tea after I had in the meantime drafted two telegrams, the one reporting on my visit with Shertok, and the other about Epstein [Elath] as ambassador. Knox and I decided that the answer to the Department's telegram of the afternoon could wait until Sunday morning since it was really in substance for our information and did not in reality envisage any change of policy by the Provisional Government.

On February 11, Elath told Shertok that President Truman would appoint McDonald as ambassador. Later that day the Israeli Foreign Ministry announced the appointment through Kol Israel radio. Elath reported the next day, "Department [is] disturbed by our premature release [of the] news [of the] McDonald appointment. This [is] usually done by [the] White House after [the] appointment [is] confirmed by [the] Senate."[67] The official presidential announcement of McDonald's nomination was made on February 25, and McDonald officially became ambassador on March 18.[68] Shertok might have acted precipitously to scotch any derailment of McDonald's appointment and to keep Moscow from raising the status of its mission before Washington could do so.

Privately, McDonald wrote Benjamin Abrams, "The President's evidence of confidence in me . . . makes me feel that my labors of the last seven months have not been wasted. Second, it enables me to carry on in what is the most absorbing task of my life. . . . I shall be given the opportunity to carry on, probably as long as I can afford it, which I hope will be until real peace has been established with Israel's

66. Quoted from Acheson to McDonald, no. 83, February 10, 1948, NARA, RG 59, 501.BB Palestine, box 2123, folder 8. Acheson wrote in a separate memorandum that the president was in full agreement. See memorandum by Acheson, February 10, 1949, NARA, RG 59, 501.BB Palestine, box 2123, folder 8.

67. Elath to Shertok, February 12, 1949, *DFPI*, v. 2, d. 384.

68. Editorial note, *FRUS*, 1949, v. VI, 769.

neighbors and the new state has dug deeper the foundations of its internal and social institutions."[69]

He added to Halsey and Janet Barrett that

> *since I am to be the first Ambassador to Israel, I become automatically, under the rigid and unchangeable rules of diplomatic protocol, the Dean of the Diplomatic Corps. Ruth, thereby, becomes the first foreign lady in the land. She will have to take the lead in entertaining the wives of the other diplomats as they arrive and to organize the affairs which I must give as the ranking resident diplomat. Fortunately, here in Tel Aviv, partly because of the continued state of lack of peace and partly because the country is so small and its leaders are so modest in their standard of living, these responsibilities will not be as heavy as they would be in most other capitals.*[70]

Saturday, February 12

Morning spent in reading and the latter half at tea at [Sam] Sacks's. The early afternoon, Shertok called to ask what was the answer about Jerusalem. I told him it was negative but that I should like to see him to explain why. He appeared to be terribly disappointed, said that he was calling from Ben-Gurion's and would get in touch with me just as soon as he came home.

[Shertok visited McDonald's residence in the early evening.] As I read him [the] paraphrase of the Department's argument, he at first took notes and then in seeming discouragement or disgust, he left off. When I finished, he expressed his regret and said that he could, as we knew, argue the case. We all agreed, however, that this would not help. Shertok then said that Ben-Gurion took our non-attendance less seriously than he had. At that point I turned the conversation by asking Shertok if it was true that Mapam had undertaken a maneuver against Weizmann's election by agreeing to support Rabbi [Meir] Berlin. He explained that this was true but that under the influence of Rabbi [Yehuda Leib] Fishman, the proposal had been rejected and that as far as could be anticipated, Weizmann should receive a nearly unanimous vote.[71] After Shertok left, Knox and I drafted the telegram on Shertok's reaction.[72]

That evening we had the first announcement on the radio from the States about my appointment. The family's reaction was one of relief that the uncertainty was over. My own feeling was divided between that of gratification that there had been this recognition of the efforts made during the past months, and pleasure at the prospect of being allowed to continue in a task which was so all

69. McDonald to Benjamin Abrams, February 16, 1949, February 28, 1949, McDonald Papers, Columbia University, box 6, folder 2.
70. McDonald to Halsey and Janet Barrett, February 18, 1949, McDonald Papers, USHMM, box 7, folder 11.
71. Mapam threatened to support Rabbi Meir Berlin [Bar-Ilan] of Mizrahi to thwart Weizmann's election. Bar-Ilan was persuaded to withdraw by fellow Mizrahi member, Rabbi Yehuda Leib Fishman [Maimon] (1876–1962), then the minister of religious affairs. Weizmann was elected by a Knesset vote of 83–15 over Joseph Klausner of Herut.
72. McDonald to secretary of state, no. 123, February 13, 1949, NARA, RG 59, MC 1390, reel 18, frame 585.

absorbing and for which to a rather extraordinary degree all that I had done previously had been direct or indirect preparation. There was also the satisfaction of the prospect of continuing until Israel was at peace. And the tangibleness of the promotion, enabling Ruth to feel that finally there was an adequate recognition and title, was an additional asset.

Sunday, February 13

The beginning of the arrival of congratulatory cables. Among these, one from Felix Frankfurter indicated that there must have been an official announcement in Washington Saturday about my appointment, though up to that time we had not yet received any official announcement from the Department beyond the earlier statement that the president had made the decision and wished the agreement of the Provisional Government.

Very pleasant luncheon with the Andruses and Bradys as guests. I liked them all, and as to the colonel, did not get the impression that he was as rigid as had been reported. His account of his handling of the Nuremberg prisoners and his explanation of the bitterly critical article in *Time* following the death by suicide of Hermann Göring were those of an able but not pompous person.[73] He and I had no time to discuss his mission here, but our talk made me feel more than before that he would not have been sent had Washington not had in mind the concept of Israel as much more important than it is large.

Major Arnon called and put Weisgal on the telephone. He was sorry about the Jerusalem decision, congratulated me on my promotion, said that there had been a battle about [Jerusalem] with strong forces in opposition but that the "old man," presumably referring to the president, stood firm. He promised to give me the full story as he had had it "from the horse's mouth." Then Weizmann came on the phone, asked why I had not been to see him, deplored the Jerusalem decision, [and] opined that it was a triumph for [the] UK. I deduced from what he said, a confirmation of Shertok's report of the day before, that he had considered a personal appeal from one president to the other. I told him that I had written a personal letter of regret, and that I hoped to see him soon. He replied that he was coming back from Jerusalem Monday night and I should get in touch with him.[74]

After dinner, four hours of uninterrupted reading, save for ten minutes of listening to Kol Israel. This enabled me to get through most of the office documents

---

73. *Time* in its October 28, 1946, issue blamed Andrus for Göring's suicide, referring to the colonel as a "pompous, unimaginative" officer who "wasn't up to his job."

74. McDonald's letter to Weizmann read, "It is with deep personal regret that, because of circumstances beyond my control, I had to deny myself the privilege of attending the historic opening of Israel's first Constituent Assembly. My regret is all the greater because I shall not hear the inaugural address in which you will so fittingly strike the keynote for your people at this epic hour." McDonald to Weizmann, February 14, 1949, McDonald Papers, USHMM, box 7, folder 11. For the speech see *Weizmann Papers*, Ser, B, v. 2, d. 100.

and to relax at the end with a chapter or two of George Adam Smith's *Geography*.[75]

Monday, February 14

Instead of going to Jerusalem, the whole morning was spent in dictation. It seemed strange to be in Israel and not be present at the historic session. With difficulty could I concentrate on current duties, because they seemed relatively trivial.

At the opening of the Constituent Assembly, which formally changed its name to the Knesset, Joseph Sprinzak was elected speaker and Weizmann was elected and inaugurated as the president of the State of Israel. Weizmann charged Ben-Gurion with forming a government, which the prime minister did on March 8, 1949.

McDonald wrote Halsey and Janet Barrett that "they have accomplished in a brief four days [in Jerusalem] the whole program which the Provisional Government outlined, and all of it was done with a legislative decorum which augurs well for the orderly development of Israel as a democratic state. [That it was] all carried through by an assembly completely inexperienced and made up of so many diverse elements and all of this without a hitch, was deeply encouraging even to the most optimistic observers."[76]

The eight o'clock BBC news broadcast from London was startling. After briefly stating that the diplomatic representatives of Britain, France and the US had not attended the session in Jerusalem, the announcement continued: "The new American ambassador explained that he could not attend because his presence might be taken as approval of the Provisional Government's stand on Jerusalem." There was no intimation that there had been a tripartite agreement. On the contrary, the casual listener must have gotten the impression that either the US, or I, or both of us had taken the initiative in this decision, which must be extremely unpopular throughout Israel.

McDonald worriedly wrote Ben Abrams, "I could almost write the editorials which will appear in the Mapam and Communist papers. These organizations always welcome an opportunity to criticize the U.S. I hope, however, that my non-attendance will soon cease to be a subject of critical comment. At any rate, I have the solace of knowing that our friends in the [Israeli] Government understand fully even if they do not agree with the considerations that led to Washington's decision."[77]

75. George Adam Smith, *The Historical Geography of the Holy Land* (1894). Smith (1856–1942) was a Scottish theologian at the University of Aberdeen who specialized in the Hebrew Bible.

76. McDonald to Halsey and Janet Barrett, February 18, 1949, McDonald Papers, USHMM, box 7, folder 11.

77. McDonald to Benjamin Abrams, February 16, 1949, McDonald Papers, Columbia University, box 6, folder 2.

Knox came for breakfast. We decided to telegraph the Department about the BBC tendentious broadcast, hoping to warn them and, if possible, to elicit some information. We also telegraphed the Department, warning of increasing tension in Jerusalem and suggesting the possibility of [the] Department asking Jerusalem to take special precautions.

At about eleven Knox called to say that the atmosphere was again murky and that he thought he ought to come out. He brought with him the Department telegram regarding Rhodes. It pointed out that Eban, on the 11th on his own initiative, had assured the US-UN representative [Ross] that only details remained to be adjusted. The same day, the 11th, word was received from Bunche through Ethridge that new difficulties from [the] Provisional Government had arisen in connection with al-Auja and Be'er Sheva. We were requested to inquire how these two conflicting statements could be reconciled.[78]

After studying the telegram and finding that only Shiloah was available (Shertok being still in Jerusalem and Eytan in Rhodes), I suggested that we ask the two colonels, van der Velde and Andrus, to meet us immediately at the Foreign Office. There we had about forty-five minutes with Shiloah. His explanation seemed to convince the military that [the] Provisional Government was making all reasonable concessions. They were agreeing to a form of armistice, which would appear as if the two sides were equal. They had accepted the mediator's November 13 line (Bunche's interpretation of the November 4 resolution), but of necessity had to maintain on the eastern line facing the [Arab] Legion troops, and others under the Legion command, until Transjordan agreed to an armistice. They could not, however, accept in the armistice any political terms which would weaken their claim to the Negev. More difficult, according to Shiloah, than the questions of amounts of troops to be left in the area or questions arising from al-Auja or Be'er Sheva, was that of the site of the armistice commission. [The] Provisional Government would not consent to three rotation sites, al-Auja, Bir 'Asluj, and Be'er Sheva, unless there were to be agreement for three additional sites on the Egyptian side of the frontier. [The] Provisional Government wanted one site, al-Auja with the armistice commission having, of course, the right to investigate on both sides of the line as far north as al-Arish and as far south as Faluja. Moreover, [the] Provisional Government did not want any UN representation in the Negev. It was bad enough to have it in Jerusalem. It was one thing to have UN representation in Israel, when the military was headed by an American, Brigadier General Riley, but it

---

78. Eban's optimism likely stemmed from his real reason for talking to Ross, namely to push for Israeli UN membership. Ethridge reported that the Israelis in Rhodes refused to accept troop withdrawal from Be'er Sheva or the neutral zone proposal for al-Auja. They based their refusal on the need for strategic freedom for the upcoming negotiations with Transjordan. Acheson to McDonald, no, 88, February 14, 1949, *FRUS*, 1949, v. VI, 748–749; Eban to Elath, February 11, 1949, *DFPI*, v. 2, d. 381.

would be something altogether different should, as might happen, a Britisher be named.

By the end of the conference it was after one o'clock, and since Bentwich was waiting for me at home, and in any case I was not really needed, Knox and the two colonels consented to draft a telegram, to add their comment and to send it off.

In reporting on Shiloah's comments, McDonald added, "Mission believes that [the Provisional Government] has been withholding further compromise during [the] last six days awaiting outcome [of] Histadrut elections [of] 13 February and [the] opening of [the] Assembly in order [to] clear [the] political atmosphere here. Shiloah's arguments [regarding] Beersheba [are] understandable. Mission opinion is that [the Provisional Government's] latest proposals constitute [a] reasonable basis [for] compromise and will possibly elicit favorable Egyptian response. Likely these proposals are as far [as Provisional Government] can go."[79]

The lunch with Bentwich was pleasant, but contained nothing that was noteworthy except his enthusiastic estimate of Dr. Mordecai Eliash, whose scholarship, industry, orthodoxy and extraordinary brilliancy make him an ideal choice for London.[80]

Wednesday, February 16

Knox called and asked if he might send off a telegram of inquiry to the Department asking for instructions about change of status. Ruth and I were out to Weizmann's from 4:20 until 6:00 or a little after. We found Weizmann concluding a conference with Simon and another official about the next day's procedure when the president was to be inducted (this of course on the assumption that the constitution were adopted later during today and the president then elected). A few minutes after our arrival, Meyer Weisgal came in.[81] Towards the end of our stay Mrs. Weizmann came down from her nap (she apologized for not having known that Ruth was there), and finally, just as we were ready to leave, in came Dr. Paul Ruegger, president of the International Red Cross, his wife and entourage.[82]

79. McDonald to secretary of state, no. 129, February 15, 1949, *FRUS*, 1949, v. VI, 752–753.
80. Mordechai Eliash (1892–1950), legal scholar and expert on rabbinic law; had insisted on the use of English in Jewish courts during the mandatory period; became Israel's representative in London in April 1949 and assumed rank of minister in May. Bentwich, also an Anglophone lawyer, knew him well.
81. Weisgal's position was executive vice president of the American Committee for the Weizmann Institute of Science (formerly the Daniel Sieff Research Institute), which was to open officially in May 1949 to coincide with Israel's first anniversary. He was in Israel partly to coordinate a visit to the United States by Weizmann in April 1949, in which there was to be a meeting with Truman. JTA *Bulletin*, February 6, 1949.
82. Paul Ruegger (1897–1988), Swiss jurist and diplomat; president, International Committee of the Red Cross, 1948–1955; toured Middle East to inspect distribution of food and necessities to refugees and needy residents of Jerusalem's Old City, February 1949.

Much of the talk at tea concerned my not going to Jerusalem on Monday. Weizmann had received my personal letter of regret and was very understanding. He said that he was sorry for me personally and regretted very much that I had been placed in such an unfortunate public position. He did not hold Truman responsible, being of the opinion that the president had not understood the situation and had been presented by a tripartite arrangement initiated probably by France but possibly by Britain. Weisgal confirmed my understanding that we had had assurances the previous Friday that permission would be granted. I made clear that almost at that same time the refusal came—there was nothing more that I could do. Weizmann cited as evidence of the government's scrupulous avoidance of utilizing the occasion to anticipate a UN decision about Jerusalem, the avoidance in his speech of any tendentious reference, an avoidance which had simultaneously been proposed by him and Shertok.

Our talk about the States centered on my report of the news that Silver and Neumann had just resigned from the [Jewish] Agency.

Rabbi Abba Hillel Silver (head of the American section of the Jewish Agency Executive) and Emanuel Neumann (president of the Zionist Organization of America) resigned their posts in the Jewish Agency on February 16 after having lost the struggle for more independent Diaspora Zionist agencies. On March 1, 1949 Henry Morgenthau Jr. accepted the general chairmanship of the United Jewish Appeal and appointed Henry Montor, Silver's primary adversary, as the UJA's executive director. Silver condemned Jewish Agency interference in UJA business.

Both Weizmann and Weisgal rejoiced at this, and thought it was the beginning of the end of the dominant role at home of these two men. Weisgal realistically recognized, however, that there would be a period of "convulsions" before a new order was established. Weizmann credited Henry Morgenthau "in his quiet and slow manner" with having been the influence that defeated Silver and Neumann.[83] As to the motives which led these two to take such a risk, Weizmann and Weisgal attributed it to "lust for power," arrogance, vanity and a misunderstanding of public opinion both in Israel and among Jews at home.

Weisgal said that a story current at home was: Israel had been recognized de facto and de jure by 30 to 40 countries and was now waiting for recognition by the ZOA [Zionist Organization of America]. Another of Weisgal's was: the ZOA has no relations with the White House, it is not admitted to the State Department, and is in revolt against Israel! Weisgal, continuing, said that many non- or even anti-Zionists now found that the existence and success of Israel had won for them a new degree of respect from their non-Jewish neighbors and that they were ready to support Israel as never before, but felt no need

83. Morgenthau once again became the head of the United Jewish Appeal by invitation of the Jewish Agency Executive on February 16.

for any such go-between as the ZOA. Hence, the success of Israel tended to weaken the ZOA by undermining its hitherto recognized role.

Another of Weisgal's amusing tales was that, when discussing with the president the postponement of the Weizmann visit, the former had said in effect: If necessary I'll send an American plane for Weizmann, perhaps I ought to send the Dewey plane. (This is the million-dollar plush job plane which reportedly was ordered and completed by and for the Air Force for the personal use of Dewey after he was elected.[84])

There was some talk about the probable action of the Constituent Assembly that afternoon and the plans for Weizmann's installation the next day. He, however, disclaimed any special interest in the political alignments at the Constituent Assembly. Nonetheless, I am sure that he is thrilled at the prospect of his election on the first ballot and his role in the establishment of the new state.

As we were leaving I spoke for a few minutes with Dr. Paul Ruegger. He thanked me for my kindnesses to his representative, Dr. Wolf, and added that he would [like to have come and seen] me but he was in Tel Aviv for only a few hours. In this hurried exchange, I had no opportunity to say anything to him about de Reynier.[85]

Thursday, February 17

Ruth and I to lunch at the Greenbergs (of General Electric). Others there were Mr. and Mrs. Persitz and Mr. and Mrs. Meir Grossman, the Revisionist leader.[86] Most of the talk was with him. He was dogmatically critical of Goldie Meyerson and of almost everything connected with the Provisional Government and the Constituent Assembly. He thought that David Remez was Ben-Gurion's logical successor. Beyond this I got very little that was definite out of Grossmann. If, however, he and his party [HaTzohar] are as dogmatic and as doctrinaire as he showed himself at lunch, I could understand their defeat at the recent elections and could feel that the country was not worse off for this.

Staff conference at tea from five to seven. Everybody accepted Knox's and my idea that staff members should refrain from "getting into bed with the British" when they came. Even if there was no tendency on the part of individual Britishers to misuse or misinterpret such close association, it would certainly be misinterpreted and disliked by the Israelis and thus weaken the status here of our personnel. The chief subject of the conversation in general terms before and

---

84. Specially outfitted Lockheed Constellation prepared by US Air Force in 1948 and named "Dewdrop" on the assumption that Dewey would win the presidential election. Truman rejected its use as a presidential aircraft, and it was used for VIPs and cabinet officers.

85. See entry of October 16, 1948.

86. Meir Grossman (1888–1964), Ukrainian-born Zionist; moved to London, 1919; settled in Palestine permanently, 1948; leading figure in Jabotinsky's Union of Revisionist Zionists; opposed founding of Begin's Herut party as a betrayal of his seniority within the Revisionist movement. His own HaTzohar group failed to win the requisite 2 percent of the vote to sit in the Knesset and merged with Herut. See entries of August 17, 1948, and September 22, 1948.

in more specific terms after the arrival of Barnes was the office [and] housing problem [for US personnel]. There was consensus of opinion that it would be worthwhile for me to inquire assiduously about the possibility of American private financing of a building for our office use.[87] Quiet evening at home finishing some documents and continuing my [reading of] George Adam Smith.

Friday, February 18

Mr. Levinus Painter[88] and Mr. and Mrs. Delbert E. Replogle[89] of the American Friends Service Committee [AFSC] came to the house for an hour and a half before lunch. Painter told of new work done and being planned in Acre and Lebanon. Without any intention to be critical, he reported the enforced evacuation by the Jewish military of the inhabitants of some of the villages bordering on Lebanon to towns or cities in south Galilee. He recognized the military purpose but deplored the hardship.[90]

Painter and his colleagues had difficulty restraining their criticism of the ICRC and its bureaucratic methods in the triangle. Their officials seemingly were still busy getting offices and such other organizational work, and had not yet had time to begin seriously the care of refugees. The Friends confirmed what I had heard earlier about the ICRC and Dr. Depage.[91] The Replogles told of their work in the Gaza-Rafah strip, the near completion of their census, which they thought would show about 230,000 [refugees]; the nearly unanimous desire to return to their homes if they were convinced they could do so without danger; the desire of the Quakers to persuade the Israeli authorities to permit experimental repatriation and retraining; their anxiety to talk to Shertok, which was arranged for the following Monday; the beginning of at least subsistence feeding; the burrowing into sand dunes for shelter; and the general

87. This problem was never resolved while McDonald was in Israel. The editors have deleted parts of these discussions throughout the diary.
88. Levinus K. Painter (1889–1983), pastor and social activist; part of AFSC mission in the Middle East, helping establish food and clothing distribution efforts in 1949 and 1950.
89. Delbert E. Replogle (1896–1963) and Ruth Replogle helped lead the AFSC's refugee effort in Acre, Faluja, and Gaza. Lorton Heusel, *Friends on the Front Line: The Story of Delbert and Ruth Replogle* (Greensboro: North Carolina Friends Historical Society, 1985); Nancy Gallagher, *Quakers in the Israeli-Palestinian Conflict*, 105–106, 123–130.
90. Refers to aftermath of Operation Hiram in October–November 1948. Of the 50,000 to 60,000 inhabitants in the Upper Galilee pocket before October 28, 1948, only 30 to 50 percent remained after the fighting. Most villages whose inhabitants actively fought the IDF were depopulated. Most of those displaced were Muslims who fled to Lebanon; most of those who stayed were Christians. After the operation, villages on the Israeli side of the border with Lebanon were cleared for security reasons. Reliable populations such as Greek Catholics in Iqrit were moved southward, and other such transfers of Arab populations continued into 1949. Morris, *The Birth of the Palestinian Refugee Problem Revisited*, 473–517; also David McDowall, *Palestine and Israel: The Uprising and Beyond* (Berkeley: University of California Press, 1991); and Dan Rabinowitz, *Overlooking Nazareth: The Ethnography of Exclusion in Galilee* (New York: Cambridge University Press, 1997).
91. Entry of January 21, 1949.

wretched condition of most of the refugees. As to Egypt, they confirmed the impression which had been given me by Pickett a few days earlier.[92]

To dinner at the Harry S. Davidowitz's. It was a very pleasant family party, which included two daughters and a son-in-law. The food was excellent, and the talk afterwards even better. Dr. Davidowitz, formerly a rabbi and a distinguished authority on Hebrew, gave a group of us an intensely interesting "lecture" for an hour or so on the Mishnah, the Gemara, as making up the Talmud.[93] He sketched, too, the role of the several editors and codifiers of Jewish law and commentary, his analysis of the pre-rabbinic discussions about the rules affecting daily life, showed that the present controversy between the Orthodox and the non-Orthodox was but a recurrence in new form of the millennial-old controversy.

In replying to a departmental inquiry of February 15, McDonald reported the "action of [the] Constituent Assembly [on] February 16, under [the] leadership [of] Shertok, inside tracking [the] Herut motion [to] declare Jerusalem Israel capital despite undoubted popular appeal is [the] best evidence [of the] government's desire [to] postpone decision [on] Jerusalem in hope [of] working out [an] arrangement with PCC and UN."[94]

Saturday, February 19

Worked all morning on my refugee report.[95] Robert Szold [chairman of the Palestine Economic Corporation (PEC)] spent two hours in the late afternoon with me on the roof.[96] He liked the idea of the PEC erecting our building and is going to check into it.[97] He confirmed that Feinberg was extremely close to the president, that Clifford retains his key influence, that Dave Niles hopes to fly over for a short time possibly in connection with the Weizmann visit. He thinks that Silver and Neumann have made their basic mistake by not recognizing the changed status of the ZOA and their personal leadership vis-à-vis Israel. We agreed that we should meet before he left to return to the States.

92. Earlier in February the Replogles with Clarence Pickett visited Arab leaders in Cairo. These included the grand mufti, who insisted that Arab refugees should not return to any Jewish-run entity, and Abd al-Rahman Azzam Pasha of the Arab League, who insisted that 500,000 Arab repatriations were essential for any peace settlement. Gallagher, *Quakers in the Israeli-Palestinian Conflict*, 99–101.

93. Entry of October 15, 1948.

94. McDonald to secretary of state, no. 140, February 18, 1949, NARA, RG 59, 501.BB Palestine, box 2124, folder 1.

95. The report was McDonald's answer to Acheson's request of February 3, 1949.

96. Robert Szold (1889–1977), US attorney and cousin of Henrietta Szold; held government positions in the Wilson administration; part of Weizmann's Zionist Commission in Palestine, 1919; served in ZOA in 1930s and AZEC after 1942, but at World Zionist Congress in 1946 supported Weizmann's moderation over Silver's and Ben-Gurion's activism; in 1949 became chairman of Palestine Economic Corporation, a development company established in 1926.

97. This was to be a building for both the US Embassy and the PEC.

Worked all day on my refugee report. Out to Weizmann's without previous engagement arriving there about five; found him and her returning from a walk in the gardens. They welcomed me and I remained for more than an hour and a half. The first part of the talk was about the election and his inauguration. I underlined the president's congratulations, my regret at my enforced absence from Jerusalem, and my hope that he would understand. He said that he had been sorry for my sake and for President Truman, whom he could not believe responsible for the adverse decision.

Speaking cordially of Ben-Gurion and in answer to my question, Weizmann indicated that Remez was *a* if not *the* logical successor to Ben-Gurion. To him he attributed exceptional ability and geniality. Shertok he regarded as an extremely able technician, but as one who was not always wise on larger issues. In answer to my question about the Negev, Weizmann said that there was no new report on mineral potentialities, but that he would let me know when there was anything. For half an hour or so towards the end, we chatted about the UPA [UJA] battle at home, Jewish and other personalities, etc. Back to the house in time for a snack before going to *Thaïs* with the family and Mrs. Sacks.[98] It was a good performance showing improved ensemble effects.

About nine o'clock Miss Herlitz called to ask if I could come to see Shertok at 9:45. I, of course, said yes. There he outlined to me a new potential crisis in the Israel-Egyptian armistice negotiations. The previous day, Bunche's final draft had been approved unreservedly by the Israelis and by the Egyptians, with only two reservations. The one, technical, on the definition of "defensive forces," and the other, of principle, about the retention of Be'er Sheva by the Jewish forces. Shertok explained that two members of the Egyptian delegation representing the Foreign Office favored signing, but that Lieutenant Colonel Ismail Chirine, close to the court and the king favored [holding] out on Be'er Sheva, lest yielding injure Farouk's prestige.[99] Shertok thought the balance of chances favored Egypt signing, but he asked that I explain the situation to the Department and suggest that they make a final plea to Egypt not to raise new difficulties. I went directly to the office and there dictated in the presence of the military and other members of the staff a draft telegram, which after some

98. Opera by Jules Massenet based on Anatole France's novel of the same title.
99. Lieutenant Colonel Ismail Chirine (1919–1994), King Farouk's aide-de-camp; raised demand for Be'er Sheva on February 17, risking a breakdown of the conference. Prime Minister Ibrahim Abd al-Hadi Pasha (1896–1981) noted that Egypt viewed Be'er Sheva in symbolic and strategic terms and thus wanted to maintain civil administration there. See Caplan, *Futile Diplomacy*, v. 3, 49; Patterson to secretary of state, no. 186, February 22, 1949, *FRUS*, 1949, v. VI, 764–765.

changes was sent off immediately.[100] The next day we were delighted to receive from the Department copy of a representation made that day in Cairo, which in some respects was stronger than our telegram of the day before, showing that Bunche seemingly had also urged action by the Department giving additional reasons.[101]

Joel Fisher and Harry Viteles, the former counsel of the JDC [Joint Distribution Committee],[102] came to tea and to ask my help. At the recent IRO [International Refugee Organization] meeting, through British influence, Tuck had agreed to an addendum to the resolution compensating the JDC for travel expenses of refugees to Israel by providing that payments for such travel after January 31 should not be made until after Tuck had conferred with the PCC.[103] Tuck is due to meet Ethridge within the next days. My advice to Fisher was to urge New York to act so that Ethridge might have specific instructions, and, if possible, before Ethridge and Tuck confer. I also agreed to send through the UN a telegram to Ethridge about an appointment for Fisher.[104]

Tuesday, February 22

Dr. Archer Cohn and Captain Helpern of the organizations to aid Jews in Arab countries, came to ask my help in securing Washington's intervention with the Arab states. I could not be encouraging and explained why, but said I would be glad to pass on a memorandum.

Twelve to twelve-thirty in Shertok's, when we discussed briefly refugees, his recent announcement and the government's general attitude;[105] Rhodes, Shiloah's expectations (he had just returned that morning), and the probable attitude of Bunche; negotiations to start not later than Monday with Transjordan,

100. McDonald to secretary of state, no. 149, February 21, 1949, *FRUS*, 1949, v. VI, 759–760. McDonald reported Shertok's comment that Israel accepted "without reservations" Bunche's draft for an armistice agreement. Egypt's two reservations concerned the definition of defensive forces allowed in the cease-fire area and the continued call for the Israeli evacuation of Be'er Sheva. Bunche's dividing line for the cease-fire in the Negev was well west of Be'er Sheva. McDonald relayed Shertok's comment that US pressure on Egypt could result in an agreement within days: "He pleads urgent action by Department."

101. Acheson to US embassy in Cairo, no. 194, February 21, 1949, *FRUS*, 1949, v. VI, 760–761. The Egyptian government was to be told that, as a consequence of US pressure, Israel had made concessions over Gaza, al-Auja, and Bir 'Asluj; that the final status of Be'er Sheva was to be worked out in a final peace agreement; and that the US government "would deplore any action likely to create further obstacles at time when armistice agreement seems near."

102. Joel H. Fisher (1918–1997), attorney and US treasury official; served in US Coast Guard, 1942–1944; chief, Foreign Exchange and Property Control Section, SHAEF, where he tracked Nazi-plundered gold and silver, 1944–1945; general counsel for JDC, 1946–1949, providing aid for Jewish refugees in Europe.

103. The IRO, which had previously refused to pay to transport DPs into a "war zone," began transferring payments to the JDC in early 1949. Between January and March, the IRO paid the JDC $2 million to transport Jewish refugees to Israel. In April an agreement was reached whereby $10.5 million would be made available to JDC for the transfer of 120,000 refugees to Israel.

104. McDonald to Conciliation Commission [then in Damascus] February 22, 1949, NARA, RG 59, 501.BB Palestine, box 2124, folder 2.

105. Refers to Shertok's statements on refugees to the PCC during the meeting of February 7, 1949.

which might also represent Iraq; Lebanese negotiations to wait on Transjordan and might include Syria.

Tea for van der Velde at Brady's. It was a family affair; only the senior members of the staff being present and was thoroughly enjoyable. Gave van der Velde my long worked-on refugee despatch to be pouched in Athens.

On February 22 McDonald assessed the Palestine refugee problem for Secretary Acheson.[106] *He noted that, like other twentieth-century refugee crises, this one would not solve itself other than through the deaths of the refugees. The United Nations could help only if individual governments supported its efforts. In the meantime, "Neither Tel Aviv nor any of the Arab capitals . . . has yet shown primary concern for the refugees, either for their immediate care or for their ultimate resettlement. . . . On the contrary, there is a tendency discernable in some Israeli and Arab circles to play politics with the refugees."*

McDonald reported that he had received no definitive statements from Ben-Gurion or Shertok, but that the essence of Israeli policy was that responsibility for the refugee problem rested with the Arab states that attacked Israel. "All other factors," McDonald said of the Israeli view, "which may have played a part in the exodus are secondary or comparatively unimportant. Had there been no Arab attack on Israel there would have been no Arab refugees." Israel, he said, would provide technical assistance for refugee resettlement in Arab states and would consider financial contributions, but resettlement was also to be considered as part of broader peace negotiations.

McDonald added, "Though the Israeli spokesmen do not say so, the unprecedentedly rapid influx of Jewish refugees during 1948 and the plan to admit a quarter of a million more in 1949 will, if carried out, fill all or almost all of the houses and business properties previously held by Arab refugees. Arab unoccupied farms will similarly, though not to quite the same degree, be occupied by the recent or expected Jewish refugees. Hence, there will be almost no residence or business property and only a limited number of farms to which the Arab refugees can hope to return."

The Arab states meanwhile, had insisted on the return of Arab refugees before there could be general peace talks, which meant that relations between Israel and its neighbors would "protract indefinitely the present twilight which is neither peace nor war. It should be obvious to the Arab governments . . . that it is impracticable if not impossible for Israel to open its doors to returning refugees before its enemies have agreed to begin peace negotiations."

McDonald said that there were too many unknowns for anyone to create a definite plan to solve the refugee problem. But he recommended the following steps immediately. Griffis and his colleagues should have the resources to keep the refugees alive until their resettlement, meaning the $16 million requested by Truman and to be

106. An edited version is McDonald to secretary of state, no. 46, February 22, 1949, *FRUS,* 1949, v. VI, 761–764. Full version in McDonald Papers, USHMM, box 7, folder 12. See also Knox's follow-up report on the absence of Israeli blood lust toward the Arabs, No. 40, February 23, 1949, NARA, RG 84, entry 2775, box 1, folder 320.

appropriated by Congress. Meanwhile, "constant and concerted pressure" should be put on Israel and the Arab states "to eschew politics in their thinking . . . and to take account of humanitarian considerations. Emphatically these governments should be told that in the long run, the human approach will be the best policy." For the Arab states, he recommended that "lands suitable for resettlement be made available" and that resettlement costs be borne partly by Israel in compensation for appropriated refugee properties and by an international loan. In this way a very large number of Arab refugees could be resettled. For the Israelis, McDonald recommended pressure so that "serious and sympathetic study of plans for the return of those refugees who wish to return be not postponed," and that "permission to return not be tied up with such extraneous problems as permission to Jews now living in Arab countries to leave in order to enter Israel."

On April 1 the Department replied that it was pleased with the objectivity of McDonald's report, that it "has had an important influence" on official thinking, and that the Department "is in accord with your recommendations." It asked McDonald for follow-up recommendations, but in the meantime followed those developed by the Palestine Conciliation Commission.[107]

Wednesday, February 23

Received Ethridge's schedule. Long conference with Jacob Herzog at the house. Again, he explained the differences to me between the Greek Orthodox Church, with its chief constituents throughout the Balkans, and the Russian Orthodox Church, limited almost exclusively to Russia. The USSR is currently endeavoring to penetrate the control of the Greek Church through its influence on the governments and on certain key ecclesiastical personalities.[108] Rome is intensely interested in the USSR's campaign because it sees in the Middle East area the vantage point from which the whole of the Far East and the far southeast can be most advantageously reached. In particular, the frontier sections of Moslem peoples midway between Soviet Russia and China, India, Persia are crucial. Hence, too, the strategic place of Palestine and Israel.

Herzog then developed one of his favorite [complaints], that the West is failing to meet the challenge of Soviet Russia, primarily because the former relies upon material gifts to lift the standard of living, but fails to supply any moral incentives with which to win the soul of the peoples materially aided. Without spiritual penetration, the material gifts are accepted and used, but by no means necessarily to advance the purposes of the donors. This moral, according to Herzog, has particular applicability in the potential relationship be-

---

107. *FRUS*, 1949, v. VI, 764, n. 2. See also Knox's report, no. 40, February 23, 1949, NARA, RG 84, E 2775, box 1, folder 320.
108. See Daniela Kalkandjieva, *The Russian Orthodox Church, 1917–1948: From Decline to Resurrection* (Abingdon: Routledge, 2015), 264–344; for the Orthodox leaders in Alexandria specifically, see Rami Ginat, *The Soviet Union and Egypt, 1945–1955* (London: Frank Cass, 1993), 10–13.

tween Israel and the Moslem world, and more immediately, the surrounding Arab world. Israel will be fatally deceived if it relies upon military, economic, or even upon scientific strength in its relations with its neighbors. It must have for them a fundamental and harmonious spiritual value, which, being in tune with the *Weltgeist* of the Moslem, will be welcomed and be built upon.

Herzog admitted all that is said about the present corruption and weakness of the Arab states. This he attributes to their "moral aridness." He argues, however, that sooner or later, perhaps within a generation, some moral content will have been given to Arab nationalism, and that if the Jews have not helped to adapt and develop this moral motivating power, they will be crushed by the resulting strength given to their neighbors. Herzog argued that therefore the Jews, who because of their millennial necessity of adapting themselves to many and varying forms of environment, must use that adaptive power to adjust the best of the West to the natural aptitudes and inclinations of the Arabs. If the Jews do this, they will survive and be a beneficent influence to humanity. Otherwise they can hope only for a relatively brief period of security from the potential menace of the Arab sea of 40 million.

Dr. Mohn and Dr. Bagge, the Swedish Minister in Cairo, were at the house for two hours talk at teatime. This time Bagge was frank and intensely interesting.[109]

At six o'clock, Ezra Danin and Miss Herlitz came to see me, the former to report on the work of his interdepartmental committee for the study of the refugee problem. With his two colleagues Yosef Weitz and Zalman Lifshitz,[110] they had made a thorough study of the possibilities of resettlement. So comprehensive was their study, that it required and enabled me easily to make the despatch's correction to the Department of my earlier statement to the effect that "no one here had really put his mind on the problem."

In August 1948 Ben-Gurion had appointed Danin, Weitz, and Lifshitz as a transfer committee to study the Arab refugees' organized resettlement in the Arab states. Danin and Weitz, had in fact been working on the problem since May 1948, and Weitz in his JNF capacity had been involved in resettlement of Jewish immigrants in former Arab villages. On February 11, 1949, Shertok informed the transfer committee of his statement to the PCC earlier in the month that the refugees would not return. It was essential, he said, to convince public opinion in the United States and in the Arab states that return was impossible.[111]

109. McDonald to secretary of state, no. 160, February 26, 1949, NARA, RG 59, 501.BB Palestine, box 2123, folder 2.

110. Zalman Lifshitz (1901–1951), Belorussian-born surveyor; emigrated to Palestine, 1924; land expert and cartographer with Jewish Agency in 1930s; did studies of possible partition schemes, 1937; developed agricultural proposals to show that Palestine's absorptive capacity was greater than the British had asserted; adviser to Israeli government on refugee issues.

111. Morris, *The Birth of the Palestinian Refugee Problem Revisited*, 329, 554–556.

Textbox 8.1.
The Israeli-Egyptian Armistice

On February 24, 1949, the Egyptian delegation in Rhodes backed off from previous demands. After six weeks of formal and informal talks, the Israelis and Egyptians signed a general armistice agreement—the first agreement signed between Israel and one of its Arab neighbors. It was expected to lead to an eventual peace settlement.

The agreement stipulated a cease-fire. The recognized armistice lines left the Israelis with most of what they had captured; Egyptian forces pulled out of the Negev entirely. Egypt was now permitted to remove its besieged forces from Faluja. The agreement also provided for the eventual withdrawal of Egyptian forces from the Bethlehem-Hebron sector of Palestine. Egypt maintained defensive forces in the Gaza Strip. The contested strategic town of al-Auja near the Egyptian border became the headquarters of a Mixed Israeli-Egyptian Armistice Commission [MAC], which was to maintain the peace under UN supervision. Al-Auja and its environs were also demilitarized.[1]

McDonald wrote Felix Frankfurter the next day: "It was a thrilling moment yesterday afternoon when the Foreign Office called to give me advanced news [of the armistice]. It promises to be, as Shertok put it, the 'turning point.' Now . . . none of the other Arab states can argue with any show of reason that 'loyalty to the Arab cause' forbids their carrying on formal negotiations. . . . What has been achieved since May 14 is so far beyond what could reasonably [have] been expected, that the future should hold no insuperable obstacles. . . ."[2]

On March 6, President Truman issued a press statement that he was "immensely gratified over the news from Rhodes. . . . I hope that now . . . this pattern for peace will be followed rapidly in the conclusion of similar agreements between Israel and the other Arab States. The general armistice will then, I trust, lead to the attainment of permanent peace, thus freeing the talents of these Near Eastern peoples for constructive work in the development of their respective countries." The day following the signing, Eban once again petitioned Secretary-General Trygve Lie for Israeli membership in the United Nations.[3]

---

1. Medzini, ed., *Israel's Foreign Relations: Selected Documents, 1947–1974*, 167–79. The US assessment, written by Major Lawrence Brady on February 24, is in NARA, RG 84, E 2774, box 2, folder 321.9.

2. McDonald to Frankfurter, February 24, 1949 McDonald Papers, Columbia University, box 2, folder 24.

3. References in *FRUS*, 1949, v. VI, 765–66; *DFPI*, v. 2, d. 397.

Stopped by the office on my way to the airport to meet Ethridge and his PCC colleagues who were due at one o'clock [from Beirut]. Others there, when the plane arrived promptly, included [Albert] Vanthier, the French consul who amused me by his firm insistence to a French member of the UN that he be greeted as the chargé; Mohn, Gruenberger,[112] and, of course, the police and photographers.

The PCC had visited Amman, Cairo, Riyadh, Baghdad, Damascus, and Beirut. It learned of the bitterness in the Arab capitals over the military defeat and the refugee issue.[113] Ethridge reported to Acheson that the "immediate key to peace negotiations if not to peace, is [the] refugee problem. . . . Commission plans to set date for meeting with Arab representatives under its chairman to explore further [the] refugee problem. Out of that meeting, providing Israel has accepted in principle [the General Assembly] resolution as to refugees, will come discussion of other phases."[114]

After greeting Ethridge, I chatted for a little while with Yalçin, the elderly Turkish representative. I found him alert and seemingly untired. Despite its long disuse, my French seemed to serve. Finally, I drove Ethridge to the Kaete Dan for his press conference (he being the chairman for this period). At the press conference, Ethridge remained vague and non-committal on almost all questions asked. He did indicate, however;

1) While [the] official site of the PCC must, under the UN resolution, remain Jerusalem, it was free to operate anywhere where it could do so most advantageously;
2) Role is exclusively conciliatory;
3) In only one area, that of Jerusalem, does the UN resolution require the PCC to draft and submit a specific plan, that of internationalization;
4) The resolution envisaged the report at the September Assembly, but since there is to be an April Assembly, the PCC will endeavor to report as fully as possible to them.

During our trip to the Kaete Dan and later to the house, and at the short luncheon, which Ethridge and I had in my study, he made these points:

1) In all the Arab capitals there was the same story told, though with varying shades;[115]

---

112. Assistant chief of protocol, Israeli Foreign Ministry.
113. In general, Simon A. Waldman, *Anglo-American Diplomacy and the Palestinian Refugee Problem, 1948–1951* (New York: Palgrave Macmillan, 2015), 63–76.
114. Ethridge [through Burdett] to secretary of state, no. 170, February 28, 1949, *FRUS*, 1949, v. VI, 776–778.
115. Syrian prime minister Khalid al-Azm, for example, refused to offer de facto recognition to Israel. He complained about the Constituent Assembly meeting in Jerusalem, the inability

2) He had not heard of the IRO resolution requiring Tuck to consult the PCC before continuing payments to JDC for transportation costs of refugees to Israel after January 31.[116] Nor had he heard of Tuck's projected visit. His first impression was that it was not the PCC's business to inject itself into the controversial field of Jewish refugees' transportation to Israel;

3) Confirmed that PCC had asked the UN for the help of a refugee expert;

4) As to Jerusalem, I got the impression that he regarded the form of internationalization as acceptable even if the substance were partition;

5) Evidently the Arab League, though ineffective as a military instrument, had secured Arab agreement to put the refugee issue forward as a condition precedent to peace negotiations. [Ethridge had argued] with the Arabs that to insist on permission to refugees to return prior to peace would be to invite the throwing of the whole problem of peace back into the UN, where Ethridge told the Arabs, "they had always been defeated."

6) Abdullah had said that, given funds for resettlement, he would take "all" the refugees. Ethridge seemed to think that if Abdullah's willingness to take refugees became known, there might be a form of competition between the Arab states for the funds which would go with the refugees, if not for the refugees themselves.

7) Ibn Saud's capital and surroundings, except for the expensive American cars, were almost unimaginably primitive. Ibn Saud spoke with enthusiasm of Roosevelt, saying that if the latter had lived there would not have been all this trouble with the Jews.[117]

From four to after six, an interesting and worthwhile staff conference at which many problems were examined and some advanced towards solution. In the evening, the family and I to the gala symphony concert in honor of Chopin's anniversary.[118] The first two rows of the balcony were occupied by government officials and by members of the diplomatic corps. Among the guests were the members of the PCC. I was delighted to have Ethridge whisper to me that he had found Shertok "much more reasonable" than at their first conference.[119] I took occasion to pass on this item to Shertok at the end of the concert; it pleased him.

of refugees to return home, Jewish immigration, and Israel's arms imports, all of which were contrary, he said, to UN resolutions. See Ethridge [through Pinkerton] to secretary of state, no. 83, February 24, 1949, *FRUS*, 1949, v. VI, 766–777.

116. Entry of February 21, 1949.

117. King Ibn Saud's belief that Roosevelt had been on his side concerning Palestine is discussed in Richard Breitman and Allan J. Lichtman, *FDR and the Jews* (Cambridge, MA: Belknap Press, 2013), 238–261; 302–305; also Goda et al., eds., *To the Gates of Jerusalem*, 7, 22, 165–166.

118. Frederic Chopin died in October 1849.

119. Ethridge was overly optimistic. He told Shertok that, with an Egyptian armistice agreement in hand and others being negotiated, the PCC could "begin to get down to some details of peace-making." The Arab states were most concerned with two questions—the Arab refugee problem and Israel's intentions more generally. Ethridge also told Shertok that the Arab governments "have come back largely to a position where they would like to see Israel do or say

Friday, February 25

Worked at home all day. At four-thirty, Mr. Grunwald of Twentieth Century Fox[120] came in to talk about *The Iron Curtain* and the possibility of our seeing a private showing of it. I explained that we could not invite government people to see it with us (he disavowed desiring this), but that we would be happy to see it alone. It was agreed that he would show us the inauguration reel, which Tetlie had just received and *The Iron Curtain* at the same time. Grunwald also volunteered to provide us with a showing of anything we would like to see at the house.[121]

At five, Danin came in with the summary of his inter-departmental report, which he promised me on Wednesday. It was just what I needed, and I told him that I would send it almost verbatim as my recollection of his long talk with me earlier. We then went on to discuss many matters especially in the field of Arab relations.

Danin outlined the transfer committee's recommendations within the contexts of refugee numbers, the value of refugee property, mass resettlements of other refugees in Europe and South Asia, as well as uncultivated arable land, irrigation possibilities, and related social and economic conditions in the Arab states, particularly Iraq, Syria, and Transjordan. The report concluded that the return of Arab refugees to Israel would be far more difficult than their resettlement elsewhere, and not simply for security reasons. The Arab economy in Palestine was destroyed, and the means of Arab livelihood often no longer existed. Jewish refugees were arriving and the country's political structures were developing accordingly. "[The] exodus of Arabs from Israel completely changed the character of the country. . . . As a result of the flight of the Arabs, Israel developed on lines totally different from what was thought at first." If the aforementioned Arab states would make land available, the cost of resettlement would be roughly $240 million. The bulk would come from a UN-backed loan, but Israel could

something about the refugee problem, not as a condition precedent, but as perhaps, to put it, [as] evidence of their good faith or desire for peace."

Shertok replied that "we do not envisage repatriation as the major solution of the problem . . . the sooner the problem of resettlement in neighboring countries is tackled seriously and constructively, the better it is for all concerned." If the refugee issue were so pressing to the Arab governments, he asked, "then what is it that holds them back from entering the peace negotiations with us?" Israel's willingness to readmit "a certain number of Arabs . . . depends on the general spirit and also fundamental provisions of the peace settlement. It is of vital importance that we know in what kind of a world we shall be living." For the discussion, see *DFPI*, v. 2, d. 400. For Ethridge's reports and those of Burdett, see Ethridge [through Burdett] to secretary of state, no. 171, February 28, 1949, *FRUS*, 1949, v. VI, 776–778; and Burdett to secretary of state, no. 167, February 26, 1949, *FRUS*, 1949, v. VI, 772–773. Both reports were sent to all US missions in the Middle East except Tel Aviv.

120. Probably the Russian-born Dimitri de Grunwald (1914–1990), who with his brother Anatoly, pioneered selling territorial film distribution rights. Although they were independent producers, they were associated with 20th Century Fox.

121. *The Iron Curtain* (1948), a Cold War thriller based on the story of Igor Gouzenko, a Soviet atomic spy in Canada. Sometimes recognized as Hollywood's first Cold War movie, it opened in Western Europe in June 1949. Openings in New York and Paris brought violent protests by the political Left that the film was anti-Soviet and a provocation.

contribute part of the total based on the value of lost Arab property in Israel minus that of Jewish property lost during the fighting.[122]

Danin and his colleagues relied heavily on the scholarly work of Joseph B. Schechtman, who after the war studied the political problem of national minorities in European borderlands and advocated population transfers in these areas as a guarantee of lasting peace. Schechtman pointed to national minority politics as a cause of war in 1939 and to the ways in which Europe was solving the issue in the postwar period.[123]

He insisted that it was a serious mistake for the PCC to ask for a token concession by Israel because this would merely whet Arab appetite and delay the settlement. Explaining the weakness of the Arabs, Danin reported that, when he was in Egypt a few years ago, an Egyptian recruiting officer told him that they could accept only one out of seven or eight hundred possible recruits examined; later, Danin said he had learned that the number should have been reduced to 250 or 300. In somewhat lesser degree, the same shocking state of debasement of the masses of the Arab population was to be found everywhere. Danin is leaving within a day or two for London for the Israel Appeal and to be associated with the Israeli legation.

Esther Herlitz, who accompanied Danin, conveyed to Ambassador Elath in Washington McDonald's apology for having reported to the State Department that the Israeli government was not paying attention to the refugee issue. She also noted, "McDonald [is] convinced [that the] majority must be settled [in the] Arab countries and will talk to [the] Conciliation Commission accordingly."[124]

Danin had scarcely left when Ethridge, Wilkins, and John Halderman came in.[125] They had spent a part of the morning with Ben-Gurion at the latter's house with Shertok present, had subsequently seen the Foreign Minister again, and had completed their day by a social call on President Weizmann. Ethridge expressed himself immediately as delighted at the comparatively conciliatory attitude he found. He contrasted it very favorably with the professorial, didactic and "unyielding" attitude shown by Shertok at the initial five-hour session in Jerusalem [February 7]. Ethridge then outlined his session with Shertok the previous day. He had found the latter prepared to consider sympathetically the problem of refugees, instead of standing dogmatically on his earlier position that nothing could be done until the peace negotiations.

122. Printed in *DFPI*, v. 2, d. 406. McDonald's copy of the memorandum is in McDonald Papers, USHMM, box 7, folder 11.
123. Specifically Joseph B. Schechtman, *European Population Transfers, 1939–1945* (New York: Oxford University Press, 1946).
124. Herlitz to Elath, February 24, 1949, *DFPI*, v. 2, d. 404.
125. John W. Halderman (1907–1989), part of State Department's Office of United Nations Affairs; headed US delegation to PCC's Committee on Jerusalem.

He thought Shertok also less adamant on Jerusalem.[126] The conference with Ben-Gurion had opened with the latter asking a number of questions about the impressions the PCC had gained in its swing around the circle of Arab capitals. As Ethridge answered, Ben-Gurion continued to inquire, indicating, Ethridge thought, a willingness to try to make adjustments to the Arab viewpoint.[127]

Ethridge and I talked at some length about refugees, I reading portions of my despatch to the Department dated three days earlier. Ethridge commented that his own thinking was very much along the lines of my conclusion. He said that they had not yet heard whom the UN was sending as their refugee assistant. It is noteworthy in the light of subsequent decisions by the PCC to hold a conference of Arab states in Beirut March 21, that to the best of my recollection (this is being dictated March 3) Ethridge said nothing at all about the proposal of such a conference.[128] The reason I am so certain of this is that had he mentioned it I would have surely reported it to my colleagues. It would have been such a surprise to me, and would have so shocked my sense of what was politically expedient or desirable, that I could not have stopped to comment on it at the time and subsequently.

Ethridge was most cordial, but made no suggestion about my coming up to Jerusalem. Nor did I suggest this, because I wished to lean over backwards away from any move which might seem to suggest interference with the PCC. The only possible exception to this was my statement to Ethridge that I thought it would be a mistake to approve of the Department's suggestion of sending Samuel Kopper out as the PCC's American Arab expert. Unfortunately, Wilkins was not present at that moment, having gone off to see Knox and to dinner with Comay. I could not be certain whether my criticism of Kopper registered strongly with Ethridge or not.[129]

My general impression of Ethridge was that he had learned a good deal by his swing around the circle of Arab capitals, but perhaps his feeling of greater

126. *DFPI*, v. 2, d. 400.
127. Ethridge told Ben-Gurion that the refugees were the Arab states' main concern and that a humanitarian gesture by Israel would facilitate a general settlement. Ben-Gurion stressed the need for military security, which, he said, would be ensured through Jewish immigration. Ben-Gurion emphasized, however, the common destiny of Israel and the Arab states, and insisted that peace would be easy if the Arabs would "give up [the] objective of throwing Jews into [the] sea." Ethridge optimistically reported to Acheson that the Israeli government was "cooling off." Burdett to secretary of state, no. 170, February 28, 1949, *FRUS*, 1949, v. VI, 775–776 (sent to all US missions in the Middle East except Tel Aviv); Ethridge [through Burdett] to secretary of state, no. 171, February 28, 1949, *FRUS*, 1949, v. VI, 776–778. See also Ben-Gurion Diary, entry of February 25, 1949.
128. Ethridge proposed this meeting to Arab officials during the PCC tour of the Arab capitals. See Ethridge [through Pinkerton] to secretary of state, no. 83, February 24, 1949; Stabler to secretary of state, no. 72, February 24, 1949, *FRUS*, 1949, v. VI, 766–768. These despatches were sent to the US consulate in Jerusalem, but not to the Tel Aviv mission.
129. Samuel K. C. Kopper (1913–1955), part of the State Department's Office of Near Eastern and African Affairs. Ethridge was already reporting to Kopper on the attitudes of the Arab governments. See Ethridge to Kopper, January 27, 1949, NARA, RG 59, E 1434, LF 54 D 403, box 11.

"reasonableness" of the Jews now was attributable primarily to the relative [Arab] intransigence. He seemed also to have a greater recognition of the complexities and difficulties. Again, he indicated that he would settle the Jerusalem issue through a substantial partition if only the form of internationalization could be kept. He hoped for an ad interim report by the April assembly but the major one not before the September Assembly.

In answer to my direct question, Ethridge said that his instructions came from the Department or the president. He did not put it quite this categorically, but implied that since US support would be necessary to see any settlement through the UN, it was essential that the PCC's plans should have the Department's approval. Nothing was said about liaison with the British or closer liaison with the Israelis. How serious the lack of such contacts might become was evident later in connection with the PCC's Beirut conference.

Saturday, February 26

The second half of the morning given over to a conference with Max Berner of Birmingham, Felix Frankfurter's sister [Estelle], and Major Hay, Lorna Wingate's mother's friend.[130] It was a very pleasant session, with Major Hay supplying most of the amusement. When they were leaving he promised to have Lorna get in touch with me soon after her arrival here.

Sunday, February 27

A delightful party at Cashman's and Knox's for Hope. There I talked business with Miss Herlitz and enlisted her cooperation with a mutual friend about Knox. Then off to our second attendance at *Manon* with Madame de Phillipe, as usual, in the title role. The performance was an improvement on the first, though the tenor was as unsatisfactory as before.

Monday, February 28

Busy at home during early morning. Eleven o'clock to twelve at Weizmann's office in Rehovot. I found him there with Weisgal. When the latter left the room for a few minutes, Weizmann confessed that he was deeply disturbed and had hardly slept during the night because of his fear that the British were still planning under "Master Bevin's unyielding hatred," to block Israel by placing an iron ring around the south from Gaza and Aqaba northward. He wished he could speak to the president about it, for he was sure the latter would understand; he regretted that it would be more than a month before he could have this opportunity; the president had quickly grasped the significance of the

---

130. Lorna Wingate (b. 1917), widow of British Major-General Orde Wingate (1903–1944) who died in a plane crash in Burma. Orde Wingate trained and led Haganah units, 1936–1939, and became a fierce advocate of Zionism. Lorna Wingate accompanied her husband to Palestine, remained an ardent Zionist, and co-chaired the Youth Aliyah movement during and after 1949. Major Malcolm Vivian Hay (1881–1962), pro-Zionist British officer and friend of the Wingates who later wrote extensively on the Jewish Question.

Negev when Weizmann had shown him the map. Only the US could, added Weizmann, block the Bevin plan.

Weizmann's second source of worry was his conviction that the projected rate of immigration, particularly if it included a large percentage of Oriental Jews, would swamp the country and destroy its economic soundness. There simply were not funds enough for such a gigantic task of integration, and the government officials should recognize it. I was very struck by Weizmann's attitude on immigration, because he was the first official who even in private had ever dared to hint that there might have to be any partial narrowing of the open door. Incidentally, Weizmann indicated his fear lest a too large proportion of Orientals with habits and traditions so alien to those of the pioneers who had built the country would destroy its unity or profoundly change its character. Weizmann said that he was glad I had come because I had enabled him to get these fears off his chest. I argued with him that in perspective the situation could not be as dark as he feared. Speaking of the political local scene, Weizmann indicated concern about Ben-Gurion's health and said categorically that the trouble was heart and that the other complaints were incidental.[131]

Gave Weisgal some mail, which, he had promised the day before when he was at the house, that he would take. On that earlier occasion I had outlined to him the elements in the situation here following the Israeli-Egyptian armistice. I stressed the importance of a realistic attitude by the PCC on Jerusalem and the refugees. I found him somewhat less willing to put his mind on political problems than I had hoped.

Shiloah came in at five and stayed with Knox and me until nearly seven. We talked fully about many subjects and, not being hurried, were able to profit much more than we could have otherwise. The prospects for the Transjordan-Israel armistice negotiations are, according to Shiloah, only fair. The Transjordan delegation is not impressive, and there is the serious uncertainty of Britain's position. Moreover, there is no certainty that Transjordan will have adequate credentials from Iraq. Israel intends to insist that the latter shall not maneuver itself into the position of the one Arab country which has avoided recognition of Israel through negotiation. Shiloah admitted, however, that though the prospects were not too bright, the initial exchanges at Rhodes might hold out much more hope. This he and his colleagues would know better after a few days of exchanges with the Transjordanians.

After the signing of the Israeli-Egyptian armistice (Textbox 8.1, p. 400), formal armistice talks between Israel and Transjordan opened in Rhodes under Bunche's supervision on March 4, 1949. Secret peace negotiations between senior Israeli and Transjordanian representatives had stalled over a complex of issues. King Abdullah had to keep his intentions secret from the Arab world and even from members of his own

131. Summary in McDonald to secretary of state, no. 169, March 1, 1949, NARA, RG 59, MC 1390, reel 18, frame 692.

cabinet. Shiloah and Moshe Dayan, who had been involved in the secret talks, led the Israeli team at Rhodes, arriving on March 1. King Abdullah wanted to send Abdullah al-Tel, the Arab Legion commander in Jerusalem who had been heavily involved in the secret negotiations, but al-Tel declined to negotiate publicly with the Israelis. Lesser military personalities led Transjordan's delegation, including Colonel Ahmed Sidqi al-Jundi and Lieutenant Colonel Mohammed Maayte, as did the Foreign Ministry's director-general, Riad al-Muflih.[132]

The second point, which Shiloah developed at length, was the [argument] against the PCC's suggested all-Arab refugee conference. He argued that no possible good could come from such a meeting, but instead much harm. Each Arab state would tend to outbid the other in intransigency. His thesis was, in essence, almost identical with that which two days later we were to learn was the position of the British Foreign Office, Kirkbride in Amman,[133] Dow in Jerusalem,[134] and Mack.[135]

Another subject on which Shiloah talked interestingly was the disadvantages of Jerusalem as the operational site for the PCC. There it was difficult for the Arab states to be represented and at ease with Abdullah's jurisdiction. Moreover, it was wholly impossible at Government House or at the King David Hotel for delegates to have the informal, confidential or even secret conferences which had made the success at Rhodes possible. In addition, the political atmosphere of Jerusalem was not conducive to moderation or agreement. Shiloah suggested that while, of course, the PCC might keep Jerusalem as its official headquarters, it operate on specific problems from other sites, for example, Geneva or Paris. When Shiloah left, both Knox and I felt amply repaid for a long session.[136]

132. McDonald to secretary of state, no. 164, March 1, 1949, NARA, RG 59, 501.BB Palestine, box 2124, folder 2. On the Rhodes negotiations, see Bar-Joseph, *The Best of Enemies*, 196–213; Ben-Dror, *Ralph Bunche and the Arab-Israeli Conflict*, 185–217.

133. Alec Kirkbride (1897–1978), British deputy resident in Transjordan, 1927–1937; district commissioner in Palestine, 1937–1939; British resident in Transjordan, 1939–1946, British minister and then ambassador to Transjordan, 1946–1952.

134. Sir Hugh Dow (1886–1978), British consul general in Jerusalem.

135. Sir Henry Mack (1894–1974), British ambassador to Baghdad, 1948–1951.

136. McDonald forwarded these comments to Ethridge. McDonald to secretary of state [for Ethridge], no. 165, March 1, 1949, NARA, RG 59, 501.BB Palestine, box 2124, folder 2.

9. March 1949

On March 4, 1949, with Ralph Bunche presiding in Rhodes, Israel and Trans-jordan began to negotiate an armistice. Transjordan had a weak hand. Having fought a hard campaign, the Arab Legion had little ammunition and could not risk more hostilities. Yet, if Abdullah hoped to keep what was left of the territory allotted to the Arabs in 1947, he had to negotiate with Israel and risk alienating the Arab League and Palestinian Arabs.[1]

At the same time, talks between Israeli and Lebanese representatives proceeded at Ras al-Naqura [Rosh Hanikra] on the Israeli-Lebanese border. These negotiations were simpler, because both sides accepted the existing international boundary as the armistice line. The main issue was Israel's withdrawal from Lebanon's border villages that it had occupied since October. The IDF had already evacuated five of the fifteen occupied villages in January. The Israelis also insisted that Syrian troops leave Leba-nese territory, and they tried, unsuccessfully, to link the talks with Lebanon to the withdrawal of Syrian troops from Israeli territory. Syria and Iraq had yet to initiate armistice talks with Israel.[2]

The United States continued to stress the plight of Arab refugees, which it saw as the fundamental problem. The United Nations Relief for Palestinian Refugees [UNRPR], established in November 1948 and placed under Stafford Griffis, was concerned only with relief, not with resettlement or repatriation—and it was offi-cially scheduled to cease operations on August 31, 1949. Washington worried that the refugee issue made the Arab states less likely to conclude peace and more open to Soviet influence. Despite having asked McDonald for a detailed consideration of the refugee problem in early February and having received his careful assessment later that month, the State Department excluded him from most discussions in March concern-ing the refugee issue.

Tuesday, March 1

Mordecai Eliash and I talked on the roof from eleven to twelve. I found him extraordinarily intelligent, as he has the reputation of being. A brilliant lawyer, an exceptional linguist, and a strict Orthodox Jew, who has been

---

1. Benny Morris, *The Road to Jerusalem*, 194–198; Ben-Dror, *Ralph Bunche and the Arab-Israeli Conflict*, 185–217. See also Efraim Karsch, ed. *Israel: The First Hundred Years*, v. 4: *Israel in the International Arena*, 73–100, on British involvement in Israel-Transjordan negotiations.
2. Overview in Morris, *1948*, 344, 378–380; relevant documents in *DFPI*, v. 3.

intimately acquainted with the British under the Mandate, should be an ideal representative [to London].[3]

Luncheon at the Boustan Café with the members of the UJA delegation.[4] During the meal I chatted with Mayor Rokach about the unwillingness of the General Zionists to accept Ben-Gurion's terms for the cabinet membership;[5] and, of more immediate importance to us, the possibility of finding a site for the building which the Palestine Economic Corporation and possibly the Rockefeller group might be interested in. Rokach said that the municipality was ready to lease for a long period a plot near Habimah and that he would talk to Szold about it. I hope he does.[6] In introducing Viteles, I spoke for about three minutes as a form of welcome to the UJA guests. Viteles spoke interestingly about the condition of Jews in Aden, Yemen, Iran, Iraq, and Syria and the inevitability of the need to evacuate considerable numbers from Aden and Yemen.[7]

After lunch there was just time to get home and to drive to the Gat to pick up Colonel Andrus and Captain Frothingham and to go on to Habimah for Tel Aviv's first formal reception for President Weizmann. As we approached the theatre circle, the crowd was so dense and the traffic arrangement so inadequate that we got out and walked. Without the broad shoulders and impressive uniform of the colonel, we would never have made our way through a crowd. Arriving, we were ushered into the front row downstairs, where presently we were joined by Ershov [and entourage]. As we were waiting for the ceremony to begin, I noticed Vanthier, the French chargé, arguing with Gruenberger[8] and refusing to take his seat in the second row. Finally, he was brought over and placed in one of the two seats reserved for the Shertoks. Then he explained to me that, as a matter of protocol, he could not sit behind the row reserved for the diplomatic corps.

The proceedings, though all in Hebrew, were impressive. The citations to the professors, [Ernst David] Bergmann's lists of their achievements, Weizmann's brief talk, the presentation of the citations and a brief address by one of the men. Thanks to Shalom having followed us in to the theatre, we were able to find our car quickly, and were home in good time.

Wednesday, March 2

Conference with Rabbi Bar-Ilan at the Sharon Hotel, where he was resting because of a heart condition. He expressed appreciation of my coming to

3. Entry of February 15 1949.
4. The United Jewish Appeal was readying a $250 million drive for 1949, and the UJA Overseas Delegation, consisting of some forty members, was in Israel.
5. Ben-Gurion was willing to include the General Zionists in the governing coalition so long as they accepted Mapai's social and economic policies. The General Zionists accepted Ben-Gurion's defense policies, but as a party representing private enterprise, they could not accept Mapai's labor orientation. They also insisted on three cabinet posts. Medding, *The Founding of Israeli Democracy*, 57–58.
6. Entry of February 19, 1949.
7. Entries of December 27, 1948, and January 13, 1949.
8. Assistant Chief of Protocol, Israeli Foreign Ministry.

see him. We talked about cabinet making and the difficulties Ben-Gurion was having with the General Zionists and Mapam.[9] The rabbi was especially amusing in the excuse he gave for his desire to keep Goldie Meyerson out of the cabinet. It was that she was too important to be allowed to leave Moscow. He was emphatic about the vital need of continuing a prohibition of lay marriages.

His real purpose in asking to see me was, however, to express his concern about Jerusalem and his hope that I might be able to explain personally to President Truman on a visit to Washington the spiritual significance of the city to Jews.[10] I explained that such a trip was out of the question. The question then arose of a conference between the rabbis and Ethridge. I said I thought this would be useful provided, of course, Shertok approved in advance.

Mr. Harmon Goldstone[11] of the Nelson Rockefeller interests[12] came to talk about their housing project here. Thus far, after two weeks, he was still uncertain that his group would be able to function. He was interested in what I then told him of our hopes for a building here and thought that they might possibly collaborate with the PEC on it.

Knox and I then cleared up a number of accumulated telegrams. But what interested me especially was a telegram received today relayed from Washington reporting the British Foreign Office's attitude toward the PCC [Palestine Conciliation Commission] Beirut all-Arab conference.[13] To my delight, the despatch said in effect that the Foreign Office, Kirkbride in Amman, Dow in Jerusalem, and Mack [in Baghdad], were opposed to the idea of the conference because "the Arabs had a bad effect on one another."

I suggested, and Knox agreed, that we send a telegram to the Department underlining the striking identity of these English views and those expressed by Shiloah two days earlier. We concluded the message with the comment that, had we known of the project in time, we would have strongly expressed identical views. [It is hard to fathom] how the PCC happened to arrive at such a fantastic decision, which at best could be futile and at worst could delay success of the pending Israel-Transjordan and the Israel-Lebanon armistice negotiation,

9. The Hashomer HaTzair element of Mapam repeatedly voted not to enter a coalition with Mapai because of foreign policy differences regarding the Soviet Union and Mapam's more pronounced cooperative economic vision. Medding, *The Founding of Israeli Democracy*, 48–52.

10. Negotiations concerning Jerusalem at this time are in *DFPI*, v. 3, d. 216, 217, 220.

11. Harmon Goldstone (1911–2001), noted New York architect; helped design the World of Tomorrow exhibition at the 1939 New York World's Fair and the UN building in 1947; in Israel for three months at earlier invitation of Mordechai Bentov, then minister of labor and construction in the provisional government.

12. Nelson Rockefeller (1908–1979), grandson of John D. Rockefeller; served as assistant secretary of state for American republic affairs; after Roosevelt's death returned to New York and headed philanthropic and business organizations aimed at economic and social development in the world's struggling economies; returned to government in 1950 to head the International Advisory Board, which was charged with implementing Truman's Point Four program (see entry of March 6, 1949).

13. Entry of February 25, 1949.

and possibly even upset the whole present trend towards peaceful adjustment.[14] The mystery deepens when one remembers that the PCC must have cleared [the idea] with the Department, which in turn would almost certainly have cleared [it] with the Foreign Office.

McDonald reported these warnings on March 1 by recounting his February 28 discussion with Shiloah. No Arab government, he warned, would dare to adopt a conciliatory position at such a conference.[15] On the same day, the PCC invited the governments of the seven Arab League states to send representatives to Beirut for a preliminary exchange of views with the PCC, to begin on March 21.[16]

William Tuck [director-general of the International Refugee Organization] and his colleague, William Cox, came for dinner. After dinner they told me of their talks in Jerusalem with the members of the PCC. As was to have been expected, the PCC declined to adopt the baby which the IRO desired to wish upon them.[17] At first they wished not to answer the IRO's letter at all, but finally consented to give a non-committal reply. This allows Tuck to go ahead with the payments to JDC for transportation costs [for displaced persons] to Israel after January 31. Tuck was very emphatic, as was also Cox, that there must be no leak whatever prior to the end of the Beirut conference. If there were, there was the possibility that the PCC might reverse itself and come out against the continuation of the payments. I promised to warn Joel Fisher of the JDC.

Thursday, March 3

Forty-five minute talk with L. W. Ross, Socony-Vacuum[18] representative in Israel and Cyprus. He told me a number of interesting facts about the Haifa refinery, for example, that the local needs of Israel did not require more than a seventh of its capacity, that before the war it regularly received half of its crude by tanker, and that a second pipeline doubling the capacity of the first was projected; no serious damage was caused to the tanks by the Israelis draining of them;[19] a settlement with the British owners might be expected presently and also one with Iraq, the latter perhaps to follow the former; full operation of the refinery is to the interests of all parties concerned. Israel at present is receiving

14. McDonald to secretary of state, no. 176, March 3, 1949, NARA, RG 59, MC 1390, reel 18, frame 695.

15. Summary in *FRUS*, 1949, v. VI, 785, n. 1.

16. Burdett to secretary of state, no. 177, March 2, 1949, *FRUS*, 1949, v. VI, 785–786, and n. 1.

17. Refers to the British insistence that the PCC approve IRO financial aid to the JDC for the transport of Jewish refugees to Israel. See entries of February 21 and 24, 1949. See also Gerard Daniel Cohen, *In War's Wake: Europe's Displaced Persons in the Postwar Order* (Oxford: Oxford University Press, 2012), 109–110.

18. Standard Oil of New York and Vacuum Oil Company merged in 1931, creating Socony Vacuum, which later renamed itself the Mobil Oil Company.

19. Entries of August 1 and 31, 1948.

ample stocks of fuel oil and sufficient supplies of other oil products, though that of high octane is rather severely limited.[20] Ross also told me of some of his company's problems here and of its desire to cooperate with the government by not insisting on dollars for its profits or for its accumulation of stocks.

Joel Fisher came in and rode with me downtown. There was just time for me to make clear to him the importance of absolute secrecy on the IRO-PCC exchanges. I showed him the draft of my telegram to the Department for George Warren's attention urging warning to JDC.[21] He urged me to include a line making clear that he had already received the warning and was acting on it.

From four to six there was the weekly staff conference. At six-thirty, Brigadier General Morris Troper and I walked for an hour on the roof.[22] He wanted my advice about setting up a branch office here. I urged him to talk to Sam Sacks so that I might have his judgment on Sacks's idea for new financing methods here. Then I might write to David Dietz[23] and Edwin Goldwasser,[24] a prominent factor. Called Sam Sacks, who said he would be glad to see Troper either Monday or Tuesday.

Friday, March 4

Received some twenty members of the UJA delegation. Thanks to the beautiful weather and the roof, the entertainment was easy.

On March 4 the United States submitted to the UN Security Council a draft resolution calling for the General Assembly to admit Israel to the UN. The resolution passed nine to one, with Egypt voting against and Great Britain abstaining.

Saturday, March 5

Early afternoon at Tel Mond [for luncheon at Rebecca Sieff's] with the family. Rebecca Sieff's other guests were her daughter-in-law, Daphne, and her sister, Mrs. Sacher.[25] It was a beautiful day, inviting one to be outdoors. The talk covered a wide range. It was not especially noteworthy, except at the point

20. With the pipeline from Kirkuk to Haifa closed and the British halting tanker deliveries, Israel's largest purchases of refined petroleum in 1948–1949 were from Romania. However, these deliveries did not cover Israel's requirements or allow the full operation of the refinery. Socony-Vacuum was in discussions with Israel concerning delivery of refined petroleum from the United States. Bialer, *Oil and the Arab-Israeli Conflict*, 46, 54–57.

21. McDonald reported the comments made by Tuck and Cox on March 2 and asked Warren to tell the JDC that strict secrecy must be observed. McDonald to secretary of state, [attention George Warren] no. 178, March 3, 1949, NARA, RG 59, 501.BB Palestine, box 2124, folder 2.

22. Morris Troper (1893–1962), chairman of the JDC European Executive since 1920; rank derived from his service in US Army during World War II.

23. David H. Dietz (1897–1984), Pulitzer Prize-winning journalist with NBC News, 1940–1950; involved in Jewish affairs and organizations.

24. Israel Edwin Goldwasser (1878–1974), New York businessman; for many years treasurer of JDC; officer in New York Federation of Jewish Philanthropies.

25. Rebecca's older sister Miriam Marks (also sister of Simon Marks) had married Harry Sacher in 1915. See entry of July 31, 1948.

when Rebecca exploded with what was even for her extraordinary violence, at the point where I had made a flippant remark about the possibility of Bunche being needed to effect an armistice between Rebecca and Vera [Weizmann]. Later, when Rebecca had left the group, the manager of Melchett Properties explained that this intensified bitterness was probably the result of Weizmann's failure (from the point of view of the Sieffs, Markses, and Sachers) to pay adequate tribute to their role in his career.[26] Whether the men share Rebecca's feeling on this I did not learn. It would be a pity if the lifelong friendship of Weizmann with this group of men were to be jeopardized. I shall learn more when I see them here within the next weeks.

On March 6, 1949, Israeli newspapers announced that Foreign Minister Moshe Shertok had taken the Hebrew name "Sharett." The timing was determined by the impending birth of his grandson. We refer to him henceforth as Moshe Sharett.

Sunday, March 6

The Hoofiens came for tea at five. From five-thirty to nearly seven, Mr. Eliezer Hoofien,[27] at my invitation, talked to us like a college professor on the problem presented by the president's now famous fourth point.

In his inaugural address of January 20, 1949, Truman proposed ideas for achieving "peace and freedom" in the world's less developed regions. Point Four called for US scientific and technological aid for the improvement of undeveloped areas. "More than half the people of the world," he said, "are living in conditions approaching misery. Their food is inadequate. They are victims of disease. Their economic life is primitive and stagnant. Their poverty is a handicap and a threat both to them and to more prosperous areas. Our aim should be to help the free peoples of the world, through their own efforts, to produce more food, more clothing, more materials for housing, and more mechanical power to lighten their burdens." Acheson and the State Department were skeptical of Point Four. To maintain control of the program, the State Department created a Technical Assistance Group in February 1949.[28]

[Hoofien] began with an elaborate preface as to the reasons [in] back of the president's suggestion. These were basically three-fold, rooted in a desire to fight communism if possible by peaceful means, if necessary by military force.

---

26. Referring to Weizmann's recently published memoir, *Trial and Error: The Autobiography of Chaim Weizmann* (New York: Harper, 1949).

27. Entry of August 27, 1948. McDonald's memorandum with Hoofien's full remarks, dated March 6, 1949, is in McDonald Papers, USHMM, box 7, folder 12.

28. See Beisner, *Dean Acheson*, 212–213; David Eckbladh, *The Great American Mission: Modernization and the Construction of an American World Order* (Princeton, NJ: Princeton University Press, 2010), 77–113.

1) To keep the American industrial machine at top speed producing its fabulous quantities it is necessary, given the present economic concept, that the "surpluses" be exported and that there be no real expectation of substantial repayment. To deceive hardheaded businessmen on this last point several subterfuges have been utilized, for example, lend-lease, [the] Marshall Plan, and now the proposed aid to undeveloped countries.

2) Such aid would directly and indirectly strengthen the areas into which it goes and incidentally tie those areas into the American industrial system and to a greater or less[er] degree into the American political orbit. Hence, the Truman plan makes sense from the standpoint of highest statesmanship.

3) Then followed Hoofien's elaborate discourse on water control, irrigation, agriculture, land settlement, industrial development, and the over-all result of such a degree of international community of economic common interests as to reduce, if not to eliminate for practical purposes, many of the current obstacles to effective international cooperation in this area.

The Jordan Valley Authority [JVA] project, developed so as to include the waters of the Litani, the Yarmuk, and possibly the Mediterranean-Dead Sea Canal, was a practical engineering problem well within reasonable financial figures.[29] The appeal to Lebanon and to Transjordan to cooperate would be [based on] long-range self-interest. Water conservation in itself, even when followed by extensive irrigation, can be vain or even harmful if there is not adequate land available and the people essential for its cultivation. Beyond such primary production, however, there must be, particularly in this area, a local population sufficient in numbers and [in] standard of living to consume the larger proportion of the increased agricultural production. This, in turn, necessitates industrial urban development and the consequent large superstructure of tertiary and even more remote services by populations several times larger than the basic production group. These various stages, essentially interlinked, must be envisaged from the beginning if the president's scheme is not to fail.

Beyond the JVA and its related projects, Hoofien said that he had no adequate knowledge to justify more than casual comment. For example, he could anticipate that a comprehensive engineering survey of the Euphrates and Tigris River valleys would disclose the possibility of making available rich lands sufficient for cultivation by many times more millions of people than now live in Iraq. But such a conclusion would not necessarily lead anywhere because of the probable lack of adequate peasantry and, beyond that, the even greater likelihood of the lack of a potential urban industrial population and the service groups, which would be essential to make city life on a sufficient basis possible.

---

29. The JVA project, theorized by the engineer Walter Clay Lowdermilk, aimed at harnessing the Jordan River for vastly expanded irrigation west of the Jordan. See Goda et al., eds., *To the Gates of Jerusalem*, 38–39.

Nonetheless, Hoofien was of the opinion that such an overall engineering survey of Iraq and of Syria would be worthwhile.

Later, Hoofien added that it should be remembered that the JVA [planning] had been engineered by competent Americans. He also emphasized that any comprehensive program such as the JVA would be a major contribution towards the solution of the refugee problem of the Arabs. In answer to our question about the power possibilities of the JVA, Hoofien denied technical competence but raised a number of very interesting points. Power in large amounts would probably not be available except from the Mediterranean-Dead Sea Canal. The Litani, though higher than the Jordan, might present insuperable obstacles to power. In any case, Hoofien thought it possible that oil as fuel would be more economical than water, particularly since at the end of a decade or more atomic energy might become economical. In connection with oil power, he added that one should remember that the old practice of charging for oil on the basis of Mexican or Venezuelan prices would certainly not be tolerated by Israel; or, if it were, Hoofien would join with the extreme opposition parties!

In conclusion, Hoofien said that he thought his hour-or-more-long discourse had been sufficient for the first installment. He would be glad to talk to us later on different occasions if he had additional ideas. Meantime, he wanted to know whether he might tell his colleagues of his talk even though it was, of course, unofficial. We said yes. I was glad to learn from Ruth that she and Mrs. Hoofien had had an enjoyable and a gossipy visit.

Noah [Karlin] sent a message to the effect that Ben-Gurion was at the Sharon, and that if we cared to come out to supper there would doubtless be an opportunity to talk to Ben-Gurion informally. We decided, however, that there had been too full a day and that we would not go. Urgent telegram received from Morgenthau inviting me to speak at the UJA "rededication" conference in Washington launching the new $250,000,000 appeal. At first, I was inclined to feel I ought to go; later, I was more dubious.

Monday, March 7

Conference at the office [with] Mr. F. B. Denham, manager of the local office of the Ottoman Bank.[30] He anticipates the rapid growth of Jerusalem as a business center, if it can be made a "free port" through which trade from Transjordan and Israel could pass without hindrance. He thinks Jerusalem will be in essence Jewish.

A little after four, I was at the RCA office [which had secure long-distance telephone connections] for my call to Henry Morgenthau, Jr. Because of transmission difficulties, the call came through at about 4:35. I explained briefly that our conditions here were difficult. I would like to accept the UJA invitation but

---

30. Founded by Baghdadi Jews under British management in 1917, the Ottoman Bank was one of five large foreign banks operating in Israel after independence. It merged soon afterward into the Discount Bank.

that the decision had to be the Department's.[31] It was up, therefore, to New York to check with Satterthwaite, the secretary, or beyond. After family greetings, we concluded. I did, however, first ask him about Abba [Hillel Silver]. Morgenthau said that Silver had for several days been singularly quiet.

Walked across the street to the Foreign Office to join Knox and Colonel Andrus. After a few minutes we went in to Shertok's office, Miss Herlitz also present. First, I asked Shertok informally whether he had approved of the Arab [refugee] meeting at Beirut. He replied very categorically that he had not. Then, turning to the summary of his conference with Ethridge and the other members of the PCC on the 24th of February, he quoted himself as having said each tended to increase the intransigency of the others. Pressed by Ethridge, Shertok said that he had agreed to think the project over. He added that he had not felt that he could be more definitely negative than he had been without assuming a responsibility for an alternative suggestion, which he was not at that time prepared to make. Then I asked Shertok about the UJA conference. He said that the "whole cabinet" was being urged to go; that they were discussing the matter at six, and that probably Goldie could not go because she had to return to make her adieus in Moscow.[32]

Finally, we turned to the business which had brought us, the Department's hope that Israel would not insist upon a rectification of the Lebanese frontier and thus jeopardize the armistice talks.[33] Shertok explained with his usual clarity that no such rectification was intended, but merely that, pending the Syrian withdrawal of forces from portions of the eastern edge of the northern panhandle, Israel felt that the armistice line on the west should be somewhat beyond the frontier. The really difficult question was whether Syria would agree to withdraw its troops and thus permit Israel to accept an armistice line in the west identical with the frontier. Sharett did not seem to feel that hitch would be serious unless the Syrians were adamant.[34]

31. McDonald at the time thought he might combine the trip with consultations in Washington. McDonald to Prihar, March 9, 1949, McDonald Papers, USHMM, box 7, folder 12.

32. Golda Meyerson became minister of labor and social security in the new cabinet, thus resigning as Israel's first ambassador to the USSR.

33. The Israelis agreed in principle with restoring the political frontier with Lebanon, but argued that the deployment of Syrian forces in southern Lebanon near Israel's northern border necessitated continued IDF deployment on the Lebanese side of the line. Lebanon's foreign minister [Hamid Beik Frangieh] stated that Lebanon "would not yield one centimeter [of] territory and would not discuss . . . [any] revision of frontiers." Acheson instructed McDonald on March 5 to ask Sharett about Israel's position. See *DFPI*, v. 3, d. 166 (and appendix), 170 (and appendix); *FRUS*, 1949, v. VI, 787, n. 1.

34. McDonald reported that the Israelis agreed in principle with Bunche's proposals that the armistice lines with Lebanon correspond to the political frontier lines, but that Israel intended to hold the Metulla salient in Lebanon so long as Syrian forces occupied territory just to the east. Pending a Syrian-Israeli armistice, Israel preferred an armistice-in-place. The US mission, said McDonald, "has [the] impression that Israel [is] very anxious for [an] armistice with Lebanon (with which country Israel never felt it had a real quarrel as compared with other Arab states) but that negotiations [are] badly complicated at moment owing to [the] interposition of Syrian troops and [the] unwillingness [of] Israel [to] yield all bargaining points to Lebanon and be left with no cards to play. . . . This [is] obviously awkward because it places Lebanon in [the] middle of [a] possible impasse between Syria and Israel. Mission has hopes [that] time and

A pleasant and useful conference with Dr. Johan A. Nederbragt, Dutch consul-general in Jerusalem, who came to pay his respects at six, and stayed until well after seven.[35] He is a studious person interested in history of the Old Testament, a former economist. He said he had been penalized for his attendance at the opening session of the Knesset by the French consul-general's [René Neuville] breaking a dinner engagement at the Dutch consulate general. He thought Jerusalem would be Jewish because, from the beginning of the fighting, he had sensed that the Jews were prepared to pay the ultimate price rather than surrender it. He seemed skeptical of possibilities of the PCC accomplishing much. He thought Boisanger was representing a definite French plan, and that the Commission as a whole could not be said to be really one of conciliation but rather as representing three national points of view. He inquired about Ethridge. In reply, I gave as sympathetic an interpretation of the latter's views and his instructions from Washington as I could. We parted with mutual expressions of desire to meet again.

With the family to dinner at the Sam Sackses. Others present included Hope, Knox, and the Robert Szolds. The things which stand out from the hours of talk were Sam Sacks's circumstantial account of British utilization of mandatory power for the advancement of the interests of British businessmen. He illustrated his point by tales of [US] businessmen in Palestine who would vainly send for catalogue and other information material [from] the States, only to have that material "lost in the mails" and then, without having requested it, receive from British business houses' comparable information. In many other ways, too, according to Sacks, the local British authorities sought to impede American competition in Palestine.

Perhaps the most interesting, or at any rate startling, of Sacks's statements was his quotation from a neighbor's account of the killing of Mr. Hoofien's sister [Jeanette Hoofien] near Latrun in the late fall [September 22, 1948]. This [neighbor] was with the party coming down from Jerusalem when the "Arabs" attacked. He urged Mr. Lewis, the American engineer [who was also there],[36] to join him in hiding in the bushes beside the road. Lewis hesitated and was killed. Mr. Hoofien's sister had meantime taken refuge in the ditch. At this point, the informant heard two Englishmen in Arab uniforms urge their Arab colleagues to kill the woman, saying "dead men tell no tales." The informant was said to understand both English and Arabic well. He insists that the Englishmen were responsible for the death of the woman. When I seemed a little incredulous, Sacks offered to send across the street to bring in his neighbor to tell me personally the story. I declined, not thinking that it was suitable for me to follow it up then.

Bunche's skill will solve [the] problem." McDonald to secretary of state, no. 184, March 8, 1949, *FRUS*, 1949, v. VI, 802–803.

35. Johan Alexander Nederbragt (1880–1953), Dutch consul general in Jerusalem, 1946–1948; Dutch minister to Israel, 1948–1951; maintained official residence in Jerusalem. For Nederbragt's sympathies toward Israel and its claims to Jerusalem, see Dov Joseph, *The Faithful City*, 333.

36. John Locke Lewis of Knappen Engineering of Philadelphia. See entry of March 21, 1949.

Ruth, Bobby, Knox, and I arrived at the Knesset Building at about 3:50, drove up to the entrance through a police-held lane in the midst of the crowded street. We were recognized and cheered as, with news cameras and motion picture cameras clicking, we entered the building. We were shown upstairs to our seats in the diplomatic gallery.

The building, a reconditioned cinema, was done in good taste. Most of the walls and ceilings were of a light color with wide window space on two sides, which, opened in the summer would provide excellent ventilation. The speaker's dais and that of the orators, together with the desks of the secretariat, were arranged on what would have been the stage section and in the same manner as the United Nations. The whole atmosphere of the assembly was business-like and casual. When we arrived, Ben-Gurion and one or two other members of the cabinet were sitting at the long, wide table which occupied the center of the auditorium, chatting. Gradually they were joined by six or seven other cabinet members while the seats of the members slowly filled.

In Israel's first elected government Mapai led a coalition with the United Religious Front, the Progressive Party, and the Sephardic and Oriental Communities. The more extreme right (Herut) and pro-Soviet left (Mapam) were excluded from the cabinet, and Mapai continued to hold the key portfolios.

The parties were arranged in order of size, the Mapai occupying the section to the left of the speaker, then came Mapam, and successively the [United Religious Front], Herut, General Zionists, Progressives, Communists, etc. In addition to the cabinet members, I recognized among others of the Assembly, Goldie Meyerson, not yet at the cabinet table because the new cabinet had not yet been approved, several rabbis, Begin and Bergson, the former sort of a mixture of a professor and Hitlerian style, and Yellin-Mor, so recently convicted of terrorist activities.[37] From the quiet and ineffective demeanor of the members, one would have thought they had long been in an Israeli legislative body.

The proceedings were opened by a few brief sentences from the speaker, Sprinzak, referring to the formal opening in Jerusalem and its historical significance. He then called on Ben-Gurion, who, in a businesslike tone, delivered a three-quarters of an hour address during the course of which he not only

---

37. Entries of September 6, 18, 1948. Natan Yellin-Mor, the former Lehi leader, had been arrested following Bernadotte's murder, but was convicted only of belonging to a terrorist organization. In the 1949 election he was elected as part of the Fighters' List, which included other former Lehi members. The Fighters' List received less than 1.5% of the vote and Yellin-More held the party's sole seat. His eight-year sentence was commuted on his election. The Foreign Ministry explained to McDonald that political amnesty was usual in the formation of a new government and that continued imprisonment would lead to further underground activities. McDonald to secretary of state, no. 141, February 18, 1949, NARA, RG 59, MC 1390, reel 18, frame 635.

presented his cabinet but also his government's ten-point program. There was no applause during the speech nor afterwards, as he quietly walked back to the cabinet table.[38]

The second and only other speaker before the recess when we left was Kaplan, who presented for approval the American loan with a brief ten or fifteen minute exposition. His statement too was quiet and businesslike and was received without any visible expression of approval or disapproval by the assembly. At no point was there any sign of "Jewish excitability."

I should have recorded on the previous evening, Monday, on our return from the Sam Sackses, there was a message to call Sharett, who told me that Goldie [now minister of labor and social security] was not going to the UJA [conference] but that he was.

Wednesday, March 9

Out with Ruth to Rehovot. We went to Chaim Weizmann's office in the Sieff Laboratory. He was in a depressed mood, the result perhaps in part of a headache. Again, as so often in the past, he expressed his dislike of politics and politicians, but to an extent quite unusual, he praised Ben-Gurion for the latter's political leadership. Again he belittled Sharett, characterizing him as a trimmer.

At luncheon with Weizmann and Vera and Major Arnon, talked much along the same rather discouraged lines. Both he [Weizmann] and she spoke of complaints from many sources about "omissions or inadequate treatment of personalities" in his book.[39] There was an obvious, but not expressed, reference to the disappointment which Rebecca had expressed so violently at Tel Mond a day or two earlier. They spoke also of Frieda's [Warburg] disappointment that neither her father nor Max Warburg was mentioned. Weizmann's answer on both these counts was the obvious one that the book was not a catalogue and could only include reference to those personalities with whom he had worked or who had played a related part in the movement.

Weizmann expressed hope that I would accept the UJA invitation to the Washington March 19–20 conference, and that if I did, I would bring his warm personal greetings to the president. As we were leaving, Weizmann gave me the beautiful edition of the Bible, which I had previously admired. I felt a little guilty having almost asked for it but was solaced by the thought that he would possibly never read it.

To bed early in preparation for planned trip with Ethridge.

---

38. Ben-Gurion pledged that his government would uphold the UN Charter and pursue friendship with peace-loving states. Development, not war, was the government's aim. He held the door open for the General Zionists and Mapam to assume cabinet posts. He called for a doubling of the Israeli population in the next four years through immigration, for swift economic development, for the raising of Arab education levels to that of the Jews, and for programs such as social security, a minimum wage, and a progressive income tax.

39. Entry of March 5, 1949.

Up early and on the way to Haifa with Shalom, McMahon, and Tom Gilmartin[40] at 7:35. We arrived at Haifa at a little after nine and went directly to Lippincott's establishment [consulate at Haifa]. It is a perfect plant for its purposes and made me envious. It would be ideal in the summer with its relatively high location and open outlook on the sea. There was time for just a cup of tea.

At the hotel on Mount Carmel, I found Ethridge and his party, the former suffering from a throat irritation. He joined me in our car with McMahon and Shalom. The presence of the latter somewhat cramped our style but not seriously. For the purpose of this record I will first outline our trip during the day and then Ethridge's talk.

The ride north to Acre gave us a good view of the Acre coastal plain and brought us, at about eleven o'clock, just outside Acre itself with a splendid view of the walled city across the narrow strip of water. It was picturesque and beautiful, with its medieval walls in perfect condition and its many minarets and domes, the whole jutting out into the sea. I was satisfied not to enter the city because I imagined that the view from where we stood could not have been improved upon.[41] Moreover, the view across the bay to Haifa gave one a much more active sense than does the map of the crescent shape of that area. One could foresee how it might become widely famous.

We then drove directly east on the main road to Safed.[42] The first portion was through the plain and valley, up which we gradually mounted towards the higher mountains with Jebel Jarmaq to our left, 1,200 meters high as we approached Safed. The contrasting valleys and mountains were [of beautiful] effect, but as we reached the heights, a low-lying fog shut out much of the view, so that we decided for the time being to by-pass Safed and go on to the Hula area.

Descending rapidly on a well-built but tortuous road, we moved along the lowland bordering the Jordan. Without intending to do so, we reached Lake Hula at a military camp near Hulata, the latter a fishing kibbutz. We were greeted by an officer in uniform who explained that we were in a military camp. Then, as we chatted, he pointed out the Syrian lines just across the narrow part of the lake about 1,100 meters distant, and another Syrian outpost to the southeast about the same distance. In answer to our inquiry, he explained that both these were within easy range, and that his post and the Syrians had frequently exchanged artillery compliments. It seemed a little weird and anomalous that, with all our "security," we had found ourselves in this place. This

40. Security official at US mission under McMahon.
41. Acre discussed in entries of January 14, 1949, and February 18, 1949.
42. Safed [Tzfat] was a majority Arab city allocated to the Jewish State in the partition plan of 1947. It served as the primary base for the Arab Liberation Army. Arab militia loyal to the grand mufti and the ALA in April 1948 attempted to conquer the small Jewish quarter before the Haganah took it in May. The Arab population of roughly 12,000 fled as a result. Morris, *Birth of the Palestinian Refugee Problem Revisited*, 221–226.

seemed even stranger when later, in Tiberias, an officer explained the absence of checkpoints on the road leading to the lake outpost. It was, he said, customary to mine such roads so that only drivers knowing the location of the minefields could pass.

Finally, we were cordially invited for lunch. It was served in a bare barracks-like room protected from the weather only by a sheet-iron arched roof. Setting ourselves at the board tables on benches, we were served with a good soup and then a substantial plate of artificial rice and meat and gravy. Finally, a grapefruit. The food was good. As we ate, I encouraged the young officers to talk about religion and politics. All of them were anti-religious or anti-clerical. As we left the room, a whistle was blown and we saw emerging from other buildings the company of soldiers rushing to their meal, which we inadvertently had delayed. Thanks to the rain and the low-lying land, mud was everywhere, the men all wearing high rubber boots. I thought we were fortunate to be able to get in and out with our cars. The whole setting and the casual business-like air and conversation of the officers made us realize that this was a matter-of-fact and unromantic war, but one which these young men were determined at all costs to win.

We then started north up the main road but ran into very heavy rain. I persuaded Ethridge that it would be foolish to visit a kibbutz in this weather. So we decided to turn around and head for Tiberias. Fortunately the weather cleared when we were nearing Safed and therefore decided to drive again to the mountain town. The views were strikingly beautiful as we mounted the steep road. The city, too, built like an Italian mountain town with its prevailing blue walls was picturesque. We did not get out, but simply drove through and back down the same road we had come, and then took the highway to the Sea of Galilee and on to Tiberias. On the descent, as from the higher roads, we had many and varied views of the lake. One can understand why it was such a favorite throughout the ages. We reached the hotel about five and were lucky enough to have our rooms ready for us and could thus rest before dinner.

The burden of much of Ethridge's talk to me during the day was that the decision to hold the Beirut conference had not been openly opposed, but rather had been half-heartedly favored by all of the individual Britishers who, subsequently in the British Foreign Office statement, were said to have opposed [it]. In any case, Ethridge argued, the PCC had no alternative; they had to hold such a conference or give up hope of making any progress on refugees. They realized the dangers of failure, but thought they could minimize these by controlling the meeting and by putting pressure on the Arabs to be realistic. If the worse came to the worst and the meeting ended in failure, then the way would be opened for Abdullah to make his own individual offer on refugees. All of this sounded to me rather like wishful thinking, and I made no counter-argument.

As to the peacemaking, the PCC contemplated putting pressure on the several states to open negotiations as soon as armistices were concluded. Egypt,

Ethridge thought, was ready, as was Lebanon. Ethridge said he was going to ask me to take up with Sharett the desirability of Israel's prompt carrying out of its promise to present the PCC with not only a working paper, but a definite proposal on refugees. This last, Ethridge argued, was highly desirable from Israel's own point of view, and was essential to progress with the Arabs. Ethridge made the interesting comment that Yalçin [the Turkish representative to the PCC] remained annoyed with Bunche because the latter had been unable to send a UN plane for Yalçin, whereas the situation was different and permitted Bunche to send a plane for Ethridge. The Frenchman [Claude de Boisanger], Ethridge spoke of a career diplomat closely in touch with his own government. Later in the afternoon Ethridge talked interestingly about the Balkans and his work there on the Balkan Commission. In his mind, the Russians made a major mistake of policy when they set up the Cominform, thus arousing and alienating nationalism such as that of the Yugoslavs.[43]

After a quiet walk along the lake before dinner, and a quiet meal with Wilkins and the guards, followed by an hour of bridge, I went down at ten to hear the news. Passing through the dining room I ran into Ben-Gurion and Paula, who had just arrived and were having their dinner. Sitting down with them, I found Ben-Gurion in a tense and somewhat depressed mood. I thought then it was because of his long session at Knesset, but later learned that it was perhaps as much because of the US's presentation about the Negev of which I then did not know. So I did my best to entertain him with a three-quarters of an hours talk of the lighter side of American political life. He seemed more cheerful when we broke up.

On March 7, Ben-Gurion noted in his diary that armistice talks with Transjordan in Rhodes were "not promising," partly because of the British influence in Amman.[44] The same day Israeli forces launched Operations Uvda and Yitzuv, aimed at securing the southern Negev. The UN partition resolution allotted the area to the Jewish state, but Israel had not controlled it. Light Arab Legion forces patrolled the area. Israeli forces moving south were ordered to avoid crossing into the Sinai to the west, lest the armistice with Egypt be violated, and to avoid any clashes with Arab Legion troops. When, on March 10, Israeli forces reached the old police station at Umm Rashrash, the town at the southernmost part of the Negev on the Gulf of Aqaba, Arab Legion soldiers abandoned it. Israel claimed the town, which it renamed Eilat. The occupation ended the possibility that the southern Negev would go to Transjordan or Egypt and create a land bridge between the two states. And as Ben-Gurion soon pointed out, Eilat provided maritime access to Asia while making Israel the only state

43. The Soviets created the Communist Information Bureau in September 1947 to control communist parties in the Eastern Bloc. To mask Soviet dominance, the Cominform's headquarters were in Belgrade. After the Soviet split with Yugoslavia, the latter country was expelled from the Cominform in June 1948 and the headquarters moved to Bucharest.

44. Ben-Gurion Diary, entry of March 7, 1949.

in the world that did not rely on the Suez Canal to go from the Mediterranean to the Indian Ocean.[45]

The governments of Transjordan and Great Britain complained to the United States that Israel had violated UN truce resolutions and armistice provisions, that its forces had crossed Transjordan's border, and that they had engaged Arab Legion troops. Secretary Acheson feared a breakdown of armistice talks in Rhodes, a renewal of hostilities, and British intervention on Transjordan's side. On the evening of March 9, he ordered McDonald to convey the "gravest concern" to Sharett, as well as the likelihood of "serious consequences" should the incursion into Transjordan be verified.

On March 10 McDonald was away from the mission, but reported "much resentment in official [Israeli] circles [regarding] these reports which are characterized as attempt deliberately [to] incite confusion [into] negotiations and discredit Israel." He commented, "Mission has no information confirming reports and on [the] contrary has received positive denials at high military and civilian official levels. Mission considers highly disturbing [the] Transjordan assertion that it has established a military 'line' across Israeli territory in Negev and [that Transjordan] now accuses Israel of crossing that line."[46]

Friday, March 11

Breakfast with Paula and the aide, joined towards the end by Ben-Gurion, who had been up at six and had his first breakfast at seven. Again the talk was not very serious, except the references of the possibility of my going to Washington. Either then or the previous evening, Ben-Gurion expressed concern at the delay in the arrival of my full credentials. He seemed relieved when I explained the mechanism of confirmation.[47]

One other point in Ben-Gurion's conversation deserves recording. I had told him that we were at work on suggestions for the implementation of the president's fourth point in his inaugural address.[48] Ben-Gurion commented, "[I]f that is American imperialism, then we can thoroughly approve of it." He also expressed delight with Griffis's present of American political books but [was] sharply annoyed that his letter of thanks had been delayed and said he was now reading Laski's *American Democracy*.[49]

The weather continuing bad, we finessed the visit to Degania,[50] promising to go there later, and drove directly to Nazareth. It was a beautiful trip through the valleys with their wonderful views of the Horns of Hattin, more than 500 meters high on the right, and Mount Tabor, nearly 600 meters on the

45. See Ben-Gurion's Independence Day speech, May 3, 1949.
46. McDonald to secretary of state, no. 202, March 11, 1949, NARA, RG 59, MC 1390, reel 18, frames 766–767.
47. McDonald's initial appointment by Truman as special representative was a recess appointment. His appointment as ambassador thus needed Senate confirmation.
48. See entry of March 18, 1949.
49. Harold J. Laski, *The American Democracy* (New York: Viking, 1948).
50. Kibbutz in northern Israel, Palestine's first, established in 1909, south of Tiberias on the Sea of Galilee.

left, and then up the high hills to the ridge, where we stopped for a glorious view of Nazareth nestling in a saucer-like depression. From where we stood, we could better credit George Adam Smith's contention that Jesus as a boy must frequently have climbed from His home in the town up to one of the surrounding hilltops and from there to look down on the pageantry of the caravans moving east and west and north and south between the empires of his day.

Our visit in Nazareth was brief. It included first a call on the military governor, the young Mapam leader, stern and unsmiling. He explained that the large communist vote in Nazareth was the result of early initiative and greater energy by the communist leaders.[51] Later, we visited the Church of the Annunciation and had a pleasant visit with Brother Robert and his French colleague.[52]

The ride from Nazareth gave us magnificent views of the Acre plain and that of the Esdraelon with its mountains bordering from the northwest Carmel to the southeast, the mountains of Gilboa. Finding no lunch at Zikhron Ya'akov, we motored to Netanya. After a fine improvised luncheon there we said goodbye to our friends and reached home about four, they reaching Jerusalem probably about five-thirty.

At the house found an urgent message from Knox to ask me to join him at the Foreign Office, where he had been called by Sharett. Sharett began by saying that he would start from the latest development and work backwards. This afternoon the Israeli flag was raised on the Gulf of Aqaba, well within Israel territory at Umm Rashrash at the police station. The Israeli forces had scrupulously avoided infringing on either the Transjordanian or the Egyptian frontier. On their way down they had noticed Transjordanian units at Naqb al-Aqaba and at Umm Rashrash [both in Palestine]. Having positive instructions to avoid if possible a clash, the Israeli forces waited and presently the Transjordanian troops withdrew from both points. Earlier, Transjordan had announced that it had drawn a line from Naqb el-Aqaba to Umm Rashrash and that the Israelis were threatening this line. Sharett pointed to this statement as self-confession by Transjordan that their troops were on Israeli territory.

Transjordan had launched a triple "diplomatic" war: First, through the reports from Amman; second, through Britain's action; and third, through appeal to the US. All of these, Sharett said, had fallen of their own weight. Sharett protested with vigor and a show of feeling against what he said was the recent

---

51. Nazareth had held 18,000 mostly Christian Arab inhabitants at the end of the British Mandate and now had 30,000 inhabitants, the growth coming from an influx of Muslim refugees from surrounding cities. The demographics of Nazareth, which sat at the crossroads of the Galilee, necessitated special military administration to avoid friction between Christians and Muslims and to protect against desecration of its Holy Places. Military administration there lasted until 1963. In the elections of 1949 and subsequently, the Christian and Muslim population dabbled with communism. See Raphael Israeli, *Green Crescent over Nazareth: The Displacement of Christians by Muslims in the Holy Land* (Abingdon, UK: Routledge, 2002), 25–50.

52. Control over the site, where the Annunciation was to have taken place and where successive Roman, Byzantine, and Crusader churches were built, was assumed by the Franciscans in 1620 in their capacity as Custodians of the Holy Land. See Chad F. Emmett, *Beyond the Basilica: Christians and Muslims in Nazareth* (Chicago: University of Chicago Press, 1995).

inclination of the US to accept as probably true unverified reports from enemy sources, and to make representations based on such reports.[53] It was more or less at this point in the discussion that Knox and I happened to disagree openly about the interpretation of the Department's instructions to repeat to the Foreign Office the substance of the presentation made to Elath in Washington the day previous.[54] My contention was that we were obligated to carry out literally the instructions; Knox argued, probably with more wisdom than I had shown, that since the Foreign Minister had categorically denied the report which had been the basis of the Washington representation, it would be rubbing salt into an open wound to carry out the instructions literally.

I was amused by the expressions on the faces of Sharett and Eytan during Knox's and my discussion. The two men were obviously a little embarrassed and sought vainly to appear to be disinterested. But the incident did no harm, because it was obvious to them that both Knox and I wanted to be friendly and helpful. As we were leaving, Sharett said that he was going to New York and Washington and would remain for the Assembly.[55] I told him that I was staying. I took occasion to mention Ethridge's concern about the promised statement of policy in addition to the working paper of data on refugees. Sharett turned to Eytan, who assured him that the desired statements would be ready.

As we were leaving, we met Major Brady and I suggested that he return to the office and bring Andrus and any of the other military people out to the house for a conference on the first draft of the telegram which Knox prepared. I urged Knox to return with me to the house where he could work uninterruptedly. The conference lasted from about a quarter of six until after eight. Knox's first draft was an accurate report of what Sharett had said. I urged, however, a preface stating briefly the categorical denial of Sharett and his resentment at the US representation. I urged, too, a postscript, which would plead for no repetition of the "have you stopped beating your wife" attitude and a statement by the military supporting the Israeli disclaimer.

McDonald's wrote, "[In] View [of the] tenseness [of the] situation and public feeling, [I] earnestly hope that [the] Department will not prejudge Israel's intentions or actions on [the] basis of complaints received from Arab capitals. Information gathered independently by [military attachés] tends to confirm [the] Foreign Minister's statement that Israel has tried to avoid clashes and has scrupulously refrained from infringing on Transjordan territory."[56]

53. See also Sharett to Elath, March 12, 1949, *DFPI*, v. 2, d. 434.
54. The Department also expressed to Ambassador Elath its concerns regarding Israel's advance into the Negev and of the "serious consequences that would ensue should the report of the Israeli incursion into Transjordan be verified." Memorandum by Acheson for Truman, March 10, 1949, *FRUS*, 1949, v. VI, 810–811.
55. Sharett left for the United States in March 14, 1949. He undertook a transcontinental tour for the UJA's fundraising drive and also met twice with Acheson in Washington.
56. McDonald to secretary of state, no. 205, March 11, 1949, *FRUS*, 1949, v. VI, 821–823.

Colonel Andrus was emphatic that independent sources of information supported this last point. By the time we had finished, it was well after dinner time, but everyone seemed to feel that a good job had been done.

In the meantime, on March 11, the Transjordanian and Israeli delegations at Rhodes reached an agreement on a temporary cease-fire, pending a permanent cease-fire arrangement.[57]

Saturday, March 12

Knox and Hope were over to discuss a number of matters, including my attitude towards requests for representations to the Israeli authorities from Ethridge or Griffis. Knox favored the draft of the telegram, which I submitted, asking the Department for instructions and leaving the way open for Washington to forbid such cooperation. Hope, on the other hand, thought it better to leave the whole matter fluid and to use one's own judgment in each specific instance. We left the matter undecided.

Just before dinner word came from the code room that a NIACT [Night Action] urgent [telegram] was in. Unable to get Hope, who had just left, I asked the boys to bring out the text. It was an urgent appeal from Ethridge of the PCC to secure from our neighbor before he left an affirmative statement, in addition to the working paper on refugees. Unable to make up my mind, I asked Knox to come over after supper. We tried to reach Sharett on the phone. Failing in this, we wrote him a note expressing our interest in the matter and our hope that he would telephone me early Sunday morning.[58]

Sunday, March 13

Not having heard from Sharett by ten o'clock, and anxious to do the utmost to meet Ethridge's wishes, I telephoned Alon at the Foreign Office. After a brief talk, he said he would call back. This he did in a few minutes, giving me the text of a telegram Sharett had just dictated to Ethridge. It was uncompromising, disavowing any approval of the Beirut conference, expressing inability because of scheduled flight next day to see the PCC Sunday, and explaining that because of reorganization of government there had been no opportunity for cabinet to consider formulation of new policy. Whole matter now was left in hands of prime minister as acting foreign minister.[59] With this in hand, I

---

57. Text in *FRUS*, 1949, v. VI, 816–817.
58. McDonald wrote Sharett: "I have just received a message from the PCC in Jerusalem that it has requested a conference with you tomorrow, Sunday, prior to your departure for the United States, on the subject of your suggested statement on the problem of the Arab refugees. I should greatly appreciate it if you could telephone me tomorrow morning early whether it is possible for you to receive the Commission. I feel that the Commission would be guided helpfully by your views on the subject, which is considered of paramount interest in the general effort to facilitate the armistice and proceed to peace negotiations." McDonald to Sharett, March 12, 1949, McDonald Papers, USHMM, box 7, folder 12.
59. Telegram in McDonald papers, USHMM, box 7, folder 12.

promptly got through on the telephone to the King David. Ethridge had gone to the Old City to meet Wells Stabler [US vice consul in Jerusalem], but I was able to speak to [Pablo de] Azcárate and give him the message. He expressed the expected disappointment and added that he supposed there was nothing more that could now be done.

McDonald reported to Washington, "Text [of Sharett's] reply obviously unsatisfactory. Later telephoned Ethridge suggesting further approach Prime Minister with whom Foreign Minister has left [the] problem."[60]

In the early afternoon, Marcus Sieff came for tea and, during more than an hour and a half, gave me revealing details of efforts to influence the development of British public opinion during the critical first weeks of January and subsequently. According to his account, [Ernest] Bevin's maladroitness and the activities of the true friends of Israel in the cabinet, in the press, and elsewhere, were responsible for the building up of opinion in Parliament and the press, which resulted in Bevin's humiliation and the defeat of his policy. The Sunday newspapers of January 9, stimulated and aided by factual memoranda which Sharett had prepared, helped to give popular support to the opinion growing in the House that Bevin's policy was unjust and dangerous. The *Observer* was one of the leaders. In the cabinet Aneurin Bevan[61] and Emanuel Shinwell[62] were especially helpful. [Stafford] Cripps[63] was difficult to persuade, partly because it is believed, he is angling for Bevin's support for the prime ministership. In the House, Bevin's hesitations, his misleading advice from [Michael] Wright, and his fumbling speech, left the door wide open for effective attacks from Churchill, and others, including a particularly effective one from [Richard] Crossman.[64]

Marcus continued his work up to and including the first of the previous week. He is convinced that Bevin has not changed his mind, is still dangerous, but that the danger of his succeeding in provoking an incident had been greatly diminished. He is sure that the plane incident of the first Friday of the year had been planned with the two-fold purpose, or rather two alternative purposes: 1) to get information proving that the Israelis were in Egyptian territory; 2) to inflame British opinion if there were a clash in the air. The defeat of the latter was a tribute to British commonsense and fairness. Marcus quoted a friend in England to the effect that Dean Acheson, prior to becoming secretary of state,

60. McDonald to secretary of state, no. 207, March 14, 1949, NARA, RG 59, 501.BB Palestine, box 2124, folder 3.
61. Aneurin Bevan (1897–1960), British Labour politician; minister of health, 1945–1951.
62. Emanuel Shinwell (1884–1986), British Labour politician; minister for fuel and power, 1947–1950.
63. Sir Stafford Cripps (1889–1952), British Labour politician; chancellor of the exchequer, 1947–1950.
64. Refers to Commons debate on January 18, 1949. On Crossman, see entry of September 29, 1948.

had written him characterizing Bevin's Near Eastern policy as unsound. Perhaps the words used were stronger but I don't recall them precisely. As he was leaving, Marcus asked whether it would be possible for me to have him at the house sometime when the new British representative happened to be here. I said I would try to arrange it.

Billy Rose,[65] whom I had talked to on the telephone at the King David [Hotel] in the morning, came out but without Eleanor,[66] who was wearied by the trip down along the Courage Road.[67] Also arriving at the same time were the men with their recording device. Not having quite finished my text, I tried out what I had on Billy Rose and also an additional paragraph making the point that a successful Israel would contribute substantially to the reduction of anti-Semitism at home. Rose approved. While I did the recording, Ruth and Bobby entertained our guest.

He then launched into a circumstantial account of the attacks on Ethridge by members of his staff, particularly by his young secretary, Busby. It appears that Busby, in the process of getting drunk at Ethridge's party for Billy Rose, launched into a tirade against Ethridge's drinking habits, parties, late hours, etc. Some other not clearly identified members of Ethridge's staff were also critical. Busby is said to have characterized me as a "jerk." Among Ethridge's critics, according to Rose, was a tall, youngish, blond man. Though this description might fit Wilkins, I cannot believe he was guilty. I then spoke to Ethridge about our efforts, and he reiterated his disappointment. I said that since the matter was being left with the prime minister, I would take [the] occasion to urge informally the PCC position. He said he would be grateful. Then I also told Ethridge of the criticism by Busby. He seemed shocked.

Following the talk, Rose and I discussed many aspects of the local situation until after eight o'clock. As he was leaving, he said it was the best talk he had had. Worked with Bobby until about 10:30 preparing the addresses and autographing some fifty of the photographs of Ben-Gurion and me.

Monday, March 14

Long conference with Knox during which we decided on a number of problems, including the dictation of a telegram to the Department reporting on the PCC's effort with Sharett, its failure, and asking instructions about future cooperation with Ethridge and Ambassador Griffis.

The State Department initially backed Ethridge's efforts to secure Israel's agreement to the return of significant numbers of Arab refugees. Acheson told McDonald

---

65. Billy Rose (1899–1966), born William Samuel Rosenberg, American Jewish entertainer and Broadway producer.
66. Eleanor Holm (1913–2004), Olympic swimmer and later the wife of entertainer Billy Rose.
67. The road between the Shimshon and Nachshon junctions is known as Kvish Hagvura (Road of Courage). It was laid at the end of the War of Independence to replace the Burma Road. The Courage Road bypassed Latrun, which remained in no-man's land until 1967.

that early Israeli magnanimity "would contribute greatly to [the] possibility [of an] early modus vivendi *between Israel and [its] Arab neighbors.*" McDonald suggested that, as he had raised these points with Sharett so often already, he delay for a few days before raising them again.[68] A frustrated Ethridge complained, "If the [State] Department can do anything useful during Shertok's [sic] visit to induce him to make one conciliatory gesture it may save the situation. Arabs have consistently impressed upon us that they regard the refugee question as [the] test of Israeli good faith."[69]

Ethridge, however, lost all remaining credibility with the Israelis when he invited grand mufti Haj Amin al-Husseini to speak at the Beirut conference. McDonald, as well as the Israeli representatives, pointed to "this man's nefarious record as a collaborator with Nazism, [as] an enemy of the UN, and [as] a constant advocate of bloodshed in Palestine."[70] Burdett in Jerusalem backed Ethridge. "[We] have," Burdett said, "set aside one day at Beirut to hear non-governmental organizations which profess to speak for the Arab refugees. The Mufti says he does and regardless of his war record he should be heard."[71] The mufti refused to attend anyway. In the name of the Gaza government, he accused all of the participants of betraying the Palestinian cause through their armistice negotiations with Israel.[72]

On March 17, the Israeli Foreign Ministry submitted an official statement to the PCC. Composed by Zalman Lifshitz and Michael Comay, the statement blamed the Arabs' attack on Israel for the refugee problem, provided statistics of 360 abandoned Arab villages and 530,000 refugees from villages and towns [as opposed to the oft-discussed number of 750,000], and noted that though Israel was willing to allow "a certain number" to return, "the main solution is not repatriation, but resettlement elsewhere." The report included detailed resettlement possibilities in Iraq, Syria, Transjordan, and Lebanon, all of which needed "fresh manpower in order to develop their resources." Resettlement, if met with international cooperation, would "contribute greatly to stable relations between Israel and its neighbors."[73] After an unsuccessful meeting with Sharett on the issue, Acheson reported to the president, who, according to the secretary, was "disturbed over the uncooperative attitude being taken" and who said that "we must continue to maintain firm pressure."[74]

McDonald, meanwhile, tried to interest the State Department in Eliezer Hoofien's ideas for land development in the context of the president's Point Four statements, which would in turn allow the resettlement of refugees.[75] Irrigation, McDonald said,

68. Acheson to McDonald, no. 144 [copied to Ethridge], March 9, 1949, *FRUS*, 1949, v. VI, 804–805, and n. 1.

69. Ethridge [through Burdett] to Acheson [eyes only], no. 222, March 14, 1949, *FRUS*, 1949, v. VI, 825–826.

70. Acheson to Burdett, no. 159, March 14, 1959, NARA, RG 59, 501.BB Palestine, box 2124, folder 3.

71. Burdett to secretary of state, no. 220, March 14, 1949, NARA, RG 59, 501.BB Palestine, box 2124, folder 3.

72. Sasson to Eytan, March 22, 1949, *DFPI*, v. 2, d. 246.

73. Memorandum on Refugee Problem, March 16, 1949, printed in *DFPI*, v. 2, d. 443.

74. Memorandum of conversation by secretary of state, March 22, 1949, *FRUS*, 1949, v. VI, 853–856. Memorandum by secretary of state [conversation with the president], March 24, 1949, *FRUS*, 1949, v. VI, 863.

75. Entry of March 6, 1949.

"is [the] lever of [the] whole economy [of the] Middle East and . . . will reclaim land making possible better food supply[,] increasing population and [would] raise [the] standard [of] living. . . . [It] would contribute materially [to] peace [and] stability [in the] region and retard [the] rising tide [of] extreme nationalism by demonstrating [the] interdependence of [the] area. Believe Israel on its part would cooperate fully."[76]

Early afternoon Dr. [Aryeh] Altman of the [anti-Herut] Revisionists came to see me. As usual with him, he did not get to his main point until other guests had arrived. I was partly responsible for this delay because of my questions to him about the election. He found it a vindication of his warning to Begin that, only through a union of the non-socialist parties and through unqualified support of Western orientation, could the opposition to the socialists of various shades make substantial progress. He cited the fact that the Herut vote was less than that of the Revisionists in the last World Zionist Congress election.[77] This showed, he said, that Begin had failed to win over any save most of the Revisionists.

Altman said that he favored a two-party or at most a three-party system. He was confident that under proper leadership and with an unequivocal anti-socialist and pro-Western platform, an absolute majority of seats could be won. He was evidently prepared to sound me [out] on the desirability of a Western orientation bloc, but I discreetly declined to be involved. Later he said he wanted to talk to me, and I suggested also to Hope, more about his ideas, including economic needs of the country.

Then on to [Félix] Vanthier's [French chargé d'affaires]. He wanted to know whether I thought the Eilat crisis was over. I gave an affirmative guess. He added that he understood Israeli troops were now stationed on the Dead Sea's western coast within the partition area. He asked me what I thought of a plan, which would connect the idea of internationalization of Jerusalem with the grant of a sort of UN trusteeship to the Jews over the corridor area. He said it was his idea and not that of the Quai d'Orsay. I termed it interesting.

Then, in answer to my question as to his opinion about the Beirut conference, he deplored it, had told Boisanger so while telling him also of the Israelis' criticism of the plan. Boisanger was, he said, very displeased at this attitude. Vanthier went on to explain that any move towards the revival of the Arab League was contrary to French policy, which traditionally had found such attempts at Arab unity to be detrimental to French Moslem interests in North Africa and elsewhere. As Vanthier spoke, the mystery deepened for me as to the genesis of the Beirut conference. Whose idea could it have been? The French Foreign

76. McDonald to secretary of state, No. 208, March 14, 1949, McDonald Papers, USHMM, box 7, folder 2.
77. In the Palestine elections for the World Zionist Congress in October 1946, the Revisionists obtained 28,300 votes of more than 200,000 votes cast. See JTA *Bulletin*, October 30, 1946.

Office opposed, the British also opposed. Seemingly, Transjordan was also in opposition; Israel certainly was. Whence the enthusiasm for the conference?

Tuesday, March 15

After a too brief nap, the family and I went to the Ben-Gurion Purim party at Paula's house. It was mostly for Americans but among the guests were the Kaplans, Goldie and a few other members of the cabinet. Goldie seemed so busy that we decided that we would not try to get together until she returns from Moscow. Robert Szold was rather discouraging about the search for a building site [for the US Embassy], having found, he said, costs prohibitive. I told a number of the Hadassah girls that I would be glad if they would come out for tea. Kaplan was interesting about the situation at home. While admitting that ambition and vanity played a role, he said that he sympathized with Abba [Hillel Silver] and Emanuel [Neumann]'s feelings that their decades of service were being overlooked by the emphasis merely on results in the UJA. At the same time, Kaplan said, what had been done belatedly should have been done two months earlier as he then urged. Again, I was rather unpleasantly impressed by Mrs. Marian Greenberg's aggressive and strictly non-humorous manner as she pressed Goldie for a contribution to the Hadassah magazine. The Ben-Gurion grandchildren were beautiful, especially the two-or-three year-old girl, whose mother is especially attractive. Ben-Gurion was in wonderful form, seemingly completely rested. When I told him about my sending off a number of photographs, he commented again on the excellence of the likenesses and mildly deplored the number of glasses. Remembering our inability to find the Lincoln speeches when I had been at his house earlier when he was in bed [January 31, 1949], he took me over to the bookcase and showed me that the volume was in the row just below that where he thought it should have been. He thus displayed his extraordinary memory and attention to details.

On the way home we picked up a large batch of mail. There was then just time enough to open it, have a bite of supper and take a short nap before we had to go off to the Sharon for the Karlinskis' party at the Sharon's gala Purim night. The hotel was crowded with 600 guests. During the evening, I chatted with a number of people. For the first time since returning here I talked with Oved Ben-Ami[78] and his wife; he deplored our failure to get in touch with him last week when we were passing through and told us of his plans for a large modern hotel, of his ambition that Netanya should be a very large city, etc.

78. Oved Ben-Ami (1905–1988), founder and mayor of Netanya; associate of right-wing political factions; one of the founders of the newspaper, *Maariv*, 1948, which became Israel's most widely read newspaper in its first two decades.

Major Andronovich arrived at a quarter of eight for breakfast and stayed until a quarter of eleven, thus giving us our first really long talk. The following are the main points I recall from his conversation:

1) Rankin is said to be uncertain about accepting the Jerusalem consulate general because of doubt about the future of the post, doubt which Andronovich shares. He regards Rankin as an able officer.[79]

2) While not disclosing any new facts about PCC or its relations with the consulate general, Andronovich said that he was under the impression that there developed a sort of competition between the PCC and Bunche.

3) In answer to my question, Andronovich said that he was of my view rather than that of Knox's and Hope's on the issue of literally carrying out the Department's instructions re repeating what had been said to Elath about the reported Israeli violations of Transjordan's territory a few days previous.

4) Israel has been so successful and has gained all its territorial immediate desires, except possibly the rectification of the Nablus-Jenin-Tulkarm northwestern line, that Andronovich wonders whether recent reports might not indicate a preparation by the Israeli general staff of a plausible ground for operations there. This, according to Andronovich, seems more likely in view of the undoubted ability of Israel to take over if it wished the whole of Arab Palestine. Andronovich deplored any such attempt to change the triangle, arguing that in the long run this would be poor policy for Israel, since it would lessen the chances of real peace with the Arabs.

When Iraqi forces deployed to Palestine in May 1948, they occupied the Nablus-Jenin-Tulkarm triangle in northern Samaria. It was an ideal point for attacking Israel's narrow "waist," which was only ten miles wide in places, and for threatening Haifa. The Israelis attacked at Jenin, but the Iraqis held their positions. Numbering some 20,000 troops but poorly supplied, the Iraqis continued to occupy the triangle.

During Israeli-Transjordanian negotiations in Rhodes, the Iraqis prepared to withdraw their troops from the triangle, to be replaced by Arab Legion troops. The Israelis argued that the redeployment was a violation of the cease-fire and a back-door ploy by King Abdullah to control the triangle. As the IDF massed troops on the northern Samarian border, Israel complained about raids from Iraqi troops and Arab irregulars. Voices within the IDF wanted to use the weakening of the triangle area to push to the Jordan River; cooler heads aimed at simply occupying the northwestern

79. Karl L. Rankin (1898–1991), career diplomat serving in Athens; reassigned as consul general in Canton and Hong Kong later in 1949. William Burdett remained acting consul general in the meantime.

rim of Samaria in order to provide strategic depth. Ben-Gurion remained cautious, worried that the British could intervene.[80]

The State Department had McDonald inquire at the Foreign Ministry. On March 16 McDonald reported that IDF chief of staff Ya'akov Dori had warned the UN that Israel might have to take military action to halt Arab raids.[81] *He further commented,*

> [There] is no tangible evidence at [the] moment that Israel contemplates military action against Arab lines in [the] triangle other than holding operations to stop raids. However, I suggest that [the] Secretary may care to use [the] Sharett courtesy call to point out the desirability of no action which would lead to hostilities at this delicate juncture. We here have expressed to [the] Foreign Office friendly concern [in] same vein in accordance [with] instructions.[82]

King Abdullah meanwhile asked London for weapons to outfit the Arab Legion properly, and Bevin was inclined to supply them.[83] *Acheson cabled McDonald on March 19 that "principal point of concern now becomes [the] problem of [the] Iraqi front [in] Samaria. . . . [Department] believes Israel and Transjordan should proceed promptly to armistice agreement, that this armistice agreement should be extended to the Iraqi front and that Israel should interpose no objection if Iraqi troops turn over [the] Samaria front to Transjordan. . . . Request you follow [the] situation closely and do everything possible to bring about [a] rapid conclusion [of] Israeli–Transjordan armistice."*[84]

5) Abdullah will probably [not] succeed in his Greater Syria ambition, since almost certainly this cannot be carried out in the next year or two, the king will be too old later, and neither of his sons is a worthy successor.[85] Andronovich expects Transjordan to become a republic. The king is very anxious for Gaza and a corridor to it. As an alternative, there was talk of an improved road [linking] Amman, Ma'an, Aqaba, Gaza. But now this too is seemingly precluded by the Jewish occupation of Eilat. Special facilities at Haifa and through road to that port would be more practical for Transjordan but less satisfying to national pride.

80. Morris, *The Road to Jerusalem*, 200–202; Morris, *1948*, 245–251; Yoav Gelber, *Israeli-Jordanian Dialogue, 1948–1953: Cooperation, Conspiracy, or Collusion?* (Sussex Academic Press, 2004), 80–82; Bar-Joseph, *The Best of Enemies*, 207–213.

81. Ya'akov Dori (1899–1973), Ukrainian-born engineer and army officer; emigrated to Palestine, 1905; Jewish Legion of British Army in World War I; joined Haganah, 1926; chief of staff, Haganah, 1939–1946; purchased arms in United States, 1946–1947; first chief of staff, IDF, 1948–1949; resigned because of poor health; president of Technion, 1951–1965.

82. McDonald to secretary of state [attention Satterthwaite and secretary with special reference comment], no. 211, March 16, 1949, NARA, RG 59, 501.BB Palestine, box 2124, folder 3; also Memorandum by Satterthwaite for secretary of state, March 17, 1949, *FRUS*, v. VI, 844–845.

83. Acheson to Douglas, no. 945, March 18, 1949, *FRUS*, 1949, v. VI, 850.

84. Acheson to embassy in Israel, no. 173, March 19, 1949, *FRUS*, 1949, v. VI, 851.

85. "Greater Syria" denoted a vague ambition to link Syria, Transjordan, and even Iraq under Hashemite rule that began in 1920 with the French expulsion of Abdullah's brother Faisal from Syria. In general see Yehoshua Porath, "Abdallah's Greater Syria Program," *Middle Eastern Studies* 20, no. 2 (April 1984): 172–189.

6) Mufti has lost almost all his prestige. He probably receives little more than a household from Farouk and must be short of funds. Abdullah, meanwhile, has strengthened his older ties in Arab Palestine, and is in effective control.

7) It is perhaps significant that, throughout his long talk, Andronovich said nothing about Arab refugees. As he was leaving, he promised to bring his wife down before they left.

So tired in the afternoon, despite a nap, that I decided to finesse three tentative tea engagements at Mrs. Andrus's, at Peter Bergson's for Billy Rose, and at [Lee] Harris's[86] for Robert Szold, where also I sent a note of apology to the guest of honor.

Thursday, March 17

Staff conference in the afternoon. I distributed draft copies of the letter to the secretary on the possible role of US labor here and the draft of the personal letter to Clark Clifford.[87] Then a number of topics were discussed including the perennial one of housing.

Partly because of recent attacks on the United States in the Mapam newspaper Al-HaMishmar, *McDonald continued to focus on problems of labor and Israel's future orientation within the context of the emerging Cold War. On March 18 he wrote Secretary Acheson personally with recommendations based partly on Samuel Klaus's earlier proposals[88]:*

> *The great labor federation of Histadrut here, embracing almost all of Israel's workers, is controlled by elements friendly to the West. Governmentally, we can to a limited extent influence and sustain this favorable trade union opinion. For example, I repeat my earlier request for the prompt designation of a labor attaché who, speaking Russian, Yiddish and Hebrew and with intimate knowledge of western and Russian labor conditions, would soon win the confidence of most labor leaders here. But at most, even the best labor attaché will not be able to do more than the smaller portion of the job that must be done to supplement with full effectiveness our governmental activities.*
>
> *Urgently needed is a carefully prepared program energetically followed up to acquaint Israeli labor leaders and the masses of workers in the industrial centers and in the kibbutzim with the elementary facts about the conditions of American and Western workers, their standards of living, their freedom to organize and to strike, as contrasted with the regimentation of Russian and*

---

86. Lee Harris (1915–1999), ex-US Navy officer; the Palestine Economic Corporation's banking manager, 1949; facilitated business contacts from the United States and elsewhere.
87. Described later in this entry.
88. McDonald to secretary of state, March 18, 1949, McDonald Papers, USHMM, box 7, folder 12.

Russian-controlled workers. The fundamental task of education here can be carried out only by American trade unions themselves.

My recommendation is, therefore, that the Department, presumably after conference with the Secretary of Labor [Maurice J. Tobin], consider advising the President to invite to the White House a small group which would include Messers Dubinsky, Potofsky, Green, and Murray for the purpose of urging upon them the opportunity Israel offers for educational cooperation. Such Presidential support would, I am confident, persuade these men to undertake in time and on an adequate basis activities which over the years would profoundly influence mass opinion in Israel.

McDonald informed Clark Clifford of his letter to Acheson. "American labor and government," he said, "working together can help the democratic forces in Israel to keep this country Western in its sympathy and loyalty."[89]

Acheson responded, "The Department is impressed by the importance, which you underline, of the Histadrut in Israel and recognizes the desirability of taking all proper and feasible action to encourage among the labor elements of Israel a true friendship for the United States and a deep understanding of our aims and institutions." He noted, however, "It is the consensus of thought in the Department that a meeting with the President of the kind suggested in your letter would be premature at this time."[90]

Friday, March 18

Mr. and Mrs. Ford and Knox and the two Ford children came out to tea. Despite the difficulties of language, since Mrs. [Lolita] Ford speaks only Spanish, plus a very little English and more French, we had a delightful get-acquainted party.[91]

Saturday, March 19

Long session during late morning with Dr. David Senator of the Hebrew University.[92] His talk ranged over the problems of finance, the reorganization of the Friends of the University in the States about which he is more encouraged now that Joseph Schwartz,[93] who became ill, has been replaced by a more effective fund-raiser, Mr. Salpeter.[94] Senator's main purpose, however, was to try to get from me some more definite information about a possible political solution, and the time of it, for Mount Scopus. Unfortunately, I could not help him. On his part, he developed the theory of an emergency road from Bethany

89. McDonald to Clifford, March 18, 1949, McDonald Papers, USHMM, box 7, folder 12.
90. Acheson to McDonald, April 26, 1949, McDonald Papers, USHMM, box 7, folder 13.
91. Richard Ford was formally assigned on February 4 to replace Charles Knox as McDonald's counselor of embassy.
92. Entry of August 18, 1948. Senator was then executive vice president of the Hebrew University (1949–1953); interested in studying the administrative methods of US universities.
93. Joseph J. Schwartz (1899–1975), Ukrainian-born New York rabbi; chief of overseas operations, JDC, 1942–1950; chairman, United Jewish Appeal, 1950–1955.
94. Hugh Salpeter (1911–1959), New Jersey-born social welfare administrator; worked with International Rescue Committee, American Jewish Congress, and Federation of Jewish Philanthropies; fundraiser for Hebrew University and Weizmann Institute.

north connecting with the Nablus road above Sheikh Jarrah.[95] He also spoke of the possibility of a general north and northwest assignment [of Jerusalem] to Israel and a south, southeast one to Transjordan. This has its logic, but the future does not emerge clear from either proposal.

Finally, he asked me about appearing for the opening of the medical school on May 17. I told him that I would like very much to do so. I thought political considerations which prevented my attending the opening of Knesset would not apply in this non-political occasion, and that I would therefore, put it down on my calendar.

Hooper[96] and Hope came out to tea. We had a useful and friendly get-acquainted party. I think Hooper will be an admirable addition to the staff, and from what I could gather about his wife, there should be no difficulty arising from her Arab background.

In the evening to the basketball game between the Marines and a local team. Our boys, tiring in the second half, were badly beaten though they had held their own during the first half. The game was so cleanly fought and was so much enjoyed by the spectators who literally covered the rooftops, that it was an excellent public relations project.

Sunday, March 20

Worked in the morning. At four, Simon Marks, Miriam and Mrs. Solomon[97] came to tea. They seemed thrilled to visit the residence of the first ambassador to Israel. Simon gave me some of the same data which Marcus Sieff had given me more fully earlier. I urged him to come and see me later when we would have more ample time for a talk.

At Cashman's and Knox's for the latter's farewell party from a little after five until a little after seven. It went off very well indeed. Among the people whom I spoke to in addition to the members of the staff were Paula, the Hoofiens, (Mrs. Hoofien showing herself most enthusiastic about her old friend Hooper), the Persitzes, and Horowitz (also friends of Hoopers), the Kaplans, the Vivian Herzogs, Miss Herlitz and Eytan.

Miss Herlitz brought me up to date on the prospective arrival of Eddie Jacobson and on a number of other matters.[98]

---

95. Sheikh Jarrah, Arab neighborhood through which regular access to Mount Scopus from the west had been blocked. Israeli-Jordanian discussions on Israeli access to Mount Scopus via Sheikh Jarrah are in *DFPI*, v. 3, d. 216, 217, 220, 228, 231.

96. Malcolm P. Hooper, first secretary and commercial attaché, US Embassy in Tel Aviv, on temporary assignment from the Department of Commerce, effectively replacing Herbert C. Cummings; had served in similar capacity in Italy before World War II.

97. Flora Solomon (1895–1984), Belorussian-born Zionist; emigrated to London and worked for Marks and Spencer after 1934, improving conditions for workers there; helped settle Jewish child refugees in London before World War II; acquainted with Soviet agent Kim Philby.

98. Eddie Jacobson (1891–1955), New York-born Kansas City haberdasher; close friend and former business partner of President Truman; spoke with Truman on Jewish rescue during and after World War II; facilitated meetings between Truman and Zionist leaders including Chaim Weizmann. Jacobson and his wife Bluma planned a two-week visit to Israel and would stay with the McDonalds.

My really important engagement was with Eytan with whom I talked about half an hour. Here is the substance of what he said to me:

1) In answer to my expression of concern about the triangle, he said that he thought I need not worry, that he thought there would be no unilateral action, and that instead he expected success with the Lebanon armistice negotiations and then with Syria and Transjordan.[99]

On March 22 Acheson informed Sharett in their meeting at the State Department that "the President was firmly convinced that a renewal of hostilities must not be allowed to occur because of the situation on the Iraqi front." Sharett replied that Israel had no intention of resuming hostilities there.[100]

On March 23, McDonald reported that the "Mission will continue [to] urge rapid conclusion [of a] Israel-Transjordan armistice." He added, however, that regarding "Transjordan troops taking over Iraqi-occupied areas [in the] triangle [the] mission feels sure that [the] Department's views have taken into account possible complications if, by any urgings on our part, Israel agrees to a situation which will give Transjordan de facto possession [of] Arab Palestine and might encourage King Abdullah [to] declare annexation thereof with consequent irritation [of] Syria and Egypt and [a] possible awkward situation [regarding the] November 29 UN resolution. Mission desires [to] emphasize political as well as military implications of Transjordan replacement [of] Iraqi troops."[101]

2) In response to my statement that we had been instructed to urge a broader and more generous policy on refugees, and that I wondered whether in view of my having brought the matter up on two or three previous occasions with Sharett and in view of his public statement in New York, it might be sufficient if I got from him then anything that he might have further to say, rather than making another formal presentation at his office; Eytan gave an affirmative reply. He added that there really was nothing more to be said at the moment, that Sharett's Washington statement represented the cabinet opinion, canvassed just before Sharett left for the States.
3) As to Eddie Jacobson, he said that Sharett's car was being sent to the airport and that a reservation had been made for him at the Kaete Dan. From all of this, I deduced that Jacobson would not lack official attention.
4) Eytan suggested that Ya'akov Riftin,[102] formerly a member of the Foreign Affairs Committee of the State Council, was the most intelligent Mapam leader for me to talk with. The other suggestions, which I had received from

99. See also *DFPI*, v. 3, d. 246, 248.

100. Memorandum of conversation by secretary of state, March 22, 1949, *FRUS*, 1949, v. VI, 853–856.

101. McDonald to secretary of state, no. 235, March 23, 1949, NARA, RG 59, MC 1390, reel 18, frame 895.

102. Ya'akov Riftin (1907–1978), Polish-born member of HaShomer HaTzair; emigrated to Palestine, 1929; senior member of Histadrut; part of Jewish delegation sent to UN in 1947 during

the Margolins (Yitzhak Ben-Aharon,[103] Ya'akov Amit[104] and Bentov) he thought for various reasons were less important. He spoke rather slightingly of Bentov as disingenuous and of Ben-Aharon as a party boss.

Monday, March 21

At twelve Knox and I presented Hooper and Ford to Simon. Then we discussed arrangements for formal presentation of credentials. Simon said that it had been decided that there should be a cavalcade from the office joined at Habima Square by a mounted escort en route to the president's office in HaKirya. He and I were to ride in the president's car, the other officers to follow in other cars. Mrs. Weizmann, Mrs. Ben-Gurion and Ruth and Bobby were to be at HaKirya in advance and to view the cavalcade from the balcony. After the presentation of credentials it was hoped that I would make a brief statement to which Weizmann would reply. Clothes were to be formal, or as formal as we possessed. On his desk, Simon had a photograph showing a presentation cavalcade in Cairo where it is the custom of the king to send his open carriage to transport the new ambassador. At the end, Simon urged that we telephone in addition to telegraphing to Washington to speed up the arrival of the formal presentation credentials.

At Eytan's, our group had half an hour's talk, the only noteworthy item of which was Eytan's reassurance that the Syrians had agreed to begin armistice negotiations.

On March 23, the Israeli and Lebanese delegations signed an armistice treaty establishing the international boundary between Israel and Lebanon as the armistice line. Israel agreed to withdraw its forces from the Lebanese villages occupied in October 1948 and to reduce IDF forces on the Israeli side of the border to defensive strength. The Israelis had agreed that a treaty provision prohibiting the use of Lebanese territory by a third party [Syria] would guarantee Israel's security. As with Egypt, a mixed armistice commission supervised the implementation of the agreement.[105] The Israeli armistice with Lebanon opened the possibility of talks with Syria.

partition debate; political secretary, Israeli UN delegation to UN, 1948–1954; elected repeatedly to the Knesset between 1949 and 1965 as a member of Mapam.

103. Yitzhak Ben-Aharon (1906–2006), Romanian-born HaShomer HaTzair leader; emigrated to Palestine, 1928; secretary, Tel Aviv Worker's Council, 1932–1938; worked with pioneer organization in Nazi Germany and expelled by Gestapo, 1935; fought with British Army against the Germans, 1940–1941; POW, 1941–1945; returned to Palestine and joined Yitzhak Tabenkin in the Ahdut HaAvoda Party, 1945; joined Mapam when it was formed in 1948 and then became one of its leaders; member of Knesset [Mapam, Ahdut HaAvoda], 1949–1977; minister of transportation, 1958–1962.

104. Ya'akov Amit, Lithuanian-born member of HaShomer HaTzair; Mapam member after 1948; editor of *Al-HaMishmar*, 1969–1974.

105. Agreement in Medzini, ed., *Israel's Foreign Relations: Selected Documents 1947–1974*, 179–184.

Just after four, my call to Satterthwaite came through with a connection, which, except for a moment, was satisfactory. I first explained the double reason for speed about the credentials, the government and Weizmann's desire that I present them to him, and his leaving for New York the first of April. I urged that they reach here not later than the 27th for presentation on the 28th. Satterthwaite seemed inclined to accept my further suggestion that they be sent by the Israeli diplomatic pouch, which according to Eytan, usually takes but three or four days. Satterthwaite promised utmost effort to get credentials ready and signed at the White House in time. I was amused to have Satterthwaite say that, owing to the filibuster in the Senate, action there might be further delayed. He had not noticed that confirmation had been voted the previous Friday [March 18].

We then discussed the question of a statement to be made by me, which, I pointed out, was desired by the Israelis. He said that this custom was declining in Washington, but if I thought it desirable, I should send a draft for Washington's consideration. Then we turned to the problem of furnishing the house. I told him that nothing was here but borrowed items and those few which I had purchased, and I faced the possibility of living in a tent. He agreed that he would urge the authorities to speed action. The whole conversation was friendly and encouraging. But I should also note that he said that he thought George McGhee was just about to arrive in Beirut, and he was anxious I should confer with him before his return to Washington. I said I planned to go to Jerusalem for that purpose.[106]

Mr. and Mrs. Theodore Knappen, head of the engineering firm which is planning the new port at Tel Aviv and has been advising on the enlargement of Haifa and the Israeli railroad plan, were here for tea.[107] He talked interestingly of his work, of the possibility of relatively quickly enlarging Haifa's capacity by several hundred thousand tons and thus provide adequate or almost adequate facilities pending the building of Tel Aviv, which will care for between two and three million tons. On the question of implementing the president's fourth point, Knappen was very interesting but, because the subject did not come up until almost the end of the period, there was no chance for him to develop his ideas. He did, however, stress the danger of great wastefulness in any large-scale projects in countries such as Iraq, where the population is unprepared and the leaders also unprepared. He underlined that projects, or even great works, are only creative in proportion as the populations are prepared for them. This, he said, applies to public health projects, which can only be creative a step at a time, as the population becomes educated and able and desirous of taking advantage of such programs. I told him that I hoped if he came back in the next weeks we would have a full opportunity to talk.

106. See entry of March 28, 1949
107. Theodore T. Knappen (1901–1951), US civil engineer and businessman; worked on flood-control projects in the United States and then projects in the developing world after starting Knappen, Tippetts, Abbett, and McCarthy Engineers, which designed new ports in Greece, South America, the Caribbean, Haifa, and Tel Aviv.

Ruth and Bobby and I after a bite of supper went to the special subscription chamber music concert at the museum under the patronage of Mrs. Weizmann. The 17th-and 18th-century music performed by cello, oboe, flute, harpsichord, harp and soprano was a delightful program. During the intermission and afterwards, we had a pleasant visit with Mr. and Mrs. Haim Gamzu of the museum[108] and with many others of our friends, including the Simon Marks and Rebecca Sieff. So far as I could note, Rebecca and Vera, though within a few feet of one another during the whole evening, did not speak. We dropped Rebecca off at her pension.

Tuesday, March 22

Many telephone conversations with Miss Herlitz's office about the expected arrival of the Jacobsons, now announced for Wednesday at three. After supper Ruth and Bobby and I went to the opera *The Barber of Seville* at the nearby movie house. We were on top of the orchestra, and all of the trappings of the stage were clearly visible. But the spirit of the performance was so lively and informal that we all enjoyed it.

Wednesday, March 23

McMahon came to lunch to say goodbye. He explained that while Tom Gilmartin was in charge of the guards, [Eugene] Padberg[109] would be the adviser on security matters. As he was leaving, he asked me if I had any oral instructions to give to people at home. I replied in general terms, because the more specific instructions and messages are being sent through Knox and Hope. Moreover, the uncertainty about McMahon's return made it a little embarrassing for me to use him fully as a messenger.

At 6:30 Shalom telephoned from Lydda saying that the Jacobsons had arrived and asked whether they were to come to the house. I said yes. They arrived about half an hour later and after some persuasion agreed to stay, and sent for their luggage from the Kaete Dan. The supper and visit afterwards showed our guests to be simple, homey folks. While he gave away no secrets, some of his scanty remarks were noteworthy. For example:

a) There was a concerted effort by "Zionist politicians to persuade the president to name a prominent Jew." He, Jacobson, had strongly urged my appointment. There had been, he said, rejoicing in Kansas City when the news was announced. He declined to say who the "official" candidate was. He said it was not Ed Kaufmann.[110]

---

108. Haim Gamzu (1910–1982), art and theater critic; co-founder and director of the Tel Aviv Art Museum.

109. Eugene L. Padberg, Jr. (1890–1950), second secretary, US mission in Tel Aviv, assigned September 1948.

110. Edmund I. Kaufmann (1886–1950), Washington, DC businessman and philanthropist; president, ZOA, 1940–1941; friend of David Niles who led fundraising for Truman's 1948 presidential campaign.

b) At the presidential inauguration, the two flags nearest to the president other than the American were the Irish and the Israeli. This was not a mere coincidence, because though the instructions were to arrange the flags so that the colors harmonized, the position of the Israeli and Irish flags had been determined by the two men who had arranged them and who happened to be of Irish and of Jewish descent. Not unnaturally, therefore, the English flag was at one extreme end. Later, Matthew Connolly admitted responsibility for this arrangement.

Thursday, March 24

Breakfast with the Jacobsons, and more friendly informal talk. Afternoon, farewell staff conference with Knox and Hope.

Friday, March 25

About 4:30 the second call came through from Satterthwaite. He told me that the formal documents for presentation had been sent by the Israeli courier. He confirmed, too, that the text of the brief address had been corrected and would, he hoped, arrive on time.

Mr. Hoofien joined Ford and Hooper at five o'clock and gave us the second of his economics lectures on possibilities of implementing the president's point four until well after six. His discussion this time was about the project of cutting the whole of the southern end of the Dead Sea beyond the peninsula into a gigantic evaporation pan which would multiply many fold the production of potash. This southern portion, unlike the rest of the sea, is shallow—not over five meters. A dam dividing the sea was entirely practicable and need not be much more than five kilometers. While the costs were wholly beyond the resources of a private company, they were not beyond those of governments.

The project would be economical, because there was an adequate demand for potash, the cost would not be prohibitive, the production would justify, as it would necessitate, a railroad to Aqaba, and the development there of an international port. The common interests of Israel and Transjordan would be strengthened by such development. Moreover, since Britain and the United States would in all probability be largely interested in the project, it would tend to make for unity of policy between them and the two countries immediately concerned. Hoofien did not pretend that this project had reached a point of planning comparable to those which he had outlined in his earlier talk [March 6, 1949], but he insisted that, on the other hand, it was not merely a dream. I was glad of the opportunity which the talk gave to bring Ford and Hoofien together (the latter and Hooper were old friends). Moreover, it should be the basis of a despatch for the Department.

Dinner at the [Lipman] Levinsons,[111] which was to have been a farewell party for Charlie Knox, but since I had "ordered" him to see Jerusalem before

111. Lipman Levinson (1875–1950), managing director, General Engineering Company for Palestine & Levant, Ltd.

he left, he had no alternative but to ask to be excused. There were a number of interesting people present, but I was tired, and was glad of a chance to get home fairly early.

Saturday, March 26

Breakfast with the Jacobsons and later with them to morning tea at the Sam Sackses. During these hours together, Jacobson told me more about his friendship with Truman and about the latter's personality. The Jacobsons and the Sackses got on very well together.

Ruth and Bobby and I reached the Sharon about 7:30, a little early for our dinner with the Karlinskis. As we went in I saw Mrs. Ben-Gurion alone in the main hall. We chatted together for a little while and then briefly with Ben-Gurion. I told him of the telegram from the president for Weizmann urging the latter to come to Washington to see the president before or after the dinner on the 23rd. Ben-Gurion at first seemed to feel that Weizmann should not go, saying that the president of a country should not go out begging for money. I argued that Weizmann could speak to the president about Jerusalem as could no one else. Ben-Gurion replied that there were other problems too. I got the impression that he would [not] favor Weizmann's going.

The dinner was pleasant. After it, we were joined by Paula who proceeded to renew her old acquaintanceship with the Karlinskis. As we were leaving, Serge Karlinski urged us to make his home in London our home when we should be there. From the pictures he shows, we could see that it is a magnificent residence.

Sunday, March 27

Feeling indisposed, I readily accepted Dr. Kohn's advice to stay in bed in the hope of being better for tomorrow's presentation ceremony. Hence, I had to finesse the Andrus tea party and even worse, the Foreign Office evening farewell dinner for Knox. I reconciled myself by reading and sleeping in bed.

McDonald conveyed a note to Simon with a tribute to Knox: "From the very beginning, when I first met him in the State Department last June, he has been literally a tower of strength to me. Skillfully penetrating in understanding, indefatigable in energy, and absolutely loyal, he has been the model of what a counselor should be. But beyond all of this, his gift for friendship and sympathy has endeared him to all of us."[112]

On December 27, 1949, Knox, now assigned in Curaçao, wrote to a friend, William F. Penniman, who was about to take up a new assignment in the US consulate in Jerusalem:

> *You will like Ambassador McDonald, and I hope that you get to enjoy his friendship. He is a shrewd judge of character, keeps his eye on the doughnut and not on the hole, and is thoroughly informed on the historical aspects of the*

112. McDonald to Simon, March 27, 1949, McDonald Papers, USHMM, box 7, folder 12.

Palestine problem. Although "on the other side of the fence," it was he that stimulated action looking toward the Arab Refugee relief program. Beneath a benign manner he is a realist and can be tough, very tough. He likes a joke and sometimes his Scotch wit has an acid (but not unkind) quality that pricks like a barb. If some aspect of the situation puzzles you, ask him, and don't let him throw you off with a bantering vein. Hang on like a bulldog and you'll get, from his encyclopedic knowledge, a great deal of information. . . . The Israelis respect him enormously, admire him and perhaps they fear him a little on those occasions when he expresses indignation—which, I assure you, he can do, and well.[113]

Monday, March 28

Fortunately, felt better and able to prepare for the ceremony. To the office with the family a little before eleven. They and the Jacobsons went along to HaKirya while I waited for Simon and his colleagues of the protocol office. He came promptly, so that there was time for brief final rehearsal instructions before we had to march out.

The cavalcade was impressive, first a score or so of new Harley Davidson motorcycles ridden by uniformed police, then Weizmann's car, with Simon and myself, the driver and a guard, and next a score or so of motorcycle police, then other cars containing the officers of the embassy, closed by a military jeep. Most of the route was lined with friendly, cheering people. At the Weizmann office we inspected the guard of honor, men in their battle dress listened to *The Star-Spangled Banner* and then marched into the building.

Weizmann and Ben-Gurion were standing at one end of the room. I stopped within a yard or so from them with the officers of the embassy lined up behind me. Having presented my letters of credence, I read my little speech (not I confess without some difficulty). It was translated into Hebrew by Miss Herlitz. Weizmann replied in Hebrew, and his talk was read in English by Simon.

The brief speech was as follows: "My presentation of these credentials to you, Mr. President, marks another stage in the development of the relations between our two countries, which have from the beginning been based upon friendship and cooperation. . . . On this significant occasion I am happy to affirm the sympathetic desire of my government to aid in the advancement of the goal which you have set for Israel—a free people securely at peace with its Arab neighbors and cooperating with them to obtain for the common good the gifts of modern science, industry, and agriculture. The furtherance of this type of collaboration is the ideal President Truman had in mind when in his recent inaugural address he expressed the desire that the knowledge and technical skill of American scientists be shared with those of other free peoples

---

113. Knox to William F. Penniman, December 27, 1949, Truman Library, Papers of Charles F. Knox, Subject File, 1948–1971, box 1, folder Correspondence, 1948–1949.

Fig. 9.1. US ambassador James McDonald passes the honor guard during the ceremony to present his credentials in Tel Aviv, March 29, 1949. Israeli Government Press Office.

striving 'through their own efforts to produce more food and more clothing, more material for housing and more mechanical power to lighten their burden.'"[114]

Then after shaking hands with Weizmann and Ben-Gurion, the three of us talked informally.

The business part of the talk was Weizmann's projected trip. I again urged him to go, Ben-Gurion agreed that he should, and Weizmann, who apparently had made up his mind before, assented. We also talked about the contrast between today's ceremony and our earlier relationships, when none of us dreamed that we should be occupying the positions we do today.

Then followed twenty minutes or so of friendly talk with the guests, including the Simon Markses, Vera, Paula, members of the Foreign Office staff, and others. Shortly after 12:30, having signed the president's book, we formed in the same marching order in which we had entered, took the salute of the armed guard of honor, stood at attention for *Hatikvah*, and drove back to the office as we had come. There were still many people along the route who continued to show their friendliness. At the office I changed cars and drove with the family and the Jacobsons to the Armon for lunch. Was back home by a little after three, tired, but glad the ceremony had gone off with such exemplary exactness.

Lunch with the Jacobsons. Included, besides the hosts and the family were George McGhee, Knox and Hope.

114. Statement dated March 28, 1949, McDonald Papers, USHMM, box 7, folder 12.

Fig. 9.2. James McDonald, Chaim Weizmann, and David Ben-Gurion after McDonald presents his credentials as US ambassador. Israeli Press Office.

In mid-March the State Department appointed George C. McGhee as its coordinator on Palestine refugee matters.[115] He was told that the Palestinian Arab refugee population amounted to roughly 725,000.[116] For McGhee, the refugee issue affected US security interests in the Near East.

McGhee attended the PCC's all-Arab conference, which ran intermittently in Beirut until April 15. During recesses he visited Arab capitals, as well as the UN delegation conducting the Israel-Transjordan talks in Rhodes. Arab diplomats and Palestinian Arab spokesmen insisted on mass repatriation.[117] US ambassadors to the Arab states, most notably James Keeley in Damascus, insisted that the Arabs would not accept Palestine's refugees for resettlement in return for US development funds alone. Israel had to make the first gesture. In Rhodes, John Reedman argued that the lands taken by the Israelis in the war itself—from Western Galilee to Be'er Sheva to al-Majdal to Jerusalem and its environs—were all suitable for Arab repatriation.[118]

115. George C. McGhee (1912–2005), Texas-born trained geologist; US Navy intelligence staff officer with US Army Air Force during World War II; joined State Department, 1946; State Department coordinator for aid to Greece and Turkey, 1947–1948; State Department's coordinator on Palestine refugee matters, with the title of special assistant to the secretary, March–June 1949; met Sharett in New York and then arrived in Beirut on March 20. See George C. McGhee, *On the Front Line in the Cold War: An Ambassador Reports* (Westport, CT: Praeger, 1997).

116. Policy paper prepared in the Department of State, March 15, 1949, *FRUS*, 1949, v. VI, 828–842.

117. Discussed in Ethridge [through Pinkerton] to secretary of state, nos. 127 and 128, both dated March 22, 1949, and copied to US missions in Jerusalem, Damascus, Amman, Baghdad, Cairo, and Jiddah, but not Tel Aviv, *FRUS*, 1949, v. VI, 856–859.

118. McGhee, *On the Frontline in the Cold War*, 36–42.

Long session from about eight o'clock till nearly one with McGhee and Ford. The discussion centered on the problem of refugees, during which McGhee gradually developed his theory, and presumably that of the PCC, for Israel's participation in the resettlement, and the role which new economic developments might play in creating new possibilities of resettlement in Israel or in the neighboring states. It is this latter prospect which appears to be McGhee's chief concern.

As we talked, I got the impression of a capable and energetic young man who in his anxiety to get a solution was tending somewhat to overlook inherent political and economic difficulties. Nonetheless, he is basically correct in his reiterated emphasis that, unless the most strenuous resettlement efforts were made, the problem would drag out indefinitely. He seemed satisfied with his talk but gave no definite assurance that he would, as I suggested, return for technical discussions with members of the Israeli Inter-departmental Committee.[119]

McGhee and Ethridge wrote a report to Acheson without consulting with Mc-Donald. Proceeding from the assumption of 800,000 Arab refugees, they called for a far greater Israeli contribution toward repatriation than hitherto discussed—350,000 to be repatriated to the regions conquered by Israel beyond the 1947 partition lines. Because of the Arab governments' intransigence toward resettlement and the desires of the refugees themselves, "maximum possible repatriation [is] necessary." Acheson agreed with the assessment and sent the report to all missions in the Middle East including Tel Aviv for comment.[120]

At my suggestion, Ford took McGhee off to lunch. Dr. Mohn came for tea and stayed a couple of hours. His report on his visit with Dr. Bunche confirmed my earlier impression that there had been no effective contact between Rhodes and the PCC, and that there were no plans for the latter's visit to the former. Nor, apparently had the PCC considered utilizing any of the personnel of the acting mediator's staff. Dr. Mohn said that Dr. Bunche had been surprised and pessimistic about the Beirut conference, but since his advice has not been asked, he did not proffer it.

As to the armistice negotiations, Dr. Mohn told of some of Dr. Bunche's firm actions, for example, his threat to withdraw altogether and to go home unless Israel agreed to get its troops out of Lebanon; to my surprise, Dr. Mohn reported that Dr. Bunche had made no commitment that Syria would have to withdraw its troops to the international frontier, as I understood was the case from Israeli sources. On the contrary, Dr. Bunche was quoted as having opposed the Israeli suggestion; Dr. Mohn also spoke of Israeli "injustices" towards

119. Refers to the transfer committee of Ezra Danin, Josef Weitz, and Zalman Lifschitz. Entries of February 23 and 25, 1949.
120. Acheson to US missions in Middle East [with McGhee-Ethridge Report], no. 191, March 30, 1949, McDonald Papers, USHMM, box 7, folder 12.

Arabs who had been in the Faluja pocket. He admitted that this might be the result of excesses by local commanders but he deplored them nonetheless.[121]

Earlier, Dr. Mohn told me of his recent visit to Eilat and to the port of Aqaba. He was sure that the Israeli troops in reaching the gulf had had to cross the Egyptian frontier because there was no other road available to them. When he reached the gulf, there was in effect a gentleman's agreement between the local Egyptian and Israeli commanders, which permitted the two sides to pass back and forth across the frontier. Subsequently, this was rescinded by order from the higher Egyptian command. As to the Transjordanian frontier, the Jewish troops were a few kilometers to the west and British one or two to the east. There had been no incidents and apparently no prospect of any.

The Ben-Gurions came promptly for dinner, followed a little later by the Kaplans and Mrs. Sharett. The only other guests were the Jacobsons. It was an almost perfect evening. The food was good, the conversation at the table easy, and afterwards also. I gave Ben-Gurion and Jacobson an opportunity to talk together and they exchanged reminiscences, the former of his life as a boy in Israel and the latter of the early life and political career of Truman. Meanwhile, Paula and Bluma talked together. As Ben-Gurion was leaving, he said: "E.J. is no fool." Both men apparently enjoyed getting acquainted with one another.

Wednesday, March 30

In bed most of the day trying to get over a minor but annoying cold.

Thursday, March 31

Again in bed most of the day until the staff meeting in the afternoon.

---

121. According to the Israeli-Egyptian armistice, the 4,000 Egyptian troops trapped in the Faluja pocket were allowed to evacuate. The agreement further guaranteed the safety of more than 3,100 Arab civilians in the neighboring villages of Faluja and Iraq-al-Manshiya, 1,100 of whom were refugees already. The IDF, against Sharett's express wishes, created intimidating conditions. Quaker aid workers including Delbert Replogle witnessed these events. Most of the Arabs left for Hebron in Red Cross convoys, the last of which was on April 22. Five days later, Israeli forces under Yitzhak Rabin demolished the two villages. Morris, *The Birth of the Palestinian Refugee Problem Revisited*, 521–525.

10. April 1949

Friday, April 1

Morning session of an hour or two with Mr. Percival L. Prattis, Negro editor of [a] Pittsburgh paper, together with Rabbi Yitzhak Herzog and Dr. Mohn.[1] Later we were joined by Harold B. Hoskins[2] and Mr. Ford. Prattis was interesting, but there was nothing particularly new in his report of his visit to Bunche. The chief rabbi asked to speak with me alone for a few minutes. He wanted to suggest that I help him to see the president when he goes to the States. I said I would do what I could.[3]

Hoskins, who seemed surprised that he was being received hospitably and urged to stay for lunch, talked freely about his impressions of the neighboring states, and of his advice to his client, Standard Oil of New Jersey, to move cautiously in this area. He was obviously made more modest in his judgments by the defeat of the Arab states, and was, at least superficially, more conciliatory towards Israel. He said that he had not been approached by the PCC [Palestine Conciliation Commission] to serve as the liaison man with the Arab states, a possibility which I had suggested to Ethridge but which the latter had apparently not spoke of to Hoskins. I got the impression that Hoskins would have accepted. I urged Hoskins to come back, and he said that he hoped to do so now that he had found himself more welcome than he anticipated.

1. Percival L. Prattis (1895–1980), journalist for African-American newspapers, 1936–1965; in 1949 executive editor of *Pittsburgh Courier*, the leading African American newspaper.

2. Harold B. Hoskins (1895–1982), Syrian-born anti-Zionist State Department and OSS official during World War II; toured the Middle East for Roosevelt, 1942–1943; reported that support for Zionism would wreck US standing in the Arab world while triggering bloodshed there. After the war he served as vice president of ARAMCO and as president of the Board of Trustees at the American University of Beirut; complained to Lovett in November 1948 that "the development of Israel as an outpost of communism, the liquidation of the Arabs in the Middle East, [and] the antagonizing of 350,000,000 Moslems throughout the world" ran counter to US interests. Memorandum by Lovett, November 10, 1948, NARA, RG 59, 501.BB Palestine, box 2122, folder 2.

3. McDonald contacted the president's appointment secretary Matthew Connelly, writing that "Rabbi Herzog is not only a man of great distinction and influence in Israel and throughout the world among Jews; he is also a very human and practical man of affairs and speaks excellent English. He could give to the President better than I think anyone else an illuminating account of the spiritual values as the Jews see them in recent developments here." McDonald to Connelly, April 19, 1949, McDonald Papers, Columbia University, box 9, folder 17.

Saturday, April 2

Long talk with the Jacobsons in the morning and lunch with them and the family at [the] Sackses. To tea at the Rokachs' where Ruth, Bobby, and I and some fourteen other guests sat down at the table. It was a pleasant affair.

Sunday, April 3

Abe Feinberg here on the Weizmann special plane, came out for lunch. At my suggestion, he agreed to take up with Clifford the following points:

1) The president's support of my suggestion in my recent letter to Secretary Acheson that the president personally urge American labor, particularly American Jewish labor, to be active in educational work here;
2) Press for our labor attaché (this refers to Clifford's support);
3) To persuade Clifford to urge the Department to be less sticky about transportation and clerical help and, in particular, to send somebody out with authority to take decisions about our housing problem.

As to the home situation,[4] Feinberg thought that Judge Rifkind[5] was the one man who could combine all elements in the ZOA [Zionist Organization of America]; that Daniel Frisch was "too much" even for the present administration of the ZOA.[6]

After dinner Dewey Stone and his wife of Brockton, Massachusetts,[7] and Mrs. Goldenberg of Minneapolis, came out for an hour or so.[8] Stone was concerned at the report he had heard in Washington from an unofficial spokesman of 52nd Street that the Vatican might submit a memorandum to the PCC

4. In April 1949 Rabbi Silver and his followers were maneuvering to regain control of the ZOA from the rival Zionist faction that included Henry Montor and Abe Feinberg. Feinberg was interested in finding a compromise candidate to lead the ZOA.
5. Simon H. Rifkind (1901–1995), Lithuanian-born trial lawyer and federal judge; legislative secretary to Sen. Robert F. Wagner (D-NY), 1927–1933; adviser on Jewish affairs to theater commander, USFET, 1945–1946, where he tried to aid Holocaust survivors in DP camps and recommended to the Anglo-American Committee of Inquiry in 1946 that they be transferred to Palestine; headed Commission on the Future Program and Constitution of the World Zionist Organization, which argued that Israel, as a sovereign state, was owed allegiance only by its own citizens and that non-Israeli Jews remained loyal citizens of their own countries, 1949. On his work with the Anglo-American Committee, see Goda et al., eds., *To the Gates of Jerusalem*, 106–109.
6. Daniel Frisch (1897–1950), Palestine-born Indianapolis businessman, Hebrew teacher, and president of ZOA, 1949–1950; developed program to maintain ZOA influence in Israel by creating contacts between US Jewish communities and Israel, encouraging pioneering in Israel by American Jewish youth and Israeli development of a mixed economy of planned agriculture and free market urban commerce. See Ganin, *An Uneasy Relationship*, 22–23.
7. Dewey D. Stone (1900–1977), Massachusetts businessman and fundraiser for Zionist causes; friend of Chaim Weizmann and financial supporter of the Sieff Institute; financial supporter of illegal immigration to Palestine after World War II; lobbied Truman on the partition of Palestine in 1947 and on recognition of Israel in 1948; helped supply military equipment to Israel in 1948.
8. Fay Goldenberg, widow of Jacob E. Goldenberg (1882–1946); Russian-born owner of Minnesota-based Quality Wines and Spirits, one of the largest liquor distributors in the United States.

protesting against Jewish claims in Jerusalem. I told him I had heard of no such move.

Monday, April 4

Miss Herlitz called to say that the PCC was due the next day in Tel Aviv and had an appointment with Ben-Gurion on Thursday. Plans in the interim were uncertain as far as she knew. As to my inquiry about Israel's unofficial reaction to ideas recently received about refugees, she is to determine whether I should speak to Eytan or one of the members of the technical committee.[9]

Simon called to say he did not think it would be necessary to see Chaim Weizmann off at the airport. His leaving time [for the United States] is now fixed at tomorrow evening at 10:00 o'clock.[10]

In the afternoon Mr. Jack Spitzer, a local vice president of the International Ladies Garment Workers' Union, came in. I was disappointed to learn that he was not here on a mission for the group that had sent Zimmerman. It appears that he is here more or less on his own and had heard nothing of any labor committee being sent. I was then interested to get his reaction to Zimmerman's report and to that of Sam Klaus.[11] I was not surprised but a little discouraged to have him say that there was no feeling of urgency in the matter, that Zimmerman had left the impression that the Mapam leaders were comparable to the Wallaceites,[12] and that their eastern orientation did not constitute even potentially a weakness. This reaction illustrates the difficulty of getting a group of men preoccupied with their own affairs to press energetically a new and apparently somewhat remote project.

To the fashion show at The Sharon a little after eight. Despite the congestion of an overflow crowd, we and [the] Jacobsons were promptly ushered to our places in one of the front rows. Seemingly all of the society of Tel Aviv was present. Almost none of the top officials were there, however. As usual the show was delayed but was an impressive display of variety of garments and fabrics for so small a country.

---

9. Eytan reported to Eban on April 3, 1949, that Ethridge was "fed up with [the] Arabs" and hoped that Israel would make a conciliatory gesture by agreeing to take a number of refugees. This, Ethridge insisted, would place pressure on the Arab states regarding resettlement and would facilitate US agreement to make financial contributions toward resettlement and development in the Arab states. Eytan thought that the United States was moving toward a policy of mass Arab resettlement. *DFPI*, v. 2, d. 472.

10. Weizmann's visit to the United States in April was theoretically private. On April 23 he was honored in New York at the Waldorf Astoria by the American Committee for the Weizmann Institute. He also informally conducted state business during his final trip to the United States.

11. Klaus to McDonald, March 31, 1949, McDonald Papers, USHMM, box 7, folder 12. Klaus told McDonald that his 250-page report on the labor movement in Israel would be complete soon; he agreed with McDonald's March 18 letter to Acheson that the United States should send a labor delegation to Israel; and he regretted that the Israeli Foreign Ministry had declined technical assistance on the labor question to this point.

12. Reference to Henry Wallace (1888–1965), Roosevelt's vice president; 1941–1945; secretary of commerce, 1945–1946; presidential candidate of the Progressive Party, 1948. In the 1948 campaign, Wallace called for an end to antagonism with the Soviet Union, an end to segregation in the United States, and universal government-sponsored health insurance.

An hour's conference in the morning with two leading TWA officials who were brought out by Mr. Hooper. From our long and rather rambling talk, I was convinced that neither TWA nor any of its rivals is yet prepared to begin regular service to Lydda. The operations official pointed to the lack of adequate navigation facilities and to those [for] servicing or refueling. But the major hurdle will remain what it was, the threat of Arab state boycott. So far as I could judge, little or no progress had been made by TWA or the other lines towards solving this problem. TWA is planning to make a thorough study here of the technical problems and then to dump the whole issue in the lap of the State Department. The traffic official did not take serious exception to my contention that a united front on the part of the airlines would avoid penalties for any one of them from [an] Arab boycott, but he gave no sign that he thought his company would, or the group of companies, take any chance. Instead, he reiterated the current delays in customs and other regulations at Tel Aviv, to which I replied that I was sure that all these difficulties as well as the technical ones would be cleared up quickly once the hesitation of the lines on the political level was ended.

Conference with Andrus and Ford on the Israel-Transjordan armistice agreement, but no decision about word to the Department.

On April 3, 1949, Israel and Transjordan concluded an armistice agreement at Rhodes.[13] A Transjordan delegation led by Abdullah al-Tel and an Israeli delegation led by Walter Eytan, General Yigael Yadin, and Colonel Moshe Dayan had hammered out the terms secretly at the king's winter palace at Shuneh over the previous week. King Abdullah gained legal control of Palestinian territory west of the Jordan River, excluding the grand mufti.[14] Expecting to hold lands on both sides of the Jordan River in perpetuity, he officially renamed his country the Hashemite Kingdom of Jordan on April 26.

But Abdullah had hoped to gain the entire region initially slated for the Arabs in the UN partition resolution. Instead, Israel kept nearly all of what it had conquered in 1948, including the cities of Lydda and Ramle and the corridor to Jerusalem. Israel further pressured Amman into surrendering a sixty-kilometer long, five-kilometer wide rim around the Tulkarm–Nablus–Jenin triangle in northern Samaria. Sixteen additional Arab villages in these foothills, including Umm el-Fahm, Baqa Gharbiya, and Taibiya, fell on the Israeli side of the armistice line.[15]

The armistice agreement guaranteed full rights to the roughly 20,000 Arabs who now found themselves on the Israeli side of this line. The Israeli government officially

13. Treaty published in Medzini, ed., *Israel's Foreign Relations: Selected Documents 1947–1974*, 184–192.
14. *DFPI*, v. 3, d. 248 and annex; d. 265, 267, 269.
15. Overview in Morris, *1948*, 384–388; Morris, *The Road to Jerusalem*, 202–203; Bar-Joseph, *The Best of Enemies*, 222–239.

opposed expulsions.[16] *Several thousand Arabs living in the strip who already were refugees from elsewhere were induced to move into Transjordanian-controlled territory. Permanent Arab residents, understanding the uncertain fate of refugees, tended to remain. For security reasons over the course of 1949 and 1950, Israeli authorities moved those villagers into larger villages farther inside Israel.[17] Arab anger over these developments was now directed at King Abdullah as well as at Israel.[18]*

According to General Assembly resolution of December 11, 1948, Jerusalem was to come under international administration. But Article VIII of the armistice agreement called for a "Special Committee" of Israeli and Transjordanian representatives to formulate arrangements "designed to enlarge the scope of this Agreement and to effect improvements in its application." The document listed six issues concerning Jerusalem on which the Special Committee was to work. These included access to Mount Scopus, resumption of road and rail access to and from Jerusalem, and resumption of water supplies from Latrun. Israel and Transjordan intended to settle Jerusalem's status themselves.

In a report to Washington, McDonald commented that the Special Committee was the agreement's most important feature.[19] "Politically," he wrote to Halsey and Janet Barrett, "conditions continue to improve here. The signing of the Israel-Transjordan Armistice . . . marks another important step. The Syrian armistice negotiations should . . . present no insuperable difficulty. . . . Moves will then be in order to translate these armistices into peace treaties without waiting upon armistices with the remoter countries, Iraq, Saudi Arabia, and Yemen. . . . The last fortnight has been so unmarked by crises that it has constituted a welcome breathing spell."[20]

McDonald remained concerned about the Palestinian Arab refugees. He also disliked being excluded from broader diplomatic discussions concerning Israel. On April 3, 1949, he wrote Satterthwaite, "Certainly I could be more useful if I knew more about conditions, views and personalities in neighboring countries than now provided in irregular messages passed [to] Tel Aviv from other capitals. . . . [To] ensure fullest possible implementation of Department's policy [on the] Middle East, I suggest possibility of regional conference . . . of heads of Missions Beirut, Damascus, Baghdad, Amman, Tel Aviv, Jidda, Cairo and possibly Yemen."[21]

"Farewell" dinner with the Jacobsons at the Armon. During the course of it received word that their flight was postponed.[22] Persuaded Mrs. Jacobson to

16. Herlitz to Elath, April 11, 1949, *DFPI*, v. 2, d. 487.

17. Overview in Morris, *The Birth of the Palestinian Refugee Problem Revisited*, 529–536.

18. Eytan to Sharett, April 3, 1949, *DFPI*, v. 3, d. 267.

19. McDonald to secretary of state, no. 262, April 6, 1949, NARA, RG 84, entry 2774, box 2, folder 321.9.

20. McDonald to Halsey and Janet Barrett, April 5, 1949, McDonald Papers, USHMM, box 7, folder 13.

21. McDonald to Satterthwaite, no. 259, April 3, 1949, McDonald Papers, USHMM, box 7, folder 13.

22. The Jacobsons were to fly on Weizmann's plane to Paris and then to the United States, but were delayed because of a fuel leak.

go with us to the concert. It was a thrilling program; Berlioz *Fantastic Symphony* and Moussorgsky's *Pictures at an Exhibition*. We were all delighted with the leadership of Paul Paray, who received a most cordial reception.[23] Indeed, it was so generous that I was a little embarrassed for [Louis] Cohen, the previous conductor, who was present.

Wednesday, April 6

Miss Herlitz called to tell me about the PCC's plans and to arrange for the visit of [Michael] Comay and [Zalman] Lifschitz. Earlier, immediately after breakfast, Dr. Mohn came to show me the text of the "stiff" letter from Bunche to the Foreign Office demanding the immediate withdrawal of Israeli troops from Syrian territory, where a UN observer had certified they had penetrated "on the very day of the beginning of the armistice talks." Mohn asked me to bring all this to the attention of the Foreign Office. I explained the Department ruling, which required that such a request be cleared through Washington. He promised to keep me informed of any new developments.

On March 30, a group of Syrian Army officers led by Colonel Husni al-Za'im overthrew the Syrian government of President Shukri al-Quwatli. Za'im had led the one successful Syrian operation of the war, the incursion into northeastern Israel that the IDF had not been able to reverse. Za'im's coup was encouraged by the CIA, partly for the sake of ARAMCO, which had been blocked from running a pipeline through Syria to Lebanon. Za'im needed to disengage Syrian troops from the Israeli front in order to bolster his position in Damascus and to protect against potential moves by Transjordan and Egypt. He was willing to accept US money for development schemes, part of which he may have intended to divert to his own pocket. Za'im thus supported armistice talks with Israel—talks that had already been scheduled before the coup. On April 3 Israel and Syria reached a cease-fire agreement, and on April 5 armistice talks began in no-man's land on the western edge of Syrian-held Israeli territory.

Za'im, however, had to show some sort of victory to mitigate anti-Israeli sentiment in Syria. He insisted on retaining the areas occupied by Syrian troops west of the pre-1948 Palestine-Syrian frontier, most notably the enclave around the Israeli settlement at Mishmar HaYarden, and also on an adjustment of the Syrian-Israeli border westward to bisect Lake Hula and the Sea of Galilee.[24] Ben-Gurion had made

23. Paul Paray (1886–1979), French-born conductor and composer who conducted various orchestras in France and the United States before World War II; fled Paris in 1940 when the authorities demanded the names of Jewish musicians; employed Jewish musicians thereafter as conductor of the Monte Carlo Opera; musical director of the Israel Philharmonic Orchestra between October 1948 and April 1951 and returned frequently as a guest conductor.

24. In general see Ben-Dror, *Ralph Bunche and the Arab-Israeli Conflict*, 218–241; Moshe Ma'oz, *Syria and Israel: From War to Peacemaking* (New York: Oxford University Press, 1995), 20–26; Douglas Little, "Mission Impossible: The CIA and the Cult of Covert Action in the Middle East," *Diplomatic History* 28, no. 5 (November 2004): 663–701; Avi Schlaim, "Husni Za'im and the Plan to Resettle Palestinian Refugees in Syria," *Journal of Palestine Studies* 15, no. 4 (Summer 1986): 68–80. See also entry of April 19, 1949.

it clear that Israel needed peace. Yet, he refused to surrender territory to gain possibly transitory goodwill, and he also suspected that the British were behind the coup.[25] The IDF moved troops over the Syrian frontier near Kibbutz Shamir on the western slope of the Golan Heights to gain leverage. UN Secretary-General Trygve Lie expressed "grave concern" to Abba Eban, and Sharett, still in New York, communicated his own shock back to Tel Aviv regarding the army's "irresponsibility." Eytan cabled Eban at the UN: "McDonald and [the] USA military attaché [are] also on [the] warpath."[26]

To the office, where after consultation with Ford and Andrus, I drafted a telegram to the Department reporting Mohn's visit and our failure to get any information from the Israeli liaison officer or the chief of staff. In the same telegram I suggested the desirability of the PCC utilizing the services of [Henri] Vigier,[27] Riley, and if at all possible, of Bunche.

At teatime, Harry Greenstein of Baltimore, the Jewish adviser to the American commanding general in Germany, came out. He told of plans for evacuation of the DP camps in Germany and Austria.[28] Interestingly, he reported that there was the beginning of seepage [refugee migration] from Hungary into Austria. We also talked about conditions here. He promised to come back and see me again before he goes.

At six o'clock Michael Comay and Mr. Lifschitz of the Israeli interdepartmental refugee committee [transfer committee] came at my invitation.[29] I went over with them rather carefully the substance of the refugee program which McGee and the PCC had worked out and which the Department had submitted for my comment a week or so earlier.[30]

The chief points they made were:

1) The figure of more than 800,000 [Palestinian Arab refugees] was a very substantial exaggeration; there are not more than 525,000 or 550,000 bona fide war refugees. There could not be more than this number because there were not many more than the total of Arabs living in the whole of Israel-occupied Palestine before May 1948. The PCC figures were exaggerated by inflated ideas of the original Arab population and by the inclusion of 150,000 or more Arabs unemployed as a result of war conditions and the withdrawal of the British.

25. See his concerns in Ben-Gurion Diary, entry of April 3, 1949.

26. Eban to Eytan, April 6, 1949, *DFPI*, v. 3, d. 279; Eytan to Eban, April 6, 1949, *DFPI*, v. 3, d. 280. McDonald to secretary of state, no. 263, April 6, 1949, NARA, RG 59, 501.BB Palestine, box 2124, folder 6.

27. Henri Vigier (b. 1886), personal representative of the acting UN mediator (Bunche). Vigier chaired the Israeli-Syrian talks.

28. Entry of July 29, 1948. Greenstein replaced William Haber as the adviser on Jewish Affairs to US Commands in Germany and Austria, February–October 1949; worked to move Jews from DP camps in US zones, most of whom emigrated to Israel and the United States.

29. Refers to the transfer committee of Ezra Danin, Josef Weitz, and Zalman Lifschitz. Entries of February 23 and 25, 1949, and March 29, 1949.

30. See entry of March 29, 1949, for the McGhee-Ethridge recommendations to Acheson.

2) The principle that the non-November 29 Israeli-held areas should be accorded priority treatment in the return of refugees is unwanted and unacceptable.

3) Similarly regarded was the suggestion that the refugees in the peripheral areas should have priority treatment.

4) Rejected, too, was the theory that repatriation would be much more economical than resettlement. This idea, it was argued, ignored the virtually complete destruction of the Arab economy in Israeli-held Palestine.

5) Comay argued that the PCC was misinterpreting the December 11 resolution in that the language did not call for the return of the refugees immediately but that they who wished to return should be permitted to do so "at the earliest possible date."

6) They argued that there was no convincing reason for the assumption that many of the refugees would return, because of the changes in the economic situation and because of their reported fear. Following our talk I had the impression that the two men would urge Ben-Gurion to emphasize their point of view about the numbers of refugees and also the impracticability on various points of the PCC's program.

Just time to dress and have a hurried supper before the family, the Jacobsons, and I went out to the Sharon for Colonel Andrus's Army Day party. Between three and four hundred persons attended; the guests included the heads of the Army and the other armed services and many officials from the Foreign Office and other government departments. Also present were a number of Americans, the American Jewish Committee group, the Charles Rosenblooms and others.[31]

[Eytan] indicated [at this party] that Israel would accept the PCC's invitation to a "peace conference" with the Arabs in some European [city]. Eytan belittled the [Israeli] Syrian frontier violation, saying it would be ironed out. As to the PCC, Eytan thought that there was a lack of unity of purpose. Ethridge, he thought, wanted as prompt a settlement as possible with Yalçin; but Boisanger, he thought, was marking time in the hope that France's position would improve in this area. He agreed, too, that the lack of a strong secretary-general impeded the work of the commission.

Thursday, April 7

Up early and breakfast with the Jacobsons at seven-thirty. Having been handed even earlier an important night action telegram which required immediate study and action during the day, I gave Jacobson the substance of it, which he seemed to grasp better than I dared hope he could.

---

31. Charles J. Rosenbloom (1898–1973), Pittsburgh financier and lawyer; active in United Jewish Appeal and Weizmann Institute; major art collector and donor, especially to Carnegie Museum of Art.

On April 5 in Washington, Acheson and Rusk met with Sharett to relay the president's concerns. Truman, Acheson said, still held to his earlier policy that if Israel held territories beyond those allotted in the partition resolution, it would have to make territorial concessions elsewhere. The president also endorsed international control of Jerusalem, but noted that the main issue for the international community concerned the safety of and access to the Holy Places themselves. Perhaps they could come under international authority while Israeli and Arab authorities could be responsible for the bulk of Jerusalem's inhabitants. Acheson noted that "the source of greatest immediate concern for the President was the question of Palestinian refugees," which, based on the McGhee-Ethridge report of March 29, Acheson numbered at 800,000. An impasse, he continued, could wreck the chance of a final peace settlement. He suggested that Israel announce that it would repatriate a quarter of the refugees. The first repatriations would be to those regions of Israel not assigned to the Jews in the November 29 partition plan. Repatriations to Israel proper would follow afterward.

On Jerusalem Sharett stated that he wanted to leave room for direct negotiations between Israel and Transjordan for a settlement that would also take account of the Holy Places and receive international approval. On the frontiers Sharett noted that there was no political distinction between lands assigned to the Jews in November 1947 and those that Israel now controlled. On refugees, Sharett disputed Acheson's figures, noting that the total was no more than 550,000, and he repeated that the refugees' resettlement in the Arab states would benefit Israel and the Arab states alike.[32]

On April 6, the State Department sent a summary of the discussion to Tel Aviv for Ethridge and McDonald. Both were ordered to visit Ben-Gurion in their different capacities to press the Department's arguments. McDonald was to convey an additional message regarding the news of Israel's incursion into Syrian territory—that given "[the] President's deep concern for prompt peace in Palestine, this report if true would necessarily cause [a] most unfavorable impression here, particularly at a time when Israeli membership [in the] UN [is]on [the] point [of] being discussed [in the General Assembly]."[33]

Jacobson asked me what he should say to the president. My suggestions were roughly as follows. The president should continue in the driver's seat as compared with Bevin; he should recognize the unwillingness of Israel to yield territory won in battle; he should see how difficult repatriation of refugees now is; the importance of labor leadership here from the States, and the necessity of the president's urging immediate and comprehensive action by Dubinsky et al., the loyalty of the Department to the embassy; the necessity of fuller cooperation on financial and personnel levels; the impossibility of full internationalization

32. Memorandum of conversation by secretary of state, *FRUS, 1949*, v. VI, 890–894; Sharett to Eytan, April 5, 1949, *DFPI*, v. 2. d. 477.

33. Acheson to McDonald and Ethridge, no. 208, April 6, 1949, NARA, 501.BB Palestine, box 2124, folder 6.

of Jerusalem. In general, I urged a continuation of the president's policy adjustment to realities here and the strengthening of the hands of the embassy. Jacobson promised to deliver all of these messages and more. He expected to see the president about the 20th or 21st of April. As I was walking out with him to the gate, I told him of my desire to return for consultation in July and intimated the family reason for this. He said that the president would be interested in this side of the problem. We parted as if we had been lifelong friends.

Eddie Jacobson wrote McDonald from Kansas City on May 5, 1949. He reported that en route to the April 23 dinner for Weizmann at the Waldorf Astoria,

> *I stopped in Washington and had a very lengthy visit with our President. He was feeling fine and in a very jovial mood. I gave him a very detailed description of my observations in Israel, and also told him of the various things you and I have discussed. I know he was very happy to hear my story.*
>
> *In the course of the conversation, I told him of the several suggestions made by you, and he thought you were right. I also told him that it would be a very good idea to call you in so you could talk the entire situation over with him, as you were more familiar with the various phases of the entire Middle East than any other man. He said he thought that would be a good idea and I sincerely hope that he does.*[34]

To the airfield by 9:45. While waiting I chatted with [Pablo] Azcárate and told him of my urgent message for Ethridge. He agreed that I might take Ethridge away from the field promptly so that he might have a chance to study the document before the eleven o'clock conference with Ben-Gurion. After greeting the three commissioners who arrived promptly at ten, I carried off the two Ethridges and Wilkins to the house. While the ladies entertained "Willie" Ethridge and Wilkins, they read the Department's telegram and Miss Clark prepared a copy for them. There was just time then for me to take the two men to the prime minister's office.

In their two-and-a-half hour meeting with Ben-Gurion and his aides on April 7, 1949, the PCC members reiterated their views on Jerusalem and the Arab refugees. They said that the Arab states had agreed on the last day of the Beirut conference [April 5, 1949] to meet with an Israeli delegation in a neutral city under the auspices of the PCC and that the Arabs this time were not setting preconditions. It was essential, Ethridge said, that Israel take immediate steps regarding the refugee question, which "was key to solution [of the] whole Palestine problem." Yalçin added that "Israel should not, like Hitler, use methods incompatible with standards [of] Western civilization."

Ben-Gurion agreed to the conference if held in a neutral country. (The PCC decided subsequently that it would commence on April 26 at Lausanne.) But he held

---

34. Jacobson to McDonald, May 5, 1949, McDonald Papers, USHMM, box 7, folder 14.

firm on the major issues. Regarding Jerusalem, Ben-Gurion rejected the UN resolu-
tion of December 11. The UN, he said, could not protect the city's 100,000 Jews, and
Jerusalem had been the Jews' capital city since the time of King David. Ben-Gurion
agreed only to have the Holy Places themselves placed under international adminis-
tration. Ben-Gurion expressed a willingness to repatriate the small number of Arab
refugees who wished to reunite with their families, and he was also willing to com-
pensate Arabs who had actually cultivated their land. But he repeated Israel's funda-
mental policy that the multilateral attack on Israel created the refugee issue and that
most would have to settle in Arab countries.[35] *According to Eytan, "no punches*
[were] pulled [on] either side."[36]

At 12:45 Mr. Levinius Painter and one of his colleagues from the American
Friends Service Committee were at the house. Painter told me of two developments in the northwestern Galilee, which he thought discouraging because
they tended to embitter Jewish-Arab relationships and to prevent settling
down. He knew of a number of instances where the Jewish military authorities
were continuing to round up individuals or groups of Arabs and transporting
them to other parts of Galilee or even pushing them across the frontier. The
second practice, which he deplored, was that of gathering up the furniture of
absentee Arabs, technically to store and conserve the furniture, but in reality
Painter thought the goods often found [their] way into the homes of Jewish
newcomers.[37] Painter's colleague told of having been ordered to leave the Faluja
area after he had called the Jewish authorities' attention to cases of alleged injustice to Arabs. His conclusion was that a relief worker jeopardized his position by any such complaints.[38]

The two Friends disagreed on a number of points with the report of
the Israeli interdepartmental committee, which I permitted them to read
through.[39] They urged that I press as strongly as possible on the Israeli authorities to accept the principle of repatriation at least of one-fourth of the total of
refugees. Painter added that he thought we should be very lucky if in fact this
number were accepted, for he is, as I am, pessimistic about any measurable
progress at present either in repatriation or in resettlement. He suggested that
meanwhile, in a number of small ways (he promised to outline these for me in
a subsequent memorandum), the Israeli authorities could improve the lot of
some of the refugees, for example, in releasing existing bank balances. The
Friends promised to come to see me again.

Lunch with the family and Mrs. Ethridge. From the latter's chatter, I
gathered the impression that Ethridge was less encouraged by the PCC than

35. Meeting in Ethridge [through Burdett] to secretary of state, no. 274, *FRUS*, 1949, v.
VI, 902–904; See also *DFPI*, v. 2, d. 479, 505.
36. Eytan to Sharett, April 7, 1949, *DFPI*, v. 2, d. 480.
37. See entry of February 18, 1949.
38. See entry of March 29, 1949.
39. See entry of February 25, 1949.

he pretended to be, and also that he and his colleagues were disturbed by the elimination of the UN chairman from the Israel-Transjordan committee set up to iron out the unsettled points between the two countries.[40] Apparently, he fears that, by bilateral agreement, the internationalization of Jerusalem may be circumvented. Willie showed herself a vivacious and unconventional personality, who so far as I could discern, had, despite considerable reading, learned nothing fundamental about this area and who would be unlikely to learn more than a mass of trivia.

About 3:30 Ethridge joined us and reported very briefly on the PCC's talk with Ben-Gurion. He found the latter adamant on refugees but got the impression that Comay and Eytan were prepared to study the matter further with a view to urging Ben-Gurion to reconsider.[41] Later, Wilkins said that he thought there had been no advance. As to the other subjects discussed, Ethridge was so brief that I got no clear impression.

Both Ethridge and Wilkins were enthusiastic about the regional roundtable conference of mission heads and said they would get off a telegram to that effect to the department. I asked Ethridge to urge that it be held in time for him to attend. As to the PCC's European plans, Ethridge was hopeful that, through the private conferences which would thus be made possible, substantial progress might be made. All the Arab states including Saudi Arabia, except Iraq, had agreed to attend. The exact place was still undetermined.

At 5:15 I began my conference with the military attachés, and Hooper and Ford, on the Department's night action telegram. We were not able, however, to get very far before Shiloah and Miss Herlitz arrived for the discussion of the Israel-Transjordan armistice details. Shortly thereafter, I had to leave for my conference with Ben-Gurion. This was extremely [simplistic], for through it I was able to carry out literally the Department's difficult instructions to reinforce the PCC's presentation on the following points: the alleged Israeli violation of the Syrian frontier; the president's reiteration of the necessity of Israel recognizing the principle of yielding something if the military gains were to be held intact; the trusteeship idea in connection with the internationalization of Jerusalem, and particularly the president's new language to the effect that the international community was interested in the internationalization of the Holy Places rather than in the daily affairs of the people of the city; and, finally, the Department's recommendation of Israel's acceptance of its program of refugee gradualism.

Ben-Gurion was amused by my quotation from Silver's letter about our photograph. [He] was pleased with the president's Jerusalem stand; was hope-

40. Refers to the Special Committee called for in Article VIII of the Israel-Transjordan armistice agreement. For direct negotiations over Jerusalem, see for example *DFPI*, v. 3, d. 267, 269.

41. On April 13, 1949, Comay had a long meeting with Ethridge and echoed earlier Israeli statements. Ethridge reported that Israel's policies were "in direct contravention" to US policies. Ethridge [through Burdett] to secretary of state, no. 291, April 13, 1949, *FRUS*, 1949, v. VI, 911–916.

ful about frontiers, definite that the troops [would] withdrawal from Syria if they had entered; but adamant against any repatriation except as an integral part of a peace settlement. Repeatedly he stressed that the elementary right of self-defense justified this position. He argued also that there was justification implicit in the UN December 11 resolution [which called for repatriation for those refugees "wishing . . . to live at peace with their neighbors . . . at the earliest practicable date"].

Ben-Gurion said that the figure of 800,000 refugees was "a British lie." He professed to having been unaware of the incursion into Syria until earlier that day. As ordered, McDonald pointed to increasing criticism of Israel in US and global opinion. He reported Ben-Gurion's reply: "I am fully aware of public criticism but Israel [is] too small [to] make promises it cannot or does not intend to carry out. Israel['s] right [of] self-protection is paramount. [The government] must insist irrespective [of] criticism [of the] right [to] defend [the] country's existence. Not fair [to] ask it [to] jeopardize safety by repatriation now." McDonald appended his own comment: "At present I see no prospect [of] softening Israel's position [regarding] refugees. Attitude [on] Jerusalem and frontiers [is] more promising. Hence it is fortunate PCC is pressing plans [for a] European conference. I hope [the Department] decides [to] call [a] regional conference [of the] heads of American missions . . . before Ethridge, who strongly supports [the] plan [for a European conference], leaves this area."[42]

On April 12, 1949, Ben-Gurion told Foreign Ministry officials that Israel's primary goals were Jewish immigration and settlement. These trends would guarantee Israel's existence while consolidating its gains. These priorities meant that Israel needed to secure peace on its borders while decreasing its unsustainable military burden. Peace with the Arabs would also decrease interference by foreign powers, namely Great Britain, which in turn would make Arab acceptance of Israel more likely. Israel could spare no effort in achieving peace, though bilateral negotiations were still preferable to working through the UN.[43]

I returned to the conference at the house in time to hear the latter part of Shiloah's presentation. This is to be summarized by Ford in an airgram to the Department. As always, Shiloah was excellent.

McDonald reported that Shiloah was pessimistic concerning Syria. Israel would not negotiate, Shiloah insisted, if Syrian forces were on Israeli soil, and Za'im could not withstand domestic criticism should Syrian forces withdraw. Israeli troops had withdrawn from Syrian territory, he added. Regarding Transjordan, Shiloah emphasized the importance of the bilateral Special Committee that would, he said, "iron out many of the outstanding differences" concerning Jerusalem.

42. McDonald to secretary of state, no. 268, April 8, 1949, *FRUS*, 1949, v. VI, 899–900; Herlitz to Sharett, April 8, 1949, *DFPI*, v. 2, d. 482.
43. *DFPI*, v. 2, d. 490.

Concerning the prospects of general peace, Shiloah said that there were two blocs with which to contend: Iraq and Transjordan, and Egypt, Syria, Saudi Arabia, and Lebanon. Shiloah then, McDonald reported, "engaged in a little mild scolding of what he considered bungling outsiders, including Britain, France, and rather more recently, ourselves. . . . Mr. Shiloah believed that, until we conditioned our support of Arab governments upon the promise . . . that such governments would make it their primary business to raise the standard of living of their people, we could expect to see a continuation of weak and corrupt governments in the Middle East."[44]

A little after nine the AJC group including Jacob Blaustein,[45] Simon Segal,[46] John Slawson,[47] and Irving Engel[48] arrived and stayed until about eleven. I was struck by their naiveté about Israel and their assumption that the AJC had a role to play here in saving Israel from making mistakes which might jeopardize the Jewish community in the States. Their vague thought about excessive rabbinical influence left me cold. Blaustein may see me again before he goes.

The American Jewish Committee [AJC], historically a non-Zionist secular organization, struggled to define its relationship with Israel after 1948. Official Israeli statements that spoke of a Jewish nation worried the AJC, because they raised the specter of dual loyalty among American Jews. The AJC worried that Israeli policies running counter to US interests would compromise the position of American Jewry. The delegation led by Blaustein, the new AJC president, arrived in March 1949. Though impressed with everything he saw, Blaustein worried about the absorption of new immigrants, 250,000 of whom were expected in 1949.[49]

Friday, April 8

Breakfast conference with Ford. Ford reported the disturbing incident in Haifa of the enforced evacuation of Arab families by Israeli troops. I hope the *Palestine Post* account in the morning paper that the soldiers have already been removed and the families restored by the military police is correct.[50]

44. McDonald to secretary of state [restricted] no. A-93, April 12, 1949, NARA, RG 59, MC 1390, reel 19, frames 070–073.

45. See entry of June 24, 1948; Blaustein was executive chairman of the American Jewish Committee, 1949–1954.

46. Simon Segal (1900–1972), director, American Jewish Committee Foreign Affairs Department.

47. John Slawson (1896–1989), executive vice president, American Jewish Committee, 1943–1967; founder of AJC's Institute of Human Relations, 1957.

48. Irving M. Engel (1891–1978), chairman of executive committee, American Jewish Committee; succeeded Blaustein as president, 1954–1959.

49. See Zvi Ganin, *An Uneasy Relationship*, 3–48.

50. The *Palestine Post* reported that, on April 7, 1949, Israeli soldiers had forced Arabs from their homes in Haifa's Arab quarter and then occupied the houses. The Arabs involved, one of whom was a member of the Knesset (Tewfik Toubi), complained to the mayor, and Arab shops closed in protest. By evening, military police removed the soldiers, and the houses were restored to their owners. "Soldiers Removed from Houses Which They Seized from Arabs," *Palestine Post*, April 8, 1949.

Dinner with the Simon Markses at the Sharon. Others present included Marcus Sieff. Chatted for a moment with Ben-Gurion and Paula. After dinner, a long talk with Lord Herbert Samuel[51] and Simon while the rest of the group chatted with Lady Samuel. It was interesting to note how Lord Samuel clung to many of his old ideas, his opposition to the Biltmore Program, his concern about British public opinion, etc. His mind was as clear and as brilliant as ever, but one could still see much evidence for the judgment made against him that he is inherently more British than Jewish. As we were listening to the ten o'clock news, he intuitively was more enthusiastic about the item that the International Court had voted in favor of Britain on the Albania-Corfu dispute than about anything else.[52] He promised to come to see me before he left. We gave Marcus Sieff a lift home and arranged for him to speak to the staff on Tuesday the 19th.

Sunday, April 10

Elaborate tea at Shoshana's for the family and staff. My longest talk there with her father, who explained fully the work he had done here in more than the past twenty years in irrigation and in the development of farm buildings and agricultural communities. He is going to the States soon and wants my help in some directions.

Monday, April 11

Lorna Wingate came for about an hour just before lunch.[53] What an extraordinarily brilliant and attractive personality she is. I complained that she had come to see me so late, just on the eve of her departure. She promised to come back again on her return after a few months. Our chief subject of discussion was the attitude of Britain and the possibility that the latter might one day become a real friend of Israel. Her answer to my query took the form of a brilliant analysis of the traditional mindset of British leaders to the effect that to put a gun in the hand of Jew was to arm a potential enemy, plus the outmoded but persistent concepts of world strategy held by [Bernard Law] Montgomery, which regarded as secure anchors such weak points as Pakistan.[54] She insisted

51. Herbert L. Samuel (1870–1963), Anglo-Jewish Liberal politician; first (nonconverted) Jew to serve as a cabinet minister, 1909–1910, and several times thereafter; first British high commissioner in Palestine, 1920–1925. As high commissioner he tried to reconcile Arabs to the Mandate through a restrictive approach to Jewish immigration and appointment of Haj Amin al-Husseini as the grand mufti of Jerusalem in an attempt to co-opt the Husseini clan; created viscount, 1937. See Bernard Wasserstein, *Herbert Samuel: A Political Life* (Oxford: Clarendon Press, 1992).
52. International Court of Justice Case, 1947–1949, involving dispute between Britain and Albania regarding shipping rights in the Corfu Channel; court awarded damages to Britain resulting from Albanian attacks on British ships, which had caused forty-two deaths during the Greek civil war in 1946.
53. Entry of February 26, 1949.
54. Field Marshal Bernard Law Montgomery (1887–1976), commander of British Eighth Army in North Africa and Italy, 1942–1944; commander of 21st Army Group in France, which advanced into Germany, 1944–1945; chief of imperial general staff, 1946–1948; served in various

that had [General Archibald] Wavell, early in the war, utilized the available hundred thousand Jews, men and women, of Palestine, there never would have been Rommel's advance into Egypt, nor would there have been the necessity of the large British reinforcements.[55] On the basis of the record, she foresees no fundamental change in the British attitude within the next years. I asked her to write me a long letter setting forth more clearly her ideas. She promised to do that.

Tuesday, April 12

A long and interesting conference with Rabbi Jacob Herzog. He expressed disappointment that Monsignor McMahon's memorandum reflected no change of position from that which he had expressed when he arrived in Israel. Like Ben-Horin, Herzog welcomed the monsignor's statement at the end of the first paragraph where McMahon wrote, "The undersigned is happy to report that he personally, after an extended journey in the area, can testify to the genuine desire of the Government of Israel to repair the damage done and to maintain proper relations with the religious institutions within its boundaries."

Herzog spoke as if encouraged by a recent visit of Cosmo Mendez, a classmate of His Holiness, to the Vatican recently. The pope is said to have listened sympathetically to Mendez's explanation on the basis of a map, which he brought with him, that the New City was in no sense a sacred area. When the question of a possible UN mandate for the Holy City was mentioned, and France as a possible mandatory came into the discussion, His Holiness asked, "why not Italy?" Herzog then analyzed what he regarded as some of the factors which might explain the Vatican's seeming willingness to support Italy's claims. The Vatican appears to be very much [more] satisfied with the Italian government's campaign against communism than with that of the French government.[56] Moreover, any prestige added to the Quirinal now would strengthen it and since even the Italian peasants and workmen were proud of Italy's overseas domain or influence, any extension of these in the Middle East would strengthen the present government.

Illustrative of the complications, national and sectarian, in Jerusalem, Herzog told me the following story: The bishop of Liège[57] on a recent visit

Western European Union and NATO capacities, 1948–1958; taught at Indian Staff College in Quetta (now in Pakistan), 1934–1937; believed after the partition of the subcontinent that Pakistan was a reliable British ally against Soviet expansion into Central Asia.

55. Field Marshal Archibald Wavell (1883–1950), commander-in-chief, Middle East, 1939–1941; virulently opposed Jewish immigration into Palestine during the war for fear it would upset the entire region. During the Arab Revolt in Palestine (1936–1939), he was the general officer commanding [GOC] British forces in Palestine and Transjordan. One of his subordinates, Captain Orde Wingate, trained Haganah units and urged Wavell to use the Haganah more extensively so that British troops could be used elsewhere.

56. Alessandro Brogi, *Confronting America: The Cold War Between the United States and the Communists in France and Italy* (Chapel Hill: University of North Carolina Press, 2011).

57. Louis-Joseph Kerkhoffs (1878–1962), bishop of Liège, 1927–1961.

here urgently desired permission from the Israeli Army to enter Notre Dame de France[58] and make a prayer of intercession there. The military objected on security grounds, but through appeal to Ben-Gurion and his instructions to the GHQ, permission was finally granted. At that point, the French consul general [René Neuville] intervened and declared that the church property was under French jurisdiction and forbade the Belgian's prelate's entrance for the formal ceremony. The latter was then in the embarrassing position of having to explain to the Israelis why he was not able to accept their permission. Perhaps the Frenchman is more wooden-headed than usual.

Mr. Hooper came out for a conference before lunch. I was impressed by his account of his work to date and could understand better why his report on the second Hoofien conference had been delayed. At lunch, Hooper and Mrs. Lourie from Johannesburg discovered many friends in common.[59] I was intrigued by Mrs. Lourie's strong feeling about the "excessive" socialism of Israel and her assumption that after ten or fifteen years the state organizations would absorb most private enterprises.

At teatime Felix Warburg's youngest brother, Fritz, and his wife came from Givat Brenner, where they are visiting their older, married daughter. We had a pleasant visit with talk of families, graphology, and the science of the palm. Later, Fritz spoke of problems within the kibbutz but insisted that his daughter and son-in-law were completely happy. Dinner with the Rosenblooms at the Kaete Dan. Other guests were the Levinsons and Paray, the visiting French conductor. It was an excellent meal and good company.

During the evening I took occasion to talk briefly with Dr. Mohn. He said he was remaining here during the Syrian armistice negotiations, will then go to New York and probably return to Europe. As always, he was extremely interesting. He said he was pleasantly surprised by the Syrian withdrawal from Hill 223, for he had feared that the Israelis had put themselves at a disadvantage by threatening not to continue negotiations unless this withdrawal were carried out.[60] He had rather a high opinion of Husni al-Za'im, the Syrian dictator, who was, he said, a professional soldier and not as loose-mouthed as his official pronouncements might suggest. He thought it not yet clear what his rise to power would mean in the Middle East puzzle. As to Glubb Pasha's recent rather inflammatory statements, Mohn tended to play it down, saying that it was probably nothing more than a professional soldier's inept attempt to defend

58. See n. 90. The monastery, which sat near the boundary between IDF and Arab Legion controlled territory, was a critical vantage point overlooking the Old City. It is one of the highest buildings on one of the city's highest points. Raphael Israeli, *Jerusalem Divided: The Armistice Regime, 1947–1967* (London: Routledge, 2002), 124–25.

59. Regina Lourie (née Muller), wife of Johannesburg businessman Harry Lourie (1875–1942) of Katz & Lourie Jewelers; mother of Israeli diplomat Arthur Lourie; donor of 411 acres of land in Be'er Sheva to Jewish National Fund.

60. The Syrians had occupied Hill 223 east of Kibbutz Mahanayim in violation of the truce. The Israelis threatened to break off armistice talks, the UN urged withdrawal, and the Syrians withdrew on April 27. *DFPI*, v. 3, d. 282, 284.

himself against the common charge that the Jews had everywhere been victorious.[61]

McDonald drafted a letter for Bunche for Mohn to deliver. He expressed admiration for Bunche as a mediator and then expressed the hope "that you will in your conferences with the PCC stress with the members the imperative reasons behind your procedure—the only one which has or can work—of bilateral negotiations. Surely the rumored 'peace conference' in [Lausanne] will have to be led by a Talleyrand with even more gifts of genius than his predecessor at Vienna if egregious failure is not to be the result."[62]

Wednesday, April 13

Conference with Ford and Padberg on various problems of security including arrangements for our Jerusalem trip. I was impressed by Padberg's understanding and grasp.

In the evening to the [Rabbi Harry and Ida] Davidowitzes' for Seder. There were just over thirty at the table, including the two young Comay children, Jill and Peter. The latter sat at the host's right and asked the traditional questions. He also, as soon as he had gained confidence, joined distinctly with "Harry" in leading the prayers, chants and singing. He added delightfully to the festival. We were fortunate to have been included, because Dr. Davidowitz conducted the whole evening with authority, skill and sympathy. He gave us outsiders a better understanding of the significance of Passover to modern Jews than we could have received from almost any other leader. I was struck anew by the extent to which, in the case of Jews, their religious traditions and national aspirations form a singular unity. Moreover, there was the service, which though dignified and at times obviously religious, [had] nothing of the sober or rather depressing solemnity which tends to characterize so many Christian religious occasions. The way in which the whole group joined enthusiastically in the singing of the quite unreligious songs at the end showed to me how Jewish festivals and religious ceremonies could be combined with the popular and continually appealing national demonstration. The degree of religiousness in the narrow sense of the word did not seem to become at all the degree of enthusiastic participation by the different members of the group. It was as if the service united them and revivified their Jewishness without regard to their different backgrounds.

---

61. Glubb had said that the Arab Legion's role in World War II had been minimized. "There is so much Jewish propaganda about what the Jews did in the war that the British public does not realize that for her size and population, Trans-Jordan did far more." He also said that Israel's victory was a "European invasion" and a "new, vicious kind of imperialism." *Palestine Post*, March 30, 1949, April 11, 1949.
62. McDonald to Bunche, undated draft, McDonald papers, USHMM, box 7, folder 13.

Thursday, April 14

First day of Passover.

Friday, April 15

From April 15 to April 17, McDonald traveled to Jerusalem with his family for the Easter weekend. It was his first trip there since 1947 when he had been a guest of the Jewish National Fund.[63] Following State Department policy, he conducted no official business with Israeli government officials, but he made contact with US officials, including Burdett and Ethridge, in accordance with earlier Department permission.[64]

Left the house with the family about 9:45 for our start to Jerusalem. The road to the south of Rehovot was familiar. From there we continued south past Gedera, and then southeast to the Majal-Latrun Road. We followed this to beyond Hulda, where we entered a relatively short portion, only ten miles or so, of the Courage Road.[65] It was in this cutoff that we saw the most beautiful and gorgeous fields of flowers, which turned the valleys and hillsides into masses of flaming colors—red, yellow, purple. As we reached the neighborhood of Latrun and began to mount the Judean Hills at Bab al-Wad [Sha'ar HaGai], we saw more than a score of buses and other vehicles along the roadside marking the defiles through which the Israeli convoys so perilously made their way. Shalom described vividly his impressions of many drives through these hazardous narrows. As we mounted the higher hills, I was again struck with the splendid vistas from the beautifully built road. The mountainsides this time seemed less harsh because of the heavy winter rains, which had clothed them with an unusual covering of grass and flowers.

The city itself, though familiar, was deeply stirring. Reaching the King David [Hotel] and YMCA neighborhood with their magnificent views of the Old City, the contrast between the beautiful Jerusalem stone and the drab and discolored Tel Aviv stucco was startling. Across the narrow valley, the walls of the Old City stood out in sharp relief intact despite the weeks and months of shelling across them. Indeed, the walls were improved by the war through the razing of many of the buildings, which had over the centuries been erected immediately against the ancient structure. And a little later when there the road [has been built] which the Jews had promised the Arabs from the Jaffa Gate along the Jaffa Road and north and eastward to give the Arabs a clear route from Bethlehem to Ramallah,[66] hundreds of yards of the wall will be free from the incrustations of relatively modern structures. There is at least

63. Goda et al., eds., *To the Gates of Jerusalem*, 259–260.
64. McDonald to Ethridge, February 2, 1949, McDonald Papers, Columbia University, box 11, folder 20.
65. Entry of March 13, 1949.
66. Refers to new roads built to link Jerusalem with other points that would not traverse the Israeli-held New City.

this improvement to be set over against the many manifestations of the war's destructiveness.

Beyond the Old City, from the second floor of the King David, I renewed my acquaintances with Mount Scopus and the Mount of Olives. I was relieved to observe that there were few signs of destruction either at the hospital or at the university. I was told that the major destruction, that of the Rosenbloom Building, was not visible from where I stood. The medical school building for which I had broken the ground two years previously[67] appeared to be about a third to a half completed and probably suffered relatively little. To the south, the buildings in the Mount of Olives stood out sharply and showed no damage. At the Viteleses' house [where McDonald and family stayed] we were greeted by a smart but very friendly and intelligent Marine sergeant and by Miss [Estelle] Frankfurter.[68]

Called Burdett and arranged to meet Ethridge at the consulate at four. Others there besides the family, Burdett, and Ethridge [was] Halderman.[69] Ethridge talked for most of an hour about the PCC's progress and plans. He expressed disappointment that Halderman was being recalled to Washington and that [James] Barco,[70] whom he had expected, was being replaced by a young man from Halderman's office. Ethridge was hopeful that there would be a chance for Halderman to be with the group for a little while before he returned. Much of the talk was about Jerusalem. As usual, however, Ethridge was so general in his statements, and Halderman was so cautious, that I got no clear impression of either the American or the PCC's program. From the consulate we went over for a few minutes to the Eden Hotel. Then for a brief visit to the King David and home.

By mid-April, the PCC, with the help of its own Committee on Jerusalem plus the US and French consuls general in the city, had drafted a solution that tried to meld international control of Jerusalem with local Jewish and Arab autonomy.[71] Jerusalem would be a demilitarized, international city, the boundaries to be determined. A UN administrator would supervise the Holy Places, ensure free access, and protect minority rights. An international administrative council would control municipal services. The city would have Arab and Jewish sectors, which would be autonomous in all areas not reserved for the UN. Jewish and Arab delegations would facilitate commerce between the zones, and an international tribunal would settle disputes. The State Department, whose main concern was for the Holy Places, accepted the PCC

67. Goda et al., eds., *To the Gates of Jerusalem*, 259.

68. Estelle S. Frankfurter (1895–1997), sister of Supreme Court Justice Felix Frankfurter; worked as a volunteer in Israel, 1948–1949.

69. See entry of February 25, 1949. Halderman headed US delegation to the PCC's Committee on Jerusalem.

70. See entry of May 26, 1949.

71. Halderman to Cargo, March 5, 1949, NARA, RG 59, 501.BB Palestine, box 2124, folder 1; PCC and US government thinking on Jerusalem's status in 1949 is summarized in Hahn, *Caught in the Middle East*, 112–117.

plan. Ethridge shared the scheme with neither McDonald nor the Israelis, evidently hoping to resign from the PCC after the start of the Lausanne talks.[72]

Israel's liaison to the PCC's Jerusalem committee, thinking that international-ization was confined to the Holy Places alone, reported on April 20 that the United States was abandoning the UN resolution as unrealistic, favoring partition between Israel and Jordan, with UN supervision of religious interests and minority rights only.[73] With Ben-Gurion's agreement, Sharett insisted that partition of the city with access to Mount Scopus and with juridical status for the Holy Places was the only viable solution, to be negotiated directly with Transjordan, not the UN. Israeli and Transjordanian representatives negotiated directly at Shuneh on the division of Jeru-salem through April 25, 1949.[74] Ralph Bunche noted in the meantime that Jerusa-lem would be internationalized only with strong US pressure.[75]

Saturday, April 16

The family and I, with Captain Moshe Hillman[76] as a guide, went to Mount Zion. We drove to the beginning of the Valley of the Hinnom, which is no-man's land.[77] There we got out and walked across the valley in full view of the Arab Legionnaires on the top of the wall of the Old City. It was a beautiful morning and always quiet. But the very quietness reminded one vividly of what must had been the cascades of fire which had crossed and re-crossed the valley and which had so obviously wreaked complete havoc on the buildings therein. Pointed out to us, as we crossed, were the badly damaged buildings of the Montefiore sector, the first Jewish section built outside the Old City under the sponsorship of [Moses] Montefiore for the residence of pious Jews who for the most part lived on the charity of the Diaspora.[78]

When we reached the bottom of the valley, we began the rather quick in-cline up a narrow path, which looked as if it would have been impregnable. Yet it was up this very route that the shock troops of the Jews took Mount Zion. As we approached the compound of the Dominican church, the signs of destruction

---

72. Ethridge [through Burdett] to secretary of state, no. 300, April 16, 1949, *FRUS*, 1949, v. VI, 920–921; Ethridge [through Burdett] for president and secretary of state, no. 309, April 19, 1949, *FRUS*, 1949, v. VI, 923–924; Ethridge [through Burdett] to Acheson, no. 311, April 20, 1949, *FRUS*, 1949, v. VI, 924–925; Memorandum by Satterthwaite for Rusk, April 26, 1949, *FRUS*, 1949, v. VI, 948–952.

73. Comay to Eban, April 20, 1949, *DFPI*, v. 2, d. 501.

74. *DFPI*, v. 2, d. 508.

75. Austin to secretary of state, no. 509, April 20, 1949, *FRUS*, 1949, v. VI, 930–931.

76. IDF liaison officer who had been part of Bernadotte's convoy the day he was assassinated.

77. The valley, reputed in the Hebrew Bible as a place of pagan worship, runs south from the Jaffa Gate on the western side of the Old City then east toward Mount Zion.

78. Sir Moses Montefiore (1784–1885), Italian-born British financier, philanthropist, and Jewish communal leader who also aided Jews in Eastern Europe and the Near East; traveled to Jerusalem on several occasions; built the first settlement outside Old City on a hill across from Mount Zion for poor Jews to live and work. Called the Montefiore Quarter and Mishkenot Sha'anim, it was the first settlement of the new Yishuv. In 1948 it bordered on no man's land; most residents left because of Arab sniper attacks; restored after 1967.

were everywhere.[79] Threading our way through labyrinthine paths amidst the ruins of the outer structures, we finally entered the church. As we were about to enter, our guides pointed out the sign on the door reading "Sacred Property, No Entrance." They added that no one was allowed to enter except when accompanied by an officer entrusted with the care of the building. Indeed, the whole of Mount Zion is off bounds except for VIPs and other special guests. Inside the church, we mounted directly the stairway leading to the balcony, which surrounds the large dome. The view from this vantage point was breathtaking. We were well above the walls of the Old City and could look down over the whole enclosure and beyond to the Mount of Olives and Mount Scopus, farther south to the Dead Sea and the mountains of Moab in the distance. Then to the south and west, the whole panorama of Jerusalem's environs lay before us.

From where we stood, we could see clearly that most of the Jewish quarter of the Old City had been completely destroyed. The great [Hurva] synagogue was a mere shell.[80] In contrast, the pasture area immediately below us was being used as a garden by the Arabs and their sheep. On the walls, Arab Legionnaires lounged in most unmilitary negligence. One could have remained on the balcony for hours and still have found objects of intense interest.

When we reached the floor of the main portion of the church, we were shown the beautiful and almost unimpaired floor with its elaborate inlaid designs.[81] Our guides pointed out to us the beautiful inlaid work in the chapels and their almost complete preservation. Only one or two large shells had penetrated the dome. It looked as if, with relatively small efforts, this modern but impressive Greek cross structure could be completely restored. Strangely enough, the even higher campanile, which towered over the dome, seemed to be almost undamaged.

Though we were behind schedule when we left Mount Zion, we were leisurely in our re-crossing of the valley, this, despite an occasional shot, which, our guide reassured, was being fired by Israeli soldiers solely to frighten Jews from entering the valley without permission. I confess, however, that we were not regretful when, having regained our cars, we drove off.

Captain Hillman insisted on taking us to see the ruins of the colony to the south of Jerusalem on the high point [Ramat Rachel], from which one has a splendid view of Bethlehem and the neighboring town Beit Jala.[82] The view

79. Refers to Basilica of St. Stephen, part of a French-built Dominican complex near the Damascus Gate on the site where St. Stephen was reputed to have been martyred. The land was purchased in 1881 on the site where a Byzantine church was destroyed by the Persians in 614 and a Crusader chapel was destroyed in 1187. After archeological excavations, the Basilica was built in 1890.
80. Entry of August 5–6, 1948.
81. Byzantine floor mosaics still survive in the Basilica of St. Stephen.
82. Ramat Rachel, kibbutz established in 1926; overlooks the Old City, Bethlehem, and Rachel's tomb; destroyed by Arabs in 1929 riots; cut off from rest of city in May 1948 and subjected to extremely bitter fighting between Egyptian/Muslim Brotherhood/Arab Legion and IDF/IZL forces in that month. Israelis thereby secured the southern approach to Jerusalem.

there was indeed proof that this hill commanded the approach to Jerusalem from the south. The buildings showed the effects of having been taken and lost three times by the Egyptians in the battle, which finally stopped their advance towards the north. Proudly, our guides told us of the repeated hand-to-hand fighting which had made Ramat Rachel one of the historic shrines of the War of Liberation. Having never before seen Jerusalem from this particular elevation, I got a new perspective on the whole city and the outlying region. Regretfully, we turned back to town, for I was then more than half an hour late.

We drove near to the home of the chief rabbi, Yitzhak Herzog, and then walked. I was greeted by Jacob and Vivian [Herzog], who said their father insisted that I sit at the table for a few minutes. Ruth and Bobby meantime had gone on with Captain Hillman to have their view of the Old City from the roof of Notre Dame de France. The chief rabbi was at a long table with four or five men at one end and six or seven women at the other end. I was served wine and cake while we chatted for ten minutes or so.

[In the afternoon] we went over to the Novomeyskys'[83] for tea with Miss Frankfurter. For me, the most important person there aside from the host was Colonel [Moshe] Dayan. His wife said that I had been in their house when I was last in Jerusalem but I could not recall it. Colonel Dayan talked interestingly. He was cordial and friendly towards Abdullah al-Tel, whom he feared might be jeopardized by his reputation of close cooperation with the Jews;[84] Dayan had no knowledge of the PCC's plans for the city since none of the group had been in touch with him, and though he would have been glad to be of technical assistance about British policy, Dayan confessed himself quite at a loss. He could not understand why Britain had permitted Transjordan to make the armistice with the Jews which left the latter in control of the Negev. Similarly, he was puzzled by the British failure to influence the Egyptians against a comparable policy to that of Transjordan. Such failure of Britain to use its influence to block Israel without at the same time adopting a policy of genuine friendship did not make sense. He was not optimistic that the several concrete subjects envisaged for settlement by the Special Committee set up by the armistice terms would be agreed upon, some of them perhaps through the [mixed] armistice commission itself without waiting on the creation of a special committee. He added that Israel had already opposed this on the question of immediate access to the Holy Places. I was surprised to have Dayan say that he felt confident that if I wanted to go to Jerash and Petra, it could be arranged.[85]

---

83. Moshe A. Novomeysky (1873–1961), Siberian-born mining engineer, businessman, and Zionist; imprisoned by Russian authorities in 1905; developed geologic interest in Dead Sea after 1906; emigrated to Palestine in 1920; founded the Palestine Potash Company with British partners and secured mining rights to the Dead Sea area, 1929. The company was extremely productive, but because of its British partners, the Israeli government restructured the mining agreement in November 1948, leaving Novomeyski, then age 75, in limbo.

84. Dayan's negotiations with Abdullah al-Tel regarding Jerusalem are in *DFPI*, v. 3.

85. Jerash and Petra, fourth-century BC cities in northwest and southwest Jordan, respectively, each with spectacular ruins.

I hope he is proved correct. Certainly he is a most charming and intelligent individual.

From Novomeysky's we walked over to the consulate to find the cocktail party in full swing. During the course of it, Ethridge and I had a long talk. The results were not, however, in proportion to the length. He told me of what he regarded as the comparative success at Beirut because of the policy he had followed of being tough with each one of the groups with whom he spoke. He was a dice player and had learned always to try for the hard throw, a four or a ten, and recommended that I follow this practice. He talked also about plans to go to Lausanne, of his pleasure that the Israelis were sending a strong delegation, and of his hopes that there would emerge one or more peace treaties or that at any rate the basis for such would be laid. He expressed his appreciation for the attitude of [Michael] Comay, whom he likes.[86] He hopes to get from Ben-Gurion, whom he was seeing the following Monday at Tiberias, a more definite and liberal policy about refugees.[87] Repeatedly, he said he wanted me to be tough with the [Jews] at this stage, as he was. Later he would be their friend, all of this he said with an air of authority as if he could really call the tune. I wish that he could, but I was not convinced that his confidence was justified.

Finally, apparently wearied by my pressing him for more definite information about the PCC's plan, and of the interrelations of the three delegations, he excused himself and assumed his more congenial role of chorus leader. While the singing was continuing, Mrs. Ethridge and I slipped into the adjoining room. She told me of her recent experiences and impressions [of] the Old City, of her admiration for Mrs. Antonius,[88] of the latter's [Antonius's] irreconcilable hatred of the Jews, of the general Arab feeling that the Jews had been saved from destruction by the first truce and that ultimately they would be destroyed by the consolidation of Arab strength. She talked also of her impressions in the colonies, her admiration for the courage and self-sacrifice of the Jews, etc., etc. I received a clear impression, however, that she was still prevailingly anti-Jewish and would remain so. Perhaps anti-Jewish is too strong and [a] fairer expression would be pro-Arab.

We then went with the Andruses for dinner at the King David. The food was [in]different. Chatted for a moment with [Gene] Currivan [*New York Times*] and his unsuccessful belated effort to cross the line the next day. Bobby went off with Tetlie to a dancing party given by the younger people, while Ruth and I went home.

86. Comay was serving as the Israeli liaison to the PCC's Jerusalem committee.
87. For this meeting on April 18, 1949, Ethridge [through Burdett] to secretary of state, no. 312, April 20, 1949, *FRUS*, 1949, v. VI, 925–927.
88. Katy Nimr Antonius (1891–1984), Arab Christian wife to George Antonius (1891–1942). He was an Arab Christian writer, diplomat, activist, and author of *The Arab Awakening* (1938). Before the war of independence, Katy lived opulently in the Sheikh Jarrah district of Jerusalem, entertaining Jerusalem's Arab and British elite.

Routed my family out at five and tried to hurry them to meet their 5:45 date at the King David to join the group to enter through the Jaffa Gate. I was only indifferently successful, for they had a checkered time getting across the lines, having missed the group. Thanks to a rescue jeep, they crossed at the Mandelbaum Gate with Ethridge, and thus were rewarded for their dilatoriness by having better places at the service at the Church of the Holy Sepulcher than they would have had had they been on time.

I was a few minutes late for my appointment with Halderman for breakfast at the King David. I found him more interesting than I thought he would be, even though he did not disclose the details of the Jerusalem plan which his subcommittee had worked out. I deduced, however, from what he did say that he felt constrained to limit his efforts to the program outlined in the resolution, that he did not feel free to warn the Department of the generally admitted impracticability of that idea; Boisanger had presented a detailed and rigid scheme which did not have the support of Neuville, the French consul general and one of the best informed of all the officials about the city. Halderman said that they had not attempted to draw boundary lines in the city but anticipated that there might be an arrangement for regional Jewish and Arab autonomy.

As we were finishing our talk, Halderman indicated that he would be glad to talk at length about the general situation in Israel, since he was going back to head the UN Palestine desk of the Department. I had to beg off, however, because it was time for me to join Captain Hillman and his group to continue my sightseeing. I recommended, therefore, that he see Knox on his return to Washington, urging that no one could help him so well as could Knox. I added, perhaps disingenuously, that Knox as compared with me had the advantage of being impartial.

The ride to Notre Dame de France took us past the Italian Hospital, which also was one of the key points in the battle for the city.[89] Our devious way through the labyrinth of rooms at Notre Dame led us finally up two ladders to the roof. What an extraordinary point of vantage to survey the whole of the Old City, particularly the northwest and northeastern quarters and beyond these extraordinary clear views of Mount Scopus and the Mount of Olives. From this vantage point we were separated by a very narrow road from the New Gate.[90] Beyond the wall, Arabs in the streets waved to us as we watched

89. The Italian Hospital, built in the Renaissance style northwest of the Old City between 1911 and 1917 to establish an Italian presence (to compete with German, French, Russian, etc.); had the strategic advantage of a high tower; closed by the British during World War II as enemy property and used as an RAF headquarters until 1948; taken by the Haganah as the British left in May 1948 and used as forward post against Arab Legion forces.

90. Notre Dame de France, grand monastery built by French Assumptionists just outside the Old's City's northwest wall for French pilgrims and as a symbol of the French presence in Jerusalem, 1884–1888. Reputedly on the site of the first Crusader camp in Jerusalem, it was the largest building constructed in Jerusalem before World War I. The New Gate to the Old City, constructed in 1889, allowed French pilgrims easy passage. The IDF controlled the compound in May 1948 as an observation post and to defend the Old City's Jewish Quarter. The Arab Legion

troops of children being directed by friars for their organized play on the roof after the morning Easter service. The beautiful dome of the Church of the Holy Sepulcher was immediately in front of us, as beyond the Dome of the Rock and the al-Aqsa Mosque seemed almost as near as if we were actually within the Temple area. Near, too, seemed the Rockefeller Museum, unscarred except for some shell marks on the tower. The day was warm and beautiful, and I should have liked to have remained surveying the extraordinary views, but my date with General Riley forced me to go on.

The trip to the Mandelbaum Gate was a devious series of detours through the northwest areas. Arriving at St. George's Street, we received from Captain Hillman a detailed explanation of the fighting in that neighborhood and of the gruesome murder of four Jewish soldiers by the Arabs to whom a British sergeant had turned them over. In some ways the Mandelbaum Gate gave us a more intimate sense of the war than anything we had seen previously. This was in part because of the widespread destruction, the presence in the upper story of the building, only sixty or seventy feet from where we stood, of Legionnaires, and the stories which were told of the desperateness of the fighting in that area.[91]

This reminds me that the day previous, on our trip to Ramat Rachel, we twice passed the spot on the road where Bernadotte had been assassinated. Captain Hillman, who had been in the car with Bernadotte,[92] gave us a detailed picture of precisely what took place. He, thinking that the roadblock formed by the jeeps and the approaching two uniformed men with sten guns were merely part of checking operations, waved to the latter and indicated that they should clear the way. Instead, however, one of the men shot up the tires of the mediator's car, and when Hillman remonstrated, fired at the latter's feet. Colonel Begley, who was burned by the powder from the assassin's gun, was stunned and had to be strongly urged to drive to the [Hadassah] hospital under Hillman's direction.[93] The French [colonel, Andre Sérot,] had died immediately, and the mediator was dead a few minutes after reaching the hospital. Hillman's account reinforced my earlier impression that, had anyone in the cavalcade been armed, the plans of the assassins could have been thwarted. In answer to my question why there was no protection, Hillman said that Bernadotte had refused it, saying that his protection was his armband. In reply to my

shelled the monastery, but did not break through. The IDF partially occupied the monastery thereafter.

91. Mandelbaum Gate north of the Old City refers to the square near the three-story house once belonging to the merchant Simcha Mandelbaum. The gate separated the Sheikh Jarrah Arab neighborhood from the Jewish neighborhood of Shmuel Hanavi. The main Arab Legion thrust to break into Jewish Jerusalem in May 1948 took place here. IDF units, using the house as a base, repelled Legion attacks, though Legion shelling destroyed the house in July. The Mandelbaum Gate became the officially recognized checkpoint between Arab and Jewish sectors.

92. Hillman was actually in the lead car, with Bernadotte's car behind.

93. See entry of September 18, 1948.

query whether the Sternists were in charge in the neighborhood where the assassination took place, Hillman replied that they were nearby.

Parenthetically, I should insert a brief word about the Jewish officers' comments in the course of our tour on the Arab fighting qualities. They made two points: 1) that the Arabs will not fight at night if they can possibly help it; and 2) that unless they have been British-trained, they are incapable of handling modern weapons efficiently, and even those so trained have difficulty adjusting themselves to weapons or new devices with which they were not made familiar by their British instructor. My informants thought the Arab Legion now included approximately 1,200 effectives. This number is inclusive of the recent recruits from Arab refugees.

Back to the King David, where the Israelis and I sat in the sun in the garden overlooking the Old City, while waiting for General Riley to arrive.[94] He and I then talked for nearly an hour. For me it was intensely interesting. He spoke favorably of Za'im, the Syrian military ruler, who had agreed to give "to Riley" the disputed Hill 223 and to do this within the time fixed by Riley, thus clearing the way for the Syrian-Israel armistice negotiations. These may take about three weeks; the sticking point will be the question whether the lines are to follow the international frontiers. Za'im is not a creature of Abdullah, and his coming to power is not a prelude to a greater Syria. Had Abdullah attempted to march [into Syria], there would have been a war.

Riley obviously favors the plan which Ethridge said he favored, to separate Riley's functions from those of the PCC and to have the former [the United Nations Truce Supervision Organization] report directly to the Secretary-General and the Security Council. Riley added that since this scheme was also favored by Bunche, who was just arriving in New York, it would probably be adopted by the UN.

Riley was conditionally optimistic about Transjordan-Israeli relations. Everything, he thought, depended upon the Arabs in the area in the [Tulkarm-Nablus-Jenin] triangle being evacuated by the Iraqis, and Transjordanian forces being persuaded to remain. Unless the Arab residents [in the area conceded to Israel] can be persuaded they will be safe, their becoming refugees will precipitate a crisis, which might jeopardize all hope of progress between Tel Aviv and Amman. Riley urged that I impress upon the Israeli authorities the vital importance of the strictest orders to the Israeli military on the spot that nothing must be done directly or indirectly to stampede the Arab residents. I promised that I would try to impress this point of view on Ben-Gurion. Another, though perhaps less serious difficulty, is the possibility of Transjordan meeting resistance

94. Brigadier General William E. Riley was still the chief of staff for the United Nations Truce Supervision Organization (UNTSO) and now supervised the work of the mixed armistice commissions.

from the local irregulars in the northwestern fringe of the triangle who have been in the pay of Iraq and did not now wish to demobilize.[95]

Riley's task from here on is to push through the Syrian-Israeli negotiations and to supervise the activities of the several mixed armistice commissions. He hopes that his immediate tasks here can be concluded within a month or two. In view of the Israeli offer to negotiate some of the issues with Transjordan through the mixed armistice commission without waiting for the setting up of the Special Committee, Riley was now urging upon Abdullah al-Tel this procedure. As to the role of Glubb Pasha, Riley thought it was wholly technical and that Glubb Pasha did not interfere with Kirkbride.

Riley seemed to have much in view the vagueness of PCC's gain at Beirut and the vagueness of Ethridge's plans for Jerusalem. Nonetheless, Riley was hopeful of progress at Lausanne, at least of more than was achieved at Beirut. He praised Eban and Shiloah, preferring the latter to Eytan who, he said, was inclined to talk down to others, for example, the Egyptians. Later, I learned that this might be the result of Eytan's experience as don at Oxford.[96] To my surprise, Riley said that he hoped I would take occasion to express to the Department my appreciation, as I had done to him personally, of his work.

As we were parting, I urged Riley to stop in Rome to see His Holiness and promised my cooperation through Gowen and Count Galeazzi. I was sure that the pope would welcome this opportunity to learn from Riley, as he could from no one else, about conditions affecting the Old City and the problems of internationalization. As we parted, I told Riley again of my gratitude that he had made a special trip over in order to see me.

On Good Friday, April 15, Pope Pius XII issued the encyclical Redemptoris Nostri Cruciatus [The Passion of Our Redeemer]. *It noted that tranquility in Palestine was "very far from having been restored" and that "we are still receiving complaints from those who have every right to deplore the profanation of sacred buildings, images, charitable institutions, as well as the destruction of peaceful homes of religious communities." He renewed his call for the internationalization of Jerusalem and its environs, as well as international agreements that would protect Holy Places elsewhere in Palestine. The encyclical also discussed the Arab refugees. "The condition of these exiles," the pope said, "is so critical and unstable that it cannot longer be permitted to continue."[97]*

On April 19, 1949, McDonald sent a letter to William Gowen in Rome to set up a meeting between Pope Pius XII and Riley:

> *From what I know of the Pope's deep personal as well as official interest in the Holy Land and particularly in the Holy Places, I feel that he would welcome*

95. McDonald met with Eytan on this issue to relay US concerns. McDonald to secretary of state, no. 274, April 12, 1949, NARA, RG 59, MC 1390, reel 19, frames 067–068.
96. Eytan taught German at Oxford, 1934–1940.
97. All papal encyclicals are available at http://www.papalencyclicals.net.

the opportunity to get from General Riley the full and detailed accounts about conditions which could be secured from no one else. There is no one either in the military or in the diplomatic service who has been so directly and so continuously in touch with both the Jewish and the Arab authorities. Riley, therefore, could answer with authority any of the many questions which His Holiness might want to put to him either about details or about general aspects of the problem of effective and just solution of the intricate problem of Jerusalem and the Holy Places.

McDonald wrote a similar letter to Count Galeazzi.[98]

The Vatican continued to press. On April 28, Weizmann and Eban dined with Francis Cardinal Spellman in New York to discuss Jerusalem. Weizmann explained that there was no inherent conflict between the church's desire to protect the Holy Places and the allegiance of the Jewish population there to Israel.[99] *Spellman complained to President Truman afterward that the arrangement with the Israelis was very different from the one the president had privately mentioned to Spellman earlier, which Spellman said had matched the UN's and the Vatican's calls for a* corpus separatum.[100]

Returning to the Viteleses', I had a brief talk with Jacob Herzog about his father's visit to the States. I promised to write Washington about the latter's desire to see the president. We were on the road home by a quarter of three. The views down the mountain, although a replica of those going in the other direction, are more impressive because one can see more of the panorama, especially when a portion of the way down the road gives one splendid vistas of the Shefelah [Judean foothills], the coastal plain, and the Mediterranean. Returning, we took the Courage Road the whole way, thus shortening the trip by ten miles but not the time. We were back at home in just two hours.

The trip had been a complete success. For me it was a vivid renewal of my acquaintanceship with Jerusalem and an opportunity to talk with a number of essential people. For the family it was almost even more exciting, including as it did the opportunity of them to attend the Easter service in the Church of the Holy Sepulcher and visit the other parts of the Old City, including the Dome of the Rock and the al-Aqsa Mosque.

Monday, April 18

For an hour and a half the Blausteins and Mr. Segal were at the house. This time the AJC attitude was much more bearable. Blaustein and Segal had learned a good deal. Now they were concerned more about the economic future than their fears of the religious influences here.

---

98. McDonald to Gowen, April 19, 1949, McDonald Papers, USHMM, box 7, folder 13.
99. *DFPI*, v. 4, no. 2, 3.
100. See *FRUS*, 1949, v. VI, 1015, n. 3.

Ford and Hooper came out at four. At five, we were joined by Harry Greenstein and later Oscar Gass.[101] We had an interesting discussion chiefly about economic problems here. Greenstein spoke at length about his observations in the reception camps, of the fact that, in his opinion, conditions in the largest of the camps, that near Haifa where there are 16 to 18,000 people, are worse than in the camps in Germany. He added, however, that in answer to his inquires he found no expression of regret of being in Israel. He thought that 250,000 would be the approximate arrival number this year. There would be about 45,000 from central Europe, perhaps as many or more from North Africa, and the others from Eastern Europe. He thought that there would be a roof and food for everyone, with tens of thousands who would have to live in tents. He anticipated that as many as 80,000 might be at one time in the camps here. What was worse, he foresaw the lengthening of the period in the camps up to six months. Nonetheless, while some officials privately were pessimistic, a conservative banker told him that he was confident that Israel's economy would survive the expected strain.

Gass, as always, was interesting in his analysis. He pointed out that the prospective investor, seeking to establish a business, should do so through co-operation with some existing firm. Being required to bring in some 30% in cash, he could bring in the balance duty-free in the form of capital goods. He should refrain wherever possible from building a plant and instead utilize some existing structure. Gass was surprising in his statement that, despite the obvious need, he had found no sympathy for or tendency to move towards his suggested austerity program. The answers of those to whom he spoke in the several ministries was that this was not a practicable matter, that a majority could not be secured for it, and they had better move on to "the business of the day."

The war, the influx of Jewish refugees from Europe and from Arab countries, and the need for the Israeli government to borrow money led to an austerity program between 1948 and 1952. The government directed capital investment, strove for greater self-sufficiency, rationed necessary goods while controlling prices, and limited production of nonessential items. It channeled money to agricultural settlements as a way to produce more food while dispersing population over a wider area. It also developed infrastructure while encouraging the development of housing. Unemployment in 1950 was only 6.7 percent. Regardless, there still were shortages in the official markets and a growing black market for needed items.[102] Israel also was desperate for foreign exchange, especially dollars. Gass's austerity ideas favored price and wage

101. Oscar Gass (1913–1990), American economist, coauthored with Robert R. Nathan and Daniel Creamer, *Palestine: Problem and Promise—An Economic Study* (Washington, DC: Public Affairs Press, 1946), which argued that Palestine could absorb more than a million immigrants in the next decade while sustaining a growing economy; economic adviser to the Israeli mission in Washington, April 1949. Testified before the Anglo-American Committee in Washington, January 1946. See Goda et al., eds., *To the Gates of Jerusalem*, 31.

102. Paul Rivlin, *The Israeli Economy* (Boulder, CO: Westview Press, 1992).

deflation as opposed to the government's program of rationing and currency devaluation.[103]

Gass added that one must recognize that the state is new and that the job of rent, price, and other controls is being done just about as well as in the US in World War I. He agreed that the absence of Mapam from the coalition made the adoption of any such program more difficult. But none of these factors mitigated against the urgent need, both from the economic and from the morale point of view, for an austerity program. On the moot question of the comparative living standards of the day, Gass was convinced that the workers, except in the single item of housing, enjoyed in buying power a higher wage than in 1939. In housing, he admitted there had been a serious retrogression. It is true that families who have been in their apartments or houses for years are for the most part still paying very small rentals, in many cases only a fraction of the rentals now being demanded, but all new renters are faced with exorbitant if not extortionist demands.

To my surprise, Gass seemed surprised at our accounts of the continued rigid policy of restricting exit visas. I admitted that part of this rigidity might be merely a hangover and a continuation of complicated bureaucratic red tape, but I thought that more than these factors were involved. Gass admitted that with hundreds of thousands of arrivals each year, there could be no justification for extreme restrictions on exit. He would favor drastic capital export control but would allow individuals to leave freely.[104] In answer to the complaints so current that the immigration authorities, or rather the customs officials are unjustifiably harsh, Gass repeated the explanation of the chief of customs to the effect that the tendency of many immigrants to smuggle is extraordinary. For example, one newcomer sought to smuggle in several thousand pairs of gloves as personal property. In another case, when a shipload of passengers declared $100,000 worth of cash, the authorities were certain that a rigid search would have uncovered several millions. As we were breaking up, I urged Greenstein to send me promptly a copy of his report, and Gass to come back and see me again soon.

Tuesday, April 19

Busy all morning on the diary. From four to five, a full office conference.

By mid-April the embassy staff faced serious housing issues. The ambassador's residence needed a new roof, new furnishing, and a new furnace. McDonald's staff

103. Nachum T. Gross, "The Economic Regime During Israel's First Decade," in Troen and Lucas, eds., *Israel: The First Decade of Independence*, 231–242.
104. Between 1948 and 1961, Israel required limited-time exit visas for citizens traveling abroad. The restrictions were occasionally relaxed, as in August 1949, but were not abolished. Currency control was a primary reason. The process was mired in red tape and was widely resented.

members needed living quarters. The embassy group as a whole needed better office space. "The pressure on housing in Tel Aviv," McDonald wrote to Halsey and Janet Barrett, "is nearly incredible. One of the American secretaries pays, and pays gladly because she has no alternative, 140 dollars a month for [a] small room without private bath and with hot water extra."

At the same time, both McDonald and Andrus were dissatisfied with security at the residence. The civilian guards, McDonald complained, had become "more and more lackadaisical and indifferent." On seeing the US Marines at the consulate general in Jerusalem, McDonald was, "so impressed by their smartness and alertness . . . that I became determined to press for them here." But on receiving approval from the State Department to move a contingent of Marines to Tel Aviv, he noted that "before they can come we must find for them a place to stay!"[105] These "housekeeping" issues, as McDonald called them, dragged on for several months. The editors have omitted most of that discussion.

From five until nearly seven, the whole staff listened to Marcus Sieff and Eliahu Sasson. Marcus talked briefly on the development of the army, particularly during the first truce, from guerrilla bands into the beginnings of an organized fighting force; the present plans for a unified command; the scheme for demobilization; the desire of a surprisingly large percentage of the foreign flyers to remain either in the military or the projected civilian air service;[106] the rise of a more friendly group of officials in the [British] Foreign Office, and of the probability that the old guard will be replaced by those genuinely friendly to Israel. He was the more optimistic about this because of the evident bankruptcy of the traditional policy.

Sasson was interesting on several topics and on two developed his views at such length that they might constitute airgrams to the Department. As to Lausanne, he does not feel that peace treaties will emerge but that [progress] may be registered. In answer to questions about the new regime in Syria, Sasson spoke at length: several factors explained [Colonel] Husni al-Za'im's coup: 1) economic discontent and distress; 2) the defeat of the Syrian Army; 3) attempts in the parliament to place the full blame for the failure in Palestine on the army and the latter's resentment; 4) personal ambition of Za'im; 5) British intrigue.

It was this last point which Sasson developed.[107] Britain has been seeking for many months to persuade the Syrian government to sign a new [economic] treaty. Negotiations to this end in Damascus and in London had been inter-

105. Quotes in McDonald to Halsey and Janet Barrett, May 1, 1940, McDonald Papers, USHMM, box 7, folder 14. See also Barnes to McNeil, May 14, 1949, McDonald Papers, USHMM, box 7, folder 14.

106. See Jeffrey Weiss and Craig Weiss, *I Am My Brother's Keeper: American Volunteers in Israel's War of Independence, 1948–1949* (Atglen, PA: Schiffer, 2004); and Joseph A. Heckelman, *American Volunteers and Israel's War of Independence* (New York: KTAV, 1974).

107. Sasson was born in Syria and had contacts with Za'im before the coup. His comment on the British might reflect his own worries about how armistice negotiations with Za'im were progressing. See Schlaim, "Husni Za'im and the Plan to Resettle Palestinian Refugees in Syria," 71–72.

mittent, and the latest attempt had formerly broken down the day before al-Za'im moved. Britain was fearful lest the agreement by Syria on the TA-PLINE[108] with the American-Saudi oil interest would give the US a preponderant influence in Syria. Britain similarly was opposed to the suggested new French arrangements with Syria. But the French on their part were also fearful of the increased American influence if the TAPLINE program became a reality. From Britain's point of view, Za'im's rise to power was a check both to France and the US and therefore an advantage.[109]

Sasson does not anticipate any immediate change in Za'im's regime unless some fanatic in opposition should assassinate the colonel. Later, if economic conditions do not improve, the colonel may face serious difficulties. Za'im's move was not known in advance to Abdullah nor was it a part of the traditional Greater Syria move. Its effects upon that movement are not now clear.[110] I should add that the views expressed by Sasson were declared by him to be wholly personal and not to represent the opinion of the Israeli government. I believe this to be true, because from other Israeli sources I have heard views expressed quite different from those of Sasson. For example, Miss Herlitz of the Foreign Office told me a few days ago that the Za'im move had been known by Abdullah in advance and was favored by the king. Shiloah, also of the Foreign Office, did not share these views. Hence, I think Sasson's views should be evaluated as those of the Israeli expert on Arab affairs but not as representing Israeli official opinion.

Towards the end of the conference, Sasson spoke fully about refugees. First, he stressed that the number of bona fide war refugees cannot be as many as 600,000. He estimated 150,000 in the north, Syria and Lebanon, 120,000 in the Gaza-Rafah strip and another 200,000 to 300,000 in Arab Palestine and Transjordan. Those in the north and the south constitute the chief problem of resettlement. Those in the center will relatively easily be resettled once the future of Arab Palestine has been decided. He implied, though he was not explicit, that the union of this area with Transjordan would greatly facilitate this solution. He was adamant that until there is an effective peace Israel can make

108. TAPLINE was the Trans-Arabian Pipeline from Saudi Arabia to the Mediterranean, begun by ARAMCO in 1947. It was originally to end in Haifa, but after Israeli independence, it was to be rerouted through the Golan Heights in Syria to Sidon in Lebanon. ARAMCO had secured rights of way for the TAPLINE in Saudi Arabia, Jordan, and Lebanon, but the Syrian government refused passage. The CIA had encouraged the Za'im coup. In May 1949, Za'im approved the TAPLINE, and it became operational in 1950. See Douglas Little, "Mission Impossible: The CIA and the Cult of Covert Action in the Middle East," *Diplomatic History* 28, no. 5 (November 2004): 663–701.

109. The British were not aware that Za'im would agree to have the TAPLINE run through Syrian territory. See Meir Zamir, *The Secret Anglo-French War in the Middle East: Intelligence and Decolonization, 1940–1948* (New York: Routledge, 2015).

110. Za'im distrusted King Abdullah. He showed brief interest in a more formal alliance with Iraq together with a joint command, but the Iraqi government rejected the offer. Sir William Strang's Tour of the Middle East, 21st May 1949–18th June 1949, Malcolm Yapp, ed., *British Documents on Foreign Affairs: Reports and Papers from the Foreign Office Confidential Print*, Part IV, Series B, v. 8, reprint ed. (Bethesda, MD: University Press of America, 2002), 158–175.

no substantial contribution towards resettlement. He was categorical, too, that under no circumstance could considerable numbers be repatriated. It was nearly seven before the conference broke up, with several of the men impatient to get away for early dinner engagements. But I was convinced that this sort of serious and lengthy discussion is worthwhile.

Wednesday, April 20

In the morning Charles Brown of *Newsweek* came out for breakfast and informal non-interview talk. Lunch at the Sharon with the Sam Sackses. While waiting for lunch Lord Samuel, coming by where we were sitting in the lounge, suggested we talk. He had just returned from a visit the day previous to Abdullah. His account of his role back in 1922 in persuading Abdullah to forego a planned attack on the French, who had just driven his brother Faisal out of Damascus, and to settle down in Transjordan as the emir, was intensely interesting, particularly as he went on to develop his thesis that there was no ground for the common Zionist assumption that the decision of that year to proclaim formally the non-applicability of the National Home provisions of the Mandate to the region east of the Jordan was a new and unjustifiable action. Lord Samuel insisted that it was clearly understood at the time of the issuance of the Balfour Declaration and subsequently, that the National Home did not apply except west of the Jordan. Churchill's formal approval, as colonial secretary, of the pronouncement of 1922 was nothing more than a formalization of an earlier decision. Lord Samuel makes no apology for any part of his role in that year. He went on to argue that the [Sir Henry] McMahon correspondence [with Hussein bin Ali, the sharif of Mecca] was intended and was so understood by the Arabs at the time to exclude Palestine west of the Jordan from the promise of independence given to the Arabs. When Edward Grey was suggesting the contrary in the House of Lords, Lord Samuel sent him a memorandum prepared by [Brigadier Gilbert] Clayton [British chief of military intelligence in Cairo, 1914–1917] to prove the contrary.[111]

Lord Samuel said that Abdullah was very friendly, still alert, and unusually intelligent despite his seventy-three years. Neither of his sons appears to count. Lord Samuel said that he and the king discussed only general issues and refrained from those having to do with current problems. Later, I learned from the press that Lord Samuel's nominal mission had been as chairman of the board of the Palestine Electric Company, and therefore to talk about the basis for re-opening the Jordan River plant. I would have liked to continue my talk longer, but Bobby, sensing that this would have been discourteous to my host, came over and asked me to rejoin the Sackses. During the lunch the talk was mostly about Sam Sacks's business, with Mrs. Sacks showing discriminating

---

111. On the promises concerning the geography of Palestine see Elie Kedourie, *In the Anglo-Arab Labyrinth: The McMahon-Huseyn Correspondence and Its Interpretations, 1914–1939* (New York: Cambridge University Press, 1976); Isaiah Friedman, *Palestine: A Twice Promised Land?* v. 1: *The British, the Arabs & Zionism, 1915–1920* (New Brunswick, NJ: Transaction, 2000).

discernment. Incidentally, Sacks expressed something akin to contempt for Lord Samuel.

[During the afternoon], arrival of Mr. Hooper and the three representatives of the US Export-Import Bank. I took the four men into the study, where during an hour we talked in an elementary fashion about Israel, its geography, resources, etc., as preliminary to their tour. I urged Hooper to go with them up to Jerusalem, and if possible, to get them across the line for a visit to the Old City, even if they could not hope to get up to Mount Scopus or the Mount of Olives. I was impressed with the informality and the friendliness of the delegation.

Thursday, April 21

Afternoon tea party for some twenty Hadassah guests, all, save a few, Americans. They seemed thrilled by the house and garden. At the end, I stayed at home, while Miss Clark and Ruth went to Mrs. Davidowitz's to a party for the same group and some others.

Friday, April 22

To the office most of the morning in conference with Ford. Agreed upon various telegrams mostly administrative in nature. Was relieved to have the Department's assurance about the sending of the labor attaché, though unhappy at the failure to fix an arrival date for this still unknown person.

On April 12 Ambassador Edward Crocker in Baghdad reported that, in accordance with the Israeli-Transjordanian armistice treaty, all Iraqi troops had left Palestine. He further reported that Iraq would have no relations with Israel and that its attitude would be "as though Israel does not exist." The Iraqi government also wanted the UN arms embargo lifted.[112] McDonald saw Crocker's report more than a week later. He wrote to Washington that "I feel impelled [to] comment that

1. *Iraq's unyielding attitude [on the] use [of] crude oil [at the] Haifa refinery is naturally interpreted by Israel officials as additional indication [of] Baghdad's unweakened hostility.*
2. *[. . .] my colleagues and I feel US support of move in UN to lift arms embargo for Iraq would be [a] serious mistake."[113]*

Saturday, April 23

Up early and looking forward to a free day to get something done. Worked most of the day on the Riley report [to the Department].

---

112. Crocker to secretary of state, no. 181, April 12, 1949, NARA, RG 59, MC 1390, reel 19, frame 069.
113. McDonald to secretary of state, no. 300, April 22, 1948, NARA, RG 59, MC 1390, reel 19, frame 158.

Sunday, April 24

Walked on the beach at Herzliya for an hour in the morning and decided that such walks might [be] the answer to my local "vacation" problem. Went to the WIZO club to tea for Edward Norman,[114] but had to hurry away to meet Sharett at his house at six.

When Sharett had telephoned me about today's appointment I asked whether or not I should bring Ford, who had not yet met the foreign minister. The latter replied that at this first talk, he would prefer that we be alone. On the whole, Sharett looked tired but triumphant after his UJA junket and his conferences with Secretary Acheson. In the evening to the third or fourth of the *Thaïs* programs.

Monday, April 25

Continued hard at work on my two long despatches, Variations on themes by Riley and the report on Sharett conference.

On April 26, McDonald emphasized that both Riley and the embassy's Israeli sources were optimistic about Israeli-Transjordanian discussions in the Special Committee on Jerusalem. He tried to persuade the Department that the PCC might be on the wrong path: "Granted that the utmost practical pressure should continue to be brought upon the Israeli authorities to agree to the maximum internationalization of the Jerusalem area envisioned in the December 11 Resolution, I think it dangerous, because potentially self-defeating, for the PCC not to take account in its confidential studies and reports[,] the probable insuperable obstacles to a literal application of that Assembly formula."

Riley, McDonald reported, was convinced that positive Israeli treatment of the Arab villagers in the northwest rim of the Tulkarm–Nablus–Jenin triangle was critical for continued progress between Israel and Transjordan. But he also concentrated on pressing for an armistice between Israel and Syria. McDonald noted that, for Riley, "the most difficult issue is the question of Syria's acceding to the Israeli demand that the Armistice line be the international frontier. The General seemed to hope that in view of Colonel [Za'im's] concession about withdrawal from Hill 223, there was a reasonable chance of agreement on the Armistice line."[115]

. . . .

McDonald also reported Sharett's comments on opposition within the General Assembly to Israel's admission. Sharett had expected opposition from Britain and the

114. Edward A. Norman (1900–1955), non-Zionist philanthropist, president of American Fund for Palestine Institutions (renamed Israel Institutions in 1950); was in Israel for a seven-week survey, visiting officials and social welfare institutions; national secretary for the American Jewish Committee, 1949–1955. In his meeting with Norman of April 23, 1949, McDonald was unimpressed. McDonald Papers, USHMM, box 5, folder 3.

115. McDonald to secretary of state, no. 106, April 26, 1949, NARA, RG 59, MC 1390, reel 19, frames 171–176.

Arab states, but not from the Scandinavian countries or the countries of Central and South America. The Vatican, Sharett thought, had influenced the latter.

McDonald further noted that Sharett "deplored the raising of specific issues, for example the Arab refugees and Jerusalem, and making these major factors in the Assembly decision on Israel's admission. He insisted that this procedure is illegal under the terms of the Charter, unjust in essence, and confusing in practice. [He] emphasized that Israel was now being asked to consider and to indicate a policy on refugees and Jerusalem in two different places and on two different levels simultaneously, at Lake Success and at Lausanne."

Sharett said that Israeli-Transjordanian negotiations in the Special Committee on Jerusalem "are going extremely well," that negotiations over access roads to Mount Scopus for the Jews and to Bethlehem for the Arabs are "practically settled," that the Arab evacuation of the Latrun salient and the reopening of the pumping station "have been virtually agreed upon," and that other access issues concerning railroads between Israeli and Transjordanian territories were in the works.

McDonald continued, "I told him of the Department's and President Truman's concern [regarding the Arab villagers in northwestern Samaria] . . . and our Government's hope that the utmost would be done to assure that on the spot the Israeli local officials would in good faith and in practice carry out the promises made by the Israeli authorities. I told Sharett also of General Riley's conviction that unless the Arabs now resident in the area to be evacuated [by the Arab Legion] can be so assured that they will remain, their becoming refugees would so embitter feeling in Abdullah's territory that all the pending negotiations might break down and armed conflict be renewed." Sharett, McDonald reported, appreciated the gravity of the situation and mentioned that a special commissioner for the area might be in order.

"Finally, taking advantage of the friendliness and informality of our conference, I told Sharett of my increasing personal concern at what seems to me to be the deepening animosity of the Mapam and left-wing labor press towards the United States. I added that I was of course not surprised by the hostility and the misinterpretation current in the Communist press, but that I could not understand how the leaders of Mapam, many of them men of unusual intelligence, could credit or approve the fantastic misinterpretations of American policies by the party's official organ, [Al-] HaMishmar." McDonald added that US labor leaders would soon arrive and that meetings with them might change the perceptions of left-wing Israeli labor leaders. Sharett was pessimistic about the impact of these meetings, because US labor leaders were so anti-Soviet. He suggested that McDonald speak with Mapam leaders personally. "He argued," McDonald reported, "that since I am not attached to the labor movement at home and was assigned here because of my 'special interest in and relations to Jewish refugee and other problems,' my interpretations would be more nearly accepted at face value."[116]

116. McDonald to secretary of state, no. 108, April 26, 1949, NARA, RG 59, MC 1390, reel 19, frames 167–170. Also McDonald to secretary of state no. 304, April 26, 1949, NARA, RG 59, MC 1390, reel 19, frame 176. On the refugee and Jerusalem issues specifically, see also Ben-Gurion Diary, April 24, 1949.

Unbeknownst to McDonald, Truman and Acheson sat down with Weizmann on April 25 in a hastily arranged White House luncheon aimed at breaking the log-jam between Tel Aviv and Washington. The president reiterated the need for Israel to concede territory should it keep lands conquered beyond the November 1947 partition lines, to assent to Jerusalem's internationalization, and to agree to repatriate a substantial number of refugees.[117]

The next day Acheson told Eban that Israel's failure to make gestures on these issues, the refugees being the most important, would make it harder for the US to convince other delegations to admit Israel to the UN. Truman later wrote Ethridge, "I am rather disgusted with the manner in which the Jews are approaching the refugee problem. I told the President of Israel . . . just exactly what I thought about it. It may have some effect. I hope so."[118]

Simon [Marks] told me what he regarded as his great success in winning the Israeli authorities, Ben-Gurion, Kaplan and Goldie Meyerson, to his scheme for a cheap prefabricated housing project. I hope his optimism is justified.

Session with Ford and preparation of official reports. Dinner with the Fords at the [St. Louis] French hospital. An extraordinarily good meal and a pleasant experience.[119]

Tuesday, April 26

Two hour conference beginning with breakfast with the Quakers Levinius Painter and Emmett Gulley.[120]

The Quakers' discussions with Arab refugees supported the Israeli argument that the Arabs were encouraged to flee by Arab leaders. McDonald reported,

> *According to Mr. Gulley, who has since the first of January been in intimate contact with the refugees in the south, nearly all of those who have spoken to him have insisted that they would never have left their homes no matter what the danger might have been from the Israelis had not their leaders told them that they must leave and had they not been promised that they would return within a few weeks preceded by victorious Arab armies. Now, according to Mr. Gulley, they are bitterly critical of their leaders whom they feel misled them. The one desire of most of the refugees is to be permitted to return to their home.*

117. Preparatory memorandum by Rusk of April 23 is in NARA, RG 59, MC 1390, reel 19, frames 148–150.
118. Relevant documents in *FRUS*, 1949, v. VI, 943–948, 954–955, 957; *DFPI*, v. 2, d. 509–513.
119. St. Louis French hospital in Jaffa, built in 1885 by François Guinet in grand style for the nuns of the Order of St. Joseph who cared for him while he was sick with malaria.
120. Emmett Gulley (1894–1981), Quaker who had headed the Portland, Oregon, American Friends Service Committee office and was recruited to head the AFSC's Gaza office in 1949; tried to stimulate development there by promoting weaving and fishing.

McDonald also reported that the Quakers disputed Israeli estimates of the refugee numbers despite his own "cross-examination" of their statements. He further relayed the Quakers' comment that it was local Israeli commanders in the Galilee and Faluja who did not "carry out the instructions from Tel Aviv to respect the rights of the Arab residents and to treat them with consideration and courtesy." Through McDonald's strong intervention, Gulley was able on April 27 to meet with Shiloah, who promised to pass on the Quakers' concerns to Ben-Gurion.[121]

In the afternoon, Ben Friedman, the [textile manufacturer from] New York, came out with a note from David Niles.

Later Mr. [Wolf] Ladejinsky, an agricultural economist, on his way home from years in Japan, via India, proved very interesting. He knows Klaus and is going to be in touch with him after returning to Washington, where he will urge prompt action in sending us the needed attaché.[122]

In the evening, delightful concert by the orchestra under Paray. The Bach *Passacaglia*, with [which] the program opened, was stirring. Then, followed a beautiful interpretation of Schumann's Fourth Symphony; the second half made up of Mendelssohn's *Midsummer Night's Dream*, the Ravel Piano Concerto, with Éliane Richepin as soloist, and finally, Dukas's, *Sorcerer's Apprentice*.

Wednesday, April 27

Long session with Ford.

More than two hours conference with the seven members of the Housing Survey Commission invited by the [Israeli] government.[123] It was a pleasure to talk to such an intelligent and interested group. Aside from discussion of basic economic and political problems in Israel, I received from them suggestions about the house, particularly the roof. I made them promise to come back and see me at the end of their visit here.

Thursday, April 28

A delightful luncheon with General and Mrs. John Hilldring and the Andruses as guests. Afterwards, the general told me of his visit to the president [on April 1, 1949] and the latter's suggestion before he sailed. In addition to telling him about his congressional problems, the president gave my guest instructions on two points; these were messages to Ben-Gurion to the effect that

121. McDonald to secretary of state, no. 112, May 2, 1949, McDonald Papers, USHMM, box 7, folder 14. The comments on Galilee and Faluja refer to comments made by Painter on April 7, 1949.

122. Wolf Isaac Ladejinsky (1899–1975), Ukrainian-born Jewish US agricultural economist specializing in Asian problems for the US Department of Agriculture; helped introduce land reforms in occupied Japan. For several months McDonald hoped that Ladejinsky might serve as the labor attaché in Tel Aviv.

123. The group was made up of Jewish American contractors and architects, including private businessmen and academics such as Louis I. Kahn (1901–1974), Estonian-born professor of architecture at Yale.

the president was anxious to continue his friendship towards . . . Israel, but that he wants Ben-Gurion to realize that he was being much embarrassed by Israel's unyieldingness on Jerusalem and on refugees. Then the general and I had a considerable talk on the problem of implementing the president's hopes.

Hilldring spent seventeen days in Israel, meeting with Ben-Gurion, Sharett, and other Foreign Ministry officials. He became convinced that the Jerusalem sections of the UN resolution would never be implemented as written. But he told Israeli officials that the president was right regarding the refugee problem. The issue had to be settled "promptly," and "as a beginning Israel should make a generous and bold proposal as to what it was willing to contribute to the settlement."[124] McDonald was not apprised of Hilldring's discussions with the Israelis.

Hilldring was understanding. I was, however, even with him, somewhat reticent in expressing my views as to the extent to which I thought the president was being permitted to continue to be rather academic on the possibility of making good the November 29th proposals in these issues. But I did explain that the Department's telegrams clearly implied that to secure a settlement there would have to be, in fact if not in form, considerable deviation from the letter of the General Assembly resolution. Hilldring wondered whether the Department was keeping the president as fully and as realistically informed as was necessary for him to keep his ideas in step with events. At this point I invited Colonel Andrus to join us because I did not wish him to feel that he was being left out.

At about six, Shiloah and Miss Herlitz came. For nearly an hour Shiloah outlined Israel's fears lest the Israeli-Syria armistice negotiations break down. He began by saying that he thought Za'im was seeking to profit by the apparent courting which he was enjoying from the powers, and that, in any case he was indubitably seeking to secure a "rectification" of the international frontier of 1920. Za'im's argument was two-fold: first, that the natural frontier should follow the watercourse; in this case, the Jordan, the center of Lake Hula and the Sea of Galilee. His second argument was that the British in 1920 had cheated the French in the frontier then agreed on.[125] Shiloah stressed that this claim was unjust, that Israel in the case of Lebanon had withdrawn to the international frontier, and that in no case would Israel agree to Za'im's demand. He thought that the danger of a breakdown of the negotiations was imminent if the Syrian leader remained insistent. Shiloah said that the "compromise" presumably favored by the acting mediator's representative [Henri Vigier] to the

124. Hilldring's July 25, 1949 description of his mission is in *FRUS*, 1949, v. VI, 1249–1252. See also entry of July 9, 1949.
125. See proposal for the armistice line by the Syrian armistice delegation of April 21, 1949, *DFPI*, v. 3, d. 286. Syrian arguments for a line west of Palestine's international boundary were based on Israel's occupation of Palestinian areas over and above the partition plan of November 29, 1947.

effect that Za'im withdraw to the international frontier and that Israel not advance that far was unacceptable. Later, Shiloah implied that Israel might accept the demilitarization on both sides of the international frontier provided the settlers at Mishmar HaYarden were permitted to return with police protection. The result of Za'im's "intransigence" was tension on the spot and danger of adverse effects in Lausanne. Israel was determined not to talk to Syrians in Lausanne unless an armistice had been agreed upon. Israel was also disturbed by Za'im's announcement of large rearming and massing of troops "against Jordan" because these might easily be used against Israel. In any case, this rearming was a breach of the spirit of the truce and UN and US efforts at peace. Present situation might "slide" into a crisis, which all desiring peace should seek to prevent.[126]

Friday, April 29

Vanthier [French chargé] brought out his mission's commercial adviser, who is here to study the organization of the commercial activities of what may become the French legation. Most of our talk was about problems of housing and other aspects of living in Israel.

At twelve o'clock I presented Ford to Sharett at the Foreign Office. After a pleasant visit, Sharett followed up on Shiloah's talk of the night before about the frontier claims of Za'im. There was also some talk about the problems of Jerusalem and refugees.

Tea party at the Kaplans for the Export-Import Bank, Ed Lynch, the economist, John Fitch, [chief, engineering division], and Sidney Sherwood, secretary of the board.[127] With Goldie Meyerson, my longest talk, the chief topic was whether or not she should go to the States for the UJA. I told her that honesty compelled me to say that I thought her work here with Histadrut in the struggle against the housing problem and the cost of living would meant more to Israel than a few additional millions from the UJA.

Ford took me aside and showed me the long telegram from the Department, instructing me to urge strongly upon both Sharett and Ben-Gurion the president's and the Department's concern at the lack of concessions by Sharett on any of the three major issues, refugees, Jerusalem, and boundaries. The implication was clear that the lack of conciliatory attitude on these points would make difficult if not impossible the US successful solicitation of support for

126. Reported in McDonald to secretary of state, no. 314, April 29, 1949, NARA, RG 59, MC 1390, reel 19, frames 191–192. Also on the Syrian negotiations see McDonald to secretary of state, no. 111, May 2, 1949, NARA, RG 59, MC 1390, reel 19, frames 202–203; Sharett to Elath, April 29, 1949, *DFPI*, v. 3, d. 294. See also entry of May 2, 1949.

127. Sidney Sherwood (1901–1984), secretary, Export-Import Bank, 1946–1959, and assistant to chairman. The delegation was in Israel in April 1949 on a fact-finding mission connected with the bank's January 19, 1949 decision to approve Israel's May 1948 request for a $100 million loan. Sherwood argued in October 1948 that the request had not been presented in sufficient detail to show its use for specific projects. By 1951 Sherwood was convinced that "Israel will succeed in her economic program." See JTA *Bulletin*, October 28, 1948, and February 21, 1951.

Israel's admission to the UN. The telegram disavowed any intention to tell Israel what to do. Nonetheless, it was a difficult message to convey without embarrassment to the Israeli authorities.

Israel, Egypt, Lebanon, Jordan, and Syria sent delegations to the Lausanne talks, which commenced under the auspices of the PCC on April 27, 1949.[128] *Initial remarks by the Israeli delegation, led by Walter Eytan, showed that Israel had not changed its policies. The Israelis wanted to conclude a comprehensive peace with the Arab states. The Jerusalem and refugee issues, they said, could be discussed during the peace talks in Lausanne, but not as a precondition to talks, nor should these issues be discussed at the UN while talks were proceeding at Lausanne. The Arabs countered that solutions to the Jerusalem and refugee problems had to be solved before the actual peace talks.*[129] *Meanwhile, there was still no armistice between Israel and Syria. Acheson became frustrated at what he called the "unrealistic and intransigent attitude of both Israel and [the] Arab states." On April 29, he urged all mission heads in Arab capitals to press the respective governments. He issued a similar order for McDonald concerning the Israelis.*[130]

Taking advantage of Shiloah's presence, I took him into one of the smaller rooms and gave him the substance of the telegram. He was particularly disturbed by the suggestion about boundaries. He said that he could not understand what the Department had in mind. To whom were the concessions [on] boundaries to be made? When the 1947 partition was drafted, there was a clear understanding that there was to be an independent Arab state. Now, everyone understood that there was to be no such state. Was it expected, therefore, that Israel would concede portions of Palestine territory which it held to Lebanon, Syria, Jordan or Egypt? Surely this could not be Washington's purpose. But if not, what did Washington mean? I remained silent, for I had no answer. I urged upon Shiloah the importance of a new approach, if that were possible, to overcome the deadlock which had so evidently developed between the thinking of his government and Za'im. In particular, I urged that I might have an early meeting with Ben-Gurion and Sharett. He pointed out the difficulties of Shabbat, May Day, and Independence Day, but promised to talk with Ben-Gurion and Sharett.[131]

Direct from dinner [with Jacob Herzog and General Hilldring] to the Mograbi Theater for my second participation in the Union of Palestine Jour-

128. On the Lausanne meetings see Neil Caplan, *Futile Diplomacy*, v. 3, 57–126, and Caplan's occasional paper, "The Lausanne Conference, 1949: A Case Study in Middle East Peacemaking" (Tel Aviv: Moshe Dayan Center for Middle Eastern and African Studies, 1993); also Waldman, *Anglo-American Diplomacy and the Palestinian Refugee Problem*, 80–99.

129. Ethridge to Acheson, no. 136, April 28, 1949, *FRUS, 1949*, v. VI, 955–956.

130. Acheson circular, April 29, 1949, *FRUS, 1949*, v. VI, 959–960.

131. McDonald relayed Shiloah's rhetorical question about border rectification. See McDonald to secretary of state, no. 323, May 2, 1949, *FRUS, 1949*, v. VI, 966–967.

nalists *Vocal Newspaper*.[132] The other speakers were Dr. [Israel] Goldstein, Edward Norman, and Mr. Harry Rogoff of the Jewish Daily *Forward*.[133] My subject was the conduct of American foreign policy. Despite two hours or so of Hebrew, the meeting finally ended. There followed a reception at the Press Club. At the end, the family and I took Paula home.

Saturday, April 30

Having made a date to meet General William Donovan at the house for breakfast between 8:00 and 8:30, I was up in what I thought was ample time to have breakfast with him. It was fortunate I was early, because General Donovan was at the door by 7:40. But breakfast was an unqualified success because he seemed to enjoy two bowls of cereal.

Major General William J. Donovan (1883–1959) was the head of the Office of Strategic Services (OSS) from its creation until it was disbanded shortly after World War II. He returned to the practice of law, serving for a time as special assistant to Chief Prosecutor Robert H. Jackson at the Trial of the Major War Criminals at Nuremberg. After that, his experience helped guide the formation of the CIA in 1947. The Soviets learned of Donovan's visit to the US mission in Tel Aviv as they had learned of the earlier visit by Hilldring, and they became increasingly suspicious of Israel's orientation.[134]

In answer to my question, General Donovan explained that Shiloah had been one of his leading men in Cairo during the war, that the latter had talked with him until nearly one that morning about the problem of Israel's organization of its intelligence and security services.[135] General Donovan had advised strongly that the two be kept separate and distinct, because otherwise one man holding both posts might easily become dangerously powerful.

From that beginning he went on to cover a wide range of subjects until about 9:30 when we were joined by Colonel Andrus, an old friend of General Donovan. The general was emphatic that I should insist vigorously on adequate

132. The *Vocal Newspaper* was a radio program. McDonald's speech concerned how US foreign policy was made according to the US Constitution and the separation of powers. The text, titled "The Conduct of American Foreign Policy," is in McDonald Papers, USHMM, box 7, folder 13.

133. Harry (Hillel) Rogoff, (1883–1971), Belorussian-born journalist, began working at the *Forward* as reporter, 1906; managing editor, 1919–1951; editor-in-chief, 1951–1962. Said to have been the best-informed Yiddish journalist in the United States.

134. See Sharett to Namir, June 27, 1949, *DFPI*, v. 4, d. 109.

135. During 1940–1941, Shiloah (then Reuven Zaslany) had tried to establish closer bonds between the Haganah and the British Special Operations Executive in Cairo. The notion was to conduct intelligence operations into Vichy-controlled Syria. After the OSS created a small base in Cairo in 1942, Zaslany tried to interest it in dropping Jewish commando units into Europe to form resistance cells and to rescue Jews. Zaslany also provided the OSS with Jewish Agency intelligence materials concerning Palestine and the Middle East, as well as information on Europe based on debriefings of Jews who had reached Palestine. Eshed, *Reuven Shiloah*, 47–50, 67, 91–92; Friling, *Arrows in the Dark*, v. 1, 278ff.

staff and services and should not hesitate to go to the highest source if necessary with Colonel Andrus; we discussed problems of communications, bringing in Fierst to inform us on the actual situation.

The general being anxious to see Sharett, I sent Bobby next door to inquire. The date was made for noon. We then continued our conversation until I walked the general over to our neighbor's house. Despite the four hours and twenty minutes of talk, I was left without any explicit information about the purpose of the general's visit. I assume, however, that it is not unconnected with his old job as head of the OSS. When I took him to Sharett, I told the latter of the telegram received just after our visit with him on Friday and of my desire to discuss its contents with him and Ben-Gurion.

Late afternoon, Ruth and Bobby and I went to the exhibit of Madame Chana Orloff.[136] I was very favorably impressed particularly with her more realistic figures. She said she would like to do a bust of me, but I would prefer one of Bobby. There was no commitment on either side.

Over to the Greenbergs for tea, where we had an extra portion of her wonderful cake to bring home. I read for duty's sake a very long letter from the government of Israel, outlining the basis of their proposed taking over the English interests in the business in Israel. I was not competent to make any technical comment, but I did venture to question whether Kaplan would go as far as was there suggested in guaranteeing complete freedom in the export of dollar profits.

In the evening to Paray's performance of the Beethoven *Pastorale*, the Tchaikovsky No. 1 Piano Concerto with Éliane Richepin as soloist, and finally, Ravel's *La Valse*. Though the last was a brilliant performance, I enjoyed most Beethoven. Despite Miss Wilkins urging that we stay for the [Edward] Norman reception on the stage, we begged off and came home.

136. Chana Orloff (1888–1968), Ukrainian-born Jewish sculptor who spent time in Paris and Israel. The Tel Aviv Museum held thirty-seven of her works in 1949, when she also created sculptures of Ben-Gurion and more abstract heroic figures.

11. May 1949

In the middle of the afternoon, Colonel Andrus and Major Brady came at my request. We discussed the May Day celebration. I urged them to make as full observation as they could of the demonstration with a view to estimating as accurately as possible the strength of the communist element.

After supper I dictated to Bobby and later to Miss Clark, some letters for our courier Ben Friedman, who promised to deliver them in the States the following Thursday.

On May 1, McDonald wrote David Niles in the White House.

Dear Dave,

This note, being carried to you by our mutual friend, Ben Friedman, is for two purposes.

First, I want you to know that we are doing everything that can possibly be done on the major issues that concern the President so deeply. Progress is being made on the major counts, and I am confident that if there is no unexpected development there will be real peace within another year and, in the meantime, measurable gains in the solution of the tragic problem of the Arab refugees. The political issues and that of Jerusalem are in my opinion inherently much less difficult than refugees and will be resolved along lines which the President will approve.

My second purpose is to solicit your friendly good offices so that I shall be enabled to go home 'for consultation' for at least two months at the end of my first year here, i.e., the last week in July or the first week in August. . . . [McDonald's daughter Janet was expecting McDonald's first grandchild at that time]. I have not yet taken up this matter with the Department and do not expect to do so for another three or four weeks. . . .

There are also important considerations of public policy which make it desirable for me to be at home long enough to get a more intimate feel of the President's and the Department's reactions to present developments and policies, not only in Israel, but in the Middle East.

Niles, after making the relevant inquiries, responded positively to McDonald's request on May 16.[1]

1. Letters in McDonald Papers, USHMM, box 7, folder 14.

Drove down to the Kaete Dan at about 9:30, where I met Dr. Mohn, who was sitting with General Donovan. While the latter saw to his luggage, I chatted with Mohn about Za'im and the latter's demand. Mohn seemed not to be very well informed or much concerned. This was a significant item for me in the light of the telegram I found at the office from the Department later that morning.

The general [Donovan] and I sat on the beach for thirty to forty minutes discussing American policy in this area. He reiterated his earlier impression that my views about what was practicable were more realistic than those of the "desk" at home. He was concerned that the secretary was not being kept sufficiently informed on the changes here which tend to outmode the November 29 General Assembly resolution. Again, he was very flattering in his comments on my work. He promised to say a word in the right places at home with a view to assuring us more adequate secretarial and technical assistance. I hope he will. We were out to the airport by 10:25. The plane was already there and took off promptly at 10:40.

To the office, in reply to a telegram from the Department answering the Israeli suggestion [of April 28] that the US intervene to persuade Za'im to withdraw his demand for the "rectification" of the international frontier, in which the Department suggested that for the moment, the matter be left to Dr. Mohn. I told the Department that I thought this wholly inadequate and gave the reason. Again, I urged the Department to act to save the Israel-Syrian negotiations.

On May 2, 1949, McDonald reported to Washington: "Dr. Mohn's efforts [to] influence Za'im are potentially weak. . . . I feel that US efforts with Za'im [are] needed now if Syria-Israeli armistice talks are not to be gravely jeopardized."[2]

On the same day, James Hugh Keeley, the US minister in Damascus, criticized McDonald's earlier report [April 29]: "[Regarding] McDonald's comment [regarding] Israel's sincerity yet unwillingness to yield even to [the] extent of leaving disputed frontier areas for subsequent determination, might it not properly be asked what profit it [is] for Syria to enter into peace negotiations with Israel if [the] only benefits Syria can hope to obtain therefrom, [a] slight rectification of [the] frontier, is relinquished without any quid pro quo or other guarantee before talks begin[?] . . . Surely if Israel's professions of desire for peace are genuine, she should be willing to make some concession."[3]

2. McDonald to secretary of state, no. 322, May 2, 1949, NARA, RG 59, 501.BB Palestine, box 2124, folder 7.
3. Keeley to secretary of state, no, 259, May 1, 1949, *FRUS*, 1949, v. VI, 961–962; also Keeley to secretary of state, no. 261, May 2, 1949, *FRUS*, 1949, v. VI, 965–996. Za'im later made more substantial demands, including the panhandle of northern Palestine and parts of the Galilee. Ethridge [through Vincent] to secretary of state, no. 699, May 9, 1949, *FRUS*, 1949, v. VI, 988–989.

A very busy teatime period. The first visitor was Jean Nieuwenhuys, the Belgian consul general in Jerusalem, who had come to pay a courtesy call during his visit to Tel Aviv for the independence celebrations. We had an interesting talk about problems of living in Israel now, but the really noteworthy item was Nieuwenhuys's categorical statement about John MacDonald, with whom he had worked for months on the Jerusalem Truce Commission. The American consul general according to Nieuwenhuys suddenly "went to pieces," began to drink to great excess, and to make a spectacle of himself in public cafés, particularly in that frequented by the Sternists. On one of these evenings when MacDonald appeared, Nieuwenhuys overheard newspapermen whom he knew say to one another, "There's MacDonald. He will soon be so drunk that we shall learn what he and his colleagues have been doing." So flagrant were Mac-Donald's lapses that, towards the end, Nieuwenhuys and his colleague[4] could no longer speak frankly in the Truce Commission in the presence of MacDonald, because the latter could no longer be trusted to keep confidences. The above report fits so exactly into earlier accounts of other sources that it must represent a true picture. The only surprising facet of Nieuwenhuys's statement was that he said he had not suspected that the incident resulting in the death of young Herzog, liaison officer with MacDonald, was a factor in the latter's disintegration.[5]

Before Nieuwenhuys left, the Rosenblooms arrived and then, within a few minutes, the delegation of the American Christian Palestine Committee.[6] The noteworthy fact was the concern of the group about the agitation among Protestant ministers against Israel because of the Arab refugees. They were all very interested in my quotation of the Quakers, Gulley and Painter, to the effect that the basic reason for the Arabs leaving was instruction to that effect which they had had from the Arab leaders and from the British.[7] They asked if they might quote me, but I said that they should secure such a statement from the Quakers. They spoke in particular of the editorial of Dr. Coffin.[8]

After a light dinner, we all went to the Sam Sacks party. In addition to members of the staff, there were a score or so people from town. My chief talk was with Shenkar, the elderly chairman of the Manufacturers Association,

4. French consul general (and archaeologist) René Neuville (1894–1981), the third member of the Truce Commission.

5. See entries of August 16 and 17, 1948.

6. The American Christian Palestine Committee [ACPC], led by liberal, pro-Zionist Protestant leaders, was formed in 1946 by the merger of the American Palestine Committee and the Christian Council on Palestine. The delegation in Israel was led by Reverend Karl Baehr, Congregationalist minister and executive secretary of the ACPC, and it included a number of academics and journalists.

7. Entry of April 26, 1948.

8. Refers to Henry Sloane Coffin (1877–1954), president of Union Theological Seminary and leading member of the anti-Zionist Committee for Justice and Peace in the Holy Land. As editor of the periodical *Christianity and Crisis*, Coffin in February 1949 wrote the editorial, "Perils to America in the New Jewish State." See Caitlin Carenen, *The Fervent Embrace: Liberals, Protestants, Evangelicals, and Israel* (New York: New York University Press, 2012), 65–66.

who surprisingly spoke of the austerity program with approval.[9] He was optimistic about the future and insisted that, as the price of success, there must be sacrifice all around.

Tuesday, May 3

Lord Samuel came to the house about 11:45 and stayed half an hour. I was much interested to note the extent to which his views had changed since I first saw him shortly after his arrival a few weeks ago.[10] Now there was no talk of refugees or expressions of acute concern at the adverse reactions to Israel's failure to accept a repatriation program. In answer to my question, Lord Samuel said that his chief impressions now were:

1) the changed landscape. When he came, Palestine was almost treeless except for a few groves near Hadera. Now millions of trees made a striking difference;
2) the extent and variety of present-day industry. Twenty-seven or [twenty-]eight years ago there was no industry except for brick and cement works and some very small traditional hand industries. Now there was a very large variety and some very modern and comparatively large industries.[11] He cited the Mueller textile mill in Haifa employing about 1,200 people;[12] I countered by citing that of our friend Sam Sacks;
3) the vastly changed and improved health conditions of the people. He would have gone on, but he had to rush back to the Sharon for dinner before a formal appearance at the Knesset in the afternoon.

The Kopul Rosens[13] came promptly for tea at 4:30. He outlined to me his project for a high school here for overseas English-speaking Jewish boys and girls. The curriculum will be modern, but impregnated with the traditional Jewish spirit. He was confident that the land would be made available, exemption from customs duties would be granted for building materials, that there would be as many if not more students as the school could care for even if it

9. Aryeh Shenkar (1877–1959), Ukrainian-born textile manufacturer; emigrated to Palestine 1924; purchased the Lodzia Textile firm in Tel Aviv; founder and first president of the Manufacturers Association of Israel (previously the Industrialists' Union in the Land of Israel), which eventually represented all manufacturers, public and private; later a director of Bank Leumi; politically well connected.

10. Entries of April 8, 20, 1949.

11. Industrial growth came during the mid-1930s, with Jewish immigrants from Germany, Austria, and Czechoslovakia. The Ha'avara [Transfer] Agreement allowed the Yishuv to import German technology and industrial equipment to Israel.

12. Refers to the ATA—Arigei Totzeret Artzeinu [Fabrics Manufactured in Our Land]—textile factory conceived and built by the Czech-Jewish industrialist Erich Mueller in 1934. In 1948 ATA became the supplier of uniforms to the IDF.

13. Kopul Rosen (1913–1962), London-born Anglo-Jewish rabbi; appointed chief rabbi of the Federation of Synagogues in London, 1946; in 1948 devoted himself to Jewish education, founding, with his wife Bella, Carmel College, a Jewish boarding school eventually located in Oxfordshire; left rabbinate, 1949.

reached the numbers of 5,000. The board should be as representative as possible, but he did not hope to include Agudat or the extreme Left. He thought of the school as being a bridge between the English-speaking Jews and Israel and as a means of mutual influence. He hoped that I would be willing to take more than a benevolent interest.

Jacob S. Potofsky[14] and his colleague Maxwell Brandwin[15] arrived. Our first fifteen minutes or so was general conversation about Israel. Then when [Rosen] had gone, my two visitors asked me to tell them more about the program I had in mind. Potofsky said at this point that the deciding influence in his affirmative decision to come out was my letter.[16] I invited them to the roof where, for nearly an hour, we talked about the problem of the future orientation of [the] labor movement here, and of the possible role of American trade unionists in influencing it. Both my visitors were emphatic that their group, more than Dubinsky's,[17] could count with the left wing, but they were not wholly optimistic that they would be given a full opportunity. They asked me many questions about the political and economic as well as personal aspects of the several party groups, which I answered as well as I could. I utilized my inability to answer some of the questions to point [to] the moral of my main thesis, that what we could do through diplomatic or other governmental channels was more limited than what we hoped the labor people themselves could do.

We talked about personnel. They spoke of a nephew of [Sidney] Hillman's, the new labor attaché in Prague, as a possibility. I said that this was one of the men whom Sam Klaus had in mind but had not been permitted by the Department to visit.[18]

Earlier, in the course of our political talk, Brandwin asked me about the Syrian situation and whether they could be helpful. I explained the Za'im demands and the possible usefulness of a word in the right quarters. From the nearly two hours of talk, I got the impression that these men would study thoroughly and probably act energetically. Brandwin was the more empathic both in his analysis of the vital stake of Jews and Jewish labor in the developments here and in his words as to what Jewish labor should try to do. I got the impression, however, that Potofsky was just as interested but by nature more cautious in expression. Both were very grateful, they said, for our long time together, and we promised to meet again at length before they left.

14. Entries of January 28, 1949, and March 17, 1949.
15. Maxwell Brandwin, adviser to CIO delegation in Israel.
16. On the need for an educational program from US labor leaders in Israel in order to stave off communist penetration. McDonald to Potofsky, January 31, 1949, McDonald Papers, Columbia University, box 3, folder 35.
17. Entry of November 29, 1948.
18. The labor attaché in Prague was Milton Fried (1917–1971), the son-in-law of Sidney Hillman, president of the Amalgamated Clothing Workers of America, 1914–1946, who founded the American Labor Party with David Dubinsky in 1936. Samuel Klaus suggested Fried to the State Department in late December 1948. See entry of January 8, 1949.

With the [Richard] Fords, Ruth, Bobby and I arrived at the Sharon for the state dinner at 8:40, a few minutes late because of unusual traffic incident to the pre-Independence Day celebration.[19] We were greeted with flashlights and camera men and Mr. Giveon[20] on behalf of the Foreign Office. Mr. and Mrs. Sharett had already greeted a portion of the diplomatic corps, among whom we mingled while the delicious hors d'oeuvres and cocktails were being served. Having chatted with the Russian chargé [Mikhail Moukhine], I introduced him to Mrs. Ford, with whom he then chatted freely in Spanish.

The table was three sides of a rectangle. At the head, to the right of the foreign minister sat Ruth, myself, Goldie Meyerson, Vanthier, and his wife. To the left the Russian chargé, and others in order of precedence. The arrangements seemed to me satisfactory, but according to Mrs. Ford, the wife of the Greek consul spent most of the dinner complaining about the seating arrangements. Vanthier, who brought in the Dutch consul general's wife, was very glum at first when it seemed that he was going to be seated below what he regarded as his proper place; how his face lit up when he was placed at the head of the table.

I was fortunate in being seated next to Goldie Meyerson who, for me, was, next to Sharett, by far the most interesting personality at the table. We talked about her experiences in Russia, of the difficulty and sometimes impossibility of foreign diplomats seeing leading Soviet personalities. She stressed that social life among the members of the diplomatic corps was very active, in part because there was nothing else for them to do. Again, we recurred to the question of her going to the States, and we were in essential agreement that it was better for her to remain here, at least during the present crisis. Perhaps going to the States in the fall.

I told her of Potofsky's visit, and we talked about the prospects of successful American labor educational efforts. She doubted that Potofsky and his colleague would be given an opportunity to reach the masses of the Mapam followers. The leaders would listen but would probably not be persuaded. Moreover, she thought that the leaders would not permit Potofsky to speak to the masses. Nor was she optimistic of the possibility of my having perceptible influence on the leaders. Nonetheless, she agreed that the effort was worth making on both levels, labor and diplomatic.

She spoke of an amusing exchange with the rabbis here. They said to her that they hoped since she went to synagogue in Moscow, she would do so in Tel Aviv.[21] She replied that she would whenever the rabbis permitted her and the

---

19. Commemorated on the fifth day of Iyar in the Hebrew calendar.

20. Zvi K. Giveon, assistant chief of protocol, Israeli Foreign Ministry.

21. In October Meyerson had attended Moscow's main synagogue for Rosh Hashanah and Yom Kippur services, to the delight of Moscow's Jews. The KGB interrogated Jews who attended the services, and Stalin's final crackdown on the Jewish Antifascist Committee followed. Yossi Goldstein, "Doomed to Fail: Golda Meir's Mission to Moscow (Pt. 1)," *Israel Journal of Foreign Affairs* 5, no. 3 (September 2011): 131; and Aryeh Levin, *Envoy to Moscow: Memoirs of an Israeli Ambassador, 1988–92* (London: Frank Cass, 1996), 95–97.

other women to sit in the main auditorium and ceased to herd them into galleries or out of the way aisles. In reply they made no promise.

During the dinner, I took occasion to ask Sharett about the Syrian negotiations. He said that there was to be held a private meeting of the two sides without international observers and at the request of Syria. He regarded the meeting as crucial. Sharett told me also that Israel was issuing a new refugee statement soon either in New York or Lausanne, depending upon the advice of Eban and Eytan.[22]

After the meat course, and before the dessert, I gave my very brief toast, to which Sharett replied briefly in Hebrew, French, English and Russian. My words were: "On its first birthday my wish for Israel is that it may through the millennia be worthy of the age-old heroism of the Jewish people and of the spiritual creativeness of the Jewish prophets. Long live Israel at peace in a world at peace." Later, several persons were kind enough to say that the toast was appropriate and poetic. I would be inclined to accept the first adjective. At about eleven, the dinner was concluded, and after brief farewells we set the pace for leaving, although a number of persons had previously gone.

Wednesday, May 4
Independence Day

Ford and I reached the presidential office at five minutes before twelve, recognized the honor guard, were photographed and were greeted by the foreign office staff. Soon everyone had arrived; Giveon called out the names and the countries in French in order of precedence. We formed a half moon, Sprinzak entered, I took my place near him and the microphone and gave my greetings as follows: "Mr. President: It is a great privilege and a distinguished honor on behalf of my colleagues of the diplomatic and consular corps and on my own behalf to offer our cordial greetings and felicitations to the government and people of Israel on this auspicious occasion. My colleagues, I am confident, share my sense of personal pleasure in being permitted to represent our respective governments on Israel's first anniversary. We have followed with sympathetic interest your extraordinary progress during the past formative year. Our hope is that your young and vigorous country may be blessed with prosperity and peace in a Middle East at peace."[23]

Sprinzak replied briefly in Hebrew, which was translated into French. Thereafter, the members of the diplomatic corps were in turn greeted by Sprinzak, to whom they gave their governments' verbal messages of congratulations. The conversation then became informal in groups of twos and threes

---

22. McDonald relayed Sharett's comments to the State Department. "He pleads," McDonald said, "for US good offices [to] urge Colonel Za'im not to insist on 'rectification' of frontier. . . . I hope Department can act promptly." McDonald to secretary of state, no. 332, May 4, 1949, *FRUS*, 1949, v. VI, 977.
23. This statement was preapproved by the State Department.

Fig. 11.1. Israel's first Independence Day parade seen here at Allenby and Ben Yehuda Streets in front of Mugrabi Cinema in Tel Aviv. Israel Government Press Office.

until getting the signal from Simon. I said goodbye, and the meeting began to break up.

Quarter past three we started to drive to the grandstand [at Mograbi Square] for the parade. The last two blocks we walked. As we approached, we noticed that the stairs leading up to the stands were jammed, but with the aid of our special policemen and two or three others, and by holding hand to hand, Ruth and Bobby and I finally got up and gradually worked our way down towards our seats. Bobby found hers in the fourth row fairly quickly, but ours in the second row had to be evacuated by the Hadassah gals, none less than Mrs. Greenberg and Mrs. Rosensohn,[24] whom Giveon forced to move. By sliding over the railing, Ruth and I finally got to our places. Such confusion and milling about of the uncontrolled crowds.

As the time passed and the armored cars and police cars and motorcycles failed to keep the street open, and as the Spitfires zoomed down dangerously over the heads of the spectators, frequently causing those on the roofs to duck, I wanted only to get out of the crowd. Finally, at about the time the parade was

24. Etta Lasker Rosensohn (1885–1966), Texas-born child of German Jewish immigrants; joined Hadassah after World War I; Hadassah representative to Hebrew University after 1939 and chair of the Hadassah Medical Organization Committee; president of Hadassah, 1952–1953; member of Hadassah National Board for two decades.

to have started, word was passed around that it had been cancelled.[25] Then a squad of military police cleared an avenue through the crowd [so that we in] the lower rows of the grandstand [could] get away. What a relief! Then, thanks to the courtesy of Mr. Novomeysky and his car, the family with Mrs. Ford and Mrs. Rosensohn were soon at the house for an hour's rest before the garden party.

I was much surprised to note the extent of the garden in back of the president's office and of the grass and gardens which adorned it. The weather was perfect, becoming cool as the sun went down. Refreshment booths located in widely separated sections of the garden helped to keep the crowds dispersed. Acting more or less as a freelance, I managed during the hour and a half we were there to see and chat briefly with many people, including members of the Orthodox bloc, who spoke to me about coming to see some of their new communities; several South Africans, including the redoubtable Sarah Gertrude Millin,[26] who was in a state of nerves, and threatening to return to South Africa directly or go on to London; the Braudos, long enough for Madame to tell me that I was ruining their lives; the members of the Export-Import Bank Commission and many, many other Americans. In chatting with Sharett and Kaplan, both of whom I was surprised to note were looking refreshed as if they had not been two hours earlier struggling futilely with the milling crowd, [I said] that I thought they, "as managers of parades, were excellent foreign minister and minister of finance." All in all it was a most successful party.

Thursday, May 5

Dr. Mohn came out primarily to tell me about the crisis in the Israel-Syrian armistice negotiations and to solicit my and the government's intervention. I told him that the Department had already indicated its interest. We then went on to talk about the general situation in the Middle East. Mohn then developed at some length his thesis, which I reported in a despatch, that the Western powers were foolishly and blindly supporting reactionary cliques in the Arab countries, while the masses of the Arab people remain sunk in illiteracy and wretchedness. This situation, Mohn thought, facilitated communist progress in all these countries. No headway could, in his opinion, be made against the latter except through a determined effort by the West to make their economic aid contingent upon social reforms.

McDonald reported Mohn's concern that the "Arabs resident in [the] section of [the] northwest triangle to be turned over to Israel under the armistice terms with

---

25. The military parade was canceled because of the far larger-than-expected crowds on the parade route. See JTA *Bulletin*, May 5, 1949.

26. Sarah Gertrude Millin (1889–1968), renowned Lithuanian-born Jewish South African novelist and biographer; strong advocate of Zionism who visited Palestine and openly opposed South African restrictions on Jewish immigration in the 1930s; at work on a history of the Jews at the time of her death.

Transjordan should [not] be stampeded and asked if the [Department] or I could do anything. I assured him of [Department's] awareness of importance of issue but did not disclose more."[27]

McDonald added, *"Dr. Mohn has been, at least since he came to the Middle East in 1947 with the UN Commission, a close student of conditions in this area. He is not pro-Jewish or pro-Zionist; on the contrary, he has usually inclined to give the benefit of the doubt to the Arabs in their differences with the Zionists and later with Israel. Hence, his criticisms of Western policies in the Arab countries cannot be attributed to an anti-Arab bias."*[28]

The Abramses called from the Sharon and we agreed to go out for lunch. Delightful lunch with the Abramses. They were evidently both, and especially Biddy [Ben Abrams's wife], [pleased] by their trip to date and by their first impressions of Israel.

McDonald's old friend Benjamin Abrams, one of the most influential Jewish leaders and supporters of Israel in the United States, had sent word in January 1949 that he and his wife would visit. In New York, Abrams already had met Abba Eban, Eliahu Ben-Horin, and others, encounters that McDonald had helped arrange.[29]

Long staff conference from four to seven. First, we discussed the May Day parades and their possible significance; the reactions of the men varied. Most of them agreed that the communist numbers are still small, but there was a general feeling that the beginnings of the traditional communist penetration methods could be discerned, and that, therefore, now was no time for overconfidence. I stressed my conviction that one of our chief jobs here is to do the best possible reporting that we could.

Friday, May 6

Breakfast with Mr. Harmon Goldstone of the Rockefeller organization.[30] He talked at length and interestingly of his three-months stay here and his general impressions. He thought that the authorities might be gradually working their way out of the housing morass. He had found much needless obstructionism from government functionaries, which he in part attributed to the fact that he had come out at the personal invitation of Mordechai Bentov, no longer in the government,[31] and in part because of the natural reluctance of lower

---

27. McDonald to secretary of state, no. 355, May 6, 1949, NARA, RG 59, 501.BB Palestine, box 2124, folder 7.
28. McDonald to secretary of state, no. 121, May 9, 1949, McDonald Papers, USHMM, box 7, folder 14.
29. See exchanges in McDonald Papers, Columbia University, box 2, folder 6.
30. Entry of March 2, 1949.
31. Minister of labor and construction in the Provisional Government (Mapam); left out of the first postelection government because Mapam did not join the governing coalition.

officials to cooperate with someone whose exact role they were suspicious of. He was hoping that within the next day or two, before he left for home next week, he would receive from Goldie Meyerson, whom he regards very highly, answers to questions which he has been vainly seeking from the lower echelon for weeks. Parenthetically, I might add his enthusiasm for Kaplan is not as great as that for Goldie.

One of the major hurdles is the government's desire to build up its infant industries, a desire which conflicts with the need to bring in from abroad everything needful [for] housing, which can be purchased overseas cheaper than they can be produced here. In the last analysis, Goldstone thought that the basic difficulty was the lack of decision to date as to where the burden of paying for housing is to fall. Once that is determined, and with the advantages which will have come from the advice of the many experts and approved techniques, real headway can begin. He is rather skeptical of the extent to which foreign direction will be accepted in the long run. He suspects that Israel will somehow insist on finding its way under its own power and by its own means. It was clear that whatever may have been his degree of success in business here, he had been thrilled by his period here and was going back to give the Rockefellers an enthusiastic picture of Israel. I asked him to tell Nelson [Rockefeller] and his father [John Rockefeller Jr.] about the [Rockefeller] Museum.

Housing in Israel worried US observers. Richard Ford, in a long report to Washington of May 3, noted that 200,000 new immigrants had arrived in the ten months since Israeli independence—which in comparative terms would mean an influx into the United States of 35 million. Eight thousand, he said, had arrived in the past seventy-two hours.[32] *The newcomers, who came from Europe, the Middle East, South America, and even Shanghai, were assigned initially to one of twenty-two overcrowded reception camps, which now, because of the housing shortage, were expected to accommodate new immigrants for months rather than weeks. "Tempers," Ford said, "are becoming daily more frayed."*[33]

For tea to meet the elite of Hebrew letters. The language difficulties were somewhat embarrassing, but at the end we found ourselves discussing, as a subject of common interest, the possibility of two quarterly magazines, the one containing Hebrew translations of current American verse, short stories and

---

32. Between Israeli independence and the end of 1949, 340,000 immigrants arrived in Israel. Recent immigrants comprised one-third of Israel's population by that time. Despite criticism, Ben-Gurion refused to consider immigration restrictions. Instead he sought long-range employment and housing solutions and urged the kibbutzim to accept more immigrants. See Dvora Hakohen, *Immigrants in Turmoil: Mass Immigration to Israel and Its Repercussions in the 1950s and After* (Syracuse, NY: Syracuse University Press, 2003), 118–120.

33. Ford to secretary of state, no. 115, May 3, 1949, NARA, RG 59, MC 1390, reel 19, frames 220–226.

essays; the other, comparable translations of Hebrew literature into English. Tentatively we agreed to continue the discussion at another time.

Saturday, May 7

I decided to write Paula about the garden party and to include in the same letter an urgent request to see Ben-Gurion the next day. The results were completely satisfactory, because she called, pleased about my comments on the party and her dress and hat, yellow and black respectively, and fixed the time for a date with her husband, Sunday at 9:30. We earlier arranged for the dinner date for the Lehmans and the Abramses, with Ben-Gurion accepting for May 15.

Over to the Sackses' for very late morning tea. Afternoon tea, the family and I went with the Abramses to Kaplan's. During the course of a talk about the hard core of the refugees, Kaplan with rather wry humor spoke of the American-Austrian zone authorities' objection to the Israeli cutting down a little on the departure of refugees for this country.[34] A day or so later I saw a reflection of this in a despatch from the Department requesting us to take up this matter with the Foreign Office. I was encouraged to hear Abrams say that he thought the JDC might add to its responsibilities that of the hard core of refugees.

Sunday, May 8

Despite work on one of the HaKirya roads, which required us to detour, I arrived at Ben-Gurion's office on time [9:30] and was immediately ushered in. He looked to me tired but was cordial as usual. I told him that I had political matters to discuss with him but that I wanted first to tell him of our critical housing [and office space] needs and solicit his intervention and aid. He made notes, added up the number of rooms and seemed overwhelmed by the need for seventy-three rooms. I told him of our first hopes about tax abatement and our subsequent dependence on governmental aid through requisitioning. When I mentioned the Hill [Ramat Gan], he demurred, saying they were releasing those houses. To this I objected that, in the emergency, the government might aid us by the possibility of requisitioning to secure a possible series of rental contracts. Finally, he said that the situation seemed to require the naming of a special officer to work with our people. I agreed and urged that this be done promptly and implied that I hoped he would have the requisite authority. Later, I wrote a note to Ben-Gurion to tie the matter up.

On the general problem of housing [for Israelis], Ben-Gurion said that he was beginning to be more encouraged. He thought that within six months or a

---

34. Jewish DPs in Austria were not moved out until 1950, and only in that year did the Zionist offices there close. The Israelis estimated that a third of the Jews who came to Israel from East and Southeast Europe in these years came through the Austrian camps. Thomas Albrich, "Way Station of Exodus: Jewish Displaced Persons and Refugees in Postwar Austria," in *The Holocaust and History: The Known, the Unknown, the Disputed, and the Reexamined*, eds. Michael Berenbaum and Abraham J. Peck (Bloomington: Indiana University Press in association with the United States Holocaust Memorial Museum, 1998), 272–273.

year a real beginning could be made. He thought Levitt, with his $5,500 housing when built in numbers of three or four thousand, would break the black market and the key-money racket.[35]

I then spoke of the three points, refugees, Jerusalem and boundaries, raised in the Department's recent telegram.[36] It was evident that Ben-Gurion had nothing to add on the first two to the statements made by Weizmann and Eban.[37] On the third, he said he could speak at length, but regarded discussions as futile until the United States indicated what specific boundaries it had in mind and what specific countries it thought concessions should be made to.

This led naturally to Ben-Gurion's discussion of the Israel-Syrian armistice impasse. He said that he was greatly disturbed by Za'im's unyieldingness, that warlike peace is indivisible, that an outbreak in the upper Jordan might jeopardize the whole peace structure and the hopes of the US and the UN. He was convinced, he said, that Za'im would not hold out as he was doing were he not supported by outside powers, the French, perhaps others. He pleaded for the exercise by the US of pressure on Za'im to leave Israel territory comparable to that used on Israel by the US to leave Lebanese territory. I promised to transmit this message as literally as I could.

As I was leaving, I had him write down in his notebook the dinner date at the house for the Lehmans and the Abrams at 8:00 pm on Sunday the 15th.

McDonald reported to Acheson, "Evident Israel not now prepared to go in public beyond recent statements on refugees and Jerusalem. [Regarding] boundaries it will not publicly suggest possibility yielding territory now held. This does not preclude bilateral talks with [Jordan] at Lausanne."[38]

Acheson insisted that McDonald raise Za'im's desire to speak with Ben-Gurion—a possibility raised by Za'im himself on April 28. There was strong US interest in such a meeting.[39] Riley told the Israelis that Za'im wished a comprehensive yet honorable settlement whereby he would resettle 300,000 Palestinian Arab refugees. Ben-Gurion insisted that the Syrians had to withdraw to the international border first.[40]

35. Refers to William J. Levitt (1907–1994), American Jewish pioneer of mass-produced, prefabricated, inexpensive houses after World War II. Levitt also made substantial financial contributions to Israel and attempted to duplicate his home construction success there.

36. Entry of April 29, 1949.

37. May refer primarily to Eban's May 5 statement to the UN General Assembly's Ad Hoc Committee on Israeli membership. Statement in *DFPI*, v. 4, d. 5 appendix.

38. Reference to McDonald to secretary of state, no. 342, May 9, 1949, *FRUS*, 1949, v. VI, 1031 and n. 1.

39. Acheson to McDonald, no. 282, May 9, 1949, *FRUS*, 1949, v. VI, 990; Keeley to secretary of state, no. 256, April 28, 1949, referenced in *FRUS*, 1949, v. VI, 980.

40. See Ma'oz, *Syria and Israel*, 20–26; Aryeh Shalev, *The Israel-Syria Armistice Regime, 1949–1955* (Boulder, CO: Westview Press, 1993), 28–36; Avi Schlaim, "Husni Za'im and the Plan to Resettle Palestinian Refugees in Syria," 68–80.

In the evening Ruth and I enjoyed the luxury of the front porch for the first time in beautifully cool and refreshing weather.

Colonel Andrus and Ford arrived shortly after General Riley unexpectedly came out to stay for lunch. The four of us then discussed Colonel Andrus's draft of a telegram about the Israeli-Jordanian turnover operations on the northwest border of the triangle.

Following lunch, Riley and I discussed further the Syrian-Israeli impasse; his hopes now given up that a high-level conference might have led to peace negotiations; his feelings that both sides were logical and from their point of view correct; and his conclusion that the matter would probably go to the Security Council. Earlier I had been pleased to have the general's assurance that there had been no hitches in the turnover.

Again this time, as in our conference in Jerusalem on Easter, I got the impression that the general was genuinely concerned lest his long stay out here disadvantage him in his career. I reflected this feeling in my telegram the next day to the Department.

One of the highlights of the general's visit was his retort to my comment on "Keeley's eloquence in defense of the Arab cause." General Riley replied quickly, speaking to me, "You're not so bad yourself." Laughingly, I insisted that I was always objective, but in any case, I never began a despatch saying that I had been received by an Israeli official "with deferential cordiality."

McDonald, in reporting Riley's visit, made the following comments:

On the turnover in the Tulkarm-Nablus-Jenin triangle: "My impression from Israeli officials, including Ben-Gurion, supports Riley's hope. I continue to seize every occasion to emphasize US concern that [the] Arabs remain."

On the Israeli–Syrian armistice: "I [am] unable [to] estimate Syrian willingness [to] compromise but [I] am sure Israel will continue [to] refuse [to] accept any armistice line which might foreshadow 'rectification' of international frontier."

On Riley: "I think it [is] impossible [to] exaggerate [the] importance [of] Riley remaining [in] this area and continuing as center [of] Israeli-Arab negotiations and armistice supervision. I sympathize with his feelings that such continuance might disadvantage him personally. I venture, therefore, [to] urge that Department and Riley's military superiors take full account of his unique present and prospective services for peace and that they act to convince him that his continuance [in] Middle East will not disadvantage him." [41]

---

41. McDonald to secretary of state, no. 346, May 10, 1949, NARA, RG 59, MC 1390, reel 19, frames 292–293.

After a too-brief nap, began the late afternoon and evening series of conferences. First came Jacob Landau with a too long story about press associations and particularly his own. I said I would consider whether I could have a group at the house in connection with [the] JTA anniversary.[42] I demurred at speaking at a dinner, but said I thought I could come to a cocktail party. Decided to ask advice [of] Department.

Before Landau left, Colonel Andrus and Colonel Ben-Artzi arrived. There was hardly time for us to begin our talk at tea before Potofsky, Brandwin, and Curran came.[43] Perhaps not too considerately, I raised in the presence of the others the question whether Ben-Artzi's colleagues here were as cooperative now as they had been with van der Velde last year. I cited the closeness of the liaison relationships in December with the present feeling of our people that they were not being kept adequately informed. Ben-Arzi countered by telling of long delays in Washington to his requests for information even when, for example, it concerned merely such an unrestricted subject as measurements of army uniforms. I had to confess that, comparatively, we were still better served than he was, but I nonetheless hoped for an improvement in the present relationship here. I asked the colonel to be sure to come back to see me before he left.

About an hour with the labor men on the roof. Potofsky told interestingly of his first contacts and impressions here. I hope that his optimism about cooperation from Mapam leaders in enabling him to talk with Mapam kibbutzim is justified. He is later going to give me a list of the Mapam leaders with his personal estimate of each. He and the other men had been very much impressed by the response of the [Mapam] committee leaders to the "surprisingly frank" statements made to them by Ben-Gurion, Kaplan, and Joseph at the Saturday night meeting. Their reaction was an augury, my guests thought, of wholehearted labor cooperation. Curran spoke of the advantage here of the lack of interlocking jurisdictions, which so confused the building trades at home. On the economic prospect, the men were rather optimistic, but they were cautious in their appraisal of prospects of communist penetration, particularly in case economic conditions here sharply worsened. They agreed that nothing should unnecessarily be left to "nature."

On the question of our labor attaché, Potofsky was very enthusiastic about Hillman's nephew [sic], Milton Fried, now holding that position in Prague. As to Sam Klaus, he was less than enthusiastic. Nor did the others show enthusiasm.

---

42. Jacob Landau (1893–1952), Vienna-born journalist; established the first Jewish news agency (the Jewish Correspondence Bureau) in The Hague in 1917. Under the name Jewish Telegraphic Agency, it moved to London and then to New York in the 1920s. He was still the managing director of the JTA, which received its funding from other Jewish groups.

43. Joseph Curran (1906–1981), former merchant seaman; founder and first president of the National Maritime Union; supporter of Israel.

Breakfast with Sidney Sherwood, secretary of the Export-Import Bank, who had asked to see me prior to seeing his group the next day. I did not discover, however, why he thought it desirable or necessary to have this advance meeting.

Lunch at the Andrus's for Hilldring. I regretted that I felt so tired that I had to leave immediately after the meal, despite the very interesting conversation, which I was listening to, among the military men who were reminiscing about Eisenhower, Montgomery, et al. I was impressed anew by the extent to which the young Israeli liaison officers had enjoyed the confidence and association of leading British officers during World War II.

To Mr. and Mrs. Albert Matalon's dinner for General and Mrs. Hilldring. General Hilldring was his usual cordial self and, on his own initiative, promised to stress on his return home to the Department and the president our needs and work here.[44]

Wednesday, May 11

Most of the day was given over to extended talks with Ray Hare,[45] who came out during the late morning. At lunch, we were joined by Ford; in the afternoon, by the Export-Import Bank group. My talk with Hare continued until the arrival of Governor Lehman at 5:30, was resumed after the latter left, and was extended until the time to leave for the Hilldring dinner given by the Foreign Office at the Kaete Dan.

The conference with the Export-Import Bank group centered chiefly about their impressions as to the viability of Israel's economy. Doubts were expressed as to the willingness of labor to make concessions necessary to the enlargement of production. Stress was laid on the restrictive and guild-like monopolistic practices of some of the cooperatives. Extortionist charges for haulage were cited as an example of Histadrut's unintentional, but nonetheless serious, obstructionism. Nonetheless, on balance the group was moderately optimistic. Up until now, the chief allocations of the loan had been for irrigation pipe, trucks and other forms of transport, agricultural machinery, and communication equipment. Subsequent allocations would depend largely upon choices to be made by the Israeli authorities.

All the members of the group were of the opinion that the export control boards of the Department of Commerce had been academically rigorous in the questions raised about the pipe allocation. They pointed out that it was absurd to expect Victorian freedom of bidding and old-fashioned competition among

44. Hilldring's report to the president on July 18, 1949 is in Hilldring to secretary of state, July 25, 1949, *FRUS*, 1949, v. VI, 1249–1252; also entry of July 9, 1949.
45. Raymond A. Hare (1901–1994), deputy director, Office of Near Eastern and African Affairs, Department of State, 1948–1949. See Paul J. Hare, *Diplomatic Chronicles of the Middle East: A Biography of Ambassador Raymond A. Hare* (Lanham, MD: University Press of America, 1993).

the American suppliers and the Israeli purchasers. They had, after consultation with Hooper, sent off a strong telegram protesting against such delay in tactics, but it seemed to me, without pretending to understand the intricacies of the controversy, that the purposes of the loan would be to a considerable extent defeated if the export control authorities were not to change their policy illustrated in the pipe case.[46]

The conference with Governor Lehman was interesting but so general in its nature that it need not be recorded. The dinner for Hilldring was gay and delightful. The young Israeli officials and their wives made excellent company.

Thursday, May 12

The morning given over to Hare and to the dentist; the afternoon, to an extended staff conference [on the housing issue with Hare].

Today is notable because the Marine Guard took over from the civilians. What a relief!

Friday, May 13

Morning through luncheon, trip with Hare to Rehovot and Givat Brenner. He was visibly impressed by our visits and particularly by the personalities of Mrs. Leah Berlin at the Givat Brenner Rest Home, and by that of the [leader] of Givat Brenner.[47] In saying goodbye, he was most cordial and appreciative of what we tried to do for him.

The following is a brief summary of my several talks with Hare and my impressions of his points of view. He emphasized that he was here not to bring instructions, but to learn. In keeping with this point of view, he listened much more than he talked. Nonetheless, he disclosed views on some topics.

As to Jerusalem, Hare showed surprise that there had seemed to us to be some differences still between the White House and the Department. I explained that I was not sure this was true, but that one might deduce this from such word as that which Hilldring brought me to the effect that the president was standing squarely on November 29th. Hare admitted, of course, that the Department had gone far beyond that now.

Hare said that McGhee's role was to coordinate under the secretary the efforts towards a settlement of the refugee problem. He made clear, however, that the president's inaugural Point Four should not be interpreted to mean American expenditure in terms of freedom, but rather as pump-priming for technical and scientific research into possible projects which might directly and indirectly help to find permanent new homes for refugees. He was obviously interested in Israel's position on boundaries and was perhaps somewhat surprised

46. Half of the $35 million loan for agriculture went to the purchase of irrigation pipe for projects irrigating the Negev. See *Congressional Record*, 1950, v. 96, pt. 13, A3449.
47. Large kibbutz south of Rehovot, founded in 1928 by Jews from Poland, Lithuania, and Germany.

when I underlined this government's replies to the Department's rather vague boundary appeals.

Hare, who had been associated with Shiloah during the Second World War and who likes and admires him, spent several hours with Shiloah.[48] The latter talked mostly about the impasse with Za'im. Hare recognized the clumsiness of the PCC organization and cooperated with us in trying to find worthwhile suggestions to pass on to the Department for a strong successor to Ethridge. Hare's visit was useful to us, and should be even more useful if he should carry back to Washington the impression which he gave us here. We felt, too, that he had learned a good deal. He was sympathetic to my hopes to return for a couple of months in the fall and will, I think, use his influence if necessary to help arrange this.

With the family to the Kaplans for their dinner for the Lehmans. Goldie Meyerson was the only other guest. Afterwards, the talk was interesting but covered so largely old ground that I do not record it.

Saturday, May 14

Worked during the morning and afternoon tried to get caught up in my back reading.

A final two-hour conference with [Donald] McNeal.[49] We read through his elaborate final memorandum and listened to his explanation of the program to be followed.[50] Now he was much more encouraged about Ben-Gurion's instructions, the result of my visit to the latter the previous Sunday, than he had been at the staff conference on Thursday. He warned however that the offer of [Israeli] governmental cooperation was to be kept in the strictest secrecy and not to become known except to those already aware of it. McNeal was anxious that we be patient at seeming delays from Washington and that we should assume that his influence there would tell. It was agreed that we should channel our complaints or disappointments through him in London. Our parting was personal and cordial. He said he was particularly gratified to have the autographed photograph of Ben-Gurion and myself.

48. During World War II Hare had been second secretary in the US Embassy in Cairo working on Lend-Lease transports to the British and the Soviets, and he was convinced of the Middle East's strategic importance. Hare told Shiloah that, in his view, the Arabs were willing to forget the Palestine issue and do business with the United States, but that the refugee problem had to be solved for domestic purposes in Arab countries. *DFPI*, v. 4, d. 23.

49. Donald McNeal, European supervisor for the State Department's Office of Foreign Buildings Operations (FBO), stationed in London. After World War II the FBO expanded US representations abroad to correspond with the new US global role. The need for general updating and trends in modern architecture slowed individual projects. McNeal visited Israel for two weeks in April–May 1949 and periodically thereafter. See Jane C. Loeffler, *The Architecture of Diplomacy: Building America's Embassies* (New York: Princeton Architectural Press, 1998).

50. McNeal to Barnes, May 14, 1949, McDonald Papers, USHMM, box 7, folder 14. McNeal would later recommend that the Department pay for the repairs to the ambassador's residence (deducting a portion from the rent payments); that quality furniture for the residence be purchased from Italy and France; that a residence be purchased for the counselor of embassy (Ford); and that, though the Israeli government would aid the mission in securing office and staff housing space at acceptable rent rates, the purchase of spaces would be explored.

A long walk and talk with Potofsky at Herzliya. He accepted our invitation for dinner that night with the Ben-Gurions, and we planned to meet a little early. This we did. I then had him read the letter from the secretary outlining the Department's views as of April 26 of my suggestions of labor cooperation here.[51] He was in full agreement with those views and added that in this area of international cooperation, there need be no fear of lack of working together by CIO and AF of L. Potofsky said that he was more optimistic than before about the potential influence of American labor here even among the Mapam rank and file. He had decided, however, not to say anything to Ben-Gurion about the possibility of Mapam being brought into the government. He was impressed by the extent to which differences between Mapam and Mapai were personal and by the way in which the Mapam leaders nearly all tended to say that, "it is up to Ben-Gurion." Potofsky would limit what he had to say on the score of reconciliation to his talk with Goldie.

The talk at tea with Mr. Matthew Schoenwald, nephew of Mr. David Dubinsky,[52] consisted mostly of his emphasis upon the impossibility of Israel remaining neutral as between East and West. He cited the experience of American labor as proof of this impossibility. I was chiefly interested in his interactions because of my feeling that they in part reflected Dubinsky's position.

The dinner for the Ben-Gurions, the Lehmans, the Abramses, Goldie Meyerson, Mrs. Sharett, Potofsky, and the family required adroit management but was, I think, a success. Everyone arrived on time except the Lehmans, who were late because of his broadcast to the States. This delay and the inevitable slowness of the service caused me to be nervous about our having time for the private talks afterwards, which several of the guests expected.

After dinner, I arranged for Lehman to sit with Ben-Gurion. They talked at first about the possibility of an international loan and then continued on other subjects, so long that I became fearful lest no one else would have a chance to talk to the prime minister. Finally, after a half hour or so, I broke up this tête-a-tête by saying to the governor that I had to talk business for a few minutes with the prime minister.

We spoke first about the possibility of his meeting Za'im. His answer, as previously, was that he saw no advantage in this unless previously an agreement had been reached involving the Syrian withdrawal to the international frontier. I followed up with the suggestion that such a meeting of the heads of the two states might, as had been indicated, lead to peace discussions. The prime minister thought this improbable. I then asked Ben-Gurion whether he did not think that the latest Bunche proposal of compromise was satisfactory. This was for the Syrians to withdraw beyond the international frontier, the Israelis also

51. Outlined in entry of March 17, 1949.
52. Mathew Schoenwald [formerly Szejnwald] (1915–1993), vice president, ILGWU. Dubinsky had arranged a visa for him to come to the United States from Lodz in 1935.

to withdraw westward but to have the right to keep civilian administrators in the area, thus demilitarized, which would remain subject to UN supervision.[53] Apparently Ben-Gurion had not heard or had not taken in the details of this compromise suggestion. He asked, therefore, for an opportunity to study it. But he seemed impressed that this might possibly be a way out. I again underlined the potential advantages of such a partial agreement in its effects on Lausanne.

> McDonald reported, "Showing strong dislike and suspicion of Za'im personally and characterizing [the] latter as 'little Mussolini,' [the] prime minister said he is willing to meet Za'im after Syrian withdrawal beyond [the] international frontier but see[s] no advantage [in an] earlier meeting." Ben-Gurion, McDonald said, was "deeply interested" in Bunche's proposal and "seemed impressed by [the] Department's interpretation and by emphasis that it would give Israel substance and facility [of a] general settlement at Lausanne." He commented, "For first time I feel there is even chance [of an] armistice agreement [between] Israel–Syria."[54]

Then I brought Ben Abrams over for his opportunity to talk.[55] At the same time, I suggested to the governor that he give Potofsky the opportunity the latter desired to discuss the possibility of Lehman's cooperation.

Monday, May 16

After not unexpected delays, the Abramses and we started off with Shalom for Jerusalem. They were very excited by the unfolding landscape culminating in the Judean Hills and Jerusalem itself. After a brief visit to the King David with its wonderful view of the Old City wall and a bite of lunch in a magnificent suite of our friends on the third floor, we went off to Novomeysky's.

The rest of the day was quiet and uneventful except for the visit on behalf of Rabbi Zelig Reuven Bengis, chairman of the Bet Din [rabbinical court] of the Jewish Orthodox community,[56] of two younger men, one a rabbi and the

53. Bunche had told the Syrian UN delegation that this was the best arrangement they were likely to get and that they would likely get worse terms if the question went to the Security Council. Austin to secretary of state, no. 587, May 12, 1949, FRUS, 1949, v. VI, 1000–1001; DFPI, v. 3, d. 303–305.

54. McDonald to secretary of state, no. 371, May 16, 1949, NARA, RG 59, 501.BB Palestine, box 2125, folder 1.

55. McDonald wrote Abrams the following month: "If you should at any time need a lift, simply recall to your mind the following message, which I assure you is authentic: Paula [Ben-Gurion] on her own initiative told me the other evening at the Sharon . . . that her husband regarded you as the ablest and finest American he had met. Paula did not bother to exempt even the American ambassador from this comparison! This tribute is the more noteworthy because [Ben-Gurion] is not free with his compliments." McDonald to Benjamin Abrams, June 28, 1949, McDonald Papers, Columbia University, box 6, folder 2.

56. Rabbi Zelig Reuven Bengis (1864–1953), born near Vilna; prodigious scholar even as a child; emigrated to Palestine, 1937, to become chief rabbi of the small, anti-Zionist ultra-Orthodox community in Jerusalem; spoke to the UN in 1947 opposing creation of a Jewish state but favoring expanded immigration of Jewish refugees to Palestine and internationalization of Jerusalem as a Holy City; called for the ultra-Orthodox not to participate in Knesset elections.

other an interpreter. Speaking in Yiddish, the rabbi first apologized for his chief's absence, saying that he had suddenly become ill this afternoon. Then they gave me their leader's blessing and asked me if they might deliver his message. They spoke of my "interest in and knowledge of" Jewish Orthodoxy and expressed the hope that I would influence the Israeli government towards a more Orthodox policy. I demurred that, while I was interested, I could not claim to have knowledge, and that it is beyond [my] province to undertake to influence governmental policy. Continuing, they said that because of the lack of Orthodoxy in the government and in the administration and control of Jewish funds, Orthodoxy was having a difficult struggle. At the beginning of their appeal to me, they referred to the fact that Cyrus, not a Jew, had been decisive in the rebuilding of the Temple. They added that there are two temples, the visible one and that which is the soul. They felt that I could and would contribute towards the building of the latter. Gradually, they worked round to the need for visitors' visas and exit visas. I said I could be helpful with the former but could do absolutely nothing about the latter since this was a matter exclusively for Israeli authorities. I asked them about [the] distinction between their group and the Agudat and the Mizrachi, to which they replied that these matters were so delicate that they would have to be left to the chief rabbi himself. I said I would welcome the explanation later.

When we entered the room from the porch, Ben Abrams moved forward to meet the Orthodox. Their appearance and manner brought back childhood memories of his own Orthodox home and caused him to decide to take home to his Orthodox mother some religious objects, which had been blessed by a famous Orthodox rabbi. The rest of the evening spent at the Novomeysky's since I discovered that I was, after all, not invited to dinner at the Berl Lockers'.

Tuesday, May 17

Most of the morning spent at the consulate general with Burdett. English[57] was present during most of the talk, but took no part. Indeed, when at one point Burdett spoke of "we" having some new ideas and I asked him who "we" were, he was embarrassingly silent. Later, English explained that he was never consulted on any political matters. To my great enlightenment, Burdett let me study the working paper [on Jerusalem] submitted by the US group to the PCC April 15.[58]

The Department in a subsequent telegram approved [the] working paper in principle as a sound basic approach and expressed the hope that it may be made the basis of work of [the] PCC in preference to [the] French draft, with following suggested modification. Approves idea of compulsory arbitration of international tribunal, which is to have jurisdiction over violations of administrator's

---

57. Possibly Clifton P. English, US consul at Basra.
58. See entry of April 15, 1949.

authority [in] either zone. Court decisions should be for present purposes "we now think" legally binding. Department understands that UN will bear expense of administrator and staff and guard, and of international tribunal. Local authorities to bear expenses of local zone and each its cost of participation [in a] mixed tribunal.[59]

On May 11, the General Assembly voted 37 to 12 to admit Israel into the United Nations. The US, the USSR, and France voted in favor. Great Britain and Turkey abstained. The Israelis argued during the debate that they had done their best under the circumstances to bring their policies into conformity with UN resolutions.[60] The Arab delegations in Lausanne were disillusioned after the vote. Ethridge, who had hoped to use UN membership as a negotiating chip with Israel, complained to Acheson that US sponsorship of the membership vote "in absence of assurances at Lausanne requested by us has weakened our position and muffled my voice."[61]

Truman believed that membership, once resolved, would make Israel more cooperative on outstanding questions of peace.[62] Pressure from the State Department on the refugee issue resumed after Israel's admission, and this time included the call for Israel to begin actual repatriation to areas outside the Israeli boundaries as defined in the November 29 resolution, including Western Galilee. Acheson called this "concrete proof of Israel's desire for a lasting settlement [that would] provide the impetus to bring the Lausanne talks to a successful conclusion."[63]

A draft of the PCC's Jerusalem plan appeared at the Lausanne Conference on May 18.[64] In response to Cardinal Spellman's complaints to Truman of April 29, Truman replied on May 19 that the UN resolution of December 11 as written was not practical. The Holy Places, not the day-to-day lives of Jerusalem's inhabitants, concerned the international community. The president supported Israeli-Jordanian responsibility for a large share of municipal functions under UN supervision, with primary UN responsibility for the protection of access to the Holy Places.[65]

As we were talking, Burdett threw off the idea that there might be a new solution, in effect [an] Israeli trusteeship for Arab Palestine. It was at this point he said that "we," apparently Burdett, had been thinking of such a scheme. He had been led to this by the feeling that [the] interests of Arabs in Palestine under Abdullah were being sacrificed, as for example, a) railroad settlement

---

59. Acheson to PCC [through legation in Switzerland], no. 566, May 2, 1949, *FRUS*, 1949, v. VI, 967–968.

60. Elath to Acheson, May 11, 1949, *FRUS*, 1949, v. VI, 996–998.

61. PCC [through Troutman] to secretary of state, no. 150, May 12, 1949, *FRUS*, 1949, v. VI, 1003; Ethridge to secretary of state, no. 157, May 18, 1949, *FRUS*, 1949, v. VI, 1028–1029.

62. Elath to Sharett, May 10, 1949, *DFPI*, v. 4, d. 17.

63. Acheson to US delegation Lausanne, May 12, 1949, *FRUS*, 1949, v. VI, pp. 1004–1005; Acheson to Elath, *FRUS*, 1949, v. VI, 1021–1022. Also Elath to Ministry of Foreign Affairs, May 11, 1949, *DFPI*, v. 4, d. 19; Elath to Sharett, May 20, 1949, *DFPI*, v. 4, d. 31.

64. Preliminary Draft, Com. Jer/W.18, May 18, 1949, *FRUS*, 1949, v. VI, 1023–1028.

65. Truman to Spellman, May 19, 1949, *FRUS*, 1949, v. VI, 1016–1017.

[concerning access to and from] Jerusalem; and, b) Colonel Dayan's refusal to admit Arabs within the triangle to cultivate their land across the border as defined in the armistice terms, except for the crops now being harvested.

Over to the King David for lunch with the Abramses; found them late, and lunched instead with the Rosenblooms. I was over to the Russian compound and the former [British] government hospital well in time for the organization of the procession that was to march to the platform reserved for speakers and guests of honor for the ceremony marking the opening of the Hebrew University-Hadassah Medical School.[66] It was an impressive, dignified service.

During the ceremony, I chatted occasionally with Ben-Gurion, at whose right I sat, and with Mrs. Halprin at my right. Thanks to the sensible procedure of not translating the talks, all of which but Ben-Gurion's were short, the ceremony was concluded by twenty minutes of six. For the record, I should add that my only interpolation in my talk was the following: "I, too, shall speak English, but English as it has been 'improved' in the United States." This quip was more generally understood than I thought would be the case. When I had finished, Ben-Gurion commented, referring to the above: "The last part of your speech was 'improved' by the Department of State." I laughingly told him that he was mistaken, because the Department had not seen my text in advance.

McDonald's remarks were as follows:

> *This is an auspicious occasion. The opening in Jerusalem of the Hebrew University-Hadassah Medical School, in which I have so long been deeply [and] personally interested, is a promise to Israel and its neighbors of more than physical healing; it foreshadows and brings nearer the day when Jew and Arab will freely work together for the advancement of all the peoples in the Middle East. . . .*
>
> *The world needs now as never before the reconciling influences of the constructive sciences. Of all these influences, that of medicine most directly tends to draw men together. The advance of this medical school will thus be welcomed by men of good will everywhere. It is my hope and prayer that, sooner than now seems possible, Jewish and Arab doctors, students and patients will be integral parts of this institution grown to proportions sufficient to serve directly and through related Jewish and Arab institutions the whole of the Middle East.[67]*

After the usual photographs and prolonged autograph-giving, a brief visit to the general reception, the Rosenblooms and Ruth and I went to the Agronsky tea. There, Ben-Gurion spent most of his time examining the host's interesting library. In the course of this, Ben-Gurion recommended in the strongest terms Robert Travers Hereford's *The Pharisees* [1924] as the best thing that has been written on this subject.

66. The opening ceremony took place on the temporary grounds just outside the Old City that housed the school until it could be moved to Mount Scopus.
67. Extracts of remarks made by James G. McDonald, May 17, 1949, McDonald Papers, USHMM, box 7, folder 14.

To the Novomeyskys to rest for a little while before the Locker dinner. Others present were Leon Simon and his wife, [Marian] Greenberg and [Rose] Halprin. During dinner I half-jokingly took Mrs. Halprin to task for having twice bothered Ben-Gurion personally about her lost ticket for the parade on Independence Day. She was intrigued to know where I had learned about this, but stood her ground that her twenty-year friendship with Ben-Gurion justified her appealing to him as a friend, even though he was prime minister. She is intelligent, and for a Hadassah gal, personally attractive. Mrs. Greenberg began to press me about the visitors' visas for the young agricultural leaders, but I stopped her by telling her that I was doing everything that could be done. All the latter part of the evening was given over to the discussion of Jewish topics, religion, rabbinical "leadership" in the US.

Wednesday, May 18

[Back in Tel Aviv.] Somewhat more than an hour and a half with Oscar Gass.[68] During the larger part of the time, Ford was present and during the last few minutes, Ben Abrams. It was an extremely interesting and worthwhile session. Following are the main points Gass made, set down not in a carefully organized fashion, but as completely as I can recall them, to be used as the basis of a possible despatch to the Department:

1) As compared with his previous experiences here in 1945 and 1947, Gass finds conditions today more hectic, more centralized, and more confusing. This, he thought, was in part because of the nature of the changes in the problem, its increased immediacy and vastly extended scope, and partly the result of the personalities most directly concerned at the top level.

2) Gass regards Kaplan as the ablest of all the men in the government. The extraordinary degree of centralization in the treasury Gass attributed primarily to the fact that governmental operations in nearly all the departments here are still on a provisional basis of at most two to three months, sometimes six weeks, instead of an annual budgetary basis, as with us.[69] This means necessarily that nearly all the departments must come to the treasury every month or two or three months to get approvals of the next short-term period and also to get approval currently for individual operations. Thus, the treasury plays a much larger part in the day-to-day work of all the departments than it does in a government such as the United States. A second reason for this treasury centralization is the superiority of Kaplan's knowledge and judgment over most of his colleagues, even in the fields of their special interests. Moreover, Kaplan has extraordinary capacity to

68. See entry of April 18, 1949.

69. During the Mandate period, the Jewish Agency prepared an annual work plan and a corresponding budget. The 1949 budget would have been discussed and approved by spring 1948, but the second half of 1948 and 1949 brought war, mass immigration, and other unexpected developments. Short-term budgets were necessary for the time being.

learn from the people who talk to him and from memoranda submitted to him, which he reads critically and understandingly. A third, but the least important, reason for such centralization is Kaplan's willingness to take responsibility and perhaps the tendency to prefer to do this rather than leave matters to lesser men in other departments.

3) On the question of monopolistic tendencies by cooperative organizations, Gass said that there are manifestations here of many of the same symptoms which marked the medieval guilds at the height of their power. His account of the Egged Bus Drivers Cooperative was illustrative.[70] This cooperative, before it would consider admitting new members to meet the increasing strain both on drivers and passengers, decided to distribute its surplus among its members, which amounted to a substantial total per head (the figure mentioned was either 3,000 pounds or 3,000 dollars). Such savings were then used by the individuals in various ways, including speculative purchases of land, etc. The problem of breaking such monopolistic practices or setting up competing bodies, Gass thinks, is extremely difficult, though not necessarily impossible. Fortunately, the trucking organizations are potentially more competitive, though at present they are extortionist to a degree. The government can, however, by allocating new trucks to new companies, to veterans as individuals or to groups, and to individual industries for their own operation, make headway against the current extortionist charges.

4) Kaplan and other men in the government are encouraged at the prospect of making clear to the workers in the "closed" industries the need for higher productivity at the same wages if the immigrants are to be housed. But Gass admitted that in practice it was going to be extremely difficult to secure higher productivity until the government has simultaneously succeeded in reducing what the workers regard, with much justification, as the excessive profits of traders, merchants and importers.

5) To make headway against costs of food and clothing, Gass thinks that the government must impose a utility program on most manufacturers of articles essential to all people such as clothing, shoes, etc., and also impose rigid price controls on these items. Gass feels that if, however, the attempt to control prices is extended throughout the whole gamut of articles used in this economy, the effort will break down of its own weight. The OPA[71] at home failed, and here, the thin layer of competent administrators would be inadequate. Once the government was able to assure the workers that their essential needs could be met at a certain total cost, which would be not more, and probably less, than current costs, it could then with a reasonable chance of success appeal to the workers for larger production at present rates of pay.

---

70. Founded in 1933 as a driver-owned transport cooperative.
71. Office of Price Administration, created in the United States in August 1941 by executive order; instituted price controls and rationing; officially abolished in March 1947.

6) As to housing, Gass did not say much. He was interested in a contract recently let involving about fifty workers in which they agreed to take about sixty percent of their wages in cash at existing rates and the rest in an equity in the houses under construction. Through this device, it is hoped to reduce the immediate expenditure for labor and at the same time to give an added incentive to higher productivity. We did not go into other questions of housing.

7) Gass stressed that, increasingly, the authorities were impressed that the number one problem was employment for the newcomers, in and out of the camps, and for the demobilized soldiers. Gass estimates that demobilization at present might be 25% from the peak. This includes, of course, women, married soldiers with dependents, et al. Normally, to encourage the required increase in employment, a government would take measures, some of which could be expected to be directly or indirectly inflationary in their effects. This government, Gass argued, could not afford inflationary measures, even to reduce unemployment. He, therefore, personally was opposed to using idle labor on roads or other capital work except to the very minimum, because this involved expenditure with no immediate increase in productivity in terms of usable goods. The country is simply too poor to put its money now into these long-term improvements. On the contrary, efforts should be concentrated on putting labor into agricultural production and into as many other forms of production for use as is possible. Only through such increase in the production of things to be used can headway be made towards price stabilization or reduction.

8) As to railroads, Gass favors the immediate construction of the required deviations at Tulkarm and Qalqilya in order to put the line from Haifa to Lydda into prompt operation, and to do the same with whatever improvements are necessary to get the trains started on the line from Jerusalem to Lydda and Tel Aviv.[72] The railroad enthusiasts are less anxious about the deviations referred to, because they fear that the government will then not be interested in the more basic Hadera route. Gass denies that the government is cool towards this route. The chief advantage of the railways would be to reduce the pressure of trucking on the highways in the carriage of heavy goods. It might also be one factor among others in preparing the way for the reduction of the present extortionist trucking charges.

72. Tulkarm and Qalqilya were just east of the Israel-Transjordan armistice line in the Tulkarm-Nablus-Jenin triangle. The armistice line cut across the road and rail network (Tulkarm had been a major rail junction since 1908), necessitating the construction of bypasses on the Israeli side of the boundary. See David Newman, *Boundaries in Flux: The Green Line Boundary Between Israel and the West Bank* (Durham, UK: International Boundaries Research Unit, 1995), 8–9.

In answer to my request for some concluding generalizations, Gass gave them somewhat along the following lines:

1) Here on the spot, he realized, as he had not been able to do from Washington, the determination of the people to carry through, no matter at what cost, the unrestricted immigration program. Hence, he was convinced that the open-door policy would be maintained to the utmost extremity.
2) He was amazed here to learn what seemingly impossible amounts had been spent by the government on its war effort. Had anyone suggested a year ago that so much could be taken from the national economy, past, present and prospective, he would have been considered fantastic. The war had been paid for through incredible depletion in the people's savings, in their and the government's foreign balances, in borrowing against the future, and in other ways.
3) Gass had been surprised, too, to note the very considerable amount of foreign capital, mostly in goods, which were coming into the country. Larger amounts would come if their encouragement were better organized, but in any case the capital inflow could be expected to continue.
4) In broadest terms, Gass expects that Israel's problems of production and absorption will be solved. The methods used will be uneven, often badly organized or at cross-purposes, but no one will starve, and gradually more and more will be employed and housed. Parenthetically, he said the housing rate, to be adequate, should be between three and three-and-a-half times the present rate. The course of development would be uneven, not neat or pretty, but the essential ends would be served. Already it is clear that the country is growing steadily in economic strength. Assuming the avoidance of the renewal of war or other catastrophe, this increase in economic strength may be expected to continue.

On the way out to the gate, I urged Gass to quote me privately in Washington to the effect that I hoped such technical restrictive administrative measures as had threatened to block the shipment of irrigation pipe would not be allowed to so delay the coming into effect of the Export-Import Bank loan as to make it of substantially less value than it would be if the proceeds were to be quickly available. Gass asked me when I expected to be home. I said I hoped to be there during September and October. Gass kindly agreed to take some of our mail, to be airposted in Paris.

McDonald wrote Acheson on May 20 regarding the economy and its political effects.

[The] wave of anti-government demonstrations by discharged soldiers and idle new immigrants [is] continuing and was publicly linked in [the]

Knesset [on] May 19 with [the] Israel Communist Party, which was accused of organizing and financing these demonstrations, and which did not, repeat not, deny [the] accusation. . . .

Government circles and press continue to highlight austerity measures. . . . It appears wages will be frozen at present levels and perhaps voluntary reductions may follow. . . .

Jewish Agency announced 32 foreign enterprises had been and are in course of being established here involving investments of 1,617,000 [Israeli pounds]; 13 are textile and 6 building materials and metals. The new investments represent prospects from Latin America, South Africa, England, US, and Western Europe.

Annual rate of nearly 300,000 immigrants continued through April. 55,950 lodged in 24 transit camps as of May 7. Effort being made [to] persuade kibbutzim and colonies [to] accept immigrants on employment basis (too early to ascertain whether old-time policy of kibbutzim will admit this radical change in spite of exhortation by [the] Prime Minister).[73]

Thursday, May 19

Teatime, Mr. and Mrs. [Knox] Helm came for a courtesy call.[74] I liked them both at first and her at the end. She is a friendly, homey person. Both of them were of course primarily interested now in housing possibilities. Apparently, despite the prolonged efforts of the representatives of the Board of Works who preceded the minister to Tel Aviv, he was still houseless and would have to remain in the Kaete Dan until the end of June when the small house next to the Andruses would be ready. But this would be only a stopgap.

McDonald confided his sense of irony to Eddie and Bluma Jacobson the next day. "It is hard . . . for British diplomats . . . to find that in Israel, where only a few years ago they were the rulers, they must put up with inadequate and noisy quarters."[75]

My unfavorable impression of Helm came when they were leaving. I asked him to come in to see my study, and as we were looking at the maps, I said quite casually that the large one of the Jerusalem area would be useful to him. At once he became the tight-lipped traditional diplomat saying almost sharply, "Oh, no, I shall have nothing to do with Jerusalem. That is all for the PCC." I half-jokingly replied that I was willing to bet that presently he would change

73. McDonald to secretary of state, no. 386, May 20, 1949, McDonald Papers, USHMM, box 7, folder 14. On the government's disappointment with the kibbutzim concerning their absorption of immigrants see Hakohen, *Immigrants in Turmoil*, 201–205.

74. Knox Helm (1893–1964), career British diplomat; served in Addis Ababa, 1937–1939; Washington, DC, 1939–1942; Ankara, 1942–1946; and Budapest, 1946–1947; British chargé and later minister to Tel Aviv, 1949–1951.

75. McDonald to Eddie Jacobson, May 20, 1949, McDonald Papers, Columbia University, box 13, folder 10. Helm's very jaded complaints concerning Tel Aviv are in Helm to Bevin, May 23, 1949, Yapp, ed., *British Documents on Foreign Affairs*, pt. IV, Ser. B, v. 8, 27–29.

his mind, but he with complete seriousness kept insisting that it would be outside his jurisdiction to raise any question about Jerusalem with HaKirya. We shall see.

Farewell dinner at the Abramses. Evening was lovely, and everybody had a good time. Both he and she, she somewhat more obviously, were emotionally stirred at the party.

Friday, May 20

Before lunch came Mr. Binyamin Mintz and an interpreter to try to persuade me to give some sort of an endorsement to Agudat's plan to complete the purchase of a large farm in the southern "religious triangle," where some 500 immigrant children could be brought up in the Torah and the traditional Jewish way of life.[76] They explained that the pressure was now so great that the Jewish Agency had, at its meeting this week, decided that it could no longer carefully allocate immigrant children to those particular types of communities for which their upbringing had prepared them. Hence the additional need for the Agudat farm. In reply, I explained the obvious UJA difficulty, but said that if they would write me about the plan, I would carefully consider whether I could write a reply which would be of some use to them.

Saturday, May 21

Up before seven and worked on the McGhee letter. Drafted a telegram as preliminary to a fuller despatch. McGhee's analysis seemed to me to have much merit but at the end to leave the poor refugees about where they were.

On April 26 George McGhee completed a lengthy analysis of the refugee problem.[77] McDonald received it three weeks later by pouch.[78] McGhee filled in the details of the State Department's policy recommendation of March 15, which assumed the existence of 750,000 refugees and called for a settlement that involved both repatriation and resettlement.[79]

76. See entry of November 11, 1948. Mintz had been the Agudat representative to the Jewish Agency's Rescue Committee in Europe, 1942–1946; worked to have Jewish children who had been rescued by gentiles in Europe sent to Palestine rather than to the United States; elected to Knesset, 1949 as member of United Religious Front; sought to have Orthodox-raised children who were in Israeli reception camps receive Orthodox education and to live in Orthodox settlements immune from state interference. Emunah Nachmany Gafny, *Dividing Hearts: The Removal of Jewish Children from Gentile Families in Poland in the Immediate Post Holocaust Years* (Jerusalem: Yad Vashem, 2009), 143–148; and Ze'ev Drory, *The Israeli Defense Force and the Foundation of Israel: Utopia in Uniform* (New York: Routledge, 2005), 173–178.
77. Memorandum by McGhee to secretary of state, April 26, 1949, *FRUS*, 1949, v. VI, 934–944.
78. See McDonald to McGhee, No. 88, May 24, 1949, McDonald Papers, USHMM, box 7, folder 14.
79. Policy Paper Prepared in Department of State, March 15, 1949, *FRUS*, 1949, v. VI, 828–842.

McGhee discussed the need for Israel to resettle at least 200,000 refugees "as a precedent to any ultimate and satisfactory solution of the refugee problem;" the need to prioritize refugees who had lived in predominantly Arab areas that Israel had conquered in the war, such as Western Galilee, that were not part of the Jewish territory as agreed by the UN on November 29; and the need for UN developmental aid, provided in part by the United States and Great Britain, for Arab states that would accept large numbers of refugees for resettlement. These countries included Syria, Iraq, and Jordan.

Recognizing the political difficulties, McGhee insisted that "continuing and vigorous pressure will have to be exerted on Israel and the Arab states if their agreement . . . is to be secured." The PCC was to exercise this pressure in the Lausanne talks while adding the necessary technical experts. He expected that the financial outlay from the United States would continue for three years.

At eleven, Messrs. [Adolph] Held,[80] [Louis] Hollander,[81] and a group of ten men and women, the men constituting the Jewish Labor Committee, spent over an hour at the house.[82] The talk was general, and I did not read to them as I intended the Department's letter.[83] They promised to come back and report to me at the end of their stay. It seemed to me that most of them were thinking in terms of what Amalgamated[84] could do here, rather than of what the trade union movement could do. Hollander appeared to be particularly suspicious of Mapam as either communist or potentially so.[85]

Afternoon tea we had as guests Mr. and Mrs. William Fondiller[86] and Mr. and Mrs. Harry F. Fischbach.[87] Both men are here in connection with a project to extend the work of the Hebrew Institute of Technology (Technion).[88]

80. Adolph Held (1885–1969), Polish-born news editor of Jewish Daily *Forward* [*Forverts*], 1907–1912; communal and labor leader; socialist member of the New York City Board of Aldermen; welfare director of International Ladies' Garment Workers' Union after 1945.

81. Louis Hollander (1893–1980), Polish-born Jewish trade union leader; vice president of Amalgamated Clothing Workers of America, 1932–1976; head of New York State CIO in 1949; strongly anticommunist.

82. Jewish Labor Committee, New York-based organization founded in 1934 to promote labor union interest in working-class Jewish communities; supportive of Israel despite its Bundist roots; organized fact-finding delegation to Israel, May–July 1949.

83. Refers to Acheson's letter of April 26, 1949, described in entry of March 17, 1949.

84. Amalgamated Clothing Workers of America, founded in 1914, led by Sidney Hillman, 1914–1946; then by Jacob Potofsky, 1946–1972.

85. See Hollander's comments that were critical of Histadrut's power. JTA *Bulletin*, July 21, 1949.

86. William Fondiller (1885–1975), Belorussian-born electrical engineer and important inventor; vice president of Bell Laboratories; redesigned the telephone into a compact single unit; long associated with the Haifa Technion; in Israel to receive an honorary doctorate from that institution, 1949.

87. Harry F. Fischbach (1891–1977), Romanian-born New York philanthropist and financial contributor to Technion whose gifts helped build the department of electrical engineering.

88. Originally known by the German name "Technikum," founded in Haifa in 1912 as a Zionist project to provide Jews with a university education in science and technology; expanded with Israeli independence to include faculties of electrical, mechanical, and aeronautical engineering.

Again the talk was general but more intimate than it had been in the morning.

In the evening the first concert of the orchestra under Izler Solomon[89] with Jennie Tourel as soloist.[90] Following the second Brahms, Tourel sang arias from Purcell, *Dido and Aeneas*, and from Rossini's *The Barber of Seville*. The second half of the program was made up of three tone poems for voice and orchestra by Ravel, Sibelius's *Pojhola's Daughter*, and a piece by Toch. The Fords, who were our guests, seemed to enjoy much the concert.

Sunday, May 22

Sunday early morning got through an accumulation of papers and then to the Herzliya beach for an hour and a half. Afternoon, more papers. Tea at the Bradys' and still more papers, until time for a bite of supper and the opera. This, the third performance of Offenbach's *Tales of Hoffmann*, was a spirited and engrossing performance. At the end, after vigorous applause for the performance, a large part of the audience turned and cheered Madame de Phillipe, who took the bows gracefully from the front row in the balcony.

Monday, May 23

Hard at work all morning achieving a distant view of a clear desk. Rabbi Yitzhak-Meir Levin[91] and an interpreter came to talk about the imminent visit of young FDR.[92] They had had a cable from the New York representative of Agudat that FDR had accepted the chairmanship of a Committee for a Children's Village here. Not unnaturally, they were anxious to remind FDR of his responsibilities, and to utilize his visit for publicity purposes. They wanted me to agree to bring the young man to the rabbi's office soon after his arrival. I said I would try to do so. An interesting exchange during the conversation was occasioned by the rabbi's remark that I was known to be "an authority on and sympathetic with Orthodoxy." I demurred on the first count and said that, as to the second, he would understand that I had to be neutral as among the several parties in Israel. He replied that he knew this but that he was glad to know that in my heart I was sympathetic to their cause.

---

89. Izler Solomon (1910–1987), American conductor; guest conductor of Israel Philharmonic, 1949.

90. Jennie Tourel [née Davidovich] (1900–1973), Belorussian-born mezzo-soprano; fled with family to Danzig and then to Paris during the Russian Revolution; then to Lisbon and the United States in 1940 just before the German occupation of France.

91. Still minister of welfare in Ben-Gurion's first and second elected cabinets, representing the United Religious Front.

92. See entry of December 9, 1948.

A pleasant but not reportable visit from David Woodward, who is here as press attaché to the British legation. Padberg brought over the new vice consul, Charles McVicker, who impressed us all as an attractive young man.[93]

Tuesday, May 24

Brief session with Barnes after breakfast. Discussion with Padberg about the agricultural instructors whom the Jewish Agency wishes to send to the States. We agreed upon a procedure by which Haifa would be asked to grant the visas and Washington to check on the activities of the visitors.

Saw Peter Bergson for about forty minutes. After an informal discussion about housing, he talked interestingly about the current report that there may after all be no written constitution for Israel. I had previously heard this possibility from the chief clerk at the Knesset. Bergson said that Ben-Gurion was the leader in this way of thinking (it could hardly yet be called a movement). Ben-Gurion's idea is that it would be disadvantageous and might be even worse for the country to be faced with the necessity of making decisions about religious questions and the role of the rabbis and traditional Jewish law, issues which might split the country wide open.[94] Bergson admitted that there was merit in this point of view, but added that his party [Herut] would oppose it and, moreover, was going to submit a draft constitution of its own. Thus does politics make reason silent!

Bergson's real purpose in planning to see me was to urge the prompt granting of a visitor's visa to Aryeh Ben-Eliezer, a member of the Freedom [Herut] Party in the Knesset.[95] Ben-Eliezer had been detained by the British on suspicion of terrorism but had not been brought to trial. Apparently, because of

93. Charles P. McVicker, third secretary and vice consul; appointed to Tel Aviv mission on April 12, 1949.

94. The November 1947 UN partition resolution called for the prospective Jewish and Arab states in Palestine to adopt constitutions by October 1, 1948. Israel's Declaration of Independence of May 14, 1948, promised that Israel would do so, but war made it impossible. The election of January 25, 1949, was for a constituent assembly that was to draft a constitution, but this assembly, which named itself the Knesset on February 16, served as a legislature. Because of the rapidly evolving nature of the new state and its needs, Ben-Gurion was ambivalent concerning a written constitution. In particular it would split Orthodox and secular Jews over the issue of religious law. Orthodox leaders insisted that the laws of Judaism be the laws of Israel, particularly with regard to the family. Ben-Gurion tried to meet them halfway, offering Saturday as the official day of rest and autonomy for educational institutions, but he did not allay Orthodox concerns. Israeli leaders worried about a *Kulturkampf* over the issue. The British model of unwritten constitutional development was adopted instead. See Philippa Strum, "The Road Not Taken: Constitutional Non-Decision Making in 1948–1950 and Its Impact on Civil Liberties in Israeli Political Culture," in Troen and Lucas, eds., *Israel: The First Decade of Independence*, 83–104; Nir Kedar, "Ben-Gurion's Opposition to a Written Constitution," *Journal of Modern Jewish Studies* 12, no. 1 (March 2013): 1–16.

95. Aryeh Ben-Eliezer (1913–1970), Vilna-born Revisionist Zionist leader; emigrated to Palestine, 1920; at the outbreak of World War II he went to the United States, where he worked with Peter Bergson; returned to Palestine in 1943 and joined the Irgun; arrested and exiled by British, 1944; involved in arms smuggling from Europe; returned to Israel, 1948; founding member of Herut.

this detention and his membership in the Irgun, the consulate had felt impelled to ask Washington to make the decision.

Going beyond this particular case, Bergson argued that it was not sound for the Department to query people or to hold up their visitors' visas on the ground that they had been members of the Irgun. This organization had striven to overthrow a "foreign" government, and not their own government. It was against this latter action that the American law, argued Bergson, was meant to apply. Moreover, account should be taken of the fact that the Herut was the one group which was more avowedly pro-American than any other in Israel. Without telling Bergson so, I was impressed by his presentation. I promised to discuss the matter with the consul promptly and to call Bergson on Friday.

At teatime came David Courtney (Roy Elston) and his wife. As [did] similar sessions, this one lasted over two hours. Again, I was strikingly impressed by the versatility and accuracy of Courtney's mind. With Hooper listening in, we traversed a wide gamut. The following are the main points:

1) Courtney rather surprisingly was not unsympathetic towards Colonel Za'im. On the contrary, he recognized that Sasson, who had spoken to us a couple of hours recently in criticism of the Syrian dictator, had been influenced by the fact that Za'im did not belong to his favorite group in Syria. Courtney added that Sasson was more Arab in his thinking than Jewish. He thought, too, that perhaps Turkey was ambitious to work out some arrangement with Syria for the extension of Turkish influence in the Aleppo area, and hence Yalçin's recent article in a Turkish magazine suggesting closer Syrian-Turkish relations. Meantime, Courtney said that of course France was seeking to recover something of its traditional position in Syria. He added that it was stupid of the French to try to advance themselves by hitting at the British.

2) Courtney spoke in a friendly manner about the new British minister [Sir Knox Helm], whom he knows, but not well. He regards him as a competent official but one whose record discloses nothing strikingly original. Commenting on my report about Helm's reaction to my large map of the Jerusalem area, Courtney said that Helm had probably had specific instructions to be rigidly correct and to eschew all controversial issues so far as this is possible.

3) As to the Israeli-Jordanian negotiations, Courtney had the impression from HaKirya that these were going better. He added that he had no specific data on which to base such a conclusion. In striking contrast to this feeling was the telegram from Amman of the 23rd in which Stabler reported that Jordan was stiffening in its attitude in part because of the conviction that, given the armistice, Israel could not take up arms to impose its will.

4) In answer to Ford's question, Courtney said that the negotiations between Mapam and Mapai were continuing but he did not believe the gap could be bridged because Mapam wanted the Ministry of Defense. This difference was the more insuperable because of the sharp contrast in the two parties' plans for the army of the future. Mapam thought in terms of a perpetuation of the Palmach organization and tradition, while Mapai envisions a unified national force.

6) As to the views of *Al-HaMishmar*, Courtney said these were dictated by the Mapam party command. Sneh he had lately found less leftish and willing to recognize that, for the time being at least, foreign capital and private initiative should be encouraged.[96]

7) Courtney was particularly interesting about the possibility of no new constitution. He thought that the support for this was rather broad. Not only Ben-Gurion but also Goldie and Kaplan favored delay. On the other hand, Joseph and some of the other Mapai leaders thought the issue should be faced squarely. Courtney personally deplored the possibility of [a] *Kulturkampf* at this time [that] might deeply divide the country. He recognized that Leo Kohn's draft was excellent and that it had not included more concessions with the Orthodox bloc than a man of Kohn's predilections would feel to be absolutely necessary.[97]

8) But the most exciting point in Courtney's long talk was the disclosure that Ben-Gurion and the JNF were working together on a program for the repatriation of perhaps as many as 300,000 or more Arab refugees. These, according to the information, would include those from the Gaza-Rafah strip [textbox 11.1] if and when that area was turned back [*sic*] to Israel. Apparently, too, the JNF is planning to help the returning refugees to modernize their industry and in this way to enable them to establish themselves with about 1/3 the land previously used in the looser form of cultivation. Courtney, on the other hand, recognized that there were strong forces here genuinely so fearful of the return of the refugees that they would oppose it with the greatest vigor, and therefore, Ben-Gurion and his colleagues would have to move with extreme caution. Perhaps this would account for the secrecy. Courtney promised to check and give me further details. This [was] welcome and exciting news, though I could hardly credit it as an adequate reason for delaying my hardly well begun despatch about McGhee's program. I, therefore, wrote instead a letter to McGhee, telling him of this report and promising him my long commentary for next week.

96. In general see Pinhas Ginossar, "From Zionism to Communism and Back: The Case of Moshe Sneh (1948–1967)," in *Dire Times, Dark Decisions: Jews and Communism*, ed. Jonathan Frankel (New York: Oxford University Press, 2004), 236–254.
97. In 1947–1948 Leo Kohn had prepared a draft constitution that sought middle ground between modern liberalism and Jewish tradition. See Amihai Radzyner, "A Constitution for Israel: The Design of the Leo Kohn Proposal, 1948," *Israel Studies* 15, no. 1, (Spring 2010): 1–24.

Textbox 11.1.
The "Gaza Plan"

The official meetings at Lausanne began inauspiciously on April 27, 1949, and reached an impasse by mid-May.[1] Ethridge insisted on major Israeli concessions from the start, namely a grand Israeli gesture on refugees—he had mentioned the repatriation of 250,000—as well as Israeli territorial concessions to offset its conquests, preferably in the southern Negev. Although Ben-Gurion had rejected both ideas in a meeting with Ethridge on April 18,[2] Ethridge was nonetheless stunned when Walter Eytan, who headed the Israeli delegation at Lausanne, also rejected preconditions for peace negotiations. "Intransigence of Israeli position," Ethridge reported to Secretary Acheson on May 4, "came as [a] complete surprise to PCC." The Arab delegations were equally immovable. They refused to meet the Israeli delegation formally, they continued to insist that Arab refugees be allowed to return before peace negotiations could begin, they demanded that Israeli troops evacuate conquered areas (Jaffa, Lydda, Ramle, Be'er Sheva, Western Galilee, and Jewish Jerusalem), and they wanted territorial concessions as well.[3]

On May 5 at Lake Success, Abba Eban, during his presentation on Israeli admission to the UN, had hinted that all questions, including that of refugees, could be settled at Lausanne. Israel, Eban said, "would be ready to make its own contribution to a solution of the [refugee] problem," though he cautioned that "it was not yet ascertainable how many Arabs wished to return under conditions that might be prescribed by the Assembly or how many Arabs Israel could receive in the light of existing political and economic considerations." Eban added, "The Government of Israel had already announced its acceptance of obligations to make compensation for abandoned lands." Israel's hope, said Eban, "was that with the clear prospect of a settlement . . . the Governments concerned would enter into peace negotiations which would lead to

---

1. In general see Caplan, *Futile Diplomacy*, v. 3, 57–126.

2. Ethridge [through Burdett] to secretary of state, no. 312, June 20, 1949, *FRUS*, 1949, v. VI, 925–927.

3. On May 9, Ethridge reported that the Syrians wanted the panhandle, the Eastern Galilee, and the Western Galilee to Acre; Transjordan wanted Gaza with a passageway through Be'er Sheva; and Egypt wanted the southern Negev. Meanwhile, the Arab delegations at Lausanne were, according to early Israeli reports, "at each other's throats," the main disagreement coming over King Abdullah's desire to annex formally Arab Palestine. Ethridge to secretary of state, no. 676, May 4, 1949, *FRUS*, 1949, v. VI, 975–977; Ethridge [through Vincent] to secretary of state [personal attention], no. 699, May 9, 1949, *FRUS*, 1949, v. VI, 988–990; Ethridge to secretary of state, no. 165, May 23, 1949, *FRUS*, 1949, v. VI, 1043; Eytan to Sharett, May 3, 1949, *DFPI*, v. 4, d. 4.

an agreed formula on the exact contribution to be made by each Government concerned and the amount of assistance required from the international community." But by May 20, after Eytan insisted that these statements did not mean a return to the status quo ante, Ethridge predicted a breakdown of the talks. "[Unless] Israel modifies her demands," he reported, "there is no possibility of peace on any basis heretofore envisioned by the State Department."[4]

The Gaza Strip idea, mentioned by Courtney to McDonald on May 24, seemed to offer a way out. The Strip was reluctantly occupied by Egypt and coveted by Transjordan. It also housed the grand mufti's All-Palestine government. Transjordan's control of the Strip would mean the need for an Arab land bridge across the Negev that could cut Israel in half. In their April 18 meeting at Tiberias, Ben-Gurion mused to Ethridge that if Egypt did not want the Gaza Strip, Israel would accept it. Refugees there, said the prime minister, would even be able to return to their homes. With Sharett's approval, Eytan proposed Israeli acceptance of the Gaza Strip at Lausanne on May 29. US negotiators, particularly Ethridge, thought that the idea could break the logjam. Israel, they thought, would accept a significant number of Arab refugees and would be expected to compensate Egypt with territory in the southern Negev. But Israel had underestimated the number of refugees in the Gaza Strip by more than half (the United States estimated 230,000 refugees with another 80,000 permanent Arab residents), Egypt was loath to surrender more territory to Israel, and Israel would not surrender the southern Negev in return for the Gaza Strip.[5] Israel quickly backed away from the plan.

---

4. Ethridge [through Vincent] to secretary of state, no. 769, May 20, 1949, *FRUS*, 1949, v. VI, 1036–1038. On subsequent Israeli statements see *FRUS*, 1949, v. VI, 1065–1071; *DFPI*, v. 4, d. 34.

5. On the Gaza idea, see Mordechai Gazit, "Ben-Gurion's 1949 Proposal to Incorporate the Gaza Strip with Israel," *Studies in Zionism*. v. 8, n. 2 (1987), 223–43; Morris, *The Birth of the Palestinian Refugee Problem Reconsidered*, 561–71; Caplan, *Futile Diplomacy*, v. 3, 89–100.

McDonald immediately wrote McGhee, noting that Courtney was "an unusually reliable source" and that "this news is . . . startling and so encouraging," but "this plan is said to be still in the top secret category."[98]

Wednesday, May 25

Busy all morning getting ready for the pouch. Conference with Dr. Harry Davidowitz, who agreed to serve on the screening board, along with the representative of Israel, of the five cases of documents sent from the German-occu-

---

98. McDonald to McGhee, no. 88, May 24, 1949, McDonald Papers, USHMM, box 7, folder 14.

pied area by OMGUS [Office of Military Government United States]. By inquiring of Viteles, I learned that the initials JCR Inc. stood for the Jewish Cultural Reconstruction.[99]

Enjoyed a relatively free day, which gave me a rare opportunity to make progress in the accumulated reading and dictation. Having before breakfast read the full text of *A Midsummer Night's Dream*, I enjoyed even more than I would have done the Habimah production of Dr. Davidowitz's translation. The staging was elaborate and beautiful; the dancing in harmony with the play and the acting spirited but not overdone. Afterwards, we stayed a little while for the reception.

Thursday, May 26

After a couple of hours work, off with Bobby and Ruth to the beach for the rest of the morning. James W. Barco[100] came for forty minutes or so. He is the Department's replacement of Halderman. He reached Lausanne the day the PCC arrived there. He is now in this area for a quick survey. First of all, he denied vigorously that he had ever said that the Jews were making the problem with the Arabs more difficult by their stubbornness about the internationalization of Jerusalem and the problem of Arab refugees. Beyond that, our talk covered a wide range including the following points:

1) He had had no knowledge about Ray Hare's appointment as assistant to Ethridge's successor. About the latter, he also knew nothing.
2) He agreed that probably the French were dilatory in their PCC tactics, hoping that time would work in their favor as against the British.
3) He, too, thought that the Yalçin statement, or rather his article in the Turkish magazine, urging closer Turkish-Syrian relations, was ill advised.
4) He was in accord with my idea that the PCC needed a strong secretary to function as had Bunche on the UNSCOP. Moreover, he thought that such a person would be acceptable to the Commission, but that Azcárete could never do the job.

99. Jewish Cultural Reconstruction, founded in April 1947 as a corporation, under the presidency of Salo Baron, for the restoration of Jewish cultural objects (books, manuscripts, religious objects) in the US occupation zone of Germany. In February 1949 OMGUS agreed to transfer unclaimed Jewish cultural objects to the JCR, after which the JCR was to act as trustee and redistributor for roughly 250,000 such objects at the US military depot at Offenbach. Some 40 percent of the books and manuscripts were allocated to the Jewish National and University Library in Israel. McDonald refers to inventories. Eighty-seven cases of actual material went to Israel. See Michael J. Kurtz, *America and the Return of Nazi Contraband: The Recovery of Europe's Cultural Treasures* (New York: Cambridge University Press, 2006), 161–73.

100. James W. Barco (1916–2008), Harvard Law School graduate, 1941; US naval officer, 1942–1946; joined State Department, 1946, becoming part of the Office of United Nations Affairs; deputy US representative to Palestine Conciliation Commission, 1949–1951; author of the Barco Plan in 1951 for Israeli compensation for Palestinian refugees; later a vice chairman of the board of trustees of the American University in Cairo and a Washington lobbyist for that institution.

5) After his interviews in Amman, he was pessimistic about the Jordan-Israel Special Committee talks.

6) On the subject of Jerusalem, he thought the working paper and the Department's comments, which I had seen in Burdett's office [May 17, 1949], offered a practicable basis and continued to be the US program.

7) He thought Burdett's idea of trusteeship for Arab Palestine to be given to Israel was fantastically impractical. He had heard it from nobody and thought it must be wholly personal to Burdett.

8) He was intrigued by my report of the possibility of Ben-Gurion and the JNF working on a large-scale refugee repatriation plan. He thought this might break the back of that problem.

9) He was seeing Comay here and promised he would come back to see me again before he completed his tour.

Long and interesting talk with Louis Johnson, head of civil aviation in the American zone in Germany. For the first time I understood the Department's program of discouraging the satellite [East European] air services. This is on the grounds that these are simply covers for Russian services. As to Israel's possible Russian air relations, he thought that the obvious best solution for the government here would be to insist on reciprocal facilities. This would, in his opinion, close the door, because Russia has fixed policy not to permit such reciprocity with outside countries. It was intriguing to hear Johnson talk about the possibility of Pan American [Airways] entrance here as, in effect, the Israeli authorities' "chosen instrument."

Friday, May 27

Busy with dictation and telephones all morning. In the afternoon Harold Field, business manager of *The Nation*, came in for a few minutes. He will come back again before he leaves.

Saturday, May 28

Most of the day at the Mendes Sackses. Took occasion to ask [Mendes] Sacks about [Louis M.] Kesselman's desire of a letter from me which could be used with American industrialists.[101] Sacks spoke well of Kesselman, but doubted that it was proper for me to give personal endorsement to an individual who was engaged in a competitive business. What I did for Kesselman I could not properly refuse to another businessman going to the States. At teatime we were joined at Sacks's by Bernard Waley-Cohen and his wife, by the Jaffes, and by Edward Norman, whom Miss Clark had diverted from his appointment at the residence.[102]

101. Louis M. Kesselman (1888–1965), Milwaukee banker and insurance agent active in Zionist causes; established fellowships for young American Jews to travel to Israel.
102. Sir Bernard Waley-Cohen (1914–1991), businessman son of Robert Waley-Cohen of Shell Oil; Lord Mayor of London, 1960–1961; director, Palestine Economic Corporation. Mark Jaffe was chairman of the PEC in May 1949.

The Jennie Tourel recital was wholly delightful. During the intermission I chatted with Mr. [Jan] Lewando of the Marks and Spencer staff.[103] He told me interestingly of his conviction that given peace with Israel's neighbors, this country would become rapidly self-supporting. He based this optimism on his observation in several modern plants here, including that of Sam Sacks and the plant of a manufacturer of ladies shoes. He also found encouraging "know-how" in other plants, including one making underwear and socks. He thought that with some new machines and an adequate supply of raw material for the truly efficient plants, Israel could soon begin to earn substantial foreign exchange. He is coming to see me later.

I should have noted above that Mendes Sacks argued against the present tendency in some quarters to make Israel self-sufficient . . . in those lines of industry in which costs here must inevitably remain substantially higher than the imported product. He thought that in agriculture, too, Israel should specialize in things which it can do especially well, while leaving other areas to be supplied by imports.

Sunday, May 29

Quiet working morning interrupted by visit of Ford with a top-secret despatch containing text of extremely strong note to be presented at the earliest in the name of the president to Ben-Gurion. Expressing deep disappointment at the failure of Eytan at Lausanne to make any of the desired concessions regarding refugees or boundaries, the note interpreted Israel's attitude as dangerous to the peace and as indicating disregard of November 29 and December 11 resolutions. The Department reaffirmed insistence that compensation should be made for territory taken in excess of November 29 and that tangible refugee concessions should be made now as essential preliminary to any prospect for general settlement. The "operative" part of the note was the implied threat of reconsideration of the US attitude towards Israel. Nothing was said about comparable notes to the Arab capitals, but I think that these were probably sent.[104]

Bilateral talks were breaking down. The Israeli-Jordanian Special Committee reached an impasse on Jerusalem by May 20. King Abdullah, facing extremely harsh criticism from Palestinian Arabs because of the surrender of territory in the Tulkarm-Nablus-Jenin triangle, now insisted on retaining full control of the Arab quarters of Jerusalem. His negotiators held Israel's access to Mount Scopus as a negotiating chip. As US diplomats saw matters, an Israeli land route to Mount Scopus would leave the

---

103. Jan Alfred Lewando [formerly Lewandowski] (1909–2004), Manchester-born cantor's son; joined Marks & Spencer as trainee in 1929 and managed individual stores in 1930s; coordinated production and supply of artillery and ammunition for War Office Technical Branch during World War II; rejoined Marks & Spencer after the war and led development of company's textile exports; knighted in 1970. Simon Marks sent Lewando to Israel in 1949 to advise the Israeli government on industrial development.

104. No similar notes were sent to the Arab governments.

Arab parts of Jerusalem at Israel's mercy. Abdullah also pressed the British for arms deliveries.[105]

Armistice talks between Israel and Syria had been suspended since May 17. By May 23, Ralph Bunche argued to the Israelis that Za'im needed a territorial quid pro quo for the sake of his domestic political position and that if the Security Council took up the matter, it would not favor Israel. On May 24, the Israeli cabinet discussed a detailed proposal from Za'im whereby the Syrian-Israeli armistice would be based on the truce lines, but an actual peace, to be made in three months' time, would be based on the international frontier. Za'im still pledged to take 300,000 Palestinian Arab refugees provided that they came with developmental aid from the United States. Sharett took the initiative seriously, but Ben-Gurion, still worried about a trap concerning the armistice line, demurred. He insisted that the Syrians withdraw to the international frontier before talks begin.[106]

The biggest failures were in Lausanne. The PCC was incensed with what it viewed as Israeli intransigence. On May 27, the State Department told President Truman that he must act in order to save the Lausanne talks, and suggested that, as leverage, Truman might withhold the $49 million credit as yet unallocated by the Export-Import Bank. Bunche, who privately remarked that Israeli demands at Lausanne would wreck all negotiations, concurred, as did General Riley.[107] *Truman by now had approved of PCC proposals for more limited international authority over the Holy Places in Jerusalem.*[108] *But he was exasperated on the issues of refugees and frontiers, and agreed to send a very strong letter to Ben-Gurion, much of which was drafted in the State Department by May 28. The US mission in Tel Aviv was excluded from these discussions. On May 29 McDonald received an urgent cable from the State Department, ordering him to deliver a lengthy letter from Truman to Ben-Gurion.*

The letter read in part, "The US [Government] and people have given generous support to the creation of Israel because they have been convinced of the justice of this aspiration. The US [Government] does not, however, regard the present attitude of the Israeli Government as being consistent with the principles upon which US support has been based." It was up to Israel, said the president, to provide a sound basis for the Lausanne talks to continue. "The [Government] of Israel should entertain no doubt whatever that the US [Government] relies upon it to take responsible and positive action concerning Palestine refugees and that, far from supporting excessive Israeli claims to further territory within Palestine, the US [Government] believes that it is necessary for Israel to offer territorial compensation for territory which it expects

105. Burdett to secretary of state, no. 370, May 20, 1949, *FRUS*, 1949, v. VI, 1039–1041; Burdett to secretary of state, May 23, 1949, *FRUS*, 1949, v. VI 1042–1043; Stabler to secretary of state, no. 216, May 26, 1949, *FRUS*, 1949, v VI, 1056–1057.

106. Austin to secretary of state, no. 627, May 23, 1949, *FRUS*, 1949, v. VI, 1046; Schlaim, "Husni Za'im and the Plan to Resettle Palestinian Refugees in Syria," 68–80.

107. Memorandum by Webb for the president, May 27, 1949, *FRUS*, 1949, v. VI, 1060–1063; Austin to secretary of state, no. 64, May 25, 1949, *FRUS*, 1949, v. VI, 1055–1056.

108. Elath to Sharett, May 4, 1949, *DFPI*, v. 4, d. 7.

to acquire beyond the boundaries of the [November] 29, 1947 [resolution] of the [General Assembly.]"

Truman's letter concluded: "If the [Government] of Israel continues to reject the basic principles set forth by [resolution] of the [General Assembly] of [December] 11, 1948 and the friendly advice offered by the US [Government] for the sole purpose of facilitating a genuine peace in Palestine, the US [Government] will regretfully be forced to the conclusion that a revision of its attitude toward Israel has become unavoidable."[109]

Immediately upon receipt of this despatch, Ford and I went to HaKirya and explained to Esther Herlitz the urgency of an appointment with Ben-Gurion. This was fixed for 3:30, and we sent off an urgent telegram to the Department notifying them as they had requested of the conference time. Ford and I met Sharett as we were going into the Ben-Gurion residence. Immediately, the four of us were together in Ben-Gurion's tiny study. Without preliminaries, I handed over copy of the note, explaining merely when it had reached us and in what form.

Sharett then slowly read the text out loud. Only once or twice did Ben-Gurion interrupt at points where the reading was not quite clear. At the conclusion, Ben-Gurion said, "This will have to be properly answered. It is very serious and very stiff." Then the prime minister made a brief statement of first reactions, which I was to report, but these were not to be [a] substitute for a formal reply. In effect, Ben-Gurion said that the note was unrealistic and unjust. It ignored the facts that November 29 was no longer applicable, since the basic conditions presupposed in that plan have been fundamentally and unalterably destroyed by the Arabs' aggression against [the] November 29 [partition] and the Jews' successful defense. Hence, to suggest that there must be compensation for territory held beyond November 29 was to ignore the facts. Moreover, to whom should compensation be made? As to refugees, Ben-Gurion reiterated earlier statements that until there is peace there can be no return in any numbers. How can we permit potential enemies to come back so long as the Arab states openly threaten a new war of destruction? To whom should we turn if Israel were again attacked? Would the US send arms or troops? Finally, in an even more passionate tone than he had used previously, Ben-Gurion said "off the record" [that] the US was a powerful country, we are a small and weak one; we could be crushed, but we will not on our own initiative commit suicide.

There was really nothing to say in reply, for I had no authorization to add or detract from the note's text; so I remained silent. Ford, however, who was visibly moved, said to Ben-Gurion and Sharett, "I sympathize with you." Then I said, "We have been through too many things together; there is no need for

109. Webb to McDonald, no. 322, May 28, 1949, *FRUS*, 1949, v. VI, 1072–1074; McDonald to Ben-Gurion, May 29, 1949, *DFPI*, v. 4, d. 42.

me to offer any comment." To the office with Ford, where I drafted and he checked a factual report of the conference.

To the State Department, McDonald reported additional comments by Ben-Gurion. The first was that the November 29 resolution was never implemented by the United States, the UN, or the Arab states: "Prime Minister unable to recall any strong action by US or UN to enforce November 29 or prevent aggression by Syria, Egypt, Lebanon and Iraq. . . . Had Jews waited on US or UN they would have been exterminated. Israel was established not on basis November 29 but on that of successful war of defense. Hence note's suggestion is today unjust and unrealistic for it ignores war and continued Arab threats which make November 29 boundaries impossible." The second was the impossibility of repatriation of Arab refugees, who, in a renewed war, would fight on the side of the aggressors.[110]

McDonald's own comment to the State Department was as follows: "Manner of Prime Minister's response and unusual reticence of Foreign Minister indicated extreme seriousness of their reception [of the] President's note. When Prime Minister opined that this was strongest representation yet sent by US to Israel, I agreed but otherwise made no comment. There [are] no grounds however, for confidence [that] Israel will accept without substantial reservations fundamentals of US position. I anticipate Israel's formal reply soon." Truman, when told of McDonald's report by acting secretary of state James Webb, expressed, according to Webb, "real interest." Webb reported, "I feel very sure that he has no doubts as to the wisdom of the course being followed."[111]

McDonald reported the next day that Eytan was being recalled from Lausanne for consultations concerning Israel's reply to the Truman letter. In addition, McDonald added the following comment: "Embassy's complete lack of authoritative knowledge [regarding] current talks [in] Lausanne seriously hampers our work. We are frequently embarrassed in dealing with Israeli officials who openly express surprise that they are at times better informed [on] US policies on refugees and other issues than are we. Hope, therefore, [that the] Department will repeat regularly to Tel Aviv (I assume Arab capital missions equally need such repeats) [of] basic telegrams and despatches."[112]

Monday, May 30

Memorial Day, but no holiday for us. Worked intensively all morning on my refugee despatch, dictating portions to Bobby and later to Miss Clark. At teatime, Helm made his "formal" call following his presentation of credentials.

---

110. Ben-Gurion's language in his personal account of the meeting reflects even greater irritation with the US note than he conveyed to McDonald. See Ben-Gurion Diary, entry of May 29, 1949.

111. McDonald to secretary of state, no. 406, May 29, 1949, *FRUS*, 1949, v. VI, 1074–1075; Memorandum by Webb, May 31, 1949, *FRUS*, 1949, v. VI, 1075.

112. McDonald to secretary of state, no. 407, May 30, 1949, NARA, RG 59, 501.BB Palestine, box 2124, folder 2. From Damascus, Keeley said "amen" to McDonald's plea for better information from Lausanne. Keeley to secretary of state, no. A-175, June 11, 1949, NARA, RG 59, 501.BB Palestine, box 2124, folder 5.

He found me in my shirtsleeves, and I bludgeoned him into taking off his coat. We then had a pleasant forty-five minutes together. But both of us refrained from any talk about Israel. More work on my refugee despatch.

Miss Herlitz came and stayed for nearly an hour's talk on the roof. First, she gave an account of the background of the "Gaza plan." This, she said had first been suggested to Eytan by Ethridge.[113] Subsequently, the Israeli cabinet had discussed it. Despite considerable opposition and two abstentions, the vote had been in favor of accepting sovereignty over the strip and responsibility for the inhabitants. She added that Egypt had indicated its approval.

As to the genesis of the Truman note, she attributed it not to any particular personality or new influence in the Department, but rather to Ethridge. She thought he had become impatient, fearful lest nothing be accomplished before he left and had, therefore, convinced Washington that a bludgeon should be used to break the deadlock. She felt that Lausanne was not desperate, that the reports of Arab delegations leaving were tendentious and were belied by reports that they were renting houses at Lausanne.

We then talked about Washington and our mutual friends, Hilldring, Potofsky and Knox. I deplored any move to send me back for consultation now. After supper continued work with Bobby on the refugee despatch.

McDonald's report on the meeting with Herlitz added her comments that the task of repatriating the "vast number" of Arab refugees proposed by the US was "gigantic," and would involve "severe personal sacrifices [for] all Israeli people." McDonald added as a postscript: "As Herlitz talked I remained silent feeling that [the president's statement] could not be strengthened by any commentary of mine."[114]

Ethridge responded on receiving these comments: "I regret McDonald . . . is apparently refraining from using his influence with Israeli Government to underline President's and Department's approved position regarding Palestine. . . . We need all [the] help we can get, particularly in Tel Aviv."[115]

Tuesday, May 31
Usual pre-breakfast conference with Ford; with Miss Clark, finished the draft of the refugee report.

Late morning, M. Alfred Escher, commissioner of the International Committee of the Red Cross [Commissariat for] Aid to Palestine Refugees, and his wife called. Escher had no special mission to me. He said that it was obvious that relief would have to be continued beyond the time planned. Supplies might be stretched to last until the end of October or November, though the later date

---

113. As the Israelis cooled to the Gaza idea, they disowned any ownership of it. Morris, *The Birth of the Palestinian Refugee Problem Reconsidered*, 565–566.
114. McDonald to secretary of state, no. 406, May 31, 1949, *FRUS*, 1949, v. VI, 1076.
115. Ethridge to secretary of state, no. 181, June 2, 1949, *FRUS*, 1949, v. VI, 1085; also Ethridge to secretary of state [attention McGhee], no. 180, June 2, 1949, *FRUS*, 1949, v. VI, 1086.

would mean diluting excessively the present sparse diet. He estimated that, in addition to the American $16 million, $8 million had been contributed to the relief funds. His committee was prepared to continue into next year but wished at least some moral assurance that a beginning would be made on repatriation and resettlement, for their committee was not "in the relief business."[116]

Ruth and I reached the Weizmann's promptly at 1:00, at the same moment as did the Helms. The revealing incident as we were entering the house was: I suggested to Helm that he stop for a moment while I asked Major Arnon to read with me a telegram about the arrival of FDR, Jr., and I checked as to whether Weizmann was expecting the young man. Helm, however, quickly demurred saying, "You are accustomed to this sun but I am not." What a timid soul to think that a minute or two in the mild sun of that day could have done him any harm.

Others at the luncheon besides the hosts, McDonalds, Helms, and the major were, Mr. and Mrs. Harry and Hannah Levine, active in the support of the Institute and interested in this visit in the building of a small plastic plant,[117] and Weizmann's son.[118] We were greeted affectionately, but I deliberately left the host to the Helms, and chatted with [Weizmann's] son about the grandson. Mrs. Weizmann was dressed in an elegant manner suitable to the occasion. [It was a] delicious, perfectly served luncheon.

The talk at the table was not political. It was only afterward that Weizmann told me of his shock on the reading the Truman note and of his feeling that it should be "properly answered." He threw out the idea, but without any encouragement from me, that he might write a personal note to the president.

After tea, Courtney and I sat on the roof for nearly an hour. He told me more about the Gaza plan and of the government's very serious consideration of it. He had been surprised, as I had been, by the disclaimer in the *Palestine Post*. That despatch from Lausanne had been killed in the other papers, but the Palestine Information Office had been unable to reach the *Post* in time. He understood that Egypt had formally rejected the plan, as of course, had also the other Arab states.[119]

---

116. To augment aid to Palestinian refugees, in November 1948 the ICRC established the Commissariat for Aid to Palestine Refugees. Escher, a Swiss diplomat, who at the time was serving in London, was placed at its head. The Commissariat focused on refugees in Arab Palestine excluding Gaza, where they were aided by the American Friends Service Committee. In 1950 Escher reported that conditions for the Red Cross-aided refugees, whom he numbered at roughly 425,000, were improving in terms of food, clothing, shelter, medicine, and education. Catherine Rey-Schyrr, "Le CICR et l'assistance aux réfugiés arabes palestiniens (1948–1950)," *Revue Internationale de la Croix-Rouge* 83, no. 843 (September 2001): 739–761; *Revue Internationale de la Croix-Rouge et Bulletin Internationale de Sociétés de la Croix-Rouge—Supplement*, v. III: *1950* (Geneva: ICRC, 1950), 63–67.

117. Harry Levine (1895–1977), president of New England Plastics and Commonwealth Plastic; helped import weaponry into British Palestine, 1946; founded Serafon Plastics Company in Rehovot, 1949; became major donor for the Weizmann Institute of Science.

118. Refers to Benjamin Weizmann (1907–1980); Weizmann's younger son, Michael, served in the Royal Air Force and was killed in combat in 1942.

119. "Israel Ready to Take over Gaza Arabs," *Palestine Post*, May 29, 1949, discussed Israeli willingness, but placed blame on the Egyptians for rejecting the idea.

The rest of our talk covered a wide range. Courtney thought it advisable that there should be a public clarification of the current misconceptions in this area about the "McGhee Plan" and "Point Four." I agreed and said I would attempt to get permission to this end. Courtney stressed the divergences among the Arab states. For example, Egypt's opposition to Jordan's taking over Gaza was greater than to Israel's doing so.

A few minutes after Courtney left the Fords arrived and we went over to Sharett's for dinner. Besides ourselves and the host were present the Ben-Gurions and the Berl Lockers. Most of my talk during the evening was with Ben-Gurion. The following are the noteworthy points:

1) He was much interested in the size of our staff and particularly in the work of the military attachés. I explained this as well as I could. He made special inquiries, too, about the role of the Marines here. I stressed that these were used as guards by many of our missions in different parts of the world. He had seemed surprised that we did not depend upon native guards and was pleased when I assured him that our practice in Israel was not exceptional.

2) Ben-Gurion was also interested in the problem of effectively coordinating the work of the three defense services at home.[120] He expressed surprise that there had been so much difficulty in having the president's authority made effective.

3) Repeatedly Ben-Gurion indicated warm admiration for Lincoln, whom he regards as the greatest man of the 19th century in public life. Time and again he said, how could this miracle have occurred? Then as if thinking of his own experience as war leader, he said: "It is relatively easy to lead in a war against a foreign enemy, for then the people tend naturally to unite, but how much more difficult it was for Lincoln to lead in a terrible civil war with so many elements of strength in the south and so many divisive and corruptive elements in the north." He also indicated intense admiration of Lincoln's style, which he attributed to his concentration on the Bible.

4) Our talk about the American founding fathers and their extraordinary breadth of intellectual interest led Ben-Gurion to comment on the uniqueness of the presidential office. In answer to my comment that the very scope and responsibility of that office tended to enlarge the capacities of the holders of it, Ben-Gurion commented rather dryly: "Any system would succeed in America."

In sharp contrast with Paula, who seemed very tired and made no effort to hide her boredom, Ben-Gurion was unusually spritely and seemed to me more refreshed than he had been at any of my recent meetings with him.

---

120. Ben-Gurion's interest in streamlined organization was based on his conviction that the Arab states would again attack Israel. See Ben-Gurion Diary, entries of June 19 and June 26, 1949.

As we were leaving, I asked Sharett to refresh my memory about the steps in the proposal from [Henri] Vigier that Sharett meet Colonel Za'im.[121] Sharett explained that he had accepted to meet "deep in Syria," that the Syrian foreign minister[122] was then substituted for Colonel Za'im, but still Sharett accepted, but later when "small" people constituting a delegation were substituted for the Syrian foreign minister, Sharett withdrew and urged that Bunche put forward his latest proposal.

Za'im's chauvinistic foreign minister, Adil Arslan, flatly refused to break ranks with the other Arab states. When Za'im proposed on May 25 that Arslan meet with Sharett, as suggested by the United States and the UN, Arslan refused and prohibited any other members of the Foreign Ministry from taking his place. Arslan told US ambassador Keeley, "I have never been fooled by the bluffs of the Jews and I am the last among the Arabs to make concessions to them."[123]

I should have noted above that Ben-Gurion had given an almost extended discourse expressing his admiration for Bunche. The latter "had extraordinary quickness of mind, sharp discernment and ability to draft that was highly exceptional." "Bunche is more intelligent than Acheson."

---

121. On May 26, 1949 Bunche had asked his deputy Henri Vigier, who moderated the Israeli-Syrian armistice talks, to use his good offices to facilitate a meeting with Sharett.
122. Adil Ibn Hamud Arslan (1887–1954), Syrian Druze pan-Arabist politician and diplomat; closely linked with Haj Amin al-Husseini since the 1920s; sentenced to death by the French three times in the 1920s; sympathetic to Nazi Germany; Za'im's foreign minister, April–June 1946.
123. Shalev, *The Israel-Syria Armistice Regime*, 31–32; and Schlaim, "Husni Za'im and the Plan to Resettle Palestinian Refugees in Syria," 75–76. See also Sami M. Moubayed, *Damascus Between Democracy and Dictatorship* (Lanham, MD: University Press of America, 2000), 40; and Eugene Rogan, *The Arabs: A History* (New York: Basic Books, 2009), 272–274.

12. June 1949

Wednesday, June 1

Usual pre-breakfast conference with Ford. He approved two drafts to the Department, the one asking for authority to clarify "Point Four," and the other reporting on Sharett's account of the previous evening and taking exception to Keeley's persistent anti-Israel propaganda.

Called Miss Herlitz and arranged to call her later about Garland Hopkins. During the approximate two hours that Mr. Hopkins was with me, I showed courteous interest in his account of his views and of his plans and those of his "liberal Arab friends."

Garland Hopkins represented the Committee for Peace and Justice in the Holy Land, a lobbying group founded in March 1948 by Virginia Gildersleeve[1] and Kermit Roosevelt Jr.[2] that opposed the partition and the creation of a Jewish state. He and Kermit, Hopkins said, "were the recognized leaders of American thinking on Arab superiority in the Middle East."[3] McDonald reported to the State Department that Hopkins was "dangerously incendiary."[4] During his visit to the Arab states and Israel, Hopkins wanted to meet Ben-Gurion and Sharett, but both refused.[5] In a long discussion with McDonald, Hopkins insisted that he was working for a unitary Palestine under nominal Jewish hegemony and with autonomy for Arab communities. The following exchange, noted in McDonald's diary, was indicative:

---

1. Virginia Gildersleeve (1877–1965), dean of Barnard College, 1911–1947, where she pioneered women's higher education while reducing Jewish enrollment; member of US delegation to UN founding conference in San Francisco, 1945; blamed UN partition plan and formation of Israel on the Zionist control of the media; continued after Israeli independence to lobby against US aid for Israel.

2. Kermit Roosevelt Jr. (1916–2000), grandson of Theodore Roosevelt; OSS agent in Cairo, 1942–1943; member, Institute for Arab-American Affairs; executive director, Committee for Justice and Peace, and its successor organization American Friends of the Middle East, 1948–1951; Central Intelligence Agency, Middle East Division, 1950–1958, during which time he engineered a plot to overthrow Mohammed Mossadegh in Iran, 1953. Publicly debated McDonald on the partition of Palestine, 1947. See Goda et al., eds., *To the Gates of Jerusalem*, 257. In general see Hugh Wilford, *America's Great Game: The CIA's Secret Arabists and the Shaping of the Modern Middle East* (New York: Basic Books, 2013), 90–93, 114–115.

3. Ford to McDonald, June 1, 1949, June 2, 1949, McDonald Papers, USHMM, box 7, folder 14.

4. McDonald to secretary of state, no. 402, May 28, 1949, NARA, RG 59, MC 1390, reel 19, frame 387.

5. McDonald to secretary of state, no. 140, June 7, 1949, McDonald Papers, USHMM, box 7, folder 14.

McDonald: "Did you confer with the Mufti on this tour? Hopkins: "Yes, of course, he is an old friend."[6]

He did not ask me questions about American policy, nor did I volunteer any information about the present state of negotiations at Lausanne. Off the record, I have seldom met a person who I felt instinctively so resentful towards as towards Hopkins. He was, to put it bluntly, so dishonest that it was a reflection upon one's intelligence to have him assume that his listener would be taken in by his half-truths. Yet, he will probably return home and there be listened to by responsible churchmen and others as an authoritative and objective reporter on Near Eastern affairs! Thus is the truth spread! His open criticism of me in his conference with Ford, whom he had never met previously, is a proof of the man's value as an amateur diplomat.

Dinner for the Kaplans, Levinsons, Persitz, Padberg, and the family. It was a very friendly and successful party. The only serious talk was mine with Kaplan briefly about the Point Four program and the "McGhee Plan." He said that he knew nothing about it except what he read in the papers, that Elath would probably be better informed, and that, nonetheless, he thought it would be useful if I could be authorized to make a clarifying public statement here.

Thursday, June 2

Franklin D. [Roosevelt], Jr. came out for an hour shortly after his arrival. He wanted a background picture for his study during the next week. I told him everything I could, including a discreet reference to such issues as refugees and boundaries. He modestly talked almost not at all about his congressional victory. He promised to stay with us the last night before he left, Thursday morning, the ninth. Shavuot dinner party at the Davidowitz's.

Friday, June 3

Theoretically a holiday, but because of my homework, I was busy most of the day. In the late morning Mr. Lewando from Marks and Spencer, on loan to Dov Joseph as efficiency expert in production and control.[7] He explained to me more fully than before his progress in streamlining production in some of the key industries, particularly textiles. Here, an eight-man board, to include our friend Sam Sacks and other textile leaders, would set standards of practice in the hope to largely increase production and lower costs. As an example of current evil practices, he cited one substantial purchaser of yarn overseas, who

6. The "liberal Arab friends" included Musa al-Alami [see entry of July 15, 1949], whose views Hopkins misrepresented when with McDonald. Wells Stabler of the US legation in Amman later learned that al-Alami would accept a unitary Palestine only if based on conditions as they existed before partition. See Stabler to secretary of state, no. 63, July 8, 1949, NARA. RG 59, MC 1390, reel 19, frames 698–700.

7. In the new cabinet, Dov Joseph was the minister of agriculture and also the minister of rationing and supply, a portfolio created in April 1949 that lasted until November 1950.

had been paying through an agent in New York a price three times that charged by the manufacturers of yarn in the States. An investigation was being made to determine whether a portion of this shocking differential was being left to the manufacturer's account in dollars. Lewando said that he was sure that given an efficient purchasing system, the further modernization of some of the more efficient plants, and the supplying to these of full quantities of raw materials needed for [an] increase of working hours to two shifts, they could not only produce all that was needed for Israel home consumption, but could begin to win hard currency abroad. He was hopeful that marked progress could be made. Meanwhile, he was warning Joseph's office against general rationing and the use of a coupon system, which in England had resulted in wasteful bureaucratic paperwork.

Saturday, June 4

Jacob Landau of the Jewish Telegraphic Agency called to ask if I would attend some affair for him and his organization in Tel Aviv. I said yes, but then explained that the Department had specifically instructed me not to personally or officially sponsor anything for them.[8]

Pleasant social lunch at the Ford's with the Mendes Sackses. At teatime Adolph Held, Abe Feinberg, Lewis Hollander, and Dr. Samuel Silverberg[9] of the American Jewish Labor Committee came for a farewell visit.[10] The replies of my visitors to my questions indicated that they, too, were worried about the sharp cleavages in Histadrut between Mapam and Mapai. They had not been able to see many of the Mapam leaders, who looked upon them, because of their Dubinsky association, as "red-baiters." They were somewhat hopeful that Mapam might split into its constituent elements, thus reconstituting a stronger labor bloc against the two extremes. On the whole, I had the impression that the men had learned a good deal, but probably had not been able to affect opinion here. Indeed, the more I talk to visiting American labor leaders, the more complex and difficult the problem here appears to become and, hence, the greater urgency for the presence of [a labor attaché], through whom I could hope to keep better informed. I told the group something of the present political situation, and they are to see the president promptly on their return, early in July. As they left, they were very warm in their words of appreciation of my "helpfulness."[11]

8. Entry of May 8, 1949.
9. Samuel Silverberg (1887–1975), medical doctor and president of the pharmaceutical firm, Sterling Magnesia, Inc.; founded the Workman's Circle division of the Jewish Labor Committee and headed it for two decades; in retirement served as president of the Forward Association, which published the Jewish Daily *Forward*.
10. Entry of May 21, 1949.
11. See also McDonald's report to secretary of state, no. 96, June 4, 1949, McDonald Papers, USHMM, box 7, folder 14.

Leo Kohn came at teatime, at my request, to talk about the progress, of the lack of it, in the drafting of the constitution.[12] But before we got to this, he began to ask me questions, as part of his inquiry into foreign government practices about their foreign service. I told him about the American interlocking consular and diplomatic services, which seemed to me admirable, and about non-career men in most of the highest and other exceptional posts, for example, Israel. I indicated how these latter men, if of exceptional ability, had often proved superior to what might have been expected from even the top career men. On the other hand, I confessed the weakness of using diplomatic posts as compensation for political financial gifts.

Dr. Kohn admitted that Ben-Gurion was increasingly of the opinion that it might be better to do without or at least postpone a written constitution.[13] His reasons include the following:

1) The most important is the danger of a *Kulturkampf.* This arises because of the possibility of splitting the country on ideological and especially religious issues, such as civil marriage, reference to the Deity, and the place of the Torah in the fundamental law of the land. It would be, Ben-Gurion argues, deplorable if not worse to split the present coalition by debate on these abstractions.
2) The pressure of the immediate and vital tasks which must now be disposed of is so great that there is no time or energy left for the arduous exhausting debate which would ensue on the constitution.
3) As a practical matter, why should not Israel follow the British example of building from precedent to precedent without a written constitution?

Over against these considerations, Dr. Kohn argued:

1) Israel needs a constitution more than most countries because of the diversity of the backgrounds of the people who make it up and the consequent necessity of a basic unifying authoritative law on which the superstructure of the governmental organizations could be built.
2) It is needed to place a restraint, though not a decisive check, on the power of the legislature and of an administration.
3) It is needed to protect the special status of religious and other minorities of the state.
4) It is needed to give assurance to the world that Israel will not become authoritarian.

After Kohn had set out all these affirmative arguments, he admitted that, much as he believed there should be a constitution, he would favor its post-

12. Entry of May 24, 1949.
13. Entry of May 24, 1949.

ponement if he were convinced that to press the issue now would so divide the country as to weaken disastrously Mapai and its cooperating parties and open the door of power to the extremists of the left and right. He recognized that these extremists, irrespective of their personal or group views about the need for a constitution, would use the debates on the issue for selfish party advantage. In answer to my question, Kohn said that he thought that, despite Ben-Gurion's position, most of the Mapai leaders favored a constitution, as did the leaders of most of the other parties. From this talk with Dr. Kohn, the latest of a number I have had with other Israelis, I received confirmation of my earlier impression that serious debate on the constitution is likely to be postponed for several months, if not for a much longer period.[14]

Monday, June 6

At ten I was at [Walter] Eytan's office, whom I had asked to see before he went back to Lausanne.[15] A few minutes later, I was joined by Ford. Then followed about an hour and twenty minutes of Dr. Eytan's racy account of Lausanne. Not included in [McDonald's report to the Department] are his several stories about the Arab bluffs about leaving Lausanne; his impressions of Ethridge, particularly the latter's habit of becoming brighter during the course of the day until in the later hours he becomes brilliant for reasons which were not mentioned. Illustrative of one of these brilliant moments was Ethridge's reply when he was pressed by Dr. Eytan to say to whom compensation by Israel of territory should be made; "To Lebanon? No; To Syria? To Jordan? Not necessarily; To Egypt, because of its war record? Certainly not. Then to whom?" Eytan's quick answer was, "Why not to Dean Acheson?"

Another significant point, this one in connection with Dr. Eytan's view that the US insistence on "compensation" was to secure British indirect control of the southern Negev, was the argument advanced at Lausanne that the Arabs would be much more conciliatory if Jewish control of the southern Negev had not driven a wedge between Egypt and the other Arab states. According to Dr. Eytan, this argument approached the extreme metaphysical.

Illustrative of Arab callousness about refugees, Dr. Eytan cited a Lebanese remark: "What does it matter if there is a million more or less Arabs?" At Lausanne, the Arabs spend most of their time watching one another. The Gaza plan was definitely first suggested to Dr. Eytan by Ethridge, though Dr. Eytan doubted that it was Ethridge's original idea. Not a single new idea had come from the Arabs during five weeks. At Lausanne there was "an air of complete indolence as compared with Rhodes." The PCC had no ideas of its own and put no pressure on anyone. Boisanger [was] apparently willing to stay in Lausanne

14. Report in McDonald to secretary of state, no. 155, June 20, 1949, McDonald Papers, USHMM, box 7, folder 14.

15. Eytan, the head of the Israeli delegation in Lausanne, was mentioned prominently in the Truman letter of May 29 for his rigidity. He was called back for consultations in the first week of June 1949 to help with the Israeli response.

indefinitely. System at Lausanne [was] hopeless, Arabs [were] using refugee issue as single means of maintaining unity and arousing world opinion against Israel. They reiterate that Israel must take all and can take them despite knowledge that this is not to be expected and that they must take many. Extremism on this issue "is our tactic," said [the] head of Egyptian delegation [Abd al-Mun'im Mustafa],[16] though he admitted it to [be] unreal. Al-Mun'im said, "Israel must take them even if they slaughter them all."

Returning to [Truman's] ideas, Dr. Eytan thinks that the president is convinced that [a] British land bridge from Egypt to Jordan is essential to peace. According to Dr. Eytan, Ethridge held out bait of large-scale development scheme in the Middle East up to $300 million, with [the] US bearing [the] brunt, this to help refugees but basically to serve [an] American peace program in this area. To secure US presidential approval, "territorial compensation" and [a] refugee offer [are] essential. Ethridge said, "[the] plan is in my safe," but [the] president won't endorse [it] unless [the] plan will lead to peace. Essential principles of plan [are] to have [the] broadest possible base, including [the] whole Middle East, to be financed by International Bank, Export-Import Bank, Britain, UN agencies, and [a] congressional grant, the latter possibly $300 million. Britain and US [would be] major partners, American director and British assistant director, France and Turkey [will be] included "for form."

Next step would be organization of a technical committee, already authorized under the December 11 resolution of the UN General Assembly; chairman American, vice chairman, British. From this a development [a new] committee is to grow, replacing [the] purely technical group. A Mr. [Herbert] Kunde, now in Geneva, [is] mentioned as American chairman. Technical Commission, Ethridge said four weeks ago, might be leaving any time.[17] Later there were hitches. Then delays attributed to UN and to the Turks.

Returning then to the general subject, Dr. Eytan said that the future of Lausanne does not lie in Lausanne. Fate [of negotiations] must be decided elsewhere. As to background of recent [May 29] US note, Dr. Eytan said Ethridge [was the] only dynamic person at Lausanne, fed up by lack of progress, probably recommended strong representation in Tel Aviv and Arab capitals. On the way out from Dr. Eytan's office, met Herlitz and gave her note for Franklin Delano, Jr.

In the evening the piano concert of Abraham Sternklar. In addition to pieces by Handel, Mozart, Debussy, he played two major pieces of his own, the

16. Abd al-Mun'im Bey Mustafa (1899–1979), director-general of Arab Affairs in Cairo and head of the Egyptian delegation at Lausanne. He was uninterested in concluding peace, believing that time was on Egypt's side. See Shlomo Ben-Ami, *Scars of War, Wounds of Peace: The Israeli-Arab Tragedy* (New York: Oxford University Press, 2006), 67–68.

17. The December 11, 1948, resolution authorized the PCC to use technical experts to help it discharge its functions. Herbert A. Kunde (US), Jean-Albert Lucas (France), and Rifki Zorlu (Turkey) formed the Technical Committee of the PCC, which was to study the refugee problem on the ground. The Technical Committee left for Jerusalem on June 18, 1949.

one heard for the first time here. He is a brilliant pianist, but I am not able to judge his works. His mother came to speak to us to thank us for attending.

Tuesday, June 7

Up early and completed the checking of the despatch about Garland Hopkins and preparation of the telegram reporting on the talk with Dr. Eytan.

Wednesday, June 8

In the light of the four separate stories in the *Palestine Post* pointing to the southern Negev land bridge as the heart of the US purpose, I decided first, to write a letter to Clark Clifford pointing out the danger of such a *démarche*. On fuller consideration, changed the letter to a telegram for the personal attention of the president and the acting secretary.

The Palestine Post *reported that certain elements in the British Foreign Office and the State Department were encouraging the Arabs in their most intransigent demands and that Dean Acheson had given his blessing to raising "the old question of the division of the Negev" between Britain's allies, Egypt and Jordan.*[18]

Here is the substance of this [telegram]: current press reports from Washington, New York, and Lausanne tend to confirm the judgment of Israeli officials, given to me privately, that the US is moving toward a policy which will ask of this country the surrender of at least a portion of the southern Negev as "compensation" for its retention of the territories the Israeli armies have conquered outside the November 29 partition area. Though the Department has given no specific indication that demand for the surrender of the Negev tip is its policy, I can see no other territories to which this insistence could be logically applied. From the point of view of American and British strategic interests, it would be advantageous if Britain could be guaranteed land bridge (either through Jordanian or Egyptian occupation) from the Sinai Desert to Jordan; and the only such possible bridge is, of course, the southern Negev.

Two considerations should, however, I think give us pause before the Department and the president commit themselves irretrievably to this policy: 1) I am as convinced as I have ever been of anything that the Israeli government will not yield any portion of the southern Negev unless it is forced to do so; and this force will have to be military force or such a degree of economic pressure as would be tantamount to war; 2) In its resistance to giving up the southern Negev tip, Israel would have at least the full moral support of the Soviet Union.[19]

18. "Deadlock Blocks Peace Settlement with Arabs," *Palestine Post*, June 8, 1949. See also memorandum by Satterthwaite, June 8, 1949, *FRUS*, 1949, v. VI, 1094–1095; Ethridge to Acheson, June 8, 1949, *FRUS*, 1949, v. VI, 1096–1097; Ethridge to secretary of state, no. 188, June 12, 1949, *FRUS*, 1949, v. VI, 1124–1125.

19. This was the basis of McDonald to secretary of state, no. 439, [personal attention president and acting secretary], June 8, 1949, *FRUS*, 1949, v. VI, 1100.

In addition to the above, I got off telegrams to Ethridge, Hare, and Mc-Ghee. The first two were greetings, the third was a word of appreciation about the article in the May 23 issue of *Current Economic Developments* on Point Four.

In the midst of lunch with Dr. Novomeysky, I went next door at about the time when I knew Sharett and FDR, Jr. would be arriving. There I had a few minutes with Sharett, who in answer to my questions, said that the "land bridge" might be the heart of the matter but he would not say this with dogmatism. If it were, this would then be the fourth round in the attempt to deprive the Jews of the southern Negev; the first was November 29, when the president personally intervened to save it; the second was the defeat of the trusteeship idea; the third was the defeat of the Bernadotte scheme at Paris; and now would come the revival of that scheme. Chatted for a moment with FDR, Jr. and confirmed the appointment of the evening.

Evening conference [arranged by McDonald] at the house was attended by FDR, Jr., Herlitz, Simon, Rosenne,[20] Comay, Leo Kohn, [Gershon] Agron, and Dov Joseph. Since Franklin had to leave at a few minutes before ten in order to do a broadcast on Kol Israel, and since he had not seen Joseph except at lunch, the whole of nearly an hour was given over to his searching questions and to Joseph's brilliant and comprehensive replies. From these I got, as indeed did most of the other auditors, for the first time a clear picture of the aims, the procedures to date of the Office of Price Controls and Rationing. It was an encouraging account. From it, one could clearly discern why Joseph had been so powerful an administrator in Jerusalem during the months of crisis there—and also why he was not too popular with the Truce Commission or any of its three consular members.[21] The others stayed for more than an hour after Franklin left. We listened to his broadcast and were impressed by its clarity and simplicity.

Then I brought the discussion around to the discussion of British policy, particularly at the present moment. Most of the comments were too general, for example those from Agron and Joseph, to be of much value. But from Comay and Rosenne, I received a wealth of detailed citations of the debates preceding [the UN General Assembly resolutions] November 29 [1947] and December 11 [1948], which threw much light on the meaning of those resolutions or at last on their intent. Particularly pertinent was Comay's recounting of the debate and proposed amendment, which preceded the adoption of the refugee part of December 11. In the light of those preliminaries, Comay was sure that the words "as soon as practical" meant substantially when peace had been established.

20. Shabtai Rosenne (1917–2010), London-born legal scholar and diplomat; served in RAF, 1940–1946; Political Department, Jewish Agency, 1946–1948; legal adviser to Israeli Foreign Ministry, 1948–1967.

21. On June 17, 1949, McDonald reported that the price index had lowered on everything from clothing to lodging, timber and iron entered the country duty free, and the government was guaranteeing mortgages at 50% of their value. Joseph remained unpopular, however, because new rationing cards were issued and wholesale retail profits were being controlled. McDonald to secretary of state, no. 108, June 17, 1949, McDonald Papers, USHMM, box 7, folder 14.

He and the others were also emphatic that December 11 did not support the contention that the boundaries of November 29 were sacrosanct.

But to my mind, the most brilliant and searching of the answers on British policy and American policy came from Rosenne, whom I must see more of. He argued that the fundamental [goal] of British policy was the maintenance of north and south, east and west communications through Palestine, but he added that he was convinced that the US had again "been sold a bill of goods" by the British. This was, of course, in reference to our latest démarche. As they were leaving, Simon said it was high time that I had the first tea party for the diplomatic corps, that Helm had complained that no one was calling on him.

Shortly after nine, a messenger from the Foreign Office brought the text of the reply to the president's note to Ben-Gurion. Ford and I excused ourselves, went through it hastily, were impressed by the brilliance and cogency of the argument, though depressed by its length. Ford took it off to the office where it will occupy the code clerks for most of the night.

Truman's note, which McDonald had delivered on May 29, 1949, threatened a reevaluation of US-Israeli relations. US demands for Israeli concessions at Lausanne had angered the Israeli government and had caused the worst crisis in US-Israeli relations since Israel's independence.[22] The Foreign Ministry replied that Israel was seriously trying to negotiate peace with the Arab governments. It argued that the stalemate at Lausanne was the fault of the Arab negotiators, who were holding out for terms that would weaken the Jewish state.[23]

Israel specifically addressed Washington's individual complaints. Territorial compensation to the Arabs, particularly in the Negev, had not been mentioned in the December 11 resolution, and it was made obsolete by the Arab rejection of the November 1947 resolution and the war. As for refugees, the December 11 resolution said that those "wishing to return to their homes and live at peace with their neighbors should be permitted to do so at the earliest practicable date." That date, the Israelis said, had to depend on "the touchstones of security and economic realism." The refugees were "members of an aggressor group defeated in a war of their own making." Meanwhile, "all the energies of Israel are focused on the absorption of the large-scale immigration now in progress. . . . New social and economic processes are gathering momentum in Israel, and the wheel of history cannot be turned back."

Israel, the note continued, had offered compensation for abandoned Arab land, was willing to allow the reuniting of Arab families separated by the war, and was willing to contribute financially to Arab resettlement. Certain limited repatriation measures "have actually been carried out in recent months."[24] As for more substantial

22. *DFPI*, v. 4, d. 49, 50, 60, 61, 63.

23. Sharett to McDonald, June 8, 1949, *DFPI*, v. 4, d. 64; also printed in *FRUS*, 1949, v. VI, 1102–1106.

24. Owing partly to US pressure, the Israeli cabinet in June 1949 accepted the idea of considering requests by Arab citizens to allow back wives, sons younger than 15 years old, and unmarried daughters. In the following months the government received requests for 3,957 refugees to return: 3,113 entry permits were granted, of which 1,965 were used. Morris, *The Birth of the*

repatriation within Israel, a peace agreement with the Arabs was a prerequisite. The Arab states, meanwhile, had to accept their portion of responsibility for resettlement and to acknowledge the changed political realities.

On reading the Israeli note, President Truman said that "the Israelis appeared to be reacting well" to US objectives, but that, "unless [the Israelis] were prepared to play the game properly and conform to the rules, they were probably going to lose one of their best friends." On June 10 Stuart Rockwell in the State Department[25] suggested that the United States reject Israeli requests for training and experts, halt the allocation of the remaining \$49 million earmarked for Israel by the Export–Import Bank, end tax exemptions for American Jewish charities that contributed to Israel, and reply strongly to the Israeli note, reiterating US expectations.[26]

Thursday, June 9

FDR, Jr., despite having been up (according to Esther Herlitz) until after two, kept his appointment with me at 7:30 promptly. We then had an hour and half together at breakfast. He showed an extraordinary breadth of knowledge [concerning] the economic and political centers of problems here. Our talk was mostly about the political. He intends to see the president immediately on his return and will then explain the situation as he sees it, the danger of our present démarche involving the possibility of an open clash with Israel and the strengthening of the leftward influences here. But he reiterated that they ought to have an affirmative program to present. I suggested:

1) The quiet withdrawal from the latest démarche;
2) The withdrawal of the bar on bilateral negotiations (he was surprised to know that there was any such). Such a withdrawal, I pointed out, need not be inconsistent with the continuation of Lausanne;
3) Sending Bunche to Lausanne, or, if that were impossible, to have him go either for the UN or US on a roving mission to this area.

In response to FDR, Jr.'s suggestion that he might ask the president to let me return for consultation, I was only mildly enthusiastic in view of my desire to go back for a longer stay later, but I could not discourage FDR, Jr. too much, for that would have seemed to be selfish. At the very end he asked to speak to me alone (we had been joined at breakfast successively by Ford, Miss Clark, and Ruth.) Then he reported two comments from the Israelis:

Palestinian Refugee Problem Revisited, 572. Sharett announced the policy in the Knesset on June 15. See *DFPI*, v. 4, 132.

25. Stuart W. Rockwell (1917–2011), career foreign service officer; stationed in Jerusalem when war broke out in 1948; reassigned as Officer in Charge, Palestine-Israel-Jordan Affairs, 1948–1950; warned Israeli diplomats that their policies would spawn antisemitism in the United States. See Hahn, *Caught in the Middle East*, 106.

26. Memorandum by Rusk for Webb, June 9, 1949, *FRUS*, 1949, v. VI, 1107; memorandum by Webb, *FRUS*, 1949, v. VI, 1109; memorandum by Department of State for the president, June 10, 1949, *FRUS*, 1949, v. VI, 1110.

1) Knox had been in the habit of going to the Foreign Office once a week to talk at length and there to be briefed in detail; Ford, though a friendly person who they realize has had discomforting household problems, has not yet gotten into this useful habit. I assured FDR, Jr. that I thought that Ford would soon recover this ground.

2) Second, and more serious was that the Israelis regard Colonel Andrus as dumb and as incapable of learning, and as a man to whom they feel they cannot safely confide. They contrasted him most unfavorably with Colonel van der Velde, whom they adored and trusted implicitly. Illustrative of Colonel Andrus's slowness, FDR, Jr. said that he was confident that he himself already knew more of the geography of Israel and its military problems than did Colonel Andrus. The Israelis had recently been shocked by his formal request for a detailed statement of their forces, locations, and strength. This request, they said, any military man should have known could not have been acceded to and should never have been made.

FDR, Jr. also spoke of an Israeli invention, which was being much sought after by the Russians, and which he thought would be freely shared with us by them [the Israelis] if they were properly approached. He also reported that they had told him that the request for places in our military training for two or three top Israelis had been declined for this year on the ground that the schools were full. This, FDR, Jr. thought, was fantastic, and [he thought] that we should invite these people and thus bring about a closer liaison [than] could be achieved in any other way. He left the impression of a young man of extraordinary capacity and drive. I sent with him warm greetings to his mother.

On his return to the United States, Roosevelt, together with Congressmen Abraham Multer, Emanuel Celler, and Jacob Javits, visited McGhee to express concern regarding State Department pressure on Israel.[27] *Roosevelt later wrote McDonald, "I have done everything humanly possible to impress the powers that be that the southern Negev must remain in Israeli hands."*[28]

McDonald also asked Ben Abrams to contact David Niles. On June 14, Abrams wrote McDonald, "I met D.N. last Friday [June 10] and after a long discussion relating to my trip [to Israel in May] and my impressions in which as usual you played an important part, I again received his assurance that there is nothing at all to be concerned about. I am certain that you will receive the same reassurance when you come back for a visit in August." McDonald replied, "I appreciate your words about

27. See Multer and Celler to McGhee, August 31, 1949, NARA, RG 59, MC 1390, reel 20, frames 136–137.
28. Roosevelt to McDonald, July 25, 1949, McDonald Papers, Columbia University, box 3, folder 45.

DN. They are the more encouraging coming in the midst of what has been a rather difficult period."[29]

Young Rabbi Jacob Herzog was at the house for about an hour at his suggestion. He did most of the talking about the following:

1) The return of Monsignor McMahon, who is bringing with him a delegation from the Vatican. This time McMahon will apparently have a more definite status with authority over a large area in the Middle East. Herzog lent me McMahon's Catholic Near East Welfare Association report, which he said contained, despite its mild language, some sharp criticisms of the Israelis.[30] Herzog said he was looking forward to long talks with McMahon, too.

2) Herzog thinks that the Vatican has not yet clarified its view, or at any rate is not yet ready to indicate what that view is, about Jerusalem. He suspects that it would be a preference for a Catholic mandatory, France or Italy, with the latter having the first place. I pointed out to him the probability that such a proposal would be unpopular with non-Catholic leaders, especially those in the United States who are always quick to sense danger in any Catholic or Vatican move.

3) Garland Hopkins is regarded by Herzog as a menace, unscrupulous, and un-Christian.

4) Herzog spoke again of the success of his father's mission in the States and of the president's statement that his half-hour with the chief rabbi had been one of the most thrilling of his lifetime.[31]

5) Herzog had opposed Colonel Dayan's policy of refusing permission to various people, including Catholic prelates, to cross the lines as a means of persuading the Jordanians to work out a more comprehensive and satisfactory agreement for the trans-line traffic [in Jerusalem]. Subsequently, the permission to Catholic priests had been given, but not until a public protest had been made.

29. Abrams to McDonald, June 14, 1949, McDonald to Abrams, June 28, 1949, McDonald Papers, Columbia University, box 6, folder 2.

30. The report was also sent directly to McDonald by Francis Cardinal Spellman of New York, who argued that the Israelis were behaving illegally in rejecting internationalization for the entire city. Spellman added that "only by international status for Jerusalem and the Holy Places can there be any lasting guarantee for the future of Christian interests in the Holy Land, whereby they would be protected against any future change of policy within Israel." Spellman to McDonald, June 11, 1949, McDonald Papers, USHMM, box 7, folder 14.

31. See entry of April 1, 1949. Rabbi Yitzhak Herzog was in the United States in May 1949 for the eighth annual meeting of Agudat Israel in New York and for UJA-sponsored events. He met President Truman on May 10. Herzog read Psalm 126 to Truman: "When the Lord restored the fortunes of Zion." Truman in turn read from the Book of Isaiah: "And He shall judge among the nations, and shall rebuke many people; they shall beat their swords into plow-shares, and their spears into pruning-books; nation shall not lift up sword against nation, neither shall they learn war any more." Herzog further told the president, "God put you in your mother's womb so that you would be the instrument to bring about Israel's rebirth after two thousand years." Truman was deeply moved. Paul C. Merkley, *The Politics of Christian Zionism, 1891–1948* (New York: Routledge, 1998), 191.

The rest of our talk was more general and not noteworthy, perhaps primarily because I was then so preoccupied with the pending US-Israeli crisis that I had difficulty concentrating on the rabbi's philosophical discussion.

In the later afternoon, Ford and I spent an hour and twenty minutes at Sharett's office. Sharett elaborated first the boundary point in the Israeli answer to the president's note. He explained that the phrase used by Secretary Acheson in their talk in New York,[32] "mutual adjustments," had been understood by Sharett in the sense of "minor adjustments" and not at all as "compensations or exchanges." Sharett thought of it as referring to "mutual adjustments" between Israel and Arab Palestine, [and] is "sorry if [the] secretary misunderstood."[33]

As to refugees, Sharett elaborated [the] phrase in his letter "under urgent consideration" as including permission to "round out families" and "more general permission [for the] return of women and children of Arabs [at] present in Israel." As to [the] phrase "measure of repatriation actually carried out," approximately 24,000 [have] already returned, divided equally between north and south. Total Arabs in Israel-held territory now 150,000.[34]

Sharett, noting press reports from Washington quoting the acting secretary [James Webb], said: "We here [are] besieged for news" but the Foreign Office has admitted merely "exchange of views" [with the US]. Will wait on US initiative for fuller statement. "Would not oppose publication of notes." Regarding Department telegram of June 8, quoting Shiloah as unable see any justification for [the] charge of rigidity in connection with [the] Gaza plan, Sharett said that neither in that, nor otherwise in Lausanne, had Eytan been rigid.[35] Regarding the Bunche compromise proposal, involving Syrian withdrawal to [the] international frontier and for demilitarization of Ein Gev, Sharett said [the] latter point would be difficult, but rather left impression of acceptance.[36] I argued that this would be wise.

32. Meeting of April 5, 1949, Waldorf Towers, memorandum by Acheson, *FRUS*, 1949, v. VI, 890–894.

33. Sharett added that Israel's views of the territorial settlements with Lebanon, Syria, and Egypt were based on international frontiers, subject to any settlement over Gaza, which might allow for mutual adjustments. Sharett to Eytan, June 10, 1949, *DFPI*, v. 4, d. 67.

34. Specifically Sharett mentioned that, since the war, 12,000 refugees were authorized to return and live in Galilee and 12,000 in the Negev, with a further 800 under consideration for return to the Galilee (wives, minor children). Sharett added that, to avoid spreading false hopes, Israel did not publish figures.

35. McDonald refers to Webb to McDonald, no. 344, June 8, 1949, *FRUS*, 1949, v. VI, 1095–1096, which discussed a comment by Shiloah in Washington to the effect that Truman's reference in the May 29 letter to "rigidity" concerning "excessive Israeli claims to further territory" was triggered by Israel's Gaza offer at Lausanne. Webb ordered McDonald to "leave no doubt" to the Israelis that the May 29 note was occasioned by their "rigidity" at Lausanne over existing refugee and boundary questions. Ethridge believed that the Israeli Gaza proposal could be used as a basis to pry Israeli concessions in the Negev. See Ethridge (through Bruce) to secretary of state, no. 2413, June 12, 1949, *FRUS*, 1949, v. VI, 1124–1125.

36. Included in Mohn to Sharett, June 8, 1949, *DFPI*, v. 3, d. 329, and map on p. 523; Webb to McDonald, no. 347, June 8, 1949, *FRUS*, 1949, v. VI, 1100–1102. The armistice line was to run within Israeli territory between the points of Lake Hula and Lake Tiberias. The disputed area that contained the Mishmar HaYarden settlement was to become a fully demilitarized zone, and civilians could return to areas in the demilitarized zone that they had evacuated.

After the meeting, McDonald reported to Washington that the US publication of the May 29 note and the Israeli response would be "unfortunate" insofar as it would "arouse strong [Israeli] public feeling;" that "Sharett feels Israel [is] wrongly charged with 'rigidity;'" that regarding the Arab refugees, "Sharett's manner of presenting these admittedly limited concessions was possible indication [of] Israel's softening on refugees;" and that there was an "even chance" that Israel would accept the Bunche compromise regarding the armistice with Syria.[37]

Friday, June 10

Vanthier came out to see the text of Bunche's compromise Israel-Syrian armistice proposal. It had been arranged that his government would in this way save cable charges. Vanthier tried to sound me out about the US-Israel negotiations, but I remained reticent. Vanthier also asked about housing. I told him frankly what we were paying here. But when he asked me whether I could tell him of any villas in this neighborhood for the French minister, I could not refrain from laughing at his optimism and lack of realism.

Saturday, June 11

To the beach in the morning. At work the rest of the day on documents. In the evening, to Jennie Tourel's final concert. I have never heard her to such advantage, whether she was singing English, French, or Russian songs. She did them all beautifully, giving to each distinctive and individual color. She is more exciting than Marian Anderson. Kaplan during the intermission spoke with something akin to a contempt about the British reported "easing of the arms embargo for the Arab states."[38]

The substance of the President Truman's May 29 note had leaked and was broadcast on June 10, 1949, by syndicated columnist Drew Pearson. McDonald, in a cable to the Department for the president's personal attention, described the adverse press and public reaction. He urged that "further US views not be expressed in terms of imperatives . . . unless President and Department are prepared to use extreme measures [the] ultimate [effect] of which no one could now foresee."[39]

Later that same day, McDonald wrote another cable to the State Department for the personal attention of Clark Clifford: "[The] Department, with best intentions of

37. McDonald to secretary of state, no. 443, June 10, 1949, *FRUS*, 1949, v. VI, 1110–1112. Webb replied that no publication was envisioned, but he wanted additional information on Israeli repatriation plans. Webb to McDonald, no. 363, June 13, 1949, NARA, RG 59, 501.BB Palestine, box 2125, folder 5.

38. The British wanted to supply certain quantities of arms and ammunition to Egypt, Iraq, Jordan, and if necessary other Arab states for what they called internal security and training purposes. They planned to begin supplying Jordan the second week of June. London still hoped for Israeli concessions in the Negev. Webb informed all US missions in the Middle East except for Tel Aviv. Webb to missions in Arab capitals, unnumbered, June 7, 1949, *FRUS*, 1949, v. VI, 1092; Holmes to secretary of state, no. 2205, June 8, 1949, *FRUS*, 1949, v. VI, 1099.

39. McDonald to secretary of state, [personal attention president and acting secretary], no. 445, June 11, 1949, *FRUS*, 1949, v. VI, 1115.

causing Israel to make what seems to Washington 'reasonable and necessary concession'
on refugees and boundaries . . . [has] so embittered Israel opinion that Ben-Gurion and
Sharett would be forced despite their will and better judgment to resist US demands. Is-
rael concessions on refugees are possible if [the] request for these is not again put in form of
demand. But under no circumstance except use of overwhelming force will Israel yield
any part of the Negev. Weizman[n] always moderate in views and ardent admirer of
President Truman has told me 'Negev will be held until the last Jew.'" McDonald added
to Clifford that his recent despatches *"have been written in full remembrance of your*
final words to me when I was leaving [the] White House before coming [to] Israel."[40]

Sunday, June 12

Pleasant visit at tea with Mr. [Reuven] Rubin.[41] We chatted about Bucharest, but he told me nothing noteworthy. Prior to that, I was intrigued by
his evident interest, which he at first rather tried to hide, in the Israeli pictures
which constituted our exhibit.[42] I led him around to note each of them before
I answered his repeated question as to whether we had purchased them. As I
was explaining the arrangement, Ruth came in at the psychological moment
and suggested that the house would not be complete without a Rubin flower
picture. I added, of course we had to have a picture of Israel's "most famous"
painter. He said that most of his pictures were stored where he could not get at
them, but he hoped that one flower picture would be available.

We were all pleased with Mrs. Hooper, a tall, dark sophisticated woman of
the world, speaking English with a marked English accent. Despite the social
occasion, I took Hooper into the study and brought him up to date, and then
later had a long talk with him, Fred and the colonel [Andrus]. The latter [An-
drus] is confident that the Israelis are powerful enough to have their way not
only with Syria, but also with Jordan, and that there is a strong feeling that this
is the simplest way out. He does not think they are worried, nor is he, about
international repercussions. He is inclined to tie the Dayan stiff statement to Vigier with the movement near Government House and the leave cancellation [for
soldiers in IDF].[43] He thinks that together they constitute a clear foreshadowing

40. McDonald to secretary of state [personal attention Clifford], no. 446, June 11, 1949,
Truman Library, Clifford Papers, Subject File 1945–54, box 13, folder Palestine—Correspondence—Miscellaneous, 1 of 3. McDonald afterward reported that "extremely sensitive Israeli
government, including all shades [of] opposition in [the] Knesset and elsewhere, is viewing each
move arising out [of the] recent exchange of notes and will be quick to take offense at any indication of partiality of treatment. . . . [If] authorization has been given to publish notes [I] should
appreciate being so informed since I feel repercussions on our position here may be grave." Mc-
Donald to secretary of state, no. 453, June 15, 1949, NARA, RG 59, 501.BB Palestine, box 2125,
folder 5. The State Department denied leaking the information to Pearson and blamed it on Shiloah's constant discussion of the note in the United States.

41. Reuven Rubin (1893–1974), Romanian-born Israeli artist and first Israeli ambassador to
Romania.

42. In April 1949 McDonald had arranged to borrow works from the Tel Aviv Museum to
help decorate the residence.

43. The enclave around the old British Government House to the south of the Old City
served as a Red Cross and then UN safe haven during the fighting in Jerusalem. It remained
demilitarized under UN protection following the Israeli-Jordanian armistice agreement of

of stronger Israel policy. Hooper reported substantial French material being supplied to Syrians, but no one seemed to think that this would be used effectively against the Jews.

Monday, June 13

Usual breakfast conference with Ford. Under his influence I reduced my draft telegram to the Department about leave cancellations to the brief statement that we were discussing matters intimately with the colonel [Andrus], and [that] it looked as if the Israelis were preparing [for resumption of hostilities], in the event that Za'im refused to talk about Bunche's proposal.[44]

Samuel Kopper called from Jerusalem at eleven twenty-five and said he was ready to come down, and I urged him to do so at once to arrive in time for lunch.[45] He accepted to spend the night at the house. We waited lunch until 2:15, but he did not arrive until after half past. He had had a slow driver and had gotten lost in Tel Aviv. There was time only for informal friendly talk during the meal, until we were joined by Ford near the end. Even then during the half an hour or so we had together in the study, Kopper was far from outgiving. About 6:30, Kopper, who had returned and gotten ready for his dinner with the Hoopers, joined me and Ford on the roof. We then talked for well over an hour, with Kopper beginning to give a little more.

At teatime members of an economic mission representing the Industrial Institute of Israel, Inc.[46] spent about an hour discussing economic conditions and possibilities here. The group included Ralph Friedman,[47] Morton S. Wolf,[48] David S. Rosenthal,[49] and Dr. Josef Cohn.[50] The discussion was mostly about

April 1949, but because it abutted the Israeli and Jordanian zones in Jerusalem, the two sides decided to divide the area, save the Government House compound itself, which housed UN officials. On June 6, in response to an attempt by Jordanian troops to take positions in their allotted section, Israel installed troops in its allotted area and began to fence it off. The US missions in Damascus and Amman saw the incident as a harbinger of what they called Israeli aggression. Moshe Dayan, who oversaw the operation, argued that the Israeli-Jordanian armistice obviated earlier truce agreements and UN resolutions. McDonald reported Andrus's analysis that Israeli forces were now astride the Hebron-Jerusalem road and controlled Arab communications in Palestine. McDonald to secretary of state, no. 440, June 8, 1949, NARA, RG 59, MC 1390, reel 19, frame 477.

44. Keeley reported from Damascus that Za'im might not accept the Bunche compromise. Keeley to secretary of state, no. 322, June 11, 1949, *FRUS*, 1949, v. VI, 1119–1120.

45. Samuel Kopper, the Near East Division's assistant director, was making a tour of the Middle Eastern capitals. He arrived in Tel Aviv on June 13.

46. Industrial Institute of Israel, organization created in 1949 by major American executives, including William S. Paley (CBS) and Maurice Wertheim (Wall Street banking), to channel American capital and industrial expertise to Israel. Samuel Rosenman was the first chair of the executive committee.

47. Ralph Friedman (1904–1992), Brooklyn-born financial executive and philanthropist; first president of Industrial Institute of Israel; chairman, American Jewish Committee National Board, 1964–1966; headed Bank Leumi operations in North America, 1963–1970; worked for improved Jewish-Catholic relations.

48. Morton S. Wolf (1907–1976), founder and head, Spencer-Taylor real-estate development and management company in New York, which ran some of New York's major hotels.

49. David S. Rosenthal (1898–1982), New York garment industry and real estate leader and philanthropist; co-founder, Albert Einstein College of Medicine and Brandeis University.

50. Dr. Josef Cohn (1904–1986), Berlin-born political scientist; adviser and secretary to Chaim Weizmann; represented Weizmann Institute in Europe; helped establish scientific coop-

textile possibilities. One of the members also spoke at length about the possibilities of chemical manufacture here, particularly through the extension of the potash works and development of fertilizer from the air. The former, he thought, was largely a matter of communications and the latter of power. I should have noted in reference to textiles that the specialist expressed serious doubt about the capacity of Israel to meet Western competition in the foreign markets. I urged the group to come back to see me before they went away.

Tuesday, June 14

Kopper joined me at breakfast about 7:30, and later, with Ford also present, we talked until after nine. I then sent him off to Jerusalem with Shalom. By that time much of Kopper's reserve had melted, and he confessed to a desire to have stayed longer and to having learned much while he was here. Others whom Kopper saw besides Ford, Mr. and Mrs. Hooper and myself, were Miss Herlitz and [unknown] for an hour and twenty minutes Monday afternoon. He also met the Helmses Monday night, and talked with Sir Alexander [Knox Helm] for half an hour, bringing back from the latter an intimation that I [sensed] to be rather cool.

The following are the main points, not arranged necessarily in any special order, which I recall from the five or six hours I spent with Kopper. At first, he seemed coldly but firmly satisfied both with the manner and the substance of the Department's communication of May 29. In reply to my comment that the document left very little more to be said, he commented dryly: "That was the intention." The clear impression was that action was envisaged instead of more writing. Ford interpreted this, in the light of what Kopper had said to him, as meaning a possible suspension of the Export-Import loan. In defense of the Department's position, Kopper argued that there was no alternative. The PCC was getting nowhere; it was necessary to break the logjam. Moreover, Israel had been told by Rusk on the night before the vote was taken to admit [Israel] to the UN that the US was counting upon concessions on the two main points, refugees and boundaries.[51]

As to refugees, Kopper had in mind, apparently from McGhee, a figure of 230,000. He argued that the acceptance of this number by Israel now, or the promise to accept them, would put the onus upon the Arabs and advantage Israel in the eyes of world opinion. During the session at the Foreign Office, where the "Gaza plan" had been discussed (to Kopper's surprise, Miss Herlitz insisted staunchly that the initiative for this plan had come definitely from Ethridge—Kopper had gotten quite different impression from Ethridge),[52]

eration between West Germany and the Weizmann Institute, the first Israeli scientific enterprise to accept German scientists.

51. On the night of May 9, 1949, Rusk telephoned Elath and said that Israel, if it did not take immediate steps to contribute to the refugee issue, would antagonize the whole world. Rusk did not mention this step as a quid pro quo for Israeli membership in the UN.

52. Ethridge repeatedly pointed out that Ben-Gurion first raised the idea at their meeting in Tiberias on April 18, 1949.

Kopper pressed the Israelis with the argument that if Israel, as a part of the deal about Gaza, should take and resettle approximately 250,000 refugees there, then they could take that number irrespective of Gaza. When Kopper made this point to me, I gave the answer which I think should have been obvious to him, that the political and territorial advantage of rounding out Israel's territory in the southwest would be an enormous incentive to make the sacrifices necessary to take the refugees in the strip, whereas without those incentives, it would not only be much more difficult for the Israeli government to say yes to the acceptance of a comparable number; it would be immeasurably more difficult for public opinion to brace itself to pay the necessary price of such an influx. Nonetheless, I am not sure that Kopper was convinced, because towards the end of his stay, he raised the question whether we ought not send off a telegram to the Department making the point that he had tried to make with the Israelis.

As to boundaries, Kopper was non-committal. When I told him of the impossibility of our answering the Israelis' insistent questions: "To whom shall we make territorial concessions?" he admitted that "This is a weakness in our armor." He then added: "The Department has not yet thought the matter through. We have not yet made up our mind what the adjustment should be." When the discussion reached this stage at one or two points, I decided to press the matter and to see if I could not get an expression of opinion, at least negatively. To do this, I expressed with emphasis my conviction, which Ford when he was present said was also his, that Israel would never yield the southern Negev, no matter what economic pressure was put upon it to do so. I quoted Dr. Weizmann, Ben-Gurion, and others to the effect that it could be taken from them only when the last Jews in the area had been killed. I told Kopper that I had expressed this view to the Department because I regarded it as my duty to report as frankly as I could, not to pull my punches because the report might not fit into Department's preconceptions. To my elaborations on this point, Kopper remained silent but obviously very attentive. It seemed to be a new idea to him that Israel would not be sensible and yield some territory in order to gain the advantage of a quicker peace and uninterrupted collaboration of the US.

It was during the exchanges on these points on Tuesday morning that Kopper finally put to me the $64 question: "You agree, don't you," he said, "that Israel intends just as soon as possible to seize the whole of the territory west of the Jordan?" He seemed so certain of my answer, that he misunderstood my first words of reply to mean an affirmative. Immediately, I made it clear that I did not share that view at all, that on the contrary, I was convinced that the present government had no intention of seizing the territory held by Abdullah. I underlined that, instead, those now in power were concerned to get a settled peace and to win a victory over their greatest present task, the adequate absorption of the immigrants, success with housing, transportation, and living costs. These, I said, were the tasks which were absorbing the imagination and the energies of the government. What ten, twenty, or thirty years would hold, I have no idea, but that I was sure that if left alone, the Israelis were confident that they would be able to make peace with Abdullah, and that this, rather than further conquest, was their aim. That my exposition shook Kopper's conviction, which he had had before he began this trip and which had doubtless been strengthened by nearly everything he had heard in the Arab countries, I could not tell. It was fairly clear, however, that he was taking account of my interpretation and weighing it, although not necessarily as heavily as it deserved, against his earlier mindset.

On the problems of refugees, Kopper was naturally more frank. He showed me a most interesting memorandum, which had been approved at the White House and is now being processed by the [Department of the] Treasury and Bureau of the Budget. It envisions an expenditure of from $250 to $275 million during the next three years on the resettlement of the refugees. Of this amount, the US might make available forty to fifty million a year for the three-year period. The outline suggested the following estimates from the International Bank, $15 to $50 million; Export-Import, $30 to $50 million; others $25 to $50 million; US government, $117,500,000. The expenditures were to be in the order of $30 million for work in Israel and $160 million in the Arab countries.[53] These figures were quite new to me and showed the further development of the Department's planning [more] than I had anticipated was the case. Kopper made clear, too, that these figures were regarded as additional to those contained in the Department's recent secret memorandum on the estimates for the first stages of the implementation of Point Four. On this last, I explained to Kopper why, despite the Department's recent permission, I was not now inclined to make a public speech here on Point Four. My reason was not that there was now less need than before to debunk current exaggerations, but rather that this would be an inappropriate time in the midst of current public resentment at "US pressure" for its representative to make any public statement.

On the subject of refugee administration, I told Kopper quite frankly that it was evident to me that the PCC was almost the worst possible basis for subsequent operations. He did not take any direct exception to my repetition of the current characterization of the PCC as "an inefficient post office." Instead, he admitted that the policy of France on the commission had been negative, if not intentionally obstructive. He said that the French evidently thought they were riding a favorable tide which, given time, would bring them back to influence and prestige in the Levant states.[54] About Yalçin, Kopper was of the opinion

53. The cost projections of this repatriation and resettlement program, by which Israel was to repatriate 200,000 of the estimated 700,000 refugees, had been discussed between Acheson and Truman. See the George McGhee memorandum on the Palestine Refugee Problem, May 4, 1949, *FRUS*, 1949, v. VI, 984–987.
54. Za'im's coup in Damascus was viewed in Paris as a positive sign in this regard. The French PCC delegate Claude de Boisanger insisted that the November 29 partition resolution form the basis of the Lausanne talks as a means by which to assuage Syria and Lebanon. Eytan to Sharett, May 9, 1949, *DFPI*, v. 4, d. 13.

that the old man had neither the desire nor the ability to press matters forward. He also agreed that against French non-cooperation and Turkish inaction, Ethridge, despite his utmost efforts, had been able to accomplish almost nothing.

I then told him that I was going to suggest to McGhee by a telegram, and then elaborate in a letter, my conviction that the PCC must not be dependent upon [the UN] as a base for subsequent refugee operations, but instead the Department ought to consider having the UN broaden the base of Griffis's office's mandate, and try to secure as the latter's successor a younger Hoover who would be willing to devote the next three years to the refugee task. Kopper made no objection.[55]

We spoke briefly about Garland Hopkins. Though Kopper was rather noncommittal, I gathered from what he said that the American missions elsewhere were not enthusiastic about Hopkins, despite his marked pro-Arabism. Kopper was shocked by Hopkins's acceptance of the idea of the assassination of Abdullah as a method in *Realpolitik*.[56]

Speaking of Israeli personnel, Kopper was enthusiastic about their energy and devotion. They made, he said, many of the Arab officials look like amateurs. He was obviously impressed by the thoroughness with which the governmental job was being tackled here.

In connection with the earlier reference intimated by Kopper, that in a deepened crisis I might be recalled, I told him that I was anxious not to go home until I could have a couple of months there beginning in later August. We spoke briefly, too, about my earlier suggestion about a regional conference of chiefs of missions. He agreed that despite the visits to this area of so many men from the Department, it would be desirable to hold such a conference. He agreed that it was obvious that there never would be a time in which there would not be a certain inconvenience at one or more posts to having the chief attend such a conference, but that this was a [price], which was small in proportion to the advantage of such a meeting. I did not press the issue further with him, partly because I thought such a conference probably would not be called at the moment following so closely after the visits of the men from Washington, and partly too, because I did not want it to interfere with my projected trip home. Finally, as I saw Kopper off in the Oldsmobile, I had a feeling that his visit had been, from both his point of view and ours, valuable.[57]

55. McDonald to George McGhee, June 15, 1949, *FRUS*, 1949, v. VI, 1140–1141. In his memorandum of April 27, McGhee had suggested that the PCC oversee refugee resettlement and repatriation efforts.

56. Hopkins thought that Abdullah would not accept Hopkins's plans for Palestine, but that he soon would be assassinated by less pragmatic Arabs anyway.

57. Kopper next met with Moshe Dayan in Jerusalem and then visited all of the Middle Eastern capitals. He submitted his report on June 27 from Athens. He respected the Israeli leaders and was disappointed with the Arab leaders, yet argued that "settlement continues to depend on moderation of both Arabs and Israelis—particularly the latter since the former are powerless to be otherwise. More important however is [the] necessity for Israel [to] understand firmness [of] our position and that representations recently made were not hollow words. Israel [is] frankly

At 11:30 Menachem Begin came to the office and remained about [forty] minutes. After some general talk about pending budget discussion in the Knesset, and the possibility of postponement of consideration of a written constitution,[58] he came to the two subjects which were obviously those which he was most interested in: 1) American "pressure" about refugees; 2) "pressure" about boundaries. His argument on both these points was a familiar one.

Begin argued that the November 29, 1947, UN resolution was never implemented because of the subsequent Arab attack and that there was no Palestinian Arab state to be compensated. Begin also argued that among the returning Arab refugees would be a fifth column engaged in guerilla warfare. Israel would have to protect its security and these Arabs would be worse off. He rejected the Gaza plan because it would come at the price of the southern Negev, and "there was no occasion . . . to ask Israel to take back part of its own territory in order to be burdened at the same time with some 200,000 Arab refugees.[59]

He also spoke about the application of his colleague Ben-Eliezer for a visitor's visa and made a plea for the American [Al] Rosoff who had been on the *Altalena* and who had lost his papers and was now derelict. On the Ben-Eliezer matter, I told him of what had been done and promised to let him know the results as soon as possible.[60] On the other I said I would make inquiry and let him know the status of the case. Throughout his talk, Begin was calmly professorial, giving no suggestion of the terrorist. Also, though less directly than Bergson, he sought to convey the impression of friendliness to the US.[61]

Wednesday, June 15

Over to the office of the British legation, where for an hour I talked with Helm. After the usual preliminaries about housing and other housekeeping matters, I gave him a factual and frank, though not (as was inevitable) complete account of the developments between the US and Israel since Saturday, May 28: the arrival of the communication, the talk with Ben-Gurion and Sharett, the fact that the former had made a brief statement, Sharett's subsequent explanation that the "finalization" of the formal reply would wait on the arrival of Eytan, who was being recalled for consultation, the date and the length of the Israeli

---

hoping for change [in] US attitude. If Israel were able to continue unfettered attainment [of] their desires Arab states would have no recourse in long run but gird for long struggle which would be very detrimental to US interests." Burdett to secretary of state, no. 430, June 16, 1949, NARA, RG 59, MC 1390, reel 19, frames 544–545; Kopper to secretary of state [through Grady for McGhee and Mattison] no. 1249, June 27, 1949, NARA, RG 59, MC 1390, reel 19, frames 614–619.

58. Herut, the General Zionists, and Mapam favored a written constitution.

59. Memorandum by Ford, June 14, 1949, McDonald Papers, USHMM, box 7, folder 14.

60. Entry of May 24, 1949.

61. Reported in McDonald to secretary of state, no. 157, June 20, 1949, McDonald Papers, USHMM, box 7, folder 14.

reply, our talk with Sharett the next day, Thursday, June 9, the late development of Drew Pearson's disclosure, its report through Reuters and the Cairo radio, the Foreign Office's reaction, and that was about all.

In answer to Helm's question as to the nature of the Israeli reply, I was general in my terms. In answer to my question, he disavowed having any information from London about these exchanges. He doubted that the British had seen the American communication in advance. His only specific contribution to the exchange of tangible information was to call my attention to the trans-oceanic news service report that Moscow was not calling Ershov back as a demonstration of its displeasure at the "attitude of Israel in regard to diplomatic relations." Helm could not have been friendlier. I should have added that he told me of the regional conference of British heads of mission in the Middle East to be held in London in July. He was evidently delighted to have this reason to get back to London.

Our large dinner was made somewhat more exciting by the discovery that I had invited the Greenbergs without the knowledge of the family. With the others, the Davidowitzes, the Mendes Sackses, Hoopers, Miss Herlitz, and the family, we added up to fourteen. Everybody seemed to have a good time. In a discussion on the porch, Sam Sacks and Davidowitz differed sharply on the productivity of Israel labor, Sacks arguing that the salary scale, several times that prevailing in England, [made it] wholly impossible for Israeli products to compete in the world market. I took occasion to chat with Miss Herlitz briefly. She said there was nothing new except that she and Ford had arranged for weekly meetings. She added that he was really getting into his stride.

Thursday, June 16

Top-secret [despatch] which was of special interest because of denial that [was] broadcast from Egypt, "quoted extensively."[62] Apparently only [the] final paragraph in [the] "slightly garbled version" was carried by Drew Pearson's column [of] June 13. Assurances to be given to neighbor [Sharett] that there has been no "publicity" to date and [that there] would be none without prior consultation. No knowledge of Pearson's source, but not surprising [that] knowledge of communication became known "in view [of] leakage [in] Tel Aviv and Lausanne" and Shiloah's discussion of it in US.

Afternoon, first meeting of the diplomatic corps. Those present besides Ford, Hooper and myself were: the British minister, Sir Knox Helm; the French chargé, Albert Vanthier; the Russian chargé, M. L. Moukhine; and the Dutch consul general, J. A. Nederbragt. It was a pleasant social occasion lightened by the Russian's compliment to my wife that she speaks more clearly than I do. Directly from the diplomatic tea we went to a reception at the Sieffs' in Tel Mond. There seemed to have been hundreds of people present at Rebecca's WIZO party. During the late afternoon and evening, I chatted with a large

---

62. Concerns Israel's proposal concerning the Gaza Strip.

number of people, but there is little to report. Rebecca reminded me that she had not been to the house for a meal. She made a speech, not too long, we chatted [with] Elath[63] and the Lockers. To the latter, I reported about the visas for the agricultural leaders.

Friday, June 17

At 11:15, Elath came for more than an hour. First, I asked him to explain to me the reasons for the recent US representation [Truman's May 29 note]. He attributed these to the following factors:

1) Rockwell on the Palestine Desk, who is intelligent but unsympathetic;
2) to Rusk, who also has never been very friendly;
3) and to the president's humanitarian concern about refugees.
4) Back of these was the feeling that something had to be done to check Israel's "aggressive spirit" (these last were not Elath's words but they convey his meaning). He did not think that the president had changed his attitude, but on the contrary was still proud of his part in creating Israel. Moreover, the president, now having complete confidence in the Department and especially in the secretary [Acheson] and the under secretary [Webb], both his men, neither he nor Clark Clifford pays the personal attention which they did formerly to the workings of the Department on Palestine questions. Still another factor is the newness of the under secretary, who, in the nature of the case, would have to accept the judgment of the technicians. On the whole, he did not regard the situation resulting from the representations as being [as] serious as it seemed to people here. As to what followed immediately thereafter in Washington, he pleaded lack of knowledge in light [of] his absence from the city within a few days thereafter.

In answer to my question about Jewish personalities and the White House, Elath confirmed my earlier impression that none of the official Zionists was influential. He included among those close to the president: Potofsky, Dubinsky, and a name completely new to me—Jack Arvey, labor leader of Chicago.[64]

On the problem of refugees, Elath, while of course supporting the position of the government, confessed that he felt that something more should be done to give tangible, visible proof of some of Tel Aviv's good intentions. In particular, he thought that more should be done in the reunion of families than had been done, and this promptly. He "expected to be unpopular" here because of his insistence on this point.

---

63. Eliahu Elath, Israeli ambassador to Washington, was recalled for consultations following the delivery of the Truman note of May 29, 1949.

64. Jacob "Jack" Arvey (1895–1977), reform-minded liberal politician in Chicago and chair of Cook County Democratic Party, 1946–1950; instrumental in election of Mayor Martin Kennelly in 1947 and in elections of Governor Adlai Stevenson and Senator Paul Douglas in 1948.

As to his relations in Washington, he found Acheson friendly. He attributed his excellent [relationship] with the secretary to Felix Frankfurter.[65] Similarly, he found Webb friendly. The latter is known as an excellent administrator, put into the Department by the president with a thought thereby of assuring congressional support for whatever budgetary requirements were put forward. Only young Rockwell did he find unsympathetic and in a gentlemanly way, "satirical." In leaving, Elath promised to come back to see me again within a few days.

At four, left with Sam Sacks in his Dodge for Mount Carmel. The trip was long, two hours and a half, and never before did I realize how rough the road was. I wished repeatedly for our Oldsmobile or the old Packard. Arrived about six-thirty, greeted cordially by Dr. Bodenheimer and office staff.[66] How wonderful Mount Carmel is. At this location, one of the furthest buildings, one has a feeling that he is in the Adirondacks save for the magnificent ocean view. The air was crisp, and during the night one needed a blanket or so.

Saturday, June 18

Went for a long walk, gradually mounting the hills at the site of the old army camp and then beyond. I returned in time for our twelve o'clock date to leave for Acre and Nahariya. The former is intensely interesting, especially architecturally and also socially, because of the obvious depressed state of the Arabs. It is, however, as [an] excellent example of ancient architecture that the city merits most study. Nahariya was delightfully clean and well ordered.[67] We were treated as honored guests by the Cohens.[68] Madame showed me their guest book with the autographs of my Anglo-American Committee of Inquiry colleagues Crossman, Phillips, and Aydelotte back in March 1946.

Back to Bodenheimer's in time for lunch and a nap. After tea, we drove and drove higher and higher on Mount Carmel until we reached its crest on the Arab [Druze] village Isfiya. There a monastery marks, I think, the traditional site where Elijah brought down the fire from heaven to confute and destroy the prophets and idols of Baal.[69] We looked in vain, however, for my longed-for view of the Emek. The best we got was a magnificent view of the Acre plain to the north and Mount Tabor and I think Gilboa to the east.

65. Acheson studied law under Frankfurter at Harvard, and Frankfurter helped arrange a clerkship for Acheson under Louis Brandeis. Frankfurter and Acheson were best friends when Acheson was secretary of state, but they never discussed Israel, about which they disagreed. See Alden Whitman's obituary of Acheson in the *New York Times*, October 13, 1971.

66. Wilhelm Lion Bodenheimer (1890–1980), German-born physician; fled Germany for Palestine with his wife Else Biram, 1933; built the Bodenheimer Sanitorium on Mount Carmel in the Bauhaus style at an elevation of 300 meters with a spectacular view of the sea and surrounded by a nature park, 1937.

67. Israel's northernmost coastal city founded in 1935 to receive German Jewish immigrants. Contains Byzantine ruins.

68. Richard and Grete Cohen, German Jews who had run a guest house in Nahariya since 1937. Guests included Weizmann, Ben-Gurion, Sharett, Ralph Bunche, and others.

69. Could refer to the Monastery of Our Lady, described in the entry of December 16, 1948, which is near Isfiya.

Left at ten, after making a tentative promise to return with Bobby and Ruth in a fortnight. The trip down was as rough as the one up. In the late afternoon, I put in an official appearance at the really impressive exhibition, American Artists for Israel. This fine show of more than a hundred American paintings had been made possible through gifts by the artists and by the American Fund for Israel Institutions.[70] [Spoke with] Elias Newman, chairman [of the Committee of American Artists for Israel].[71] There were three brief talks including mine, in which I, in three or four minutes, praised the generosity of the artists and the fund, said that the show would give to the Israelis a fuller picture of American cultural interests, and my hope that there would be a comparable show of Israeli artists in the States.

In the evening, Miss Herlitz came [at McDonald's request] and stayed for two hours, giving me a full and, I think, accurate report on the long conference held the previous day in Washington in the office of the acting secretary of state. In addition to Webb, the Americans present were Rusk, Rockwell, Ethridge, and perhaps one other. The Israeli representatives were Aubrey Eban, Reuven Shiloah, and Uriel Heyd, [the Israeli] chargé d'affaires.[72] According to Miss Herlitz, the first hour was taken up by Ethridge's apologia for the failure of the PCC.

On June 12, Ethridge left the Lausanne Conference. Five days later, after meeting with President Truman, he resigned from the PCC. Raymond Hare of the State Department's Near East Division replaced him. On his way back to the United States, Ethridge stopped in Paris, where he blamed the Israelis for the stalemate at Lausanne. Ethridge suggested adjourning the Lausanne meetings and reconvening them in New York a month before the meeting of the UN General Assembly in September.[73]

He blamed Israel for making its offers [Gaza] too little and too late. Then he made the extraordinary suggestion that "there might be peace in fourteen

70. The exhibition by more than 100 American artists ran in New York from December 1948 to January 1949; the works were then donated to the Tel Aviv Museum, the Bezalel Academy of Art and Design in Jerusalem, and the Ein Harod Museum of Art.

71. Elias Newman (1903–1999), Polish-born painter; moved to New York in 1913 and traveled to Palestine/Israel often after 1925; painted biblical themes and American landscapes. See Elias Newman, *Art in Palestine* (New York: Siebel Company, 1939); idem., *American Artists for Israel*, exhibition catalog (December 21, 1948–January 30, 1949) (New York: American Fund for Palestinian Institutions and the Jewish Museum, 1948).

72. The Israelis called the meeting to add context to their government's reply of June 8 to the Truman note of May 29, particularly regarding the refugee and frontier issues. Eban's account, dated June 17, 1949, is in *DFPI*, v. 4, d. 84. The US memorandum is in *FRUS*, 1949, v. VI, 1148–1153.

73. Ethridge [through Bruce] to secretary of state, no. 2413, June 12, 1949, *FRUS*, 1949, v. VI, 1124–1125; memorandum by Webb [Ethridge meeting with president], June 16, 1949, *FRUS*, 1949, v. VI, 1146.

days if Israel made confidential offer [to the] PCC on refugees." Also talked generally about putting "McGhee Plan in operation as reward."

Rockwell made case against Israel's peaceful intentions on [the following] grounds:

1) "Reported concentration of troops at every point;"
2) appearance [of] Dayan at Jerusalem in armored car (this Miss Herlitz belittled, but I learned later from Riley's memorandum about the discussions at Jerusalem, that under the armistice terms armored cars were not admissible to demilitarized zone);
3) Shiloah's stopping in Prague to buy arms (on this Miss Herlitz commented that this was not Shiloah's business, that purchases were made by a special agency and everywhere where practicable);
4) Comay's frequent expressions of intransigence (this seemed to me as well as to Miss Herlitz quite out of keeping with Comay's character);
5) aggressive purposes attributed to Israeli offers because of alleged bellicose statements.

Rusk then brought up the question of "territorial compensations." Miss Herlitz said that Rusk admitted that this obligation had been deleted from the December 11 resolution "largely through Arab votes." Miss Herlitz put a question mark as to the meaning of this last point. She wondered whether US might be planning to raise [the] question again at UN in September. Ethridge then spoke about Jerusalem, saying that the US plan was not very far removed from that of Israel or what Israel might accept.

Eban judged that the atmosphere of the conference was less sharp than that indicated in the exchange of notes.[74] He was impressed that the Department had been fed on "a constant stream of malicious misinformation."[75] Eban stressed [at the meeting] various concrete proposals Israel had made, its desire for peace talks either through the PCC or directly with individual Arab states. He reported too that the Gaza proposition still existed, though vaguely.

I explained to Miss Herlitz in general terms how I thought the prevailing impressions in Washington might have been created. In particular, I told her of what I regarded as the disservice to Israel and the US involved in the Israeli army's present policy of "not giving out" to our military attachés, that this forced them to report rumors, which might cumulatively give quite false impressions at home.

---

74. Referring to Truman's communication of May 29 and Sharett's reply of June 8, 1949.

75. Eban also reported to Sharett that the "malicious" information had a negative effect at the White House; that an explanatory letter from Weizmann to Truman was urgent; that the Gaza proposal should be kept in play because the United States was interested in it; that Ethridge's frustrations were having a disproportionate effect; and that a McGhee plan for mass repatriation as well as the resettlement of refugees did exist. Eban to Sharett, June 17, 1949, *DFPI*, v. 4, d. 84.

McDonald told Herlitz that he would speak to the US attachés and tell the State Department that he disagreed with the attachés' reporting. He also gave details of the McGhee plan's financing (as revealed to him by Kopper) as it was to occur over three years. McDonald, as Herlitz reported to the Israeli embassy in Washington, then "read out his cables [to] Webb, Truman, Clifford, marked personal and dated [June] 11th, in which [he] strongly objects [to] contents, tone [of] note, asks why [there is] one-sided pressure, states Israel [is] unable [to] accept imperatives like last paragraph [of the May 29th] note.... In conclusion, [he] asks whether [the] President [is] prepared [to] draw [the] conclusions [that are] threatened. Also states [that] Israel [is] likely [to] give in slightly [on] refugees but never on [the] Negev, quote[s] moderate Weizmann in this respect."[76]

Ben-Gurion called and asked if I had any ideas about where he could get quickly an authoritative statement on the forms of organization of armies throughout the world. He was not concerned with strength, numbers, etc. but with organization as such.[77] I promised to do what I could. Worn out, I decided to drive over to see the Andruses and to check at the Sharon. Returned in an hour refreshed and to meet at the gate the family and the Fords, just back from the concert, which I had had to finesse.

Monday, June 20

At the office during the morning. Dictated telegram to the Department, indicated approval of Burdett's Jerusalem ideas for the superseding of the [Special Committee] by the Mixed Armistice Commission, and also the details of these programs, which followed closely the earlier working paper of the PCC.[78] In this, I also reported on the presentation to the Foreign Office of the Department's memorandum on the above subject. As [a] related subject, sought to play down alarmist reports about troop concentrations and aggressive designs here.

On June 17, Webb ordered McDonald to tell the Israeli government that the situation in Jerusalem in the Government House zone was a threat to peace in Palestine; that the United States wanted the Mixed Armistice Commission to take over negotiations concerning Jerusalem from the Special Committee established by the Israeli-Jordanian armistice agreement; and that General Riley, now occupied with the Israeli-Syrian negotiations, should chair the meetings of this Israeli-Jordanian commission in the hopes of defining the Jewish and Arab zones, public utilities services, and modes of access to the city's sensitive areas such as Mount Scopus.

McDonald later reported that the Israeli government rejected the notion that the Government House problem constituted a threat to peace. It accepted the proposal for

76. Herlitz to Heyd, June 20, 1949, *DFPI*, v. 4, d. 89.
77. Entry of May 31, 1949.
78. Burdett to secretary of state, no. 436, July 14, 1949, NARA, RG 59, 501.BB Palestine, box 2125, folder 8.

the Mixed Armistice Commission, adding its desire that only Riley preside over the meetings. Meetings of the Mixed Armistice Commission concerning Government House under Riley's chairmanship had in fact already begun.[79]

At the Kaete Dan spoke briefly with Mrs. Hoofien and finally with Dr. Mohn. I also met Major Stallings to whom I gave the second telegram to Riley. He promised it would be sent off promptly. In the evening delightful birthday party for Ford at his house.

Tuesday, June 21

Ford and I were at Sharett's office at five and remained with him for about an hour and a quarter.

At 11:00 a.m., McDonald had sent a top-secret telegram to the Department for the special attention of the president and the acting secretary. He provided five reasons why Israel would not attack its neighbors, including Israel's need to stabilize the economy and absorb the 250,000 immigrants expected to arrive annually and its need not to alienate global opinion.[80] *McDonald began his meeting with Sharett by reading the contents of the same telegram.*[81]

First, I outlined succinctly my estimate to the president and the acting secretary my reasons for not crediting current fears of Israel aggressive purposes. Taking account of extremist statements in army and Knesset and also of Israel's ability [to] impose its will, nonetheless following reasons are decisive: a) Ingathering task; b) battle against cost of living; c) wrecking influence of hostilities; d) [Israeli] confidence in Riley; e) world opinion and possible sanctions. Moreover, leaders [are] aware even quick victory would be self-defeating. They are not reckless, but intelligent and practical, desiring American support and president's friendship. Sharett's response was: "May the Lord reward you for your common sense understanding." These quiet words were the more remarkable in the light of the rest of the interview.

79. Webb to McDonald, June 17, 1949, *FRUS*, 1949, v. VI, 1153–1154; Sharett to McDonald, June 23, 1949, *DFPI*, v. 4, d. 98; McDonald to secretary of state, no. 489, June 25, 1949, *FRUS*, 1949, v. VI, 1184.

80. See McDonald to secretary of state [personal attention president and acting secretary], no. 471, June 21, 1949, *FRUS*, 1949, v. VI, 1163–1164 and n. 1. Rusk dismissed the message as "only McDonald's view." Acheson afterward told McDonald that his telegram was "read by the President with much interest," and that to the Department the "points you enumerate make out conclusive case against further Israeli mil[itary] adventures from realistic point of view of Israeli self-interest." Acheson wondered, however, whether "such considerations appear as decisive to Israeli leadership as to outside world." McDonald mused afterward: "There was satisfaction in [Acheson's] telegram, even though in a sense, my arguments were being used to point in the direction opposite from that intended." See Acheson to McDonald, no. 397, June 24, 1949, *FRUS*, 1949, v. VI, 1173–1174; McDonald Papers, USHMM, box 5, folder 3.

81. A detail he omitted from his report on the meeting. McDonald to secretary of state, no. 478, June 22, 1949, *FRUS*, 1949, v. VI, 1165–1166.

With marked show of resentment at what he termed "[Deputy Under Secretary of State] Rusk's peremptory fifteen-minute summons" to Israeli chargé [Uriel Heyd] on June 14,[82] Sharett outlined in great detail successive steps from May 25 to June 9 to secure personal conference with Za'im or [Foreign Minister Adil] Arslan and of Syrian "endless evasions and delays."[83] Sharett exclaimed that to be accused of imminent aggression in the midst of such Israeli "patient conciliatory procedure" was "shockingly unjust," and made Za'im's intransigency a model with Arab states.

As to present Syrian-Israeli relations, the foreign minister hopes [the] Mixed Armistice Commission negotiations will succeed, but warned that Za'im could not expect indefinitely to avoid withdrawal from Israel territory.[84] "US should understand that Israel will exhaust every peaceful means through the Mixed Armistice Commission, UN, direct negotiations, etc. to secure mutual agreement, but if Za'im persists in refusal to accept the Bunche proposal, Israel does not intend [to] remain quiescent."[85] Foreign minister is evidently under heavy strain as a result of bitter criticism in the press and the Knesset that the government's pro-American policy "had resulted in national humiliation." I believe his words are meant to emphasize with the US that justice and expediency require pressure on Za'im to evacuate Israel territory "comparable to that exerted on Israel [to] evacuate Lebanese territory."

Sharett took strong exception to opening sentence in Department's *aide mémoire* [of June 17] to the effect that the actual situation in Jerusalem [at the Government House] is a threat to peace. As to the substance [of] the Department proposal, Israel is "quite prepared to consider this important suggestion."[86] Foreign minister took exception also to importance given in acting secretary's conference with Eban, et al. [on] June 17 to the report that Dayan had arrived at Government House "in armored car." This was not—repeat—not a fact; Dayan "never uses armored car." By mistake, an armored car did appear at Government House, but Dayan "immediately ordered it away."[87]

Regarding reunion [of] Arab refugee families, Sharett explained this principle being maintained and procedure "being worked out." Decisions will be in individual cases with "security considerations paramount." I fear this foreshadows

82. Regarding IDF leave cancellations and troop movements in Jerusalem and on the border with Syria, presumably to force a settlement. See Webb to McDonald, no. 367, June 14, 1949, *FRUS*, 1949, v. VI, 1137.
83. Entry of May 31, 1949.
84. Ben-Gurion remained willing to reach peace accords with Syria only after the international border was restored. See Ben-Gurion Diary, entry of June 16, 1948.
85. The Syrian government argued that the Israeli incursion into the demilitarized Government House zone in Jerusalem showed that the Israelis did not respect demilitarized zones. Thus Damascus did not trust the Bunche proposal for the Israeli-Syrian armistice, in which Israel was to leave Syrian-evacuated territory in Israel demilitarized.
86. See also Sharett to McDonald, June 23, 1949, *DFPI*, v. 4, d. 98.
87. This accusation was made by Rockwell. *DFPI*, v. 4, d. 84.

relatively few reunions [in the] near future.[88] Regarding the Gaza proposal, foreign minister said that prime minister "disclaims conception at Tiberias,"[89] but Israel "still willing [to] accept strip including refugees."

As we were leaving, I said: "I trust nothing will happen to give ground for fear about Israel's pacific purposes towards Syria." Foreign minister replied: "If all peaceful means fail, we can't preclude possibility of ultimate use of force." I believe this remark to be a move in Israel's efforts to secure that [the] US influence Za'im to accept the Bunche formula. Certainly, non-armistice with Syria weakens all peace efforts with other Arab states. Support, therefore, of Bunche's proposal is "key log" in present jam.

Stupidly, I arrived at the Gat Rimon at 8:15 for my talk with Jacob Landau, though the dinner did not get under way until after 9:00 and was not finished until well after eleven. Landau talked about his plans, and, by questioning, I got something of a picture of the financial problem. Jacob Blaustein was formerly his chairman but was now very critical. According to Landau, the reason is Blaustein's unwillingness to make substantial financial contributions to the Jewish Telegraphic Agency.[90] Nonetheless, as Landau talked, my initial unpleasant impression of the man increased. I asked him whether he did not need someone to go to South America and elsewhere to raise money. The answer was yes. Then I suggested Mrs. [Yolande] Harmer and that he get in touch with her in Paris. He seemed impressed by the reasons I suggested for her probable success, and promised to look her up in Paris.

Before and during the dinner, I chatted with a number of people, but my talk with Sprinzak, speaker of the Knesset, needs to be noted. There had been a near crisis in the chamber that afternoon when one of the communist members undertook to use the excuse of asking a question to begin a speech, the thesis of which was that Israel would enjoy a more cooperative attitude from the East European countries in the matter of immigration of Jews if its policy were oriented more to the East.[91] Sprinzak interrupted the speaker and adjourned the session. From what Sprinzak and others said, it became more evident to me that the government has been under very heavy fire in the debate on foreign affairs, largely because of the disclosures about the US "demands." This news helped me to understand better Sharett's tenseness during our interview a few hours earlier.

88. Eban told Webb in the June 17 meeting that this step could lead to 50,000 Arabs being repatriated. See memorandum by Webb, June 17, 1949, *FRUS*, 1949, v. VI, 1149. Morris, *Birth of the Palestinian Refugee Problem Reconsidered*, 572.

89. Concerns Ben-Gurion's raising the Gaza Strip idea to Ethridge at Tiberias on April 18, 1948.

90. See entry of April 7, 1949. Blaustein had been chairman of the Jewish Telegraphic Agency during World War II and was now executive chairman of the American Jewish Committee. He was concerned that JTA reporting of official Israeli comments could be misconstrued as throwing doubt on the loyalty of American Jews to the United States. Funding from the AJC was critical to the JTA. See Ganin, *An Uneasy Relationship*, 27–47.

91. When Israel gained independence, 2.5 million Jews were living in Eastern Europe, 80 percent of them in the Soviet Union; 152,802 were able to emigrate to Israel between May 15, 1948 and the end of 1949—none from the USSR—and most in return for secret payments or trade arrangements. Bialer, *Between East and West*, 57–67.

When the dinner was nearly over, Elath came in, and we got into brief huddle. He said that he was depressed by the emotional tenseness he had found here, the direct result of the disclosures about the American note. Its effect had been as follows:

1) Weaken if not destroy all present hope of peace because of the prestige it gave to Za'im and his intransigence. One result has been to upset all optimistic calculations and to increase dangerously the possibility of incidents.
2) Israeli resentment was so bitter that it made difficult calm consideration of pending issues.
3) He was forced to reexamine his earlier views as to possible motivation of American attitude. He could see no logic in it unless there was an intention in Washington to destroy Israel—a purpose which he could not possibly credit knowing well as he does the men shaping American policy. Nonetheless, those in authority ought to understand the effect of their actions, whatever may have been their purpose.
4) His own position here is incomparably more difficult than he had thought it would be. I explained to Elath why I could not be at the dinner given for him by Miss Herlitz Wednesday evening. He understood, and I think was glad that I was keeping the Jerusalem appointment.

On June 24, McDonald reported to Washington the

> *recent prediction [in] some quarters that "tottering" Ben-Gurion Government may crash under weight [of] violent attacks [of] both left and right opposition centered primarily on Government's "pro-American" foreign policy and to considerably less extent on its domestic program. . . . While [it is] undeniable [that] the Government has been visibly shaken and both official and public resentment at US representation [of May 29] remains acute and profound, [I] am convinced Ben-Gurion will safely weather present storm but that he and other members [of] his Government will continue to smart from political lashing.[92]*

Earlier in the day a message came from General Riley that he could meet me for dinner at the King David Wednesday evening at seven—he would be arriving in Jerusalem at four, or he could come down to Tel Aviv Thursday morning. I wired that I would meet the general in Jerusalem at the time he suggested.[93]

Wednesday, June 22

My trip to Jerusalem during the morning, from a quarter past eleven until a few minutes after one, was pleasant. The Shephelah and the Judean Hills were increasingly brown as we mounted towards the plateau. Gone were the

92. McDonald to secretary of state, no. 486, June 24, 1949, McDonald Papers, USHMM, box 7, folder 15.
93. McDonald had urgently suggested the meeting. McDonald to Riley, June 20, 1949, McDonald Papers, USHMM, box 7, folder 14.

last traces of the variegated colored spring flowers and the green, which hid the bareness of the rocks this spring. At the King David, I was supplied with a beautiful suite overlooking the Old City. Over to the consulate a little after five, where I met Burdett and Roberts[94] on their way to the Millers' tea at the "Y."[95] The tea party was a success. The Millers were charming and had a number of interesting guests, including Brother Patrick and one of his Franciscan colleagues.[96] We chatted also about Garland Hopkins, whom he had known during the war. He thought him a very ambitious man; he was interested in my account of Hopkins's latest maneuvers, and said he shared my regret that Hopkins had managed to see His Holiness.

A few minutes before six, I met Riley in my sitting room.[97] He had changed from his uniform and wore a silk or rayon Russian-type blouse with a monogram on the pocket—the very embodiment of coolness. He seemed glad to see me, having expressed his appreciation that I had come up, because it would have been rather difficult and possibly embarrassing for him to come to Tel Aviv. I told him that I wanted to talk to him about a number of matters, some specific and some general. When he told me that he had not seen the text of the president's note, I gave him the substance of it and of the Israeli reply. To this I added my fear that those who had drafted the American text had not, as they should have done, warned the president:

1) of the inevitable sharp repercussions at home and;
2) more important, the probability that the Israelis would reject our demands.

Without commenting directly on this statement, Riley said that he too was somewhat troubled by our government's attitude. Later, I was to learn that he was thinking of something other than what was in my mind.

First, General Riley told me about the Israeli-Syrian negotiations. He deplored a new issue raised by Israel, that of the citizenship of the Arabs to be allowed to return to their small villages [in Israel]. He thought it difficult for Za'im to accept the contention that these should be considered Israelis and under local Israeli police, instead of retaining at least theoretical Arab citizenship under local Arab police.[98] General Riley also was inclined to be somewhat critical of Sharett for "trying to impress Za'im that he, Sharett, was more influ-

94. Perhaps Randoph Roberts, US vice consul in Haifa, assigned in March 1948.
95. On Alvah Miller and the YMCA, see entry of December 28, 1948.
96. Brother Patrick, Franciscan. The *Palestine Post* in an article of October 26, 1948, refers to a Father Patrick, a monk from Baltimore who brought gift parcels from Cardinal Spellman to Roman Catholic institutions in Jerusalem.
97. Summarized in McDonald to secretary of state, no. 166, June 27, 1949, NARA, RG 59, MC 1390, reel 19, frames 623–624.
98. Israel refused to accept Syrian civil administration within the proposed demilitarized zone within Israeli borders, insisting that Israeli civil administration be reinstated. Bunche insisted that all administration in the demilitarized zone be local only, depending on the population of the village in question, and that broader citizenship and sovereignty issues be raised only after the armistice was in place. *DFPI*, v. 3, d. 339, 341, 342, 343.

ential and more important than most foreign ministers."[99] On the other hand, General Riley's opinion of Za'im's foreign minister, Arslan, was not very different from that of Sharett's. General Riley regarded him as a "terrible person." On balance, however, General Riley held the Israelis primarily responsible for the delay in reaching an agreement with Za'im.

About Government House, General Riley was inclined to be critical of Dayan as "unnecessarily stiff." The latter had appeared at the Government House Mixed Armistice Commission conference [under Riley's chairmanship] accompanied by two armored cars. An example of Dayan's alleged stiffness, mentioned also by Burdett, was that Dayan refused to have the line, which would be tentatively drawn to divide the area, deviate as little as sixty or seventy yards in order to permit an Arab house to remain on the Arab side. On the question of status of civilians, particularly those of the UN, Dayan was also, General Riley thought, "stiff." The general admitted that the question whether UN officials should be kept out of the area was a nice one, because the armistice terms were silent. Nonetheless, he had taken the responsibility of insisting that such officials could not be banned, since there was no provision for such action within the armistice terms. Nonetheless, he was anxious to avoid having the issue sharply drawn because he was not certain that a judicial finding would be favorable. An example of possible Israeli violations in the Jerusalem area was, according to General Riley, the concentration there of some 3,000 men, instead of the approximately three hundred envisaged by the armistice terms. When this matter was brought to the attention of Dayan, he explained that he was not sure about the number, and that in any case he had not read the annex in which the permitted numbers were set forth.[100]

General Riley stressed the importance of settlement at the Government House and other Jerusalem area problems, because unsettled, they continued to be potential friction points; moreover, as time passed, with more and more Jews occupying Arab sections and with an increase of Jewish strength in proportion to that of the Arabs, the Jews were inclined to ban new concessions.[101] General Riley indicated that he was willing to accept the enlarged responsibilities which would be his if the Special Committee were replaced by the Mixed Armistice Commission, as had been suggested by Burdett, and later formally by the Department to Tel Aviv and Amman. I reported to General Riley Sharett's acceptance in principle, the day before, of the Department's *aide mémoire* on this substantive point. General Riley emphasized, however, that he had pointed out to the Department that he did not wish to be subordinate to or to have to report to the Sub-Committee of the PCC on Jerusalem, on which Barnes is the

99. Concerned Za'im's earlier refusal to meet with Sharett, because Sharett was not of equal governmental rank. See entry of May 31, 1949.

100. Annex II of the Armistice agreement provided for Israel and Jordan to maintain defensive forces in their sectors of Jerusalem, defined as two battalions of 800 men for each side.

101. Most Arab residents of Jerusalem living behind what became the Israeli armistice line had been evacuated during the previous fighting. Jewish refugees, including Jews from Jewish neighborhoods in Jerusalem, were settled there.

American member, but the existence of which might have been forgotten in Washington.

Latrun was an issue, said General Riley, which should and could be settled quickly. It required the yielding by Israel of only eight or ten small villages either in that area or in the Hebron area as a quid pro quo for the Legion's withdrawal beyond the crest of the ridge, which in Jewish hands, would give the latter control of the road. But on Latrun, as on other problems which the Special Committee was to have settled, and on which there appeared to be agreement weeks ago, Jordan had asked for a month or so delay in order that Arab opinion in Palestine and in the neighboring states might quiet down and be less resentful of Jordan's "surrender of Palestine territory in the northwest fringe of the Triangle to the Jews."

On refugees, General Riley was skeptical of present much-talked-about plans. He was inclined to think that the financial demands from the Arab states would be prohibitive. Nor was he surprised by my view that Israel (unless the Gaza [Strip] were returned) would probably take relatively few. He was skeptical, too, about the reported latest Israeli estimate of Arabs in Israeli-occupied territory, 200,000. I told him that Sharett had given me a few days earlier the figure of 150,000.[102] Towards the end of our talk, General Riley indicated that his chief question about US policy was its continued reference to November 29. This, he thought, raised "false hopes" among the Arabs. He had sought to disabuse them of these expectations by saying that it was too late to have hopes of recovering Western Galilee or Ramle or Lydda. He added that he had not been thinking in terms of the southern Negev.

General Riley then developed what is apparently one of his central theses about Israel. It is that increasing unemployment and the pressure of the immigrants have created a situation where the demobilization scheme of last December or January cannot be carried out. This means the retention of an army of approximately 80,000 in a relative state of idleness, a dangerous position. Implied in General Riley's analysis was the fear that the Israeli government might choose to use the army rather than allow it to become possibly dangerously discontented. This thesis led General Riley directly to the point that of course the Israelis have the power to take what they might want, even up to the whole of Palestine west of the Jordan. I was a little surprised at the general's complete acceptance of this thesis.[103]

102. Eliahu Sasson, who studied demographics as part of the Foreign Ministry's transfer committee, thought that there were 130,000 refugees. Morris, *The Birth of the Palestinian Refugee Problem Revisited*, 556–557.

103. Demobilization began in March 1949, the timing determined by the economic strain of continued mobilization and the need to stimulate the civilian economy. It accelerated after the armistice agreement with Jordan. On April 4, the number of soldiers was 82,000 [Ben-Gurion Diary, entry of April 16, 1949]; on May 23, 66,000 [Ben-Gurion Diary, entry of June 13, 1949]; and on June 27, 50,000 [Ben-Gurion Diary, entries of early July 1949]. Ben-Gurion envisioned an army of between 20,000 and 25,000 [Ben-Gurion Diary, entry of July 4, 1949]. We are grateful to Tuvia Friling for these references.

The more I thought about these views of the general, the more they seemed to fit into a dangerous pattern: US support of November 29, feeding Arab false hopes; the pressure on Israel to get through with armistices and to achieve peace; and its power to enforce its will. This combination leaves the US in the ungrateful position of seeming to encourage Israel's enemies while at the same time constraining Israel from forcing those enemies to terms. In the course of our long talk, particularly when we were joined by Burdett and Vigier before dinner, I, in answer to their question, underscored my belief that the Israelis would not yield any of the territory [they] now occupied, and in particular would not under any circumstances, except at the end of a disastrous new war, yield the southern Negev. I was a little surprised that Riley had not taken fuller account of the Israeli attitude towards the southern Negev. My only explanation is that he is so preoccupied with his more limited and highly important task that he has deliberately chosen not to confuse them by thinking beyond them.

As to refugees, I was frank to tell the group that I could not yet discern any will on Israel's part to make any large contribution by repatriating any substantial numbers unless these came in as a part of the "Gaza plan." Needless to add, they were not surprised. General Riley told me that Mr. Keeley had told him that my first long despatch on refugees was one of the most brilliant comprehensive and sound documents that he had seen, that he had called it to the special attention of his staff and ordered them all to make it required study.[104] In reply, I could only gasp that I admired Keeley's energy, and that his despatches, which I always read with great care, gave me a fuller picture of Syria than I was able to get of the other countries from the despatches of the other men. I explained to General Riley about Gowen's letter.[105] He replied that as soon as the Syrian armistice was signed he planned to go to Rome for a long enough period to give the Vatican authorities the required few days' notice.

Awake before five and unable to sleep, did some reading and made some notes. But I was more and more absorbed by the emerging synthesis of the present US role. I thought that I might write this interpretation as a despatch or as a private letter to Clifford. Certainly it is high time that someone looks beyond the immediate situation and sets down frankly what he sees. The trip down was pleasant and at times exhilarating. I stopped at the office and was home a little after ten, in time to bring my diary almost up to date before lunch. The afternoon staff conference concentrated on plans for July 4, the new office possibility on the hill, security, Captain Frothingham's inquiry about the USS *Cone*,[106] and my brief exposition about the general situation resulting from the US recent representation.

104. Entry of February 22, 1949.
105. Entry of April 17, 1949. Gowen had written McDonald on May 11, 1949, that he would arrange a meeting for Riley with Pope Pius XII. McDonald Papers, USHMM, box 7, folder 14.
106. Destroyer deployed in Mediterranean from March–October 1949.

Max Wolf of the International Red Cross of Geneva came for a half an hour or so of talk on the roof. As to the future refugee organization, he said he was wholly of my view about the impossibility of the PCC as a basis for such future work, and of the need for leadership of the sort I had urged in my communications with McGhee. The ICRC's technical work here he was trying to wind up. There were still about five hundred Arab prisoners-of-war in Israel from the Gaza Strip. Israel was ready to return them, but there was no Gaza authority ready to receive them.

As between Israel and Syria, there was [a] small prisoner-of-war problem, ten or twelve on each side. At this point, Wolf told me an amazing story about an alleged cousin of Za'im, who was said to have been captured by the Haganah on May 30, 1948. All inquiries about his present whereabouts made by the ICRC have been unanswered. It was suspected that he was in a Haifa hospital or prison, but there was no certainty. Za'im is said to have said: "Let them return my cousin and there will remain no problem between Syria and Israel." Wolf did not know whether Riley was aware of this cousin complication. I suggested that he get in touch with General Riley. He promised to send me the cousin's name.

Wolf also promised to send me a copy of a letter in which the ICRC expressed its gratitude for the Department's move to unblock about ten million Swiss francs in Switzerland and thus make these available to the ICRC.[107] Wolf said that he was sure my expression of opinion in favor of this policy last fall had been helpful in persuading the Department to act so promptly.

Saturday, June 25

Eight hours of reading during the day, with a three-hour break at Mendes Sacks's. From there we were driven home by the British commercial attaché, Mr. Studley, whom I brought into the house for a brief visit. He was much impressed by its spaciousness and by the gardens.

Sunday, June 26

Continuation during morning of hours of uninterrupted reading, resulting in the clearing up of all back documents except one sizable batch on Point Four. And that I did not worry much about, however, because of my decision not to venture a public address until tension had eased here.

At Tetlie's large cocktail party, I chatted with many people, but need to record only one or two of the conversations. Padberg was much disturbed at our tentative plans to invite a limited number of Americans to the residence for the Fourth. He argued almost vehemently that I had to choose between having none or all. My answer was "none." I was the firmer in this decision as he explained to me that in the other posts where he had been, the embassy party was

107. Entry of November 1, 1948.

very elaborate, orchestra, dancing, baseball game, and "not merely lemonade." Together we checked with Barnes and tentatively agreed that except for the diplomatic corps, whom I would invite for the morning, no invitations would be issued, [and] that we would be at home to anyone who came.

To the concert in the beautiful amphitheater on the hill to hear the orchestra under [Izler] Solomon,[108] [play] Dvorak's New World Symphony; Tchaikovsky's First Piano Concerto, Alexander Unisky as pianist.[109] The final piece was Copland, Jazz Ballet Music. Brought Mrs. Sharett and Mrs. Kohn home.

Monday, June 27

During the morning finished drafting two or three despatches. I should have reported under yesterday's date, the receipt of the Department's reply [of June 24] to the Israeli note of June 8. Its tone was quite different from that of May 29. It stressed an identity of interests between the US, Israel, and the Arab states—"the early accomplishment of an equitable settlement of the Palestine question, an interest which is in fact shared by all of the Members of the United Nations."

The US answer still maintained earlier US arguments concerning Arab refugee repatriation; continued to argue for frontier rectification since Israel held territories exceeding those allocated in the UN partition resolution; and insisted that the military phase of the Palestine question must be terminated. Any government that renewed hostilities, or threatened to do so, would incur a "grave responsibility before the community of nations."[110]

Further comment promised. Having analyzed the above four or five times, I am impressed and amazed by the failure of the Department to have the language tightened before filing. About 5:30 Esther Herlitz came in with Ford. I let her read the text of the June 24 reply since their copy had not yet reached them. It is coming through Shiloah at the end of the week. When she had finished, she gave us a paraphrase of the Israeli chargé's report of the talk between him and Rusk after the delivery by the latter of the US reply. According to this, Rusk said in effect: Gaza plan is worth serious consideration, because once peace is made with Egypt, that with other Arab states would follow. To secure peace with Egypt, territorial compensation might be required. Also might [be] required with other Arab states. Rusk then spoke of the need for speedy action on refugees in order to have plan ready before August budget meeting. Then

108. Izler Solomon (1910–1987), St. Paul, Minnesota-born conductor, guest conductor with Israeli Philharmonic.
109. Alexander Unisky (1910–1972), Ukrainian-born American pianist who moved to Paris in 1923.
110. The aide-mémoire was handed by deputy undersecretary Rusk to Israeli chargé Uriel Heyd on June 24, 1949. Copies in Acheson to McDonald, no. 398, June 24, 1949, *FRUS*, 1949, v. VI, 1174–1177; *DFPI*, v. 4, d. 105.

Rusk is said to have returned to his suggestion of Israeli-Egyptian bilateral negotiations. He mentioned, as possibilities, Washington as a site with Eytan and Egyptian representatives, or New York, with Eban and Egyptian representatives; or Tel Aviv, with McDonald and Israel, with parallel talks in Cairo. Or, finally, if Israel preferred direct talks with Egypt, [it is] ok with US.[111]

I then brought the talk back to refugees, and said that I regarded it as unfortunate that in spite of my known friendliness to Israel I could not in honesty report that it was showing or promising anything substantial. I recognized the difficulties, but still thought that from Israel's own point of view, it should promise and do more.[112] Miss Herlitz made the usual counter argument but was, I think, in a measure impressed.

McDonald's report of this meeting to the State Department contained a stronger statement regarding Arab refugees, wherein McDonald paraphrased himself as follows:

> *No amount of friendship for Israel can hide [the] fact that it has [regarding] refugee repatriation, been poor in promise and poorer in performance. Recognizing all difficulties, there are no justifications [for] Israel's relative inaction. Impossible [to] exaggerate human tragedy if Israel persists [it its] failure [to] cooperate. If Israel in good faith proposed [to] absorb the more than 200,000 refugees [in the] Gaza Strip, it must have envisioned ways to do this. Hence [there is] no logic in Israel's argument [that] it [is] unable to repatriate more than [a] few tens of thousands (as also stressed to Foreign Office by Kopper on his recent visit). Unacceptable everywhere except in Jewish circles, will be [the] argument that ingathering of exiles makes repatriation [of] Arabs impossible. Israel self-interest requires refugee cooperation asked [for] by [the] Department.[113]*

Ford and I briefly then compared notes on the apparent change of Department policy regarding opposition to bilateral negotiations. We were not sure whether this was really a change, or if Rusk might have forgotten to take cognizance of the earlier instruction.

Harry Viteles, in a conference at the residence, proposed new emigration from Aden. The British authorities in Aden were now urging the JDC to reconstruct their reception camp in Aden—it had been dismantled by the British following the completion of the JDC "Magic Carpet" program by which 2,500 [*sic*] Yemenite Jewish refugees had been flown to Israel[114]—and to use it as a

---

111. The less expansive US memorandum by Rusk on his discussion with Heyd is in *FRUS*, 1949, v. VI, 1177–1178. McDonald was informed.
112. Acheson had told McDonald on June 27 that, in discussing the issue of refugees with the Israeli government, he was to adhere to the State Department policy as expressed in Lausanne. Acheson to McDonald, no. 406, June 27, 1949, NARA, RG 59, 501.BB Palestine, box 2125, folder 7.
113. McDonald to secretary of state, no. 495, June 28, 1949, *FRUS*, 1949, v. VI, 1189–1190.
114. Entry of December 27, 1948. By March 1949, the problems of fuel procurement for Operation Magic Carpet had been overcome, and the armistice with Egypt was in place. Sixty-

base from which to fly to Israel perhaps as many as 20,000 more Jews who, it anticipated, would flee from Yemen if the opportunity were offered to them. The JDC was seriously considering undertaking this new heavy responsibility through the same Alaska Airlines which had transported the earlier refugees.

Mr. Viteles explained that the British concern in this matter arose presumably through the fear that if [an] opportunity for evacuation were not given to these Jews, they would be in danger of pogroms in Yemen. That there is such a danger was no occasion for surprise. The surprising fact is that, according to Mr. Viteles, the Israeli government has classified this project as a rescue operation, has given it priority, and has urged the JDC to carry it through. This decision is the more remarkable in view of the present unacknowledged policy of Israel to reduce the inflow of refugees.

The situation for Jews in Yemen continued to deteriorate, this time with accusations of ritual murder. Yemeni Jewish emigration to Aden resumed in April 1949. The JDC, in response to a request by the British authorities in Aden, was willing to build a larger transit camp and undertake another airlift from Aden to Israel, on the condition that Israel take all Yemini refugees, including the old and sick. The Israeli government agreed. The entire community, consisting of tens of thousands of impoverished and terrorized Yemeni Jews, was ready to leave. Instead of the expected flow of 700 refugees per month, hundreds of Yemeni Jews arrived in Aden each day, overtaxing the new transit camp. As late as August 1949, there were 3,000 in the camp, many of them ill, and the air transports had not yet begun.[115]

Tuesday, June 28

Spoke to Davidowitz about his participation in the project of screening the sets of books and manuscripts rescued from Germany by the American military authorities and now awaiting distribution in Jerusalem.[116] He said he would be prepared to begin work in about three weeks.

Out to Weizmann's for lunch. Before meeting Weizmann, I chatted briefly with Meyer Weisgal and Harold Goldenberg in the former's office at the Institute, and then with Abe Feinberg, his wife and children. With Weisgal and Goldenberg, I talked briefly about the recent exchanges and the more encouraging present situation. Feinberg said he hoped we would come out to dine with them at the Sharon. I urged them and the others to come to see us at the house.

seven Alaska Airlines flights had moved 5,207 Yemeni Jewish refugees—almost all of the Yemeni Jewish refugees then in Aden—to Israel by early March. Between March and May 1949, additional flights brought 1,779 Adeni Jews to Israel.

115. By September 1950, some 47,000 Yemeni Jews had been transported to Israel; these included the 5,207 who had been flown in earlier. During the operation in Aden, hundreds of refugees died of disease, and thousands arrived in Israel sick with malnutrition and related illnesses. Parfitt, *The Road to Redemption*, 191–215.

116. Entry of May 25, 1949.

During our brief talk in Weizmann's office he showed himself, as before, adamant on the problem of Arab refugees.

McDonald reported Weizmann's reply to US pressure on the refugee issue as follows: "Your people don't understand these refugees are our enemies and [a] potential fifth column. Don't your people read repeated threats from Arab capitals [concerning] renewed war?" When McDonald asked how Weizmann reconciled this statement with the earlier Gaza offer, Weizmann replied, "That would be more than we ought to do but it certainly is [the] utmost that is possible."[117]

He had written a personal letter to the president, which was now in Washington, in Eban's hands, with authority to deliver it or not. I got the impression that probably it would be held up.[118] Weizmann was rather depressed, perhaps because the heat has begun to take its toll. At any rate, he is looking forward to two months in Switzerland.

Wednesday, June 29

Up early and working from shortly after seven with Miss Clark on a despatch about the ten working papers on refugees from the Department, and a telegram about the talk with Weizmann the day before. Spoke on the telephone with Burdett, giving Davidowitz's message, which he said he would transmit to Germany.

Thursday, June 30

Max Wolf of the ICRC came to see me at the office. He stressed anew the urgency of the time element, the absolute necessity of the right man, and the enormous difficulties inherent in the refugee problem. Speaking of the man, he said he thought I was he. I replied first that the Arabs would not have me, second, that I could not and would not take it.

Interestingly, Wolf talked of Abdullah's extraordinary loss of prestige in Arab Palestine and of the increasing lack of order and discipline in that area. Every night shooting goes on in the Nablus area between the various and conflicting Arab groups. All of this made me feel that there might be something in the earlier report of the danger to Abdullah's life. Wolf estimated that there are still some 1,500 Arab prisoners of war in Israel; 750 who are native to soil occupied by Israel and 400 native to the Gaza Strip. As to the latter, Wolf is going to Gaza within the next days to try to arrange for the Egyptian reception of these. Wolf said that Alfred Escher, ICRC Commissioner for Arab Refugees,

---

117. Reported in McDonald to McDonald to secretary of state, no. 498, June 29, 1949, NARA, RG 59, 501.BB Palestine, box 2125, folder 7.
118. Weizmann to Truman, June 24, 1949, *DFPI*, v. 4, d. 104. Eban made the final corrections to the text. He did not hand the letter to Truman until July 6, 1949.

and perhaps Dr. Lehrner (Prisoners of War in Israel) and Dr. Munier (Prisoners of War across the lines) might be coming to see me.

Nearly two hours in the afternoon with the ZOA delegation headed by Mr. and Mrs. Daniel Frisch.[119] I was more impressed with him than I expected, and during our evening talks at the opera my respect deepened. I learned that he had not seen the president, that he anticipates cooperation at home, and is here primarily to establish more cordial relations with the Israeli authorities (he did not say this, but I got this impression), to open a ZOA house or arrange for it to be built in Tel Aviv, and to secure, if possible, permission to take over, on behalf of ZOA, the rehabilitation work among incoming [Jewish] refugees (this is the task which the JDC offered to handle and which it, much better than the ZOA, is prepared to deal with). Asked how much money the ZOA had for this purpose, Frisch said they would raise it. Then, he admitted that the primary purpose for his anxiety was that the ZOA might have a challenging project. At the moment, I was depressed by this latest manifestation of organizational ambition at the expense of refugees.

With Ruth, Bobby, and Shoshana to the apartment of the artist Yitzhak Frenkel.[120] On the whole, it was a depressing experience. The very small living room was cluttered up with pictures of all sorts, hodge-podge bric-a-brac, and semi-antiques. The few chairs, the couch, and the whole atmosphere was shoddy. Throughout, I kept pitying Mrs. Frenkel. He did a brief sketch of me, as a basis for my inclusion in the fresco painting for [the] Knesset. The ladies chose a picture for us to borrow, one of Safed. As we left, I'm sure that Ruth was more than ever satisfied not to have married an artist.

For a few minutes we stopped in at the apartment of the Per Sorensens who are living at the Rubins'.[121] I had interesting brief talks with his water engineers about the problems of Tel Aviv's supply, which is threatened with salt because of the excessive use of wells near the sea. I was intrigued by what they had to say about a possible nearer source of water for Jerusalem than the present springs near classic Antipatris. The move to have a closer Jerusalem supply is motivated by strategic considerations, in order to avoid the vulnerability of long pipe lines and the several remote pumping stations such as Latrun. I should like to hear more about these water problems. The engineers agreed with my impression that there was a great waste of water in Tel Aviv, where the per capita use is as large or larger than in an American city. This is a basic misuse, which Israel can ill-afford.

---

119. Entry of April 3, 1949.
120. Yitzhak Frenkel (1899–1981), Odessa-born painter; emigrated to Palestine, 1919; settled in Safed in 1934, where he painted scenes of the town and surrounding countryside; won the Dizengoff Prize for painting, 1948.
121. Per Sorensen was the project engineer for the Knappen Tibbetts Engineering Company of New York, then engaged in developing the port of Tel Aviv.

To the opera a little after nine in the amphitheater. We seemed to enjoy the *Tales of Hoffmann* more than we had in the theatre. Pleasant visits during the intermission with the Frisch group. Home after midnight.

On June 10, Clark Clifford had written McDonald, "I have kept in constant touch with developments in Israel and I am highly gratified at the splendid job you are doing for us." On June 24, McDonald replied, "The first paragraph of your note was deeply heartening, especially coming at the particular moment it did, when to us here it seemed as if American–Israeli relations had reached an almost unprecedented low." McDonald repeated his hope to return to the United States for consultations from mid-August through mid-October: "Dave [Niles], in a personal note of some weeks ago, implied that the President already knew of my hopes and that he was sympathetic. . . . Never have I felt so acutely as now the need to talk heart-to-heart with the President and with you." [122]

---

122. Clifford to McDonald, June 10, 1949; McDonald to Clifford, June 24, 1949, McDonald Papers, USHMM, box 7, folder 14.

13. July 1949

Shiloah was at the house with Ford from 6 to 8, directly at my invitation but also because Sharett had indicated to me that Shiloah was much upset by his Washington experiences.[1] For nearly the whole of the first half of the session, Shiloah unburdened himself uninterruptedly. He had been shocked and hurt by the deep and widespread conviction he had encountered in official circles that Israel was preparing for aggressive action. He complained that all of its pledges were disregarded or evaluated as mere subterfuges. This reaction was, of course, he said, not indicated in so many words but was clear enough. As proof he cited the sharp tone used by Rusk and others, including even the new undersecretary [Webb]. He resented the petty or unrelated evidence cited, such as Dayan's reported use of an armored car en route to Government House, his (Shiloah's) visit to Prague "as if a senior Foreign Office official did not have the right to visit Israeli missions," etc. On the negative side was the US government's ignoring of the Arabs' intransigence, their unwillingness to make peace, their avowed preparations for war, their strengthening of their armies, etc. When Shiloah had finished his indictment (I should have included his report that he had been closely shadowed by three plainclothes men during the whole of his stay in the States), he said that his chief concern now was to discover the why of the American attitude; wherein had Israel failed? Had its representatives been too friendly and frank with the US? Had they failed to play the diplomatic game with sufficient cunning? It was, he said, of the highest importance that the cause should be unearthed and the dangerous situation remedied.

In our turn, Ford and I attempted to think the problem through with Shiloah. In addition to the unyieldingness of Israel on refugees and boundaries, we suggested that its very success tended to breed suspicion, but I suggested also that the failure of the Israeli army recently to tell our military attachés anything of value may have driven these men to pick up from unofficial sources their data and to make out of this more than was justified by the facts. I pleaded, therefore, that there should be a return to the frankness and good relationships of the days when van der Velde was the military attaché (I was delighted to be told a few days later that there had been a definite improvement). I cited also as a contributing factor the seemingly authentic reports that Dayan and others

---

1. See also Heyd to Herlitz, July 1, 1949, *DFPI*, v. 4, d. 115.

had used language about Za'im and on other occasions which tend to create uneasiness.

I cited, too, the fear of General Riley (I did not mention his name) that the economic strains of the [Jewish] refugees and the inability to demobilize, because of the lack of homes and jobs, might encourage military aggression. To this Shiloah gave a contemptuous reply, saying that it was fantastic—that all that prevented demobilization was the lack of peace and at the moment the lack of an armistice with Syria. He explained that an army is [a] closely integrated complex organism, which makes piecemeal demobilization impossible.

It is noteworthy that Shiloah played down the importance of personal prejudices in his assessment of the Washington scene. Rusk, he said, was not particularly friendly, but the suspicions of the Department and the White House were too deep to be explained by the usual reference to anti-Semitic or anti-Israel personalities.

It was clear from Shiloah's talk that the American note of May 29 and the feeling of suspicion of Israel's intentions on which it was based had shaken Elath's position in Washington. He had not anticipated the US attitude and therefore had not prepared his people for it. I could understand better his consternation because, though my own position was not affected proportionately, it was weakened by the suddenness and uncompromisingness of the US note.[2] Our talk could have continued profitably beyond the two hours, but the peremptory order from Lolita [Ford] and my wife's reticent desire to go on with supper caused me to break up the session at eight.

Saturday, July 2
In the late morning Jack Loewenthal of TWA [Trans World Airlines] came out with Hooper, Ford also present. First we had a brief discussion about the US policy of aerial containment of USSR through shutting out as far as possible civilian aircraft of the Iron Curtain satellites from western and southern Europe and western Asia. I learned that my old friend, [Francis] Deak, was in Switzerland in charge of this operation.[3] A new test of policy was imminent in the reported reopening of Czech airlines to Israel via Rome, Nicosia, and Lydda. I had noted earlier telegrams dealing with this problem. I had noted in one what seemed to me the naïve suggestion that at Nicosia there should be a pretense of technical difficulties, landing limitations, etc., and indeed any excuse which would have plausibility. I indicated that we had no specific instructions and hoped to have none because of our conviction that Israel would not willingly be a part of our program. This [is] not because of any unfriendliness to

---

2. Summary in McDonald to secretary of state, no. 511, July 3, 1949, *FRUS*, v. VI, 1197.
3. Francis Deak (1898–1972), Hungarian-born US international lawyer and diplomat; US civil air attaché for Central Europe based in Bern, 1946; negotiated with Hungarian government for landing rights for Pan American Airways in Budapest on flights from Vienna headed to Belgrade and the Middle East; assignment likely a response to the Berlin blockade that ended in May 1949.

the US, but because of carefully reasoned unwillingness to get caught in this issue between the US and the USSR. Loewenthal's tone was wholly uncompromising.

As to TWA's immediate relation to Israel, Loewenthal admitted that sufficient progress had been made to reopen the [regular TWA] flight [to Lydda], that he was still filled with a good deal of dissatisfaction at the failure to assure assent to specific requests [including foreign exchange issues, a private telephone between the Lydda airport and the TWA office in Tel Aviv, and the use by TWA of its radio system with Rome and Paris]. I tried to give Loewenthal something of a background picture of Israel's attitude towards TWA, of its place in the troubled Middle Eastern area, and of the current pressure on it in the political arena, which in the nature of the case does not make its leaders particularly responsive to US appeals in air matters now.

Loewenthal said that he was appreciative of my information but that TWA was the US's "chosen instrument" in this area. In an important sense its requests were governmental. I promised that when this or other matters had passed beyond the stage where there was no more hope of securing assent from the lower echelon of Israeli officials, I would gladly raise the question with Sharett and Kaplan and even with Ben-Gurion if that were necessary. Loewenthal expressed his appreciation. As to a reception on the arrival of the TWA plane on the 5th, we agreed that in the light of the Department's instructions, I would not go out to the field but that Ford would invite [Israeli officials] to a luncheon.

Because of foreign currency shortages and the desire to build up the Israeli carrier El Al, the Israeli government restricted the activities of foreign airlines, including TWA. El Al's director, Aryeh Pincus, the US Embassy thought, was also learning the commercial air business from scratch and attempting too much, given El Al's under-capitalization.[4] Malcolm Hooper at the US Embassy helped with negotiations. TWA resumed weekly flights to Lydda on July 5, 1949.[5]

With the family out to Herzliya for the sunset. Abe Feinberg and I talked for about an hour. He told me of his impressions in Washington before he left, of the president's annoyance that he had not been able to get Israel's full acquiescence on any one of his three policies, Jerusalem, refugees, boundaries. He had sensed the hardening of the US attitude in his talks with Dave [Niles] and Clark [Clifford]. He then suggested the possibility that it would be desirable

---

4. Louis Aryeh Pincus (1912–1973), South African-born lawyer; legal adviser and managing director, Israeli Ministry of Transport and Communication; first director of El Al Airlines, 1949–1956.

5. See Hooper to secretary of state, no. 78, February 8, 1950, *Confidential U.S. State Department Central Files. Palestine and Israel Foreign Affairs, 1950–1954*, 6 reels (Frederick, MD: University Publications of America, 1984) [hereafter USSDCF-PIFA, 1950–1954], reel 6, frames 886–887.

for Israel to offer non-aggression pacts to the Arab states. He is going to try to convince the Israelis of this desirability.[6] Feinberg felt that Elath's position in Washington was a weak one, but that the change of US attitude was not Elath's fault.

At a recent small dinner given for President Truman by forty or forty-five people active in the campaign, Feinberg and David Niles had taken Assistant Secretary [John] Peurifoy[7] aside and had gotten his ok on my return in the fall.

Sunday, July 3

Sunday a quiet day with progress with a new batch of reading which came in the pouch. Cocktail party at the Greenbergs but little to report.

Dinner again with the Feinbergs at the Sharon. Feinberg told me that Joseph Levy had advanced cash of $375,000 and purchased [Palestine Economic Corporation] stock and advanced another $125,000, thus making a total of $500,000 for the projected PEC office building, two-thirds of which we hope will be occupied by the embassy.[8]

An important item was Feinberg's request that I have him and a Mr. May, attorney for Henry Ford II, out to the house when [May] arrives early this month. The purpose is to help prepare May to recommend to Ford and the latter's foundation the investment of $20,000,000 in housing in Israel. Feinberg is planning to urge a very important American industrialist to interest himself in Israel. He cited as possibilities, Ambassador Davies[9] and Edwin Pauley,[10] who had recently secured large concessions in Saudi Arabia and in Mexico. They might be persuaded to consider setting up a new refinery here. At any rate, this was the type of man whose cooperation here would do much to lay [to rest] the communist bogey.[11]

Monday, July 4

6. On July 5, 1949, McDonald reported that a "reliable private American, whom I trust completely" informed him that Weizmann would meet with Ben-Gurion and Sharett on July 6 to urge that Israel offer a nonaggression pact to the Arab states. The State Department was interested, but wanted further details as to how such an offer would fit into a final settlement. McDonald to secretary of state, no. 512, July 5, 1949, *FRUS*, 1949, v. VI, 1202.

7. John E. Puerifoy (1907–1955), deputy undersecretary of state for administration.

8. See entry of February 19, 1949. The idea for US embassy office space was that the Palestine Economic Corporation would construct a new building, which the embassy would share. Joseph Levy, clothing manufacturer and philanthropist, formed a partnership with the PEC to construct, manage, and hold a 75% interest in the first US-owned office building in Tel Aviv, which would cost $500,000 to build. The deal was announced on June 10, 1949. JTA *Bulletin*, June 10, 1949.

9. Joseph E. Davies (1876–1958), ambassador to USSR, 1936–1938; Roosevelt's envoy to Moscow, May 1943; special adviser to Truman at Potsdam Conference.

10. Edwin Pauley (1903–1981), American oil magnate, friend of Truman, and leader in the Democratic Party.

11. McDonald continued to report on communist statements, particularly in the Knesset, but also noted that the Knesset was investigating communist comments in Eastern Europe against Israel. McDonald to secretary of state, no. 509, July 1, 1949, McDonald Papers, USHMM, box 7, folder 16.

The morning official reception of the diplomatic and consular corps went off quietly. [Attendees included Sir Knox Helm and Colin Crowe of the United Kingdom; Vanthier of France; Mikhail Moukhine, the counselor of the Soviet embassy, plus representatives from Switzerland, Denmark, Czechoslovakia, Uruguay, Belgium, Guatamala, and Norway.]

The afternoon reception began early by the arrival about 3:30 [of additional diplomats, including William Burdett; numerous private individuals, including the de Sola Pools and other Hadassah figures; businessmen including Mendes Sacks; Estelle Frankfurter; and others]. There were so many people to talk to that there is little to report. I asked Father Terence [a friend of Eddie Jacobson] about Monsignor McMahon. Father Terence rather took exception to my suggestion that McMahon had larger than his announced charitable mandate in this area. Father Terence did not seem to be surprised at the report by Stabler about the visit of two Orthodox priests to the Old City and their success with the Greek Orthodox group.[12] Father Terence naturally made no comment on the additional suggestion these Russian successes grew out of Orthodox fear about Roman Catholic plans for Jerusalem. He promised me that we should have a longer chance to talk when he was back in this neighborhood in a fortnight.

Tuesday, July 5

[Herbert] Kunde, the American member of the technical refugee subcommittee of the PCC [Palestine Conciliation Commission], came out for a long visit this afternoon. I found him a bright young man whose background on the staff of the old International Migration Service[13] and whose later work have given him knowledge of refugee problems. He told me of some of the difficulties in getting an agreement on their terms of reference. At the moment they are concentrating on preparations for a conference with the three operating agencies to be held in Beirut on the 12th. There they hope to secure agreement on the definition of refugee and to secure a common policy on refining the estimates of refugees. He recognized that the inclusion of persons impoverished by the war but not displaced by it had increased the estimates of refugees probably from some 600,000 to 900,000. His group had secured permission from Israel not only to conduct an investigation of Arab citrus orchards in Israeli-held territory but also to employ a neutral expert in the evaluation of the state of those properties. I volunteered to try to help them find such a person. On the broader problem of resettlement, Kunde, without saying so, seemed to

12. Stabler reported the presence in Jerusalem of two Russian prelates loyal to Moscow who were there to discuss with the Israeli authorities the return of Russian church property. He mentioned the worry of Timotheus, the Orthodox Patriarch in Jerusalem, that the mostly Arab Orthodox congregants would accept Moscow's leadership. Stabler to secretary of state, no. 50, June 14, 1949, NARA, RG 59, MC 1390, reel 19, frames 521–523.

13. The International Migration Service was founded in Geneva 1924 to aid with the movement of Europeans to North America. Its concerns included reuniting families, child custody, and adoptions. Its name was changed to International Social Service in 1946.

share my view about the inadequacy of the PCC. He promised that he would return for a longer talk before or immediately after the Beirut meeting.

Wednesday, July 6

Off to the tea at the Gat Rimon for the resident head of the ICRC [International Committee of the Red Cross]. I had very little time there, but chatted briefly with Dr. Mohn, who was hopeful about the signing of the armistice between Israel and Syria after which time, no longer having any duties as political representative of the acting representative, he would leave Israel. Speaking of the international situation here, Mohn stressed that of course the Arab states now had no incentive to make formal peace. They felt that they could . . .[14] hold off indefinitely, while Israel, for reasons of self-interest, would wish to carry through peace negotiations. As he said this, Dr. Mohn was not particularly cheerful, for somehow he has never been sympathetic to Israel.

Back home, in time to dress before any of the guests arrived for dinner. These were: Sir Knox and Lady Helm, the Colin Crowes,[15] the Fords, Hoopers, Rebecca Sieff and the McDonalds.

Thursday, July 7

[In the middle of the afternoon the talk with Dr. Rita Morgan[16] and Ray Hartsough[17]] went on for nearly two hours. Dr. Morgan told graphically of her experiences in the Gaza Strip, the harshness of the Egyptian officers, their indifference to the suffering or death of the refugees whom they looked upon as little more than animals, the hopelessness of work under these circumstances when no future whatever could be envisioned for the homeless. She estimated that the numbers of bona fide displaced in the south were about 230,000, a reduction of about 30,000. She told also of the surprising amount of movement by the refugees from one area to another. For example, the coming into the Gaza Strip of several hundreds in one group and remaining for a short time, having heard that the food ration was 1,500 calories instead of 800 in the Hebron region where they had been. She confirmed, too, reports we had had from other sources of illegal but more or less regular Arab mail services across the Jewish lines.

The Friends were anxious to have my opinion as to whether Israel would really welcome their type of social experiment in cooperative living between Jews and Arabs. Until now they had not been able to get satisfactorily definitive answers. Now they were planning to remain in Israel on their next trip down from Acre until they got a final reply. I told them that I thought that they

14. The word "not" was deleted from the original in keeping with the context of this passage. The editors believe it was included by mistake.
15. Sir Colin Crowe (1913–1989), first secretary, British mission in Tel Aviv, 1949–1950.
16. Rita Morgan, Quaker volunteer in Gaza Strip, who was sympathetic to Israel.
17. Raymond Hartsough (1911–1991), Congregationalist minister who became a Quaker and spent nine months with UN and AFSC in Gaza in 1949.

would be permitted to carry on because of the general recognition that they were wholly non-political. In the political realm, I thought that their ideas quite impracticable. They inquired about the possibility of an internationalized area in the south where a substantial number of the Gaza Strip refugees might be settled. I commented that such a project seemed to me quite impossible. Their suggestion about retraining refugees for integration into the more modern life of Israel were undoubtedly sound, but again, they would require so much time and money as not to be applicable. They, too, seemed to agree with my views about the need for the replacement of the PCC by something which would be able to function with authority. They invited us to come to see them in Acre.

Worked late on an analysis of Burdett's amazing despatch in which he dogmatized about Jewish responsibility for lack of progress in peace negotiations [as well as] the discrediting of the US position among both Arabs and Jews unless this time Washington made good its threats. As I analyzed it, I found that only three of its twelve paragraphs could be accepted as sound. All the others seemed to me only partially sound or wholly misleading. Yet as I studied it, I had the uneasy feeling that it would have a more sympathetic reception in the Department than would our analysis.

In his despatch of July 6, 1949, Burdett argued that the favorable opportunity for peace that existed after the Israeli-Egyptian armistice had passed: "Willingness on the part of the Arabs to end, at least for the time being, the fight over Palestine has been replaced by a general hardening of attitude and reaffirmation of their earlier conviction that it is impossible to do business with the Jews." Israel's insistence on embarrassing concessions from Jordan in the Tulkarm-Nablus-Jenin triangle was responsible: "Thus Israel has missed an opportunity to start on the long and difficult road toward at least a working relationship with the Arabs." The Arab states were now thinking of "long-range plans" for the resumption of war with Israel.

Burdett discussed the plight of Arab refugees, their desire to return home regardless of which government was in control, and the movement of Jewish immigrants onto Arab property. The UN had failed them by not enforcing its own resolutions. Having lost everything, the refugees could turn to communism. Meanwhile, disappointment with the United States was growing throughout the Arab world.

Burdett continued, "Israel eventually intends to obtain all of Palestine" and "is convinced of its ability to 'induce' the United States to abandon its present insistence on repatriation of refugees and territorial changes." The United States, he concluded, should undertake "the necessary punitive measures against Israel to force her to consent to a reduction in territory and repatriation of refugees" or "admit that the US and UN are unable or unwilling to take the required measures, and therefore that US policy on boundaries and refugees cannot be carried out."[18]

18. Burdett to secretary of state, no. A-94, July 6, 1949, *FRUS*, 1949, v. VI, 1203–1205.

Paul Davidovici, the Romanian chargé, made a courtesy call. He gave me the usual story of housing difficulties and then a romantic picture of the perfection of life in Communist Romania, where each is treated according to his desserts and where charity such as that of the UJA [United Jewish Appeal] is no longer needed or desired. He became almost rhapsodic as he talked about the "charm, graciousness, brilliance of Ana Pauker," the redoubtable Communist Romanian foreign minister.[19]

At the end of a long working day, brought the diary up to this point.

Saturday, July 9

[For] nearly two hours during the morning Ford and I labored to get our ideas straight about the pending Jerusalem negotiations, particularly the many despatches from Burdett, Stabler and the Department, the fitting together of which was a major jigsaw puzzle. We also had to make clear to the Department in a carefully worded telegram why it had been impracticable to follow through with representations by Jerusalem [Burdett] precisely as it had urged. We ended the telegram by pleading for a conference of Riley, Burdett, and myself in Jerusalem. This seemed to us the more essential because [of] the frequent delays and misunderstandings arising from poor Jerusalem-Tel Aviv telegraphic communications.[20]

Continued my reading Saturday morning until 12:30 when I went out for a conference with Abe Feinberg at the Sharon. After I had brought Feinberg more or less up to date, he divulged to me the following main developments:

1) Weizmann, Ben-Gurion, and Sharett had had their first official meeting on Friday and had then discussed among other questions the possibility of the offer of a non-aggression pact to the Arab states. Against it was urged the point of he who disavows too often his aggressive intent gives the impression of guilt. Nonetheless, the decision was in principle to accept the idea and to leave to Sharett and Eban the form and the time of making the offer.

2) Startling was the information that President Truman had asked General Hilldring to communicate to Israel the information that it would have to choose between a break with him and making of a constructive contribution

---

19. Ana Pauker (1893–1960), Jewish-born Romanian communist; trained by Comintern in late 1920s; became a Romanian communist leader in exile during World War II in Moscow; returned to Romania as part of four-person directorate of Romanian Communist Party loyal to Stalin, 1944; Romanian foreign minister, 1947–1952; overtly anti-Zionist but helped facilitate emigration of 100,000 Romanian Jews to Israel in return for Israeli payments to Romania; arrested partly owing to supposed sympathy for Zionism, 1952; released on Stalin's death in 1953. See Radu Ioanid, *The Ransom of the Jews: The Story of the Extraordinary Secret Bargain Between Israel and Romania* (Chicago: Ivan R. Dee, 2005).

20. McDonald to secretary of state, no. 524, July 9, NARA, RG 59, 501.BB Palestine, box 2125, folder 6.

to the refugee solution. He asked General Hilldring to get a definite answer. Feinberg asked whether I was aware of this move and was told [by McDonald that] I was not and that I was not supposed to know of it.[21] This influence and the warnings which had come from many sources—Eytan, Eban, Elath, Feinberg and the embassy—were beginning to have their effect. Careful consideration was being given to the possibility of an offer to take 100,000 (this presumably quite independent of the Gaza plan).[22] Feinberg warned, however, that not even Ford was to be told of this because if there were a leak, it would be traced to Feinberg.[23]

On July 5 Sharett proposed to the cabinet that Israel pledge to accept 100,000 Arab returnees, including the 25,000 who had already returned illegally and the 10,000 more who were now expected to return through the family reunion idea. The proposal would be part of a comprehensive settlement that did not include absorption of the Gaza Strip, but that retained Israel's present boundaries. Sharett was hopeful that such a compromise offered a pragmatic "way out" of the refugee impasse that might "dispel escalating tension between the United States and ourselves." Ben-Gurion was skeptical, but the cabinet agreed that Sharett should sound out the United States' reaction before raising the idea at Lausanne.[24]

3) Feinberg anticipates that the next phase of the drive against Israel in the States will be on the ground of alleged communism or its possibilities here. Already an unpleasant attack had been made on David Niles. Others were to be anticipated on other personalities. Feinberg warned the conference of the danger of these developments. They agreed to begin by giving instructions to speakers in the States to desist from their recent practice of balancing any favorable comment about aid from the US with a comparable favorable comment about aid from [the] USSR.

4) Feinberg asked if I did not think that it was desirable at this point to write a personal letter to Clark Clifford. I agreed that I would try. He said he would undertake to have it sent by a safe hand.

Late afternoon continued my work on the reply to Burdett's amazing despatch of July 6 on "General observations . . . regarding the current situation in Palestine." The more I studied this astounding series of dogmas, the more startled

21. Entries of April 28 and May 10, 1949.
22. The 100,000-refugee plan is explained in Morris, *The Birth of the Palestinian Refugee Problem Revisited*, 570–580.
23. On July 6, McDonald reported a statement by Herlitz to Ford of the previous day that Israel probably would accept fewer than 25,000 Arab repatriates under the family reunification idea. McDonald to secretary of state, July 6, 1949, NARA, RG 59, 501.BB Palestine, box 2125, folder 6.
24. See Sharett's extensive comments in the Israeli Delegation Guidelines, July 25, 1949, Fischer, ed., *Moshe Sharett: The Second Prime Minister, Selected Documents (1894–1965)*, 396–397. See also *DFPI*, v. 4, p. 206, d. 136; Morris, *The Birth of the Palestinian Refugee Problem Reconsidered*, 572–574; Waldman, *Anglo-American Diplomacy and the Palestinian Refugee Problem*, 96–98.

I am that one in a responsible position should be so violently prejudiced. Drafted my reply, which I am not sure I shall send but in any case keep for the record.

Sunday, July 10

Worked during the morning on my documents and on drafts of the letter for Clark Clifford and reply to Burdett.

McDonald attacked Burdett's points one by one. Burdett's argument that Arab attitudes had changed because of Israel's gains in the triangle, McDonald said, "is not supported by any evidence. In fact, the attitude of the Arab States other than Trans-Jordan on the issue of peace with Israel was intransigent before as well as after *the Israel armistice with Trans-Jordan." McDonald argued, "Mr. Burdett's implication that these Arab plans for resumption of war are solely the fault of Israel is manifestly unjust unless the very existence of Israel be deemed justification for Arab plans to destroy the new State by war."*

Concerning Burdett's argument that Israel had no intention of allowing an appreciable number of refugees to return, except perhaps in return for additional territory, McDonald argued, "On the contrary, at the time his despatch was filed, intensive consideration was being, and continues to be given, by Israeli authorities in Tel Aviv to repatriation of a large number of Arab refugees without involving additional territory for Israel." McDonald noted that Burdett "would be more persuasive [regarding Israel's violations of UN resolutions] if anywhere in his despatch he took account of the Arab states' violation on vital UN decisions, notably the basic partition decision of November 29th."

McDonald further noted that Burdett's argument concerning Israel's purported wish to conquer all of Palestine "is consistent with his central thesis that this State alone is the devil of the piece, but he cites no proof of Israel's alleged expansionist program." McDonald continued, "Similarly, it would be interesting to have the evidence on which Mr. Burdett bases his statement" that Israel planned to "induce" the United States to abandon its insistence on repatriation and territorial concessions. "He gives no proof of this flat declaration." Moreover, Burdett was "unsound and defeatist" in his statement that the United States had but two choices: to use punitive measures on Israel or admit an unwillingness to take the required measures. "I have no fear that the State Department or the President will be tempted to impale themselves on either horn of this destructive dilemma."[25]

The reception at Weizmann's, in good time, accompanied by the Fords. We chatted for a few minutes with Chaim Weizmann, Vera and David and his mother, since the bulk of the crowd had not yet arrived. Vera commented that Bobby looked so much more mature than when she had come to Israel. She, Vera, on her part, was looking splendid.

25. McDonald to secretary of state, no. 180, July 13, 1949, *FRUS*, 1949, v. VI, 1221–1223.

Everybody who was anybody was at the party. Most picturesque of the guests were the dignitaries of the Eastern Churches, the Russian Archimandrite Leonidas, formidable and elegant, with his robes, magnificent cross, silver-headed cane, maroon gloves, red beard, etc.; the Greek archimandrite of Haifa, also elegant but much more spiritual in appearance; the representatives of the Copts, swarthy with semi-turban, refined face and gentle eyes; the Armenian prelate, also elegant, and their several secretaries. Also picturesque were the Arab dignitaries, including a Druze leader. Rabbi Jacob Herzog and Dr. Vardi were busily engaged introducing the prelates and avoiding incidents. There was, so far as I could see, no Catholic representative present.

I spoke to a great many people, but there is nothing that needs to be recorded except Feinberg's statement that he could transmit safely the Clark Clifford letter on Thursday. Of incidental interest, too, was Meyer Weisgal's urging me to come back on the *Queen Elizabeth* leaving New York on October 14, saying that it would be good business for me. I suggested that [Gershon] Agron come out some late afternoon for a long talk, which he said he would do. I made a similar suggestion to Eytan who may or may not accept. Also recordable is the fact that during the course of a passing conversation with Helm and Courtney, I only half jokingly told the latter that it was high time he learned at first hand something about the West because, after all, Western statesmen were not completely stupid. He grinned but I think was not amused, particularly since this was said in the hearing of Helm. My remark was deliberate, however, because I had felt that his two or three recent pieces [in the *Palestine Post*] after his vacation had been particularly unfair. Then having tried gentleness, I thought I would try the opposite and see what happens.

The way out from the Weizmann's jammed. But fortunately the evening was exquisitely beautiful so that I almost wished that we might have stayed until darkness. The concert of the Philharmonic at the amphitheater, with [Menahem] Pressler as soloist in the Schumann concerto, was delightful.[26] The other [compositions] we heard were the Mendelssohn Italian Symphony, and [Johann] Strauss, the *Fledermaus* overture.

Monday, July 11

Early conference with Ford forced a break in my recent practice of biblical reading to my wife while she has her tea. Ford and I studying together the pertinent documents prepared for our nine o'clock session with Sharett.

The conference at the Foreign Office was about thirty-five minutes. Briefly but forcibly I presented the US Government's views on Jerusalem and then later on refugees.

---

26. Menahem Pressler (1923–), German-born pianist, fled with immediate family after Kristallnacht to Italy and then Palestine; most of his relatives were murdered; became famous as a member of the Beaux Arts Trio.

On July 9, 1949, the Department ordered McDonald to press Sharett to allow the Israeli-Jordanian Mixed Armistice Commission more jurisdiction in the Jerusalem settlement. At issue was the Israeli return of Arab neighborhoods in the city. The State Department also wanted an agreement on Jerusalem to be incorporated into the Palestine Conciliation Commission's recommendations. The Department also ordered McDonald to repeat its stance on the right of refugees to return. McDonald replied that he "presented with utmost earnestness [the US government's] strong views." [27]

Sharett's answer on the first subject was succinct: the net effect of American pressure was to discourage implementation [of] Article VII of the armistice [with Jordan]. This was unfortunate in principle and practice. He did not say definitely that Israel would not agree to [the] broadening of [the] Mixed Armistice Commission's jurisdiction as suggested by the Department, but he clearly saw through the arguments which he seemed to understand were behind the US position. As he talked, I could imagine what a devastating reply the Foreign Office could give to the Burdett memorandum.

As to refugees, his answer was even shorter: it is not our responsibility, it is very difficult, we may not have said our last word, but it should be understood that obvious and frequent evidence of US pressure makes Israel's [concessions] from the domestic point of view more difficult. The last point was made without a smile.

Concerning Sharett's statement on refugees, McDonald reported, "I hope but I am not sure that Sharett's words foreshadow more constructive refugee proposal by Israel than any heretofore." [28]

Worked hard with Miss Clark on the letter to McGhee in answer to his airgram received three days earlier.

Evening, dinner for the Elaths and the Fords. After the meal the two men and I talked on the porch for well over an hour. Elath was almost the only speaker. The following is a summary of what he said:

1) The Arab states. He thought that recent [developments] within and among the Arab states should occasion no surprise or special comment. Za'im, he thought, had been very successful in winning general recognition and support largely through a policy of threatening. His prestige was now comparatively high, and because of his desire not to risk weakening it in an open conflict with Israel, he may consent to sign an armistice. His rise to power was easy so long as he controlled the army, because the civilian regime had been corrupt and weak. It could be pushed over by any firm hand. But this

27. Referenced in McDonald to secretary of state, no. 528, July 11, 1949, *FRUS*, 1949, v. VI, 1215–1216.
28. Ibid. Also *DFPI*, v. 4, d. 132.

should not lead to a conclusion that Za'im was a fixture, for dissatisfaction within the army will in time grow and possibly eventually lead to his overthrow or to his assassination. In any case, nothing fundamental is likely to be changed within Syria.

Iraq continued to be extraordinarily corrupt and weakened by dissatisfaction of the tribes, including the Kurds. Abdullah's regime is extremely unpopular in [Arab] Palestine, and were he not continuously guarded by Circassians, he would probably be assassinated by agents of the mufti. One of the chief reasons for the king's unpopularity in Arab Palestine is his failure to have appointed to high office leaders of the Palestine Arabs. Instead, he chose to name for those posts Arabs who had been so long associated with the mandatory regime that they are looked upon as foreigners. The mufti, whose policy has been a failure, has not given up hope that, either through a fortunate assassination or through the outbreak of war, he will be permitted to regain his prestige. At present, he is maintaining only a small entourage with funds received almost certainly for the most part from Pakistan.

Egypt, of all the Arab states, is the least likely to make real peace with Israel and the most apt to launch a renewal of war. This is because of Egypt's pride in its size and what it feels to be its strength, wealth and prestige; the latter was so seriously damaged by defeat in Israel that there is among the Egyptians a feeling that only victory over the Jews can recoup that loss.

2) Israeli-American Relations. Elath stressed almost poignantly what he regarded as the sharp deterioration of the close contacts and mutual confidence between the two governments and people. On his return here he had found opinion at the highest and lower levels so affronted by the US "pressure" that for many days he felt it unwise to raise the issue with those to whom he spoke. This feeling is much deeper and keener than is evident in the press, except the extremist press. But he urged that we not misinterpret this moderation.

In explanation of his country's pained reaction to the change of American policy, he said that small and new states were always more sensitive about their independence; that it was the part of the larger powers to take this sensitiveness into account to avoid open pressure. On his return next week (he deplored that he had to go back so early after having had hardly any vacation) he would concentrate on resuming the close and friendly and, he felt, trusted relationships which he had previously had with officials from Acheson on down.

3) Conditions in Israel. He said he was optimistic about this country, and despite present acute difficulties domestically, he could discern increased elements of strength wherever he went. These seemed to him more marked than he had thought would be the case.

In view of Elath's expansiveness, Ford and I had occasion to say very little. Parenthetically, I got the impression that Elath had been able to persuade Kaplan et al. to expand the Washington staff more nearly in proportion to its enlarged duties.

Delightful conference at twelve with Professor [Abraham] Fraenkel from the [Hebrew] University and a younger man, Fraenkel's associate in the local B'nai B'rith.[29] Fraenkel talked interestingly and lightly about higher mathematics, its relation to physics and philosophic theory and about two new sciences about which I had never heard, econometrics, the science of exact measurements in economics, the center of which is the University of Chicago; and, mathematical measurements, the center of which is Columbia University. The latter is now an essential prerequisite for advanced agricultural studies. He told of one of his lectures at the Institute of Technology, Pasadena, where there were four Nobel Prize-winners in his audience. Another interesting story was that recently when he was to lecture at [Revivim] in the Negev, he asked the members of the kibbutz what subject they preferred. They replied: "Is the world infinite or finite?" In answer to my question as to the reply he gave he said: "The world we know is finite, but the larger world is infinite." I should like to see more of him.

Abe Feinberg was at the house for a half hour or so. He thought my letter to our mutual friend Clark Clifford was excellent. He was shocked by the analysis of my friend on the Hill [Burdett] and approved of my rejoinder.

McDonald's letter to Clifford was "written for your eyes and—if you think he would be interested—for those of the President. It is a frank report on four basic misunderstandings about Israel which are, I am told, becoming so widespread in Washington that they could menace the good relations between our governments and also the general peace."[30]

Truman's "unceasing insistence" on the primacy of the Arab refugee issue was "gradually, though still too slowly, forcing the Israeli authorities to the conclusion that they must, despite all the difficulties involved, make a substantial contribution to the solution of this tragic human problem. My personal association during my sixteen years with refugees has from the very first weeks of my mission in Israel lent fervor to my representations to Ben-Gurion and the others on behalf of these war victims."

Second, "the concern lest Israel harbor aggressive designs to use its military superiority to seize the whole of Palestine west of the Jordan is, I believe, unjustified," because of Israel's need to build the state. Ben-Gurion and his colleagues "do not intend to break the peace but . . . instead . . . are anxious to negotiate binding peace treaties with the Arab States."

29. Abraham Fraenkel (1891–1965), highly accomplished German-born mathematician and Mizrahi Zionist; professor at University of Marburg, 1922–1928; took position at Hebrew University, 1930; later first dean of mathematics there.
30. McDonald to Clifford, July 12, 1949, McDonald Papers, USHMM, box 7, folder 16.

Third, McDonald noted, "It is true that Israel insists on retaining most if not all the territory it won outside the lines of the November 29 partition as well as the territory then assigned to it; in particular, Israel will not surrender any part of the southern tip of the Negev with its access to the Gulf of Aqaba unless forced by overwhelming strength to do so. This insistence, however, is in my judgment, not evidence of future aggressive purposes but rather of a dogged determination to keep what was won in the war—a war which Israel firmly believes was forced upon it."

Fourth, McDonald noted, "The future of Jerusalem is a problem of great but not, I think, of insuperable difficulties."[31] *Blame for the slowness of the settlement in Jerusalem was partly on Israel and Jordan, but also partly on "the insistence in some influential Western quarters that the settlement be satisfactory not only to Israel and Trans-Jordan, but also to other Arab states. There can be no such universally agreed solution. To insist on this impossibility is to play into the hands of the Russians, whose claims, both political and religious, to participate in the settlement and administration of Jerusalem [becomes] stronger every week that a settlement is delayed."*

McDonald concluded as follows:"Continued American pressure—applied equally to both Jews and Arabs, or in proportion as either side on any specific issue shows the larger measure of intransigence can—if carried out with acute discernment and infinite patience—make a decisive contribution toward the achievement of the President's aim; peace with justice that will lay the basis for the gradual modernization of the whole of this vast Near East."

Mr. Hooper brought in A.C. Embracht, representative of the manufacturing associate of International Telephone and Telegraph. In addition to the $5,000,000 worth of equipment being purchased through the Export-Import Bank, there is pending a contract for $7,500,000 more communications equipment which, if put into operation, would complete the modernization of Israel's system. He admired, he said, the extent to which Israeli technicians repaired their equipment and made use of what was available including considerable portions of the earlier shipments. He thought the chief weakness in the Israeli communication field was the extent to which the top people were overworked and by the lack of sufficient technical staff. But considering these limitations, he had much praise for their efforts.

In the evening, Ruth and Bobby and I went with Shoshana as her and Yosef's guests to see the Chamber Theater's production of *Dear Ruth*. We enjoyed it. I was impressed with Yosi's acting in the small part, that of the sergeant. I shall be curious to see him in the main role in the forthcoming production *Born Yesterday*.

31. Entries of April 15 and May 17, 1949.

Amused to read in the Department's account [of] May 25, 1949, Review of the Second Part of the UN [General Assembly], April 5–May 19, the frank statement that the [Near Eastern Affairs] group had opposed active support of Israel's application for [UN] admission, instead had favored merely a 'yes' vote accompanied by "absolute quiet" and "the most complete silence." I was interested, too, to the extent to which the group leaned on Ethridge and also their statement that the delegation decision to move actively was taken to secure admission before they had a chance to express their "views." They added that so far as liaison with the Arabs and other Asiatic states was concerned, "we as representatives of the US were again put in the ridiculous position of saying one thing one day and having [to] reverse [it] the next."

Dr. [William M.] Schmidt came (unfortunately late) just before lunch. He is retiring to join the Harvard faculty of public health.[32] He is not enthusiastic about a functional mission for the JDC here but would limit its activities to subventing health programs of the government, which he thinks should carry the responsibility and can do so with increasing efficiency as its technical staff increases, especially nurses. He is against multiplication of private functions in the public health field. His account of the Jewish communities in North Africa, the worship of saints and local shrines, their backwardness in matters of hygiene and agriculture and industry, combined with their mystical devotion to Israel and the determination of many of them to come here, made an absorbing tale which I wish might have been extended, but there was no time.

Thursday, July 14

Usual breakfast conference with Ford, which by now has become as regular as breakfast itself. Major Brady came out with the news that Riley was arriving with a session at eleven to try to clear up the deadlock about Samakh on the southern end of Lake Tiberias [Sea of Galilee], which had deadlocked the Syrian armistice negotiations. I at once sent a note to the Foreign Office for Riley, urging him to let me talk with him while he is in town.

Ford came out with a telegram with the text of Bunche's appeal to Sharett regarding Syria. It was a beautiful example of diplomatic writing.[33] I at once called the Foreign Office, which arranged for me to carry out my instructions with Sharett the next morning.

Both sides had accepted a demilitarized zone defined by the Israel–Syrian border in the east and a western line that included parts of Israeli territory, including a bulge

32. William M. Schmidt (b. 1907), overseas medical director of American Jewish Joint Distribution Committee, 1946–1949; instrumental in reducing tuberculosis and malnutrition among Jewish refugees, making it possible for them to leave Europe; took up faculty position at Harvard University, School of Public Health, 1949, where he spent the rest of his career.
33. Mohn to Sharett, July 14, 1949, *DFPI*, v. 3, d. 356; Rosenne to Mohn, July 14, 1949, *DFPI*, v. 3, d. 357.

around Mishmar HaYarden and the eastern part of the Sea of Galilee. Syrian reservations concerned Samakh, a former Arab town in Israel where Syrian citizens also once had access. Bunche urged the Israelis to accept the Syrian reservations since the main Israeli concern, the exit of Syrian forces from Israel, had been met. Riley was sent to Tel Aviv on Bunche's request to work out the final differences with Sharett.[34]

Down to the Kaete Dan a little before two to meet General Riley and to get from him, if possible, a full account of the Jerusalem situation. While waiting for the general, who was lunching with his colleagues and I think the Israelis, [Mordechai] Maklef[35] and Shiloah, I had a long talk with Major Stallings, first about the southern Negev and also Petra and its neighborhood, in which regions he had worked for the UN during many months. His account of Petra made me the more anxious to visit it.

Riley joined me on the porch at about 2:30 in his usual extremely friendly and cheerful mood. About the Syrian negotiations, he said that he was optimistic. He had been most cordially received by Sharett and had just had a telephone call from Shiloah that there was "nothing to worry about." He argued that since Za'im had agreed to withdraw to the international frontier, the latter's three reservations were not unreasonable and were a small price for Israel to pay to get the issue settled.

After I had told him my views of the May 29 stern note and the subsequent changes, and the embarrassment which the policy of near ultimata, without subsequent steps having been clearly anticipated, had caused, he proceeded to give me his view of the Jerusalem problem. He admitted that technically the Israelis were correct in their contention that the six points under Article VIII of the armistice terms should have been carried out independently of other issues. But, he contended that because in fact the Special Committee had not been able to go beyond agreement in principle, it was most desirable that a neutral chairman through the Mixed Armistice Commission [MAC] should aid. The broadening of the scope of MAC considerations, while technically a concession to Jordan, was in fact an advantage to Israel because it was the one way to move

34. In 1926, in return for accepting the 1923 boundary line that left all of the Sea of Galilee in Palestine, Syria received railroad access to Samakh, an Arab town on the southern shore of the Sea of Galilee, to provide, among other things, access for Syrian fishermen and a rail route for pilgrims to Mecca. Samakh was in Jewish-designated territory in the UN partition resolution. The Syrians captured and then lost it during the war, and the Arab population fled. The argument in July 1949 was over whether Samakh should be demilitarized, whether the Arab residents should return, and whether Syrian citizens should have access to it. The Israelis did not compromise on Arab return, but part of Samakh was included in the demilitarized zone, and Syria received fishing and agricultural concessions, easing the way to the conclusion of the armistice before the resumption of the Lausanne talks. See entry of July 20, 1949 and in general Ben-Dror, *Ralph Bunche and the Arab Israeli Conflict*, pp. 233–234.

35. Mordechai Maklef (1920–1978), Palestine-born general; fought with the Palestine Regiment of the British Army, and subsequently the Haganah; commanded the Carmeli Brigade and took part in Operation Hiram, 1948; represented Israel at the armistice negotiations with Lebanon and Syria, 1949; deputy chief of staff, IDF, November 1949–1952; chief of staff, IDF, 1952–1953.

towards peace, which Israel needed more desperately than do the Arab states. In this connection General Riley made the interesting point that Israel's internal economic difficulties are being used in the Arab capitals to support the theory that domestic difficulties here will weaken if not destroy the state, and that hence, the Arabs can afford to wait. From this General Riley concluded that Israel had a better chance to move towards peace now than it might have later.

The broader issues [in Jerusalem], General Riley defined as:

1) The definition of permanent division lines. On this he repeated Burdett's earlier argument that unless such final partition is soon fixed, there will be no opportunity for the Arabs to return to Katamon, [a] previous[ly] predominantly Arab section of the city.[36] Without such return, he implied that there could not be peace.

2) The second of the broader issues would be the laying of a basis for internationalization, neutralization, and, though he did not specifically mention it, I presume demilitarization. Presumably, too, he had in mind the preparation of agreement on these issues as preliminary to a proposed Jerusalem settlement by the Palestine Conciliation Commission.

3) A third broad issue was, according to General Riley, freedom of access. This he did not specifically define.

As to the six Article VIII points,[37] General Riley said five of them were predominantly favorable to Israel. As a part of his argument in favor of a broader base under a neutral chairman, General Riley emphasized that the Israeli negotiators on the spot in Jerusalem and with Syria had been and were continuing to be rigid and dictatorial in the manner of their presentation to the opposite side. They spoke not as if they were negotiating but as if they were presenting ultimata. The young Jordanian [representative] now heading his country's delegation found this attitude nearly unbearable and had repeatedly complained to General Riley. The latter thought that this Israeli manner was at least in part responsible for the bogging down of the work of the Special Committee. In any case, it made essential, in his view, the presence of a third person as neutral chairman.

I brought up the subject of Burdett's July 6 airgram, which General Riley had not seen. On the issue of Israel's fundamental intentions, General Riley seemed inclined to share Burdett's views about expansion throughout the

36. Katamon, neighborhood in south central Jerusalem established by affluent Arab Christians; taken in April–May 1948 by Palmach from Arab fighters, including Arab Legionnaires, in heavy combat.
37. Refers to (1) free movement of traffic on vital roads, including the Bethlehem and Latrun-Jerusalem roads; (2) resumption of the normal functioning of the cultural and humanitarian institutions on Mount Scopus and free access thereto; (3) free access to the Holy Places and cultural institutions and use of the cemetery on the Mount of Olives; (4) resumption of operation of the Latrun pumping station; (5) provision of electricity for the Old City; and (6) and resumption of operation of the railroad to Jerusalem.

whole of western Palestine. When I pressed him, however, he had no tangible basis for his views except to say: "They are planning to build their state, aren't they?" In answer to my question, General Riley said that his views got to the Department only indirectly through heads of our missions in this area or through Bunche. I questioned whether some of Burdett's interpretations of General Riley's views were in fact accurate. General Riley said that he had been misquoted by Stabler on occasion, but so far as he knew not by Burdett. I told him that I refrained from passing on his views about the disadvantage of the Department's continued reference to November 29 as a basis; that I took the line that if he wished to express this general view to the Department, he would do so. I think he was appreciative of this restraint.

As to the PCC, General Riley seemed to share fully my view about its virtual impotence. He denied the views reported by the Israelis that he had been asked and declined to serve on the PCC. He had not been asked, and he gave me the clear impression that he would not accept if he were asked, because his efforts there would be futile. [In] speaking of the PCC and its weaknesses, [General Riley] referred to [Pablo de] Azcárate as a futile executive who unfortunately was more and more controlling the PCC and, I thought he said, building a bureaucracy.

Returning for a moment to Syria, General Riley said that the retirement of [Foreign Minister Adil] Arslan, who was "a fool," had been a definite gain; he added that [Prime Minister Mushin al-] Barazi[38] had told him that definitely Syria would sign an armistice.

At the beginning and end of our talk we referred to the Vatican and my anxiety that the way, which I had prepared there, should be used.[39] Jokingly, I told General Riley that I did not wish my status at the Vatican to be weakened by the non-cooperation of "any shanty Irish." He laughingly assured me that he would put in his appearance there.

Friday, July 15
Ford and I stopped for a moment at Miss Herlitz's office, and I read her Charlie Knox's last letter.[40] The three of us then had about thirty-five minutes with Sharett. I opened by telling him that, as far as I was concerned, I would require only a few minutes, but that of course if he wished to "make an oration," we should be attentive. In reply to my support of the Bunche appeal [on Syria] Sharett agreed with me that not only was this statement by Bunche but all statements by him were models of perfection. Then briefly, he said that they had accepted two of the three Za'im reservations and 50% of the third, which should satisfy Za'im. On the issue of the continued utilization of Government

---

38. Muhsin al-Barazi (1904–1949), prime minister of Syria, June 25–August 14, 1949; close adviser to Za'im.
39. Entries of April 17 and June 22, 1949.
40. Not found.

House for the UN Headquarters he said that he agreed that it should be so used *pro tem* "which might be for a long time."

There seemed to be some time left, and I quoted Riley about the "dictatorialness" of the Israeli negotiators. To this Sharett replied in substance: Most of them are inexperienced in the ways of diplomacy and are not practiced in understanding that the impression their words create is more important than what they intend. On the other side, he urged with considerable feeling that the limitless procrastination of the Syrians and the Jordanians was enough to destroy the patience of anyone. As an example, he cited the Israeli suggestion that the Jordanians draw their own map of the Government House area. This done, and the Jordanian product accepted unaltered by Israel, Jordan rejected its own work and presented a new and wholly unacceptable version. Returning to the house, we drafted our telegraphic report and then went off to the office.[41]

In a conference with Colonel Andrus, I was again shocked by the slowness of his mind and by his lack of understanding of the current documents. For example, when he told me of his conference at Cyprus Thursday morning with the US military attaché from Damascus and the British military attaché, I learned that his account of Israeli-Jordanian relations took no account of the latest developments, about many of which he could have informed himself before he left.

In a brief talk with Hooper, I criticized his having brought up to [Aryeh] Pincus, even parenthetically, any reference to the possibility of Israel keeping out the Czech airlines. With difficulty I made him see that this, being a part of the high-level policy of "containing the USSR," could be spoken of to the Israelis only under specific instructions from Washington and then by me. It had nothing to do, as Colonel Andrus mistakenly thought, with any "TWA planned monopoly."[42]

Incidentally, a horrible example of Hooper's lack of security mindness was his answer when I asked him if the folders on his desk were classified. He replied he did not have to take them with him because they were in covered folders.

At six o'clock Shiloah, at his suggestion, came to the house and remained for two hours. He had prefaced his visit by saying that there was nothing terribly important in what he wanted to say but he thought it might be desirable for us to have an informal chat. The following are the chief points he made during our free give and take:

1) He was going within a few days to Lausanne to head the Israeli delegation, replacing Eytan, who was needed at HaKirya to carry on his administrative

41. McDonald to secretary of state, no. 540, July 15, 1949, NARA, RG 59, 501.BB Palestine, box 2125, folder 8.
42. Entry of July 2, 1949.

duties in the Foreign Office.[43] In answer to my question, Shiloah said that this change was not a lowering of the rank of the delegation but rather could be interpreted as a substantive strengthening because of his connection (a very close and confidential one) with the prime minister.

2) He was taking, he said, with him a more elastic program than that the delegation had formerly followed. He had hopes that if the PCC would bring the two groups together, substantial progress might be made before the PCC would have to report to the UN General Assembly in September.

3) In particular, he added that, on the problem of refugees, his government had decided as a result of many influences (he did not specify that of the United States but it surely was among the most important) to suggest a definite number for repatriation "as part of a general refugee settlement." In the course of our discussion on this point, Shiloah said: "What number do you think it would be best for us to suggest?" I replied that I could only speak with diffidence since it was not my responsibility to instruct his government on such a difficult question. I understood from sources not American that the cabinet was toying with the idea of an offer of 100,000 on the assumption that the Gaza plan remain inoperative.

I added that it seemed to me that Israel would be advantaged and the refugee problem brought much nearer an overall solution if Israel's offer was the 200 or 220 thousand, which would be close to if not equal the number suggested by Ethridge. I presented a number of arguments in support of this position, all of them in terms of Israel's self-interest. I think Shiloah was somewhat impressed. At any rate, it was clear from what he said or did not say that the government here now recognized refugees as the key log in the jam of Israel-Arab relations.

At this point, Shiloah asked me another and more difficult question: "From what areas would you think it most advantageous that the Arabs to be repatriated should be selected." In the course of asking this question, Shiloah seemed to indicate the feeling that the situation of the refugees from the Gaza Strip was more desperate and hopeless than that of those elsewhere and that, therefore, the southern group should be preferred. Unwilling to give any definite answer to Shiloah's question, I recognized the desperateness of the condition of those in the south but reminded Shiloah that there were more Christian Arabs among the refugee groups in the other sections. He assented to this statement of fact, saying that probably there would be only a few hundred Christians in the south. I did not press my point because he understood the implications of my statement of fact.

4) Shiloah, in reply to my question about the reasons for the reported decline of Abdullah's prestige, said that this was due only in part to the concessions

43. Decision made in Israeli Foreign Ministry on July 13, 1949. *DFPI*, v. 4, d. 136.

which the king had made to the Israelis on the northwestern fringe of the Triangle. Indeed, he added that the Arab villages which had come under Israel's control in that area were now enjoying an "unprecedented prosperity" through the twice higher prices which the Israel authorities were paying for eggs, poultry, etc. than was being paid in the Triangle. Parenthetically, he said that the fifteen hundred Arabs who had been expelled [after the Israeli annexation] had been refugees in those villages and that it had been the mukhtars [heads of villages] who had insisted that they cross the line [back] into the Triangle proper.[44] The resulting issue was being ironed out by the Mixed Armistice Commission. More important than these concessions was the rise of Za'im as a factor in reducing Abdullah's status. With the Arabs everything was comparative, and Za'im's rapid rise tended to cast a shadow over Abdullah.

5) In answer to my question about the danger of the reported possible assassination of Abdullah, Shiloah spoke about the general use of such danger or alleged danger by Arab governments as a political weapon. For example, he said in Iraq, Nuri Said, the prime minister, is a candidate for assassination because he is accused of being "a corrupt British tool"; in Egypt the present prime minister is a similar candidate because he outlawed the Muslim Brotherhood[45] and is "playing with the British"; King Farouk is in the same category because "he is fattening on the blood of the fellahin"; Abdullah is in like case because "he is a tool of the British and is being bribed by the Jews"; Za'im too is in this category because of incipient opposition in the army and because of the undying enmity of those he drove from power. Moreover, even when such danger is relatively slight, Arab governments find it profitable, Shiloah added, to use the allegation of danger as a convenient weapon to eliminate political opposition and to justify arbitrary regimes.

6) Taking advantage of our friendly talk, I reiterated to Shiloah my quotation to Sharett of that morning of what General Riley had said to me the day previous about the "dictatorial attitude of Israeli negotiators" with Syria and Jordan. Shiloah listened with close attention and will, I think, use his influence with Ben-Gurion to soften the manners of the Israeli negotiators. He said that he was going to Jerusalem in a day or two and would talk to Bergman and Dayan; while there he hoped also to get better acquainted with Burdett.

7) Towards the close of our talk, it shifted to current impressions abroad, including Washington, that Israel is a potential aggressor. We covered much of the ground which I had on previous occasions discussed with Sharett and

44. Entry of April 5, 1949.
45. Ibrahim Abd al-Hadi Pasha (1886–1981), Egyptian prime minister, December 28, 1948–July 29, 1949. His predecessor, Mahmoud al-Nukrashi Pasha, was assassinated by the Muslim Brotherhood. During al-Hadi's premiership, Hassan al-Banna, the founder and head of the Brotherhood, was assassinated, and al-Nukrashi's assassin was arrested and hanged.

others in the Foreign Office. Shiloah's chief new contribution in reply was to say that this critical thesis and the arguments [in] back of it were almost identical with this thesis and the arguments supporting it in Musa al-Alami's new [article].[46]

8) Shiloah asked my advice as to whether Anton Daoud, the Arab driver of the American consulate-[general] car which had contained the explosive which wrecked the Agency building, would be extraditable.[47] The whereabouts of Daoud is known; he is in a country with which the US is on excellent relations [Egypt] and has an extradition treaty. Some Israelis have urged direct action against Daoud, but the government's decision has been to move through legal channels. My reply was of necessity indefinite because of my lack of technical knowledge and my desire not to be committed. I pointed out that the case was highly exceptional. The mandatory regime within whose jurisdiction the crime was committed had no generally recognized successor in Jerusalem, and moreover, I doubted whether our government could act in such a case. I suggested that Elath be instructed to talk quite informally with some of the technicians in the Department about the technical problems involved. Shiloah agreed that this would be best.

Comment. Again this long talk illustrated the value of an extended informal discussion out of the office, giving the kind of opportunity for detailed analysis which never comes in the more formal talks with Sharett or others in the Foreign Office.[48]

The day after Shiloah met with McDonald, Arthur Lourie, the Israeli consul general in New York, informally discussed the 100,000 returnee proposal with General John Hilldring, who had visited Israel at Truman's behest in April. Hilldring raised it with Truman on July 18. The Israelis learned that the president was pleased with Israel's flexibility and hoped it would break the deadlock. The State Department did not reject the proposal, but continued to press for 250,000 returnees.

Hilldring also told Truman that Jordan would block proposals to place Jerusalem under international control. In addition, he noted that "after the experience of the 100,000 Jews in Jerusalem during the siege of 1948, no government in Israel which

---

46. Musa al-Alami (1897–1984), Jerusalem-born, Cambridge-educated Arab nationalist; worked in the British mandatory administration in the 1930s; engaged in talks with Ben-Gurion and Sharett, 1934; contributed to the talks behind the White Paper of 1939; headed the Arab office after 1946; lost most of his property in Jerusalem and the Galilee in 1948 and moved near Jericho. The piece referenced is probably "The Lesson of Palestine," published in English in *Middle East Journal* 3, no. 4 (October 1949): 373–405, which argued that Jewish ambitions included the rest of Palestine and beyond.

47. Refers to car bomb explosion in the courtyard of the Jewish Agency/JNF compound in Jerusalem, March 11, 1948, which killed thirteen people. Daoud worked as a chauffeur for the US consulate and gained easy access to the compound as a result. He was believed to have acted as an agent of the grand mufti.

48. Briefer summary in McDonald to secretary of state, no. 545, July 16, 1949, NARA, RG 59, 501.BB Palestine, box 2125, folder 8.

agreed to [international control] would last five minutes." The United States and UN could guide movement toward peace in the Middle East, but could not force it on the belligerents.[49]

Saturday, July 16

Worked in clearing up documentation most of the day. At five Eytan came and stayed for an hour and a quarter. Much of the ground he covered was a repetition of what Shiloah had said. An interesting personal sidelight was the seeming desire of Eytan to play down the importance of Shiloah's going to Lausanne. Eytan returned to a couple of points which he had mentioned to me earlier. Mark Ethridge's tendency to become brighter as his drinking day developed, citing Ethridge's alleged remark in answer to Eytan's question to whom compensation in territory should be made, with the words: "Turn the territory over to Dean Acheson." Eytan quoted Ethridge also as having said that "all of Willie's brains are in her feet" in connection with her habit of dancing every night until one or two or later.[50] According to Eytan, the younger Americans, [Fraser] Wilkins, [Paul] Porter,[51] et al., religiously kept up with Ethridge's drinking but quickly desisted when Ethridge had left Lausanne.

On the more serious level, Eytan said that during the past [meetings] none of the delegations to the PCC had been forthcoming, nor had the American representatives put their cards on the table. Illustrative of his general reticence was the American insistence on [an] Arab-Israeli refugee agreement before any clear indication could be given of what financing might be possible and the part the US might take in this; on the other hand, Israel and the Arabs were unwilling to say what they might do in repatriation or resettlement until they knew what funds would be available. Eytan told of long talks with [Raymond] Hare on this matter, Eytan stressing the need of having the financial arrangement known in advance and Hare insisting on the other way procedure.

Eytan also spoke of a "more forthcoming" program by Israel at Lausanne, of his hope that the Arabs could make a similar contribution and that the American delegation would similarly be less reticent. He added that it was important for all concerned that the PCC be enabled to have a success at the UN General Assembly.

Henry Montor came to the house before Ford's and my conference with Eytan had been concluded. He sat in with us, and later he and I talked, making an engagement for a fuller conference on next Wednesday.

After dinner, Ruth and Bobby and I went out to the Sharon. I had a brief talk with Abe Feinberg alone. He said that he hoped to have the exact data about conditions at the end of this week from one source and from another at

---

49. Hilldring's account is in *FRUS*, 1949, v. VI, 1249–1252. See also *DFPI*, v. 4, p. 206, d. 124, 139; entries of April 28–30, 1949.
50. Willie Snow Ethridge, Mark Ethridge's wife.
51. See entry of July 19, 1949.

the end of next week. We agreed then to compare notes. Feinberg said that one of the reasons Eytan was being replaced at Lausanne was his comparative standoffishness. As an example was cited Eytan's non-attendance at the bar in the Beau Rivage during the long evenings where he might profitably have been talking with Hare instead of having the latter sit often alone. This account of Feinberg fit in closely with Eytan's statement to me earlier that he "never" went to this bar.

For a half hour or so, our family joined the Feinbergs and Mr. and Mrs. May of Ford's. Home by a little after eleven.

Sunday, July 17

A free morning for work.

Thanks to Shalom's skillful navigation, the Fords and Bobby, Ruth and I were in our seats in the front row of the diplomatic section of the grandstand for Army Day at 3:15, a full three quarters of an hour before the opening. The Russians, who came later in a party of six, found the whole front row occupied and were divided up into groups of two.

The ceremonies were impressive, the brief order of the day by [IDF chief of staff Ya'akov] Dori, the awarding of the medals for heroic actions (pathetically touching were these awards posthumously received by mothers or sisters). The main show, however, was the march-by, which lasted about an hour and a half. All the branches of the service were represented, including the Navy, and the heavier tanks, as well as the cavalry. Miracles of miracles, not a vehicle stalled.

For us, however, the most exciting part of the day was wholly unplanned. Shalom, as usual, had his car ready for us when we came out, and we thought we would be the first home. Instead, we found ourselves immediately behind the last tank and became an integral part of the parade all the way from the grandstand through the whole of Tel Aviv to Jaffa, where we finally were able to turn out and head for Ramat Gan. Immediately following us for the first part of the procession was the Belgian diplomatic car and behind it an Israeli car. Somehow these two cars were passed by the Russian diplomatic car, which then clung to us tenaciously the whole way.

For approximately four or five miles the route was flanked on either side by masses of people, eight to ten or more rows deep and with thousands of persons perched precariously on balconies, trees, roofs, etc. As soon as the American flag was noticed, there were friendly cheers and greetings to the American representative. I returned these greetings with as consistent animation as I was capable of for so long a pull. At no single point did I discern the slightest indication of unfriendliness or of anything other than cordial warmth. It was a heartening experience.

The Russian representative, evidently desirous of watering down as much as possible these spontaneous greetings to us, continued to wave energetically to the crowds, which in more measured tones responded. Or, perhaps there were spontaneous greetings from the crowd for the Russians. Their car followed so closely after ours that it was difficult to discern where applause for us ended and that for them began.

Hot as it was whenever (and this happened frequently) we were forced to pause because of congestion in the procession, and despite my almost morbid fear that the crowd would at some time realize that the parade was over and break through the police lines and engulf us, I found the trip definitely worthwhile. In addition to my discovery that the newspaper criticism of recent weeks found no reflection in these friendly crowds, I was glad of the chance to study at close range the people as they had waited so patiently, many of them probably for hours to see this visible demonstration of Israel's power. The variety of physical types impressed me anew.

In the light of the embarrassing debacle of the Independence Day attempted parade, Army Day was an extraordinary showing of perfect organization, perfect control by the police and the home guard and complete self-discipline by the people. Everyone concerned had [the] right to be proud.[52]

We were finally home about ten minutes before eight. There was just time for bath and change and a bite before the Fords and we went off to the Army reception at HaKirya. We stayed only about a half hour and were back home a little after eleven.

Monday, July 18

Arranged with Sam Sacks to go to Haifa in time for dinner for Justice Douglas and to stay at Bodenheimer's that night. Justice Douglas called me from Rehovot and confirmed that he and his son would stay with us. About four the Douglases arrived, hot and tired from their trip down from Jerusalem. After they had had a rest, we had a brief visit at teatime.

William O. Douglas (1898–1980), US Supreme Court justice (1939–1975), had said that Justice Louis Brandeis had converted him to Zionism. During his visit to the Middle East, he also visited the Arab states and consulted with the US missions in those capitals. McDonald and the Israeli government laid out the red carpet for his two-week visit to Israel. "Douglas," McDonald wrote Janet and Halsey, "as a close friend of the President and in his own right is expected to receive almost regal honors here."[53]

[Herbert] Kunde of [the] PCC Technical Committee came at four and remained for more than an hour. He reported progress in preparing for a census of the refugees. He now estimated their number at something more [like] 700,000 rather than the 900,000-plus of the earlier estimate. He told me too of

---

52. Fuller comments in McDonald to secretary of state, no. 560, July 22, 1949, McDonald Papers, USHMM, box 7, folder 16.
53. McDonald to Halsey and Janet Barrett, July 13, 1949, McDonald Papers, Columbia University, box 14, folder 13.

the hope that the census could be taken by graduate students of [the American University of] Beirut under the direction of [a] professor of economics there. On my part I brought him up to date on what seemed to me the encouraging developments here.

At our dinner for Douglas were present besides the justice, Mr. and Mrs. Ben-Gurion, the Sharetts, the Smoiras, the chief judge of the [Israeli] supreme court,[54] the Judge Wyzanskis,[55] the Fords and the three McDonalds, making a crowded table of fourteen. The meal was excellent and admirably served. During it the prime minister seemed to have an enjoyable time, as did the justice.

After dinner Ben-Gurion divided his talk almost equally between the justice and Wyzanski. Ben-Gurion seemed to be intrigued by what both of them had to say. [Douglas] told him about Frankfurter's "decline," which he said was more apparent than real because Felix had never been much of a liberal under his own power and returned to his natural conservatism after the influence of Brandeis and Holmes had waned.

My task as host kept me from concentrating on any one person. I did, however, finally bring the conversation around to the general subjects which I had discussed so fully with Shiloah and Eytan and got enough response from the two men, Sharett and Ben-Gurion, to feel confident that the two younger men had not been talking through their hats. As the party was breaking up Ben-Gurion took me aside in the study and said something to the effect that he deplored any misunderstanding about his inquiry to me earlier on the function of the different members of the military attachés' offices. I explained that any misunderstanding which might have existed had been cleared up and then talked rather freely about the colonel [Andrus]. When the party was over, the McDonalds all had the feeling that it had been an unqualified success.

On July 19, McDonald reported that after the dinner Ben-Gurion had "confirmed Israeli plans for more conciliatory and broader approach at Lausanne."[56]

54. Moshe Smoira (1888–1961), German-born jurist and labor Zionist; emigrated to Palestine, 1921; law partner of Pinhas Rosen; lecturer at Jerusalem Law School; attorney for Histadrut; president of the World Zionist Organization's Court of Honor; president of Israel's supreme court, 1948–1951; married to Esther Smoira (née Horovitz); related to Zalman Shazar, current minister of education and later president of Israel, 1963–1973.

55. Judge Charles Wyzanski Jr. (1906–1986), US jurist; solicitor-general, Department of Labor, 1932–1935; special assistant to attorney general, 1935–1937; US District Court for Massachusetts, 1941–1971, and chief judge on that court, 1965–1971; worked to allow more Jews into the United States under the immigration quotas in 1930s; initially questioned the fairness and legitimacy of the International Military Tribunal proceedings at Nuremberg in late 1945–early 1946, but publicly reversed his opinion several months later; married to Gisela Warburg (1912–1991), daughter of Max Warburg; worked with Youth Aliyah in Germany; emigrated to the United States, 1939; longtime board member of Hadassah, and active in UNICEF.

56. McDonald to secretary of state, no. 549, July 19, 1949, *FRUS*, 1949, v. VI, 1237–1238.

Breakfast with Douglas. He talked very interestingly about [Judge Joseph] Hutcheson, his early brilliance and his later decline, largely through his violent antipathy to the New Deal and the administrative tribunals set up under it. Nonetheless, Douglas recognized Hutcheson' s deep honesty. He reported that the Palestine mission had been an intellectual rebirth for Hutcheson.[57] Speaking of Frankfurter, Douglas said that the former lacks inner security and that this probably explained his embarrassing attacks on lawyers in the [Supreme] Court, attacks which made his colleagues feel ashamed.

At teatime Rabbi Soltes,[58] formerly of McGill [University], and Dr. Voss,[59] Professor Payne[60] and another member of the New York University Katznelson Seminar, were out at the house.[61] Though the talk was long there is not much to report, except Voss's impression about the reaction at home on the Arab refugee problem. According to him, the Protestant reaction was intermittent and not the most serious. It was and is led, as far as the Federal Council is concerned, by [Henry Smith] Leiper.[62] The Foreign Missionary Boards, particularly those active in the Middle East, and the Gildersleeve-[Kermit] Roosevelt Committee[63] are also among the leaders. Voss regards, however, the Catholic criticism as being more telling. The statements issued from time to time by official or semi-official Vatican sources, for example, the Vatican City broadcasting section, have and continue to receive wide publicity, particularly in the *New York Times*.

Ruth and Bobby and I were at the Kaete Dan at 8:30 and remained until 11:15 for the dinner for Spyros Skouras[64] and Murray Silverstone[65] of 20th

57. Judge Joseph Chappell Hutcheson Jr. (1879–1973), Texas-born federal judge; sat on US Court of Appeals for the Fifth Circuit, 1931–1964; accomplished and colorful legal writer with two books and nearly 2,000 judicial opinions; US chairman of Anglo-American Committee of Inquiry, 1945–1946, treated extensively in Goda et al., *To the Gates of Jerusalem*.

58. Rabbi Avraham Soltes (1917–1983), New York-born Reform rabbi and musicologist; Jewish chaplain at McGill, Cornell, and West Point; chairman of the National Jewish Music Council; assistant to the president of Tel Aviv University, 1974–1977; hosted the program "The Music of Israel" on WQXR (New York), 1974–1983.

59. Dr. Carl Hermann Voss (1911–1995), US Congregationalist minister; founder and head of the American Christian Palestine Committee, which, during World War II, called for founding a Jewish state; closely associated with Rabbi Stephen S. Wise; held academic positions in England, Israel, Switzerland, and the United States; encouraged US aid to the new state.

60. Enoch George Payne (1877–1953), preeminent liberal educator; scholar and dean in New York University School of Education; developed program in educational sociology.

61. Katznelson Seminar, summer workshop, Kfar Saba, July–August 1949, co-sponsored by the New York University School of Education and the Katznelson Institute; named after Berl Katznelson (1888–1944), a founder of Histadrut and the newspaper *Davar*, opponent of partition, and advocate for peaceful coexistence between Arabs and Jews; seminar led by Abraham I. Katsh (1906–1998), Hebrew and Judaica scholar who taught at NYU.

62. Henry Smith Leiper (1891–1975), New Jersey-born missionary and Protestant theologian; executive secretary, Federal and World Council of Churches; outspoken opponent of Nazi persecution of Jews; called for a boycott of the 1936 Olympics in Berlin.

63. The Committee for Justice and Peace in the Holy Land. See entry of June 1, 1949.

64. Spyros Skouras (1893–1971), Greek-born businessman: merged Fox and Twentieth Century film studios, 1935; chairman, 20th Century-Fox, 1942–1962.

65. Murray Silverstone (d. 1969), Polish-born film executive; foreign manager of 20th Century-Fox; with wife Dorothy founded Intercultural Center for Youth in Jerusalem to promote interaction between Jewish and Arab children, 1960.

Century-Fox. It was interesting sitting next to Skouras, who has had wide personal contacts throughout the world. He was very enthusiastic about Paul Porter, whom he regards as extremely able.[66] Shiloah, who sat on the other side of Skouras, said that he had reported fully to Ben-Gurion and Sharett on our long talk the previous Friday. From the way he spoke I got the impression that these two men at the top are in accord with what he said to me about the more forthcoming policy of Israel and his hopes of PCC action before the Assembly. He added that probably Eytan was not going back to Lausanne because of his child's illness [meningitis].

McDonald noted, "I believe Israel now [is] willing [to] contribute to and hopeful of progress at Lausanne prior [to UN General Assembly]. . . . Appointment [of] Porter [to the] PCC creates excellent impression. Vital [that] Riley remain chairman [of the] four MACs because no adequate substitute [is] available. He deserves highest praise, which I hope [Department] will pass to Riley's superiors."[67] The Lausanne talks formally resumed on July 18.

My general impression of Skouras was that of a human dynamo, or to mix the figure, a high-powered plane rushing from capital to capital. Incidentally, he asked about going to the Old City tomorrow. Shiloah undertook to call Dayan last night and to have it followed up Wednesday morning so that the arrangements could be perfected by the time Skouras reached Jerusalem, where they are remaining for only part of the day. He is returning in time to take off from Tel Aviv in his private plane for Stockholm Wednesday.

Wednesday, July 20
Received letter from McGhee approving of my return home. [George McGhee became the assistant secretary of state for Near Eastern and African affairs after a departmental reorganization in summer 1949 in which the Office of Near Eastern and African Affairs became the Bureau of Near Eastern, South Asian, and African Affairs (NEA)].[68]

Wednesday, July 20
Accepted for the Technion dinner on the 21st for Justice Douglas.

---

66. On July 16, 1949, during the recess at Lausanne, the White House announced that Paul A. Porter (1904–1979) would succeed Mark Ethridge as the US representative to the PCC. A Missouri-born lawyer and senior Democratic Party official, Porter headed the publicity campaign in the 1944 elections and afterward served as Roosevelt's chairman of the Federal Communications Commission [FCC]. Truman appointed him to head the US economic mission to Greece in 1946 with the rank of ambassador.

67. McDonald to secretary of state, no. 553, July 20, 1949, NARA, RG 501.BB, box 2126, folder 1.

68. *FRUS*, 1949, v. VI, 1418.

On July 20, 1949, the Israeli-Syrian armistice agreement was signed near Mishmar HaYarden.[69] Cease-fire conditions were now officially applied to all fronts. McDonald reported that "attention will now focus on composing [solving] Israel-Jordan differences. Arab Legion has evacuated strip of territory along north edge of "Triangle" from Zububa to Jordan River in accordance with agreement. Jordan is delaying about Latrun but it now stands alone as last to concede to Israeli demands."[70]

Thursday, July 21

Long breakfast conference with Colonel Archibald. He reported rather fully about his Washington impressions. These were in large part replicas of those of van der Velde; suspicion of our objectivity, suspicion of Israel's purposes, etc. He spoke of Symington's interest in the Middle East and of his friendliness.[71] The colonel seemed confident that he would be able to get permission to fly us to Paris and is promptly making the necessary moves. Told the staff of our plans for leaving on [August] 8th and offered to perform various services at home but not to act as a general carrier for supplies.

McDonald and his family went to Haifa on July 21 to hear Justice Douglas speak at the Technion dinner.[72] They, along with Sam Sacks, Abe Feinberg, and Selig Brodetsky, stayed at Bodenheimer's.

The trip to Haifa was pleasant and shortened by the cutoff through the local [Jewish] refugee camp. In itself this was a most depressing camp, with thousands of refugees huddled together four to eight cots in a single small tent, etc.[73] Bodenheimer's and Mount Carmel were a blessed relief. I arrived in time to change and get to the Technion dinner for Douglas at a nearby pension before seven. The justice was, I think, glad that I came.

The dinner was in complete contrast with that the previous Tuesday at Kaete Dan. This night the meal was finished and the brief talks concluded by a little after nine. In his few remarks the justice spoke of the assurances he had

---

69. Text in *DFPI*, v. 4, 723–734. See also Ben-Dror, *Ralph Bunche and the Arab Israeli Conflict*, 234–237.

70. McDonald to secretary of state, no. 560, July 22, 1949, McDonald Papers, USHMM, box 7, folder 16.

71. See entry of July 21, 1948. Archibald spoke with Symington, the secretary of the Air Force, about housing issues among other matters.

72. The affair had been arranged by the American Technion Society. Douglas's talk at the Technion concerned Israeli economic and technological development and the need for Israel to share its expertise for the development of the Middle East in general. See Thomas S. Bloodworth (US vice consul in Haifa) to secretary of state, no. 43, July 27, 1949, NARA, RG 59, MC 1390, reel 19, frames 779–787; JTA *Bulletin*, July 13, 1949.

73. Israel had established twenty-three immigrant camps by March 1949; several were around Haifa. Some 1,000 immigrants arrived each day. By October there were 92,000 immigrants in the camps, amidst deteriorating conditions. See Hakohen, *Immigrants in Turmoil*, 35, 89, 92.

received on all sides about the American ambassador. Rode back to Bodenheimer's with [Selig] Brodetsky.

Friday, July 22

On July 22, the McDonalds made an excursion across northern Israel with Sam Sacks and Abe Feinberg. Justice Douglas toured other parts of the country, including the Negev.

A pleasant morning exploring [Mount] Carmel and the new refugee center in the old British army camp.[74] It was in welcome contrast with the camp in Haifa proper, but as I scrutinized the wobbly temporary box-like structures, which were little more than tents, I pitied those who would have to live there in the midst of the winter winds and rains, the former being especially hurricane-like on [Mount] Carmel. I inspected the restoration work going on in the largest building on the hill, which is to be a new school. Its site is so commanding as to be literally sensational; it looks out over Haifa to Acre and the bay, over the whole of [Mount] Carmel and out to the Mediterranean.

Friday afternoon we all went to visit the Jewish boy- and girl-scout camp near Nahariya. While there we met General McNeill, on whose land the camp had been laid out.[75] He is another of those eccentric, but not by any means unique, Englishmen who have become so at home abroad that they prefer to live there rather than return to their native heath. He explained to us that he had been living in the nearby villa with his wife and one Arab servant for the most of eighteen years. He was smartly dressed and gave no evidence of being peculiar. The camp itself was primitive, the children sleeping on the ground with merely mats separating them from the earth. We were invited to stay for supper, but though the food looked tempting, the flies in the open-air kitchen were forbidding, so back we went to Bodenheimer's.

Saturday, July 23

Left about a quarter past nine for Mount Tabor. Our route was unusually interesting. Instead of going down through Haifa proper, we went on up [Mount] Carmel and this side of the Druze villages with their famous monastery on the reputed site of Elijah's triumph over the gods of Baal. We turned off and wound down the mountain on a spectacular road, which brought us out on the Haifa plain just above the cement works. We then took the main road to Afula, entering the Emek [Jezreel Valley] and skirting the valley on the north

74. Reference to the Sha'ar HaAliyah camp south of Haifa, which opened in March 1949, on the site of a rebuilt British army camp, to serve as the registration and medical screening center for new immigrants before they were sent to immigrant camps, hospitals, or housing. See Hakohen, *Immigrants in Turmoil*, 89–92.

75. Refers to town of Mazra'a between Acre and Nahariya. Brigadier-General Angus McNeill (1874–1950), commandant of British Gendarmerie in Palestine, 1922–1926; officer-in-charge of British Army horse breeding in Palestine, 1927–1931; resident of Mazra'a, 1932–1949, having decided to remain after termination of the Mandate.

to Megiddo, where we turned sharply to the left and crossed the Emek to Afula. From there we went directly to Mount Tabor at the foot of which we found McVicker waiting for us in a jeep. As we climbed the mountain, we were grateful for the jeep. The view from Mount Tabor would on a clear day be stupendous, but even today when a distant haze hid the farther mountains, Mount Gilboa, and the northern Galilean mountains and Mount Hermon, one had a wonderful panorama of all the nearer-by regions.

The church, a relatively new basilica, is in excellent taste with beautifully appropriate mosaics. The monastery itself is in a harmonious style, which the Greek Orthodox Church does not obtrude. The two Franciscans, one from Bari and the other from Sicily, were most courteous and helpful. After we had had a snack with tea, we bade them a grateful goodbye.[76]

Our drive to Tiberias was uneventful, except for the increasing heat as we went below sea level. For a moment in the town when our car refused to start, and it was activated only as it was pushed downhill towards the sea, I thought that Ruth's and my end had come when the driver appeared not to notice that he had to put on the emergency brake to avoid running off the pier.

Our search for Capernaum was rather painful, because the last kilometer or so of the road was torturing to the car and nearly dissuaded us from pushing on. Finally, however, we reached the sea and there were greeted by the same friendly Franciscan who had been so courteous to us in 1946. He remembered that trip and spoke with enthusiasm of Judge Hutcheson and the latter's biblical knowledge.

The drive up to Safed was, as always, thrillingly beautiful. Fortunately, through a friend of Sam Sacks we found [Moshe] Castel's studio, a delightfully old place where he greeted us most courteously.[77] The drive from Safed to Acre was as usual one of the most thrilling that one can enjoy anywhere in the world. We were back to Bodenheimer's in time for dinner. I hope on some later time to do that trip more leisurely so as to be able to stop and see the lake and its surrounding mountains from all several points of vantage.

After dinner, there was [an] animated discussion in which Sam Sacks and some of his industrial friends joined issue with [Ezriel] Carlebach of *Ma'ariv*[78] on the attitude of the government towards industry. The businessmen argued

76. Refers to the Church of the Transfiguration, part of a Franciscan complex built in 1924 on the ruins of a fourth- to sixth-century Byzantine and a twelfth-century Crusader church, where Christ's transfiguration is said to have occurred. McDonald also refers to the neighboring Greek Orthodox Church of St. Elias, built in 1845.

77. Moshe Castel (1909–1991), Jerusalem-born Israeli artist descended from Spanish Jews who migrated to Palestine after the expulsion of 1492; studied and held exhibits in Paris in 1920s; settled in Safed, 1940; known for Sephardic themes in 1930s and 1940s.

78. Dr. Ezriel Carlebach (1909–1956), German-born journalist and novelist; covered Jewish communities throughout Europe in the late 1920s; arrested by the Nazis in January 1933 perhaps for journalistic attacks on Joseph Goebbels; fled to Poland where he wrote exposés on Nazi seizure of power and numerous other stories for the Yiddish newspaper *Haynt*; emigrated to Palestine as correspondent for *Yiddishe Post* of London, 1937; founded and became editor-in-chief of *Ma'ariv*, 1948–1956, which became Israel's most widely read newspaper and opposed Ben-Gurion's government.

with what seemed to me much cogency that the government through its non-sympathetic attitude towards industry was making impossible the reconstruction of the country and work for the immigrants. Sacks continued to underline the desperate need of raw material and the failure of the government to find the exchange or to permit the industrialists themselves to find it. He and the others in this group asserted that Zionist leadership had traditionally been anti-industry and pro-agriculture. They argued that by the erection of industrial buildings at a fraction of the cost spent on kibbutzim the whole problem of industrialists with small capital would be made incomparably simpler. Later, Sacks said that he was sure that one of the reasons for Kaplan's failure to see the danger of present policies was the influence of Hoofien, who had been traditionally anti-industrialist and who was thinking primarily in terms of maintaining the present fictitious value of the pound. Carlebach's reply was, in effect, that the government had not yet made up its mind which industries were to be preferred.

Sunday, July 24

Back home before noon after an uneventful trip. All the way down Sam Sacks chattered amusingly, though always with evidently sincere criticism, of the government's sins of omission and commission.

In the evening to the first performance of *La Bohème*. Paula [Ben-Gurion] went along with us. Though uneven, the performance was on the whole pleasing. It had verve, the orchestra was well led, and most of the singers including Madame de Phillipe handled their roles competently. The young tenor was excellent in most of his songs, while the woman new to the company who took the second role was excellent.

Monday, July 25

General Riley came out for nearly an hour in the late morning. He was more exuberant and optimistic than I had seen him at any previous time. First, we arranged for a telegram to Gowen and a letter to Galeazzi, the latter to [be] taken by General Riley, telling that he would spend Wednesday night of this week in Rome en route to Lausanne and giving the days of the week following that he would be available for a private audience with His Holiness.

General Riley said that he thought there was now a possibility that the armistice with Syria would be followed by peace leadership under al-Barazi. Parenthetically, he said he was of the opinion that the proposed meeting of Ben-Gurion and Za'im was both too late and premature. Had it come when Za'im was a personal ruler, it might have been useful, but to come now before Lausanne had any chance, it would be unfortunate.[79] As to the armistice itself, he saw dangers arising from the provision for the permission of Arabs to

79. This was also the assessment of Ben-Gurion, who told Shiloah that Israel should not press Za'im for a separate peace unless it was clear that general peace could not be reached with the Arab states at Lausanne. Ben-Gurion Diary, entry of July 26, 1949. The editors are grateful to Tuvia Friling for this reference.

return to the demilitarized zone and from other technical aspects of the terms. He was hopeful, however, that these difficulties would not be insuperable and that Syria could be made the leader in transforming armistices into treaties of peace.

As General Riley talked on the above point, I had a mental reservation arising from his statement that the Syrians were still anxious about the "rectification" of the northeastern frontier. He himself said that, of course, the watercourse [of the Jordan River] would be a more logical boundary. But he admitted that, at present, there would be no possibility of the Israelis effecting such a change. General Riley added that he anticipated a furor in the Knesset when the debate on the armistice took place and that probably Sharett would have a difficult time. We were both of the opinion, however, that with Ben-Gurion's help a crisis could probably be gotten over.[80]

General Riley thought that, on his return, Latrun might be ironed out with three or four weeks of talk. He did not seem so confident about [Mount] Scopus. He was, he added, increasingly aware of the importance of the southern Negev, the significance of which he at first learned from me. He was glad to have my report that I had emphasized to Sharett and Shiloah and Eban his points about the manners of the Israeli representatives in negotiations with the Arabs. As the general was leaving, he signed our guest book in such a way as to add to its value to us.

A little after 2:30, I was awakened up from my nap by mysterious sounds of goings on around and outside the house. Only about half awake, I went out into the hall to discover that the Douglases were just going out to the Sharon. I thought the justice was rather cool and casual as he said goodbye. It was not until he had gone that Miss Clark disclosed the enormity of the crisis.

On his return from the Negev an hour or two earlier, the justice had exploded successively to Archibald, Tetlie, and Miss Clark about the unwillingness of his guides in the Negev to let him see what he wanted to see or to talk to those in whom he was interested. "This was," he declared, "a police state in which you were shown only what they wanted you to see." And there was much more of the same. Before he got away from the house, however, Miss Clark was able to elicit from him a half-hearted promise to keep his evening speaking engagement before the Israel-America Friendship League.[81]

Douglas later complained to State Department officials that "his Israeli guides had whisked him through the Negev and down to Aqaba so fast that he had not been

---

80. Ben-Gurion and Sharett indeed faced harsh criticism in the Knesset on this issue on August 2, 1949.

81. The Israel-America Friendship League, founded in Haifa in 1949 with club rooms by early 1950 in Tel Aviv, Jerusalem, and Petah Tikvah. Initially under the chairmanship of Uriel Friedland of the Shemen factory in Haifa, it aimed to promote trade and cultural exchange between the United States and Israel, hosted guest speakers from the United States, and worked with the public affairs officer in the embassy in Tel Aviv. See Waller to secretary of state, no. 51, April 25, 1950, USSDCF-PIFA, 1950–1954, reel 6, frames 90–91.

able to see anything or talk to anyone." He later protested to the Israeli Foreign Ministry and "was suspicious that troop movements were taking place and [that] his journey had been hastened for that reason."[82]

Until nearly 9:30 there were diminishing fears that he might not appear. Thanks, however, to Astar's imagination (instead of taking the justice directly to the Sharon, he showed him during four hours many of the types of institutions which he had failed to see in the south) and to Tetlie's pleading, the justice came to the meeting at 9:30 and delivered an interesting and, at points, even stirring address on the American judicial and political system. I sensed in his speech something of a Lincoln quality.

The rest of the meeting was about as satisfactory as one could expect. The League will be, I think, a useful if not very influential body. In my few remarks I welcomed the League, paid a tribute to Douglas, and said I would be glad to help personally in the League's effort to build a library. The most horrific event of the evening was a local judge's introduction of the justice which, judging from the size of the script would have lasted more than half an hour had not the jeers of the crowd persuaded the speaker to end his rambling discourse about the superlative merits of Brandeis and the high qualities of the latter's "disciple" Justice Douglas.

After the meeting Ruth and I took the justice out to the hotel. He talked interestingly in answer to my questions about the Supreme Court's decisions on questions involving the use of school buses for children to denominational schools and the use of schoolrooms for religious teaching.[83] He thought that a young Catholic judge, [William D.] Campbell of Chicago,[84] very close to Cardinal Stritch,[85] might be strongly backed for the post as successor to the late Justice Murphy.[86] Justice Douglas said it was certain that the [Catholic]

---

82. Memorandum of conversation, August 8, 1949, NARA, RG 59, 501.BB Palestine, box 2126, folder 3.

83. Refers to *Collum v. Board of Education* (1948), concerning use of taxpayer funds for religious instruction in public schools during "extra time" during the school week. The Supreme Court voted 8–1 against the Champaign, Illinois, public school district, arguing that the district promoted religious sects and violated the principle of church–state separation. Douglas was part of the majority opinion. In general see M. Charles Wallfisch, "Justice William O. Douglas and Religious Liberty," *Journal of Presbyterian History* 58, no. 3 (Fall 1980): 193–208.

84. Judge William D. Campbell (1905–1988), judge, US District Court, Northern District of Illinois, 1940–1959 (nominated by Roosevelt); chief judge of that court, 1959–1970.

85. Cardinal Samuel Strich (1887–1958), archbishop of the archdiocese of Chicago, 1940–1946; raised to cardinal by Pope Pius XII, 1946–1958; opponent of the antisemitic priest Father Charles Coughlin; oversaw creation of first US chapter of Opus Dei.

86. William Francis "Frank" Murphy (1890–1949), US attorney general, 1939–1940; US Supreme Court justice, 1940–1949; died unexpectedly, July 19, 1949; part of the more liberal faction of the then-divided Supreme Court, which included Douglas and Hugo Black; dissented from Supreme Court ruling in *Korematsu v. United States*, which declared constitutional the internment of Japanese Americans; replaced by Tom Campbell Clark (1899–1977), Truman's attorney general and political supporter, who strengthened the more conservative faction under Chief Justice Fred Vinson, which upheld Cold War legislation on loyalty oaths and on affiliation with subversive groups. The appointment triggered charges of cronyism.

hierarchy would interest itself actively in this place [on the court]. The bishops had been disappointed a number of times by Murphy's being a part of the majority in decisions which they regarded as inimical. He added that some of the attacks on Murphy by the bishops had been as strong as any he had known. Justice Douglas concluded that the new appointment would have great importance because, if the new judge were conservative, he would fundamentally alter the balance in the court.

We did not talk at all about the justice's experiences in the south [of Israel]. I preferred to entertain the fiction that I knew nothing of it. Our only reference to Israel was my rather brief statement about the PCC, to which the justice listened without comment. His goodbye to us when we left him at the hotel was correct, but Ruth thought it lacked cordiality. Perhaps this was merely his manner.

In the middle of the afternoon the Feinbergs came in to say goodbye. Abe would have taken the two Castel [paintings] at 250 [Israeli] pounds, but Mrs. Feinberg's lack of enthusiasm kept me from encouraging him.

The ambassadorial residence did not receive new furniture until November 1949. In June, however, McDonald arranged with the Tel Aviv Museum and Israeli artists to borrow paintings for display there."[87] *Works of contemporary Israeli art in the residence at different times included Arieh Lubin's* Tel Benjamin Landscape*; Nachum Gutman's* An Old Synagogue at Tiberias*; Ludwig Schwerin's* Olive Trees *and* Jaffa*; Yitzhak Frenkel's* Safed*; Moshe Castel's* Sephardic Marriage *and* Jacob's Dream*; Menachem Schmidt Shemi's* Safed Landscape*; and Anatoly Kaplan's* Nostalgia.[88]

Feinberg was much upset when I told him about the justice. He said he would speak to Agron at 4 and Ben-Gurion at 4:30. Feinberg reported that he had learned from the Foreign Office the following:

1) Through the French assistant secretary-general of the UN,[89] Israel had offered to take 100,000 refugees (this figure is in lieu of and conditional to those that might be taken if the Gaza project became a reality); Dean Acheson said that it was "unsatisfactory"; but when the Department was asked if the offer should be withdrawn, Israel was asked not to do this.[90] Feinberg

---

87. McDonald to Halsey and Janet Barrett, July 13, 1949, McDonald Papers, Columbia University, box 14, folder 13.
88. Full list in McDonald Papers, Columbia University, box 13, folder 6.
89. Henri Laugier (1888–1973), Sorbonne-trained doctor who studied the psychology of work; helped organize flight of French scientists during the German occupation; assistant secretary-general for social affairs (one of six assistant secretaries-general), 1946–1952; helped draft the Universal Declaration of Human Rights, 1948; helped create the World Health Organization; became part of executive council of UNESCO, 1952.
90. On Acheson and the Israeli refugee proposal see Sharett to Elath, July 21, 1949, *DFPI*, v. 4, d. 144.

said that HaKirya was alarmed at the refugee figures in Gaza Strip, which they now estimate at nearly 280,000 (including, I assume, the native Arabs, many of whom have probably become destitute), instead of their earlier estimate [of] more than 100,000 less. In Feinberg's opinion, there will be a dangerous revolt against the government in the Knesset if the proposal to take large numbers of Arab refugees comes before that body for approval.

2) Through unofficial sources, Israel had assured the Department that it regarded the armistice lines as sacrosanct and was firmly of the intention not to use force to go beyond this. This statement, though encouraging, had a reverse aspect, which the Department may have regarded as an indirect warning that Israel would not tolerate, or at any rate would not agree to, Arab or international pressure to change the armistice line.

3) He spoke at some length of Paul Porter as one of the political intimates of the president, though not necessarily of the very closest grade. He was very close to Bob Hannegan.[91] His appointment should be considered as a presidential one and he representative of the president rather than the Department.

3) Another fact tending to support Feinberg's view that the president is personally giving the Israeli directives these days is the injunction unofficially given Porter that he is to talk to no American Jew other than Feinberg.

4) Feinberg was going to telephone Porter [in] London to find out whether the latter wished to see him. Otherwise he would not go to Lausanne, but whether he went or not, he would find out whether I was going to be asked to go. He thought this likely in view of my passing by there at such an opportune moment.

All in all it was a very interesting talk.

Tuesday, July 26

Up unusually early and worked on the Chinese puzzle, the recent despatches and telegrams, and finally drafted a strong telegram urging again that in the light of the apparent hardening of the attitude of the Arab states, of the desire of Israel to keep all its wartime gains, of the manifest self-stultification of [the] PCC (see its more than seven months' record), and finally of the need for concerted, decisive and rapid action, the US should begin a campaign for action by the UN General Assembly to replace the PCC by one-man authority, even if Bunche were not available to do the job. Ford strongly urged sending it.[92]

91. Robert E. Hannegan (1903–1949), St. Louis politician and Truman supporter; helped ensure Truman's reelection as US senator in 1940, despite Truman's association with Kansas City boss Tom Pendergast, by mobilizing St. Louis Catholic vote; Roosevelt's commissioner of internal revenue, 1943–1944; chairman, Democratic Party (on Truman's suggestion to Roosevelt), 1945–1947; recommended Truman as Roosevelt's running mate and helped secure Truman's nomination, 1944.

92. McDonald to secretary of state, no. 566, July 26, 1949, excerpted *FRUS*, 1949, v. VI, 1245.

Friendly visit from the new French minister and Mrs. Guyon. They indicated clearly that they would prefer our house to their more ornate Jaffa mansion. His attitude towards Israel's inaction in aiding foreign missions with their foreign problem reflected the impatience of the representative of a great power towards a small one.[93]

Received at breakfast the wonderful news of the safe arrival of Donald [McDonald's grandchild], exactly a year less two days from the tragic event [Janet's miscarriage] of last year.

Miss Herlitz called and said Sharett would like to meet me at his office at 7:15 on Wednesday.

The Sharett reception for Justice Douglas was very pleasant, the weather cool and grounds beautiful and the guests in good humor. It was particularly gay for us because of the very sincere congratulations of everyone to us on Donald's arrival. It was amusing to note how many people, on learning that it was a boy, would exclaim: "Double Mazel Tov."

There were so many people to see that there was no time to say anything which evoked comment worthy of being reported. I was glad to note that the justice seemed to have recovered completely from his Negev-caused ill humor. I managed to remember to tell him that his address the night before had seemed to me to have a Lincolnesque quality. He good-humoredly replied that this might have been because he was so extremely tired.

On August 8 Douglas met with Rusk, McGhee, and Wilkins in Washington. The Arab refugees, he said, sincerely wished to return to their homes even though they might decide afterward to leave Israel on seeing the changed conditions there. Douglas had expressed skepticism to Sharett that even 250,000 returnees would balance the Arab desire to return, and that "if Israel does not now permit their repatriation this action will forever rankle in their hearts and be the source of future trouble." Douglas further reported that the Israelis would give up no part of the Negev. He spoke highly of the US ministers in the Middle East, particularly Keeley and Burdett. He remarked that he "considered it unfortunate that Ambassador McDonald at Tel Aviv, whom he considered a fine man personally, was biased" and spoke "as though American and Israeli interests were one and the same."[94]

93. Édouard-Félix Guyon (b. 1902), career French diplomat, served Vichy regime in Bucharest and as general secretary in Quai d'Orsay; in secret contact with French Committee of National Liberation in Algiers in 1942; minister plenipotentiary in Bern, 1946–1948; ambassador to Israel, 1949–1952. France gave de facto recognition to Israel in January 1949 and de jure recognition in May of that year. Guyon presented his credentials to Weizmann on July 19, 1949. Guyon reported in late August 1949 that "the manner in which Israeli leaders have proceeded recalls Hitler's Reich, when after the occupation of the Baltic countries by Soviet troops in 1940, [Germany] repatriated Baltic Germans. . . . The Israeli leaders have acted no differently, though admittedly with less method and scientific rigor." In general see David Pryce-Jones, *Betrayal: France, the Arabs, and the Jews* (New York: Encounter, 2008), 82–83.
94. Memorandum of conversation, August 8, 1949, NARA, RG 59, 501.BB Palestine, box 2126, folder 3.

Dr. Joseph Schwartz of the JDC came to the house promptly at 7:45 and remained until 9:00. The first fifteen minutes or so was spent in his telling me of the Jewish scene at home. Montor and Morgenthau had resigned from the Palestine Economic Corporation [PEC] in part because of difference of opinion about personnel and policies and perhaps more because not being in a position to give time to the PEC after they had returned to the United Jewish Appeal [UJA], they were not able to perform the function which had been initially envisaged for them.[95] As to Montor's future, Schwartz thought that he should continue with the UJA because he could not be satisfactorily replaced. Neumann and Silver are temporarily almost completely out of the main currents. Daniel Frisch, who was only at the last minute Silver's candidate and who was not even on speaking terms with Neumann, had made his own candidacy [for presidency of the ZOA], and was seeking to establish his independence and demonstrating willingness to work with the progressive Zionists.

Schwartz thought that it would be desirable for the JDC to have a special project in Israel, that of the institutional cases among the refugees, but not that it should itself administer the program; rather, it should enable existing agencies to do more and better the work which they have already undertaken. Most of the rest of the time was spent in my reporting on conditions here and recent international developments. Schwartz did, however, speak of Jack Arvey of Chicago as the extraordinary new personality in Midwestern politics. As the reform Democratic boss, he had elected a reform mayor, his governor Adlai Stevenson,[96] and his senator, Professor Douglas.[97] Despite his success, Arvey continued to labor in the ranks of the UJA workers.

Schwartz also spoke about the new personality in Philadelphia, the clothing manufacturer who had played such a prominent role with Abe Feinberg, Arvey and others in the Truman campaign.[98]

The middle of the morning Rabbi Jacob Herzog came in to talk to me before the arrival of Monsignor [Thomas] McMahon. The latter, though technically concerned only with refugees is, Herzog is convinced, representative of the Vatican also on the political level. The two have had hours of discussion together. From this, Herzog got the impression that the propaganda which he attributes to the Vatican and which he says has reached "almost incredible proportions," will continue unless Israel yields on refugees and internationalization of Jerusalem. Herzog argued that this attitude from the Vatican's own point of view is fundamentally mistaken because: 1) It will not succeed; 2) It

95. The PEC on June 10, 1949 announced that Morgenthau resigned his position of chairman of the board and Montor his position as vice president.

96. Adlai Stevenson II (1900–1965), governor of Illinois, 1949–1953; Democratic nominee for president, 1952, 1956; US ambassador to UN, 1961–1965.

97. Paul Douglas (1892–1976), prominent liberal Democrat; professor of economics, University of Chicago; Chicago city councilman, 1939–1942; US congressman; 1945–1947; US senator, 1949–1967.

98. Possible reference to Albert M. Greenfield. See entry of September 26, 1949.

risks alienating Jewish opinion throughout the world at the very moment when the church is engaged in a desperate battle with the forces of materialism and; 3) It opens the door to Russian penetration in Jerusalem. Herzog was hopeful that I would be willing to talk with the monsignor about these related problems.

Herzog was also very interesting in his report of Monsignor McMahon's statement that "the Catholic Church considers that it is engaged in a life and death struggle for survival in the States." The public statement about Mrs. Roosevelt was issued only after the most careful consideration and it may be taken as the opening effort to combat the anti-Catholic forces.[99] There is said to be danger of a recrudescence in the near future of Klu Klux Klanism in the South. Almost in proportion as Catholic influence and strength have increased, there has increased either actual or potential hostility. According to Herzog, Justice Douglas "whom Israel has been feting" was characterized by Monsignor McMahon as one of the Church's main dangers because of the attitude and influence he showed in the Supreme Court. Felix Frankfurter is also regarded as hostile.[100]

My talk with Monsignor McMahon lasted from about 11:30 until lunch about one, when we joined the family. At first, we chatted about his impressions in the nearby Arab states which he had visited, the role of the several relief organizations working under Griffis, the latter's leadership, soon to be relinquished which, though it had not been perfect, had been much better than that of Dodge would have been. The latter, according to McMahon, though physically energetic, seems incapable of making up his mind. As to the International Committee [of the Red Cross], McMahon had much the same view as mine.

Monsignor McMahon talked at some length about his refugee work, their effective utilization of the religious personnel, thus reducing overhead to a minimum, their desired concentration on education and social work rather than on feeding, but that the inadequacy of the UN feeding made them participate in it; they operate, however, only in the villages and towns and never in the camps. He denied most vigorously that there was any attempt to use relief or other services as leverage for conversion or transfer of loyalty from Orthodox to Roman. He said that the Church still refused to give any support to favoritism on behalf of Christian refugees as over against the Moslems.[101] He admit-

99. Eleanor Roosevelt engaged in a public debate with Spellman over federal funding for religious schools. Responding to her June 23, 1949, "My Day" column, which warned of "religious control of our schools," Spellman, in an open letter of July 21 stated that "whatever you may say in the future, your record of anti-Catholicism stands for all to see;" that her record was "unworthy of an American mother;" and that "I shall not again publicly acknowledge you." The controversy contained further exchanges and was major news. See James Hennesy, *American Catholics: A History of the Roman Catholic Community in the United States* (New York: Oxford University Press, 1981), 297–299.

100. See for example Wallfisch, "Justice William O. Douglas and Religious Liberty."

101. The Vatican provided extensive funds for Arab refugee relief after the 1948 war, the money flowing through Archbishop Gustavo Testa, the apostolic delegate to Palestine and Jordan, as well as the nuncio to Syria and the internuncio to Egypt. Money also went through other Catholic organizations, including the Catholic Near East Welfare Association, of which McMahon was the national secretary. The money helped fund schools in Amman and elsewhere.

ted, however, that in fact the Israeli authorities might be favoring the Christians.

Again as in previous talks, Monsignor McMahon emphasized that the real issue in Israel was not the spoliation or desecration of one or more churches or other religious property but rather the right of the refugees to return and the establishment of an international regime in Jerusalem. As to the form of this latter regime, Monsignor McMahon was not very definite. He knew of the PCC working paper and of the State Department's acceptance in principle.[102] He argued that there was much exaggeration in the Israeli estimates of the cost of Jerusalem's administration. For example, police could not cost anything like 30 million dollars, because the whole of Palestine under the Mandate was only ten million dollars for police. Useful information could be secured by checking on the mandatory administration record.

McMahon recognized the complication of the Russian interest in Jerusalem. He admitted, too, the efforts of the Russians to capitalize on the Orthodox and other possible fears of the Latins. Nevertheless, he was of the opinion that the Russians could be kept out if internationalization were put on the basis of the status quo. By implication at least, McMahon admitted that there was another and possibly serious danger if, as might happen, the Greeks came under Russian influence or control. The Greek patriarch had historically the best title to preeminence. At present there is an interregnum in the Latin Patriarchate.[103] Another weakness in the Latin position was the recent death of the nuncio to Cairo.[104]

McMahon gave me a long letter from the cardinal [Francis Spellman], which he had been carrying for some time. He suggested, too, that probably the cardinal would expect to see me.[105] Incidentally, McMahon left the impression that one effect of the Jewish state which causes concern is that Jewish control will make it more difficult for Christian Jews to remain practicing Christians and would tend to discourage additional conversions.

Mrs. [Sima Rubin Arlosoroff], a friend of Max Wolf, and wife of [Chaim] Arlosoroff, political head [sic] of the Jewish Agency who was assassinated by

Frank L. Hutchison, *Refugees from Palestine: The Church's Continued Concern* (New York: National Council of Churches, 1963).

102. Entries of April 15 and May 17, 1949.

103. The Greek Orthodox Church was the oldest Christian institution in Jerusalem, but faced financial difficulties stemming from Israeli assumption of control of its property as "abandoned" during and after the war. Catholic institutions stepped into the void with regard to charity and the education of Christian children. The Greek Church opposed the internationalization of Jerusalem because of fear of Catholic domination there. Bialer, *Cross on the Star of David*, 178ff.

104. Archbishop Arthur Hughes (1902–1949), internuncio in Egypt from August 23, 1947 to his death on July 12, 1949.

105. Not found. Possibly a response to McDonald's letter of May 11, 1949, which enlisted Spellman's help in securing an audience for General Riley with Pope Pius XII. McDonald to Spellman, May 11, 1949, McDonald Papers, Columbia University, box 4, folder 13. See also entry of September 23, 1949.

terrorists in '33.[106] Her later husband and she had been members of the [Judah] Magnes group favoring reconciliation with the Arabs. She is now a feature writer on the *Palestine Post*. She came to talk to me about her fears lest non-reconciliation between Jews and Arabs would lead to ultimate disaster for the Jewish state. She thought the test would be the treatment within Israel of the existing or future Arab minorities. Since she was obviously an intelligent and sincere person, I discussed some of the problems with her frankly, but warned her that what I said must not be used in any way publicly, or if it were, I would have to disavow it completely. She promised solemnly that she would not use it in any public way.

Ford and I were at Sharett's office promptly at 6:30. He received us immediately. We first spoke for a few minutes about the success of his party the day before for Douglas and of Donald. The purpose of his call was to explain to us formally what was being explained with equal formality by Elath to Rusk this same day.[107] It was that Israel, without changing its fundamental stand that it is not responsible for the refugee problem and that this should be settled as part of an overall peace arrangement, was offering to take a total of 100,000 Arab refugees on condition that the Arab states were willing to enter into peace negotiations and would accept the Israeli contribution of 100,000 as part of a general refugee settlement. The procedure at Lausanne was to be gradual, and the Israeli offer would be made formally only if the Arabs agree to discuss peace. If they did, Israel would agree that refugees be considered first. Moreover, Israel's offer was to be made with the understanding that the refugee problem would be attacked together with that of peace.

In his preliminary statement, Sharett referred to Eban's words on refugees on page 41 of the latter's address before the Ad Hoc Committee of the UN last spring.[108] Sharett continued that his government had been impressed by one argument that the refusal of both sides to define what either would do created an impasse, because without an initial offer there could be no scheme, and without a scheme there could be no financing and no proposal to Congress for long-range or even for interim financing. Israel felt obligated to try to dislodge PCC from [the] present "dead point." Another factor was Israel's desire to meet the wishes of the United States. Sharett stressed that there were no reservations

---

106. Sima Rubin Arlosoroff (1901–1986), Estonian-born wife of Chaim Arlosoroff (1899–1933), a founder of Mapai who was political director of Jewish Agency, 1931–1933, was optimistic about Jewish-Arab cooperation, and who negotiated the 1933 Ha'avara Agreement with Nazi Germany concerning the rescue of some Jewish assets through German exports to Palestine. Arlosoroff was assassinated in Tel Aviv on June 16, 1933. The culprits were never determined despite later Israeli state inquiries.

107. Memorandum of conversation by Rusk, July 28, 1949, *FRUS*, 1949, v. VI, 1261–1264.

108. Eban addressed the Ad Hoc Political Committee of the General Assembly on May 5, 1949, in connection with Israel's application for UN membership. In the address, he discussed the refugee issues about which the PCC had expressed dissatisfaction. For Eban's excerpted statement see Lapidoth and Hirsch, eds., *The Jerusalem Question and its Resolution: Selected Documents*, 100–102.

as to territory connected with the offer. On the other hand, it did involve very serious risks for Israel even within a formal peace framework; so much so that outside of such framework, the offer was unthinkable. The maximum of 100,000 was not subject to bargaining. Moreover, it would include approximately 1/3 of that number already returned.

In general explanation he reiterated: 1) that the offer does not admit any responsibility of creation of problem; 2) [it] is not to be interpreted as lack of interest in solution; instead that interest compels Israeli action within Israel's capacity, of which it is the final judge. As a footnote, Sharett referred to Egypt's non-answer of US proffer of mediation on the Gaza Strip. He cited as also discouraging the failure of the Arab states to reply favorably to his July 1 offer on broken families.[109] Finally, he returned to the very real danger which the government was running in making this offer, a danger at once political in [the] Knesset and militarily should there be a resumption of hostilities.

Thursday, July 28

Mr. Ford brought in two drafts of a telegram on last night's meeting with Sharett. I approved it unchanged.[110]

In the afternoon at tea time I had a pleasant visit with an elderly Rabbi Silberfeld, of Newark. He is a warm admirer of Silver and Neumann and he was kind enough to add, of myself. He thinks that peace has been made in the ZOA.[111]

Later, three of the friends of Joe Chamberlain[112] and Mrs. Borg[113] came. They were Herschel Alt,[114] Dr. [Peter] Neubauer[115] and Miss Aline Cohn,[116] who are here as a group on behalf of [a] Hadassah study of child welfare. The most interesting point in our conversation from my view was Alt's statement, supported more or less by the other two, to the effect that the fear of charge of

---

109. See entry of June 8, 1949.

110. McDonald to secretary of state, no. 571, July 28, 1949, *FRUS*, 1949, v. VI, 1265.

111. Rabbi Julius Silberfeld (1877–1958), rabbi at Temple B'nai Abraham in Newark, then the largest Conservative congregation in New Jersey, 1902–1939.

112. Joseph Perkins Chamberlain (1873–1951), professor of public law, Columbia University, 1923–1950; US representative to League of Nations High Commission on Refugees, 1933–1934; chairman, National Coordinating Committee of JDC, 1934–1938; chairman, National Refugee Service, 1939–1946; member, President's Advisory Committee on Political Refugees, 1938–1945; chairman, American Council of Voluntary Agencies for Foreign Service (a relief group of twenty-two agencies that sent food to Europe and was the precursor to CARE) after World War II.

113. Madeleine [Mrs. Sidney] Borg (1878–1956); Columbia University expert on juvenile delinquency and child psychology; founded Jewish Big Sister movement, 1914; became president of New York Federation of Jewish Philanthropies, 1939; head of the Women's Division and vice president of the Federation for the Support of Jewish Philanthropic Societies of New York.

114. Herschel Alt (1897–1981), Ukrainian-born social and child welfare expert; named to Jewish Board of Guardians in 1940s; advised Israeli government on child welfare.

115. Peter Neubauer (1913–2008), Austrian-born child psychiatrist; escaped to Switzerland after Anschluss in 1938; led the New York University Child Development Center and the Jewish Board of Family Services in New York City.

116. Aline Cohn (1917–1968), US social worker; assistant executive director of American Council of Voluntary Agencies for Foreign Service (chairman was Joseph P. Chamberlain); specialty was stateless DPs.

dual allegiance was growing in certain Jewish circles at home following the creation of the Jewish state.

Friday, July 29

Usual breakfast conference with Ford.

Saturday, July 30

Chester Williams of the Town Hall group came for breakfast. It was clear from what he said that the Department is much interested in the Town Hall tour.[117] Reception in the evening for some twenty [members] of the Round the World Town Meeting and Town World Seminar [which included leaders from the American Civil Liberties Union, the League of Women Voters, the American Legion, the American Association of University Women, the American Farm Bureau, and Walter White and Chester Williams of the NAACP] and twelve or fifteen members of the local committee and their wives. It was a pleasant informal occasion. Some of the visitors expressed personal pleasure and surprise that at an American Embassy reception no liquor was served.

Sunday, July 31

Nine-thirty session with Eytan of the Foreign Office. I delivered the Department's message about its anxiety for progress at Lausanne, and its survey of its attitude during the past two years, and its reasons for not favoring bilateral negotiations at this time because they might undercut the PCC.[118] We then went on to discuss other matters, with Eytan doing most of the talking. He thought the optimistic reports from Lausanne were hardly justified. Certainly the agreement of both sides on a vague formula meant little. Moreover, there were no indications as yet that Porter was going to press for a more affirmative program than has Ethridge.

McDonald reported that Eytan was skeptical about Arab counterproposals to Israel's family reunification offer. Eytan said that the words "based on [the] oriental concept of family units" weakened the chance of agreement.[119]

I was at Habimah at three for the rehearsal and recording of a 13-minute [Town Hall] NBC program with [Brooks] Emeny[120] as moderator and

---

117. "Town Hall" was a radio program that ran on the National Broadcasting Corporation station after 1935 and promoted divergent political views through on-air "Town Meetings." The Town Hall Seminar group was on a world tour in 1949, and McDonald and Tetlie facilitated their travel to Tel Aviv. Chester Williams represented the NAACP with the Town Hall group.

118. Acheson to McDonald, no. 476, July 26, 1949, *FRUS*, 1949, v. VI, 1256–1257. Repeated to US missions in Arab capitals.

119. McDonald to secretary of state, no. 577, August 1, 1949, NARA, RG 59, 501.BB Palestine, box 2126, folder 2.

120. Brooks Emeny (1901–1980), scholar and president of the Foreign Policy Association, 1947–1957.

[Robert W.] Hansen[121] and [George H.] Wilson[122] the other two participants. It was not too bad, but on the whole I was inclined to agree with Wilson that it was rather wishy-washy because of its lack of critical material. This, however, was a difficulty which probably could not be overcome without creating other and greater difficulties. I was glad to have a chance to persuade Brooks Emeny to eliminate from his preliminary remarks reference to the Arabs, which would have been invidious.

The recording of the Town Hall Program was workmanlike and very satisfactory. One might have thought he was in the town hall itself, what with George's elaborate traditional introduction and all the mechanical paraphernalia of NBC. The main talks were to the point and sufficiently controversial to give interest. [Kenneth] Bilby [*New York Herald Tribune*] opened with a moderate plea for restriction of immigration in the interests of the immigrants themselves and of Israel. [David] Horowitz countered by arguing that the history of restrictions on Jewish immigration, plus the basic purpose of the state of Israel, made any restriction on the ingathering of the exiles impossible. Moreover, he contended that free immigration is self-regulating. Dr. [Carl Hermann] Voss followed with an even milder plea for restrictions than that of Bilby, and combined it with a plea for support to enable Israel to take more refugees. [Israel] Rokach supported Horowitz with blunt variations on the former's themes. The questions from the platform and from the audience were sufficiently varied and direct to give a spark to the discussion. Towards the very end George asked me if I had anything to say. I replied that I was glad to welcome the meeting to Tel Aviv and that I wished on my own behalf and that of my government to express thanks to Israel and especially the mayor for their generous and cordial hospitality. When the recording was completed George made a four-minute statement of the Town [Hall] meeting policy, which I thought with one exception was excellent. This was his rather gratuitous statement that communists, because they did not really believe in the discussion method, were not included in its programs. Several other persons told me that they had a similar reaction to mine.

In the evening to the local amphitheater to hear Handel's *Judas Maccabeus*. Despite some obvious inadequacies, I enjoyed the performance. During the intermission I chatted with Miss Gertrude Samuels of the Sunday *New York Times*[123] and, in answer to her question, explained why I thought it would be unwise and [a] hazard for her to try to carry out Markel's[124] assignment to do a piece on the Arab refugees in the Arab countries.

121. Robert W. Hansen (1911–1997), member of Fraternal Order of Eagles and later a justice on the Wisconsin Supreme Court.

122. George H. Wilson (1905–1985), director of American Farm Bureau Federation and later an Oklahoma congressman and judge.

123. Gertrude Samuels (1910–2003), English-born photojournalist for *New York Times* and other publications; toured displaced persons camps; wrote *B-G: The Fighter of Goliaths. The Story of David Ben-Gurion* (New York: Crowell, 1961) and *The Secret of Gonen: Portrait of a Kibbutz on the Border in a Time of War* (New York: Avon, 1969).

124. Lester Markel (1894–1977), editor of *New York Times* Sunday edition, 1923–1964.

14. August 1949

Monday, August 1

From four until nearly six, I continued my conference with Thomas Hickok, [Foreign Service] Inspector from the Department.[1] Although he said very little, I deduced the following tentative conclusions about him:

1) He should be helpful in speeding up the reorganization and strengthening of the Jerusalem and Haifa consulates. If he and Ford and Barnes can agree on what is needed at Haifa, his recommendation and ours should carry weight. The same I think should apply to recommendations about personnel here.

2) He is a hardheaded individual who manifested no sympathy or understanding of, but rather an underlying critical attitude towards, Israel. I could not make out whether this was the result of his residence in the Middle East before '36 or was an outgrowth of his months of work since last February in the Arab countries.[2] Probably both factors have their influence. He was willing to criticize departmental personnel methods and also its informational relationships with missions in the field. In particular, he was sympathetic towards criticism, which he said he understood I had first made and which was supported by some of the neighboring missions, of the lack of adequate information from the Department on its formulation of policies in advance of their pronouncement or even subsequent to their being made known to foreign powers. I was glad that I had asked him to come down and regretted that the time was so short. I think, however, that Ford and Barnes will be able to work with him advantageously.

Rabbi [Ben Zion] Bokser[3] and three of his colleagues representing the Conservative Rabbinical Association at home spent an hour at the house. After we had exchanged views about religious trends in Israel, the special attention to the present, and prospective attitudes of the sabra, they asked my advice as to whether they should begin "missionary activities among the Jews." They meant

---

1. Thomas A. Hickok inspected numerous missions in the Middle East, Far East, and Southeast Europe in 1949.
2. Hickok had been the vice consul in Jerusalem in the early 1930s and studied, among other things, the development of the port at Haifa.
3. Rabbi Ben Zion Bokser (1907–1984), Polish-born leading Conservative rabbi and social activist in the United States; author of several books on subjects ranging from the Talmud to Maimonides to Israel.

the possibility of setting up one or more typical Conservative synagogues with related social and other seven-day-a-week programs as foci from which to propagandize on behalf of the Conservative conception of Judaism. In reply, I pointed out that obviously I could not advise, but that personally I thought that if they wanted to begin somewhere, they might advantageously begin with a community center and its social activities, leaving the synagogue proper for later.

After dinner to the opening performance of *Born Yesterday*, with Shoshana's husband in the leading role.

Tuesday, August 2

A young Mr. Cox of Miami came to see me about his business project and his city's desire to have an Israeli consulate. He told me too that he had talked with someone in the Near East Division of the Department, and that it was interested in his group's plans for Arab refugees. He spoke about transfer of populations in this area to the Tigris-Euphrates and back again. When I asked him how his group expected to figure, he said that they had an aluminum house to sell. As the young man was leaving, he said that his Miami group had placed in escrow $50,000,000 which was to be used to build a model resort town at [the] former Caesarea, north of Hadera, on the coast. Work was delayed only by some pending questions with the government; in particular, they were not sure that the government would give them a free hand on building styles, etc.[4]

Julius Hochman,[5] international vice president of [the] International [Ladies'] Garment Workers' Union and a close associate of Dubinsky, for thirty or forty minutes gave me his impressions of the labor movement in Israel. I was particularly intrigued by his views that the rank and file of Mapam were more leftward than the leaders. He thinks that there is very little that can be done by American organized labor to correct the Mapam romantic view about Russia and [its] "vicious" view towards the US. This pro-Russian attitude is not the logical one; it is an expression of deep emotions, which are not subject to reason.

As to a program here, Hochman seemed defeatist. Perhaps this impression was because I raised this point shortly before Hochman had to leave. As to Dubinsky, Hochman thought that he should come after perhaps a year. Meanwhile, the labor group would be happy to "carry out my program." I can't take this too seriously because Hochman is here unofficially. It is evident, however, that I must follow through on this with Dubinsky and others at home. Though

4. Ebert D. Cox, (1892–1984), entrepreneur representing AMKO Buildings; tried to interest the Israeli government in a trailer-house made of masonite and plywood that could accommodate a family of four.
5. Julius Hochman (1892–1970), Bessarabian-born labor organizer in the garment industry; vice president of the ILGWU and close associate of David Dubinsky; responsible for the "Union Label" campaign, 1958; one of the founders of the Liberal Party and the American Labor Party, as well as vice president of World ORT.

Hochman seemingly has had little time to read while he has been here, he gave me the impression of having gotten a rather intimate feel of the psychology of the people. As to the future of Mapam, he is convinced that the party will split. Those inherently communistic will, when the issue is made clear, perhaps when it is forced by Ben-Gurion, go over to the Communist Party. Hochman is sure, however, that they will never be able to make a dangerously popular appeal.

During the next hour or more of tea, we had a varied and interesting discussion with the following group: Dr. [Bernard] Weinryb of Brooklyn College;[6] Professor Max Laserson[7] of Columbia University and [James T.] Shotwell's[8] department of the Carnegie Endowment, he bringing a letter from the latter; and Mr. Borowski, who is the director of an organization of the advancement of Hebrew study [and] publishes a weekly Hebrew journal.[9] The talk was mostly about lines of cleavage, religious and other, in Israel. Professor Laserson, who is to do some work for Shotwell on the significance of the truce and other negotiations, their successes and failures here, asked me if I thought this worthwhile. I replied in the affirmative.

Wednesday, August 3

After the usual breakfast conference with Ford, he dropped me off at Ben-Gurion's office. I was a little early but was received at once. After some personal chat about Donald [McDonald's new grandson] and Bobby, (the prime minister was much interested in Bobby's decision to stay and in her study of Hebrew), I told him that I had nothing to say to him, but that since I might see the president when I return home, I wondered if he had a message to give me.

In substance his message was as follows:

1) "Please express to the president our deep appreciation of all that the US and he did for us before and after the establishment of Israel. We shall never forget this assistance. Never."

2) "Please emphasize to him that Israel needs and wants peace, first with its Arab neighbors and throughout the whole Middle East and throughout the

---

6. Bernard D. Weinryb (1900–1982), Polish-born economic and social historian; librarian at the Breslau Jewish Seminary, 1931–1933; emigrated to Palestine, 1934, and then to the United States, 1939; taught at Brooklyn College, 1948–1951, and subsequently at Columbia University, 1950–1956; economist at the State Department, 1951–1955; author of *The Yishuv in Palestine* (1947) and *The Jews of Poland: A Social and Economic History of the Jews of Poland from 1100–1800* (1973).

7. Max Matatiahu Laserson (1887–1951), Latvian-born academic; lectured in politics at Columbia University, specializing in Soviet legal philosophy and the Jews in the USSR, 1946–1951.

8. James T. Shotwell (1874–1965), Canadian-born history professor; taught at Columbia University; promoted human rights in international arena, advocated US membership in League of Nations, International Labor Organization, and the UN; president of Carnegie Endowment for International Peace, 1949–1950.

9. Samuel J. Borowski (1895–1966), Russian-born communal educator in the United States; Hebraist; Zionist leader; executive at the National Council for Jewish Education; president of Young Judea.

world. The US can do much to help in the attainment of this goal of peace. I earnestly hope that the Great Powers will succeed in avoiding war among themselves. Israel dares not take sides, for it would be crushed."

3) "It is vital that the living standards of the mass of the people in the neighboring Arab countries be raised. Only through giving them a stake in their countries' welfare can communism be forestalled. It will not be enough to pour money into the Arab states. What is done for them must be so designed that it will benefit the masses and not profit merely the effendi and the pashas. For example, the British during the 19th century did wonders in Egypt in flood control, irrigation, etc. But all these achievements profited not at all the masses of the people, who continued sunk in ignorance and enfeebled by disease [with] the average life expectancy [at] some 20 years."[10]

When Ben-Gurion had finished his message, I spoke to him about Lewis S. Rosenstiel and [Jack] Laban, their industrial empire, the potential advantage of their visit here, as contrasted with the visits of many smaller financial figures.[11] Ben-Gurion said he had had my note but did not see on what basis the invitation could be issued. It was left that I would, if the occasion were opportune, speak to them in the States, and then if I suggested it, the invitation would be forthcoming.

Then I explained to Ben-Gurion that the chief reason, aside from Donald, for wanting to go home now and for having suggested it to the Department and having used my White House influence to get permission, was that I wanted to find out directly and indirectly from the president whether he regarded my presence here during the next year or so as really important, for I added, if I were to be merely a messenger boy, that could be performed just as well by any one of several career men.

Seemingly a little startled by this frankness, Ben-Gurion said, "Why should you want to go home? Are you homesick?" To this I said no. "Aren't you happy?" I said yes, but that the measure of one's satisfaction naturally depends on the extent of his usefulness.[12] Ben-Gurion left no room for doubt that he

10. In his diary Ben-Gurion recorded these comments at greater length. Regarding the building of Israel, he noted, "We wish to make this country bloom, and make it a shelter for all Jews who cannot remain where they are, and I believe America can assist us in both matters. We do not ask for charity, but rather, America's capacity for action, its methods of procuring equipment, American work processes, and financial assistance that will be repaid in full." Regarding peace with the Arab states he added, "America can also be of assistance in matters of peace, surely in Lausanne, but perhaps more so by allowing us to operate directly vis-à-vis the Arab states, with each and every Arab state. If Lausanne remains the only channel—chances are slim, because when all Arab states are involved in talks, the state least interested in peace and most hostile will determine the position of all the rest. But if we speak with each individually, we might find an open ear in one country, and the country that makes peace with us will be a catalyst for others." Ben-Gurion Diary, entry of August 3, 1949. We are grateful to Tuvia Friling for this reference.

11. Lewis S. Rosenstiel (1892–1976), owner of Schenley Industries, a whiskey distilling conglomerate; friend to J. Edgar Hoover and gangster Meyer Lansky; became noted philanthropist. See entry of August 31, 1949.

12. In his diary Ben-Gurion recorded these comments, paraphrased as follows: [McDonald] said he was mainly going to assess his own standing with the president, on which his personal

thought I ought to stay on. As I was leaving and he showing me out of the room, the omnipresent and indefatigable [Paul] Goldman snapped us twice.[13] I was then sent home in the prime minister's magnificent Cadillac.

Spoke to Martha Sharp[14] on the telephone and explained that I was very busy and that besides, there was no reason for her to see me personally because it was quite impossible that I should do anything at all about getting her friend Mrs. Cohen across the [demarcation] line [in Jerusalem] for a study of Arab refugees. Indeed, I doubted whether she would be able to manage it for herself, but that in any case, I could not move in the matter, that it was for the Jerusalem consulate. I added that if she would write me a letter, I would pass it on to Burdett with the recommendation that he do his utmost.

At teatime three of the Quaker group, Don Peretz,[15] Ray Hartsough, and the representative from Philadelphia, Colin W. Bell,[16] stayed an hour and a half. It was a very pleasant session. After discussion of the authorship of the Epistle to the Hebrews and of the origin of the Quaker aversion to taking oaths (this goes back beyond the Epistle of James to the words of Jesus recorded by Matthew), they then told me of their determination not to continue in the feeding business and of their anxiety to get on to constructive rehabilitation if at all possible on a joint Arab-Jewish basis. They confirmed the figures for the south [Gaza Strip] as 235,000 plus another large number of the native Arabs, bringing the total to approximately 285,000. Our discussion went beyond refugees to the general question of government policy. I was surprised and encouraged to see that the experience of the younger men here had made them realize the futility of attempting to turn the hands of the clock back.

plans depend. He does not see the use of being here as a mere "letter carrier." If the president would like to assign him a certain mission, and he gains a certain standing with the president—then he is willing to stay at least another year, until peace is declared. . . . He knows Clifford, secretary to the president [*sic*], who is fulfilling the same role as [Samuel Rosenman] had for Roosevelt, quite well. But he [Clifford] is closer to the president than [Rosenman] was to Roosevelt, and far more than David Niles. He will find out from him if there is purpose to his continued stay, and if he has some assignment from the president. He may also see the president himself, though I am not sure of it. Ben-Gurion Diary, entry of August 3, 1949. We are grateful to Tuvia Friling for this reference.

13. Paul Goldman (1900–1986), Budapest-born journalist who documented Israel's early years.

14. Martha Sharp (1905–1999), American philanthropist married to Unitarian minister Waitstill Hastings Sharp. The couple went to Czechoslovakia after the Munich agreement in 1938 and helped those wanting to emigrate, working closely with the American Friends Service Committee; relocated operations to Lisbon in 1940, where they aided Jews in escaping from Vichy France; in 1943 began work to help orphaned Jewish children emigrate to Palestine through Hadassah's Youth Aliyah.

15. Don Peretz (1922–), professor of political science at SUNY Binghamton; wrote numerous books and articles sympathetic to Palestinians and highly critical of Israel; represented the AFSC at the UN; served as the AFSC representative to United Nations Relief for Palestinian Refugees in Western Galilee, 1949.

16. Colin W. Bell (1903–1988), British business executive who joined the AFSC in China, 1943; directed AFCS efforts in Gaza Strip under UN supervision.

A pleasant visit with my young friend Morris Goodman of Miami.[17] His impressions after four weeks or so here were interesting and at times amusing. He regards the sabras as immature and, despite their informality, he finds them rather rigid as to dress. He was unfavorably impressed by the "overemphasis on [Mapam] party's [education] this extending even to the very young." He disliked, too, the "*Al-HaMishmar* attitude." I asked him how there could be any other attitude in the light of the continued danger from the Arabs. Somewhat reluctantly he admitted that only this spirit could have won the war against the Arabs.[18]

Thursday, August 4

I was very much interested in the British proposal reported in a despatch of July 22 about the Haifa refinery and pipeline. Feeling was that a direct approach to Israel offered little hope. As alternative, considered worth study the following: Now that [the] armistice with Syria [has been] concluded, "time is approaching when it may be propitious lift the arms embargo." [British] Foreign Office thought French might so recommend. Simultaneously therewith or when action had been taken to lift embargo "Britain would let Egyptians know that permission to [Israeli] tankers [to] pass through Suez would facilitate arms. . . . Iraqi[s] might then agree [to] reopen line since [this] could point to Egypt's action as deciding factor, thereby saving own face." Foregoing represents thinking rather than [a] decision, and noted that French could not be satisfied because they [are] interested in crude [oil] rather than refined.[19]

Amused and satisfied by [the] Department's circular of July 22nd, promising fuller information to Middle East, obviously the result of complaints by Stabler, Keeley, myself, and others.[20] Also amusing, but in a grimmer vein, was reference in one of Crocker's[21] telegrams from Baghdad outlining the grave financial crisis in Iraq, containing the following: understand finance ministry is urging the granting of permission to Jewish businessmen to begin operations again because the elimination of Jewish activities is considered one of the causes of Iraq's financial crises.[22]

At the office for part of the morning. Conference with Hillel Kook [Peter Bergson]. I promised to urge reconsideration by the Department of its attitude

---

17. Morris Goodman, Miami businessman active in United Jewish Appeal drive for 1950; chair of Greater Miami Committee for Bonds of Israel, 1951–1952.
18. Refers to Mapam newspaper's advocacy of Israeli-Arab coexistence, its opposition to the destruction of Arab villages and expulsions, and its opposition to Israeli settlements on former Arab lands.
19. Entries of August 1, 1948, and March 3, 1949.
20. The State Department began to send general updates on the talks in Lausanne when there seemed to be meaningful developments, but it did not share discussions between Washington and the US delegation in Lausanne.
21. Edward S. Crocker (1895–1968), US ambassador to Baghdad, 1949–1952.
22. See entry of January 14, 1949.

on visas for former members or sympathizers of the Irgun.[23] I could not, however, at face value [agree with] Kook's estimate of the potential value of [Herut] as the one out-and-out pro-American party. It was intriguing nonetheless to hear him expound the thesis that, from Israel's national self-interest, it is important that there be such a pro-American party. It was interesting, too, to listen to Kook's interpretation of [David] Courtney's activities as a devious but carefully planned British effort to oust the United States or, at any rate, to keep the rising power of the United States in some sort of check.

Staff meeting, notable chiefly because of the disclosure of the sharp cleavage between the servicemen's [attachés'] attitude towards Israel and my own. Archibald, showing none of his usual signs of geniality, declared that he would recommend no concessions whatever to Israel's request for training facilities for their men in American military schools until there was some reciprocity on the part of Israel. He complained bitterly about the reticence and non-cooperation of the Israeli military, and in this he was joined by Andrus and Frothingham. The tales they told of non-cooperation seemed real enough, but to my mind, they all were allowing something akin to personal pique resulting from this Israeli attitude to cause them as military attachés to forget the higher interests of the US. Surely policy motivated by pique, no matter how justifiable the pique, is the height of un-wisdom. During and after the conference how I longed for van der Velde.

Most of the rest of the conference was given over to housing, with special concentration on what should be said to [Frederick] Larkin.[24] It was agreed that I should set forth as forcibly as possible our present difficulties office-and housing-wise and the certainty that these will be much more insurmountable at the end of a year and a half or so, when the existing leases on the houses expire and cannot be renewed. There was not consensus of opinion, however, as to whether the major recommendation should be for building or buying.

Ford's farewell dinner was a distinct success despite the non-appearance of Goldie Meyerson. The failure to show was not explained during the evening. Those present, besides the Fords and the McDonalds, were only the Ben-Gurions and the Sharetts. The house was resplendent with light, silver, and other objects of art. The Israeli guests were overwhelmed by the view, the likes of which Ben-Gurion said he did not know there was in Tel Aviv, nor had he imagined there was such a house.

During the dinner, since I was placed between Paula and Goldie's vacant chair, I had a full portion of talk with Paula. After dinner, conversation was particularly interesting for me, because Ben-Gurion and Sharett went off into a long discussion of languages, particularly the relations between Arabic and

23. Menachem Begin visited the United States in December 1948 [see entry of October 29, 1948] because Truman ordered that there be an exception made to US visa laws. The Immigration and Naturalization Service continued to refuse visas for former Irgun members until 1951.
24. Frederick Larkin (1918–1992), chief, Division of Foreign Buildings Operations, Department of State.

Hebrew. They both deplored the loss, through Western influence, of some of the finer nuances of pronunciation in Hebrew, which formerly had been, for comparable words identical or almost so, with Arabic. This latter, uncontaminated by the West, has remained pure. The most traditional Hebrew, they agreed, was that pronounced by the Yemenites.

The two men disagreed about Jesus's probable common language. Ben-Gurion insisted it was Hebrew, and Sharett said it was Aramaic. Ben-Gurion argued that if you read the New Testament in the original Greek, you must be convinced that the words attributed to Jesus could only have been spoken in Hebrew, so characteristically Hebrew is the sentence structure. To this, Sharett countered that this might be true but that it came about not because Jesus spoke Aramaic, but because his Aramaic vernacular was written down in classic Hebrew.

At one point I told of the visit of four American Conservative Jewish rabbis who wanted my advice on this question: "Should we undertake missionary activity in Israel?" Sharett laughed and said there is no use asking Ben-Gurion about it because he has not been in a synagogue in forty-five years and knows nothing about distinctions and conflicts between various kinds of Judaism and rabbinism. Yet Ben-Gurion did express himself to the effect that, contrary to my and Sharett's opinion, Chief Rabbi [Yitzhak] Herzog could be blocked, if he attempted to keep the American rabbis from performing marriages, [by] an appeal to the Mandatory law which permitted dissident Jewish groups to set up their own congregation. I laughingly retorted that the prime minister would hardly dare publicly use the British Mandatory law as a basis for an argument against the chief rabbi. Seriously, both men were inclined to agree that my advice was sound, that the American rabbis, if they wished to begin operations here, should do so from the social or community center starting point.

For the first time in several parties, Paula was not yawning and urging her husband to leave early. After they had gone, Lolita jokingly indicated that she thought she and Paula were getting together by saying that opposites tend to meet. Nonetheless, she was quite critical of Goldie for not having come or sent word, and for Miss Herlitz's similar action a few weeks earlier, and was not inclined to accept our excuses for the ladies.

Friday, August 5

Two guests for breakfast. My friend Sam S. Mintz and the redoubtable Sam Klaus. The former was obviously deeply touched by being able to visit someone he had worked with and who had now become first American ambassador to Israel. He was very full of his conviction that this was a view shared by millions of Jews. Later, he asked me a lot of questions, some of which I could not answer, and forced me to beg off about an engagement in Pittsburgh.

Sam Klaus, as usual, was full of information, conviction, and plans. His new information was about the labor attaché and of the way in which [Joseph] Potofsky's "blunders," by assuming the right to offer the job to [Milton] Fried in Prague, had aroused the opposition of [David] Dubinsky.[25] Klaus is contemptuous of Potofsky. Klaus thinks, however, that Fried will still be named.

About the Department, Klaus thinks well of [Raymond] Hare and [Stuart] Rockwell; [George] McGhee, he thinks, is ambitious and inclined to talk and plan only in large figures, but without any prejudice against Israel. According to Klaus, the villain in the piece is [Dean] Rusk, while Acheson is rather indifferent. He thinks that the old crowd is in complete command.

He explained briefly his work in Turkey and his plans here, and went off a little after ten to see Miss Herlitz. I will learn more from him later. One additional point, however; he returned several times to his earlier thesis that the basis of closer relations in the long run between Israel and the US should be found in an exchange of technicians, most of whom could be supplied by the US in such fields as housing, sanitation, police, and military. He was still almost furious with Sharett's rejection of some of the earlier proffers from the US. When first suggested, the military had been enthusiastic, at least so far as their attitude was represented by the Department. He thought that I ought to work hard to get these plans into operation.[26]

I should note here some of the points made by [William] Burdett in his telegram of July 27th to the Department. [Burdett urges] that it is impossible to have the PCC plan realistically [provide for] for "'effective UN control'" [of Jerusalem] without inclusion of points [in] Article VIII [of Israeli-Jordanian armistice treaty], [namely] demarcation zones, access to Holy Places, [access to the] Jewish cemetery on [Mount of] Olives, and Jews in [the] Old City. Unless these points [are] settled, no proposal of PCC [will be] acceptable. Moreover "demarcation lines will play [the] major part in determining stability [of the] UN regime and certain Christian nations have great interest in exclusion [of] their institutions from Jew zone." He then urges PCC action parallel with bilateral negotiations, with a view to pooling results for [the] UN.[27]

Also noteworthy was the summary in the Department's Council on Foreign Relations July 20th summary of UK's Foreign Office suggestions to PCC. These include

1) acceptance [by] both sides [of] refugees for resettlement and repatriation;
2) acceptance [of] Israel Gaza proposal, provided [it contains] safeguards for refugees and for territorial compensation,
3) if southern Negev [goes] to Jordan or Egypt as territorial compensation, Israel should have freedom [of] access to [the] Red Sea and Arab States freedom [of] communication through Gaza and Haifa;
4) free port [in] Haifa so that oil [is] freely exported in return [for] Iraq provision [of] normal supply [to the Haifa] refinery;

25. Entries of May 3 and May 9, 1949.
26. Entry of April 4, 1949.
27. Burdett to secretary of state, no. 495, July 27, 1949, *FRUS*, v. VI, 1259–1260. McDonald quoted directly from Burdett's despatch, and the editors have corrected his slight mistakes.

5) agreement [that] Israel and Arab states share Jordan and Yarmuk waters. US comment: agree [with] free zone [for] facilities [at] Haifa, but doubt possibility [of] free port outside Israeli control. Have urged both sides [to] utilize PCC [to the] fullest. Urge freedom of negotiation particularly regarding Jerusalem, territorial settlements, and refugees. Turkey has agreed [to] support this approach, and it is hoped France will do likewise.

Report that Syria asked US [for] financial aid [to] resettle [a] quarter million refugees, whose deteriorating position makes them increasingly ripe for communist propaganda. Without US initiative, international action would be too slow. Syria will categorically refuse direct French aid [for] refugees. Already talk of such aid has stimulated active nationalist propaganda.

Regarding [the] reported British attitude, I should record this point, [of the] statement made [to] Ford and me by Sharett Saturday the 6th as follows: UK [is] not supporting US position [on] territorial compensation; is not opposed [to] Israeli retention [of] Negev tip, [there] should be provision [for] freedom [of] Egyptian and [Jordanian] transit [to] Negev tip; possibly held out joint Jordan-Israeli development [of] Aqaba port; considers Israeli refugee offer reasonable; showing more conciliatory attitude [in] discussions [of] blocked funds, no longer riding high horse. Sharett interpreted all this as evidence [of a] sharp change [in] Bevin's policy. Certain [that Ambassador Mordechai] Eliash has reported accurately.[28] Is keeping fingers crossed regarding future. Driving back to the house, Ford and I agree that it looked as if UK was setting model for us in delicacy of approach, whereas we seem to be suffering from great power-itis. Perhaps UK, having burned its fingers so often, has learned more than we [have].

Saturday August 6

General Riley was a quarter of an hour early to his 11:00 appointment to the house, which he had suggested.[29] He was in fine form, saying that his visit to the Vatican was the most thrilling experience of [his] life. Showed me [the] memorandum of what he said to His Holiness; chief point of this was [Riley's] statement that November 29th [General Assembly resolution] internationalization for Jerusalem was now impossible. He said that he also discussed the Russian danger. I received the impression that the visit had been well worthwhile. Certainly, he was delighted and grateful [for] my initiative. General Riley was interesting in his account of the cabled request from Sharett to Rome that Riley explain to [the Vatican] Israel's position regarding Jerusalem and secure views [of the] former on [the] latter. General Riley seemed pleased when I said at

28. See Eliash meeting with Bevin, July 19, 1949, *DFPI*, v. 4, d. 140. Bevin's statements on these issues to McGhee, which centered on international control of the Iraqi oil flow to Haifa, are in memorandum of conversation, September 13, 1949, *FRUS*, 1949, v. VI, 1376–1378.

29. Very brief summary in Ford to secretary of state, no. 597, August 8, 1949, NARA, RG 59, 501.BB Palestine, box 2126, folder 3.

once that, obviously, he could not have acceded to this request even if he had received it in time. To have done so would have been to have affronted the Arabs and then [to] pull Israel's chestnuts unjustifiably out of the fire.[30]

It was at this point that I asked General Riley if he wished to see Sharett. At my suggestion Bobby acted as messenger. Sharett came over and stayed for about a half an hour. According to the report of both men later, they had a frank exchange of views. General Riley said that Sharett understood why he could not have acted as messenger in Rome. As to Lausanne, General Riley was moderately optimistic. The acceptance in principle by the Arabs of the Israeli refugee proposal, with its emphasis on peace negotiations, was encouraging.

Shiloah arrived at Lausanne on July 27 to head the Israeli delegation after the July recess. On August 3, he formally introduced Israel's offer to allow the return of 100,000 Arab refugees, explaining that this would create an Arab population in Israel of 250,000. Shiloah further explained that the offer was predicated on Israel's retaining all territories that it now held. On August 2, Paul Porter reported from Lausanne to Washington that the Arab states accepted Shiloah's offer as a basis for discussion. The next day he backtracked, stating that the Arabs had not formally obligated themselves.[31]

Paul Porter was energetic and intelligent. He is the president's man. His chief weakness is his inability to spend more than his vacation on this job. He is working therefore to finish his part in time for the Assembly. Both Raymond Hare and I thought this a serious weakness.

As to the detonation problem in Jerusalem, General Riley said that he did not think that the danger of spontaneous explosion was serious and that, therefore, the Israelis were not certainly [un]-justified in carrying through the detonation arbitrarily. In any case, this was a matter for General Riley, not for Burdett or diplomatic intervention. General Riley did not seem to feel that the explosion would seriously damage the Old City or the Church of the Holy Sepulchre, which is about 300 yards distant. He again expressed some resentment at certain reports by Stabler and Burdett.[32]

Delightful and interesting luncheon at [Leo Kohn's]. Sharett and his daughter Yael were the chief entertainers. The leading topic was Jewish reli-

---

30. Detail in Shlomo Ginossar [Israeli ambassador to Rome] to Sharett, August 2, 1949, *DFPI*, v. 4, d. 173; Gowen to secretary of state, no. 24, August 13, 1949, *FRUS*, 1949, v. VI, 1308–1309, and n. 3. Sharett asked about the Vatican policy concerning Jerusalem, adding that, although Israel would agree to internationalization of the Holy Places or even the Old City under certain conditions, Israel would not agree to the internationalization of the entire city. It was the State Department that rejected Riley's acting as intermediary between Israel and the Vatican.

31. Porter to secretary of state, no. 260, August 2, 1949, *FRUS*, 1949, v. VI, 1276; Porter to secretary of state, no. 261, August 3, 1949, *FRUS*, 1949, v. VI, 1281–1282.

32. The Israelis blew up an ammunition dump on August 23, 1949. The planned detonation did no damage to any Holy Places in Jerusalem. Residents in the area were evacuated beforehand. JTA *Bulletin*, August 24, 1949.

gious experience. Yael frankly avowed her irreligiousness, but at the same time proclaimed that the Reformed service seemed to her nauseous. Obviously, Yael is more influenced by traditionalism than she knows. Sharett was thrillingly interesting in his account of his religious childhood and his and his brother's and sister's demand for more prayers and ceremonies, from which their father was in the habit of choosing which of the ceremonies he would lead. To him, these were more national than religious. Striking was Sharett's statement to me, as we were walking home, that as a young man he prayed regularly and always said a special prayer before he went to the Russian government school as a safeguard against the latter's demoralizing influence. But once in Israel, or rather in Palestine, he never prayed again, no longer feeling the need for prayer since he was among his own and no longer living in a hostile world.

The cocktail party was almost overwhelming in numbers. I chatted with [Ralph] Curren from Cairo[33] about the problems of the bilateral air agreement and the probability that Israel's legalism would make difficulties.[34] The representative of the International Telephone and Telegraph told me that he thought Israel's delay in signing [the] proposed seven-and-a-half million dollar [agreement] for communications equipment was the result of British pressure to use blocked pounds to get the contract for British interests. A few minutes later I chatted with Kaplan and casually mentioned this delay. He said, "There is now much interesting competition, particularly an offer from Sweden." Later, I reported this to the IT&T man, who was not convinced.

Sunday, August 7

Another long breakfast conference of a couple of hours with Sam Klaus. He reiterated his feeling that Israel was making a mistake not to cooperate by asking for more American advisers as a means of building technical bridges between the two countries and thus gradually, but surely, influencing State Department feeling. I promised to speak to Sharett. The other portion of our talk, which should be reported, concerned the elusive labor attaché. Milton Fried will not be released by [the] Czech desk in the Department. Klaus thinks he might be pried loose.

At twelve o'clock, Ford and I were received by Sharett and remained with him a full hour.[35] Main purpose [for] his call was to register formally [a] courteous but very firm protest against US injunction against Israel-Arab bilateral negotiations as potentially undermining [the] PCC. Both he and Ben-Gurion had been gravely disturbed by [the] US government communication which I presented to Eytan Sunday July 31st.[36] Reiterating Israel's determination to

---

33. Ralph B. Curren (1901–1968), first secretary to the US Embassy in Cairo and civil air attaché, assigned December 1944; also assigned to Baghdad, Beirut, Damascus, and Jidda.

34. See entry of July 2, 1949.

35. Brief summary in Ford to secretary of state, no. 602, August 8, 1949, NARA, RG 59, 501.BB Palestine, box 2126, folder 3.

36. See entry of July 31, 1949.

work for peace through [the] PCC, Sharett underlined solemnly that, as sovereign state, Israel must be free to choose its means to achieve peace so long as it in good faith works with and does not impede the UN efforts. I have seldom seen Sharett more serious. He stressed that what he was saying was also the view of the prime minister [and] that the latter had intended to speak to me on this point when I called to say goodbye, but had decided to do it through the foreign minister.[37]

Sharett then turned to explain that on the refugee issue Israel is at variance with Washington mathematically. Through McGhee and Rusk, [the] State Department recently spoke of 750,000. Israel holds this [to be] an impossible figure. Total number of Arabs in Israeli-held territory [in] April 1945, mandatory official figures, [was] 736,000. On basis [of] actual tests of villages remaining intact, Israel [is] convinced [that the] official estimate [in] '45 [was] 6% too high, real figure therefore approximately 736,000 less 43,000. Subtract from this the estimated number of Arabs now in Israeli-held territory gives maximum figure [of] 523,000 as highest legitimate total. Israel holds that the discrepancy is accounted for by a) flight of Arabs within Arab territory (not Israeli-held); b) Arabs who have gone to camps to gain relief while destitute; c) system of headmen inflating figures to get extra rations. Arab states say they are dissatisfied with Israel's offer [for the repatriation of 100,000 Arab refugees]. Israel replies, 'take it or leave it.' Moreover, the longer [the] Arabs delay, the greater will be [the] increase of demand within Israel for withdrawal of offer. Will be more difficult [to] resist [a] demand for withdrawal than it was to defend offer in Knesset.[38]

On leaving, I raised question of American [labor] advisers, Sharett replied a) there was a limit to how many foreign advisers could be digested; b) government must not [needlessly invite the] charge of American control through advisers. [Israel is a] new and small state, [and] must be more careful. Sharett at first thought I referred to military advisers and to Israel's request to have people trained. This led to an exchange of views about military attachés and Miss Herlitz's reiteration of older charge that military attachés had asked for secret information. She thought it had been easier during [the] fighting to give information, as was done to van der Velde. Sharett was visibly annoyed and surprised that this issue had not been cleared up.

On leaving, Ford and I again discussed what I should do about [the US] military attachés [while] in Washington. Though Ford was not dogmatic, I gathered the impression he thought [the] present evil less than [a] possible future one. What he seemed to have in mind was that I might fail to get better

37. Sharett elaborated on this point in Sharett to Mordechai Eliash, August 10, 1949, Fischer, ed., *Moshe Sharett: The Second Prime Minister, Selected Documents (1894–1965)*, 399–400.
    38. Refers to the heated critique of August 1 in the Knesset concerning the government's policy of repatriating a limited number of Arabs. See Sharett's discussion of the Knesset debate in Sharett to Eliash, August 10, 1949, Fischer, ed., *Moshe Sharett: The Second Prime Minister, Selected Documents (1894–1965)*, 399–400.

personnel and, even worse, I might give added ground to those who seek to discredit me as pro-Israel and unwilling to tolerate objective reporting. Very pleasant farewell luncheon at the Fords. After the meal Hooper took me aside to say that he was outraged by the military attachés and by their remarks at the last staff conference. They seemed, he said, not to realize that the ambassador is master. Evidently, he thinks they ought to be replaced.

Late in the afternoon, Ford brought in two disturbing telegrams from Burdett to [the] Department, one charging that the Knesset opposition to Israel's refugee offer [on August 1] was staged for effect abroad; and more serious, a long, five-page telegram tendentiously arguing that Israel's suggestions, including the refugee [suggestion], are disingenuous and that, as a means of assuring Arab refugees a measure of justice, the PCC should undertake to rectify existing armistice lines and thus provide lands for Arab refugees.[39] Ford was so outraged by this proposal to change the frontiers adversely to Israel that he sputtered his determination to answer. I drafted, and he will send, the last of the telegrams over my signature. Comments on both [of] the above [charges]. As to the first, I said that there was no ground whatsoever for the charge; as to the second, I indicted the whole despatch as partial and the specific suggestion as one which Israel would resist if necessary by force of arms.[40] The rest of the day in visits from friends and in packing.

Monday, August 8, 1949

The trip via Athens was uneventful. We arrived in Rome the late afternoon of a very hot, stifling day.

Tuesday, August 9

Early takeoff, and again an uneventful trip, arriving in Paris early afternoon.

August 11–13 [Paris]

The most important events during these days were my four telephone calls to [Clark] Clifford, [Abe] Feinberg, [Donald] McNeal,[41] [Frederick] Larkin, and Shiloah's visit from Lausanne.

Clifford and I first talked about our families. In answer to my suggestion, he promised that I could see the president early after my arrival. I told him of the personal message I was bringing from Ben-Gurion. He suggested that I call the White House soon after docking so that the date might be fixed.

---

39. See Burdett to secretary of state, no. 500, August 2, 1949, *FRUS*, 1949, v. VI, 1276–1277. The other reference is to Burdett's no. 505 of August 3, 1949.

40. Ford to secretary of state, no. 607, August 9, 1949, *FRUS*, 1949, v. VI, 1292. McDonald's report on the Knesset debate is in McDonald to secretary of state, no. 594, August 5, 1949, McDonald Papers, USHMM, box 8, folder 1.

41. Entry of May 14, 1949.

With Feinberg, I talked about the dangers inherent in the general principles which were influencing the thinking and action in the highest quarters. He told me that he had offered to go down to Lausanne from Paris to see Porter but that the latter had said this was unnecessary. He was even ready, he said, to return from the States if he could be useful. [The talks with McNeal and Larkin concerned ongoing housing issues concerning the US representation in Tel Aviv.]

Shiloah made a special trip to Paris from Lausanne to bring me up to date on the situation there. He spoke highly of Paul Porter, the latter's realism, and his keen intelligence.[42] He was pessimistic about any accomplishment at Lausanne, but said he would remain as long as there was any hope at all. He looked very tired and complained of his heart.[43]

After this meeting, Shiloah reported to Sharett that McDonald seemed dejected, feeling that his standing in Washington was deteriorating. McDonald complained of not being consulted on policy, and he told Shiloah that, on his arrival in Washington, he would ask if his mission had become pointless.[44]

The Louvre was as wonderful as ever, but at each new visit I feel more acutely the need for a wheelchair to enjoy it fully.

August 13–19—voyage

The trip was pleasant, the weather fine, the ship luxurious, and the food very French and very good. We met a number of people but the only notable ones were Rex Harrison and his wife, who were returning from their summer vacation in England for the reopening of play "Anne of the Thousand Days;"[45] the other was Sam Shubert.[46]

The big event of the day [of landing], after seeing Janet and Halsey, was of course our introduction to Donald Vail [Barrett]. He proved to be a husky and beautifully-formed baby, who already had almost as much or more hair than his father; though perhaps I could not prove it, I felt that though he looked a good deal like his father, he more nearly resembled his grandfather. Janet looked better than I had seen her in many years.

42. Shiloah's opinion of Porter and his lament that Porter's authority was circumscribed are in Shiloah to Sharett, August 7, 1949, *DFPI*, v. 4, d. 186.

43. For detail see Shiloah to Sharett, August 5, 1949, *DFPI*, v. 4, d. 180; Shiloah to Sharett, August 7, 1949, *DFPI*, v. 4, d. 186; Shiloah to Sharett, August 9, 1949, *DFPI*, v. 4, d. 191. Sharett did not worry about the PCC moving Palestine-related discussions to the UN General Assembly, because he did not believe that the United States could create a two-thirds majority there against Israel. *DFPI*, v. 4, 192, 193, 198, 200.

44. Shiloah to Sharett, August 15, 1949, *DFPI*, v. 4, d. 214. On August 12, 1949 the newspaper *Yediot Ahronot* reported, "Our enemies in the United States seek to replace McDonald."

45. Rex Harrison (1908–1990), British stage and film actor. *Anne of the Thousand Days* (about Anne Boleyn), which opened on Broadway in October 1948, won him his first Tony award.

46. Could be conflated with Jacob J. Schubert (1879–1963), brother of Sam S. Schubert (1878–1905). The family owned numerous theaters in New York.

My first golf in the morning. It was exhilarating to be walking on turf and in the midst of beautiful trees. In the evening, out with the Abrams to Sam Katz's for dinner.[47] The dinner, though informal, was as luxurious as the surroundings and made me little nauseous, so much did it contrast with the austerity of Israel. I had this feeling more markedly when, after dinner, sitting in the elaborate gardens beside the swimming pool with the floodlights illuminating the grounds, Katz "modestly" demurred at my statement that his place was luxurious.

I was especially interested in the discussion between Ben Abrams and Katz on the issue of the possibility of a successful Israeli loan in the States. Katz was confident that much larger sums could be raised that way than through the UJA. He said, for example, that his firm would buy as much as a quarter of a million dollars' worth of bonds, whereas he felt able to contribute only $50,000.

Sunday, August 21

Tea at the Warburgs' where I found Frieda in fine form. Also present were Gisela and her husband.[48] They were full of their visit to Israel, and both of them again expressed their pleasure at our including them in the dinner for Justice Douglas.[49]

Monday, August 22

Arrived in Washington shortly after nine, having flown down. Went directly to the Department, where a desk in the "Ambassadors' Suite" was waiting for me. A Miss Zerbee was to act as secretary for me and the ambassador from Saudi Arabia [J. Rives Childs], who shared the room with me.

Lunch with [Herbert J.] Cummings and Carl Wood of the Near East unit of the Department of Commerce. Chief discussion was about the possible labor attaché; [Louis] Silverberg, Fried, and [Horace] Stern were most talked of.[50] Cummings also told me about the prospective visit of the House Sub-Committee on Executive Expenditures, headed by [John] Blatnik [D-MN]. There was no opportunity, however, for intimate discussion about policies.

Dinner with Elath and Mrs. Elath at the Shoreham [Hotel], where they are living in a pleasant and comfortable, but not at all showy apartment. We dined out of doors in the lovely hotel park. During dinner John Foster Dulles, who was at a nearby table with his family, came over to us and said he would like to see me while I was home (unfortunately my schedule proved to be such

47. Sam Katz (1892–1961), Polish-born partner in Balaban & Katz luxury cinemas in Chicago and similar chains; vice president in charge of production at MGM since 1936.
48. Entry of July 18, 1949.
49. Ibid.
50. Louis G. Silverberg (1887–1975), public affairs officer in National Labor Relations Board. Horace Stern (1879–1969), justice on Pennsylvania State Supreme Court, 1935–1956; adjudicated and arbitrated labor disputes; active in Jewish affairs.

that there was no opportunity for this talk). During the dinner it was evident from Elath's conversation that he was under a heavy strain and was on the verge of being jittery.

On August 9, George McGhee, the assistant secretary in charge of the Bureau of Near Eastern, South Asian, and African Affairs, told Ambassador Elath that the Arab states had rejected Israel's offer at Lausanne to take in 100,000 refugees as completely inadequate; he further emphasized that Israel's proposal concerning refugees and boundaries was not in accordance with the General Assembly resolution of December 11, 1948, or with US policy. McGhee pressed for 230,000 Arab repatriations to Israel, and the State Department continued to discuss Israeli territorial concessions. Elath reported to Tel Aviv that McGhee's statements represented a "new turn [in developments in] view [of] Lausanne impasse."[51]

Later the same day, Elath met with Clark Clifford. By now the State Department had worked to close the gap in thinking between itself and the White House.[52] *Clifford told Elath that Israel would have to be flexible with its boundaries and that this was "also [the] President's view." Clifford was receptive to Israel's arguments concerning refugees, but he also noted that Porter and the Lausanne talks were "carrying great weight with the President." Elath reported to Sharett, "I warned [Clifford] against pushing Israel into [a] position of having to refuse [to] cooperate [with the] U.S.A.," but that the discussion with Clifford "proved [the] seriousness [of] our situation [in the] White House."*[53]

On August 11, Elath wrote Sharett that "close relations [between] President-Acheson [are] presently facilitating Department efforts [at] preventing White House interference [in] Lausanne."[54] *On August 18, McGhee handed Elath the president's reply—drafted by Fraser Wilkins—to Weizmann's letter of June 24.*[55] *It expressed confidence in the PCC and noted, "I would be less than frank if I did not tell you that I was disappointed when I read the reply of your Government to our note of May 29."*[56] *McGhee stressed what he called "the unity of the White House and the Depart-*

51. Elath to Sharett, August 9, 1949, *DFPI*, v. 4, d. 194. The Arab states insisted in Lausanne on August 15 that all Arab refugees coming from land allotted to the Arabs by the November 1947 partition plan be allowed to return, a statement that Stuart Rockwell described as "unrealistic and unhelpful." See Acheson's telegrams to the US Delegation in Lausanne, no. 224 and 225, August 11, 1949, *FRUS*, 1949, v. VI, 1297–1298, 1301–1302; Rockwell to secretary of state, no. 277, August 16, 1949, *FRUS*, 1949, v. VI, 1319.

52. On August 3, 1949 the State Department learned that Eban had told Shiloah that, according to a source close to the White House, Truman found the 100,000 proposal "very reasonable" and would oppose any attempt to deprive Israel of the Negev. On August 9, the State Department ordered the US delegation in Lausanne to inform Shiloah that there was no difference of view between the president and the State Department on these issues. Clifford was informed of these developments. Porter to secretary of state, no. 263, August 3, 1949, and Acheson to US delegation in Lausanne, August 9, 1949, Truman Library, Clifford Papers, Subject File 1945–54, box 14, folder Palestine—Telegrams and Cables, 1 of 2.

53. Elath to Sharett, August 9, 1949, *DFPI*, v. 4, d. 195.

54. Elath to Sharett, August 11, 1949, *DFPI*, v. 4, d. 201.

55. Weizmann to Truman, June 24, 1949, *FRUS*, 1949, v. VI, 1168–1173; Truman to Weizmann, August 13, 1949, *FRUS*, 1949, v. VI, 1305–1308.

56. Entry of June 8, 1949.

ment regarding recent developments concerning Palestine" and suggested that Israel would not benefit from trying to play the White House against the State Department or by trying to mobilize American Jews.[57]

Tuesday, August 23

Made a date for meeting with the [American] Friends [Service Committee] in Philadelphia.

My first introduction to McGhee's [Bureau of Near Eastern, South Asian, and African Affairs]. Present must have been twenty or twenty-five Department and Foreign Service officials, representing not only different portions of McGhee's vast domain, but also liaison representatives from the Departments of Commerce, Agriculture, Labor, and perhaps others. For example, Cummings represented [the Department of] Commerce.

An interesting report was made by a man just back from the work of the Pakistan truce commission [*sic*]. As he spoke, I thought as if the subject [was] Israel and the Arab states, rather than Pakistan and India in controversy over Kashmir.[58] I was called upon, but since the time was obviously very short, I spoke for only four or five minutes.

Later in the morning, had the first of several very brief talks with McGhee. He denied that the Department had discouraged bilateral negotiations between Israel and individual Arab states "except when duress was being used." I took sharp exception to this doctrine, arguing that it is not possible to eliminate what might be termed by one side or the other as "duress" in negotiations following a war. I added that I, as a former professor, had studied many peace treaties and could recall none which had been negotiated in such peaceful an atmosphere that one side or the other might not charge duress.

Later, I had a brief and formal interview with [James E.] Webb, the new under secretary. He was friendly and willing enough to talk. I could not discern, however, that he knew very much about our part of the world. First, he explained to me the nature of the latest Departmental reorganization. Each of the assistant secretaries was an executive vice president and was given large responsibility in his area. As to Israel, Webb's only comment which impressed itself upon me was in the form of a question: "When will the Israeli officials grow up to their responsibilities as heads of a state?" I took as sharp exception as seemed safe to this obvious underrating of the caliber and capacities of the Israeli leaders. I explained, but I am afraid without making a convincing impression, that I regarded Ben-Gurion, Sharett, Kaplan, and others as the equals of any leaders I knew elsewhere. I left the conference with the uneasy feeling

57. Memorandum by McGhee, August 18, 1949, *FRUS*, 1949, v. VI, 1323–1326; Elath to Clifford, August 15, 1949, *DFPI*, v. 4, d. 217; Elath to Sharett, August 18, 1949, *DFPI*, v. 4, d. 225; Elath to Sharett, August 19, 1949, *DFPI*, v. 4, d. 229; Sasson to Sharett, August 25, 1949, *DFPI*, v. 4, d. 241.

58. Refers to United Nations Commission on India and Pakistan, established on January 20, 1948, to investigate fighting over Kashmir and Jammu. A cease-fire line was established on July 27, 1949. William L. S. Williams was the US delegate to the UN Commission.

that Webb would be completely in the hands of his technicians. I should perhaps add for the record that I told Webb that though my personal views on some issues might differ from those of some of the men in the Department, I made it a practice to carry out the Department's instructions with the most exacting correctness, adding nothing and subtracting nothing.

Just before leaving the office, Elath called me in high excitement to say that the Department representative had vetoed the Export-Import Bank allotment of the portion of the loan requested for the Haifa harbor development. I attempted vainly to assure him that the matter could not be of such great moment, but he insisted that it was, and that he was sure Tel Aviv would be "gravely disturbed." I promised to check about the matter, about which up to then I had heard nothing. Immediately I got Wilkins on the telephone, who said that he knew nothing of the matter. Later, he explained to me that he had to give this reply, which was false, because there was sitting at his desk at the time a curious and alert newspaperman who would have had an important scoop if he had discovered the situation. Then I went in to see Hare. He admitted that something had to be done, but he suggested that I had better take the matter up with McGhee. Fortunately, the latter was still in his office, and we had an opportunity for substantial talk.

On August 15, 1949, the State Department decided to "postpone" the allocation of the $49 million balance of the $100 million Export-Import Bank loan to Israel. Five million of the balance had recently been allocated for the development of Haifa harbor. The secretary of state, who was on the board of the Export-Import Bank, would also, according to this decision, rule on Israeli requests for funds thereafter. The Department reasoned that the slow progress of the PCC talks justified the new procedures. Export-Import Bank officials opposed the decision, but on August 23, bank officials notified the Israeli embassy of the new policy.[59]

McGhee, while admitting the Department's action, sought to interpret it as of no great moment. He said in effect, the Department had long been considering such an action but had not taken it until now because this was the first request by Israel for an allocation since the possibility of a request for delay had been in the minds of the Department officials. The action did not mean refusal or rejection or suspension but merely holding up the grant for the time being. His defense of this action was:

1) Peace was further away than at the time the loan was granted. (To this I took exception, saying that in my opinion, war was further away.)
2) There is no present prospect that an improved Haifa harbor will be available to the Arabs, since there is no prospect of a suggested free zone there.

59. Memorandum by McGhee and Thorpe, August 15, 1949, *FRUS*, 1949, v. VI, 1311–1312 and n. 1; also Gass to Kaplan, *DFPI*, v. 4, d. 240.

3) Israeli officials were inclined to be exigent (this last is not the word McGhee used, but the impression he gave was as strong if not stronger than that).

I expressed surprise that such a decision had been taken at this time. There was nothing in the situation to justify what would be regarded in Israel as an unfriendly act,[60] [and] that on the contrary, Israel's cooperation with the Clapp Commission made the present a particularly unseemly time to interpose a loan veto. McGhee may have been somewhat shaken in his opinion of the action, but he made no admission of the fact.

Porter had suggested to Washington the creation of an expert committee that would study the refugee problem from the perspective of the economic absorptive capacity of each country, focusing on Israel, Syria, and Jordan. On August 23 the UN, based on a State Department recommendation, established the United Nations Economic Survey Mission to the Middle East [ESM]. It was to make recommendations to the PCC concerning repatriation, resettlement, and development. The mission, under the chairmanship of an American, Gordon Clapp (1905–1963), who had headed the Tennessee Valley Authority, included three deputy chairs from the United Kingdom, France, and Turkey, as well as eight experts.[61]

The Economic Survey Mission represented a potential retreat from the 250,000 repatriation figure pressed by McGhee. Israeli officials expected their arguments to impress the group. Porter told Shiloah that the ESM's creation had averted a crisis in US-Israeli relations. The mission established its headquarters in Beirut in September 1949.[62]

Cocktails with van der Velde and his bride at the Mayflower. She is a good-looking and intelligent woman. Van der Velde could tell me nothing more about the reasons for his recall.[63] Dinner with Fierst and general discussion of the whole situation. He is still suspicious of the leadership in [Near Eastern Affairs], particularly that of Rusk.

Wednesday, August 24
[Morning discussion at the State Department's Office of Foreign Buildings Operations concerning housing expenses in Tel Aviv]. Dinner with [Charles]

60. Sharett warned two days later that the postponement was a blow to US-Israeli friendship and that the United States underestimated Israeli determination if they expected the step to change Israeli policy. Sharett to Elath, August 25, 1949, *DFPI*, v. 4, d. 242.
61. In general Caplan, *The Lausanne Conference*, 104–107; Waldman, *Anglo-American Diplomacy and the Palestinian Refugee Problem*, 101–114; also UN Conciliation Commission for Palestine, *Final Report of the United Nations Economic Survey Mission for the Middle East: An Approach to Economic Development in the Middle East* (Lake Success, NY: United Nations, 1949).
62. Heydt to Sharett, August 14, 1949, *DFPI*, v. 4, d. 211, and esp. n. 6; Eban to Sharett, August 15, 1949, *DFPI*, v. 4, d. 216; Memorandum of Feinberg-Porter meeting, August 18, 1949, *DFPI*, v. 4, d. 226; Shiloah to Sharett, August 23, 1949, *DFPI*, v. 4, d. 236.
63. Entry of September 21, 1949.

Knox. He analyzed the situation within the Department, reaching the same general conclusion as had others that Rusk was, in effect, the maker of policy.

Thursday, August 25

Before seeing the president I had a brief but friendly talk with Clark Clifford. At the beginning of our talk [at 11:15] I asked the president, "When are you coming to Israel?" He replied, in effect, that he was afraid that he had other more pressing duties. I then spoke of Eddie Jacobson's visit [in January 1949]. The president commented: "Yes, he told me all about it." Without thinking of the current scandal about General Vaughan, his aide and intimate,[64] I said: "One of the fine things about Eddie is that he does not capitalize on his friendship with you."

The president said he was pleased to have me say that I was receiving full cooperation from the State Department. A little earlier, when I had told him that Secretary Marshall had opposed my appointment, the president commented: "General Marshall didn't exactly oppose it; he had a similar attitude towards Stanton Griffis when the latter was named to Poland.["] Six months later, however, General Marshall had gone to the president and said that he wanted to send the best man he could find to Cairo and then indicated that he had Griffis in mind. In answer to the president's jibe that "you must have changed your mind a lot about Griffis," General Marshall had replied, "Yes, and about McDonald, too."

At about this point I took the opportunity to express my serious regret that the Department had vetoed the Export-Import Bank Haifa port allotment of the Israel loan (Clifford had told me that David Niles had slipped in to tell the president earlier that morning about the veto). When I had finished with my brief argument, the president said, "I am seeing Secretary Acheson at our regular conference today. This matter can probably be worked out." Then, after some general talk during which the president was very cordial and wished me well, I left [at 11:40].

Truman, according to Niles, expressed extreme displeasure that he had not been consulted on such an important issue as the Export-Import Bank loan to Israel. After his meeting with Truman, McDonald told Elath that the president promised him that the matter would be resolved.[65]

Hurried over to the Pentagon for my appointment with Secretary [Louis] Johnson.[66] He was immediately receptive when I told him of my desire to reduce the staff of the military attaché.[67] He called in a civilian assistant and then

---

64. Brigadier General Harry H. Vaughan (1893–1981), friend and confidant of Truman since they had served together in World War I; had been accused of taking improper gifts and of influence peddling.

65. McDonald, *My Mission in Israel*, 186–187; *DFPI*, v. 4, d. 243, n. 3.

66. Louis A. Johnson (1891–1966), secretary of defense, March 1949–September 1950.

67. Meaning that McDonald wanted a military attaché better qualified than Colonel Andrus. McDonald, *My Mission in Israel*, 189.

referred this and related problems to Major General James H. Burns.[68] The latter was very cordial and cooperative.

Reached the Metropolitan Club a little late for the luncheon with McGhee, Elath, and Hare. After the usual generalities, the discussion centered on the State Department veto of the [Export-Import Bank] loan. McGhee made his usual defense [that the loan had not been suspended or canceled, but was being reviewed in light of the disappointments at Lausanne] but without any effect on Elath, who launched the most vigorous counter-attack that I have listened to in my entire experience. I had not thought him capable of such brutal frankness. Again and again he returned to the charge that the veto was morally, if not legally, a breach of contract. Argument after argument he piled up against a nearly defenseless McGhee, while Hare and I remained discretely silent.[69]

Parting with Elath, the three of us rode back to the Department together. My comment was that Elath's vehemence was the more impressive because of his recognized gentleness of manner and of nature. Later, I was to learn that in a sense, Elath had "put on an act" because he confessed to me that he kept watching my face—I sat opposite to him—as the gauge of how far he could go.

A little to my embarrassment, McGhee asked me if I had spoken to the president about the loan. I had no alternative but to confess that I had. My only regret was that I had not told this to McGhee before he asked me. Later in the afternoon, when I was talking to McGhee about something else, he referred to the subject of the loan and asked me whether I really thought the Department veto was a mistake. I told him that I was confident it was. He seemed to be somewhat less sure of his position.

On August 26, Acheson and Truman discussed the suspension of the loan.[70] Later the same day, McGhee informed Elath that Acheson had instructed him to restore normal procedures with the Export–Import Bank loan to Israel.[71]

Friday, August 26
Conference with General Burns and other sessions with [Charles] Knox and another brief one with McGhee.

68. Major General James H. Burns (1885–1972), Johnson's assistant for foreign military affairs.

69. See also official memorandum by Hare, August 25, 1949, *FRUS*, 1949, v. VI, 1328–1331; Elath to Sharett, August 25, 1949, *DFPI*, v. 4, d. 244. Elath told McGhee that the suspension was the "worst blow we have ever suffered at hands U.S.A. government," that it would shake Israeli faith in US commitments, and that it would weaken Ben-Gurion's government, making success at Lausanne less likely. Elath reported to Sharett that McGhee was "obviously confused when answering my queries regarding practical differences between postponement and suspension," and he suggested to Sharett that Israel was in a "strong moral position [to] use loan veto as turning point to force improvement [of] our relations and compel [the] U.S.A. Government [to] relinquish methods [of] coercion and blackmail."

70. *FRUS*, 1949, v. VI, 1332 and n. 2.

71. Elath to Sharett, August 26, 1949, *DFPI*, v. 4. d. 247, and August 30, 1949, d. 253; Elath to Eytan, September 14, 1949, *DFPI*, v. 4, d. 287.

At home most of the time with Janet and Halsey and Donald.

At lunch on the 29th, I spent half an hour or so with [Samuel] Leidesdorf's UJA group.

Lunch with Jack Laban at [Lewis] Rosenstiel's office together with Leidesdorf and the general counsel and public relations chief of Shenley's. It was disappointing not to have Rosenstiel himself, who had begged off on the ground of illness and had remained in the country. Rosentiel's two colleagues listened with very close attention to my account of the situation in Israel and of the possibilities of an imaginative approach by their chief to a large-scale medical investment in the country. They promised to urge it sympathetically on Rosentiel. At the end Laban escorted me downstairs.

Dinner in the evening with Eddie Cantor and Manny [Goldman].[72] It left me with the uneasy feeling that Eddie was not well.

Back in Washington. Another brief conference with Secretary Johnson. He said that Israel should have American support because of our strategic interests, but that he thought Israel should "take back more refugees." I did not get the impression that he was really informed on this problem; nonetheless, his offhand comment was doubtless illustrative of prevailing opinion in the highest Washington quarters. Lunch with Congressman Multer, with whom I was again very well impressed.[73]

Long conference with Philip Kaiser, assistant secretary of labor, and in charge of international labor relations.[74] He urged that I see Stern, one of the candidates for the post of labor attaché. He did not give him the strongest endorsement. Nonetheless, I agreed to see him.

Either on this day or about this time, I had my first conference with Arthur Z. Gardiner, a special assistant in the [State] Department who was acting as administrative officer in the organization of the Clapp mission.[75]

72. Emanuel Goldman of New York, McDonald's haberdasher and good friend.
73. Entries of September 9, 14, 19, 1948.
74. Philip M. Kaiser (1913–2007), assistant secretary of labor for international affairs; promoted trade union movements in Western Europe and Japan; instrumental in promoting the new office of labor attaché; later an ambassador in the Kennedy and Carter administrations.
75. Arthur Z. Gardiner (1901–1975), special assistant, Bureau of Near Eastern, South Asian and African Affairs, Department of State, 1945–1954; McGhee's adviser to the Economic Survey Mission.

15. September 1949

Thursday, September 1[1]

Long conference in the morning with [Arthur Z.] Gardiner and [Gordon] Clapp about the latter's mission. I was very much impressed by the latter, his open-mindedness, his non-political approach, and his complete objectivity. He seemed to me also unusually able and discerning.

Another indecipherable note about Arthur Armstrong, CIA, [with] whom I agreed to speak. [Conference] with the CIA people at their headquarters. I was pleasantly surprised by the realism and the lack of cloak-and-dagger atmosphere in this session. The group as a whole and the men in charge of it seem to be genuinely appreciative of my frankness.

Learned in the Department during the day that Burdett had replied to our number 607 of August 9th in a secret communication no. 522 received in the Department August 18.[2] I did not mind his criticism but thought it would have been fairer if he had circulated copies to me.

Burdett charged that McDonald "in effect recommends abandonment or emasculation of US policy on boundaries and refugees. . . . Solution imposed by Israel with force or threats of force on UN, US and Arab states will hardly contribute to lasting peace, or fail to strike at vitals of moral authority upon which UN and US world leadership hinges."[3]

Larger reception in the afternoon for Clapp at the Mayflower [Hotel]. It was significant that, in view of the Department's invitation to Elath, the Arab representatives unitedly declined to attend. Instead, they went as a group to the Department and made their apologies. It was an interesting party for me. I had a good talk there with [John] Snyder, secretary of the treasury, who indicated more knowledge and sympathy with my work in Israel than I had anticipated.[4] Talked also with [Sidney] Sherwood over [at] the Export-Import Bank. He

1. McDonald's diary for September 1949 probably was dictated on his return to Tel Aviv. The original is considerably out of order, and the editors have resequenced material where appropriate.
2. See entry of August 7, 1949.
3. Burdett to secretary of state, no. 522, August 16, 1949, *FRUS*, 1949, v. VI, 1319–1321.
4. John W. Snyder (1895–1985), secretary of the treasury, 1946–1953; close friend of Truman who had helped McDonald with access to the White House in July 1946. See Goda et al., eds., *To the Gates of Jerusalem*, 244.

confirmed that the bank officials had been unanimous in their support of the Haifa port loan allocation and had been surprised and dismayed by the Department's abrupt political veto. Sherwood said he would be glad if he were assigned to the Clapp Mission. Brief talk with the president of the international bank.[5] Also passing but not very significant chats with [James] Webb, [Dean] Rusk, and other members of the Department.[6]

Friday, September 2

During previous days I had talked to several of the men of the [State] Department about our labor attaché problem and received the discouraging impression that it was everybody's business and nobody's business, and that the prospects of a prompt and favorable decision were remote. So many people have to be consulted that no one seems to be willing to take any responsibility or any initiative.

From many persons I heard praise of Dillon Myer, who is to be one of Clapp's chief assistants and a man whom the Department has in mind as a possible central executive for Arab refugees and possibly with an even wider responsibility.[7]

Wednesday, September 7

Luncheon at the *New York Times*. In Arthur Sulzberger's absence, Iphigene[8] was hostess. The discussion was less satisfactory than usual because of the extraordinary contrast in the level of knowledge of the members of the group, ranging all the way from General Adler,[9] who knew nothing, to Anne O'Hare McCormick, who is very well informed. The questions were so varied and so unrelated that at the end I felt exhausted by my efforts to follow them.

Friday, September 9

Talked with [Paul E.] Fitzpatrick of the Democratic National Committee[10] about the desirability of meeting with the mayor.[11] He thought it desirable to leave the whole thing to him.

5. Could refer to Herbert E. Gaston (1881–1956), chairman of the Export-Import Bank, 1949–1953.

6. Representative Emanuel Celler was also at the reception. Elath was hopeful regarding Clapp, characterizing him with the following terms: "progressive, social-minded, clear views." He also reported that Snyder was friendly. Elath to Sharett, September 2, 1949, *DFPI*, v. 4, d. 260.

7. Dillon S. Myer (1891–1982), director of the War Relocation Authority, 1942–1946; director of the Federal Public Housing Authority, 1946–1947; president of the Institute of Inter-American Affairs, 1948–1950. Did not serve with the Clapp Mission.

8. Iphigene Ochs Sulzberger (1892–1990), daughter of Adolf Ochs, who had bought the *New York Times* in 1896; married Arthur Sulzberger, 1917; became trustee of the *New York Times* after 1935.

9. Major General Julian Ochs Adler (1892–1955), nephew of Adolf Ochs; general manager of *New York Times*, 1935–1955.

10. Paul E. Fitzpatrick (1897–1977), New York State Democratic Committee chairman, 1944–1952.

11. William O'Dwyer (1890–1964), mayor of New York City, 1946–1950.

Talked to [Zalman] Friedman[12] of the Red Mogen David about negotiations with Rosenstiel. He again volunteered to act as carrier.

Telephoned [Clark] Clifford's office about his mother.

Late morning at the Jewish Hospital in Brooklyn, where Max [Abelman][13] had made General Marshall the central figure for publicity purposes.[14] I had a brief chat with the general and with his accompanying host, General [Walter] Bedell Smith, who, not unnaturally, was not flattered by [the] failure to associate him with Moscow, where he had been the American ambassador until very recently.[15]

Rode as far as borough hall with John Cashmore.[16] He is in fine form, enjoying his dual role of borough president and borough [Democratic] party leader. He had no doubt about his own reelection this fall, but is worried about [Governor Herbert] Lehman. The aftermath of the Roosevelt-Spellman controversy, into which the governor had injected himself, might make the difference between success and defeat.[17]

According to John, he was the one major Democratic leader who never wavered in his support of the president for the nomination. Haig of New Jersey[18] had done his utmost to weaken John's loyalty, but he insisted on bringing the largest single bloc of delegates into the convention unwaveringly on the president's side. As a result, the president is very grateful and has told John that he is one of the few men who never need make an appointment at the White House.

Lunch at the Sulgrave with Arthur Lourie, [Gideon] Rafael, and Eban, who arrived late from Lake Success. The latter expressed himself optimistically about the prospects of the attitude of the Latin-American states on the problem of Jerusalem. He had the impression that at least some of the Latin representatives were so disappointed by the repeated ineffectiveness of UN resolutions

---

12. Zalman J. Friedman (1915–1999), executive director of Magen David Adom; wished to have Magen David Adom included in the League of Red Cross Societies.

13. Max Abelman (1887–1960), secretary to board of trustees of Jewish Hospital in Brooklyn.

14. General George Marshall was made an honorary citizen of Brooklyn on September 13. A reception was held for him at the Jewish Hospital in Brooklyn before the formal ceremony.

15. General Walter Bedell Smith (1895–1961), US ambassador to the USSR, 1946–1948; director of central intelligence, 1950–1953.

16. John Cashmore (1895–1961), borough president of Brooklyn, 1940–1961.

17. Refers to the public argument between Eleanor Roosevelt and Cardinal Spellman. Lehman had publicly condemned Spellman's attack on the former first lady. See entry of July 27, 1949.

18. Frank Haig (1876–1956), mayor of Jersey City, 1917–1947; vice chairman of the Democratic National Committee, 1924–1949; notoriously corrupt politician.

that they would now hesitate to vote for the imposition of the PCC plan of internationalization. Eban insisted, too, that there had been no real discussion of this plan at Lausanne.

On September 1, 1949, the Palestine Conciliation Commission [PCC] submitted to the secretary-general its "Draft Instrument Establishing a Permanent International Regime for the Jerusalem Area."[19] *On September 16, the PCC concluded its meetings in Lausanne. It planned to reconvene in New York during the meeting of the General Assembly on October 19.*

The PCC's Jerusalem proposal was an expanded version of the plan that McDonald had seen in May.[20] *It called for local autonomy for the Jewish and Arab zones, with a UN commissioner and a UN council to oversee the Holy Places and common civil issues, as well as full demilitarization of the city and its environs. But at the insistence of French PCC representatives, it also prohibited immigration that might alter the demographic balance between the two zones.*[21] *The proposal limited Israeli prerogatives far more than the Israeli government had expected. The Israelis viewed Jewish Jerusalem as an integral part of Israel and agreed with UN supervision only of the Holy Places.*

From Tel Aviv, Richard Ford reported "strong and even violent opposition to plan . . . from every quarter." Washington, remembering Count Bernadotte's fate, worried about a resumption of right-wing violence in the city.[22] *On September 16, Moshe Sharett gave a press statement rejecting the PCC's Jerusalem instrument, which he called a "metaphysical abstraction" given the facts on the ground; he derided the demographic restrictions as "utterly fantastic."*[23]

The State Department proceeded regardless. On September 21, during his address to the General Assembly, Acheson praised the efforts of the acting mediator and the cessation of active hostilities; he expressed hope in the work of the PCC; he called for all sides to recognize their responsibilities concerning Palestinian refugees; and he called for the General Assembly to act successfully on the PCC's recommendations concerning Jerusalem.[24] *The General Assembly placed Jerusalem on the session agenda the next day.*

19. In general Slonim, *Jerusalem in America's Foreign Policy, 1947–1997*, 121–171; Hahn, *Caught in the Middle East*, 112–117. The fifty-page draft instrument was officially published in November 1949.
20. See entry of May 17, 1949.
21. See http://unispal.un.org/UNISPAL.NSF/0/426AB77C3C1B506D852563B90070 23D8, accessed June 2014; Eban to Sharett, September 13, 1949, *DFPI*, v. 4, d. 284, 285; Burdett to secretary of state, no. 611, October 7, 1949, NARA, RG 59, 501.BB Palestine, box 2127, folder 1.
22. Ford to secretary of state, no. 142, September 16, 1949, McDonald Papers, USHMM, box 8, folder 2. Also McGhee to Rusk, September 22, 1949, *FRUS*, 1949, v. VI, 1396–1397; memorandum by McGhee, September 22, 1949, *FRUS*, 1949, v. VI, 1396–1397; Burdett to secretary of state, no. 576, September 17, 1949, NARA, RG 59, 501.BB, box 2127, folder 3 and other documents in this folder.
23. *DFPI*, v. 4, d. 293; Burdett to secretary of state, no. 573, September 16, 1949, *FRUS*, v. VI, 1390–1392.
24. United Nations, *Official Record of the General Assembly, Fourth Session, Plenary Meeting, Summary Records of Meetings, 20 September–10 December 1949*, 6.

Thursday, September 15

Morning conference with Emanuel Neumann at the latter's office. He, now being out of power, was almost pathetically grateful for my call. Lunch with [Eliahu] Ben-Horin. Tea with Herbert May. Evening train for St. Louis.[25]

Tuesday, September 20

[Back in New York] A day of odds and ends. Met Chaim Sacks and the woman with whom he stays at teatime. Dinner with Miss Schulkind and her husband. To the theatre with Janet, Ruth, and Halsey to see *Kiss Me, Kate*. Earlier we had seen *Anne of the Thousand Days* with Rex Harrison as Henry VIII.

Wednesday, September 21

Morning conference with the Quakers in Philadelphia. In addition to asking me general questions, they wanted my judgment on an agricultural cooperative project in [the] Galilee, among Arabs and [Jews].

Luncheon given by Judge Levinthal to a group of twenty or so Jewish jurists.[26] The only non-Jew was Curtis Bok.[27] It was a pleasant session. Immediately afterwards, I took the train for Washington.

Back in Washington. Having arranged for an appointment with Charlie Knox at cocktail time, he and I went together to Elath's large party at the Shoreham for Miss Herlitz[28] and the Israeli embassy's new counselor [of embassy, Moshe Keren]. There one met nearly everyone. I was somewhat amused by Rusk's comment. Evidently impressed that the British ambassador [Sir Oliver Franks] and his staff were present, [Rusk said] Miss Herlitz, obviously is having a wonderful time. I was pleased, too, to meet the attractive wives of Wilkins, Kopper, McGhee, and Rusk.

Dinner with the [Colonel Eugene] van der Veldes and [A. Guy] Hope. Van der Velde continued to be very much disturbed at the possibility that there is a black mark against him at the Pentagon for his work in Israel. He was anxious, and Hope seemed to agree, that it would be correct for me to write a letter to the secretary of defense, thanking him for his courtesies to me, his instructions about the reorganization of the attachés in Tel Aviv, and then, parenthetically, to praise van der Velde and to point out that his forecasts about [lack of] Russian penetration in Israel had been borne out by subsequent developments. I promised

25. From September 16–20, McDonald and Ruth traveled to and from Kansas City to attend the wedding of Eddie and Bluma Jacobson's daughter. En route, they visited Clark Clifford's mother, Georgia, in St. Louis.
26. See entries of September 8, October 2, and October 6, 1948. Levinthal was still a judge on the Court of Common Pleas in Philadelphia.
27. Curtis Bok (1897–1962), presiding judge on the Court of Common Pleas of Philadelphia; Quaker and philanthropist; prolific writer.
28. Esther Herlitz had recently been assigned to head the American desk at the Israeli Foreign Ministry and had left for the United States on August 31. Elath had taken her to meet George McGhee on September 20.

to write such a letter if on fuller consideration it seemed that I could properly do so.

McDonald wrote the Pentagon in hopes that van der Velde might be reassigned to Israel to replace Andrus, whom he viewed as ineffective. The Army refused for what they called "military reasons." Van der Velde replied to McDonald, "I appreciate your asking for me very much and your suggestion to [the] Army that they consult with me. They have not done so and probably will not. . . . I believe you know that I worked as hard and as sincerely for the Intelligence Division as I could when I was in Israel. It is therefore doubly discouraging to have my efforts fall on such barren soil."[29]

Thursday, September 22

I had a serious half-hour conference with Clifford on the 22nd in his office. After we had talked about his mother and her driving, I gave him a sort of lecture on the necessity for realism in dealing with Israel. I argued that however sound theoretically might be the general principle on which the Department's and the president's policy might be based, such principles in fact were not applicable and led only to actions which were self-defeating.

He then made himself, as it were, the advocate of those principles by asking me a serious question: "Had not the Jews recognized the complete internationalization of Jerusalem in the November 29, [1947] resolution? Had they not at the same time accepted the November 29 territorial plan? Had they not also accepted the refugee program in the December 11, [1948] resolution? What would happen to the UN if its decisions could be 'flouted'?" Although he put these questions in the mouths of others, I sense that he shared the views expressed or implied in them.

My answer in substance was as follows: These principles for the most part had ceased to be [relevant]. Moreover, the Arabs, by their attack on the November 29 partition [resolution] and through the subsequent war, had helped to create conditions which released the Jews from their obligations under that resolution. In any case, the partition was conceived on the basis of an independent Arab state in Palestine, a condition which no one any longer expected to be fulfilled. As to the December 11 resolution, its refugee provision was vague, and in any case, the Jews, for good reasons or bad, simply would not accept the large numbers being suggested to them.

I then elaborated my fundamental thesis that peace would not be secured in the Middle East except through bilateral negotiations. I underlined that the Department, by conditioning its approval of such negotiations to those in which "no duress is used," was in effect negating all effective bilateral negotiations. I quoted my argument to McGhee that in such negotiations following a war there will always be some side which will claim on some occasion that the

29. Van der Velde to McDonald, September 19, 1949, McDonald Papers, Columbia University, box 20, folder 11.

other is using "duress." What is needed is insistence by the UN and US that the armistices be translated into peace treaties; the best procedure towards this end would be to copy the Bunche procedure which had secured the armistices.

Turning from these generalities, I explained to Clifford the contents of the American note of May 28–29, the Israeli reply of eight days later [June 8], and the Department's counter-reply of sixteen days later [June 24]. I pointed out the embarrassment to the president and the weakening of our government's position through the use of the president's name save in the gravest crises, and only after a policy has been most carefully considered and the follow-up steps decided upon in the event that the initial démarche was rejected. I suggested that he read these documents and then decide for himself whether it was not true that the president's name had been misused and the American position rashly endangered. Perhaps I used the word prestige rather than position. At the end of our talk, Clifford suggested—I am not sure whether I had first suggested it—that he come back into the US-Israel picture. He said that he had been very favorably impressed with Elath when he had met him a few weeks earlier and that he would like to talk with him again. I promised to pass on this word. I left Clifford with the impression that he might resume his former role, at least to the extent of checking on any policy which involved the use of the president's name. He did not indicate that he resented my argumentative frankness.

Much bother about the change in my travel orders [McDonald extended his stay from two weeks to nearly five]. Brief meeting with [John] Peurifoy, assistant secretary [for administration]; he promised that if the Czechoslovakians made difficulty about the transfer of [Milton] Fried [as US labor attaché in Israel], he would clear the matter. He was interested in my illustration of power organization within the Department. That morning one of the most junior members in the [Bureau of] Near Eastern Affairs had come to ask me to tell him of our personnel needs in Israel. He was, he said, working on a project that had been assigned to him about personnel needs in this general area. I asked him if he had studied Hickok's report. He said he had not known that the Department's inspector had been in this area, but at any case this report was for the personnel division.

Peurifoy said that he was working to break down this kind of inefficiency, that more and more power in reference to personnel was being given to the operating division. Moreover, each division is to have an administrative officer, who will have overall supervision of personnel problems for his division. We also talked briefly of the need in Tel Aviv for an economic adviser. I left with the impression that the visit had been worthwhile, because I thought it would leave me in a position to make a direct appeal to Peurifoy later if that should be necessary.

Back to New York by air in time for the first few minutes of the FPA [Foreign Policy Association] board meeting.[30] Everyone was very cordial, but Eustace

---

30. McDonald had been chairman of the board of the FPA, 1919–1933.

Seligman could hardly hide what seemed to me to be his chagrin that he, a brilliantly successful and rich lawyer, was not an "ambassador."[31] Brief cocktails with Judge [Morris] Rothenberg,[32] whom Miss Schulkind insisted I must see alone. Early dinner with Emanuel Neumann and some of his friends. Neumann's remarks were very friendly, but a little labored in contrast with the brilliant and brief but meaningful statement [by] Eban. Others present included Arthur Lourie [and Louis] Lipsky.

To the theatre with the family to see *South Pacific*. Its wonderful music, perfect settings and cast, including Pinza and Mary Martin, made it perfect entertainment.

Friday, September 23

Met Mendel Fisher at the Commodore and later had a bite of lunch with him.[33]

Nearly an hour's conference with Cardinal Spellman and Monsignor [James] Griffiths[34] at 50th and Madison. This session had been preceded by a luncheon the previous week at the cardinal's residence, but which at the last moment he had been unable to attend because of a funeral in Boston.

On his own initiative, McDonald visited Cardinal Spellman's residence twice in September to discuss the PCC's draft instrument on Jerusalem. McDonald's diary first describes the first meeting at the Spellman residence, which Spellman could not attend, but which included Griffiths and Archbishop James Francis McIntyre of Los Angeles.[35]

At the earlier meeting at 50th Street and Madison the discussion showed no spirit of compromise. The monsignors (the archbishop had little to say) were adamant in their refusal to admit any argument against the PCC scheme for Jerusalem's internationalization. They denied that it would open the door to Russian intrigue, contending that this point was put forward by the Jews merely for debating purposes, that the latter had shown no real disposition to oppose Russian penetration, that on the contrary, [the] "turning over" [of] the Russian church property in the New City to the Moscow-controlled Russian church representative [Archimandrite Leonidas], was proof of co-

---

31. Eustace Seligman (1899–1975), corporate lawyer with Sullivan and Cromwell, 1914–1970; senior member of Foreign Policy Association; writer on international affairs.
32. Entry of August 11, 1948.
33. See entries of August 11 and August 27, 1948.
34. James Henry Ambrose Griffiths (1903–1964), named titular bishop of Gaza, October 15, 1949; consecrated by Cardinal Spellman in that role, January 18, 1950; named auxiliary bishop of archdiocese of New York by Pope Pius XII, 1955.
35. Archbishop James Francis Aloysius McIntyre (1886–1979), born in New York; archbishop of Los Angeles, 1948–1979; elevated to cardinal in 1953.

operation with the Soviets, or at least of an unwillingness to oppose them in Jerusalem.[36]

Similarly, the monsignors gave no indication that they were convinced that internationalization would abet the Russian intrigues with the Greek Orthodox. The monsignors were pleased by the PCC's report, and by Acheson's general endorsement. They were critical of Ben-Horin especially for his recent article in the [World Jewish] Congress Bulletin, entitled "The Catholic Empire" or some such title. They objected to the implication in this title, and to his quoting Monsignor Griffiths "in such a way as to distort the latter's meaning." As I was leaving the luncheon, Archbishop McIntyre said that he was sure the cardinal would want to see me. I said I was at the latter's disposal. Not being sure, however, that the archbishop was not being merely courteous, I called Tom Murray[37] and asked him to check for me. The word that came back bore out the archbishop's statement.

My conference with [Cardinal Spellman on September 23] lasted from five until nearly six o'clock. The only other person present was Monsignor Griffiths. As we talked, it became clear to me that the cardinal was more realistic in his approach to the problem of Jerusalem than was his younger colleague. As I set forth the difficulties of the problem as I saw them, the cardinal two or three times said in substance that he shared my point of view. In contrast, Monsignor Griffiths clung tenaciously to the arguments which he had advanced at the earlier meeting. He was inclined to discard the reports that Cardinal Tisserant favored a compromise.[38] As to the Vatican's view, the cardinal reiterated that he knew only what His Holiness had set forth in his two encyclicals [October, 24, 1948; April 15, 1949]. These, of course, called for a much broader and more absolute internationalization than that of the PCC. As I was leaving, the cardinal expressed in very cordial terms his feelings about my work in Israel.

In a speech on September 26, Eban presented an alternative plan for Jerusalem whereby the Old City alone would be internationalized as a kind of religious-historical museum. Israel made its arguments to other countries on the self-determination of Jews in Jerusalem, the PCC's lack of any provision for implementation, and Israel's respect for the international nature of the Holy Places. Israeli diplomats were

36. See entry of January 20, 1949; Bialer, *Cross on the Star of David*, 144–153. Israeli legal experts had concluded that the Soviet government was the legal heir to tsarist Russian church properties as well as other former official tsarist Russian properties in Jerusalem. The legal turn-over process was completed between June and August 1949.

37. See entry of January 7, 1949. Murray was an influential Catholic layman in the New York archdiocese and close to Cardinal Spellman.

38. Cardinal Eugene Tisserant (1884–1972), head of the Congregation for Oriental Churches. The Israelis contacted him and learned that his views on Jerusalem "were close to those of Israel and [that] he had made them known to the Pope." The Israelis hoped Tisserant would help prevent an open breach with the Vatican and that, as a French bishop, he would also have a positive effect on the French government. A confidant of Tisserant in Jerusalem urged the Israelis to back the French government insofar as international control of the Holy Places was concerned. See *DFPI*, v. 4, d. 273, 296, 314; in general Bialer, *Cross on the Star of David*, 13–14.

optimistic that most of the Latin American states, despite Vatican pressure, would support the Israeli idea. Argentina, for instance, was more interested in a commercial treaty with Israel. Even the secretary-general, who worried about the legality and expense of the PCC's Jerusalem plan, urged the Israelis to draw up an alternative scheme.[39]

Saturday, September 24

On the eve of sailing there were too many chores to permit a last round of golf.

Pre-luncheon conference with Jimmy [James N.] Rosenberg. He would like to be brought into the Israel picture and suggested that I might tell Eban or Elath about it. This I shall do.

The afternoon and evening delightful visit from the Philadelphia McDonalds. We regretted only that Ellen and Jack were unable to come.

Sunday, September 25

To the Abramses for a brief lunch. In the afternoon Mrs. [Hanna] Colt had her tea party for us, which was graced by the presence of Donald at his first public formal appearance. His behavior, while being shown off, left much to be desired, for he cried out his lungs. But later, when he was put in his carriage out of doors, he slept like an angel.

In the evening to see [Abe] Feinberg for a moment. We agreed about the roles of Rusk and Burdett and about the necessity for facing the prospect of a long series of difficult battles on specific issues.

Monday, September 26

Lunch with Mendel Fisher, who despite his terrible operation, seemed almost as well as usual. He urged me to let him arrange my initial post-ambassadorial tour, saying that he would be able to get me many, many engagements at handsome fees.

Tea with Rose Halprin and members of the American group of the [Jewish] Agency and including Nahum [Goldmann], [Marian] Greenberg and others. They asked me questions about the Washington situation and were a little taken back when I told them frankly that—in answer to Mrs. Halprin's question—I saw no role for them. The official representation, as they knew, was that of Elath and the embassy. The unofficial representation, so far as this is effective, is in the hands of individual Jews who happen to be *persona grata* to the White House, but who are nearly all outside the regular Zionist organizations. I cited the examples of Abe Feinberg, Albert M. Greenfield,[40] Jack Arvey, Eddie Jacobson, David Dubinsky, Joseph Potofsky, et al.

---

39. Published documents in *DFPI*, v. 4, d. 275, 283, 289, 291, 377.
40. Albert M. Greenfield (1887–1967), Ukrainian-born Philadelphia-based real estate developer, banker, investor, philanthropist, and supporter of the Democratic Party; served as treasurer for the Democratic Party in 1948 and was a confidant of Truman to whom the president

Little Forum meeting in Bronxville.[41] Almost immediately after my talk I had to leave for the night train to Washington.

Tuesday, September 27

First thing on the morning of the 27th I spoke to Dave Niles and said goodbye to him.

Then followed my final and most satisfactory conference with [colleagues from] the Foreign Buildings Operations [concerning renovations and repairs to the ambassador's residence in Tel Aviv].

At twelve o'clock I met McGhee and Wilkins for what I assumed was to have been a comprehensive conference, since it was to be my last. We had hardly had fifteen minutes together, however, when a call came from Rusk. McGhee immediately excused himself and let Wilkins carry on. At that point, McGhee's secretary said that Rusk wanted Wilkins also, and that was the end of our talk. McGhee began by asking me what groups I had been seeing in my period of consultation, which had been made the justification for the change in my travel orders from approximately two weeks to approximately five weeks. I told of meeting with various Jewish organizations, the Quakers, the Catholics. McGhee questioned me about the Catholic attitude towards Jerusalem, but I had no time to reply fully when the conference was broken up. Wilkins made the point that it was not true, as the Israelis insisted, that the PCC Jerusalem plan had not been fully discussed in Lausanne.

Lunch in Washington as the guest of Elath. Present were most of the men from the [Bureau of] Near Eastern Affairs and Rusk. It was a pleasant, informal party. At the end, Elath spoke briefly but warmly of our association and my work. I, not wishing to be serious, spoke very briefly. In concluding, I said I did not know what the purpose of the Department's system in treating visiting chiefs of mission was, but I was sure of its effect; it was to make the chiefs glad to get back to their posts. Later at the Department, chatting with Stanton Griffis, he said that he was in complete agreement with my interpretation. Griffis, who is being briefed for his mission to the Argentine [reassigned in 1949], was pessimistic about the Arab refugee situation and the delay in naming his successor. At the luncheon I had told Elath of Clifford's desire to see him again.

After the Elath luncheon, on the way back to the office with McGhee, the latter said to me: "Well, there has been a great deal left undiscussed, hasn't there?" Naturally, I had to agree. He said, "Well, we will just have to 'sweat it out.'" Had a brief informal talk with [Wells] Stabler,[42] who said that the Department, despite current British urging, was unwilling to lay down a specific

offered a cabinet post or ambassadorship in 1949. See Dan Rottenberg, *The Outsider: Albert M. Greenfield and the Fall of the Protestant Establishment* (Philadelphia: Temple University Press, 2014).

41. Little Forum in Bronxville, a rotating monthly dinner and lecture series held in various homes to which about forty people were invited. Guest speakers varied, with heavy emphasis on Protestant clergy.

42. Reassigned to the Near Eastern Affairs department after his return from Amman.

territorial program. Also, the Department had no specific plans about refugees. Had there been more time, I think Stabler would have told me more.

Mid-afternoon, an hour or so conference with high Air Force officers at the Pentagon. Their questions showed a wide knowledge, [and] much less concern about Russian penetration in Israel than I had anticipated. From that conference, despite the rain and mist, I decided to take the plane. I was rewarded by clear skies very soon after leaving Washington, and my arrival in New York, not only in time for dinner but to clear up some odds and ends at the office. Talked to [Abba Hillel] Silver on the telephone in Washington. He seemed unusually appreciative of my remembering to get in touch with him. Tried again vainly to reach Felix Frankfurter. Dinner at Halsey and Janet's.

Wednesday, September 28

Very important luncheon with Albert M. Greenfield at the Biltmore. My first impression of Greenfield was that of a very successful, but rather vain businessman. Later, from his questions and his reactions to my points, I concluded that he, though not a Zionist, is deeply interested in, and discriminately informed on, central problems of US-Israel relationships. I told him with frankness of my fear that undue emphasis on general principles and [the] unwise readiness to use the president's name were disadvantageous to American interests and, in effect, unfair to Israel. Specifically, I told him of two personalities whose activities I regarded as especially detrimental. He was careful to note the names and to have me be so explicit that he could fix the details in his mind. He promised to speak to our mutual friend, and I am sure that he will do so.[43] I regarded the conference as particularly useful.

Tea with the Tom Murrays at their palatial home on Park Avenue, directly opposite Hunter College. Our talk was partly about family, their three Jesuit sons, the married children, and our children. I promised to tell His Holiness of my visit.

Spoke to Gerold Frank and left for him at the FPA an autographed photograph—that of Ben-Gurion and myself. Pleasant visit on the phone with John D. Rockefeller III, who returned my call.[44] He may be coming out to the Middle East.

Went directly from the Murrays' to the Biltmore, where Mr. [Samuel] Leidesdorf and his group of UJA workers were waiting for me. I made there my only semi-public address during my stay at home. On my arrival, the UJA had been very insistent that I speak at the national conference in Washington and at one or two other key meetings, particularly Boston. But after a couple of conferences with the Department, it was decided that since I could speak only from an approved text, it would be better for me not to speak at all.

43. Surely a reference to the president. Greenfield met with Truman at the White House in January 1949 and January 1950.
44. John D. Rockefeller III (1906–1978), philanthropist with special interest in Asia; prime mover behind the creation of Lincoln Center in New York City; brother of Nelson Rockefeller.

My talk, which followed the showing of a brief, almost gruesome UJA film depicting [Jewish] refugee conditions in Israel,[45] recognized frankly the enormous difficulties inherent in Israel's present situation but nonetheless struck a moderately optimistic note based on the following chief considerations: 1) the desperate need; 2) the willingness of the people themselves to sacrifice; 3) the energy, devotion and intelligence of the Jews in Israel; 4) the extraordinary capacity and devotion of the Israeli leaders; and 5) finally, my confidence that world Jewry and especially American Jewry would continue steadfast in their support. Afterwards Ben Abrams told me that he regarded it as the best UJA talk heard that year. Leidesdorf was seemingly deeply moved and said to me, "Anything you want will be done." Ben urged me to dine with him and a small group but I had to hurry over with Max Abelman to my dinner with Manny [Goldman] at the Pavilion.

UJA fundraising efforts were falling short of goals, and Israeli officials dealing with the absorption of new Jewish immigrants were worried. On September 8, Haaretz reported that, with Jewish Agency funds running low, the absorption system could break down because the Agency "will be unable to feed those [some 71,000] now living in reception camps."[46]

Manny's guests included one of his brothers, his sister and her husband, Hymie Ross, and a group of Irish friends, together with Mr. [Maximilian] Moss, the president of the Jewish Hospital.[47] The food was excellent but the prices so fantastic that they somewhat spoiled my enjoyment. Afterwards, Manny drove me home and gave me a gift for Ruth.

Home by about ten and up until midnight packing.

Thursday, September 29

Up very early, packed and ready to leave in Manny's car by about a quarter of nine. It was hard to say goodbye to the family and perhaps most of all to Donald, who will have changed so by the time we next see him.

Ben and Biddy Abrams were at the dock. The former asked me to give messages to Sharett, Kaplan, and Ben-Gurion.

45. Refers to the last part of *Homecoming, 1949*, produced by Joseph Krumgold and Norman Lourie.
46. Ford to secretary of state, no. 141, September 9, 1949 and no. 143, September 23, 1949, McDonald Papers, USHMM, box 8, folder 2.
47. Maximilian Moss (1897–1964), Brooklyn-born lawyer, judge, and fundraiser for many Jewish and non-Jewish causes; president and chairman of the executive committee of Jewish Hospital in Brooklyn until his death.

16. October 1949

The Voyage, September 29–Tuesday, October 4

Cabled [William] Gowen on the 30th regarding possible audience with His Holiness on the 9th or 10th.[1]

Young Henry Ford was on board with a party, but I made no effort to renew my acquaintance with him.[2] Later, I thought this might have been a mistake; a talk might have opened the way to some suggestion about his foundation operating in Israel.

Almost the only conversation during the voyage which deserves careful recording is that with George Warren, who together with General Wood,[3] were on their way to the IRO [International Refugee Organization] meeting in Geneva. Warren, as he had been in Washington, was pessimistic about the efforts which would have to be made to secure funds for the Arab refugees' maintenance during the next year. He recognized that the result of the Clapp Mission [Economic Survey Mission—ESM] might be to supply a more plausible basis for these appeals by suggesting the beginning of work relief. Nonetheless, Warren thought that the effort would be very difficult.

As to the Department, Warren shared my view about the increasing complexity of this organization and the ever-larger distance between the technicians in the Department and the men in the field and the top officials. He regards [Dean] Rusk as the dominant personality in the formation of day-to-day political policies and thinks that he has a special interest in, and fixed ideas about, US-Israeli relations. Rusk's extraordinarily quick rise to his present position, skipping the post of assistant secretary,[4] and his heretofore nearly continuous success with his superiors, (first in the War Department and then later with Marshall and Lovett and now with Webb and Acheson) has given him a degree of confidence that may cause his audacity to trip him up.

---

1. See entry of October 19, 1949.
2. Henry Ford II (1917–1987), president of Ford Motor Company, 1945–1960, and simultaneously president of the Ford Foundation, 1943–1950. McDonald had discussed with the elder Ford the settling of Jewish refugees on Ford-owned land in Brazil in 1941.
3. Major General John S. Wood (1888–1966), fought in France during World War I; professor of military science, University of Wisconsin, 1939–1940; 1st Infantry Division, Third Army, 1940–1941; led 4th Armored Division in Operation Cobra in France following the Normandy landing; after retirement led IRO in Austria, 1947–1950, and worked for the UN in the Far East, 1952–1953.
4. In May 1949 Rusk was promoted from director of the State Department's Office of Political Affairs (the UN desk) to deputy undersecretary of state.

What Warren had to say about Rusk tended to confirm the impression which the Israelis had told me they had. They had cited Rusk's vigorous initiative during the first weeks of May 1948 in trying to "bludgeon" the Jewish authorities into non-declaration of the Jewish state.[5] This interpretation also made more plausible [John] Waldo's[6] statement that the May 28–29 note had not gone through the regular channels of the [Bureau of Near Eastern Affairs] but had been drafted in Rusk's office and sent out without the prior knowledge of the lower echelon. This would help to account for its lamentably loose language.

As to his own role in the Department, Warren said that he was left very much to himself. He was not usually consulted even in the areas of his special competence, he had no fixed superior, [and] he drafted his own instructions in connection with IRO or related problems. Sometimes the Department seemed surprised that he insisted—as he had in the matter of requesting [William Hallam] Tuck to reconsider his resignation,[7] a move favored by the British and nearly all the states members of the IRO—on adhering firmly to those instructions.

I should have indicated earlier that, one day in the Department, I was told casually that [a] decision had been made to hold a regional conference of the chiefs of mission in this area. No reference was made, of course, to the fact that my suggestion of such a conference six or eight months ago had been summarily rejected by the Department.[8] I was asked merely what would be my preference of a place for the meeting. I strongly objected to Beirut, which had been mentioned, on various grounds, and suggested instead Cyprus as much more neutral and as being just [as], if not more, convenient.

Paris, Tuesday, October 4–Saturday October 8

The landing and luggage arrangements of the White Star Cunard at Cherbourg could not have been improved upon; the trip to Paris, though, a little over five hours. We were met at the station by the incomparable Mr. Bolton,[9] who whisked us to the [Hôtel de] Crillon in no time. There we found a suite for which, during the one night we kept it, we had to pay only the rate for a double room.

Telephoned Clifford through the embassy and told him that the more I had thought about our talk [of September 22], the more important I thought it that he should read the [Truman] note of May 28–29 and the two others which grew out of it. He said he would send for them and study them. I added that I

5. Brecher, *American Diplomacy and the Israeli War of Independence*, 12–13; Tal, *War in Palestine*, 84–86; Cohen, *Palestine and the Great Powers*, 303.

6. John A. Waldo, Bureau of Near Eastern, South Asian, and African Affairs, Department of State.

7. Entry of August 9, 1948.

8. Entries of April 6, April 9, June 14, July 9, July 11, 1949.

9. Kenyon Bolton (1912–1983), attaché, US embassy, Paris.

was anxious that he should make up his own mind whether or not the president had been well served.

Cabled my Philadelphia friend [Arthur M. Greenfield] and asked him to call me, which he did, shortly after the Clifford call was completed. He was very much interested in what I had said and in my forthcoming visit with His Holiness. He seemed, too, to be most appreciative that I had suggested he call.

Lunch and dinner with the Benins as their guest with no mention by him of business.[10]

Benin said he was optimistic about Israeli-Egyptian relations; many Jews had returned to Egypt and had resumed unmolested their managerial and other business positions; there was an increasing recognition among Egyptians that the Jews were essential to Egyptian prosperity.[11] He had the impression that Egypt might be the first to break with the Israel boycott policy.

Met Ambassador [David] Bruce[12] at the airport, where he had come to greet the returning French Foreign Minister, [Robert] Schuman.[13] Bruce told me of an amusing defeat suffered by [Frederick] Larkin [chief of the Division of Foreign Buildings Operations (FBO)] at the hands of Mrs. [Perle] Mesta, the new US representative to Luxembourg. This society gal had gone shopping in Paris at the most expensive places for items for her residence and then presented the bill to Larkin. The latter, horrified at such "extravagance," said that Congress would never approve. Mrs. Mesta is said to have replied: "I have more friends in Congress than you have."[14]

Quite unexpected and pleasant meeting with [Chaim] Weizmann on the Rue de Rivoli. He was looking unusually well.[15] [Brief] visit at the JDC headquarters with [Joseph] Schwartz, [Moses A.] Leavitt,[16] and one or two others. There I had in the strictest confidence suggested my impression that some of the authorities in Israel had come to be a little disregardful of foreign opinion. I mentioned Sharett as one of the men who no longer "listened well."

10. Menahem Musa (Maurice) Benin, Jewish-Egyptian entrepreneur; property confiscated in 1949 and later returned. See Levin, *Locked Doors*, 90–99.

11. During the war against Israel the Egyptian government arrested several hundred leading Jews, including non-Zionists, and placed their businesses under state supervision. Sporadic violence by the Muslim Brotherhood against ordinary Jewish enterprises broke out in response to Israeli victories in the summer of 1948. Between July 1949 and February 1950, the government released leading Egyptian Jews and restored their assets. Still, between 15,000 to 20,000 lower and middle-class Egyptian Jews—a fifth to a quarter of the Jewish population in Egypt—left the country between 1949 and 1951. Gudrun Krämer, *The Jews in Modern Egypt, 1914–1952* (Seattle: University of Washington Press, 1989), 211–218.

12. David K. E. Bruce (1898–1977), US ambassador to France, 1949–1952.

13. Schuman was returning from the UN General Assembly meeting in New York.

14. Perle Mesta (1888–1975), noted socialite known for lavish Washington parties; political supporter of Truman; US ambassador to Luxembourg, July 1949–1953. McDonald was in the process of purchasing furniture in Rome for his Tel Aviv residence.

15. Weizmann had been in Switzerland since July for eye treatments. He returned to Israel from Paris on October 10.

16. Moses A. Leavitt (1894–1965), JDC executive vice chairman after 1947; helped formulate JDC policy decisions after the war concerning aid to Jewish refugees; helped channel immigration to Israel; also active with the Palestine Economic Corporation.

I heard nothing in Paris about Mrs. [Yolande] Harmer or her son, so I assume that, as they had planned when we met them in Paris in August, they had gone to Cairo for her convalescence and preparatory to their "exodus" to Israel.

Colonel Archibald was very unhappy when, at our first talk in Paris, I told him of my appointment with His Holiness in Rome for the 10th, which would delay our return. He was fearful of embarrassment to his crew and his Israeli guests through their possible lack of funds for the extra days. Actually, they were all delighted, but nobody was so delighted as Curtis Barnes, who greeted each new announcement of delay as a condemned man might each new day's reprieve. My two or three visits to the Louvre gave me an even larger-than-before impression of the richness of the galleries.

The trip to Rome was not nearly as unpleasant as the colonel had threatened it would be. The plane was cold, and we took turns standing up to the heaters. But the weather was not very rough nor the bucket seats too uncomfortable.

Met at the airport by the always-cooperative Mr. Adam,[17] we were at the Excelsior by 5:30, while the others went to what is for me the grim and forbidding Ambassador [Hotel].

Rome [and Greece], Saturday October 8–Wednesday, October 12

Within a few minutes after our reaching our room, the Israeli minister to Rome [Shlomo Ginossar][18] called to say that he had received instructions from Tel Aviv to see me as soon as possible on the most urgent business.[19] I put him off until 9:00 pm.

Ambassador [James] Dunn[20] invited us to a cocktail party at 6:00. We arrived—all of us—at seven, but still in time. Everybody was impressed by the elegance and luxury of the residence. Dunn and I had a good talk. He complained that the FBO, which had allowed him to spend his own money in making the house livable and furnishing it before it was government-owned, now was annoying him and his wife by wanting to tear it apart.

Dunn and I found ourselves in the same corner on the issue of the Department's consistent failure to consult the men in the field in advance of the formulation of basic policies. He said that he, for example, was never asked about the Italian colonies.[21] And when I complained that the Department had not confided in me as to its future policies in Israel, he commented in almost identical

17. Archibald Adam, attaché in US embassy in Rome.
18. Shlomo Ginossar (1890–1969), Israel's minister to Italy, who presented his credentials in July 1949; son of famed Zionist philosopher Ahad Ha'am.
19. Meeting likely focused on Israeli concerns regarding the Vatican and Jerusalem.
20. James Clement Dunn (1890–1979), US ambassador to Italy, 1946–1952.
21. The peace treaty with Italy in 1947 provided for the victors to follow the recommendations of the UN General Assembly concerning Italy's former colonies, including Libya, Italian Somaliland, and Eritrea. The General Assembly debated the issue in the 1949 session, calling in November for independence for Libya, independence after UN trusteeship for Italian Somaliland with Italy as the trusteeship authority, and further study regarding the status of Eritrea. The Italians pressed their allies for a continuation of colonial rule.

language to that used by Knox on the same subject: "this is not a reflection upon you; it more likely means merely that the Department has not yet got a policy."

The audience with His Holiness was in most respects a repetition of that at Castel Gandolfo in August of last year.[22] This time Ruth was with me during the whole talk, and Colonel Archibald and Captain Cashman were presented at the end. The latter seemed to make a special impression on His Holiness.

After the usual civilities, I said to His Holiness that, returning to Israel as ambassador, I was present in my personal capacity with no instructions from Washington. Then, having received his tacit permission to talk about Jerusalem, I told him that it was my personal impression that the essential interests of both Church and Israel were "not irreconcilable." My double negative seeming to bother him, I reiterated my thought in simpler terms. He then pressed me for a few minutes with questions all directed to determine whether or not the Israeli authorities, in my opinion, would give satisfactory guarantees and would adhere loyally to them. I gave a personal affirmative answer to all such questions, adding that I felt that the Israeli authorities would welcome an opportunity for direct negotiations, whenever the Vatican indicated that these seemed desired.

A very revealing question was put by His Holiness in connection with my account of my recent visits to 50th Street. I said that it seemed to me that Cardinal Spellman was more realistic in his attitude than were some of his monsignor colleagues. The pope quickly said: "Do you mean Monsignor Griffiths?" This I thought remarkable, because it had been Monsignor Griffiths who had led the uncompromising argument, and yet he is but one of several monsignors around the cardinal. Obviously, His Holiness's knowledge of 50th Street is more than casual. The pope seemed pleased by my friendly and favorable comment on the personality and work of Monsignor McMahon. His Holiness said in effect: "I hope he can work out a settlement." This, though not proof, was to me another indication that Monsignor McMahon's role in this area is not exclusively philanthropic. I was pleased with what seemed to me to be the pope's improved appearance since we were with him fourteen months before. He seemed more rested and even more alert.

The Borghese Gallery with its beautiful Titian, Raphaels and its gorgeous Correggio, and the Vatican galleries, were as always richly rewarding. Visits with Noah and Eli [Karlin] were entertaining.

Weather having delayed our departure, we were out to the airport and ready to take off at ten on the morning of Wednesday, the 12th. The flight to Athens was pleasant. We were met at the airport and taken directly to the Grand Bretagne Hotel.

[Leslie] Rood and his wife Dorothy, who had been with us on the Anglo-American Committee of Inquiry, had a bite of lunch with us and took us out to

22. Entry of August 10, 1948.

the Acropolis. This gave us an opportunity for a comparison of notes on developments since the spring of 1946.[23] The large reception given by the Gradys at their palatial-like residence to the congressional committee[24] was enlivened by Mrs. Grady's effusions to the effect that she could hardly bear to have us leave Athens without having a meal with them. I could hardly refrain from telling her that on our several visits to Athens, her husband had quite restrainedly managed to refrain from inviting us to the house.[25]

One of the American generals with whom I was talking [to] with Rood had an extremely interesting theory to the effect that Soviet expansion throughout Asia and a comparable expansion possibly through Europe would weaken, rather than strengthen, Soviet power in an armed conflict with the US. American air power, he calculated, could and would successfully cut off the communications of the outlying Soviet posts and at the same time reduce Soviet production potential. To my question whether the Soviet planning staff itself realized this potential weakness, the general could give no competent answer.

Thursday, October 13

The trip from Athens to Tel Aviv was broken by lunch in Cyprus and so passed quickly, bringing us to Lydda exactly at 4 o'clock. It was good to be home even in the midst of the painters' mess at the house. The reception at the Ford's gave an opportunity for meeting many old friends.

Friday, October 14

Jacob Herzog came in to talk about Israel's relations with the Vatican and promised to come back and tell me later more of developments since I had left.[26]

McDonald told Herzog that Cardinal Spellman in New York was "frightened" of the Greek Orthodox link with the Soviets in Jerusalem, which Spellman said was born of the Greek Orthodox fear of Roman Catholic domination there. He further told Herzog that the pope "enquired at length [concerning the] efficacy [of] Israeli guarantees [regarding the] Holy Places."[27]

---

23. Leslie L. Rood (1930–2010), served as one of the US staff members on the Anglo-American Committee of Inquiry and helped protect the integrity of the Committee's recommendations; assigned to the US Embassy in Athens after May 1949. See Goda et al., eds., *To the Gates of Jerusalem.*

24. See entry of October 18, 1949.

25. See entry of November 17, 1948. Henry F. Grady, US ambassador to Greece, 1948–1950; served as head of US Cabinet Committee that traveled to London to discuss Palestine with the British government in 1946; opposed by McDonald and the rest of the US members of the Anglo-American Committee of Inquiry for ignoring their recommendations; unceremoniously recalled by Truman from London. See Goda et al., eds., *To the Gates of Jerusalem,* 239–250.

26. For these see also Herzog to Eban, September 29, 1949, *DFPI,* v. 4, d. 314.

27. Herzog to Eban, October 19, 1949, *DFPI,* v. 4, d. 354. Elath reported later in the month that, according to French sources, McDonald was overly optimistic concerning the pope's personal attitude, which, Elath said, still leaned toward internationalization of all Jerusalem and its environs. Elath to Sharett, October 26, 1949, *DFPI,* v. 4, d. 371.

Just before sunset we belatedly reached the journalists' reception at HaKirya.

Saturday, October 15

In the morning Mr. [Emanuel] Bornstein and Mr. Probst came to tell me of their difficulties with the government and the disinclination of the latter to give any public support to the CARE [Cooperative for Assistance and Relief Everywhere] campaign. I promised to talk to [Golda] Meyerson and Kaplan and possibly Ben-Gurion to discover if there was any way to break down the economic and political arguments against full Israeli cooperation.

Lunch with the Karlins and tea with the Fords. I should have recorded that, at the Thursday evening party at Ford's, I talked at length with [William] Cleland, the new intelligence adviser to [George] McGhee.[28] With his two decades or more of residence in Arab countries and close association with the Arab people, he nonetheless remains so reticent about his sympathy towards their cause that I felt more suspicious than if he had been an open advocate. Returning to Beirut the next day, Cleland promised to carry my apologies to Gordon Clapp for the circumstances—my audience with the pope on the 10th, which precluded my return to Israel in time for Clapp's visit here.[29]

Sunday, October 16

Dr. Ernst Jokl, a civil servant in the South African government, returning from a physical development international convention in Stockholm, told me the very interesting story of that organization's proposal to sponsor in Israel a research project in backward (physically and psychologically) persons among the immigrants and Arab refugees, along the lines of the poor white study conducted in South Africa years earlier, which had been financed by the Carnegie Corporation. His desire was that I transmit and if possible endorse the organization's appeal to the Carnegie people for funds. I promised that if Ford approved, I would do so.[30]

28. William Wendell Cleland (1888–1972), scholar of Egypt at the American University of Cairo in the 1930s who studied the Egyptian rural economy, worked with the Office of War Information in World War II, and pressed for closer cooperation between the American University of Cairo and the State Department. In 1947 he was a member of the Department's Division of Research for the Near East, and he opposed the UN partition scheme for Palestine. Afterward he served with the Department's Office of Intelligence Research, where he functioned as an intelligence adviser for the Bureau of Near Eastern, South Asian, and African Affairs.

29. The Economic Survey Mission, headed by Clapp and his three deputies, made a two-day preliminary visit to Tel Aviv in mid-October. Clapp reported to Ford that there was no progress on repatriation or compensation for Arab refugees, but that the visit was useful for future discussion. Ford to secretary of state, joint weeka no. 42, October 14, 1949, McDonald Papers, USHMM, box 8, folder 3.

30. Ernst Jokl (1907–1997), German-born expert on physical development; left Germany for South Africa in 1933; helped with training of South African athletes; advised the South African armed forces during World War II; worked in Ministry for Medicine and Instruction, 1943–1950.

Breakfast with Robert Nathan.[31] There was not time for an elaborate discussion. Nonetheless, I was very glad to hear his general impression after six-years' absence and in the light of his close association with Israeli affairs in Washington. On the whole, he was moderately optimistic. There is no problem in Israel, he said, which money will not solve. He believes that more and more capital will come into the country for investment, but the only question is whether it will come in sufficient amounts and rapidly enough to permit the continuation of the present rate of immigration, or if that inflow will have to be checked. He thought that the handling of potential capital was being steadily improved. What surprised me most in his talk was his declaration that the Arab boycott was not a basic hindrance to Israel's progress.[32] He thought that there was no danger of this economic exclusion being fatal. Speaking of the abortive proposal to postpone the Haifa port allocation, he had the same views about the disastrous effects of publication as had Elath.[33] He even seemed to go further by saying that the news would have jeopardized all forms of American economic cooperation on a loan basis.

Monday, October 17

At 11:30 Ford and I began with [the] Sharett conference (Shiloah and Comay also present), which lasted for an hour and a half. Ford first paraphrased the Department's despatch of some days earlier on Jerusalem. He had previously had Comay's and Shiloah's replies to the same despatch.[34] Sharett's comment did not differ substantially from those of his colleagues earlier. The PCC plan had stirred up sharp reactions in Israel, not because the government wished these, but because feelings were so strong. These were sharper because of the attacks in the Catholic press throughout the world, attacks which, he was glad to note, seemed to have diminished.[35] The PCC report, Sharett said,

---

31. Entry of June 23, 1948. Nathan was to meet with government officials and businessmen to discuss ways of increasing the flow of private investments from the United States. JTA *Bulletin*, September 27, 1949. Nathan's role from 1944 to 1946 is discussed in Goda et al., eds., *To the Gates of Jerusalem*, 53.

32. Dean Acheson encouraged all representatives to try to break the impasse between the Israelis and the Arab states. He noted that Arab representatives had to be told that the Arab states, "while counting unrealistically upon econ[omic] boycott to obtain political objectives, are sacrificing opportunity for econ[omic] development and for social reform." Acheson circular airgram, October 14, 1949, *FRUS*, 1949, v. VI, 1428–1429.

33. Entries of August 23 and 25, 1949.

34. Refers to Department telegram no. 637 of September 30. On October 4, 1949, Ford relayed to Michael Comay the State Department's argument that the PCC draft instrument on Jerusalem provided a realistic approach to a permanent international regime there, and its earnest hope that Israel would cooperate. Comay relayed the official Israeli belief that the proposal "does not represent common ground," as well as Shiloah's comment that Israel was working on a counter-proposal. Ford to secretary of state, no. 726, October 5, 1949, *FRUS*, 1949, v. VI, 1419–1420; Ford to secretary of state, joint weeka no. 41, October 7, 1949, McDonald Papers, USHMM, box 8, folder 3. Eban's steps at the UN concerning a counter-proposal are in *DFPI*, v. 4, d. 337, 341, 347, 348, 349, 351, 364.

35. Sharett later learned that the easing of Catholic press criticism was on Vatican orders, but Elath cautioned that the Vatican might have toned down its rhetoric only for the lead-up to the UN debate on Jerusalem. Sharett to Elath, October 26, 1949, *DFPI*, v. 4, d. 370 and n. 1.

was a "provocation" because it was anachronistic and impracticable. The idea of a neutral chairman named by the UN over a joint Israel-Arab board would give to the chairman absolute control. Second, the limitation of immigration was wholly unacceptable; third, demilitarization was impracticable and unreal, except as a potential long-range ideal.

On the merits of the question, he recognized the rights of all the three great religions, and had to point out that the major shrines of all three were in Arab hands. Israel was prepared to give every guarantee for internationalization of the Holy Places, but such [an] international body [was] not to have any territorial authority. He hoped for an agreed solution. He was still uncertain whether he personally would go to Lake Success. Then he showed us pictures of the devastation of the Jewish portion of the Old City. It was then my turn to summarize my Washington impressions and those I had gained in Rome. Sharett said he was grateful for my frankness, but I interrupted to say that I had not been wholly frank. Sharett hoped that I would tell Ben-Gurion my opinion of Elath.

When I finished, Sharett came to what was evidently really occupying him. He launched into a long tirade against the reported prospective Iraq-Syrian Federation. It will, he said, change the whole background of the Middle East and might have explosive effects. Each country is, he continued, already comparatively large, underdeveloped, with vast unsolved internal problems, including those of recalcitrant minorities. [A] federation would probably result in less efficiency and less honesty. In Israel, such a federation does not "breed counsels of stability." Israel accepted [the] November 29 [partition scheme] on [the] theory of [a] small independent Arab state. Now with a larger neighbor, Israel has greater need for territory, and no neighbor has comparable claim. Moreover, there is a "larger cake to be divided." Now, there is danger of the whole basis being destroyed. Personally, he does not want a discussion of enlarged Israel frontiers. [An] Iraq and Syria Federation foreshadows absorption of Jordan. Under such circumstances [the] ideal of peace seems impractical. He is taking up with [the] British and French [the] possibility of their opposing. Egypt and Saudi Arabia are certain to, and Turkey might, oppose. Parenthetically, he told us that Israel and Turkey had agreed to exchange "diplomatic representatives."

Repeatedly, Sharett stressed that Nuri [al-] Said, the Iraqi [prime minister], was looking forward to the federation as an essential step towards the second round of the war with Israel. Nuri's 1942 *Blue Book* ideal of an Arab power stretching from the Persian Gulf to the Mediterranean was never so close to realization.[36] Temporarily the Iraqi regent[37] might be [the] king of

36. Refers to Nuri al-Said's *Blue Book*, which called for Arab unity beginning with the states in the Fertile Crescent in such a way that would reconcile nationalists with monarchists and the Hashemites with their dynastic rivals in the Middle East. He called for an Arab league that would have a common defense and foreign policy. See Louis, *The British Empire in the Middle East*, 313–315.
37. Crown Prince Abdullah (1913–1958), who acted as regent for King Faisal II (1939–1958), who officially reached majority in 1953.

Syria, and the king of Iraq [would] remain as king there. But unity for military and foreign purposes would be achieved.

On August 14, 1949, Syrian strongman Husni al-Za'im, who had resisted King Abdullah's idea of a Jordan-dominated "Greater Syria," was overthrown in a military coup and executed, along with his prime minister, Muhsin al-Barazi. Discussions began afterward between members of the new Syrian government and members of the Iraqi government concerning union of the states.[38]

Sharett had Elath and Eban inform the State Department that such a union would destabilize the Middle East as prelude to an Arab "second round" against Israel and that it would bring calls for Israel's annexation of the remainder of Palestine. He informed them further that, with McDonald, he had raised no specific requests so as to prevent the United States, as a quid pro quo, from demanding Israeli concessions over Jerusalem, refugees, or frontiers.[39] McDonald reported to Washington that no useful purpose would be served by raising the Jerusalem issue in Tel Aviv again before the General Assembly discussed it. The Israelis would not change their minds, and Sharett was more concerned with the Syria-Iraq union.[40]

Meanwhile, there were grave developments within Iraq; a new wave of persecutions, arrests and torture, talk of confiscation of property with probably 2,000 Jews in prison.[41] He hoped for moderating influences from the outside and that possibly the United States would act again as it had eight months ago [*sic*] following the execution of [Shafiq] Ades, an Iraqi Jew.[42] A reported recent Iraqi proposal of an exchange of 100,000 Iraqi Jews for a comparable number of Arab refugees seems sinister in the light of the above. Shiloah intervened to say that this proposal might even be a smokescreen to placate Iraqi minorities by suggesting to them attacks on local Jews.[43]

---

38. Overview in Daniel Pipes, *Greater Syria: The History of an Ambition* (New York: Oxford University Press, 1990).

39. Sharett to Elath, October 16, 1949, *DFPI*, v. 4, d. 345; Sharett to Elath, October 17, 1949, *DFPI*, v. 4, d. 346; Memorandum by McGhee, October 18, 1949, *FRUS*, 1949, v. VI, 1440–1441.

40. McDonald to secretary of state, no. 756, October 18, 1949, *FRUS*, 1949, v. VI, 1444–1445.

41. See entry of January 14, 1949. Sharett refers to the most recent wave of anti-Jewish persecution in Iraq in October–November 1949, beginning with arrests of Jews in Baghdad on Yom Kippur (October 7), and the torture of some for confessions as to their supposed Zionism. From December 1949 to March 1950, 4,500 Jews left Iraq for Israel. For the Israeli statement and press reports, see enclosures 1 and 2 of McDonald's despatch no. 252, October 23, 1949, McDonald Papers, USHMM, box 8, folder 3; McDonald to secretary of state, no. 44, October 25, 1949, McDonald Papers, USHMM, box 8, folder 3. In general, Moshe Gat, *The Jewish Exodus from Iraq, 1948–1951* (London: Frank Cass, 1997), 51–143; and Bashkin, *New Babylonians*, 185–228. British and US responses in *DFPI*, v. 4, d. 380–382.

42. See editorial note in entry of January 14, 1949..

43. On October 19, 1949 McGhee, Wilkins, and Stabler met with Elath and tied the Iraqi persecutions to Israel's intransigence on Arab refugees and the recent Israeli shooting incident concerning Arab refugees near Beit Hanoun (see October 20, 1949). Elath to Sharett, October 19, 1949, *DFPI*, v. 4, d. 357. On October 28, Weizmann asked McDonald personally to request State

I should have included in my talk with Sharett his exposition of the 34th chapter of Exodus, 17th verse, which he developed as the original Ten Commandments.[44]

At teatime, Dillon Myer of the [Economic Survey] Mission and his two colleagues, one of them [Herbert] Kunde of the PCC technical committee, were at the house for about forty-five minutes. I was very glad to get from Myer my first direct information about the progress about the Survey. As was to have been anticipated, the work to date has concentrated on the preparation of the preliminary report (Clapp hoped it might be ready by November 1), to be used as material to secure favorable action on refugee relief from the UN and US. The next stage, which Clapp hoped would be completed by December, was the presentation and evaluation of all the resettlement schemes which had been seriously considered by any of the governments.

Myer was personally much interested in the possibility of the revival of the Gaza-Rafah Strip project. He wanted to know whether we thought that Israel would again consider it favorably. In reply, Ford first gave a very pessimistic estimate. I could not do other than agree in substance with Ford. In the light of the difficulty which the cabinet had in the first instance in securing approval, the subsequent contemptuous refusal of the proposal by Egypt, the political use of Israel's 100,000 offer, and now Sharett's interpretation of the Iraq-Syria union, [all this] made the prospects of Israel's acceptance of the earlier idea very, very slight. I tried to get Myer to commit himself as to whether he would accept larger responsibility in this area in the field of refugees and possibly conciliation as well if it were offered him. He was non-committal. He gave me a very favorable impression.

Gordon Clapp and the Economic Survey Mission held meetings in Tel Aviv with Sharett, Eliezer Kaplan, David Horowitz, and other Israeli officials from October 9 to 11. Sharett, Clapp reported, now doubted that Israel could fulfill its earlier offer to repatriate 100,000 Arabs because of public reaction against the idea.[45] Discussions in Syria, Lebanon, and Jordan fared no better. "Opinion in Arab states," Clapp said, "remains so violently opposed to abandonment of rights of refugees to repatriation in Palestine that contemplation by Governments of settling them elsewhere would likely make governments more shaky. . . . Whatever [the] ESM or its successors in the near future can accomplish will depend on the divorce of its activities, in Arab eyes, from any connection with political settlement of the Palestine war." Acheson ordered the US missions on the Middle East to urge all sides to promote the Economic Survey Mission as a means to reduce the refugee problem to a level at which it would

Department intervention on behalf of Iraq's Jews. McDonald to secretary of state, joint weeka no. 44, October 28, 1949, McDonald Papers, USHMM, box 8, folder 3.

44. Exodus 34 describes the creation of the two stone tablets that replaced those Moses had smashed, onto which Moses himself wrote the Ten Commandments. Verse 17: "You shall make for yourself no molten gods."

45. Entries of July 15, 25, 27, 1949.

no longer constitute a threat to peace, which meant "substantial resettlement and repatriation"[46]

Later [William J.] Levitt,[47] [Monroe] Goldwater,[48] and a group of eight JDC people came for tea. It was a pleasant visit, the discussion was mostly about possibilities for the importation of capital. Goldwater seemed to be fearful of the socialist regime here; Levitt much less so.

Tuesday, October 18

Charlie Bender, the cowboy Zionist of west Texas, came with a letter of introduction from Sydney L. Herold. Never have I had so appreciative a listener.[49] Then came the redoubtable personality, Mr. [Samuel] Keener of the Salem Engineering Company, Salem, Ohio, present in Israel with his DC-4 traveling engineering laboratory.[50] His sense of outrage at having been dispossessed at the Sharon in order to make room for the visiting congressmen was a lurid spot in an otherwise rather drab day.

Delightful dinner at the Archibalds'. Afterwards, he and I went to the Fords to greet the visiting congressmen [led by John Blatnik, (D-MN)] who were having supper there.[51]

Wednesday, October 19

The first of three afternoon and evening parties was at cocktail time at the Kaete Dan, where Mr. Viteles was host to the JDC group. I was struck by the depth of feeling of [Moses A.] Leavitt about Israel. The second party, cocktails at Lady Helm's, was friendly and pleasant. The hosts grow on one. As I was leaving, Sir Knox asked me if Sharett had brought up his fear of the Iraq-Syria Union, adding that there seemed to be opposition to it all around. I replied that

46. Clapp [through Pinkerton, Beirut] to secretary of state, no. 539, October 13, 1949, *FRUS*, 1949, v. VI, 1425–1426. Clapp [through Pinkerton] to secretary of state, no. 549, October 18, 1949, *FRUS*, 1949, v. VI, 1442–1444. Israeli policy explained in Eban to Yalçin, October 27, 1949, *DFPI*, v. 4, d. 372.

47. Entry of May 8, 1949.

48. Monroe Goldwater (1885–1980), chairman of JDC's reconstruction committee and president of UJA.

49. Charles Bender (1888–1970), Odessa (Ukraine)-born businessman; moved to Dallas, 1912 and founded the Star Bottling Company and the Texas Young Zionists of Dallas; later moved to Breckenridge, Texas, founded a department store and the city's first synagogue, of which he served as president; sent both sons to school in Israel, promoted Israeli bonds, and helped fund the Charles and Bertha Bender Laboratory in Israel, which did aeronautics research. Bryan Edward Stone, *The Chosen Folks: Jews on the Frontiers of Texas* (Austin: University of Texas Press, 2010), 189–191.

50. Samuel Keener (d. 1954), Ohio engineer and entrepreneur, founded Salem Engineering Company, 1935, which built steel mill equipment and industrial plants. To promote Salem's capabilities, in 1949 he took the company's engineers on a round-the-world trip that included twenty-four countries.

51. The congressional delegation that visited Israel in October 1949 included Herbert C. Bonner (D-NC), Harold D. Donohue (D-MA), Anthony F. Tauriello (D-NY), Ralph Harvey (R-IN), Edward A. Garmatz (D-MD), and Peter F. Mack, Jr. (D-IL).

Sharett had urged the matter most strongly and that there did appear to be general opposition, but that in some quarters, the attitude of Britain was considered to be in doubt.[52] I had a pleasant and not very revealing talk with Kaplan, who looks extraordinarily well.

The dinner for the visiting congressmen at the Sharon went off very well despite my initial consternation when I discovered that Padberg's protocol seating had placed women on both sides of our three chief Israeli guests and had deprived Goldie Meyerson of worthy dinner companionship. It was then too late, however, to change the seating. But after the first course had been served, I asked my wife to change places with the chairman of the group [Blatnik], which brought him in between Sharett and Ben-Gurion. Then I had Mrs. Hooper change places so that Kaplan could be flanked by two congressmen. Finally, I asked Mrs. Archibald to change with Congressman Garmatz so that Goldie Meyerson would have a congressman on either side. An amusing result of these shifts was that I had four or five ladies on either side of me. But the important thing is that the Israeli officials had new, and, for them, interesting people to talk to.

All our American guests seemed to enjoy the dinner and the company. At the end, I offered a brief toast to the president of Israel; Ben-Gurion responded with one to the president of the United States; I then said a few words of welcome, to which Sharett very briefly but with extreme correctness added his greetings. The response was by Blatnik, who threatened to be a little long. We rose from the table about eleven, but it was some time after that before the party broke up. Ben-Gurion was one of the most reluctant to leave. Before dinner, I had a brief talk with Ben-Gurion, to whom I stressed my high opinion of Elath's qualities, including that of strength. Ben-Gurion said he would be glad to see me after he came back to town the middle of next week.

On October 24 McDonald wrote Elath as follows: "Since my return here, I have already taken advantage of several talks with your associates to give them my impressions of the Washington situation and particularly of your affirmative role there." McDonald urged Elath to meet with James N. Rosenberg, a leading lawyer and publisher who had helped found the Joint Distribution Committee. "When you and Mr. Rosenberg meet, I think you will discern some of the reasons why I regard him as one of my ablest and most valued friends."[53]

The congressmen, who of necessity even at the end of the dinner had vague ideas about Israel and its governmental personnel (Blatnik, for example, during his brief talk referred to Sharett as the prime minister), were seemingly pleased

52. On the rather confusing British policy see Louis, *The British Empire and the Middle East*, 608, 620–631.
53. McDonald to Elath, October 25, 1949, McDonald Papers, Columbia University, box 11, folder 22.

with their reception and can, I think, (especially Blatnik through Herb Cummings) be useful with the FBO [Division of Foreign Buildings Operations]. I was amused at the obvious dullness, if not stupidity, of the Department's liaison man, Mr. [J. Edward] Lyerly. Surely it was stupid of the Department not to supply a competent man to such a committee whose recommendations on American administration and expenditures abroad must carry large weight in the House.

I should have indicated above, under my Rome dateline [October 8–12], my talks with Gowen, particularly about the attitude of the Vatican towards Jerusalem. The preference would be, as indicated in the pope's two encyclicals, for the broadest possible internationalization with sovereignty and real authority in the international body, on which it would be hoped France, Italy and Spain would play a large part. The much more limited program put forward by the PCC is, however, regarded as inadequate and unworkable. It is recognized that without clear authority and the means to make that authority felt, the partial internationalization must fail. According to Gowen, Monsignor Montini, acting secretary of state [sic], has the largest influence with His Holiness. Monsignor Tardini is also important.[54] Cardinal Tisserant, who has repeatedly [and] openly expressed his skepticism about the PCC plan, is in charge of religious interests in this area.[55]

Thursday, October 20

I was delighted to have General Riley call me and to agree to come out. After he had had his two cups of straight tea [. . .] Riley and I had nearly an hour on the roof.[56] Following my brief report on Washington and on Rome, the general opined substantially as follows:

1) He had been disturbed by the Israelis' recent action in the border region between the Gaza-Rafah strip and the Jewish area near Gaza. It is true that the permission which the Jews had accorded to the Arabs owning land in that region to move out from the Egyptian area to cultivate their fields in the daytime and return at night was clearly contrary to the armistice agreement. But clearly also, the Jews had no right to send in jeeps and Sten guns to shoot the Arabs in their fields. After the first incident, Shiloah had pledged

---

54. The Israelis had learned from Raffaele Cantoni that Monsignor Domenico Tardini (1888–1961), Vatican acting secretary of state for special affairs, strongly advocated Jerusalem's full internationalization and had great influence with the pope. Monsignor Giovanni Battista Montini (1897–1978), head of the general branch of the Vatican secretariat of state and the future Pope Paul VI (1963–1978), was, according to Cantoni, less obdurate but not opposed to Tardini. See *DFPI*, v. 4, d. 296.

55. On Tisserant, see entry of September 23, 1949. The Israelis were in contact with Tisserant, who seems to have had an influence on the recent more moderate position expressed by the French government in the General Assembly. *DFPI*, v. 4, d. 314.

56. Riley's cautious optimism concerning the developments of the armistice agreements and his suspicions concerning Israeli aims are in entries of July 15, 25, 1949, and August 6, 1949.

that it would not occur again, yet but two days later an even worse incident had occurred. Riley had not yet had a chance to talk to Shiloah about this.

On October 7 and October 14, Israeli forces launched successive attacks on 'Abasan and Beit Hanoun in the Gaza Strip. These were the first attacks by the IDF on Arab villages since the 1948 war. The aim was to prevent Arab infiltration from the villages into the adjacent fields and orange groves, which lay on the Israeli side of the border. Riley had reported the attacks to the UN.[57]

2) The Jews did not like, but had agreed to, the institution of joint patrols along the southern frontier.

3) The report in the morning's *Palestine Post* to the effect that Riley had said that peace could be made through the Mixed Armistice Commission[s] was misleading in that it did not include the words used by Riley "provided there is a spirit of conciliation and adjustment on both sides."[58]

4) The Arabs are inclined to keep a "box score" of armistice violations. There is no doubt that the Jews are guilty of the greater number of these, but the mere keeping of the score has no serious value.

5) The Iraq-Syria suggested union is not likely to come to more than a military alliance. Za'im's successors in Damascus, particularly the man who sits in his chair,[59] are not as strong as the previous regime. It was not the intention to kill Za'im but merely to dispose of al-Barazi. Za'im, unfortunately for himself, resisted and was shot. Enmity had been directed against al-Barazi because he was considered as the power behind Za'im, who had undertaken to disperse the Army leaders among remote posts. The Syrian Army is about thirty to forty thousand, but very poorly equipped. It has five or six planes, including two or three jets. These latter will probably last about fifteen minutes in flight with fatal results to the pilots.

6) There is talk in some Arab quarters of preparing for the second round of the war.

7) It was on Jerusalem that Riley was most interesting. He sees no possibility of internationalization. The PCC's scheme is impractical, as also would be the larger and more complete program included in the November 29th resolution. Even partition he now sees as difficult, unless the separating line is made a very tortuous one. In a recent talk, [John] Glubb said that he favored agreement on Jerusalem between Jews and Arabs as the only practi-

57. The State Department conveyed its displeasure to Elath. See Acheson to McDonald, no. 673, October 20, 1949, *FRUS*, 1949, v. VI, 1448. In general, see Benny Morris, *Israel's Border Wars, 1949–1956: Arab Infiltration, Israeli Retaliation, and the Countdown to the Suez War* (Oxford: Clarendon Press, 1993), 186–188.

58. Riley's comments were to the Rotary Club at the Jerusalem YMCA. "M.A.C.'s Can Settle All Issues—Riley," *Palestine Post*, October 20, 1949.

59. Colonel Sami al-Hinnawi (1898–1950), chief of staff of the Syrian Army who overthrew Za'im with aid of fellow members of Syrian Social Nationalist Party, which called for a "Greater Syria" scheme.

cable solution. Similarly, the Egyptian military chief has indicated the same view.[60] Riley added that this, of course, did not necessarily represent the political point of view. Riley had talked to Burdett a number of times;[61] the latter also saw difficulties, but Riley did not see Burdett's despatches. In answer to my inquiry, Riley said that the Department never asked him for his views. He continues to be directly responsible to the secretary-general of UN, but I did not gather that the Security Council had [lately] asked him for his views. This seemed to me a waste of excellent material, and I resolved to suggest to the Department that it secure Riley's views. As Riley was leaving, he asked me when I would come to see him in Jerusalem.

McDonald cabled the State Department on October 21: "Personal Attention McGhee. Had long interesting talk [at] residence twentieth with General Riley. Hesitate to quote him[,] instead suggest you secure his personal views [of the] practical aspects [of the] Jerusalem Problem[,] on which he has [the] highest competence."[62]

8) I almost forgot to record General Riley's views on the reported threats to the Clapp Mission. Riley regarded these as from quite irresponsible individuals, and he does not now consider that there is danger to UN or other foreign representatives.[63]

Friday, October 21

Jacob Herzog came for a long talk. He told me of recent conferences between Monsignor McMahon and Sharett and the prime minister. He left for me to read a copy of a highly confidential memorandum summarizing these talks.[64] This is to be returned when he next calls. He told me that the papal nuncio, [Monsignor Alcide] Marina at Beirut, had in strictest confidence told an Israeli official that the Vatican was ready for secret exchanges of views, provided the authorities here would give certain guarantees.[65] This strengthened

60. Colonel Mohammed Ibrahim Seif al-Din, head of Egyptian delegation at the Rhodes armistice talks.

61. For example, Burdett to secretary of state, no. 627, October 18, 1949, *FRUS*, 1949, v. VI, 1446–1447. Riley conveyed concern over the long-term durability of the armistice agreements and suggested using the Mixed Armistice Commissions for direct negotiations for de facto agreements on practical issues, if not actual peace treaties.

62. McDonald to secretary of state [personal attention McGhee], no. 765, October 21, NARA, RG 59, MC 1390, reel 20, frame 312.

63. Refers to various threats from right-wing fringe groups, and also a death threat made to Riley in early October from the New Underground for the Freedom of Jerusalem. See *FRUS*, 1949, v. VI, 1444, n. 3.

64. McMahon's talks with Israeli officials on July 28, 1949, and afterward are covered in *DFPI*, v. 4, d. 179 and d. 215 and appendices 1 and 2. The memorandum of the July 28 discussion, filed under October 19, 1949, is not printed in *DFPI*.

65. Alcide Marina (1887–1950), apostolic nuncio in Beirut; returned from Rome during the first week of October 1949 with message that the Vatican could not undertake official contact with Israel because of the Jerusalem question but that unofficial contacts to discuss the refugee and Jerusalem issues were possible. Marina passed along word that the Vatican expected a more favorable tone from the Israeli press plus the restoration of Israeli-requisitioned church properties. Herzog to Eban, October 13, 1949, *DFPI*, v. 4, d. 335.

Herzog's feeling that the time was coming when such an exchange would be possible and useful. He stressed that Monsignor McMahon was unyielding basically because of the latter's doubt of the continuance of a moderate regime here, being fearful that Mapam might, with its leftward and markedly anti-clerical views, take over. This is a possibility which Monsignor McMahon feels that the church dare not risk.[66]

Herzog argued that from the church's own point of view this was a fundamental mistake, because of the advantage which the Russians are taking of it. According to Herzog, it is driving the Greek Catholics [sic], who are the most important Christian group in the Middle East, into the arms of the Moscow-controlled Russian church. The Greeks are fearful of any form of international-ization because of their dread that this would give the Latins a preponderant place. They are the more troubled by the possibility because of the Vatican's known desire to have Italy, France, and Spain represented on the international-ization board. From the point of view of US interests in the Middle East, Herzog argued that support of internationalization undermined American influence in all the Greek communities in the Middle East. From the point of view of this area, the Greek[s] are more important than is the Vatican.[67] Herzog doubted that the underlying fundamentals of this situation were understood by the US or even sufficiently by Elath to enable him to put the case with maximum efficacy. Even here at home, Herzog was skeptical about full understanding at the highest level, for example, in the Foreign Office. He thought Ben-Gurion had a better grasp of the essentials than did Sharett.

I suggested that we continue our discussion as soon as he had any additional data to present to me. Before he left, however, he stressed that Cardinal Tisserant had recently declared that he was going to continue his fight against internationalization because of his conviction that the Church interests would be jeopardized by it. Herzog was almost rhapsodic in his praise of Ben-Gurion's presentation to McMahon.

Afternoon conference with Padberg.

Mr. Embrick of the IT&T [International Telephone and Telegraph] came to tell me of the allocation of funds by Israel for communication equipment. The American interests seemingly have done well. As he left, however, he said that he hoped I would, if I could, put in a good word for the transfer of the tentative contracts of the British for "switching equipment" to his company.

A long and pleasant talk with Julius Simon of the PEC [Palestine Economic Corporation]. He insists that he is moderately optimistic about Israel's

66. See also Herzog to Eban, September 29, 1949, *DFPI*, v. 4, d. 314, which explains in more detail McMahon's worries concerning an Israeli political swing to the right or left based on new Jewish immigrants, as well as the possible overthrow of Abdullah by nationalist elements in Jordan.
67. Herzog refers to Greek Orthodox prelates' comments that they would ask for Soviet assistance rather than see the Vatican dominate Jerusalem, and he pointed to recent contacts between the Greek and Russian churches in Jerusalem. *DFPI*, v. 4, d. 314.

economic future, but is skeptical about loan possibilities in the States at present.

Ruth and I ate supper at the Sam Sackses'.

Saturday, October 22

At work during the morning on drafts.

In the afternoon, while the family went to Mendes Sacks's, I had first an hour's conference with Harry Greenstein, [John] McCloy's Jewish adviser.[68] He is most enthusiastic about the new High Commissioner [in Germany]. He told me in detail of the latter's active intervention to secure the acceptance by the West German state of the new law providing for a measure of compensation for victims of the concentration camps.[69] Greenstein was hopeful that this would ultimately mean tens of millions of dollars of restitution to Jewish victims or to their heirs.[70] Greenstein is soon to return to the States, and his office is to be discontinued, because the [displaced persons] camps have been almost completely liquidated. Moreover, there now remain in Germany only a few tens of thousands of Jews, only approximately half of [whom] desire to leave.[71]

Belatedly, [Harry] Montor and fourteen or fifteen members of the UJA group arrived. Crowded into my disordered office, we had an hour or so discussion of conditions here and at home. They were full of enthusiasm for their campaign next year. They expressed warm appreciation for our conference. Out to the Sackses' very late but had a delightful time.

Ben-Gurion had asked US Jewish organizations for financial help with Jewish refugee resettlement—100,000 Jews were expected to spend the winter in reception camps—and with the industrial development needed to support the growing population. Montor's UJA team made a week-long tour of Israel after meeting with McDonald. They agreed with Ben-Gurion that Jewish immigration should not be halted,

68. See entry of April 6, 1949. After the end of the occupation regime in Germany in October 1949, Greenstein became adviser on Jewish Affairs to High Commissioner John J. McCloy, aiming to liquidate DP camps.

69. McCloy made German restitution to Jewish victims a priority, and in 1950 the West German government agreed to a lump sum settlement of nearly DM 23 million. See Thomas Alan Schwartz, *America's Germany: John J. McCloy and the Federal Republic of Germany* (Cambridge, MA: Harvard University Press, 1991), 175–184.

70. Greenstein believed that permanent Jewish communities could be reestablished in Germany funded by recovered Jewish assets. He organized conferences on the continuation of Jewish life in Germany. See Jay Howard Geller, *Jews in Post-Holocaust Germany, 1945–1953* (New York: Cambridge University Press, 2005), 70–76; and Steven M. Schroeder, *To Forget It All and Begin Anew: Reconciliation in Occupied Germany, 1944–1954* (Toronto: University of Toronto Press, 2013), 78–79.

71. From January 1 to October 15, 1949, 54,700 Jews were moved from US camps in Germany and 12,500 from US camps in Austria; of the total number 40,300 migrated to Israel and 23,500 to the United States. In addition, 33,000 Jewish DPs remained in the US zone of Germany and 10,000 in the US zone of Austria; see Report by Mr. Harry Greenstein, November 1, 1949, www.ajcarchives.org/AJC_DATA/Files/DP59.PDF, accessed January 2014.

McDonald said, "even momentarily." Rather, the UJA would seek $250 million in contributions for 1950.[72]

Sunday, October 23

Continued drafting in the morning until we went for an hour's walk at Herzliya.

A little after seven in the evening we were at the French minister's [Edouard-Félix Guyon] reception. Naturally, we were intrigued by the Arab house, which they had done so much to make livable. Nonetheless, despite its fine garden and splendid view, I much prefer our house. Mr. and Mrs. Guyon were very cordial.

I should perhaps add that Sharett said to me, "We are spilling the beans tomorrow morning." When I asked him how, he explained that the Foreign Office was issuing a statement on the alleged Iraqi persecution of the Jews there.[73] As to the reported Iraq-Syrian union, I mentioned that General Riley had been skeptical about this. Sharett admitted that there seemed [little] likelihood of its confirmation now. Delightful family dinner at the Andruses.

Monday, October 24

A busy morning with almost continuous dictation interrupted only by workmen of various sorts. A nearly two-hour afternoon staff conference at the office. I gave a full and confidential account of my activities and impressions in Washington. In the discussion period, [Oliver] Troxel[74] brought out the disquieting report that a local photostat office had access to and was photostating documents from the embassy. According to his informant, all of these documents were of lower classification, not going beyond restricted. There followed a brief discussion of the security problem, but I suggested that we postpone full consideration until we could have a special conference on this subject.

A long and comprehensive talk with Noah Karlin. Ruth and Bobby and I spent half an hour at Mr. and Mrs. Avram Levin's cocktail party for the [Paul] Parays. Ruth and I had a pleasant visit with [Zino] Francescatti.[75]

Family dinner with the Karlins. Much talk about Serge, which gave me a much fuller picture of this extraordinary man.

72. McDonald's joint weeka reports nos. 43, 44 of October 21 and 28, 1949, McDonald Papers, USHMM, box 8, folder 3.
73. On October 24 the Israeli government publicly called on Great Britain and the United States to intervene with the Iraqi government concerning the new wave of anti-Jewish persecutions. JTA *Bulletin*, October 24, 1949.
74. Oliver L. Troxel (1919–2013), second secretary and vice consul, US Embassy Tel Aviv, assigned May 10, 1949.
75. Zino Francescatti (1902–1991), French violin virtuoso, performed with Israel Philharmonic, 1949.

The house still in a state of complete confusion, but progress perceptible inside, outside, on the roof and walls and in the basement. Mr. and Mrs. Dewey Stone of Boston were at the house for tea.[76] Before they left, Mr. [Samson] Weiss and his colleagues of Young Israel arrived and remained for nearly an hour.[77] Weiss et al. desired me to speak at the ground-breaking of their new headquarters in Tel Aviv and also to do a piece for them. I declined both invitations on the ground that I could not associate myself with any one of the Jewish organizations that held a controversial position or whose activities could be the source of debate.

Much enjoyed the orchestra concert under Paray. The opening symphony by Mahler-Kalkstein, a local composer, would probably [have] meant more to me had I read the program notes concerning its biblical inspiration from the life of David.[78] The other numbers by De Falla, Paganini's violin concerto played with amazing virtuosity and feeling by Francescatti, and the final Liszt rhapsody, were all exciting; the most memorable being the Paganini.

Mr. Embrick of IT&T, who was at the concert with Mrs. Kaplan following a dinner at her house, said that Kaplan was resisting all efforts of the European competitors to change the basic communication allotments.

Brief talk with Jacob Herzog. He told me that he was going to Rome within a day or two on a "secret mission" to meet with Veronese of the Italian Catholic Political Action Party at the suggestion of papal nuncio Marini at Beirut.[79] At this stage there was no question of a direct approach to the Vatican. This latter would have to wait on a settlement of Jerusalem problems.

Herzog said that he would keep in touch with Gowen and would take advantage of Galeazzi's earlier invitation to get in touch with him whenever Herzog is in Rome.[80] He added that he would keep me informed through a confidential communication in the Israeli diplomatic pouch, and that this memo might serve the purpose of the earlier ones he had promised me. He repeated earlier expressions of warm appreciation for my "help."

Mr. [Arthur Z.] Gardiner of McGhee's office, and the latter's representative on the Clapp Mission, reached the house from Beirut in time for tea. [They] and I had an hour or so of talk before we went to Padberg's for dinner. There on

---

76. Entry of April 3, 1949.
77. Samson Weiss (1915–1990), Orthodox rabbi; served as Young Israel's director, 1947–1956. The National Council of Young Israel planned to build a $250,000 social and recreational center in Tel Aviv on land donated by the Jewish National Fund. A delegation of the group including Weiss arrived in October.
78. Mendel Mahler-Kalkstein (1908–1995), Ukrainian-born conductor and composer; later took the name Menahem Avidom; director of Israel Philharmonic, 1945–1952. McDonald refers to his Symphony No. 2.
79. Vittorio Veronese (1910–1986), Italian lawyer and bank director; president of Azione Cattolica Italiana, 1946–1952; connected with Vatican personalities.
80. Entry of October 27, 1948.

the balcony of his luxury apartment to the soothing melodies of *South Pacific* and *Kiss Me, Kate* played on the new long-playing records, we continued our Clapp Mission discussion.

Thursday, October 27

Gardiner came to the house with Padberg in time for a final hour's summation of our exchange of views on the Clapp [Economic Survey] Mission. Mr. Gardiner's summary of the Clapp Mission's work to date and its plans were substantially as follows: The interim report will be sent to Washington about November 5 for probable release on approximately November 10. We are to receive advance copies in order to be in a position to give an advance clarification to the Israeli authorities. This report will concentrate on the problem of beginning the shift from mere relief to work relief. [The Economic Survey Mission] will be able to make more concrete suggestions than seemed possible at the beginning and at a cost of perhaps not more than 2 ½ million as compared with 2 million dollars a month. It is hoped that this amount, given the new approach to the problem, can be raised on much the same basis as was the somewhat smaller sum for the past twelve-month period, that is, the US to match what will be made available from other countries. Great Britain is expected to contribute four million dollars.

Clapp anticipates that there will be disappointment in Israel at the diminished emphasis, as compared with the initial announcement, on fundamental resettlement schemes. He urges that we here explain that this is the result partly of the fact that this is only the first report and that some measure of this disappointment will be allayed by the subsequent report. Gardiner added that the soft-pedaling of the fundamental program had been necessitated also by the Arab resistance to it as a means, they thought, of relieving Israel of its responsibility for the refugees. The later report, which will be due before the end of the year, perhaps by December 15, will envisage fundamental rehabilitation schemes in many parts of the Middle East and seek to show their interrelation both in the physical sense and in the sense that political peace throughout the area and political and economic cooperation among the several states are essential to large scale progress.

During the first year or so, very little will be undertaken in this basic area. None of the many plans which have been put forward, or almost none, have reached the engineering stage. Hence, even if large funds were available (they are not), there would be no opportunity to spend them advantageously. Probably at most, there will be available only about five million dollars for engineering.

On the problem of organization, Gardiner said that Clapp and the Department were still in the exchange-of-views stage. Clapp favored a single organization for both the fields of activities envisaged above. He felt that there would not be enough for one organization to do in the basic field and that the two fields are really parts of one. Among the names that had been suggested as executives were Lawrence Wilkinson, formerly in Germany under [General Lucius] Clay; and [John] Blanford, deputy chief ECA [of Economic Cooperation Authority][81] in Greece and housing administrator during the war, formerly of the TVA [Tennessee Valley Authority], [and] liked by Clapp. With the setting up of the new organization, plans will be put under way for the elimination of the three agencies now operating in the refugee field.[82] It is felt that the more than $300,000 being spent monthly in relief administration is excessive and that the maintenance of a central office in Geneva is little short of scandalous. Padberg and I urged that the new central office should be on Cyprus.

To one of the suggested characteristics of the new organization, I took sharp exception. This was the idea that the executive should have associated with him national representatives corresponding to the members on the PCC. This would, I told Gardiner, be fatal, for no executive can function efficiently if he must at each step take account of national points of view. I pointed out that Bunche's work would have been wholly impossible with such an organization and that the same applies to Riley. I was pleased to have Gardiner report that Clapp and the Department appear to be agreed that there should be a one-man conciliator with broad powers. He may be responsible in the first instance to the PCC, but that triple-headed organization [should] not be able to hamper his tactical moves. Gardiner repeatedly emphasized that, of course, final decisions on all plans remained with the General Assembly. Though this is of course true, it is well that Clapp and the Department have gone this far in envisioning a truly workable organization. I urged Gardiner to tell Clapp that we are anxious to do everything we can to facilitate his work, that we are delighted that he is coming back this way, and that I hoped he would give us sufficient notice so that we could adequately prepare for him.

Meantime, Gardiner urged that we do the following:

1) Learn from the Israelis their estimate of the value of Arab refugee property. He suggested we exclude the blocked bank funds, the problem of which is being separately investigated [by] the PCC.
2) As indicated above, it is desirable that we prepare the Israeli authorities in advance for possible disappointment in the scope of the first interim report.
3) Check on the possibility of extension of [the] gentlemen's agreement for the giving of permission to Arabs to cross the lines to work their fields.
4) Sound out the Israeli authorities on their possible willingness to renew or extend the 100,000 offer, and to determine their present attitude towards the earlier Gaza Strip proposal.

81. Economic Cooperation Authority, created in 1948 to administer aid from the European Recovery Program.
82. Gardiner Refers to the United Nations Relief for Palestinian Refugees (UNRPR), the United Nations International Children's Emergency Fund (UNICEF), and the World Health Organization (WHO). The Quakers and Red Cross were still active in Arab refugee work.

Taking advantage of Gardiner's close association with McGhee, I asked him some questions about Departmental organization. In particular, I asked him what he thought was the best procedure to secure from the Department the additional personnel which we so urgently need. He said that the best procedure would be through a direct appeal to McGhee. He thought that the Peurifoy program of transferring larger measures of personnel control and decision [making] to the geographical units had now become sufficiently effective to make the approach to the Division head preferable to that through the Division of Foreign Personnel.

An hour at the groundbreaking ceremony of the children's village in Zikhron Meir, really a [section of] Bnei Brak. The village is financed by New York and Los Angeles groups. From the former were present Edith Levin and Mrs. A. Gellis, representing the Good Will Welfare League of Brooklyn. Among those who spoke while I was present were the chief rabbi [Yitzhak Herzog], the Sephardic rabbi [Benzion Uziel], and the minister of interior, Moshe Shapira. The whole project is under the direction of Rabbi Kahaneman on behalf of Orthodox refugee children.[83] I was amused that when I had had my picture taken with two American women representing Brooklyn, the rabbi insisted that I have my picture taken at another spot so that the Los Angeles banner would be shown. Otherwise, as he put it, he would "never be forgiven by LA." An excellent cup of tea at Lady Helm's, where I picked up Ruth.

I was delighted with the opening of the [United States Information and Education] Library.[84] [Richard] Tetlie and his acting librarian [Ora C. Zuckerman] have done a wonderful job. The building is attractive; the reading room and stacks as they should be, but what impressed me most of all was the admirable selection of books. For the first time, I am really impressed by the possibilities of the USIS [United States Information Service].[85] I was interested in the reaction of a young Israeli major who, not finding the military technical magazines he was looking for, wondered if they could be made available. I told Tetlie that I hoped it would be possible for him to invite suggestions from visitors of desired publications or books. He said he would keep a suggestion box at the entrance.

Brief but pleasant dinner with the Karlins.

Friday, October 28
Probst of CARE called to say that he had spoken to Goldie Meyerson, who had been less than enthusiastic. She promised, however, to speak to Kaplan.

83. On Kahaneman, see McDonald's previous excursion to Bnei Brak, entry of November 2, 1948.
84. On October 27, 1949 the United States Information and Education Library opened on Bialik Street in the heart of downtown Tel Aviv. Richard Tetlie of the embassy had prepared it for the opening.
85. Entry of January 27, 1949.

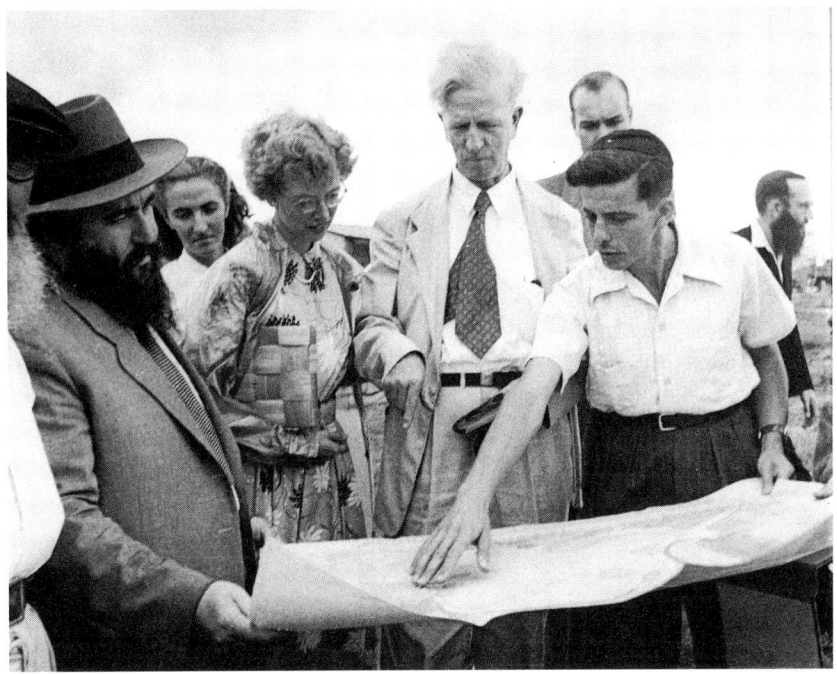

Fig. 16.1. Ambassador James McDonald and his daughter Barbara examine a building plan at Bnei Brak. United States Holocaust Memorial Museum.

As to my part, I told Probst that I had not yet had what seemed to me a suitable opportunity to raise the problem with the officials.

I should have noted above Gardiner's suggestion that [Judd] Polk, the economic adviser to the embassy in Cairo,[86] might usefully be borrowed by the embassy here. Gardiner also suggested that Charlie Kuhn, of the Federal Reserve Board, now on special assignment to the Clapp Commission [*sic*], would be admirable to make a study of economic conditions here. Gardiner regards him as extraordinarily able.

Hickman Price and his colleague Mr. Gage of the Kaiser-Frazer Corporation for more than an hour explained to me on the roof the intricacies of the plan through which they hoped to set up a Kaiser-Frazer assembly plant at Haifa. Kaiser-Frazer would put in approximately half a million dollars' worth of equipment.[87] Auxiliary to this project, it is hoped there may be a tire plant installed by an American company. Our friend [Akiva] Persitz is to be one of

86. Judd Polk (1912–1975), financial attaché, US Embassy in Cairo.
87. Kaiser-Frazer Corporation, automobile maker founded in July 1945; had brief success after World War II. Hickman Price (1911–1989) was vice president and director in 1949. Israeli entrepreneur Efraim Ilin, a prominent industrialist and member of the Revisionist movement, convinced Price to invest in Israel and, along with Kaiser-Frazer established Kaiser-Ilin Industries Ltd., which became Israel's first substantial automobile manufacturer. Kaiser-Frazer invested a half-million dollars, Ilin invested two million, and the assembly plant in Haifa began operating in 1951.

the Israeli participants in what will be an Israeli company. The formal presentation is to be made to Horowitz on Sunday. Price told me that the Ford project for an assembly plant had come to nothing. He added that he felt the Ford people never intended to do more than get rid of excess inventory at a good price, with not too generous terms.

Ruth Gruber came out to say goodbye, but because of the presence of Price and Gage and the Archibalds, who had come to say goodbye, there was little chance to talk. She did tell me, however, of her trip to and from Aden in one of the Yemenite refugee planes and of her vivid impressions of a people being bled by the Yemenite sheiks.[88] We also chatted about our mutual friend Bart [Crum], who she thinks suffered a serious blow to his pride in his newspaper [*New York Star*] failure.

Saturday, October 29

Fred Monosson of Boston, here to arrange for the building of the ZOA House, told me of his problems and of his hopes that the house would be ready within six months or a year.[89]

Sunday, October 30

Shiloah called up about five, and at my urgent invitation, came out for an hour's talk. He was just back from ten days at Bodenheimer's, his first rest in years. He looked much rested. He appeared to have nothing special in mind. We, therefore, covered a number of subjects in our general talk:

1) In answer to my question about Mapam-Mapai relations, Shiloah admitted that these were still strained, and that the prospects of agreement at the forthcoming meeting of the negotiating committees of the two parties next Thursday were not good.[90] Also in answer to my specific question, Shiloah admitted that there was a difference of approach to this problem as between Ben-Gurion on the one side, and Sharett, Kaplan and some other members of the cabinet on the other. The prime minister, though recognizing that the need for ending the cleavage is great, does not believe it can now be achieved and holds, therefore, that the cabinet should concentrate on making a success

88. Ruth Gruber (1911–2016), Brooklyn-born journalist with the *New York Post* and *New York Herald*; covered many Palestine and then Israeli topics; in 1949 reported on the airlifting of Yemenite Jews to Israel. See Ruth Gruber, *Witness: One of the Great Correspondents of the Twentieth Century Tells Her Story*, reprint ed. (New York: Schocken, 2007), 179–194. For her coverage of the Anglo-American Committee of Inquiry on Palestine, see Goda et al., eds., *To the Gates of Jerusalem*.
89. Fred Monosson (1893–1972), Belorussian-born raincoat manufacturer and philanthropist; treasurer of the Zionist Organization of America, 1949–1952; in Israel undertook several building projects including Neve Monosson, a settlement near the Lydda airport, in 1953.
90. Earlier in the month Mapai leadership wanted to include Mapam in the governing coalition and had offered several cabinet portfolios, but this offer was rejected. Differences concerned Israel's Western orientation, its frontiers, its economy, its governance, and more. October 1949 negotiations between party leaders are reported in McDonald's weekly reports in McDonald Papers, USHMM, box 8, folder 3.

of its program, after which it will be in a much stronger position to deal with Mapam. Ben-Gurion is of the opinion that at such a time the moderate elements in Mapam, which are on matters of basic policy in essential agreement with Mapai, would then break away and rejoin the parent organization. Those members of the cabinet who do not share the prime minister's view are said to regard the continued Mapai-Mapam split as too serious as to permit of the delaying policy favored by their chief.

2) In answer to my question about the Palmach incident recently, Shiloah gave the following explanation: As at first planned, the Palmach demonstration was so political in tone, involving marching in military formations and the carrying of so many anti-governmental banners, that it was impossible for the general staff to authorize participation [of] soldiers in the active army. The general staff would have been willing to have permitted such participation and told the Palmach leaders, provided the political aspects of the demonstration were eliminated. This was refused. At the last moment, however, when it was too late for the general staff to authorize such participation, the Palmach changed its plans and made the demonstration so innocent in appearance that the military authorities were made to appear unwilling to cooperate in what then became a quite legitimate demonstration by a famous unit. Shiloah admitted wryly that the authorities had been out-maneuvered. He admitted, too, that ill feelings had been left but added that this was "just one of those things."[91]

3) Despite Za'im's assassination, it is Shiloah's opinion that the reforms initiated by Za'im, such as participation—for the first time in an Arab country—by women in the voting, would not be undone. The new Syrian regime is, according to Shiloah, very weak. The military leader, fearful of assassination by the families of Za'im and al-Barazi, is seeking to appear merely as the agent of the civilian group [that is] in control. The prime minister is old and ga-ga and a mere tool of the controlling [military] clique.[92] The latter is for the most part favorable to the Iraq-Syrian unity program. Currently, there [are] taking place technical discussions between a large

91. In Tel Aviv on the weekend of October 15, members of the Palmach, the elite Jewish forces during the British Mandate, held a conference that included military parades. The tone was expected to be antigovernment because of the leftist sympathies of some Palmach commanders and the belief of others that the armistice agreements left Israel vulnerable. Army chief of staff Ya'akov Dori prohibited current IDF soldiers and commanders from participating, because doing so would represent loyalty to an armed force outside the IDF. Regardless, a number of officers who later were among the IDF leadership attended, including then-Lieutenant Colonel Yitzhak Rabin (IDF chief of staff [1964–1967] and prime minister [1992–1995]); Major Haim Bar-Lev (IDF chief of staff [1968–1971] and minister of trade [1973–1977]); and Major David Elazar (IDF chief of staff [1972–1974]). Dori only reprimanded them because of the circumstances and their past service. See Dori to Ben-Gurion, November 1, 1949, IDF Archives. We are grateful to Tuvia Friling for this reference.

92. Hashim al-Atassi (1875–1960), former Ottoman official, Syrian nationalist, and former ally of Shukri al-Quwatli, who had been overthrown by Za'im; after Za'im's death, prime minister of a provisional government to reestablish civilian rule, August–December 1949; president, 1936–1939, December 1949–December 1951, and 1954–1955.

group of Syrian military men who are visiting their opposite numbers in Iraq. According to Shiloah, the Iraqis are better equipped than the Syrians but are poorer fighters.

4) Referring to recent reports of jet and other military planes being sent by England to Egypt, Shiloah expressed concern at the growing plans among certain sections of Arab opinion for the "second round" in the war with Israel. These plans, he said, are of serious concern to the Israeli authorities and, if unchecked, would constitute a grave menace.

Monday, October 31

I should note here for my personal record that, according to a London telegram under date of August 27, no. 4309 regarding Egypt and the Suez, the king is reported as favoring opening free passage [of the Suez Canal] in return for supplies [of] arms, but Sirri Pasha[93] gave an emphatic negative unless and until the Iraq-Haifa pipeline were opened. He would give Nuri al-Said no excuse for accusing Egypt of breaking the "Arab front." Israel, it was reported from London, was unwilling to give a public pledge of non-aggression in return for the opening of the pipeline, but would formally give the desired pledge [though] not for publication. Israel also made clear its wish to reconsider the tax situation on the oil prices in connection with the refinery. It does not intend to establish a general free zone in the Haifa port, but, through bilateral negotiations with individual countries, to provide for free zones for those who are willing to trade with Israel. Unless some progress were made about Suez or the pipeline, Israel was considering appealing to the UN.[94]

Also for my record, from a telegram from [the] UN delegation in New York regarding [the] conversation by Abd al-Mun'im of Egypt with [a] UN secretariat member.[95] If concession to Egyptian prestige in Palestine settlement can be made, Egypt is prepared to leave Israel to work out settlement with other Arab states. Egypt is fed up with bickering among Arab states and anxious to draw away in order to work closer with [the] US and UK. [Nuri] Eren (Turkey)[96] expressed the view that Arab states would profit by recognizing reality of Israel's existence and by the fact that such a modern and Western-oriented state would be generally beneficial, that its Western culture and modern influence would serve to make the Arab states reform their economic and social structures.[97]

93. Hussein Sirri Pasha (1894–1960), Egyptian prime minister and minister of foreign affairs, July 1949–January 1950.
94. Printed documents on British desire to reopen the Haifa pipeline and refinery are in *FRUS*, 1949, v. VI, 1–185.
95. Abd al-Mun'im Mustafa Bey, head of Egyptian delegation to the Lausanne Conference, called in October 1949 for the repatriation of Arab refugees to be handled separately from other outstanding issues between Arab states and Israel.
96. Nuri Eren, Kemalist member of the Turkish delegation at United Nations, author of *Turkey Today—and Tomorrow: An Experiment in Westernization* (New York: Praeger, 1963).
97. McDonald originally attributed the remark to Mun'im and sought clarification from the State Department. The editors have changed the names accordingly. See McDonald to secretary of state, no. 791, November 1, 1949, NARA, RG 59, MC 1390, reel 20, frames 377–378.

[H. J.] Loewenthal of TWA came for a long talk in the late afternoon. Loewenthal's purpose [was] to secure my support for TWA's effort to break down Kaplan's refusal or inability to make good on his promise about [currency] conversion. Loewenthal spoke of the Israeli plan for increase in the number of its own planes in the foreign service with a view to "winning dollars." This, Loewenthal is sure, can never be achieved, at least not for many years. Yet, he is inclined to believe that the governmental authorities are in more optimistic frame of mind. He told me of the opposition to TWA's plans to increase their flights to three a week. He regards this opposition as a trading point in order to win concessions from TWA.

Towards the end of his talk, Loewenthal said that he was fearful that, in view of TWA's large losses last year, $6,000,000 or $7,000,000, largely as a result of conversion difficulties, for example in Egypt, where almost a million pounds had been accumulated, management of TWA might decide that it would be better to pull out of Israel rather than risk accumulating another large non-convertible amount. Later I learned that Loewenthal had himself— whether on his own initiative or not, I do not know, given the Israel authorities a kind of ultimatum. I made no commitment to Loewenthal except that I would speak to some of the Israeli authorities. I am anxious not to be used unjustifiably by TWA to pull their purely business interests out of the fire. I did underline to Loewenthal that obviously TWA's withdrawal now would create a very bad impression even though, as I was fully prepared to believe, such withdrawal were decided solely on business grounds and with no anti-Israeli or no anti-Semitic motivation.[98]

Sir Knox [Helm], the British minister, came at 5:45, and we talked until a quarter past seven. Most of the talk was on my part giving Helm frankly a good deal of background material, which he seemed not to have had. He is an excellent listener. He told me that on his way out here initially it had been planned that he should stop and see the pope, but that this was changed by the foreign secretary himself, because he feared that Helm's visit to the Vatican en route to his post would give rise to misunderstanding in Israel. Helm had been sorry, but had to agree. He was able to get to His Holiness, however, whatever he had to say about the Cardinal Mindszenty trial and other conditions in Hungary through talking to Monsignor Martini at a dinner in Rome, given by the British representative to the Vatican.[99]

Following my report to Helm on my talk with His Holiness about Jerusalem, Helm said that he considered the present PCC plan quite unworkable. This fits in with a telegram from Burdett reporting that [Sir Hugh] Dow, [the] British representative in Jerusalem, was of this same opinion. Burdett's coun-

98. See also entry of July 2, 1949.
99. József Mindszenty (1892–1975), fiercely anticommunist archbishop of Esztergom and leader of Catholic Church in Hungary; elevated to cardinal by Pius XII in 1946; arrested for high treason in December 1948 and sentenced to life in prison after show trial in February 1949. The pope held a secret consistory to protest the cardinal's condemnation.

ter-argument in his comments indicated his fixed intransigency. He declared his unwillingness to consider Israel's non-acceptance of the plan and the difficulty of enforcement as adequate reasons for failure to support it. Reading this comment, I was the more delighted to note in the press that Burdett is being replaced as [acting] chief of the consulate general by a senior officer from Salonika.[100]

More than once during our talk I was struck by what I considered Helm's, or what appeared to be, his inadequate briefing. He knew of Crossman, but he had not read his book,[101] nor did he appear to be as well documented in other respects as one would have expected. On the other hand, I received a more favorable impression that I had had earlier of him as a colleague, [regarding] his friendliness and his probable cooperativeness.

100. Raleigh A. Gibson, the consul general in Salonika, was reassigned to Jerusalem on October 28, 1949. He replaced Burdett, who had been acting consul general since the quiet recall of John J. MacDonald in the fall of 1948.
101. Richard H. S. Crossman, *Palestine Mission: A Personal Record* (New York: Harper, 1947).

17. November 1949

Tuesday, November 1

Lunch with Troxel. He seemed to me an extremely well informed, hard-working, and penetrating fellow. I was interested in the possibility of his doing a despatch on the prospects for a citizenship law here and the difficulties involved therein. Sound, too, seemed to me his suggestions that we should encourage the negotiations of an extra-territorial treaty with Israel. This, he thought, was the logical next step after an agreement on a bilateral air pact. The general theory was that it would be good for the United States to be the first country to sign treaties with Israel in several spheres. On the whole, he seemed mature and thoughtful for his years. Nor did I find in him any suggestion of that lack of sympathy with local conditions, which mars the attitude of some members of the staff.

Wednesday, November 2

Ruth and Bobby and I left for the Weizmann Institute at 9:45 but were not in our places for the dedication ceremony of the Institute until five minutes after eleven, being seated just before Dr. Weizmann was ceremonially escorted in and the proceedings began.[1] The program, which opened with a brief statement by Meyer Weisgal,[2] continued for a little over an hour under the chairmanship of [Selig] Brodetsky.[3] The speakers included Ben-Gurion, [Avraham] Granot of the JNF,[4] Sprinzak for the Knesset, [William E.] Rappard from Geneva, who gave a brilliant two-minute improvisation, Dr. [Ernst] Bergmann and the administrative officer of the Institute, and, finally, Weizmann himself. All the speeches sounded variations on the central theme, the vital relation between Israel's success and knowledge. Also, most of the addresses lauded Weizmann as leader in the organization of the state and in the development of its creative intellectual life. It was a truly notable occasion.

---

1. On November 2, 1949, the Daniel Sieff Research Institute in Rehovot, founded in 1934, was formally rededicated as the Weizmann Institute of Science. The aim, aside from the official renaming as a tribute to Weizmann on his 75th birthday, was to create an expanded "City of Science" for applied research beginning with the already existing Institute of Physics and Physical Chemistry.
    2. Weisgal was chairman of the Council for the Institute.
    3. Entry of August 18, 1948. Brodetsky succeeded Judah L. Magnes as the second president of the Hebrew University in 1949.
    4. Avraham Granot [formerly Granovsky], see entry of August 27, 1948.

Immediately after the cornerstone laying for the new [Institute for Biology and Biochemistry], a buffet luncheon was served to the 2,000 or more guests. We were fortunate enough to find a place at the table with the government officials for Ruth, while Bobby and I ensconced ourselves comfortably on the branches of a friendly tree. Chatted for a little while with Leo Kohn. He told me of his present hopes to get a portion of the constitution acted upon by eliminating the bill of rights and related sections. He said that he would be glad to talk to me further about his scheme. Rappard told me an amusing tale to the effect, that when the Russians had received the American Committee's[5] invitation to today's ceremony in English, a legation representative had gone to the Foreign Office to say that it would be impossible for them to accept such an invitation and would not the government or Dr. Weizmann send them another invitation in Hebrew. This was done.

I should record a Department telegram containing views on the Iraq-Syria proposed union substantially different in tone from those expressed in a telegram of a couple of weeks earlier. It reiterated the earlier approval of union anywhere in this area if reached by democratic processes with the full assent of the peoples concerned. It contained, however, a qualifying paragraph, which, in effect, ruled out American support of the Syria-Iraq proposal. It listed opposition as follows: from Abdullah because of fear of loss of Jordan's independence; Egypt because of suspicion of a new Arab bloc which might lessen Egypt's preeminence; Saudi Arabia, fearful of Hashemite ambitions on the Hejaz; Lebanon, nervous about its independence; and the French, fearful of the union's effect on their position as compared with that of the British.[6]

The drive out to Rehovot for the "command performance" of the [Israel Philharmonic] Orchestra was surprisingly short—25 minutes compared with an hour and twenty minutes in the morning. The program was a repetition of the one we heard in the second of the regular series, with [Zino] Francescatti playing so admirably the Paganini. After the concert we went to Meyer Weisgal's new house. We were all surprised and full of praise for the house itself and for its furnishings. It gave the impression of a fine villa in Florida. At the concert and at the reception, I chatted with many of the American visitors here for the Institute dedication. Harry Levine[7] said that the group was planning to invade the embassy residence, nearly one hundred strong. This sent the McDonalds into a huddle. It was finally agreed with Dewey Stone that he would check with the group and telephone us if it were possible for them to come in some time on Sunday, Ruth and Bobby having decided that we could somehow manage this formidable number.

---

5. American Scientific Planning Committee for the Weizmann Institute of Science.

6. State Department thinking on the proposed union between Iraq and Syria under the Hashemite monarchy is in *FRUS*, 1949, v. VI, 180–185.

7. On Levine, see entry of May 31, 1949. Levine was a friend of Weizmann and a charter member of the American Committee for the Weizmann Institute of Science.

Made tentative arrangements with Horowitz that he would come to the house some evening at our mutual convenience for a general talk about economic problems. Home about twelve. For the record, I should report that we were the only diplomats present for both the evening affairs. Even at the concert the only other chief of mission that I saw was the Dutchman, [Johan] Nederbragt. Though none of the Israelis complained at this slight, I am sure they felt it.

Thursday, November 3

Long conference at and following breakfast with Ford and Padberg. In addition to discussing with them a number of current problems, which incidentally brought Ford up to date after his two weeks' absence, I emphasized my concern that no members of the staff should either publicly or in discussions with their fellows give vent to expressions of opinion or feeling which could be picked up and subsequently quoted as evidences of lack of sympathy with Israel and its people. I cited as proof of the need to be doubly careful my own mistake some months ago when I unwisely coined the phrase that I did not wish our people to "get into bed with the British." I pointed to the fact that this quotable phrase had been broadcast and remembered, with results unfortunate for me and [for] our relations with the British. In this talk I also made clear anew what I thought had been clear before, that I wanted no political despatch or telegram to be filed without my having had an opportunity to read it and to approve or disapprove. This was said for Padberg, especially because, as I told him, both Knox and Ford had invariably followed the practice which I was now insisting on. I said also that I thought we ought to do more reporting and that, if this necessitated, sending in ad interim despatches rather than waiting additional weeks for more definitive data.

Afternoon, Professor [Benjamin] Akzin recently arrived for his post at the Hebrew University where he is to teach political science, came in for a visit at teatime.[8]

Ruth and Bobby and I, overestimating the time required to get to Rehovot, arrived there in good time for dinner. It was a typical Weisgal affair admirably carried through. During dinner most of my talk was with Professor Rappard and with Rebecca Sieff. Rappard was intensely impressed by what he had seen and heard in Israel. There were many, too many, speakers even though only two of them, Rappard and President Weizmann, spoke at any length. Rappard was brilliant, and the president was, as usual, much more effective in his informal and extemporaneous talk than he ever is when he reads a prepared speech. His main theme was that for 2,000 years his people had been strangers

8. Professor Benjamin Akzin (1904–1985), Latvian-born political scientist and Revisionist Zionist; served as secretary to Ze'ev Jabotinsky; lobbied in Washington for the Jewish state during World War II; served on War Refugee Board and called for bombing of Auschwitz; joined faculty of Hebrew University, as professor of political science and constitutional law, 1949; founded department of political science, 1950; later helped found University of Haifa.

more or less welcome throughout the world, [and] who had never been in a position to return the hospitality received. Nor had they been able to carry out the creative work in their own name. He did not quote, but he might have appropriately used as an illustration the following: "Einstein is reported to have said when he was living in Germany and working on his basic theory; if I succeed, the Germans will call me a German and the French a man of the world, but if I fail, the Germans will call me a Jew and the French a German."[9] Perhaps the most striking phrase in Weizmann's address was: "We are welcoming the debris of Jewish communities throughout the world. The first generation may be a liability, but the second will build Israel."

The other speeches need not be recorded. Kaplan spoke in Hebrew; Rebecca was very brief; the Dutch professor paid tribute on behalf of the scientists to Weizmann; the American officers of the Committee—[Harold] Goldenberg,[10] Harry Levine, Dewey Stone—made what in effect were brief appeals. We were home a little after midnight.

Friday, November 4

Mrs. [Julia] Dushkin of Hadassah[11] urged me to attend the Sunday opening in Jerusalem of Hadassah's new Institute for the Fashion Industry. I begged off but agreed to write a note.

Nearly an hour and an interesting talk with Joseph M. Mallah, ad interim representative of Greece.[12] His country supports the PCC's scheme for Jerusalem, but Mallah doubts its practicability, and fears that it, if enforced, would be used by the Russians both within the city and throughout the Middle East as an instrument against the [Greek] Orthodox Church. He said that the Greek Patriarch in Jerusalem[13] was opposed to the internationalization for these reasons and because of his fear that it would advantage the Latin Church. Mallah said that the other patriarchs of the Orthodox Church were also opposed. He spoke too of the propaganda use already being made by the Russians among the Greeks of the internationalization proposal.

Mallah explained his country's coolness towards Israel on two grounds: 1) Greece's very large interest in Egypt; and 2) the unsolved problem of Greek [Orthodox Arab] refugees from Israel. As to these latter, Israel was prepared to let the refugees return but could or would not facilitate the return of their prop-

9. Quotation in Michael Brenner, *A Short History of the Jews* (Princeton: Princeton University Press, 2010), 323.
10. Harold J. Goldenberg (1907–1978), vice president of Palestine Economic Corporation; in Israel since June 1949 to establish a chemical and plastics factory.
11. Julia Aronson Dushkin (1895–1975), vocational education chair in Hadassah; occupied with child welfare; wife of Professor Alexander Dushkin, who from 1949 to 1960 directed the School of Undergraduate Studies at the Hebrew University and served as an educational consultant to Hadassah.
12. Joseph Mallah (1889–1982), Sephardic merchant, legislator, and diplomat from distinguished Salonikan family; delegate to the League of Nations; resistance fighter in France; Greece's first representative to Israel, arriving May 1949.
13. Timotheus I, patriarch, 1935–1955.

erties.[14] Mallah, who has long been resident in Paris, said that he did not anticipate remaining long in Israel.

Shmuel Katz of Herut[15] came to talk about the Department's ruling on the non-admissibility of former Irgunists or Irgunist sympathizers.[16] He made the interesting and revealing point that [Ephraim] Margolin, who has been held at Ellis Island for some weeks because of his Irgunist connections, was, with his father, a leader in the pro-Western bloc of the Herut. Katz is anxious that the present ruling be reversed, and pending such reversal, he and his colleagues in Herut do not intend to apply for further visas.[17] Even before Katz made his case, I explained to him the efforts we were making from here and the even more direct ones which I made when I was at home. I asked him to make clear to his colleagues that we were doing our utmost to change the ruling and that we were hopeful of success. Parenthetically, however, I pointed out to him the slowness of our government in making any change in an established policy. He seemed convinced that we were doing the best we could.

Early dinner with Sonia and Misha Karlinski, after which all of us, our hosts and Ruth, Bobby, Miss Clark, and I went to the meeting of the Vocal Newspaper.[18] [Gershon] Agron and Brodetsky were both short. My reception was as cordial as I could desire when I was introduced. My [talk] was a six or seven [-minute] account of personal impressions of Weizmann.

Saturday, November 5

Several hours spent in catching up on my document reading. I was particularly intrigued by the Haifa Refinery file. A despatch, [of] September 8, 1949, [Thomas] Bloodworth[19] to Department made clear that the Iraq Petroleum Company [IPC], which operates the [pipeline], in "expectation of an Arab victory" had within four or five days before the end of the Mandate made an arrangement to pay to the successor state, expected to be Arab, a substantial royalty for "protection of pipeline" through Palestine. Bloodworth's despatch also reported the significant fact that the British government was not making itself [the] protector of the IPC's "secondary interests," for example, operating conditions of the refinery, the Israeli claims for lower oil prices, the allotment

14. In general see Michael R. Fischbach, *Records of Dispossession: Palestinian Refugee Property and the Arab-Israeli Conflict* (New York: Columbia University Press, 2003). Also see J. Henry Carpenter, "The Arabs Can't Go Back," *Christian Century* 68, no. 26 (June 27, 1951): 763–766.

15. Shmuel Katz (1914–2008), Revisionist Zionist; associate of Ze'ev Jabotinsky; member of first Knesset as member of Herut; adviser to Menachem Begin, 1977; author of numerous books including a two-volume biography of Jabotinsky (1993).

16. See entries of October 29, 1948, and August 4, 1949.

17. Ephraim Margolin (1926–), German-born former member of IZL; detained in Ellis Island while his case was under study by the Immigration and Naturalization Service, August 1949; released on November 8, 1949; graduated from Yale Law School, 1952; renowned criminal defense attorney in San Francisco.

18. Weekly event featuring different speakers sponsored by the Israel Journalists Association and held at the Mograbi Cinema in Tel Aviv.

19. Thomas S. Bloodworth (1922–1991), US vice consul in Haifa after November 1948.

of substantial quota of the product through the Israeli government, the concessions in the Haifa oil docks, etc.

Ford's despatch to the Department under the date of September 28 is also an intensely interesting contribution to the Haifa jigsaw puzzle. Now it appears that Israel and Britain have completely changed places on the question of whether Israel is a "successor government" to the mandatory. A year ago Israel argued "yes" and Britain "no." Today they take diametrically opposed positions. The reasons for these reversals are obvious. A year ago Israel was anxious to claim the advantages of being a successor state, and now it is anxious to avoid them. Ford confirms that on May 10, 1948, the IPC and the Consolidated Refinery Ltd.[20] made an arrangement with the mandatory for the payment of 35,000 pounds annually for pipeline protection; presumably this amount would be paid over to the Arab successor state. Unfortunately for this arrangement, the successor state was Jewish.

The several telegraphic reports from London, giving a rather detailed picture of the schemes, naïve and otherwise, through which HMG [His Majesty's Government] vainly sought to intrigue Egypt into setting the pace for Iraq in making oil available for Haifa, were both amusing and discouraging; amusing that a great government should think that these obvious devices would fool or persuade Egypt or Iraq; and discouraging because so obviously the devices have not worked.[21] The device of using the promise of relaxing arms shipments as a bribe to persuade Egypt to let a few tankers through was futile. Similarly, the idea of sending a few tankers from the Caribbean to show that the [refinery] could be operated without Iraq oil had no effect. Farouk's seeming willingness to have Suez opened was either deliberate deceit or it was overruled by [Hussein] Sirri Pasha, the prime minister [and foreign minister], who stubbornly refused to "give Iraq an excuse for claiming Egypt had 'broken Arab solidarity.'"

On a par with the almost childish maneuvers of HMG to persuade Egypt and Iraq to carry out their legal obligations were the arguments of the Iraqi representative that Britain should move the refineries to Syria at the "modest cost of $14,000,000." Israel, on its part, refused the British suggestion of early October made through Helm, that it disclaim any aggressive intentions in [its] desire to see the reopening of the Haifa refinery, and pointing out [that] the financial advantage would be confined to dues and taxes allowed by prior connections with oil companies (approximately 80,000 Israeli pounds annually).

Interesting in Ford's despatch of September 28 is the fuller development of Israel's claims about Haifa, including, according to Mr. Z. W. Ross, manager for Israel and Cyprus of the Socony-Vacuum Oil Company, "a much wider field

20. Consolidated Refineries, Ltd. (owned by the Anglo-Iranian Oil Company and Royal Dutch Shell) owned the refinery in Haifa.
21. The British hoped to have Egypt open the Suez Canal to tankers moving to and from Haifa and to have Iraq reopen the pipeline to Haifa. Because neither Arab state wanted to be accused of breaching the boycott against Israel, London suggested that Egypt and Iraq act simultaneously, but this suggestion failed. Discussions between McGhee and Michael Wright on Haifa, November 17, 1949, *FRUS*, 1949, v. VI, 80–82.

than should reasonably apply to a purely refining activity, encompassing matters of internal supply, price structure, finance, and distribution . . . for instance, it has been estimated that [the] Israeli government would like 100,000 tons of crude annually to be refined by CRL [Consolidated Refineries, Ltd.] and distributed by a designated national authority for 'government' purposes." Shell is worried about how such an arrangement would affect its interests as a distributor. It is clear from both Bloodworth's and Ford's reports that the IPC is unhappy because HMG is limiting its support to its basic interest and is not taking a strong line to persuade Israel to accept operating conditions pleasing to CRL.

Sunday, November 6

Brief chats with Sharett, who said he was leaving at the end of the week for the States, the UN and the UJA, with Kaplan and Goldie. The latter told me that she regarded Ashkelon [formerly al-Majdal] as the most beautiful seaside city in Israel. The government is planning substantial building there and at Be'er Sheva. In a talk with Rappard, the latter expressed his near amazement at the extraordinary accomplishments in Israel and at the high level of intelligence among the leaders. He, too, had gotten the impression that Ben-Gurion was the most creative and the most powerful of the men today. He urged me to visit him in Geneva. Jokingly, Rappard, as well as one of the other Swiss professors, referred to my quotation from Bobby about Geneva being "finished." They both admitted, however, that in a certain comparative sense Geneva is "finished."

Monday, November 7

At four went with Colonel Archibald to the Air [Force] reception, where we met other members of the staff. High air officials showed us the extremely interesting exhibit. It should do much to stimulate public interest and air-mindedness. It is another illustration of how much the Israelis are able to accomplish with so very little.

With the Fords and Ruth and Bobby to the Russian Revolution anniversary party. The building was [as] crowded as last year,[22] but with less of a festive air because, perhaps chastened by the refusal of the Mapam to "dress," there were no instructions this time that formal clothes should be worn. Almost immediately after we arrived, [Ambassador Pavel] Ershov led the diplomatic corps and Israeli officials into one of the buffet rooms.

During the evening, I chatted with many of the guests, but, as is usual on such occasions, there was no time for sufficient talk with anyone. Ben-Gurion said jokingly in Ershov's and my presence that the Russians and the Americans were people who knew only one language. Weizmann remarked jokingly that Israeli receptions were like a play; you kept seeing the same characters all the

22. Entry of November 7, 1948.

time. Paula, sitting next to the Archimandrite [Leonidas],[23] and visibly unhappy, signaled me repeatedly to join her.

Because of the press of the crowd and warmth of the evening, nearly everyone was impatiently awaiting the Weizmanns' withdrawal, which had been delayed until after nine by the non-arrival of their car. As last year, we followed closely after the Weizmanns and the Ben-Gurions on the leave-taking. The Fords insist that the applause on arrival and on departure was as great if not greater for the American party than for that of the president or the prime minister. Home by 9:30 or 9:45 and glad that the affair was over.

Tuesday, November 8

I note here that in Burdett's telegram to [the] Department of October 18, he reports Glubb Pasha as anxious for a settlement and as moderately optimistic that this will be possible by direct negotiations, if the Israelis are reasonable.[24] Burdett also reported that [Colonel Mohammed Ibrahim] Seif al-Din expressed similar views as to direct Israel-Egyptian negotiations. In his comments, Burdett asked the Department for instructions as to the encouragement of bilateral negotiations and as to the usefulness of the MAC [Mixed Armistice Commission] for this purpose. He concluded with the judgment, which I share, that Israel is not likely to yield any territory, except possibly minor "rectifications," or to take back substantial numbers of refugees. I sent a telegram to the Department agreeing with these general conclusions and expressing appreciation of Jerusalem's full reporting distribution.[25] Incidentally, I contrasted [this] with Keeley's recent suggestion that the mission should receive copies of the exchanges between the Department and the Economic Survey Mission.

Useful office conference. Major Brady again showed his unusual thoroughness by being the one staff member to give a categorical statement that the Egyptian armistice agreement ceases to be operative at the end of the year. He is to check and give me the exact language in this and the other armistice agreements.[26]

Arrived late to the Weizmann farewell reception for Americans visiting the [Weizmann] Institute. I was surprised, or perhaps I should not have been, by Levine's and Stone's critical attitude towards Israel. They were not specific, but they indicated that their nerves had worn thin and that they were happy to be on their way home. One of them asked what they could do to make life

<hr />

23. Archimandrite Leonidas, senior-most Russian Orthodox cleric who acknowledged the supremacy of the patriarch of the Russian Orthodox Church in Moscow; resided in the Soviet legation in Tel Aviv until the Israelis returned Russian church property in summer 1949. See entries of July 10 and September 23, 1949.

24. Burdett to secretary of state, no. 627, October 18, 1949, *FRUS*, 1949, v. VI, 1446. See also entry of October 20, 1949.

25. McDonald to secretary of state, no. 810, November 8, 1949, referenced in *FRUS*, 1949, v. VI, 1146, n. 3.

26. Relevant materials in McDonald Papers, USHMM, box 8, folder 4.

for us more bearable in this bleak country. I suggested that anything which would help us enjoy music at home would be gratefully received.

To the opera to hear *Rigoletto*. The Andruses, the Karlins, and Madame de Phillipe were in the row with us. It was a well-integrated and enjoyable performance.

Wednesday, November 9

Planned to go out to deliver personally to Weizmann at Rehovot a personal letter received that morning from President Truman but was told that Weizmann was indisposed and therefore sent the letter to his office at HaKirya.[27]

Three-ringed circus at teatime. The first group was the sub-committee of the Economic Survey Mission headed by Royall Tyler of the International Bank for Reconstruction and Development (World Bank);[28] Sidney Sherwood, of the Export-Import Bank; Charles A. Coombs, Federal Reserve Bank; and Paolo Contini [legal adviser to the Economic Survey Mission]; all Americans. They are here to secure from the Israeli government basic statistics about the financial and economic situation. After we had had an hour's visit, I urged them to come back and see me before they left in order to give me their judgment.

Before they left, Joseph and Mrs. Schlossberg of the Amalgamated [Clothing Workers of America][29] and Dr. A. S. Juris of Histadrut,[30] arrived. Schlossberg is engaged now in work on behalf of Histadrut in the States. I urged him to urge his colleagues to get on with their educational program here.

Thursday, November 10

At dinner at Ford's, I had interesting talks with both Goldie Meyerson and [Reuven] Shiloah. With the former it concerned possible interpretation of the extremely critical attitude of some of the most important of the American members of the Weizmann Institute Committee [*sic*]. Without mentioning names, I had quoted Mr. and Mrs. Levine to the effect that they would be so glad to get back home that they would want to kiss the soil and their question to me: "What could they have sent to us which would make life more livable in

27. Truman to Weizmann, August 13, 1949, *FRUS*, 1949, v. VI, 1305–1308, already received by Elath on August 18, 1949.

28. Royall Tyler (1884–1953), US historian of early modern Europe and Byzantium; US peace delegation in Paris, 1919; League of Nations economic adviser to Hungary, 1924; served during World War II in US consulate in Geneva where he aided Allen Dulles (Bern) in intelligence work because of his European contacts; after the war served with the World Bank until his death.

29. Joseph Schlossberg (1875–1971), Russian-born Zionist and general-secretary of Amalgamated Clothing Workers of America; traveled to Palestine in 1930 and 1937 to study Jewish labor.

30. Avraham Shmuel Juris (1890–1971), Jewish Agency emissary to Latin America, 1940–1942; tried to obtain admission for Jewish refugees, with some success in Ecuador; later a Histadrut official.

this 'godforsaken country'?" Goldie's basic interpretation was that they were spoiled and had been disillusioned by difficulties of living in Israel.

My talk with Shiloah was more important. It concerned chiefly [Robert] McDowell,[31] who is to be one, if not the chief, adviser of McGhee at Istanbul.[32] Shiloah was most enthusiastic about the intelligence, the honesty, and the directness of this former intelligence officer in Egypt during World War II. Shiloah regards him as one of the most knowledgeable and soundest men on this area. He earnestly asked me to urge McDowell to visit here. A few days later Sharett cordially seconded Shiloah's invitation.

Friday, November 11

More than an hour's conference in the morning with Royall Tyler, Sherwood, and Contini, whom I had seen Wednesday. This time they told me of their long conferences with Horowitz and other experts of the HaKirya. They said that they had been given full, and they thought, correct information, but that the available data inevitably was inconclusive because no figures [had been] given as to probable receipts from the States on the UJA and related accounts during the next fiscal year. Nor, of course, could there be any calculation in the event that the peace was disturbed. Tyler, therefore, refused to hazard even a guess about the future. Sherwood, in the light of his larger knowledge extended over nearly a year's period, was more optimistic but was also conservative.

Saturday, November 12

Worked on documents during the morning. At the Sackses' for brief Shabbat tea. Dinner with the Karlins and later to the Chaplin movie, *Monsieur Verdoux* (1947). It was interesting, but I am not at all sure that it could be considered a great production. Chaplin showed flashes of his old genius but the piece as a whole did not hang together.

Sunday, November 13

On the way out from dinner [at the Sharon] I chatted for a moment with the Italian secretary, Gasparini, who introduced me to the new minister [Enrico] Anzilotti and their women folk.[33] It was pleasant to hear them speak perfectly good English. I told the minister that I was inviting him to come to the house on Thursday for the meeting of the diplomatic corps. He doubted whether he was eligible until he had presented his credentials, which would not be until a week later. I urged him not to stand on protocol.

31. Colonel Robert Hayden McDowell (1903–1979), Balkan specialist from the University of Michigan; OSS desk officer in Cairo during World War II; in 1944 headed mission to Chetniks in Yugoslavia.
32. Refers to State Department's conference at Istanbul, during the third and fourth weeks of November, for US mission chiefs in the Eastern Mediterranean and Middle East.
33. Baron Gasparini, interim Italian counselor of embassy; Enrico Anzilotti (1898–1983), Italian minister to Israel.

Fig. 17.1. Ambassador James McDonald hands out food packages from the United States to toddlers at a WIZO Mothercraft Training Center in Tel Aviv. Israeli Government Press Office.

In the evening with the family to a special concert of the orchestra. [Paul] Paray opened with the Weber Oberon Overture, then continued with Bach's Concerto for Violin in A, and, in the second half, Brahms's violin concerto. Francescatti played both with a complete mastery, which had won him such enthusiastic support here. The applause at the end was as great as that which Leonard Bernstein received in 1947 in Jerusalem. Francescatti was so touched that despite his two concertos he played as an encore Kreisler's Scherzo and Caprice. Afterwards, there was a brief reception on the stage which the family and I attended, giving us a good opportunity to make our farewell to the Francescattis.

Monday, November 14
An hour at HaKirya with Sharett; also present were [Michael] Comay and Shiloah. Sharett's talk covered a wide field and was general rather than specific.

I expressed the hope that Sharett would [during his impending trip to the United States] meet and talk with [Albert M.] Greenfield and [Jack] Arvey, explaining to him why these men were particularly important. I suggested, too, that he see David Niles to give him a picture of conditions here particularly as they affect me personally in relation to other individuals who ought to be more sympathetic than they are.[34]

Comay and I had a brief talk on our way out about problems discussed. . . . I told Sharett of the [US] military changes, emphasizing that these were part of a world-wide program of retrenchment and consolidation. I also told Sharett of the arrival of [Milton] Fried and of my reasons for hoping that he would be valuable in not merely his technical role as labor attaché, but also as close counselor and adviser.

McDonald reported the following on his discussion with Sharett[35]:

"1) [Foreign Minister] expects to argue [in the General Assembly] against postponement [of Jerusalem] decision; will plead that UN delay solves nothing [repeat] nothing [and] that instead 'natural forces which can not [repeat] can not be halted will continue to make current PCC and related suggestion anachronistic.'

2) As one of the initiators of MAPAI-MAPAM negot[iation]s [Foreign Minister] said 'authoritatively' that no [repeat] no progress was made. Immovable obstacle is not [repeat] not foreign policy but is MAPAM 'dogmatic insistence on (a) revision cost living index with meanwhile no reduction wages and (b) capital levy.' Both these demands [Foreign Minister] said are 'fantastic and wholly unacceptable.'

3) Communism in Israel is no [repeat] no threat and [Foreign Minister] added '[I] am confident Israel Gov[ernment] is realistic in its appraisal this issue.'

4) [Foreign Minister] guesses that [Michael] Wright of UK [Foreign Office] urged [on] Dep[artment] UK-US leadership 'outside UN or with mere nominal UN sponsorship' in [Middle East] development projects. Israel 'strongly opposes such move. Will cooperate fully with any UN Agency in [Middle East] but could not [repeat] not do so with UK-US sponsored Agency outside UN because this would jeopardize Israel['s] relation[s] with Russia.'

5) [Foreign Minister] under impression that Dep[artment] regional conference [in] Istanbul will discuss '[Middle East] security pact' [and] emphasized 'danger of any such pact unless Arab states cease talk about preparations for 'second round' [of] war with Israel.' US or UK support [of] such [a security] pact prior to Arab-Israeli peace would strengthen Arab instransigency and make Israel cooperation with pact impossible. (Disclosed nothing [repeat] nothing to Sharett about Istanbul agenda).

34. Sharett was to address the UN, meet with Secretary Acheson, and help launch a critically important United Jewish Appeal fundraising campaign.
35. McDonald to secretary of state, no. 820, November 14, 1949, NARA, RG 59, 501.BB Palestine, box 2127, folder 4.

6) As I was leaving [Foreign Minister] said he hoped to discuss above points and others [with Secretary of State].
Comment: [Received] impression Sharett optimistic about UN action or inaction on [Jerusalem] and on other issues directly involving Israel."

Tuesday, November 15

At five o'clock Shiloah came to take me to the home of the new chief of staff Rav Aluf [Major General] Yigael Yadin, the youngest chief of staff of any army in the world.[36] He is thirty-two. We were greeted at the door by Mrs. [Carmella] Yadin, who in her house slacks looked like a high school girl. The apartment is small, apparently three or four rooms, but none of them larger than my study at the residence. The furnishings were scant and modest.

After the usual preliminaries, and tea, Yadin launched into approximately an hour's talk about the military in the Middle East. He began by emphasizing the danger to what he assumed is the American program—peace and stability—inherent in the rapid Arab rearmament. Until now a sort of equilibrium of military strength had been established between Israel and its Arab neighbors. Any unsettling of this balance would precipitate an armaments race, which would inevitably increase the chances of a renewal of hostilities.

Yadin did not give figures, but characterized Jordan's rearmament as intense and that of Egypt as very rapid. As to Jordan's air force, Yadin admitted that it was just in the beginning stage but insisted that it was potentially dangerous. It was, however, Egypt which Yadin considered the most serious menace. The government there is spending large sums on modern equipment, including jet planes. This is the more significant because without Egypt's participation there will be no Arab attack on Israel. But, given Egyptian aggressive leadership, that attack would be certain.

At this point I asked Yadin about the reports that there is a strong body of opinion in Egypt in favor of withdrawal from Arab involvement, with a view to freeing the country for a fuller collaboration with Britain and the US and in the advancement of Egypt's leadership in Africa. Yadin said that of course there were leaders who favored this program, for example, the recent prime minister [Hussein Sirri Pasha] and others, but there were no convincing evidences that this point of view is in the ascendancy. The present meeting in Cairo of the representatives of the general staffs of the several Arab states, taken together with the Egyptian sponsorship of an Arab security pact, gave additional ground

---

36. Entry of November 14, 1948. Yadin served as IDF chief of staff from November 1949 to December 1952. McDonald reported that he succeeded Ya'akov Dori on November 9 because of Dori's ill health and that the change "confirms that IDF General Staff and command reorganization has been completed; reportedly after much bickering and many changes since [March] 1949." Yadin retired from military at age 35 over disagreements with government and returned to his chosen field of archaeology. McDonald to secretary of state, joint weeka no. 46, November 10, 1949, McDonald Papers, USHMM, box 8, folder 4.

for uneasiness.[37] Yadin said that there was no danger from Lebanon or from Syria singly, but that the rearmament of Iraq was more serious. The talk of a Middle East security pact was in itself mischievous, because it aroused hopes of revenge in the Arabs by giving seeming promise of Western aid. Such a pact prior to real peace between Jews and Arabs could only be regarded as, in effect, anti-Israel.

There is, Yadin added with great seriousness, an increasing uneasiness not only in the Israeli Army but in the Israeli government and public, lest the country be unprepared for the much talked of Arab second round. There is a minority party within the Army which, fearful of the advantage which would come to the Arabs through the completion of their present rearmament, would prefer to take the initiative and to "settle once for all with the Arabs."[38] He, Yadin however, and the majority of his colleagues prefer to maintain the peace on the basis of the status quo. These moderates, however, would have to reconsider their position if the Arabs continue their present program. If the war broke out again, it would be the aim of Israeli forces to drive deep into enemy territory. As the prime minister publicly stated, Israel this time intended that the war should be fought on enemy soil. Moreover, if the war were to come, Israel could not afford to let the Arabs strike the first blow. On the contrary, Israel should anticipate at least by a day or a few hours such a blow.

After this not very-encouraging talk, Comay, who had been present throughout, Yadin, his wife, and I visited on the balcony—stretched over our heads in Israeli fashion were the family clothes lines—about Yadin's former profession, archaeology. He said there were no present diggings going on in this field under foreign auspices. He recommended, however, as interesting the excavations near the mouth of the Yarkon, which have disclosed civilizations as far back as Solomon.[39]

37. In the Arab League meetings of October 1949, Egypt—to obviate talk of an Iraq-Syrian union—called for a collective security pact among the Arab states. See draft defensive security pact among the states of the Arab League, Cairo, *FRUS*, 1949, v. VI, 1506–1508; Michael Barnett and Etel Solingen, "Designed to Fail or Failure of Design? The Origins and Legacy of the Arab League," in *Crafting Cooperation: Regional International Institutions in Comparative Perspective*, eds. Amitav Acharya and Alastair Iain Johnston (New York: Cambridge University Press, 2007), 198–208.

38. UN Security Council Resolution 73 of August 11, 1949, expressed satisfaction with the armistice agreements and pointed to the Palestine Conciliation Commission as the route toward peace in the Middle East. On August 12, 1949, Dean Acheson told the Egyptian chargé in Washington that the new resolution "in effect removed the arms embargo imposed by its resolutions of May 29 and July 15, 1948." Limited sales to the Arab states by Great Britain and the US took place afterward, based on the principle that the weapons should serve the aims of self-defense and the maintenance of internal order. See *FRUS*, 1949, v. VI, 1302; *FRUS*, 1950, v. V, 685; Peter Hahn, *Caught in the Middle East*, 72–73; idem, *The United States, Great Britain, and Egypt, 1945–1956: Strategy and Diplomacy in the Early Cold War* (Chapel Hill: University of North Carolina Press, 1991), 77–83.

39. The excavations north of Tel Aviv on the banks of the Yarkon, which began in 1948, were the first in independent Israel and created ancient links to the contemporary Israeli state. See Yaakov Shavit and Mordechai Eran, *The Hebrew Bible Reborn: From the Holy Scripture to the Book of Books* (Berlin: Walter de Gruyter, 2007), 449.

In the evening to a delightful piano recital by Bobby's teacher, Mrs. Edith Kraus Bloedy. The recital at the museum gave us another opportunity to see pictures in [Yitzhak] Frenkel's show.

On November 22, 1949, McDonald wrote his former military attaché, Robert van der Velde, now working in US Army intelligence at Fort Meade. After praising Yadin as more forthcoming with information than his predecessor, he noted, "In several of the neighboring states there is continuous talk about a second round, with news from Egypt, Trans-Jordan, and elsewhere of rearmament. The attempts to implement Article VIII of the Trans-Jordan–Israel Armistice have thus far proved abortive and there are signs of conditions becoming less favorable. You will be able to interpret this better than will most people because of your experiences here."[40]

Wednesday, November 16

At ten at the [WIZO] Mothercraft Center, I participated in the CARE publicity distribution of the contents of one of their large packages to the children. As always for me, when children were involved, it was a pleasant experience.

In the evening, we had to hurry away from the Andrus-Frothingham cocktail party in order to get to Rebecca Sieff's in Tel Mond. Present at the latter, besides Rebecca and her niece, were [Leo] Istorik of the Anglo-Palestine Bank, [I. J.] Linton, formerly Israel representative in London, and the Helms. Almost the only noteworthy item in the talk was Helm's insistence that, if his experience in the British Middle East regional conference were a guide,[41] I certainly would not be allowed to hold, as I had said I planned to, a listener's brief during our Middle East session in Istanbul.

Thursday, November 17

The first full meeting of the diplomatic corps, held at the residence in the fitting environment of our elegant new furniture,[42] was much more interesting than I had supposed such a meeting could be. It was attended by Ershov for Russia, and the representatives of France, the Argentine, Romania, Great Britain, Italy, Holland, Belgium, Greece, Poland, Switzerland, Czechoslovakia, and Iran. First, we discussed the rather academic question whether or not we favored a diplomatic club. Happily, there was no enthusiasm for it and the matter was laid on the table. The second topic, the real purpose of the meeting, was to discuss plans for the diplomatic corps' formal presentation of its felicitations to President Weizmann on his 75th birthday. There was, of course, no objection

40. McDonald to van der Velde, November 22, 1949, McDonald Papers, Columbia University, box 20, folder 11.
41. Held in London in July 1949 to discuss political, social, and economic developments in the Middle East insofar as they could promote British strategic aims. See Louis, *The British Empire in the Middle East*, 578–583, 604–612.
42. Arrived November 15 through Haifa from Rome after numerous delays and arguments with McDonald's landlords, the Braudos, over his continued use of their furniture.

to this, and most of the points involved were quickly settled. Ershov agreed to act as the corps' spokesman in my absence and would speak in Russian. The president, I explained, would respond in Hebrew. But when I added that the Foreign Office preferred not to have any translation of either statement, Monsieur Guyon, the French representative, objected on the ground that the diplomatic corps should maintain the tradition in these matters and that this required a translation into the accepted language of diplomacy, implying, but not specifying, that this would be French. I explained that I had made this suggestion, but that the Foreign Office had rejected it. Undismayed by this, the corps then proceeded to express itself strongly and unanimously in favor of French translations. This was then decided upon. [Long discussion followed on housing problems for the diplomatic corps].

In the afternoon to the office for a long staff conference on a number of topics including housing. I took occasion to speak of the letter received that day from Secretary of Defense [Louis] Johnson thanking me for my strong letter of commendation of Colonel van der Velde.[43] Parenthetically, I also referred of my letter of commendation of Hooper to the Department as another illustration of my practice of supporting my colleagues. Turning then to the military situation, I reported briefly on the new chief of staff's talk with me two days earlier and asked the military their reaction to their luncheon with Yadin that same day. In general their reactions were similar to mine, that the political situation had worsened, that elements in the Israeli Army and cabinet would welcome aggressive initiative by the Arabs which would "open the door for a decisive victory," but that probably there would be no overt breach of the peace in the near future. The attachés were of the opinion that Yadin, the world's youngest chief of staff, would be more cooperative and more informative than had been his predecessor [Ya'akov Dori].

Friday, November 18

Mr. [Leo] Istorik, of the London office of the Anglo-Palestine Bank, came out to talk about the present impasse between the UK and Israel on the pounds blocked in England and the claims of one government against the other.[44] We discussed the possibility of the present stiff policy of the UK being influenced by political consideration and by the immediate financial stringency of the local authorities. At the end of our talk, however, I was still not clear as to Istorik's purpose in coming to see me. He said he had nothing he wished to ask me to do. Perhaps he was simply desirous of getting what information he could. In the course of our talk, he stressed that the great majority of shares of the

43. Entry of September 21, 1949.
44. Israel had made claims against the Anglo-Palestine Bank in London, but Great Britain refused to discuss the transfer of Israeli sterling balances because of unresolved claims and counterclaims resulting from the end of the Mandate. See entries of December 7, 1949, and March 22, 1950.

Anglo-Palestine Bank were held by non-Jews; only the voting shares were controlled by the Zionist Organization.[45]

Francis Ofner of the *Christian Science Monitor* and Constantine Poulis of the ONA [Overseas News Agency] and *The Nation* came out to ask me if they might fly with us to Istanbul. I hesitated to give a definite answer but was not encouraging. Later, after talking with Colonel Archibald, I told them that the answer had to be negative. The air attaché had argued that to take these two men would be to open the door for requests from all of the other journalists. Ruth [made] an additional point which had not occurred to me, that taking these two men might appear to my colleagues at Istanbul as a publicity stunt on my part.

Saturday, November 19

Goldie Meyerson brought out with her a young Jewish girl recently escaped from Baghdad. The latter's tale, as she gradually gained confidence, was depressingly familiar. It sounded just like the stories I used to hear of refugees during the first years of Hitler, before his assault on the Jews had become overt and unashamed. Common now is arbitrary arrest; conviction on the evidence of two Moslems on vague charges of Zionism or communism, with resultant penalties of three to seven years imprisonment; frequent blackmail by officials or private Moslems threatening to denounce their victims to the authority; discrimination in business, as for example through the refusal of import licenses to the extent of destroying businesses altogether in some fields; arbitrary dismissal from governmental posts, and in general such a veiled reign of terror as to make the whole Jewish community feel as if it were at the beginning of a persecution which would destroy it. The young lady had the impression the American embassy in Baghdad was not well informed. On the contrary, the American embassy in Teheran had the reputation among the Jews of being both well informed and very cooperative.[46]

At the Sam Sackses', where I arrived late for our usual midday Shabbat tea, there was the usual talk of housekeeping arrangements. . . . Of more significance was the casual reference by our hosts to a rather disquieting situation in the local schools. Their two boys, six and twelve, who go to the Ramat Gan public school, which is essentially General Zionist in its orientation, are from time to time called "members of the bourgeoisie" with contempt by their friends or neighbors who attend the labor-sponsored schools. In retort, the older boy called one of his detractors a "son of a mule." This very strong rejoinder is said to have silenced his detractor. To illustrate how far-reaching such party feeling among youngsters engendered by the party school system might go, the Sackses said that one of the reasons they had sent their older boy to the States for

45. The Zionist Organization created the Anglo-Palestine Bank in 1903 to help finance Jewish land purchases and development in Palestine.
46. See entry of October 17, 1949.

high school was his sensitiveness to these "class" jibes of his fellow youngsters. Almost startled by this casual revelation of one of the effects of the lack of a single public school system in Israel, I began to think that perhaps the effects of the present system may be more unfortunately divisive in fundamental ways than I had before thought likely.[47]

Sunday, November 20

Brief visit to the residence section of the Weizmann Institute at Rehovot. Our visit to Ashkelon was of extraordinary interest.[48] The orchards, now in a state of dissolution because of neglect following the fighting, and the other vegetation, are so luxuriant as to give one a more vivid impression of the almost tropical possibilities of Israel than any other part of the country, with the possible exception of some portions of the Jordan Valley. We were invited by the guards to take our fill of the grapefruit and oranges just approaching maturity. We also brought back a large bunch of figs, but the bananas unhappily had suffered so from neglect that none worthwhile were available. Depressing were the neglected wells, which with their ancient and primitive wooden apparatus for drawing the water from the fifteen or thirty meters below the surface, had through probably thousands of years maintained this rich oasis in the desert.

Equally interesting, but in a quite different way, were the ruins uncovered by the archaeologists of the ancient Crusader, Roman, and pre-Roman Ashkelon. The remains of the massive walls, which had once enclosed the city, were still visible on two or three sides. As we wandered about, my mind went back to David's famous lament on the death of Saul (Samuel II, 1:19–20): "The beauty of Israel is slain upon thy high places: how are the mighty fallen! Tell it not in Gath, publish it not in the streets of Ashkelon; lest the daughters of the Philistines rejoice, lest the daughters of the uncircumcised triumph." This extract shows how as early as David's time, a thousand BC, Ashkelon was a famous Philistine city;[49] it was one of the centers of the Philistine-dominated southern Palestine plain which resisted Jewish attempts at conquest even at the time of the largest expansion of Jewish power under David and Solomon. An incidental but a major advantage of work in Israel are the opportunities it affords for these excursions into ancient history, so intensely absorbing to anyone who has any historical sense.

47. Political parties had a major role in education in Israel's early years. Ben-Gurion later rejected their involvement as a divisive holdover from the Mandate and called for state-centered national education. The State Education Law, which instituted a national curriculum, was passed in 1953.

48. Ashkelon, formerly al-Majdal in the northern portion of the Gaza Strip, thirty miles south of Tel Aviv. The Egyptians had made it a base for attacks to the north and east in late May 1948. The IDF captured it in November as part of Operation Yoav. Egyptian forces and most of al-Majdal's 10,000 inhabitants then fled to Gaza. In 1949 Jewish settlers began to move in and remade the town. Perhaps 2,000 Arabs lived there in 1950 before being transferred in that year. Morris, *1948*, 333–334.

49. The Philistines captured the city from the Canaanites in about 1150 BCE; it was taken by the Crusaders in 1153 CE.

In the evening the family and I had a farewell dinner with Captain Froth-ingham and the Bradys and Hooper at the Gat.

Monday, November 21

Comay of the American desk of the Foreign Office called and offered to supply me with any documents I might need before I left for Istanbul. I said I would check with him again. Gurdus of the French press called to ask if I had any statement about Istanbul. My answer was no.

At teatime [Walter] Eytan and Comay came and remained for two hours. After they had admired the furniture, we all, including Ford, settled down in the study. My first question to Eytan concerned communism in Israel. His reply was substantially as follows: Both government and people are staunchly opposed to communism. It would be difficult to imagine a more anti-communist government than the one headed by the prime minister. Ben-Gurion is by instinct and with every fiber of his body anti-communist. His recent frank speaking is an illustration of his true feeling. He, like leaders of the Labour Party in England and the Socialists in France, is more violently opposed to communism than are, for example, the moderates or conservatives.

The people of Israel, except for a very small minority, are inherently anti-communist. The Jews by nature are opposed to the regimentation inherent in communism. Although there are many among the population who are liberal or even interested in leftish or radical concepts, they do not support communism—on the contrary, they regard it as blocking their hopes of economic and political freedom. Even the rank and file of Mapam is not sympathetic with commu-nism. Observers are apt to be misled by the editorials of *Al-HaMishmar* and by the theoretical speeches of some of the Mapam leaders. The significant fact, however, is that the Mapam appeal to the masses is invariably on domestic issues such as wages, cost of living index, etc. Another misleading factor has been Sharett's practice of issuing public statements to "keep the record bal-anced" following anti-communist pronouncements such as the recent ones of Ben-Gurion.[50] These statements, however, should not be regarded as more than formal.

According to Eytan, the carefully drafted terms of the several armistices do not permit—as Bunche clearly intended that they should not—any escape by either party from the terms of the agreement. The armistices can be ended only by treaties of peace. It is notable, too, that the Security Council is specifi-cally brought into the arena, but that even the Security Council cannot release either party unilaterally from its armistice obligations.[51] The binding nature of these agreements is a fine tribute to the skillful draftsmanship and the con-sistent and farsighted purpose of Dr. Bunche.

---

50. Ben-Gurion's most recent anticommunist statements to the Knesset are recorded in McDonald's weekly reports from November 1949, McDonald Papers, USHMM, box 8, folder 4.
    51. See entry of November 8, 1949.

In reply to my query about the attitude of Abdullah, he said: Abdullah is the one Arab ruler who is genuinely anxious and ready to make peace terms with Israel; of course, on conditions acceptable to him. There is no reason to suppose that, if left to himself, Abdullah would not be able to agree with Israel. His anxiety and willingness to negotiate on realistic terms vary with his comparative status vis-à-vis his Arab neighbors; when he feels strong, he is more ready, when he feels weak, he withdraws. At the moment, he is in a sort of midway. There has been no meeting recently between Abdullah and any Israel representative; Abdullah met Novomeysky a few weeks ago, but this was in no sense a political talk, nor did Novomeysky represent the Israeli government.[52]

On the issue of Jerusalem, Abdullah is staunchly opposed to any form of internationalization. In his arguments with the Arab leaders, he reminds them that they too are really opposed, but give verbal support only because the Jews are opposed. Abdullah argues, too, that internationalization involving demilitarization, and thus the withdrawal of the Legion, would leave the whole city open to Jewish occupation; in possession of that strategic center, the Jews would then dominate the whole of Palestine—a situation which none of the Arab leaders is willing to contemplate.

As to Iraq, Eytan pleaded lack of personal information, since it is the one Arab state which he has never visited. The regime there he characterized as corrupt, backward, and inefficient. The only progress in recent decades has been that forced by the British for their own purposes upon Iraq. Remote from Israel and in no conceivable fear of Israeli aggression, Iraq is free to indulge its hatred, even though this involves, for example, through the loss of the pipeline oil revenues, "cutting off its nose to spite the Jewish face." Eytan does not anticipate any change in the position of Iraq in the near future.

The Syrian election according to [Eytan] was indecisive and will probably not change the regime.[53] The pressure from Damascus for the union with Iraq has slackened, presumably because of the unexpectedly strong opposition from several quarters. At the moment, there appears to be a marked tendency towards a pro-US orientation. Heretofore, Syria during its short history as an independent state has kept itself free from political commitments to the outside. Now, however, because of the economic pressure, Syrian leaders are beginning to contemplate the possibility of "paying the US's price for financial aid." I made no comment on this appraisal.

In Lebanon, there is the sharpest contrast between desires and words. Beirut ardently desires peace; it was intensely frightened by the drive for Syrian-Iraq union because this would at best mean the loss of certain parts of its terri-

---

52. Abdullah met Novomeysky in London on August 31, 1949, and continued to use him as a conduit for peace negotiations. See Mary Christian Wilson, *King Abdullah, Britain, and the Making of Jordan* (New York: Cambridge University Press, 1987), 202–203; *DFPI*, v. 4, editorial note, 636.

53. Syria held elections for its constituent assembly on November 16, 1949. The Syrian People's Party, the most powerful at the time and which pushed for union with Iraq, won 63 of the 114 seats.

tory, and at worst the loss of its independence; it would therefore welcome peace on the basis of the status quo. But it is so fearful of Arab opinion and so anxious to prove that, despite its approximately 50% Christian population, it is loyal to the cause of "Arab unity," that it goes so far as to announce its policy to be "opposition to whatever Israel favors."

As to Egypt, I expressed the following opinion. The present "caretaker" government is most unlikely to do more than maintain the status quo.[54] To underline this point, Eytan told the story of Switzerland's negotiation, or rather attempted negotiation, with Cairo for the renewal of a treaty for the protection of its interests in Egypt. This treaty had been repeatedly renewed in the past and raised no new questions. Nonetheless, the obviously stalling tactics of Cairo had finally persuaded Bern that there was no use in pursuing the matter now. The Swiss, therefore, have postponed further exchanges until after the election. Eytan added that there was, of course, divided opinion in Egypt as to the future orientation of the country; the anti-Arab entanglement school headed by Sidqi Pasha[55] probably had more support than the public attitude of the present government suggests. The recent Cairo initiative on behalf of an Arab security pact was pressed only while the Syrian-Iraq union was being strongly urged; when the latter faded into the background, the Egyptians were apparently glad of the opportunity to drop the security pact propaganda.

On the role of Ambassador [Jefferson] Caffery,[56] Eytan was almost startlingly interesting. I do not refer to his confirmation of one of the reported personal habits of the new ambassador, but rather to the role which he thinks the latter has been playing. Mr. Caffery has, according to Eytan, taken a high hand even with the king, comparable to that of Sir Miles Lampson when the latter was British ambassador.[57] This attitude, together with Caffery's general manner and his rank as senior career ambassador, has caused the Israelis to suspect that the US is following a policy aimed to replace Britain as the most important foreign influence in Cairo.[58] Ford and I in complete good faith sought to dissuade Eytan of this interpretation.

Speaking in general terms of Israel's relations with its neighbors, Eytan said it was significant that only those with frontiers common with Israel had

54. Under Hussein Sirri Pasha, independent prime minister between the king's disbanding of the parliament on November 7, 1949, and new elections on January 3, 1950.

55. Ismael Sidqi Pasha (1875–1950), nationalist prime minister, February–December 1946; called for full British withdrawal and Egyptian control of the Sudan; failed to come to mutual defense arrangement with Great Britain; opposed Egyptian entrance into war with Israel in 1948.

56. Jefferson Caffery (1886–1974), US diplomat since 1911; US ambassador to Brazil, where he pressed for Brazilian acceptance of Jewish refugees, 1937–1944; ambassador to France, 1945–1948; ambassador to Egypt, 1949–1955. Philip F. Dur, *Jefferson Caffery of Louisiana: Ambassador of Revolutions* (Lafayette: University of Southwest Louisiana, 1982).

57. Sir Miles Lampson (1880–1964), Lord Killearn, British high commissioner to Egypt and the Sudan, 1934–1936; ambassador to Egypt and the Sudan, 1936–1946; forced King Farouk to replace pro-German cabinet in February 1942 with an anti-Axis Wafd cabinet under Mustafa al-Nahhas Pasha by presenting a personal ultimatum and surrounding the king's palace with tanks.

58. See Hahn, *The United States, Great Britain, and Egypt, 1945–1956*.

bothered to sign armistices. Only these were significant in the problems of peace, at least in the near future. Comay brought with him extra copies of the Hebrew-English text of the four armistice agreements and a summary statement of Israel's position on Jerusalem. The full memorandum of the Israel delegation at Lake Success dated November 11, a thirty-five-page lawyer's brief,[59] was left for me to read during the evening while I lent them my one text of the Clapp Interim Report, received a few hours earlier.[60] It was agreed that we would exchange these documents on Tuesday through [whomever] would come to the house from HaKirya.

Gordon Clapp's Economic Survey Mission (ESM) counted 757,000 Arab refugees—652,000 of whom were in need. But it concluded on the basis of meetings with Israeli and Arab officials that neither repatriation nor resettlement programs were possible for the foreseeable future because of the unsettled political situation. The ESM recommended an eighteen-month program that would move refugees into local developmental work projects centered on land reclamation, road building, water distribution, and the like—and off UN and other relief programs by the end of 1950. The cost would be $54.9 million, half to be financed increasingly by the states where the refugees found themselves and where the projects would be done. The British had already agreed on an interest-free £1 million loan to Jordan for this purpose.

Tuesday, November 22

I should record here that Ford, in a conference on Monday, confirmed my impression that the list which included the names of the career consuls as well as the diplomatic representatives whom I invited to the residence last week to discuss the presidential birthday reception had been prepared by HaKirya and sent to our office by Giveon, in charge of protocol during Simon's absence. Hence it is clear that HaKirya is responsible for the proposed separate treatment of the honorary consuls.[61]

Wednesday, November 23

Awakened by the noise of heavy thunder, which with the brilliant flashes of lightning, made me so pessimistic about our getting off that I telephoned the colonel to inquire about the possible delay [in trip to Istanbul]. Happily, however, the storm was local, and we were able to avoid it by detouring a few miles

---

59. United Nations General Assembly, Delegation from Israel, *Memorandum on the Future of Jerusalem: An Analysis of the Palestine Conciliation Commission's Draft Instrument* (New York: United Nations, 1949). See also memorandum by Stabler, November 17, 1949, *FRUS*, 1949, v. VI, 1495–1498. For additional Israeli efforts in November 1949 concerning the Jerusalem settlement, see *DFPI*, v. 4, d. 401, 403, 405, 413, 415, 417, 419, 420, 420, 434, 439, 446.

60. The ESM Interim Report was completed and signed in Beirut on November 6 and submitted to the UN secretary-general by the PCC on November 16. *United Nations Economic Survey Mission for the Middle East, First Interim Report* (Washington, DC: Department of State, 1949). Summarized in the later discussion.

61. The eight honorary consuls in Israel were not invited to the presidential birthday reception, causing some irritation among them.

to the north. Not having to stop in Cyprus, we made the trip to Athens in five hours.

Thursday, November 24

The trip from Athens to Istanbul was less interesting than it would have been had we been permitted to fly over the Dardanelles. Nonetheless I was glad of the opportunity to see the northwestern corner of Anatolia, over which we flew at relatively low height. The view coming in over the Sea of Marmara was excellent but a little too distant for us to see Istanbul clearly.

We were met at the airport by Mr. Baldwin, the consul general,[62] and members of his staff. From that moment until we left five days later, we received every possible courtesy from the local mission. The drive into the city through the old walls, some of which go back to the early Middle Ages, through the older city with its striking mosques and minarets, across the Golden Horn to our hotel, the Pera Palace, gave us fascinating impressions. The hotel, however, which had been deluxe fifty years ago, was rather depressing, with its rather tawdry grandeur which had never been in very good taste. Nonetheless, we were to be very comfortable there. The Baldwins gave a large cocktail party for the visitors and local staff. I was delighted to meet there most of the men with whom I was to spend the next five days.

From November 25 to 29, Assistant Secretary of State George McGhee, who headed the Bureau of Near Eastern, South Asian, and African Affairs, hosted in Istanbul the US mission chiefs in the Near East.[63] As he put it later, "US defense policy in the Middle East continued to focus on Greece and Turkey. A broader defense policy on behalf of the entire region was not yet part of our Cold War strategy."[64]

The US defense establishment had determined that the region had become key to US security for two reasons: It offered an outer rim of strategic bases through which to contain the Soviet Union, and US military deployments and European economic recovery depended on Middle Eastern petroleum reserves. The northern tier of states—Greece, Turkey, and Iran—had been subjected to communist pressure since the end of World War II. The Arab states and Israel provided strategic depth. Yet with the United States' growing strategic commitments to Western Europe with the formation of NATO in April 1949, and to the Far East with Mainland China having fallen to the communists in October, it could not make a substantial military commitment to the Middle East, the countries of which were suspicious of one another in any event. Britain was even less able to manage the strain.[65]

The State Department and the British Foreign Office wanted to coordinate Anglo-American strategy for the Middle East. Senior US and British officials led by

---

62. LaVerne Baldwin, assigned to Istanbul in July 1949.
63. Preparatory documents in *FRUS*, 1949, v. VI, 165–168.
64. McGhee, *On the Frontline in the Cold War*, 32.
65. In general see Cohen, *Fighting World War Three from the Middle East: Allied Contingency Plans, 1945–1954*.

McGhee and Michael Wright, Bevin's assistant undersecretary for foreign affairs, held intensive talks in Washington earlier in November 1949.[66] They tried to harmonize Middle Eastern policy to ensure the Western, anticommunist orientation of the Arab states and Israel. In part, this aim called for economic development to create conditions for peace and democratic progress. A US-UK imposed peace, it was reasoned, would create bitterness between the Middle Eastern states and the West. The sooner the regional parties came to grips with the problem of peace, the sooner it might emerge. In the meantime, a collective security arrangement among the Arab states, as proposed by Egypt, or the mergers of states, as discussed by Syria and Iraq, might do more harm than good.

McGhee and his deputies traveled to Istanbul after the meetings with Wright. McDonald kept a very detailed record of the talks there. To the best of the editors' knowledge such a record is not available elsewhere. The editors have abridged the lengthy discussion of Greece, Turkey, and Iran.

Friday, November 25

While Ruth and Bobby took the easy way—an automobile tour through the city—Mr. Clapp and a few of us did a real sightseeing tour with Mrs. Hutton.[67] The Blue Mosque, Santa [Hagia] Sophia, and the Mosque of Suleiman the Magnificent were our three chief objectives. Visiting the three edifices at the same time enabled one to understand the theory that Moslem religious buildings in Istanbul were deeply rooted in the practice of copying the basic features of Santa Sophia. As we gazed at the façade of the latter, stripped bare of all its marble and mosaics—these now constitute the façade of St. Mark's in Venice, the spoils of the Crusaders [looted in 1204]—one was reminded again of how cannibalistic successive generations and cultures are. The inside of Santa Sophia, with its sections of brilliant mosaics uncovered by Professor [Thomas] Whittemore[68] and his colleagues, gave us a suggestion of how brilliantly beautiful this great church must have been. The remains of Moslem overpainting tend to accentuate the perfection of the earlier surfaces. Our visit would have been even more wonderful if we had been able to have Professor Whittemore as our guide.

Late afternoon George Wadsworth gave a cocktail party at the consulate, the former embassy where he keeps an elaborate apartment.[69] The evening dinner given by Wadsworth in the name of McGhee marked the beginning of

---

66. Major documents from the McGhee-Wright discussions in *FRUS*, 1949, v. VI, 50–90.
67. Wife of Paul C. Hutton (1903–1983), US consul in Istanbul.
68. Thomas Whittemore (1871–1950), Harvard Byzantine scholar; established Byzantine Institute of America in Boston with field office in Istanbul, 1930; beginning in 1931, with the permission of Mustafa Kemal, uncovered the Byzantine mosaics at Hagia Sophia that had been discovered during the massive restoration under Sultan Abdülmecid (1839–1861) and then covered over again at his behest.
69. George Wadsworth (1893–1958), US minister to Lebanon and Syria, 1944–1947; US ambassador to Iraq, 1947–1948; US ambassador to Turkey, 1948–1952. His antipathy to Zionism is discussed in Goda et al., eds., *To the Gates of Jerusalem*.

our work period. The Wadsworth-McGhee dinner was limited to the chiefs of mission. During the meal, I talked with Ambassador [John] Wiley[70] and Bill Porter.[71]

At the conclusion, McGhee talked at considerable length but extremely well about the plans for and his hope for the conference. He began by expressing thanks to Wadsworth and his guess [that] the conference would be an annual affair. Exchanges at it should be frank and free without restraint or platitude. The US is emerging as a major power in the Near East area, in part as an inheritor of British responsibilities which the UK is no longer desirous or capable of bearing and partially because of the increasing necessity for the containment of the USSR. Oil is, of course, a major consideration, but there is wide misunderstanding on this issue. In wartime, either side is expected to be able to deny the other the full, if not the partial, use of these vast resources. Control of them is vital in [the] peacetime economy and in the Cold War; it is expected to be of little value in a shooting war. McGhee sketched our current relations with the UK, and in particular, plans for future collaboration in our area. This he was to elaborate the next morning. The assistant secretary emphasized the Department's objection to the US's participation in additional regional pacts, underlining that such pacts without the will and the power to make them effective are futile and misleading. Hence, chiefs of mission should discourage their governments from expectations of such pacts.

American aid would be available through the anticipated US support of the Economic Survey Mission [ESM] program, which McGhee outlined briefly, and through the Point Four Program.[72] As to the latter, McGhee indicated that the amount available for the Middle East would be five million dollars, to be limited to the payment of technical experts to work on the operational level. While the amount of money might seem small, it could buy, it was anticipated, the services of 250 experts. The technical skill of this number, rightly utilized, could make a vast difference in the improvement of living standards. Thus, at the very beginning [it] was made clear that the large and vague expectations of the so-called McGhee Plan would have to be radically inflated by some 90%.[73]

At the conclusion of this summation, [McGhee] called upon each of the chiefs of mission to state his country's problems as he sees them in the light of

---

70. John Cooper Wiley (1893–1967), US ambassador to Iran, 1948–1950.

71. William J. Porter (1914–1988), foreign service officer; served in Baghdad, 1937–1941, in Beirut, 1941–1943, and in Damascus under Wadsworth, 1943–1946; on the Palestine desk in the State Department's Division of Near Eastern Affairs, 1946–1947; US consul in Nicosia, 1947–1950.

72. See entry of March 6, 1949. McGhee also had discussed using the Point Four Program for long-range development in the Middle East with Michael Wright on November 17, 1949. See discussion in *FRUS*, 1949, v. VI, 76–80.

73. Meaning that McGhee's initial offer of $5 million of Point Four funds would not be sufficient for Middle East development.

national conditions. Caffery, who was first called upon, spoke rather briefly but well. Thus, from the first, I was pleasantly surprised by Caffery, who neither that night nor on any subsequent occasion lived up to his "billing" as an eccentric. On the contrary, he showed himself matter of fact, shrewd, abstemious, and restrained. Caffery spoke of his very friendly reception in Cairo, of his direct entrée to the king, and of the Egyptian appreciation that a senior ambassador had been sent there. He thought the Egyptians divided in their minds as to their future role as between becoming a great African power and remaining the chief Arab state. He doubted that the present so-called caretaker government would take any initiative in international affairs and that therefore any lead by Egypt would have to wait until after the January parliamentary elections.

Ambassador [James Rives] Childs of Saudi Arabia explained the very special status of his country, the patriarchal and absolute rule of King Ibn Saud, the problem of the succession to the throne,[74] the desire of the king for a special guarantee from the US against potential aggression, either Hashemite or Israeli. He urged that very prompt action was needed if the king were to be satisfied that the US would justify its special status in Saudi Arabia.[75]

A. David Fritzlan[76] talked shortly but well about Jordan, the king's concern for agreement with Israel, his determination against internationalization of Jerusalem, his problem of succession, his opposition to the Syrian-Iraq union, and his program for the absorption of Arab Palestine.

James Hugh Keeley, Jr., of Syria, despite a very heavy cold, which should have kept him in bed, lived up fully to his reputation for definiteness of opinion and volubility and strength of expression. He described, with vividness and feeling, Syrian resentment at the US's "partiality" in favor of Israel and at our country's unwillingness to force the Jews to live up to the UN resolutions. McGhee took exception to the charge of partiality, saying that at least during the last six months the US had held an even hand. In nearly each of the subsequent sessions, we were to hear from Keeley other versions of his central theme, that if the US wished to recover any of its former prestige in the Syrian and Arab world, it would have to "give evidence by deeds, not words, of confession of past sins and of a sincere repentance and a desire to make amends."

74. Saudi Arabia had no established rules for royal succession and the king, aged 73, had not designated an heir.

75. Refers to oil concessions through ARAMCO and the air base at Dhahran. See Irvine H. Anderson, *Aramco, the United States, and Saudi Arabia: A Study of the Dynamics of Foreign Oil Policy, 1933–1950* (Princeton, NJ: Princeton University Press, 1981); and Aaron David Miller, *Search for Security: Saudi Arabian Oil and American Foreign Policy, 1939–1949* (Chapel Hill: University of North Carolina Press, 1980).

76. A. David Fritzlan (1914–1996), US second secretary and vice consul in Jordan, 1949–1952; acting head of mission, November 1949; strongly anti-Zionist. In a 1990 interview Fritzlan described McDonald as "a well-known, ardent Zionist, though not a Jew, who could never see anything but the Jewish and Israeli side of things, who was completely and utterly sold out. I don't say that he was literally bought, but sold out his principles, his thinking, and everything to the benefit of the Zionist cause. So our relationship with the Tel Aviv embassy under his stewardship [was] nothing, didn't exist, just pro-forma. See United States, Department of State, *Jordan, Country Reader*, www.adst.org/Readers/Jordan.pdf.

Edward S. Crocker II, ambassador to Baghdad, took in general Keeley's line, but with somewhat less earnestness or vividness. He is on the whole a much less colorful or attractive person than is Keeley. He also spoke of the special problems of his government, of his personal anxiety that the loan being contemplated by the International Bank should go through as promptly as possible, and that British unavowed opposition to the loan should be thwarted.[77] He characterized Britain's role in Iraq as that of a colonial power discouraging initiative of Iraqis or by any other outside group. He thought we should ask the British to slide over and give us a chance to help the country advance more rapidly.

Ambassador George Wadsworth spoke with enthusiasm of Turkey, of its willingness and ability to fight and for the period at least to hold up the Soviet juggernaut. He indicated the outline, which he was to fill in later, of the large role which the US was playing in increasing Turkey's military potential.[78] His repeated emphasis that Turkey's position in the whole area was unique brought from his colleagues good-natured jeers. Rather to my surprise, Wadsworth said nothing which would indicate that he had spent much of his career fighting eloquently the cause of Arab countries against the Jews.

Ambassador John C. Wiley of Iran began on the high line, which he followed throughout the conference, that Iran, though a Moslem country, was actively disinterested in Arab internal differences or in their quarrels with Israel. His country he regarded as in the same light as Turkey and Greece, except that it was almost wholly neglected by the US. With a few brief strokes he pictured the threat to his country from the north and the importance that it should be strengthened to the point where it should at least act as a series of roadblocks against Russian advance. The young shah whom Wiley regards as our best bet . . . is modern-minded, genuinely interested in the welfare of his people and desirous to advance their future well-being.[79]

My turn was next, by which time it was already far past twelve o'clock. I therefore was among the very briefest. I sought to fit the Israel portrait into the general gallery without unnecessarily raising controversial issues, for I had decided that I would hold a listening brief as long as possible.

William J. Porter, consul at Nicosia, then spoke briefly about the large communist development on Cyprus and of British toleration of this movement as a makeweight against the native Greek desire for absorption in the Greek

---

77. The Iraqi government applied for a loan from the British and then, after the British refused, from the International Bank for Reconstruction and Development, which demurred because of the unbalanced Iraqi budget. The Iraqis next tried the Iraq Petroleum Company, which would agree only on the condition that Iraq reopen the pipeline to Haifa. Matthew Elliot, *Independent Iraq: The Monarchy and British Influence, 1941–1958* (London: I. B. Tauris, 1996), 74.

78. For the US-Turkish defense relationship see Ekavi Athanassopoulou, *Turkey–Anglo-American Security Interests, 1945–1952: The First Enlargement of NATO* (New York: Frank Cass, 1999).

79. Mohammed Reza Shah Pahlavi (1919–1980), ruled Iran, 1941–1979; backed by United States and Great Britain; promoted secularization and westernization of Iran.

motherland. He thought representations should be made by the US to Britain on this issue.[80]

Finally, William C. Burdett, Jr. of Jerusalem and Lowell C. Pinkerton of Beirut spoke briefly, as befitted a near one o'clock hour.

Saturday, November 26

The first of our regular business sessions began promptly at ten at the consulate, the former embassy, which was very near to our hotel. In addition to the chiefs of missions, the following were present during all or most of the sessions: Burton Y. Berry, McGhee's lieutenant for Near East and Africa;[81] Gordon H. Mattison, in charge under McGhee of our area, Israel and the Arab states;[82] Jack Blanchard Minor, an associate of [Henry] Grady;[83] Philip W. Ireland from Cairo;[84] William Langdon Sands,[85] Gordon Clapp of ESM, who was present throughout all the sessions except those of the last two days when he was ill, and an associate of Mr. Wiley.

After a few minutes spent in discussing housekeeping matters, McGhee gave a résumé of his talk of the night before and elaborated at considerable length a report on the recent talks with Michael Wright, of the UK Foreign Office, in Washington. Several hours a day had been spent by department officials with Wright in a comprehensive survey of Anglo-American relations in our area. Complete agreement in principle was reached on every important issue, and plans were laid for further meetings.[86] Regional agreements [have been made] on the working level. Both countries were recognized to have the same general objectives, though in certain countries specific interests might not be identical. For example, in Iraq, India and Africa, Britain's strategic interests and her traditional position are not identical with ours. There are, as McGhee indicated, "points of asymmetry."

Wright agreed as to the general unity of Anglo-American interests. He underlined that the Middle East is the key to the struggle with Russia. Its

80. After the war the British aimed to maintain control of Cyprus, a crown colony with a mostly Greek population that wanted unification with Greece, as a key strategic fallback position in the Eastern Mediterranean. The United States reached agreement with Britain in late 1947 to use Cyprus as a bomber base. The CIA set up monitoring bases there in 1949. Louis, *The British Empire in the Middle East*, 205–225; Yiannes P. Roubatis, *Tangled Webs: The U.S. in Greece, 1947– 1967* (New York: Pella, 1989); and Monteagle Stearns, *Entangled Allies: US Policy Toward Greece, Turkey, and Cyprus* (New York: Council on Foreign Relations, 1992).

81. Burton Y. Berry (1901–1985), career diplomat and also OSS officer during World War II in Istanbul (1943) and Bucharest (1944); had ties in Istanbul with Teddy Kollek, Ehud Avriel, and other Yishuv delegates; director, Office of African and Near Eastern Affairs (which was moved into McGhee's Bureau of Near Eastern, South Asian, and African Affairs), 1949–1952; ambassador to Baghdad, 1952–1954; noted collector of Middle Eastern coins, gems, textiles, and other antiques.

82. Gordon H. Mattison (1915–1999), deputy director, Office of African and Near Eastern Affairs.

83. Jack Blanchard Minor, attaché in the Office of Administration under the US High Commissioner in Germany.

84. Philip W. Ireland (b. 1902), first secretary, US embassy, Cairo.

85. William L. Sands, consul, US legation, Beirut; later editor of *Middle East Journal* for twenty-five years.

86. Documents in *FRUS*, 1949, v. VI, 50–90.

control by the USSR would break [the] British road to Asia; would so advantage Russia as to work irretrievable damage to the UK and that, therefore, it is essential that the US assume a larger role in the area. McGhee agreed because: oil; estimated 130,000,000,000 units as compared with 20,000,000,000 units in the reserves of the US. The Middle East reserves are by far the most vast in the world.

It will not be easy to ward off communism; must do more than back the governments in power; we support nationalism against communism. Wright agreed that nationalism was a vital makeweight against communism. He agreed that there should also be the abandonment of colonial type of exploitation in this area. There is no longer any place for the type of policy associated with French, Belgian, and Dutch colonial administration.

[The] US is to keep its policies on [a] UN basis. It is not to propose overall solution[s] which would not be acceptable to either side [in the Arab-Israeli conflict], but would bring blame from both [onto] the US and embarrassment to the UN. Hence, [the] US continues [to] support [the] PCC; while recognizing [the] latter's lack of progress, [the US] considers it useful . . . for [the] long pull, coordinating direct talks, in addition to our support of such direct talks. It is desirous to keep separate political [questions] from relief and development programs. As to Jerusalem, [the] US supports [the] PCC report but would consider conciliatory amendments; but [the US] will not take the initiative in altering [the] PCC [draft] resolution. [The] US agrees with Wright on inclusion of Arab Palestine in Jordan in due time.

Wright explained British long-range plans for Middle East and Far East. [He] presented detailed studies for [a] 15-year program [of] public works in several of [the] Arab countries. Plans for public health, etc., [are] designed to increase standard of living. With this program, [the] US [is] in essential agreement. [The] UK recognizes it has not done enough, that [its] Middle East office with its eight technicians [is] insufficient. Most of these [projects], it is indicated, are ordinary, except Owen Falls.[87] An example of [the] failure to implement early plans is Iraq, where no ground has been broken despite completion of Haigh Report five years ago.[88]

[The] US and UK see alike on Point Four. Moreover, [they agree on the] beginnings of UK-US coordination in [the] Clapp [Economic Survey Mission] recommendations during [the] first years. Nothing is to be said about these plans or to our respective [host] governments. [The] US and UK agreed that it would be undesirable to try to parcel out spheres of influence [in the Middle East]. The UK would in fact be willing to "move over" to give us room. It was recognized that private capital would [play] little role.

---

87. Owen Falls Dam, hydroelectric power project on the Nile in Uganda, built 1950–1954.

88. F. F. Haigh, *Report on the Control of the Rivers of Iraq*, published in 1952, was a 1944 comprehensive survey of irrigation in Iraq completed by British engineers. It also contained development projects such as marsh draining. See Joseph Sassoon, *Economic Policy in Iraq, 1932–1950* (New York: Frank Cass, 1987), 143–145.

As to the ESM, [the] UK and US [are] in basic agreement and have both approved the draft General Assembly resolution.[89] [The] UK had agreed to the transfer [of responsibility from the UN Relief for Palestine Refugees (UNRPR)] proposed in the resolution and approved of the idea that, while UN auspices were maintained, there should not be UN administration.[90] [The] phrase used was "as thin a UN coating as possible." As to financing, it was agreed in general that the US fund one half of the $53 million suggested by the ESM, the UK a fourth, and France, 15%. Wright suggested the desirability of using sterling balances.

On the subject of Arab unity, Wright had spoken at length. [The] UK had deplored [the] 1919 fragmentation, which violated [the] Arab desire for unity. Extreme nationalism was against [the] Western powers. If now unity were blocked by the West, [the] Arabs would again fall into intense bitterness. There is also deep desire for change and reform. For [the] West to block unity would be interpreted as blocking reforms. [The] UK would, therefore, not oppose any change by peaceful and constitutional means. [The] US and UK should combat [the] French idea of status quo [at all costs]. [The] US's position was not to oppose union by constitutional and peaceful means. [The US] was concerned, however, [about] the several sources of opposition to [a] Syrian-Iraqi union. Is essential that [such a] union should express desire of people and should not be aimed at any single state. The British point of view was almost identical. [McGhee is] convinced that Britain had not instigated [the] Syria-Iraq move. France had been directly opposed [to it] and had asked the US also to oppose [it].

On the subject of pacts, McGhee said it was too early to express any view about Egypt's inclusion in a general [security] pact. Moreover, a Middle East pact on the Atlantic model [is] not now the US policy, [and] was also not desired by [the] UK.[91] [The] US now wishes to maintain [a] balance between [the] Arab states and Israel. There should be no military assistance except to Saudi Arabia. [In the] meantime, [the] US gives general support to UK treaties [in] this area.

McGhee added that the US is in the process of examining its treaty relations with all the Arab states. As to the Haifa refinery, US and UK agreed on the desirability of its opening [as soon as possible]; [they] agreed to [apply]

---

89. Working Draft Resolution Prepared by Department of State, November 21, 1949, *FRUS*, 1949, v. VI, 1500–1502; called for financial contributions to realize proposals in the Economic Survey Mission Interim Report.

90. The Working Draft also called, per the ESM interim report, for the establishment of a Near East Relief and Works Agency with a director who was responsible to the General Assembly and who would choose his own staff. UN General Assembly Resolution 302, enacted on December 8, 1949, established the United Nations Relief and Works Agency [UNRWA] for Palestine to carry out the ESM's proposals, with a director to be appointed by the secretary-general. The UNRWA replaced the UN Relief for Palestine Refugees [UNRPR], established in the General Assembly Resolution 212 of November 19, 1948.

91. The United Kingdom, as had been its policy, preferred bilateral agreements with the Arab states.

continued pressure, but not to the extent of provoking a crisis. [The] US is supporting UK representation.

In general, McGhee said that on the London level there was almost complete UK-US agreement. [The] UK [was] a little taken aback by the US suggestion of 250 technicians for the Near East under Point Four. [The] general idea of coordination is on [the] model of [the] Latin American coordinator in Washington.[92] Wright's idea was for the use of British planning under American direction with long-range educational objectives, [and] coordination of the US [with the British] Middle East Office while maintaining separate approaches.[93]

McGee said no report[s] on his talks with Wright were to be made to Tel Aviv but [were made] fully to [McDonald's] UK colleague [Helm]. At the end of his long account, McGhee announced that each of us would be asked to outline the basic political trend in our several countries, and called on Caffery to begin.

Caffery said that Farouk had initiated the replacement of [Ibrahim Abd al-Hadi Pasha] by Sirri Pasha. [The] present caretaker government [is] representative of all parties, [and is] to maintain [political] balance pending [the] election [in January 1950] and the redistricting by decree. The campaign would be virulent, with the possibility of riots. If [the] election [is] free, [the] Wafd would win, but Nahhas Pasha[94] would never be forgiven by the king. Farouk says he will not interfere in [the] elections. [The next] prime minister will back [full] independence [from Britain]. [The] king [has] not yet decided on his policy. As to [the] campaign issue, all parties make about [the] same speeches regarding fellahin, Suez, and Sudan. Prime minister [Sirri Pasha] is Western-minded and, being an engineer, is less political than most Egyptians. For [a] time, [the] prime minister flirted with Nuri al-Said[95] [as secretary-general of the Arab League] against Azzam Pasha, but Azzam won because of Egypt's opposition to [the] Syria-Iraq union.[96] [The] prime minister invoked [a] collective security pact against [the proposed] Syria-Iraq union. At first there was no draft, merely a request for a vote in principle. As a counter-move, Iraq called for close federation. [There is] no doubt of [the] intensity of Egypt's opposition to Iraq-Syria union. All parties have talked themselves into opposition to [the] British remaining [in] the Suez [Canal zone]. [A] Wafd victory would be disadvantageous

92. Refers to the Office of the Coordinator of Inter-American Affairs, established during World War II to coordinate economic and social policy toward Latin America. This office was abolished in 1946, and its functions were assumed in 1949 by the Office of American Republic Affairs in the State Department.
93. The Developmental Division of the British Middle East Office, itself within the Foreign Office, had only eight or nine technical experts, but had completed a great deal of survey work.
94. Mustafa al-Nahhas Pasha (1879–1965), Wafd leader; prime minister 1942–1944; helped found Arab League in 1944; clashed with King Farouk over the limitation of royal prerogative.
95. Nuri al-Said, prime minister of Iraq, January–December 1949.
96. Refers to seventh session of the Arab League, held in Cairo, October 17–30, 1949.

because of swarm of new employees and because of [their] anti-British bias. [In the] meantime, [the] budget continues to show [a] surplus. [The] king has complete control of the army, and though he has lost in popularity, he really runs the country. [He] would prefer [the] Wafd and all other parties in [the] government, with Sirri Pasha remaining as prime minister. [The] British have lost considerable prestige, but are not as much hated as [the] newspapers would indicate. Ronald Campbell,[97] unlike his predecessor, Sir Myles Lampson, is well liked by [the] king.

In answer to my question whether there were Arab [military] staff meetings in Cairo, Caffery replied affirmatively, but said nothing would come out of these partial conferences. Egypt does not desire that there should be any definite agreement and does not think there will be. In answer to McGhee's question about Egypt's attitude toward [the] Arab states, Caffery replied that Egypt was contemptuous of the others, wished to remain a dominant figure, but to avoid too much involvement. [It] prefers [a] policy of divide and conquer. During the [Egyptian] debate on the security pact, there was almost no mention of Israel or Russia. It was aimed at Syria and Iraq.

Despite much talk of improving condition of [the] fellahin, nothing substantial is being done. [There is a] general admission of need of improvement, but no will or program to secure real reform. Talk of reform [is] motivated by fear of Russia. [The] only sign of progress in recognition of [the] trade unions was [the] government's consent that a representative should go to the London meeting of the Free Trade Unions Congress.[98] Meantime, no federation of Egyptian trade unions [was] permitted. [The] king was aware of need for modernization but "our pretty talk" [was] not enough to influence him beyond support of a few model villages. Farouk would like to play [the] US off against Britain. He respects our industrial might. In answer to McGhee's question, Caffery said we should help build up the British because there is no substitute, but that we should do nothing before the elections.

Caffery said Egypt has no interest in North Africa and cited its poor treatment of Abd al-Krim.[99] In answer to McGhee's question, he said Egypt should be encouraged to take a more constructive attitude towards the Arab states. At this point Childs intervened to say that Saudi [Arabia] was drawing on Egyptian educators. To McGhee's question whether [the] Arabs could be made [into] a constructive influence under Egypt's leadership, Caffery answered, "not now." There had hardly been any talk about Israel at all. Egypt had agreed on that "silly note" (the one presented a few days earlier by several Arab

---

97. Ronald Campbell (1890–1983), British ambassador to Egypt, 1946–1950.

98. The founding meeting of the International Confederation of Free Trade Unions [ICFTU] opened in London on November 28, 1949. Sixty-three national trade union centers were represented. The ICFTU advocated collective bargaining, but rejected communism.

99. Mohammed Abd al-Krim (1882–1963), Rif independence fighter in interwar Spanish and French Morocco; captured in 1926 and imprisoned on Réunion; released and arrived in Egypt with extended family, May 1947; eventually given two villas by King Farouk; became spokesman for independence of Maghreb from France, but was not aided by Egypt.

states to the US) but had recognized that it was unrealistic, and had added, "what else can we do."[100]

Wadsworth reported that a Pakistani leader had said that the basis for constructive [co-] operation was resistance to communism. Caffery agreed that we should attempt to get the Arab League to be more constructive. On this point Parker said, "[The] weakness of [the] Arab League is the same as [the] weakness of [the] individual Arab states." Their internal weaknesses [are] exaggerated six-fold in the League. We should attempt reforms within each country.

Reverting to the Egyptian election, Caffery told of the king's prayer to Allah, who had replied that it was "God's wisdom that certain seats should not be contested."[101] Caffery agreed that there might be certain democratic forces which could be encouraged, but should not be [aided] directly. As to whether anyone was motivated by unselfishness, Caffery cited the king, Azzam and Sirri. Islam, however, he said, is against progress.

Caffery thought there was no danger that we might be discredited later with new forces that might arise. Caffery thought the possibility of communist developments was remote. In all our approaches to king or [to the] government, [the] ambassador should be allowed to "play it by ear." [The] best argument for reform is fear of revolution. Caffery thought that Sidqi Pasha's recent demand that Egypt face toward Africa was primarily a personal expression.[102] On the question of educational aid, Caffery thought we could help Egypt, but only in specialized areas. He agreed that we should also express a desire to learn from them.

When Caffery had finished, Keeley asked permission to read a fifteen-minute indictment of American policy, which had been expressed by the Egyptian representative to Damascus. Keeley said he wished to find out if this were representative of Egyptian opinion. When the reading was finished, Caffery said drily: "Yes, Egyptians will talk like that, but they know they are not realistic." McGhee commented that "The US can't satisfy Mr. Keeley's friend, who demands an open confession of sin and concrete evidence of repentance." McGhee denied, too, staunchly, that the US had shown partiality during the past six months. Keeley interrupted to demand that the Jessup Plan be enforced.[103]

---

100. Refers to note from the Arab League to the US government in mid-November 1949 following the October 17–30 meetings of the Arab League Council in Cairo. It argued that the Arab states had cooperated with the United States and UN in an effort to bring peace to Palestine and that US aid was needed in persuading the Israeli government to comply with the peace conditions outlined by the Palestine Conciliation Commission.

101. The Egyptian elections in December were to be the first free elections there. The Wafd was the sole party with a national organization and broad support. Deep antagonism existed between Farouk and the Wafd (and its leader Nahhas Pasha) dating from February 1942 when the British had imposed a Wafd ministry on the king.

102. Ismail Sidqi Pasha (1875–1950), former Wafd politician; prime minister of Egypt, 1930–1933, 1946; wished in 1946 to unite Egypt and Sudan under Cairo's rule.

103. Philip C. Jessup, deputy US delegate to the UN Security Council in 1948, suggested in June 1949 that Israel keep the whole of the Galilee in return for ceding part of the Negev. The

McGhee replied: "We stand by the Jessup idea of compensation but what does it mean? We never indicated any specific amount of territory. Any transfers which would satisfy the parties would satisfy us." When Mr. Keeley's turn came, he launched into a vivid indictment of the US "partiality" which had prejudged the case in favor of Israel to such an extent as to alienate Arab opinion.

After lunch Crocker began his story. The regent is self-seeking in Iraq. Nuri [al-] Said has grown to lack favor [as a consequence of the depressed economy in Iraq], and a military coup is always possible, provided only a leader of sufficient strength appears. It is important, indeed vital, to Iraq and to the US position there that the small loan of eight or nine million dollars contemplated by the International Bank should be made. Crocker implied that the British were discouraging the loan and were utilizing their special treaty position to keep Iraq in leading strings [partially subservient] and to restrict rigorously American activity.

McGhee asked: what would be an advantage of a revision of the British-Iraq treaty? Crocker replied that such revision would loosen [the] British hold and open the door to the US. Crocker admitted that the airfield[s] should remain under British control.[104] Referring to the exceptionally low royalties paid [for oil] in Iraq [by the Iraq Petroleum Company], Crocker said he did not understand the reason. McGhee gave an interesting possible explanation to the effect that since US, British, and French interests share in Iraq's oil, each group was more interested to develop resources elsewhere which were in their own exclusive control.[105] This is more likely to be the case, he continued, because now oil is "a glut on the market." Continuing, McGhee replied that there was no possibility of curtailing production in [the] US.

Crocker then urged a general survey of potentialities in Iraq, which he estimated might, over many years, require the expenditure of $200,000,000. McGhee replied that under Point Four, technicians might be made available for this purpose; but Clapp interjected that such wide general studies could be self-defeating, and that it would be better to limit the efforts to smaller and specific projects. On the issue of Iraq's treaty relations, Wadsworth said [that the] Portsmouth Treaty had been an improvement.[106] Crocker said Iraqis did not suspect us. On the problem of alleged persecution of Jews in Iraq, Crocker summed up the official Baghdad view but did not seem to me to know very

"Jessup Principle" from this point forward referred to the exchanges of territory that Truman and the State Department ultimately favored.

104. Refers to Habbaniyah in north and Shaiba in the south, which the British held by treaty provision since 1930 and which were critical for protection of its oil logistics. An attempted revision in January 1948 for base sharing between the British and Iraqis had failed.

105. The Iraqi government negotiated with other oil companies in 1949, but all insisted that the pipeline to Haifa be reopened. The British government suggested that the IPC grant loans to Iraq, but the IPC refused. The Iraqi economy improved in 1950 because of improved harvests and higher oil royalties paid by the IPC. Sassoon, *Economic Policy in Iraq, 1932–1950*, 99–101.

106. Treaty signed in January 1948 by the British and Iraq governments for the sharing of British bases there, ultimately rejected by Iraqi nationalists and scuttled when not ratified.

much beyond. Nor did he add much when McGhee asked him if the US could do more than it had done.[107] In general, Crocker impressed me as a pleasant but not very able man.

Ambassador Childs spoke interestingly about Saudi Arabia, where he said there are "no elections, no political parties and no trade unions." The king is as "secure as an oriental ruler ever is"; his authority is unquestioned; his administration highly centralized. Personally, the king is well for his years. There is not likely to be trouble about the succession. The crown prince Saud[108] is being given larger power. There is no real rivalry with Faisal,[109] who is losing interest in public affairs. On the other hand, Mohammed,[110] who gets out among the tribes, might cause trouble. External situation is happy. King feels his destiny linked with that of US. Britain he suspects because of link with Hashemites. Parenthetically, Childs took what I agreed was [a] justifiable question to the use of the term "reactionary" in the working papers. For example, I cited its use as applied to the Orthodox Bloc [United Religious Front] in Israel as being misleading.

In answer to McGhee's question as to what is the minimum that we can additionally give the king, Childs replied [that the] king has emphasized his isolated position; the Hashemite "threat;" the Yemenite differences, the lack of proper arms for the military, and the need, therefore, for sufficient modern equipment to insure internal order and defense against foreign aggression. Childs argued that military aid would: 1) Have stabilizing effect by discouraging [the] Hashemites and Yemenites; 2) would enhance US prestige; 3) have [a] stabilizing effect among Moslems outside of Arabia by being taken as evidence that failure to support the [Nationalist] Chinese, among whom there are many Moslems, is not to indicate that the US does not intend to support its friends; 4) would strengthen our hand in encouraging social reforms in Saudi Arabia through the education of youth in military training. This is the one avenue for us to have influence on Arab education; [and] 5) would strengthen existing balance of power.

McGhee agreed that something should be done. Referring [to] General O'Keefe's report,[111] [he] asked whether the king would be satisfied with a small military mission and the right to buy arms. Such aid could be secured by a special act of Congress. Childs agreed that there was no need for a separate treaty, but [that the] king wants special assurance against [the] Hashamite "menace"

---

107. On the US embassy, McGhee, and the Jews of Iraq, see also *DFPI*, v. 4, d. 89, 390, 436.
108. Saud bin Abdul Aziz al-Saud (1902–1969), second son of Ibn Saud, king from 1953–1964.
109. Faisal bin Abdul Aziz al-Saud (1906–1975), third son of Ibn Saud, king from 1964–1975.
110. Mohammed bin Abdul Aziz al-Saud (1910–1988), fourth son of Ibn Saud, crown prince from 1964–1965.
111. Air Force Brigadier General Richard J. O'Keefe (1906–1993), commanded the Dhahran air base; headed a military mission to Saudi Arabia in 1949 to assess Saudi security requirements.

and that there is [a] need for some specific formula. Wadsworth said that such aid would be basic to stability. McGhee thought that the National Security Council could advise the president to this effect. Childs said that the existing airbase is almost as good as a treaty, but [that the] king wants military aid and training now. Wadsworth again agreed, and Childs insisted that [this was] the one way open to us. However, in answer to McGhee's question, Childs admitted that technicians under Point Four might usefully make water surveys and reclamation studies.

Towards the end, Childs made the interesting suggestion that the "social possibilities" of improvements through the Arab League had been neglected.

Sunday, November 27

McGhee was apologetic about working on Sunday, but we continued throughout the whole day. Following up on Childs's discussion of the day before, McGhee raised the question of the desirability of a visit of Ibn Saud to the States. There was consensus of opinion that though such visits of heads of states should be discouraged, this particular one should be favored.

Pinkerton spoke briefly but very informatively about Lebanon. There, he said, is the best chance for the US to exercise influence. There is no xenophobia; the conflict of French and British interests leaves the US untouched. The American colleges have been very helpful. Their graduates would be more influential in the government were it not for [that] the small pay leads to graft or to non-entrance into the service. Lebanon's needs are not great; it is overpopulated and therefore should export young men; [it has] need of better cultivation of land and hence could use technicians and experts in irrigation, seeds, fertilizer, etc. There is talk of Lebanon as a free zone area. It would offer several advantages; labor is reasonable, it has the good will of the other Arab states, and could work with Israel. On the political side, Lebanon has no territorial or political ambitions. It fears for its sovereignty and frontiers. Its long Moslem hinterland and memories of the massacres of 1860[112] and jealousy of a prosperous Lebanon by other Moslems occasion concern. It also fears [a] dynamic Israel, particularly for the Litani and for a second partition.[113] Lebanon would, therefore, desire US assurance about sovereignty and [the] frontier; a mere public declaration would be sufficient, preferably by [the] US, UK and France.

Wadsworth agreed that there was [a] need for this guarantee but queried: "If Lebanon were to ask for it, could we give it?" McGhee replied, "Others have asked for it and have been refused: Greece, Turkey, [and] Saudi Arabia. How [can we] make an exception for Lebanon?" Parenthetically, Pinkerton said

---

112. Sectarian fighting between Druze and Maronite Christians that resulted in 7,000–11,000 Christian deaths.
113. In 1919 the Zionist Organization proposed maps of the Palestine Mandate in 1919 that included the Litani River as a primary water supply. For background see John J. McTague Jr., "Anglo-French Negotiations over the Boundaries of Palestine, 1919–1920," *Journal of Palestine Studies* 11, no. 2 (Winter 1982): 100–112.

some Christian Lebanese fear Moslems more than Israel. Answering McGhee's question, Pinkerton said the only possibility of Lebanese leadership is cultural. This Wadsworth supported, but [he] suggested the additional possibility of a free zone area. Clapp praised the Lebanese for [their] willingness to break the Arab boycott of the ESM, and for their generally liberal leadership. Wadsworth added that Beirut was a natural trading center.

Keeley's exposition about Syria was long [and] interesting but inclined to be repetitious. He praised the working papers, but said that in some respects they were oversimplified. Syria is the most highly politically developed Arab state except Lebanon. [The] people are as "proud as pigs on ice." They regard Damascus as the center of the Arab world. He protested against what he called "all-Arab" circulars from the Department, arguing that each circular message should have leeway to get best results locally.

The Za'im coup was prepared militarily but not otherwise. Za'im had fantastic idea of building up a peacetime army of 50,000 and in war 300,000, and wanted American aid for this purpose. Keeley told him any American aid must wait on [a] settlement with Israel. Za'im replied, "Then, let's get on with Israel. I'll meet Ben-Gurion and settle all issues." Arslan refused, but al-Barazi accepted, and [the] armistice [was] finally signed. Za'im's downfall [was] due to [these] elements; [his] soak-the-rich program, modernization [and] terms with Israel, and [the] failure to satisfy the military. This last [was] the least important. The new government is weak and may be the victim of a third coup.

[The] Syrian opinion [is] unanimously anti-Israel and fearful of Israel's ambitions. Recently [the] Syrian foreign minister[114] summed up [the] situation as follows: [the] need for [the] US [to have a] long-range and fixed policy; Russia's interest [is] to destroy [the] Arabs' faith in the US; British and French interests can't be hurt by Russia, because no faith in their disinterestedness is felt by Syrians. They would like to side with [the] US and would do so except for Israel. Their fear of the latter is so great that they even talk of preferring a communist to a Zionist world. [The] US should take a positive lead to right the wrong as the Syrians see it. This involves at least recognition of the tragedy of the refugees and insistence on Israel's carrying out the UN resolution. Russia is bluffing about Western Europe; its real threat is in the Middle East. Syrians think of Israel as US's strategic or imperialist instrument. They admire our strength but want [a] partnership.

Clapp's pilot plants, if accepted, might be [a] beginning. Childs interrupted to say that he was inclined to think that the Russian strategy would be [to move] southward for oil, and in order not to let their soldiers note the comparison between Russian and Western standards of living. Then followed an exchange between McGhee and Keeley in reference to the latter's charge that the Syrians blamed us for not helping them as we had helped the Jews, when in

114. Nazim al-Kudsi (1906–1998), foreign minister in first post-Za'im cabinet under Hashim al-Atassi; carried on unification negotiations with Iraq.

fact the Syrians had never asked. Wadsworth urged need for assurance against future Israeli aggression and said that this would lay [the] basis for cooperation with [the] Arabs. I took exception to the assumption that all that mattered was the Arab fear of aggression.

Fritzlan talked interestingly and briefly about Jordan and Abdullah. The latter, theoretically absolute, is limited by UK and by his own government. The king is inclined to be effusive and to take ill-considered, irresponsible, and arbitrary actions. The real issue is when will Jordan [officially annex] Arab Palestine and what will be the basis of representation. As to Israel, [the] king and [the] people are anxious to liquidate [the] affair. [The] king hopes for some concessions and does not feel bound to work with other Arab states. [The] king's hope for Greater Syria is for the distant future; [he] brings it up now only in moments of stress. He has no designs on Saudi Arabia; in any case, Britain would not permit him to carry them out. Britain's position is paramount and, in [the] US interest, should be continued. [The] king opposes internationalization of Jerusalem because in part he fears this would lead to Jewish control.[115]

Burdett spoke powerfully, but I thought mistakenly, in favor of requiring Israel to cede territory for the settlement of refugees and to accept the PCC's plan for Jerusalem. He argued that there was a substantial minority of Jews, including members of Agudat in Jerusalem who would, if they were free to express their genuine views, favor the plan. He criticized Israel [for] taking over of "nearly all Christian institutions" and the prevailing and increasing anti-foreign atmosphere. The Old City, he said, is dead and can be brought back to life only [through] the plan. There is no love for Abdullah or Jordan in Arab Palestine, where the feeling, particularly in the [Tulkarm-Nablus-Jenin] triangle, is especially bitter against Israel.[116] He deplored the use of religious communities by foreign powers and the turning over of the Russian Orthodox property to the Russians [USSR].[117]

Following Burdett's suggestion that the crown prince[118] was a nonentity, Wadsworth questioned who would succeed Abdullah. McGhee interrupted to ask whether, in view of the latter's role as a "destructive element," he should be displaced. Burdett replied that concessions should be won in the direction of constitutional government before [a] union with Arab Palestine was effected. Pinkerton interrupted to comment that "Kirkbride is impossible."[119]

115. Abdullah's views on peace are elaborated in reports to Washington in November 1949, *FRUS*, 1949, v. VI, 1483–1486, 1502–1504, 1509–1510, 1512–1514. Jordanian and Israeli officials once again began secret peace talks at Shuneh on November 27. See *DFPI*, v. 4, editorial note, 636, d. 424, 426, 441, 444.

116. Entries of April 3 and April 17, 1949.

117. Entries of January 20 and September 23, 1949.

118. Talal bin Abdullah (1909–1972), king of Jordan, 1951–1952, forced to abdicate because of his schizophrenia.

119. Kirkbride had been a British official in Transjordan and Palestine since 1920; British minister in Amman, 1946–1952. Pinkerton had been the US consul general in Jerusalem, 1941–1945.

Burdett reverted to the problem of internationalization, arguing it was the one point on which the UN had consistently agreed and that it should not be dissuaded by Israel's threats. Among the Jews who would favor internationalization should be included also small tradesmen. In addition 70% of the Arabs plus the Christian [Arabs] and the religious heads would also be on their side. Burdett continued [that the] US should favor [the] PCC plan to deter "Israel aggression" and to prove that Christian influence counts. Failure to implement plan would mean [an] Arab reaction against Christianity. McGhee then restated the Department's position, support of the PCC plan but not liking the population division insisted upon by France;[120] [he] had not been impressed by the violence of the Jewish opposition. The Department would favor any changes in the PCC plan which would make for agreement. Then followed a general discussion of internationalization until the lunch interval. Stole off with McGhee and Professor Whittemore, Clapp, and Mrs. Wiley to see two of the very old churches which were in the process of being restored by Whittemore. He was very enthusiastic about the mosaics which he uncovered.

Beginning of the afternoon session. McGhee again summed up the Department's position. In the past, the US government had taken specific positions; e.g., the Jessup statement, but these had proved futile. It is now disengaging, leaving initiative to UN. Obviously, there is not to be one neat solution for refugees, territory and Jerusalem. The latter [Jerusalem] presumably will be decided by the [UN General] Assembly. The PCC is to be kept in being with Ely Palmer,[121] the new US member, to stay on the job permanently. The US government is, of course, giving full support to the ESM.

Although [the] Arab position is now in favor of the acceptance of partition, the Department is accentuating its earlier policy of favoring bilateral negotiations, arguing that time is running against both sides. [The] Arabs have suggested mediation. [The] PCC has acceded and waits on Israel. As to direct talks, McGhee emphasized that [the] US had always favored these except [for] the proposed Za'im-Ben-Gurion talk.[122] The Gaza-[to]-Israel proposal had been hopeful and had been pressed hard by Patterson.[123] Now Abdullah was ready apparently for negotiations. He hoped that Egypt would be ready and a face-saving formula could be found. McGhee then outlined these possibilities for US: 1) continue as during last six months to try gradually to bring Arabs and Israel together; 2) [a] US initiative has obvious disadvantages; 3) [there is] no hope for [an] overall solution, hence, any practical settlement is best. Many

120. The French government signed onto the PCC's Jerusalem proposal, but earlier in 1949 had proposed a complete *corpus separatum* in Jerusalem and its environs separated from Israel, with a separate currency, citizenship, and police.
121. Ely Eliot Palmer (1887–1977), foreign service officer; had served as US consul general in Jerusalem, 1933–1935, and Beirut, 1938–1941; head of US mission in Afghanistan, 1945–1949; officially replaced Paul Porter as US representative to Palestine Conciliation Commission on November 4, 1949.
122. See entry of May 8, 1949. Acheson had favored these talks at the time.
123. Jefferson Patterson (1891–1977), counselor, US embassy in Cairo, 1946–1950.

of the demands on Israel arise out of collective Arab interest. As a group, the Arab states create difficulties, which would not arise in bilateral negotiations. Compensation [is] less important than [the] refugees or [a] territorial adjustment. McGhee would have pressed for refugee resettlement [in the Arab states] rather than [the] handing over of territory to someone else.

Summing up the chances of bilateral negotiations, McGhee said: "Abdullah is anxious to settle. Egypt probably will do so if face could be saved. Syria has little except prestige and sentiment at stake. Lebanon would gladly settle [with Israel] if Arab opinion outside would permit it. The principal variable is whether it is possible for the US alone to inject itself into moves for settlements. If bilateral negotiations fail, let [the] PCC go ahead and [the] US will support it. [The] US should inject itself only as a last resort. Grady asked whether [the] two sides had not reached impasse on [the number of] refugees. I pointed out that [the] total number of the latter was more nearly the 652,000 named in the ESM report than the 940,000 or more commonly spoken of.

Caffery said Egypt desired guarantees against Israeli expansion and favored [the] internationalization of Jerusalem. It would be willing, but not anxious, to negotiate with Israel.

McGhee then asked me whether Israel would still be willing to make the Gaza offer. I told him I did not know. He later suggested to me that Caffery and I get together to talk over possible ways in which we could advance Israel-Egyptian direct negotiations. Childs then reverted at length to Keeley's thesis that it would be very difficult for the US to now "sell anything to the Arabs." How can we have assurance against "limb being sawed off behind us" again? Each circular message has interest in maintaining American "good name." Should [the] US not strengthen [the] UN by pressing for enforcement of [the] UN resolution [of December 11, 1948]? [The] Arabs say [that the] US hesitates to act favorably, and [they] contrast [this with] our position in favor of Israel. [The] Saudis would welcome guarantees against Israeli expansion. Moreover, if [the] Arabs lose their refugee fight, they will have lost all.

Clapp said the Gaza Strip refugee problem [was] the most difficult of all. He thinks resettlement will have to concentrate in Jordan and Arab Palestine. Refugees need the experience of mobility. We need not be too pessimistic about their assimilability. Joe Palmer from the embassy [in] London,[124] charged with [the] Near East, said [that the] British desire [is] to remove obstacles to incorporation of Arab Palestine in Jordan. McGhee indicated that [the] US government favored such absorption and would not object to the extension of the British [defense] treaty [to include the West Bank if annexed to Jordan]. Crocker said that Iraq does not recognize Israel but will ultimately accept what other states have done in reference to Israel. McGhee's question, "Will Iraq hold against [the] US [its] non-action against Israel?" evoked incon-

---

124. Joseph Palmer II (1914–1994), second secretary and consul, US embassy London, assigned May 1949; specialization was sub-Saharan Africa.

clusive debate. In the discussion about Lebanon and Israel, I affirmed that the latter would guarantee the former's frontiers. McGhee returned to the thesis that the Gaza solution would settle both territory and refugees.

Burdett interjected, "there is need for punitive measures to force Israel to yield." McGhee contended that the present US policy is a completion of earlier policy, not a change. It is easy, he said, to suggest redress by taking from Israel, but [a] more practical suggestion would be to give something additional to those [countries] which felt aggrieved. As to sanctions, "we don't use special means to enforce UN resolutions elsewhere, e.g., Southwest Africa."[125] [McGhee] granted that [suspension of] the Export-Import Bank loan to Israel had been an exception to the rule against political considerations; should we now use that loan to undo the earlier policy?[126] Or should we not, rather, make funds available to the other side? We can't be expected to undo an earlier policy by sanctions now, in contrast with non-action towards other states.

Turning to Burdett, McGhee asked him "what should we do?" Burdett replied in effect, [the US should] enforce financial sanctions by stopping UJA contributions [to Israel]. The obvious answer was given; it was not legal. Burdett retorted, "If Israel could be made to agree to [the December 11, 1948] UN resolution, [the] US could again be confident of lessening Arab intransigence. If it is not possible to force Israel's acquiescence in the principles and the resolutions of the UN, [then] the US should revise its ideas." McGhee answered, "What would be the advantage of such revision even if we can't enforce the earlier principles?" Burdett answered, "Let's scrap the principles and say frankly that we favor direct negotiations." McGhee countered, "We are not scrapping the principles. Jessup was not specific [on territorial compensation]. We adhere to the principles but favor their interpretation in a practical way. [There is] no use in introducing artificial elements into the problem. We will accept [the] results of bilateral negotiations made on the basis of desire by individual [parties] and on the basis of their respective bargaining positions."

Wadsworth asked whether Burdett thought Abdullah could agree with Israel. Burdett answered affirmatively but added that the settlement would not be stable. I interjected that I wondered how Burdett could be sure. McGhee added that it was not certain that Israel was in the stronger bargaining position in view of its "desperate financial position." Clapp said, "I could not in good conscience recommend repatriation unless you could combine it with the withdrawal of sovereign status; that is, by putting Arabs back on territory [to be] taken from Israel." Clapp [is] uncertain about such intervention because [Israel's] economic plight might be more serious than in places where refugees now are. [He] doubts [that] Israel is or will soon be viable. [Israel's] resource base [is] too small, assuming [the] present standard of living. If

125. Relevant General Assembly resolutions from 1946 through 1949 rejected the union of Southwest Africa with the Union of South Africa.
126. Entries of August 23–25, 1949.

[Israel's] area is to be further reduced by taking away productive regions, this might be excuse and reason for recurrent crises. [The] more basic problem is how to make economic adjustments between Israel and Jordan. Clapp had changed his first views, which had been in favor of repatriation, though he now realized more clearly that more than economics are involved in problem of absorption. When Clapp had finished, I satisfied myself by saying that his had been an admirable presentation that it required no addition from me, for I completely approved of it.

McGhee then said that he regarded the Gaza proposal as the best bet. But Burdett returned to his thesis that there should be land made available for refugees near Nazareth and Hebron. McGhee thought the resulting political problem would not be worth the 100 or 150,000 that might be so settled. Clapp reiterated his objection to the return of large numbers of refugees to Israeli sovereignty. I added, how would you do it anyhow. Burdett replied, "with punitive action." Clapp returned to his basic question, "What form of resettlement really settles or merely invites future trouble?" Israel's future may be very dark and that of Arab Palestine and Jordan [are] not very promising. Nonetheless, on the basis of Jordan's traditional standard of living, there is a chance of improving it by the combination with Arab Palestine. Moreover, there will be a certain amount of self-settlement as soon as political conditions are stabilized. Territorial adjustments could not be the answer. A more realistic approach is for the people of Israel to realize they will have to lower their living standards.

Pinkerton said that he agreed with me on the question of issues between Israel and Lebanon. American interests will be served by agreements at the earliest possible date, and these can be reached only by bilateral negotiations, which must be kept separate. Burdett's glance at Pinkerton said in effect: here is one more Machiavellian diplomat prepared to sacrifice justice and the rights of the refugees for political expediency. I later told Burdett that I could sympathize with his feeling, but as a practical matter his objectives could not be achieved. [Grady] said that [though] he agreed that whatever we might wish, we are faced by the necessity by dealing pragmatically with the problems. He favored the Department's program of bilateral negotiations. Stressing the economic side will help to solve psychological difficulties, [he] thought that Israel should be discouraged in its hope of [the] unrestricted "ingathering of the exiles."

McGhee then asked whether anyone thought we should at this stage assume an interventionist role. Childs said that McGhee's comments had been very helpful, but that he wanted to think the question through. We should, in any case, maintain impartiality. McGhee finally said, "[The] big question is what will make for stabilization. [The] decisive new fact is Israel. Pushing it back a little would not count for much. We should concentrate on affirmative solutions."

Breakfast with McGhee and Berry and Mattison. Our discussion covered housekeeping [office and apartment space] as well as political problems. McGhee was shocked by my account of how Charlie Knox had been forced to do without a confidential secretary until within a few weeks of his leaving. Berry's prospective visit to Tel Aviv will give an opportunity to drive home our [space and funding] needs. Another problem I reported on was the delay in the communications through Tel Aviv owing apparently to the lack of 24-hour, seven-day-a-week service there and at relay stations.

On questions of policy, McGhee urged that I talk with Caffery about the possibility of expediting bilateral talks between Israel and Egypt, and with Fritzlan about relations between Jordan and Israel. Subsequently, I did talk to both men. Caffery was cooperative, but felt that there would have to be some delay until after the [Egyptian] elections [of January 3, 1950], and that even then he would have to "play it by ear." We agreed to keep one another informed by pouch. Fritzlan was similarly cooperative, and we agreed that we would try to meet either in Jerusalem or Tel Aviv. Throughout our talk McGhee showed the same kind of detailed knowledge that had so impressed me during the larger meetings. He is a natural leader.

From breakfast, we went directly into our morning sessions, which concentrated on security. McGhee set the theme and elaborated it as follows. The basic problem is the Russian threat. In the current Cold War, the pressure on Arab states and Israel is much less than on GTI [Greece, Turkey, and Iran]. [The] problem of [the] army in other countries is less. It would be a great mistake to give military assistance to Arab countries and Israel other than Saudi Arabia. In [a] shooting war, GTI would be important through [their] degree of resistance, thus buying time, encouraging resistance elsewhere, and stimulating underground activities. The time that will be bought is difficult to assess. Turkey can hold for perhaps three weeks; Greece and Iran; the former for a few days, and the latter perhaps not more than a few hours. In Iran, communications are more important than potential resistance. It is not desirable to build up armies in Arab states and Israel for a shooting war.

On the subject of pacts, McGhee was clear and categorical. Commitment under [the North] Atlantic Pact not determined until we know what Western Europe can do for itself.[127] We do not enter into treaties unless we have [the] force to back them up; this is basis of our answer to GTI. Generally in the Near East, we cannot be expected to have forces comparable with the British. We might wish to consider [the] UK's extension of its treaties along the line of that [of the US treaty] with Turkey and [a] revision of [its] treaty with Iraq. As to

---

127. For background see Lawrence S. Kaplan, *NATO 1948: The Birth of the Transatlantic Alliance* (Lanham, MD: Rowman & Littlefield, 2007).

the suggestion of a new general pact for the region, it could mean little more than the UN since, as is the case, we are not prepared to back it up.

[Reports by Grady on Greece, Wadsworth on Turkey, and Wiley on Iran]. McGhee then summarized in a striking phrase the comparative situation in [the] GTI countries. Turkey is supplied above the need for [a] cold war; Greece below that for [a] hot war but above that for [a] cold war; Iran less than needed for [a] lukewarm war.

In the next exchange Wiley argued for an expenditure of approximately $40,000,000 for training and supplies for the Iranian army, but McGhee answered that all this would buy is an orderly withdrawal to the mountains, according to the shah. Later Wiley was to say cynically that the leader of whichever tribe in which the shah took refuge would be the next shah. Wadsworth asked whether [the] Arab states and Israel would feel more secure if [the] US were to meet Iran halfway. Keeley replied, "If Syria gets nothing then, [it] will regard Iran aid as pro-Israel." My answer to Wiley's question was "yes." McGhee asked the group whether [there was] any thought [that] there should be military aid to the Arab states other than Saudi Arabia. All except Keeley answered no. Keeley continued to argue, but Pinkerton countered that any aid to Syria would throw Lebanon into the arms of France.

Tuesday, November 29

[After discussions concerning Turkey and Cyprus] McGhee then suggested that we should each in turn discuss the following points: the Clapp resolution,[128] communism, governmental minorities, position of foreign powers, USIE and cultural program,[129] [and the] intelligence program. Caffery added little that was new in his statement. Childs reiterated that there would be no reconciliation between Saudi Arabia and Israel in our lifetime. Saudi Arabia's second enemy is Russia. Its favorite is Egypt, and then Lebanon and, until recently, Syria. Keeley characterized conditions in Syria as being order over disorder.

When my turn came, I praised Clapp's resolution with its provision for a single head, responsible directly to the General Assembly and with only a bow to the sponsorship of the PCC. I spoke briefly about the reports of the Communists' center in Haifa, saying that we had not been able to confirm. I was frank about the position of the Arab minorities in Israel, admitting that the Israeli practice towards them was probably less correct than the government's formal pronouncement. I praised the USIE and suggested the usefulness of more scholarship. My comments on the intelligence program were critical. I added that probably our new labor attaché[130] would be able to supply us with much more really useful information than any member of intelligence or

128. To be based on the interim report of the Economic Survey Mission.
129. United States International Informational and Educational Exchange Program, formed in 1948 to operate from US missions abroad as a means of cultural diplomacy.
130. Milton Fried, assigned December 2, 1949.

security officers. There was a considerable discussion about intelligence and security, but [less] on consensus of opinion. Some of the men were less concerned about independent reporting than I [was].

McGhee then raised the general problem. What role does and should the US play in this area? Referring to the president's statement on Clapp's appointment,[131] he underlined that the US stands ready to lend a firm and helping hand. He queried what this means and explained that it did not involve new military aid, except possibly in the case of Saudi Arabia. Perhaps his question, he said, would answer itself. We are being pushed into this new role by [the] force of circumstances. If the chiefs of mission agree that this is true, how can we best do our job? In the light of our program, of which we are not ashamed, what shall we do? Considerable time was given to the discussion of the Arab security and other possible pacts. McGhee said that in general, the US wished to support any pact designed to strengthen the peace.

As preliminary to Clapp's report, McGhee stressed the extraordinarily low comparative level of economic life in the Middle East, other than [in] Israel, where the average income was only about eighty dollars as compared with $556 [per month] in the US. He stressed the importance of increasing trade with these countries, but deplored that our standard treaty of Commerce, Friendship, and Navigation had not been accepted by any of the twenty states under his jurisdiction.[132] There was a consensus of opinion that the treaty was too complex and should be broken up into its natural constituent parts.

Clapp gave an extremely interesting and comprehensive report. He emphasized that the interim refugee effort was important for the longer range. The methods suggested were designed to get the Arab states to accept some measure of responsibility. Moreover, the sort of works suggested for temporary employment—roads, watersheds, terraces, forestry—are all related to longer-range goals. He hoped that after a year the number of dependents might be reduced [from] 652 to 300 thousand. Presumably by that time the Arabs would be themselves undertaking the bulk of the responsibility, with the majority in the Gaza Strip. His final report will draw a parallel between Arab refugees and other Arab inhabitants. [The] obstacles to full economic development or advance[ment] are water and peace. There has been much excessive and naïve propaganda for [the] JVA [Jordan Valley Authority]. It is not an emergency program. The Hayes-Savage scheme[133] would require an international agreement between Israel and the Arabs.

Among other obstacles to progress [are]: 1) lack of technical competence among Arab governments. Israel has [competence] to an extraordinary degree; 2) inadequacy of technical data in many of the general surveys. The Gibb

131. Entry of August 23, 1949.
132. Standard treaty of bilateral relations establishing common principles and standards.
133. Plan for irrigation and development by James B. Hayes and J. V. Savage, building on earlier ideas by Walter Lowdermilk for a Jordan Valley Authority. Referenced in Goda et al., eds., *To the Gates of Jerusalem*, 38.

survey, for example, is a good catalogue, nothing more;[134] 3) lack of capital or [a] broad tax system and the vast chasm between rich and poor. But if all were taxed, the wealth would be inadequate; 4) lack of electric energy. Where some is available, it is quite inadequate. [Clapp's] proposals: [the] Western world facing facts as they are and joining in selecting [a] pilot project in countries willing to cooperate, around which technical training and the beginning of tangible achievements can be had.

In Lebanon, [Clapp] suggests the careful survey of the Litani; as to Syria, the project [is] not settled. Israel is full of them; Egypt is carrying on, with the British, its own major projects. The advantage of pilot projects includes being small enough to succeed; [they are] related closely to frontier conditions, [and] can be made [a] basis for teaching and preparation for larger work. He hopes that [the] establishment of development boards will enhance [the] prestige of technical skills, and that they will cooperate with an international development board. He thinks of $45,000,000 during three years beyond the immediate work project. [He] will not estimate settlement costs. There should be an international technical assistance agency [for] planning regional water schemes on [a] neutral basis, cooperating with [the] development boards of each government, which would coordinate the pool of ideas and research in each country. Point Four and [the] BMEO [British Middle East Office][135] could be related with these. McGhee then raised the suggestion of an Institute of Near Eastern Affairs [INEA] in the State Department, comparable to the Institute of Latin American Affairs. As an agency of coordination, the INEA could bring to bear directly or indirectly many governmental resources.

My comments on the points raised earlier by McGhee were, briefly, as follows: [there has been] no consideration as yet in Israel for the US standard treaty of Commerce, Friendship, and Navigation,[136] but we were considering conventions on extradition and double taxation; everything possible was being done to stimulate trade; social legislation and trade unions were extremely advanced through the Histadrut, high wages, Kupat Holim,[137] etc.; I expressed enthusiasm for Clapp's program and commented favorably on McGhee's suggestions about Point Four and the INEA.

When the turn of the GTI countries for full explanations of their positions came, Grady was extremely revealing in his analysis of the US policy in Greece, its organization, and [its] results. There we had taken full responsibility

134. Sir Alexander Gibb & Partners (consulting engineers), *The Economic Development of Syria* (London: Knapp, Drewett and Sons, 1947), discussed by the Economic Survey Mission.

135. Refers to the Development Division of the British Middle East Office, which after 1945 aimed to accelerate economic and social development there through small-scale pilot projects. See Paul W. T. Kingston, *Britain and the Politics of Modernization in the Middle East, 1945–1958* (New York: Cambridge University Press, 1996).

136. The Israelis requested such a treaty in April 1950, and it was concluded in June 1951. See USSDCF-PIFA, 1950–1954, reel 6, frames 558–652.

137. Kupat Holim, comprehensive health insurance program formed by Histadrut for its members when the organization was founded in 1920. A smaller alternative civic health network had been available since 1931.

for the country. In a spirit of enlightened self-interest, we had and were intervening. Our policy was midway between [a] free gift of money and Russian imperialist control. Our middle ground preserved Greek sovereignty and self-respect. [A] difficult course, but principles clear. We worked on three fronts, military, political, and economic. The political had no set form but worked very closely with the government, which took advice on all essential questions. It is [neither] corrupt nor dictatorial. Our military control [is] exercised through our mission and [through the] supply of equipment. The most difficult control has been economic, exercised through [a] Greek currency committee and foreign trade organization.

Generally Grady's technique has been to remain in the background, but [he] has recently made [a] series of six speeches throughout the country. There was an interesting exchange between Grady and Wadsworth [on] the question of ambassadorial control of the ECA [Economic Cooperation Administration], which under congressional dictum, is independent. McGhee agreed that the Greek experiment offered a number of lessons, but pointed out that there were basic differences, which lessened the applicability of these [lessons] elsewhere. The Greek situation had been a desperate emergency, it was European, there was lots of money, and it was democratic. The exchange among Grady, Wadsworth, and McGhee on the issue of counterpart funds and the imperative necessity, as McGhee emphasized, of refraining from dollar expenditures for local labor or local products left me rather confused, but with a general idea of this limiting factor of American financial aid abroad.

Wiley's main presentation was more political than economic, but was grippingly interesting. Our object in Persia, he said, is to keep the Russians out. But we have no tools; we have done nothing. Ours has been a policy of "aggressive non-intervention and dynamic inactivity." The press is inconsequential. The country [is] wholly feudal. Parliament has been only an instrument of turbulence and vested interests.[138] People are of superior intelligence, but the internal situation is strained and fuzzy. There, you rarely know where you are going, or why. The Iranians mount and gallop off in all directions. For example, recently in the field of public health, nine separate and unrelated important initiatives were undertaken at the same time. Theoretically [Iran] has favorable foreign exchange, but this is unreal and could not be used [as] an excuse for our inaction. Iran has done much for itself; [it] has got Russia out of Azerbaijan [and] eliminated puppets, but should it be penalized for this when [the] American cornucopia is gushing all around?[139] Aid for Iran's military [is] important for

138. Mohammed Reza Shah Pahlavi called for parliamentary elections for a new Majles, the bicameral legislature, which were held in July 1949. He appointed royalists to the upper house, as provided by the constitution, but was accused of rigging the elections for other parliamentary seats. Protests under the leader of the progressive National Front, Mohammed Mossadeq, broke out in October 1949.

139. The Soviets occupied the northern provinces of Iran after 1941 and encouraged separatist Azeris and Kurds there. By agreement, the Soviets were to withdraw six months after the end of the war. In 1945 a separatist uprising began in the northern Iranian province of Azerbaijan, and the

morale, internal security, and roadblock[s]. Something has been done by the two very small missions,[140] [but] more is needed. In Iran, there are [the following] British representatives: the ambassador, the intelligence [apparatus], and the Anglo-Iranian Oil Company [(AOIC] and Anglo-Iranian Imperial Bank. All of these are separate even though Britain owns 62% of the AIOC. Relations between Iran and Israel are zero. No recognition in foreseeable future out of deference to Moslem world, but Iran [is] not interested in [the] Arabs' troubles.[141]

Political setup of [the] shah [Mohammed Reza Shah Pahlavi] is good.[142] He has sense of responsibility, favors land reforms, democratic processes and has a measure of popularity with people. Greatest danger is organized terrorism, made worse by shah's imprudence.[143] Probable heir, Prince Ali, is unstable[144] whereas a young Abdul Reza shows great promise.[145] In general, there is hope in the younger generation trained in the West. Meantime, there is danger that the shah, in his modernism, may fall between the two stools of East and West. Persia has about 100,000 Jews, very few of whom are rich. There is no anti-Jewish feeling. Only the members of the Bahai are looked upon with suspicion as schismatics.

In answer to McGhee's question [as to] what were the interests of Iran in the Moslem countries, Wiley replied, there is almost none. First in interest is Britain, then [the] USSR, and the US, followed by Pakistan. Relations with Iraq [are] routine. [The] shah regards Turkey as [a] menace. [The] prime minister[146] says this is nonsense. Relations with Turkey will improve. [The] shah has [a] "father" complex; [he] thinks in dynastic terms. He fears Turkey [and] thinks Turkish troops will liberate Persia from Russia and will not leave. [He] hopes to retire to [the] mountain triangle and return after the war. [The] shah is much interested in [the] Seven Year Plan with the Overseas Consultants, Incorporated, headed by Max Thornburg, formerly vice president of Standard [Oil] of New

Soviets would not allow Iranian forces to quell it. The Soviets withdrew in 1946 in response to pressure from the United States and the UN, where the Iranians had filed a complaint. Angry Soviet propaganda followed the 1947 Iranian decision not to grant an oil concession to the USSR. See Jamil Hasanli, *At the Dawn of the Cold War: The Soviet-American Crisis over Iranian Azerbaijan, 1941–1946* (Lanham, MD: Rowman & Littlefield, 2006); and Kristen Blake, *The U.S.-Soviet Confrontation in Iran, 1945–1962: A Case in the Annals of the Cold War* (Lanham, MD: University Press of America, 2007).

140. United States Mission to the Iranian Gendarmerie (GENMISH), initially sent in 1942 and remaining as an advisory mission in 1949; US Army Mission (ARMISH) sent in 1947 to help coordinate Iranian Army command and Iranian Ministry of War. See Blake, *The U.S.-Soviet Confrontation in Iran*, 17, 45, 48–49.

141. See also *DFPI*, v. 4, d. 402.

142. Shah Mohammed Reza Pahlavi (1919–1980), shah of Iran, 1941–1979.

143. There had been an assassination attempt against the shah in February 1949.

144. Ali Reza Pahlavi (1922–1954), brother of the reigning shah; lived mostly in Europe, spent much of his life hunting, and died in a plane crash.

145. Abdul Reza Pahlavi (1924–2004), half-brother of the reigning shah; held a number of government posts in Iran.

146. Mohammed Sa'ed (1883–1973), prime minister of Iran, November 1948–March 1950.

Jersey.[147] Plan [is] very broad, [and] was drafted by Allen Dulles.[148] [The] US has [a] benevolent attitude but no responsibility towards [the] plan. Wiley stressed the basic need of getting Iran away from "ditchwater." Until this is achieved, not much else can be done. In answer to McGhee's question, "Can we escape giving more aid?" Wiley replied, "We have little appeal. I am anti-pact and anti-guarantee, but we must show ourselves on their side. Token aid [is] not enough. We should all read Hajji Baba, still a masterpiece."[149]

The dinner, given by McGhee at the city's finest casino, was gala in the best sense. Everybody dressed and, with a sense of much work done, prepared to enjoy the evening. The food was excellent; McGhee's chairmanship during [the program afterwards] was adroit. The responses of Caffery and Grady were a little heavy, Grady's particularly so for an Irishman. Childs and Porter were good, Mrs. Crocker was better, and Keeley the gayest of all.

My effort was two stories only. Wadsworth was much touched by his colleagues' presentation to him of a really beautiful silver tray. During the dinner he and my wife seemed to be having the gayest of times.

Wednesday, November 30

Under McGhee's driving leadership, despite some signs of disintegration of the conference, most of us continued to work until McGhee and Grady went off to catch the 6:00 o'clock train for Ankara. The products of the day were the approval of the two basic statements, one for our [respective] foreign offices and the other for the Department[150] and the presentation by several of us to McGhee of our answers to his question: "What role can the US representative play in his particular country during the next weeks and months?" My reply was drafted during the lunch period, during which time I also drew up and sent off with Mattison my emergency letter to Clifford. Here is the first:

My main task during the next weeks and months should be to urge the Israeli government:

---

147. The Seven Year Plan was a modernization blueprint drafted by the Iranian officials in 1947 and passed into law by the Majles in March 1949. Max W. Thornberg (1892–1962), a wartime petroleum adviser to the State Department and oil executive and consultant, was instrumental in the final drafting. Overseas Consultants, Inc. (OCI) was the US oil consortium retained by Thornburg to survey Iran's needs and steer the plan. The plan was mostly technical, and neither the Iranian government nor OCI called for basic social or land reforms. After very little success it was suspended in 1951, and the contract between OCI and the Iranian government was terminated. Linda Wills Qaimmaqami, "The Catalyst of Nationalization: Max Thornburg and the Failure of Private Sector Development in Iran, 1947–1951," *Diplomatic History* 19, no. 1 (1995): 1–31.

148. Allen Welsh Dulles (1893–1969), diplomat and lawyer; chief of OSS station in Bern, 1942–1945; co-chaired intelligence review committee to evaluate US intelligence system for NSC, 1948; deputy director of plans in CIA, 1951–1951; director of central intelligence, 1953–1961.

149. Reference to novel by James Justinian Morier, *The Adventures of Hajji Baba of Ispahan* (1924), which portrayed the Muslim world as derisible.

150. The general summary of conclusions for the respective foreign ministries and the more detailed summary for the Department are in *FRUS*, 1949, v. VI, 168–178.

1) To see the problem of the internationalization of Jerusalem in perspective, to recognize the overriding interests there of the international community, and to take into account the US's conviction that Israel's essential interests will be assured under the UN regime;

2) To show realistic moderation in the current and prospective bilateral peace negotiations which will have the full moral support of the US;

3) To soften—on grounds of enlightened self-interest if not on those of common humanity—its rigid refugee policy;

4) To face the fact—it is so regarded by American experts—that continued unrestricted "ingathering of the exiles" will mean economic disaster for Israel.

5) In general, I should make indubitably clear that the American government's continued benevolent cooperation would be gravely jeopardized if Israel should fail to take into account the above suggestion[s].

McDonald's letter to Clifford is as follows:[151]

Istanbul, Turkey
November 30, 1949
Dear Clark:

This note is being written during the last hours of our Chief of Mission Conference and being sent via [Gordon] Mattison who is flying back this p.m.

What a wonderful leader McGhee has proved to be! His energy is unlimited; his comprehension of the general lines of U.S. policy and even of details of our relationships in this area [is] amazing; and his judgment seems to me to be extraordinarily sound. We are lucky that he is in charge in this part of the world.

My only present reservation on our current policy is re[garding] Jerusalem. I recognize the validity of the reasons for the U.S. support of the PCC resolution; but I dread what might happen if an attempt were made under UN auspices [to] force Israel to accept immediately a UN administrator. A repetition of the Bernadotte tragedy would not be improbable if internationalization were to be implemented before there has been an overwhelming demonstration of world public opinion, backed by such tangible evidence of effective material support as would discourage Jewish extremists and make it possible for the Israel Government to yield without destroying itself.[152]

My hope, therefore, is that UN action—if this should receive the required vote in the Assembly—will be limited at this UN session to a formal declara-

151. McDonald to Clifford, November 30, 1949, McDonald Papers, USHMM, box 8, folder 4.

152. In the Knesset debate on November 7, Ben-Gurion openly rejected the PCC's Jerusalem scheme and insisted that Jewish Jerusalem was part of Israel. Menachem Begin called for the "Jerusalem Law" in that session and again raised Jerusalem in the Knesset debate of November 22.

tion of principles and purposes. This procedure would give time for passions to cool and for reason—as well as self-interest—to assert itself in both Jerusalem and Tel Aviv.[153]

McGhee expressed himself as warmly appreciative of my draft program. Berry later said that it was one of the finest things that came out of the conference. McGhee earlier, possibly as part of his general friendliness, told Ruth that I had been a "tower of strength." His wife [Cecelia], who arrived only that morning, proved also to be a very charming person. The farewells to our colleagues at the conference were genuinely friendly indicating one of the incidental gains of the meeting.

As we were breaking up, I had for the first time since I took office what seemed to me a clear picture of our government's policy. Its incorporation in the formal statement which was to be forwarded to us from Washington (there was no time to secure a clean copy in Istanbul) was an essential embodiment of this.[154] I felt, too, that the Departmental mechanism in Washington was now geared to effective action. Although Berry and Mattison had said almost nothing during the meeting, it was clear that without them McGhee could not have functioned as he did. These three men, together with Hare, Wilkins, et al., make a formidable combination.

In the evening, Ruth and Bobby and I went for a couple of hours with Eliachar, the Israeli consul, to meet a small group of the Jewish community. There was, of course, no talk about the conference and very little about Israel. Most of it was about the Jewish community locally. It seemed from the talk to be far removed from both the ardent Jewishness of Israel or the many-voiced Jewishness of the West.

---

153. Marginal note by McDonald next to final paragraph: "I cannot put this too strong."
154. "Agreed Conclusions of the Conference of Near Eastern Chiefs of Mission," *FRUS*, 1949, v. VI, 168–179. With regard to Israel, the conclusions stressed the need for overall stability and economic development in the Middle East, the enhancement of US prestige, US impartiality in the Arab-Israeli conflict, US endorsement of the Economic Survey Mission Interim Report, the desirability of Israeli-Jordanian peace negotiations, the willingness of the United States to see Jordanian-occupied Palestine annexed to Jordan, the importance of avoiding military pacts in the Middle East, and the desirability of an Institute for Near Eastern Affairs.

18. December 1949

The usual semi-confusion of getting away from the hotel and the usual delays at the field. Nonetheless, we were in the air before noon and in Athens in time for the traditional ice cream.

After less than half an hour on the ground [in Nicosia] we had a pleasant trip to Lydda, where we arrived just after sunset. When we reached the residence, we were delighted at the progress that had been made during our absence.

Busy trying to get caught up.

Ford and I had a long hour-and-a-half conference with Eytan and Comay. I gave them the agreed-upon account of Istanbul, and answered their questions as far as I was able. They were naturally concerned chiefly about Jerusalem. The best summary of our talk is in my despatch of the next day to the Department.

In his despatch McDonald described his hour-long meeting with Ben-Gurion and the ninety-minute meeting that followed with Eytan and Comay.[1] In Istanbul, McGhee and McDonald had agreed on five points to relay to the Israelis. On Jerusalem, Ben-Gurion noted that "Christianity still cannot accept nor tolerate fact that Jewish State now exists and that its traditional capital is Jerusalem." Israel, Ben-Gurion said, would guarantee free access to the Holy Places, but he warned that "it [would] take an army to get [the Jews] out of [Jerusalem]; and the only army I see willing to occupy [Jerusalem] is Russia's." In his diary entry of December 6, McDonald added,

> Ben-Gurion could not have been more emphatic about Jerusalem, on which . . . he
> indicated an unyieldingness which could hardly have been more firmly expressed. . . .
> In the course of his analysis of the possible Vatican motivation for its strong stand,
> Ben-Gurion said that if it was fear of a leftward orientation in Israel, he would like to

1. McDonald to secretary of state, no. 859, December 5, 1949, *FRUS*, 1949, v. VI, 1521–1522. See also Ben-Gurion Diary, December 4, 1949, for the former meeting.

say that "Rome would be communist before Jerusalem." Ben-Gurion added that just as the Jews had fought for nearly three thousand years against regimentation so they would also fight now as they had fought against the Romans and other invaders in their defense of Jerusalem.[2]

Ben-Gurion seized on McDonald's suggestion for direct Israeli-Egyptian talks, noting that "peace with Egypt [would] mean peace and stability throughout entire [Middle East]." But Ben-Gurion warned that King Abdullah badly wanted Gaza, so an Egyptian takeover of Gaza as part of an Israeli-Egyptian accord was impossible.[3] *Ben-Gurion confirmed that secret talks were in progress with Jordan (they had begun in Shuneh on November 27,)*[4] *and according to McDonald, Ben-Gurion "seemed sanguine about the outcome." Eytan added that the success of these talks hinged primarily on Gaza and a corridor to the area. Other outstanding issues, including the partition of Jerusalem, were manageable.*

Ben-Gurion summarized, "[The] US must in its own interests work out with or without [the] British an American [Middle Eastern] policy; we think we see it beginning to take shape." McDonald reported that "throughout the two and a half hours of our two talks, formalities were dispensed with and our exchanges were forthright." After the meeting Comay reported to Elath that

> *McDonald [is] most encouraged by State Department views disclosed at [the Istanbul] conference, [he] sees no conflict with Israel except on Jerusalem, concerning which he stressed Washington [is] remaining moderate against heavy pressure. Alleged pro-Israel slant [is] strongly attacked by [the] pro-Arab faction composed [of the US] representatives [from] Damascus, Baghdad, Jiddah, Jerusalem, who called it [a] betrayal, but McGhee ably argued existing realities. . . . Ben-Gurion told McDonald: (1) We welcome [the] U.S. initiative [to] promote peace with Egypt which [is] key to situation. (2) He would have Israel leave U.N. rather than accept binum [internationalization of Jerusalem].*[5]

Monday, December 5

Very pleasant visit in the afternoon with the new librarian, Miss Davis, who was brought out by Tetlie. She will be an excellent addition to the staff. I was much impressed by her obviously excellent preparation for her work here.

Tuesday, December 6

In the afternoon a long and, as usual, extremely valuable conference with Shiloah. After I had reviewed for him briefly Istanbul (there was no need to do this at length because he had already had a summary from Eytan and Comay), he told us in considerable detail about the Jordan negotiations. The Jordanian suggestion about the southern Negev having been rejected, the discussions had

---

2. McDonald's original diary entry of December 6, 1949, in McDonald Papers, USHMM, box 8, folder 5.
3. Ibid.
4. See *DFPI*, v. 4, d. 441.
5. Comay to Elath, December 5, 1949, *DFPI*, v. 4, d. 460.

concentrated on Gaza and the access thereto.[6] In answer to the Israeli insistence that they would do nothing about Gaza which was not satisfactory to Egypt, the Jordanians had replied that that was a family matter between them and Cairo.[7] Israel on its part was trying to find a formula which would satisfy Jordan without violating Israel's determination not to yield sovereignty over any corridor which would divide the country into A and B sections.

It became clear from Shiloah's talk that the Israelis are much concerned about the possible extension of the British treaty to Cis-Jordan. Shiloah admitted that in sober reality such extension would make little difference in the power which the UK could wield. Nonetheless, he was insistent that from the domestic political point of view, it would be impossible to permit British installations, the stationing of troops, and the movement of them [through] Israeli territory. This spelled out more fully what the prime minister had said on Sunday night about the need to discuss such extension "with the British themselves." Shiloah told us that the next meeting with the Jordanians had been fixed for Thursday [December 8], that it might be crucial, and that he was a little hopeful that it might be followed by formal negotiations.

Wednesday, December 7

At 6:15, the family and I went to the Helm's. While I talked until 7:30 with Sir Knox, the ladies, having examined the new furniture, visited with Lady Helm. I gave him a full and frank account of Istanbul. He showed the greatest interest when I was reporting on the Israeli views expressed by Shiloah and Ben-Gurion about the possible extension of the British treaty to Cis-Jordan. When I had concluded, I said it was now his turn to bring me up to date, since our governments had agreed that we should put the cards on the table for one another. He laughingly said that I was much better informed than he, that there was little for him to tell me. He then went ahead, however, and brought me up to date on the projected resumption of Israel-UK talks on financial matters and blocked sterling.[8] On the larger issues, the Israelis had in the first talks been so unyielding that there was no hope of agreement. As illustrative of this attitude he cited the Israeli position on pensions for former British civil servants in Palestine. As to the Israeli charges that the UK is using the sterling balances as a club to force agreement on Israel's obligations as [a] "successor state," he said that there had been no direct connection between the two issues, but that naturally if the UK had to deal with two prospective customers,

6. Abdullah had insisted in the initial round of negotiations on November 27, 1949, that the Negev be ceded to Jordan in order to link Jordan with Gaza. In the second round of talks on December 1, Jordanian negotiators abandoned their claim to the Negev. *DFPI*, v. 4, d. 441, 449.

7. Specifically, Shiloah had told the Jordanians that Israel could not become embroiled with Egypt should Egypt oppose Jordan's receiving Gaza and that Jordan could have access to Gaza without Israel having to cede territory.

8. The British had argued in July 1949 that the Israelis owed 20 million pounds for expenses related to the liquidation of the Mandate. The Israelis had counter-claims stemming from Jewish Agency deposits in London. See *DFPI*, v. 4, d. 443, 455; editorial note in entry of March 22, 1950.

one of whom was conciliatory on a large related issue and the other [of which] was quite the opposite, naturally this attitude [affected] the UK on the smaller matter.[9] He quoted the Israeli authorities as having said that there is little hope for partial agreement and that, therefore, they should strive for a settlement "across the table" on all outstanding issues. Talks are to be resumed within the next few days on both categories of questions.

Thursday, December 8

Long staff conference at the office. After brief reports by other members, I spoke for more than an hour about Istanbul and answered questions. This period was followed by a round-the-table discussion led by Major Brady[10] on the possibility of Jerusalem complications in the event the decision on internationalization were affirmative. Brady showed intimate knowledge and made several penetrating and suggestive comments, but was not able to convince most of his colleagues that there is any considerable likelihood that the local authorities will move to advance their frontiers. The consensus of opinion was that this, while perhaps a good military task, would be almost suicidal from the economic point of view.

Friday, December 9

Long and pleasant tea conference with Jack Loewenthal, who brought out his successor, Dr. D. B. Yovanovich, who has been with TWA for several years. He is a Yugoslav who has been absent from his country for eight years. He is planning to establish his citizenship in the States. Loewenthal reported that relationships with the Israeli authorities and El Al were satisfactory, that by mutual agreement TWA had given up for the time being the third weekly flight, preferring that to accepting an unsatisfactory traffic arrangement with El Al. Moreover, passenger traffic had fallen off by 65% from the peak of the summer and fall. They had no definite answer other than seasonal for this slump.[11]

Saturday, December 10

Over to [Sam] Sacks's for a brief visit before lunch. The late afternoon [Gene] Currivan [of the *New York Times*] came in to talk about the Israeli-Jordanian negotiations and about Jerusalem. It appears that he is almost the only important American correspondent left here.

---

9. The Israelis believed that London was using political questions to solve the financial issues. London had pursued improved relations, telling the Israelis that Britain accepted Israel as a reality, that London understood that most Arab refugees would have to be settled in Arab countries, that London would pursue a policy of friendship to the Arab states and Israel both, and that London no longer supported the detachment of the Negev from Israel. Yet now, with the financial disagreement, the detachment of the Negev was being raised again in London. *DFPI*, v. 4, d. 455.

10. Colonel Burton Andrus, the military attaché, was reassigned to Brazil on November 30, 1949. Major Lawrence Brady assumed the post of military attaché in Tel Aviv. Captain Frothingham, the naval attaché, was reassigned on December 2, and his post was left vacant.

11. See entries of July 2 and October 31, 1949.

At 5:45 Dr. [David W.] Senator[12] came to talk about the University and the possibility of opening the [Mount] Scopus road in exchange for the opening of the Bethlehem road. He told me first of his mission to American universities, of the support he got from the presidents of Chicago, [Johns] Hopkins and Yale, but of his failure with Eisenhower [president, Columbia University] and [James] Conant [president, Harvard University]. He had found Hector McNeil[13] very sympathetic, prepared to admit the reasonableness of agreement on restricted areas and prepared to write to London to that effect. This he did but to no avail. When Senator later followed up with him, McNeil reported that there had been some hitch from the Israeli side. Following that, Eban had secured double confirmation from Sharett, but still the British seemed to hesitate. I told Senator that it was my guess, it could not be a judgment, that probably there would be no partial settlement of this sort, because Scopus was potentially too valuable to the Jews. He argued that so long as the Arabs held the German Hospice on the Mount of Olives, Scopus had little or no military value, and that in any case, only unarmed students and professors would, under the proposed agreement, be permitted to pass through the Sheikh Jarrah lines. I replied that the Arabs would be dubious about the efficacy of the latter restriction, and that they might feel that the presence of hundreds of young men at the university would endanger the Hospice and the Mount of Olives, and thus open the way to the control of the Jericho road from the northern heights. Ford came in about that time and said that he shared my view that it was not likely that either the Israeli government or the British or American would make special efforts to secure this limited, though admittedly important, settlement.

Shiloah then came for our second talk about the Jordanian-Israeli negotiations and about Jerusalem. He explained that the meeting, the second, had been held the previous Thursday (I think it was the third [meeting]).[14] The atmosphere had continued to be friendly, but Shiloah was less optimistic primarily because he thought the Jordanians were in no position to negotiate about Gaza. During the last talk, he had pressed them for some more definite statement of the basis for their answer that this was "a family affair." The response was unconvincing, and the negotiators showed embarrassment. The Israelis had then reiterated their earlier statement that they would make no settlement about Gaza which was not satisfactory to the Egyptians.

On the question of a "corridor," the Israelis had finally made their proposal beyond which they were not prepared to go, that is, to grant to the Jordan's "jurisdiction" over the road through Israeli territory on the analogy of the grant of jurisdiction over a road to Panama through the canal zone. Towards the end of the discussion it had been uncertain whether there would be another meeting. Shiloah had suggested two alternatives: 1) fixing another date; and 2) leav-

---

12. Entry of August 18, 1948.
13. Entry of July 30, 1948.
14. The third meeting was on Thursday, December 8. See *DFPI*, v. 4, d. 469.

ing the exchanges unconcluded but temporarily interrupted. The second alternative would permit either side to suggest a resumption when either had something new to offer or merely wished to take up where they had left off. It was then that, according to Shiloah, Abdullah interrupted to say that this suggestion was not wise because, once broken off, it would be much more difficult to resume the negotiations. It was therefore decided to meet again, the exact time to be fixed as was customary in these exchanges, by mutual agreement a few days hence.

As to Jerusalem, Shiloah thought it might make Abdullah more anxious to achieve at least a local settlement with Israel in order, to that extent, to forestall the Trusteeship Council's internationalization plan. On the other hand, he pointed out what neither Ford nor I had thought of, the possibility that Abdullah's defeat in the UN might be used against him by the mufti and his adherents who, if they were supported more actively by Egypt, might embarrass the king.

Speaking of Saudi Arabia's possible fear of Jordan, Shiloah told a very interesting tale. This had to do with the tendency of defeated Saudi Arabian troops to justify their withdrawal by tall accounts of the incredible ferocity and mechanical aids of the enemy. The victory of the Jews would be attributed to demoniac devices and aids, which made resistance by ordinary mortals impossible. The relation of all this to Jordan is that, since the Legion was the one Arab army which had successfully resisted the Jews, it must share the unnatural strength of the Jews. This conclusion would lead to the fear that the Legion would be invincible and that Ibn Saud must have protection against it. Naturally, I said nothing to Shiloah about the detailed discussions at Istanbul about [the] American special guarantee for Saudi Arabia.

In his report to the State Department, McDonald added Shiloah's statements that peace negotiations with Egypt were "dear to my heart" and that Shiloah hoped the United States would bring the sides together; that in any partition of Jerusalem, "we shall, of course, expect part of the Old City;" and that Israel would insist that Britain, despite its treaty with Jordan, station no troops west of the Jordan River.[15]

. . . .

On December 7, 1949, the UN's Ad Hoc Political Committee presented two draft resolutions to the General Assembly. One concerned aid to Palestinian refugees based on the recommendations of the Economic Survey Mission. General Assembly Resolution 302 passed 48–0 with 6 abstentions. It allocated some $52 million dollars for direct relief and works programs through June 1951 and established the United Nations Relief and Works Agency for the Palestinian Refugees [UNRWA].[16]

15. McDonald report on this meeting with Shiloah is no. 869 of December 7, 1949, printed in *FRUS*, 1949, v. VI, 1528–1529.
16. On this issue, see memorandum by the acting secretary of state, [Webb], February 27, 1950, *FRUS*, 1950, v. V, 763–766. On January 30, 1950, President Truman recommended to

The other December 7 draft resolution, authored by Australia, concerned international control of Jerusalem. It recalled the earlier resolutions of November 29, 1947, and December 11, 1948, and insisted that the entire city and its environs be "established as a corpus separatum *under a special international regime*" to be administered by the UN through [the] Trusteeship Council, which would begin by drawing up a new governing Statute of Jerusalem. It was approved on December 9 as General Assembly Resolution 303 by a vote of 38–14 with 7 abstentions.[17]

The Israelis had lobbied hard against this resolution, and the vote surprised the government. From New York, Sharett described an "unholy alliance" between the Arab states (minus Jordan), the Soviet bloc (which argued that the partition of Jerusalem would validate British dominance in Jordan), and the Latin American states, which were pressured by the Vatican.[18] The United States (with Truman's approval) and Great Britain both voted against the resolution, arguing that it could not be implemented.[19] Acheson labeled it an "extreme" position. The PCC's compromise proposal, he argued afterward, would have left most purely local affairs in Jerusalem to the Israeli and Jordanian authorities.[20]

On the night of December 9, after the General Assembly vote, McDonald received a night action telegram from Acheson ordering him to "take all possible steps in your discretion to urge upon Israeli [government] and its officials [the] importance of preventing any statements or action which would inflame [the] situation in Near East, particularly in view of current Israeli-Jordan talks and possible further Israeli conversations with [the] Vatican."[21]

On the same evening, McDonald wrote David Niles in the White House:

> The developments since we left Istanbul on the Jerusalem issue have deepened my fears of what may happen if the attempt were made to enforce political internationalization on the city. . . . We have to confess surprise that the vote on the Australian resolution was so nearly decisive. Indeed the result was almost as surprising as the combination of forces which brought it about. . . . Now we are waiting anxiously to see what will happen during these next days. In our pessimistic moments we are beginning to picture possible crises comparable to those of a year ago; but in our more cheerful moments, we still hope that a head-on collision between a UN decision and embattled people can be avoided. Certainly an open clash would serve no one's purpose except the Russians.[22]

Congress that the United States contribute half of the costs estimated by the UN. In general, see Waldman, *Anglo-American Diplomacy and the Palestinian Refugee Problem*, 166–185.

17. Text in *DFPI*, v. 4, 693–694.

18. On Vatican pressure, which the Israelis tried to alleviate in Rome days before the UN vote, see especially *DFPI*, v. 4, d. 479. The Vatican did not answer Israeli appeals. On the Soviets, see *DFPI*, v. 4, d. 484.

19. Memorandum of conversation by the secretary of state, December 7, 1949, *FRUS*, 1949, v. VI, 1524–1527. For Israeli efforts against the resolution, see *DFPI*, v. 4, d. 446, 447, 450, 466, 467, 468.

20. Acheson's comment in Acheson to Truman, December 20, 1949, *FRUS*, 1949, v. VI, 1551–1555.

21. Acheson to McDonald, no. 755, December 9, 1949, *FRUS*, 1949, v. VI, 1531–1532.

22. McDonald to Niles, December 9, 1949, McDonald Papers, USHMM, box 8, folder 5.

McDonald's concerns were well founded. The Israeli public was outraged. The government, particularly the Mapai element, came under heavy criticism even within the cabinet itself. Ben-Gurion even worried about renewed IZL and Lehi violence against UN officials. More fundamentally, he believed that a defeat on Jerusalem would lead to international intrigue in Israel more generally, as well as successive defeats on other security issues such as Israel's frontiers and the Arab refugees. Despite the diplomatic risks, Ben-Gurion decided to fight the UN resolution head-on.[23] He publicly reiterated Israel's position on Jerusalem, and he held the government together as it forged a response to the UN resolution.

Sunday, December 11

Ford and I were at Eytan's office before the agreed time, 10:30. I gave him a paraphrase of the [night action] telegram, which had reached me the day before. Eytan said that he thought the government would stand on Ben-Gurion's statement of three sentences in the morning paper.[24] He did not venture an opinion, any more than had Shiloah, as to whether the government would merely refuse to cooperate with the PCC or its committee or agents, or might refuse them admission to Jewish Jerusalem. He seemed to think that the issue would not arise for some weeks.[25]

Eytan seemed more optimistic than had Shiloah about the possibility of at least a limited agreement in the very near future with Abdullah. He thought the exchange of the two roads to Scopus and Bethlehem might be very near. He told us that the date for the next Israeli-Jordanian talks had been fixed for the 13th. He seemed surprised at the suggestion that the UN decision might be used by the mufti or Egypt against Abdullah. He was more inclined to think that Abdullah could gain by posing now as the defender of the Arab Holy Places against the infidels to whom, for selfish political and nationalist reasons, the leaders of the other Arab states had been blindly willing to open the door. Eytan reiterated the Israeli view that the Moscow-Vatican marriage of convenience could not endure. He frankly expressed the expectation and hope that Russia would be so intransigent in its demands for participation in the governing body of the UN organ created for Jerusalem that agreement would be impossible.

I took the occasion of this talk to complain personally but bitterly about the anti-American bias of the *Palestine Post*, as illustrated by the gross distortions in [Jesse Zel] Lurie's pieces in recent editions.[26] I said that it should now

---

23. See Ben-Gurion Diary, entry of December 12, 1949. The editors are grateful to Tuvia Friling for this reference.

24. "Israel's position on the question of Jerusalem found a clear and final expression by the Government and all parties in the Knesset on December 5. Jerusalem is an inseparable part of Israel and her eternal capital. No U.N. vote can alter this historic fact." *Palestine Post*, December 11, 1949.

25. The Israeli cabinet met later that day and decided that Israel's position concerning Jerusalem was unchanged by the UN vote and that the government would continue moving its offices to Jerusalem. *DFPI*, v. 4, d. 472.

26. For example, Jesse Zel Lurie, "Vatican Made Latins Switch," *Palestine Post*, December 9, 1949, which blamed the United States for not counteracting Vatican influence and sug-

be clear to the Israeli officials that there was only one great power which was willing to let its friendship for Israel play a role in shaping its policy, that there is only one which had chosen its representative because of his known friendship for Israel. [For this reason it is conspicuous] that a newspaper which must in one way or another be partially or largely subsidized by Israel should abuse that government's friend. Eytan made no defense of the *Post*. On the contrary, he said that the Foreign Office complained almost daily about one or [an]other sin of omission or commission. Cables had been exchanged frequently with Sharett about [Lurie's] articles. I still pressed my point and said that I intended to urge with Sharett and Ben-Gurion, when I saw them, consideration by them of the obvious fact that Russia is concerned only with its own interests and cannot be counted upon for any friendship or generosity towards Israel.

In his report of December 11, McDonald quoted Eytan:

> "Israel may refuse access [to] Jewish Jerusalem to [Trusteeship Council] representatives or merely refuse cooperation." McDonald added the following comment: "Whole [of] Israel [is] shocked and pro-Russian sections stunned by success [of] Russian-Vatican-Moslem combination. Russian cynicism is [a] bitter pill for all, but especially for [the] Leftists. Ben-Gurion and [the] Cabinet now see [the] absurdity [of] Sharrett's policy [of] insisting on balancing Russian 'friendship' with that of [the] US. I pressed this point cruelly with Eytan and intend to do the same with Ben-Gurion and Weizmann, urging them [to] speak and act accordingly."[27]

Out to the Fords for lunch in my borrowed Plymouth station wagon. The lunch was noteworthy because of Hadassah Samuel's presence and the extended discussion about the Weizmanns' too frequent entertainment of [the] Russian minister and chargé. This talk began because of the Weizmann luncheon the previous day for the dual piano team Vronsky and Babin.[28] The frequent invitations to the Moukhines[29] were in striking contrast to the complete lack of invitations for the Fords.

Monday, December 12

For the record, I note an extraordinarily surprising report that under date of December 9 our friend [Gowen] tells the Department that [the Vatican] believes [the] USSR is attempting to block [the UN] Jerusalem action by

---

gested that the United States was willing to see the resolution pass as a means to pressure Israel on boundaries and refugees.

27. McDonald to secretary of state, no. 878, December 11, 1949, *FRUS*, 1949, v. VI, 1532–1533. Eytan's report to Sharrett of December 11, 1949, added that McDonald, "speaking with great feeling, said he realized Israel [is] bound [to] maintain correct relations with Russia but [the] time had come for her to appreciate that [the] U.S.A. was [the] only power which [is] prepared help her even against [her] own interests [and] where [the] head of state [is] always approachable and ready to lend [a] friendly ear." *DFPI*, v. 4, d. 473.

28. Vitya Vronsky (1909–1992) and Viktor Babin (1908–1972), noted Russian Jewish piano duo who performed worldwide. Both died in Cleveland, Ohio.

29. M. L. Moukhine, Soviet chargé d'affaires, Tel Aviv.

supporting it, in knowledge [that] this will frighten votes. [Vatican is] surprised [by the] US present attitude [in] view of [US] support [for the] November '47 resolution. Fears another war [over] Jerusalem because of Arab-Jewish intransigence.

Worked at home all morning and afternoon. At teatime Ford brought [Burton] Berry in for nearly an hour-and-a-half's visit. After sketching out his plans for tomorrow, during which I emphasized the importance that he see as much of the historic part of the country as possible, we discussed housekeeping problems with special emphasis on personnel and housing.

There was some but not much discussion of policy. Earlier, Berry had told Ford that he and McGhee thought that my statement of my program here was the clearest and most constructive suggestion that had been made by the chiefs at Istanbul. In reporting to Berry, I underlined the fact that, already in my talk with Ben-Gurion and in my several talks with the other men of the Foreign Office, I had followed closely the line agreed upon. In particular, I told him that I was using the present Israel embarrassment about the Russians to drive home the basic fact that only the US government, of all the great powers, had evidenced any willingness to influence its policy by considerations of friendship for Israel. Berry agreed that this was [a] timely strategy.

Hurried off with the Fords to keep [our] date with Eytan, which [the] latter had suggested two hours earlier. When we reached [the] Foreign Office, Eytan seemed a little embarrassed because the Ben-Gurion statement which he had expected to hand us had been postponed until Tuesday [December 13]. He did not or could not give us the exact reason.[30] The decision to postpone had been made too late for him to get us on the telephone. The visit was worthwhile, however, because Eytan gave us an indication of the line Ben-Gurion was to take. It had been decided that the government must assume leadership, or else [initiative] would be seized by one or other of the intransigent groups. The prime minister was, in form at least, following the line suggested by the Department's plea to avoid any inflammatory statement or act. In substance, however, I gathered that the prime minister would indicate no yielding but rather a continuation of action as during past months. Presumably, this would mean the continuation of transfers of parts of departments to Jerusalem and the encouragement of emigration to the city. Ford agreed to draft the telegram to the Department while I went for high tea to Brady's.

---

30. The reason lies partly in Sharett's message to Ben-Gurion of December 12, 1949, from New York urging caution regarding Jerusalem until US policy was formulated (Truman was then in Florida). Sharett urged that the government refuse cooperation with the UN Trusteeship Council, that it hasten peace with Jordan, and that it "sit tight" for the time being concerning Jerusalem's status. Eban insisted on the same day from New York that the resolution be allowed to die a "natural death," because the UN had "no serious intention" of sending representatives to take over administrative functions in Jerusalem. *DFPI*, v. 4, d. 470, 471, 476, 478, 482, and pp. 709–710.

From there I went to Ford's to check his text, which Padberg then took to the office for filing.[31]

The Sackses and I arrived at the Ohel Theatre well before Elisabeth Bergner began her recital.[32] The audience which packed the hall was predominantly German in background and almost without sabras. Most of the intellectuals were there. Her first reading from the [novella] *Fräulein Else* by Arthur Schnitzler lasted an hour and a quarter, but despite my inadequate German, was very dramatic and absorbing. After the intermission, she read extracts from the Bible in English and, surprisingly, from the New as well as the Old Testament. The last number was the final examination scene from [George Bernard] Shaw's *Saint Joan*, with an Israeli actor reading in Hebrew the Inquisitor's role, while Bergner read in English. Her technique is to make no pretense of not reading. Her acting is quiet but varied and touching. At moments she seems literally to be the 19-year-old girl she represented as Else or the even younger Joan [of Arc].

It was revealing that when I asked Mrs. Kaplan why Atara had not come, her mother replied that she hated German and did not know or want to know a word of it. Mrs. Ben-Gurion, who sat immediately in front of me, showed boredom before the end of Bergner's long first number. I could not be sure whether or not this was merely a pose.

Tuesday, December 13

For the record I insert here that under [the] date of December 8 the Department informed [me] that "Colombian delegation alleging authority to speak for Vatican informed Latin American caucus, Vatican would prefer UN adoption [of] Australian resolution even though realizing could not be implemented."

Harold Hoskins came out for eight o'clock breakfast and stayed until twenty minutes of ten when he left with Ford.[33] Fortunately, I had been able to secure an appointment for him with Eytan, which he accepted with good grace in lieu of his impossible request for interviews with Weizmann and Ben-Gurion. He purports now to be interested in some practical working arrangements between the Arabs and Israel, but says that he finds among governmental Arabs no one prepared to move. All are fearful of losing their jobs or in some cases their lives. Abdullah, he thinks, has lost so much status with Arab leaders that he cannot regain his prestige, while his appeal to Arab popular opinion as a defender of the Holy Places against the infidel is not likely to reach the masses. I asked Hoskins about the objectivity of the *Middle East [Journal]*. He rather cynically replied, "It is about as objective as is possible in view of its anti-Zionist

31. McDonald to secretary of state, no. 880, December 12, 1949, *FRUS*, 1949, v. VI, 1534–1535.
32. Elisabeth Bergner (1897–1986), Ukrainian-born German-language stage and film actress who fled Germany for England in 1933.
33. On Hoskins, see entry of April 1, 1949.

premise."[34] During our nearly two hours together we covered many subjects. I spoke with considerable frankness in the hope, if not the expectation, that I would not be misquoted. Hoskins seemed satisfied with his visit.

For the record I note that a Department [telegram of] December 9 cites Egyptian sources to [the] effect that "Vatican turned tide [Jerusalem] particularly by influencing wavering [Latin American] states . . . Bunche, Riley uneasy over possible [General Assembly] action; Riley fearing will upset armistice; Abdullah cabled [Secretary General] would consider Austral[ian] resolution as menace to Jordan's security." Under date [of] December 11, Burdett reports that Colonel Coverdale, acting UN chief of staff,[35] "does not anticipate any disturbances but notice[s] considerable underlying tension among both Israel and Arab officials." Thinks Arabs in MACs are stiffening attitude and "much less willing to yield to Israel demands and expects continuation [of] this change. Believes Israel will react with increased aggressiveness."

Mr. Simon of protocol called to say that Mrs. Weizmann was anxious that the president send a message on the occasion of the opening of two recreation centers named after Mrs. Truman and Eddie Jacobson in a military hospital at Tel Litwinsky.[36] Mrs. Weizmann quotes Mrs. Truman as having assented to the use of her name[37] and as favoring the presidential message. After talking the question out with Hooper and Ford, we agreed the next day that we should recommend against the presidential message and so telegraphed the Department. Our reasoning was that now is [not] an opportune time for such a message, and that in any case, it is not suitable that the president should spread his messages so thin.

At teatime Norman Jacobs from Manchester came for [an] unofficial visit.[38] At the same time Harry Rosenfield of the US Displaced Persons Commission was at the house. The latter is coming to see me again before he leaves Israel.[39]

The family and I were at dinner at Eytan's. The other guests included the Guyons[40] and the Vivian [Chaim] Herzogs. After dinner, Guyon delivered a considerable lecture on Israel's failure to aid the diplomatic corps in securing

---

34. The *Middle East Journal*, which first appeared in 1947, was and is the journal of the Middle East Institute in Washington, DC (founded in 1946). See Matthew F. Jacobs, *Imagining the Middle East: The Building of an American Foreign Policy, 1918–1967* (Chapel Hill: University of North Carolina Press, 2011), 38–50.

35. Colonel Garrison Barclay Coverdale (1905–1988), chairman of the Israeli-Jordanian Mixed Armistice Commission.

36. Now the Sheba Medical Center in the renamed town of Tel HaShomer. This hospital was initially built by the US Army to treat Allied casualties in the North African campaign. The Royal Air Force assumed control in 1944. Israel reopened the hospital during the War of Independence as Military Hospital No. 5. The recreation rooms, dedicated to Truman's late mother and Eddie Jacobson, were funded partly by B'nai B'rith and officially opened in January 1950.

37. Vera Weizmann mistakenly refers to Truman's wife Bess. Truman's mother Martha had died in July 1947.

38. See entry of November 8, 1948.

39. See entry of December 25, 1949.

40. Édouard-Félix Guyon, French ambassador to Israel, 1949–1952. See entry of July 26, 1949.

proper housing. Eytan's reply was to ask what specifically Guyon would have the government do. Guyon seemed to feel that I ought to follow up on the diplomatic corps meeting, but I am not inclined to do so, because it might easily be misunderstood and even used as a basis for misinterpreting my action, since it would be difficult to limit the discussion at the house to matters strictly related to housing in Tel Aviv. Inevitably someone would raise the question about the government move to Jerusalem, and then whatever one said or did not say could be used against him. A couple of days later, when I was discussing this matter with Helm, he was emphatic that it would be dangerous to hold the meeting. Ford agreeing, I decided definitely to follow their advice.

The only substantial new item which Eytan added to the discussion was that Ben-Gurion was leaving the next morning at 9:30 "to choose prime minister's office in Jerusalem."

After several discussions the Israeli cabinet on December 13 decided on the transfer of government offices and of the Knesset to Jerusalem.[41] *In the Knesset Ben-Gurion reiterated that the UN General Assembly resolution was "utterly incapable of implementation. . . . We respect and shall continue to respect those wishes of all those States which are concerned for freedom of worship and free access to the Holy Places, and which seek to safeguard existing rights in the Holy Places and religious buildings in Jerusalem . . . [but] for the State of Israel there has been and always will be one capital only—Jerusalem the eternal. So it was three thousand years ago—and so it will be, we believe, until the end of time." The Knesset approved its own move to Jerusalem.*[42] *Ben-Gurion was uncomfortable defying the UN, and he worried about US sanctions, especially because US policy had yet to crystallize. But he also felt that he had no choice because of Jerusalem's place in Jewish history, the desires of the 100,000 Jews living there, and the belief that compliance with the resolution would weaken Israel on other security-related issues.*[43]

McDonald commented, "Eytan's prognostications given [to] me [on] December 12 . . . that [the] Prime Minister's speech would contain 'no inflammatory statements' [are] hardly borne out in such remarks." Ben-Gurion's statements, McDonald explained, were "obviously made (1) to forestall more drastic demands by government's violently outspoken right-wing critics such as [Herut] and (2) to confound Communists and leftist Mapam elements supporting or apologizing for [the] USSR stand on internationalization. Ben-Gurion [is] evidently confident of instant favorable reaction to his bold directive."[44]

41. Sharett, who had urged a more careful policy and came under heavy attack as a result, submitted his resignation privately to Ben-Gurion, who nonetheless convinced Sharett to remain in the government. Fischer, ed., *Moshe Sharett: The Second Prime Minister, Selected Documents (1894–1965)*, 402–404.

42. Statement in *DFPI*, v. 4, 709–710. See also *DFPI*, v. 4, d. 482.

43. See his diary entry of December 14, 1949, printed in *DFPI*, v. 4, d. 487.

44. McDonald to secretary of state, no. 882, December 13, 1949, NARA, RG 59, MC 1390, reel 20, frames 619–621; McDonald to secretary of state, no. 885, December 14, 1949,

Confidentially, McDonald wrote his friend Ben Abrams as follows: "I must limit myself to the vague generality that we are hoping for the best and struggling to avoid the more serious possibilities inherent in this crisis. . . . This one can say with no possibility of being controverted: There is never a dull moment in Israel. Moreover, the Jewish people in proportion to their numbers cause more stir in the world than any other folk."[45]

The Knesset held its first session in Jerusalem on December 26, 1949.

Wednesday, December 14

James M. Silberman, chief of productivity and technological development branch, US Bureau of Labor Statistics,[46] talked to me about his visit here on invitation from Goldie Meyerson. He has been working in the Western European countries under [the] ECA [Economic Cooperation Administration] to increase industrial productivity. The response here had been friendly both from Meyerson and Kaplan, as well as from the manufacturers association and from the secretary general of Histadrut.[47] Silberman thought that if Israel made an application, there would be made available a grant of $30,000 from the [Division of] Scientific and Cultural Cooperation [in] the Department to finance the work of American production experts here. The Israeli governmental officials had seemed inclined to pay for such experts. I am to follow up with Goldie Meyerson.

Thursday, December 15

Helm was at the house with Ford for more than an hour. I outlined to him in detail my recollection of Shiloah's reports on the Israeli-Jordanian exchanges, while Helm listened attentively. At the end, he told me something of the reports he had had from across the river. These were much more pessimistic than those we had received. I wondered, as he spoke, to what extent the report of Jordan's "insistence" on the Negev was a reflection of British desires and interests.

Helm then brought me up to date on the negotiations about the blocked sterling and the broader financial picture between the two countries. He emphasized that the Israeli initial position on financial obligations, for example, in reference to pensions, was "wholly unacceptable." He added that he expected that he would be very busy during the next weeks on this problem.

FRUS, 1949, v. VI, 1541–1542. Further reports in McDonald to secretary of state, no. 894, December 15, 1949, McDonald Papers, USHMM, box 8, folder 5.

45. McDonald to Benjamin Abrams, December 15, 1949, McDonald Papers, Columbia University, box 6, folder 2.

46. James M. Silberman (1913–2016), chief, Productivity and Technology Development, US Department of Labor, 1948–1950; responsible for the Marshall Plan's Productivity Assistance Program.

47. Pinhas Lavon (Lubianker) (1904–1976), secretary-general of Histadrut, 1949–1961.

Eytan telephoned, not knowing that Shiloah had been here the evening before to express his pleasure at the progress which was being made in the exchanges with Jordan.

Mr. Givens of General Electric came to say goodbye and to tell of the problem which is bothering him in connection with the persistent refusals of the Arab states to admit GE experts who have Israeli visas. He said that it was impossible for his company to send two sets of experts to this area and that, therefore, he wished to urge again the issuance by the US of dual passports to cover these special situations. I told him that I would check with Ford and suggested that the US issue dual passports for these special purposes.

Mr. Bezner, Director of Foreign Exchange,[48] came out with Mr. Hooper. The most noteworthy part of our talk was that which concerned the *Palestine Post*. I told him frankly of my conviction that it is deliberately and maliciously anti-American and gave him examples of the reasons for my opinion. He insisted that the paper is not publicly owned but seemed really to know very little about it. He was obviously so disturbed by what I said, however, that he promised to tell both Horowitz and Kaplan of my views.[49]

Spent the rest of the day trying to clear up my documents so as to get away for the weekend to Jerusalem. During the whole of the week we had been waiting with a measure of anxiety for word from Washington of our government's response to Israel's announcement of December 13 that the Knesset and the prime minister were moving to Jerusalem and that other central offices would soon be added to those already there.[50] Meantime, Israeli opinion appeared to be almost unanimous that the Ben-Gurion decision was overdue and that it should have been taken earlier, when it could have been carried through, as was commonly assumed, with less trouble.

Friday, December 16

On December 16, McDonald and his family went to Jerusalem, he to examine conditions as they related to the armistice there.

48. Yitzhak Bezner (1908–1952), controller of foreign exchange, Ministry of Foreign Affairs; later headed reparations negotiations with Federal Republic of Germany.

49. Bezner's account of this meeting is in *DFPI*, v. 4, d. 499. He reported McDonald as adding that only the United States and its six million [*sic*] Jews could help Israel in its precarious economic position. Thus Israel should abandon its professed neutrality and participate in the Marshall Plan, which would bring about economic prosperity. Concerning Jerusalem, Bezner recorded McDonald's comment that the United States and Britain would not appoint any representatives to the UN governmental machinery charged with implementing the UNs resolution, but that, for the next few months, the United States and Britain would not be able to act in defiance of the resolution, lest they damage UN prestige. Thus members of the US mission to Israel could not transfer to Jerusalem or even visit Israeli officials there, and the transfer of the Israeli Foreign Ministry to Jerusalem would cause substantial diplomatic damage as a result.

50. McDonald noted on December 16 that six full ministries were already in Jerusalem as well as individual departments from three others, while three principal ministries (foreign affairs, finance, and defense) remained in Tel Aviv. McDonald to secretary of state, joint weeka no. 51, December 16, 1949, McDonald Papers, USHMM, box 8, folder 5.

The ride [to Jerusalem via Petah Tikvah with Ford and Hooper] through Lod (or Lydda) and Ramle was interesting because of the historical association of these areas, and because I had not been through them since '46.[51] Everywhere there were evidences that the Arabs, though they had been Christians, had almost completely disappeared, and that they had been almost completely displaced by Jewish refugees. The road had been so improved that, except for about ten kilometers, it was almost as good as the old Latrun route. We reached the King David at a quarter of two; a quarter of three we were at the consulate and at three under the guidance of young Root,[52] the grandson of Elihu, crossed the line and went to the American Colony. About a quarter past six, Burdett came by for me to take him to the Dayan weekly tea party and open house. Their large apartment was comfortably crowded while Mrs. Dayan served delicious tea.

I had two conferences worthy of being recorded. [To] Shiloah I reported briefly that the accounts of the current negotiation as given by the British were in sharp contradiction with his account. In particular, the UK report quoted the Jordanians as adamant about the Negev, for example, and about the Arab sections of Jerusalem. In reply, Shiloah said that perhaps the Jordanians were "boasting to the British," but that in any case his report had been accurate. He offered to show me the text, as written out in Arabic, of the points on which there had been a measure of agreement in principle. Again as always, in my contacts with Shiloah, I was impressed by his knowledge and sincerity.

The Israelis (including Shiloah) and Jordanians (including King Abdullah) initially reached a draft agreement in Shuneh on December 13. It included the partition of Jerusalem, with Israeli control of the Jewish Quarter and Western Wall and access to Mount Scopus; Israeli sovereignty over the west bank of the Dead Sea to the potash works on the northern end; reciprocal border changes in accordance with the needs of both; and Jordanian sovereignty over a corridor from Hebron to Gaza, this corridor to be excluded from the Anglo-Jordanian defense treaty, and with the Israelis keeping the right to cross the corridor into the southern Negev. The Jordanians continued, however, to demand additional concessions, including the southern Negev itself.[53]

The other talk was with Ted R. Lurie, editor of the *Palestine Post*. I told him with brutal frankness my personal opinions of his brother's dispatches citing as an example, that of the previous Friday in which an attempt was made to explain the UN adverse vote without even a mention of the Russian and satellite support of the Australian resolution. I characterized other portions of the paper as being also deliberately tendentious and characterized by overt or indirect attacks on the US. I emphasized that my government had not interested

---

51. Goda et al., eds., *To the Gates of Jerusalem*, 121–190.
52. John B. Root, vice consul in Jerusalem, assigned March 1949.
53. *DFPI*, v. 4, 716.

itself in the *Post* or even mentioned it to me but that I, as a friend of Israel, anxious for the country's success, could not refrain from saying that the paper, by its anti-Americanism, is doing Israel a very poor service at the moment when it needs the US more than ever. I paid my respects also to Courtney but made a distinction between a columnist who, in the nature of the case, would be expected to express personal views, as compared with a correspondent who presumably is supposed to report news rather than editorialize in his dispatches.

Lurie attempted to argue that the *Post* is an independent journal and not the organ of any party or group and that, therefore, it is free to express at least editorially and to report those aspects of the news which it regards as important or of special interest to its readers. I replied that it could not be regarded in the same light as a party paper, that it was at least in part a public organ, was commonly regarded as close to the government and therefore, had a responsibility for objectivity which could not be expected from the party organ. One of Lurie's defenses was that his brother reported nothing more adverse to the US than could be found in American papers, for example in Thackrey's *Compass*.[54] Despite Lurie's refusal to admit any validity in my charges, I think he was shaken.

After the tea, Root, Burdett, and a third officer from the consulate and I had dinner at the King David. Afterwards we had a long and pleasant visit during which I talked to them about my appointment and my early relations with the Department.

Saturday, December 17

Long talk with Ruth Jacobs of Manchester[55] and Norman Bentwich. Lunch with Mrs. John Gunther.[56] This was rather painful, because I could not quite make out whether she was still to be taken seriously as a writer and also because of her relations with her former husband.

Tea with a Mr. Gladstone from Toronto and a very interesting Scotsman now in charge of the electrical plant in Jerusalem. The latter had been in Persia and elsewhere in the Middle East for many years. Because of his knowledge of the local languages and his intimate acquaintanceship with some of the countries, particularly Persia, he was absorbingly interesting. In particular, I listened with closest attention to what he had to say about Persia in order to compare his impressions with those of Ambassador Wiley. He was even more pessimistic than the latter about the possibility of Iran organizing effective roadblocks against the Russians. He thought it possible that the shah, with his

54. *Daily Compass*, established by Ted Thackrey in 1948 to replace *PM Daily*. It ceased publication in 1953.
55. Ruth Jacobs, daughter of Zionist leader Norman Jacobs; one of first students in the United Kingdom to receive a bachelor's degree in modern Hebrew.
56. John Gunther (1901–1970) and Frances Fineman (1897–1964), journalists who covered Europe in the 1930s and who divorced in 1944. Fineman, the daughter of Russian Jews, settled in Israel in 1949 and, inspired by Martin Buber, was interested in Israeli-Arab reconciliation. The 1947 death of their son John from a brain tumor is the subject of John Gunther's *Death Be Not Proud* (1949).

marked preference for things modern and American, might lose support at home, particularly since he did not possess the physical power of his father. Again, as I listened to this Britisher talk, I was struck by the extent to which the UK is well served by its adventurous pioneers.

Sunday, December 18

Despite the rain and the cold, Ruth Jacobs and I used Shalom advantageously to visit Ramat Rachel[57] with its splendid view of Bethlehem and Beit Jala. We then drove slowly, stopping at various points, to the southern section of Jerusalem, thus helping to fix in my mind Talpiot, Baka, Mekor Chaim, the Greek and German colonies, Katamon, Kiryat Shmuel, Talbiya, Rehavia, Neve Sha'anan. After stopping for tea at the Eden, we drove out to the Herzl Hill, on the road to Ein Karem.[58] It would have been difficult to find a more spectacular sight than from Herzl Hill. From it one takes in the whole horizon. But because of the overcast and lowering clouds, I decided to return in the afternoon.

Lunch with Colonel Coverdale, Riley's substitute, two of his French colleagues, Mr. Fisher of the UN, press representative for the PCC but now serving with Riley, an American woman who is finance officer for Riley, and a Mr. Shapiro, in Jerusalem for a brief visit from the Public Relations Office of the UN in Geneva.

Dinner with Burdett. He told me nothing about the difficulty which had arisen between him and the other members of the consular corps as a result of his (according to Helm) "unauthorized" letter to Abdullah suggesting a meeting between the latter and the corps. Ford told me about this on Tuesday, having heard it from Helm Monday night.

Monday, December 19

Breakfast with the lady financial officer of Riley's mission. Afterwards, a brief and pleasant visit with Burdett while waiting on Root to bring the family across the line. By this time Burdett had become almost warmly friendly. While he is glad to go to London,[59] I had the impression that he is a little sad at the prospect of losing his unusual position as a political reporting officer.

My several talks with Burdett brought out nothing startlingly new. He seems to feel that nothing effective will be done to block the Jewish transformation of the New City into their national capital. He anticipates complications from the problem of issuing new exequaturs for the new members of the diplomatic corps. He doubts that the question will be raised specifically in the case of [Raleigh] Gibson.[60] He thinks that Israel may raise it in general.

---

57. Kibbutz south of Jerusalem named for Rachel's tomb and overlooking Bethlehem.
58. Mount Herzl, approximately 2,800 feet above sea level; burial place of Theodor Herzl, reinterred in August 1949.
59. Burdett was officially assigned as a second secretary in the US Embassy in London in November 1949.
60. Raleigh Gibson, US consul general in Jerusalem, assigned October 1949.

The chief value of my stay in Jerusalem, in addition to my survey of the southern sections of the city, was the opportunity it gave me to enjoy for hours the views of the Old City and the area beyond from the windows of the King David. Having my *Westminster [Historical] Atlas [to the Bible]* with me, I utilized this opportunity to study the history of the city.

McDonald described the view in a letter to Janet and Halsey Barrett:

> *My room faced the Old City across the narrow Hinnom Valley. Literally for hours, I sat or stood at my window studying the medieval walls and the historic landmarks, which to a historically-minded person takes one back to the Jebusites from whom David took the ancient city nearly three thousand years ago. How exhilarating it was to contemplate the site which had been the scene of the labors of the great from David to Solomon through Nehemiah, Ezra, the Maccabees, and Jesus and the Apostles, to Allenby, Weizmann and Ben-Gurion. I never tired of watching the play of light and shadow on those battlements.*[61]

Our morning visit to the Herzl Hill was brief, but it strengthened one's sense of the impressiveness of the site. The trip down was uneventful but was, as always, full of vantage points from which one got unforgettable impressions of this historic land.

In the late afternoon a long conference with Ford while the evening was spent in studying [a] document Ford had brought.

McDonald reported that on

> *[December] 19 the coming of the millionth Jew to Israel was marked by "Ingathering of Exiles Day" celebrations throughout the country. Ben-Gurion, in congratulating [the government] and [the] Jewish Agency on [their] accomplishment, warned that in bringing in [the] second million a "shortcut" must be sought as "there is no complacency or security so long as we are only a million." . . . Ben-Gurion, in spite of recommendations of some [government] officials based on foreseeable economic disaster to halt temporarily immigration, has not been persuaded.*[62]

Tuesday, December 20

Conference at breakfast with Ford. We agreed that, during his absence, Padberg would generally be the liaison officer between the office and the residence, but that I would work with individual members of the staff depending upon the particular problem involved. We decided to send [a] telegram to the

61. McDonald to Halsey and Janet Barrett, December 21, 1949, McDonald Papers, Columbia University, box 14, folder 13.

62. McDonald to secretary of state, joint weeka no. 52, December 23, 1949, McDonald Papers, USHMM, box 8, folder 5. He added that, according to the Jewish Agency Executive, 337,444 immigrants had entered Israel since its founding; that about 227,000 had been absorbed, mostly in the cities (27,000 in settlements); and that 100,000 still were in immigrant camps.

Department regarding the reconcilability of Jordanian and Israeli accounts of the current negotiations as contrasted with the much more pessimistic reports from British sources.[63]

The Argentine chargé called. The talk was rather slow and a bit difficult until learning from him that he was stationed regularly in Damascus, I persuaded him to talk about the present dictator, Colonel Adib Shishakli.[64] He thought the movement primarily military without any definite political significance. The new colonel is a vigorous, violent personality without clear or constructive political ideas. Syria, according to my visitor, is politically and socially in the stage of feudalism. There are no, or at least very few, leaders who are at all representative of the popular will. The army, on its side, has few strictly professional leaders. Nearly all of the higher officers are a combination of military and political. Personalities rather than principles are dominant. He doubts that this coup, any more than the two previous ones, would secure peace or stability. There was, my informant said, a general impression that any movement towards federation between Syria and its neighbors had British support, while contrary movement had US support. He implied that there were some observers who thought that [in] back of all these upsets was some outside sinister influence. He was not specific enough to give the clue as to the alleged "culprit." The Argentine was very enthusiastic about Keeley.

On December 20, the UN Trusteeship Council voted to censure Israel for its recent movement of government offices to Jerusalem. The vote was 5–0 with 7 abstentions that included the United States, the USSR, Great Britain, and Australia (which had proposed the December 9 Jerusalem resolution in the first place).[65]

Acheson understood the impracticality of the December 9 resolution. On December 20 he suggested to President Truman that a new Jerusalem Statute based on the resolution be drafted by the UN Trusteeship Council; afterward in informal talks between Israel, Jordan, and the Vatican, it could be negotiated into something workable and the General Assembly then might revisit the issue. "Our underlying objective," he told Truman, "is to achieve a solution of the Jerusalem problem which will meet with a considerable degree of concurrence by the world community and be

63. Geoffrey Furlonge (1903–1984) of the British Foreign Office confirmed McDonald's suspicions when he admitted that, for the United Kingdom and for Jordan, a corridor to the Mediterranean was key and that the extension of the Anglo-Jordanian treaty to such a corridor was none of Israel's business. McDonald to secretary of state, no. 903, December 20, 1949, NARA, RG 59, MC 1390, reel 20, frame 643; Holmes to secretary of state, no. 5062, December 20, 1949, NARA, RG 59, MC 1390, reel 20, frame 644.

64. Colonel Adib al-Shishakli (1909–1964), launched a coup in Damascus in December 1949, the third coup of the year, seizing power from Sami al-Hinnawi. It became clear with time that Shishakli opposed all momentum toward a Syrian union with Iraq, but the situation was watched closely, particularly in Israel.

65. Resolution printed in *DFPI*, v. 4, p. 756. Eytan's response of December 24, 1949 in *DFPI*, v. 4, d. 515. General Israeli reaction in McDonald to secretary of state, joint weeka no. 52, December 23, 1949, McDonald Papers, USHMM, box 8, folder 5.

acceptable to the two nations which are most directly involved." Truman agreed in principle.[66]

Acheson ordered McDonald on December 20 to convey the following official US response to Ben-Gurion's announcements of December 13: *"As a friendly [govern-ment] which has followed with interest and sympathy Israel's development,"* the United States *"considers particularly unfortunate any step or course of action on part of Israel likely to prejudice or complicate [the] settlement of Jerusalem question, espe-cially at [a] moment when [the] problem of Jerusalem is being studied by [the] Trus-teeship Council."*[67]

McDonald carried out his instructions on December 21. Eytan, he said, gave no response other than that *"he would inform the Prime Minister."*[68]

Wednesday, December 21

Staff conference in mid-afternoon. 4:45 session with Eytan. In answer to Ford's question, Eytan told us that the next meeting of Shiloah and his [Jorda-nian] colleague would be Saturday, the 24th.

I then took occasion to speak of the obvious leak in the Israeli and Ameri-can press following our previous presentation, that of December 11. *Hador* had had almost a verbal reprint of our text and there had been comparable state-ments in the *New York Times* by Gene Currivan and from Lake Success. Eytan commented that he was not surprised because as soon as any secret was pre-sented to the cabinet there was the probability of such a leak.

The Davidowitz family Hanukkah dinner was the usual success.

Thursday, December 22

This day was an unusually busy one, including as it did three major social affairs, two of them official, as well as individual conferences.

Ford and Hooper came by for our usual morning talk on their way to the office. At 10:30, Gene Currivan of the *New York Times* came out for our session about recent serious leaks to the press. I reminded him of the article in the Mapai party daily *Hador* and of the two dispatches to the *Times*, one his own from here and the other from Lake Success, all of which had with disconcert-ing accuracy quoted the substance of our representation to the Israel Foreign Office on December 11. I explained to Currivan that, of course, I did not expect him to disclose any of his own sources of information, but that I would be grateful if he would tell me his opinion of the vulnerability of the Foreign Office in such matters. He frankly said that there was hardly such a thing as secrecy at HaKirya; that instead, whenever we or any other mission had an important conference at the Foreign Office and the substance of our talk had

66. Memorandum from Acheson for Truman, December 20, 1949, *FRUS*, 1949, v. VI, 1551–1555.

67. Acheson to McDonald, no. 768, December 20, 1949, *FRUS*, 1949, v. VI, 1555.

68. McDonald to secretary of state, no. 908, December 21, 1949, NARA, RG 59, 501.BB Palestine, box 2127, folder 5.

become known to five or six persons there, it would in one way or another become the common property of journalists in the know. He added that the same description would apply to despatches from the Foreign Office to Lake Success. Shortly after these reached Israel's UN delegation, the substance of the telegram would be known to journalists. This statement by Currivan left me rather confused as to what, if anything, we could do to protect ourselves against such disclosures. Problem was made more difficult by Currivan's insistence that the State Department is just as vulnerable as the Foreign Office here.

At noon the Fords, Bobby, Ruth, and I drove out to the Weizmanns' at Rehovot for lunch.

We could not refrain from stopping for a few moments on their terrace to take in the glorious view of the Judean Hills sharply etched against the blue background and the brilliant green foreground of the vast expanse of orange grove brightened by their masses of ripening yellow fruit. Besides the three McDonalds, the Fords, and our hosts, there were no other guests except the president's aide, Major [David] Arnon, and Mrs. Weizmann's brother. Our hosts could not have been more gracious or friendly. They were especially kindly towards Bobby, whose going home they both deplored with evident sincerity. She had won with them, as she has with so many others here, a place of affectionate regard.

The talk before and during the meal—the meal as always there was delicious—was on a light, and for the most part, non-political level. Nonetheless, Dr. Weizmann did not hide his personal concern about recent developments, particularly when he spoke to me privately about the government's seemingly inadequately considered retort to the UN internationalization resolution. As we were leaving, Dr. Weizmann and I agreed that we should talk privately soon. As we left, it was obvious that the Fords as well as we had had a perfect time. The Weizmanns' farewells to Bobby were very warm.

In the late afternoon Bobby and Ruth and I went to the British minister's housewarming cocktail party. We were delighted with the Helm's three children, who had arrived by air from England the day previous for their Christmas holidays here. The only business I did was to check with Kaplan, Goldie Meyerson, and Mrs. Sharett about their coming to our dinner to be given New Year's Day for Jack Ewing and the prime minister. I also had a brief talk with Shiloah.

We went directly from the Helms' to the Sam Sackses' for the benefit concert for the crippled children. The party was a great success. The musical talent was excellent and varied. Bobby's teacher played the piano brilliantly. The harpist from the orchestra was excellent, and the granddaughter of Max Nordau sang Hebrew and other folk songs with a delightful sense of intimacy and taste.[69] Before the concert and during the intermission, there were the usual

---

69. Max Nordau (1849–1923), Hungarian-born physician, author, and Zionist; early associate of Theodor Herzl; helped Herzl found the Zionist Organization in 1897.

brief friendly exchanges with many friends and acquaintances. The elite of Ramat Gan and Tel Aviv were there. We were all pleased that our good friend Ruth Sacks had been the hostess for such a successful affair.

Friday, December 23

My Italian Jewish friend [Raffaele] Cantoni made a date for eleven o'clock but was confused about the place and is coming out tomorrow.

Saturday, December 24

Cantoni was at the house for about an hour and gave me a vivid account of his talks with Vatican dignitaries in the office of the secretary of state[70] about the internationalization of Jerusalem. He had received the impression that those authorities did not seriously believe that the internationalization would be literally carried out.[71]

While the family completed their Christmas preparations, I spent most of the day reading Harry Emerson Fosdick's intensely interesting new book *The Man from Nazareth as His Contemporaries Saw Him*.[72] The more I read in this volume, the more I was pleased—and frankness compels me to add surprised— at the author's sympathy and understanding of the Jewish environment of Jesus's day and of the latter's intimate relation to that environment. It is to be regretted that Dr. Fosdick's understanding of Jews of that day seems not to be equaled by his understanding of Jews of today. In particular, so far as I have discerned, he has not seen that the dynamism of Jewish apocalypticism of the first century is matched by a comparable though different Jewish apocalypticism in and connected with Israel today. I shall write him on this point.

A friendly pre-Christmas evening at the Archibalds'.

Christmas Day

As befitted the day, I deviated in my morning reading to Ruth from St. Paul's Epistles to Luke's story of the Nativity.

Two hours of the morning was spent in the un-Christmaslike talk with Harry Rosenfield about politics at home.[73] Among the many items of inside information he gave me were the following:

---

70. Pius XII had no secretary of state after the death of Cardinal Luigi Maglione in 1944. Domenico Tardini and Giovanni Montini shared these duties.

71. On the Vatican and the carrying out of the Jerusalem resolution, see also *DFPI*, v. 4, d. 504, 508.

72. Harry Emerson Fosdick (1878–1969), liberal-modernist Baptist pastor and author who ministered in New York City arguing against literal interpretations of the Bible. *The Man from Nazareth* was published by Harper Brothers in 1949.

73. Harry N. Rosenfield (1911–1995), Brooklyn native; associate of Fiorello LaGuardia; appointed by Truman as commissioner of the United States Displaced Persons Commission, 1948–1952, which helped settle displaced persons in the United States following the Displaced Persons Act of 1948.

1) Charles Murphy, formerly assigned to the Hill, has been in preparation to succeed Clark Clifford.[74]

2) Jack Ewing[75] wants to be governor [of New York] and has long been preparing for it. The chief complication is that Paul Fitzpatrick,[76] without admitting it, also wants to be governor. [William] O'Dwyer also has the same ambition.[77] No one of them seemingly wants to be senator. Lehman may therefore again be drafted. William Boyle also appears in that picture.[78]

3) Among the people closest to the president are: Leon H. Keyserling, vice chairman of Council of Economic Advisors;[79] Charles Brannon, now secretary of agriculture, who more than anyone else won the farm vote for Truman[80]—he had been quick to capitalize [on] Stassen's mistake in coming out against the maintenance of farm parity during the campaign;[81] Dr. John Steelman, assistant to the president,[82] a warm personal friend of John Lewis—Steelman together with John Snyder are the leaders of [the] conservative section of the presidential family. For Dean Acheson the president has a deep personal regard. Greenfield and Rosenman are at the White House occasionally. Baruch is out of the picture. Matt Connelly[83] and Charles Ross[84] are, of course, important. Proskauer is occasionally at the White House. Morgenthau has a great influence there through David Niles. Monroe Goldwater[85] exercises considerable influence through Ed Flynn.[86]

74. Charles S. Murphy (1909–1983), office of legislative counsel, US Senate, 1934–1946 (where he helped Senator Truman in the drafting of legislation); administrative assistant to the president, 1947–1950; special counsel to the president, succeeding Clifford, 1950–1953.

75. Entries of June 26 and December 6, 1948.

76. Paul E. Fitzpatrick (1898–1977), chairman, New York Democratic State Committee; supporter of Jewish state in 1947–1948.

77. William O'Dwyer (1890–1964), mayor of New York City, 1946–1950.

78. William Boyle (1902–1961), secretary and executive assistant to Senator Truman, 1942–1944; executive vice chairman, Democratic National Committee, 1944–1945, 1949; chairman, Democratic National Committee, 1949–1951.

79. Leon Keyserling (1908–1987), legislative assistant to Senator Robert F. Wagner (D-NY), 1933–1937; general counsel to various federal agencies, 1937–1946; vice chairman (1946–1949) and then chairman (1949–1953) of Council of Economic Advisers, which advised the president.

80. Charles F. Brannon (1903–1992), secretary of agriculture, 1948–1953; favored price supports for farm products; tried in 1949 to enact "Brannon Plan" that would guarantee farm incomes.

81. Harold E. Stassen (1907–2001), governor of Minnesota, 1939–1943; repeatedly sought Republican presidential nomination; debated and then supported Thomas Dewey in 1948; tried to help Dewey during national campaign by accusing Brannan of raising food prices through government purchases for export. Brannan publicly accused Stassen, the Republican-controlled Congress, and Dewey of attacking government price supports for agriculture.

82. John R. Steelman (1900–1999), first White House chief of staff under Truman, 1946–1953.

83. Matthew J. Connelly (1907–1976), executive secretary to the vice president, 1945; appointments secretary to the president, 1945–1953.

84. Charles G. Ross (1885–1950), White House press secretary, 1945–1950.

85. Monroe Goldwater (1885–1980), leading New York Democrat and senior partner in law firm Goldwater & [Edward] Flynn; headed JDC Reconstruction Committee, which aided Holocaust survivors; delegate to Democratic national conventions after 1924; president of the UJA for greater New York after 1944.

86. Edward J. Flynn (1891–1953), New York attorney and Goldwater's partner; Bronx political "boss" 1922–1953; secretary of state of New York, 1929–1939; chairman, Democratic

Dave Dubinsky and Murray are influential in domestic matters. Ann Rosenberg is still appointed to important posts but is less influential following the eclipse of Baruch. Albert Lasker is in the picture as helping Jack Ewing financially in the latter's fight against the AMA [American Medical Association]; Mary Lasker also figures.[87]

At length and very interestingly, Rosenfield told me the story of Jack Ewing's increasing interest in and influence in matters affecting Palestine policy. Very early in '47 Rosenfield had warned his boss Jack Ewing that New York, Illinois and Pennsylvania [would be lost] if the president did not clear up the US government's attitude towards Palestine. At first, Ewing was skeptical but later so convinced that he threw himself more and more into the campaign to effect that change. Gradually, he became the center of the moves which led to the US government's prompt recognition of Israel.

Illustrative of Ewing's role was Rosenfield's story that just before May 15th [1948] Loy Henderson had a meeting with the president attended by Marshall, Clifford, Dave Niles and Ewing. Henderson had said that Shertok (as he then was) had told him that the Jews would accept a compromise less than the Jewish state. Ewing slipped out, learned from Niles (I now recall that Niles was not in the conference) that Sharett (to whom Niles had quickly telephoned) had "not spoken to Henderson for months." Ewing returned to the conference with this news, and Henderson was subsequently transferred to India.

As Rosenfield gave me the story of Ewing's political ambitions in New York, I could discern at least one reason for Ewing's visit to Israel. In answer to my question as to Ewing's status with the Catholics in New York, Rosenfield said this was good, but that in a speech on St. Patrick's Day a year or so ago, Ewing had committed the blunder of reading a speech prepared by his new public relations man which contained something to this effect: "Here in New York we have moved a long way since the time Irish Catholics conducted pogroms against New York Negroes." Much explaining had supposedly cleared up the matter with the cardinal [Spellman], but there might be sore spots left. There were also dramatic differences of opinion in Catholic circles about Ewing's socialized medicine program and his fight against the AMA. All-in-all, Rosenfield's tales constituted an interesting background for my friend Jack Ewing's forthcoming visit. At the end of two hours there was no time for me to ask Rosenfield his impressions of Israel. Anyhow, as I told him frankly, he had more to tell me about home politics than about Israel.

National Committee, 1940–1943; close associate of President Roosevelt who attended Yalta conference; among Democratic political leaders who urged Truman to recognize Israel; important factor in Truman's 1948 election victory.

87. Albert Lasker (1880–1952), businessman and advertising innovator; Mary Lasker (1900–1994), president of the Birth Control Federation of America. Noted philanthropists, especially in the medical field, whose work helped expand the National Institutes of Health and its medical research; founders of American Cancer Society; supported idea of national health insurance.

Eggnog party at the Ford's. Delightful Christmas dinner at the house for those officers of the staff who had not gone to Bethlehem. The gala concert of the Philharmonic Orchestra was brilliant. Ella Goldstein played with fine taste Beethoven's Fourth Piano Concerto. The Ninth Beethoven [symphony] was excellently done, even though the chorus was weak in male voices. It is a tremendous work.

Monday, December 26

Work all day on material for Halsey.

At the end of December McDonald wrote a long memorandum concerning his future as US ambassador to Israel. It went not only to Halsey and Janet Barrett but also to Abe Feinberg and Joseph Proskauer, and it was surely shared with some others, including Jack Ewing. McDonald had hoped, he said, to remain at his post until peace was in sight. But fatigue, as well as financial, and family reasons, had brought him to request resignation. He wanted to return home in the fall of 1950.[88]

The dinner in the evening was a success. Besides the Fords, who were the guests of honor, we had the Mendes Sackses, the Sam Sackses and the Max Greenbergs.

Tuesday, December 27

In the afternoon Harvey Rosen, deputy fire commissioner of New York City, and his secretary came to the house for an hour.[89] One glance at Rosen convinced me that I could learn nothing from him about his observations in Israel during the previous fortnight, but that he probably could tell me a good deal about New York politics. He certainly could and did. Associated with O'Dwyer for six campaigns, Rosen enthusiastically described his work during the recent campaign. He thinks that Jack Ewing may not be able to overcome Fitzpatrick's rivalry. The latter, though coy, is a formidable candidate. Another possibility is Farley,[90] who has not relinquished his old ambition. John Cashmore is finding increasing difficulties in being both borough president and borough leader. Rosen had no definite information about Ewing's standing with the cardinal but had heard something of the St. Patrick's Day faux pas. As to the senatorship, Rosen thought that there would probably be a draft movement

---

88. McDonald to Halsey and Janet Barrett, personal and confidential memorandum, January 1, 1950, McDonald Papers, Columbia University, box 14, folder 13; McDonald to Abe Feinberg, December 27, 1949, McDonald Papers, Columbia University, box 11, folder 3. See also entry of April 3, 1950.

89. Harvey Rosen (1911–2003), New York labor leader; deputy fire commissioner under Mayor William O'Dwyer of New York City.

90. James A. Farley (1888–1986), leading New York politician, close to President Roosevelt; postmaster-general and chairman of Democratic National Committee, 1933–1940; appointed by Truman to the Hoover Commission on Organization of the Executive Branch of Government.

for Lehman not only because of the state situation, but also for its effect on the next presidential campaign.

The philharmonic concert was excellent. The second of these, Tchaikovsky's Second Symphony, is definitely a lesser work than Tchaikovsky's last three symphonies. The soloist of the evening, Mrs. [Yosefa] Schocken has a truly operatic voice, which she uses with artistry.

Wednesday, December 28

Another, the seventh [day] or so, of torrential rains. Morning conference at the house with Helm. After I had told him of the Department's [telegrams] about Syria, he confirmed that he had had nothing from the Foreign Office and that the UK government did not share the Department's concern. Helm then outlined in detail his talk with Eytan a few days earlier. Eytan had suggested that [the] UK government make "its contribution" towards Israel-Jordan peace by not asking for the extension of the treaty to Cis-Jordan.[91] To this Helm had replied that the treaty was exclusively a matter for the UK government and Jordan. Then with that tone which is characteristic of a superior to an inferior, Helm said, "that was *Schluss*." Eytan then expressed the hope that the UK would not wish to establish bases or maintain troops in Cis-Jordan. Helm replied that there was no such intention. According to Helm, Eytan seemed relievedly [*sic*] grateful.

At 11:30 Ford and I were with Eytan for about a quarter of an hour. While waiting for Ford, I returned to Eytan two documents which had been left with us, the Israeli printed statement on Jerusalem, which had been circulated privately,[92] and the memo on Monsignor McMahon's conference with Ben-Gurion, which had been left me by Jacob Herzog.[93]

I presented the Department's point of view about the report from Syria. Eytan replied categorically, "Israel has no intention of sending a single soldier into Syria." He then added that Helm was reported to have said the other evening: "Conditions in Damascus have reached such a pass that a single foreign soldier would topple the government over." Eytan added, "We don't intend to supply that soldier." Eytan then developed the Israeli thesis that, despite all denials, Abdullah and Iraq are considering moves against Syria. He told us, too, of the offer by the Syrian minister of defense, [Abdullah] Atfeh,[94] before, under, and following Za'im to work with Abdullah to seize Syrian power. Abdullah had inquired if the suggestion was serious and had received word that Atfeh was returning from Paris to Damascus via Cairo and Amman. Eytan asked me if I would like to hear more about their information on the Syrian maneuvers.

91. See also *DFPI*, v. 4, d. 509 for Israeli efforts in London on this issue.
92. Could refer to the very pessimistic memorandum by Yosef Tekoah, legal adviser in the Israeli Foreign Ministry, dated December 19, 1949, *DFPI*, v. 4, d. 507.
93. Entry of October 21, 1949.
94. Abdullah Atfeh (1897–1976), first army chief of staff after Syrian independence in 1946 until Syria's defeat in 1948; defense minister under al-Za'im and al-Atassi, 1949; replaced after most recent coup by Akram al-Hourani.

I said yes enthusiastically. It was then arranged that [Shmuel] Divon, Sasson's assistant, would come to the house.[95]

Cecil Brown of Mutual Broadcasting and his wife came at 4:30 and stayed until nearly 6:30. Before the other guests arrived, I gave him what help I could on his two ambitious projects, to interpret Israel to the States through wire recordings, which he would make during a week here.[96]

The [Reuven] Rubins came at five, and Miss Herlitz at six. The tea party talk was general. Miss Herlitz told of her adventurous flight home and the Rubins of their life in Bucharest. There the diplomatic corps is a society unto itself. Everyone takes advantage of any excuse to "go abroad," for example, to Vienna. Rubin was most friendly but made no binding commitment about a picture. They are asking us to their house presently.

Shiloah came a little after seven and remained with Herlitz until after eight. Ford was with us until about a quarter of eight. The first period of time was given over to Shiloah's account of the last Israel-Jordan meeting, December 23. It had been "sticky because of Samir [al-Rifai's][97] bringing up anew and in a firmer form Jordan's demand for the Negev or a very wide corridor." To illustrate the difference, Shiloah quoted the Jordanians as saying "you speak of a corridor in terms of meters, we in terms of kilometers."[98] Speculating about the Jordanian change of tactics, Shiloah said that it might be that they had from the first intended to fall back on those more extreme demands and that, therefore, they had not been serious in wishing agreement. He was inclined to doubt this, however, because they had gone quite far in putting down in Samir's own Arabic script on the king's stationery a rather far-reaching tentative agreement in principle. Sasson had taken exception to Samir's Arabic style but agreed that the substance was an advance.

In answer to my question, Shiloah said that he could discern no signs of British interference in the negotiations. The only probability he could see of UK discouragement of progress might be in connection with a possible British condition put to the Jordanians, before the negotiations began, to the effect that a land bridge from the sea to the Persian Gulf must be assured. Shiloah thought that if this had been made a condition, Jordan had probably been left free on all other points.

Shiloah said he had suggested at the conclusion a suspension of the talks but that the king had urged their continuance, apparently against Samir's

95. Shmuel Divon (1917–2003), acting director of Middle East Division in Ministry of Foreign Affairs.

96. Cecil Brown (1907–1987), CBS radio correspondent and writer in Rome and Singapore during World War II and associate of Edward R. Murrow; resigned in 1943 because of journalistic disagreements with CBS management and joined Mutual Network.

97. Samir al-Rifai (1901–1965), Jordanian minister of court and King Abdullah's chief negotiator; prime minister six times between 1944 and 1963.

98. Specifically the Israelis offered a corridor 50 to 100 meters wide. King Abdullah and al-Rifai openly argued with one another during the meeting, the king urging compromise and al-Rifai holding firm and hinting that a wide corridor would be used to settle Arab refugees then in Gaza. *DFPI*, v. 4, d. 530.

preference for suspension. At this point Shiloah suggested another possible explanation of the stiffer Jordanian terms—that they might have decided to use these as an excuse for delaying agreement pending possible developments in Syria, since it would look very bad to the other Arab states if Jordan began an adventure in Syria after having "cleared the way" by peace with Israel. Shiloah then launched into a very interesting statement that he was sure Abdullah and Iraq were engaged in discussions about possible moves in Syria. He thought it was quite possible that the regent and his uncle could agree on [a] division of spoils, that the king would not require an order from Kirkbride, but merely the latter's tacit or [c]overt permission.

Shiloah then stressed with great seriousness the "unsettlement" of the current "precarious balance in the Middle East" which would be brought about by any move of Syria's neighbors towards Damascus. Israel could not, he said, be expected to stand idly by while a Hashemite empire were being set up across its frontiers. He recognized that there were historical forces making for such a union, but in view of the balance which had been established since World War I, it might be disastrous to unsettle it. He was certain that Saudi Arabia and Egypt would vigorously oppose any form of northern union.

In answer to my question whether, if that union were achieved "peacefully and by democratic processes," Israel would be more reconciled, Shiloah replied, "there is no possibility of democratic processes, and whatever the form, it would be arbitrary action and interference by one state in the affairs of another." Then I tried to pin him down as to whether, if Iraq and Jordan moved overtly or otherwise in Syria, Israel would move militarily along the northeastern frontier. Shiloah refused to be drawn, merely repeating in different forms what he had said previously, and thus leaving the impression that Israel would not remain quiescent.

Worked until after midnight on my memorandum to Halsey.

Thursday, December 29

Up early and cleared a mass of documents and prepared the draft of telegram to Department on Shiloah before Ford's arrival at 8:30.[99]

The late afternoon Divon, the assistant to Sassoon as Arab expert, talked with me for about an hour. Ford joined us during the latter part, but had to leave before the end. Divon was frank and informative, speaking out of an intimate knowledge of conditions within the Arab states. As had Shiloah, he expressed confidence in the new Syrian cabinet, especially in the leader, Khalid al-Azm, prime minister and foreign minister.[100] Azm is a businessman, modern-minded

---

99. McDonald to secretary of state, no. 918, December 29, 1949, *FRUS*, 1949, v. VI, 1561–1562; McDonald to secretary of state, joint weeka no. 53, December 30, 1949, McDonald Papers, USHMM, box 8, folder 5. McDonald commented in no. 918 that "Ford and I agree that . . . Shiloah is expressing firm views of his government based on sincere concern lest union jeopardize Israel's hopes [to] move gradually toward peace through bilateral negotiations."

100. Khalid al-Azm (1903–1965), senior Syrian independent nationalist politician from leading family; prime minister in 1941, 1946, and December 1948–March 1949; afterwards

and honest. The men he had associated with him are broadly representative and as good as can be expected in Syria.

Divon's analysis of internal conditions in Syria was sympathetic and, I think, substantially sound. He credits the Syrians with having been the center and real leaders in the Arab nationalist movement. Unfortunately, those leaders had been almost exclusively negative in their policies, anti-French, anti-British, anti-foreign, anti-imperialist, anti-Zionist, etc. There were, however, among the younger generation possible leaders with more affirmative ideas.

Divon said he was convinced that the British do not desire the development of a strong independent Syria. According to him, just as the British via Tel Aviv succeeded in having their way in the Sudan; through Baghdad [they] were short-circuiting Abdullah; and through Amman [they] were unsettling Damascus, so the UK government continues everywhere in this area to discourage genuinely independent nationalist movements. The British want, he contends, to extend to Syria a regime comparable to that in Iraq or in Jordan.

Divon argued that Syria's sense of confidence should be built up, thereby lessening the dangerously high political temperature. He thought this could be done if Western powers would now encourage the present Damascus regime. He though there should be tangible evidence given by Washington, Turkey, and by some of the other Western powers of their friendship and support of the Azm government.

Divon did not give as much credence as Eytan had seemed to do to the story that Atfeh, former Syrian minister of defense, had made serious proposals to Abdullah for cooperation in setting up a new regime in Syria. He thought that Atfeh was rather irresponsible and relatively unimportant.[101] As to the future of Syria's internal situation, Divon was only moderately optimistic. He thought there was a movement underway, sponsored by Egypt, for the return of former president [Shukri] al-Quwatli[102] and Jamil Mardam,[103] the former strong man in Syria. Both these men are now in Egypt. Divon cited this maneuver as but one phase of the war of nerves in which Syria is a more or less hopeless pawn. He is inclined to think that an outside power, presumably Britain, is instrumental in fomenting this psychological uneasiness. From Divon I did not get the impression that Israel would welcome any move by Abdullah against Syria or by anyone else. Perhaps I had misunderstood Eytan when he seemed to be rather willing that Abdullah should achieve his ambition to be "King in Damascus."

imprisoned by Za'im; again prime minister of Syria, December 27, 1949–June 4, 1950; enemy of pro-Hashemite factions in Syria.

101. See note 94 in this chapter.

102. Shukri al-Quwatli (1891–1967), nationalist politician, president of Syria 1943–1949 (when overthrown by al-Za'im), 1955–1958; treated in Goda et al., eds., *To the Gates of Jerusalem*.

103. Jamil Mardam Bey (1894–1960), nationalist politician, Syrian prime minister 1936–1939, 1946–1948, treated in Goda et al., eds., *To the Gates of Jerusalem*.

Reverting to Syrian nationalism, Divon emphasized that there would always be strong opposition in Syria to any form of close association with Iraq or Jordan, because both these countries are regarded as British puppets. Granted that certain cliques might welcome the Iraqis or the Arab [Legion] leaders, the former would be in a disadvantageous position because of their long lines of communication. Moreover, there would certainly be some degree of open resistance as well as much covert opposition to either Iraqi or Jordanian penetration. As he left, Divon promised to send me a list of some books in English or French on Syria and the neighboring Arab states.

The Brady party was a great success, as was to have been expected, and the food was the best available in Israel. I chatted for a little while with Sharett, who said that he was mentally much more tired than he was physically. He regretted that in his foreign affairs statement in the Knesset he would be stopped from telling of the factors which had really been decisive at Lake Success.

The late evening spent working with Bobby.

Friday, December 30

At 3:30 I had forty-five minutes with Sharett at the Foreign Office with Eytan and Shiloah present. Sharett said he wished to put somewhat more formally than had Eytan and Shiloah in their earlier talks, the present situation of the Jordan exchanges. December 23 meeting had resulted in a virtual impasse through the Jordanian insistence on a corridor [of 10 or 15] kilometers in width, whereas the Israelis had assented to an 80 or 100 meter width.[104] Sharett argued that much more was involved than might appear. This was not only because the wider corridor would really cut the country in two, but also because that wider area could be used for mass settlement and as a base for operations against Israel. He feared that the demand for this was indicative of purposes inconsistent with peace.

Sharett suggested that I send word to the Department that he hoped the US government would be willing to indicate its hope that Jordan would not break the negotiations through such an impossible demand (Shiloah had suggested a suspension following the December 23 meeting but the king's suggestion that another meeting be held was accepted, though, as usual, the date was not then fixed) and that Abdullah would not permit his Syrian ambitions [to] interfere with peace with Israel.

As I was leaving, I mentioned the information which we had had from Washington that the embassy at Cairo was informed that leading advisers to Farouk would suggest that, without waiting for the election, the king move towards a final frontier and peace with Israel.[105] Sharett was so interested that he would like to come over the next day to talk further. I, of course, assented.

---

104. See also McDonald to secretary of state, no. 923, December 31, 1949, NARA, RG 59, MC 1390, reel 20, frame 680.

105. See Acheson to McDonald, December 27, 1949, McDonald Papers, USHMM, box 8, folder 5. The telegram also reported that Lebanon's foreign minister indicated that his country would follow any state except for Jordan in negotiating a peace treaty with Israel.

In his reporting to the Department, McDonald commented that "Sharett obviously desires conclude peace with Jordan but I am sure [that the] cabinet [will] dare not yield on [a] wider corridor"[106]

Saturday, December 31

At the conference with Sharett in the afternoon at the house, I asked him if I had correctly heard him the day before say that the Jordanians were demanding a corridor with [a width of] 40 to 60 kilometers. He replied in the negative and added that they had spoken or rather implied that they wanted a width of tens of kilometers not of scores of kilometers. I then decided that I would have to send a correcting telegram. This I later drafted and left with Troxel at the New Year's Eve party, together with one about the item described in the paragraph below.[107]

Sharett was obviously intrigued by the intelligence from Cairo via Washington. He asked me in effect to say to Washington that Israel was anxious to open negotiations with Egypt and to make peace. He hoped that the Department would instruct Caffery and me to take whatever initiative seemed to us most promising. Immediately after Sharett left, I drafted a brief telegram to the Department to this effect.

Very pleasant brief visit at the Rubins' about a quarter of ten. They served delicious champagne and equally good caviar, both brought from Romania, the former the gift of the French representative in return for a drawing from Rubin. Rubin had on his easel a large landscape showing Nazareth in the background and olive orchards with pickers in the foreground and harvesters in the near foreground. He said this was the picture which someone should buy for us to place over the mantle, where it would fit perfectly. Bobby interrupted to say that there would be a better chance of its being bought if it could be seen by a prospective purchaser in its destined position on the wall. The Rubins laughed, but he did not offer to send it over, and we naturally did not press the matter. They could not, however, have been more friendly. He even told me the amount of his loss while minister.

Over to the staff's party for half an hour or so. Fortunately, we had to leave after a brief visit in order to get some sleep before I had to be up to meet the Ewing plane scheduled then for arrival at 6:00 am, New Year's Day.

---

106. McDonald to secretary of state, no. 922, December 31, 1949, *FRUS*, 1949, v. VI, 1565.
107. *FRUS*, 1949, v. VI, 1565, n. 2.

19. January 1950

At 9:15 the Ewings' plane arrived. Jack was in good form, but his wife [Helen] seemed to me to be feebler than when I had last seen her. After the brief period required to get the luggage, I drove the Ewings to the house. There Mrs. Ewing decided to spend the day until we were to leave for Weizmann's. Jack and I drove down to the Dizengoff office, where I left him in charge of the Israeli couriers.

In February 1949 McDonald had invited Ewing to Israel. Considering a run for the governorship of New York, Ewing had known McDonald since their under-graduate days at Indiana University.[1] After visiting Ambassador Elath in Wash-ington before the trip, Ewing wrote McDonald, "I will be primarily interested in the health, education, and social security activities of the Israeli Government. Also I would like, if possible, to visit some of the holy places, including perhaps some of those in the old city of Jerusalem."[2]

McDonald planned a more ambitious itinerary. "I rarely go to the airport to meet VIPs," he wrote Janet and Halsey, "but this time I wanted for old friendship['s] sake to do so." For the afternoon, McDonald had arranged for Ewing to meet President Weizmann.[3]

Mrs. Ewing, Ruth, and I were at Weizmann's a little after 4:30. Jack and Padberg had previously arrived. Vera had laid herself out, with the result that the tea was perfection. After brief general talk, Jack, Weizmann, Leo Kohn, and I retired to the study. There, Weizmann gave Jack a full-dress indictment of the Egyptian rearmament program being carried through with the tanks and planes from the British. Weizmann talked impressively about the menace to Middle Eastern stability and to world peace if this development were not checked. He finally urged Jack to give the following message to the president: first, an expression of warm gratitude for the large role—the largest played by any living man—by the president in aiding in the establishment of the state. Second, he urged the president to discourage the British from continuing this

1. See also entry of June 26, 1948.
2. Ewing to McDonald, November 28, 1949, McDonald Papers, Columbia University, box 11, folder 3.
3. McDonald to Halsey and Janet Barrett, January 3, 1950, McDonald Papers, Columbia University, box 14, folder 13.

"stimulation of armament race in the Middle East."[4] He urged too, that the president seek to dissuade Farouk from rash adventures.

Weizmann was scathing in his characterization of Farouk as man and ruler, underlining Egypt's need for social advance rather than large expenditures on armament. As to the British motivation, Weizmann did not pretend [not] to be dogmatic. He charged that while Egypt had been involved in Palestine, Britain had, in effect, forced the Egyptians out of the Sudan.[5] The British effective control of the Sudan would give to London a deadly grip on the throat of Egypt because extensive diversion of water from the upper Nile could destroy the livelihood of millions of Egyptians. Another possible explanation of British policy was, Weizmann said, Bevin's vindictiveness. The latter had three chief hates: the Jews, the Russians, and the Americans. Weizmann doubted that Bevin had in his heart given up any one of these hates. Weizmann said that he was preparing a letter, or at least a statement, on the Egyptian rearmament, which he hoped Jack would take to the president. It was to be ready by Monday evening and delivered to the residence, so that I might give it to Jack in Haifa. The Ewings were delighted with the party and so, I think, were the Weizmanns.

Our guests for dinner arrived promptly. First, the Kaplans, then the Sharetts, the Ben-Gurions and Goldie Meyerson. The dinner was excellent from the culinary point of view and seemed to go off well otherwise. Afterwards, I arranged so that Ben-Gurion and Jack might have a private talk together, and later Jack and Sharett. I suggested in each case that the Israelis give him their views of the Israel-Egyptian situation.

Ben-Gurion was less dramatic than Weizmann had been, but stressed, as had the president, that Egypt's rearmament constituted a major threat to the interests of all who desired peace in the Middle East. He repeated in different form Weizmann's statement that peace between Israel and Egypt meant peace in the Middle East, that it was only Egypt which could threaten war, that without Egypt's leadership and support, the other Arab states were militarily innocuous. A calm, quiet, and almost detached attitude of Ben-Gurion impressed Jack. The Sharett talk I did not [hear], but from what Jack told me of it, I concluded that it had been a more vivid presentation than the prime minister's, but

---

4. In July 1949 the Egyptian government had announced a three-year rearmament plan that was to include the construction of armaments factories in Egypt itself. Expenditures in 1949–1950 amounted to some $400 million, a six-fold increase over Egypt's military spending before the war against Israel. The Egyptians were successful in buying weapons in Western Europe, and especially in Great Britain, which sold them Vampire and Glostor Meteor fighter jets, as well as tanks and frigates. Paul Jabber, *Not War Alone: Security and Arms Control in the Middle East* (Berkeley: University of California Press, 1981), 130–131; Hahn, *Caught in the Middle East*, 71–73.

5. British-Egyptian security negotiations after 1945 were blocked partly by disagreements over the fate of the Sudan. Egyptian nationalists called for unity of the Nile Valley, but local British officials aimed to maintain control of the Sudan, partly by using nationalist elements in the Sudan against Egypt. Louis, *The British Empire in the Middle East*, 253–261, 700–707.

less immediately alarmist than the president's. At any rate, Jack is obviously much impressed with the foreign minister.

Monday, January 2

Called at six, had breakfast ready for the Ewings at 6:30. During the first day together, I was able to deduce that, despite his reticence, Jack is probably [a] candidate for the governorship. In answer to my jocular remark that: "I wish I could go back home to campaign for you," he had replied simply that he also wished I could. Jack's comment about [William O'Dwyer] was that "Bill" had missed the political boat by not accepting the vice presidency candidacy offered him at Chicago. As to [Paul] Fitzpatrick, Mrs. Ewing made a flattering remark, but Jack remained silent.

Throughout Jack's talk with the Israelis, which I heard, I could not discern that he had learned much about conditions in Israel or its problems. [He] had rather confirmed my earlier impression that his chief interest had been in the political situation at home.

After their breakfast with McDonald, the Ewings traveled to Jerusalem. McDonald prepared to escort his daughter Bobby to Haifa the next day for her journey back to the United States, where she was to take up graduate study in history at Columbia University.

Tuesday, January 3

On the way in the station wagon, Ruth and Bobby, and all of the latter's effects by ten. Despite a stop at Bodenheimer's, we were at the consulate before one and at the pier a few minutes later. We were on board by a little after one and were having a delicious lunch with [Fred E.] Waller [US consul in Haifa] by the time the boat got under way from the breakwater to the pier.

To make up for what Bobby seemed to regard as my almost discourteous lack of interest in Mr. Waller's suggestion that I visit the consulate, I spent considerable time chatting with Waller on the deck. Our talk was mostly about the administration of the Haifa port and the problem of Mr. Stebbins, the technical director. The latter, a carry-over from the mandatory regime [and] a competent man, is harassed by seeming divisions of counsel in political circles in Haifa and even in HaKirya. It is doubtful if he will remain. We also talked briefly about the oil situation.

By four-thirty or five a number of people from the office had begun to arrive to see the air technician's family off. We all sat around in the bar with welcome Cokes until the Ewings came about six o'clock. Mrs. Ewing seemed completely gone, but after a brief rest, struggled into the bar. Jack and I discussed his impressions. He was thrilled by the day in Jerusalem and by the trip up north.

A little earlier I had received from Major Arnon two letters from Weizmann, one for Ewing himself, and the other to be carried by Ewing to the president.[6] The former was a recapitulation of Weizmann's data about Egyptian rearmament, given to Ewing at the Rehovot tea a few days earlier. The latter was an eloquent argument for the Jewish position on Jerusalem. It concluded with a brief reference to Egypt. It was a powerful statement, but again, as in earlier letters of this sort, it seemed to me too much of a lawyer's brief, at least in its length. When I handed them to Ewing, he assured me that the president would not be deterred by the length, but would read it, coming as it did from Weizmann.

Ewing delivered the letter to the president on his return. But the State Department and the Pentagon were anxious to cooperate with the British on regional security in the Middle East. Truman said that he would discuss the issue with Acheson, but that Israel could not be left empty-handed. Concerning Jerusalem, Truman wanted Israel to work with Jordan and the Vatican on a final settlement.[7]

Came 6:30 and we had to decide whether we would stay and have dinner with Bobby, the Ewings and the captain, or keep our date with the Sackses. Decided on the former. This decision gave us more than two hours more with our friends and Bobby. The dinner was like the lunch—excellent, this time delicious steak replacing the earlier roast beef. Jack and I talked during much of the meal, but he continued to play rather close to the cushion; as to the gubernatorial campaign, he said he was not saying or doing anything about it until the time approached for action much later. There were too many things that might happen in the meantime. My impression was that [of] willingness, but of a present disinclination to make any commitment.[8]

As we finally said goodbye to Bobby about nine, we had the impression that she would have a pleasant trip. The group at the table should be interesting, and the breaks in the journey at Athens, Naples, and perhaps elsewhere should greatly shorten it.

McDonald wrote to Clark Clifford on January 3, 1950.

> *Dear Clark,*
> *I have just heard from our mutual friend, Jack Ewing, who is visiting us here now, that you have finally decided to look after your family and have left the*

---

6. Weizmann to Truman, January 3, 1950, printed in *DFPI*, v. 5, d. 3; *FRUS*, 1950, v, V, 658–661, and n. 5. Truman asked the State Department to file Weizmann's letter. The president also was said to have agreed with the comment by his secretary William S. Hassett that it had been inappropriate of Ewing to have acted as a courier between Weizmann and the White House.

7. Elath to Sharett, February 1, 1950, *DFPI*, v. 5, d. 65.

8. Labor leaders supported Ewing for the Democratic New York gubernatorial nomination because he had backed Truman's national health insurance initiative. By the time of the Democratic convention in Rochester in 1950, however, Congressman Walter A. Lynch received the party's nomination with the backing of New York party leader Ed Flynn. Republican Thomas A. Dewey won the general election easily over Lynch.

White House. The President will miss you sorely. I hope, however, as no doubt does he, that you will be nonetheless available from time to time for "emergency" jobs. I shall be watching the papers to see whether you are returning to St. Louis or settling down in Washington and commuting to New York.

From what I hear about your successor, Mr. [Charles S.] Murphy, the President has chosen wisely.[9] I have never met him but everyone who has spoken to me about him praises him as brilliant, discreet and loyal, all of which qualities are essential in the place which you fill with such distinction.

May I ask you a favor? It is that some time you tell Mr. Murphy about the way in which I came to be in my present post and of my special relation to the whole problem of political refugees. There is no occasion now for me to ask Mr. Murphy to pass on anything from me to the President but I am anxious that he should learn from you that it was the understanding before I left Washington the first time that the President would welcome direct communication from me when in my judgment the exigencies of a particular crisis seemed to warrant. I hope you will feel justified in telling Mr. Murphy that I have not abused this privilege.

With all best wishes to you and all your family. . . .

Cordially Yours,
James G. McDonald

Clifford wrote back to McDonald on January 31: "I have already talked at some length with Mr. Charles Murphy about the details surrounding your appointment and the understanding that exists with reference to it. I am sure you will find Mr. Murphy intelligent and cooperative."[10]

Wednesday, January 4

Most of the morning spent at the [Haifa] consulate, where I admired and was envious of the completeness and modernness of the office arrangements. I was pleased, too, with all the members of the staff whom I talked to.

Mr. Ross, the local Socony-[Vacuum] representative, came over, and we talked for about an hour. Ross does not seem sure that the British are yet prepared to do their utmost to get the Iraq line open.[11] The situation is complicated by the present surplus of oil, which tends to make Haifa a peripheral

9. Entry of December 25, 1949.
10. Letters, including a similar exchange between McDonald and Murphy, in McDonald Papers, USHMM, box 8, folder 6.
11. On Ross and Socony-Vacuum, see entries of March 3 and November 5, 1949. Most of Haifa's capacity belonged to the British companies Shell and AIOC, but 25 percent to 30 percent belonged to the US company Socony-Vacuum. Following many attempts to spur the Iraqi government to allow oil to flow to Haifa from Kirkuk, and to persuade the Egyptian government to allow tankers en route to Haifa from the Persian Gulf to pass through the Suez Canal, the Haifa refinery halted operations on December 23, 1949. With the shutdown of refining operations, Israel had enough refined oil products to last two to three months. See Bialer, *Oil and the Arab-Israeli Conflict*, 12–13, 59–82.

plant and comparatively uneconomic. Ross thinks that the highest UK authorities are carefully assessing what would be the minimum terms they could accept from the Israelis and then, in the light of these, proceed to negotiate for whatever additional gains could be won. Ross thought that [Maurice] Bridgeman,[12] recently here, is really [the] top UK official and that he had talked to some of the men in Tel Aviv as he would to schoolboys.[13] Ross doubted the wisdom of this but thought it typical of one of Britain's carryover and unfortunate habits.

Ross stressed that under no circumstances could the Israelis expect to secure oil products at less than world prices, since it was not a prime producer. On the other hand, there might be ways of making adjustments through royalties or in other ways. As he talked, Ross disclosed that, from the point of view of Socony, his chief concern was that an Israeli-British agreement not be permitted to penalize the American company in the local market. I told him that I would be glad to help in any practicable way, but that I was very anxious that he should be wholly above board with me and that no attempt should be made to use me to secure any special advantage. I had earlier told him of my desire to work as closely as possible with my British colleagues but that I was most anxious not to be "used."

Lunch with the Sackses, a brief nap and tea and the trip home, arriving at seven.

Thursday, January 5

To the office to check and complete [the] telegram to [the] Department regarding [the] American press [UP] report that Sharett had said in Knesset that Israel and US were united against Jerusalem internationalization. We sent [the] full pertinent text, and also on the Russian subject, with the explanation that Sharett had deliberately used language which permitted exaggerated interpretation of [the] US attitude, and that the language about Russia had been intended to avoid annoying Moscow and to secure if possible Russian support or at least abstention when [the] issue [was] raised again in UN Assembly.[14]

A French proposal in the UN Trusteeship Council known as the Garreau Plan[15] *upheld the principle of internationalizing Jerusalem. The plan concerned the Old City's Christian and Jewish quarters and certain additional areas, including Mount Scopus, the Mount of Olives, and the former Government House. This "international*

12. Bridgeman was AIOC's director of relations with governments; see Bialer, *Oil and the Arab-Israeli Conflict*, 53, 79.

13. Bridgeman pressed the Israelis to make sovereignty concessions in Haifa as a way to convince the Iraqis to resume the flow of oil there. *DFPI*, v. 5, d. 49.

14. McDonald to secretary of state, no. 8, January 5, 1950, McDonald Papers, USHMM, box 8, folder 6.

15. Named for Roger Garreau (1891–1991), Free French representative in Moscow during World War II; in 1949–1950 French representative to the UN Trusteeship Council and its chairman.

city" would be under the purview of a UN commissioner, who would also guarantee access and freedom of worship in Jerusalem's Holy Places outside the Old City.[16] On January 3, the Israeli cabinet rejected the plan. In response the State Department called for a proposal acceptable to Israel, Jordan, and the Vatican. Sharett's January 2 statement in the Knesset argued that the United States "showed great understanding for the logic of the situation created in [Jerusalem] by the events of the past two years," but that it was still not clear "how the US interprets the application of the principle of international supervision of the Holy Places." The Israeli government hoped that "as a result of additional discussion we shall arrive at [a] complete understanding."[17]

Middle of afternoon Padberg brought interesting word from my southern colleague [Jefferson Caffery] indicating [Egyptian] willingness to talk, but urging utmost secrecy. My neighbor [Sharett] came in an hour or so later. As a result, we were able to reply to [the night action telegram] with one of our own reporting promise of prompt and secure action. Used Ruth as messenger to the office.

Egypt's parliamentary election of January 3, 1950, brought a convincing victory for the nationalist Wafd Party, which pressed for the removal of British influence from Egypt and Sudan. Caffery reported confidentially that the new Egyptian cabinet, created on January 12 under Mustafa al-Nahhas Pasha,[18] was interested in secret bilateral talks with Israel when the PCC resumed its meetings in Geneva at the end of January.[19]

Sharett reported to Elath the next morning: "Mc[Donald] yesterday informed me [that] Egypt agrees [that] their man, our man, should talk [in] Geneva. Insists [on] complete secrecy as Azzam[20] [is] violently opposed [to] any direct negotiations not through [the] PCC . . . Mc[Donald] added [US] Cairo Embassy warns [that] if [the] matter leaks Egypt will 'run for cover.' Self replied [that] we accept proposal."[21]

Friday, January 6

Breakfast with Padberg. Later received detailed but expected instructions from the Department regarding my and Burdett's relations in Jerusalem. Reiterating its non-recognition of "Israel sovereignty in Jerusalem," [the] Department said I might not visit the city officially or transact any official business there. My personal visits are to be limited to those of absolute necessity.

---

16. Most Holy Places were on the Jordanian side of the line. The Israeli side of the partition line in Jerusalem included, by the Israeli reckoning, the Dormition Abbey on Mount Zion, the adjacent Franciscan Cenaculum on Mount Zion, and the Church of the Annunciation in Nazareth as the only Holy Places. *DFPI*, v. 5, d. 47, 94.

17. On the Garreau Plan and responses, *DFPI*, v. 5, p. 7, d. 4–5, 15, 18, 22–23.

18. Entry of November 26, 1949. Nahhas Pasha became Egyptian prime minister for the fifth time, January 12, 1950.

19. For example, Caffery to secretary of state, January 2, 1950, *FRUS*, 1950, v. V, 658, and n. 6; *FRUS*, 1950, v. V, 661–664.

20. Entry of October 3, 1948.

21. *DFPI*, v. 5, d. 12.

Burdett, on his part, while he may attend social functions with Israeli officials, may not act as US representative with Israel except on strictly consular matters affecting Jerusalem only.[22] To this telegram I replied that it was exactly what I had expected and added that there were no indications that the Israeli government would try to maneuver us into acts which would be tantamount to de facto recognition of Jerusalem as the capital.

Gene Currivan brought with him Allen of the AP,[23] successor to Long. It was a general get-acquainted meeting, which was interrupted by the arrival of Shiloah, whom I had to see. Unfortunately, before I concluded with him, Currivan and Allen had left.

The purpose of Shiloah's visit was to ask me if we could find out the name of the Egyptian representative.[24] A secondary purpose was to warn us of a coup being planned with Iraqi encouragement against the present regime in Syria. This is said to be on a broader basis than heretofore, involving some of the tribes. Shiloah was hopeful that we might directly or indirectly do something to discourage this movement.

Troxel was at the house for more than an hour. Apparently, [he] had indicated a week or so previous that he might have time and would like to work on some commercial subjects. I told him that at the moment we were being so pressed by the Department for biographical information [on Israeli government personnel] that I was going to ask everyone to turn in and help. About that time McVicker came in. The three of us then had a long discussion of Koestler's book and related subjects.[25] Both young men proved interesting conversationalists. McVicker and I agreed that he should carry out his offer to do a despatch on the [January 4] Knesset debate [on Jerusalem]. He said he would do it Saturday morning and bring it out to me before lunch. Spent most of the late evening with Koestler's book.

Saturday, January 7

Daniel Frisch called up and reminded me of the ground-breaking exercises of the ZOA [Zionist Organization of America] building on the 24th.[26] I promised to be there and to make a few remarks. Most of the day spent in getting through the accumulation of documents. Midday visit to the Archibalds, whom we invited over for the evening. In the late afternoon McVicker brought out his despatch. Our discussion of this and other subjects lasted until Ruth invited him for supper, which he helped to prepare.

22. Acheson to US embassy Tel Aviv [drafted by Raymond Hare], January 4, 1950, *FRUS*, 1950, v. V, 667–668.

23. Laurence Edmund (Larry) Allen (1908–1975), Pulitzer Prize-winning correspondent in Europe, 1938–1944; reported from Poland, 1945–1947; AP bureau chief in Moscow, 1949; correspondent in Israel, 1950.

24. Abd al-Mun'im Mustafa. See entry of January 8, 1950.

25. Arthur Koestler, *Promise and Fulfillment: Palestine 1917–1949* (New York: Macmillan, 1949).

26. See entry of January 13, 1950.

A little later, while the ladies and McVicker played bridge, the colonel [Archibald], the major [Brady], and I had a long and serious discussion of problems related to their liaison relationships and those of biographical data [of their Israeli liaisons]. Once again, the colonel complained of lack of responsiveness from the Israelis and emphasized how this worked to their disadvantage. I said that I could not again intervene unless I could be guaranteed against the kind of a repetition of the stupid reaction [of the] the late summer [when] I had spoken to Sharett.[27]

Our discussion of biographical data and the military attachés' possible cooperation resulted in their volunteering to aid. In the course of his talk, the colonel gave a revealing indication of having felt left out and unused. Without seeming to give the point special attention, I said that I had had no confidence in Andrus's judgment and had gotten out of the habit of [the] close consultation which had marked my relations with the military attachés earlier. It may prove that I have been neglecting valuable sources of helpfulness. At any rate, I shall change my tactics and test out my colleagues.

At about ten we joined the ladies and had a pleasant, friendly visit until about eleven.

Sunday, January 8

Having decided that McVicker's text needed amendment so as to include Ben-Gurion's statement about Jerusalem as the de jure and de facto capital, I was able to reach Miss Barry at the office where she was typing. Later [Troxel] brought out the despatch for me to sign.[28]

Shiloah came at a little after five and at my request stayed until nearly seven.[29] First, I asked him about the report from Amman that there would be a meeting of [King Abdullah] and Ben-Gurion. He explained that at the end of the December 23 meeting, the king had suggested a talk between Samir [al-Rifai] and Ben-Gurion, but that when Shiloah had explained that Sharett would be back, the king had agreed to a meeting between the foreign minister and Samir.[30]

Through the MAC [Mixed Armistice Commission] word had come that the Egyptian representative would be Abd al-Mun'im Mustafa, and an inquiry

27. Entry of August 7, 1949. The attachés complained that month about Israeli military secrecy.
28. McDonald reported that, in the Knesset debate of January 4, Ben-Gurion stated that no legislative act was necessary to declare Jerusalem Israel's capital; it was the de jure capital from the moment the state was declared, and now, with the transfer of offices there, it was the de facto capital as well. "He expressed his confidence," McDonald said, "that world would recognize [Jerusalem] as Jewish and as [the] capital of Israel if Israel recognized [the] rights of 'Christian and Moslem worlds.'" McDonald to secretary of state, joint weeka no. 1, January 6, 1950, McDonald Papers, USHMM, box 8, folder 6.
29. Official report of this meeting in McDonald to secretary of state, no. 16, January 9, 1950, *FRUS*, 1950, v. V, 677–678.
30. McDonald's report on Israeli-Jordanian deadlock regarding Jerusalem demarcation in joint weeka no. 1, January 6, 1950, McDonald Papers, USHMM, box 8, folder 6.

had been made about the name of the Israeli representative.[31] Shiloah expressed concern about a possible breach of secrecy. He thought he might go to Geneva and said that he knew and respected Mustafa. As to later talks, Dayan might represent Israel with Jordan.

Shiloah expressed concern about what he interpreted as US government acquiescence in the UK policy of rearming Arab states, for the purpose of "domestic security." Such rearmament did not so contribute [to domestic security], and weapons such as tanks and jet planes so openly supplied to Egypt for domestic security had no relation to it. The assurance that Egypt has no native pilots competent to handle their new jets was met by the argument that they are engaging German and other foreign skilled pilots.[32] As to assurances that Egypt has [only] small supplies of munitions, Shiloah said that a contract has recently been entered into with an important Swiss firm for the setting up of an arms plant in Egypt.

The British, Acheson explained in an open letter, upheld the arms embargo in 1948, but had treaty obligations to Egypt, Iraq, and Jordan, all of which had "legitimate security requirements." The United States would use its influence to prevent a renewal of war in the Middle East, but based on information available to the United States, fighting was unlikely.[33] The British, meanwhile, dismissed Israeli objections. Israel, said John Sheringham in the Foreign Office, was "merely an irritant in the Middle East" and Britain was "compelled to base [its strategic planning] on Arab goodwill."[34] The Israelis concluded that the United States was preoccupied with broader Cold War issues concerning Europe and the Far East and was possibly recalibrating its relationships in the Middle East.[35]

I told Shiloah of my instructions about Jerusalem. He assured me that no attempt was going to be made to press for foreign representation in Jerusalem. In answer to my statement about the unsatisfactory liaison relations between the military attachés and the army, Shiloah said that he was confident the appointment of Ted Kollek as the head of the North American [Division at the Ministry for Foreign Affairs] would straighten out a number of minor irritations.[36] This was, he said, no reflection on Miss Herlitz, because

31. Entries of June 6 and October 31, 1949.
32. In general see Richard Breitman and Norman J. W. Goda, *Hitler's Shadow: Nazi War Criminals. US Intelligence, and the Cold War* (Washington, DC: National Archives, 2010), 25–27; and Nicholas Kulish, "Old Nazis Never Die," *New York Times*, January 10, 2015.
33. Acheson to Javitz, January 12, 1950, *FRUS*, 1950, v. V, 684–685; also memorandum of conversation by the secretary of state, January 9, 1950, *FRUS*, 1950, v. V, 671–674. Elath later attributed Acheson's support of Arab rearmament to suspicion of Israeli expansionism, general support of Great Britain, and the US need to show concern for the Arab states. Elath to Sharett, January 26–27, 1950, *DFPI*, v. 5, d. 48.
34. Paraphrased in *DFPI*, v. 5, d. 25.
35. *DFPI*, v. 4, d. 39.
36. Theodore "Teddy" Kollek (1911–2007), Hungarian-born, Vienna-raised labor Zionist; emigrated to Palestine as a pioneer, 1934; helped smuggle Jews out of Nazi-occupied Europe, 1938–1941; central figure in Jewish Agency Political Department's special assignments division,

Kollek's relation with the general staff and all the higher-ups was such that he could put to them informally matters which Miss Herlitz could only raise formally.[37] As to our need for [biographical] information, Shiloah said he would be glad to talk to Colonel Archibald, but that he thought in general it would be better if these matters were cleared through [the Ministry of Defense].

Late evening spent in the near completion of Arthur Koestler's book.

Monday, January 9

In the afternoon a long and rather painful staff conference. The pain arose from the necessity of driving unpleasantly hard at the task of getting the biographical information file underway. Apparently, Ford had not stopped to envision the difficulties involved, or to make sure that Padberg had the time and resources to do the job. Finally, it was agreed that different members of the staff would do different parts of the task.

Troxel brought up the interesting questions of relationship on the technical level with bureaus such as [the] Custodian [of] Absentee Property,[38] now located or soon to move to Jerusalem. I took the line that we should adhere strictly to the recently received instructions from the Department. It was agreed that we would re-examine those instructions and then put the problem up to the Department, asking them for an official interpretation or for new instructions.

Home after six, tired and rather out of sorts, and therefore, glad to accept [Samuel Guy] Inman's last-minute invitation to dine with him and his colleagues.

Samuel Guy Inman (1877–1964) was a Texas-born Christian missionary, academic, and an architect of Roosevelt's good neighbor policy between the United States and Latin America in the 1930s. As the League of Nations commissioner to the Latin American republics in 1935, he had aided McDonald in trying to find places in Latin America for Jewish refugees from Germany. Now he was part of a fact-finding mission from the American Christian Palestine Committee, which aimed to resolve the status of Jerusalem.

At the Gat, the dinner was good and we had a pleasant visit. They had not been able to get into the Old City but had talked with one of the Legion officers just within the Arab lines. Thus, they could say they had been on Arab

working largely on rescue operations in Istanbul, 1943–1945; served in the Bricha, 1945–1946; helped procure ammunition for the Haganah in the United States, 1947–1948; mayor of Jerusalem, during which he developed Jerusalem as a modern city, 1965–1993. See Ruth Bachi-Kolodny, *Teddy Kollek: The Man, His Times, and His Jerusalem* (New York: Geffen, 2008).

37. Esther Herlitz became the deputy director of the North American Division at the Ministry for Foreign Affairs and thus the deputy to Kollek.

38. Israeli government office created in July 1948 to administer the property of those who fled Palestine during the War of Independence.

soil. They could have entered had they not desired to return. They were all much intrigued by the Yemenite [immigrants'] camp[39] and by their very satisfactory tea with Dr. Weizmann. They showed me their press release. It was an argument for non-internationalization of Jerusalem. Considering the very short time they had been in the country—Inman just a week and a day—their "fact finding report" had a certain impressiveness.[40] Inman took a last-minute letter to Bobby. He is due home on Friday and is to speak at the Public Forum in Bronxville on Monday.

I took occasion to tell Miss Herlitz, who, with another Israeli official had come to say goodbye, that I intended to continue "to work with her."

Tuesday, January 10

Barnes and Padberg came out. We decided that we should go back to the Department and ask for the second vice consul, and to urge the early arrival of the three American clerk-secretaries. It was felt that with these it would be possible to supply the needs of [Milton] Fried and the extra needs of Hooper and the work on the biographical file.

At teatime, Zvi Kolitz[41] and Hermann Segal[42] visited for nearly an hour and a half. Segal, who is an active Revisionist and a close colleague of Jabotinsky, did most of the talking. He began by admitting the demise of the Revisionist [HaTzohar] Party; then he outlined at length the program which he and a group of "free enterprise" men have for the development of a "film city" at Ashkelon. There they intend to exploit in pictures the millennia-old historical heritage of Israel. Simultaneously, they hoped to develop other forms of Israeli art and to do all of this on a sound commercial basis. Demonstration of such commercial success would, they hope, ultimately help to strengthen non-socialist elements in the state. Segal is soon leaving for a six-month trip through Europe, North Africa, the States and South America to secure financial and other support for the project. He is counting heavily on the cooperation of Hollywood.

From these subjects we drifted onto the more interesting area of reminiscences about Jabotinsky. One story which Segal told deserves recording. He had been, as we all know, often accused of impracticality and of not seeing

---

39. Refers to the Rosh HaAyin immigrant camp, which housed Yemeni immigrants.
40. Inman and colleagues believed that forced internationalization would be disastrous because of strong local opposition and that Israeli-Jordanian peace had to come first. Lapidoth and Hirsch, eds., *The Jerusalem Question and Its Resolution: Selected Documents*, 100–102.
41. Zvi Kolitz (1912–2002), Lithuanian-born Revisionist Zionist and writer/producer; best known for his Holocaust short story, "Yosl Rakover Talks to God" (1946); his film, *Hill 24 Doesn't Answer* (1955), about the War of Independence (Israel's first feature-length film); and his co-production of Rolf Hochhuth's *The Deputy* in New York in 1964.
42. Zvi [Hermann] Segal (1901–1965), Polish-born Revisionist Zionist leader; emigrated to Palestine from Danzig, 1938; important figure in illegal immigration from Europe before and during World War II; signatory of Declaration of Independence and member of the Provisional State Council, 1948; after formation of the Herut Party resigned from politics and focused on real estate; had ambitious plan to build a film city and casino complex in Ashkelon.

the realities of a given situation. To answer his critics, Jabotinsky once told the story to illustrate his point that sometimes situations become so confused and the outlook so dark that the ordinary practical person can see no way through. One day during the war and the blitz, London was so densely enveloped in fog that all movement in the streets had to stop. At this moment a man came out of one of the hotels frantically crying for someone to show him the way to the hospital where his wife was gravely ill. His hand was grasped by a stranger whom he could not see and who led him quickly, despite the fog, to the hospital. When they reached their destination, he turned to his guide and said, "How could you see to lead me through this terrible fog?" The reply was, "I am blind."

Wednesday, January 11

Pleasant visit in the morning with the Turkish minister [Seyfullah Esin] and his wife.[43] They proved to be just as charming as our mutual friends in Istanbul had said they would be.

Colonel Archibald came in rather excitedly to tell me that his radio operator, who had been drinking heavily for weeks, and who had gotten in the habit of publicly announcing that the Americans would someday follow the Nazi example and "make lampshades out of Jewish skins," had been seriously beaten up in a drunken brawl the night before. I urged the colonel to speed up the replacement.

Young Adan Graetz[44] came to say goodbye and talked to me about the problem of the relations between his family's new shipping line and the Israeli line [ZIM]. He deplored the latter's remaining outside the [North Atlantic Passenger] Conference and worried lest a rate war begun by the older Israeli lines might be disastrous to Israeli shipping. He deplored, too, the Israeli tendency to use financial controls as a means of diverting freight from foreign lines. He thought this in the long run would be self-defeating. As he was leaving, he finally agreed to take letters home and to get in touch directly with Bobby.

Maurice Benin[45] and Barnes were here for lunch from one to three. Earlier, Curt [Haut][46] had told me of his surprise and almost consternation at the

---

43. Seyfullah Esin (1902–1982), Turkish diplomat since the 1920s; first Turkish head of mission (legation) in Israel; presented credentials to Weizmann on January 7, 1950.

44. Adan Graetz (1928–2000), son of Heinz Rudolf Graetz, last surviving partner in Meir Dizengoff & Company, a leading shipping firm in Israel. The company purchased additional cargo ships in 1950 and competed with ZIM Israel Navigation Company, which was founded in 1945 by the Jewish Agency, Histadrut, and the Israel Maritime League. ZIM purchased Meir Dizengoff & Company in 1955. See www.hma.org.il/Museum/Templates/showpage.asp?DBID=1&LNGID=1&TMID=84&FID=1753&PID=5153, accessed September 2014. See also entries of May 1 and July 27, 1950.

45. On Benin, see entries of October 4–8, 1949.

46. Curt Haut, commercial analyst, US Embassy, Tel Aviv.

report from Benin that [Frederick] Larkin[47] had told the latter that the [US] embassy ought to proceed at once to anticipate the time when it would have to have land for official buildings in Jerusalem. I was frank to tell Benin that at this time there was no possibility of any move in that direction. I then outlined the substance of the current Department's instructions against giving, by any actions or inactions, support for the view that Washington was weakening in its non-recognition of Israel sovereignty in Jerusalem or of its support of the UN principle of the Jerusalem internationalization. Benin said that he recognized this situation, but thought that, nonetheless, I would like to see the unusual plots which he held in Jerusalem, which he would sell to us. From his map it was obvious that he does possess just the sort of property that we would need. I agreed that Curt might, wholly in his personal capacity, go to Jerusalem with Benin.

Very interesting was Benin's report on the softening process taking place in Egypt towards Israel. He himself is returning to Alexandria before he goes back to France. He told of how his partner Hassan Youssef[48] had influenced [permission for] the calling of an Egyptian ship at an Israeli port as a beginning of a breach in the non-intercourse deadlock. Benin had been disappointed that the Israelis, instead of assenting at once to this call, had raised difficulties and had insisted upon reciprocity. Benin is planning to speak to the [Israeli] Foreign Office about this. Benin is optimistic that the Wafdist regime under Nahhas will be inclined to follow, and perhaps speed up, the recent Egyptian tendency toward rapprochement with Israel. As Benin was leaving, I urged him to bring out his mother and brother to the house. He seemed touched that I had thought of his mother.

Lady Helm and Donald, Ann and Isabelle, came for tea. The presence of the children made it doubly enjoyable.

At 6:00 Daniel Frisch was at the house for about an hour. He deplored the cleavages in the Zionist movement at home and the difficulties which he had found here. In answer to my question "which of the Israeli leaders have you found to be most cooperative?" he replied unhesitatingly, "Ben-Gurion." The latter, more than nearly all the others, took a broad and impersonal view, never showing pettiness or resentment. In general, Frisch's view of Ben-Gurion was just the same as my own, that is, that Ben-Gurion is one of the great natural leaders of our time. Again, as in my earlier talks with Frisch, I got the impression of a man of more discernment and ability than he is credited with by most US observers. I hope that my favorable judgment on this point is not unduly influenced by his generous estimate of my work here.

47. See entries of August 4 and 12, 1949; October 4–8, 1949.
48. Acting chief, Egyptian Royal Cabinet.

The concert to which we took Eli [Karlin] and Dr. [Misha] Karlinski was delightful, especially the first half. The new French conductor [Charles] Bruck[49] had the orchestra admirably under control, while the young violinist, Miss [Ida] Haendel[50] played the Sibelius Concerto[51] so as to give me at least greater pleasure than had [Jascha] Heifetz's recordings.[52] The opening short symphony by one of Bach's children was excellently performed. The second half was less interesting, but I enjoyed the closing number, Stravinsky's *Firebird*. I was pleased to see that the doctor got such a thrill out of the concert.

Thursday, January 12

Two hours or so with Harold Glasser, here for a six-months study of economic and other conditions for the Jewish National Welfare Fund [*sic*].[53] He is well acquainted with Coombs of the Federal Reserve Board,[54] whose estimate for Clapp of Israel's viability was so pessimistic. Glasser thinks that such pessimism ignores favorable imponderable elements. At home, Glasser finds no younger lay leadership to replace the older generation, except as this is found in the younger generation of professional social workers.

At four-thirty Mr. [Robert] Gottlieb[55] and Harry Wolfson[56] of the Palestine Jewish Colonization Society [PICA] were at the house for an hour. The latter was very informative in his estimates of Israel's economic possibilities. He denied that there had been a disproportionate emphasis on agricultural settlements as compared with industry. He argued that Baron [Edmond James de] Rothschild[57] had been duly interested in industry but, had not there been the

---

49. Charles Bruck (1911–1995), Romanian-born French conductor; active in resistance in World War II.

50. Ida Haendel (b. 1928), Polish-born violinist; began recording in 1940; performed for Pope Benedict XVI at Auschwitz-Birkenau, 2006.

51. Jean Sibelius wrote one violin concerto, in D minor.

52. On Heifetz, see entry of May 17, 1950.

53. Harold Glasser (1905–1992), economist who worked with the US Department of the Treasury, Department of State, UNRRA, and Marshall Plan; Soviet agent (codename "Ruble"), providing economic intelligence, 1937–1945; under FBI investigation after 1945 for espionage; forced to resign from US government, 1947. From 1948 to 1953, director of the Institute on Overseas Studies, part of the Council of Jewish Federations and Welfare Funds, which studied agricultural expansion and the degree to which it kept pace with immigration; resigned because of revelations concerning his communist connections. See www.documentstalk.com/wp/glasser -harold-1905-1992, accessed September 2014.

54. Charles A. Coombs (1918–1981), Ph.D. in economics; served in OSS in Middle East during World War II; joined Federal Reserve in 1945, specializing in foreign exchange questions.

55. Robert Gottlieb (1902–1968), Alsatian-born government attorney and judge; recruited by the Rothschilds to work for the Jewish Colonization Association (ICA), which was restructured in Palestine as PICA by Baron Edmond James de Rothschild in 1924; director of ICA in Paris, 1936–1940; fled to Palestine, 1940; managing director of PICA in Israel in 1950, replacing Harry Wolfson.

56. Harry L. Wolfson (1910–1974), general manager of PICA, 1934–1950.

57. Baron Edmond James de Rothschild (1845–1934), strong early supporter of Zionism; in 1924 founded PICA, which acquired more than 125,000 acres of land in Palestine and established several agricultural settlements and wineries. On PICA, see Goda et al., eds., *To the Gates of Jerusalem*, 161–162.

large emphasis on returning to the land, there could have been no sound basis for the Jewish state. Wolfson was interesting, too, in his vivid interpretations of Jewish personalities. It would be worthwhile to see more of him.

The Archibalds' cocktail party was a success. I made an occasion to talk business with Shiloah. He was anxious to know whether the person and the date previously spoken[58] of would be adhered to for Switzerland. I promised to inquire. He said also that he expected the Jordan talks to be resumed with the return of Samir. Again, he expressed lively concern about the possibility of [the] UK government planning to extend its treaties [with Jordan] in the event that Israel recognized Abdullah's annexation of Arab Palestine. He hoped that in the latter [case], even the US government would be willing to try to dissuade the British. He argued that self-denial by London would be interpreted throughout the whole Middle East as a proof of non-imperialist intentions.

A little earlier, Padberg had given me a sealed envelope which, I discovered when I opened it somewhat later, had essential answers for Shiloah, to the effect that [al-Mun'im] Mustafa was delaying his departure until the 16th or 17th in order to have "pertinent discussions" with the new foreign minister [Muhammed Salah al-Din Bey]. By the time I had opened the envelope, Shiloah had gone, but I was able to send the necessary message through Esther Herlitz so that it would reach Tiberias in time.

Friday, January 13

Impressive ceremony at the groundbreaking of the ZOA House. [Fred] Monosson as chairman, though his manner was not attractive, was restrained in his own speeches and got through the planned schedule expeditiously.[59] The first speaker was the prime minister, who redefined world Zionist relations to Israel. I was second, and stuck strictly to my typewritten text. Then followed brief talks by [Berl] Locker, head of the [Jewish] Agency; [Joseph] Sprinzak, president of the Knesset; [Avraham] Granot, Jewish National Fund; and finally, [Israel] Rokach. Then, Paula participated in the actual cornerstone laying and the meeting was over. Again it was noteworthy that though several rabbis were on the platform, none of them participated in the ceremonies. As we were breaking up, I took occasion to whisper to Ben-Gurion that I thought there were encouraging developments to the South [Egypt]. He apparently had not yet been informed.

Troxel came out in the afternoon to talk about his complicated assignment of guessing at the numbers and classifications of Americans in Israel. I was surprised that his calculation of the number would not exceed a couple of thousand.

58. Presumably Abd al-Mun'im Mustafa. See entry of January 5, 1950.
59. On Monosson, see entry of October 29, 1949. He chaired the building committee for the ZOA House in Tel Aviv, which was to serve as an information center for American Jewish visitors and for Israelis interested in Jewish life in the United States.

In the late afternoon I spent about an hour and a half at Goldie Meyerson's cold and severe apartment on upper Yarkon Street. There was no heat, and the cold ocean winds found their way through the shuttered and thickly curtained French window. First, we talked about the suggestion of James N. Silberman[60] that the scientific and cultural cooperation work of the Department might—quite apart from Point Four—make available approximately $30,000 worth of technical assistance to Israel. Goldie recalled clearly her conversations with him and confirmed his impressions that Israel would welcome and might even pay or at least contribute towards the cost of such experts.

We then discussed Point Four possibilities, and I went over with her the revised schedule of possibilities recently sent us by the Department, which listed twenty-four experts and forty-five trainees at estimated costs of $272,800 and $165,930 or a total of $448,730; adding to this for "material costs" 30%, the total would be $569,730. Goldie was obviously desirous of securing this assistance, which she said was sorely needed. She belittled the possibilities of political criticism. She seemed to think that Sharett's earlier coolness towards Sam Klaus's suggestion of technical assistance[61] was a political maneuver which would not again be repeated, at least not in such a discouraging form. My talk with her on the general subject of American expert assistance left me confused both as to what the US is really offering and as to the attitude of HaKirya.

Goldie's reaction to my informal complaint about the use by the shipping and the air people of the Tel Aviv financial forms to discriminate against foreign planes and ships was that [Eliezer] Kaplan would be quick to understand the self-defeating aspects of such procedure. She was illuminating about the [Jewish] Agency and the common charge that it has outlived its usefulness, and that its personnel is made up almost altogether of older leaders who have not been found fit for the Israeli government. She denied that the Agency could be dispensed [with], arguing that its functions overseas of stimulating contributions and regulating emigration could not be handled by the government. While admitting that its colonization efforts were inadequate, she doubted that much could have been done by an overworked and harassed government. As [to] the personnel of the Agency, Goldie argued that there were strong men on it. Locker, she said, was an able chairman and one of the best leaders in Israel. The secretary Shlomo Eisenberg[62] is able, but especially so is the treasurer, Levi Eshkol.[63] This latter, working quietly, is "very effective."

60. James M. Silberman (b. 1913), held US federal government jobs during the New Deal beginning at the Bureau of Labor Statistics; later technical expert on the Marshall Plan, Point Four, and other overseas aid programs, including the Peace Corps.
61. Entries of April 4, August 5, and August 7, 1949.
62. Shlomo Eisenberg (1899–1959), emigrated to Palestine from Poland, 1926; general-secretary of Jewish Agency; later managing director of ZIM and El Al.
63. Levi Eshkol (1895–1969), emigrated to Palestine from Ukraine, 1914; Haganah command, 1940–1948; treasurer and head of Settlement Department, Jewish Agency, 1948–1963;

We jokingly discussed some of our mutual friends including Nahum Goldmann, Abba Hillel Silver, and Emanuel Neumann. On all, our views were more or less identical. She confirmed my understanding of the contrast between Ben-Gurion and Sharett; the latter highly strung unable to relax or get away from his work, the other quiet, well balanced and able to relax with his Greek philosophy. Goldie said that she would supply the biographies I requested of the Histadrut and labor leaders.

Saturday, January 14

Finished my documents during the early morning.

At Sam Sacks's I met again the publisher of the *Jewish Biographical Encyclopedia* [*sic*], Mr. [David] Tidhar.[64] Three volumes in Hebrew have been published, and a fourth is at the binder. I told him that I would send a memo to the office asking them to purchase one set of the volumes. Rather to my dismay, I discovered through a chance remark by Tidhar that he is bitterly critical of Shiloah, whom he charged with having been instrumental, through the British CID [Committee of Imperial Defence], in having a couple of hundred [Jews] put in [the British detention camp in] Latrun.[65]

At teatime the Australian minister O. C. W. Fuhrman and his wife[66] were with us for about an hour and a half. We enjoyed them. He said that he hoped he could come from time to time to talk about technical matters. I replied that he would always be welcome.

Sunday, January 15

For a walk with Ruth to Napoleon's Hill.

[Gideon] Rafael of the Israeli UN Delegation came for more than an hour in the afternoon.[67] He had just returned from an all-day session at Tiberias with Sharett and other members of the Foreign Office.[68] He was rather surprisingly and disquietingly pessimistic about the initiative from the South. He was inclined to regard it—whether in this he was reflecting the opinion of his colleagues or not I could not judge—as a possible maneuver to muddy the

minister of agriculture, 1951–1952; minister of finance, 1952–1963; minister of defense and prime minister, 1963–1967.

64. David Tidhar (1897–1970), Jaffa-born policeman and detective who provided information concerning Arab affairs to Jewish Agency and British authorities; turned to publishing after 1950. *Enziklopedyah le-Halutzei ha-Yishuv u-Vonav* [Encyclopedia of the Founders and Builders of Israel] was his major work begun in 1947. It reached nineteen volumes, all appearing in his lifetime.

65. Refers to British arrests of some 2,700 Yishuv leaders and underground figures during Operation Agatha in June 1946.

66. Osmond C. W. Fuhrman (1889–1961), Australian librarian, scholar, and diplomat; served in consular positions in China before becoming Australian minister in Tel Aviv, 1949–1953.

67. Entry of November 22, 1948.

68. For this meeting *DFPI*, v. 5, d. 27.

waters of the Jordan.[69] He indicated, however, that the Foreign Office was going ahead and that my friend Shiloah might be leaving soon.

Rafael's chief concern appeared to be that the PCC, for lack of something better to do or through instigation by the French for their own purposes in Syria, might take the initiative in suggesting a territorial settlement. This, Rafael thought, would be disastrous. I told him that I thought it quite unlikely that the US government would be a party to any such move, particularly since at Istanbul there had been a clear and unequivocal pronouncement in favor of bilateral negotiations without any reservations save that these should not be influenced by the threat of force. Rafael urged that I should ask the Department to be on guard.[70]

Regarding the Garreau plan for Jerusalem[71] [it] was interpreted by Rafael as a device to diminish the chances of Israeli-Jordanian agreement and to weaken Abdullah so that he might not intervene in Syria. According to Rafael, the French fatuously refused to give up their hopes of reinstalling themselves in Syria. All their actions in this area must be read in the light of that mirage. Rafael was also inclined to think that the French are anxious to forestall the strengthening of Egypt and the concentration by the latter of its attentions in North Africa. Paris is fearful of Egyptian extension into Libya and towards Tunisia. Rafael is hopeful that the Wafd may decide to cut their losses of prestige in Asia and concentrate on their contest with the British for the Canal and the Sudan. In this event, Cairo would be the more willing to make real peace with Israel. On the attitude of the Department, Rafael felt that there was no longer any anti-Israeli bias at the top level. He had found Rusk, McGhee, and the others sympathetic and cooperative, though he thought there might be remnants of the older attitude at the lower level.

Rafael gave me no support for Inman's theory that the overwhelming victory of the Vatican on December 9 had caused echoes which might reverberate adversely in the event a repetition of that success were undertaken. There were evidences of Protestant fears but not of any organized or powerful action. Granting that Rome must have realized that the extreme resolution of December 9 would fail of that degree of unanimity which a milder resolution would have received, Rafael thought that the Vatican had insisted on a showdown in order to demonstrate the strength and determination to fight in the political arena to the last. This determination, he thought, had been evoked by recogni-

69. Meaning that the Egyptian feelers were a ploy to wreck peace talks then in progress between Israel and Jordan.
70. Elath visited Burton Berry and John Waldo, McGhee's deputies in the Office of Near Eastern and African Affairs, on January 9, 1950. He called for a postponement of the PCC meetings in Geneva. The PCC, said Elath, could wreck bilateral negotiations then in progress between Israel and Jordan, and he accused the British of encouraging obstacles. The State Department pressed the Jordanian government to proceed with its bilateral negotiations in the spirit of compromise. It also told the British government that, "[in] view of [the] PCC experience," Israeli bilateral negotiations with the Arab states would "probably be more conducive [to] successful outcome." *FRUS*, 1950, v. V, 674–677, 680–682, 699, 700–702.
71. Entry of January 5, 1950.

tion that both Jordan and Israel were determined to oppose to the last internationalization. Though our talk was interrupted by the arrival of the barber, we continued much as if he were not present. I hope to see Rafael again before he leaves. He is to be here a month.

For tea came Gerry Thornton and his wife Irene, P. G. Yovanovitch and his wife, all of TWA. During an interval of the social visit, these two men and Mr. Hooper (who had come with his wife) and I talked business. Thornton seemed optimistic that the Israelis, learning from experience, would desist from undue utilization of financial restrictions to disadvantage the foreign air and shipping lines.[72] His recent talks with the new director of foreign exchange had been encouraging. Moreover, he anticipated that with the coming of spring and the extraordinary traffic due to the holy year,[73] there would be so much demand for space that all the lines would be satisfied. Indeed, the Israelis had already indicated the possibility of giving permission for the third flight.[74] Thornton seemed pleased at my promise that I would talk to Kaplan in general terms. All the men agreed that it would be desirable to get on with the bilateral air agreement between the US and Israel.

Monday, January 16

Hooper, who had been good enough to go out to meet Henry Morgenthau and his party, reported on their arrival. I sent a note to the Sharon, and when Morgenthau returned my call, he made a date for the afternoon.

Morgenthau, the general chairman of the United Jewish Appeal, arrived in Israel on January 16. McDonald reported that Ben-Gurion had invited him "to discuss major financial and economic problems with him and other [government] heads." According to McDonald, Morgenthau "called for enormous increase in American Jewish support through [the] UJA."[75] McDonald reported that 243,547 immigrants had arrived in 1949 and that funds at the Jewish Agency's disposal for their resettlement only amounted to 110 Israeli pounds per person—less than a third of what was needed for their absorption.[76]

---

72. Entries of July 2, October 31, and December 10, 1949. To build foreign exchange and increase the business of El Al, the Israelis in February 1950 allowed only nine flights out of Lydda to points west by TWA and Air France with a total of 327 passengers between them (many on return flights with tickets purchased elsewhere), while El Al flew thirteen monthly flights out of Lydda, with 518 passengers. Foreign airlines also were required to reinvest their Israeli revenues into Israel, above and beyond normal expenses such as aviation fuel. The French government was particularly furious and wanted a joint approach to the Israelis. Bruce to secretary of state, no. 890, February 24, 1950, USSDCF-PIFA, 1950–1954, reel 6, frames 894–895.

73. The Jubilee year in Christianity occurs every fifty years.

74. The third weekly TWA flight was granted in February 1950, to the irritation of Air France and KLM, which were not granted the same. Hooper to secretary of state, no. 78, February 8, 1950, USSDCF-PIFA, 1950–1954, reel 6, frames 886–887.

75. McDonald to secretary of state, joint weeka no. 3, January 20, 1950, McDonald Papers, USHMM, box 8, folder 6.

76. McDonald to secretary of state, joint weeka no. 2, January 13, 1950, McDonald Papers, USHMM, box 8, folder 6.

In the late morning Shiloah came over with Mr. Kollek. I thought they had come to speak about the Acheson statement on Near East rearmament. Instead their purpose was to solicit our cooperation in determining whether Mun'im's mission was approved by the Wafd regime, and if so, when he would set out [for Lausanne]. I promised to try to get the desired information. We then talked for a little while about the Acheson statement.[77] Shiloah repeated arguments which he had made previously but did not emphasize the case, saying that the Foreign Office was waiting for the full text.

I then took occasion to ask Shiloah about Sam Sacks's friend, Tidhar. At first, Shiloah did not recall the man, but then explained that Tidhar had been caught in an unsavory attempt at near extortion at the time a number of Italian Jews were still being interned by the British mandatory authorities shortly after Italy entered World War II.[78] At once, it was clear why Tidhar was not enthusiastic about Shiloah. On the other hand, Shiloah's story, which was confirmed by Kollek, made one wonder at the stupidity of Tidhar in attacking Shiloah in such a way as to bring the old story back to life. I also began to question the [general activities] of Tidhar even though Shiloah had said that he knew of no reason to doubt Tidhar's present activities were legitimate and worthy of support. As the two men were leaving, I invited the two men and their wives to dinner for Morgenthau this Thursday evening at eight.

A little earlier Morgenthau had accepted for Thursday and asked to bring Mrs. Klotz.[79]

Although Morgenthau volunteered to come to see me, I drove out to the Sharon in the continuing rain and through several rather ominous-looking lakes across the road. I found Morgenthau in conference with a group of Israelis, so we went to his room for nearly an hour's private talk. He told me first [about] his conference just before leaving Washington with Acheson and [Stuart] Rockwell.[80] The secretary and Rockwell had explained the Department's policy of approval of Britain's "carrying out its treaty obligations" in rearming the Arab states. Acheson expressed confidence that this would not unsettle Near East conditions and that the UK government was as anxious as the US to strengthen Near East peace. Rockwell was emphatic that no "large arms" were being supplied. Morgenthau said that he was unconvinced by these presentations but that since he was no longer in the government, was not engaged in a

77. See editors' description in entry of January 8, 1950.
78. McDonald, in a letter to Samuel Klaus, later explained his reservations about Tidhar. Most important was "Shiloah's comment . . . that his only contact with Tidhar had been during the last days of the Mandate when he [Shiloah] was acting as liaison between the British Government and the Jewish internees confined by the Mandatory. Tidhar was, according to [Shiloah], caught in an attempt to get money from the families of internees by promising them to use influence to speed up their release." See McDonald to Klaus, May 17, 1950, McDonald Papers, USHMM, box 8, folder 10. On the detention of Axis aliens in Palestine see Daphna Sharfman, *Palestine in the Second World War: Strategic Plans and Political Dilemmas* (Eastbourne: Sussex Academic Press, 2014), 28–37.
79. Morgenthau's longtime assistant, Henrietta Stein Klotz (1900–1987).
80. Memorandum of meeting printed in *FRUS*, 1950, v. V, 671–674.

political mission, and did not possess the technical data necessary to argue, he let the matter rest. He was not, however, persuaded that the US policy was sound or justified. On my part, I told him of the fears here and of my own doubts about the wisdom of UK policy. In strictest confidence I also told him of the political developments to the East and of the possibilities to the South.

He was amusingly interesting about the political situation in New York State. According to him, Jack Ewing's press conference here [January 3] had not caused a ripple in the New York press. Morgenthau had not seen a line about it. Moreover, Ewing is so slightly known that he would have a very heavy handicap to overcome. Morgenthau thinks that Fitzpatrick is ambitious but is inclined to bet on FDR, Jr.[81] The latter was very active in the Lehman campaign, especially upstate, and he succeeded in introducing himself favorably to many of the smaller communities.[82] Morgenthau regards him as extraordinarily intelligent, and the ablest of the boys. [FDR]'s new wife Morgenthau regards as a large asset.[83] She is old-fashioned, intelligent, and will not stand for any nonsense.

Morgenthau then reported from a personal source in which he has complete confidence the nearly incredible statistics that within a recent brief period in an upstate city a thousand Catholics had been converted to Protestantism and that in one small town in the Hudson Valley seven Catholics had joined the Episcopal Church. Morgenthau's informant said that "for the first time the Catholic Church is worried about the situation at home." I had to recognize the seriousness of his source and information, but I remained skeptical. As to Jerusalem, Morgenthau had found no support for Inman's report that Protestant support would, because of fear, fall away so sharply that there would be no chance of a repetition of the bolt of December 9.

Back to the house in time to meet with Colonel Archibald and Padberg. Having had the opportunity to think a good deal about the Acheson statement, I was less inclined than I had been in the early morning to do more than to send an urgent appeal to Washington for the full text. After a considerable discussion, a telegram to this effect was drafted. Then at the colonel's suggestion we passed on to the Department Vivian [Chaim] Herzog's report that Egypt had sent a "number of planes" to Damascus. We requested Keeley to check.

Ruth and I had dinner at the Helm's with the family, including the children and the Anglican bishop of Jerusalem.[84] The latter impressed me as a little less sanctimonious and political than when I met him first in 1946 at the Anglo-American Committee of Inquiry hearings in Jerusalem and had failed to attend the afternoon when His Grace held forth.[85] Deliberately during the

---

81. Roosevelt served in Congress until January 1955. He sought the nomination for the governorship of New York in 1954, ran for attorney general of the state that year having failed to win the nomination, and lost to Jacob Javits.
82. Herbert H. Lehman was US senator from New York, 1949–1957.
83. Suzanne Perrin (b. 1921), New York socialite and Roosevelt's second wife.
84. Weston Henry Stewart (1887–1969), Anglican bishop of Jerusalem, 1943–1957.
85. Goda et al., eds., *To the Gates of Jerusalem*, entry of March 26, 1946.

dinner and afterwards, I tried—and with considerable success—to keep the conversation away from the political aspects of Jerusalem, and to draw the bishop out on ecclesiastical and related Jerusalem matters. He was interesting but not, it seemed to me, at any point profound in his comments on the several churches, their points of conflict, [or] their relations with Rome or Moscow.

The most important conclusion he drew was that the Greek Catholic [Uniate Church] would [not] become the dominant church, because Rome has the wisdom to appoint Arab bishops and to avoid the besetting weakness of the Greek Orthodox Church, with its insistence on Greek bishops and its practice of keeping the native clergy in virtual ignorance and deprived of any save the scantiest means of subsistence. His Grace said that from time to time representatives of the Uniate Churches (he cited a recent example of the Maronite) appealed to him against Rome and its alleged abuses of Uniate rights. He made it a practice, however, merely to listen and not to take seriously the offers sometimes made by such Uniate leaders to bring their flocks into the Episcopal fold. This, he said, they would not be able to do in any case.

On the moot questions of Russian church property and current Russian penetration in the Greek Orthodox [Church], His Grace was interesting and to a point informative.[86] He argued that the mandatory's last-minute decrees about property [remaining in current hands] had in fact been binding despite their non-publication in the official gazette.[87] According to his information, the text had been stolen by Jews from the printer, but that the attorney general[88] had been able to have them printed in a pamphlet together with a covering decree validating the other. His Grace added that he understood the Knesset had recently taken formal action to invalidate the whole group of decrees. As to Russian penetration, His Grace agreed the attempt was being made and would be continued, but he doubted its present or future success. He did not believe that Russian money was being spent to win Greek Catholics through arms.

There was no talk between Helm and me about business, except that he, in answer to my question, reiterated his earlier opinion that there was no need, and that if he were in my place, he would not now call a meeting of the diplomatic corps. As we were leaving, Sir Knox, having said that [David] Balfour[89] was making a full study for the mission of the Russian Church property problem, laughingly pretended to be envious of my ability to talk biblical and ecclesiastical subjects with His Grace.

Tuesday, January 17

For the record I here paraphrase [the] London embassy telegram of December 22, [1949]: [Geoffrey W.] Furlonge [Head, Eastern Department in

---

86. Entries of December 28, 1948 and September 23, October 14, October 21, and November 27, 1949.
87. *The Palestine Gazette: Official Gazette of the Government of Palestine.*
88. Sir Leslie Bertram Gibson (1896–1952), attorney general of Palestine, 1944–1948.
89. David Balfour (1903–1989), counselor, British legation in Tel Aviv.

British Foreign Office] said Israel was told that "question extension to any area [acquired by Jordan] concerned only UK and Jordan." UK has "no intention [of] establishing any bases [so acquired] in time peace" but "war or threat of war was another question [as to] which UK could not express its intention at present time." British [in] Amman [instructed] to inform Jordan about [policy] but "to add for Jordan's own confidential information" UK's "firm intention [. . .] to apply treaty to any areas [acquired by Jordan] so soon as they have been incorporated within their state." It was to apply also to any corridor.

[Furlonge had said that] Jordan had been told when talks with Israel began that [the] treaty was [the] principal item [of] interest [to the] UK, which desire[d] to "maintain hands-off attitude" [toward Jordanian-Israeli talks]. However, Foreign Office had given "Kirkbride some comments 'mostly of technical nature' on [the] question of corridor for his guidance in event he is asked" [by Jordan]. In response to question "if [the] establishment of [a] corridor would pose any particular problems for UK, Furlonge replied in negative but stated [the Foreign Office] did not think corridors were ever completely satisfactory arrangements."[90] As to the above, I would not go quite so far as Ford's comment written on the margin: "double-dealing dastards."

Dr. Aryeh Altman[91] came at five for what he termed a "philosophical talk." He had prepared notes and evidently had thought carefully about what he would say. Altman's central thesis appears to be that the Jewish people, whether organized in a state as during biblical times dispersed through the Diaspora, or now in Israel, have exercised and will exercise an influence for good or ill far out of proportion to their fewness or to their small territory. He cited the "revolutionary" influence of individual Jews. Rome, he said, had fallen because of many influences but primarily because of Christianity. From the time of Jesus until that of [Ferdinand] Lassalle, Karl Marx, [Leon] Trotsky, [Grigory] Zinoviev, and Ana Pauker, [Jews] had wielded, directly or indirectly, atomic power. Often this power was negative or even destructive, because the Jewish individuals were fighting blindly against forces in the midst of which they could exist or live only precariously. Given the opportunity, Jewish influence in the world could be a balancing force for peace and reconstruction.

Dr. Altman said that it was obvious that there were now but two great powers, the US and Russia. In Western Europe the decline which [Oswald] Spengler had foreseen was already underway, and at a rate more rapid than was believed possible at the time Spengler wrote. Hence, Britain and France and other Western European powers could at most be merely auxiliaries of the US. The same could be said of Eastern powers in their relation to the USSR. Given the relative balance of power between the US and the USSR, Israel, though hardly more than microscopic in comparative size, might be able to alter the

90. Holmes to secretary of state, no. 5079, December 22, 1949, *FRUS*, 1949, v. VI, 1556. Sent simultaneously to US embassy in Tel Aviv.
91. Revisionist leader of HaTzohar; see entries of August 17 and September 22, 1948; February 17 and March 14, 1949.

balance. It was this thesis and its elaboration which he thought he could prove almost mathematically. We tentatively agreed upon another appointment.

Wednesday, January 18
First conference with Rabbi Jacob Herzog since his return from Rome and Lake Success. Regarding his conversations with the Vatican, I quote from the memo of conversation which Herzog had with John Ross on December 5, at which Eban and Sharett had also been present. Herzog's account to me was in essence the same as the above. He added, however, some points: In addition to [Vittorio] Veronese,[92] there are two other laymen who are important contacts for the Vatican, my friend Count Galeazzi and a Mr. Gedda.[93] Herzog had tried but vainly to see Count Galeazzi, but Veronese was insistent that all the talks, five in number, must be with him only.

About his impressions of Lake Success, Herzog talked freely. There was not time for a full exposition. He confirmed that Eban and his advisers had been quite mistaken in their estimate of the final situation. They had confidently expected, even after the Ad Hoc Committee vote, that in the Assembly, the Australian resolution would be defeated. Herzog attributed the final decision to the last-minute Vatican influence. He thought that the pope himself had not been convinced until the very end that the Australian position could be maintained. He credited Monsignor McMahon and Griffiths with very large influence, and Cardinal Spellman with having played the major role in the closing days.

Herzog summed up his estimate of the Vatican motivation as follows: 1) desire to make Jerusalem a place of refuge for Christians; 2) to advance the relative position of the Latins in Jerusalem at the expense of the Orthodox; 3) to establish a bulwark against communism; 4) to establish the principle of internationalization even if it were not finally implementable; 5) an underlying opposition to Jewish possession of so large a part of Jerusalem, stemming primarily from non-reconciliation to the Jews' non-acceptance of the Messiah.

For the first time Herzog seemed to me very pessimistic. He was sure that the December 9 vote could not be reversed, despite an increased anxiety in many Protestant circles over the Vatican's demonstration of political power. He did not agree, however, with Inman that this concern would issue in political action. Herzog did not agree with the general opinion at HaKirya that it was better to have had the UN adopt the Australian position against the votes of US-UK-Canada et al., than it would have been to have had the UN adopt nearly unanimously the milder internationalization. Herzog argued that the

92. See entry of October 26, 1949 for Herzog's plan to meet Veronese, the president of the Italian Catholic Action party and a financial and political adviser to the Vatican.
93. Luigi Gedda (1902–2000) Venetian-born physician and influential Catholic layman; medical adviser to Pope Pius XII; president of Catholic Action before Veronese, 1934–1946; engaged in organizing various Catholic youth groups.

UN action would be used and was so intended by the Arabs and possibly the Vatican to make Israel a pariah among the nations. This, he thought, would fit neatly into the Arab plans for a second round.[94]

The dinner at the [Michael] Simons' was pleasant despite the bleak coldness of their very small apartment. The food was better than Padberg had reported, and the conversation was pleasant and interesting. The guests included the new Czechoslovakian minister Dr. Eduard Goldstücker[95] and his wife, the Turkish representative and his wife, and the heads of the Western European and East European desks. Most of the time during the dinner I chatted with Mrs. Esin about life in Turkey, the reforms of Atatürk, and her painting. After dinner my talk was mostly with Esin. The general conversation had to do for a considerable time with the problem of translations in general and, in particular, from Arabic into Western languages.

Throughout the evening, the Czech representative behaved in a very civilized manner, displaying none of the secretiveness or reticence commonly associated with Iron Curtain countries. For example, he spoke about Koestler without indicating either prejudice or resentment. He promises to be the most attractive of the East European representatives.

Thursday, January 19

Bart Crum failed to arrive.[96] Morning conference with Hooper.

An hour's talk on the roof in the wonderful sun with Mr. [Joseph] Hooding of Cincinnati. A businessman, he is a friend of Sam Katz and, like the latter, active in the UJA. He was somewhat qualified in his enthusiasm of what he had seen in Israel, though he admitted that, considering the inherent difficulties, miracles had been performed. He was concerned by the role of the Orthodox here and by the propaganda use which the Council for Judaism in Cincinnati is making of the resulting restrictions here on activities of Reform Jews.[97] He admitted that [Eliezer] Kaplan had given a reasonable answer to the effect that not everything could be done at once, and that if a specific case arose, ways would be found to permit civil marriage or marriage by a Reform rabbi. My comment was that you could hardly expect Israel in the midst of all its urgent

---

94. In general on Herzog and the Foreign Ministry concerning Jerusalem, see Bialer, *Cross on the Star of David*, 27–37.

95. Eduard Goldstücker (1913–2000), joined Communist Party in Czechoslovakia in 1933 after having been member of HaShomer HaTzair; in 1939 escaped to Great Britain, where he studied German literature and worked for the Czech government-in-exile; Czechoslovak ambassador to Israel, 1948–1951; arrested and imprisoned as part of Stalinist purge, 1951–1955; became professor of German literature at Charles University, specializing in Kafka; went into exile after Soviets crushed Prague Spring in 1968 and returned in 1991.

96. Crum arrived in Israel with Gerold Frank on January 21, 1950.

97. The American Council for Judaism was an anti-Zionist Reform Jewish organization formed in 1942. On the early relationship between Reform Judaism and Orthodox clerics in Israel, see Richard G. Hirsch, *Reform Judaism and Israel* (New York: Commission on Israel, 1972); and S. Zalman Abramov, *Perpetual Dilemma: Jewish Religion in the Jewish State* (Cranbury, NJ: Associated University Presses, 1976).

tasks to adjust its program in what would certainly prove to be the vain effort to avoid giving ammunition to the Council for Judaism. Hooding agreed.

Before dinner Padberg brought out a [top-secret despatch] from Caffery[98] telling us that Mun'im would go to Geneva, but that the new foreign minister[99] wished to study the files before making a commitment. Padberg also spoke vaguely about another Department telegram, which he had seen on the coding strip. It concerned, he said, the US's desire that there should be no outside intervention in Syria in the event of another coup there. Unfortunately, as it later proved, Padberg missed the boat badly by not waiting to bring the text to me.

Mr. and Mrs. Shiloah and Kollek, without his wife, arrived twenty-five minutes early for our dinner for Morgenthau. This was fortunate, because it gave us time to get Eli Karlin to fill the fourteenth place. Others at the dinner were the Eytans, the Simons, Mrs. Klotz and Mr. Ware,[100] and Padberg. The food was excellent, but despite heroic efforts on my part, there was no general conversation. Morgenthau resolutely refused to speak for more than thirty seconds on any one of the several domestic and foreign subjects I asked him about. Whether overtired or not feeling well (this last possibility seemed to be belied by his good appetite), he was dumb.[101]

After dinner, I took Shiloah and Eytan in the study and gave them the message from the South. They were pleased with the quick service and asked me to query Caffery again about possible late developments. I told them, too, about the Department's concern about Syria but admitted that I had not seen the text and had, therefore, to be un-usefully vague as to whether this latest expression of concern was based on new information.

Eytan then made the adroit suggestion that since the several missions had repeatedly complained about HaKirya's "failure" to aid them in their search for houses and offices, he proposed that I, as dean of the diplomatic corps, should let the members know that the government is now prepared to cooperate fully if the missions would merely indicate what their needs and desires are for houses and offices in Jerusalem. I then told him of my instruction, which precluded our mission's recognition of Israel sovereignty or its capital in Jerusalem and that, therefore, I did not think that Washington could take advantage of his offer. He then emphasized that he was speaking to me not as American

---

98. Dated January 18, 1949, *FRUS*, 1950, v. V, 679, n. 3.

99. Muhammed Salah al-Din Bey. The Israelis had similar information. *DFPI*, v. 5, d. 27.

100. Leonard Ware, attaché, US Embassy in Tel Aviv, assigned as public affairs officer, October 1949.

101. Morgenthau's comments to Ben-Gurion on the following evening explain his mood. He complained that the Israelis asked him only for money and not for political advice. He then described the US strategic focus on the Soviet Union, which to Morgenthau meant the abandonment of Israel, and Acheson's personal irritation with Sharett for speaking to him as a teacher would to a student. Israel, Morgenthau said, had to declare openly its allegiance to the West. Ben-Gurion responded that it was impossible to know when such a war might break out and that Jewish immigration from Eastern Europe had to remain Israel's primary goal. See Ben-Gurion Diary, entry of January 20, 1950. The editors are grateful to Tuvia Friling for this reference.

ambassador but as dean of the diplomatic corps. I promised to check with Washington to learn whether I could act.[102]

After dinner I renewed my efforts to draw out the guest of honor, but again in vain. The guests went home by 10:30.

Friday, January 20

Ross of Socony at Haifa, the Wallers, and Mr. Hooper were here for lunch. For an hour before the meal we listened to Ross explain some of the intricacies of inter-company and company-government and intra-governmental oil relations in the Middle East. Ross agreed with McGhee's dictum at Istanbul that the IPC (Iraq Petroleum Company) was disadvantaged by its triple ownership [British, US, and French interests] during a period of oil struggles, when, not unnaturally, each of the participating interests would have preferred to develop preferentially the areas in which each has an exclusive control. Ross pointed out, however, that this generalization had to be qualified by taking account of the dollar-pound problem and the related problems of dollar-pound areas.

On the question of the diversion of the 36-inch pipeline now building from Haifa to Sidon, Ross indicated some of the complicating factors. The French desire of this diversion is motivated in part by its relative lack of interest in [Consolidated Refineries Ltd. in Haifa]. The American companies are not much interested because the Haifa refinery is in any case for them not an essential [one]. Britain regards the Haifa plant as a marginal operation, particularly in view of the erection recently of several large refineries in Western Europe. In connection with this last point, Ross pointed out that the modern strategic concept is that refineries are much less vulnerable if they are in the consuming country rather than in the country of origin of the crude, particularly if, as in the case of the Middle East field, these are especially vulnerable.

On a second of McGhee's general dicta that the Middle East fields are useful in peace but probably would not be in war, Ross made the reservation that it was very difficult to destroy "a hole in the ground." He argued that "a good deal of oil could probably be gotten out" despite the efforts of the enemy. On the question which interests me most—is the UK making its utmost efforts to have the Iraq line open and to get the Haifa refinery into operation—Ross was enlightening but not dogmatic. He argued that since the Haifa refinery is almost marginal from the economic point of view, and since there are so many international political factors involved, it may well be that the UK authorities are prepared to do their utmost only if and when they are convinced that they can make a "paying deal" with Israel. According to Ross, the UK holds nearly all the trump cards. These include the Israeli blocked sterling,[103] influence with Iraq, and the ability to leave the Haifa refinery closed. The only business

102. McDonald to secretary of state, no. 40, January 20, 1950, referenced in *FRUS*, 1950, v. V, 706, n. 3.
103. See editorial note in entry of March 22, 1950.

consideration which Ross could see which would tend to influence Britain to come to terms would be Britain's fixed policy of never giving up a market if it can possibly be saved. Here in Israel the non-opening of the Haifa refinery would certainly lose Britain the local market.

Ross returned again to the point made in our Haifa talk[104] that his company was concerned lest Britain make terms with Israel which would "sell Socony down the river." By this he meant such an arrangement as would seriously disadvantage Socony in this market. Much of our talk was devoted to the baffling problems of dollar and sterling balances and areas and their intricate ramifications.

As to potential or possible oil resources in this country, Ross was pessimistic. He did not deny that there might not be some oil here but said that it was the consensus of opinion of the oil geologists that the fault which has created the vast deposits in the Middle East begins to the East of here and will leave to Israel only a relatively small share. He admitted, however, that this might be large enough to supply Israel's needs. Whether it could be produced economically and refined economically could only be tested in fact. He stressed that such an operation would, of course, have the advantage of not involving the expenditure of dollars or of British pounds.

Saturday, January 21

Brief tea visit to the Sam Sackses'. Just as we were going out to the Ben-Gurions' for the Morgenthau luncheon, Padberg called to say that he wanted to come over right away to discuss a matter which might require him and Brady to go to Jerusalem that afternoon. When I had looked at the Department telegram concerned, I told him to go ahead. He had forgotten that he was duty officer for the weekend. In any case, theirs proved to be a wild-goose chase, because no one was there who could give them authoritative information about the position or number of the Israeli tanks alleged to be out of bounds.[105]

At the Ben-Gurions' besides the hosts, ourselves and the guests of honor were Mrs. Klotz, Mr. Ze'ev Sherf, director-general of the cabinet and his wife,[106] [and] Mr. and Mrs. Joseph Jacobson. During the luncheon I chatted with Jacobson about his Coca-Cola concession, and he said he expected work to begin within six months. Then jokingly, I asked him what economic advantage there was for Israel in its straitened condition to have a Coca-Cola plant here. He replied that it would give the people a good drink and make some people "richer." Perhaps in fairness I should add that this last statement might have been mine rather than his. Anyhow, the subject became for a moment general conversation, with my question about the economic validity of the project from

104. Entry of January 4, 1950.
105. Entry of January 24, 1950.
106. Ze'ev Sherf (1904–1984), Ukrainian-born socialist-Zionist; emigrated to Palestine, 1925; member of Haganah command during World War II; helped create apparatus of new Jewish state in 1947; secretary of government, 1948–1957; held ministerial posts in 1960s.

Israel's point of view. Facetiously brought to the prime minister's attention, Jacobson, in the friendly spirit of the conversation, jokingly said that his company had planned to send the ambassador gift cases of Coca-Cola, but "would not now do so in view of his sabotage in the presence of the prime minister."[107]

More serious was Jacobson's talk of the coming of Frank Ryan of the World Commerce Corporation to Israel. Jacobson evidently expects to secure a $10 million investment from this corporation, created a few years ago by [Edward] Stettinius.[108]

After the lunch there was fortunately an opportunity for me to talk briefly with Ben-Gurion. I told him of our problem of communicating with departments which had moved to Jerusalem, and of our desire to use the Foreign Office as the post office for these communications. He agreed at once saying, "We have no desire to be petty in this matter; we are not worried about foreign non-recognition now; we are more concerned to establish ourselves in Jerusalem."

As to Egypt, Ben-Gurion thought that the king might be obdurate because of his loss of face in the war and that this matter might be left to the palace by [Prime Minister Mustafa al-] Nahhas because of the latter's predominant interest in the Sudan and the Suez. He added, "it is necessary that we should be patient with Egypt and give the new government six months to find itself." He added pessimistically that he did not believe that Britain wanted peace between Israel and Egypt, because so long as there is no peace, the UK can use Israel as a means of diverting Egyptian attention from the Sudan and the Suez.

During the lunch I had half-seriously complained to the prime minister of the difficulty of getting translations of his and other important speeches and of Sharett's insistence on revising whatever translations of the foreign minister's speeches have been made. The prime minister jokingly asked me about the comparative age of English and Hebrew and about the number of people in the world who used English. Afterwards, Sherf assured me that the translations of the prime minister's speeches would be made available to us promptly.

At teatime the Halprins and Nahum Goldmann were at the house. The talk was in part about the December 9 defeat. Mrs. [Rose] Halprin said that the last-minute changes of votes had surprised everyone, including the Americans. She was inclined to share the view that the US has not made an all-out effort. I reminded her with emphasis that it was not reasonable to expect the US to

107. For the Coca-Cola franchise in Israel in 1950, see Arnold Forster, *Square One: A Memoir* (New York: Donald I. Fine, 1988), 269.

108. The World Commerce Corporation (WCC) was formed in 1945 under the name, British American Canadian Corporation, to provide investment capital for industrial development and free trade, beginning with occupied Germany. Former Secretary of State Edward Stettinius Jr. was not one of the founders of the company, but he held a large stake in it. The company used former OSS chief William J. Donovan's law firm for its legal representation. Donovan himself became chairman and a major shareholder, as did other US and British intelligence officers from World War II. Frank T. Ryan, a former OSS officer who served in Spain, became president in November 1947, when WCC took its new name. By that time it had representatives in forty-seven countries.

make of Jerusalem one of those rare issues on which it would use its utmost pressure to get out the votes. I pointed out that such pressure could be used but rarely if its usefulness were not to be exhausted, and that it was unreasonable to assume that the US had not done everything which could fairly be expected of it. Later, a member of the staff had joined our discussion and said that he was disturbed by the seeming practice of American Jews "to put Israel first." I explained that I did not think that this was a fair statement, but that they did frequently seem to lose sight of the fact that the US has other essential interests than those of Israel.

There was considerable talk led by Nahum Goldmann about the attitude of the UK government. Does Britain really want peace between Israel and its neighbors or not? Nahum, with his usual tendency to optimistic over-refinement, spoke of what he believed to be the conflict of views between the "more friendly" [Hector] McNeil and the "traditionally hostile" Michael Wright. I refused to accept this dichotomy, explaining that during Wright's recent visit to the States[109] he had spoken on behalf of the Foreign Office and not as presenting [his] personal or group's view. Moreover, in the agreement then reached in Washington, there must have been the underlying assumption that Wright's final statement of agreement with the US on all major issues in the Middle East represented the considered judgment of the British cabinet. After Nahum had to leave, we discussed Jerusalem and the US position thereto. At the end the Halprins promised to come back to see me before they left for the States early in February.

I should have noted . . . that in my talk with Ben-Gurion, following [the] luncheon at his house, after we had finished our serious talk about Jerusalem, I said jokingly: "You know I can't go to Jerusalem until you make it possible for us to build our house on Mount Scopus." Ben-Gurion gaily replied: "Your suggestion is all we need, Dayan has just been waiting for an excuse to act. Now I have a witness"—Ben-Gurion was [directing his comment] to Sherf, who had overheard my words—"that you suggest that we move." Proof that my joking remark was not taken seriously is found in the fact that Ben-Gurion, later reporting to the people in the Foreign Office—according to them, made no reference to our exchange about Mount Scopus but did speak about Egypt and his concern about the British and the king.

Sunday, January 22

I exploded when Padberg brought in the Department's delayed telegram about Syria. He had seen it first on Thursday, but had not regarded it as important enough to bring out promptly. Therefore, on the night of the Morgenthau dinner I had been able to speak about it in only general terms to Eytan and Shiloah. By the time I saw the text I had read almost the whole of it in the morning *Palestine Post* in a [UP] article from Washington. Padberg's delay was

109. See entry of November 26, 1949.

the less excusable because he had gone on an ill-considered wild-goose chase to Jerusalem on Saturday with Major Brady to check the tank story with Riley or his American colleague, neither of whom was in Jerusalem. Moreover, Padberg had forgotten that he was duty officer over the weekend. I lectured him roundly on the danger of assuming that a telegram was unimportant and that action on it could safely be delayed.

When we reached Eytan's office in the midst of the deluge, he greeted Padberg and me, laughingly asking in effect whether the Foreign Office here was the only sieve. I replied that I assumed that he had already read in the *Palestine Post* the substance of the instructions which I had been asked to deliver. Then, very carefully I paraphrased the instructions, emphasizing at the end the final point that nothing in them was to be interpreted as meaning that the Syria-Iraq union was going to be effected.

The instructions [stated that] the continuing uncertainty of [the] situation in Syria makes desirable [a] reappraisal of possible union with Iraq. [The] US neither favors nor opposes [a union] but [is] concerned that there be no foreign intervention. [The] Department appreciates Israel's disavowal of intention [to intervene], since such action [not only] would undo all progress achieved to date with [the] Arab states and prejudice further chances of settlement, but might have catastrophic effects throughout the Middle East. [The] Department [is] concerned that Shiloah's statement [that] Israel could not be expected to remain quiescent in view of menace to its security and also by [the] statement [by] Elath that [a] union would, in [the] words of [the] Israel ambassador, place extremists in Israel in [a] position to urge intervention before an attack could be launched from the new unified state. [The] Department considers existing agreements [as] keystones to Middle East peace [and] will continue [to] exercise its influence directly and through [the] UN to secure full observance. [The] US [is] confident [that] Israel intends to respect [the] armistices and avoid action which would provoke retaliation throughout [the] entire Arab world. Hence, [the] US hopes Israel will firmly resist [the] urgings of extremists or any other elements that [want precipitate] action [to] be taken in situation arising out of events in Syria. The closing paragraph in the light of the story in the *Post* of January 22 would have been humorous if it had not been serious: "Dep[artment] desires M[cDonald] to discretely convey above to F[oreign] M[inister], Shiloah, and other appropriate high Israeli officials." It should be emphasized that [the] "foregoing does not indicate US has concluded that [a] Syrian-Iraq union [is] probable."

Eytan said that his government had no intention of breaching the peace or intervening in Syria. He then told us that there was to be another meeting of the Israeli-Jordanian representatives on the night of January 24, and that the Israelis were optimistic that progress might be made.[110]

---

110. The Israeli-Jordanian meeting of January 24 at Shuneh is in *DFPI*, v. 5, d. 40.

Sunday afternoon, Ruth and I went to the Tel Litwinsky Hospital for the opening of the Martha Truman Recreation Room [for Disabled Soldiers]. Originally, this hospital had been built by the Americans during World War II and then had been abandoned and was now in use by the Israelis.[111] Vera [Weizmann], in her address, stressed her gratitude to the president for his permission to use his mother's name and Israel's gratitude for his consistent support. I spoke briefly.[112] The other speakers were [General] Yadin and Professor Fraenkel.[113] Bart Crum and Gerold Frank were present during the ceremonies, the latter in his role as publicity agent of the B'nai B'rith.[114] They promised to come to see me on Wednesday.

Sunday night, Padberg having brought out a Department telegram from Caffery indicating that the king's advisers still wanted to go ahead [with negotiations at Lausanne] but were uncertain about views of the new cabinet, I called Eytan, and it was arranged that someone would come to the house early the next morning.

Monday, January 23

Shiloah and Ted Kollek came at 8:15 [at McDonald's invitation]. After I had given them the message from the South, Shiloah asked if I would be willing to inquire whether the Israeli representatives should get in touch with Mun'im in Geneva. They emphasized that they did not wish to embarrass either the king or Mun'im. I said I would inquire.

Then I brought up the question of Syria, the Department's instructions, and there followed an animated discussion. Shiloah was insistent that there was convincing evidence of a plot now brewing with Iraqi instigation, which would seek to stir up popular revolt and which would not be as bloodless as the three previous ones. At this point, Kollek interposed to say that, as a resident of Ein Gev,[115] he was painfully conscious that once Bedouin tribes were stirred into action they were no respecters of frontiers; moreover, once border incidents were launched there would be no way to certainly prevent their spreading. Hence, the two men wished me to warn Washington that it was not enough to counsel non-intervention. Shiloah insisted that the US should take account of the extent to which [the] Syria-Iraq union, no matter how achieved, would upset dangerously for Israel the precarious Middle East balance. I promised to transmit his views.

McDonald also reported Shiloah's "moderate optimism" concerning negotiations with Abdullah. UN sources had told Shiloah that Abdullah was willing to give up his

111. Entry of December 13, 1949.
112. Remarks in McDonald Papers, USHMM, box 8, folder 6.
113. Dr. Oscar Fraenkel, chairman of the B'nai B'rith District Grand Lodge. B'nai B'rith held its annual convention in Israel in January 1950. His speech reported that the organization sent $4 million in goods, mainly prefabricated housing, to Israel.
114. Entry of September 10, 1948.
115. On eastern shore of the Sea of Galilee.

insistence on a corridor through Israel and instead would accept frontier rectifications and free access to Israeli ports.[116]

[In] the early afternoon the Turkish minister [Esin] came, he said, to check with me on his impression of conditions here and, as became evident later, to ask me if he might send diplomatic mail through our pouch. On this point I told him that I hoped the answer would be yes but that I would have to query Washington. Esin's appraisal seemed to me shrewd. He inquired diplomatically about relations to the East and to the South. I told him as much as I thought I properly could. He said he was grateful for the confidence which I had indicated in him. This, I think, was a genuine feeling on his part. He indicated adroitly that he doubted that the present Israeli frontiers could endure. He was suggesting that Israeli dynamism would inevitably force a modification of the present unnatural bulging frontier.[117] I replied that one would have to take into account, however, the influence of Britain on the other side of the line and the weight which it would naturally bring to bear to bolster Jordan's strength.

The Gibsons and Burdett arrived shortly after five. A little later Miss Herlitz came and, rather unfortunately, stayed until nearly seven, thus leaving me no time to talk with the Jerusalem men before dinner.

McDonald emphasized to Herlitz that, though the United States voted against the December 9 UN resolution on Jerusalem, it had not given up on making Jerusalem international along the lines proposed earlier by the Palestine Conciliation Commission. The Israelis, he said, had been overconfident on the eve of the General Assembly vote. Further, they believed that, because the United States opposed the resolution, it would also engineer a vote against it behind the scenes. In fact, the Jerusalem issue was not vital to the United States, thus precluding strong action either for or against the Vatican before the UN vote.[118]

On January 23, the Knesset approved a government resolution reaffirming Jerusalem's status as Israel's capital. Ben-Gurion announced, however, that for the time being the Ministry of Defense and the Ministry of Foreign Affairs would not move to Jerusalem. As Ben-Gurion put it, "We do not want to cut ourselves off from the world, not from Russia, nor America, nor Czechoslovakia, who have sent their ministers to Israel, if not to its capital."[119]

The Wallers arrived a little after seven. The other guests had come earlier, the Hoopers, the Archibalds, the Bradys and Mr. Ware. The whole atmosphere

116. McDonald to secretary of state, no. 50, January 23, 1950, USSDCF-PIFA, 1950–1954, reel 1, frame 353.

117. This concern was also expressed by Turkish prime minister Semsettin Günaltay on January 13, 1950. *DFPI*, v. 5, d. 26.

118. Herlitz-McDonald meeting, January 23, 1950, *DFPI*, v. 5, d. 41.

119. Reported in McDonald to secretary of state, joint weeka no. 4, McDonald Papers, USHMM, box 8, folder 6.

was informal and strangely American. We were finished before the after-dinner guests arrived. These were Tetlie, Padberg, Troxel and McVicker.

We [McDonald and Gibson] talked about liaison between here and Jerusalem. I was delighted to have Gibson say that he would pass on to us promptly any developments which he thought would interest us. When the pouch would be too slow or communications through Washington impracticable, he would use commercial. I got the impression of a man who is thoroughly competent technically, and who will exercise a much larger degree of imagination and initiative particularly in his cooperative relations with us than did Burdett.

Tuesday, January 24

Early conference with Goldmann the photographer and a representative of *Haaretz* to discuss a group of pictures for a special edition to show "the Ambassador at Home." We agreed on the following shots: in the study, at tea, illustrating a hobby, my wife sewing, with the gardener, with some sabras, etc.

Left for Jerusalem at five minutes after eleven with Ruth [and] Sonia [Karlinski].[120] We reached the King David at about 12:45. [General] Riley [and McDonald had] tea in his beautiful corner suite at the King David. As always, he was most friendly. I told him of the thus-far futile exchanges with the South and asked him about the leak in connection with his role as messenger. He replied that he did not know what had happened. The letter he carried was from Sasson to Chirine.[121] It was a simple statement putting the question whether the time had not come when the two countries might not begin to talk.

I then put to him the $64 question: whether, in his opinion, the British are in fact doing their utmost to secure peace in this area? He replied that though he could not document his feeling or put his finger on concrete evidence, he was of the opinion that the answer should be in the negative. Then he, in effect, expressed the same opinion as that so consistently put forward by the Israelis; in effect, that the UK still acts on the theory that unsettlement strengthens its position in the Arab states. General Riley promised to come down to see me after his planned weekend visit—or rather visit during the weekend—to see Abdullah.

Eli [Karlin's] lecture [at the Hebrew University] was impressive, beautifully organized and perfectly presented with the poise of a veteran. I must confess, however, that there were several times during the short period when I could not follow the argumentation. After the lecture, I suggested to Sir Leon Simon[122] that the young man might be used for something more at the univer-

---

120. On Sonia Karlinski, see entry of August 1, 1948.
121. Entry of February 21, 1949; Colonel Ismail Chirine was brother-in-law to King Farouk and a member of Egyptian-Israeli Mixed Armistice Commission.
122. Sir Leon Simon (1881–1965), English Zionist and Weizmann protégé who helped draft the Balfour Declaration; British civil official until 1944; afterward chairman of the executive council of the Hebrew University of Jerusalem; notable scholar of ancient Greek and Hebrew literature.

sity and indicated in that connection that his Uncle Serge [Karlinski] might be interested in a grant to the university.

The dinner with the family after the lecture [at the King David Hotel] had the air of a celebration. For Sonia, it was a family triumph. When Riley and Gibson came in, they stopped to speak to our table. A little later I went over and chatted with Morgenthau and Goldie. I tentatively asked Morgenthau about acting as messenger for me to the president. Later, I was convinced that I ought not send the message I had in mind, except through the pouch. Stopped at Steinglass's table and chatted with him for a little while.[123] He was not very definite about Morgenthau's relations with the president.

Stopping at Colonel Cloverdale's table, I took him aside for a moment and received from him confirmation that during his trip earlier during the day he had found that the Israeli tanks in the disputed area west of Be'er Sheva had "all been removed."[124] This statement and an earlier one of Riley about tanks and the general's support of my concern about British intention made my day complete.

At 9:35 we left the King David and had a pleasant drive in the moonlight reaching the outskirts of Tel Aviv in an hour and five minutes. The absence of traffic rather than high speed was the explanation. Sonia seemed so thrilled by her son's success as to forget her physical troubles.

Wednesday, January 25

Mr. Benin and Barnes discussed the desirability of the latter's meeting with [Donald] McNeal[125] to settle on the site for what would be the consulate general here in the event of a territorial separation of consular and embassy functions. I stressed again that I could do nothing under present instructions to encourage the idea of moving to Jerusalem, but that I would ok the telegram to the Department for Barnes's trip to Rome.

The afternoon was spent in getting caught up on the diary.

Thursday, January 26

Up early and out to Lydda by 8:30. Chatted with a number of the Israelis and briefly with Bart. As he was saying goodbye he was, even for him, unusually laudatory. I walked out to the plane with Morgenthau and explained to him that I decided not to burden him with any personal message to the president.[126] A

---

123. Meyer F. Steinglass (1908–1997), director of publicity for the United Jewish Appeal; helped found Israel Bond Organization in 1951.
124. Involved five to seven tanks in a semi-demilitarized zone west of Be'er Sheva.
125. Entries of May 14 and November 13, 1949.
126. Morgenthau may not have been in the best mood. Outside the Israeli reception for him in Jerusalem on January 25, there were communist protests against the "warmonger, anti-Soviet, anti-Jewish, pro-Nazi Morgenthau," partly in reference to Morgenthau's advocacy of a Middle East regional defense pact that included Israel. McDonald to secretary of state, joint weeka no. 4, January 27, 1950, McDonald Papers, USHMM, box 8, folder 6; *DFPI*, v. 5, d. 81, 85.

few minutes earlier I had talked with Steinglass, the UJA press representative, whose reaction on the above score was negative. He kindly agreed to take some mail, including a photograph, home. I autographed the Ben-Gurion "serious conversation" photograph [figure 2.1, p. 74] for him and for Mrs. Klotz. Miss Herlitz and I think also Comay, who saw me autographing these pictures, expressed a desire for one, which I promised them as soon as they came to the house.

Brought Gerold Frank back with me. He said that Weizmann had commented to him and Bart that Morgenthau had failed since the death of Mrs. Morgenthau,[127] that he was slow and unimaginative. Frank added that last spring following the retirement of Silver, Morgenthau had been booed at a meeting of UJA leaders (no particular friends of Silver) when Morgenthau had said that he was glad that "a certain Cleveland rabbi had just made his 'swan' song." Frank said that Bart's autobiography had reached the point of about 300 pages dictated to a stenographer, that it was difficult going. Apparently there is no early prospect of its completion.

Frank and I stopped to see the offices on the hill.[128] Though rather grim and cheerless now, they should be wonderful in the summer for some eight months and then satisfactory next winter when the heat is on.

Shiloah and Kollek came at about 5:30 and stayed nearly an hour.

Shiloah discussed the January 24 Israeli-Jordanian meeting concerning the partition of Jerusalem, with the Jordanians remaining firm on the issue of Mount Scopus.[129]

I gave them first the message from the South in which my colleague [Caffery] modified, in a somewhat more optimistic way, his telegrams of the previous days.

Caffery reported that the new Egyptian foreign minister, Mohammed Salah al-Din Bey, informally expressed the following policy on Palestine: Egypt would never attack Israel because the army was being reorganized to provide security in the broader East-West conflict. But neither would Egypt ever make peace with Israel, recognize Israel, or collaborate with Israel. Any other policy, he said, would destroy morale throughout the Arab world, which looked to Cairo for leadership.[130]

---

127. Elinor Fatman Morgenthau (1891–1949), to whom Morgenthau had been married since 1916, died after a stroke in September 1949. She was politically astute and very involved in promoting her husband's career. Edna S. Friedberg, "Elinor Morgenthau," *Jewish Women's Archive*, http://jwa.org/encyclopedia/article/morgenthau-elinor, accessed September 2014.

128. Refers to new US Embassy offices in Ramat Gan, which opened on Monday, January 25, 1950.

129. McDonald to secretary of state, no. 63, January 28, 1950, USSDCF-PIFA, 1950–1954, reel 1, frame 354.

130. Caffery to secretary of state, no. 73, January 25, 1950, *FRUS*, 1950, v. V, 702.

Shiloah commented that he could well understand why the new government might hesitate to take an avowedly conciliatory line. It would almost certainly have to move in the direction of a new treaty with Britain, which would probably involve some seeming concessions about the Suez and Sudan, both unpopular with public opinion. Under these circumstances it would be almost too much to expect that the new regime should simultaneously move in the direction of peace with Israel. At the end I had the impression that Eban would discreetly sound out Mun'im in Geneva.

The PCC began informal meetings with Arab negotiators in Geneva that week. Mun'im, according to US interlocutor Ely E. Palmer, stated that "there could be no question [of] direct conversations [with Israel] since for Egypt, Israel did not exist." Palmer told Gideon Rafael, the lead Israeli delegate, that the United States "strongly favored" bilateral negotiations between Israel and the Arab states, and would assist wherever possible.[131]

Then I gave my guests a paraphrase of the Department's recent statement on arms shipments for this area.

Acheson had written McDonald:

> [Department] continues to believe [that the] shipments [of] arms to Arab States and Israel [should] be limited to those necessary for maintaining internal law and order by [governments] concerned and for providing for reasonable requirements of self-defense. . . . [Department] has received no info justifying [the] conclusion [that] Egypt or any other Arab State has serious intention or immediate plans for renewing hostilities. You should assure Israelis that US [government] will continue [to] keep close watch on [the Near Eastern] arms situation and if convincing evidence [is] received of preparations by any party [to] renew conflict, US will not hesitate [to] use its influence [to] attempt [to] prevent such plans from being carried out.[132]

[In] effect, the Department asked Israel for a factual statement of the basis for its charges that the British arms supplies to Egypt and to the other Arab states constitute a menace to the peace. Shiloah evidently considered this last of great importance and asked me for a written paraphrase. I promised that it would be available Friday morning, while he on his part promised the desired reply promptly.[133]

On January 25 the Israeli government issued a press release maintaining that the weapons purchased by Egypt—including jet fighters and tanks—went beyond

---

131. Palmer to secretary of state, no. 149, January 28, 1950, *FRUS*, 1950, v. V, 707–708.
132. Acheson to McDonald, no. 16, January 17, 1950, *FRUS*, 1950, v. V, 696–697.
133. Shiloah also told McDonald he would consult Yadin and bring back proof of aggressive Arab intentions on January 28. McDonald to secretary of state, no. 62, January 27, 1950, McDonald Papers, USHMM, box 8, folder 6.

legitimate internal security or defense requirements. They could instead "facilitate re-newed aggression against Israel," especially because the Arab press was constantly calling for a "second round." As a result, Israel had to increase its own defensive capacity.[134]

McDonald commented to the State Department on January 26 that these statements were based on "1) almost angry surprise at [the] Department's statement; 2) fear of being outdistanced in armaments race in preparation for [a] 'second round;' 3) desire of [the] Army to secure public support for additional appropriations to expand defense forces."[135]

At the reception given by the Australian minister, I was amused by Fuhrman's reply to my question about the progress he was making in finding house and office in Tel Aviv. He said, "We haven't done very much here because of the possibility that we might be moving to Jerusalem." This, from the representative of the state which had taken [the] aggressive lead on behalf of complete internationalization, was ironic.[136]

Chatting with [Edouard-Félix] Guyon, I told him of Eytan's suggestion that the foreign missions now indicate to the government what their needs and desires are for houses and offices in Jerusalem. He commented, "That's naïve." To this he added, "These people are very provincial" in a tone of semi-contempt, which was perhaps not surprising from a diplomat as *protocolaire* as the French minister.

[Gene] Currivan said that there was a rumor current that the US was offering to Israel technical assistance which would amount to about half a million dollars a year. I said that I was glad for once to be able to give him some definite information, though it was not then for publication. I told him briefly of the Department's revised estimate of some forty-five experts and a larger number of trainees. I stressed that this was still only a Budget Bureau estimate and had not reached the stage of Congressional consideration.

Friday, January 27

In the late morning Otto Frederick Nolde, director of the Commission of the Churches on International Affairs [CCIA], established by the World Council of Churches and the International Missionary Council,[137] and Max Habicht,[138] the husband of my old friend Elizabeth Petersen, came to the house

134. *DFPI*, v. 5, d. 44.
135. McDonald to secretary of state, no. 59, January 26, 1950, *FRUS*, 1950, v. V, 705–706; McDonald to secretary of state, joint weeka no. 4, January 27, 1950, McDonald Papers, USHMM, box 8, folder 6.
136. "Evidently," McDonald commented to Washington, "Fuhrman has no such categorical non-recognition Jerusalem instructions as [were] sent to me." McDonald to secretary of state, no. 63, January 28, 1950, USSDCF-PIFA, 1950–1954, reel 1, frame 354.
137. Otto Frederick Nolde (1899–1972), human rights pioneer for peace within the World Council of Churches; acted as a human rights diplomat during and after World War II and influenced the language of the UN Charter.
138. Max Habicht (1899–1986), Swiss-born advocate of international law and human rights; served with League of Nations as a legal officer until World War II; as legal adviser for

with two Israeli officials. Habicht is representing the Lutheran interests in their relations with the Israeli government; Nolde is on a similar but broader and less technical mission on behalf of the Protestant churches.

Taking advantage of my visitors, I asked Nolde about the effects upon Protestant opinion of the Vatican's activities in favor of the December 9 vote in the UN Assembly. He denied Inman's interpretation. He admitted that there was an increase of Protestant uneasiness about Catholic political influence, but he did not believe this would seriously weaken the Protestant support of internationalization.

Habicht explained the desire of the Lutheran Church to work out its problems with the Israelis by informal and direct negotiations, rather than by resort to public appeals for action through the UN or other government or intergovernmental bodies. He stressed, therefore, that he and Nolde were calling on me not to elicit governmental participation, but to inform me and to be courteous and friendly. I expressed my appreciation and urged that one or both of them continue to keep me closely informed.

Padberg and Archibald and Brady came in with what they regarded as an important telegram from Damascus. According to it, a "controlled source" reported that the Syrians were fearful of moves by the Israelis on the northeastern frontier. My reading of the telegram was that it was merely a report of a rumor, and that the concluding sentence, in which the Damascus legation promised further investigation, showed that it called for no action by us. Nearly half an hour was required, however, for me to convince Padberg that this was so. Finally, the military [officers] agreed that since they were going to see Riley on Sunday, they would not make inquiries [in advance to] the Israelis.

Because of the unanticipated session with Padberg and the military attachés, there was little time to talk with Ware before the arrival of David Woodward and his wife for tea.[139] During the tea we talked about our common problems of translations of Israeli speeches, laws, decrees and other documents. Ware and Tetlie agreed that the embassy's contact with the PIO [Palestine Information Office] should be handled by the USIE.[140] There was a consensus of opinion that possibly an Anglo-American pooling arrangement might save time and money in the translation of the Knesset material, but that each of us would continue to need our own man to translate the Hebrew press and do individual jobs.

After the Woodwards had left, Ware and Tetlie stayed until after eight o'clock. The talk was of a general nature about staff organization, Ware's role, etc. He agreed at my suggestion to postpone his regular visits to the hill [new US Embassy offices at Ramat Gan] for the study of documents until after our staff conference this Wednesday afternoon at the house. At the close I had a

Swiss embassy in US during the war, he inspected POW camps in the United States; became a leader in world federalist organizations after World War II.
139. David Woodward, first secretary and press attaché, British legation, Tel Aviv.
140. United States International Informational and Educational Exchange Program.

favorable but still not very definite impression of our new public affairs officer. I hope he will prove to be a counselor of major value.

Saturday, January 28

An hour and a half at teatime with Nahum Goldmann. He, as always, was interesting and informative. His analysis of Henry Morgenthau was the best I have heard. He regards Morgenthau as a man of limited imagination, moody and at times irascible, but at others charming. Nahum confirmed Gerold Frank's report about the Morgenthau "swan song" reference to Silver. According to Nahum, Morgenthau's value in the UJA has become relatively less year-by-year, but even now it should not be underestimated. His devotion, his earnestness, and his willingness to put on the heaviest pressure make him a valuable assistant to [Henry] Montor. It is the latter, however, who, according to Nahum, is the driving force of the UJA.[141] His limitless energy, creative imagination, and the enthusiasm which he evokes—especially in the group of younger leaders such as [Abe] Feinberg, who had not previously been very active—make him irreplaceable.

Nahum's characterizations of Israeli leaders were discriminating and colorful. In particular, I was interested in his analysis of Dr. Moshe Sneh, whom he had known as a young man in Poland. Sneh is motivated by "an insane hatred" of Ben-Gurion. Ben-Gurion's removal of Sneh from [the] Haganah "without ceremony" had bitterly alienated this former favorite of the prime minister. Sneh is very brilliant but has allowed his determination to destroy Ben-Gurion politically to lead him to a much more leftish position than he genuinely believes in. Even now, Sneh is not fully trusted in Mapam, partly because of his General Zionist background and partly because of his ambition.[142]

[Daniel] Frisch's election [to presidency of the ZOA], according to Nahum, was made possible by Silver's support and Frisch's own earlier active campaign and by his appeal to the rank and file on the platform that he was one of them. Perhaps Frisch can be reelected despite Silver's present coldness or possible animosity arising from resentment at Frisch's independent life and his enthusiasm for Ben-Gurion.

As Nahum talked, I wished that he were remaining longer in Israel, because he could be invaluable in giving us, if he were willing as I think he would be, his personal characterizations of Israeli leaders for our biographical file. He is returning in April for a longer stay.

Sunday, January 29

Worked in the afternoon and then out to the Sharon for a walk along the beach during the afterglow of a gorgeous sunset.

---

141. Montor technically served under Morgenthau, the general chairman, as the executive director of the United Jewish Appeal.
142. Entry of October 13, 1948, May 24, 1949.

814 | Envoy to the Promised Land

I put in an appearance at the B'nai B'rith convention at the Ohel Shem at 9:30, as I had promised Fraenkel's assistant to do. The professor was just finishing his presidential address. I suggested that I not go on the platform until he had concluded, but the manager insisted. The applause was generous then and when I was introduced a little later. My remarks were very general and brief.

Monday, January 30

Lunch with Dr. [Benzion] Kounine.[143] He was as fluent and as dogmatic as ever on questions affecting Israel and especially on British policy. As to the latter, he was especially interesting. He interpreted UK policy as pragmatic and adjustable to changing circumstances. Always the [British] Foreign Office kept in mind an alternative to its publicly professed policies. Hence, the seeming frequent inconsistencies, which in fact are merely current adjustments of an essentially fluid and unprincipled program. Persistently, the Foreign Office approaches each question from the point of view of what will advance British economic and political interests. It is the addition of these many day-to-day adjustments and deviations which constitute British policy.

According to Kounine, the above explanation solves the mystery of local British diplomats occasionally not seeming to know what UK policy is. Though they, of course, receive from time to time specific instructions and also general statements of policy, they are not informed of the unexpressed, and perhaps at times not fully conscious, reservations in the minds of the top Foreign Office officials and cabinet members.

Kounine was very interesting about Weizmann's book. He illustrated its inaccuracy by the story of a luncheon discussion with the widow of General Wingate,[144] her mother and a close family friend, Mr. Hayes. They had been outraged by Weizmann's claim that he had been instrumental in restoring Wingate to favor in the army, whereas in fact it had been Kounine who had done this. The family [was] anxious that Kounine publish the documents, but he laughingly told them that he would do nothing of the sort. Nonetheless, Kounine agreed that Weizmann is inherently ungenerous.

I should note here that, according to Amman's report on the conference of a week ago [January 24, 1950] between Jordan and Israel, Shiloah said that Israel would withdraw from the UN rather than surrender Jerusalem, and that Samir [al-Rifai] had made a claim for a partition of the city which would have given Talbiya, the Greek Colony, and the Baka regions back to Jordan.[145]

---

143. Benzion Kounine, Russian-born physician and Zionist; became a naturalized British citizen, 1934; knew leading Zionists before and during World War II; close friend of Orde Wingate, a pro-Zionist British Army and intelligence officer who helped train the Haganah.

144. Lorna Wingate. See entries of February 26 and April 11, 1949.

145. Samir at the Israeli-Jordanian meeting of December 13, 1949, had recognized Israeli interest in the Western Wall and in access to Mount Scopus, and he expressed Jordan's interest in regaining, from the Israeli side of the armistice line through the city, Jerusalem's Arab quarters and the Bethlehem Road. The request for Talbiya, the Greek Colony, and the Baka regions were new demands made at the meeting of January 24, 1950. The Jordanian negotiators, led by Minister of

At the Foreign Office at five, I reported to Eytan Washington's instructions refusing me permission to present to members of the diplomatic corps Israel's offer of cooperation in helping missions to prepare for their housing in Jerusalem.[146] Eytan replied that Israel would now do nothing further in this regard unless specifically asked by individual missions or by the group as a whole.

Eytan thought that the Trusteeship Council consideration of Jerusalem would be intermittent during this session of the [PCC], thus allowing time for exchanges in the lobbies.[147] Eytan and Kollek promised to ask Eban to come and see me before he goes on to Geneva. Kollek promised that the arms statement tentatively scheduled for last Saturday would be ready within a day or two.

Sir Knox was at the house for about an hour. We compared notes on a number of subjects including the Jordan negotiations. As to Jerusalem and Eytan's offer of housing, Sir Knox was frankly contemptuous. Sir Knox's chief concern appeared to be the Israeli agitation about the arms supplies to Egypt and the other Arab states. He purported, in a spirit of righteous indignation, to be unable to credit that the Israelis could genuinely be worried. The "gypsies" could not, as the Israelis must know, possibly be effective no matter what arms. Sir Knox took most energetic exception to Ben-Gurion's remarks quoted in the morning *[Palestine] Post*: "not all the planes which fought us in the Negev were manned by Egyptian crews."[148] This Sir Knox considered a deliberate insult, which he bitterly resented in part because it was so "gratuitous."

Then Sir Knox asked repeatedly how the Israelis [could] seriously believe their expressions of fear. "What," he said, "could be [in] back of their charges. I would give anything to know the truth." I was unable to enlighten him. Nor was I quite able to credit 100% his expressions of indignation at Israel's "arms campaign."

Tuesday, January 31

Dr. Eduard Goldstücker came for his formal courtesy call. We talked mostly about young [Jan] Masaryk, whom he knew very well and of whom he said he was very fond.[149] He stressed the alleged elements of instability in the

Defense Fawzi al-Mulqi, wanted to tie the Jerusalem settlement to a broader Israeli-Jordanian settlement, but, because of the threat of UN action, were willing to consider a separate Jerusalem agreement. Fritzlan to secretary of state, no. 7, January 25, 1950, *FRUS*, 1950, v. V, 703–704.

146. Acheson responded to Eytan's earlier suggestion that McDonald, in his capacity as dean of the diplomatic corps, help establish foreign mission offices in Jerusalem. McDonald was told to inform Eytan that "in [the] US view it is not consistent with [the] present status [of the] UN consideration [of the] Jerusalem question for Israel to establish its capital in that city." Acheson to embassy in Israel, no. 41, January 26, 1950, *FRUS*, 1950, v. V, 706–707.

147. Garreau of the Trusteeship Council formally presented his plan for Jerusalem to the PCC in Geneva when it opened its fourth round of talks on January 30, 1950.

148. Ben-Gurion emphasized the need for quality in the armed forces. See "Test of Quality," *Palestine Post*, January 30, 1950.

149. Jan Masaryk (1886–1948), son of Czechoslovakia's first president Tomáš Masaryk (1850–1937); foreign minister of Czechoslovakia's government-in-exile in London and then in

Masaryk family strain. A young brother of Jan [Herbert Masaryk, d. 1915] is supposed to have committed suicide, and elsewhere in the family were alarming indications of psychological unbalance. Jan had never recovered from the breakup of his marriage.[150] Moreover, he was an extraordinarily sensitive personality, made more so by a secret fear that he might go mad. His outward gayness and cynicism were a cloak to cover his inner uneasiness.

Most of this analysis had an air of plausibility and may be near the truth. I would have been more inclined to credit it did it not fit in so neatly with the official Communist view that Jan committed suicide. At any rate, I found Goldstücker the first of the Iron Curtain representatives with whom I could carry on more than the most perfunctory conversation. Possibly this means that he is a front, rather than the effective Czech representative.

Mr. Benin came in for a few minutes to say goodbye. He was decidedly optimistic about increasing moderation in the foreign policy of Egypt. He thought the foreign minister, despite his public intransigence, to be less important in determining policy than his colleague Serag Eddin.[151] Meantime, Jewish businessmen were being allowed to return to Egypt to carry on their activities unhampered.

liberated Czechoslovakia's communist-dominated cabinet; found dead in courtyard of Foreign Ministry, March 1948. His death was ruled a suicide by the Czechoslovak Ministry of the Interior. Evidence that his murder was ordered by the Soviets emerged in 1990s and 2000s.

150. His marriage to Frances Crane ended in 1931.

151. Fuad Serag Eddin (1910–2000), leading figure in the Wafd Party, minister of interior and finance minister in the Nahhas cabinet.

20. February 1950

Wednesday, February 1

Dinner at the [Major Lawrence] Bradys'. We did not sit down to dinner until after 9:15. During the cocktail period Sir Knox, possibly because of the influence of a very strong martini, but more likely because of his reporting what someone else had said to him, spoke animatedly and in detail. Shiloah had just been to see him to give him an account of the meeting the week previous between Jordan and Israel [January 30, 1950].[1] I do not here report Sir Knox's account, because presumably, I shall get a first-hand account from Shiloah presently. I could discern no inclination in Sir Knox's account to color the picture. Sir Knox, in answer to my question spoke about the [Haifa] refinery strike settlement as had Waller, as a complete victory for the company [Consolidated Refineries Ltd.].[2]

Thursday, February 2

At four o'clock, the arrival of Lee Harris marked the beginning of a long afternoon and evening. Harris came to explain that the PEC [Palestine Economic Corporation] was managing [Gerard] Swope's itinerary.[3]

By 6:30 we reached the residence of Dr. [Victor] Grünwald,[4] just before the buffet was opened for the reception in honor of Dr. Goldstücker. Many Israeli officials were present, and the Iron Curtain country representatives were out in force. I chatted briefly with the Kaplans and several others and at length with the Russian minister [Pavel I. Ershov]. He was in a gay humor as we talked about several wholly non-political subjects, such as the French pictures in Moscow. My most interesting talk was with the young son of Grünwald, aged twenty, and his girlfriend, eighteen, both sabras. The girl was more radical and more anti-religious than the boy. They agreed that they would come to the house sometime when I had a small group of sabras. When I happened to say

---

1. Memorandum in *DFPI*, v. 5, d. 55.
2. A general strike at the Haifa refinery was to have begun on February 1, 1950, over the issue of criteria for workers' dismissals, but it was called off by the Haifa Labor Council.
3. Gerard Swope (1872–1957), president of General Electric, 1922–1939, 1942–1944; chairman, New York City Housing Authority, 1939–1942, working on large apartment buildings in Brooklyn and Queens for middle-income families; in 1949 and 1950 traveled to Israel and became chairman of the PEC board of directors; lauded the standard of living in Israel, urged greater generosity to United Jewish Appeal, and later created generous endowments for the Technion and Hebrew University.
4. Victor Grünwald, Czech consul in Tel Aviv.

that I had not met Dr. Moshe Sneh and would like to do so, my young friends brought him over. At the end of our chat, Sneh said he would be glad to come to the house to talk.

At 9:30 Ruth and I were at the nearby motion picture theatre for the celebration on the occasion of the recognition of Ramat Gan as a city. Shortly after I arrived, I was asked to say a few words. I spoke for three or four minutes, paying tribute to the social-minded leadership of Mayor [Avraham] Krinitzi, expressed the warm appreciation of the [US] staff and myself to the municipality for its unfailing generous cooperation, and wished long life to the mayor and success to his plans for his community. I was glad that so many of the staff, headed by Hooper, Barnes, and the military men, were in attendance. Their presence and mine will, I think, prove to have been good business, because of the appreciation which the leaders of the municipality will feel all the more, since ours was the only group of foreign service people present.

Friday, February 3

Morning especially interesting because of two long conferences first with Eban and later with Shiloah.

On January 31 Eban, Kollek, and Sharett had discussed ways of improving Israel's relations with the United States. Eban argued that Israel's main problem was the US reluctance to anger the Arab states and that Israel's clashes with the UN and the Roman Catholic Church over Jerusalem were also harmful. Israel, Eban said, must show that it was striving to integrate itself better into the Middle East.[5] Eban then visited McDonald before leaving for Geneva to head the Israeli delegation to the PCC.

Eban stayed for about an hour and a half. In answer to my questions, he first commented interestingly on a number of our American colleagues as follows: [John] Ross is able in the UN, but he fails to carry the impression of weight and of being truly representative of the power of the US, as was [Philip] Jessup;[6] McGhee is a man of large capacity and grasp of his area—he is believed to be friendly to Israel; Rusk's present role vis-à-vis Israel is uncertain; Niles is playing a larger role with more confidence now that Clifford has withdrawn; Clifford continues to be in and out of the White House, but his absence is sorely missed; Abe Feinberg is seemingly [the] outstanding Jewish personality in the White House picture; Felix Frankfurter gives no indication of playing a more active role; Murphy is, from Eban's point of view, still an unknown quantity, but Eban feels that Clifford will continue to be missed; [Stuart] Rockwell

5. Memorandum of meeting in *DFPI*, v. 5, d. 62.
6. John C. Ross replaced Philip C. Jessup as the deputy US representative on the UN Security Council in February 1949. Jessup became Acheson's ambassador-at-large.

is active and seemingly not friendly; at any rate, he continues to make unsympathetic remarks.

Eban spoke of Bunche hoping that the [Trusteeship Council], after recognizing the impracticability of the December 9 resolution [on Jerusalem], would draw up, if possible with Israel's and Jordan's benevolent approval, a compromise scheme as the basis for Assembly discussion. If this were not done and the matter were referred back to the UN Assembly merely with the report that the December 9 action could not be implemented, Israel would be in a very disadvantageous position.

In answer to my question about the effect on Protestant opinion of the Vatican December 9 success, Eban gave much the same report as that which Nolde had given.[7] He did not share Inman's view.[8] Eban said that there were evidences of undercurrents of Protestant concern, that certain leaders such as [Reinhold] Niebuhr and [Garfield] Oxnam had spoken out, but that there was no organized movement.[9]

As we both referred to the success, newspaper-wise, of the Inman mission, which despite its very scanty visit here, received headline treatment throughout the country, Eban interpreted this as a reflection of a popular uneasiness about the December 9 decision and the forces behind it. Eban thought that it would be desirable to have a number of leading clergymen come to Israel one by one rather than as a group, and, wherever possible, on their own financial responsibility or rather that of their bishop[s].

On the story of December 9, Eban had no apology for his and his colleagues' miscalculation. Hardly anyone had expected the result; [. . .] there had been some votes for the resolution motivated in part by the conviction that it would not pass. He admitted that the leadership of [Charles] Malik, who utilized so skillfully the cable to him from the Vatican, and who played so adroitly on the sensibilities of his Arab colleagues, was in large part responsible for the final result.[10]

Eban [was] interesting, too, in his evident disapproval of the spectacular reaction here to the December 9 resolution. It was easy to see that he thought the speeding up and the dramatization of the movement of offices to Jerusalem

7. Entry of January 27, 1950.
8. Entry of January 9, 1950.
9. Reinhold Niebuhr (1892–1971), American Protestant theologian and anticommunist intellectual; supported Jewish immigration to Palestine and a Jewish state in 1946. See Goda et al. eds., *To the Gates of Jerusalem*, entry of January 14, 1946. Garfield Bronley Oxnam (1891–1963), Methodist anticommunist theologian. Both Niebuhr and Oxnam stood with the Roman Catholic Church in its anticommunism, but both were concerned regarding the Church's interventions in Jerusalem and both were invited to Israel later in 1950. See Carenen, *The Fervent Embrace*, 71–78; and Jonathan P. Herzog, *The Spiritual-Industrial Complex: America's Religious Battle Against Communism in the Early Cold War* (New York: Oxford University Press, 2011).
10. On the eve of the December 9 vote in the General Assembly, Lebanese delegate Charles Malik sent a cable to the Vatican citing rumors that the Vatican was not vitally interested in the Jerusalem question. The pope answered immediately to the contrary and urged Malik to ensure that all delegations understood the Vatican's concerns. Sharett credited the pope's message with swinging the vote against Israel. Bialer, *Cross on the Star of David*, 25.

and the subsequent Knesset declaration were unnecessary and, in part, self-defeating. Many countries, he said, had been voted down in the UN Assembly without raising such a fuss about it. On the other hand, Eban agreed that Ben-Gurion is the outstanding, natural leader, that he had saved Sharett in [the] general debate, and that probably some action had been required of the sort Ben-Gurion took.[11] I had [the impression] that Eban was suffering from the effects of overstrain, but this impression may be the result of my lack of intimate acquaintance with him.

The Shiloah interview, which began at one and lasted for an hour, concerned the meeting the previous week with the Jordanian delegates at the king's winter palace [January 30, 1950]. The inclusion this time of members of the Jordanian cabinet broadened the base [and] gave it a more official character, but tended to make negotiations more difficult.[12] At the beginning, Jordan failed to agree with Shiloah's proposal that the two delegations present a united front to the [Trusteeship Council] on Jerusalem. Then, the discussion centered for the rest of the period until after 2:00 am on schemes for [the] Jerusalem partition. The most difficult point appears to be the Jordanian demand for the return of the former Arab sections in the south. To meet this, Shiloah and Dayan presented three possible plans: 1) [financial] compensation to enable the rebuilding of Arab areas elsewhere; 2) mild adjustments of existing lines; 3) a solid Jewish access to [Mount] Scopus with Arab compensation to the southeast. A so-called "kissing point" in the north would protect the Arab Nablus Road and that of the Jews to Scopus.[13]

Before I drafted my telegram, I had read Amman's telegram to the Department, which reported without recommendation Kirkbride's suggestion that the time had come for UK-US "assistance" in the negotiations.[14] I made a contrary recommendation in my comment.

McDonald reported Shiloah's statement that Abdullah displayed "great anxiety for progress," that the king seemed willing to abandon the idea of a corridor across Israel, and that he appealed to both sides to "work and work and work until success."

11. Refers to the Knesset debate of December 13, 1949. Begin and others blamed the UN vote on Sharett's moderation and miscalculations. Ben-Gurion ignored the criticisms. Netanel Lorch, ed., *Major Knesset Debates, 1948–1981*, v. 2, 560–565.
12. The cabinet members present were Samir al-Rifai, Fawzi al-Mulqi, and two Palestinians, Khulusi al-Khayri (minister of public works) and Radi Hijdawiv (mayor of Jerusalem). The problem, as McDonald reported, was that all were not equally trusted by the king.
13. See also the proposals and counterproposals in the meeting summary in *DFPI*, v. 5, d. 55; McDonald to secretary of state, no. 76, February 4, 1950, USSDCF-PIFA, 1950–1954, reel 1, frames 360–362. The Jordanians refused to allow Israeli sovereignty over the Jewish section of the Old City and insisted that, though the Israelis could have access to Mount Scopus, it would remain part of Jordanian territory.
14. The US embassy in Amman thought that negotiations over Jerusalem would succeed but that general peace negotiations were deadlocked. The State Department believed that the main stumbling block was the issue of Jordan's proposed corridor to the Mediterranean, but disagreed that US intervention would bring agreement any more quickly. Fritzlan to secretary of state, no. 12, February 1, 1950, *FRUS*, v. V, 716–718; Acheson to US legation in Jordan, no. 13, February 3, 1949, *FRUS*, 1950, v. V, 721.

Abdullah urged the Israelis to consider the pressure on him from Palestinian Arabs and thus to be generous. McDonald commented, "I doubt [the] wisdom [of] any UK or US intervention . . . at [the] present stage."[15]

Saturday, February 4

At teatime Sir Robert Waley-Cohen and his son, Bernard,[16] with Eli [Karlin], were at the house. Sir Robert's chief contribution was his insistence that the time had come when the US government should put pressure on American capital to invest largely in [the] Near East, and at the beginning, chiefly in Israel as the most immediate and creative region. I was a bit amused to note his rather stubborn insistence that despite his present enthusiasm, he is not sure that he is "a Zionist."

Sunday, February 5

Took Eli with me on the way to the Foreign Office at 4:30, where I saw Eytan while Eli went on down to the hotel. Eytan, I thought, was a little casual about the *Hador* leak.[17]

As to the two islands at the mouth of the Gulf of Aqaba which the Egyptians had a few days previously informed the American embassy that they had taken over with the full approval of [the] Saudi Arabian government, because of "certain pretentions of the Israelis,"[18] Eytan replied he "had to strain his memory" to recall their names. He had noted them when flying over the mouth of the gulf on his visit to Aden, but he assured me that his government had "no interest whatsoever in them." I was not quite convinced.[19]

As to the meeting of the night before of the two [Israeli and Jordanian] delegations [February 3, 1950], this time in new Jerusalem, [Eytan] said he thought I had better get the complicated story from Shiloah.[20] Eytan thought

---

15. McDonald to secretary of state, no. 76, February 4, 1950, USSDCF-PIFA, 1950–1954, reel 1, frames 360–362.

16. Robert Waley-Cohen (1877–1952), British Jewish oil magnate, philanthropist, civic leader, and president of the United Synagogue. An anti-Zionist, he nevertheless founded the Palestine Economic Corporation. See Breitman et al., eds., *Advocate for the Doomed*, 272, 280, 417; Breitman et al., eds., *Refugees and Rescue*, 2, 55; Goda et al., eds., *To the Gates of Jerusalem*, 53. On Bernard, see entry of May 28, 1949.

17. Entry of December 21, 1949. Following McDonald's informal protests to Eytan concerning the leak in the Mapai newspaper *Hador* on December 21, 1949, the State Department ordered him on February 3 to make a more formal protest, pointing to possible damage to Israeli-Arab talks at Geneva. Acheson to McDonald, no. 52, February 3, 1950, *FRUS*, 1950, v. V, 721.

18. Tiran and Sanafir, located in the Straits of Tiran, linking the Red Sea with the Gulf of Aqaba. The islands were occupied by Egypt with the agreement of Saudi Arabia on January 28, 1950, ostensibly to protect them from Israel. The straits already had been closed to Israeli shipping and remained so until 1957. Caffery to secretary of state, no. 102, January 30, 1950, *FRUS*, 1950, v. V, 711; and Eitan Barak, "Between Reality and Secrecy: Israel's Freedom of Navigation Through the Straits of Tiran, 1957–1967," *Middle East Journal* 61, no. 4 (Autumn 2007): 657–679.

19. Ben-Gurion officially disavowed Israeli interest in the islands on January 9, 1950. Eytan to McDonald, February 14, 1950, McDonald Papers, USHMM, box 8, folder 7.

20. Entry of February 7, 1950.

that the decisive meeting would be this week, perhaps Tuesday or Wednesday. Eytan had no comment on the Export-Import Bank loan allocation for development in new Jerusalem.[21]

Our large dinner for the Swopes went off well. Besides the guests of honor were present the Max Greenbergs [of General Electric], the Kaplans, the Persitzes, the [Harry] Vollmers, [and] Sam Sacks. Swope and Kaplan had an excellent opportunity for talk.[22] The guests as a whole enjoyed the good meal and the ladies very especially the warmth of the living room. This last was the more sensational because of the historic blizzard, which had then begun.[23]

Monday, February 6

Frigid in the house, with very little power and no furnace in operation. The heavy snow and thick hail-like snow drops in the later morning made the outdoor scene one reminiscent of an old-fashioned American winter. But how the country must be suffering. Huge losses in orchards and gardens, and pitiful exposure in the [immigrants'] camps in tents and unheated barracks. To cap the accumulation of near disasters came Shalom with his graphic tale of the burning of the El Al DC-4 in the early morning hours at Lydda and of the miraculous escape of all the passengers and crew.[24] Busy all day with Miss Clark despite the frigidity. In the late afternoon welcomed the returning heat and the restoration of telephone service.

Tuesday, February 7

An hour's conference with Shiloah. He outlined the meeting with [the] J[ordanians] on the night of the third. Samir [al-Rifai] and [Fawzi al-] Mulqi[25] (without the Palestinian [delegate], whose absence Shiloah thought helpful), proposed access to Jewish quarters [of the] Old City and Wailing Wall and to [Mount] Scopus, if [the] latter remained [part of] Arab territory.[26] This [offered] less than proposed in [the] Garreau scheme.[27] In answer to [the] Jorda-

21. On February 3, 1950, the US Export-Import Bank announced a credit installment of $20 million, which brought the total money allocated to $93.35 million out of the initial loan agreement of $100 million. The February allocation was to be used for housing and infrastructural developments for recent immigrants, including in Jerusalem. A memorandum by Troxel noted internally that this announcement ran counter to the State Department's policy toward Jerusalem, which was to avoid any step implying acknowledgment of Israeli sovereignty over the city. He continued, "It makes our caution look downright ridiculous. If the Ambassador should decide to ask for a relaxation of the restrictions imposed on our actions, he has an excellent talking point. The recognition implied by the Bank's action is probably greater than any we could take short of moving the Embassy to Jerusalem." McDonald Papers, USHMM, box 8, folder 7.
22. Reported in McDonald to secretary of state, no. 78, February 6, 1950, McDonald Papers, USHMM, box 8, folder 7.
23. Snow measured forty centimeters in Jerusalem and seventeen centimeters in Haifa on February 6, 1950.
24. The airplane, named *Herzl*, crashed on takeoff for Europe and burned.
25. Fawzi al-Mulqi (1910–1962), Jordanian minister of defense, 1950; later ambassador to London and prime minister, 1953–1954.
26. For meeting see *DFPI*, v. 5, d. 73.
27. The Jordanians offered Israeli access to Mount Scopus, the Jewish Quarter, and the Western Wall. The Garreau Plan offered access to these points, as well as to the Mount of Olives.

nian question, Shiloah repeated three alternate plans, suggested at previous meetings. The first of these, the radical solution, making the north [of Jerusalem] Jewish and the south Arab, was rejected, and in its [place] Samir suggested [a] combination of [the] second and third plans, by which there would be partial restoration of Arab property in the south with compensation for that not returned.[28] This concept was accepted by Shiloah, but only on condition that it be clearly understood by both sides that the property returned be nominal, and that the settlement be final for the city.

In support of their position, Shiloah argued that the first Jordanian proposal would satisfy not at all the Israeli demand[s][29] and would do nothing to preclude political internationalization. It was finally agreed that another meeting would be held within a few days, this time to try to break the deadlock of repeated inconclusive meetings by finding a practical basis of agreement, which could then be worked out in detail by continuous session[s] over several days.

Shiloah thinks the king is influenced by three considerations: desire for final settlement, financial offer, and his worry about [the] Garreau plan. Shiloah thinks [the] king will be able to get [the] P[alestinian] A[rab] group to support [a] settlement.[30] Rather to my surprise, Shiloah seemed to think that UK and US intervention might be helpful. In this connection he told me what I had not known before, that he had spoken to Riley about his [Riley's] taking the initiative in seeing the king. Later, however, Israel had written directly to the king suggesting reopening negotiations, so that Abdullah might not feel that his approach to the UN, to Trygve Lie, to Eban, were being used to humiliate him.[31]

Both the Israeli government and King Abdullah hoped to reach agreement on Jerusalem before the UN Trusteeeship Council began its discussions in Geneva on February 6. Abdullah was said to favor acceding to Israeli demands. On February 11, however, Abdullah's governing cabinet rejected the concession of territory to Israel in the Old City.[32]

28. Shiloah's three proposals are outlined in McDonald to secretary of state, no. 76, February 4, 1950, USSDCF-PIFA, 1950–1954, reel 1, frames 360–362.
29. The Israelis demanded for the first time sovereignty over the Old City's Jewish Quarter and the Western Wall, as well as full sovereignty over, and not just access to, Mount Scopus. The Jordanians rejected these demands, though they remained willing to grant access, and King Abdullah remained hopeful that an agreement could be reached. For additional details, see Fritzlan to secretary of state, no. 17, February 7, 1950, FRUS, 1950, v. V, 727–728.
30. To sweeten the pill of Jordan's annexation of Palestinian territory, Abdullah had awarded three cabinet posts to Palestinian Arabs in 1949, and during the Shuneh negotiations with the Israelis that began in December 1949, the Jordanian delegation had two pro-Hashemite Palestinian Arabs from the prominent Tuqan clan, Khulusi al-Khayri and Jamal Tuqan.
31. In his report McDonald suggested informal parallel approaches by the United Kingdom and United States to King Abdullah and Ben-Gurion, respectively. McDonald to secretary of state, no. 86, February 7, 1950, USSDCF-PIFA, 1950–1954, reel 1, frames 366–368.
32. Fritzlan to secretary of state, no. 20, February 10, 1950, FRUS, 1950, v. V, 735; Fritzlan to secretary of state, no. 22, February 13, 1950; Gibson to secretary of state, no. 50, February 16, 1950, FRUS, 1950, v. V, 741–742, 745–746.

I was surprised rather that Shiloah had no criticism to make of Kirkbride's suggestion of possible UK-US intervention. He intimated that he would favor US action, but said that any suggestion to this effect would have to come from the prime minister or the foreign minister. As to the PCC, Shiloah limited himself to speaking enthusiastically about [Paul A.] Porter and favorably about [Ely E.] Palmer and [James W.] Barco.[33] The latter [Barco] he termed open-minded and thorough. He even had good words to say about Mark Ethridge. In connection with [the] Middle East, Shiloah confessed that, in his opinion, a good deal of the responsibility for the PCC's early attitude of seeming hostility to Israel, and of the Department's coldness towards Israel, lay with Ben-Gurion and Sharett. Granted that Israel expected little from the PCC, it was, Shiloah argued, all the more important that it be treated with respect in this consideration. It was especially important that individuals on the PCC should not have felt that they were being handled casually and as if they were of no consequence. In this analysis Shiloah showed again his usual intelligence and understanding.

Before Shiloah left, I drew him out on the relations between Ben-Gurion and the Mapam. Shiloah thinks that the leaders of Mapam—other than Sneh, [but including] [Yitzhak] Ben-Aharon,[34] Yisrael Galili,[35] Yitzhak Tabenkin,[36] Ya'akov Chasan,[37] and Mordechai Bentov are anxious for a settlement.[38] They have a sense of frustration in opposition, and their whole record would lead them to want to work affirmatively. Sneh, because of his intense bitterness towards Ben-Gurion, would fight [an] agreement, but rather than go into the wilderness or openly join the Communists, he might remain in the party.

In answer to my inquiry about Sharett's health, Shiloah commented that they were more concerned that Ben-Gurion should get a rest. The latter characteristically had expressed the desire to go to Greece, where he could continue

<hr />

33. See entries of May 26, 1949, November 27, 1949. From Geneva, Rafael and Eban had reported that Palmer and Barco were cautiously optimistic concerning the possibility of direct Israeli-Egyptian negotiations and that they planned to appeal to the Egyptian government to grant Mun'im the authority to negotiate. They also communicated their hope that bilateral negotiations between Israel and the Arab states would be more effective than multilateral talks. *DFPI*, v. 5, d. 76, 86, 90.

34. Entry of March 20, 1949.

35. Yisrael Galili (1911–1986) Ukrainian-born left-wing politician; emigrated to Palestine, 1914; head of national Haganah headquarters, 1946–1948; member of Knesset 1949–1951 (Mapam), 1955–1977 ('Ahdut HaAvoda); minister of information, 1966–1969.

36. Yitzhak Tabenkin (1888–1971), Belorussian-born left-wing politician; emigrated to Palestine, 1912; helped found kibbutz movement; withdrew from Mapai, 1944; member of Knesset, 1949–1951 (Mapam, 'Ahdut HaAvoda).

37. Ya'akov Hazan (1899–1992), Belorussian-born left-wing politician; emigrated to Palestine, 1923; member of Knesset, 1949–1974 (Mapam, Alignment).

38. In February 1950 Mapam negotiated with Mapai leaders to join the governing coalition. Mapai negotiated with the General Zionists as well. The Orthodox Bloc was boycotting cabinet meetings because of differences over religious education in the immigrant camps. McDonald reported that the threat by the Orthodox Bloc to wreck the coalition had induced Mapam and the General Zionists to ask for additional concessions from Mapai. Mapam broke off negotiations in March 1950. McDonald to secretary of state, joint weeka no. 7, February 20, 1950, McDonald Papers, USHMM, box 8, folder 7.

his Greek studies. This being obviously impossible, plans were being made for him to take a fortnight off somewhere in semi-hiding on the Sea of Galilee.[39]

At teatime came Ware and Tetlie with four members of the Executive Committee of the Israel-America [Friendship] League[40] [including] S. Z. Abramov,[41] Dr. Baruch Osnia,[42] and Dr. Aryeh Altman. The first half hour or so was devoted through my initiative to talk about Mapam and Mapai with special attention to the diverse elements in Mapam. One received the impression that the three sections of Mapam had not coalesced; that there was no single leadership and that therefore, Ben-Gurion might succeed—if that [is] his purpose—in splitting the party.

Dr. Osnia spoke at some length about the educational purposes of the Israel-America [Friendship] League, mutual education, etc. I said that I was sure that Ware and Tetlie would aid in every practicable way. Halfway through, Altman launched into a detailed and frank discussion of the society's political but not partisan purpose, to work towards a Western orientation of Israel's foreign policy. His colleagues joined him in this presentation. They seemed much encouraged by Sharett's friendly reception of them a day or two earlier, at which time he had told them that he wholly approved of their political purpose, that since Mapam and the Communists were avowedly working for an Eastern orientation, it was desirable that there should be efforts made in the other direction.[43]

At the end of the long session, I still felt that the Israel-America [Friendship] League, while useful and desirable, is not likely to exercise any large influence. Abramov seemed to me the most original of the four. Tetlie tells me he is worth cultivating. Later, I was intrigued by McVicker's ingenious, but I am not convinced sound, theory that Sharett's friendly reception to the Israel-America [Friendship League] was motivated in part by Sharett's desire to gain support in what McVicker says (that he has heard [in] rumors) is the threatened, if not growing, cleavage between the foreign minister and Ben-Gurion.

39. For McDonald's account of this meeting see McDonald to secretary of state, no. 86, February 7, 1950, *FRUS*, 1950, v. V, 729–730.
40. Entry of July 25, 1949.
41. Shneor Zalman Abramov (1908–1997), Minsk-born politician; emigrated to Palestine, 1920; headed Israel-America Friendship League, 1950–1964; member of Knesset, 1959–1977 (General Zionists, Gahal, Likud).
42. Baruch Osnia [formerly Eisenstadt] (1905–1994), Pinsk-born politician; emigrated to Palestine from Danzig, 1933; member of Knesset, 1951–1969 (Mapai).
43. Recent communist agitation included demonstrations in Tel Aviv on January 28 and 30 that led to the use of police force; a bitter subsequent debate in the Knesset on February 1; a communist sit-in at the Jewish Agency office in Tel Aviv leading to police removal of the demonstrators on February 5; and a similar sit-in at the Histadrut Agricultural Center from February 7–12. McDonald to secretary of state, joint weekly no. 5, February 3, 1950; McDonald to secretary of state, joint weeka no. 6, February 10, 1950, both in McDonald Papers, USHMM, box 8, folder 7.

Mr. Bornstein of CARE came to tell of the arrival next week of Paul Comly French, executive director.[44]

Rabbi Isaac Klein, recently religious adviser to the US Army in Germany, and his wife [Henrietta] came for tea.[45] He is going to study here especially religious developments. Klein was pessimistic about German opinion towards the West and peace. He found even "good Germans" quite "unreconstructed." Illustrative of basic Teutonic psychology, he quoted extracts from the writings of Dr. Kohler, the distinguished Jewish [*sic*] authority on international law, to the effect that German civilization, education and intelligence were all vastly superior to those of the West.[46]

Nearly an hour's talk with [Raleigh] Gibson [US consul general, Jerusalem] before lunch. I found Gibson most sympathetic and understanding. Gibson indicated, without saying so directly, that he would be happy when [William] Burdett had gone. The latter had so concentrated on the political side of his mission that regular consular functions had been neglected. Moreover, Burdett's very strong bias is probably an embarrassment to Gibson. I am sure that working with Gibson will be much easier and give much better results than with his junior predecessor.

At five Kollek and Miss Herlitz came in for a long, nearly an hour conference. They brought with them the delayed data about Arab rearmament "in preparation for the second round." It was in the form of [a] carefully drafted lengthy aide-mémoire. After we had read it out loud and a number of questions had been asked about it, Colonel Archibald led in a rather slashing attack on the Israeli policy of secrecy about its own armaments, which, he argued, made it difficult, if not impossible, for the US government to argue effectively with the British about their policy of rearming Egypt and the other Arab states. This led to a discussion of the practicability of a less secretive Israel policy, with Kollek admitting some weaknesses in his colleagues' attitude and promising to work towards a larger openness.

As to the aide-mémoire, it was agreed that we would airgram it to the Department, but would reserve our comments until the colonel and the major had a chance to talk to the Israeli Army.

The Israeli aide-mémoire discussed rearmament programs in the Arab states in light of recent public statements, including one by Egyptian Foreign Minister Mu-

44. Paul Comly French (1903–1960), Quaker activist, pacifist, and writer; executive director of CARE, 1947–1955.
45. Isaac Klein (1905–1979), Hungarian-born US Conservative rabbi; holder of Harvard Ph.D. in Judaic Studies and a leading scholar on Jewish law; chosen by President Truman to advise on Jewish religious affairs for US High Commissioner in Germany, 1950–1951.
46. Possibly Josef Kohler (1849–1919), eminent German jurist and authority on comparative legal systems.

hammad Salah al-Din: "*The primary condition for the return of the Arab refugees is the ejection of the Jews from Israel. The Arabs are preparing for their return to their homeland as masters, not as slaves. In other words, they are preparing to finish off the State of Israel.*"[47]

McDonald commented, "Israel prefers [to] cling to [the] doubtful benefit of [a] policy of complete secrecy on all [military] matters. Prognostications of [a] 'second round' might be [an] attempted formula [to] obtain more dollar assistance from [the] US and/or actual anxiety [to] stop [an] arms race because [of an] inability to compete successfully."[48]

On February 13 in Washington, Ambassador Elath, using the arguments of the aide-mémoire, *formally requested additional licenses for the purchase of arms.*[49]

Friday, February 10

Surprising telephone call from Kollek to tell me of the Near East Broadcasting report from Cyprus that the Egyptian Minister of War [Mustafa Nasrat Bey] had announced that there would be peace negotiations between Israel and Egypt beginning February 26, the first anniversary of the armistice. Later Kollek called to say that Reuters had an even more optimistic story, but that the UP and AP had what Kollek regarded as a more realistic one.

In answer to my question as to what background the Foreign Office had, Kollek replied in effect "none." He added that it seemed likely that this news meant that the Egyptians had merely intended to refer to the armistice anniversary as the logical time for resumption of negotiations. Kollek thought it encouraging that an Egyptian spokesman talked so optimistically about the MAC [Mixed Armistice Commission] and the current relations along the frontier.

McDonald reported to Washington Sharett's comment that evening that Mustafa Nasrat's statements concerning peace talks were a "complete misunderstanding" and that "Israel knows nothing [repeat] nothing about such [negotiations]." Sharett regarded the rumors as "merely [a] mistake by [an] uninformed [Egyptian] official."[50]

47. The aide-mémoire, "Arab Threats of a Second Round," is in McDonald Papers, USHMM, box 8, folder 7.

48. McDonald to secretary of state, joint weeka no. 7, February 20, 1950, McDonald Papers, USHMM, box 8, folder 7.

49. Until then the United States had granted export licenses to Israel and the Arab states only for equipment deemed necessary for defense and the maintenance of internal order. Elath reported that, though Truman seemed sympathetic to Israel's arguments, the president was unwilling to contradict Acheson. In the State Department's view there was no evidence of serious Arab preparation for another round of war. Moreover, the Arab governments were protesting US arms sales to Israel, claiming that Israel had aggressive intentions. *DFPI*, v. 5, d. 88, 98, 99, 104, 117; see also memorandum of conversation by Stuart Rockwell, February 6, 1950; Elath to Acheson, No. 1240/50, February 13, 1950, *FRUS*, 1950, v. V, 723–726, as well as 736–741, 759, 763–766, 773, 776, 778–781, 789–793, 799–802.

50. McDonald to secretary of state, no. 95, February 12, 1950, McDonald Papers, USHMM, box 8, folder 7; see also McDonald to secretary of state, no. 105, February 13, 1950, USSDCF-PIFA, 1950–1954, reel 1, frame 370.

Saturday, February 11

Work on the manuscript[51] until the UJA group, headed by Louis Nizer, arrived.[52] The group included representatives from nine or ten of the industrial or trade groups of New York City.

At night the first real diplomatic party in Israel was given by the French minister [Guyon] in their large Arab house in Jaffa. There must have been eighty or more present—the diplomatic corps less those from the Iron Curtain countries, higher officials from the Foreign Office, and a few Tel Aviv private citizens. The buffet was in the best pre-war French tradition, with champagne served lavishly.

The only business I transacted was to have Eytan tell me that the report of Egyptian-Israel "peace negotiations" on the anniversary of the armistice was "news to him."

Sunday, February 12

With Ruth to the symphony to hear the program which we had missed. The Beethoven Third was well played. The new Israel Concerto by [Paul] Ben-Haim[53] with [Frank] Pelleg[54] at the piano was better than I had heard it described. The final Berlioz Benvenuto Cellini Overture would have been more impressive had it followed a less noisy piece.

Monday, February 13

Koussevitzky arrived on the early morning plane with his wife and assistant conductor [Howard Shanet].[55] At the same time came Edward G. Robinson.[56] I satisfied the protocol by sending letters of welcome to both celebrities, urging Koussevitzky to come for supper and Robinson as soon as he could.

Late morning Rabbi Jacob Herzog came to talk about the Jerusalem situation and its implications. He is sorely troubled by the turn of events, and is convinced that the [Roman Catholic] Church feels that a third world war is inevitable and [that the Church is] the only means of checking communism. He quoted one of our mutual friends to this effect. He is convinced that those

---

51. McDonald began drafting his memoirs during his free hours.
52. Louis Nizer (1902–1994), London-born New York trial lawyer; general counsel to the Motion Picture Association of America and representative of numerous celebrities; philanthropist active in Jewish causes, particularly the United Jewish Appeal, in which he headed the speakers committee. Nizer headed a delegation of New York businessmen who traveled to Israel in February 1950 to survey current needs.
53. Paul Ben-Haim (1897–1984), Munich-born Israeli composer; emigrated to Palestine, 1933; composed Israeli national music. McDonald may be referring to his 1950 piano concerto.
54. Frank Pelleg [formerly Pollak] (1910–1968), Czech-born Israeli pianist, harpsichordist, composer; emigrated to Israel, 1936.
55. Serge Koussevitzky, at the time the conductor of the Boston Symphony Orchestra, was to conduct the Israeli Philharmonic for four weeks. Howard Shanet (1918–2006), Brooklyn-born US conductor and composer who conducted with Koussevitzky after World War II and with Leonard Bernstein in the 1950s.
56. Edward G. Robinson (1893–1973), Romanian-born American actor; supported Israel through United Jewish Appeal.

who hold this view find in Jerusalem the unique slogan around which to rally world opinion. No other issue could possibly be so useful.

Herzog sees this issue being used to cut across all party lines at home and as a means to whip the president into an acquiescent mood. Herzog thinks the threat endangers the unity of the Democratic Party. In his opinion the whole strategy is self-defeating because [. . .] it will open for Communist penetration [. . .] this part of the world and [because of] the disruptive effect it will have upon the Greek Orthodox Church, which in desperation will have no choice except to turn to Moscow. The only possible check to the strategy, he fears, would be for the US government to refuse to play the game in Jerusalem. I could have no doubt of Herzog's sincerity, no matter how much I might question the soundness of his interpretation.

At 4:30 General Riley came and stayed until after six. Our talk covered, among others, the following items:

1) The [Egyptian-Israeli] MAC issues in the south centering about Umm Rashrash [now Eilat] and Bir Qattar [outpost seven kilometers north of Eilat].[57] On the first, [Riley] took the Israeli point of view because Umm Rashrash was east of the dividing [Egyptian-Israeli] armistice line; on the second point, he sided with the Egyptians since the occupation of the disputed Bir Qattar was a clear violation of the armistice.[58] In a recent talk with Sharett, General Riley had urged the Jews to evacuate both points if they wished to have a chance to start direct peace talks with Egypt. In reply, Sharett had said that he could not believe that to yield in this way to "Egyptian intransigence" was the way to peace. Riley countered by stressing the importance to Israel of such peace talks.
2) The Jordanian-Israeli talks had virtually broken down in Riley's opinion. Neither side was willing to make any large concessions essential to agreement.[59]

57. On February 5, 1950, the Egyptian government accused Israel of having violated the Egyptian-Israeli armistice during the previous year's occupation of Umm Rashrash (reestablished as Eilat) and Bir Qattar (renamed Ein Netafim) during Operation Uvda. The latter had been a border post between the Ottoman and British Empires before World War I. The Egyptians said that peace was impossible unless the Israelis ended their occupation. Caffery to secretary of state, no. 126, February 5, 1950, *FRUS, 1950*, v. V, 722.

58. Riley's reasoning was that Bir Qattar's occupation took place in March 1949 after the Egyptian-Israeli armistice agreement. Bir Qattar was located within the Jewish state's 1947 boundaries, but was in the western zone of the Negev as defined by the armistice. Israeli forces were to have been withdrawn from this zone, save for defensive forces in the settlements, so the legality of the Israeli occupation was disputed in the Egyptian-Israeli MAC. See Riley's progress report to the UN Secretary-General, S/1459, February 20, 1950, McDonald Papers, USHMM, box 8, folder 8.

59. Jordanian-Israeli negotiations on the status of Jerusalem continued in Shuneh, but their talks in the PCC had deadlocked on the issues of general borders, refugees, compensation, corridors across Israeli territory, and the division of Jerusalem. King Abdullah faced Palestinian and general Arab anger if he made peace without broad Israeli concessions. See *DFPI*, v. 5, d. 74, 97, 100.

3) Riley was also pessimistic about [the] possibility of the Trusteeship Council making a practical Jerusalem proposal. He thought the Garreau scheme was clearly beyond the competence of the Trusteeship Council since it was so inconsistent with the December 9 resolution. That decision was also unworkable, and therefore he [saw] no light ahead.[60]

4) General Riley does not believe that there will be a "second round"; neither side wants it or can afford it; the Egyptian and other Arab states' rearmaments are largely replacements and are not sufficient for offensive purposes.

5) I was somewhat surprised that General Riley thought that the two islands which the Egyptians occupied a fortnight or so ago were in the Gulf of Aqaba itself, instead of being at the narrow bottleneck channel from the Gulf to the Red Sea. I suggested that General Riley call at the office the next morning, where the attachés would show him the recent Israel arms memo.

[Edward G.] Robinson with his entourage came in time to overlap a little [with] Riley's [visit]. There is little to report about Robinson's stay, except that he seemed intensely and intelligently interested in Israel and grateful for our talk. The [Reuvin] Rubins were acting as his hosts. Robinson asked if there was anything he could possibly do for me, and I answered in the negative.

Tuesday, February 14

At 9:00 Sir Knox came in to ask whether I had any specific program in mind to supplement my suggestion to the Department a few days before, that it might consider consulting with the UK about offering good offices on both sides of the Jordan. I had suggested parallel [intervention] on the East [Jordan] and unilateral on the West [Israel]. I replied that I had nothing definite in mind, but that in the light of Kirkbride's earlier suggestion and Shiloah's receptiveness, it might be useful to show US-UK encouragement.

In the late afternoon Major [Abraham S.] Hyman, assistant for several years to the advisers on Jewish affairs to the US military commanders in Germany, visited the house.[61] He was very pessimistic about any betterment of German opinion [and] cited a number of examples of complete intransigence and even of German Jews prepared to follow in the old Hitlerian pattern.

Wednesday, February 15

At twelve, Morris Morgenstern, a banker of New York, here with the UJA delegation but unable to come the previous Saturday because of his unwillingness

---

60. Both the Israeli and Jordanian delegations at the PCC opposed internationalization, and the other Arab states opposed the Garreau Plan. The State Department, meanwhile, argued that an Israeli-Jordanian arrangement was sufficient only if it had Vatican approval. See *DFPI*, v. 5, d. 94, 95, 97, 101, 110.

61. Abraham S. Hyman (1904–1995), artillery officer; assistant adviser on Jewish Affairs to Commander of US Forces in Europe, August 1946–October 1949; adviser on Jewish Affairs to US High Commissioner for Germany, October–December 1949.

to ride on Shabbat, was a welcome visitor.[62] In an old-fashioned but extremely friendly way he expressed warm appreciation of "the honor" done him by permitting him to come.

At 5:30, Hooper brought in Messrs. Frank Ryan and K. W. Banta[63] of the World [Commerce Corporation] set up by Stettinius. At the same time came Charles C. Crooks of the ECA [Economic Cooperation Administration]. Crooks told of the sharp rise in efficiency of the Haifa port expected with the new equipment supplied by the Export-Import Bank.[64] The other visitors spoke of their negotiations with Kaplan and Shertok for $10,000,000 worth of surplus American food commodities.

Thursday, February 16

Terribly sorry to have Padberg call me with the news of the sudden death of his father.

Shiloah and Kollek came at six forty-five [at McDonald's request].

Their meeting concerned the next round of Israeli-Jordanian negotiations, to commence the following day. McDonald reported, "Shiloah said he is not optimistic. Confident King still wants agreement but fears he may not be able to build [a] Cabinet willing to take responsibility for agreement with Israel."[65]

The press ball was so extraordinary that no one could possibly wish to have it repeated. Over 2,000 people crowded Habimah for the rather interesting program of local stars. The highlight, however, was Edward G. Robinson, who spoke briefly in Hebrew, a little longer in Yiddish, and dangerously long in English. I thought the speech too wordy and sentimental for its audience, but when I heard portions of it a second time on Kol Israel, I thought it better. At any rate, it was well received.

Friday, February 17

Conference at 12 with Begin and [Shmuel] Katz. I promised them that I would follow up on the effort to get a reversal by the Department of its policy of exclusion of former Irgunists. In return, Begin promised not to raise, as he

---

62. Morris Morgenstern (1882–1969), financier and philanthropist; set up the Morris Morgenstern foundation in 1949.

63. Kenneth W. Banta (1893–1969), New York officer for World Commerce Corporation; corresponded with, among others, Hermann Joseph Abs, a German industrialist formerly associated with Albert Speer. Christopher Kobrak, *Die deutsche Bank und die USA: Geschäft und Politik von 1870 bis Heute* (Munich: C. H. Beck, 2008), 582, n. 98.

64. The Haifa port was congested partly because of the large volume of US machinery imports and Israeli citrus exports. Crooks, a member of the ECA staff in Paris, visited to advise the Israeli government on the best ways to expand operations with the harbor equipment purchased from the United States with money from the $100 million Export-Import Bank loan. JTA *Bulletin*, February 20, 1950.

65. McDonald to secretary of state, no. 119, February 17, 1950, *FRUS*, 1950, v. V, 747–748.

had planned to do, the issue in the Knesset. We then talked about a number of subjects, including [David] Courtney. Begin holds that Courtney is a part of UK intelligence. In reply to my expression of disbelief, Begin argued that there are basic differences of interest between [the] US and UK; that the latter is fearful of American aims in Egypt, Iraq and Syria; and that the UK has not reconciled itself to the US special position in Saudi Arabia. I listened with much interest, but continued indications that I was not convinced.

[Turkish Minister Seyfullah] Esin wanted, as usual, to check his impressions. He was of the opinion that the Arab states have not given up their hopes of revenge. His people's reports from Egypt, Iraq, and elsewhere were not reassuring. As usual, he listened with flattering attention to my appraisals of current developments.

Saturday, February 18

Paula called to ask why I hadn't been to see "the old man." I replied that I had not wanted to bother him [while he took a three-week leave of absence for health reasons]. She urged Ruth and me to come over. At the house I found Ben-Gurion in flannel pajamas and a heavy woolen bathrobe working at his desk. I chatted to him about American politics and my friend Jack Ewing and his race with FDR, Jr. for the governorship. Ben-Gurion talked about the constitution, indicating his unyielding opposition to it and the probability that he would take part in the debate.[66] I took advantage of the opportunity to press my opinion about the *Palestine Post* and Courtney as working to the disadvantage of both Israel and the US. He agreed so emphatically that I am hopeful he may do something about it. He did not, however, agree with Begin's charge that Courtney was a part of UK intelligence. Rather, he thought Courtney was merely "a disillusioned fellow traveler who sought to find solace for his disappointment by charging the United States with the same sort of faults that he had reluctantly discovered in the USSR."[67]

Sunday, February 19

In the afternoon, Shiloah and Kollek came to report briefly that [at the] Jordan-Israel meeting [at Shuneh] the previous Friday night [February 17] there had been present only the king and Samir and the Israelis, led by Shiloah [and Dayan]. After a friendly agreement on both sides that formal peace was not

66. February 1950 marked the one-year anniversary of the first sitting of the Knesset. It brought renewed debate, which Ben-Gurion had tabled the previous year, over Israel's constitution. Herut demanded a constitution. The Orthodox Bloc argued that Jewish law should be the basis of civil society in Israel. Mapai and the governing coalition wanted to postpone the drafting of a constitution until more stable times. In a Knesset debate of February 20, Ben-Gurion, leaving his sickbed for the day, said that drafting a rigid constitution at this point would be harmful. *Palestine Post*, February 21, 1950.

67. Courtney's most recent "Column One" opinion piece in the *Palestine Post* (February 10, 1950), criticized the US decision to develop the hydrogen bomb, likened Acheson to a "caveman," and spoke of the United States "striding the world on her hydrogen bomb like an atomic witch on an atomic broomstick."

now possible, the king brought forward his proposal for a five-year non-aggression pact. It included suggestions for extension beyond the five-year period; the maintenance of present frontiers; freedom of access across the frontiers for persons and trade; [an] international zone at Haifa; setting up of study committees on individual problems; [and] mutual guarantees to [the] UN regarding maintenance [of] freedom [of] access and protection [of] Holy Places. [In] the following discussion, the king suggested [a] financial concession to Arab property owners, while Israelis raised question of access [to Mount] Scopus. [The] king seemed to feel this could be arranged. [The] king's initial proposal was taken down in Arabic by Shiloah, read back to [the] king, and accepted by him. When written down, it was somewhat less definite than when first made because of [the] king's desire to keep [a] flowery literary style.

My impression, as I reported to [the] Department, was that [the] Israelis were pleased. Shiloah said that Ben-Gurion and Sharett were inclined to recommend [the] plan as [a] basis [of] principle for discussion. Shiloah hopes to return to Amman Tuesday or Wednesday, 21 or 22 [February], and to begin [to] continue negotiations until agreement reached.

The US legation in Amman reported that the Jordanian cabinet was unaware of the king's idea and that it likely would not agree to it.[68] On February 6 the Trusteeship Council had begun drafting a statute for the boundaries and governance of the city. On February 21, the Iraqi delegation to the PCC, speaking also for Egypt and Syria, announced that it "stood either for a purely Arab Jerusalem or complete internationalization." Anything in between, they said, "was unacceptable."[69]

Monday, February 20

Three-hour "emergency conference" with Gibson, Waller, Hooper and Barnes on housing and personnel. After the luncheon with Gibson and Waller, I still felt that both would be glad to help, but in the tradition of the Foreign Service they are looking out for their own posts first. Gibson was grateful to our reference to his needs in the letter to McGhee.

Tuesday, February 21

Teatime conference with the [Walter] Lowdermilks.[70] He spoke interestingly about the British groundnut scheme in Tanganyika, from where he had just returned as consultant.

68. McDonald to secretary of state, no. 28, February 20, 1950; Fritzlan to secretary of state, no. 28, February 20, 1950; US delegation to Trusteeship Council to secretary of state, no. 262, February 21, 1950, *FRUS*, 1950, v. V, 752–755.

69. US delegation to Trusteeship Council to secretary of state, no. 267, February 22, 1950, *FRUS*, 1950, v. V, 754 and n. 1.

70. Walter Clay Lowdermilk (1888–1974), chief, US Soil Conservation Service; world expert on soil erosion and reclamation; arrived in Israel from Tanganyika as the guest of the Ministry of Agriculture to provide advice on irrigation projects that would make possible the settlement of more immigrants. His main focus during the visit was a tour of the Negev. But in

Wednesday, February 22

The reception [at the residence for George Washington's birthday] was large—estimate 350 guests—and, according to the frequently expressed opinion, definitely a success.[71] Happily, by sheep dog methods with the cooperation of the staff, everybody had gone at 7:20. Shiloah told me that he expected to go to Jordan the 23rd or 24th. It was a great relief when the party was over.

The first Koussevitzky concert was accurately described in the *Palestine Post* [on February 25] as the most distinguished musical event since Toscanini [conducted Verdi]. Koussevitzky had an ovation at the start, at the intermission, and a tremendous one at the end. The orchestra showed the electric effect of the new conductor, as was described to me afterwards by the concert master. He said that the moment Koussevitzky gave his first downbeat the orchestra felt his inspiring leadership. We enjoyed very much both the Prokofiev Fifth and the Tchaikovsky Fourth. The reception afterwards at the Kaplans was, for us, brief. After Koussevitzky had embraced us both, I took Ruth home because she was very tired. In bed by twelve or thereafter.

Thursday, February 23

Arranged with the Helms to accept Comays and Kollek's invitation to fly to Eilat on Thursday, the 2nd [March], leaving around ten and back about six.

Went off to the first formal meeting of the Israel-America [Friendship] League. Eytan told me as he was leaving, in answer to my question, that Shiloah expected to go across the river again within two or three days.[72]

Friday, February 24

At teatime the UJA group from San Francisco came and stayed for about an hour at the house. The leader was Lloyd W. Dinkelspiel.[73] The talk followed the usual course. I had, however, the impression that the group had been rather disillusioned, if not disheartened, by their four days. Perhaps this was inevitable in view of their background and comparative lack of previous knowledge of Israel. Dinkelspiel gave me a most cordial invitation to San Francisco.

June 1950, work based on his advice was undertaken to use the Jordan River for increased irrigation by using the Yavniel depression as a reservoir. His testimony before the Anglo-American Committee of Inquiry on Palestine concerning irrigation possibilities is discussed in Goda et al., eds., *To the Gates of Jerusalem*, entry of January 12, 1946. See also McDonald to secretary of state, joint weeka no. 22, June 2, 1950, McDonald Papers, USHMM, box 8, folder 11.

71. Guest list, including Israeli government officials, diplomatic and consular personnel, religious and cultural figures, as well as business personalities, is in McDonald Papers, Columbia University, box 6, folder 7.

72. Reported in McDonald to secretary of state, no. 137, February 24, 1950, USSDCF-PIFA, 1950–1954, reel 1, frame 380.

73. Lloyd William Dinkelspiel (1899–1959), San Francisco attorney and Jewish leader; president, National Jewish Welfare Board; vice chairman, American Jewish Joint Distribution Committee; member, National Campaign Cabinet of the United Jewish Appeal.

I was especially interested to read Michael Wright's report regarding Israel arms claims. The UK [Foreign Office] took almost identically the same line as the attachés here. The despatch closed with the significant phrase "the Israelis speak of paying in dollars."[74]

I was intrigued and a little troubled by a Geneva telegram of February 21, which indicated that Eban had suggested pressure on Jordan regarding [the] Holy Places,[75] particularly [since] this seemed inconsistent with the very encouraging news received that morning in a personal note from Sharett.

Sharett telephoned in what McDonald reported was a "cheerful voice," and his son Chaim brought McDonald a secret handwritten note: "I am pleased to inform you that a non-aggression pact was last night initialed between Israel and Jordan. Shiloah is coming to report on details in course of today, and I will ask him to call on you to tell you the story. For the time being details are unknown."[76]

King Abdullah initiated the move toward a non-aggression pact as an interim step toward peace. The Israeli cabinet approved a simple draft agreement with Jordan. To Ben-Gurion and Sharett, the agreement removed the UN from Israeli-Jordanian negotiations, including those regarding Jerusalem. It also seemed to point the way for positive developments with other Arab states while weakening the Arab League.[77]

Started early to Weizmann's so that we might have time to take the back road past Ras al-Ain and skirting the hill country under Arab control. The anemones were frequently in evidence, but not in the profusion I had expected. The luncheon was small. Besides the hosts, the Koussevitzkys and ourselves, there was only Miss Wilkenson and Weizmann's new liaison with HaKirya. Ruth and I were both greeted in the most cordial Russian manner. Before the meal I spoke to Weizmann about the Sharett news. He had already heard it. To no one else except the liaison man did I mention the matter. Talk at the meal was rather political but not very specific. Both the Weizmanns were critical of Russia's attitude towards its Jewish population and its general policy of re-

74. In a discussion with the US ambassador in London, Michael Wright of the Foreign Office stated that British arms supplies to the Arab states were based on their legitimate security needs, the desire to avoid an arms race in the Middle East, and on existing Arab arms stocks, which allowed London to set ceilings on arms shipments. The British Chiefs of Staff, he said, were against sending arms to Israel, partly because there was no information on what the Israelis currently possessed. Holmes to secretary of state, no. 963, February 18, 1950, *FRUS*, 1950, v. V, 750–751.

75. US delegation to Trusteeship Council to secretary of state, no. 262, February 21, 1950, *FRUS*, 1950, v. V, 753–754.

76. Sharett to McDonald, February 25, 1950, McDonald Papers, USHMM, box 8, folder 7; McDonald to secretary of state, no. 140, February 25, 1950, USSDCF-PIFA, 1950–1954, reel 1, frame 381.

77. *DFPI*, v. 5, d. 74, 97, 100 and n. 4, 105, and editorial note p. 139; *FRUS*, 1950, v. V, 757; Fischer, ed., *Moshe Sharett: The Second Prime Minister, Selected Documents (1894–1965)*, 411–412.

pression.[78] Koussevitzky did not make any defense—on the contrary, he gave indications of having been disillusioned.

At my request Ruth read her letter from the president [Truman], and Vera gave her blessing to its utilization at Tel Litwinsky. As we were leaving, I asked Weizmann if he had any word from the letter sent to the president through Jack Ewing.[79] He said no, but that he understood he was to have a reply.

The luncheon was notable chiefly for the opportunity it gave to study and compare Weizmann and Koussevitzky, both Russian-born Jews whose careers had been so different and so brilliant, and who, towards the end of their lives, are joining in a common enthusiasm for Israel. Koussevitzky was rhapsodically enthusiastic about the beauty and exhilarating effect of the country. His visit here will undoubtedly be one of the most dramatic experiences of his life.

The surprise party at the Bradys' for the major and for Captain Cashman was a success. The only business transacted was 1) to discover that Ambassador Kirk[80] is due in this area early in March. The air attachés had had [a] technical inquiry about the clearances for Kirk's plane, but had not told me of it, assuming that I would not be interested. Nor had they bothered to report that the Jerusalem field was not the preferred one for DC-3s. I was upset and annoyed.

Sunday, February 26

Sunday morning, a couple of hours reading a fortnight's accumulation of translations of the Hebrew press left me with the feeling that Israel is now in the winter of its discontent. The many editorials on the black market and on the religious education row left a bad taste.[81]

It was doubly heartening, therefore, to have Shiloah and Kollek come about one and to give me so encouraging an account of the meeting with Jordan the previous Friday night [February 24].[82] This idea of the king [for a five year non-aggression pact], which had been accepted in principle by Israel, was developed into a set of principles, which both sides initialed. These are further steps towards peace; they do not represent any change in existing lines, but set up sub-committees to find solutions for all issues. Partition of Jerusalem and

78. Joseph Stalin undertook anti-Jewish measures under the rubric of anti-Zionism beginning in 1948, but persecution intensified between 1950 and Stalin's death in 1953. See *DFPI*, v. 5, d. 87. Genaddi Kostyrchenko, *Out of the Red Shadows: Anti-Semitism in Stalin's Russia* (Amherst, NY: Prometheus Books, 1995); and Jonathan Brent and Vladimir P. Naumov, *Stalin's Last Crime: The Plot Against the Jewish Doctors, 1948–1953* (New York: Harper, 2004).

79. Entries of January 1 and 3, 1950.

80. Ambassador Alan Goodrich Kirk (1888–1963), US Naval Academy graduate; senior US naval commander in Operation Overlord, June 1944; after retirement from Navy in 1946 served as ambassador to Belgium, 1946–1949, and to the Soviet Union, 1949–1951.

81. The Orthodox Bloc still boycotted cabinet meetings, insisting on exclusively religious education in immigrant camps for Yemenite and North African Jews. On March 21 it agreed to a compromise, which called for a unified school system comprising religious, academic, artisanal, agricultural, and trade schools. It remained in the coalition. McDonald to secretary of state, joint weeka no. 7, February 30, 1950, McDonald Papers, USHMM, box 8, folder 7.

82. Entry of February 25, 1950. Shiloah and Dayan's meetings were with King Abdullah, Samir al-Rifai, and Fawzi al-Mulqi.

outlet to sea [are] specifically mentioned. First sub-committee to attempt [the] partition of no man's land without prejudice to final settlement; initiation of normal trade and economic cooperation, and grant of free port for Jordan in Haifa; Israel to start payment now of compensation to Arab Jerusalem property owners; access to be provided to [Mount] Scopus and Bethlehem; access to and freedom of Holy Places to be provided by joint guarantee of two countries to [the] UN, and by their acceptance of international supervision.

Shiloah claimed that he had had to work hard to get Jordan to accept this idea of supervision. He had pleaded that their two countries "must satisfy reasonable members of [General] Assembly." He thinks [this] agreement should go [a] "long way towards relieving doubts of faith of two countries toward Holy Places." [He] hopes [a] pattern will be set for arrangements with other Arab states, and meanwhile [for] open commercial intercourse with Jordan. He added: "it is not yet in the bag, but we are optimistic." My only comment to the Department was that Shiloah [was] "obviously delighted with progress to date."[83] [Shiloah added that the next meeting with the Jordanians was to be February 28.]

The main report finished, Shiloah told me that Fawzi al-Mulqi, the Jordanian defense minister, said that Colonel Mitchell, the US Army attaché,[84] had offered to accept five Jordanian officers in US Army schools and to pay portions of their expenses. The offer was declined with thanks, since the British offered more. Shiloah did not wish Mitchell's offer to be reported to Washington, but he thought it significant in view of the meager admissions of Israel officers to US Army schools. My two visitors were interested in [Ambassador] Kirk's possible visit.

Reception at the Ritters', which we attended with the Hoopers, was the usual party.[85] I told Helm that I had news for him about Israel-Jordan, and he is to come in Monday morning.

Monday, February 27

Morning session with Archibald. He showed me the list of arms requested by Israel, made his usual criticisms of the Israeli secretiveness, stressed the air of suspicion in the Pentagon about Israel's purposes, a suspicion which he attributed in large part to adverse reports brought back by UN observers who had not been wisely handled by Israeli officials. Though the colonel admitted that the impressions he had gotten in the Pentagon were not borne out by the facts as he found them in Israel, he seemed loath to blame the UN observers for any

---

83. See McDonald's report of this meeting, McDonald to secretary of state, no. 142, February 26, 1950, *FRUS*, 1950, v. V, 757–758. He also reported that according to Shiloah, the king, "showing joy," said he "would not go back on his word" and would replace his governing cabinet should the present one reject the agreement.

84. Colonel Lawrence C. Mitchell (1893–1975), US military attaché in Amman, assigned March 1949.

85. Paul Albert Ritter, Swiss consul general in Jerusalem and first Swiss envoy to Israel, 1949–1951.

measure of prejudice. He promised that this week he and Brady would work out the evacuation report if Troxel gave the necessary data.

Before I finished breakfast, Sir Knox Helm came in. He was pleased to have the details of Shiloah's report. As to arms, he said that he had a few days ago told the Israelis that they weakened their case for arms supplies by refusing to disclose to their best friend, the US, the exact amounts they now possess. As he was leaving, he agreed to meet at the time and place which he would report to us for the trip to Eilat [on] Thursday.

In the afternoon Messers [Donald] Stevenson[86] and [Frank] Hunt[87] [of the American Friends Service Committee] were at the house for more than an hour. They seemed primarily interested in their inter-racial project for Acre[88] and one or more of the Galilee communities. They said that they had received encouraging support from the Israeli authorities at their meetings this morning and yesterday. They had surprisingly little to say about the general problem of refugees and the Quaker plans for the continuation of their share of the responsibility. They seemed pessimistic about the UN slowness, both from the point of view of setting up an organization and from that of finance. They understood that eight or nine men had been asked to head the new organization, but all had declined.

In the evening all of us went with Mrs. Sacks to see Gary Cooper and Patricia Neal in *The Fountainhead*.[89] It was always interesting because of its unusual plot, but she was rather a disappointment to me.

Tuesday, February 28

Koussevitzky's special concert was a thriller. The Bach suite was played with loving care and made a profound impression. The [Modest] Mussorgsky *Khovanshchina* was given the perfect execution which it deserves. Debussy's *La Mer* seemed almost boisterous in contrast with the first two pieces. Beethoven's Seventh seemed to me admirably done, the last movement sweeping one to his feet. Spoke to Koussevitzky briefly after the concert. It was obvious that he had been as thrilled as the audience and the orchestra.

---

86. Donald Stevenson, AFSC liaison in Beirut; highly distrustful of Israel and convinced that communism was strong there.

87. Frank Hunt (1925–1973), British Quaker, worked with Jewish DPs in Austria after 1945; served in Gaza Strip and the Galilee for the AFSC.

88. In March 1949 the AFSC had undertaken a relief effort for Arab families in Acre that was aimed also at reconciliation. Stevenson complained earlier that Arab families expelled from Acre's old city could not return without police permit and that the Israeli authorities were limiting AFSC activities. Gallagher, *Quakers in the Israeli-Palestinian Conflict*, 134, 161.

89. *The Fountainhead* (1949), based on the Ayn Rand novel of the same name.

21. March 1950

Mrs. Ben-Gurion called to say that she and her husband were going away for a vacation and that therefore she would not be able, as she suggested yesterday, to go to Eli [Karlin]'s lecture. It is probably just as well!

During the course of the day I talked to Kollek about the possibility of using the Foreign Office's extra copy, if there was one, of the Trusteeship Council's draft statute for Jerusalem. Later in the day, Kollek called to say that Shiloah had returned [from Shuneh] and was very tired; he suggested tomorrow for a talk. It was fixed for 9:30.

Kollek and Shiloah an hour at the house reporting on the Jordan meeting February 28. Next [meeting] will be tonight. Shiloah said the leak of the first "probably not serious." Israel's draft of [the] 28th was "except for minor changes mere formalization" of [the] agreed statement. In contrast, Jordanian draft "removed all meat from that statement." It eliminated: 1) non-aggression pact, substituting mere modification of armistice; 2) five-year provision; 3) freedom of commerce and trade, this last because [of] "fear to break Arab League boycott." Jordanian draft emphasized [the] right to corridor outlet to sea and free port [at] Haifa and [a] committee to study these.[1]

Then followed three hours [of] vigorous argument, [the] king not present, Fawzi al-Mulqi [as the] chief Jordanian representative, Samir [as] "observer," and Jamal Tuqan, Palestine Arab [representative], mostly silent. At midnight Shiloah said, "No sense repeating ourselves" and proposed [to] leave note for king "explaining impasse." Jordanians strongly objected and instead decided to "wake His Majesty." [The] king, who had not seen [the] Jordanian draft, was "very annoyed" and "told Jordanians off." "He intended to adhere to his plan." Then he described Jordan's difficulties and "sufferings of both countries due [to] lost trade." "Only alternative to agreement is war, and Jordan [is] in no position [to] resume war." King's criticism was so forthright and strong as to be "bit

1. Israeli and Jordanian representatives initialed the simple draft agreement on February 24. They disagreed on more detailed drafts when alternative forms were examined on February 28. It was agreed to suspend talks until March 3, 1950. For the alternative drafts, see *DFPI*, v. 5, d. 112.

embarrassing." He [was] "emphatic he would get [a] new cabinet if necessary." At [the] conclusion, [the] king "commanded" both parties to come back on Friday. Position must be clarified. He appealed [to the Israelis] to take account [of] Jordan's difficulties. Shiloah said in reply [that] his draft [is] "not bargaining, but also not Ten Commandments."

As to access [to] Wailing Wall and passage [to] Latrun, Shiloah said these [are] covered by general language providing "access for all faiths to Holy Places and [the] proposal to divide No Man's Land." His language [is] "purposely vague" to make Jordan's acceptance "easier." Shiloah thinks chances [of an] agreement depend on strength of [the] king. He thinks Kirkbride [is] helpful. Regarding Eban's account [of] his talk with [Abd al-] Mun'im [in Geneva], Shiloah thought it "interesting." Then he suggested that "a little more direct influence from US in Cairo might be decisive." I cabled Department substantially as above.

In his cable McDonald included Shiloah's comment that US pressure on Egypt would be helpful.[2] Egypt's chief negotiator in Geneva, Abd al-Mun'im, insisted on Israeli concessions in the southern Negev to establish a border with Jordan and ostensibly to provide a buffer against Israeli aggression. Time, al-Mun'im told Eban, was on Egypt's side. Ambassador Caffery replied, "I am continuing to try to lead [the] Egyptians in the desired direction . . . but McDonald tell Israelis please, 'no more leaks.'"[3] Sharett, meanwhile, ordered Eban to push for a non-aggression pact with Egypt, and he worried about Egyptian designs on the Negev. On March 19 he told Eliezer Kaplan that everything—from increased settlement to development of infrastructure—should be done to reinforce Israel's hold on the southern Negev.[4]

Very pleasant tea with [the] Koussevitzkys in their new Italian house off the new Herzliya Road opposite the new parade grounds, in the new section of Tel Aviv. I was invited to act as courier for the Koussevitzkys' Thursday and Friday tour of the north next week. I said I would like very much to go, but I was very doubtful that I could in view of absence of five [embassy] officers.

Saturday, March 4
Worked all day Saturday on [the manuscript] and in [the] file room.

Monday, March 6
A crowded, busy day. After an hour or so's work, Sir Knox arrived about nine, and I recounted to him the talk with our Israeli friends the previous Friday. He had not heard anything substantial that was new about the subsequent

2. McDonald to secretary of state, no. 155, March 3, 1950, *FRUS*, 1950, v. V, 774–775.
3. Caffery to secretary of state [relayed to Tel Aviv], no. 216, March 4, 1950, USSDCF-PIFA, 1950–1954, reel 1, frame 389. The reference was to a March 1 *Palestine Post* article titled, "Cabinet Discusses Pact with Jordan."
4. *DFPI*, v. 5, d. 118, 119, 124, 125, 129, 142.

crisis in Amman, but what he told me fitted reasonably into Shiloah's information and that we had had from Amman.

King Abdullah, having told his negotiating team to sign the agreement or resign, accepted the resignation of Prime Minister Tewfik Abu al-Huda on March 2. Israeli sources said that the king would try to form a new government with Samir al-Rifai at its head.[5] By March 4 the US legation in Amman reported that al-Rifai was unable to form a new cabinet. The king thus asked al-Huda to withdraw his resignation, and the just-dismissed cabinet remained in office. The king assured them that negotiations with Israel would not resume before parliamentary elections, to be held in April.[6]

At the Foreign Office at Sharett's request, in presence [of] Shiloah and Kollek, [the] foreign minister outlined [the] following: crisis in Amman "more than local test between [the] king and [the] opposition. It is [a] clash between negative and affirmative forces. Now Amman is [the] crossroads [of the] Middle East. Decision there will affect [the] whole course [of] history [for the] next few years." Strong forces at play in and out. "Example [of the] latter is presence [in] Amman [of] Iraqi Deputy Prime Minister Salih Jabr.[7] Abdullah does not need pressure but needs moral encouragement in his present ordeal."

[The] foreign minister stressed that Israel and [the] king favor [an] accord, though [are] not yet agreed on exact provisions. Sharett earnestly pleaded that [the] US encourage [the] king by official but secret assurance of US moral and economic support and hopes for his success. Sharett added there is also [a] practical problem. [The] king's willingness [to] resume trade relations with Israel involves more than break with [the] Arab boycott. It necessitates legislation to undo Jordan's part in [the] boycott. There is [the] possibility Egypt and Iraq might cut off Jordan's supplies as [a] penalty. Abdullah would be reassured if US would suggest possibility [of] American supplies of sugar and rice to replace those from Egypt, not as gifts, but on commercial basis. Foreign minister "ventured [to] suggest that if [the] Department agreed it would be most helpful if President Truman gave [the] king [a] personally encouraging message." Sharett emphasized [that he] was "acting solely on own initiative; king not involved."[8]

In his report to the State Department, McDonald added, "Sharett will probably appeal also to Britain. It is obvious that Israel attaches highest importance to success of

5. *DFPI*, v. 5, d. 122, 126.
6. Drew to secretary of state, no. 36, March 5, 1950, *FRUS*, 1950, v. V, 777–778.
7. Sayyid Salih Jabr (1896–1967), Iraqi Shi'ite leader and prime minister, 1947–1948; opposed peace with Israel and was behind the Iraqi law of March 1950 stripping citizenship from Iraqi Jews. Ya'akov Meron, "The Expulsion of the Jews from the Arab Countries: The Palestinians' Attitude Toward It and Their Claims," in *The Forgotten Millions: The Modern Jewish Exodus from Arab Lands*, ed. Malka Hillel Shulewitz (New York: Continuum, 1999), 112, n. 30.
8. This passage including direct quotes uses cleaner wording from McDonald to secretary of state, no. 158, March 6, 1950, *FRUS*, 1950, v. V, 781–782. Sharett had urged Elath to press for US aid as well on March 5, 1950. *DFPI*, v. 5, d. 127.

[the] King in [the] present 'tug of war,' because his success would 'remove key logjam which still prevents peace in Middle East. . . . This may be overly optimistic but surely [the] King as [the] first Arab ruler to show courage to face realities does deserve US encouragement in this crisis."[9]

In a separate despatch for the eyes of Truman and Acheson also sent on March 6, McDonald was more forceful:

> For [the] first time in many months I ask your personal consideration. If [the] projected Israel-Jordan five-year non-aggression pact can be saved, [the] US policy of peace and stability in [the Middle East] will be immeasurably advanced. Abdullah sorely needs and fully deserves our moral and economic support as he struggles against intransigent forces which hope for Israel's economic collapse [and which] demand indefinite continuance [of the] anti-Israel boycott. Personal messages of sympathy and support from [the] President to [the] King might be decisive. Also [a] friendly word of counsel in Cairo urging sympathetic understanding [of] Abdullah's stand would diminish greatly [the] forces threatening [the] King's program [of] conciliation. I think Dr. Bunche would agree that now is [the] opportune moment [to] save Arab extremists from themselves.[10]

In the State Department, Raymond Hare advised Acheson that "it is our belief that, motivated by his own personal interests, King Abdullah has gone as far as he could in attempting to reach an agreement with Israel. . . . A message from the President to the King would in our opinion not help the King vis-à-vis his Government." Instead, the mission in Amman should discreetly encourage further negotiations. Hare rejected McDonald's suggestion for intervention with the Egyptian government.

Acheson relayed these concerns to Truman and added that, should a letter from the White House to Abdullah be leaked, the president would become the chief issue in the upcoming Jordanian elections. Truman agreed with the secretary's recommendations. Acheson told McDonald, "Abdullah's greatest difficulties appear [to] arise from opposition [in] his own [government] and from public opinion in Jordan and Arab Palestine. If Jordan-Israeli conversations resumed [an] opportunity will be offered to work out [a] formula more susceptible to being accepted by Jordanians."[11]

[Paul] Blanshard is here for the *Nation* to do some stories "from new angles" on the Holy Places. He has come from and is returning to Rome. We had only a few minutes' talk together.[12]

---

9. McDonald to secretary of state, no. 158, March 6, 1950, *FRUS*, 1950, v. V, 781–782.

10. McDonald to secretary of state [personal attention president and secretary], no. 161, March 6, 1950, USSDCF-PIFA, 1950–1954, reel 1, frame 395; McDonald to secretary of state [personal attention Charles Murphy], no. 165, March 7, 1950, USSDCF-PIFA, 1950–1954, reel 1, frame 404.

11. Penniman to secretary of state, no. 65, March 8, 1950; Hare memorandum to Acheson, March 8, 1950; conversation with the president, March 9, 1950; Acheson to US embassy Tel Aviv, no. 115, March 9, 1950, USSDCF-PIFA, 1950–1954, reel 1, frame 396, 399–400, 409, 413; also *FRUS*, 1950, v. V, 782.

12. Paul Blanshard (1892–1980), left-wing and anticlerical associate editor of the *Nation* in 1950s; published *American Freedom and Catholic Power* (New York: Beacon Press, 1949). His visit to Israel resulted in the articles "Second Round for Israel?" *Nation*, April 15, 1950; "Israel: Church and State," *Nation*, May 27, 1950; and "The Vatican and Israel," *Nation*, July 1, 1950.

Miss Herlitz's visit was interrupted by Sir Knox and Lady Helm "popping in." He and I talked briefly, I reporting to him Sharett's plea to me of the morning. The foreign minister had not yet gotten in touch with Sir Knox. Then the latter, on his own, developed a thesis, which deserves to be carefully set down. It was evoked by Sharett's statement that the issues involved in Amman were far-reaching and crucial. In substance, Sir Knox said the following: ever since I have been here, I have been trying to figure out the Arab position. Now that I have gotten my feet on the ground, I feel strongly that the success of the Arab intransigence would be a disaster for the US and the UK's vital interests in this area. Such success, which I regard as extremely unlikely, could only take the form of breaking Israel's political power. If this occurred and Israel were eliminated as a state, there would certainly be war among the Arab states for the control of Palestine. Moreover, if there were such a defeat of Israel and, as might be the case, there were the threat of Jewish massacre in Tel Aviv, Haifa, Jerusalem and elsewhere, the US and the UK would be forced by their own public opinion to intervene in defense of the Jews. This in turn would inflame Arab opinion against US and UK. Either of these eventualities, Western intervention or Arab intra-warfare following Jewish defeat, would play directly into [the] USSR['s] hands. The moral from all this is that US and UK interests demand a strong Israel at peace with its Arab neighbors. I have been urging this policy as strongly as I can upon the Foreign Office at home. The above was spoken with an evident sincerity, which carried conviction. Sir Knox also said that he thought Kirkbride, in his helpful attitude in Amman, must be speaking with the approval of the Foreign Office.

McDonald summarized Helm's argument for the State Department and added this comment: "I think [the] opinion of Helm, who is able and objective with no Palestine background to confuse his judgment, is sound."[13]

At nine o'clock Kollek and Shiloah came. Shiloah stressed news that [the] Syrian prime minister [Khalid al-Azm] had that afternoon announced his government is "considering closing Syrian frontier with Jordan if [the] five-year agreement [between Jordan and Israel] becomes effective; other Arab governments already conferring what action to take."[14] Shiloah hoped US would: 1) regard such statements as interference [in the internal] affairs [of Jordan and

13. McDonald to secretary of state, no. 164, March 7, 1950, *FRUS*, 1950, v. V, 783–784.
14. US minister Keeley in Damascus confirmed this based on statements by Prime Minister Khalid al-Azm on March 6. Keeley was subsequently ordered to convey that the United States "deplores [the] attitude" revealed by the prime minister, because an Israeli-Jordanian non-aggression pact would be a major step toward peace and stability, and to impress on the Syrian government the US desire that Syria not interfere in the negotiations. *FRUS*, 1950, v. V., 804–808.

Israel] and blows to peace and stability in [Middle East]; 2) urge neighboring Arab capitals [to] permit [Israel and Jordan] [to] settle own affairs.[15]

Regarding present power [of the] king, Shiloah's views differed from those expressed in Amman legation telegram.[16] According to Shiloah: 1) king has sent Israel message "Abdullah son of Hussein does not break his word;" 2) Samir [al-Rifai] did succeed in getting cooperation of more than "third-rate politicians" [for a new cabinet] 3) two members [of the] old cabinet asked to be included in Samir's; 4) Tewfik [Abu al-Huda] has promised [the] king to work out solution with Israel; 5) another [Israel-Jordan] meeting tentatively fixed for night March 7, but may be postponed.[17]

Tuesday, March 7

Earlier in the morning I had unpleasant conference with Colonel Archibald in presence [of] Major Brady and Captain Cashman. Answering the colonel's question, I frankly admitted my opinion that Colonel van der Velde would get more for us.[18] The talk dragged on without much that was new developing. The two [junior attachés] sat silent as the grave. What a wondrous institution is military discipline!

Invited Major [Brady] for lunch. We talked shop privately, and he was throughout "correct." Nonetheless, I was not happier about the status quo [concerning Archibald's performance as senior attaché]; on the contrary, I, between the lines, gained confirmation of Curtis Barnes's fears. I was glad, therefore, that I had sent off my telegram to Jerusalem[19] following the Foreign Office conference. I should have included in my account of my talk with Colonel Archibald that at one point in his criticism of the Israelis he said in substance: "Why, their liaison for me is not a very bright major." The emphasis on the major was stronger than on the other characteristics of the man. How far rank-consciousness can lead men!

Thursday, March 9

General Riley at the house for an hour, and [he] would have stayed longer but for the arrival of Shiloah and Kollek. General Riley listened sympathetically

---

15. The request originated with Sharett after Arab League General Secretary Abd al-Rahman Azzam Pasha called for closure of the Syrian border with Jordan, lest an Israeli-Jordanian peace wreck other Arab states' boycott of Israel. The inclusion of Grand Mufti Amin al-Husseini in calls against a Jordanian peace with Israel was especially worrisome in Tel Aviv. See *DFPI*, v. 5. d. 131, 162. McDonald reported his meeting with Shiloah and Kollek on March 7, *FRUS*, 1950, v. V, 783. The State Department asked the other missions in the Middle East for comment. *FRUS*, 1950, v. V, 791.

16. Drew to secretary of state, no. 36, March 5, 1950, *FRUS*, 1950, v. V, 777–778, entry of March 3, 1950.

17. See also McDonald to secretary of state, no. 164, March 7, 1950, *FRUS*, 1950, v. V, 783–784. In a meeting of March 5, 1950, King Abdullah told Drew that negotiations with Israel would resume. Government circles in Amman suggested that any resumption would have to be after the April 2 election.

18. Entries of February 9 and September 21, 1949.

19. Not found, probably to General Riley. See entry of March 9, 1950.

as I told him my problem with Colonel Archibald. He agreed that the latter was not intelligence material and illustrated this by the following: at the luncheon or dinner in honor of [Yigael] Yadin, when he was recently promoted, Colonel Archibald, sitting at one end of the table, out of the blue said: "I have just decided that the Arabs [and] not the Jews began the war." And, later again, in a most untimely way, said: "After all, the armistices are of no damned use." According to General Riley, these remarks were both stupid and unseemly. We turned then to the immediate question of how I should make my request. The letter, which I finally drafted, represents General Riley's views. He cautioned me particularly against saying anything which would make anybody in the Pentagon take up a defensive position. This I strove to avoid.

That same day McDonald wrote Stuart Symington, the secretary of the Air Force, to ask that Archibald, who was also the senior military attaché at the embassy, be replaced: He noted that Major Brady, the Army attaché was "one of the most brilliant intelligence officers I have ever met," but that Archibald, though "a charming gentleman and a loyal and devoted officer," was not working out. "This country I regard as one of the richest potential intelligence sources in this part of the world. Colonel Archibald is not capitalizing fully [on] these possibilities."[20]

On the political issues, General Riley said that he had never expected the [Jordan-Israel] talks to lead to agreement, because Abdullah "simply does not dare to step out and take the initiative in moving towards peace or opening trade with Israel." General Riley emphasized that only Egypt can make the beginning. From this, he developed the thesis that Israel was unwise in trying "to play off Jordan against Egypt." He thought that if someone like Bunche were on hand to push a settlement between Egypt and Israel it could be arranged. As to the PCC [Palestine Conciliation Commission] and the Trusteeship Council, they are "useless" and are "confusing the issues."

General Riley complained that Israel was making a mistake in not withdrawing from the disputed point Ras al-Naqeb, which is undoubtedly to the west of the Negev line.[21] This concession would improve the chances of negotiations with Egypt. He scoffed at the Israeli proposal that they would accept being declared in violation so long as they were allowed to remain.

When General Riley met Shiloah, they embraced [in] European fashion. In answer to my question, Shiloah vigorously contested General Riley's point of view about Ras al-Naqeb: to yield it would encourage the Egyptians to ask for the whole of the southern Negev as a prior condition to negotiations. Even if the Israeli army decided to yield it, Shiloah would press for their reconsideration.

20. McDonald to Symington, March 9, 1950, McDonald Papers, USHMM, box 8, folder 8.
21. Strategic pass on southern Egyptian-Israeli frontier, disputed owing partly to placement of border marker pillars in 1906, ultimately resolved in favor of Egypt in 1988.

Shiloah [in answering Riley's argument that Israel should make peace with Egypt first, was] not encouraged by Eban's letter.[22] In it, or rather in Mun'im's reply to Eban's queries, [Shiloah] restated all the old objections. Shiloah thinks Egypt, or at least the king and the foreign minister, while willing to talk softly, prefer to prepare for the second round.

Shiloah said that the meeting on March 7 [with the Jordanians] at Shuneh had ended not in a rupture, but a postponement, the king being pleased that his government had accepted his plan and that Tewfik would proceed with it. In return, he had agreed to the delay. Tewfik had read out a *note-verbale*, which the Israelis copied. It stressed the idea of mere delay and of continuity. Shiloah repeated his earlier suggestions about the desirability of encouragement for the king and his hopes that the negotiations could be resumed fruitfully. Meantime, nothing could be done towards presenting the Trusteeship Council with a *fait accompli*. He hoped that Drew and Kirkbride would encourage the king during their five-days' camel vacation with the king.[23]

In the afternoon to [Ludwig] Schwerin's one-man show at the Katz Gallery.[24] He had two new interesting types of pictures; one plain black and white and the other in brilliant colors. He and his wife urged us to come to his studio.

Friday, March 10

Talk with [Walter] Lowdermilk, who was rather critical of what he termed the division of responsibility for land settlement between the [Jewish] Agency and the Ministry of Agriculture.[25] He was also critical of the work of the British Colonial Development Corporation in Colonial Africa.

Pleasant tea party with the [Paul] Uhlmanns from Kansas City, who came with Dr. Cohen of the Weizmann Institute.[26] Others were the Rosenblooms, with whom we promised to have dinner in Jerusalem on the night of March 21 before the Koussevitzky concert, at the King David.

Saturday, March 11

At tea were present Ralph B. Curren, civil aviation [attaché] from [the US Embassy in] Cairo, here to discuss a bilateral air agreement with Israel, but in fact absorbed in trying to [convince the] Israeli government to rescind its recent regulations affecting TWA limiting its traffic out of Israel and requiring

22. Probably referring to the transcript of the Eban-Mun'im meeting of February 27, 1950 (described earlier), dated and sent on March 3. *DFPI*, v. 5, d. 125.
23. Reported in McDonald to secretary of state, no. 170, March 9, 1950, *FRUS*, 1950, v. V, 796–797.
24. Ludwig Schwerin (1897–1983), artist and illustrator; fled Germany for Palestine via Switzerland, 1938.
25. Probable reference to agreement between Israeli government and the Jewish Agency whereby the latter transferred duties to the former, but kept responsibilities concerning immigration, settlement, and connections to world Jewry.
26. Paul Uhlmann (1884–1969), Danzig-born Kansas City grain operator and Jewish community leader; invited by Weizmann and Kaplan to advise on Israeli industry.

investment here of [Israeli] pounds secured from sale of tickets beyond the amount required for local expenses.[27]

The dinner at the Argentine house was notable for several points: 1) our first view of Lolita [Ford]'s furniture in its new setting; 2) the extraordinarily good Argentine food; 3) and finally, the upsetting news of the death of [Mordechai] Eliash, which was telephoned to Dr. Simon, who passed it on to the Sharetts.[28]

Sunday, March 12

The late morning out to the beach south of Bat Yam. It is a magnificent expanse of sand, reaching seemingly endlessly southward. The view from the top of the dune gave one a comprehensive picture of Jaffa.

I visited the A. S. Epstein factory for concrete slabs for walls. The product, waterproof and heat-resistant, was in sharpest contrast with the traditional bricks being made in the traditional way just across the street, a method as primitive as that which the Jews had used in Egypt more than 3,000 years before. I could not understand why, given the desperate need for housing, Israel had not in the beginning concentrated on brick-making machinery which would have enabled them to build houses of some durability. Chatted at the plant with the management, with Goldie, and with the editor of the *Atlanta Constitution*.[29]

Curren, civil aviation attaché in Cairo, and Yovanovich of TWA came at teatime to tell me of their conclusion, after hours of study, of the Israeli recent proposed regulation of sale of tickets by foreign airlines and restrictions of their transfers and requirements of investment in Israel; they reported, too, that [Aryeh] Pincus was leaving on Wednesday for the States, stopping en route for a day at the TWA conference in Rome. In Washington, he was to try to get permit for landing of El Al Israel-US flights.[30] As the men talked, it became obvious to me that it would be better not to wait [for] the normal process by which the discussions would drag on at the lower levels, with each side probably hardening in its original position.

At Kaplan's apartment we first chatted a moment about Weizmann and about Eliash. As to the latter's sudden death while reading the Torah [*sic*], Kaplan, who also has a heart condition said: "What a wonderful way to end." I

27. See entry of January 13, 1950. McDonald had urgently requested Curren's visit. "Aviation matters are developing to [a] critical point and Curren's experience would be most valuable here." McDonald to secretary of state, no. 147, February 28, 1950, USSDCF-PIFA, 1950–1954, reel 6, frame 899.

28. Entry of February 15, 1949. Ambassador Eliash died suddenly in London on March 11, 1950, of a heart attack during private Talmud study.

29. Ralph Emerson McGill (1898–1969), editor-in-chief of the *Atlanta Constitution*, 1942–1960, and then its publisher until his death; from Vienna covered the Nazi annexation of Austria; advocate of civil rights in United States; author of *Israel Revisited* (Atlanta: Tupper and Love, 1950).

30. See entries of July 2 and October 31, 1949.

agreed. I stressed with him the unacceptability of the proposed regulations and argued that they were self-defeating because under them El Al would never gain landing rights in the States. Moreover, insistence on them would risk disrupting air traffic at the very peak of the tourist season. Even if a substantial amount of foreign exchange had to be released, it would be but a small proportion of that brought in by the tourists. It was obvious from his manner and from what he said that he was impressed by my plea, not so much by its technical aspects, which I barely mentioned, but by my evident sincerity. He knew, of course, that I would not have gone out of my way to raise the issue at this stage had I not been completely convinced that the best interests of both our countries would be served by scrapping the proposed regulations. He said he would talk to [Aryeh] Pincus that night and would have one of his own men sit in on Curren's conferences with Pincus. He saw clearly that Pincus could not hope to wangle through political influences in the States a modification of the cabinet's fixed policies. Immediately thereafter, I reported to Curren and Yovanovich, both of whom were encouraged.

On March 22, McDonald reported to Washington, "In view [of the] sincere co-operative attitude shown by Israelis here this week, [I] urge [the] Department [to] give utmost consideration [to] expediting [the] air agreement." The agreement was completed in its essentials by May and signed in June, thanks largely to McDonald's intervention.[31]

Monday, March 13

I arrived at Lydda about twenty minutes after three, well before the scheduled time of the landing of the plane bearing the body of Eliash. Chatted for a few minutes with Herlitz and Kollek and Sharett about the arrival [of labor attaché Milton] Fried and the difficulty of our finding a house for them. Kollek thought there might be something in the officers' block of houses near the army field and promised to let me know.

Milton Fried, the long-awaited labor attaché recommended by Samuel Klaus, was the only Jewish member of the US mission staff. McDonald later said that Fried "has one of the most penetrating and subtle minds I have ever met. His years of experience in Czechoslovakia are invaluable to him in Israel. He is the one almost irreplaceable man." Owing to Fried's value and his poor health, McDonald took extra effort to secure housing for him. Nevertheless, Fried and his family were obliged to remain in a hotel for their first five months in Israel.[32]

31. McDonald to secretary of state, nos. 200 and 201, March 22, 1950, USSDCF-PIFA, 1950–1954, reel 6, frames 906–909. See entry of June 13, 1950.
32. McDonald to Monnet Davis, February 5, 1951, McDonald Papers, Columbia University, box 10, folder 3.

Up to the office on the hill for a moment to check on the morning tele-grams and back to the house in time for the meeting of the diplomatic corps. The discussion covered a wide range of complaints that protocol was badly administered, either through ignorance or lack of staff, that missions had been delayed as long as seven or eight months in getting a telephone or in securing some other elementary and essential service. Considerable bitterness was ex-pressed by some. My suggestion that the food committee be authorized to take up these various complaints with the Foreign Office was rejected and the matter left in my lap. An ungrateful task! The discussion of a possible diplomatic club or other organized facilities for recreation and getting together of members and their families had little support and was finally rejected, with only the loophole that I might ask some of the juniors to give their judgment on the matter.

The Recknagels came in about five-thirty, driving down from Haifa. He is here from Sofia and will have his office at the consulate. His mission is classi-fied. I liked him and her, both seemingly simple and intelligent young people.[33] Presently, Milton Fried, the long-looked-for labor attaché, arrived, fortunately without his wife, baby, or boxer dog. Earlier during the day, I had been harass-ing Barnes to try to find a place for Fried to spend the first night, but without success. He stayed with us.

On our way to dinner at the Helms' we stopped at the Koussevitzkys' re-quest "to give him advice." He greeted Ruth and me with warm Russian em-braces, she only a little less enthusiastically. He told me with emotion of his impressions of the Galilee, the thrill of his trip on the Sea of Galilee, his visit to Ein Gev, Nazareth, and elsewhere. He was amusing in his estimate of his talk with Ben-Gurion. The latter, he said, seemed uninterested and at no point opened up. It was Koussevitzky's conclusion, probably correct, that Ben-Gurion thought a musician had nothing of interest for him. Ben-Gurion is not in the least musical. Koussevitzky then asked my advice on two counts. First was whether he should accept the invitation of the [Israel Philharmonic] Or-chestra to conduct five concerts in their American tour next winter. He said he would do so, but only if these were in the large cities, which he would choose. Naturally, I agreed that he was correct in his decision; and besides, I really thought he was. The other question was whether he should accept the invitation of the Yugoslavs to conduct at Belgrade. After some talk as to whether this would involve him dangerously with Moscow, we all agreed that he ought to say no.

33. Bulgaria severed its relations with the United States on February 20, 1950, after charg-ing US officials with espionage, and gave the US representation three days to leave the country. Thomas M. Recknagel (1918–2015) had been a vice consul in the US Embassy in Sofia. He was assigned as second secretary and vice consul in Tel Aviv on February 23. Recknagel was a specialist on the Balkans and on refugee issues, and his job in Israel was to debrief Jewish arrivals from Eastern Europe. See the interview of Recknagel from 1986, The Association for Diplomatic Studies and Training Foreign Affairs Oral History Project, http://lcweb2.loc.gov/service/mss/mfdip/2004/2004rec01/2004rec01.pdf, accessed September 2014.

After renewed embraces and promises to attend his final concert in Jerusalem on the 21st, we left for the Helms'. I should perhaps note first, however, that Koussevitzky, in talking about his impressions about the north, said, "Here thousands of years of history roll back and leave one in the land of the Bible. It is for me one of my greatest experiences. I am a little tired, but exulted." I should also perhaps note an amusing item: Koussevitzky's disclosure that Lenny Bernstein is becoming less willing to carry out his gentleman's understanding always to do his full share at Tanglewood. Koussevitzky, granting Lenny's great talent, claimed not unnaturally that his patronage had given Lenny ten or twenty years advance over where he would be otherwise.[34]

At the Helms', besides the hosts and ourselves, were a Sir Hutchins, [British] Foreign Office Inspector; Rebecca Sieff; the Shiloahs (I had not seen her for some time); Kollek and Miss Herlitz. The only business transacted was two-fold, my promise to Sir Hutchins that he was welcome to use our elaborate "hardship post" report [on the problem of housing for the US staff], and second, Shiloah's statement to me that there was nothing at all in the day's rumor that peace had been signed between Jordan and Israel. Shiloah also parenthetically asked me in a hurt tone of voice why no American consular representative had been present at the Eliash funeral in Jerusalem, which had been attended by other members, including British and Belgian, of the consular corps. This absence had been noted and commented upon. I had no explanation.

Wednesday, March 15

Luncheon conference with McVicker, during which he reported on Cairo. Of chief interest was his word from my colleague [Caffery] that he was still hopeful that Farouk was still desirous of peace and had the power to have his way on this issue. My colleague deplored the *Hador* leak and pleaded for non-repetition.[35] He was concerned, too, at statements attributed to Eban at Geneva critical of Egypt's rearmament and possible participation in a "second round." All of this, together with a tendency of Israel "to play off Egypt against Jordan," made progress very difficult.[36]

Just before I left the office in the morning, the code room handed me a telegram from Damascus reporting that the Foreign Office there had told of unimpeachable evidence, photographs, etc., that Abdullah and Ben-Gurion had

---

34. Tanglewood in the Berkshires had been an estate belonging to the Tappan family, donated to the Boston Symphony Orchestra in 1938 to be used for annual summer music festivals. Koussevitzky was its first conductor and music director. In 1940 Koussevitzky allowed Bernstein, then only age 22, to conduct and teach at Tanglewood, and Bernstein did so off and on until his death in 1990.

35. Entries of December 21, 1949, and February 9, 1950.

36. On March 18, Caffery reported that the Egyptian foreign minister handed him a personal note complaining about "the political and territorial ambitions of Israel" and US encouragement of these ambitions in the form of arms sales to Israel. Caffery to secretary of state, no. 260, March 18, 1950, *FRUS*, 1950, v. V, 810.

signed peace. I did not believe a word of it, but felt that before I wired I must have confirmation beyond what Shiloah had told me the previous evening.

At four o'clock I met Shiloah, Kollek and Herlitz at the latter's office. Shiloah told me that there was no ground whatever for the rumor, that my telegram to the Department of March 9 reporting the "adjournment" of the talks was the last word.[37] Moreover, Ben-Gurion had not seen Abdullah since late August, and Ben-Gurion had not been within a hundred miles of Eilat at any time during the period he was alleged to have signed with the king. These recurrent rumors Shiloah attributed to Syrian and Egyptian campaigns to discredit Abdullah before the Jordanian elections. The net result of such efforts, Shiloah thinks, is to make the Jordanians more and more aware of the need for and practicability of peace.

I then asked the advice of the three as to how I should carry out the diplomatic corps' injunction to protest to the government against the inefficiency of protocol and the slackness of the government in supplying essential services to the corps. They advised a stiff protest to the Foreign Office through Eytan, after having given Simon courteous notice. They thought that Eytan would then be in a position to make the administrative heads of the other departments function more intelligently and expeditiously.[38]

At supper Fried told us that almost astounding story of the American embassy residence at Prague, which is such a white elephant that it requires a ton of coal a day to heat during the winter. It has more than sixty rooms. The successor to [Laurence] Steinhardt, under whom the place was bought, became almost a mental wreck because, being a career man without additional funds, he simply could not maintain the place. Briggs, the second successor, being a tougher person, is browbeating the Department into granting additional funds or permitting him to move out.[39]

Fried's plans to avoid all receptions for him, and to move quietly while he gets acquainted, meet with my complete approval. Fried declined Ruth's and my invitation to go with us to the Kaete Dan to see the new Israel picture *The Magnetic Tide*. We enjoyed it. It is to have its premiere in New York within a few months and, in advance, three of the most popular columnists and radio commentators have agreed to give it major publicity. This is the picture that [Murray] Silverstone's wife [Dorothy] and daughters [Barbara and Susan] made here last year.[40]

---

37. Entry of March 9, 1959; McDonald to secretary of state, no. 170, March 9, 1950, *FRUS*, 1950, v. V, 796–797.

38. See also McDonald to secretary of state, no. 181, March 15, 1950, USSDCF-PIFA, 1950–1954, reel 1, frame 427.

39. Laurence A. Steinhardt (1892–1959), ambassador, 1944–1948; Joseph E. Jacobs (1893–1971), ambassador, 1948–1949; Ellis O. Briggs, ambassador, 1949–1952.

40. *The Magnetic Tide* (1950), twenty-two-minute color documentary concerning European Jewish refugees' arrival and settlement in Israel; soundtrack provided by the Palestine String Quartet and the Tel Aviv Opera.

[Menachem] Begin and his colleague in the Knesset, [Shmuel] Katz, came at twelve and stayed until nearly 1:30. We had coffee on the roof. Begin seemed pleased by my report that the Justice Department had changed its ruling affecting admissibility of Irgun members and the likelihood that the State Department would soon follow suit. I promised to follow up and see if I could get a ruling in time to prevent delay in issuance of visa for Katz, who is going to the States to prepare [the] English publication [of] Begin's book.[41]

Begin, commenting on my half-serious statement that "[Gershon] Agron did not interest me because he never told me anything," said, "Well I had better not commit the same fault." He then developed [the] thesis that Britain, despite my quotation of Helm's recent pronouncement, could not be considered friendly to Israel or favorable to a strong Israel so long as it continued to rearm the Arab states and to refuse to support Israel's "right to viable frontiers." Naturally, I could not engage in a full debate on this subject, but merely reiterated my conviction that Knox Helm was sincere and that my impressions were that the UK was sympathetic to and was supporting current efforts at bilateral negotiations.

Conference at the chancery [in US Embassy offices] of staff, who listened to Chartrand's exposition of the United States Information and Education [USIE] program. It evoked quite divergent reactions. Undoubtedly, much is being accomplished, but it was rather startling to have Chartrand suggest that some participants in the program favored an expenditure upwards towards $300 million annually. Obviously, many times that could be spent, but the question of the US being able to afford it is paralleled by the question whether such manifold activities would be welcomed in the countries to which they are addressed. Moreover, as in our own case, there is the issue of how many members of a mission are appropriate at any particular post. Here, we have been waiting for and desperately needing a labor attaché and another top officer for more than a year only to have the Department delay, sometimes on the grounds of finance. It is surely out of line to have USIE talk about hundreds of millions when the Department can't find the money for essential officers or even secretaries in the political missions. Also, even if one assumes that the directives for the USIE's work would be formulated with the highest intelligence, there still must be considered the fundamental fact that American goodwill abroad must depend basically upon American political and commercial policies and the wisdom with which these are formulated, rather than upon any amount of "information or education."

Friday, March 17

At chancery, where I became definitely upset about what seemed to me the poor security arrangements in the file room. After consultations with various

---

41. Menachem Begin, *The Revolt*, was published in the United States by Henry Schuman in 1951. It is Begin's autobiographical history of the IZL.

people concerned, including the people working in the room, I drafted a very stiff order. Before issuing it, we shall discuss it at a staff conference.

Cy Sulzberger[42] and Currivan came to tea. The former told of his impressions that the king [Farouk] had the power and wanted to secure peace with Israel. In this realm [Prime Minister] Nahhas is Farouk's agent. I was not quite convinced on either count.[43] Sulzberger is making a survey of countries bordering Russia.

H. Alexander Straus of RCA[44] came to tell me of his two weeks' study of commercial and industrial possibilities. He is leaving with a divided mind.

Edwin Samuel came to tell me of his program to go to the States as representative of the group participated in by the government to prepare and administer the "[Conquest of] the Desert" international exhibition in Jerusalem in the spring of '51.[45] He hopes for US participation and support. I explained that, until the political hurdles were overcome, I could be of no use and that I doubted if the US would take part. I urged him, however, to go to the States there to find out for himself, for any worthwhile negotiations would have to take place there in any case.

Sunday, March 19

Our first all-day trip to the country this spring. In all we covered more than 250 miles. Even the ride up the Haifa road to Hadera was pleasant, so lovely was the whole countryside. From Hadera we drove through the foothills across the Emek to Afula and up to Nazareth, thence on through the mountains and down to Tiberias. There we accepted Paula's invitation.

The talk with Ben-Gurion covered a number of topics. As to Egypt, he doubts Farouk's will to peace, but grants that he has power. Israel "cannot" advance peace by concessions in the Negev. Was pleased at progress in US-Israel civil air negotiations. Admitted difficulty in finding adequate successor to Eliash. Expects soon in Israel [a] visit from [Gérard] Bloch, "an old personal friend,"

42. Cyrus Leo Sulzberger II (1912–1993), Pulitzer Prize-winning (1951) journalist and fiction/nonfiction writer; nephew of *New York Times* publisher Arthur Hays Sulzberger; senior foreign correspondent for *New York Times* in 1940s and 1950s.

43. On March 19, 1950 the Israeli press reported that Sulzberger had been assured in Egypt that the government was not interested in resuming war with Israel and wanted to find a way to sign a de facto peace. Sulzberger told officials in the Israeli Foreign Ministry that he had spoken to Azzam Pasha and Ambassador Caffery while in Cairo. Ben-Gurion responded that Israel wanted peace with Egypt based on de facto frontiers. McDonald commented to the State Department that the Israeli government "apparently feels [the] time [is] ripe [to] begin [an] open peace offensive campaign." McDonald to secretary of state, joint weeka no. 12, March 24, 1950, McDonald Papers, USHMM, box, 8, folder 8.

44. Hans Alexander Straus (1901–1977), German-born employee of RCA who worked in Japan, 1932–1940, and then emigrated to the United States; lived in Locarno, Switzerland, after 1959.

45. The "Conquest of the Desert," Israel's first international exhibition, opened in Jerusalem in September 1953. Focusing on land reclamation in deserts, it was sponsored by the Israeli government, the Jewish National Fund, and the Jewish Agency. Thirteen foreign countries including the United States participated. However, the United States skipped the opening ceremony in keeping with its refusal to acknowledge Jerusalem as Israel's capital.

[from the] Yugoslav Federation.[46] Finds [Isaac Deutscher's] "Life of Stalin" [*sic*] "fascinating."[47] Is returning "to work" March 20. As Ben-Gurion and I talked, Ruth kept Paula busy. It was a pleasant luncheon.

After lunch we drove down to the southern end of the lake, and [I] was more impressed than on previous visits by the volume of the Jordan as it pours out of the sea. We were interested in Degania and noted its war memorial, the [Syrian] tank which had been destroyed by an elderly member of the kibbutz with a Molotov cocktail.[48] Then, while Shalom and Ruth gathered brilliant colored anemones and other wild flowers, I had a quick nap in the car. From Tiberias we drove up to Safed for tea. The recurrent views of the sea and the Jordan and Syrian mountains beyond were rewarding. After tea, we drove down the mountain, stopping from time to time to enjoy the views of [the] water and [the] mountain, but instead of taking the main road on to Acre, we turned south and drove through one of the richest and most beautiful parts of Galilee that I have seen—mile after mile of olive groves closely cultivated by Arabs and with views to the west through the mountains and through the east to the sea and Jordan beyond. We were well on our way to Hadera before dark. Notable on the trip down from Safed was the impressiveness of Mount Tabor in the twilight, standing out from its broad valley as the natural scene for the Transfiguration. Spring certainly is the time to see Israel and especially the Galilee. Everywhere was green; even the Moab Mountains have for the time being lost their somber brown, which comes with the first heat of the summer and remains until the winter rains. We are looking forward to our next trip, this time up to the extreme north when we hope to skirt the Lebanese frontier. Home tired but mentally rested and refreshed by the day.

Monday, March 20

Introductory chat with Samuel Gorlitz, Department [of State] economist, who is here checking for the Department and the Export-Import Bank on the utilization of American funds.[49] Talked with Ware, who agreed that the fourth USIS officer ought not come.

At Eytan's office at four to discuss the diplomatic corps' complaints. Eytan had decided not to ask Simon to be present. I presented the case as well as I could, illustrating it with specific examples, while deploring the unhappy role my deanship placed me in. Eytan expressed concern, but less than I thought was suitable. He said that they had been trying to increase Simon's staff, but

---

46. Gérard Bloch (1920–1987), Yugoslav functionary and writer; vilified the USSR in 1950 as a deformed and degenerated state; in turn vilified by Soviets as a Trotskyist.

47. Isaac Deutscher (1907–1967), *Stalin: A Political Biography* (London: Oxford University Press, 1949).

48. Refers to destruction of the Syrian Army Renault R35 that penetrated into the Degania kibbutz, Battle of Degania, May 20, 1948. The tank remains as a monument there.

49. Samuel J. Gorlitz (1918–2007), University of Chicago-trained economist who became the State Department's economic expert on the Middle East and Africa; formed Federal Realty Investment Trust, 1962.

had succeeded to the extent of only half a girl when in fact he needed a leg-man.

Ruth and I stopped for a moment to see Sheldon Schoeneberg's pictures at the Katz Gallery.[50]

At the Argentine reception for Senator Molinari[51] the food was good but not up to the billing. The cordiality of the hosts and the guests was cheering. The only talk of any length I had was with Helm. After I had told Sir Knox of my talk with Ben-Gurion on Sunday, he related to me his unhappy experience trying to get Paula to arrange for Ben-Gurion to come to the Helm house. Two or three tentative invitations and inquiries as to when the prime minister would be free had drawn from Paula what the Helms interpreted as rather surly and discouraging responses, and they have given up pressing the matter. Until now he has not had a long talk with the prime minister. He seemed pleased when I said I would try to arrange at our house an occasion when the two men could have a really long talk.

Tuesday, March 21

On the way to Jerusalem, Ruth, Eli, and I [leaving] by ten [and] arriving at 11:45. The countryside all along the way was beautiful. I went directly to the consulate and found that Gibson and the senior officers were across the line. I called Riley and made a date for four o'clock at the King David.

My tea conference with Riley lasted from four until twenty minutes to six. It was one of the most comprehensive I have had with him. The following are among the points discussed:

1) He reiterated and argued for his favorite thesis that the Israelis are not doing enough to make successful peace negotiations probable. Though conciliatory in tone, they are in fact offering no substantial concession at any point to any one of their neighbors. Examined critically, it becomes evident, he said, that the "concessions" made to Abdullah in the recent talks were more nominal than substantial. This characterization would apply even to the Israeli offer to "pay compensation immediately" to Arab property owners [in Jerusalem], because the payments would in fact not begin until after possibly extended investigation, and the term "within five years" was a measure of the "promptness" of the payment. Similarly, Israel was refusing to make any concession to Egypt at Bir Qattar. The recent MAC [Mixed Armistice Commission] meeting on this point had shown not the slightest yielding by Dayan. As to Syria, the attitude of Israel is comparable, because there is no willingness on Israel's part to accept Syria's claim for the "natural water

50. Sheldon C. Schoeneberg (1929–2012), American Jewish artist who visited Israel several times, painting murals celebrating Palestine's early Jewish pioneers.
51. Argentine senator Diego Luis Molinari (1889–1966), son of Italian immigrants; prolific historian and politician; strongly pro-Zionist chairman of Argentine Senate foreign affairs committee, then on a tour of the Middle East and Asia.

frontier." I argued each of the three points but found the general to be firm in his conviction that Israel was ruining the chances of peace by not being more tangibly conciliatory.[52]

2) General Riley was inclined to hold that even a successful negotiation with Jordan would be bad for Israel, because it would lock and seal the doors to peace with the other Arab states. Moreover, it might result in an intensified boycott of Jordan and a worsening of the situation of Abdullah.

3) General Riley was sometimes inclined to question whether Israel really wanted peace now. Her actions were interpretable as indicating a desire to keep conditions in a state of flux, in the hopes that later, more could be gained than now. Evidence of Israel's determination to keep all is found, for example, in the strengthening of frontier settlements in the northeast and along other frontiers. The more these are built up, the more difficult will any concessions become.

4) The Trusteeship Council discussions of the proposed Jerusalem statute are a solemn farce. They can hardly be seriously meant by most of the participants in the current meetings. Obviously, the US, Britain, and perhaps other countries represented intend to mark time in the hope that the December [9] decision of the last Assembly can be demonstrated to be inapplicable.

5) General Riley again deplored the unwillingness of [Roger] Garreau to delay his compromise plan until after an effort had been made by the Trusteeship Council to implement the Assembly decision.[53] Garreau's insistence on presenting his compromise plan at the very beginning, while proof of his own conviction that the Assembly's resolution was inapplicable, tended to destroy the chance of getting a compromise solution later. "You cannot expect to have support for a compromise move before efforts have been made to apply the principles under which the Trusteeship Council was obligated to offer it." There is a bare possibility that, despite Garreau's mistake in tactics, a compromise can still be reached. Perhaps the best solution would be for the Trusteeship Council to approve the revised draft statute in principle but take no action to implement it, except perhaps to authorize a subcommittee to persuade the two parties directly interested, Israel and Jordan, to consider it sympathetically. Then the matter could be reviewed at the June meeting of the Trusteeship Council. If, as a result of that review, it could be maintained

52. McDonald reported on March 24, 1950, that a subcommittee of the Israeli-Syrian MAC, appointed eight months earlier to delineate the Israeli-Syrian border, had completed its work and that the delay in the approval of its report lay in the "Syrian contention for the commanding ground." In the final settlement Syria was to withdraw its forces from Tel Azazyat (partly inside the demilitarized zone) by March 24 and to demolish its fortifications there by April 4, 1950. McDonald commented, "This reportedly completes [the] demarcation [of the] Israel-Syrian frontier." On March 31, 1950, McDonald reported that the Israeli-Egyptian MAC reached agreement to establish joint border patrols and for the Egyptians to use the water wells in Israel at the south end of the Gaza Strip. McDonald to secretary of state, joint weeka no. 12, March 24, 1950, McDonald Papers, USHMM, box 8, folder 8. McDonald to secretary of state, joint weeka no. 12, March 31, 1950, McDonald Papers, USHMM, box 8, folder 8.

53. Entry of January 5, 1950.

that the Assembly's proposal was impracticable, the Trusteeship Council could so report at the fall Assembly and at that time propose a compromise solution.

6) General Riley was emphatic that the present handling of Jerusalem and the related problems of peace negotiations were being so mishandled as not only to minimize the chances of success, but also to discredit the existing international mechanisms for conciliation and indeed the very thought of such conciliation. This led us then to a consideration of what could be done about it.

7) General Riley and I were agreed that a one-man conciliator is essential. He could be brought into the picture through a slight modification in the Mixed Armistice Commissions by simply adding to the role of the chairman the authority to propose the implementation of Article VIII in the Israel-Jordan agreement and comparable powers in the other agreements. The difficulty here is that this would require assent of both parties in each case. The obstacle to a general conciliator lies in the terms of reference of the PCC, which under its statute has this authority from the Assembly. This observation brought us back to the familiar theme that the PCC is not only futile, but is a major obstacle to progress.

8) I asked General Riley what he thought about attempting to persuade the US and the UK to take the lead in facing realities about the PCC and in securing its replacement by Bunche or by someone of his type. In particular, I asked General Riley if he thought it desirable that he talk with Helm. I asked him also if he had spoken with [Hugh] Dow or with [John] Glubb. Riley's answer on all of these counts was negative. He said that he thought he had to stick to his last and not go beyond his technical role, except in his talks with me or other American official representatives in this area. He did not however, discourage me from trying to formulate a program and urge it on the authorities in Washington.

9) I left him with the feeling that perhaps the most important single effort that I could make in the near future would be to put up to Washington strongly the imperative necessity of the new approach. Perhaps preliminary to this, I should have a long talk with Helm to explore the possibility of our making a joint approach or at least taking parallel action.

Katz, Begin's associate, met me at the hotel and showed me the "text" of my note to Begin when the Anglo-American Committee was in Jerusalem. The language quoted was obviously in some respects not mine because it was so uncolloquial. After the two of us had tried to figure out what I had probably really written, we decided that a paraphrase would be better than the quotes. In substance, this is what Katz agreed to insert instead of the "text" of my note:

> Mr. McDonald wrote that there was a good chance of persuading the
> British to change their policy towards Israel [*sic*] and Zionism. He

hoped that during the period of the Committee's work nothing should be done by Begin and his associates to diminish the chances of the Committee's success.[54]

Having disposed of this, Katz and I talked of other matters, including his request for a visa. I told him that I hoped there would be no difficulty on this latter score.

Pleasant dinner with the Rosenblooms and then to the concert.[55] The hour previous had been enlivened by the report that Koussevitzky had taken cold but he made his appearance, and at the end received an ovation, which did not cease until he motioned the orchestra off the stage. I was greeted at the concert by a number of people, including Sharett, as if my appearance there were a sort of recognition of the status of Jerusalem as Israel's capital.

Wednesday, March 22

To the Bradys' cocktail party. Delightful affair, which gave [the] opportunity for transacting six or seven separate items of minor business. One of these, not so minor, was my talk with Shiloah about the desirability of Helm's having a full chance to talk with Ben-Gurion. I offered to invite the two couples to dinner at our house if that would be acceptable. I mentioned that, of course, nothing should be said about Paula's part in the previous failures.

In the last week of March 1950 the British and Israeli governments signed a financial agreement settling claims and counterclaims dating from the termination of the Mandate. Israel's payment of three million pounds over fifteen years would settle all British claims concerning Crown property, as well as British-owned industrial equipment that transferred to Israeli hands, the Mandate's financial deficits, pensions of British mandatory officials, and so forth. The Israelis were satisfied with the agreement—British officials had claimed Israel owed twenty million pounds as recently as July 1949.

But Bevin spoiled the moment. On March 28 in the House of Commons he upheld the legality of Iraqi and Egyptian policies of blockading crude oil deliveries to Israel, and he blamed Israeli violations of UN resolutions for Iraqi and Egyptian behavior. McDonald commented to Washington, "In the past year Israel-Brit[ish] relations have been steadily strengthened mainly by clever handling [of the] situation by Brit[ish legation] staff [in] Israel. Settlement [of] financial issues together with ensuing trade agreements might have brought about complete rapprochement. However, [the] Bevin statement together with hard feelings over Brit[ish] rearmament [of the]

54. See entry of April 13, 1950. There is no reference in McDonald's diary from 1946 to having met or corresponded with Begin in Palestine. See Goda et al., eds., *To the Gates of Jerusalem.*
55. Charles Rosenbloom (1898–1973), Jewish financier in Pittsburgh and leader with the local Jewish federation, the United Palestine Appeal, and the Weizmann Institute.

Arab States has clipped wings of [the] financial agreement in its secondary role of 'dove of peace.'"[56]

Thursday, March 23

The reception for Monsignor Gori, the new Latin Patriarch of Jerusalem, was well managed, dignified and brief.[57] Helm, Esin and some of the other diplomats were somewhat reluctant, as I had been, to be a part of the procession, but we all marched sedately. The Argentine [Minister Pablo Manguel] was not present, giving as the reason the necessity of seeing Senator Molinari off at the airport that morning. A contributing factor may have been his being a Jew.[58] The representatives of the government, including in addition to those from Protocol [Simon], Eytan, and representatives from the Ministry of Religious Affairs, joined us in greeting the patriarch at the French Hospital but then rode to the church and awaited the procession there.

The reception at the French Hospital in Jaffa was a formal affair that included official greetings by Simon on behalf of President Weizmann and the official presentation of the diplomatic corps to the patriarch by McDonald. A full processional of the patriarch's subordinates, choir boys, and foreign diplomats made its way to the Church of St. Antoine, where the patriarch, sitting on his throne, allowed church representatives and members of the diplomatic corps to kiss his ring. Foreign Minister Sharett received the patriarch at HaKirya on March 24.[59]

Friday, March 24

At ten I was completely taken by surprise by the visit of Monsignor Gori, accompanied by Monsignor Vergani,[60] Father Terence Kuehn,[61] and [three] other priests. During coffee, in addition to the usual courteous talk, I raised the question of the soundness of Jacob Herzog's thesis that Israel and the Church have common interests against materialistic Moscow. The responses were not encouraging. The monsignor [Gori] and Father Terence stressed instead the irreligious or unreligious nature of many of the Israeli leaders, the unwillingness of the Orthodox, as well as the other Jews, to recognize the reality of the Messiah, their sublimating of the state as the Jewish messiah, the uncertainty of the ambitions of the leaders for the state and other manifestations of complete unwillingness to accept central truths, make anything like a common

56. McDonald to secretary of state, joint weeka no. 12, March 31, 1950, McDonald Papers, USHMM, box 8, folder 8.
57. Monsignor Alberto Gori (1889–1970), custos of the Holy Land, 1937–1949; pressed hard for the internationalization of Jerusalem; elevated to Latin Patriarch of Jerusalem by Pope Pius XII, 1949.
58. Dr. Pablo Manguel (1912–1984), Jewish Argentine labor lawyer and diplomat; founded Organización Israelita Argentina (a Perónist organization), 1947; minister to Israel, 1949–1954.
59. *Palestine Post*, March 23, 25, 1950. The ornate French Hospital, built from 1879–1885 and bequeathed to the local nuns, is now a luxury hotel.
60. Entries of October 17, 1948, December 16, 1948, and January 4, 1949.
61. Entry of July 4, 1949.

front impossible. My visitors seemed rather optimistic that among the so-called "schismatic[s]," that is the Greek Orthodox and others, there was a tendency to recognize the truth of the Church and the primacy of His Holiness. Reference was made several times to the traditional willingness of the Church to forgive the sinner but not the sin. Monsignor Gori was kind enough to suggest that I come to visit him in Jerusalem. When I explained the official difficulties, he suggested that I make it a personal visit.

Shiloah and Kollek came at 3:30 to urge that the American representatives in Cairo and the other Arab capitals be instructed to discourage attacks on Abdullah. I promised to pass on the word to the Department. Both men, but particularly Kollek, were intrigued by the concept that Israel might be for modern Jews a substitute for the personal messiah.

McDonald passed the request to Washington and to US missions in the Arab capitals later that day. From Damascus, Ambassador Keeley characterized Israel's desire for US pressure on other Arab states as "the best example of misplaced zeal that this Legation has seen" and argued, "Nothing . . . could be better designed to stiffen resistance to peace with Israel than such US intercession."[62]

At the Arab League's twelfth session, which began in Cairo on March 25, 1950, there was immediate hostility toward King Abdullah's annexation of Arab Palestine and his desire for peace with Israel. Before formal meetings began, Egypt backed statements by Grand Mufti Haj Amin al-Husseini and by Abdullah al-Tel attacking Abdullah, and on Egypt's insistence, the League Council invited members of the grand mufti's Gaza government to participate in League meetings. Portrayed as the enemy of Arabism, Abdullah was isolated and threated with expulsion from the Arab League.[63] *McDonald commented, "Majority of popular thinking is that Abdullah will make peace in spite of any Arab League decision provided [that the April 2] general election in Jordan allows him to form [a government] which will support his plans."*[64]

Sunday, March 26

Late morning visit from Colonel Archibald and the two air inspectors, [one of whom was] Lt. Colonel [Norval C.] Bonawitz.[65] Talk was mostly about the difficulty of housing, but I did manage to press Colonel Archibald about

62. Keeley to secretary of state, no. 207, April 7, 1950, USSDCF-PIFA, 1950–1954, reel 1, frames 471–472. This file has numerous statements by Arab leaders rejecting an Israeli-Jordanian peace and threatening retaliation against Jordan.

63. Michael Barnett and Etel Solingen, "Designed to Fail or Failure of Design? The Origins and Legacy of the Arab League," in *Crafting Cooperation: Regional International Institutions in Comparative Perspective*, eds. Amitav Acharya and Alastair Iain Johnson (New York: Cambridge University Press, 2007), 197–198; and Ronen Yitzhak, *Abdullah al-Tall, Arab Legion Officer: Arab Nationalism and Opposition to the Hashemite Regime* (Eastbourne: Sussex Academic Press, 2012), 92–94.

64. McDonald to secretary of state, joint weeka no. 12, March 31, 1950, McDonald Papers, USHMM, box 8, folder 8.

65. Norval C. Bonawitz (1914–1995), United States Air Force.

the evacuation report. In the afternoon I decided that I must see Bonawitz alone and, with some difficulty, managed it on the roof. He told me that Washington was aware of the situation[66] [and] that this was one of the reasons they [the air inspectors] were here. I judge from what he said that the Department is anxious to improve the reporting from here and that Colonel Bonawitz had not received satisfactory answers to his questions. He spoke highly of Major Brady and said that the Army was pleased with him.

Two days later, McDonald sent a note to Colonel Bonawitz: "I was glad that we had a few moments alone on the roof before you left. I hope that you and your colleagues will see fit to act promptly, for the longer we delay, the longer we miss utilizing, as fully as it ought to be, the large possibility here for intelligence information."[67]

On March 27 Acheson cabled the US embassy in Tel Aviv stating that Israeli armament requests needed to include more detailed information concerning the size of the Israeli military establishment. The Israeli embassy in Washington had informed the State Department that, although Israel would not make official statements as to its military strength, it would provide information on an informal, discreet, and personal basis. Colonel Efraim Ben-Artzi, the former Israeli military attaché in Washington, would meet with the US service attachés in Israel. The Israelis requested purchase licenses for, among other things, eighteen jet fighters and forty-five Sherman tanks, plus rifles, machine guns, and artillery pieces.[68]

Monday, March 27

Visited Goldie Meyerson with Fried. As part of my effort to bring her out, I repeated criticism I had heard of Histadrut's monopolistic tendencies and the "capitalistic abuses" of some of the cooperatives, for example, the bus cooperative. Her replies were masterly in their clear analysis and effective phrasing. She will, I think, be very helpful to Fried. She approved his plan of going quietly about his work. She stressed that nothing could be rushed, especially not with the Left. I suspect that, after we left, she telephoned [Pinhas] Lubianker's office, head of the Histadrut, who had delayed seeing Fried; within an hour or so Lubianker's office called to make a date for Fried.[69]

Talked to Leo Kohn about some memoranda on three aspects of Orthodoxy; the local political one, the religious and cultural side here in Israel, and the effect on Judaism throughout the world. Kohn will do something on all.

66. Referring to Archibald's unsuitability as senior military attaché, reported by McDonald on March 9, 1950.

67. McDonald to Bonawitz, March 28, 1950, McDonald Papers, USHMM, box 8, folder 9.

68. Acheson to US embassy in Israel, no. 147, March 27, 1950, *FRUS*, 1950, v. V, 818.

69. Pinhas Lubianker [later Lavon], (1904–1976), East Galician-born politician; emigrated to Palestine, 1929; secretary of Mapai, 1935–1937; member of Knesset (Mapai), 1949–1961; secretary-general of Histadrut, 1949–1950; held ministerial posts, 1950–1954, including minister of agriculture in Ben-Gurion's second cabinet, November 1950, and minister of defense under Sharett, 1953–1955.

We were joined by Kollek and Shiloah during a discussion of possibility of Catholic-Jewish reconciliation. Kohn was firmly negative on the ground that [perceived] Jewish stiff-necked sinfulness had been too long a central [Catholic] dogma. He foresaw no possibility of affirmative change. As to Israel being a sort of sublimation of the Jewish concept of the messiah, Kohn was prepared to discuss it but not inclined to accept it. There was also some talk about an alleged present effort to unite the forces of some Christian groups with the more extreme elements against Israel and the Jews. Nothing, however, was set forth that was very tangible on this rather startling point.

Decided to finesse the cocktail party [at Swiss Consulate] for President Paul Ruegger of the ICRC [Red Cross] and drove instead to Netanya for the very pleasant small tea party of the Ben-Amis[70] for Nathan Straus.[71] The hosts have a very large house. He said that the new road would be finished in two months and that, shortly thereafter, Netanya would be on its way towards [a] 50,000 population. Straus said that he had practically completed arrangements in Washington for an interview, which he would get from Abdullah across the line. He had consulted Hare, who said it must be quite unofficial, and Straus had said he would do nothing without talking to me. At the moment he is simply waiting to hear from Amman. We drove Rebecca Sieff back to her house. Marcus Sieff and Simon Marks are coming soon.

Tuesday, March 28

In the afternoon Eli [Karlin] and I held our first "sabra seminar." Akiva Kounine[72] brought four of his friends, Amos Elon,[73] Benjamin Tammuz,[74] Shabtai Tabechkin[75] and Ya'akov Malkin.[76] The talk, which lasted from five o'clock until after seven, was very interesting and revealing. Perhaps they did not show as much of the native sabras' reactions as would have been the case if our guests had not all been intellectuals.

70. Ovid Ben-Ami (1905–1988), founder (1927) and first mayor of Netanya.
71. Nathan Straus Jr. (1889–1961), New York journalist and civic leader; son of the American Jewish philanthropist Nathan Straus (1848–1931), who donated much of his fortune to the development of health care in Palestine and for whom Netanya was named.
72. Akiva Kounine (1929–1997), son of Benzion Kounine (see entry of January 30, 1950); trained in economics at Oxford and Yale; foreign loans adviser to Palestine Economic Corporation and Israeli Ministry of Finance.
73. Amos Elon (1926–2009) Vienna-born journalist for *Haaretz* and author; best-known book *The Israelis: Founders and Sons* (1971) was critical of the Zionist pioneers; early advocate of a Palestinian Arab state.
74. Benjamin Tammuz (1919–1989), Russian-born writer; emigrated to Palestine, 1924; spent time in Paris thereafter where he became a communist; literary and cultural critic for *Haaretz*.
75. Shabtai Tabechkin [later Teveth] (1925–2014), the only actual sabra of the group; historian and journalist with *Haaretz*; son of pioneer Dov Tabechkin; biographer of Ben-Gurion who, he claimed, never authorized the expulsion of Palestinians in 1948; conducted research into the Chaim Arlosoroff assassination and concluded that it was the work of Revisionists, a conclusion rejected by Menachem Begin.
76. Ya'akov Malkin (b. 1926) Warsaw-born intellectual; emigrated to Palestine, 1933; educator, literary critic, and leading atheist philosopher; affiliated with Habimah and Cameri theaters and Tel Aviv University.

The opening statement was made by "the Canaanite," as his fellows nicknamed this advocate of the historical and archaeological approach to Israel's problem and its future. A second of the group, a member of Mapam, argued [that development] can follow only after the economic integration of the new settlers. A third of the group contended that Israel is a modern version of the American melting pot and that its chief need is for the rebirth here of the spirit of the pioneer. I shall append a fuller account of the session later.

When it was over, Eli and I decided that our next group should be somewhat younger and less sophisticated sabras. I should note here, however, that one of the group developed the interesting thesis that Judaism as a religion was a development of the Diaspora. It began as a cult in Babylonia and was developed in exile by the rabbis. Hence, the Jewish religion as we know it is not the basis of the Jewish faith, and need have little to do with the future Israel. Other members of the group took exception to this particular interpretation, but none made any defense of Orthodoxy.

The ingathering of the exiles developed diverse points of view. These ranged from the emphasis on national self-interest to the recognition that Israel could not impose quotas, since the Zionists had so long fought British quotas. On all the many questions discussed, there were large, sometimes sharp, differences of opinion. It was obvious from this first session that one danger to be avoided in our chapter on sabras is the acceptance of popular clichés and oversimplification. It was notable that this first group showed little interest in party politics as such.

The performance of *Carmen* was good, but Madame de Phillipe, though she looked completely unlike herself or any of her other characters, was not as exciting as I had thought she might be. The performance was more elaborately costumed than any of the previous ones. In the intermission before the third act, I spoke briefly over Kol Israel preliminary to [the] broadcasting of the third act.

Wednesday, March 29

Our misadventure to Eilat. We were at the airport a few minutes before nine but, because of the management's failure to have word about weather conditions at Eilat, we did not take off until after eleven. The pilot during the warming up seemed to have trouble with one engine, but after nearly fifteen minutes it seemed to perform perfectly. The trip down was quiet and, fortunately, [the] clouds broke away before we reached the more picturesque mountainous area. From there on the countryside was scenically reminiscent of the Colorado canyon upside down. It was utter desolation but impressively beautiful. As we approached Eilat, the passengers became more and more quiet, many of them longing for a prompt landing. I was among these.

As the pilot ran over the landing strip and headed out over the gulf, I was undisturbed because I thought he was turning into the wind for his landing. Even when he circled the field a second time, I thought this was just a usual maneuver. But by the time he had circled a fourth or fifth round, I lost interest.

After forty-five minutes and repeated conferences between some of the VIPs, particularly Mr. Nicolai Kirschner,[77] on behalf of the management and the pilot, we headed back for Lydda a few minutes before one [o'clock], where we arrived just before two. Never had I expected the sparse vegetation of the northern Negev and the scattered kibbutzim to look so like home, bringing as they did the promise of relief within a few minutes.

When we landed, all our Israeli friends were full of apologies and they kindly invited us to lunch. But I was in no mood for visiting and hurried home for a cup of soup and a desperately needed nap. Mr. Kirschner, who rode back with us, and I vainly sought to solve the mystery of the forty-five minute "philosophical discussion" between the pilot and Lydda control tower while we were circling over Eilat. Later, I asked Cashman to get hold of the pilot and get the latter's story. The mystery was further deepened the next day when, at a cocktail party [for] Mr. Kirschner, Brigadier Dayan, who was waiting for us in Eilat with a "bountiful lunch," told me that there had been no rain in Eilat and that the runway was in perfect condition.

Thursday, March 30

Visit with Thurston of Moscow at the office in the morning.[78]

Esin came to compare notes about Jordan-Israel-Arab League relations and wondered if possibly Jordan might not turn towards other Islamic countries outside [the] Arab League.

Somewhat depressed by Fried's characterization of the office as a "high school fraternity." Urged McVicker and Hooper to eliminate personal use of phone and break up business-hour parties.

Brief visit at [Moshe] Castel's show of his new style pictures. They are very colorful and decorative and some of those representing ancient manuscripts one might like to keep, but the others are not nearly so attractive as those in his older style.

At Mrs. Irron's party for her father, Mr. Kirschner, received more apologies about the Eilat trip. Was glad to note that Thurston seemed to be having a good time. Shiloah, whom he had met in Jerusalem, concentrated on trying to make [Thurston] see that the British arms program and its support by the United States [had a negative effect on] the US urging on the Arab states the policy of peace.

Friday, March 31

To Eytan's office, where he handed us his government's *note-verbale* warning against a favorable vote on the Jerusalem draft statute. I am keeping a copy for my record.

---

77. Nicolai Kirschner (b. 1886), former president of the South African Zionist Federation for twenty years.
78. Ray L. Thurston, first secretary and consul, US embassy in Moscow; later ambassador to Haiti and Somalia.

During March 1950, the UN Trusteeship Council in Geneva, as charged, drafted a new Jerusalem statute based on the UN General Assembly Resolution of December 9, 1949. The draft called again for internationalization of Greater Jerusalem as a corpus separatum. *In theory, the General Assembly would debate the draft when it convened in June.*[79]

On March 28, Nahum Goldmann in his capacity as chair of the American section of the Jewish Agency, told Secretary Acheson that US support for the statute would be disastrous. Because the United States was on the Trusteeship Council, it could not vote against the statute. Instead, the United States abstained on the provisions concerning Jerusalem's boundaries and its legislative council, and Acheson pressed for a separate UN agreement to consult Israel and Jordan on the statute's implementation. The French were wary, not wishing the statute to become a dead letter. The final Trusteeship Council vote on the draft statute as a whole was scheduled for April 4.[80]

The Israeli note-verbale *of March 31, handed to the US, the UK, French, Argentine, and Belgian ambassadors, reflected Israel's frustration. It pointed to the possible "grave consequences" should the Trusteeship Council adopt the Jerusalem statute as written. The imposition of a foreign regime ran contrary to the wishes of the Jewish majority in Jerusalem, as well as the wishes of the two countries controlling the area; it would disrupt economic connections between the city and Israel; it would make the Jewish population there vulnerable to attack; and all the while failing to protect the Holy Places, which was ostensibly the reason for the statute in the first place.*[81]

We then discussed the suggestion that Eytan had made, that Ben-Artzi would give informally the information which our people wanted as a basis for considering Israel's arms appeal. Eytan said that Kollek knew more about that. The latter was to see Major Brady later in the morning, but had to postpone the date because of a call from Kaplan. We talked also about El Al, the Eilat fiasco, and the need for a civil aviation director. Eytan said he had agreed some time ago and had spoken about it to Remez, Ben-Gurion, and others. Kollek was not flattering about [Aryeh] Pincus, or his ability.

Shocked, but not surprised, by Bobby's information that the Fords might not arrive until the end of May. I sent another telegram to [the] Department, urging that in view [of the] excess strain on other officers during Ford's absence, he should return at the end of April.

Shocked and displeased at the news that Archibald had ordered his men not to work on the [Joint Weekly Report] overtime. I ordered the men to get it out today irrespective of time, and intend to make clear to the colonel that we are here to get work done, and not to watch the clock.

---

79. *DFPI*, v. 5, d. 123, 149, 152, 153; also *FRUS*, 1950, v. V, 811–812.
80. *DFPI*, v. 5, d. 155, 159; also *FRUS*, 1950, v. V, 776–777, 790, 805–806, 814–815, 819–821, 827–829.
81. Printed in *DFPI*, v. 5, d. 163; *FRUS*, 1950, v. V, 829–830.

22. April 1950

Saturday, April 1

Left a little after ten, arriving in Tiberias at 12:30. The countryside was beautiful. To our delight, Mount Hermon stood out sharp and clear as we rounded the last hill before dropping down to Tiberias. The lake was like a jewel, set in its surrounding hills and plateaus, all for a few brief weeks brilliantly green and with snow-capped Hermon towering above the northern end of the lake. After lunch and a nap at the Galil Kineret [hotel], we crossed the lake at four. During the crossing we enjoyed Kollek's excellent courier [tour guide] service as he pointed out the historic spots.

The spring festival of the gathering of the first fruits of the harvest, in which the young children all participated, was an interesting prelude to [the] seder.[1] The seder itself, in spite of its heavy overcrowding, was worthwhile. It was so very different from the traditional seders we had attended at the Davidowitz's. The intermingling of the traditional and the new, the participation by many persons, some newly arrived, the intense interest with which the young people followed the reading and the singing, made it seem a richly national ceremony.

The recrossing of the lake in the bright full moonlight was enlivened by the gaiety of four young Bulgarian refugees, all of whom had been here long enough to feel at home.

Sunday, April 2

Long and pleasant visit with the Louries, Arthur's father and mother. We enjoyed the lake and the views of Mount Hermon and the mountains. The Louries' account of deepening hatred [in South Africa] between the Afrikaners and the natives did not surprise me. Seemingly, [Daniel] Malan[2] and his colleagues have accomplished nothing beyond adding fuel to the native resentment.

At four we started back to Tel Aviv. It did not seem possible that the countryside in the milder light was even more beautiful than the day before. We

---

1. The harvest festival as a prelude to Passover is practiced in some kibbutzim.
2. Daniel François Malan (1874–1959), head of the National Party in South Africa and prime minister of South Africa, 1948–1954; known for the implementation of systematized apartheid.

dropped Miss Jaffe of the *Jewish Morning Journal*[3] at Afula and continued the short way home via the Magda road to Hadera. There was a sense of timelessness in thus traversing this historic route of conquerors during thousands of years. Home by 6:30.

Monday, April 3

Busy all morning at the house. Long visit with [Rudolf] Sonneborn at teatime.[4] He explained to me the reasons for Morgenthau's present irreplaceability in the UJA, chiefly because Morgenthau is so genuinely willing to sacrifice himself for the cause. No successor is in sight. I was intrigued by Sonneborn's account [of] Senator [Herbert H.] Lehman's unwillingness to make any comparable sacrifice.[5] This cheered me a little because it made less invidious Lehman's declinations on the two or three occasions when I had asked him for help. Sonnenborn confirmed that David Niles is still the best approach in these matters to the president. Abe Feinberg continues to have access,[6] as, of course, do Dubinsky, Potofsky, et al. Sonnenborn said he was delighted with the news of Mr. [Sidney] Herold's visit.[7] I should include him when we give a dinner for Herold.

On April 3, McDonald sent a personal and secret message to David Niles, excerpted below.

> Dear Dave,
> You know so well my loyalty to the President and his policies and you have always been so helpful to me that I naturally turn to you for advice on a crucial decision.
> You will recall that when President Truman asked me to represent him in Israel, I calculated that I would be able to carry through his three specific instructions—set out in his letter to me of July 21, 1948—within a year or so. Now, after nearly twenty-one months, all three have been accomplished; but his major goal—peace and stability in the Middle East—is still far off. I hope, however, that before the end of this year some at least of the present armistice agreements between Israel and its neighbors will have converted into peace treaties.

3. Jean Jaffe (1898–1958), Lithuanian-born Yiddish-language journalist for the *Jewish Morning Journal* [*Morgen Zhurnal*] of New York. See entry of February 3, 1950.
4. Rudolf Sonneborn (1899–1986), leading American Zionist and fundraiser who was close to Ben-Gurion and Weizmann; aided after World War II with movement of Jewish refugees to Palestine and with weapons procurement for Haganah, the latter after hosting a group of supporters in his New York apartment at Ben-Gurion's request in July 1945; the "Sonneborn Institute," founded during this meeting, was the codename for arms purchases in the United States.
5. Herbert H. Lehman, governor of New York, 1933–1942; US senator from New York, 1950–1957. See entries of December 2, 1948; September 13, 1949; January 16, 1950.
6. Elath confirmed that Feinberg had access to Niles as well as to Secretary of Defense Louis Johnson, particularly on the issue of arms sales to Israel. Elath to United States Division, April 26, 1950, *DFPI*, v. 5, d. 211.
7. Entry of July 23, 1948.

In view of this probability and because of what seem to my wife and to me compelling family reasons, I hope the President will permit me to retire before January, 1951. Ruth and I both physically show some of the effects of our strenuous 'tour of duty' here. . . .

Ruth and I expect to take our accumulated leave at home in the Fall and—if the President approves—we shall not return to Israel but instead retire soon after early November.

If the schedule is agreed upon, I shall be glad, during my home leave in September and October, to make as many non-political speeches as may seem desirable on Israel's achievements and on President Truman's decisive contributions towards these.

Please write me frankly what you think about the above. Until I hear from you this whole possible program will remain exclusively between you and my family.

Cordially Yours,
James G. McDonald

Tuesday, April 4

At the office filed a telegram regarding [the] possible visit of Garreau or Bunche to Jerusalem and a despatch of praise on Crocker's report on the Jewish situation in Iraq.

Wednesday, April 5

Dov Joseph[8] called to tell me of his US plans. He expects to be gone about a fortnight.

Staff meeting and beginning of tightening of regulations.

Called for Paula to take her to the [Israel] Philharmonic concert, crowding seven people into the Oldsmobile. [Paul] Paray was well received, but not, of course, with the enormous enthusiasm which greeted Koussevitzky. He played Beethoven's Fifth, the other chief work was Bartok's piano concerto with the French Mademoiselle [Éliane] Richepin.[9] She was excellent.

Thursday, April 6

Emanuel and Mrs. Neumann came in just before lunch and stayed for nearly an hour. Neumann thought [Lazar] Braudo a routinier whose future would not be determined until the next meeting of the ZOA. On the question of the successor to Weizmann, Neumann made the amazing statement "it will of course be Ben-Gurion." To my question why the latter should give up the prime ministership

8. In the current government the minister of rationing and supply and also minister of agriculture.
9. Éliane Richepin (1910–1999), French pianist and child prodigy; specialized in Chopin, Ravel, and Debussy; founded the Annecy Music Festival; in Israel at the invitation of the conductor Paul Paray.

to become a president without power, Neumann reported that Ben-Gurion would, of course, change the constitution. He indicated no specific plans for Silver.

At 3:30 [Claude de] Boisanger and [Pablo] Azcárate with a French assistant came and stayed for nearly an hour. He [Boisanger] had seen Sharett with Eytan, Shiloah, and Leo Kohn present. Later Azcárate had seen Eytan alone. Boisanger's general reaction was one of restrained disappointment. He said that he had not expected Israel to give unqualified acceptance to the PCC's new procedural program but that Sharett would indicate conditional acceptance. The response had been less than that; Sharett had stressed that an essential prerequisite of any progress was a change on the part of the Arab states foreshadowing at least a desire to discuss peace.[10] Boisanger then talked at considerable length about the commission's procedural plans, interpreting them as a reasonable compromise between the Arab request for mediation and that of the Jews for direct negotiation. He said he hoped I would express to the Foreign Office interest in the success of his mission. I told him I had not yet received any instructions, but would be happy to do what I properly could.[11]

It was just about at that moment that McVicker arrived with a telegram from the Department, dispatched on the 3rd and dated as received here on the 5th, but which for some reason had not been previously delivered to me. It instructed me to express the hope that the PCC's proposal would be sympathetically received and considered as a means towards progress.

Listening to Boisanger, one would never have guessed that he and his colleagues had been on the job for over a year with nothing accomplished, so leisurely did he appear to be.

On March 29, 1950 the Palestine Conciliation Committee called for reorganization into mixed committees, each negotiating on a specific topic and composed of representatives from the various states and guided by PCC members. US missions in the Middle East were to encourage a friendly and dispassionate hearing of the PCC's plan in the hope that it could advance a settlement.[12]

On April 4 the Arab League issued a resolution in Cairo: "It is forbidden for an Arab state belonging to the League to negotiate or conclude a separate peace or a political, military, or economic accord with Israel. The state which contravenes this principle will be considered as excluded from the League."[13] The Arab League Council also instituted procedures to break diplomatic and economic relations with Arab states that

---

10. Sharett's account to Eban of his meeting with the PCC delegates is in *DFPI*, v. 5, d. 173. He refused to commit unless the Arabs showed a readiness for peace through declarations and by sending representatives with full powers to negotiate to Geneva. Otherwise, he said, the entire scheme would allow the Arab states to continue evasion while escaping blame.

11. Report in McDonald to secretary of state, joint weeka, no. 14, April 7, 1950, McDonald Papers, USHMM, box 8, folder 9.

12. Acheson circular to US missions in Middle East, April 3, 1950, *FRUS*, 1950, v. V, 835–836. Further clarification in memorandum by James M. Ludlow, August 17, 1950, *FRUS*, 1950, v. V, 971–973.

13. Included in Caffery to secretary of state, no. 332, April 4, 1950, *FRUS*, v. V, 839–840.

negotiated with Israel; reaffirmed the closure of the Suez Canal to ships bound to or from Israel; reaffirmed a travel ban for anyone with an Israeli visa; called for Jerusalem to adhere to the status prescribed by the UN resolution of November 29, 1947; issued a resolution to the effect that any Arab armies in Palestine were there temporarily without the aim of annexation or partition; and provided for the head of the All Palestine government—Grand Mufti Haj Amin al-Husseini—to attend future meetings.[14]

Friday, April 7

At the Foreign Office at 8:45 to see Eytan. Gave him message from the Department. He in turn explained Israel's point of view, stressing that it was prepared to accept any form of [PCC] procedure, but that mere procedure would be useless until the Arab states indicated a willingness to make peace. He said that Boisanger was procedural-minded and exaggerated the possibilities [of] mere machinery. He also implied, as I had heard earlier and as [Gideon] Rafael was subsequently to elaborate, that Boisanger was anxious to drag out the PCC's existence for personal reasons.

On April 7 McDonald reported on his meeting with Eytan, which, he added, occurred despite the Passover holiday. Eytan, McDonald said, hoped that Abdullah could possibly find the PCC scheme helpful in that it would allow him to negotiate with Israel in the open. McDonald also reported his own comment to Eytan that the Israeli leak to the Palestine Post *of Boisanger's discussions at the Foreign Office— despite Boisanger's request for secrecy—could jeopardize Boisanger's chances of securing any procedural agreement in the Arab capitals.*[15]

The Egyptians, on behalf of the Arab states, agreed in principle with the PCC's proposed procedures, but only if Israel accepted the General Assembly resolution of December 11, 1948, particularly as it regarded the return of Palestinian Arab refugees. Boisanger took this as a positive step. But the Israelis made clear in the third week of April that the Arab answer was "bogus." Israeli acceptance of the PCC procedure, said government officials, hinged on declarations by Arab states that they were ready to make peace without Israeli concessions in advance.[16]

An interesting dinner at the Kaete Dan with Miss Dubinsky. Others besides Ruth and myself were Mrs. Harris, Fried, and Mr. and Mrs. [Rachel] Margolin, she of Histadrut.[17] I tried to learn what I could from Mrs. Margolin by addressing her many questions on possible successors for Weizmann and for Ben-Gurion. I was a little disturbed by her obvious and marked Mapai partisanship. She seemed unable to conceive of a future president from any

14. Editorial notes in *FRUS*, 1950, v. V, 856–858.
15. McDonald to secretary of state, no. 255, April 7, 1950, *FRUS*, 1950, v. V, 849–850.
16. *DFPI*, v. 5, d. 191, 194, 197, 203, 209; *FRUS*, 1950, v. V, 867–868.
17. Rachel Margolin, member, Central Control Committee of Histadrut, 1937–1944; member, Histadrut Executive, 1945–1949; director, East European Division, Ministry of Foreign Affairs, 1950.

group to the right of Mapai. She would have nothing to do with Rokach or any of the mayors. She would have nothing to do with Professor [Joseph] Klausner because of his earlier alleged Revisionist association.[18] As to Ben-Gurion's successor, she thought, and on this point I am inclined to agree with her, that Pinhas Lubianker, [secretary-general] of the Histadrut, was logical. Throughout the evening Fried listened attentively.

Saturday, April 8

On April 5, Shiloah informed McDonald that King Abdullah had told US ambassador Drew in Amman that Jordan was ready to resume negotiations with Israel. On McDonald's inquiry as to why he had heard nothing from the State Department, Acheson replied on April 8 that "Abdullah has adequate means [of] contact with [the] Israelis, and . . . it is therefore unnecessary and undesirable for US [to] assume role [of] intermediary." Jordan, Acheson added, was under strong attack from the Arab League for negotiating with Israel, and Israeli press leaks would not improve matters.[19]

Sunday, April 9

Un-Easter-like, except for the beautiful weather. Ruth went to church, but I worked during the morning.

At cocktail time a reception for the representatives of the Bank of America, R. G. Smith of New York,[20] Nelson Monfort of Paris,[21] and Philip S. Ehrlich, the bank's lawyer from San Francisco.[22] I fortunately had opportunities to talk briefly with all three men. I was sorry to hear that they had no definite plans about establishing a branch, but they are sending soon a technician who will spend two months here studying the possibilities.

Monday, April 10

Afternoon ceremony to welcome the arrival of the *Henrietta Szold*, an addition to the Israeli fleet of cargo ships. Mr. [Heinz] Graetz was the chairman, for his company had bought the ship.[23] Both he and Sharett, who was the other speaker, took as their text Israel's need to be more nearly self-sufficient in transportation, particularly because of the news that morning from Cairo [concerning] the economic embargo of the Arab states against Israel's unaltered firmness in

18. Joseph Klausner (1874–1958), Lithuanian-born historian; emigrated to Palestine, 1919; professor of Hebrew literature at Hebrew University after 1925; Revisionist Zionist sympathies; stood against Chaim Weizmann for president in 1949.
19. Acheson to McDonald, no. 45, April 8, 1950, and n. 2, *FRUS*, 1950, v. V, 850.
20. Russell Gordon Smith (1894–1990), San Francisco-born head of Bank of America's international banking department, 1946–1958.
21. Nelson Wicks Monfort (1891–1976), Brooklyn-born vice president, Bank of America from 1947; with Consolidated Foods, Chicago, from 1966.
22. Philip S. Ehrlich (1889–1979), Hawaiian-born attorney; on boards of San Francisco Symphony, Mount Zion Hospital, and the Jewish Community Federation; as legal adviser to Bank of America, he claimed in interview to have arranged in 1949 a $15 million loan to the Jewish National Fund by advising the Giannini family, founders of Bank of America, that they could mitigate their reputation as antisemites by making the loan.
23. Entry of January 11, 1950.

meeting such boycotts by new affirmative action. One feature of the ceremony was the presentation of a [Torah] scroll in the name of Henrietta Szold to one of the Sephardic immigrant groups.

Tuesday, April 11

Mr. [Lazar I.] Estrin of the Irving Trust [bank] came to see me.[24] To my surprise, he gave the local banks and their system rather high praise. He did not think that their interest rates were unduly high and said that they were offering certain services which were not within the customary procedure of the American banks, such as several years' long-term credit. His bank has no intention of organizing a branch here; his purpose has been to discuss with the treasury Israel's financing methods in the States and to point out that [Oscar] Gass and his associates had, in the judgment of the Irving Trust, been penny-wise and pound-foolish by trying to save a fraction of the percent by shopping around among the banks.[25] What was thus saved, he was sure, was more than lost by the resulting diminution of bank goodwill toward Israel, which he holds is especially important now because the banks are advisers to nearly all the interests which may contemplate private investments in Israel.

Professor [Francis] Freeth,[26] free-lance of the Imperial Chemical Inc., at Eli [Karlin]'s suggestion came to the house. He is a distinguished organic chemist and is intimately acquainted with chemical research in most parts of the world. Hence, I put to him this basic question: "Has Israel the possibility of making itself more nearly economically self-sufficient through chemical developments here?" Freeth's answer was in the affirmative. This, he said, was because of the high quality of many of the research people here and their intensity of interest, and also because of unique chemical materials in the Dead Sea. On the whole, he gave a rather surprising and optimistic interpretation.

[Gideon] Rafael came at six and stayed until after seven.[27] As usual with him, he was detailed and intensely interesting in his information. Two broad topics—the recent activities and future prospects of the PCC and the recent work of the Trusteeship Council on the Jerusalem internationalization statute.

His description of the activities, or rather inactivities, of the PCC was amusing. In addition to giving and receiving dinners, the PCC was accustomed to hold two *pro forma* meetings a week, the second always in time to permit an early weekend takeoff, and the first late enough in each week to permit the extension of the weekend until at least Monday night. There were, of course, occasional conferences between individual members of the PCC and the Arab and the

---

24. Lazar Estrin (1892–1978), Russian-born banker; emigrated to the United States, 1916; worked with Irving Trust Bank and then Iran-America Chamber of Commerce, 1946–1950.

25. Entries of April 18 and May 18, 1949.

26. Francis Arthur Freeth (1884–1970), British chief chemist and research manager, Imperial Chemical Industries; specialized in explosives and did secret research for British Special Operations Executive in World War II.

27. Rafael was in Israel for a few days from Geneva to report to the government on the PCC and the Trusteeship Council at Geneva before heading to the Israeli embassy in Washington.

Israeli representatives, but these never came to anything; nor did the PCC ever seriously try to bring the two parties together. This dilly-dally procedure Rafael attributed primarily to the desires of Boisanger and Azcárate to prolong the PCC's life. Azcárate, an old time League of Nations official trained in the defeatist technique of taking no chances in the hope that something will turn up, likes his present job for it involves no risk, little labor, and is extravagantly paid. The budget of the PCC is $7,000,000 a year, a huge amount for three principals and a staff of six or eight. The members receive a $50 *per diem*, and presumably the staff are paid proportionately well.

Boisanger's desire to "perpetuate" the PCC is attributable to his uncertain position vis-à-vis the Quai d'Orsay. His brother, said to have been guilty of collaborationism, is in trouble, and seemingly Boisanger finds it advantageous to stay away from any return to Paris as long as possible.[28] Moreover, the excellent pay and the opportunity the job offers to Boisanger to exercise his "genius for proceduralism" enlarge his desire to remain. Yalçin, too, is found by Boisanger to be indifferent to the lack of rapid progress. He has now been in Ankara for some time and is remaining there for some weeks in connection with the elections.

In sharpest contrast with Boisanger and Yalçin, Rafael finds [Ely] Palmer, the American representative, and his assistant, [James] Barco, to be excellent—the best American representative to date on the PCC. Palmer, unlike [Paul] Porter, who was giving up his vacation to the work, is a retired foreign service officer prepared to outwait the waiters, and to struggle on until something is done or the PCC is buried. Palmer has been a serious student of the problem and has become sympathetic to the Israeli point of view about the necessity for direct negotiations. His colleague, Barco, is also sympathetic and unusually intelligent.

As to the future of the PCC, Rafael feels that Boisanger's failure on this recent trip, the zero record of the mission itself, and the intransigent attitude of the Arab states justify and should lead to the PCC's recommendation to the next Assembly for its own demise. Rafael would like to see it replaced by a one-man conciliator with wide powers, preferably, of course, Bunche. Rafael thinks that any open moves towards ending the PCC should wait until after Palmer's visit here and preferably should, in form, be initiated by the PCC itself. He did not disagree with my interjection that such initiative could be hoped for only if the US, France and UK, and preferably also Turkey, were agreed that the PCC should so act.

Rafael's discussion of the Trusteeship Council and the Jerusalem statute was briefer. He praised [Francis B.] Sayre[29] for intelligence and understanding

28. The brother was Yves Bréart de Boisanger (1896–1976), financial official who served on the German-French Armistice Commission in 1940 and then as governor of the Bank of France, 1940–1944; responsible for the transfer of Belgian gold reserves—for which France was the custodian—from French West Africa to the Reichsbank in Berlin. Annie Lacroix-Riz, *Industriels et banquiers français sous l'Occupation: la collaboration economique avec le Reich et Vichy*, revised ed. (Paris: Armand Colin, 2007), 14.

29. Ambassador Francis Bowes Sayre Sr. (1885–1972), son-in-law of Woodrow Wilson and career diplomat; high commissioner to the Philippines, 1939–1942; US delegate to Trusteeship

but questioned the wisdom of the latter's "too punctilious and too literal" carrying out of the Department's instructions to "cooperate loyally" with the PCC. By this Rafael meant that Sayre's full discussions of the many articles of the statute gave, not unnaturally, an exaggerated impression of the United States' "enthusiasm for the statute." On the other hand, Sayre had always been realistic about the impossibility of the statute becoming a reality and had encouraged the Department to permit him to abstain on the final vote on the statute's adoption. He had also been consistent in his opposition to a specific and definite implementation clause.[30]

On April 4 in Geneva, the Trusteeship Council approved the Jerusalem statute 9–0–2 with the United States and Great Britain abstaining. The same day, Sayre offered the following explanation to President Truman:

> *Since complete internationalization as provided by the General Assembly resolution of December 9 is manifestly impracticable and realizing that the question of Jerusalem must therefore eventually be referred back to the General Assembly, the United States Delegation devoted its efforts to support a program calling for the transmittal of the completed Statute to the Governments of Israel and Jordan . . . [and] thus to give the two Governments the opportunity of expressing their views on the completed Statute and also, if possible, of reaching some common agreement of a nature to protect Christian and world interests in the Holy City. The Trusteeship Council agreed unanimously to this program.*

The Israeli reaction to the latter step was positive.[31]

As to the future, Rafael was hopeful that by the next Trusteeship Council meeting [in June] someone, preferably Bunche, would have made a trip to this area and would have directly or indirectly been the means of presenting, through the PCC to the next Assembly, an alternate plan.

Towards the end of our stay, we talked about possible new ministers to London. In passing, I made my remark about Elath, that he deserved to be relieved of the harassing burden of his too many Jewish organizational and personal advisers in Washington. I added that I could not, of course, make any suggestion, because it might be interpreted as an indirect reflection on Elath, who, in my opinion, is perfectly adjusted to his Washington environment and is doing a wonderful job. Rafael said he thought any word from me on this would be welcome at HaKirya, but I insisted that I could not take any initiative.

Between the time Rafael left and the arrival at 8:30 of our sixteen-or eighteen-man delegation of the [American Christian] Palestine Committee,

Council in Geneva, 1950.
   30. Entry of March 31, 1950.
   31. Sayre to Truman, April 4, 1950, *FRUS*, 1950, v. V, 837–838, 841–842; memorandum by the secretary of state, April 5, 1950, *FRUS*, 1950, v. V, 842–844. Also see the US position paper in preparation for the seventh session of the Trusteeship Council, May 19, 1950, *FRUS*, 1950, v. V, 899–902.

Ruth and I had a bite of supper. This group, headed by Daniel Poling[32] and including [Howard] LeSourd, the director,[33] and Dr. [Harry S.] Rogers of Brooklyn Polytechnic,[34] stayed for about an hour and a half, asking many questions which I answered as fully as I thought I dared.[35] Ruth served them coffee, and afterwards they left with many expressions of appreciation. Ruth and I felt that it had been a day!

The April 11, 1950, Jordanian elections for forty parliamentary seats included voting by citizens of Jordan itself and by the Arabs in Jordanian-controlled Palestine. Antigovernment Palestinian candidates won parliamentary seats. Still, gerrymandering, army voting, and other government measures helped ensure a pro-Hashemite legislature that would approve Jordan's official annexation of Arab Palestine.[36]

McDonald reported to Washington on April 13, 1950:

> Now that the Jordanian elections [are] successfully concluded, [the] Israelis hopefully await [the] possibility of resuming [negotiations] with Jordan. Israel press and public still believe [that] agreement will be reached with Jordan. They hope [the Arab League]'s threatened economic boycott of Jordan can be offset by supplies from Britain and the US. Israelis consider direct [negotiations] with Arab States only possibility of achieving peace. Agreement with Jordan [would] act as spearhead.
> COMMENT: [Arab League's] anti–Israel measures and [the] successful Jordan elections now require Israel to make more enticing concessions to Jordan if [the] latter is to continue peace efforts despite [the Arab League].[37]

Wednesday, April 12

Staff conference at which I presented the two new "stiff" orders about absences during working hours. The other chief item was Major Brady's interesting discussion of recent Israeli army reorganization.

32. Reverend Daniel A. Poling (1884–1968), US evangelical pro-Zionist; president, American Christian Palestine Committee; testified in 1946 to Anglo-American Committee of Inquiry, calling for the establishment of a Jewish commonwealth in Palestine, linking Christian conscience to antisemitism, Jewish national homelessness, and the mass murder of Europe's Jews and stating that Palestine was "divinely selected as the site of the Jewish nation." See Goda et al., eds., *To the Gates of Jerusalem*, 39; In general see Carenen, *The Fervent Embrace*, 44–124.
33. Howard M. LeSourd (1889–1972), Methodist minister and longtime religion professor and dean at Boston University; also known for struggle to make Hollywood a force for moral education.
34. Harry S. Rogers (1891–1957), dean, Brooklyn Polytechnic, 1933–1957.
35. Among other things, Poling's committee announced during its April trip to Israel that it would participate in the development of memorial forests for those murdered during the Holocaust.
36. Joseph Andoni Massad, *Colonial Effects: The Making of National Identity in Jordan* (New York: Columbia University Press, 2001), 231–232.
37. McDonald to secretary of state, joint weeka no. 15, April 13, 1950, McDonald Papers, USHMM, box 8, folder 9.

I was supposed to call young Chaim Sharett to continue our political discussion of a year and a half ago, but the pressure of immediate duties prevented [it]. David Horowitz, fresh from his triumphant settlement of the blocked sterling and other financial problems with Britain[38] and his visit to New York, spent an hour at the house, nominally, at least, merely to report to me on his US trip. As the talk developed, I was waiting for him to ask me to do something, but he did not, so I assume that his purpose was to bring me up to date and perhaps also to prepare the way for some form of intervention by me later, should current rumors of a new request by Israel for a US loan become a reality.

In Washington, Horowitz had talked with Gardiner of McGhee's office about refugees.[39] This had mostly to do with technical organizational matters. Horowitz talked also with Secretary of Agriculture [Charles F.] Brannan and subsequently continued with men on the lower level the discussion of the possibility of Israel purchasing at nominal prices some of the US surpluses. Already arrangements have been made for purchase at [a] nominal price of quantities of egg powder, etc.

Horowitz talked also with [Eugene] Black of the World Bank for Reconstruction [and Development].[40] No request for a loan was made, these talks being purely exploratory. A condition precedent to Israel's possible request being granted would be its joining the [International] Monetary Fund. This is being studied. Being a member of the [IMF] would automatically impose a certain measure of bank control on Israel's decisions about possible devaluation. Horowitz said he did not object in principle to the [World] Bank's influence in this respect, but he doubted whether its rules for determining sound currency valuations would be appropriate for Israel, where economic and financial conditions are so radically unorthodox. He did not close the door to joining the [IMF] but was attempting to weigh the pros and cons. I got the impression that the pros would prove the more influential if the [World] Bank indicated that a loan would be possible. In general, Horowitz seemed delighted with his American trip.

His chief mission had been, however, to the British treasury. He was enthusiastic about Stafford Cripps, whom he found to be intelligent, sympathetic and broad-minded.[41] All issues capable of causing friction between the two countries had been eliminated. Those that remained were minor and could be readily solved. Horowitz is confident that in Britain now, relations with Israel are handled by different government departments, without relation to one another. For example, he is convinced that the Foreign Office, quite unlike the

38. See editorial note in entry of March 22, 1950.
39. See entries of August 31, September 1, and October 26, 1949.
40. Eugene "Gene" Robert Black Sr. (1898–1982), president, World Bank, 1949–1963.
41. Cripps (see entry of October 8, 1948) was chancellor of the exchequer and the chief British official involved in negotiations concerning outstanding financial questions concerning the Mandate's termination. See Howard M. Sachar, *Israel and Europe: An Appraisal in History* (New York: Random House, 1999), 11–14.

Treasury, is still motivated by concepts not very different form those which dominated when Bevin was violently opposing the creation of the state. That psychology continues, and the young men trained under Bevin are "maintaining in essence if not in form the old line."

Horowitz became less the calm economist when he let himself go in outlining what he considers the stupidities of Britain in making major concessions to Iraq and Egypt, for example, without first receiving any quid pro quo from them. He argued that this policy is obviously self-defeating, [and] that it could only be carried out by men who are dominated by the "old illusion" that British interests do not permit anything which would annoy the Arabs. Horowitz cited Britain's weak acquiescence in Egypt's closing of the Suez [to ships bound for Israel], despite the heavy blow this involved [on the] British economy.[42] He urged that this constitutes a dangerous precedent of a relatively weak country "thumbing its nose at one of the large powers." I am afraid I could not argue very effectively against this contention, nor could I demonstrate that the US had been much more heroic than Britain.

At eleven o'clock came the new Belgian minister, Jean Eugene Dubois,[43] and at eleven-fifteen, the Iranian Representative, Mr. Reza Saffinia.[44] The Belgian is an attractive younger man with whom it should be interesting to work. The Iranian, on the other hand, I could not make out, perhaps because our common language, French, is not too comfortable for either of us.

The diplomatic corps meeting which was attended by, in addition to the two above, the representatives of Britain, France, Australia, Turkey, Russia, Yugoslavia, Czechoslovakia, Romania, and the US, was to have been routine, and would have been except for Ershov.

Ershov objected to McDonald's proposed Independence Day reading of a short statement to Weizmann on behalf of the diplomatic corps, which would note that at Israel's first anniversary, the diplomatic corps had seven members, whereas now it had fourteen.[45]

I explained that of course each representative would greet the president personally and would then have the opportunity to make his own individual

42. Despite the Israeli-Egyptian armistice of February 24, 1949, Egypt, following the logic that it was still at war with Israel, closed the Suez Canal to ships bound for Israeli ports. Israeli complaints to the Mixed Armistice Commission were ineffective, because the Egyptians argued that the canal closure was not an "aggressive action" as defined by the armistice agreement. See Shabtai Rosenne, *An International Law Miscellany* (The Hague: Martinus Nijhoff, 1993), 730–736.

43. Belgium officially recognized Israel on January 15, 1950. Dubois (b. 1887) was a career diplomat and Belgium's first ambassador, arriving from his previous post in Bucharest.

44. Iran conferred de facto recognition of Israel on March 14, 1950, becoming the second Muslim country to do so (after Turkey). An important impetus of the recognition was Iran's desire for a counterweight to the Arab states and its opening of its borders to Jews fleeing Iraq. See Jacob Abadi, *Israel's Quest for Recognition and Acceptance in Asia: Garrison State Diplomacy* (London: Frank Cass, 2004), 29–53.

45. McDonald Papers, USHMM, box 8, folder 9.

address if he chose to do so, and of course to give it to the press. I am sure that Ershov was not happy, but he finally seemed to acquiesce, and, after some other pleasantries, the meeting broke up.

After the others had gone, Helm, Fuhrman, Esin, Guyon and I held a bit of a rump session to comment on the morning's demonstration of our "cold war in miniature." We were not certain whether Ershov's attitude was motivated by fear lest Moscow would criticize him for being party to an arrangement to which I spoke on behalf of the diplomatic corps, or because he was fearful of adverse criticism if my little talk gave any advantage to the US in the press reports of the celebration.

[Shmuel] Katz, Begin's colleague, came in to ask about the visa situation, which I explained to him fully, emphasizing that we had again followed up with the Department to persuade it to implement the Department of Justice's permission to admit former Irgun members. As to Begin's reference in his book to my request to him in March '46 to discontinue terrorist activities at least during the period of our Anglo-American Committee of Inquiry work, [it] is to be included in the form of a paraphrase. This is, I think, more satisfactory than quotes from a note which I never wrote. Begin mistook apparently a personal message I sent him in verbal form, and which probably was handed him as a note from me.[46]

A three-ring circus at teatime. Mr. Feldman from Florence, Alabama,[47] Judge Rothenberg and his wife of the UPA,[48] Emery Reves[49] and several others. Still later came Sidney Herold and his brother from Shreveport, Louisiana.[50] As always, it was a pleasure to talk with this wise and learned elderly statesman of the Zionist movement.

That evening Ambassador and Mrs. McDonald, joined by Mr. and Mrs. Sam Sacks and Paula Ben-Gurion, attended the concert given by Yehudi and Hephzibah Menuhin.[51] In 1947 Yehudi had, as a self-described act of reconciliation, performed with the Berlin Philharmonic conducted by Wilhelm Furtwängler, who had conducted that orchestra throughout the Nazi period.

The fears that there might be demonstrations against Yehudi did not materialize, possibly because of the excellent police arrangement, but more likely because of Yehudi's generosity in turning over the proceeds of all his concerts here, some ten or twelve in a fortnight, to various local causes. In the intermission,

---

46. Entry of March 21, 1950.
47. Albert Feldmann (1876–1968), merchant from Florence, Alabama.
48. Entries of August 11, 1948, and September 22, 1949.
49. Emery Reves (1904–1981), born Revesz Imre in Hungary of Jewish parents; educated in Berlin, Zurich, and Paris; founded the anti-Nazi Cooperative Publishing Service, 1933; became Churchill's literary agent in 1937 and subsequently arranged to publish a number of his books outside Britain; sent to the United States by Churchill to bolster British propaganda effort; chief advocate for world federalism after the war.
50. Voyage entry of July 1948.
51. Yehudi Menuhin (1916–1999), American-born violinist; Hephzibah Menuhin (1920–1981), American-born pianist, writer, and human rights activist.

Paula insisted on going backstage, and I obediently followed after her in the path she made with her broad shoulders through the packed aisles, stairway and lobby. The Menuhins were very friendly. Hephzibah is particularly attractive, more so even than Yehudi's new wife. For once, I could fully share Paula's views as she later waxed enthusiastic about Hephzibah.

Friday, April 14

Mr. [Sidney] Herold and his brother came at lunch. We covered a lot of ground, but since I did most of the talking, the record can be very brief. What a joy to talk to a man to whom you need merely suggest your point of view to have it fully understood.

At four Mr. [Alfred] Perlman, a Denver railroad man who is here studying Israel's railroad problems, gave me his first impressions.[52] He is not yet certain whether Israel should try to skip the railroad economy. If the country is to be highly industrialized, he thinks the railroads will have to be completely rebuilt, for at present their freight capacity is so small that, as he put it, a single freight train on the Burlington railroad can haul as much freight as all of the freight trains in Israel in a month. He finds Israel predominantly anti-railway minded. For example, at the port in Tel Aviv there are no tracks, and in Haifa freight cars may not be spotted on the port tracks except at night in order "not to interfere with the truck loading and unloading." Both officialdom and the public are still unfriendly to railroads. This is in part a carry-over from the Mandatory days when the Jews as a matter of policy discouraged use of the railway in order to develop their own control of truck transportation. Perlman said he would come back and give me his final views before he left Israel in a fortnight.

From four thirty until a quarter past six, Albert Lasker and his two sisters, Mrs. Rosensohn and Loula were at the house.[53] Albert Lasker, to my surprise, was prepared to listen. After I had made my "speech," I tried to learn about some conditions at home. All my guests stressed the absurdity and extremism of [the] current [anti-] communist witch-hunt. Lasker told me much that was interesting about [Jack] Arvey, the boss in Chicago, who naturally is of interest to me because of his relations to the president.

Saturday, April 15

On April 15, McDonald toured the north of Israel with the Herolds and the Karlinski/Karlin family, including Eli Karlin, Eli's mother Sonia, and his uncles Serge and Misha Karlinski from London.

52. Alfred E. Perlman (1902–1983), civil engineer and railroad development engineer who had developed numerous railroad lines in the United States.
53. Albert Lasker (1880–1952), Chicago banker and advertising mogul; active in Jewish affairs and a member of the American Jewish Committee; Etta Lasker Rosensohn (1885–1966), social worker and philanthropist; member of the Hadassah national board for more than two decades; Loula Lasker (1886–1961), social worker; member of the Hadassah board, 1949; editor of the Hadassah newsletter, 1952–1955.

This will be a memorable day in our experiences of Israel. With Eli and Sonia, we were on the road to Haifa at 8:35. With almost no traffic, Shalom reached the outskirts of Haifa in an hour and five minutes flat. We stopped at Nahariya for a drink and to see this bit of Deutschland in Israel,[54] and then on to the frontier point Rosh HaNikra [on the border with Lebanon]. There we were joined by Major Fogel and his colleagues, who remained with us throughout the whole day. They took us first to the frontier itself and even across the line for a few yards. From here, the "Ladder of Tyre," we had a magnificent view of the coast to the north and south and through much of Lebanon and Galilee. After a brief and reassuring conference about the state of the road, we set out in convoy.

Our road skirts closely the frontier at points almost touching it, as it traverses the high valleys. At Sasa, we stopped for lunch at a new American kibbutz.[55] The view from there in all directions is startlingly beautiful. The highest Israeli mountain, al-Jarmaq [Mount Meron], 1,208 meters, was nearby to the south, while to the east one had a clear picture of Safed. After an adequate lunch, we drove on towards Manara. The road continued closely along the frontier, and as we approached the Hula we traversed a rich, lush valley divided between Lebanon and Israel. Just short of the police station at al-Nabi Yusha[56] we began to climb sharply up the mountain to Manara. I had not exaggerated its spectacular location. Even Eli was in raptures. Spread out below us from our vantage point on the bluff were the upper reaches of the Jordan, the Hula Valley, swamps and lake, the lush fields of the many kibbutzim; to the north was Mount Hermon still covered with snow; and to the south, the winding Jordan on its way to the Sea of Galilee. Dan and Metula were so clearly visible that I persuaded my clients that we need not go there. Since my last visit, Manara has grown remarkably. It is now one of the major frontier posts. Graphically, our officer guide showed us how Fawzi al-Qawuqji's threat to Manara had been the means by which Israel had cleared the whole of Galilee.[57] My only regret during our visit was that I did not meet the young girl leader who had previously shown us around.

In order not to have to spend the time the next morning, we went directly to Tiberias for tea. Then, in the setting sun we visited briefly Degania, showing our guests this oldest colony and the Jordan as it races out of the Sea of Galilee. Our trip up to Safed was in the dark and a little nerve-wracking to the back-seat drivers as Shalom took the curves. Our hotel, the Mines [House], brand new, was on a high point overlooking Safed proper. There we were greeted as celebrities.

54. Nahariya, founded initially as an agricultural village in 1934, expanded with the purchase of additional land from Arab landowners; became a haven for German Jews after 1935. Several successful German Jewish entrepreneurs rebuilt their lives and businesses there.
55. Sasa, founded on the land of the depopulated Arab village of Sa'sa in January 1949 by US members of HaShomer HaTzair. It was one mile from the Lebanese border.
56. Former Shi'ite village, also depopulated in the 1948 war.
57. Entry of November 19, 1948.

Following a brief trip into Safed, we explored by taking the road back through Sasa and around the high mountains, coming back to the main road through Peki'n[58] and Rameh.[59] Bobby will remember Peki'n, which she visited with the [Eddie] Jacobsons. I am determined to return there, so picturesque is this ancient village, which had its Jews before the Exodus and is now a Christian Arab center, hidden away in one of the most picturesque spots imaginable. Coming down the mountain and just before we reached Rameh, we paused to get the view west to the Mediterranean, and east to Kinneret. In the mid-morning lights and shadows, Switzerland could not have been more beautiful. The rest of our drive was familiar. The new road southward to the main Tiberias-Nazareth Road. We paused outside Nazareth for the general view and then drove straight south through Afula to the Megiddo Pass. As always, this route of the conquerors in history thrilled me. We reached Rebecca Sieff's at Tel Mond at a quarter of one. Shalom took the Karlins on to the hotel.

I record here very briefly the substance of Helm's talk with me at our house Tuesday morning, April 11, following his return from a week in Cairo. He went by way of Amman, from where he flew in a small bi-plane to Egypt. In Cairo [for] just a week, he saw only the British or other foreigners, including, of course, American diplomats. He was to, but did not, talk to Azzam Pasha, secretary general of the Arab League.

Just before Helm left Tel Aviv, Sharett called him to the Foreign Office and elaborated the Israeli thesis that Egypt, under the leadership of the king, was rearming for the second round.[60] In Amman, Helm was told by Kirkbride, the British minister there during the past decade or more, that Farouk did not lead in foreign policy. Kirkbride anticipated that Abdullah would resume negotiations with Israel after the Jordanian elections. In Cairo, Helm found the consensus of opinion to be: the king, if not decisive in foreign affairs, is very influential; Nahhas Pasha, leader of the Wafd, is past his prime and not in complete control of his party; the most influential members of the cabinet are the ministers of foreign affairs [Mustafa Salah al-Din Bey] and defense [Mustafa Nusrat Bey], the latter markedly anti-Israel. Helm was shocked at his British colleagues' lack of close and detailed information about Israel. They appeared to share somewhat the Arab view that Israel could not become viable.

---

58. Majority Druze town in the Northern District of Israel, the Jewish community of which, according to tradition, has lived there since the period of the Second Temple.

59. Muslim and Druze city in the Northern District of Israel; received local council status in 1954.

60. On April 10, 1950, Sharett argued to Helm that London's policy was contradictory in that it furnished the Arab states with arms without setting any conditions concerning peace with Israel, while telling Israel that it could import British weapons only if it made peace with the Arabs. Helm countered that Israel could get its weapons elsewhere, while the Arab states' military establishments were tied to Britain's regional defense needs. See *DFPI*, v. 5. d. 181.

Helm did what he could to show them the truth. As Helm talked, I was impressed anew by the sharp divergences of view among the experts on Egyptian policy. Each of the views indicated to him was supported by men whose judgment should have been authoritative. Perhaps the truth would be found in a combination of all the seemingly conflicting views.

In response to the Arab League's resolutions, the British cabinet considered a statement to the effect that Britain would take strong steps in an effort to prevent aggressive moves by the Arabs or Israelis in the Middle East. At the same time, London refused to supply arms to Israel for fear of upsetting the Arab governments.[61] On April 20, 1950, Helm tried to clear the air with Sharett. He understood, he said, Israeli anger at Britain's policy on arms sales to the Arab states and concerning Bevin's March 28 statement in the House of Commons legitimizing the Arab boycott of Israel. Helm hoped that Israel would nonetheless appreciate how far Israeli–British relations had come. Sharett responded that Israel's desire for improved relations had been complicated by Bevin's policy of distrusting Israel while exonerating its enemies.[62]

On April 3, 1950, Major Lawrence Brady, the US military attaché, had met with Teddy Kollek and Israeli military officials, failing to gain much data on Israeli military capabilities. Kollek told Brady that McDonald must have overstated Israel's willingness to supply sensitive military information. Brady countered that this information was needed because of State Department and Pentagon concerns that Israel was very possibly an aggressor state; the United States did not want to accept international responsibility for fueling aggression. On April 5, Chaim [Vivian] Herzog, the head of Israeli military intelligence, informed Brady that Israel could not provide detailed military information until after the United States promised to sell Israel the arms it requested.[63]

At teatime, Ware brought in Sidney Glazer of the Voice of America, who wished to talk about problems incident to the project of establishing a Hebrew daily broadcast to Israel.[64] He was seemingly intrigued by my combination of radio experience with my work in Israel and intimated that there might be an editorial job awaiting me in connection with the Voice of America, which

61. Memorandum by Stuart Rockwell, April 6, 1950, *FRUS*, 1950, v. V, 844–847; Acheson to US embassy in Egypt, A-152, April 7, 1950, *FRUS*, 1950, v. V, 848–849.
62. *DFPI*, v. 5, d. 202.
63. Elath concurred that Acheson's subordinates suspected Israel of aggressive intentions and that the Pentagon's opposition to supplying Israel with arms was due to its negative assessment of Israel's place in US regional security plans. He also reported Jack Ewing's comment that Truman, though sympathetic to Israel, would not overrule Acheson's idea of peace through political pressure rather than through arms sales. By April 26 Elath learned from Niles that the president and Acheson agreed that Israel should be treated with "consideration and fairness." The main source of difficulty, Elath said, was now Secretary of Defense Louis Johnson. *DFPI*, v. 5, d. 174, 177, 200, 211, 212.
64. Sidney Simon Glazer (1911–2002), New York-born scholar of the Arabic language; helped decipher Japanese codes during World War II with US Army; acting chief of the Near East Division of the Library of Congress after the war; headed the Hebrew broadcast section of the Voice of America, 1948–1974.

would pay as well as a diplomatic post. I was not displeased with this thought, but neither was I tempted.

Stopped by and chatted for a little while with the Helms and then with the Hoopers.

Tuesday, April 18

Sidney Herold and his brother came during the morning to say goodbye. They had been tremendously impressed by their visits in this neighborhood and up north. After a few days in Jerusalem they are returning on Monday morning by air to Paris and then by boat home. Herold expressed very warm appreciation of my "helpfulness" and said he was sure I was "much appreciated" everywhere in Israel. I was delighted that he had been so pleased and relieved that he did not press me about the appointment with Ben-Gurion.

In the afternoon Rabbi and Mrs. Fox of Chicago came for tea. He is a Silverite. A little later Mr. and Mrs. Oscar Gass and David Ginsburg came out.[65] After tea these two men and I went to the roof and talked for more than an hour.

Wednesday, April 19

In the morning talked with [Colonel] Archibald about the answer to the Rome top secret letters regarding cooperation with Britain and details of our communications. As to the latter, an inquiry has been sent to a regional center; as to the former, it was the colonel and the major's view, which I shared, that we could give a partial answer, but that in doing so we should indicate that a full reply was impossible without first disclosing to the British the whole purpose.

Ruth and I in the evening went to the Ohel Shem expecting to hear the Mozart Requiem with the Kol Israel Orchestra and a local chorus. Unfortunately, the first hour and a quarter together with an intermission was occupied by the playing of two Mozart symphonies, so that the main feature did not begin until a quarter of ten. Since we felt we had to leave at 10:15 to get to the Sam Sackses' for a few minutes before their America Israel [Friendship League] meeting broke up, we heard only about half of the Requiem. The orchestra and chorus were adequate and the four soloists excellent. We were very sorry to leave in the midst of it. As it was, we arrived so late at the Sacks' that only a few of their guests were still there.

Thursday, April 20

A little before ten Monsignors McMahon and Vergani, [who] stayed until about a quarter of twelve. Fortunately, I had no other appointments and only one telephone interruption, which took me away for only a moment. McMahon

65. Charles David Ginsburg (1912–2010), prominent New York-born attorney; held a series of New Deal posts, especially concerning price controls after 1935; helped reorganize the German economy after World War II; advised Chaim Weizmann in 1948 and helped smooth the path to Truman's recognition of Israel.

explained that he had not been home but had been here continuously (that is in the neighboring countries or in Israel), except for two weeks in Rome when Cardinal Spellman was there. First we talked about refugees and the new UN organization [the United Nations Relief and World Agency for Palestine (UNRWA)]. McMahon has not met either General [Howard] Kennedy or Mr. [John B.] Blandford.[66] He understands that the three cooperating organizations, the International Red Cross, the Quakers, and the League of Red Cross Societies, are as organizations, to withdraw, but that a portion of their personnel will continue to operate in the field as part of the UNRWA. McMahon thought that little progress towards the transfer from relief to work could be expected during the first year. Monsignor Vergani thought that nothing could be done towards such transition in the Gaza Strip. Short of its abolition, constructive purposes there are hopeless. Throughout the discussion on this point of refugees, McMahon showed an intimacy of knowledge, which follows naturally from his more than a year of active work in the refugee field.

After a little while I brought up my favorite topic of the possible replacement of the PCC by a one-man conciliator. My two visitors were, as at least indicated by their manner, quite sympathetic to my criticisms of the PCC record, the personalities, and work habits of Boisanger and Azcárate and the mild interest in the subject and the absenteeism of Yalçin. McMahon, however, had his doubts about replacement by one man. He questioned the possibility of finding an adequate person who would not become involved in the "intrigues which have so unsettled this whole area." In particular, he was critical of Bunche, suggested that Bunche's work had been overrated, and that he would not be an ideal choice. As to Riley, whose name I threw into the discussion, McMahon spoke enthusiastically of Riley's record in the armistice enforcements, thought Riley could hold his own with military men anywhere, but wondered whether in the broader field he could be comparably effective. As if thinking aloud, McMahon added that, of course, Riley had learned almost everything about the specific problems at issue, but there still remained the questions as to Riley's ability to meet the extreme difficulties of the situation.

As if to emphasize these difficulties, and as it were to parenthetically explain, if not justify, Arab intransigence towards Israel, McMahon spoke substantially as follows: What we see now in the Middle East is in a sense a continuation of the last world war, which never really ended here. Instead, it was followed by a number of small potential or actual conflicts just as World War II had been preceded by such "small wars." In a sense one could say that the decision to set up Israel was the beginning of a new world conflict, which, much as one might abhor it, seemed now inevitable. The world willy-nilly was divided, and there was no longer any possibility of so-called neutrality. The Church was accused in some quarters of helping to cause this division, but that was not true. The fact that it was in the Western camp was the result of no desire on its

66. See editorial note in entry of June 4, 1950.

part but because of bitter experiences in the Iron Curtain countries, where today some thirty-eight bishops are imprisoned.[67]

McMahon contrasted with such treatment the much more favorable handling of Church problems by Israel. Broadly speaking, conditions are good here. While not everything which should have been done has been done, there is always the possibility here of an appeal to the officials of the Ministry of Religion, who, in their turn, appear to do their utmost to secure just compensatory actions by whichever ministry is concerned. Moreover, the existence of one central agency to which the Church can appeal is a great saving of time and energy. At this point, Monsignor Vergani interpolated that Jacob Herzog and [Chaim] Vardi and their colleagues in the Ministry of Religion did from time to time on their own initiative stimulate governmental departments to acts of justice.

Then, as if preparatory to the main purpose of his visit, the discussion of Jerusalem, McMahon stressed the view that the Church had never opposed the creation or the development of Israel. Any suggestion that it had was based either on lack of knowledge or was tendentious. From the Church's point of view there was no connection between Israel's legal claims and its ambitions in Jerusalem. On the subject of internationalization of Jerusalem, McMahon made the following major points:

1) Legally, internationalization is prescribed by the successive actions of the UN Assembly, November 29, 1947, December 11, 1948, and December 9, 1949.
2) The elaboration of the draft statute by the Trusteeship Council during its recent session in Geneva was the required [progress] of the express judgment of the UN.
3) A plebiscite of the Jerusalem population as of November 1947 would give a majority for internationalization. And legally and morally, Israel's enforced changes in the city should not affect the situation. For example, the latecomers should not be counted in a plebiscite, the changed political situation should not be permitted to influence the UN, and the corridor driven to Jerusalem similarly can have no legal or moral bearing on internationalization.

Continuing with his detailed discussion of the Jerusalem internationalization, McMahon stressed that the change of front by Russia had removed the chief remaining Israeli [argument] against internationalization. It also made McMahon more comfortable. Israel was now reduced to feeble or non-existent arguments to support its case.

67. Overview in Stéphane Courtois et al., *The Black Book of Communism: Crimes, Terror, Repression* (Cambridge, MA: Harvard University Press, 1999), 409–412.

On April 17, the Soviet Union abandoned the UN resolution of December 9, 1949, because it failed to satisfy either the Jewish or Arab populations of Jerusalem. This change in Soviet policy encouraged the Israelis to approach the United States with an acceptable alternative to the Jerusalem statute. On April 19 in Washington, Elath and Eban proposed UN control of Jerusalem's Holy Places, which, they added, would depend on Jordanian agreement. State Department officials were encouraged, but urged the Israelis to continue talks with Jordanian and Vatican officials. In the meantime, the State Department pressed Jordanian representatives to meet international concerns concerning Christian and Muslim Holy Places in Jerusalem's Old City.[68]

McMahon was, by implication, critical of the US policy at Geneva under the Trusteeship Council. He recognized that "much good work was done" in refining the several provisions of the statute, but [argued] that the US had been seriously at fault in "following the British lead" in refusing to vote for the statute as a whole or to favor any concrete or immediate plans for implementation. Nonetheless, these great power failures had not altered the legal situation, nor had they weakened the Church's position in favor of full internationalization.

Knowing from my friend Jacob Herzog of McMahon's critical attitude towards the British in this area, I deliberately brought the talk around to the policy of Britain. McMahon was sharply critical, charging that the British had sacrificed the world interest in Jerusalem (though he did not put this in so many words) by sabotaging the statute's implementation. Moreover, Britain has managed to reinstate itself in this area in an almost miraculous fashion in the last two years. Today it has gained dominance in Syria, and through its control of Jordan and its support of the latter's ambitions west of the Jordan, has regained its old position here. Indeed, its direct gain in Israel in the last year has been extraordinary. These gains illustrated, McMahon said, Britain's genius for muddling through and for utilizing others' strength to advance its own imperial interests.

To try to get McMahon to clarify his ideas of an American program in the Middle East, I asked him what he thought the US ought to do here. His answers were not specific. He clearly intimated, however, that he thought the US should quit playing what he regarded as second fiddle to the British, that we should take our own line. McMahon praised [George] McGhee and what he understood to be the latter's Middle East policy. Naturally, I refrained from divulging anything about the Department's earlier and its most recent directive regarding closer and closer cooperation between US missions in this area and the British [missions]. McMahon spoke of McGhee as a capable and far-sighted and idealistic leader. But nothing he said gave any clue to the basis on which presumably McMahon reached the conclusion that he and McGhee were in essential agreement. Perhaps his impressions of McGhee's policy are

68. *DFPI*, v. 5, d. 186, 190, 193, 199, 208; *FRUS*, 1950, v. V, 861–865.

based upon a talk with the latter of more than a year ago before McMahon came out here.

On the broader problem of the general international situation, McMahon was pessimistically fatalistic. He saw no likelihood that the split between East and West could be healed and seemed to expect, much as he deplored it, a third world war. This portentous conclusion McMahon used as the opening for his summation. [Returning] to the question of internationalization of Jerusalem, he argued that to divide it between Jordan and Israel would serve no world interest and would deny the interest of the world community. It would serve Britain's imperialist interest by deepening its hold in this area, but it would be likely to intensify irritations between Jordan and Israel and certainly would exacerbate relations between these two countries and the neighboring Arab states. Assuming that Jordan and Israel made peace and that ultimately the other Arab states followed Jordan's example, the peace would be unquiet and would give no security. On the other hand, an internationalized Jerusalem would, according to McMahon, serve as a cushion between Israel and Jordan and the other Arab states. More important, it would serve as a rallying point for Western civilization against totalitarianism. With almost passionate earnestness, he closed with an only thinly veiled appeal to me to use my influence towards implementation of the Jerusalem statute.

Early in his talk, McMahon categorically denied that he had any political representative capacity in this area, asserting again as in all our earlier talks, that he is here solely as the representative of the Church's interest in refugee and social work. But everything else that he said, his extraordinary depth of knowledge and his worldwide comprehensive outlook, gave the impression that irrespective of his technical status, he is the Vatican's chief political and diplomatic agent. Whether our mutual friend Jacob Herzog's judgment will be proved correct, that McMahon is some day to be papal secretary of state, I of course don't know, but I share Herzog's high opinion of the perspicacity and breadth of intelligence of McMahon. I should have noted above that McMahon disclaimed any institutional interest by the Church in the proposed Jerusalem internationalization. He said that the Church's preponderance of institutions, educational, eleemosinary, and religious, was so substantial that there was no need for political reinforcement.[69]

At the very end of our talk, we spoke of [Ronald] Knox's translation of the Bible and particularly of the concluding volume of the Old Testament, which I had received only that morning from Tom Murray. McMahon much prefers Knox to the Confraternity Edition. Whether the new papal translation from

69. In the last week of April, Roger Garreau discussed the Jerusalem statute with Domenico Tardini, the acting Vatican secretary of state, and with Pope Pius XII himself. Garreau told the US ambassador in Rome that Tardini was adamant that the UN must find a way of implementing the December 1949 resolution and that the pope, sounding more moderate, called for "any reasonable solution." Dunn to secretary of state, no. 1736, April 28, 1950, *FRUS*, 1950, v. V, 878–879.

all the original sources will ultimately replace the vulgate and the Douay Editions, McMahon said, would depend on the judgment of the pope in office when the new work is completed. Already it has been underway for more than twenty years, and the scores of translators are only half through the Old Testament.[70]

Friday, April 21

The new Belgian minister [Dubois] came for his formal call, but stayed forty minutes for a substantial talk.

Colonel Archibald came in with news about the reply from Teheran. I asked him to send off appropriate letters to Rome about both communications and cooperation with the British.

Saturday, April 22

To the office with two telegrams and for conference with Hayden. The latter reported on what had been told him about Israel by the US chiefs of mission in the Arab capitals. These contained nothing that was new. I gave him as much data as there was time for. Although he did not commit himself, I got the impression that the National City [Bank] might be interested in a branch here. He did say that he would probably recommend one for Cairo and, as to Israel, he raised the embarrassing question about possible transfer of profits. The answer to this, I told him, he would have to get from Kaplan or Horowitz. The latter he had met that morning, and [he] had been much impressed by the terms Israel had won in the recently concluded negotiations in London.

Arrived with the Hoopers at the Sharon at 8:30 for the foreign minister's dinner [celebrating Israeli Independence Day]. There were all the usual preliminaries, photographers, greetings with one's colleagues and friends and not sitting down to the table until well after nine. About ninety guests were present, including foreign diplomats, foreign office officials, and others. The food and service were excellent and the menus notable, because each one contained a lovely reproduction of some recent painting by an Israeli artist.

I had the good fortune of being seated next to Golda Meyerson. Our talk was mostly about the pending discussions between the government and the [Jewish] Agency. She deplored what she called the childishness of debating procedures when so much substantial work remains undone. She was not, she said, interested in "quarreling about the credit for failures!" She thought that a compromise might be reached through the setting up of a development corporation in which both [the] government and Agency would participate.[71]

---

70. On the various versions see F. F. Bruce, *The English Bible: A History of Translation from the Earliest English Versions to the New English Bible* (Oxford: Oxford University Press, 1970); and David Rooney, *The Wine of Certitude: A Literary Biography of Ronald Knox* (San Francisco: Ignatius Press, 2009).

71. For this dispute see entry of April 30, 1950.

Her private views about organizational leadership in the States were very much the same as mine. She, too, thinks that the great mass of the Jews, whether Zionists or not, are but slightly interested in the several organizations as compared with their vital interest in the new state. She agrees also that millions of Jews receive deep vicarious satisfaction through the achievements of the Jews in Israel on the land, in government, and in war. She holds, as I do, that these satisfactions will be enduring and will give assurance that Israel can continue to count upon the support of world Jewry. Meyerson spoke admiringly of the abilities of Rose Halprin and Nahum Goldmann. As to the latter's weaknesses, we were also in agreement.

Illustrative of Golda Meyerson's quality and deserving of being recorded fully is the following. During her January 1948 visit to the States, when Israel was fighting the desperate undeclared war with the Arabs, she found little support for her efforts to find the needed $25,000,000 in cash from the organizational head[s]. Particularly, she found Dr. Israel Goldstein discouraging. Nonetheless, by telling the story of Israel's needs in that critical hour and by overriding the timid counsels of organizational-minded men, she got the money in time. Israel thereby was enabled to purchase the arms essential when the time of open warfare came.[72]

Contrary to the earliest reports, my toast was the only one of the evening. Speaking on behalf of the corps, I said:

> Israel, made possible by thousands of years of Jewish heroism, may it fulfill the glorious mission envisioned for it by the Prophets. To this hope, I ask you to raise your glass.

Sharett replied briefly and spoke successively in French, English, Russian, Turkish and Hebrew.

After the dinner I chatted briefly with General Riley, who spoke highly of Monsignor McMahon. Ruth called over Serge [Karlinski] and Eli [Karlin], who were pleased to meet the general. There were many other brief visits with other guests, but the only reportable item was Shiloah's whisper to me as Ruth and I were leaving: "We have word from Amman that our contacts are to be resumed next week."

Told by the protocol people that Ruth and I were supposed to leave first, I with difficulty dragged her away at midnight, but did not get her to the door in time to avoid having Ershov drive off first. He has no respect for protocol when it works against him!

---

72. Meyerson was the acting head of the Jewish Agency's political department and was raising money, primarily for armaments. Goldstein was then the head of the United Jewish Appeal. During the six-week fundraising trip from January 23 to March 17, 1948, Meyerson met with several American Jewish organizations and raised $50 million, double the $25 million target. Meron Medzini, "Israel's Midwife: Golda Meir in the Closing Years of the British Mandate," in *Israel at Sixty: Rethinking the Birth of the Jewish State*, eds., Ephraim Karsh and Rory Miller (New York: Routledge, 2009), 62–66.

With Hooper off to Rehovot early, stopped at the office to leave the telegram reporting what Shiloah had said to me.[73]

The official [Independence Day] proceedings were carried out as planned, the Russians making no attempt to speak independently. Copies of my statement on behalf of the diplomatic corps and Dr. Weizmann's response are included in my document file. Following translations, Weizmann shook hands with each of us. Then he and I, after embracing, talked briefly. He was very appreciative of the US aid in making "the day possible." Since he referred to Britain and the US in the same general way, I asked Helm to join us. Weizmann then told the latter of his conviction that, without the UK, Israel independence would have been long delayed. I left the two of them to finish their talk. Subsequently, each of the chiefs of mission spoke briefly to the president.

We drove downtown through the crowded streets as far as the Gat. Everywhere were signs of continuing gaiety. Along the beach, on the "boardwalk," and in the nearby parks and squares, youngsters were still indefatigably and seemingly gaily dancing. According to Misha [Karlinski], the dancing had not ceased in front of his hotel until five o'clock that morning. There can be no doubt Israel's second anniversary of independence stirred its people deeply.[74]

Monday, April 24

Jacob Herzog called me from Jerusalem to say that Monsignor McMahon would be in Tel Aviv on Tuesday, and in answer to my question, said that he thought that McMahon could be reached through the Church authorities in Jaffa.

Ruth and I—I in a white tie for [the] first time in Israel—were on our way to the president's ball at Rehovot by 8:30, arriving about 9:15. Despite the one-lane road from the gate to the house, the traffic was so well-arranged that there was a delay due to congestion of only fifteen or twenty minutes.

The whole house was open. The Weizmanns received in the drawing room, from where the guests gradually drifted out onto the lawn and from there past the swimming pool through the main hall and the dining room onto the large terrace where there was dancing until midnight. The weather was perfect, cool but not too cool, with the recent khamsin only a distant memory.

My social activities were, as I like them to be, combined with business. Guyon, having told me that he was going to buttonhole Eytan and deliver his government's message expressing the hope that Israel would give an unqualified acceptance to the PCC's plan as delivered recently to the government here by Boisanger, I decided that I would save time and do the same if the opportunity arose. Presently, when Guyon had concluded his talk with Eytan, the

---

73. McDonald to secretary of state, no. 286, April 23, 1950, *FRUS*, 1950, v. V, 873, n. 1.
74. Report in McDonald to secretary of state, joint weeka no. 17, April 28, 1950, McDonald Papers, USHMM, box 8, folder 9.

latter and I walked in the rose garden. He said that my message came at a timely moment because his government was considering its answer this week. He seemed confident that it would be affirmative. Except for Israel's note of November 18, 1948 (which he reminded me I had so often spoken of with admiration),[75] all of Israel's answers to the UN or its agencies had been affirmative. He said also that Herlitz's statement to McVicker as to the government's reasons for delay in answering was her "personal" interpretation.

I took advantage of the talk with Eytan to offer a kind of apology for the Department's refusal to accept more completely the results of the civil aviation negotiations, which [Ralph] Curren from Cairo, Hooper, and I had labored on with the Israelis for weeks. Though Eytan had signed the letter from the Foreign Office on this matter, it was evident that he was not really well informed about it.

I chatted with Shiloah, who reiterated what he had said earlier about the probability of a renewal of contacts with Jordan this week. He expects Abdullah to try to raise the ante in the light of the hostility of the Arab League, but Shiloah has "some answers ready." He is looking forward "eagerly" to the talk.

On April 24, 1950, Jordan announced its formal annexation of Arab Palestine. Both houses of the Jordanian parliament proclaimed the "complete unity between the two sides of Jordan . . . and their union into one state which is the Hashemite Kingdom of Jordan."

On April 25, 1950, McDonald reported that the Israelis had issued a "formal" protest concerning the annexation because no final political settlement was possible without peace between Israel and Jordan. But, as McDonald reported, the protest had been shown to Abdullah in advance and Shiloah did not expect it to hinder bilateral negotiations. Israel would continue to abide by the armistice in the meantime. McDonald also reported that Shiloah expected to see King Abdullah that week, anticipating that the king would ask for "additional concession[s] to compensate for [Arab League] threats." The US legation in Amman predicted that negotiations would not resume in the near future because of Arab League pressure and opposition from within the Jordanian government.[76]

I asked Helm what he was going to do about the Hebrew University invitation to attend its 25th anniversary in Jerusalem. He said he had declined without consulting his government, on the assumption that his general instructions were sufficiently clear. I decided that I had better ask Washington for instructions.

75. Eytan to Mohn, November 18, 1948, *DFPI*, v. 2, d. 160, replying to the UN Security Council resolutions of November 4 and November 16, 1948, regarding an Israeli pullback in the Negev to the October 14 battle lines.

76. McDonald to secretary of state, nos. 293 and 298, April 25, 1950, USSDCF-PIFA, 1950–1954, reel 1, frame 483; Drew to secretary of state, no. 84, April 26, 1950, *FRUS*, 1950, v. V, 873–874.

Got off my various telegrams and despatches during the morning. Among the telegrams were one to David Niles and another to Halsey regarding the suggested November plan. All is still uncertain [concerning McDonald's proposed resignation].[77]

Decisive letter received from the president's friend [Stuart] Symington.[78]

Troxel, Recknagel and I worked in the living room. The three of us settled a number of matters about Recknagel's program.[79] He is to write [Sam Klaus] to inquire whether the schedule might not be arranged for Recknagel to return here after his enforced statutory leave. We decided also to suggest the possibility of utilizing more fully men such as Recknagel in countries such as Israel for reporting purposes.

Wednesday, April 26

Afternoon staff meeting.

[Teatime included Judith Gottlieb,[80] Simcha Even-Zohar,[81] and Madame de Philippe and was interrupted by the arrival of Mr. and Mrs. Solomon Trone.[82]] Henceforth, the subjects ranged from engineering to philosophy and religion. Having known Trone years ago and recalling the contents of Loy Henderson's despatch about Trone's work in India and in China, I sought for an opportunity to induce Trone to indicate his basic points of view about Communist China and Soviet penetration. I was only partially successful. He did speak of the "great progress that can now be expected" in China now that the new regime has replaced the Kuomintang corrupt dictatorship. He referred to Formosa as "a horrible place." In answer to my specific question, he said that he was of very much the same point of view about what should have been done in China as was Professor [Owen] Lattimore, with whom he has been closely in touch.[83] Trone's only reference to India was his statement that "unless we

77. McDonald to Niles, April 25, 1950, McDonald Papers, USHMM, box 8, folder 9.

78. Symington to McDonald, April 7, 1950, McDonald Papers, USHMM, box 8, folder 9, announced officially the replacement of Colonel Archibald as air attaché and senior military attaché in Tel Aviv by Colonel Samuel C. Gurney Jr., scheduled to graduate from the Industrial College of the Armed Forces on June 18 and then to receive a forty-five-day orientation in intelligence activities. Symington expected Gurney to arrive in Tel Aviv in August and noted that "he has a temperament which should prove valuable in his relations with the Israelis."

79. Entry of March 14, 1950.

80. Judith Gottlieb (d. 2003), designer for Gottex, an Israeli clothing manufacturer founded by her mother Lea Gottlieb (1918–2012).

81. Simcha Even-Zohar, secretary to the Executive and Coordination Committees of Histadrut; with Edis de Philippe founded the Israeli National Opera; married her in August 1950, thereafter giving up his Histadrut post and becoming the opera's chief administrator.

82. Solomon Abramovich Trone (1872–1968), Latvian-born Jewish businessman and engineer sympathetic to Marxism; managing director of General Electric in Russia before 1917, aiding with electrification of USSR in 1920s; representative of the American Jewish Joint Distribution Committee charged with moving Jews to the Dominican Republic, 1939–1941; US technical adviser in India and China after World War II.

83. Owen Lattimore (1900–1989), US scholar of China and adviser to Chiang Kai-shek during World War II; accused of espionage in Senator Joseph McCarthy's Senate hearings,

watched our step we should lose India as we had China." Trone promised to see me again before he left Israel.

Thursday, April 27

Very interesting late morning talk with Shiloah at his HaKirya office across the street from the prime minister's. Shiloah had seen Abdullah Tuesday night, April 25. The latter was cheerful and confident that his people and government wanted peace with Israel and would support his moves to secure it. He intends to carry out his earlier principles. He agreed on the need for pushing the negotiations until they were concluded and calculated that the adjournment of his parliament within a week would enable him to organize and brief his delegation with the aid of the government, so that at the end of a fortnight negotiations could begin. The only point on which Shiloah could discern an inclination of the king to ask for more generous terms from the Israelis was in his emphasis on the need for resettling the refugees in enlarged Jordan with outside funds. On the Israeli side, the only reservation that Shiloah reported was regarding the annexation by Jordan. Israel did not oppose this move, but could recognize it only as a part of a general settlement. Shiloah is going off on an Israeli freighter [for two weeks' vacation] and returning in two weeks for the negotiations.[84]

Miss Herlitz telephoned to ask if she might come to tell me a secret before I learned it from a visitor [Helm] later in the day. Naturally, I welcomed her. I was not terribly surprised when she told me that the decision was identical with a suggestion which I had rashly thrown out some weeks ago. Helm came at four o'clock, was at first obviously a bit disconcerted, if not displeased, by the fact that I knew what Herlitz had told me. He emphasized the absolute need of complete secrecy if the UK authorities were not to be embarrassed. I emphasized my reasons for thinking the choice admirable.

Helm then let me read the excellent statement by the UK, which was being announced in the Commons this day at 5:30 Israel time. There were no surprises in the document, unless it was the complete clarity and forcefulness of the language. Obviously, the Arab League has received a heavy blow. Helm emphasized this by saying in effect: "it is high time that these silly Arabs be taught a lesson." It was evident that he was hoping for strong support from the US.

On April 27, 1950, Great Britain announced recognition of Jordan's annexation of Arab Palestine. Its military alliance with Jordan would extend to the region, but Britain had no plans to establish bases west of the Jordan River. The government also

March 1950; exonerated after numerous subsequent proceedings; later taught at Johns Hopkins and Leeds.

84. In his report, McDonald added that, according to Shiloah, Abdullah hoped that the negotiations might resume by May 10, 1950, and continue until concluded. McDonald to secretary of state, no. 309, April 27, 1950, *FRUS*, 1950, v. V, 877. See also *DFPI*, v. 5, d. 213; Abdullah met with Shiloah without informing his cabinet. US minister Gerald Drew was not informed either, and the British minister Alec Kirkbride was informed only days later. Drew to secretary of state, no. 90, May 3, 1950, USSDCF-PIFA, 1950–1954, reel 1.

announced that it was changing its recognition of Israel from de facto to de jure, but deferring its stance on Jerusalem and on Israel's boundaries, as these were defined by temporary armistice agreements. The government statement concluded, "In announcing these two acts of recognition, His Majesty's Government wish to reaffirm their conviction that the problem of Palestine is capable of solution by peaceful means, given good will and understanding on the part of all the parties concerned."[85]

An hour or two later I received the [*en clair*] telegram from the Department giving the press statement by the secretary on the annexation. What a flabby and inconsequential pronouncement it was. It took notice of the Jordanian expansion and stated that in general we were sympathetic to unions of people by mutual understanding and agreement, but that this case requires study since it involved problems which we were hoping might be solved through the UN and that for the moment this was all that there was to say.[86]

Just after lunch Ruth received a delayed telegram from our family telling of her mother's death on Monday. The funeral was Thursday afternoon.

Friday, April 28

Struggle with the [joint weekly report] because of differences of views about the Russian volte-face on Jerusalem, and because McVicker was not au courant on the British statement about Abdullah's annexation, Jerusalem, and de jure recognition of Israel. Was again delighted with Fried's quickness and brilliance in drafting.

McDonald reported as follows on April 28, 1950:

> *Now that the pleasant shock of Russia's* volte face *on [Jerusalem] issue has worn off, most Israelis, while grateful and relieved that [the] Soviet action will probably kill internationalization in [the] UN, are consciously and subconsciously examining Russia's possible motives. . . . [The] Russian* volte face *appears to be [a] further step in [the] long-run effort [to] undermine [British] influence in [Middle East]. Convinced it had nothing to gain from internationalization which to them meant Anglo-American-Vatican domination in [the] area, and aware it [could] not continue indefinitely [to] support both internationalization of [Jerusalem] and [an] independent Arab State [in Palestine] it shrewdly capitalized on [the] anticipated annexation by Abdullah and chose this time for [abandoning the idea of an] independent Arab State while simultaneously denouncing [the] British in [the] Arab world for latest example [of] British imperialist expansion via Abdullah.*[87]

Still shocked by the Department's [press] statement of the 26th. I wired urging prompt and specific statement, strongly supporting Jordan action on

85. Hansard, Parliamentary Debates, House of Commons, April 27, 1950, v. 474, c. 1137–1141; *DFPI*, v. 5 d. 215, 216.
86. Printed in *FRUS*, 1950, v. V, 874–875.
87. McDonald to secretary of state, joint weeka n. 17, April 28, 1950, McDonald Papers, USHMM, box 8, folder 9.

Jerusalem similar to [the] UK. I reported that the other statement [was] "not dignified here even by mention in *Jerusalem Post*" and concluded "we can no longer advantageously hide behind UN action or inaction."

Conference with Ware about a number of USIE matters.

Saturday, April 29

To the Sam Sackses' for eleven o'clock tea. There [was] Mr. David Tidhar, an old friend of Sam's who is going to the States in connection with his *Encyclopedia [of the Founders and Builders of Israel]* and offers to be of assistance to those protecting the US against certain forms of penetration. I made no commitment, having in my mind what my friend Shiloah had said about the offer by Tidhar to secure the release of certain persons from custody under the mandatory in return for cash payments.[88] I sounded out Tidhar on his relations with Shiloah and was told, "I have nothing against him [Shiloah] but I just don't like him." I will talk to Fried before I write to Sam Klaus about Tidhar.

On the way to the Philharmonic concert Ruth and I stopped at the Gat. There I ran into Dr. Mayer, the New York bone surgeon, who has been busily engaged here in a series of operations during his stay of four weeks.[89]

On our way out we noted the soloist Mademoiselle Richepin waiting for a delayed taxi, so we took her along with us. At the hall, the management explained that they were changing our seats so that we would sit beside Lenny Bernstein. He was most sympathetic towards Ruth. As to the concert, he was very critical of the soloist and not enthusiastic about Paray until the end of the last piece, Berlioz's *Symphonie Fantastique*. The ovation given for Paray at the end was stupendous. Not even Koussevitzky or Lenny [was] ever cheered more by an Israeli audience. Finally, after more than ten minutes of spontaneous applause, Paray was so moved that he made a little speech in French. Everyone seemed to feel that this was a fitting tribute to his musicianship. . . . Perhaps now he will accept the orchestra's offer to return next year for two months.

Sunday, April 30

At work all morning. At eleven Nahum Goldmann came and remained until a little after twelve. His account of his interview with Acheson a few weeks ago substantially confirmed the *aide-mémoire* of conversation, which we received about it shortly thereafter.[90] The significant fact is that the secretary appears to like Nahum and to welcome him as a spokesman not only of the Jewish Agency but also of Jewish groups at home. It may be that Nahum's suggestion that he save the secretary's time by being [a] kind of shock absorber will work out. Nahum admitted that it would be more difficult to serve in this way

88. Entries of January 14 and 16, 1950.
89. Leo Meyer (1884–1972), New York pioneer and leader in orthopedic surgery; organized orthopedic rehabilitation care in Israel; supporter of United Jewish Appeal.
90. See entry of March 31, 1950.

between the president and Jewish groups because the president is in the nature of the case, or at least traditionally, more obligated to receive delegations.

About the American Zionist scene, Nahum was confident that he would be able to checkmate any divisive program which Abba [Hillel Silver] might have in mind. The latter, he thought, was still hopeful of being elected head of the World Zionist Congress—a hope obviously unrealizable. Nahum thinks that [Israel] Brodie may be renamed as ZOA head if, as he hopes may not be the case, former Judge Rifkin declines.[91]

On the issues between the [Jewish] Agency and the [Israeli] government, Nahum was optimistic that a mutually satisfactory arrangement would be worked out. He said that Ben-Gurion and Golda, who alone represented the "extreme position," had already modified their stand. The Agency did not want to "direct" the activities of all American private organizations in Israel but rather to "coordinate" these. Already a beginning had been made in this direction, through the requirement that no contract could be made by a governmental agency with a particular American organization without the approval of the Agency. One of the chief problems of the Agency was its chairman, Beryl Locker, who not only was not as strong as he might be, but also had never in recent years been as friendly with Ben-Gurion as was requisite to the fullest harmony between Agency and government.

Nahum is himself torn between his desire to remain in the US and continue his leadership in [the] Agency and ZOA there and the suggestion being made to him by Ben-Gurion and others that he establish himself here and head the Agency from Jerusalem. I talked to him briefly about my own desires, and he promised to take them up with Dave Niles discreetly.

To the Cashmans for a late afternoon visit; stayed for supper and I for the first part of a movie, and Ruth until the end. I was interested to learn from Colonel Cashman that [the] military attachés had already received word that [Colonel Archibald's] replacement would be Colonel Samuel C. Gurney, Jr. in November. Thus the only difference between the colonel's information and mine is the time of the replacement, mine being August.[92]

91. Israel Benjamin Brodie (1884–1965), Lithuanian-born Zionist leader in the United States; chairman of ZOA, 1931; co-founder of Palestine Potash Co.; member, board of directors, Palestine Economic Corporation. Judge Simon H. Rifkind (1901–1995), Lithuanian-born jurist; legislative aide to Senator Robert F. Wagner, 1927–1933; adviser on Jewish Affairs to Commander of US Forces in Europe, October 1945–May 1946. Treated in Goda et al., eds., *To the Gates of Jerusalem*, 106–109.
92. See entry of April 25, 1950.

23. May 1950

Monday, May 1

Was amused and a little sorry for [Gerald] Drew [in Amman] to note that in his telegram of April 27 to the Department he showed no knowledge—indeed, on the contrary, his information was quite different—of Abdullah's talk with Shiloah the previous Tuesday night [April 25], which I had reported fully in my telegram to the Department of the 27th, copy of which sent by telegram to Amman.[1]

Mr. [Heinz] Graetz of Dizengoff spent an hour or more at the house telling me of his shipping plans and shipping difficulties. It appears that the semiofficial line [ZIM] has not adhered to its promise to limit the number of its ships in the American trade to four. In other ways [it] had used its governmental relationship to deprive Graetz's ships of their anticipated share of the American trade.[2]

To the woodwinds concert at the Tel Aviv Museum. As usual, Bach and Mozart were the highlights of the program.

Tuesday, May 2

Esin, the Turkish minister, came at twelve and stayed until lunch for another of his regular visits. This time at the very beginning, I said, "At all of our previous meetings I have done the most of the talking. This time I hope you will tell me what I don't know." He replied that I was so much better informed but then continued making the following points:

1) Ankara is concerned about internal development[s] in Iran, lest there be local disturbances that might threaten international relations.
2) As to Syria, his information was that there was an increasing amount of communist agitation there, more in Aleppo than in Damascus. The center of communist propaganda for the region, he thinks, is in Beirut.
3) In Egypt, he feels that Farouk is the dominant influence in foreign affairs, that Nahhas Pasha is past his prime, and the leading members of the cabinet are the minister of defense [Mustafa Nusrat Bey] and the minister of foreign affairs [Mustafa Salah al-Din Bey].

---

1. See entry of April 27, 1950; Drew to secretary of state, no. 90, May 3, 1950, *FRUS*, 1950, v. V, 880.
2. See entry of January 11, 1950, for Heinz Graetz and ZIM.

Pleasant lunch with Professor Silverman and his wife of Dartmouth.[3] Brief visit in the late afternoon to the new children's village north of Tel Aviv. The national Hadassah officers were present because of their financial participation in the construction. Wonderful buffet dinner at the Archibalds' for thirty-two people. Everything was perfect. The only talk which needs to be recorded is that which I had with Helm, who indicated his disappointment at the coolness of the Israeli reaction to the recent British statement on de jure recognition and the annexation of Abdullah.[4]

Wednesday, May 3

Joseph J. Schwartz of the New York JDC [Joint Distribution Committee] and Charles Passman, the director of the Israel-JDC Committee dealing with the hard-core cases, spent an hour at the house.[5] Aside from general talk, Schwartz was interested to get my views, which were necessarily very sketchy and tentative, about what might be expected from Baghdad and Teheran to facilitate the exodus of Jews from Iraq.[6] A second Magic Carpet was preferable, except that it did not permit [the] bringing by the exiles of their personal effects, and there was a possibility that it could not be arranged because of Iraq's policy of opposition to any direct air travel between Baghdad and Lydda. Shipping also was difficult, hence efforts were being made to secure permission to fly the émigrés nominally to Cyprus. A few days later I saw telegrams from Baghdad indicating a serious difficulty might be anticipated in this Baghdad-Cyprus scheme.

3. Louis L. Silverman (1884–1967), Lithuanian-born mathematician; emigrated to the United States, 1892; professor of mathematics at Dartmouth College; known for expertise on divergent series of numbers; founder, Menorah Society; later taught at the Tel Aviv University.

4. Refers to Sharett to Helm, May 2, 1950, *DFPI*, v. 5, d. 218. Sharett expressed "deep satisfaction" on the part of his government, but noted that "the Government of Israel has already had occasion to express its misgivings concerning the apparent contradiction between the United Kingdom's declared policy and the inevitable effect of some of its actions." Specifically he pointed to British arms sales to Arab states without a condition that they conclude peace with Israel together with London's refusal to sell Israel arms.

5. Charles S. Passman (1888–1971), Russian-born Zionist; emigrated with parents to the United States at age 12; settled in Palestine, 1920; co-founder of Herzliya, 1925; aided with Jewish relief in Hebron, 1929; joined JDC at start of the war; JDC chief in Istanbul, helping rescue Romanian Jews, 1942; traveled to Teheran to organize relief for surviving Polish and Soviet Jews, 1944–1945; headed JDC "Mediterranean" division, aiding Jewish emigration from Italy (met McDonald in Bari in that year), 1946; headed JDC office in Munich, 1946–1947; one of seven members of the Jerusalem Emergency Committee set up to prepare the city for the exit of the British, 1947; headed the JDC in Israel with special responsibility for the Malben organization tasked with helping older refugees coming to Palestine, 1948–1957. See Dalia Ofer, "Defining Relationships: The Joint Distribution Committee and Israel, 1948–1950," in Troen and Lucas, ed., *Israel: the First Decade of Independence*, 713–72; and Zertal, *From Catastrophe to Power*, 187, 189, 199.

6. Between January and March 1950, despite official prohibitions on Jewish emigration from Iraq, some 4,000 Iraqi Jews fled the country through Iran for Israel, causing embarrassment for the Iraqi government. In March 1950, Iraq acknowledged that Jews could emigrate, but claimed their assets. The State Department did not press Iraq hard on the treatment of Iraqi Jews, the Israelis thought, because of the importance of the Iraq Petroleum Company (IPC). Fischbach, *Jewish Property Claims Against Arab Countries*, 132ff.

At 3:45 I called on Sharett at the Foreign Office and remained for an hour. He elaborated on the *aide-mémoire*, which he asked me to pass on to the Department.

Israel still was unable to buy arms in the United States to defend itself. Quantities and types of weapons supplied by Britain to the Arab states exceeded Arab defensive needs, and Britain required no steps toward peace in return for these deliveries. Israel had requested that the United States use its good offices to check the sales of arms to the Arab states, but the United States had not yet answered.[7]

George McGhee noted, "The recommendations of the Department of Defense in all cases referred to it where the Israeli Government was the recipient have been for denial of the export applications [on grounds that Israel was too strong militarily]. The reverse has been true for all recommendations concerning arms for the Arab states." He recommended that the Pentagon's policy be reconsidered and "that limited amounts of the arms requested should be permitted to go to the Arab states and Israel."[8]

Then he explained his reasons for being troubled about the attitude of Britain despite the latter's de jure recognition [of Israel]. He was fearful lest London discourage Abdullah in his peace-making plans. One possible indication of this was a letter from the king intended to be shown to the Israelis in which enlarged political and territorial claims were made.

I told Sharett of the charges from some of the neighboring [Arab] capitals that the US was pulling Israel's chestnuts out of the fire. He replied that if it served any useful purpose he could make a long list of the instances where I, speaking for the US government, had been very stiff with the Foreign Office.[9]

Sharett said that at the meeting a few days earlier, between him and Helm, there had been almost sharp exchanges of views.[10] Sharett had put forcibly Israel's views about the unilateral annexation and the UK's extension of the

---

7. See *DFPI*, v. 5, d. 224, also 225, 226. McDonald to secretary of state, no. 330, May 4, 1950, *FRUS*, 1950, v. V, 882–883. Elath's efforts in Washington to procure arms in May 1950 are described in *DFPI*, v. 5, d. 222–226, 231, 233–235, 238.

8. Memorandum by McGhee, undated, [drafted by Rockwell May 16, 1950], *FRUS*, 1950, v. V, 891–892.

9. Anti-American sentiment increased throughout the Arab world. The Egyptian newspaper *Al-Ahram* condemned the United States' "bare-faced support of Israel." On April 9, Syria's economics minister insisted, "If the American Government continues its pressure on Arab states in an attempt to make the Arab people subservient to the Zionist cause, I hope a plebiscite will be taken in Arab countries so that it may be known whether the Arabs prefer a thousandfold to become a Soviet republic rather than a prey to world Jewry." On May 18, Acheson suggested that Truman "reaffirm in a public statement our friendship to the Arab governments and peoples." *FRUS*, 1950, v. V, 895–899.

10. Recounted in *DFPI*, v. 5, d. 221. For the heated reaction in London, see Kidron to Comay, May 16, 1950, *DFPI*, v. 5, d. 239; Sharett to Kidron, May 23, 1950, *DFPI*, v. 5, d. 246.

treaty and its persistence in the arms shipment. Helm had replied forcibly. The meeting, however, had ended amicably.[11]

Marcus Sieff came for somewhat more than an hour and told me interesting stories of the role of certain personalities in the UK Foreign Office.[12] We were joined midstream by [Milton] Fried. In substance, Marcus said [that] Michael Wright is unreconstructed. He and [John] Sheringham and those who think like them had decided to go all out to build up Egypt in order to secure a treaty affecting the Suez and the Sudan. To achieve this, they were prepared to make almost any concessions to Farouk and his colleagues no matter how these might affect Israel. Hence, the arms shipments, which were far beyond any required by treaty obligations; the designation of Farouk as a full general in the British Army;[13] the rumors that in the event of war Farouk might be designated as honorary commander of the British forces in Egypt; and the general softness of the UK impressing its views about the free passage of the Suez, etc.

During Bevin's absence in the hospital [April 12–May 8 for a minor operation] the recent declaration about Abdullah and de jure recognition had been worked out. These were, to a degree, a reversal of the Michael Wright-Bevin intransigent pro-Egyptian policy. Unfortunately, however, Bevin was returning soon to the Foreign Office, and there was danger that there would be a relapse into his anti-Israel policy. There is considerable opposition in Parliament and in the press to the Michael Wright-Bevin program. Eden and Churchill, as well as some of the liberals and the [Richard] Crossman Labour section, are opposed. The *Times*, after hearing Marcus, had made its own inquiries at the Foreign Office, and had then written a stiff editorial criticizing the Foreign Office's policy.

Marcus indicated here that if by fall the Egyptian air force had been raised to the strength now planned, the king might launch an all-out air blitzkrieg, which during its first stages could be expected to work havoc in Tel Aviv. Later, he anticipated that the tide would turn but not until Israel had suffered severely. He had asked a prominent and friendly Britisher what would happen if, after the tide turned, Israel pressed on into Egypt. The latter had replied that "he supposed the UK would have to fight Israel."

Dinner at the Sharett's. Present besides ourselves were the Hadassah group: [Rose] Halprin, [Etta] Rosensohn, [Marian] Greenberg and [Tamar] de Sola Pool; also, the [Gershon] Agrons and the Davidowitzes. The house was attractive and the food good by Israel standards. The only political item was

11. McDonald commented to Washington, "UK *de jure* recognition would have been much more enthusiastically received had it not been linked with recognition of annexation and extension of treaty which, though known to be inevitable, were embarrassing to Israel Government." McDonald to secretary of state, no. 327, May 4, 1950, hereafter USSDCF-PIFA, reel 1, frame 490.

12. Entries of August 4, 1948, and March 13, 1949.

13. Farouk's appointment as an honorary general in the British Army in March 1950 was an attempt by Bevin to encourage Farouk to renew the 1936 Anglo-Egyptian treaty and was widely criticized in Parliament.

Sharett's inquiry whether other Tel Aviv diplomats were going to the [Hebrew] University celebration. I told him that Helm had said he was not going, but I did not know about the others.

McDonald remained under official instructions not to attend official functions in Jerusalem, but on May 5, 1950, he attended the twenty-fifth anniversary ceremony at the Hebrew University in Jerusalem. During the War of Independence, the Hebrew University had moved from Mount Scopus to the Terra Sancta building (rented from the Franciscan Order) and other buildings in Rehavia, where it remained until 1960. It was there that the ceremony, described next, took place.

Friday, May 5

Left at 7:40, Ruth, Miss Davis [embassy staff] and I, for Jerusalem, where we arrived at 9:20. Almost directly we went to the Terra Sancta, where the women entered the grounds while I joined the others, who were to sit on the platform and who had convened at a neighboring house. I chatted with four or more of the faculty and visitors. The only noteworthy talk was mine with Ben-Gurion; the latter took exception to my inability to respond properly to his Hebrew salutation, and said half seriously that "it is shameful that I have learned so little." I replied that I would have understood him better if he had spoken with Sharett's more classic accent. Then, more seriously, I said that I had more important business, and then recounted the reports from neighboring capitals that "Israel had the US in its pocket." Ben-Gurion's comment was "we must have a very big pocket."

The Dutch minister [J. A. Nederbragt] and I, the only two diplomatic representatives present,[14] were seated in the front row along with the top governmental and university dignitaries. The speaking lasted nearly two hours and, except for a few paragraphs, was wholly in Hebrew. The following is the order of speaking: Sir Leon Simon, who presided, spoke briefly and then read Weizmann's address. The last paragraph of this, an appeal for Israel-Arab friendship, was translated into English. Then [Selig] Brodetsky spoke for twenty minutes. We could follow this forceful statement because an English translation had been distributed. The prime minister spoke for the same length of time, but since we had no translation we had to wait to read his summary in the *Jerusalem Post*. Others who spoke briefly were [Yigael] Yadin, [Dr. Simcha] Assaf (the rector),[15] [Zalman] Shazar, minister of education,[16] and a student.

---

14. Nederbragt, the Dutch minister to Israel, also served as the Dutch consul general to Jerusalem; thus his presence at the ceremony.

15. Simha Assaf (1889–1953) Minsk-born professor of rabbinic studies at Hebrew University; emigrated from Odessa, 1921; rector, Hebrew University, 1948–1950; appointed to the Israeli Supreme Court, 1948.

16. Zalman Shazar [formerly Rubashov] (1889–1974), Belorussian-born labor politician and poet; emigrated to Palestine, 1924, and worked with the Histadrut; editor of *Davar* 1944–1949; member of the first Knesset, and minister of education in Ben-Gurion's first government

At lunch, the food was excellent; Gibson expressed himself as critical of [Alva] Miller and the YMCA, who he says is unnecessarily unsympathetic with the Jews.[17] On the other hand, Gibson said that he thought, judging from items in the *[Jerusalem] Post* that, almost as if they were paid for it, certain Jewish writers were so critical of Abdullah, whenever the latter made a conciliatory move, as to endanger if not destroy whatever progress had been made. Gibson said he hoped to have a long visit with opportunities for a searching talk soon.

Saturday, May 6

Breakfast with Jimmy Parkes.[18] He is disturbed by "ignorant and vicious" anti-Israel propaganda in British church circles. He has written an essay to endeavor to counteract this. He showed me his little book of maps of Jerusalem, which I should have.[19]

Took Kingsley Martin of the *New Statesman*[20] out to Ein Karem. It is a very beautiful section in the ravine southwest of Jerusalem.[21] It reminds one of sections of Italy. The monks and nuns who chose it as a center for their institutions had a keen eye for its possibilities.[22] Today the terracing, the cypresses, and the orchards make it a heartening example of what parts of Israel could become. Lunch with Serge [Karlinski] and his family, and back to Tel Aviv immediately thereafter.

I should have noted that Friday evening, before dinner, I had a brief but important talk with General Riley in the lobby of the King David. Earlier that day, Jacob Herzog had told me of the "tense" interview between Monsignor McMahon and Sharett, on the Tuesday [April 25] following the former's visit at our house.[23] According to Herzog, there has been almost passionate talk about a third world war, breakup of the UN, the internationalization of Jerusalem, etc. General Riley's understanding of the views of McMahon did not fit into Herzog's account; particularly, the emphasis was not the same. General Riley believes that there will have to be a compromise and that the Vatican will accept it, but that, naturally at this point, McMahon was not indicating this.

(Mapai). After chairing the Jewish Agency Executive, he became the third president of Israel, 1963–1973.

17. See entry of June 22, 1949.

18. James Parkes (1896–1981), Anglican priest and scholar of Christian-Jewish relations who worked to remove antisemitism from Christian tradition; author of *The Emergence of the Jewish Problem, 1878–1939* (London: Oxford University Press, 1939); testified before Anglo-American Committee of Inquiry in 1946 where he met McDonald. See Goda et al., eds. *To the Gates of Jerusalem*, entries of January 26, 30, 1946. See also Haim Chertok, *He Also Spoke as a Jew: The Life of Reverend James Parkes* (London: Vallentine Mitchel, 2006).

19. Refers to James Parkes, *The Story of Jerusalem* (London: Cresset Press, 1949).

20. Kingsley Martin (1897–1969), British left-leaning journalist; editor of *The New Statesman*, 1930–1960.

21. Ein Karem, village near Jerusalem and legendary birthplace of John the Baptist.

22. Refers to the monastery Les Soeurs de Notre Dame de Sion, founded in the nineteenth century.

23. See entry of April 20, 1950.

This was a full workday. Cleared up a number of matters during the early morning. Later, McVicker came in with a number of telegrams. The only one which required careful thought and action was that asking for our view on a suggested non-aggression statement by US, UK and France.[24] We decided to indicate that it would be well received, but without great enthusiasm, and expressed the hope that it might be made more specific by being extended beyond technical concepts of violation of existing frontiers or armistice lines. I called attention to Israel's fear of an Arab blitzkrieg by air.

At teatime the Frieds and Michael were at the house and later Mrs. Edward Norman[25] and Dr. [Israel] Wechsler.[26] The only noteworthy item was Dr. Wechsler's opposition to the united [fundraising] drive of the Hebrew University, the Haifa [Technion], and the Weizmann Institute. From what Wechsler said, I judged that the idea was [not] Wechsler's, and had been forced through by Brodetsky during his recent trip to the States. As usual, Wechsler was vague about what the Friends [of the Hebrew University] under his leadership had intended to do. He talked generally about the desirability of his group being a cultural link between the two countries but gave no indication that now, more than before, was he willing or able to undertake the essential financial effort.

Ruth and I lunched with General Riley at the Sharon. The food was almost as good as I have ever tasted at an Israeli hotel. Riley and I did not talk business formally, but a number of items including the following are worth recording: he does not share the Israeli fear of an Egyptian air blitzkrieg. The king might personally be tempted, but his government would not agree because it dare not risk Israel's bombing of Cairo. He seems inclined to the view that the talk of a second round and the intensive campaign about arms shipments are parts of legitimate propaganda; Riley is hoping to be released and return home this fall, though I got the impression that he would not fight strenuously if he were asked to remain; the present Jordanian prime minister [Sa'id al-Mufti] is, he thinks, in much the same position as was the recent prime minister [Tewfik Abu al-Huda], embarrassed by Abdullah's impetuosity and his unwillingness to take the time to prepare public opinion for a resumption of negotiations with Israel; the recent floodlighting by Israel of Mount Scopus and the Hebrew University during the University anniversary celebration and the repeated talk of the University returning "home" to Mount Scopus, has created a degree of nervousness among the Jordanians. Riley is seeing Eytan, Sharett, and other officials here, including Yadin.

24. Discussed during the Foreign Ministers' Meeting in London in May 1950 and sent on May 24, 1950. See italicized insert to entry of May 21–June 2.
25. Entries of April 24, 29, 30, 1949.
26. Entry of November 26, 1948.

Riley's account of the forcing down of the plane a few days ago differed substantially from the official Israeli account.[27] According to Riley, the plane was within the corridor allocated to it by the civil authorities flying from Haifa south of Mount Carmel, when it was intercepted by two fighter planes. These latter did not fire across its bow, but did fire parallel with the plane when the pilot appeared to the fighters not to be obeying their signal. The pilot of the UN plane at once radioed Lydda and received word that Lydda knew nothing of fighter planes but would check. The latter followed the plane over Egyptian soil, when the plane turned back and landed at Lydda. The pilots of the fighters said that they thought the plane was headed for the Israeli military airfield east of Haifa. The general explained that to get around Carmel to the east and south, it was necessary for the pilot for a little while to head in the general direction of the military field. The Israelis at first threatened to make a formal protest, but after receipt of Riley's factual account they have not made any protest. Riley sought to avoid making a major issue of the incident. Riley expects to see General [Howard] Kennedy[28] soon in Amman and will then spend a few days each in Beirut, Damascus and Cairo.

I was grateful to Fried for his bringing me at teatime the Department's report from Cairo regarding the enlarged draft of the statement being worked on with the UK. We did the best we could to make suggestions which would strengthen the draft, which seemed to both of us weaker than the previous one, and to illustrate again the British capacity to persuade us to endorse their policies. We approved the French being in and suggested that the statement be a part of a geographically more comprehensive one.[29]

Kollek came to talk about the possibility of the NEAT [Near East Air Transport][30] setting up another Magic Carpet from Baghdad to Lydda via Cyprus. I suggested that Kollek talk with Hooper Tuesday and that I would join them after they had covered the initial ground. Kollek also brought some good photographs taken by our military escort during our trip along the northern frontier.

Tuesday, May 9

Conference with Kollek and Hooper at the office, at the end of which we drafted a telegram to the Department in which we suggested that it urge the embassy in Baghdad to express the hope that the Iraqi government would permit a second Magic Carpet service, this time from Baghdad to Lydda via

---

27. On May 2, 1950 two Israeli F-51 fighters forced down a UN C-47 transport en route from Haifa to Kalandia Airfield, the Jordanian-controlled strip near Jerusalem. The Israelis claimed the UN aircraft had strayed from the permitted air corridor.

28. Director of the new United Nations Relief and Works Agency (UNRWA), which began work in its headquarters in Beirut on April 25, 1950.

29. Concerns Acheson's statement regarding armament sales to Middle East countries. See the later discussion.

30. Specially created offshoot of Alaska Airlines, first put together for the transport of Aden's Jews to Israel in August 1949. See Parfitt, *The Road to Redemption*, 214–215.

Cyprus in the assumption that guarantees would be given that all arrivals in Cyprus would be carried on immediately to Israel.

On the same day, Kollek's US Division told the Israeli embassy in Washington to press the State Department to assist in setting up the transport. The message said, "Every day counts." On May 19, 1950, the first two airplanes with Iraqi Jews landed in Cyprus, and the Israelis gratefully acknowledged the "extreme helpfulness" of the State Department.[31]

Jacob Herzog came to the house about 12:45 and remained until [1:30]. First, he outlined very clearly and in some detail the replies which he had given to several groups of Americans, including those from the AJC [American Jewish Committee] and rabbinical associations, to the fears expressed that the Orthodox influence here was undemocratic and might adversely affect both Israel and Jews in the Diaspora.

In a letter of agreement of June 19, 1947, Ben-Gurion gave ambiguous assurances to Orthodox leaders regarding minimal accommodations concerning Shabbat, kashrut, marriage, and autonomy in education.[32] *Following independence Ben-Gurion resisted calls for a written constitution, understanding that arguments over halakhic versus secular law would tear the country apart. Yet he felt obliged to make certain concessions insofar as he understood these to be in the interests of the state. Some of these concessions worried non-Orthodox American Jewish groups, whereas for some Orthodox they did not go far enough.*

Here are some of the chief points which Herzog made:

1) There is not and never has been nor can there be a Jewish church in the Christian sense of the word;
2) The rabbi is essentially the teacher rather than the priest or intermediary;
3) Jewish marriage is not dependent for its validity upon the presence or the officiating of a rabbi. Two people in the presence of witnesses can marry themselves so long as they follow the Jewish law, and no rabbi in the world can declare the marriage not valid.
4) In fact the rabbi, when he performs the marriage ceremony, is little more than a public official administering the Jewish laws;
5) The requirement for religious marriage among Jews in Israel is nothing new; it is a continuation of the rule under the mandatory;[33]

---

31. *DFPI*, v. 5, d. 230, 244.
32. Overview in Menachem Friedman, "The Structural Foundation for Religio-Political Accommodation in Israel: Fallacy and Reality," in Troen and Lucas, eds., *Israel: The First Decade of Independence*, 51–81.
33. Meaning that the British retained the Ottoman millet system of religious laws for those who wished to be part of Jewish, Muslim, or Christian communities.

6) Ben-Gurion defends the insistence on religious marriage, not as the price of support of the Orthodox group, but because not to have such marriage compulsory would be to divide the community into two castes which could not marry one another. In arguing this case with some of his own party members, Ben-Gurion put it this way: if, he said, you could answer these two questions affirmatively I will change my view; a) are the children of non-religious marriages better than those of religious marriages? b) do you wish to create a situation where the religious section of the community will be unable to marry with the other half of the community because the young people of this latter group are the products of non-religious marriages?[34]

7) As to kosher food and its requirements in governmental institutions, including the army, Ben-Gurion's defense is that without it there would have to be two soldier and officer messes, and he is unwilling to divide the armed services or public officials on religious lines. Non-religious Jews can eat kosher food, but religious Jews cannot eat non-kosher food.

8) The prohibition of public service travel on Shabbat is less of a restriction on the personal liberty of citizens than is imposed, for example, by New York State on its citizens through the latter's divorce law, which recognizes adultery as the only legal basis for divorce.

9) There is no possibility under Jewish law of a theocracy in Israel. Even at the time of the priesthood, the chief priest could never be king; his proper role was to be the critic, the conscience of the king.

10) As to the criticism of the Reform rabbis that the Orthodox are tending to divide the Jews, Herzog said, it ill becomes the dissidents to blame the Orthodox, for surely the Jew who performs more of the laws' prescriptions is not less Jewish than those who perform fewer of the rules. Herzog deplored the tendency of some of the Orthodox in the States to boast that the role of Orthodoxy in Israel was proof that Orthodoxy in US is preferable to Reform.

Herzog said that, with few exceptions, the Americans who came to complain of the role of Orthodoxy here accepted his arguments and agreed either to discontinue their opposition or at least to wait and see future developments before renewing their efforts to lessen [the] Orthodox power or program in Israel. In answer to my urgent request, Herzog said that he would give me in writing, at least in outline form, the main points of his presentation.

Herzog then turned again to the interview between the foreign minister and Monsignor McMahon on April 25. Again, he emphasized the tenseness of the atmosphere and the difficulty [that] Sharett had in restraining his inclination to answer undiplomatically. McMahon, reporting that His Holiness was

---

34. The result of discussions between Ben-Gurion and Orthodox leaders, which began in earnest in 1947, was the Rabbinic Courts Jurisdiction Law of 1953. The law made halakhic marriage by Orthodox rabbis and divorce by rabbinic courts mandatory. For contemporary interpretations, see Susan M. Weiss and Netty C. Gross-Horowitz, *Marriage and Divorce in the Jewish State: Israel's Civil War* (Lebanon, NH: Brandeis University Press, 2013).

gravely troubled by the international situation and had himself taken direct charge of foreign policy, went on to indicate that there was doubt whether the time had not already passed when even an anticipatory affirmative action by the Western European powers could save Europe from being engulfed by Moscow.

I pressed Herzog on the subject of McMahon and Monsignor Gori's complaints that without the return of the Christian Arab population the Holy Places were emptied of meaning, and that, if they had to choose, they would sacrifice the Holy Places rather than the Christian population.[35] Herzog had no ready answer. He admitted that the Christian institutions deprived of their Christian Arab population and natural clientele would tend to wither. The only alternative he could urge was an arrangement by which a Christian Arab enclave would be developed to include the major Holy Places and new sections of the city to be built and inhabited by the returning former residents of Katamon, the Greek colony, the German colony, [Baka] and others, in the south of the now Jewish New City.

Herzog developed the thesis that the British had out-maneuvered the Vatican, and that the latter, by refusing to consider the Israeli proposal of functional internationalization, had played into the hands of London and Moscow. Herzog deplored the fact that Abdullah, who was much more intransigent than the Jews and who would not accept even functional internationalization, had, through his own reticence and through the cover of the British, escaped almost altogether opprobrium for opposition to the Jerusalem statute. Herzog expressed admiration for the cleverness of the British, who, while giving a form of lip service to internationalization, had been instrumental in blocking [it]. He said he was surprised that the Vatican had not seen through the British purposes.

Wednesday, May 10

I asked Nederbragt [who spent an hour at McDonald's residence] about the unusual situation created by his residence in Jerusalem now that he is the diplomatic representative of his country.[36] He anticipated that, if he were replaced, the new man would have to live in Tel Aviv. As Nederbragt was leaving, I had an example of Sir Knox's brusqueness when he is off his guard. I called him on the telephone to find out where Nederbragt was to keep an appointment with Sir Knox. The latter's tone suggested that he thought Nederbragt something of an old gaga.

To the [Nachum] Gutman show at the museum.[37] There visited with the artist and his wife and also with the Castels. All of Gutman's new pictures are of Tiberias.

---

35. See entries of March 20, 23–24, 1950.
36. The Netherlands conferred de facto recognition on Israel in May 1949 and de jure in January 1950. Previously, Nederbragt had been the Dutch consul general in Jerusalem and now also held the post of ambassador.
37. Nachum Gutman (1898–1978), Bessarabian-born Israeli artist; emigrated to Palestine, 1905; studied in Jerusalem, Vienna, Berlin, and Paris.

Dinner at Max Greenberg's. Dr. Marsh of Boston University[38] left early, clearing the way for Dr. [Solomon] Trone, who was there with his wife, to talk most interestingly about India and China for more than an hour.[39] He told of his experiences as Chiang Kai-Shek's engineering adviser, emphasized the extraordinary achievements materially of the Japanese in a little over ten years in Manchuria, denied that Chinese resentment at the Russian despoiling of Manchuria [in August 1945] had alienated Chinese support from Moscow, and affirmed that contrary to the wishful thinking of American and other liberals, Chinese communism is and will remain of the Russian brand. The talk of agrarian reform as if this were all that is involved is, he said, to nourish dangerous illusion. The Chinese communist leaders are men of great ability and are ideologically closely akin to Moscow. He deplores the failure of the West to have moved in time, but insists that once the social revolution had gotten securely under way in China, there was no possibility of checking it by Western influence. The net result of all our efforts had been to pour into China billions of dollars worth of industrial and other equipment, which is now being used by the Chinese communists. He wasted little time condemning the corruption and inefficiency of the old regime, praised Chiang Kai-Shek as personally patriotic and unselfish, but blamed him as the tool of corrupt and reactionary political military and feudal forces. On balance, he seemed inclined to the belief that the Chinese people at least would benefit from the communist regime as compared with that which they had suffered under during the past three decades, or for that matter under the Manchus.

Nothing he said, however—and I listened with great care so as to evaluate the nuances of his exposition—gave me the impression that he could with any fairness be termed communist or a fellow traveler. When Max Greenberg suggested that, when Dr. Trone returned to the States, he might be examined by Senator [Joseph] McCarthy, Trone and his wife laughed and said that would be an interesting new experience. They plan to return to the States for a few months, unless it should be decided that they go back directly to India. He promised to come and see me for a long talk before he left Israel.

Thursday, May 11

[Edouard-Félix] Guyon, the French minister, spent about an hour at the house. He was not very out-giving, but left me the impression that he thinks the Vatican has maintained an impossible position about Jerusalem, that Israel has foolishly put itself much too much in the forefront vocally on this issue and [has] therefore incurred needless criticism, whereas Abdullah under British tutelage, by remaining silent, escaped criticism for his even greater intransigence. Guyon deplored the current tendency in the Israeli press to play up

---

38. Daniel L. Marsh (1880–1968), Methodist minister; president of Boston University, 1926–1951.
39. See also entry of April 26, 1950.

and "exaggerate" the arms menace. He was fearful that this propaganda might get out of hand and that Ben-Gurion be persuaded to take offensive action if, as the press gives the impression, the second round is nearly a certainty and that time is running against Israel.

Sunday, May 14

Late morning Mrs. de Sola Pool came with Mrs. [Zipora] Sharett, Mrs. [Ida] Davidowitz, and the "Israel Mother for the Year" and her mother, together with four lovely children. I hope the photographs were good because the children were very attractive, so much so indeed that I "forgave" Mrs. de Sola Pool for bothering me on a Sunday about this matter.

Home for a bite of supper before the Bernstein concert.[40] At the last minute we decided to take Mrs. Fried in order to get her away from her troubles. Lenny's concerto contrasted most sharply with the Brahms Variations and the Mendelssohn concerto. As to the concerto, I am tempted to apply the banal characterization that it was "interesting."

After the concert at the Gat, Lenny and we embraced and he complained that we had not come backstage. He said, "We must get together," and that he would try to arrange it before Ruth and I went off to Cyprus.

Monday, May 15

Policy staff conference at the house. [Two] chief topics were discussed: 1) the internationalization of Jerusalem in the light of the Russian reversal, the British recognition of Abdullah's annexation, and the unyieldingness of the Vatican. 2) The arms race, the supply of arms by the West, and the contrast between the possible motivation of the suppliers and the purposes to which the recipients might put them. Perhaps the most helpful contribution of the afternoon was Fried's elaboration of the thesis that the arguments by Britain, supported by the US as to British purposes, were irrelevant from the point of view of either the recipient of the arms or that of Israel, against [which the arms] might be used. Fried stressed that there exists a genuine fear both in Israel and in the Arab states about the possible intentions of the other side. The very lack of genuine cooperation among the Arab states is an added reason for their fear.

There is in the Israeli government's reply of March 29, 1950 to [the] PCC [Palestine Conciliation Commission] the following very pertinent and apt expression of this problem from one point of view. Speaking of Egypt's receipt of

> large numbers of offensive weapons . . . going far beyond the requirements of internal order or local defense. . . . [t]he [Government] of Israel welcomes the assurances which have been given to the effect

---

40. Bernstein returned to Israel partly to commemorate the twenty-fifth anniversary of the Hebrew University with a concert in Jerusalem on May 9. He then performed several concerts in Tel Aviv.

that this armament is not intended to be used for renewal of hostilities against Israel. Yet it is quite possible to respect the sincerity of these assurances without being reassured or comforted by them. In a rearmament process, the intentions of the donors may not be expressed in the actions of the recipients. Moreover, even if Arab [governments] are now credited with having no intention to attack Israel, an illusion of military superiority may well breed that intention in the future.

The next day Ford told me he thought the meeting had been worthwhile, but that in the future it should be more narrowly limited to the senior officers.

Army Day cocktail party at the Archibalds'. As was to have been expected, the food was an excellent substitute for dinner. My talks, which deserve brief recording, were three. First, with [Gene] Currivan, who told me that [Lester] Markel was arriving on Tuesday and that they would come out to see me during the week.[41] He raised the question, apparently in order to sound me out, as to whether Shiloah was not engaged on some mission other than health during his more than a fortnight's absence from Israel. I honestly replied that I had no information, except that I understood that Shiloah would be back on the 16th.

My long talk was with Esin. He was much less reticent than usual. He thought that the seeming overwhelming victory of the [Turkish] Democratic Party would be cut down by the late returns from the country.[42] Despite the defeat of the foreign minister, he did not think that the election would affect foreign policy.[43] Esin [returned] several times to a thesis, which he had previously never developed so clearly, that the UK is the real influence in shaping Jordan's policy. Esin went beyond that to intimate that British policy was now dominant in Syria and that, in general, this might be said of the Arab world adjacent to Israel.

Another talk which was interesting was with Chief of Staff Yadin. In addition to developing the usual Israeli thesis about Arab rearmament, he talked interestingly about internal conditions in Syria and of the possibility that Abdullah might march to Damascus. Yadin thinks that there is a very active propaganda and intrigue being carried on by Iraqis in Syria, and that if these issued in another *coup d'etat*, Abdullah might, if Britain indicated that it would not object, move quickly. Yadin thinks that the one Jordanian brigade stationed near the Syrian frontier could reach Damascus in forty-eight hours. [McDonald noted Yadin's comment that the Syrians had a brigade on the northeast frontier of Israel, a brigade at Aleppo, and one facing Iraq]. I told Yadin about Fried's difficulty in finding a house and jokingly added that, in return for a

41. Lester Markel (1894–1977), editor of *New York Times* Sunday edition, 1923–1964.
42. The Turkish general election of May 1950 brought a 53.3% majority for the Democratic Party and a defeat for the ruling Republican People's Party.
43. In fact, the foreign minister, Necmettin Sadak (1890–1953) of the Republican People's Party, was replaced by Mehmet Fuat Köprülü (1890–1966) of the Democratic Party, who held the portfolio until 1955.

house, I would undertake to get Israel some arms. In comparable vein, Yadin replied that for such a quid pro quo the house would be provided!

I should have recorded as under our policy staff conference of this afternoon a statement by Hooper. Soon after Helm's arrival, Sir Knox said to Hooper, "I am here with long-range instructions." To Hooper's comment, "I suppose you will talk these over frankly with my chief," Sir Knox had replied, "I will not." My only comment on Hooper's report is that Sir Knox has certainly not disclosed any of his instructions to me, despite our growing friendliness.

Tuesday, May 16

Drafted at the office an answer, which was approved by Ford and McVicker, to the Department's request for comment on the US [PCC] delegation's statement of the [PCC]'s intention to press for negotiations by the Arab states with Israel.[44] The statement was a reasonable one, suggesting that PCC is at "the crossroads and that unless it can secure Arab cooperation its usefulness may be at an end." The assumption throughout the text was that Israel is cooperative. I was surprised in the US delegation's statement [of May 11] that the PCC seems to think that it can influence the several [Arab] governments to name more useful representatives. I expressed doubt on this score but added that we would not be embarrassed here, because it would be easy to telegram the [Israeli] Foreign Office of the PCC's "high regard" for Eban and Rafael. We approved of the suggestion that Abdullah and the British be persuaded to have Jordan resume negotiations with Israel, this time under PCC auspices. We doubted, however, that though such negotiations would lessen the danger to Abdullah from either domestic opposition or from the Arab states, his example would be one that would encourage other Arab states to negotiate with Israel.

The PCC hoped that negotiations might resume on May 23. On May 13, Sharett cabled Shiloah, then on leave in Paris, that his main question to the PCC—which Arab states were ready to negotiate with Israel—had been left unanswered. On May 15, Shiloah met in Geneva with Ely Palmer, the head of the US delegation. Absent a useful Arab response, he said, Israel would prefer direct negotiations with Jordan for the time being. Palmer had not expected the Israelis to send a delegation to Geneva without a satisfactory Arab answer. Sharett thereafter informed the PCC that he would "await clarification of the Arab attitude on question of direct negotiations before considering next step."[45]

Dinner at the house for the Guyons, the Esins, the Fuhrmans, Fords, Rebecca Sieff, and McVicker. Esin was interesting as he spoke about the

44. Palmer to secretary of state, no. 606, May 11, 1950, *FRUS*, 1950, v. V, 888–889.
45. Ibid.; Palmer to secretary of state, no. 619, May 16, 1950, *FRUS*, 1950, v. V, 893–894; *DFPI*, v. 5, d. 228, 236 and n. 2, 242.

Turkish election, stressing that the only surprising element was the size of the opposition victory. He doubted that, aside from a greater emphasis on private initiative in internal affairs, the election would otherwise change Turkish policy. Particularly, he was confident that it would not change foreign policy. Guyon asked me what had happened to the suggested Anglo-American-French proposed statement on Near Eastern security and arms problems. I told him I had no information.

Wednesday, May 17

At the office told David Tidhar that I would give him a note of introduction to Sam Klaus to whom I had written about him. I declined to give him any form of endorsement for his publication project.[46]

The [Jascha] Heifetz[47] appearance with Lenny Bernstein and the [Israel Philharmonic] Orchestra was, after the appearance of Koussevitzky, the high-water mark of the season. The whole program was delightful. Haydn's symphony, Roy Harris's symphony, culminating [in] Brahms's concerto. Afterwards, there was a reception on the stage. The Heifetzes were very friendly and said they would like to see us as soon as they had gotten their schedule straightened out.

Thursday, May 18

Acting as my own chauffeur and passing by the Sharon to leave flowers for the Karlinskis, Shalom and I arrived more than an hour late, about a quarter past seven, at the dedication service of the girls' home [a Beit HaHalutzot in Netanya]. Fortunately, the last speaker was about to conclude the oratorical part of the affair when I marched down the steps of the beautiful Netanya amphitheater, where the meeting was being held. I spoke for just a few minutes praising the work of the Women's League for Israel. Then followed singing and dancing by groups of girls and individuals from the several homes in Haifa, Jerusalem and Tel Aviv. The most interesting part was the quartet of Yemenite girls who played primitive pipes, which must not have been very different from those of David 3,000 years ago. Their music was hauntingly melancholy.[48]

After the ceremony, which ended about 8:15, [Mayor Oved] Ben-Ami, Golda Meyerson, and I shared the buffet supper with several hundred people. On the way home, Golda and I talked about a number of topics, the following of which are worth recording:

46. In informing Klaus that Tidhar was in the United States on a publishing venture and that Tidhar thought that he had information of use to the US government, McDonald recounted Shiloah's suspicions of Tidhar. See entry of January 16, 1950.
47. Jascha Heifetz (1901–1987), Lithuanian-born violinist; emigrated to the United States with his family, 1917; played Carnegie Hall at age 16; thought by some to be the greatest violinist of all time.
48. The Women's League for Israel, headquartered in New York, sponsored facilities for refugee and disabled women and established this particular Beit HaHalutzot in Netanya.

1) She had not heard, she said, any rumors about a possible Knesset election. Her people, Mapai, had not even raised the possibility. She saw no reason for an election at this time.

2) After I had told her briefly about the labor dispute at Sam Sacks's factory, I asked her whether it could be possible, as he charged, that the "trouble-makers," said to be members of Mapam, could be more interested in embarrassing the government by reducing production than they were in opposing Sacks's demand that they speed up the use of the new machines so as to get the utmost production out of them. Golda replied that it was a possibility.

3) Speaking of the Knesset budget debate, Golda and I had the same views about [Moshe] Sneh's speech, that it was weak and irrelevant. She added that it sounded as if Sneh were not prepared, and that a day or two later his arguments were torn to pieces by a Mapai spokesman.[49]

4) When Golda told me that she was going to the States for her son's wedding, I asked if she would do some speaking for the UJA. She said she would because "we are in rather a difficult situation." She said she was anxious to attend the ILO [International Labor Organization] meeting at Geneva, but would probably have to forego it because of the financial exigencies.

5) She said that Weizmann was much better, but admitted that there had been a good deal of discussion about [a] possible successor. She scoffed at the idea of Professor [Joseph] Klausner or Rabbi Silver but did not mention any names. As to [David] Remez, whose name I brought up advisedly, she merely said that she understood that the doctors were hopeful that his partial facial paralysis would be cured.

Friday, May 19

Talk in the afternoon with Shiloah about [Jordan].[50]

Saturday, May 20

Evening orchestra concert as guests of Madame Weizmann. The Beethoven concerto with Heifetz and Lenny was wonderful.

Sunday, May 21 to Friday, June 2, 1950

The McDonalds went to Cyprus for twelve days of vacation time in late May and early June. They traveled with Colonel Archibald, who was en route to Munich

---

49. Moshe Sneh, speaking for Mapam, attacked the government's budget proposals, geared mainly toward economic development, by saying that they were geared toward geopolitical aggression. McDonald to secretary of state, joint weeka no. 20, May 19, 1950, McDonald Papers, USHMM, box 8, folder 10.

50. McDonald reported, "Shiloah with Kollek at [the] residence [on] May 19 told me [a] message was received from Amman [on] May 16 inquiring [about] Shiloah return. Latter expects [the] date for meeting with [the] King to be fixed within [a] few days. Shiloah [is] emphatic [that the] King must personally participate during [the] early stages [of] negotiations if these are to succeed; later they might be transferred to PCC offices Geneva." McDonald to secretary of state, no. 380, May 19, 1950, *FRUS*, 1950, v. V, 902.

for a military conference. Rumors in the Israeli press accompanied the McDonald trip, but as he explained later, "We went simply for a much-needed rest."[51] *The editors have abridged this section of the diary.*

Kyrenia is a picturesque and beautiful town. The only business done at Kyrenia was with [A. David] Fritzlan [US minister in Amman], with whom I talked several times. There is nothing particular to report about these talks, except his emphasis on what he regarded as the underestimation by the Israelis of Abdullah's dependence on "[Jordanian] public opinion."

On May 25, while McDonald was in Cyprus, the United States, United Kingdom, and France issued a joint statement from London known thereafter as the Tripartite Declaration of 1950. Based on a US initiative, it stated that the three powers recognized the need of Israel and the Arab states to maintain a certain level of armed force for self-defense and for regional security and that all applications for weapons would be weighed in light of these principles. The three governments referenced their August 4, 1949, Security Council statements that they opposed an arms race between Israel and the Arab states, and they reiterated their commitment to stability and their opposition to aggression—or even the threat of aggression—in the region.[52] *In the days that followed, Washington, London, and Paris made clear to Israeli representatives that Israel need not fear a second invasion by the Arab states.*

The Israelis were not consulted about the statement in advance. It brought satisfaction insofar as it recognized the status quo in the region at least in the de facto sense while suggesting that the Western powers assumed responsibility for stability in the Middle East. The practical effect, however, remained unclear in light of Britain's treaty obligations to the Arab states, the Arabs' theoretical part in regional security, and their refusal to make peace with Israel.[53]

The Israelis pursued more particular issues with the PCC. In New York on May 26, Eban delivered to Garreau the official Israeli response to the Trusteeship Council's Jerusalem statute. Israel maintained that the statute as written was unworkable while expressing regret that no representatives from the Trusteeship Council had come to Jerusalem during the recess to survey the situation for themselves. Eban's statement suggested that there be UN jurisdiction, through permanent organs, over the Holy Places in Jerusalem. Meanwhile, the population of greater Jerusalem should be under Israeli and Jordanian governance, as they desired.[54]

On May 30, the PCC, having grown impatient with Arab demands that Israel accept the repatriation of Arab refugees before negotiations could begin, urged the Arab governments to abandon preconditions.[55]

51. McDonald, *My Mission in Israel*, 223.
52. Printed in *DFPI*, v. 5, d. 248.
53. Relevant discussions in *DFPI*, v. 5, d. 249–255; also Fischer, ed., *Moshe Sharett: The Second Prime Minister, Selected Documents (1894–1965)*, 158.
54. Printed in *DFPI*, v. 5, d. 257.
55. Contained in Palmer to secretary of state, no. 667, May 30, 1950, *FRUS*, 1950, v. V, 915–916.

24. June 1950

Saturday, June 3

Good to be home. Paula called and asked us for tea and to bring the Fords. There was the usual tea talk among the group of ten or twelve until Ben-Gurion came down. He and I sat down together and chatted about a number of things but always within hearing of the others. After twenty or twenty-five minutes, the talk having veered to South America, I invited Ford to change places with me.

As we were walking out, Ben-Gurion went along and said "Let's have an hour's talk sometime in Jerusalem. There is never any opportunity here in Tel Aviv." I murmured some noncommittal reply, but felt that he really did want to talk and that he was not being merely clever by trying to inveigle me into an official visit to Jerusalem.

Sunday, June 4

To the airport at eleven to meet the UNRWA [United Nations Relief and Works Agency]. I brought John B. Blandford[1] [US representative] and Donald Bergus[2] to the house after having left General Howard Kennedy,[3] Sir Henry Knight [UK representative],[4] M. Jacques Tarbé de Saint-Hardouin [France representative];[5] General Refet Bele [Turkish representative];[6] M. Robert de Nerciat, Mr. Edward Kunde, and M. Paul Marc Henry, staff members.

The UNRWA was formed as a result of the General Assembly resolution of December 8, 1949, and the subsequent recommendations of the Economic Survey Mission. Its first director was General Howard Kennedy of Canada. The agency's

---

1. John B. Blandford Jr. (1918–1969), former administrator of Tennessee Valley Authority, 1933–1939; deputy chief, Economic Cooperation Administration mission to Greece, 1948–1950; US adviser to UNRWA, 1950–1951; UNRWA's second director, 1951–1953.
2. Donald C. Bergus (1920–1988), Indiana-born US career diplomat who held a variety of Middle Eastern posts; initially assigned to US legation in Baghdad in 1942.
3. Major-General Howard Kennedy (1892–1967), Canadian Army, trained engineer; quartermaster-general during World War II; director of UNRWA, 1950–1951.
4. Sir Henry Knight believed that repatriation was unrealistic and focused on the need for Israel to pay compensation to refugees so that UNRWA then could tell them that return would be impossible. Jacob Tovy, *Israel and the Palestinian Refugee Issue, 1948–1956: The Formulation of a Policy* (New York: Routledge, 2013), 83, 112.
5. Jacques Tarbé de Saint-Hardouin (1899–1956), French diplomat who aided with the Allied landings in Algiers in 1942 and served under General Marie-Pierre Kœnig in the French occupation zone in Germany.
6. Refet Bele (1881–1963), Thessalonika-born Ottoman general; had fought the British in Gaza in 1918; retired from Turkish Army, 1926.

headquarters were in the UNESCO building in Beirut, and it held its first meeting there on April 25, 1950. On May 1 it formally assumed responsibility for the distribution of relief supplies to Palestinian refugees—which it counted as 652,000—that came from the voluntary agencies such as the Red Cross and the American Friends Service Committee.[7] On June 5, President Truman signed into law the Foreign Economic Assistance Act of 1950, which included up to $27,450,000 for aid to Palestinian refugees.[8] The funds were also to be distributed by UNRWA, whose top officials visited Israel from June 4–6, 1950.

During more than two hours at the house at lunch and on the following Tuesday, another hour with the two men [Blandford and Bergus], I got important first impressions of them and of their concepts of their job. These were supplemented by impressions passed on to me by the members of the staff with the two Americans on Monday. Here they are for what they are worth.

1) Blandford is an imaginative, energetic, and unconventional person who, though handicapped by no knowledge of this area, promises to be a driving force in the [UNRWA]. Bergus was mostly silent but gave the impression of being able.
2) Blandford is somewhat concerned by overlapping of [UNRWA] and PCC and seems to have gotten a view of the PCC not very different from ours.
3) [It] was clear from what Blandford said that the Department intends that he should be its agent and to carry on, if practicable, the exploratory inquiries with the Arab states on economic matters beyond the specific mandate of the [UNRWA].

My staff and I felt towards the [UNRWA] a little as old-timers in Palestine must have felt towards the many visiting commissions in their day—a feeling of skepticism mixed with cynicism and a small measure of hope. To all of us, the obvious complexities of the [UNRWA] organization and its relations to the PCC were discouraging factors.

Blandford's June 19 letter to McGhee following his meetings with McDonald, General Riley, and Raleigh Gibson gave the following assessment: Repatriation, he said, "except as it may occur through the modification of armistice lines, is unrealistic, and so long as this banner is waving, precious time and assets are wasting." Compensation, he said, "should be persistently pressed in terms of a generous contribution by Israel toward refugee resettlement rather than be lost in the contradictions of repatriation." Blandford hoped that the Mixed Armistice Commissions might take the lead

---

7. Description in US legation Beirut to secretary of state, no. 215, May 16, 1950, *FRUS*, v. V, 1950, 892. Number of refugees in Gardiner to Duce, July 13, 1950, *FRUS*, 1950, v. V, 951–952.
   8. *FRUS*, 1950, v. V, 921.

in lieu of the PCC and said that the refugee problem "should not be entombed in a period of inactivity."[9]

The evening philharmonic concert with [Alexis] Weissenberg as soloist in the Rachmaninoff piano concerto.[10] His was a brilliant performance, though my lack of familiarity kept me from getting the fullest enjoyment from it. I liked, too, Lenny's interpretation of the Shostakovitch Fifth. During the intermission we went backstage.

Tuesday, June 6

Dinner with the Novomeyskys at the Sharon. After dinner we went over to the home of the [Joseph] Levys, where the Novomeyskys and our host reminisced nostalgically about their life work on the Dead Sea.

Thursday, June 8

Afternoon, hour and a half with Shiloah at the house. Most of the talk was about Israeli-Jordanian relations. Shiloah was obviously rather discouraged, the more because the impasse was not the result of differences over any specific issue—differences which would have been tangible and therefore, perhaps compromisable. Instead, the difficulty was "atmosphere." He attributed this adverse climate to a lessening of US-UK interest in Israeli-Jordanian peace. He urged encouragement to the king to get on with the business; Abdullah needed not pressure but assurance that if he went ahead and as a result got into trouble with the Arab League, he would have US-UK support.[11]

Shiloah argued further that the British were making a mistake by putting or seeming to put all their eggs into the Egyptian basket.[12] Shiloah thinks that the Egyptian prime minister [Mustafa al-Nahhas Pasha] and foreign minister [Mustafa Salah al-Din Bey] are overwhelmingly influenced by the [grand] mufti, and their policy is shaped accordingly. The king, too, is at present intransigent. Hence, negotiations in Cairo offer little hope. A beginning with Israeli-Jordanian peace might help to resolve the UK-Egypt impasse.

Shiloah developed the related thesis that the Arab states, particularly Syria, Iraq, and Egypt, have regimes which are morally bankrupt and, in the case of the first two, financially bankrupt also. The failure of all three regimes to live up to their promises to their people or to do anything substantial to help the masses is a danger to their internal security and in the long run may open the door to communism.

9. Blandford to McGhee, June 19, 1950, USSDCF-PIFA, 1950–1954, reel 4, frames 925–927.
10. Alexis Weissenberg (1929–2012), Bulgarian-born pianist; imprisoned in Bulgaria during World War II; escaped to Istanbul and emigrated to Palestine, 1945.
11. Foreign Office views in Douglas to secretary of state, no. 3043, June 2, 1950, *FRUS*, 1950, v. V, 917–918.
12. For British comments on the importance of Israeli peace with Egypt, see Kidron to Avida, June 6, 1950, *DFPI*, v. 5, d. 271.

Shiloah disclaimed any formula to meet these dangers, but argued that the US and UK should study Middle East situations more profoundly.[13]

Friday, June 9

Joseph Sugarman of the Jerusalem Shoe [Company] and Claude M. Sweeney of the General Shoe Corporation. To my surprise, Sweeney recognized me immediately because he had been a student in Indiana when I was doing my graduate work there. Their program for their plant in Jerusalem is very encouraging.[14]

Eliezer Peri of the Kupat Holim[15] and [deputy] mayor of Tel Aviv[16] came in to talk about his trip to the States on a public health mission. He kindly said he would take a letter from Ruth to the family.

Dinner at the Kaplans'. Present besides the hosts and ourselves were Atara [Kaplan], Kollek, and the [Paul] Ritters.[17] The only item which needs to be recorded was Kollek's talk to me about the necessity he felt for tightening the exchange controls by restricting more vigorously Israelis' foreign travel. He said that many people who have gotten exit visas and have said that they needed no foreign exchange had in fact made deals abroad with foreigners coming to Israel by which the latter gave them, for example, dollars, in return for their promise to give the foreigners arriving in Israel pounds at a cut rate.[18]

Saturday, June 10

Dr. and Mrs. Harold Korn from New York,[19] with a letter of introduction from [Clark] Eichelberger,[20] came at 12:00. He is authorized by Eichelberger to represent the [American] Association [for the United Nations] at various international meetings of UN organizations. Korn is going to be spending most of his evenings in Israel making speeches.

---

13. McDonald's brief report from this meeting emphasized again Shiloah's desire for the United States and the United Kingdom to concentrate on peace between Israel and Jordan. McDonald to secretary of state, no. 425, June 9, 1950, *FRUS*, 1950, v. V, 925–926.

14. See entry of November 26, 1950.

15. Kupat Holim was the Worker's Sick Fund under Histadrut since the Mandate period and the largest of Israel's heath organizations. In 1950 it was negotiating with the government to become part of the national social security and health care system as a quasi-independent organization for health care insurance.

16. Eliezer Peri [formerly Perlson] (1894–1979), Russian-born labor Zionist and member of Mapai; emigrated to Palestine, 1921; administrative director, Kupat Holim, 1922–1928 and after 1950; founding member of newspaper *Davar* in 1925 and later its board chairman; executive committee of Histadrut since 1941; deputy mayor of Tel Aviv, 1940–1948, and city councilman after 1950; director general, Ministry of Defense, 1948–1950.

17. Paul Ritter, Swiss consul general and head of mission, 1949–1951.

18. Symptomatic of Israel's increasing problems of foreign exchange debt due to foreign loans. See entry of March 12, 1950.

19. Harold Korn (1882–1969), president of New York lodge of B'nai B'rith; active in Jewish charities.

20. Clark M. Eichelberger (1896–1980), first executive director of American Association for the United Nations, founded in 1943 from its predecessor, the League of Nations Association.

Picked up Ruth and we went to the lawn tea party of [Yosef] Sapir, mayor of Petah Tikvah.[21] It was a pleasant affair. Most of my time was given over to listening to a long explanation by Fritz Bernstein[22] of the relations between the General Zionists and Ben-Gurion and the cabinet.

In answer to my questions, Bernstein made the following points, some of which are rather new:

1) The General Zionists are genuinely anxious to "pull their weight" and make their contribution during Israel's critical formative years; there is, however, a feeling in the party that perhaps it would be better to wait before joining the coalition, on the theory that time is running in their favor. When I pressed Bernstein for tangible indications that this is the trend, his answer was unconvincing, particularly since he admitted that his party was without knowledge about the prevailing tendency among the new arrivals.

2) The prime minister and the General Zionists had agreed that the latter should have two places in the cabinet—the question was, which two. The Ministry of Commerce and Industry had presumably been offered to Bernstein and another post to Israel Rokach, mayor of Tel Aviv. Bernstein did not hint at the name of this post. He did say that his colleagues wanted the Ministry of Defense. He also spoke about the desirability of placing Mrs. [Shoshana] Persitz,[23] the able woman member of the General Zionists and chairman of the Knesset's education committee, as minister of education, to replace the Mapai [member] Zalman Shazar,[24] who is not well.

3) Bernstein said that the Ministry of Industry and Commerce was undesirable and perhaps unacceptable so long as Kaplan of the Treasury kept such a close control on industry through his control of foreign exchange and Dov Joseph, of the Ministry of [Rationing and Supply], exercised the right to allocate raw materials. Ben-Gurion had intimated that if Bernstein became minister of industry and commerce, his powers would be satisfactorily enlarged, but later, after [a] conference with his Mapai colleagues, the prime minister is said to have withdrawn this concession. Nonetheless, Bernstein gave the impression that he would have been willing to accept the post if there could have been agreement on broader issues.

21. Yosef Sapir (1902–1972), Jaffa-born mayor of Petah Tikva, 1940–1951; member of Knesset, 1949–1972 (General Zionists); held ministerial posts in 1950s and 1960s.

22. Shlomo Fritz [Peretz] Bernstein (1890–1971), German-born Zionist who moved to the Netherlands before World War I and emigrated to Palestine, 1936; president of Zionist Organization, 1930–1934; Jewish Agency's director of economics, 1946–1948; signatory of Declaration of Independence; minister of trade and industry in Ben-Gurion's provisional government; General Zionist member of Knesset, 1949.

23. Shoshana Persitz (née Rosalia Gillelovna Zlatopolsky) (1892–1969), Kiev-born daughter of Hillel Zlatopolsky, a Keren Hayesod founder who was murdered in Paris, 1932; chair of Supervisory Committee of the General School System and of the General Zionist Women's Organization, 1948–1954; member of Knesset (General Zionists), 1949–1959.

24. On Shazar, see entry of May 5, 1950.

4) According to Bernstein, more important than the question of which posts in the cabinet was the issue of the government's broad economic policy: was the prime minister willing to enlarge the area of free enterprise and private initiative? More tangible was the General Zionists' demand that the labor exchanges become national, thus depriving the Histadrut of one of its strong propaganda cards, and that the Kupat Holim also be nationalized, thus taking away from Histadrut its second-strongest means of appealing to the masses. Bernstein gave the impression that on both these major issues, Ben-Gurion, being more of a statesman than a Mapai leader, was favorable, but that on these issues he was unable to carry his party with him.

5) Although Bernstein did not specifically commit himself, I received the impression that he thinks that there is no prospect at present nor in the near future for agreement between Ben-Gurion and the General Zionists.[25]

Knowing that Bernstein is soon to go to the States to speak to the ZOA national convention, and that he is internationally influential among the General Zionists, I sounded him out about the ambitions and future of Rabbi Abba Hillel Silver. Bernstein thinks that Silver would like to be and will be the next president of the World Zionist Organization. I raised the question of the opposition of Zionist labor to Silver. Bernstein replied that this had softened. He added, moreover, that the mass of Zionists throughout the world are General Zionists. This is true, but I still doubt Silver's ability to attain this post of formal world leadership.

Sunday, June 11

Up to the office before lunch to talk with Ford about the infiltration problem. At teatime worked with Ford, Brady and Fried on the telegram regarding the above, and Miss Clark typed it out.

Arab expellees sometimes returned to Israel as snipers or to lay mines in border areas, some of which killed Israeli soldiers.[26] During the spring, impoverished Arab and Bedouin infiltrators crossed into Israel to harvest their crops or raid nearby kibbutzim for food stores, livestock, or farming equipment. They clashed with settlers, Israeli police, and sometimes IDF units, all of which pushed the infiltrators back, often without appeal to state authorities. Some 1,600 infiltrators were arrested between January and June 1950, with 227 apprehended in June alone.[27] The US consul general in

25. In the July 1951 election the General Zionists became the second largest party in the Knesset with twenty seats. The fourth government coalition (December 24, 1952–January 26, 1954) included the General Zionists, whose members held the Ministries of the Interior, Health, Transportation, and Trade and Industry.

26. See for example McDonald to secretary of state, no. 229, March 31, 1950, USSDCF-PIFA, 1950–1954, reel 1, frames 460–461.

27. Figure from Israeli sources, McDonald, joint weeka no. 30, July 28, 1950, McDonald Papers, USHMM, box 9, folder 1. Also Gibson to secretary of state, no. 142, June 30, 1950, USSDCF-PIFA, 1950–1954, reel 1, frames 531–532.

Jerusalem reported that the "fault . . . appears to lie with Jordan authorities for allowing seeding in Israel territory without realizing [the] possibility [that] Israel would not allow harvest. There was no agreement on harvest between responsible Israel and Jordan authorities."[28]

The worst of these incidents occurred on May 31, 1950. The IDF took a group of 120 Arabs by truck to the remote area of Wadi Araba between the Dead Sea and the Gulf of Aqaba and forced them over the Jordanian border. Up to thirty-three of the group died. The incidents made Abdullah look weak to the Arab world.[29]

An Israeli public statement discussed the increasing numbers of border incidents, the use of force to capture "usually armed" infiltrators, the rejection by the Israeli government of torture methods, and the responsibility of the Jordanians for having "lost control of its population in border areas." But on June 11, 1950, McDonald reported a discussion with Kollek, who confirmed that the Wadi Araba story was "unfortunately true" and that the details were "pretty horrible." On June 12, McDonald received a further statement from Eytan that confirmed Kollek's admission of abuses and conveyed that the fact that such a thing could occur "remains [a] serious source of concern and regret." The government promised the punishment of "men shown guilty [of] wanton or cruel behavior," and Major Brady confirmed that one court-martial had been completed.[30]

Monday, June 12

Up at 5:15 and on the way to Lydda a few minutes before six. It was fun to drive out that early, leaving Shalom sitting beside me as a passenger.

Made peace with [Joseph] Sieff[31] in the waiting room, but insisted that we have the [Eddie] Cantors alone tonight for dinner. He suggested that Beryl Locker be included, but I said no, this was to be solely a family party. The Air France set down a little after six-thirty, and Eddie was the first passenger off. We embraced, and then followed Ida. Next came their friends, the Marksons.[32]

After seemingly innumerable shots by the photographers, outdoors, at the breakfast table and during Eddie's press conference, we finally got away, at

---

28. Gibson to secretary of state, no. 102, May 10, 1950, USSDCF-PIFA, 1950–1954, reel 1, frame 496.

29. Acheson to embassy in Tel Aviv, no. 296, *FRUS*, 1950, v. V, 923. On the expulsions, see Wilson, *King Abdullah, Britain and the Making of Jordan*, 205–206; and Gelber, *Israeli-Jordanian Dialogue, 1948–1953: Cooperation, Conspiracy, or Collusion*, 179–180.

30. McDonald to secretary of state, no. 427, June 11, 1950; McDonald to secretary of state, no. 442, June 12, 1950, USSDCF-PIFA, 1950–1954, reel 1, frame 522. At the Mapai meeting of June 1950, Moshe Dayan discussed the dilemma facing the IDF: "The Arabs who are infiltrating to reap [the] harvest they have sown in our land are women and children and we open fire on them. . . . [W]ill this stand the test of a moral evaluation? . . . I know no other way to protect the borders. If shepherds and farmers are permitted to infiltrate, Israel could lose its borders tomorrow." Mapai faction meeting, June 18, 1950, Labor Party Archives, Beit Berel, Tzofit. We are grateful to Tuvia Friling for this reference.

31. Joseph Edward "Teddy" Sieff (1905–1982), chairman, Marks & Spencer, 1967–1972, succeeding his brother Israel Sieff; succeeded by Marcus Sieff, the son of Israel Sieff; active Zionist, particularly with the Joint Israel Appeal [JIA] in Britain.

32. Probably Ben Markson (1882–1971), screenwriter.

about a quarter of eight. But because the escorting motor policeman had instructions to take us to [Herzliya] through Lydda, Ramle and Tel Aviv, we did not reach the Sharon until nearly nine o'clock. There I left the party after Ida had pledged herself and Sieff had agreed that there would be no conferences of any sort today, until the Cantors and the Marksons came to our house for dinner at 7:30.

The remarks of my four friends in the car were interesting and sometimes amusing. They seemed quite surprised at nearly everything they saw and delighted with much. I was especially interested with Markson's discriminating remarks about housing, which Eddie told me was one of Markson's interests.

In the late afternoon [a] cocktail party given by [Aharon] Remez of the Air Force for [the] Archibalds at the aerial camp in Jaffa.[33] It was a beautiful evening. Ruth and I had to go early because of the Cantors coming to dinner. Hence, there was no possibility of my avoiding Mrs. Archibald; her tone when she spoke to me would have slain me were tones capable of fatal effects.

The family dinner party with the Cantors and the Marksons was lively and enjoyable. When they left, shortly after ten, we had agreed to meet again for dinner at the Sharon on Sunday.

Tuesday, June 13

At four-thirty, the signing of the bilateral air agreement at HaKirya. Sharett and I signed in the presence of [Minister of Transport David] Remez, who still bore the facial marks of his recent stroke. [Ralph] Curren and Hooper were also present on behalf of the staff; the Israeli group including besides Eytan, Kollek and Miss Herlitz, three or four men who had done the work. After the signing, Sharett spoke briefly and I, in reply, expressed the hope that this first formal agreement would be followed by many others binding our two peoples and countries closely together.[34]

The bilateral air agreement—the first signed by Israel—replaced ad hoc temporary arrangements and regularized equal rights for TWA and El Al in the two countries. It removed what the United States considered discriminatory practices against TWA (the one US carrier to Israel), provided protections for Israeli currency, and allowed El Al to begin long-sought passenger flights to New York. It further specified routes, tariffs, and numbers of flights. McDonald had been given authority by President Truman to sign the agreement on behalf of the US government.[35]

---

33. Aharon Remez (1919–1994), son of David Remez; Tel Aviv-born Haganah member and pilot; served with Royal Air Force, 1942–1946; rejoined Haganah, 1947–1948; commander, Israeli Air Force, 1948–1950; thereafter headed purchasing missions to Washington and served as air adviser to Ben-Gurion; ambassador to London, 1965–1970. IAF headquarters was in Jaffa until moving to Ramle in December 1950.

34. See entry of March 12, 1950. The Israelis requested Curren's presence specifically because of his role in the negotiations.

35. State Department to US embassy Tel Aviv, no. 43, June 1, 1950, USSDCF-PIFA, 1950–1954, reel 6, frame 934. The agreement itself is in frames 955–967.

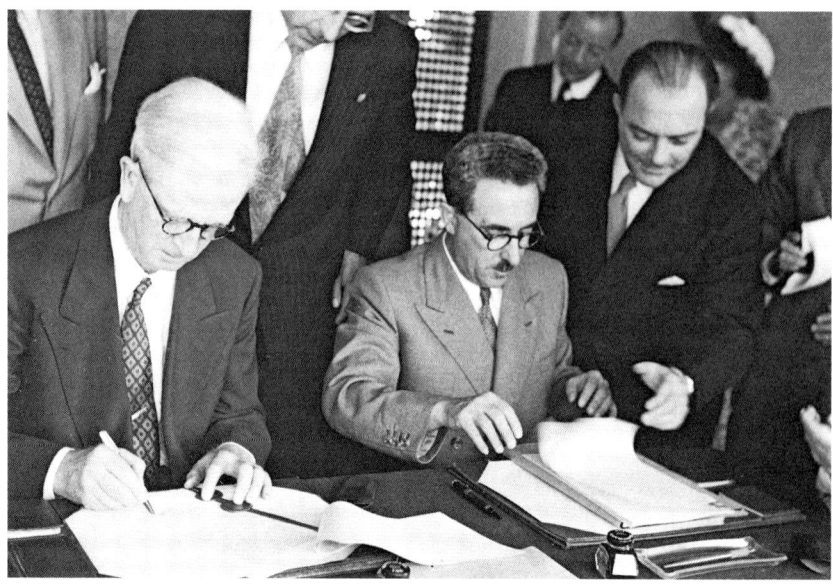

Fig. 24.1. Ambassador James McDonald and Israeli foreign minister Moshe Sharett sign the Israeli-US Air Agreement, June 13, 1950. Israeli Government Press Office.

The agreement received wide coverage in the Israeli press because, as Sharett noted, it was "the first agreement signed by us with the United States of America on any subject. It augurs well for the cementing of friendly ties between us and the United States."[36]

Acheson quickly pointed out the missions in the Middle East with which the United States already had bilateral agreements: Lebanon, Egypt, Turkey, and Syria. He further advised, "No special significance [should] be attached to [the] fact that [the] US–Israeli agreement is [the] first such formal arrangement concluded by Israel."[37]

During the refreshments, Sharett and I chatted about South Africa. His impressions were very similar to ours.

Thursday, June 15

Jacob Rosenheim, New York Agudat leader,[38] was at the house for forty-five minutes in the late morning. Aside from general talk and reminiscences, his main points were:

---

36. Israeli press release June 13, 1950, Curran to secretary of state, no. 379, June 14, 1950, USSDCF-PIFA, 1950–1954, reel 6, frames 947–949.

37. Acheson circular to certain American diplomatic officers, June 9, 1950, USSDCF-PIFA, 1950–1954, reel 6, frame 944.

38. Jacob Rosenheim (1870–1965), one of the founders of the Agudat World Association; called for US leaders to bomb railway tracks to Auschwitz-Birkenau, June 1944.

1) Israel should in spirit align itself up squarely with the West, and as far as political exigencies permit, should make clear its loyalty to and support of Western ideals. Russia, with its godlessness and its organized efforts to break down all religion and all faith in God—thirty millions are in concentration camps, an unprecedented situation in world history—constitutes the gravest crisis for civilization. The probably inevitable titanic struggle between Russia and the West may be the decisive conflict ushering in the coming of the Messiah.

2) Israel, which he has visited now for the first time, has made a tremendous impression upon him. He stressed its lights and shades and deplored particularly the irreligion of so many leaders and so many people and the common desecration of the Sabbath.[39]

3) Ben-Gurion is the one outstanding political leader who strives to understand the position and meaning of Orthodoxy and who realizes the danger of such an internal cleavage as might lead to civil war if the Orthodox came to feel that their children's faith was threatened by an imposed unified state godless education.

At 3:30 Jacob Herzog came. He was full of admiration for Ben-Gurion's present concern with the problem of Orthodoxy and the avoidance of a national cleavage on religious lines. He told of Ben-Gurion's recent long conference with religious leaders and rank and file. On one occasion the prime minister fought out the problem for three hours with a group of sixteen, or, as he put it, "one against many." He is struggling to get at the heart of the problem. He is almost alone in this understanding of the need of a profound effort to prevent, as he puts it, "Israel becoming two nations." Herzog used this illustration to underline his conviction that Ben-Gurion, never wasting his energy or attention on petty matters, has in this case again shown his instinctive concentration on a vital issue once it becomes ripe for action. Like most great leaders, he allows issues to ripen until they can be effectively dealt with.

The Knesset voted 50–38 on June 13, 1950, to adopt an evolving constitution for Israel. The United Religious Front (Orthodox Bloc) deputies abstained because they had received no assurances concerning religious (halakhic) law. The Knesset vote triggered debate over the role of religious law in Israeli society, leading to Ben-Gurion's meeting with the religious deputies. Cabinet arguments concerning kosher meat imports (which were three times as expensive as nonkosher meat amidst rationing and budget cuts) and equal rights for women irritated many Israelis.

On June 23, 1950 McDonald reported, "It is known that during [the] past few weeks [Ben-Gurion] has been engaged [in] considerable religious research. Undoubtedly

---

39. Shabbat was the official day of rest during the week, as determined by arrangements between Ben-Gurion and World Agudat in 1947, but general secular activities were not prohibited. See entry of May 9, 1950.

he is attempting to decide for himself [the] momentous question of [the] role religion [should] play in State of Israel."[40] *In the Knesset on June 26, what McDonald called the "smoldering feud within Coalition ranks" burst open. The Orthodox deputies read a long bill of particulars against Ben-Gurion ranging from complaints about religious discrimination in schools to the importing of nonkosher meat. Ben-Gurion, commented McDonald, had concluded that his coalition was unstable and that he would call new elections soon.*[41]

Herzog reported that [Andrew] Cordier, the UN undersecretary,[42] doubted that the Vatican would again be able to exercise on the Jerusalem issue comparable [to its] decisive influence at Lake Success. Yet, Herzog was disturbed by the fact that Cordier's estimate of the attitude of France on the issue had been proven wrong by Paris's reversal since Cordier had talked with [Foreign Minister Robert] Schuman.

The French government was positive, in principle, toward the May 16, 1950, Israeli memorandum on Jerusalem. Eban hoped that French support would induce other Latin states to support the Israeli proposal, especially because the Vatican refused to do so.[43] *Yet on June 6, 1950, French foreign minister Robert Schuman told Israeli ambassador Maurice Fischer that the French position was traditionally determined by the need to defend traditional Catholic interests. The French government wanted the list of Holy Places to be placed under UN protection expanded to include other religious sites throughout Israel. White House orders were, "Let someone else take the lead," because during the fourth UN General Assembly the United States had received unwelcome criticism of its policies on this issue. The State Department concurred, willing to support a new UN resolution, but not willing to draft a new one for fear of antagonizing the Arabs.*[44]

After Herzog and I had talked about my personal project, he agreed that he would take a week off in the latter part of July or first of August to do carefully what I had asked of him.[45] Our talk would have gone on but for the ar-

40. McDonald to secretary of state, joint weeka no. 25, June 23, 1950, McDonald Papers, USHMM, box 8, folder 11.

41. McDonald to secretary of state, joint weeka no. 26, June 30, 1950, McDonald Papers, USHMM, box 8, folder 11. See also entry of May 9, 1950. On June 28, 1950, Ben-Gurion had a long meeting with Orthodox deputies, including Rabbis Yehuda Leib Maimon and Binyamin Mintz, who feared the formation of two nations in Israel, but who asserted that religious priorities had been ignored. Ben-Gurion enunciated his policy of satisfying religious needs while avoiding religious coercion. He pointed to governmental acceptance of Shabbat and Jewish holidays as non-work days, but said that other issues should be allowed to sit for the time being. He disagreed that the Torah had redeemed the Jewish people, stating instead that the spirit of Israel had done so. Ben-Gurion Diary, entry of June 28, 1950. We are grateful to Tuvia Friling for this reference.

42. Andrew Wellington Cordier (1901–1975), executive assistant to the UN secretary-general, 1946–1961.

43. *DFPI*, v. 5, d. 266, 268, 270.

44. *DFPI*, v. 5, d. 274, 281, 319; *FRUS*, v. V. 918–919, 927–928, 977–978, 981–982.

45. McDonald intended his memoirs to help Americans understand Israel and its leaders. Herzog assisted by reading and commenting on McDonald's manuscript.

rival of Shiloah, but I should add that Herzog made the shrewd observation that the US would probably not want General Riley to relinquish his present key post to take another, for he is at present very valuable to the US.

Shiloah told me "in confidence and not to be repeated even to Washington" of his last meeting with his friend [June 12, 1950]. This was not at the place reported by Helm. Present also was, as usual, Dayan. Kirkbride had evidently been able to make Abdullah realize that he should not be short-circuited. Kirkbride is apparently organizing a [peace] delegation, which might become the government if the present government planned to accept a negotiated accord. Shiloah thinks that Abdullah feels unable to proceed now and needs US-UK support. Shiloah's development of this thesis was similar to his earlier talks.[46]

Shiloah doubts that General Riley would be asked to Tel Aviv, because such a shift would be interpreted as meaning that the US had been or was using the UN for national purposes. Shiloah said that he really would prefer [the] return of [Charles] Knox, if as he feared, I was not going to return. On this latter point, I told him there had been no decision and that it was up to the president, and that if I knew anything definite before I went on home leave, I would tell Ben-Gurion and Sharett before I left. The more I talk to Shiloah, the more I feel that he is, as Jacob Herzog told me a little earlier, a real friend of mine.

Cocktail party at the [David] Balfours.[47] We talked with Kollek about Eytan's letter to the colonel [Archibald]. He said that the military had gone out of their way to try to make Archibald feel better.

Arthur Sulzberger's young son, Arthur Ochs, and his charming young wife [Barbara Winslow Grant], were brought to tea by Gene Currivan. We had a pleasant visit.[48]

Dinner at the Helms'. Besides ourselves and the hosts were Mr. and Mrs. [Jon] Kimche,[49] Mrs. [Flora] Solomon[50] and [George] Weidenfeld from Weizmann's organization.[51] The food was surprisingly good and the talk interesting but not needing to be recorded. I noted Helm's seeming low estimate of intelligence services, including the British.

46. This was the general assessment in Tel Aviv. See Divon to Sharett, June 16, 1950, *DFPI*, v. 5, d. 282.

47. Entry of January 16, 1950.

48. Arthur Ochs Sulzberger (1926–2012), publisher of the *New York Times*, 1963–1992. His father, Arthur Hays Sulzberger (1891–1968), was publisher, 1935–1961, and was McDonald's employer from 1936 to 1938.

49. Jon Kimche (1909–1994), Swiss-born, British-raised journalist and historian; active in the Independent Labour Party; fought in Spanish Civil War (where he knew George Orwell); editor of the leftist *Tribune*, 1942; involved in helping Jewish refugees reach Palestine; wrote widely on Middle East subjects; brother of David Kimche, a major figure in the Mossad and in Israeli diplomacy.

50. Flora Benenson Solomon (1895–1984), Russian-born influential British Zionist who worked for Marks & Spencer.

51. Arthur George, Baron Weidenfeld (1919–2016), Vienna-born journalist; emigrated to Britain after German annexation of Austria, 1938, and worked for the BBC monitoring service; co-founded influential publishing house of Weidenfeld & Nicolson, 1948; chief of cabinet and political adviser to Chaim Weizmann, 1949; made a life peer, 1976. See also entry of August 7, 1950.

The evening we spent quietly at home, since Paula did not—as she should have done—invite us to the [Eddie] Cantor party at her house. We had previously invited them for that night for the Cantors but had agreed to ask Eddie earlier, since the prime minister insisted that he had to be the host to Eddie. But one does not expect Paula to be a respecter of the niceties of social intercourse.

Illustrative of this is the amusing fact that about ten minutes to eight the overseas telephone operator called me in a state of perturbation to inquire where he could reach Eddie Cantor for a call from New York. I explained that Eddie would presently be at the Ben-Gurion's. The reply was: "I know, but calling there I got the strangest reply from Paula." Evidently Paula had told him that she could not be bothered.

To the Weizmann's for lunch. Others present besides ourselves and the Cantors and the hosts were their son, Weizmann's aide-de-camp [Major David Arnon], and Sigi Weissenberg.[52] I was shocked by Weizmann's appearance. He had aged and weakened so in the six weeks since I saw him last. He had lost much weight, walked with a painful shuffle, and had an ashen grey color. Mentally he seemed more his old self. Nonetheless, I got the impression that he is indeed living on borrowed time.

Fortunately, Eddie was the life of the party and carried most of the conversation. Weizmann expressed the hope that I would come to see him before he left July 5 for Switzerland and that I would also come to see him there. He also deplored the rumors of my retirement, about which I was noncommittal.

On the way back, Eddie rode with me while Ida and Ruth were in his car. This gave me an opportunity to tell him something of my plans. He made one interesting suggestion that, in addition to anything else I might do, I ought to plan for a [Jewish] Agency sponsored lecture tour in the chief cities soon after my resignation. He emphasized that this would be valuable in addition to the monetary return—valuable to me and to the "cause."

Supper at the Fords', where the other guests were McVicker, the Currivans . . . and the young Arthur Ochs Sulzbergers. The young Sulzbergers are attractive, he having something of his father's and his mother's charm, and she being intelligent and unspoiled, and, as Lolita [Ford] called her, a Presbyterian.

At ten-thirty went over with the Fords to the baptism of the Cashman's beautiful new baby, Margaret Suzanne, at which Miss Clark and General Riley

---

52. Pianist Alexis Weissenberg went by the name "Sigi" early in his career. See also entry of June 8, 1950.

were the godparents. After the ceremony and a brief visit in the rectory, I drove back to Ramat Gan in Riley's car, paced by Shalom in ours.

The general had nothing new about Israel-Jordan, and bound by Shiloah's injunction to secrecy, I told Riley nothing about the meeting early in the week of the 11th. I asked him about Egypt. He made no general comment on his two visits there; he merely said that he was still of the opinion that progress could be made with Egypt if the Israelis were willing to withdraw from the hill near Umm Rashrash on the Egyptian side of the armistice line near Eilat.[53] This did not seem to me very encouraging, because I knew that HaKirya would do nothing of the sort. Riley had or said he had no information about the reports current in Tel Aviv that the Egyptian foreign minister, Mohammed Saleh al-Din Bey, as well as the prime minister, Nahhas Pasha, are "in the pockets of the mufti." As to the recent charges of torture of Arab infiltrees, Riley thought that there was probably substance in them, but added that this is the sort of thing which happens whenever police or military are dealing with that kind of situation.[54]

The most important part of our conversation had to do with the prospect of Israeli-Jordanian negotiations. Riley reiterated his earlier views that the PCC should be scrapped. He was particularly anxious that it should not attempt now negotiations on compensation, because such negotiations preceding agreement on boundary lines would necessarily be futile. Riley's preferred program would be to replace the PCC by a one-man mediator, the transformation of the MACs [Mixed Armistice Commissions] into negotiating bodies, and of the chief of staff into the mediator. He added that this was the sort of thing I could recommend to the Department where he could not. I said I would.

At five I participated in the cornerstone laying of a new WIZO nursery in Ramat Gan. It was the usual thing with numerous, but fortunately brief, speeches. Even Rebecca Sieff was brief.

Out to the Sharon for dinner with Eddie, Ida, and the Marksons. Talk during the meal itself was riotous. Eddie told with inimitable humor of their dinner the previous night at Rebecca Sieff's. He mimicked her nearly two-hour harangue at dinner, hardly interrupted by the necessity of eating. The subject was not a new one—the iniquities of Hadassah, than which there could have hardly been found a topic less interesting to her guests. Briefly before we left, Eddie and I talked further about plans at home. He promised to get in touch with Ben Abrams and Abe Feinberg promptly on his return to New York.

---

53. For explanation see entry of February 13, 1950, notes 57–58. Riley had visited Cairo during the first week of June and had tried to convince the Egyptians to renounce their demands for the Israeli evacuation of Bir Qattar and Umm Rashrash [Eilat] as a precondition of entering talks with the Israelis. The Egyptians refused, citing popular pressure. Riley thought that the Egyptian case for Bir Qattar had merit, but that they had a poorer case with Umm Rashrash. Riley also failed to convince the Egyptians to give up the return of refugees return as a precondition for talks. Caffery to secretary of state, no. 1315, June 6, 1950, *FRUS*, 1950, v. V, 922–923.

54. Entry of June 11, 1950.

Three days later McDonald wrote Ben Abrams and Abe Feinberg as follows:

> *Ruth and I are planning to go home, technically on "home leave," on the* LaGuardia *sailing from Haifa August 20. . . . Nothing has been settled beyond "home leave," which is normally two months. I anticipate that it can, in any event, be extended [by] another four weeks or so of "consultations," that is, conferences in different cities with leaders of Jewish and other organizations interested in Israel, refugees, and related matters.*
>
> *Occasionally I weaken for a moment or two in my program of retirement. After sober consideration, however, I each time am convinced that it would be for the best. It has been a long pull here with no opportunity for relaxation or even getting away from one's work. And I am tired.*
>
> *I wish I could add to the above personal account a second paragraph of real interest on our regional international situation as seen by us here. Unfortunately, there is nothing that is both new and encouraging to report. As you will have noted from the press accounts, there seems to have been a hardening of the attitude of most of Israel's neighbors. . . . Nonetheless, I have hopes that a beginning can still be made to break the logjam which now impedes all progress.*[55]

Monday, June 19

At the brain trust meeting at the office—Ford, Troxel, McVicker and Fried—we discussed the reply we should send to the departmental circular telegram reporting the utter intransigence of our neighbors to the south and to the northeast.[56] Ford had drafted a long and rather wordy reply, and I promised to bring back the next morning my draft.

At teatime I had another sabra conference. Those present were Bobby's friend Michael Grunwald and Malka Bohner, Michael Singer, Ofra Bourla-Adar,[57] and Amos Elon.[58] Much of the ground covered was not new. All of the young people disavowed any intensity of party loyalty. They emphasized that most young people of their acquaintance were now more concerned with their own careers, education, jobs, etc., than with politics or affairs of state. Nearly everyone now 19 or 20 has had six or seven years of excessive work in youth organization[s], [the] Haganah, and finally, in the army. This last seems to have been a sobering experience. On the religious issue, the group was almost unanimous. They saw no need for formal religion in their lives [and] are convinced that Orthodoxy will decline, despite the new Aliyah from Yemen, Iraq, East Europe and North Africa.

Irrespective of personal prejudices, all were enthusiastic about Ben-Gurion. Among the possible successors they named were [Yigal] Allon, the Palmach

---

55. McDonald to Benjamin Abrams, June 21, 1950, McDonald Papers, Columbia University, box 6, folder 2.
56. Palmer to secretary of state, no. 730, June 13, 1950, *FRUS*, 1950, v. V, 928–929, described later.
57. Ofra Bourla-Adar (1925–2013) writer and translator; daughter of the important Israeli author Yehuda Burla (1886–1969).
58. Entry of March 28, 1950.

leader[59]; Sharett; Goldie; and Sprinzak. As to the presidency, they seemed to feel that there is no need for the office, and that it might be abolished.

My main impression was that these young people were almost militantly emancipated from their traditional and Orthodox background, and in this they are typical of Israeli youth other than sons and daughters of Orthodox parents.

Tuesday, June 20

To the office for a conference with the staff on my draft telegram. Even the most critical of the group approved, and with minor verbal and one or two substantive changes, we sent it off. It was a very stiff recommendation for the scrapping of the PCC and its replacement by the single-man mediator. I felt rewarded for my labors late the night before and early this morning.

On June 12, the Egyptian representative to the PCC, Abd al-Mun'im Mustafa, officially replied to the PCC's March 29, 1950, proposal for mixed committees. The reply, which reflected Arab League discussions in April, insisted that the return of Arab refugees to Israel and payments to those who did not return were a prerequisite to any further negotiations, because they were provisions of the General Assembly resolution of December 1948. If Israel agreed unconditionally to their return, then Egypt would discuss this issue in a mixed committee on refugees. Egypt would participate in mixed committees on other questions after Israel and Egypt had reached agreement in principle on these issues in advance. The PCC, he said, "had dealt too tenderly with Jewish susceptibilities."[60]

McDonald and his staff wrote a comprehensive assessment that went to Washington, London, Geneva, Moscow, and every US mission in the Middle East. Reflecting the views of Riley, Bunche, and the Israelis themselves, as well as his own views, McDonald called for the dissolution of the PCC.[61] He argued that the PCC had failed, because of its poor administrative setup, ineffective representatives—particularly Azcárate and Boisanger—and a complete failure to convince the Arabs or Israelis to moderate their positions. "[The] PCC is condemned by [its] own record, and irrespective of personalities or national or UN pride [it] should be scrapped by [the] next UN [General Assembly]."

"[Near Eastern] peace and security," McDonald continued, "demand [a] radical new approach." McDonald suggested replacing the PCC with a "1-man medium . . . not hampered by an advisory commission and particularly not by [a] commission composed of national representatives responsible to their own governments." He recom-

59. Yigal Allon (1918–1980), co-founder of the Palmach, the elite unit of the Haganah; commander-in-chief, Palmach, 1945; general in IDF, 1948–1950, led several major operations during Israeli War of Independence; interim prime minister, 1969.

60. Palmer to secretary of state, no. 730, June 13, 1950, *FRUS*, 1950, v. V, 928–929. Also Keeley to secretary of state, no. 224, April 18, 1950, USSDCF-PIFA, 1950–1954, reel 4, frame 912–914; McDonald to secretary of state, joint weeka, no. 24, June 16, 1950, McDonald Papers, USHMM, box 8, folder 11.

61. For the others, *DFPI*, v. 5, d. 283, 285, 291.

mended a "strong personality, such as Riley, with conciliation powers comparable to Bunche." If these suggestions were impractical politically, McDonald suggested having the PCC focus on a single "hopeful point," namely Israeli-Jordanian negotiations. Discussions of refugees and compensation, he said, would confound the work of the UNRWA.[62]

Conference at the house with Reza Saffinia, Persian [special] representative [in Israel]. He talked very interestingly for about half an hour about Israel-Iranian relations. He knew, of course, that, at the suggestion of the Foreign Office, I had asked the Department to inquire whether the US Missions in Greece and Teheran felt that they could encourage the two governments to which they were accredited to move towards de jure recognition of Israel. The reply in each case had been discouraging for the time being.

My guest explained that his government was under fire for having established de facto relations, because Iranian citizens who had been exiled or who had fled from Israel had not had their properties returned to them. Some steps had been taken by Israel, but these were "quite inadequate." Saffinia had written strongly to Sharett, urging fuller restitution and letting the foreign minister know that the desired de jure recognition must wait on such steps.[63]

An unexpected sabra conference filled some two hours of the late afternoon. A couple of Ramat Gan boys, aged 16 or 17, came to the door and asked if they could see me. I invited them in. Shortly thereafter, Chaim Sharett came over. He proved to be the most talkative of the three. Again, most of the discussion was centered on the attitude of youth towards religion. Chaim, with the expressed approval of the other two, vigorously defended the current disavowal of Orthodoxy. He denied that this in any sense was un-Jewish or that it was a break with Jewish tradition or for that matter with Jewish religion. He emphasized that most of the modern Orthodox prescriptions and prohibitions were the products of the Jews' [lives] in the Diaspora and of the rabbis' successful efforts to make the law a powerful fence to protect ancient and medieval Jews from contamination by their Christian neighbors. But, he continued, it should be obvious that no such fence was necessary in a Jewish state. When Eli [Karlin] cited extracts from the prophets Nehemiah and Isaiah about the need of keeping the Sabbath and the fate of the Jews depending on such ob-

---

62. McDonald to secretary of state, no. 465, June 20, 1950 [sent to all US missions in Middle East, plus Geneva, London, and Moscow], *FRUS*, 1950, v. V, 935–936. See also Barco to secretary of state, no. 766, June 22, 1950, *FRUS*, 1950, v. V, 938–939.

63. Relations between Iran and Israel remained stable and, from the Israeli perspective, helped cause a split in the Muslim world vis-à-vis Israel while making it possible for Iraqi Jews to flee via Iran. In September 1950, Sharett eliminated red tape, thereby allowing Iranian Bahai sect members who had lived in Haifa to recover their property there, and in the same month Israel backed the Iranian candidate for president of the UN General Assembly. *DFPI*, v. 5, d. 336, 377. In 1948, 95,000 Jews lived in Iran. In 1950 and 1951, some 25,000 Iranian Jews emigrated to Israel with no impediment. Martin Gilbert, *In Ishmael's House: A History of Jews in Muslim Lands* (New Haven, CT: Yale University Press, 1994), 268.

servations, Chaim replied that such injunctions replied to specific situations in the times of the writers, and were not today to be taken as warrants for such outmoded restrictions as those affecting motor travel, smoking, etc., etc. on Shabbat.

As to the role of the rabbis, Chaim contended that the youth today looks to other leaders for guidance, to their youth organization leaders, to their teachers, to the statesmen, or to their parents, provided of course the parents are emancipated. One does not, he said, turn from a rabbi because he is a rabbi, but because so many of the rabbis have nothing now which appeals to youth. As to traditional Jewish holidays and ceremonies such as circumcision and bar mitzvah[s], the young men agreed that of course circumcision is essential "for health reasons" and that the others are all or many of them maintained by the "unpious" Jews. Throughout all that, Chaim said, there ran the note that the creation of the Jewish state made its perpetuation and strengthening the central "religious" duty of Jews.

In answer to our queries: "Will not the irreligion of Jewish leaders in Israel weaken the influence of the state on the Diaspora?" Chaim did not retreat from his earlier pronouncement that the state is the natural leader of the Diaspora. All Jews everywhere, he said, must be interested in Israel as a refuge for such Jews as those from Yemen, Iraq, North Africa and Eastern Europe; even American Jews could not be wholly sure of their long-range future in the US and must hence think of Israel in terms of a place of potential refuge.

Exhausted by this long session, I inveigled Ruth out for a walk before supper.

Thursday, June 22

David W. Petegorsky of the American Jewish Congress[64] came at twelve and for more than half an hour we discussed home political affairs. His most interesting item was the disclosure that he had worked with Jack Ewing through [J. Donald] Kingsley, the new head of the IRO [International Refugee Organization],[65] when the latter was a public relations assistant to Ewing. Kingsley used to turn to Petegorsky for confirmation or technical data on Jewish affairs. Petegorsky is enthusiastic about Kingsley's ability. He does not know, however, what the latter will do when the IRO concludes its work.

---

64. David W. Petegorsky (1915–1956), Ottawa-born Canadian scholar and government official; executive director, American Jewish Congress, 1945–1956; member of Executive Committee, World Jewish Congress, 1948–1956.

65. J. Donald Kingsley (1908–1972), political scholar, succeeded William Hallam Tuck as director-general of the IRO, July 31, 1949.

Shmuel Katz came to tell me of the crisis in Herut and the threat against Begin led by [Hillel] Kook, formerly [Peter] Bergson, and [Ari] Jabotinsky.[66] Kook is the brains and Jabotinsky the name. According to Katz, the differences between Begin and Kook go back to [Kook's] period in Washington, when he was organizing his many committees and setting up his Hebrew embassy.[67] Differences then arose because of divergent views about the importance of the American efforts and of the share of money raised there which should go to Israel.

On Kook's return to Israel, he persistently refused to carry his weight in the party's organizational struggles, [and] went back to the States during the Knesset election campaign. Subsequently in the Knesset, while nominally following Begin's leadership, Kook persistently undermined confidence in Begin.[68] The most important recent issue between the two men was Kook's demand for an open pro-American orientation of the party. Though this was voted down by a very large majority, Kook refused to admit defeat and continued to agitate on the ground that the party decision had been railroaded through. Moreover, Kook was critical of Begin's failure to draft for the party a clear economic program, but when Kook was asked to set down his own ideas and to lead in the drafting, he declined. Similarly, he declined to accept any committee chairmanship in the Knesset other than the political one.

A pleasant and prolonged cocktail party at the Pender-Cudlips[69] and the O'Neill's.[70] I had no serious talk except with [Gene] Currivan who, in what may have been a fishing expedition, talked about a potential new arrangement between Israel and Egypt centering about the Gaza Strip and suggested thereto [suggestions] said to have been made by Riley on his recent trip to Cairo.[71] I argued that I thought this unlikely because of my impression that Cairo, under the influence of the [grand] mufti on the prime minister and the foreign minister, had stiffened extremely. Currivan appeared to scoff at

66. Ari Jabotinsky (1910–1969), Odessa-born son of Vladimir (Ze'ev) Jabotinsky, the founder of Revisionist Zionism; active in Istanbul as part of Bergson Group, 1944, and arrested by British; Knesset member, 1949–1951 (Herut); helped form opposition to Begin within the party; became an academic after leaving the party in 1951.

67. Refers to Kook/Bergson's Hebrew Committee for National Liberation and his American League for a Free Palestine, lobbying groups that had promoted the Irgun insurgency in Palestine, 1945–1946. Discussed in Goda et al., eds., *To the Gates of Jerusalem*, 40.

68. Kook was elected to the first Knesset in January 1949 on the Herut list. He and Jabotinsky eventually split with Begin and served out their terms as independent members. Kook returned to the United States in 1951.

69. Colonel Peter Pender-Cudlip (1914–2010), British military attaché in Tel Aviv.

70. John Anthony O'Neill (1915–2008), heroic British World War II pilot who won the Distinguished Flying Cross; first British air attaché in Israel.

71. Riley proposed that Israel turn over a ten-kilometer strip along the eastern portion of the Gaza Strip, which would provide an Israeli concession while easing refugee congestion in the strip. It would have meant abandonment of several Jewish settlements, and Riley was not optimistic that the Israelis would agree. Caffery to secretary of state, no. 1315, June 6, 1950, *FRUS*, 1950, v. V, 922–923.

this and said that I was misled by despatches from [Philip] Ireland, Caffery's political officer.[72]

Saturday was a busy but quiet day. Rebecca Sieff's for large evening party for Leonard Bernstein and Jennie Tourel.[73] We stayed until nearly eleven o'clock.

Sunday, June 25
Worked during the morning.

In the evening Ruth and I as Krinitzi's guests attended the amphitheater concert of the orchestra with Jennie Tourel as the principal in Mahler's *Das Lied von der Erde*. It was an exciting performance. Afterwards we stopped for a moment to see the Cantors and the Marksons at the Sharett's, where they were for dinner.

Monday, June 26
Ruth and I picked up the Cantors at eight o'clock at the Gat; or rather, I picked up Eddie and Ruth rode with Ida. On the way out, Eddie developed his ideas about the B'nai B'rith. He also renewed his promise to talk with Abe [Feinberg] and Ben [Abrams] on his return to the States. He suggested that I write him in care of the Waldorf.

The news in the morning paper of the aggression of the Communists against Southern Korea gave us all to think not merely about the world situation but about the possibilities for us here. I began to plan about getting some material in anticipation of a possible period of virtual isolation here.

With Soviet encouragement, North Korean communist forces on June 25, 1950, attacked South Korea over the 38th parallel. Communist forces quickly advanced to within twenty kilometers of Seoul, the South Korean capital. The UN Security Council convened an emergency meeting on June 25 and issued Security Council Resolution 82, calling for North Korean withdrawal to the 38th parallel. At that time, the Soviets were boycotting Security Council meetings because of the lack of a seat for the People's Republic of China since that regime's takeover of the mainland in 1949. They thus could not veto the resolution.

Quiet evening at home reading Douglas Ball's popular *This Fascinating Oil Business*.[74]

72. Philip W. Ireland (b. 1902), US embassy, Cairo, consul and head of political section, 1948–1950.
73. Entry of May 21, 1949.
74. Max W. Ball, Douglas Ball, and Daniel S. Turner, *This Fascinating Oil Business* (Indianapolis: Bobbs-Merrill, 1940), among the first books to explain the importance of oil in geopolitics; influential in US government.

An hour and a half conference in Ford's office. Present besides Ford and myself, Troxel, Major Booth and Fried. On the world situation [caused by the Korean conflict] it was agreed that we should at once query the Department about the possibility of establishing stocks of food supplies here in addition to the emergency rations which would normally be accumulated. Troxel was instructed to check with Booth and Brady on the latter's return and prepare a draft.

As to the balance of probabilities, we agreed that the Russians [*sic*] probably [will] have taken over the whole of Korea in a day or two and that beyond the inevitable mopping up, they will call it a day and consolidate their gains before another major push. Our reaction in the States, beyond its effect in speeding up rearmament, is not likely to cause us to deliver an ultimatum. After all, we have to carry Western Europe with us, and there are no indications that this time, except in response to a direct thrust into the West, it would support wholeheartedly a final test of arms.

Later on June 27, the Security Council issued its Resolution 83, calling for military aid to South Korea to repel the attack and restore peace. Again, the absent Soviets failed to use their veto power. From the UN, Gideon Rafael reported that the Egyptian delegation abstained and that the "implication [of] their abstention [is] obvious." He said further that the United States had the strength to repel the attack and that US diplomats were sure that the USSR would not intervene. After discussion concerning the possibility of Israeli military aid to avoid diplomatic isolation from the West, Sharett decided to express verbal support for UN action against acts of aggression, while reminding the UN that Israel too was surrounded by enemies against which it might need UN support.[75]

Troxel was interesting about the new nationality law, and I urged him to prepare a telegram asking the Department for instructions.[76]

I reviewed the recent developments affecting our local situation, the General Riley reports from Cairo, the several British reports about Jerusalem partition, the Arab League, Jordan's new intransigence, Jerusalem and the PCC, and raised the question whether the time had come to ask Israel to do for refugees what was done for Jerusalem and also the question of compensation in Jerusalem. Fried's answer on the last was, I thought, conclusive. He reminded us of the Department's own suggestion that Israel save its further concessions until the [General] Assembly. Finally, I agreed to do nothing at the moment, and to review the situation in a couple of days.

75. *DFPI*, v. 5., d. 293–295, 296, 300–301.
76. Reference to the Law of Return, passed July 5, 1950, qualifying every Jew to enter Israel as an immigrant.

Lovely garden party at the Helms' for the admiral commanding the Eastern Mediterranean Fleet.[77] I had a few minutes chat with him about Korea. He said that [though] the US was not ready, neither in his opinion are the Russians, for a final test of strength.

Dinner with Lenny Bernstein, Miss Coates, and the former's young Viennese artist friend who is staying at the house. It was an interesting but not amusing meal because Lenny was so obviously overtired. Here in Israel he had been able to deny himself to no one and had worked, therefore, all day long every day. He himself recognized that he would have to choose between being so lavish with his time and concentrating on his music.

Wednesday, June 28

Dr. [Wilhelm] Bruenn,[78] a friend of Dr. [Judah] Magnes,[79] asked to come to see me to develop his humanitarian views about Israel and the Arab peoples, particularly those resident in Israel and the refugees. I begged off until later.

Thursday, June 29

More than half an hour with [James A.] Wooten of the NEAT [Near East Air Transport][80] at the office with Ford, and Troxel. Though Wooten's language is appallingly vulgar, he obviously has performed near miracles in having smoothed his way in the several Arab capitals. His graphic account of his methods and of the number and variety of officials high and low who were reachable, was most illuminating. His account of the need for sixty-six separate and individual signatures of Iraqi officials, including that of the regent [Abd al-Ilah for Faisal II] and of all of the members of the cabinet on the release papers of each emigrating Jew, would have made a successful comedy. He explained that permission to overfly Jordan had been withdrawn after the Israelis had forced down recently [a] Jordan commercial plane; he was furious about this "stupidity" and was hoping to see Sharett to tell the latter how the whole Iraqi "Magic Carpet" is jeopardized by such Israeli Air Force action. Admitting that he was overflying Syria and intends to continue to do so, he explained that he had made arrangements with someone in control of the Syrian Air Force

77. Admiral Sir John Hereward Edelsten, commander-in-chief, Mediterranean Fleet, 1950–1952. See entry of July 3, 1950.

78. Wilhelm Bruenn (1884–1950), German Jewish physician who emigrated to Ottoman Palestine before World War I, treating malaria and trachoma among Jews and Arabs; established, with encouragement of Weizmann, Magnes, and Nathan Straus, the first comprehensive health clinic in Hadera, which influenced Hadassah and other health organizations in Palestine.

79. Judah Leon Magnes (1877–1948), San Francisco-born co-founder and first president of Hebrew University, 1935–1948; helped with Martin Buber to found the Ihud Party, which called for a binational solution for Palestine. See Goda et al., eds., *To the Gates of Jerusalem*, 157–159.

80. James A. Wooten (1914–1985), director of Alaska Airlines after 1947, which was responsible for the transport of 45,000 Yemeni Jews to Israel in 1949; in 1950 director of Near East Air Transport, which ferried Iraqi Jews from Iraq and Iran to Cyprus and then to Israel. See entries of December 27, 1948, January 13, 1949, and May 8, 1950.

that he use an inaccurate [departure time], and that in any case, Syria had no night fighters. (His flights across Syria are always at night.)

Wooten was very cynical about [Edward] Crocker [in Baghdad] and [James Hugh] Keeley [in Damascus]. He deplored the latter's nervousness at the over-flying of Syria and was furious with the former, whom he charged with proto-colaire aloofness. When the British ambassador made a move which looked like a governmental appeal to Baghdad for British participation in the Magic Carpet, Wooten said he forced Crocker's hand and made him intervene on the threat of having the Department order him to do so.

As to [John C.] Wiley,[81] Wooten was enthusiastic and had offered Wiley a $25,000 a year job as president of one of his companies. The duties would be wholly "diplomatic" in relation to the several Arab governments. Wiley had discreetly and wisely replied that having been a career officer for more than thirty years, he could not imagine himself doing anything else. And he was right!

I should have liked to have talked longer to Wooten, partly because of the inherent importance of his amazing interlocking network of airlines and partly because he is so amazingly like the early piratical American industrialists who allowed no "petty considerations" to block their expansionist program.

Shiloah and Kollek during forty-five minutes outlined Israel's present position regarding Jordan. Some old ground was covered, but the emphasis was new.[82] Abdullah's seeming inability to carry through on his promises, for example, repeated promises to strengthen the Jordanian representative on the MAC [to replace Abdullah al-Tel], the promise to have Glubb meet Yadin, and, [for Glubb] to have a high officer meet and work with Dayan. Shiloah returned to his earlier thesis that the fundamental difficulty is the failure of US and UK to give the king adequate encouragement by promising aid in the event Jordan's negotiations led to Arab League sanctions.

In effect, Shiloah admitted a measure of Israeli responsibility for recent border incidents by saying that the failure of the Jordanian-Israeli promises of negotiations on broader issues had weakened his (Shiloah's) influence of a support of a continuation of leniency toward infiltrees. He admitted, too, that Israel had a responsibility for failure to set up Jordanian-Israeli joint border patrols by insisting on the prior release of three recently captured Israeli border soldiers.

McDonald reported on the meeting and commented, "Believe Israel is genuinely anxious [to] resume negotiations, because of [the] urgent necessity [to] win peace on at least one front." McDonald stated, "I recognize [the] failure [of the] King's policy [of]

---

81. John Cooper Wiley, US ambassador to Iran, 1948–1950. See entries of November 25, 28, 29, 1949.

82. Abdullah had invited Shiloah for another private talk. The king said that conditions for negotiation were more favorable than ever, but that the cabinet still presented difficulties. Moshe Sasson to Eliahu Sasson, June 27, 1950, *DFPI*, v. 5, d. 292.

negotiating without knowledge or support [of] his government." But he argued again that US and UK reassurance to Abdullah, together with a reaffirmation of Israel's earlier willingness to provide immediate compensation for Arab property in Jerusalem as well as an Israeli agreement to set up a joint claims commission for other properties, could break the logjam.

Gerald Drew, the US minister in Amman, was more pessimistic. Abdullah, he said, liked to meet the Israelis personally and without the knowledge of his cabinet. But the king could not find ministers willing to resume peace negotiations, particularly in the wake of the Wadi Araba expulsion and similar border incidents.[83]

Tea as guest of the mayor of Petah Tikvah [Yosef Sapir] in one of the town's beautiful gardens.

The meeting of the local branch of the Israel-America Friendship League was held in the attractive hall (seating about 300) of the imposing Histadrut Building. Fortunately, the preliminary speeches were very short. My talk, except for a reference to Korea, with emphasis on the US's role in supporting the UN Security Council Resolution, was largely a repetition of my Haifa talk on Point Four. We were home by eleven.

Friday, June 30

So busy during the morning reporting on the Shiloah interview that I had to give up seeing Lenny Bernstein off at the airfield.

---

83. McDonald to secretary of state, no. 485, June 30, 1950; *FRUS*, 1950, v. V, 944–945. Drew to secretary of state, no. 109, June 27, 1950, *FRUS*, 1950, v. V, 941–942.

25. July 1950

Sunday, July 2

Ford and I decided to go to see Kollek to try to find out what we could about Israel's plans in response to the UN [Security Council]'s Korean resolution [of June 25]. We were more successful than we dared hope. We learned and reported that members of the Foreign Office on Friday had decided that Israel ought to support the UN; that Saturday, Sharett had drawn up a statement and submitted it to Ben-Gurion, who decided to call a cabinet meeting, which, we later learned, was held at Weizmann's in connection with the cabinet visit there to say goodbye. We were also told that four or five Mapai members of the cabinet at a social party at Goldie Meyerson's had favored a supporting Israeli resolution.

Throughout most of July, North Korean forces drove back undermanned and underequipped US divisions toward Pusan. It was not yet known whether the attack against South Korea was the prelude to a general global communist offensive that might include the Near East. On July 7, 1950, McDonald reported, "Initial widespread [Israeli] enthusiasm over US action gave way to feelings of some doubts as news of repeated US defeats became headlines." Some labor leaders questioned UN and US support for the corrupt South Korean regime.[1]

On July 1 David Niles informed Nahum Goldmann of the White House's "disappointment and indignation" at Israel's silence.[2] Sharett drafted a resolution aimed at preserving Israel's nonaligned status while supporting the UN and United States: "The Government of Israel opposes and condemns aggression wherever it may occur and from whatever quarter it may emanate. In fulfillment of her clear obligations under the Charter, Israel supports the Security Council in its efforts to put an end to the breach of the peace in Korea and to restore peace in that area. The Government of Israel hopes that the United Nations will continue its endeavors to align all the Great Powers in a common effort for safeguarding the peace of the world."[3]

After debating the draft resolution, the majority of the Knesset endorsed the government's statement. McDonald explained to Washington that Israel's stance was forged in the "interest of Russian and Iron Curtain Jewry" and that Sharett's remarks really meant the "final abandonment by Israel of its policy [of] neutrality and complete

---

1. McDonald to secretary of state, joint weeka no. 27, July 7, 1950, McDonald Papers, USHMM, box 9, folder 1.
2. *DFPI*, v. 5, d. 302–303.
3. *DFPI*, v. 5, 419.

final alignment with the West." He also explained that Israel, fearing a second attack by the Arab states, was unable to send troops.[4] *Still, there was irritation with Israel in some quarters of the State Department.*[5]

Monday, July 3

Office conference chiefly on Korea and related matters.

Helm and his new counselor, [John] Chadwick, came at 6:15 and with Ford, stayed until after seven. It was a general introductory session. I was chiefly interested in Helm's understandable resentment of the Egyptian threat to close the Suez Canal as an act of "neutrality" in the Korean crisis. I got the impression that there is a tendency in Britain to adopt a stiffer line with Cairo.[6]

Egypt had abstained in the June 27 Security Council vote on Korea. Mapai leaders then told the US Embassy in Tel Aviv that the United States lacked the experience dealing with Arab personalities that was needed to stand up to "the obvious blackmail. . . . We are not at all sure that the democracies have learned that the friends you continually have to buy are not the most dependable in the world, especially in this area."[7]

Israel-America Friendship League dinner-dance at the Pilz Restaurant. Mercifully, the speakers were short. In mine I made a comparison between our initial years of independence and the past two years of Israel's life. I referred to the fact that pessimists were refuted in each case. Then, taking advantage of the previous speaker's reference to the US's support of the UN Security Council Resolution on Korea, I spoke of the world's interest in and gratitude for Israel's stand on this issue. I noted also that the welcome the day previous to the British admiral was an event which would not have been anticipated two years before.[8] Ruth and I were home about midnight.

Tuesday, July 4

In the morning, members of the diplomatic corps called to offer their congratulations [for US Independence Day]. Ford, the military staff, and I received

4. McDonald, joint weeka no. 28, July 14, 1950, McDonald Papers, USHMM, box 9, folder 1; McDonald, joint weeka no. 29, July 21, 1950, McDonald Papers, USHMM, box 9, folder 1.

5. *DFPI*, v. 5, d. 304–306, 323, 326.

6. Anglo-Egyptian discussions over the future of the Suez Canal zone had resumed in June before the Korean conflict broke out. The canal remained essential for the movement of troops and material to Korea. Louis, *The British Empire and the Middle East, 1945–1951*, 589; and Hahn, *The United States, Great Britain, and Egypt, 1945–1956*, 102–105.

7. Relayed by Milton Fried to McDonald, July 7, 1950, McDonald Papers, USHMM, box 9, folder 1.

8. Refers to the two-day visit to Haifa in June–July 1950 by Admiral John Hereward Edelsten (1891–1966), commander-in-chief, British Mediterranean Fleet. His was the first foreign warship to visit Israel (HMS *Surprise*); he was greeted with Israel's first twenty-one-gun salute, and British and Israeli flags flew side by side in Haifa during the visit. Edelsten continued on to Tel Aviv to meet Ben-Gurion in a somewhat tense encounter; the admiral was also irritated that the Israeli fleet was out on maneuvers during his visit. Aridan, *Britain, Israel, and Anglo-Jewry*, 67.

the visitors on the porch, serving sherry and cookies. Those present included the representatives of all the missions except those from the Iron Curtain countries. The visitors were the British, French, Dutch, Belgian, Italian, Argentine, Turk, Australian, Iranian, Yugoslav, and Romanian. The chargé of Romania came, I think, by mistake, since obviously there had been agreement among the other Iron Curtain countries not to come.

A little after six, Ford brought over [William Wendell] Cleland of McGhee's office.[9] He is making a goodwill tour of the Arab countries with a special assignment of talking to government officials and his former students about ways in which [the] Point Four technical training program can be implemented cooperatively, and preferably on a regional basis, by and in the Arab states. The assignment seemed to both me and Ford to be admirably planned. For the first hour or so I queried our guest on political conditions in the several countries he had visited. He did not add much to our information, except his emphasis on what seemed to him to be the dangerous increase in the power of Farouk.

His affirmative idea was that Israel should for its own sake and for the sake of peace in this area make a generous gesture to the Arab states. He felt that unless Arab unity could be restored and deepened, there would be no chance of cooperation in this area at all. He thought, contrary to the impression of most of us, that the Arab opposition [to] Israel had weakened and that, given a face-saving formula, all of the states would be glad to get out of the mess. I told him I was delighted to hear this and I strongly approved his desire to see Israeli officials to make this case to them, though he would of course be doing this unofficially and on a personal basis. I asked Ford to try to arrange for himself and Cleland to visit Kollek and, if possible, also Eytan and Shiloah.

Wednesday, July 5

Bart Crum, who says he is here on legal business, called and said he had a message from Dave Niles, whose position he said was stronger than ever. He implied that it would be unwise for me to go on leave as planned and would tell me more. He is going to go to Jerusalem to see Dov Joseph,[10] and I suggested that he call from there about our getting together over the weekend.

A little after noon, Ruth, Shalom and I started for Haifa. We had a bite of lunch on the way and were ready for a brief nap before the reception for the president at the pier. We reached the waterfront at 4:15 promptly. The president [Weizmann] had just arrived and was listening to a brief flag presentation service by the ship's side [in] which [David] Remez and [Joseph] Sprinzak spoke for a couple of minutes each. Then the president mounted the gangplank to the accompaniment of a 21-gun salute. After that the other guests, numbering perhaps 75 or 100, and we crowded up the gangway, milled around in the crowded

9. Entry of October 15, 1949. Cleland was McGhee's intelligence adviser.
10. Now minister of rationing and supply and minister of agriculture.

corridor, for a moment had an opportunity to say a word to the president and greet Mrs. Weizmann and then told that we were to leave.

President Weizmann left from Haifa for Switzerland on July 5, 1950, where he was to have an extended medical and sick leave. McDonald reported afterward that some believed "that he 'may never again see Israel.'"[11]

Thursday, July 6

Dr. John Paul of Yale University, epidemiological work [in] the medical school, made a farewell call. I was much interested in his report on the polio epidemic here.[12]

Friday, July 7

Ford and I [met] with Kollek and Herlitz for a half hour. They wanted to talk about Cleland. They were concerned lest the latter's emphasis on the need for strengthening the Arab League and for general Arab negotiations with Israel might represent a new Department view. We assured them that Cleland's views were personal and that, to our knowledge, there had been no change in the Department's policy of favoring direct bilateral negotiations. Whether or not our friends were convinced, Ford and I felt that, on balance, despite the risk involved, we had been justified in arranging for Cleland to talk to the several people at HaKirya.

At 12:00 Ford and I, accompanied by Kollek, had a 45-minute session with Sharett. First, I summarized the several points of view which the Department had asked us to present. Then, going beyond these, I sought to answer any questions which might be in Sharett's mind as a result of the military reverses in Korea. I emphasized that these might in the long run be helpful by the stimulus they would provide for more rapid and more complete preparedness at home. In reply, Sharett thanked me for my praise of the government's statement on Korea and his Knesset address. On the latter, he said, there would be available to us within a few days, "an authorized" translation. He elaborated the government's views, stressing its support of the UN even at the risk of being charged with having joined one of the rival blocs. From both the tone and the substance of what he said, I could only conclude that the government here sees clearly that its interests can be served and its security protected by a defeat for the aggression in Korea.

Sharett admitted that the economic plight of Israel would soon become desperate in the event of a world conflict, but he did not see how any adequate stockpiling program was practicable because of the current lack of funds. He realizes, too, I think, the danger from the military point of view if there

11. McDonald to secretary of state, joint weeka no. 27, July 7, 1950, McDonald Papers, USHMM, box 9, folder 1.
12. Dr. John R. Paul (1893–1971), virologist, Yale School of Medicine, 1928–1951; known mostly for research on polio.

were a race for strategic airfields. In his heart he probably has no illusions about his government's power to remain neutral for long if the conflict spread to the eastern Mediterranean.

When Kollek went out to inquire about when the translation of Sharett's speech would be ready, he brought back the news that Bart Crum and two business colleagues were waiting. Sharett said he would see them, but we went on leisurely with our talk.

In the anteroom, Bart was his usual enthusiastic self and introduced us to his colleagues Emanuel Reich and Jack Buncher.[13] We made a date for that afternoon at the house. Bart and his colleagues drank Bart's mixed martinis and explained to me their plans for a new package for Israel scheme. Then we discussed the general situation here. As they were leaving, I asked Bart about the personal message he said he had for me from Dave Niles. There was no time for a full answer, but from what Bart said, I doubt if there was an important message. I am supposed to see Bart again alone.

Saturday, July 8

Major Brady made his farewell call, which gave us an opportunity for a general survey of the military situation as it might affect us. He is anxious personally to be assigned to Persia.[14]

Sunday, July 9

Had a longish talk with Sharett during the course of which he reported that among the comments from their [Israel's] embassies were two points of reported criticism:

1) the US not waiting for the second UN resolution [before it deployed troops in Korea]; and,
2) the separate action regarding Formosa [Taiwan].[15] He added that Ershov had indicated no particular nervousness about the situation but had argued that of course the US was the aggressor.

Monday, July 10

Jacob Herzog was at the house for nearly an hour at teatime. He developed the thesis that the West must find some moral equivalent for the communist appeal to the masses of Asia. He suggested that thanks to Britain's withdrawal from India, Nehru was a leader who could influence Asia as no one else.[16] It was evident that he is trying also to find some way in which Israel in this crisis

---

13. Jack Buncher (1911–2001), Pittsburgh industrial and real estate tycoon.
14. Brady was not assigned to Iran.
15. Because of worries concerning the security of Taiwan, the United States sent the 7th Fleet to the Taiwan Straits to protect it from the People's Republic of China after the Korean War broke out.
16. Jawaharlal Nehru (1889–1964), prime minister of India, 1947–1964.

could act as a spiritual force and a peacemaker. I had to point out that such hopes must be vain pending peace between Israel and its Arab neighbors.

Delightful concert of the Philharmonic at the amphitheater with the Negro conductor, Dean Dixon,[17] and his white wife, Vivian Rivkin,[18] soloist in the Mozart piano concerto. The other numbers were a Handel *concerto grosso*, Schumann's Fourth Symphony; and Tchaikovsky's Romeo and Juliet. Dixon is very quiet in his conducting and unlike Lenny or Paray, he is no sort of a ballet dancer. After the concert Ruth and I stopped for nearly an hour at a pleasant reception for the Dixons at the [Joseph] Levys' in Ramat Gan.

Tuesday, July 11

Shiloah with Kollek came to the house for half an hour or more to tell me about his meeting alone with Abdullah on the night of July 7. Shiloah had asked for this meeting in order to explain to Abdullah that, if he thought it desirable, Israel was willing to postpone any further attempts at negotiations for three, six, or nine months in order to avoid possible embarrassment across the river. Shiloah added then an appraisal of the situation in the Arab states, in all of which there are more marked elements of instability than in Jordan. But Shiloah foresees that, failing peace between Jordan and Israel, Jordan, too, may suffer an economic crisis. Prompt peace would prevent this by reducing burdens on both sides by reducing Jordan's import expenses very substantially and by its receipt of compensation from Israel for Arab property in Jerusalem.

Abdullah, in reply, said that he did not want an indefinite postponement of negotiations, not even for three months, that he was working in his own way which he need not describe, that he was making progress, and though he had not received "from certain quarters" all the encouragement he deserved, he was hopeful. Then followed Shiloah's heavy meal at about two with the king's entourage. There was little salt in the food so as not to invite thirst during the ensuing eighteen hours or so of fast [for Ramadan].

In his report of this meeting, McDonald addressed the PCC's recent decision to reconvene in Jerusalem on August 5. Shiloah, though "not optimistic concerning a resumption of negotiations with Jordan, 'dreads [the] return of PCC to Jerusalem' because if PCC intervenes 'all hope of progress with Jordan will end.'"[19]

We then discussed in general terms Korea and its implications. Kollek brought up also the economic situation, which led us to a discussion of currency evasions. Shiloah suggested the need for an American expert to "catch the crooks."

---

17. Charles Dean Dixon (1915–1976), Harlem-born, Julliard-trained American conductor; left the United States in 1949 to conduct Israel Philharmonic Orchestra for the 1950 and 1951 seasons.
18. Vivian Rivkin (1912–1968), piano soloist; married to Dixon, 1947–1953.
19. McDonald to secretary of state, no. 21, July 11, 1950, *FRUS*, 1950, v. V, 950–951.

Kollek and I did not demur but pointed out the imbalance of Israel's economy as the basic cause of the currency difficulties.

In the afternoon two groups of American educators for tea. [The groups included Moshe Davis of the Jewish Theological Seminary[20] and Emil Lengyel of the New York University seminar at the Katznelson Institute.[21]] Davis was interesting in his discussion of Brandeis University, which he thinks has no great future, in part because it has not dared to be a wholly Jewish institution. He thinks the president, Mr. Sachar, is ruining his health by his financial efforts.[22] Davis is pessimistic too about the future of the UJA and doubts the possibility of successful future "catastrophe" appeals.

Wednesday, July 12

[Gene] Currivan brought [Ralph] Chapman, the new [*Herald*] *Tribune* correspondent, to see me in the late morning. The latter has been in Japan and reports that there were no troops there fit for combat service and that there is no occasion for surprise at our reverses in Korea.[23]

Messers [John] Geehan and Robert Nichols, former vice president of the American Export Lines[24] and the latter a European manager, came with Mr. [Aaron] Rosenfeld[25] to discuss company problems.

Thursday, July 13

Long talk in the afternoon with Vivian [Chaim] Herzog, who from all accounts has had a successful beginning as Israel's military attaché in Washington. Our talk ranged from questions connected with Israel's application for arms to Vivian's guesses about the current roles of important personalities in Washington. He had talked with Dave Niles just before he left and had received the impression that Niles thought General Riley would fit the bill as my successor. On the arms problem, Vivian was moderately optimistic, saying that, in principle, the way seemed to be opening, but that now the chief difficulty was the possible unavailability of the items most needed. He wondered whether the higher-up authorities had yet envisioned the strategic importance of Israel sufficiently to lead them to give it the priority essential.

20. Moshe Davis (1916–1996), first American to earn doctorate at the Hebrew University; helped found and for many years headed the Institute for Contemporary Jewry there; created the field of Israel-American studies.

21. Emil Lengyel (1891–1985), Budapest-born journalist and historian; covered Germany for the *New York Times*; then wrote extensively on the Middle East, including a biography of Mustafa Kemal Atatürk. On the NYU seminar, see entry of July 19, 1949.

22. Abram L. Sachar (1899–1993), New York-born US historian and first president of Brandeis University, founded in 1946.

23. Ralph Chapman (1904–1980), US journalist who worked for a number of newspapers, most notably as foreign correspondent for the *New York Herald Tribune*; considered an expert on Japan.

24. Founded in 1919 as the Export Steamship Corporation and renamed in 1920s; ran mainly between east coast of the United States and eastern Mediterranean ports.

25. Aaron Rosenfeld, private shipping agent and broker based in Haifa.

Secretary of Defense Louis Johnson had agreed on June 28, 1950, that Israel and the Arab states would be able to purchase limited armaments in order to serve broad State Department policy aims. He approved of the sale of AT-6 aircraft (a World War II fighter), half-tracks, machine guns, and ammunition. However, by July 27, 1950, the Israelis were told that arms were scarce because of the war in Korea, and jets were not available at all.[26]

Friday, July 14

Israeli mission chiefs abroad, including Abba Eban and Eliahu Elath, had returned to Israel for meetings regarding the Korean conflict and the upcoming Fifth UN General Assembly.

Eban and Kollek at the house for an hour and a quarter during which we canvassed a number of important topics.

1) On arms, Eban said that [the] Pentagon no longer used as negative reasons [for not selling weapons to Israel] Israel's failure to supply full information or the alleged degree of communism here. Rather, the guiding considerations were availability of items and possible political repercussions if Israel were "favored."
2) Eban had left the States just after the Korean crisis broke. Everyone was surprised and delighted with the president's firm handling of the situation. In London he found the British less excited and the Foreign Office still inclined to surrender Formosa to Communist China.
3) As to an additional loan, Eban thought the political climate was as favorable now as it was likely to be. He assumed, therefore, that [David] Horowitz had explored further and that the possibility would be followed up.[27]
4) Eban thought Dave Niles well entrenched in the White House. As to other individuals, his views seemed not unlike those of Vivian [Herzog]. [Charles] Murphy is much more technical than Clifford was; the latter, some say, has no longer entree at the White House because of the president's resentment at his leaving because of salary. Rosenman is called in emergencies, and Feinberg is still seen at the White House.

---

26. Johnson to Acheson, June 28, 1950, *FRUS*, 1950, v. V, 942–943; Keren to US Division, Israeli Foreign Ministry, July 27, 1950, *DFPI*, v. 5, d. 323.

27. On May 30, 1950 Kaplan had asked the Export-Import Bank for an additional credit of $35 million on the expectation that Israel would double its agricultural output by 1952. Oscar Gass, the economic adviser to the Israeli embassy in Washington, met with board members of the Export-Import Bank the following week. Herbert E. Gaston, the chairman of the board, replied that many doubted Israel's creditworthiness, and bank vice president Walter C. Sauer added that the $35 million loan was hardly guaranteed. The US officials would give no timetable for a decision, stating that the earliest date would be September 15. In July 1950, Israel was also negotiating credit arrangements with France and with Swiss banks. Gass to Kaplan, *DFPI*, v. 5, d. 320; Mc-Donald to secretary of state, joint weeka no. 27, July 7, 1950, McDonald Papers, USHMM, box 9, folder 1.

5) The problem of Jerusalem has, according to Eban, been improving. The US position is less difficult, because it no longer calls for an agreement between the Vatican and Jordan, but rather between Jordan and Israel with due regard to the world religious interest. The Israeli new program was at least a practical and probably a strategic gain, according to Eban. Britain is inclined to think it goes too far, that international protection should be limited to those Holy Places which are not within the area of the majority concerned. For example, [the] Dome of the Rock area should not be internationalized because it is within [the] Moslem area. Israel has found echoes of support not only in nearly the whole US lay press, but also from Scandinavia and New Zealand. The Church is expected to fight for the retention of the internationalization principle as passed at the last session, even if its implementation is recognized as impossible. The Church does not yet accept the idea that Israel is so firmly established that compromise with it is essential.

6) Eban hopes that the PCC may not come to Jerusalem, but that instead the MAC may be strengthened and Riley's role similarly.

7) Eban had the same impression [that] Dave Niles had, that is, that Dave is personally satisfied that Riley would be an appropriate successor.

8) Eban is convinced that Egypt and Farouk have no present desire for peace with Israel. They see nothing to gain by it; besides, they are looking forward to the possibility, though not necessarily believing this probable, of a second round. Eytan said that Boisanger in his recent tour here had told quite different stories to Egypt and Israel from the statements made by each of these countries as to their policy towards the other.

As we were walking out, I was glad to have Eban tell me that Edmund Kaufmann is giving his people a bargain in the Embassy House [apartments] in Washington.[28]

Sunday, July 16

Long and pleasant visit in the afternoon from the three chief officers of the *Empire State* [training vessel for the New York State Maritime Academy].[29] They invited and we accepted for dinner on the ship Tuesday night, the 18th.

Out to the Sharon with Ruth for the dinner given to the visiting group of American woman lawyers by the Israel Bar Association. It was a pleasant party, and I was pleased to chat with Judge Florence Allen again.

Monday, July 17

While serving me my tea, Pesa [embassy staff] made an amazing and rather disquieting request. She naively said in effect: "Won't you please speak

28. Entry of March 23, 1949.
29. The *Empire State* was docked in Haifa with 395 cadets and crew for a six-day visit sponsored by the Foreign Ministry, the Haifa municipality, the Maritime League, the Israel-America Friendship League, and other organizations.

to Ben-Gurion and get me a green license plate (taxi) which I could then use to make enough money so that I shan't have to worry?" I struggled to make clear the impossibility of such a move. From it two disquieting conclusions emerged: 1) that experience in concentration camps and from the sufferings of war tends to destroy any clear standard of conduct; and; 2) the evident current belief in Israel that *protectzia* is unlimited and universal. These points were not less clear because of her emphasis that my name is magic in Israel. My refusal was clear-cut, but I am afraid my reasons did not carry conviction.

At teatime Mr. Alexis M. Kaminsky came to tell me of his work in erecting the Frank Cohen Building at the Pardes Hanna [Secondary Agricultural] School.[30] His most interesting point was the confirmation of the usual reports that Israel workmen are only about 50% as efficient as American workers. He had been about to increase it to about 75% by persistent but friendly pressure.

At the [David] Balfour cocktail party for the Chadwicks,[31] I had two talks which deserve to be set down. The first was with Helm, who expressed concern at Israel's current treatment of Arabs and at Ben-Gurion's "unnecessary irritation of Mapam in the Knesset."[32] The result of these mistakes is to worsen the prospects of peace. Helm made his complaints in the tone of a friend of Israel, and I believe he is genuinely disappointed that, as he sees it, the authorities here are not more skillful.

My other talk was with Shiloah. It covered [three] points. 1) In answer to Helm's criticism, whose name I did not mention, on the point of Ben-Gurion's tactics in the Knesset, Shiloah by inference admitted Ben-Gurion's mistakes but said that there was nothing could be done about it, because these were the results of his innate honesty and his inability to tolerate dishonesty in others. 2) In our discussions about the possibility of [Lowell] Pinkerton coming to Tel Aviv, Shiloah indicated interest, but while he implied that there would be doubts in the minds of some Israel officials, he was inclined to think that Pinkerton had never been really unfriendly and that he would be a good choice.[33] 3) As to Riley, Shiloah said that for Riley to come to Tel Aviv would be in direct contradiction to his whole present program at Lake Success. There, Riley is campaigning to have the MACs [Mixed Armistice Commissions] extended and his own authority enlarged. He is meeting with some success. Bunche is supporting him, and Hare and McGhee have expressed

---

30. Founded in 1935, the school received four prefabricated buildings in February from the Esco Foundation for Palestine, which was founded by Frank (1893–1959) and Ethel Cohen, candy manufacturers and benefactors from New York.

31. John E. Chadwick (b. 1911), chargé d'affaires, British legation, July–August 1950.

32. Ben-Gurion's attacks on Mapam and the Israeli communists [Maki] in the Knesset had been frequent. In late May when Mapam and Maki representatives attacked the cabinet's support of the May 24, 1950, three-power declaration on armaments as anti-Soviet, Ben-Gurion reminded them that foreign policy was not made by the left-wing parties. On July 4, 1950, he ridiculed Mapam's pro-Soviet "peace" statements on the Korean War by arguing that Israel should not stand with those who had violated the peace but with those who restricted aggression on behalf of the UN.

33. Entry of October 23, 1948.

interest in the program.[34] As Shiloah spoke, I wondered whether there was anything more in addition to my earlier telegrams along these precise lines that I could do to aid Riley's program.

Tuesday, July 18

We arrived at Waller's [in Haifa][35] just as they were finishing lunch and joined them in their dessert of fresh peaches just arrived on the *LaGuardia*. The first of two parties on the *LaGuardia* was on the bridge deck with Geehan and Nichols of the American Export Lines. Both Geehan and Nichols chatted with me about Hooper, and I praised his qualifications for the liaison job which they had in mind here in Israel. It would be wonderful if he received it. The elder [Heinz] Graetz attempted to talk with me about the problem of the threatened shift of American Export Lines agencies here. But he was interrupted by the appearance of one of the American Export Lines officials. We are to talk later.

The party for Maude Brady lasted until after seven. At the end tears were in evidence. At 7:30 Ruth and the Wallers and I boarded the captain's launch and were first to reach the *Empire State* to be greeted by the skipper and his officers. During the next two hours on the forward deck, a bountiful and delicious buffet supper was served to nearly three hundred guests, among whom were the leading Israelis at Haifa. At our table we had a chance to chat with the [commander] of the Israeli fleet.[36] Earlier I met [Shaul] Ben-Zvi (Paul Shulman), who was the active leader of the Israeli fleet during the war. His [US] passport has been taken up by the consulate.[37]

We were back at Waller's about half past ten and on the way home by eleven. Found a message at the house to call Ford, who told me that [Raleigh] Gibson was in town and wished to see me on urgent business the next morning.

Wednesday, July 19

At 8:30 Gibson, [William] Penniman,[38] and Ford came [to the residence]. Penniman, with interruptions from Gibson, gave me nearly an hour's report. . . .

---

34. On July 5 Riley argued at the State Department that the PCC had reached a dead end in trying to deal with the Arab states jointly, that it could no longer perform any important function, that it should not move to Jerusalem, and that the functions of the PCC should be transferred to the MACs, the existence of which had been agreed to by the parties themselves. Bunche agreed with Riley's assessment, but the State Department had procedural doubts concerning the expansion of MAC functions. Memorandum by John W. Halderman, July 11, 1950, *FRUS*, 1950, v. V, 949–950; *DFPI*, v. 5, d. 319, 340.
35. See entry of January 3, 1950.
36. Shlomo Shamir (1915–2009), Ukrainian-born Haganah smuggler of weapons and immigrants after 1939; RAF pilot, 1940–1946; commander, Israeli 7th Armored Brigade, 1948–1949; commander, Israeli Navy, 1949–1950.
37. Shaul Ben-Zvi [formerly Paul Shulman] (1922–1994), Connecticut-born graduate of US Naval Academy; helped smuggle Jews to Palestine after World War II and moved there permanently in 1948; commander, Israeli Navy, 1949; afterward Ben-Gurion's naval adviser.
38. William F. Penniman Jr., vice consul, US consulate general in Jerusalem, assigned December 1949.

McDonald reported to Washington:

> *Consul General Gibson and Vice Consul Penniman gave Mr. Ford and me a detailed account of attempts, presumably by local Israeli Police, to persuade or coerce local employees of the Consulate General to disclose information about the workings of the Jerusalem office and about the work habits of the officers there. Some of these attempts suggested an interest in our cryptographic material.*
>
> *I agreed to act immediately on Mr. Gibson's request that I take up the matter with the Israel authorities, protest in most vigorous terms, and ask for the immediate cessation of all police activity in connection with the Consulate General.[39]*

At teatime Harold Hoskins was at the house for more than an hour.[40] His general reactions on this trip as compared with his last six months ago [December 1949] were pessimism both as to conditions in the Arab states and in Israel. On both sides he found worsened economic conditions and [an] apparent lessened willingness to make peace. He qualified this latter statement by saying that now, for the first time, he discerned among the Arabs a readiness to enter into peace negotiations provided Israel first made a conciliatory gesture about frontiers and at least partial compensation for refugees. As to Jordan, he thought it important that "practical exchanges should take place on a lower level than those with the king." The latter, he thinks, is quite unable at the present time to carry his cabinet with him along the lines of the recent talks with Shiloah.

Thursday, July 20

To Lydda by 9:30 to see Hoskins off and to be of use in the event he had trouble with the censor. There I also found Bart Crum. The latter seemed very tired and, except for the Brown Hotels project, rather discouraged about his visit. I did not have time to talk fully with him or his two colleagues, Reich and Buncher. There was a chance for me, however, to ask Bart about his talk with Dave Niles. As I suspected, Bart had brought no message for me beyond the general one of good wishes from Dave. Bart on his own urged me very strongly to stay on the job because of my wonderful record and of what I could do in a possible future crisis. I was almost persuaded to believe that he really meant it!

Hoskins seemed pleased that I had come. I hope he will be more friendly in his report than I suspect he has been previously.

At Sharett's, large party for the visiting Israeli diplomats, I made an occasion to talk to Shiloah about Gibson's report. The Russians were out in force at the party, but I discreetly avoided meeting them.

McDonald's report to the Department of State was as follows:

---

39. McDonald to Department of State, no. 45, July 25, 1950, McDonald Papers, USHMM, box 9, folder 1.

40. See entries of April 1 and December 13, 1949.

I took Shiloah aside, outlined the charges and urged drastic and prompt corrective action. Shiloah's first response was that he was incredulous because of the following: 1) Both the regular and the security Israel Police had "positive orders" under no circumstances to make any special "survey" of a foreign mission or of any of its employees without specific authorization from the Foreign Office. 2) No such permission had been asked for and none had been granted to "survey" the Consulate General. 3) In the case of the Consulate General, unlike that of another foreign mission here, there was no necessity or excuse for any special security scrutiny. The "only possible explanation" Shiloah could imagine was that some "eager beaver" officer had on his own responsibility undertaken to secure information about the Consulate General in the "vain hope" that he might thus win commendation or promotion. In conclusion, Shiloah promised that he would make immediate inquiries and would report to me by the middle of the following week.

On July 24 Shiloah and Kollek visited McDonald's residence. They reported that the guilty party was an Israeli police officer acting without authorization and that the officer had been suspended and would be tried and punished.

McDonald reported,

In the general talk which followed, Shiloah deplored any possible misinterpretation by the Consulate General of his frankness in telling me that on some very special occasions the Israel police had taken special measures to secure information about one or two foreign missions. Such practice, he said, is common by governments and is justified when there is reason to suspect improper activity by a particular mission. He added that Israel was in these matters more punctilious than many governments because no branch of the Police could be authorized to take action towards a foreign mission without the categorical affirmation of the Foreign Office.[41]

Friday, July 21

McDonald and Ruth visited Cyprus over the weekend of July 21.

Our plane took off at nine and we were in Nicosia at 10:30. I was delighted to learn that the [Gerald] Drews [US minister in Amman] were not at the mountains but at Kyrenia.

The following are the chief points which should be noted about Drew's views:

1) He was emphatic that the king [of Jordan] cannot alone carry off negotiations with Israel; that instead, his cabinet must be considered and probably increasingly, because of the increasing power of Palestinian Arabs in Jordan[ian] counsels. On this point he was in complete agreement with Hoskins. As an example of Palestinian Arabs' intransigence, he cited the statement of a former resident of New Jerusalem, who said that he did not want compensation for his property, that he preferred to wait even a generation or two in the hope that finally Israel would collapse and his son or grandson would receive the property.

41. McDonald to Department of State, no. 45, July 25, 1950, McDonald Papers, USHMM, box 9, folder 1.

2) He adheres in the views expressed in his despatches that it is better to go slowly and not to urge too strongly the king to resume negotiations.
3) The king is one of the world's great chess players and loves to play chess in politics, but it is important that Israel recognize that the king is far from absolute.
4) He was critical of the Cleland visit [and] saw no necessity for it or for similar "junkets."
5) We are all to be invited to Joan's wedding on September 1 in Amman.

Saturday, July 22

Drew left at eleven. Sally, Nancy [embassy staff], and I left the hotel in time to reach the airport at four and were back in Lydda at 7:15. A pleasant supper and visit with Ford.

Monday, July 24

Meeting at the office in the morning. Fried suggested on the basis of factual items presented by Troxel that we should make an inquiry of someone near the top in the [Ministry of the] Treasury about the status of the pound and the Israel economic situation. Later, it was decided to postpone this until the return of [David] Horowitz early in August.

Tuesday, July 25

At teatime Mrs. John Gunther [Frances Fineman] came for an hour. Ware and McVicker were present. Though Mrs. Gunther had some interesting and provocative ideas about the need for new leadership in Asia and the desirability of utilizing for such purpose Nehru's unique position, I could not avoid the impression that she is personally on the brink of some possible personal tragedy.[42]

Wednesday, July 26

At the office conference, there was unanimity of opinion that the Israeli fighter plane's shooting down of the Lebanese DC-3 the day previous was the logical culmination of a stupid army policy.[43] [Captain Thomas] Brubaker[44] was intensely interesting as he explained the futility of shooting across a DC-3's bow unless the attacker intends to destroy the defenseless [air]craft,

---

42. See entry of December 17, 1949. Gunther and Fineman had visited Indian and Chinese leaders in the 1930s, and Fineman, interested in global peace initiatives, visited India in 1950 as Nehru's guest.

43. An Israeli fighter intercepted a Lebanese DC-3 that had crossed into Israeli airspace north of Rosh Pina. The Lebanese pilot had ignored instructions to land. A chase ensured, partly over Lebanon, and shots were fired. Lebanese reports were that two passengers were killed and seven injured. The incident got attention in Washington and at the UN. Israeli pilots were under orders to force down all aircraft operating outside established corridors, but after this incident, they were under strict orders not to shoot at civilian aircraft. *DFPI*, v. 5, d. 323–324; McDonald joint weeka no. 30, July 28, 1950, McDonald Papers, USHMM, box 9, folder 1.

44. Captain Thomas F. Brubaker (1921–2006), assistant air attaché, US embassy, Tel Aviv.

because it is not possible for the pilot of a DC-3 to know that he is being fired at.

Thursday, July 27

Ford and I went to see Kollek, to whom informally and personally I made three points: first, I suggested that it would be wiser if Shiloah did not press the Herut issue, because it was fantastic that any American money was being made available to the organ of one of the Herut factions; second, I personally urged that he report to his superiors my private view that the Lebanese incident had cost Israel heavily in America and, in the event of a similar [event] with the result of the loss of American lives, the resulting American opinion could be grave. Kollek made no defense, except to say that it was very difficult to get the Army to admit a mistake unless the order came from the very top; third, I explained my inability to see Ben-Gurion in Jerusalem and my hope that it would be possible for him to see me somewhere else before I went home.

Mr. [Heinz] Graetz came to the house and for nearly an hour explained his relations with the American Export Lines, the role of the Israel-America Line, and his own relations to the US Steel and their Isthmian Lines.[45] Graetz is undoubtedly an able man.

Friday, July 28–29

Left for Jerusalem in time to reach the King David at about seven in the evening. The change in air was delightful. Lunch with Rabbi and Mrs. Stern of Montreal.[46]

Over to Ben-Gurion's residence to have tea with Paula and to see the house. Before going, I had been told that Ben-Gurion was on his way to Eilat for the weekend. The house is substantially larger than the one in Tel Aviv but furnished not nearly so well as is Sharett's house. Paula's personal touches have added little to it. About a quarter past five, to my complete surprise, Ben-Gurion appeared in his slippers and shirt-sleeves looking much like the traditional Santa Claus. He took a seat in my corner, and after he had had his tea and the ladies had been shooed out, we had nearly an hour's talk.[47]

45. Isthmian Lines was owned by US Steel, for which Meir Dizengoff & Co. operated as an agent in Israel. Heinz Graetz purchased three older ships from the Isthmian Lines, renaming one the *Abraham Graetz* after his father. The three ships operated under the Israel-America Line, competing with ZIM. See also entries of January 11 and May 1, 1950.

46. Rabbi Harry Joshua Stern (1897–1984), Lithuanian-born Reform rabbi and Zionist; trained at Hebrew Union College and then served at Temple Emanuel in Montreal, 1927–1972; worked for improvements in interfaith relations among Jews and Christians both.

47. McDonald's subsequent diary description of the meeting contains personal information concerning his home leave and a less clear description of the geopolitical discussion. The editors have instead inserted the relevant section of McDonald's official report to the secretary of state, no. 61, July 31, 1950, *FRUS*, 1950, v. V, 960–961. See also Ben-Gurion Diary, entry of July 29, 1950. McDonald's memoirs suggest that the talk with Ben-Gurion in Jerusalem might have been more than pure accident. McDonald, *My Mission in Israel*, 226–227.

McDonald reported to Washington as follows: "*Importance of Prime Minister's disclosure reported below will I hope excuse my accidental violation of Department's standing instructions [regarding] my actions in Jerusalem. [To] escape [the] Tel Aviv heat and attend [the] Bach concert, I was in Jerusalem July 28–30. Being informed [that the] Prime Minister was in [Eilat], Mrs. McDonald and I had tea [at] his residence with Mrs. Ben-Gurion where to my complete surprise [the] Prime Minister joined us.*"

McDonald focused on Ben-Gurion's statements concerning his desire to come to Washington to discuss 'on the highest level' Israeli participation with the United States and United Kingdom in the regional defense of the Middle East. Ben-Gurion mentioned US sponsorship of an intensified three-year period of immigration that would bring the Israeli population to two million people and the building, with American armaments, of an army numbering 250,000 men.

> Prime Minister hopes he "*can convince President Truman, Secretary Acheson and [the] US military that America's vital interest would be served by [the] proposed strengthening of Israel as [the] only country other than Turkey in [western] Asia willing to fight Russian aggression to [the] limit of [its] strength.*" Prime Minister feels [that] American Jews would give or lend money required beyond [US government] possible loans only if [the US] first sponsors intensified Israel efforts to speed up immigration.
>
> In answer to my question [regarding] Israel left-wing labor, [the] Prime Minister said confidently, "*[The] Israeli people would support crushing any form [of] Communist collaboration in [the]event [of] world conflict. Only [a] few Mapam [leaders] could possibly cause embarrassment and this locally.*" [A] Re-equipped and enlarged Israeli army "*would guarantee Israeli unity in support of [the] West.*" If Russia attacked Israel's strategic airfields, "*Israel's new army could and would hold until US and UK forces could arrive.*"
>
> Comment: Conscious of large implications of [the] effects [of the] Prime Minister's proposal upon US overall [Middle East] policy, I gave no indication [concerning] possible Washington response. Prime Minister could not have been more explicit in [his] willingness [to] commit Israel unreservedly to [the] West. His statement is doubly significant because it follows and doubtless represents consensus [of] opinion [in the] Foreign Office and [among] diplomats whose fortnight conference Tel Aviv and Jerusalem he attended. Although Israel's attitude [is] strengthened by increasing difficulties [in the] internal economy, I believe it basically represents [the] culmination of realization by Israeli leaders that Israel can survive only in [a] world freed from [the] menace of Communist aggression. To defend itself Israel would fight against Russian invaders as desperately as against Arabs.

As I was leaving, he said he would see me again before my "home leave."

In the evening back to the performance by [Frank] Pelleg of Bach, Goldberg Variations.

Monday, July 31

Some fifty members of the World [Jewish] Congress group were at the house in the late morning.

Ruth and I attended the wedding of the daughter of the Tel Aviv chief rabbi[48] in the Great Synagogue. The proceedings began an hour late because of the delayed arrival of Rabbi [Yitzhak] Herzog. The actual wedding ceremony was on the roof under a canopy under the platform of which were crowded twice as many people as could comfortably stand there, Ruth and I among them.

48. Rabbi Isser Yehuda Unterman (1886–1976), Belorussian-born rabbi who served in Liverpool, 1924–1946; chief rabbi in Tel Aviv (Ashkenazic), 1946–1964; chief rabbi of Israel (Ashkenazic), 1964–1972.

26. August 1950

Tuesday, August 1

Mr. [S. M. Levin] of South Africa and his friends brought me the framed certificate of my enrollment in the Golden Book of the Jewish National Fund.[1]

Mr. Fish of Chicago, a production engineer, came at three to tell me of his work here with Histadrut and the Manufacturers Association. Rather to my surprise, he testified that he had found no deliberate slowing up of work by the workers. The chief reason for low production, he thought, was poor machines and poor utilization of them.

John A. Waldo, Jr. of the Palestine Desk,[2] came for lunch on his way to Jerusalem to confer with the PCC.[3] This is an excellent opportunity for him to get acquainted for the first time with the field. We had a pleasant visit, but he told me very little that was new; nothing at all about my successor. I was glad to learn from him that [Burton] Berry had become second-in-command to McGhee and served during the latter's absences as acting assistant secretary.

In the late afternoon out to Netanya on the new road covering the entire distance in less than half an hour. The mayor, [Oved] Ben-Ami, gave us a motor view of the city, which enabled me for the first time to appreciate the far-sighted planning of the community. It seems to me the best planned of any city in Israel.

After an outdoor dinner, the Israel[-America] Friendship League meeting was held in the open air at the theatre. The management estimated that a thousand people were present. I would have put it at little more than half that. I spoke on the "UN in Action," contrasting the present Korean policy with the failures to meet the aggressors in Manchuria in '31 and Ethiopia in the middle '30s and Hitler's reoccupation of the Rhineland in '36.

Back home in time to go to the Fords' to visit for a little while with them and Waldo. There I had my first opportunity to see Mrs. Ethridge's book. What a cheap and tawdry performance![4]

---

1. S. M. Levin, general secretary, South African Zionist Federation office in Tel Aviv; tracked the number of South African Jews who settled in Israel.

2. In the Bureau of Near Eastern, South Asian, and African Affairs, Department of State.

3. The PCC reconvened in Jerusalem on August 5 after having concluded its Geneva meetings on June 15.

4. Willie Snow Ethridge (1900–1982), wife of Mark Ethridge and author. McDonald refers to her *Going to Jerusalem* (1950), based on her and her husband's time in the Middle East, which followed a breezy and confused anti-Zionist line and received poor reviews.

A long and useful visit with Jacob Herzog. His theory about the aggression in Korea is that Russia knew that the northern forces would cut through the South, that the US would intervene, and that the result would be to strengthen the communist propaganda in the rest of Asia that the US is the aggressor. He thought that the president, however, could not have done differently from what he did do because of the pressure of American opinion.

As to Jerusalem, he is of the opinion that Rome will try to maintain the principle of the last General Assembly even though there is no prospect of the [Jerusalem] statute being implemented. He shares the view credited to His Holiness that the communist military strength is so great that the Russian forces could drive through Western Europe in a matter of hours. He wondered whether even in a world conflict Israel and Palestine might not be respected as the Holy Land. I thought this question showed naïveté unusual in him.

[In the afternoon], Ruth and I drove to meet the New York University workshop group at the Katznelson Institute.[5] It is a delightful plant, the most modern, with the exception of the Weizmann Institute, that I have visited in Israel. It is a pleasure to meet the students. Back to the house in time to have a bite of supper and to attend the Yugoslav opera company concert tonight at the amphitheater.

Thursday, August 3

On July 31, 1950, some American Jewish leaders, including Rose Halprin, Henry Montor, Jacob Blaustein, and Dewey Stone, arrived in Israel for discussions with government and Jewish Agency members. The subject was Israel's precarious economic situation, which had been exacerbated by the Korean War, the arrival of 91,000 Jewish immigrants since January 1950, price controls and rationing of many everyday items, and a drop in contributions by American Jews, partly due to their disappointment in Israel's nonaligned status.

The group concluded that Israel would need $1.5 billion over three years to absorb 600,000–1,000,000 new immigrants and that two-thirds of the money would have to come from the United States in the form of fundraising drives, in addition to what could be raised by the United Jewish Appeal and through US government loans. On August 3, the cabinet also discussed making a tangible contribution to the UN effort in Korea. Rejecting Ben-Gurion's call to send a small contingent of IDF soldiers to enhance Israel's international image, the cabinet accepted Sharett's proposal to send medical aid to UN forces.[6]

Among the guests at [the] Sharetts for dinner besides the hosts and ourselves were the Dewey Stones,[7] Harry Levines,[8] Mr. [Irving] Raab of Boston

5. Entry of July 19, 1949.
6. *DFPI*, v. 5, 451, 457, d. 330, 352.
7. See entry of April 3, 1949.
8. See entry of May 31, 1949.

chain stores,[9] and three or four others. After dinner, as we sat out of doors, I brought up the question of the exclusion of American publications in Israel from the recent treasury [Ministry of Finance] reallocation of funds and pointed out how Russian publications had replaced ours through the Russian use of its blocked ruble account. I also explained that the British in their blocked Israeli pounds settlement[10] had included a provision for 40,000 pounds importation of British publications. I stressed that the result was wholly unacceptable to the United States. Sharett's first reply, based on the brief memorandum handed him by Teddy Kollek, was that the treasury had left the matter to the educational minister.[11] This, I showed at once, was merely passing the buck. Sharett gave the impression that he would do the utmost to have the matter rectified.

Then, capitalizing on this breaking of the ice, I brought up seriously the Lebanese plane incident[12] and argued that it had involved serious loss for Israel in American opinion, and if in [a] subsequent incident American lives were lost, it would be very serious for the UJA. Sharett gave the usual answers, the right to protect sovereignty, frequent violations, dangers of aerial photographing, [and the] need to show states unwilling to make peace that they cannot operate freely over Israeli territory. I insisted on the unfavorable reaction among the diplomatic corps and the danger to Israel if there were a recurrence. I added that among the diplomats here there is the conviction that the Army rejects advice from the Foreign Office and listens only to specific orders from Ben-Gurion.[13] Finally, I got the impression that despite his bold defense, Sharett was unhappy about the incident and fearful about a possible recurrence.

The rest of the evening until after eleven was spent in an extremely interesting exchange of views about ways in which Israel might find the essential funds additional to the UJA funds. Raab presented a number of new ideas, Sharett hinted at the three-year plan, which had been discussed with [Henry] Montor. At the end, after I had suggested that the younger men in the treasury and related departments should be assigned to study the possibilities here and in the States, Sharett said that he thought [David] Horowitz, on his return, should be freed from other responsibilities for some weeks and concentrate on this problem.

Saturday, August 5

Quiet day except in the afternoon. We met Sam Sacks for tea [and] talked about the retailers strike and the [Dov] Joseph clothing and shoe rationing

---

9. Irving William Raab (1913–2011), Boston retailer, founder of Stop & Shop stores, active in Jewish causes and philanthropy.
10. See entry of March 22, 1950.
11. Zalman Shazar; see entry of May 5, 1950.
12. See entry of July 26, 1950.
13. McDonald's assessment was correct because of the IDF's confidence in Ben-Gurion stemming from the independence period.

scheme.[14] Sam, who is a notorious private-initiative individual and chronically critical of the Histadrut, was this time sharply critical of the strikers, whom [he] considered to be jeopardizing the position of private industry in Israel by going counter to the obvious need for time and, in the case of many of them, by seeking to maintain a position where they could exploit a seller's market. Sam doubted that the industrialists would thwart the shopkeepers. Sam explained to me that Histadrut was not guilty, as commonly charged, of having forced the large cement works in the north, Nesher, to sell out.[15] Sam explained that the owners, one of them no longer interested and the other desirous of clearing up his affairs, had willingly sold out.

At the Sharon chatted for half an hour or so with Judge, former congressman, [Samuel] Dickstein, who was there with his wife and daughter.[16]

Sunday, August 6

At Sharett's house from five-thirty until after seven. Following tea with the ladies, he and I spent more than an hour in the study. First part of our talk was about my retirement and possible successor. Sharett urged that I return to stay, but that in any event, I come back to make my formal adieus. On both points I maintained a listener's brief. As to my successor, he was definite that they would not desire a Jew and would prefer a career man who had not had previous personal experience in this area.

Then Sharett developed at length for more than half an hour his ideas for a regional aid scheme from the United States, which he considers preferable.[17] This should be designed for and on a sufficient scale to resettle the refugees in Arab territories and to speed up the immigration and settlement of Jews in Israel. He argued that thus the US would avoid taking sides. I refrained from attempting to predict what the attitude of the Department might be, but suggested merely that the Arabs would surely regard his scheme as the means towards the Jewish refugee victory and of building up Israel to the point where it might menace its neighbors. If this were the Arab reaction, Sharett said, then there could be no regional plan.

He then turned to the idea of some form of Marshall aid. This, he said, could not be acceptable, however, if it were coupled with the right of US representatives at the UN to whisper [voting] instructions to Israel delegates, or the right of the US to have representatives in Israel who would have the right to

14. Among the many items rationed on Joseph's orders were shoes and textiles. Some 12,000 merchants across the country affiliated with the General Merchants Association closed between July 31 and August 8 in protest of the government's steps.

15. Nesher, the main Israeli cement manufacturing facility near Haifa, began operating in 1925 and was the major factory in the construction sector. The company planned to build a new factory in Ramle in 1950.

16. Samuel Dickstein (1885–1954), Lithuanian-born US congressman (D-NY), 1923–1945; helped establish the House Committee on Un-American Activities, but might also have been a Soviet agent; justice on New York State Supreme Court, 1946–1954.

17. Refers to Ben-Gurion's proposals to McDonald given in Jerusalem on July 29, 1950.

influence Israel's social and economic policies. [Sharett said Israel would gladly accept conditions similar to those that came with the Export-Import Bank loan.] As Sharett talked, I got the impression that his attitude is really less cocky than his words might indicate, and that what he said was only his opening proposal and that he might later, as the price of US aid, agree to concessions to facilitate peace with the Arabs.[18]

As to Ben-Gurion's proposed visit, I was not of course definite about the possibility of an official invitation, but I was not encouraging, though of course I had to admit that form would contribute most to the success of the mission. Sharett said that Ben-Gurion would go even if the attitude were merely one of welcome.

Monday, August 7

Out to Lydda to say goodbye to Rose Halprin. There was little time to talk, because she arrived late. Nonetheless, I was able to reinforce some of the points I had made to her the other day when she came to the house unexpectedly and stayed for nearly an hour.

At twelve, [Seyfulla] Esin came in for a talk before he went on leave. Of most interest were two points: 1) his report that he had urged Sharett vigorously to make some refugee concession in the interest of peace; it looks now as if Turkey were seeking to act as a sort of mediator. His second point was even more startling. He reported that George Weidenfeld[19] had said that the Israeli Army was convinced that Russia would overrun the Middle East quickly in the event of a world conflict and that, therefore, Israel should strive for a policy which would enable it to have the same relation with the conqueror, or a comparable relationship to that which Denmark had with the Nazis. Both Esin and I doubted whether this was a representative opinion. But whether it was or not, it strengthened my view that Weidenfeld is an unreliable, if not dangerous, person.

McDonald reported, "Israel–Turkish relations on all fronts are excellent. Turk[ish] Minister in Israel has been carrying out [a] quiet campaign [in an] attempt [to] convince [the] Israel Gov[ernment of the] necessity [to] permit [a] substantial number [of] Arab refugees [to] return [to] Israel as [a] possible means [of] breaking [the] present peace deadlock. Turks have nothing to lose in this effort and much to gain. [Should] by some presently unforeseen chance Israel agree[s] to [the] Turkish proposal, [the] Turkish desire [to] establish leadership in [the Middle East would] be greatly enhanced."[20]

In September, Israel backed Turkey for the seat on the UN Security Council vacated by Lebanon.

18. McDonald's report of this meeting to the State Department in embassy's no. 75, August 8, 1950, *FRUS*, 1950, v. V, 966–967.
19. Entry of June 15, 1950.
20. McDonald, joint weeka, no. 32, August 11, 1950, McDonald Papers, USHMM, box 9, folder 3.

Interesting talk with [Milton] Fried at teatime. He gave no indication of having decided to go home in October [as had been rumored among the embassy staff]. Instead, he talked about the possibility of moving into the Hoopers' place. About the future here, he was especially interesting. His suggestions for procedure deserve very close attention, as do his interpretations of the attitudes of various personalities. Fried's estimate of [Pinhas] Lubianker made me wish that I might, despite my leaving in the near future, have a visit with Lubianker. Fried's estimate was strikingly similar to mine.[21] He appraised him as a great moral force, which is being wasted in a secondary administrative post. He thought that he with Ben-Gurion were two of the people who could do most to save Mapai from the dry rot of institutionalism, which had been the death sentence of earlier social democratic parties.

Tuesday, August 8

Rabbi [Samuel] Wohl of Cincinnati[22] visited for half an hour or so, and would have stayed longer had not I been so tired and needing rest before the arrival of Palmer and Waldo. Wohl had two chief ideas—one a series of lectures at the Hebrew University or the Katznelson Institute, to be known as the James G. McDonald Lectures. I thought the idea of the lectures good, but was less than enthusiastic about the title, which, I said, in any case could not be used while I am in office.

Wohl's second idea was the establishment of an American-Israel Institute, which would feature as its rallying cry a monumental Liberty Bell on Mount Carmel comparable to the Statue of Liberty in New York. I thought the idea of striving to make the United States better known in Israel through such an institute was needed. I urged him to check with the Israel-America Friendship League people in order to learn what was being planned at present. Wohl is very well informed.

Ely E. Palmer and Jack Waldo arrived at 1:15 and stayed until 3:30. We had a very pleasant and useful visit. I did most of the talking, laying out frankly the situation here as I saw it. Palmer listened with closest attention. As to my known views on the PCC, Palmer indicated no resentment but rather understanding. He did not say whether they expected to continue beyond the next [General] Assembly. The [PCC] is planning to go to Cairo again this week,

21. Then the secretary-general of Histadrut. See entries of December 19, 1949, and March 27, 1950. In a discussion with Fried on August 2, 1950, Lubianker argued that Britain's Middle Eastern strategic interests were not served by peace between Jordan and Israel and that he had it on good authority that British officers had told members of Abdullah's cabinet to move slowly. He urged the US government to become more involved in pressing for a peaceful settlement between Israel and Jordan. Ford to secretary of state, no. 74, August 11, 1950, USSDCF–PIFA, 1950–1954, reel 1, frames 558–560.

22. Rabbi Samuel Wohl (1895–1972), Ukrainian-born rabbi serving Cincinnati's Bene Yeshurun congregation, 1931–1966; member of Hebrew Union College board of governors; labor Zionist and delegate to World Zionist Congress. He stood with Ben-Gurion when Israeli independence was declared.

and it is possible for me to see Palmer again in Jerusalem at the same time that I hope to see Riley.

The PCC reconvened in Jerusalem on August 5, 1950. After consultations there it began a series of visits to the Middle Eastern capitals. None of the discussions moved the parties toward peace. Even King Abdullah now seemed reluctant because of vocal Palestinian Arab opposition within Jordan.[23] The PCC was expected to return to Geneva in September, where it was to prepare a report for submission to the UN General Assembly.[24]

McVicker came in just before the men left. I was startled to have him speak of [Moshe] Dayan as a "madman." He backed away from it later, but the fact that he gave such an outburst was somewhat disquieting.

Wednesday, August 9

At the [staff] meeting all of us were intrigued by the frankness of Ben-Gurion's proposals[25] and by the reservations which Sharett included in his elaboration of one of his chief's suggestions.

One of the first subjects I brought up at the nearly hour's session with Eban and Kollek was the form of their chief's presentation to me. Naturally, they were inhibited from open criticism, but I got the impression that there had been elements of improvisation, if not something akin to panic in the formulation.

Both Eban and Kollek stressed that it was important that I should return, if only for a few weeks. They put this in such a way that I could not doubt that they were expressing an official opinion, or that they would press in Washington to have this carried out. After a frank analysis of personalities, both in our mission and in the Foreign Office, I urged strongly that if Kollek were to leave for the States, it would not be sufficient if Esther Herlitz were left in charge of the [North] American Desk. Their counter-proposal was that Shiloah be assigned general responsibility for the desk and that he be available for all major purposes. I agreed that this would be excellent.

Thursday, August 10

An explosive meeting at the office. I was shocked by [Major Reed] Booth's statement that he had reported to Washington, without consultation with any of us, rumors that substantial parts of the Israeli Army were so convinced that the Russians would occupy the Middle East in a world conflict that they thought it wise for Israel to prepare for making the best terms possible with the conqueror. Outraged by this lack of team play, I demanded that there must be no more reporting without my knowledge on issues of political import and reminded

23. Palmer's reports are included in *FRUS*, 1950, v. V, 973–981. Also *DFPI*, v. 5, d. 337, 338, 339, 341, 342, 356 and editor's note, p. 504.
24. Memorandum by James M. Ludlow, August 17, 1950, *FRUS*, 1950, v. V, 971–973.
25. See entry of July 29, 1950.

those present that I had sent home two military attachés [Colonels Andrus and Archibald] and was ready to send the third one home. All-in-all, it was a very unpleasant half hour and was as much of a surprise to the staff as it was to me. My only regret is that I did not find an occasion to explode in a similar fashion in the early weeks of Andrus's regime.

Friday, August 11

Shiloah came about half past twelve and stayed for more than an hour. He, as had Eban and Kollek, sought to give the impression that the prime minister's and foreign minister's recent statements to me had been informal thinking out loud. I was not persuaded.

McDonald reported to Washington that Kollek was "slightly worried" about Ben-Gurion's and Sharett's linkage of US support for mass immigration to Israeli defense commitments to the West. The informal proposal, Kollek said, would meet opposition in Mapai and groups further to the left. McDonald also paraphrased Kollek's comments that "unlimited immigration was [the] most sacrosanct tenet of present government and since it now realized [that this] policy can only be carried out with assistance [of] Western Jewry, principally American Jewry, [the] Prime Minister and those advisers consulted had decided upon [the] necessity for radical change in basic policy."[26]

Shiloah said that he would be available to Ford [in McDonald's absence], though he doubted if he could take the responsibility of the [North] American desk. This was especially difficult because there was a reorganization in the process of the Middle East desk which involves him. He plans, however, to see Ford regularly and to utilize their lunches together as a means of keeping one another informed.

On the issue of relations with Jordan and particularly that of the [prospective] meeting of Dayan and a high Jordanian officer, Shiloah said that he was convinced that the trouble in Jordan was complete confusion rather than ill-will. No one seemed to have or be willing to exercise real authority.

In connection with Jordan he returned to his favorite thesis that Britain and we are not doing enough to strengthen those who would make peace. He does not credit the reports that the opposition to peace is so strong that the king dare not move against it. On the contrary, he insists that if Britain and we indicated a firm purpose, the very people who are now most intransigent would ease their opposition. He did not, however, ask that I report again this point of view since we have told the Department of it so often; I did not include it in [the] telegram drafted later today.

---

26. McDonald to secretary of state, nos. 86, 87, August 11 and 12, 1950, summarized in *FRUS*, 1950, v. V, 967, n. 1.

On the issue of my return for at least a courtesy farewell, Shiloah was emphatic. He said that this was more than a personal matter; that I was the first ambassador to Israel and relations of Israel to the US were special and that, therefore, some formal indication should be given through a more ceremonial departure. I said that I would do whatever the president and the Department wished.

Regarding the general international situation, Shiloah confirmed the definitely pro-Western point of view that was indicated by the prime minister.

Pleasant tea with [the] Jan Peerces and with Rabbi and Mrs. Korff,[27] whom I did not identify as the notorious leader in the arms smuggling movement until the guests were almost ready to leave. I found him unattractive.

Sunday, August 13

While Ruth went with Shalom out to meet Miss Coates at the airfield, I drove the station wagon downtown for my appointment with [Pinhas] Lubianker. I found Lubianker quiet, modest and brilliantly logical. First we discussed the international situation in general terms, he giving the indication of support of the Ben-Gurion position. Regarding Mapam, there are, he said, three distinct groups, each with elements of differences within each. Nonetheless, each presents a united front within the party, and the party as a whole in return is unified in its public expressions and actions in the Knesset. It is not yet communist but may be said to be on the way. He gave an intriguing explanation of the reasoning by which intelligent people support Russia despite its clear anti-Zionism.[28] That policy is based on "misunderstanding." Efforts must be made to "clear up this misunderstanding"; after all, Zionism and Israel must loom "very small" in the eyes of Moscow, which has such vast projects in hand; hence, the Zionists should work for their ideals while sympathizing with Russia's world ideas in the hope that in the future the two lines of development will meet and support one another.

On the economic front, Lubianker was 100% for increased production through modernization of management and with the cooperation of labor. He cited the large results already achieved in ATA where Moller had agreed to let

27. Rabbi Baruch D. Korff (1914–1995), Ukrainian-born rabbi and Revisionist Zionist; as a child witnessed his mother's murder in a pogrom in 1919; emigrated to the United States, 1926; ordained a rabbi, 1934; deeply involved in Jewish rescue and ransom efforts during World War II; after the *Exodus* incident in 1947, was arrested for his involvement in a plot to carry out a reprisal bombing at Buckingham Palace; worked with IZL during Israeli War of Independence; rabbi of Temple Israel in Portsmouth, New Hampshire, 1950.

28. Explanations in Benjamin Pinkus, *The Soviet Government and the Jews, 1948–1967: A Documented Study* (New York: Cambridge University Press, 1984); and Ya'akov Ro'i and Avi Beker, eds., *Jewish Culture and Identity in the Soviet Union* (New York: New York University Press, 1991). Also see relevant essays in Zvi Gitelman, *A Century of Ambivalence: The Jews of Russia and the Soviet Union* (Bloomington: Indiana University Press, 2001); Zvi Gitelman and Ya'akov Ro'i, eds., *Revolution, Repression, and Revival: The Soviet-Jewish Experience* (Lanham, MD: Rowman & Littlefield, 2007); and Gennady Estraikh, *Yiddish in the Cold War* (London: Legenda, 2008).

the three workers who had been to the States block out a reorganization.[29] Incidentally, I discovered that Sam Sacks was a special subject of Lubianker's criticism. He terms him a merchant, not a manufacturer. On the issue of Histadrut seeking to monopolize industry or to penalize private enterprise, Lubianker denied the charge *in toto*. He said that there were rumors aplenty, and never was one proved. He was sympathetic to the need for a more efficient concentration of government brains in integrating the many ideas of stimulating capital investments here. He doubted, however, that Horowitz was the man to head the group, because he is "too much of a professor," and also too willing to be convinced that a problem cannot be solved.

When I suggested that Goldie [Meyerson] should be freed of her administrative responsibility to devote her time to moral leadership, Lubianker said, "You know too much for an ambassador." He added, "If you can accomplish this you will have done the country a great service." He seems to feel that Ben-Gurion would like to make this change, but that Goldie is unwilling to relinquish the Labor cabinet post.

Monday, August 14

At teatime, Dr. Leo Kohn told me all about UNESCO and the meeting at Florence. He deplored the US delegation's strenuous and political efforts on behalf of Germany.[30] I was surprised that he was not informed about Ben-Gurion's and Sharett's recent statements to me. He was very critical of Vera Weizmann, saying that she was responsible for Chaim Weizmann's hard trip to Switzerland, whereas it could have been perfectly comfortable during the summer in one of the nice homes in Jerusalem or in a summer home built for him on the heights nearby, but that Vera could not bear twelve months of "these Jews." He was critical, too, of George Weidenfeld, whom he characterized as a dilettante and a playboy. In answer to my question about the situation of the Israeli constitution, Kohn replied that he thought the decision to proceed in the Knesset with a series of fundamental enactments was in fact an important step towards the making of the constitution.

Tuesday, August 15

Having arrived in Jerusalem before midnight the previous evening, I was up early and had a nearly two-hour conference with [General] Riley, beginning at nine. I was delighted to meet Mrs. Riley and their daughter Kathie, just turning sixteen. I was sorry to miss the boy.

29. Refers to the ATA textile factory, founded by Erich and Hans Moller of Czechoslovakia in 1934 and the largest textile factory in Israel. In the 1930s and 1940s it produced work clothes and uniforms reflective of the Zionist ethic. The management was sympathetic to labor.

30. The fifth meeting of UNESCO was held in Florence in May and June 1950. Kohn refers to economic and scientific developments projected for West Germany and West German membership in UNESCO, which was decided in 1951. See John Krige, *American Hegemony and the Postwar Reconstruction of Science in Europe* (Boston: MIT Press, 2006), 65–71. See also the Israeli assessment of Germany's status, in *DFPI*, v. 5, d. 328.

Our talk covered a wide range. First he told me about his efforts at Lake Success and his inability to persuade the Department to move to end the PCC and to strengthen the MACs and the authority of the UN chief of staff.[31] The explanations given to him were not very different from those I had heard of here. He went on to say that unless he was enabled to do more than at present, he would not wish to continue in the area. Later, when I was telling him of the suggestion, presumably put forward by Dave Niles regarding my successor here, Riley did not say that he would not be interested. On the contrary, he remained discreetly silent. My impression was that he would accept if he were urged to do so.

He [Riley] argues strongly for action to break the present deadlock. He doubted that time would work in the favor of peace. On the contrary, he expressed fear that the [Mount] Scopus situation might blow up.[32] He explained that under Article VIII of the armistice, Jordan was obligated to discuss the opening of the roads to Scopus, that meanwhile through his (Riley's) initiative, there was a continued violation of the July 7, 1948 [Mount Scopus] agreement through the continuance of the Arab [Women's] Hospital in the [Augusta Victoria Hospital]. When he brought this to the attention of the Jordanian authorities, they answered that as far as they were concerned, the hospital could be closed.[33] This Riley was unwilling to have done because of the penalty which it would inflict upon the innocent patients there. Riley continued that the Israelis have been very conciliatory, agreeing repeatedly not to make a fuss about the hospital but he was fearful lest, should there be more delay, some incident would involve an open break. It was no secret, he said, that the recent Israel blowing up of the three houses on the border line of the frontier had been carried through in a spectacular manner in contemplation of the possibility that the Arabs would fire and that then the Israelis could proceed to take Scopus by force. This was an extraordinarily interesting interpretation, and made sense out of what otherwise seemed to me a mere useless bravado action.

Regarding Jerusalem itself, General Riley seemed to share [Raleigh] Gibson's views that the Israelis were anxious for a settlement, but that whether one was reached or not at the Assembly, there would be a strong, perhaps irresistible, demand that the Foreign Office be moved. In this event, the US would be

31. See entry of July 17, 1950; memorandum by John W. Halderman, July 11, 1950, *FRUS, 1950*, v. V, 949–950; *DFPI*, v. 5, d. 319, 340.
32. Avraham Biran (1909–2008), the Israeli Foreign Ministry's representative in Jerusalem (and one of Israel's best known archaeologists), had told Riley that Israel might take matters into its own hands in opening up the road to Mount Scopus. Riley warned that unilateral action would further unite all Arab states against Israel. It was better, Riley said, to work through Article VIII, which was designed for such issues, and then through the MAC. See *DFPI*, v. 8, d. 340.
33. The Augusta Victoria Hospital on Mount Scopus had been used by the Arab population before 1948. The hospital was leased in April 1949 by the Red Cross to aid refugees. The Israelis protested the Red Cross's use of the hospital because the Hadassah Hospital on Mount Scopus still remained inaccessible, but they were willing to allow both to be opened on the condition that Mount Scopus become accessible. Gibson to secretary of state, no. 108, April 24, 1950, USSDCF-PIFA, 1950–1954, reel 1, frames 479–482.

faced with a serious problem whether to recognize and also whether to move. Riley's view on this score was much the same as that I got later from Gibson. In general, Riley seemed to me more stirred to speed action and more sympathetic to the attitude of the Jews than at any previous time.

Towards the end of our talk we were joined by Elath, with whom I went to my room for a longish chat. Mostly it was a reiteration or a reemphasis of points of view I had heard from him previously. He, too, was inclined to play down Ben-Gurion's and Sharett's statements when I reported them to him. A little wryly, he confirmed what Eban had told me earlier, that the conference of diplomats had not discussed these matters. He is anticipating London being in a sense a continuation of Washington.

Elath was reassigned to London, where he served as ambassador until 1959. Abba Eban, already the Israeli ambassador to the UN, took up the concurrent post as Israeli ambassador to the United States, a position that he also held until 1959.

Lunch with [Jacob] Blaustein and [Simon] Segal lasted more than an hour and a half. Blaustein was better informed than when I had last spoken to him.[34] He was much impressed by Ben-Gurion but was still troubled by reports of Histadrut's monopolistic and anti-capitalistic tendencies. I urged him to see Lubianker and get an account, which should be set off against those which he had been receiving from private businessmen.

Segal wondered whether Israel might not be urged to come out more openly for the West. I replied that these problems were being studied and discussed on the highest level, and I doubted if there would be any advantage in their intervention. Blaustein was interested in what I had to say about Fried and will I think, if he remembers it, speak to McGhee. He was also sympathetic to the Israeli idea that I should return for a formal farewell.

Before tea, over to the roof of Notre Dame de France. This time I went up by the stairs, through the part turned back to the monks. An intelligent English-speaking brother acted as my guide. It was a nostalgic and exciting experience.

The tea at Gibson's was in its talk a continuation of my discussions with Gibson in his office during the morning. He is very keen for the utmost efforts to speed up Jordan-Israel negotiations.[35] By implication he seconded Riley's view that [US minister Gerald] Drew in Amman appears to be so hesitant that one is tempted to think him under Kirkbride's influence.

Discussing his views that Israel will force the move-to-Jerusalem issue, Gibson outlined ways in which he thought the embassy could fit into existing space in Jerusalem. This was on the assumption that the consulate, the military, or most of them, and some of the functions of the labor attaché and commercial

34. Entry of April 7, 1949. Blaustein was still the president of the American Jewish Committee, and Segal was the director of its Foreign Affairs Department.
35. Negotiations at the time had stalled because of opposition to Abdullah's peace initiatives by Palestinian Arab leaders in Jordan. See *FRUS*, 1950, v. V, 975–981.

attaché would remain in Tel Aviv. I was not wholly convinced, but did not examine the matter as closely as I would have done had I felt that this would be my problem.

Back to Tel Aviv a little after eight.

Wednesday, August 16

Conference with Horowitz, Ford and Hooper. [Horowitz] was very interesting about his London and Washington trips. As to the proposal that he take over the direction of the planning for the US private and public financing, he, not unnaturally, pleaded preoccupation, especially in view of the fact that Kaplan must have a vacation. He denied that he and Kaplan inadequately delegated responsibility and pointed to several areas in which neither he nor Kaplan exercised any responsibility. (Later, a well-informed person was to criticize his analysis by pointing out that many final decisions in areas where responsibility had already been delegated did in fact come up to Kaplan or Horowitz.) Horowitz will, I think, because of his assignment of balance of payments, be the one to whom most responsibility for the US financing planning will go.

Tea with Sam Sacks. Evening dinner at Ford's. At the latter's were present the Sharetts, Hoopers, Shiloahs, [and] Kollek; afterwards, there was a nice party with most of the officers and some of the secretaries joining. At the end, Ruth and I were presented with an extraordinarily beautiful silver box by the staff. Ford's speech was just the right tone, and I tried to reciprocate. We did not stay much later, however, because Ruth was so tired. Subsequently I learned that Ted Kollek and perhaps some others stayed until two o'clock. This is really taking advantage of your host.

Thursday, August 17

Last minute clearing out and burning all classified documents higher than confidential, though I was heartbroken to give up many of the pieces. Farewell conference with Ben-Gurion at his house.

On August 7, 1950, McDonald received a State Department cable drafted by the Bureau for Near Eastern Affairs and approved by President Truman the same day. It concerned Ben-Gurion's statements of July 29, 1950, and McDonald's analysis. The Department was pleased to hear of Ben-Gurion's anticommunist stance, but it also noted that the president's Point Four program, the UN Relief and Works Agency [UNRWA], and the three-power declaration on arms sales in the Middle East were designed to stabilize the region. Ben-Gurion's proposal for "three-year immigration program providing for movement [of] approx[imately] one million people and direct [military assistance] by [United States government] for [a] greatly augmented Israeli Army are concepts whose implementation [would] be contrary to present programs and policies and [which would] thereby jeopardize current progress toward area stability and peace." US commitments in Europe and the Far East, the cable continued, made Ben-Gurion's concepts impossible to implement in any event. McDonald was to convey these thoughts to Ben-Gurion before he left Israel.[36]

I was a little early but met him in the hall and we immediately began our talk. The first fifteen minutes or so was given over to my explaining, at his request, the differences between the respective roles and responsibilities of Riley, PCC and [the UNRWA].

Then, we turned to the subject of our last talk, when, in a tone I could not quite decipher (it seemed a combination of mild annoyance, shamefacedness, and regret), he said that he was surprised that I had reported the interview, for he was speaking informally to an old friend and in Jerusalem! This last point was perhaps the least impressive of all, because he had specifically suggested that we have a serious talk in Jerusalem instead of attempting it in Tel Aviv, where there is "no time."[37] He did not indicate, and I of course did not remind him directly, that none of these reservations had been either implied or expressed by him during the Jerusalem talk. Anyhow, I expressed my regret that I had misunderstood and assured him, though I confess not with complete conviction, that no harm could have been done.

The rest of the talk was given over to his plans for the States. He was not enthusiastic, but he did not reject the idea that he might head the Israeli UN delegation. At the end, he was much intrigued by my suggestion that Goldie should be enabled to become the modern Deborah.[38] He agreed that it was desirable and did not dissent from my report that I understood she was unwilling to forego a cabinet post (the next day Sharett explained this on the ground that Goldie's lack of formal education had left her with a certain inferiority complex, which made her anxious to maintain status in the cabinet comparable to the others). As I was leaving and spoke a farewell, Ben-Gurion said, "But this sounds as if you were not coming back," with an evident tone of regret in his voice.

McDonald reported that the prime minister "was obviously disappointed [in the Department's message] but made no comment." Ben-Gurion would not come to the United States unless the Department of State approved of the visit and he could meet with Truman.[39] On August 20, Richard Ford reported, "[Israeli] government leaders at last realize [that] Ben-Gurion's explanation of [his] plan to Ambassador McDonald was premature and consider Ben-Gurion's action as blunder."[40]

36. Webb to embassy in Israel, no. 52, August 7, 1950, *FRUS*, 1950, v. V, 965.
37. Entry of June 3, 1950.
38. Reference to Deborah as fourth judge of pre-monarchic Israel in the Hebrew Bible's Book of Judges. She defeated Jabin, king of Canaan, and his military commander, Sisera, in battle. To refer to someone as a Deborah is to call her a strong and independent woman.
39. McDonald to secretary of state, no. 99, August 18, 1950, summarized in *FRUS*, 1950, v. V, 965, n. 2.
40. Ford to secretary of state, no. 101, August 20, 1950, summarized in *FRUS*, 1950, v. V, 965, n. 2.

Back to the house to find General and Mrs. Riley. We had a pleasant visit, the most reportable item being his account that the PCC had been met in Amman by a proposal that Article VIII be implemented and that a Special Committee be set up promptly.[41] General Riley was amused, as was I, by the reported discomfiture of some of the members of the PCC who had never heard of Article VIII. When the Rileys had gone, my wife made the penetrating suggestion that Mrs. Riley had insisted on coming down in order to see the house and as the prospective next tenant!

To the Toscanini film but so tired as to not enjoy it much. Met [Gene] Currivan [of the *New York Times*] there and intimated to him that his scoop might be proved to be inaccurate.[42] I made no pretense of being friendly, nor did my wife later.

Friday, August 18

Usual hectic packing. Sharett came in for a farewell and to bring gifts. As he was leaving, we chatted about rumors of General Riley. He said he had heard nothing, but returning to his office, he called up to say he had just had a telegram from Washington, which indicated that Riley was the preferred one.

Perhaps to scotch rumors of this kind, Acheson met with Truman at the White House on August 28, 1950. Truman agreed with Acheson that Riley would be a poor choice as McDonald's successor. As Acheson put it, "General Riley's present task was of the most vital importance and should not be prejudiced in any way." He continued that the next ambassador "should not be a partisan. He should be concerned with the interests of the United States. While he should be sympathetic with the nation to which he was accredited, he should not cause antagonism to the Arabs."[43]

Fried came in to get my draft of a telegram about my talk with the prime minister yesterday.[44] To my surprise, he said that at the office there was talk that the Israeli energetic playing down of the prime minister's Jerusalem talk had been because I had indicated that it might have been a mistake when I talked subsequently with Eban and Kollek. This interpretation, I told Fried, I

41. The Special Committee to implement Article VIII of the Israeli-Jordanian armistice agreement concerning the division of Jerusalem and access to various points within the city had been unsuccessful virtually since the implementation of the armistice itself. In Amman on August 14, 1950, Jordanian prime minister Sa'id Pasha al-Mufti proposed to the PCC that the Special Committee be reconstituted, and Palmer relayed this (along with other Jordanian and Arab demands) to the Israelis. Shiloah found the request odd, "because we have been pressing . . . for more than a year, not only to have [the Special Committee] reconstituted but to have it constituted. For all practical purposes it has not been in existence." However, because Abdullah thought that the formation of the Special Committee could help movement toward a general peace, Shiloah agreed with the proposal. Palmer to secretary of state, no. 40, August 17, 1950, *FRUS*, 1950, v. V, 973–975; Ford to secretary of state, no. 114, August 29, 1950, *FRUS*, 1950, v. V, 984–985; meeting between Sharett and PCC members, August 17, 1950, *DFPI*, v. 5, d. 341.
42. Perhaps in reference to Ben-Gurion's proposed visit to the United States.
43. Memorandum by Acheson, August 28, 1950, *FRUS*, 1950, v. V, 981.
44. Telegram no. 99, described earlier.

regarded as fantastic, because their reaction was based on their own judgment and not on what I thought or did not think.

Eban departed for the United States on August 19, 1950, to assume the ambassadorship there. Kollek unexpectedly went with him. Ford explained that Kollek's trip was "indicative [of the] state [of] nervous agitation [in] government circles [as a] result [of] final recognition [of] Ben-Gurion's blunder." In a meeting in the State Department Kollek disowned, on behalf of the Israeli government, Ben-Gurion's proposals.[45]

Moshe Keren, now the embassy's senior official, sent a long memorandum to the Foreign Ministry. He argued that emotive appeals to the president would be fruitless in the long term. "We cannot easily expect," Keren said, "a repetition of events like the recognition of Israel by the fist of the President without his even consulting the Department of State. Every request of ours must now pass though the [State] Department," which saw Israel as part of a broader geopolitical region where stability was the primary objective.[46]

On the day McDonald sailed, the Jerusalem Post *ran an editorial, "Farewell to a Friend," on the assumption that McDonald's home leave might become permanent. It is excerpted here:*

> *If we must say goodbye to him now, we do so with a deep sense of obligation for a constant understanding of our trials, and for a frank and friendly, yet . . . statesman-like advocacy of our cause in Washington. Cordial and mutually beneficial relations with America are in the forefront of our Government's policy. . . . It may be that Mr. McDonald fought our fight too well, and another may come in his place who may conceivably help us more by liking us less. . . . For our part, we thank Mr. McDonald and remember him with gratitude as the prototype of the unaffected, in the true sense philanthropic, and democratic American.[47]*

The *LaGuardia* Trip
August 18–September 1

We were both so tired that we had no incentive to try to work. Fortunately, the weather, the food and the service united to make the two weeks unusually enjoyable. Thanks to the wonderful cooperation of Manny Goldman,[48] who sent his truck to the pier to meet us and the special arrangements made by the Department representative, plus the excellent handling of our thirty-four pieces of luggage by the ship's personnel, we were off the pier and on our way home with Halsey and Bobby within a half hour of our disembarking. The weekend was thrilling with its opportunity to get acquainted with the babies [McDonald now had a second grandson] and to meet old friends.

---

45. Ford to secretary of state, no. 101, August 20, 1950, summarized in *FRUS*, 1950, v. V, 965, n. 2; memorandum by Rockwell, August 31, 1950, *FRUS*, 1950, v. V, 986–988.
46. Keren to United States Division, August 24, 1950, *DFPI*, v. 5, d. 352.
47. Quoted in Ford to secretary of state, no. 92, August 21, McDonald Papers, Columbia University, box 11, folder 6.
48. McDonald's friend who owned Goldman Brothers men's store in New York.

27. September–December 1950

McDonald reconnected with family in New York. He then went to Washington for deliberations in the State Department, partly to air his views on US policy toward Israel, partly to learn about his successor, and partly to determine whether he would return to Israel before his formal resignation. McDonald's original diary entries for these months are cluttered. The editors have rearranged the entries chronologically and eliminated redundancies.

In the Department
September 4–11

The arrangements for me in the Department were much better than they had been on my previous leave,[1] for this time my office was in the NEA [Bureau of Near Eastern, South Asian, and African Affairs] wing, and I saw casually much more of the officers. Moreover, I had a considerable number of formal conferences and spoke at three separate group meetings, but this time, as on my previous visit, I was to leave the Department without knowing much more about its policy towards Israel and the Arab States than I had known earlier.

During this first visit to Washington I spoke first to one of the regular weekly NEA meetings, where I stressed my views that PCC should be replaced by a one-man vigorous conciliator, or that in any case PCC should be given more momentum through the naming of a strong secretary; the need for greater pressure on both Israel and Jordan to get on with the peace-making, and the urgency of a settlement about Jerusalem. I argued that on no one of these accounts was time working for us, but rather to the contrary. I was listened to attentively, but there was no clear exposition then or later of the Department's policies. Rather, there was merely an unconvincing statement that the PCC should be kept in being as of possible contingent use.[2]

On a later occasion, I spoke again at a meeting of the same group, where Ambassador [Edward] Crocker [of Baghdad] was also present. Although the reports from different parts of the larger area were interesting, I received no clearer understanding of what the Department's policy in my segment is. The

---

1. See entry of August 22, 1949.
2. The PCC announced on September 2, 1950, that it had decided to terminate its sessions in Jerusalem and the Arab capitals. It would renew its deliberations in New York on October 2, 1950. Palmer told the Israelis before leaving the Middle East that he hoped they would make contact with the PCC at that time. *DFPI*, v. 5, 517.

third occasion at which I expressed my views was a meeting of the assistant secretaries under the chairmanship of [Undersecretary of State James] Webb. Here I made the same points as earlier and was listened to attentively, but I did not receive the impression that anything would be changed by what I had said.

It was interesting to be in the Department during the days of the Naharayim crisis.[3] Seemingly the Department was temporarily swept off its feet by the Jordanian charges and moved to ask the mission in Tel Aviv to make vigorous inquiries. I asked whether they had yet received a report from Riley and received a negative reply. I mildly suggested that to act on one-sided reports, whether the charges came from Jordanian or Israeli sources, was to encourage irresponsible charges and would tend to short-circuit the Mixed Armistice Commission. Within a few days reports from Riley and from Ford, which showed that there had been no Israeli invasion, fully justified my caution.

On several occasions I chatted briefly with [Fraser] Wilkins, [Stuart] Rockwell, and some of the other junior officials. My talk with Wilkins was too short to be significant. . . . With Rockwell, during several talks, I caught glimpses of his own personal view, but was never sure that these represented the Department. He is a brilliant and independent-minded young man. I was a little surprised to note that neither of these two men appeared to be in "the know" on the question of the Department's plans for my successor. With [William] Cleland I spoke once or twice in the halls only.

George McGhee was away during this visit, and most of my talks, therefore, were with Burton Berry, who seemed always to be accessible. Despite my several long talks with Berry, we never got very far in matters of policy.[4] While we occasionally talked about policy, most of our exchanges were in reference to the Department's plans for my successor and my own plans. I was quite frank that I had no preference as between returning and staying at home, though from a purely personal point of view it would be more convenient not to go back. Berry said that it had been decided to name a top career man, in part because I had recommended this and had indicated that this was the Israeli preference. I said that I would urge it also on the president. Berry gave me the

---

3. Naharayim, at the confluence of the Jordan and Yarmuk Rivers east of the Jordan, was within the mandatory border of Transjordan, but the Israeli-Jordanian armistice maps, probably mistakenly, left it inside Israel. Israeli farmers began moving into the area on August 27, triggering a bellicose reaction from the Jordanian cabinet. On September 29, 1950, Jordan complained to the UN Security Council. British and US representatives in Israel were dismayed, with Ford postulating that the Israelis took the area to push forward talks with Jordan and so that they would have something to concede in negotiations. Washington and London suggested that Israel, though legally right, was making a settlement more difficult. King Abdullah's attempts to defuse the situation failed because of the truculence of his cabinet, and his reputation continued to decline. Shooting exchanges occurred between the IDF and the Arab Legion in December. See relevant documents in *FRUS*, 1950, v. V, esp. 1010–1029; *DFPI*, v. 5, esp., d. 381, 382, ~~400~~, 407–408, 417; and in USSDCF-PIFA, 1950–1954, reel 1, frames 574–699.

4. Berry's assessment of Israeli-Arab issues are in his memorandum of September 21, 1950, *FRUS*, 1950, v. V, 1015–1018. He recommended following all Israeli and Arab complaints closely and encouraging more conciliatory attitudes.

impression that the Department's choice was between [William E.] De Courcy in Haiti[5] and Monnett Davis in Panama.[6]

My visit to the president [Monday, September 18] also bore on this question. The president was, as usual, very cordial, expressed appreciation of my work, and told me something of his hopes for the area. He seemed to have in mind progress through regional economic and political arrangements.[7] He said he was pleased at my report that the Department and I had gotten on well together. I told him that I thought it desirable that my successor should be a career man. He listened attentively to my favorable estimate of the two men then under consideration by the Department.

As to my return, I told him that for me it was a 50-50 proposition; the Department at the time was inclined against it, but some of the more politically conscious of his advisers thought it would be well for me to be on my way back by the first Tuesday of November. The president said: "What do you want to do? I should like to have you do what you prefer." I replied that I did not think it was a decision which should be made on the basis of my personal preference. He finally said that he would talk it over with Acheson at their next weekly meeting. As I was leaving, we briefly talked politics and the president expressed his personal ambition to see [Robert] Taft[8] and [Thomas] Dewey[9] defeated. He told me a story of Taft's reputation for intellectuality, which was matched by a singular lack of political gumption.

In the president's outer office, I chatted first with Paul Hoffman, who was going in to say goodbye to the president prior to his resignation from the ECA [Economic Cooperation Administration].[10] Then, I had a longer talk with Under Secretary Webb, to whom I explained the substance of the exchange between the president and me about my return. David Niles, who was keen about my return, assured me that, after talking at the White House, the decision would be affirmative. Nonetheless, several days passed after Webb's next visit to the White House [September 21] with no word from Berry. I suspected that the Department had over-persuaded Webb. This was confirmed when I learned that Berry had argued with Webb that I had no preference in the matter and that, therefore, the president's indication in favor of my return could be interpreted

5. William E. De Courcy (1894–1981), foreign service officer for thirty-one years; ambassador to Haiti, June 18, 1948–October 13, 1950, when he relinquished his post in order to retire from the State Department the following year.

6. Monnett Bain Davis (1893–1953), foreign service officer since World War I; ambassador to Panama, 1948–1951; McDonald's successor in Israel, 1951–1953, where he died in his sleep on December 26, 1953.

7. See also Truman's friendly comments to Eban on September 5, 1950, when Eban presented his credentials as ambassador. Eban to Sharett, September 6, 1950, *DFPI*, v. 5, d. 370.

8. Robert A. Taft (1889–1953), US senator (R-OH), 1939–1953; Senate Republican Policy Committee chairman, 1947–1953; co-sponsored the anti-union Taft-Hartley Act, for which Truman's veto was overridden, 1947.

9. Thomas Dewey, then running for a third term as Republican governor of New York.

10. Paul G. Hoffman (1891–1974), president of Studebaker, 1935–1948; headed ECA where he administered Marshall Plan aid, 1948–1952; returned to Studebaker, 1953; headed UN Development Program, 1966–1972.

as not being binding. It was at this point that I wrote to Berry, but before he received the letter, he called me up to tell me of the affirmative decision on the understanding that I return home by Christmas. I suspect that the White House influence led to this reversal by Berry.

In one of my talks with Dave Niles I was amused at his strong expression of feeling about Jacob Blaustein, who was asking for another talk with the president. Despite Dave's opposition, Blaustein got the interview because, as the president's engagement secretary put it, Blaustein was a large campaign contributor.

During McDonald's absence Richard Ford, McDonald's counselor of embassy, wrote that the era of Israel's heroic birth had ended and that Israel had to live within the US's regional vision for the Middle East. The State Department should take account of the relationship between Israel and five million American Jews while convincing the Arab world to accept an "unwelcome newcomer in their midst." Criticizing McDonald, Ford argued that a new, dispassionate ambassador more in the mold of the State Department was an essential part of a needed shift.[11]

The fifth General Assembly of the United Nations opened in New York on September 19, 1950. Under Secretary James Webb told Reuven Shiloah on September 20 that, in the eyes of many, the Jews had turned from an object of world sympathy into an oppressor. Shiloah responded that the Arabs had not reciprocated Israeli steps toward peace and had to be brought to face realities. This uneasy exchange was replicated in Tel Aviv between Ford and Israeli officials, including Ben-Gurion himself.[12]

But by mid-October, US-Israeli relations were easing. The UNRWA's interim report emphasized resettlement of Arab refugees and funds for economic development. The State Department emphasized Israeli compensation for abandoned Arab property as a contribution to the reintegration fund, rather than mass Arab repatriation. The Israelis were willing to contribute under these conditions.[13] *Shiloah reported that, in Washington, Israel's good intentions were taken at face value. Burton Berry predicted that the Export-Import Bank would approve Israel's recent request for a new agricultural loan of $35 million. Israel was further invited to apply for funds under the Point Four program. Kollek, in return, discussed compensation of former Arab property holders in Jerusalem as a precursor to comprehensive peace talks, and the State Department backed Israel's stance on Jerusalem.*[14] *McDonald was not included in these discussions.*

11. Ford to secretary of state, no. 118, September 14, 1950, *FRUS*, 1950, v. V, 1006–1009.
12. Webb to US Embassy in Tel Aviv, September 30, 1950, *FRUS*, 1950, v. V, 1019–1020; Ford to secretary of state, no. 211, October 9, 1950, *FRUS*, 1950, v. V, 1027–1028; also *DFPI*, v. 5, d. 387, 406.
13. Report at http://unispal.un.org/UNISPAL.NSF/0/EC8DE7912121FCE5052565B10 06B5152, accessed December 2014. Also memorandum by Stabler, October 26, 1950, *FRUS*, 1950, v. V, 1036–1038, 1063; Eban to Sharett, October 25, 1950, *DFPI*, v. 5, d. 429–431, 435.
14. Shiloah to Eytan, October 12, 1950, *DFPI*, v. 5, d. 415; Kollek-Berry meeting, October 11, 1950, *DFPI*, v. 5, d. 416; Aide-Mémoire by US Embassy, October 23, 1950, *DFPI*, v. 5, d.

Washington, October 25 and 26

These days were given over mostly to last-minute preparations for getting away, and to my final but inconclusive talk with McGhee. I had had difficulty in tying McGhee down to a time for a real talk. Finally, when I did see him, he, as usual, was on the verge of rushing off to a conference. I told him that it was necessary that I know definitely about the Department's plan for my successor. Obviously embarrassed, he replied that everything was in the air. For reasons which he did not explain, De Courcy was not being named, and no one else had been fixed upon. I think I replied that I would, of course, be at the Department's orders.

I did not realize until weeks later, when in Tel Aviv I had an opportunity to study some of the documents, the extent to which I had, from the point of view of learning about Department policy, wasted my time in Washington.

Other than Washington
Items During
September 1 to October 30

The day before I sailed, [Henry] Montor came to see me at the Foreign Policy Association.

Henry Montor recruited McDonald to chair the advisory board of the American Financial and Development Corporation for Israel—known also as the Israel Bond Organization—a fundraising effort beginning in 1951 aimed at augmenting US and global financial aid for Israel. Montor became the chief executive officer and Ben Abrams became the chairman of the Greater New York Committee. McDonald was eager to take part, but as he wrote Abrams, "[M]y success in working with Montor will depend in part upon his acceptance of my principle that I should not become part of his administrative machine. This means a separate office and an agreement that I am not obligated to subjugate myself to innumerable and interminable staff conferences."[15]

As to the time, late winter or early spring seems to suit him as the beginning period. Similarly a year initial contract was envisaged.

Despite everything else, however, Donald and Vail [McDonald's grandchildren] were the centers of Ruth's and my interests. Their development will be absorbing.

Several efforts were made by those speaking for Brandeis University to interest me in it.[16] Dave Niles was urgent on two or three occasions,[17] but my

424; Eban to Sharett, October 26, 1950, *DFPI*, v. 5, d. 431; Eytan memoranda, October 31, 1950, and November 7, 1950, *DFPI*, v. 5, d. 435, 449. On Jerusalem, position paper of October 10, 1950, *FRUS*, 1950, v. V, 1029–1032.

15. McDonald to Abrams, November 22, 1950, McDonald Papers, Columbia University, box 6, folder 2.

16. Brandeis University had tried since July to recruit McDonald as a lecturer.

17. Niles had been a member of the Brandeis University Board of Trustees since 1949 and served until his death in 1952.

longest talk was with Dr. [Abram] Sachar, the president. I also had a very long letter from Chairman of the Board [George] Alpert.[18] At the end of all these, however, I remained unconvinced that it was the place for me.

I saw little of the Israelis in Washington or New York.[19] My longest visit with them was at Arthur Lourie's dinner.[20] But even there, largely because of the presence of David Sarnoff,[21] the talk did not become technical.

There was an interesting luncheon for Ralph Bunche given by the Israelis. I sat next to the guest of honor, who outlined to me his views about peacemaking in this area. I was glad, but not surprised, to learn that he, as did Riley and I, strongly favored a more direct approach than the PCC, that is, through a one-man powerful conciliator. He added, however, that though he and Riley had worked hard with the Department, they had not been able to win it over. Again, I was struck by Bunche's clear intelligence and singular charm.

In its October 23 report to the UN secretary-general, the PCC discussed the causes of its failures. Foremost was the Arab rejection of Israel's establishment "in territory which the Arabs considered their own," together with "anxiety felt by both Israel and the Arab States with regard to their security." The PCC called for continued UN involvement in the region for the reestablishment of stability and harmony, which it said "can result only from a compromise by which, first, the new State of Israel will do its best to counteract the dislocations caused by its own establishment among the Arabs and, secondly, the Arab counties will endeavor to adapt their policy to the new state of affairs." Stability, it concluded, depended on direct discussions between the parties and "the passage of time."[22] Eban declared the report "on the whole positive" with a "tendency not [to] be hidebound by old resolutions."[23]

The Voyage
November 1–25

McDonald sailed on October 31. During the voyage he worked to complete his memoirs of his mission in Israel with the help of his friends James N. Rosenberg and Eli Karlin. Gerold Frank had arranged for promotion of the volume, which was to be published in 1951 by Simon & Schuster. The final section, which contained reflective analytical chapters on Israel's leaders and on the ingathering of exiles, was the most difficult to write.[24]

18. George Alpert (1913–1984), first chairman of the board of trustees at Brandeis University, 1946–1954, and a board member thereafter until his death.

19. Referring to the Israeli UN delegation, led by Sharett.

20. Arthur Lourie, Israeli consul general in New York, deputy permanent representative at the UN, and member of Israeli delegation for the fifth session of the UN General Assembly.

21. David Sarnoff (1891–1971), Belorussian-born president of RCA.

22. General Progress Report and Supplementary Report of the United Nations Conciliation Commission for Palestine, October 23, 1950, http://unispal.un.org/UNISPAL.NSF/0/9303 7E3B939746DE8525610200567883, accessed December 2014.

23. Eban to Sharett, October 25, 1950, *DFPI*, v. 5, d. 427.

24. McDonald to Ruth and family, November 6, 1950, McDonald Papers, USHMM, box 9, folder 4.

For the first time in some three-score Atlantic crossings, I worked consistently. Reluctantly, but steadily, I worked with Jimmy Rosenberg in preparation for the deadline, which I had set with Gerold. Rosenberg was very valuable, though naturally I could not accept all of his ideas. The work made the crossing short but dull. Anyhow, I didn't meet anyone that would intrigue me or was especially interesting. Thus with the daily routine of work and three full days of excessive rolling, the time passed bringing us to Southampton on schedule and to our London hotel late Sunday night.

Monday, November 6

Worked all morning with Eli. It soon became apparent that Eli and Jimmy were in complete disagreement on the last section. Eli also took very strong exception to some of Jimmy's emanations. I sought to act as arbiter.

Jimmy Rosenberg and I had a very civilized luncheon at Marks and Spencer with [Harry] Sacher at the head of the table.[25] How intelligent these Jewish businessmen can be, and how wide their intellectual and cultural interests.

Tuesday, November 7

Worked all day with Eli and finished in the very late afternoon. We took an hour off for a bite of lunch and an exhilarating visit to the newly arranged galleries of the [National Gallery].

The dinner at Serge Karlinski's house was elaborately luxurious. Throughout the evening Serge was quietly but obviously the master. The house itself is almost ostentatious.

Wednesday, November 8

We were delayed nearly two hours at the airport, but finally took off about ten. The flight was uneventful. We put down in Rome for tea, and reached Lydda at eleven, Israel time. We were met by Ford and several members of the staff, but both Jimmy and I were so tired that we made early excuses to go home to bed. Thanks to Lolita [Ford]'s blankets and Pesa's housekeeping, the place was in order, though naturally not homey. The weather was almost sultry, and for a few days I was almost fearful that I would need my summer clothes.

Thursday, November 9

I attended the [Lazar] Braudo's cocktail party for Jack [Ya'akov] Geri, the new minister of trade and industry.[26] The hosts could not have been more cordial.

---

25. Entry of July 31, 1948.
26. Ya'akov Geri (1901–1974), Lithuanian-born Israeli minster of trade and industry in Ben-Gurion's second government, 1950–1951; political independent.

Friday, November 10

First visit to the Foreign Office to call on [Shmuel] Bendor, the new head of the American desk.[27] Lunch and dinner at the Fords'.

McDonald reported to the State Department on this talk. "One point," he said, "was new and will interest the Department. Israel is about to begin extensive surveys, which are expected to be followed by large-scale drainage operations in the eastern part of the Hula swamp area. Some of these operations will be within a few hundred meters of the Syrian frontier. Bendor seemed to be fearful, lest these 'wholly civil activities' might be misinterpreted by the Syrians. I asked him if the Foreign Office, through its Missions abroad, [has] informed the Governments to which they are accredited of these prospective development operations. He replied that this he had not done, but that he would suggest it to his superiors.[28]

Saturday, November 11

Jimmy Rosenberg and I had luncheon at the Chaim Weizmanns'. Weizmann was physically very weak. As I led him in from the veranda to the dining room, it seemed that he would never get through the long living room, for he was barely able to slide one foot before the other. During the meal he was alert and even amusing. His references to old friends and enemies were often marked by his old caustic wit. Jimmy had a thrilling time.

McDonald reported on Weizmann's condition to Washington: "He has lost so much weight that his clothes 'hang on him.' Nonetheless, he was mentally more alert than on some of the occasions when I saw him last spring and early summer. . . . Despite all the official efforts to deny the President's increasing weaknesses, it is certain that his margin of physical strength has become very, very narrow."[29]

Sunday, November 12

In the evening . . . to the Philharmonic. The program included Tchaikovsky's Fourth Symphony. [Eleazar de] Carvalho is proving to be a popular conductor.[30]

Wednesday, November 15

Fairly early start with Shalom for Tiberias [to visit Ben-Gurion]. The trip up was notable because we took the [Jezreel] Valley road from Afula to Beit She'an, and then up to Tiberias over the new picturesque mountain road. From the heights we had a glorious view of almost the whole of the Sea of Galilee,

27. Shmuel Bendor (1934–2007), US-educated Israeli diplomat; head of the American desk in Israeli Foreign Ministry; then minister to Prague and later to Bucharest.
28. McDonald to secretary of state, no. 240, November 17, 1950, McDonald Papers, USHMM, box 9, folder 4. See also *DFPI*, v. 5, d. 444.
29. McDonald to secretary of state, no. 240, November 17, 1950, McDonald Papers, USHMM, box 9, folder 4.
30. Eleazar de Carvalho (1912–1996), Brazilian conductor and composer who had studied under Serge Koussevitzky in the Berkshires.

the Jordan Valley, the river with its endless windings, the valley kibbutzim, the power plant; Naharayim, the scene of the recent crisis; and in the distance the Syrian and Jordanian plateaus. We reached the hotel about twelve.

Nehemia [Argov][31] came up to us (Jimmy Rosenberg had arrived just before I did) and asked us for lunch with Ben-Gurion. Later, we had tea and dinner with him also.

Israel's worsening economic situation in the fall of 1950 induced Ben-Gurion to resign as prime minister on October 15. He formed a new cabinet on November 1. Ben-Gurion abolished Dov Joseph's highly unpopular Ministry of Supply and Rationing, and Joseph was not included in the new cabinet.

McDonald and Rosenberg met for five hours with Ben-Gurion in the presence of Argov and Shiloah. The italicized comments below are from McDonald's more complete report to the State Department, and the topics, which received different numbers in the diary and the report, are renumbered here.[32]

The following are the main points of our talk.

1) Although the election results, which had just become known and which showed such marked General Zionist gains at the expense of Mapai, were on everybody's minds, Ben-Gurion remained philosophical.[33]

"Ben-Gurion admitted that the General Zionists and to a lesser extent other Rightist parties, notably the Herut, had made significant gains at the expense of Mapai and Mapam. The losses of the latter were naturally not displeasing to him. Mapai's losses he attributed primarily to the popular—and he did not deny, justifiable, reaction against [an] immature and inefficient bureaucracy. It is, nonetheless, certain that Ben-Gurion realizes more fully than before the election the imperative need for improving the bureaucracy."

2) Ben-Gurion listened with close attention to Jimmy's suggestions about specific forms of private US financial aid. When he didn't understand, he asked questions.

"Replying to Rosenberg's arguments that greater assurances to foreign capital are needed, Ben-Gurion said that these would be given. . . . After Rosenberg had explained the advantages of some of the new American banking techniques, particu-

---

31. Colonel Nehemia Argov (1914–1957), friend and military aide to Ben-Gurion.

32. McDonald to secretary of state, no. 240, November 17, 1950, McDonald Papers, USHMM, box 9, folder 4. See also Ben-Gurion Diary, entry of November 15, 1950.

33. Refers to municipal elections on November 14, 1950. The General Zionists gained 25.4% of the vote total compared to 5.2% in the national elections of 1949. They did especially well in the cities, climbing from 1% to 15.9% in Jerusalem and 7.2% to 31.1% in Tel Aviv. Mapai votes fell to 27.3% of votes cast compared to 35.7% in 1949. Orit Rozin, *The Rise of the Individual in 1950s Israel: A Challenge to Collectivism* (Lebanon, NH: Brandeis University Press, 2011), 79.

larly factoring, as aids to industry and trade, Ben-Gurion asked [Rosenberg] to see Horowitz in charge of the [Ministry of Finance] in Kaplan's absence, and later to talk with Kaplan and with the latter's American economic advisers, [Robert] Nathan and [Oscar] Gass.

The Prime Minister asked my opinion of the prospects for success of the very large efforts now being made by the American Jewish Community. I pleaded—quite honestly too—[a] lack of adequate information on which to base a judgment. He did not ask me anything specific about the prospect for an additional loan from the United States Government or its agencies.

The Prime Minister said that the preliminary report made by an American oil geologist (presumably that of Mr. Ball) had shown that there were reasonably good prospects for oil in Israel. If these materialize, they would, he added, 'solve Israel's most difficult problem, fuel.'"

3) Ben-Gurion again indicated that irrespective of the cost in sacrifice in Israel or of money costs, the ingathering of the exiles must continue until Israel can be "safe with a population of three million" [this topic omitted from McDonald's official report].

4) *Jerusalem*

"*a) I asked the Prime Minister if the Government planned to move the Foreign Office to Jerusalem in the near future and expressed my personal views that such a move would be disadvantageous to Israel. Ben-Gurion's answer to my query was in the negative. He reiterated the earlier views that what mattered in Jerusalem is not recognition or non-recognition of the New City as Israel's capital, but rather Israel's success in so strengthening its physical position there through enlargement of its population and building up of the local industry that there can be no doubt about the realities.*

b) I took exception to the Prime Minister's suggestion that it is the United States Government, which is the chief obstacle to international recognition of Israel's claim to Jerusalem as its capital. I pointed out that no government to my knowledge, except the Netherlands, had established its official diplomatic residence in Jerusalem and that other great powers, including France and Great Britain, appeared to be quite as firm in their non-recognition as the United States.

c) Ben-Gurion said he did not expect a 'favorable' decision on Jerusalem at this UN Assembly and that the 'best' Israel could anticipate was 'no resolution at all.' Shiloah disagreed with his Chief and cited indications at Lake Success that the Swedish-Netherlands Resolution might pass. To this Ben-Gurion countered: 'Maybe, but there is certain to be included some undesirable or unacceptable provisions; it is better that there be no resolution now.'"[34]

34. For Israeli comments and revisions to the Swedish-Dutch draft resolution, which called for international protection of the Holy Places only, see *DFPI*, v. 5, d. 428, 432, 433, 448, 454, 464. On November 17, 1950, word came that the Vatican, and thus the French too, would accept the resolution in principle so long as language was added to the preamble mentioning the failure

5) *"The Prime Minister indicated that he saw no grounds for hope that there would be an improvement in Israel-Egyptian relations. He cited [as] discouraging signs 'recent intransigent statements by Farouk, Nahhas Pasha.'"*

6) *"Israel and its other Arab Neighbors: About the prospects of peace with these, the Prime Minister was also pessimistic."*

7) Ben-Gurion's most cheerful comment was when he was telling us that his book agent in Germany had found, after a long search for him, a complete set of the 50-volume of commentaries in the original Greek on Aristotle.

8) Ben-Gurion showed much interest and knowledge of nearly all the personalities and the local US Zionist situations which Jimmy Rosenberg brought up.

9) *"The Palestine Conciliation Commission: The Prime Minister said that he thought the PCC was becoming more realistic in its approach to its problems and that he is moderately optimistic about its future usefulness. Both he and Reuven Shiloah spoke highly of Mr. [Ely] Palmer and his part in the PCC."*

10) *"My Return to Israel: The Prime Minister was kind enough to say that he would 'never have forgiven me' had I not come back. I could not, of course, enlighten him either about the name or the time of the arrival of my successor. He seemed relieved, however, at my expression of opinion that the President and the Department planned to name a 'top' career man. He seemed relieved that there would probably not be a political appointment."*

Ben-Gurion could not have been more cordial or outgiving. He was obviously tired, but was nonetheless keenly alert and as anxious as ever to learn.

Thursday, November 16

Shalom and I drove up to Safed and then up to the higher hill nearby from which we had magnificent views, not only of the Sea of Galilee, Syria and Jordan, but also of nearly the whole of northern Israel. Then instead of coming directly home, we continued northward to [the village of Peki'n]. This one village, which traces an unbroken line of Jewish villagers since the destruction of the Second Temple, welcomed us through the mukhtar [Arab village elder]. He led us to his primitive house where in the main room, about the size of my study, and apparently the meeting place of the elders, he served us tea. Gradually the Druze, and other religious leaders came in. With them was an elderly Jew. For nearly the whole time the conversation was in Arabic, with Shalom the efficient interpreter.

We were given the story of Jewish relations there and were told of the elders' friendly relations between Druze and Jew. At the end the mukhtar, in a dignified but not stilted speech, sent greetings on behalf of his fellow Druze to President Truman, and I replied. Then we walked through the village to the

---

"so far" of previous UN resolutions on Jerusalem. *DFPI*, v. 5, d. 464–465, 470, 473, 479, 658; *FRUS*, 1950, v. V, 1064–1065, 1066–1067.

small central square where the year round mountain spring waters flow through three or four largish basins. There the Druze women were washing their clothes, rubbing them with smooth stones on the large stones below.

As we were leaving, a young boy of three or four was in the group with the mukhtar. When I extended my hand to the boy, he took it and instead of shaking it carried it towards his mouth. I stupidly drew my hand away remembering that a few weeks earlier my older grandson had tried to bite his mother's hand when she was correcting him. Here in the Galilee, this "uncivilized" Druze boy had simply intended to kiss my hand, so shamefacedly I gave him my hand again.

Saturday, November 18

[Seyfullah] Esin came at eleven and we had a long general talk.

Lunch at Rebecca Sieff's. Talked mostly with Marcus Sieff about his work for Ben-Gurion. This is twofold, to break down red tape and to bring businessmen into governmental administration. He is hopeful that with Ben-Gurion's support and the cooperation of Geri and Lubianker [now minister of agriculture], much can be done.

Sunday, November 19

Jimmy Rosenberg gave a dinner at the Sharon Hotel for the officials of the PEC [Palestine Economic Corporation] and the labor organizations. It was very informative. Each man stating briefly but frankly how he viewed the international situation and the possibilities of PEC or other American financial aid.

Wednesday, November 22

A most interesting hour and a half at the Residence-Museum of Dr. [Walter] Moses, who is planning to take a portion of his extraordinary collection of ancient Israeli glass, jewelry and other art objects on an exhibition tour to the States.[35]

To the concert where Carvahlo played the Beethoven Leonore Overture, the Brahms Second Concerto, Copland's Appalachian Spring, and Rimsky-Korsakov's Easter Music [Russian Easter Overture].

Thursday, November 23

I met the [John] Blandfords at Rehovot at about eleven. Showed them the [Weizmann] Institute and took them to lunch at Givat Brenner. I enjoyed feasting with them, and they enjoyed seeing the country. They were impressed with everyone. Dinner with the Blandfords at the [Major Reed] Booths. It was an excellent Thanksgiving meal. After dinner, Blandford and the group dis-

35. Dr. Walter Moses (1893–1955), German-born industrialist; emigrated to Palestine, 1926; collector of glass antiquities. His collection is now in Tel Aviv's Eretz Israel Museum, founded in 1958.

cussed current problems, particularly those related to Arab refugees. Again, I was impressed by the ambassador's intelligence and realism.[36]

Friday, November 24

To the Foreign Office with Blandford to meet [Gershon] Meron[37] at nine. For an hour and twenty-minutes Blandford explained the present program of the [UNRWA] and discussed with Meron and Bendor, who was also present, the problem of liquidating the refugee status of some twenty or twenty-five thousand Arabs in Israel.

Because of the necessity of getting off an urgent telegram to the Department about Ben-Gurion's projected private visit to Greece and Great Britain, Shalom and I didn't get off to Haifa until about eleven. Had an enjoyable lunch at the LaGuardia [Hotel]. Back home before the arrival of Justice [William] and Mrs. Clark[38] of the [Court of Appeals] in the American Zone of Germany. She was the former Sonia Tomara of the *Herald Tribune*.[39] After sherry at home, I took them to the Sharon for dinner.

Saturday, November 25

To Jerusalem with Miss Watson and Miss Zakas [embassy staff]. We used the newer section of the road, and then for the second half went over the mountains.

Jacob Herzog and I went to see Paula Ben-Gurion at the Hadassah Hospital and visited with her for more than an hour. She had a small, old, grim room. I was forced to tell her an untruth about her husband, whose plans to go to Greece and England [for needed rest] were unknown to her.

Afterward Jacob and I walked through some of the eastern Jewish sections of the city, portions of which were not unlike the Old City. We ended up at Jacob's father's [Chief Rabbi Yitzhak Herzog] house for Shabbat greetings. Lunch with the Novomeyskys. Walking out of the King David, just before dinner, I was picked up by a Mrs. Freedman, who wanted to sell me a lot.

Sunday, November 26

To the [Jerusalem Shoe Company] factory, where my friend [Claude M.] Sweeney showed me with great pride his production lines. But most of all he was proud of the people who, coming from remote and backward sections of the world [Eastern Europe and North Africa], had within a few months been

---

36. Blandford emphasized the political importance of Israeli contributions to the UNRWA's development fund. *DFPI*, v. 5, d. 429, 430.

37. Gershon Meron (1904–1958), director of the Economic Division, Ministry of Foreign Affairs.

38. Justice William Clark (1891–1957), chief justice of Allied High Commission Court of Appeals in Nuremberg, 1949–1954, which oversaw the eleven judicial districts that had replaced the Military Government Courts of the Department of the Army.

39. Sonia Tomara (1897–1982), Russian-born foreign correspondent who worked for the *Herald Tribune*, 1928–1945.

trained to work productively at the most modern machines.[40] I was glad to meet again his wife and two charming children.

In the middle of the afternoon Jacob Herzog insisted upon my seeing some of the sages, including leading Kabbalists. Each one was more exotic than the one before. Late tea at the [Raleigh] Gibsons'. Picturesque moonlight ride, down the mountains. A pickup supper at the house.

Monday, November 27

Ten o'clock escorted Colonel [Samuel C.] Gurney[41] to the HaKirya for a round of meetings beginning with that with [Gershon Agron][42] after we had met [Michael] Simon. The meeting with Meron I had to leave in order to go out to Rehovot.

I reached the president's house a few minutes before noon to bring him greetings on his 76th birthday on behalf of the diplomatic corps. The proceeding was wholly informal. We sat before the fire and chatted about old friends and enemies. He spoke amusingly about Jimmy Rosenberg, but seemed to have forgotten that I had brought the latter out. He commented upon the municipal elections saying in effect that it had been a lesson to Ben-Gurion. Driving out towards the main road, we were nearly pushed into the ditch by the speeding military escort and car of [Yigael] Yadin on their way to the president's.

Tuesday, November 28

In the afternoon the Persian minister [Reza Saffinia] paid us a formal call.[43] At seven, dinner at Greenberg's where as usual, the food was excellent. Unfortunately, I had to leave at nine in order to attend the Iwo Jima film [*Sands of Iwo Jima*, 1949] at the Esther [Cinema]. With what brutal realism it portrays the horrors of modern war!

Wednesday, November 29

In the afternoon the Gurneys and Booths came to tea. At the Yugoslav party on the national anniversary,[44] I chatted with Shiloah, who told me of the roadblock crisis on the Eilat Road.

The issue concerned Israel's months-long military use of a 4.5-kilometer stretch of road seventy kilometers north of the Gulf of Aqaba as a bypass connecting the two parts of the main highway from Be'er Sheva to Eilat. The bypass avoided a sandy stretch of highway. On November 29, the Arab Legion blockaded the road. Shiloah was not sure whether the bypass was on the Israeli or Jordanian side of the armistice

40. See also entry of June 9, 1950; McDonald, *My Mission to Israel*, 234–235.
41. Colonel Samuel C. Gurney, senior military and air attaché, assigned to Tel Aviv, September 1950.
42. Agron still headed the Israeli government's official information service.
43. Entries of April 13 and June 20, 1950.
44. Republic Day in Yugoslavia, commemorating the establishment of the postwar republic on November 29, 1943, by the Anti-Fascist Council of National Liberation.

line, and he believed that the crisis had been precipitated by conflicts between Abdullah and his cabinet. From Greece, Ben-Gurion voted to run the blockade. Eytan argued that it was impossible to determine whether the road was on the Israeli or Jordanian side of the armistice line since the armistice map was marked with thick pencil. Sharett worried about running the blockade if the road was on Jordan's side.

On November 30, IDF Chief of Staff Yadin sent a convoy to run the blockade if Arab Legion troops did not withdraw by December 1. The Mixed Armistice Commission called an emergency meeting but was unable to avert the crisis, for while the Israelis said they would attend an emergency meeting and abide by any MAC decision, the Jordanians refused. On December 2, the two sides opened fire in the disputed area. Following a ceasefire order by the UN truce supervisory officers, the Arab Legion withdrew and the Israeli convoy proceeded, pending investigation in the MAC, which called for a new land survey of the border. The British and Americans learned afterward that Defense Minister Tewfik al-Mulqi had kept King Abdullah in the dark and was subsequently sacked. But Abdullah was also incensed with the Israelis for—he said—sending a warplane to circle his palace during the crisis.[45]

McDonald reported the aftermath of the crisis, including the December 6 killing of an Israeli officer on the Eilat road during an ambush (presumably by Bedouin refugees) and the resumption of Israeli convoys to Mount Scopus, which the Jordanians had halted in November.[46]

The Eilat Road crisis was McDonald's last. On November 29, as the argument played out, he wrote the following letter to President Truman:

> Dear Mr. President,
>
> Two and one-half years ago when you named me as your first Representative to the new State of Israel, I anticipated that my tour of duty would be relatively short, six months or at the most a year. The indications of confidence which you and Secretary Acheson have given me and the exigencies of the work, however, have made me glad to stay on.
>
> My experience here has been personally very rewarding. It has enabled me to watch closely the emergence of democratic Israel from a provisional regime which, even while at war with several of its neighbors, was struggling to build itself into a modern progressive state. Elections for the Knesset were held early in 1949, and were followed promptly by the establishment of a representative government. This transformation was simultaneous with the signing with all of Israel's immediate neighbors of armistice agreements which were primarily the result of the brilliant mediation of Dr. Ralph Bunche. Since then, the rebuilding and enlarging of the economic life of the country [have] been carried on indefatigably and at amazing speed.

45. *DFPI*, v. 5, d. 486, 489; *FRUS*, 1950, v. V, 1065–1066, 1068–1071; documents in USSDCF-PIFA, 1950–1954, reel 1, frames, 733–843.
46. McDonald to secretary of state, no. 332, December 7, 1950, USSDCF-PIFA, 1950–1954, reel 1, frame 799.

But the most heartening of all of these developments has been Israel's open-door policy of 'ingathering the exiles' into a Jewish population of less than seven hundred thousand at the time the State was set up. Israel has already gathered more than one-half million refugees. Even our own hospitable country at the peak of its policy of unrestricted immigration never received proportionately so large an influx.

The absorption of these newcomers and of the approximately two hundred thousand expected to follow annually will be Israel's major task during the next five or ten years, This gigantic program entails immense economic burdens. But success will mean the rescue from inhospitable or perilous situations of many additional hundreds of thousands of Jews, who will then so strengthen their new-old homeland that it will be freed to concentrate fully on constructive work of peace. Thenceforth—and I hope in co-operation with its Arab neighbors—Israel will become an increasingly potent influence for the democratization and modernization of this whole strategic area.

Interesting and challenging though my work continues to be, I feel that for personal reasons I should soon return home. I hope that you will agree to make effective my resignation on or about January 1.

I am deeply grateful for the confidence you have shown me, and if there should be any task in the future in which you should find that I might be helpful I should be very happy to serve.

Very Sincerely,
James G. McDonald

President Truman replied on December 18, 1950.

My dear McDonald,
I have received your letter of November twenty-ninth and in light of your earlier correspondence expressing your wish to be relieved of your assignment as Ambassador to Israel, I reluctantly accept your resignation, effective December thirty-first.

I wish to extend my deep appreciation for the outstanding service you have rendered as Special Representative of the United States to the Provisional Government of Israel and, since March, 1949, as first American Ambassador to Israel.

Your effective performance of duty resulted in the establishment and operation of our Government's first diplomatic Mission in that new State and enabled you to maintain a most valuable relationship with the officials of that Government and the people of that country as well.

With best wishes,
Very sincerely yours,
Harry S. Truman

Thursday, November 30

Lunch at the Sharon. Then, on for a brief visit to the Kfar Truman, a new individual holding settlement [moshav] in the process of being established just beyond Lydda and within a couple of kilometers of the Jordan frontier.[47]

At the inevitable tea, in response to my question about the politics of the group, one of them replied, "Our first loyalty is to agriculture." I was photographed, I hope successfully, with an extraordinarily husky and beautiful baby. I want to send the picture home to show my daughter how a baby should be brought up.

Friday, December 1

[Édouard-Félix] Guyon came to the house for more than an hour. We discussed all aspects of our local situation including the sources of irritation between the diplomatic corps and the HaKirya. Guyon continues to put much of the responsibility on Simon.

Saturday, December 2
Sunday, December 3

Saturday was spent on a very interesting trip to the south, which Miss Watson, Mrs. Sheehy, and Miss Zakas [embassy staff] went on. On [the] route to Revivim[48] we visited an Orthodox kibbutz, Sa'ad,[49] overlooking Gaza only three or four kilometers away. It was a model of cleanliness and order. We enjoyed our tea with rich cream. The babies were typically husky. Then on down to Be'er Sheva to [Bir] 'Asluj,[50] where we visited briefly a new Mapam kibbutz, which was an example of seeming disorder and lack of cleanliness.[51] The gals were a little shocked by the informality of the dining hall.

Revivim itself had not changed much since I was there in 1947. Wholly surrounded by the Arabs during the war, its agricultural and water experiments had been of necessity retarded. Moreover, it is in the process of moving a kilometer or so to a new site where most of the new buildings are ready for occupancy. I walked over to the dam and had explained to me its operation. During the first year, the floods came before it was finished. During the war it was partially destroyed by a floating bomb or a mine. In a normal winter they hoped

47. The settlement was established in 1949 by former soldiers of the Palmach as B'nai Harel and renamed for Truman in 1950.
48. Kibbutz in Negev desert, south of Be'er Sheva, founded in 1943 by immigrants from Italy, Germany, and Austria; southernmost Jewish settlement until 1950; notable residents included Golda Meyerson.
49. Founded in 1947 by members of B'nai Akiva, badly damaged by the Egyptian Army in 1948 and later rebuilt.
50. Bedouin village of Bir 'Asluj (inhabited by the Azzazma tribe), strategically located on the al-Auja-Be'er Sheva road; site of fierce battles between Egypt and Israel, 1948; captured by the Negev Brigade on December 25–26, 1948, and renamed Be'er Mash'abim. See n. 139 in chapter 7.
51. Mash'abbe Sadeh, twenty-five kilometers south of Be'er Sheva, founded in 1949 and named after Yitzhak Sadeh, one of the founders of the Palmach.

to impound enough water for about four months' use. The process is to divert the portion of the floods into a new channel leading to two reservoirs.

The trip back home took us through the rich coastal plain, and I was impressed anew by the extraordinary growth of the settlements and the villages all the way down to Gaza. Arrived home about six.

The visit to the Foreign Office and cables to Washington regarding the Eilat Road kept me busy most of the day.[52]

Shmuel Bendor's summary of this meeting contains McDonald's comments on Jerusalem, which were based on his meeting with Ben-Gurion on November 15.[53] "The ambassador (McDonald) relayed that he spoke with [Roger Garreau] who told him there was no hope for the Sweden-Holland plan. There is a proposal to appoint a UN representative in Jerusalem without claiming any authority. Jordan opposes this proposal. He, McDonald, told [Garreau] it was probable that Israel opposes it as well. To me, he added that he hopes we allow the Arabs to sabotage the proposal and not hurry, as we often do, to intervene prematurely." McDonald also commented that he "hopes there will not be a decision [by Israel] regarding Jerusalem. The current situation is more convenient than any law and the potholes it might include. . . . The ambassador added it would be foolish of us to transfer the [Ministry of Foreign Affairs] to Jerusalem without the UN decision, as we would be alienating ourselves from diplomatic contact with many countries. The United States embassy would not move to Jerusalem under these circumstances, and neither will England, France, Argentina, and others. These countries will pull their chief representatives and only third secretaries would remain."

Dinner at the Sharon with Martha Gellhorn.[54] Her piece on Israel for the *Saturday Evening Post* is to be, she thinks, mostly about the extraordinary contrasting types of people who are building Israel.

At about ten at Eytan's invitation, we joined his party for Helm and the latter's guest Sir Thomas [Rapp]. Martha had a cherished opportunity to talk with Yadin. I chatted with Eytan, who told me of the cabinet crisis in Amman, with evident pleasure.[55] He also told me that Israel was going to contribute a million pounds [to the UNRWA development fund]. Whether in cash or kind was not made clear.

52. On the night of December 2–3, 1950, an IDF armored patrol broke through the Jordanian blockade. The Jordanians opened fire and the IDF returned fire. One Jordanian armored vehicle was destroyed. UN intervention achieved a swift cease-fire. *DFPI*, v. 5, d. 489.
53. Shmuel Bendor Report, December 3, 1950, Protocols, Ben-Gurion Archives. The editors are grateful to Tuvia Friling for this reference.
54. Martha Gellhorn (1908–1998), American war correspondent who covered many conflicts including the Spanish Civil War, World War II, and later the Six-Day War; married to Ernest Hemingway, 1940–1945.
55. On December 3, 1950 the cabinet under Prime Minister Sa'id al-Mufti resigned and was replaced by a new cabinet under Samir al-Rifai, who held the portfolios of prime minister and foreign minister. The British believed that the change indicated a move toward a settlement if Israel would not aggravate relations with Jordan. *DFPI*, v. 5, d. 492.

Monday, December 4

In the afternoon to Eytan to deliver a message from the Department on the Eilat Road. We also talked about the new financial aid program, concerning which I urged prompt action by HaKirya. Back to the office and sent off a report telegram.

Tuesday, December 5

I should have noted under yesterday's date that finally I got off a telegram to [Burton] Berry and McGhee asking them for travel orders if the "back home before Christmas" plan still held, and for new instructions if there had been a change. Then I waited suspended in mid-air.

Out to Lydda with the military to meet General Riley. His plane was precisely on time. There was not much chance to talk, but he did say that he hoped that the Security Council Resolution [No. 89] would strengthen his hand. Later as he was leaving, he promised to come down within a few days. He looked well, but tired. What a relief to have him back!

UN Security Council Resolution 89 of November 17, 1950, called on all sides to use the Mixed Armistice Commissions for their grievances ranging from Jordan's protests regarding Naharayim to Egypt's complaints concerning the mid-September expulsions of Bedouins from the Negev into the Sinai and Arabs from Ashkelon [al-Majdal] into the Gaza Strip. It called for no expulsions to take place without consultation with the MACs and took note of an Israeli pledge to evacuate Bir Qattar, as called for by the Egyptian-Israeli MAC in March 1950.[56]

Wednesday, December 6

At the office during the morning to welcome Ford and to check with him on developments since he left. He reported some Jerusalem gossip about General Riley, which I was not inclined to take too seriously. In any case, it does not affect his value here. Ford seemed pleased at my report that I had made, the recommendations about his transfer to Spain or South American posts.

Dinner at the [Akiva] Persitz's with the new Danish minister. I do not envy the latter his dual assignment to Ankara and Tel Aviv.[57]

The concert was exciting. Lenny [Bernstein]'s sister Shirley was in our party. Despite the vigor of the [Carlos] Chávez Indian Symphony and the power of the Brahms Fourth, Mozart's Linz Symphony was the most beautiful item on the program.

After the concert, I drove the [Reuven] Rubins to Lenny's house for a reception. This gave me a chance to talk with Lenny and Shirley. They are

---

56. Resolution at www.un.org/en/ga/search/view_doc.asp?symbol=S/RES/89%281950%29, accessed December 2014.
57. Dr. H. P. Hoffmeyer, first Danish minister to Israel (nonresident), based in and accredited to Turkey. Not until 1961 was a Danish envoy, Paul Daniel Steenberger, a resident in Israel.

planning to sail either on the *Liberté* on the 27th or on the *Queen Mary* on the 28th. I made a mental note of these sailings as possible alternates for the 16th.

Thursday, December 7

Delegation headed by Rabbi [Zemach] Green of Washington urged me to attend the dedication of the Givat Washington, "a new agricultural school" near Kibbutz [Kvutzat] Yavne.[58] In the afternoon the new Danish minister [Hoffmeyer] made a formal call. An interesting staff meeting.

Friday, December 8

That morning I finally received word from McGhee that the "home for Christmas" plan still held. The day before and the previous Monday I had urged the Department to give me a definite answer.

Immediately upon receipt of the Department's telegram I went to the Foreign Office to see Eytan. He expressed his regret and, I think, with sincerity. I asked him whether he had heard anything about my successor, and he said that he had not.

Sunday, December 10

To Jerusalem early. Visited with the Gibsons and with the Sweeneys. Had a last look-around the beautiful and historic city.

On the way home stopped at the Givat Washington. The site is historic because it was there [Kvutzat Yavne] that Jewish culture and agriculture took refuge after the destruction of the Second Temple.

Monday, December 11

At noon with Gurney to the military exhibit, which was impressive. Tea at the Weizmanns.' It was [both] sad and gay. Farewell dinner at the Fords'. Dinner was interrupted by my visit to the WIZO meeting in Ramat Gan where one of the speakers told the following story: "At a group meeting of boys in our neighborhood, the question was debated "who is the most popular man in Israel," Weizmann, Ben-Gurion, Sharett, and I were put forward, but no agreement could be reached. Finally, one of the boys suggested that the question be "who is the most beloved." The decision was unanimous in favor of the American ambassador. Believe it or not!

Tuesday, December 12

Finished at the office in the morning. The afternoon and evening included farewell visit to Paula, a call at the consulate (for my sins I forgot the library), reception at the Israel-American Society, met Riley at seven, who disclosed

---

58. Givat Washington, an Orthodox youth village established in 1946 by Jewish groups in Washington, DC, for orphaned Holocaust survivors. Rabbi Zemach Green headed the effort and named the settlement for the first US president. Kvutzat Yavne, a religious kibbutz founded in 1941 by German Religious Zionists. See also entry of December 10, 1950.

considerable impatience at the current stand of the Israelis about the maps to be used in determining the road in the south.

The Foreign Office dinner was representative and dignified, but I thought it was a little slow. I hope my family likes the statue, which was given me.

Wednesday, December 13

Moderately hectic farewells.

McDonald's diary ends with this entry.

On December 14, 1950, the UN General Assembly voted to adopt Resolution 394, based on a draft submitted by the US, Great Britain, France, and Turkey. It called on Israel and the Arab states to enter into negotiations under PCC supervision in order to settle all outstanding issues. The PCC was also to establish an office to create a procedure for the valuation of refugee property and the awarding of compensation. The resolution made no mention of refugee repatriation despite Arab efforts in the General Assembly.[59]

The General Assembly was unable to agree on a new resolution concerning Jerusalem. The Swedish-Dutch draft resolution, which called for UN supervision of the Holy Sites only, failed to attain the necessary two-thirds vote. For the moment, General Riley carried on as an intermediary between Israel and its neighbors on issues ranging from Israeli access to Mount Scopus to the opening of the Suez Canal to Israeli shipping. Israel's diplomats in Washington discussed a new loan for agricultural development with the State Department, and the purchase of arms with the new secretary of defense, General George Marshall.[60]

On December 12, 1950, the day before McDonald sailed, Moshe Sharett, then in New York, telegraphed a tribute to McDonald:

> Deeply distressed my absence abroad prevents me from being with you all on [the] occasion [of] farewell to Ambassador McDonald and [from] paying personal tribute to his personality and work. My association with the Ambassador goes back to [the] 1935 Zionist Congress in Lucerne, where his appearance as High Commissioner for Refugees made a profound and indelible impression on me. To me, as to most Jews and Zionists privileged to know him, he has always personified that type of Gentile to whom special veneration and thankfulness are reserved in Jewish tradition under the name "Khassidey Umot HaOlam" [Righteous of the Nations of the World]. All Israel was thrilled when [the] President of the United States, having extended recognition to Israel on [the] very day of its establishment, proceeded to give further eloquent token of his sympathy and friendship for the new State by appointing James G. McDonald as First Ambassador to HaKirya. In this capacity it was given to Ambassador McDonald to play [a] foremost part in laying [the] foundations for American-Israel friendship. On [the] basis of intimate knowledge gained over many years, he succeeded in conveying and interpreting to Washington with sympathy and understanding the spirit and problems of Israel. At [the] same time he served as an inspired exponent to [the] people

59. For printed resolution, see http://daccess-dds-ny.un.org/doc/RESOLUTION/GEN /NR0/059/92/IMG/NR005992.pdf?OpenElement.

60. *DFPI*, 5, d. 503, 509, 510–512, 516, 517, 523; *FRUS*, 1950, v. V, 1077–1086.

of Israel of all that is noble, liberal, and progressive in [the] great American tradition. His terms of service, which to our deep regret now comes to an end, will forever remain associated with [the] most dynamically creative stage in [the] history of Israel rebuilt. [The] people of Israel take leave of him and his wife with feeling of deep affection and gratitude. His striking figure will be greatly missed at our public functions and popular gatherings. Though he now relinquishes a post of unique importance in the association of [the] United States with [the] fortunes of Israel, we all feel confident that the cause of friendship and understanding between our two nations will always find in Ambassador McDonald a warm understanding and active supporter. Our affection and good wishes go out to him and his family for continued prosperity in their home country and for happy memories of Israel.[61]

61. McDonald Papers, USHMM, box 9, folder 5.

Epilogue and Conclusion

In his 1951 memoir of his years in Israel, McDonald tried to allay American apprehensions about the new state. He introduced Israel's first generation of leaders, from Chaim Weizmann to Golda Meyerson. They were, McDonald said, "an extraordinary group of human beings, any of whom was equal, and some of whom were far superior, to their opposite numbers in many great nations of the world."[1] He predicted success in "the attempt of modern Israel . . . to achieve a secular, democratic State" and argued that "religion will . . . become as it is in America, permitted, encouraged, welcomed, but not officially enforced by the State."[2] He discussed the historical meaning of mass Jewish immigration to Israel and its place in the continuum of Jewish history going back to the Book of Isaiah, emphasizing not only the arrival of Jewish refugees from Europe but also of Jewish expellees from Yemen and Iraq. He debunked "the old bogy of dual allegiance" in the Diaspora, particularly in the United States.[3] He calmed readers concerning Israel's relationship with the Soviet bloc, which he said was limited. He was even optimistic about the achievement of a formal peace with the Arab states within the decade.[4]

McDonald had earlier done fundraising for the United Jewish Appeal, but Israel's difficult economic circumstances called for a new approach. In February 1951 a new nonprofit organization called the American Financial and Development Corporation for Israel began to sell and underwrite Israeli bonds. The government bonds promised purchasers a return of up to 4 percent on maturation. The Israeli government expected that the bonds could raise a billion dollars in just three years.[5] The initial campaign was for $500 million.

The Development Corporation depended on tens of thousands of volunteers and was run by a board of governors that included more than two hundred prominent American Jews. Henry Montor, whom McDonald knew well and who recruited him for the new organization, was the chief executive officer. Ben Abrams, McDonald's old friend, was the bond chairman for greater New York. James McDonald was the single Gentile in a leading role. From the

1. McDonald, *My Mission in Israel*, 272.
2. Ibid., 278–279.
3. Ibid., 289.
4. Ibid., 282.
5. See Allen Lesser, *Israel's Impact, 1950–51: A Personal Record* (Lanham, MD: University Press of America, 1984); and Allon Gal, ed., *Envisioning Israel: The Changing Ideals and Images of North American Jews* (Detroit: Wayne State University Press, 1996), 193–270.

Fig. 28.1. James McDonald speaks at a fundraising banquet on behalf of the State of Israel. United States Holocaust Memorial Museum.

launch of the bond program in 1951 to his retirement in 1961, he served as the chairman of the corporation's advisory council.[6]

The position was more than honorary. In addition to writing numerous letters to Jewish leaders to urge the purchase of bonds and to undertake bond drives, McDonald traveled and spoke to an extent that belied his age. Hundreds

6. McDonald's activities with the Development Corporation for Israel are documented in McDonald Papers, Columbia University, boxes 34–36.

of audiences all over the United States and Canada, from big cities such as New York and Vancouver to smaller places such as Baton Rouge, El Paso, Davenport, and Pierre, heard McDonald speak of his experiences and of Israel's needs. In 1955 he undertook a South American tour that included Panama, Venezuela, Peru, Brazil, Argentina, Chile, and Curaçao, and in 1958 he traveled to Australia and New Zealand. He was an attraction wherever he went. Vera Cohen, the area manager of the Atlantic City Committee, wrote him in 1955 with a compliment that American Jews would well understand:

> You will never know how worthwhile your being at Temple Beth Israel was and still is. For several days after, people were still discussing the profundity of your talk. I realized that there was a sizable crowd who came to hear and see you—but what I did not know until just recently, was that this was a larger audience than even for the High Holy Days.[7]

The US presidential election in 1952 created a new situation for Israel and for McDonald. Dwight D. Eisenhower had not expressed enthusiasm for Israel and was elected with almost no Jewish support. He entrusted his foreign policy to John Foster Dulles, who had worked with McDonald in late 1948 at the UN. But Dulles had changed his views toward Israel in the interim, perhaps owing to the communist victory in China in 1949, the shooting war in Korea after 1950, and the development of NATO in Europe. The United States, he believed, had to think more globally. American support for Israel's creation, Dulles thought, had alienated the Arab world with its millions of people, its strategic bases, and its oil, the last of which supplied Western Europe and Japan. Eisenhower and Dulles hoped to win back the Arab world for the struggle against the Soviets through a policy of "friendly impartiality," which could, they believed, create a bloc of Arab states loyal to the United States.[8]

It was not a promising policy. In July 1951, a member of the Palestinian Husseini clan assassinated King Abdullah of Jordan in Jerusalem. Abdullah's grandson Hussein, who witnessed the assassination and then assumed the throne in 1952 at age 18, declined to resume negotiations with the Israelis. Egypt offered even worse prospects for peace. In 1952 military officers overthrew King Farouk, and by 1954 Gamal Abd al-Nasser, a lieutenant colonel who had been trapped by the Israelis in the Faluja pocket in 1948–1949, emerged as Egypt's leader. Seeing himself as an anticolonialist champion of the Arab world, Nasser distrusted the West, primarily Britain, and refused to consider peace with Israel. Meanwhile, armed infiltrators from western Jordan and Gaza had become

---

7. Letter of November 16, 1955, McDonald Papers, Columbia University, box 34, folder 4.
8. On this complex of problems see Hahn, *Caught in the Middle East*, 147–222; Isaac Alteras, *Eisenhower and Israel: U.S.-Israeli Relations, 1953–1960* (Gainesville: University Press of Florida, 1993); Abraham Ben-Zvi, *Decade of Transition: Eisenhower, Kennedy, and the Origins of the American-Israeli Alliance* (New York: Columbia University Press, 1998); and Cohen, *Fighting World War Three from the Middle East*, 239–323.

a growing problem, killing 420 Israelis between 1950 and 1953 and triggering Israeli military reprisals.[9]

Dulles managed to conclude a 1954 arms deal with Iraq, which the next year joined the Baghdad Pact, a bloc of four "northern tier" states (along with Turkey, Iran, and Pakistan) plus Great Britain. As the Israelis pointed out, Iraq was the one Arab belligerent from 1948 that had not even signed a cease-fire agreement with Israel, and it continued to block the flow of oil to Haifa. Dulles refused to press Egypt to open the Suez Canal to Israeli shipping, declined to sign a bilateral defense treaty with Israel, and rejected any US-Israeli arms deal for fear of alienating the Arabs. Washington pressed Israel for major sacrifices, including deep territorial concessions in the Negev to allow contiguity between the Arab states; an end to plans to divert northern waters for irrigation in the Negev; and a slowing of Jewish immigration, which key State Department officials saw as the root of Arab anxiety. As Eban put it to Dulles in September 1953, a "cloud had fallen over the [US-Israeli] relationship."[10]

Though busy with annual Israel Bond campaigns, McDonald weighed in. In March 1954 he wrote a long memo to Eisenhower and Dulles on the need for realism in the Middle East. "The first—and a constant—task of a states-man," he wrote, "is to distinguish between realities and illusions;" any faith in Arab commitment to democracy, Arab unity, or Arab help against the Soviets was an illusion. He continued,

> Arab unity is a myth. Despite the facade of the Arab League the Arab states are radically divided by dynastic rivalries, fanatical nationalism and, in the case of the Lebanon and its neighbors, by the Lebanese Christians' fear of Moslem fanaticism. . . . The only real measure of Arab unity is the negative attitude of the Arab states toward Israel . . . [but] [e]ven in the war against Israel, the Arab states were never effectively united. . . .
>
> Israel, compared with the Arab states, is tiny both in area and in population. To assume, however, that this differential is any measure of the comparative military potential, would be an illusion. . . .
>
> The way to make peace is through negotiations. But the Arab states stubbornly refuse to recognize or discuss peace with Israel. They insist on maintaining a boycott of the new State.[11]

Eisenhower replied politely that he would pass the memorandum to Dulles. Dulles did not reply at all.

---

9. Benny Morris, *Israel's Border Wars, 1949–1956: Arab Infiltration, Israeli Retaliation, and the Countdown to the Suez War* (New York: Oxford University Press, 1993).

10. Alteras, *Eisenhower and Israel*, 88–89.

11. "Realism and the United States' National Interests in the Middle East," memorandum for Eisenhower and Dulles, March 27, 1954, McDonald Papers, Columbia University, box 14, folder 6.

McDonald returned to Israel frequently as a private citizen and spoke to his old contacts there, including Ben-Gurion and Sharett.[12] En route to Be'er Sheva from Lydda in 1954, he saw that "the fields . . . were green with rather luxurious grass and barley and rye nearly ready for the harvest." He marveled at the development of Ashkelon and Haifa. He visited the new dams, pumping stations, canals, and reservoirs in the north. He also worried about the border areas, which had become increasingly dangerous. McDonald's driver came within three kilometers of the Gaza Strip. "In answer to my further inquiry about possible infiltrators," McDonald recounted, "he assured me that there was no danger. Exactly four hours later, at 8 o'clock that evening on that very spot, or within a kilometer or so of it, Arab infiltrators killed one Israel soldier and wounded eight or so more. You see, life is never dull in Israel."[13]

In May 1956 McDonald wrote Ben-Gurion, who had returned to the prime ministership from a temporary retirement at the Sde Boker kibbutz in the Negev desert. He warned that his recent travel for Israel Bonds suggested that "Israel, as compared with the Arab states, is losing dangerously in American public opinion." Dulles, McDonald added, was "quick to sense and to take advantage of Israel's declining prestige with our public." The only influential Jewish Republican was Rabbi Abba Hillel Silver, who had met with Eisenhower as recently as April 1956 and, according to McDonald, had offered "to play the role of the influential friend of the President and the Secretary of State." But Silver's efforts alone would not be enough. Israel, McDonald told Ben-Gurion, needed a better public relations program in the United States. "I am not," he said, "one of those Americans who exaggerates the efficacy of public relations experts, but I cannot underline too strongly that Israel desperately needs the cooperation of such experts."[14] That same year the American Zionist Council registered as an official lobbying group for Israel. In 1959, it changed its name to the American Israel Public Affairs Committee (AIPAC).

By then the Soviet Union had reversed its initial policy of support for Israel. Stalin had implemented anti-Jewish policies earlier, including the anti-cosmopolitan campaign that began in 1949, the halt of Jewish emigration from Eastern Europe in spring 1952, and the purge of "Zionist" elements in the Czechoslovak Communist Party later the same year. In February 1953, shortly before Stalin's death, Moscow severed relations with Israel. The decision by Stalin's successors in 1955 to sell jet fighters, bombers, and tanks to Egypt wrecked the May 1950 Tripartite Declaration between the United States, Britain, and France, which aimed to prevent a Middle Eastern arms race, while establishing a Soviet foothold in the Arab world. Nasser's continued blockade of Israeli ships from the Suez Canal, in defiance of a UN resolution of 1951,

12. Weizmann had died in 1952.
13. McDonald's description of this trip is in his letter to Barbara Ann McDonald, April 24, 1954, McDonald Papers, Columbia University, box 19, folder 10.
14. McDonald to Ben-Gurion, May 16, 1956, McDonald Papers, Columbia University, box 1, folder 8.

and his closure of the Straits of Tiran (which closed off Eilat from the Red Sea) in September 1955 portended additional threats. Meanwhile, Nasser declared that stepped-up raids from Gaza "will cleanse the land of Palestine;" that "we demand vengeance, and vengeance is Israel's death;" and that "my task is to deliver the Arab world from destruction through Israel's intrigue."[15]

An anti-Nasser coalition formed, but it did not include the United States. The French government under Premier Guy Mollet, furious with Nasser for his support of the Algerian rebellion that had begun in 1954 against French rule, agreed to sell Israel tanks, jets, and antitank missiles. Under the Conservative government of Anthony Eden, the United Kingdom joined the effort to remove Nasser after July 1956 when Egypt nationalized the Suez Canal. The canal was no longer manned by British troops, but it was partly owned by the British government, and Britain depended on it for trade. On October 29, 1956, Israel launched a successful campaign against Egypt.[16] It captured the Gaza Strip, crippled Egyptian forces in the Sinai, and broke the Egyptian blockade of the Straits of Tiran and the Gulf of Aqaba. The British and French bombarded strategic targets in Egypt, and on November 5 they landed paratroopers, seeking to push toward the Suez Canal zone and to topple Nasser.

Although unhappy with Nasser, Eisenhower and Dulles were even angrier with the Israelis, French, and British. They had kept their intentions secret from the United States, launching their campaign during the crisis over Hungary's attempt to leave the Warsaw Pact and just days away from the US presidential election. The United States immediately secured a UN General Assembly resolution calling for withdrawal of all invading forces from Egypt. US economic pressures on Britain forced British and French troops to halt short of the Suez Canal and withdraw from Egypt entirely by December 22. Israeli forces withdrew from most of the Sinai after heavy pressure from Moscow and Washington. But Israel retained control of Sharm al-Sheikh in the eastern Sinai, which controlled the Straits of Tiran, and it maintained control of the Gaza Strip. It refused to withdraw until its security was guaranteed. Eisenhower and Dulles insisted that Israel could not set conditions on its withdrawal, and they worried that US-backed security guarantees for Israel would alienate the Arab world, which now looked to Nasser as a hero. In February 1957 Eisenhower submitted a resolution to Congress, later known as the Eisenhower Doctrine, which called for military and economic aid for Middle Eastern countries resisting armed communist aggression. The White House meanwhile threatened to back any sanctions approved by the UN against Israel and considered halting US government aid and even private Israel Bond purchases.

---

15. Quoted in Abba Eban's address to the UN General Assembly, November 1, 1956, in Mezini, ed., *Israel's Foreign Relations: Selected Documents, 1947–1974*, 547–549.

16. Israel's Sinai campaign of 1956 and the Suez Crisis are assessed in several collections of essays. See Simon C. Smith, ed., *Reassessing Suez 1956: New Perspectives on the Crisis and its Aftermath* (Burlington, VT: Ashgate, 2008); David Tal, ed., *The 1956 War: Collusion and Rivalry in the Middle East* (London: Frank Cass, 2001); and William Roger Louis and Roger Owen, eds., *Suez 1956: The Crisis and Its Consequences* (New York: Oxford University Press, 1989).

Sympathy for Israel's security needs and Democratic congressional opposition to sanctions against Israel led to heated debate on Eisenhower's resolution. McDonald testified for two days—February 8 and 11, 1957—before a joint meeting of the Senate Foreign Relations and Armed Services Committees.[17] He supported the president's resolution in principle as a means to stop Soviet aggression, though, as he pointed out, the Soviets were more likely to infiltrate the Arab states than attack them. Mostly, however, he criticized recent US policy toward Israel. The attack on the Sinai, McDonald said, was poorly timed, but undertaken out of real security concerns. "So long as the Arab states," he said, "stridently proclaim their refusal to recognize Israel and their determination to destroy it, Ben-Gurion and his colleagues are not unreasonable in demanding, before the withdrawal of their troops from Gaza and the Tiran Strait, firm guarantees against renewed Egyptian commando raids and [the] blockade of the Gulf of Aqaba."

As for the prospects of peace, McDonald recommended true evenhandedness: "I would like to knock the heads of Israel and the Arab States together; but it seems to me that it is self-defeating to knock the head of Israel alone. It is this which is implied in the current talk about sanctions, which I hope is only talk. . . . I think we must make up our minds that the Arabs need us quite as much as we need them. . . . Actually the Arab States are capitalizing on their inherent weakness with astonishing success. . . . I think the Arabs understand firmness, and I think I should like to see it applied not merely to Israel but to the Arabs." Fears of Israel's expansion, he testified, were overblown. "I have . . . talked to [Israeli leaders] many times off the record," he said. "They have always said to me that what they wanted to do was to intensify the development of the area which they now have. They have taken in a little less than a million Jewish refugees, and have integrated them into the land. They think they can become a second Switzerland, a second Belgium, a second Holland, and that to meet the necessities of their people they do not require additional territory."

McDonald's broadest testimony answered questions concerning the Arab refugees from Senator Richard B. Russell (D-GA), the chair of the Armed Services Committee, and Senator William Fulbright (D-AR). Scholars then, such as Joseph Schechtman, and now, such as Benny Morris, place the refugee issue in context.[18] Shortly before Israel's creation, tens of millions were forcibly transferred in Europe and in South Asia amidst terrible violence. Palestine's refugees were far smaller in number. But with no place willing to resettle them, the question remained, and still remains, unresolved. McDonald too understood the plight of Palestine's refugees in context:

17. *The President's Proposal on the Middle East: Hearings before the Committee on Foreign Relations and the Committee on Armed Services, United States Senate, Eighty-Fifth Congress, First Session on S.J. Res. 19 and H.J. Res 117*, Part II: *February 5, 6, 7, 8, and 11, 1957* (Washington, DC: Government Printing Office, 1957), 827–856, 914–937. The editors have edited and reordered parts of the testimony based on subject matter.
18. Morris, *The Birth of the Palestinian Refugee Problem Revisited*, 42–43, and n. 11, 37.

The first thing to remember about refugees is that almost always they are the result of war. . . . The second point is that I knew many of the Israel leaders before there was an Israel—Dr. Weizmann, Ben-Gurion, Sharett and others. . . . Before Israel was set up and before the war with the Arab States, I never found one Israeli leader who even hinted at any expectation that the Arabs would leave Palestine. . . . All of the Jewish talk and plans were on the assumption—I do not say there was not some secret plans I did not know about, but everything I heard was on the assumption—that the Arabs would stay in Palestine, and that the Jews would gradually, by accentuated immigration, become the majority, but never that the Arabs were to be driven out.

Then came the war. . . . By the time the first truces were signed in the middle of 1948, a substantial number of Arabs, maybe five or six hundred thousand at that time, had left the country. About 150,000 or 175,000 remained. . . . The refugee problem has increased by natural means. The chief occupation in the camps is begetting children. Surprisingly, though the standard of refugee living is low—they are kept on a dole, as you know, by the U.N. organization and mostly with United States money— . . . the health of babies is better than those of many peasants in Arab countries. . . . Then too there have been increases of the [refugee] lists, by Arabs . . . U.N. people have done the best they can to avoid the padding of their lists, but only with partial success. . . . I don't wish to minimize the problem—it is a tragic problem—whether the number of bona fide refugees is 600,000 or 900,000.

The Israeli Government has not done everything that it might have done. I used to repeatedly try to fix Ben-Gurion's mind, or that of Dr. Weizmann or Foreign Minister Sharett, on the problem, but they were usually thinking more about the 6 million Jews who had been murdered in the war. Moreover, they argued that they were not responsible for the plight of Arab refugees. This responsibility, they always contended, rests upon the war begun by the Arabs. . . .

On the other hand, I am sure that there can be no settlement of the refugee problem except as part of an overall peace problem. When the Arabs say Israel must first settle the refugee problem before they will talk peace, this is equivalent to saying that the Israelis must yield on all major issues before there can be peace negotiations. . . . Actually, I do not think the Arab leaders in their hearts worry much about the plight of the refugees. After all, in Egypt an appalling percent of the fellahin die in their twenties and early thirties of endemic diseases. The infant mortality is also appalling. . . . The refugees constitute the best argument the Arabs have in their debate before public opinion with Israel.

The presidential resolution was passed on March 9, 1957. As a consequence of White House and UN pressure, Israeli troops withdrew from the Gaza Strip on March 7 and Sharm al-Sheikh on March 12. But owing to congressional pressure on the White House and because of Ben-Gurion's tenacity, the Israelis left with certain assurances that held up for a decade. Egyptian civil rule returned to Gaza, but the Egyptian military did not, and the United Nations Emergency Force (UNEF) remained in Gaza until 1967, helping ensure that the border with Israel remained quiet. A similar UN force remained in Sharm al-Sheikh, helping keep open the Straits of Tiran, which in turn allowed Israeli development of Eilat, as well as a new pipeline from Eilat to Haifa. It too remained until 1967.

In the meantime, McDonald could feel hopeful, yet apprehensive. In January 1958 in the year of Israel's tenth anniversary, he gave the fourth annual Chaim Weizmann lecture at the Jewish Theological Seminary in New York City. His title was "Israel—The Next Decade: Problems and Aspirations." He outlined Israel's unique issues, ranging from the absorption of double its population from countries as diverse as Hungary and Yemen, to the problem of religion "in its most rigid, fanatical, and intolerant form . . . developing in a state which is based on modern concepts," which, he said, would demand exceptional statesmanship, tolerance, and good will. McDonald discussed Israel's economic problems and its need to become more financially independent of foreign sources of money, such as German reparations and US grants-in-aid.

McDonald also expressed concern that Israel's intransigent enemies could now build a relationship with the USSR, in a coalition that might ultimately destroy Israel. In the meantime, Israel would be a state perpetually on the razor's edge, and Israelis would have to manage that tension: "The solution of these problems is not only decisive politically to allow Israel to live a normal life, not surrounded by millions of enemies who wait for a moment to be able to destroy Israel. . . . [It] would have tremendous consequences for the whole spirit, for the whole intellectual atmosphere . . . in which the young generation especially will grow up if Israel will be allowed, one day in the second decade, the luxury of living in peace with normal relations with its neighbors."[19] The day that McDonald mentioned did not come in the second decade. Indeed, it has yet to come.

. . . .

McDonald retired in 1961. He lived his remaining years in Bronxville, New York, where he made his home. He died in 1964 after a long illness. He is buried in Albany, Indiana, the small Midwestern town in which he grew up.

On the surface, McDonald was ill-suited to his mission to provide US diplomatic support to the new state. He was a scholar, not a trained diplomat, and his appointment angered the State Department. Yet in another sense, McDonald was very well matched because of his fundamental decency, intellectual curiosity, and past history. McDonald understood the Jewish plight from two decades of having watched and studied it as no one in the State Department had. He appreciated, as very few non-Jews did, that the Jewish people needed a state, and that having finally regained one and having bled to defend it, they would do nothing to see it endangered and everything to see it preserved and developed.

19. "Israel—The Next Decade: Problems and Aspirations," January 5, 1958, McDonald Papers, Columbia University, box 26, folder 5.

McDonald could thus play a determinative role on many levels. Day to day, he undertook many activities that few ambassadors would, despite the paucity of the US mission's budget. He held discussions at the residence nearly every day, hosting everyone from Revisionist Zionist leaders such as Menachem Begin to writers such as Arthur Koestler, to traveling US businessmen, to young Israeli intellectuals. He constantly traveled to Jewish settlements, examining everything from shoe factories to bakeries. He spoke at opening ceremonies at institutes and schools, attended numerous cultural events from symphonies at the Israel Philharmonic to art shows at the Tel Aviv Museum, visited artists' studios as far away as Safed, and reveled in special occasions as simple as Rabbi Harry Davidowitz's first Passover seder in Israel. Even those who had never met McDonald felt they knew him personally. In March 1949 James Rosenberg wrote McDonald that a friend from Virginia, having returned from a six-month visit to Israel, exclaimed, "James G. McDonald? Why the people there are absolutely crazy about him. Soldiers down in the Negev talk about how wonderful he is. He's a real hero to the people of Israel."[20]

McDonald's diplomacy was all the more impressive for his being cut out of the State Department loop for much of his mission. But McDonald had the trust of the president, which, if employed correctly, could offset State Department hostility. And because he had no plans to stay in the Department after the conclusion of his mission, he could do his job largely as he saw fit. McDonald developed a network of friends, family members, businessmen, and even congressmen who could relay messages and apply pressure when need be. He engineered a revolt against the State Department's technicians during the 1948 Paris General Assembly meeting, averting the threat of sanctions against Israel while helping Israel keep the Negev. He conducted private diplomacy with the Vatican concerning the fate of Jerusalem and on his own set up meetings for Israeli representatives with his contacts in Rome. He could not defuse the political conflict over Jerusalem, but he surely kept the conflict from becoming worse. Having worked with refugees over much of his career, he was deeply concerned for Palestine's Arab refugees. He talked at length with Quaker and Red Cross officials charged with their welfare, and he helped create the UN machinery that would provide vital aid. Though he understood that the Israelis might have done more to relieve the crisis, he never forgot that the Arab states had attacked Israel, refused to accommodate most refugees, and used the refugees as a political issue in the years that followed.

McDonald also helped build the foundations of a US-Israeli relationship based on the recognition of common values. He initiated research projects through trusted experts to show the State Department that Israel was not, nor would it be, communist—no small feat given the linkages sometimes conjured in the popular imagination between Jews and communists in the mid-twentieth

20. Rosenberg to McDonald, March 28, 1949, McDonald Papers, Columbia University, box 4, folder 3.

century. He set up liaisons between major US labor leaders and labor leaders in Israel at a critical point in world history, while calling for, and eventually getting, a qualified labor attaché for the embassy. In Israel he helped start educational programs about the United States and provided continual support to American Jewish groups in Israel.

McDonald built positive relationships with Israel's leaders while telling the State Department uncomfortable truths about the realities on the ground. UN truce machinery, he said, sometimes worked and sometimes did not; UN peacemaking machinery, he argued, was hopelessly flawed. Israel, McDonald argued repeatedly, would remain, and it would remain as it was. Any US policy that pretended otherwise while not taking advantage of what Israel offered—the promise of a stable, democratically minded, modern, and honest friend in the Middle East—would be foolish. It was a position he maintained after his ambassadorship, even if it meant challenging the Eisenhower White House.

. . . .

On a visit to the Orthodox settlement at Bnei Brak on November 2, 1948, the local council welcomed McDonald with this comment: "It is hard to be a diplomat," they said, "but even harder to be a friend of Israel."[21] James McDonald was one of Israel's first true friends and one of the most steadfast. His friendship was born of the hard-learned belief that persecuted Jews needed a place of their own and that with time that place would, despite its growing pains, become a beacon. The peace that McDonald wished for Israel has not yet come to pass. Yet McDonald and his deep conviction, tireless work, and genuine interest in everything he saw helped ensure that, of all the foreign representatives in Israel's foundational decade, he was the most instrumental in building the global diplomatic supports on which the new state could stand.

21. In McDonald Papers, USHMM, box 7, folder 8.

INDEX

Page numbers in italics indicate maps and figures.

Note: The initials JGM refer to James G. McDonald, and BAM refers to Barbara Ann McDonald.

tion of view of, 95–96. *See also*
    refugees, Arab; *specific states*
Arab villages in Israeli territory, 69–70,
    453, 484, 485, 675–676
Archibald, Colonel Edwin P.: as air
    attaché, 287, 302, 707, 845–846; Air
    Force reception and, 697; at audience
    with pope, 666; Bonawitz on, 862;
    on Israeli arms, 827, 838–839; JGM
    conferences with, 610, 884; on JGM
    visit to Rome, 665; on Joint Weekly
    Report, 866; liaison relationships of,
    632, 782; replacement for, 897; trip
    to Dead Sea area by, 346
Argov, Nehemia, 981
Arlosoroff, Chaim, 621–622
Arlosoroff, Sima Rubin, 621–622
armament of Israel: Acheson on,
    862; Archibald on, 838–839;
    D. Ben-Gurion July 29 proposal
    on, 955, 960, 963, 964, 969–970,
    971–972; by Czechoslovakia, 94,
    232, 370; Elath on, 828; secrecy
    about, 564–565, 581, 827, 883;
    M. Sharett on, 900; war in Korea
    and, 946–947. *See also* arms embargo;
    Czechoslovakia; rearmament of
    Arab states; second round, Israeli
    fear of; Shiloah, Reuven
armistice agreements: Comay and,
    712; expiration of, 698; Eytan on,
    709; with Jordan, 892; with Syria,
    610, 613–614. *See also* armistice
    negotiations
armistice lines, *xvii,* 617
armistice negotiations: with Abdullah,
    362, 363–364, 407–408; D. Ben-
    Gurion on, 505; Bunche and,
    327, 376, 395, 396, 407, 409, 709;
    Dayan and, 303, 327–328, 408,
    452; with Egypt, 313, 327, 329,
    349–351, *352,* 357, 372–373,
    375–376, 389–390, 395–396; Eytan
    and, 327, 329, 438, 439, 452; Herlitz
    on, 349–350; with Lebanon, 409,
    417, 439; Mohn on, 501–502, 586;
    Nablus-Jenin-Tulkarm triangle in,
    433–434, 506; Negev in, 389; PCC
    and, 364; M. Shertok on, 329–330,
    361, 395; Shiloah on, 303, 327,
    375–376, 389–390, 407, 488; with
    Syria, 439, 453, 454, 475, 476,

488–489, 501–502, 506, 568,
    570–571, 586, 610; with Transjor-
    dan, 303, 317, 362, 407–408, 409,
    427, 452–453. *See also* armistice
    agreements; Mixed Armistice
    Commissions
arms embargo, 14, 31, 64n82, 81,
    116n81, 198, 245n91, 483, 552, 631,
    704n38, 783,
arms race in Middle East, 910–911, 915
Armstrong, Arthur, 649
Army Day, 605–606, 911
Arnon, David, 315, 928
Arslan, Adil Ibn Hamud, 538, 571, 599
Arvey, Jack, 561, 619, 658, 702
Assaf, Simcha, 902
Atassi, Hashim al-, 687
Atfeh, Abdullah, 768, 771
Austin, Warren, 16
Australia, recognition of Israel by, 358
Axelrod, Harry, 323, 346
Azcárate y Flores, Pablo de, 344–345,
    362, 458, 599, 870, 874
Azm, Khalid al-, 770–771, 844
Azzam Pasha, Abd al-Rahman, 137, 160,
    169, 180, 780

Babin, Viktor, 750
Baer, Arthur B., 11
Bagge, Widor, 261, 264, 399
Baghdad Pact, 998
Bailey, Moses, 196, 200–201
Balaban, Abraham J., 20
Baldwin, LaVerne, 713
Balfour, David, 796, 927
Bancroft, Harding F., 272
Banta, Kenneth W., 832
Barazi, Mushin al-, 137, 599, 613, 671, 676
Barco, James W., 529–530, 825, 874
Bar-Ilan (Berlin), Meir, 82, 88, 386,
    410–411
Barkley, Alben W., 334, 357
Barnes, Curtis W.: on Archibald, 845;
    assassination of Bernadotte and,
    131; on entertainment, 81; furniture
    for mission and, 293; JGM contacts
    with, 128, 170; on JGM visit, 665;
    July Fourth plans and, 575; as
    mission staff, 17, 21; safety of, 143;
    on site for consulate in Jerusalem,
    809; Special Committee on
    Jerusalem and, 572

Barrett, Donald (grandchild), 618, 640, 658, 977

Barrett, Halsey (son-in-law), 11, 85, 258

Barrett, Janet McDonald (daughter), 39, 147, 493, 618

Barrett, Vail (grandchild), 977

Baruch, Bernard, 110

Beeley, Harold, 28, 166–167, 232, 257, 298

Begin, Menachem: Altman and, 67n102, 431; comparisons with Hitler, 104; and Arab refugees, 559; Herut Party of, 142, 352; J. Herzog on, 340; as Irgun leader, 67n102, 104, 119, 853; JGM meetings with, 210–211, 559, 832–833; Koestler on, 135; reference to JGM in book of, 858–859, 879; threat against leadership of, 934; on US pressure, 559; US visa application of, 199, 201, 211, 212, 220; US visit of, 632

Begley, Frank, 131, 474

Beilin, Harry, 210

Beisner, Robert L., 2

Bele, Refet, 916

Belgium, recognition of Israel by, 878

Bell, Colin W., 630

Ben-Aharon, Yitzhak, 98, 439, 825

Ben-Ami, Oved, 432, 863, 913, 957

Ben-Artzi, Efraim, 207, 243, 507, 862

Ben-Artzi, Victoria, 243

Bender, Charlie, 673

Bendor, Shmuel, 980, 990

Ben-Eliezer, Aryeh, 524–525, 559

Bengis, Zelig R., 512–513

Ben-Gurion, Amos, 136

Ben-Gurion, David, *446*; on alliance with West, 954–955; anti-communist statements of, 709; on Arab states, 983; on armistice negotiations, 505; BAM on, 5; on Bernadotte assassination, 132; cabinet and, 360, 419–420, 981; at congressional delegation dinner, 674; on constitution for Israel, 524, 542, 833n66; criticism of government of, 569; on economy, 981–982; on Egypt, 803; Ethridge on, 404; Ewing and, 775; at Foreign Office reception, 207; Frisch on, 787; Griffis meeting with, 368; health of, 407; on Hebrew language, 632–633; Helm on, 949;

J. Herzog on, 353; on Y. Herzog, 633; on housing issues, 504–505; immigration and, 679–680, 760; on Israeli approach at Lausanne, 607; on Jerusalem, 65, 459, 742–743, 982; Jewish Agency Executive and, 12; on JGM, 629–630, 902; JGM contacts with, 64, 106–109, 175, 176, 236–237, 241–242, 281, 294–295, 303–305, 460–461, 854–855, 970; JGM formal presentation to, 73, *74*; JGM on, 423; July 29 proposal on immigrants and arms of, 955, 960, 963, 964, 969–970, 971–972; Kohn on, 354; Koussevitzky on, 850; leave of absence of, 833; Lehman meeting with, 511; on Lincoln, 358, 432, 537; Morgenthau and, 793; move of office of, to Jerusalem, 754; at movie party, 367; on Negev, 107, 196, 242; on negotiations with Syria, 511–512; Operation Hiram and, 209; on organization of armies, 565; Orthodoxy and, 906, 907, 925–926; PCC and, 458–459, 460; peace negotiations and, 106, 108, 533; as prime minister, 1, 4, 388; provisional government and, 13; Purim party of, 432; radio address of, 361; refugees and, 461, 526, 533; rumor of attack on, 147; at Russian party, 230; on Security Council resolution, 194–195; Shiloah on, 825–826; at state council meeting, 154; on Syrian coup, 454–455; Truman and, 230, 271, 316, 424, 443, 487–488, 514, 628–629; UN Resolution 303 and, 749, 754; on US founding fathers, 537; C. Weizmann and, 51, 420, 443; at Weizmann Institute of Science dedication, 691; Za'im and, 613; at Zimmerman reception, 282. *See also* Mapai Party

Ben-Gurion, Paula: farewell visit to, 992; at Foreign Office reception, 207; garden party of, 501, 504; Helm on, 856; on housekeeping service, 195; JGM contacts with, 237, 985; JGM on, 64, 176, 201, 281, 632–633, 928, 954; at Menuhin concert, 879–880; V. Weizmann and, 231; at ZOA House groundbreaking, 789

Ben-Haim, Paul, 829
Ben-Horin, Eliahu, 248, 254, 260, 263, 282, 318, 342, 653, 657
Benin, Menahem Musa (Maurice), 664, 786–787, 809, 817
Ben-Ovadia, Isaac, 158, 159
Bentov, Mordechai, 98–99, 439, 502, 825
Bentwich, Norman, 293, 390, 758
Ben-Zvi, Shaul (Paul Shulman), 950
Bergman, Avraham, 199, 295, 317, 320
Bergmann, Ernst David, 63, 74, 410, 691
Bergner, Elisabeth, 752
Bergquist, Kenneth P., 280
Bergson, Peter (Hillel Kook), 89, 104, 181–182, 199, 524–525, 631–632, 934
Bergus, Donald C., 916, 917
Berlin, Meir. *See* Bar-Ilan (Berlin)
Berlin crisis, 39, 40, 45, 294
Bernadotte, Folke: and Arab refugees, 70; 183; assassination of, 7, 128, 129–130, 131–132, 140, 141, 144, 185, 237, 264, 474–475, 740; appointment as mediator, 9; authority of, 64–65; Ben-Gurion on, 106; de Reynier on, 185; and Jerusalem fighting, 64–65, 115, 126, 129; and Jewish immigration, 69, 97n15, 122; JGM on, 71, 79, 86, 111–112, 144; Kaplan on, 114; MacDonald on, 115; Mohn and, 68–71; peace negotiations and, 111–112; refugee aid and, 183; M. Shertok and, 65, 122; transfer of headquarters of, 129; UN Truce Commission and, 9. *See also* Bernadotte Plan
Bernadotte Plan, 26, 128–129, 180, 209; British government and, 42, 44, 128, 137, 141, 146, 162, 247, 253, 261, 344; Czechoslovakia and, 263n157; erosion of, 270, 277, 546; Israeli government on, 114, 138, 148, 164n24; JGM and, 66, 69, 197, 375; Mohn on, 180; Multer on, 134; pope and, 53; E. Roosevelt and, 221; Mohn and, 72; M. Shertok on, 26; support for, 28, 42, 141–142, 143, 144, 146, 151, 197, 253; UN General Assembly and, 137; US response to, 28–29, 75, 102, 112n71, 117, 128, 137–138, 172, 248, 253,

259n145; USSR and, 150n84, 271; Weizmann and, 48; White House and, 148–149, 197, 264
Bernstein, Leonard (Lenny): appearances with Heifetz, 913, 914; BAM on, 6; concerts of, 158, 186, 194, 213, 240, 910, 918; JGM contacts with, 149–150, 937, 991–992; Koussevitzky and, 193, 851; parties for, 935
Bernstein, Mrs. Peretz, 75–76
Bernstein, Shirley, 991–992
Bernstein, Shlomo Fritz (Peretz), 91–92, 201, 920–921
Berry, Burton Y., 718, 733, 741, 751, 957, 974–976
Bevan, Aneurin, 428
Bevin, Ernest: on arms embargo, 198; on Bernadotte Plan, 137, 141–142, 151; L. Douglas on, 39; Israel and, 9, 28; JGM and, 37–38, 43, 47, 48, 859–860; Kohn on, 354; Locker on, 213; Lovett and, 33; on Negev, 50; release of Jewish internees from Cyprus and, 337–338; M. Seiff on, 167, 428, 901; on US policy toward Israel, 253; views of, 44–46; warning to Israel from, 247; C. Weizmann on, 775
Beyer, Roland C., 246, 280
Bezner, Yitzhak, 756
Bidault, Georges, 49
Bilby, Kenneth W., 105, 145–146, 307, 625
Biran, Avraham, 967
Bir 'Asluj, 350, 372, 389, 396n101, 989.
Bir Qattar, 830, 856, 929n53, 991
Bisgyer, Maurice, 164
Black, Eugene R., Sr., 877
Blandford, John B., Jr., 683, 885, 916, 917–918, 984–985
Blanshard, Paul, 843
Blatnik, John, 673, 674–675
Blaustein, Jacob, 14, 15, 32, 462, 478, 568, 958, 968, 976
Bloch, Benjamin, 74, 81
Bloch, Gérard, 854–855
Bloedy, Edith Kraus, 705
Bloodworth, Thomas S., 695–696
Bloom, Sol, 369, 373
Blum, Léon, 49
Bnei Brak agricultural settlement, 216–218, 684, *685*

career of, 231; JGM meeting with, 471–472; municipal election rumors and, 373; Riley on, 571; on trip to Eilat, 865

Deak, Francis, 582

De Courcy, William E., 975

de facto/dejure recognition of Israel. *See* recognition of Israel

Deir Yassin, 12, 72n120, 121, 179

De Luce, Daniel, 84, 150

de Nerciat, Robert, 916

Denham, F. B., 416

Depage, Pierre, 345, 393

de Philippe, Edis, 6, 100, 119, 213, 229, 239, 287, 613, 864

de Reynier, Jacques, 183–186, 345, 369

de Rothschild, Lionel and Anthony, 41

Descoeudres, Pierre, 235

de Sola Pool, Tamar, 99, 901, 910

Dewey, Thomas, 17, 46, 101, 110, 198, 202, 218, 975

Dickstein, Samuel, 960

Dietz, David H., 413

Dinkelspiel, Lloyd W., 835

diplomatic corps: complaints of, 852, 855–856; on Israel aggression, 959; meetings of, 560, 705–706, 850, 878–879

displaced persons, 4, 57, 69, 165, 168, 239, 286, 450n5, 455, 504n34, 679. *See also* refugees, Jewish

Divon, Shmuel, 769, 770–772

Dixon, Charles Dean, 945

Dodge, Bayard, 250, 251–252, 255, 256, 257, 275

Donovan, William J., 491–492, 494

Dori, Ya'akov, 434, 605, 704

Douglas, Lewis W.: in Bevin meeting, 45, 46, 47; British position and, 37–38; JGM meeting with, 39–40; JGM on, 274; Lovett and, 33; Marshall despatch shared with, 98; on Negev, 198, 238; E. Roosevelt on, 25; on size of Jewish state, 28

Douglas, Paul, 619

Douglas, William O., 274, 282, 606, 607, 608, 610, 614–616, 618, 620

Dow, Hugh, 408, 411, 689

Drew, Gerald, 898, 939, 952–953, 968

Dubinsky, David I., 267, 272, 357, 511, 561, 634, 658, 765–766

Dubinsky, Jean, 267, 269, 271, 871

Dubois, Jean E., 878, 889

Duffus, Robert L., 24

Dulles, John Foster: JGM contacts with, 202, 255, 258–259, 272, 273, 278–279, 641–642, 998; JGM on, 264, 274, 999; radio speech of, 265; role of, 101; as secretary of state, 997, 998; at UN General Assembly, 137, 248, 249, 254

Dunn, James C., 665–666

Dushkin, Julia Aronson, 694

Eastern Europe, immigrants from, 335n100

Eban, Abba: Ad Hoc Political Committee of UN address, 622; as ambassador to US, 968, 972; on Bernadotte Plan, 26–27, 137; on Bevin, 28; British government and, 146, 326; biographical note, 8n4; on Griffis plan, 276; on Jerusalem, 657–658, 948; JGM contacts with, 259, 300, 651–652; on JGM retirement, 963; on Korean crisis, 947; Lovett and, 333; PCC and, 915; on refugees, 527–528; as representative at UN, 8; Rusk and, 172; M. Shertok on, 226; on State Department meeting, 564; trip to US, 306, 307; at UN General Assembly, 249, 257; on UN Resolution of December 9, 820–821; on US relations, 327, 819–820

Economic Cooperation Administration, 755, 832, 975

Economic Survey Mission to the Middle East (Clapp Commission), 645, 648, 662, 681–683, 712, 734

economy of Israel: American Jewish leaders visit related to, 958; austerity program, 495–496, 520; Economic Cooperation Administration and, 755; Feinberg on, 584; Gass on, 478–479, 516–519; government attitude towards industry, 612–613; Greenstein on, 478; Hochman on, 627; Hoofien on, 414–416, 442; JGM on, 435–436, 519–520; Kollek on, 945–946; Lewando on, 531; Lubianker on, 965–966; Nathan on, 669; Office of Price Controls and Rationing, 546; opinions on,

Goren, Asher, 382–383
Gori, Alberto, 860–861, 908
Gorlitz, Samuel J., 855
Gottlieb, Judith, 893
Gottlieb, Robert, 788
Gowen, Franklin C., 52, 53, 54, 203, 204, 675, 681
Gower, William L., 184
Grady, Henry F., 246, 667, 718, 736–737
Graetz, Adan, 786
Graetz, Heinz, 872, 898, 950, 954
Granados, Jorge García, 106
Granovsky/Granot, Avraham, 82, 99, 153, 164, 691, 789
Gravitzky, Joseph, 239
Great Britain: Abdullah on, 363; Begin on, 853; Dayan on, 471; defense policy in, 713–714; Eban on, 146, 326; Egypt and, 298, 300–301, 326–327, 696, 775, 783, 811–812, 878; E. Epstein on intentions of, 313; financial matters between Israel and, 744–745, 755, 859–860; Foreign Office suggestions to PCC, 634–635; on frontiers of Israel, 39, 208, 210; Goldmann on, 804; Horowitz on policy of, 877–878; JGM on diplomats from, 520; JGM on policy of, 134, 262, 323–324, 338, 631; Jordan and, 796–797, 821–822, 824–825; T. McMahon on policy of, 887; military reinforcements in Aqaba from, 313; peace negotiations and, 299; public opinion in, 428; rearming of Arab states by, 238, 245, 312, 434, 552–553, 688, 774–775, 783, 794–795, 811–812; recognition of Israel by, 39, 40, 42, 48, 49, 366, 894–895; reconnaissance flights of, 318–319, 321–322, 344, 354–355, 428; refugee program of, 47; Riley on policy of, 808; Rosenne of policy of, 547; L. Ross on, 801–802; Royal Egyptian Air Force and, 189; on sanctions for Israel, 222, 232; M. Sharett on policy of, 635, 900–901; M. Shertok on, 102–103, 146, 208, 226; Syria and, 480–481; Transjordan and, 198, 423–424; Tripartite Declaration of 1950 and, 915; Truman on, 326–327; UN General Assembly

proposal of, 271; C. Weizmann on, 324–325, 406–407. *See also* Bernadotte Plan; Bevin, Ernest; British Mandate of Palestine; Douglas, Lewis W.; Helm, Knox; McNeil, Hector; Wright, Michael
Greater Syria, 434, 475, 481, 671, 676n59, 728. *See also* Iraq-Syrian Federation
Greece, 694–695, 717–718
Green, Zemach, 992
Greenberg, Marian G., 308, 376, 432, 500, 516, 658, 901
Greenberg, Max, 909
Greene, Joseph N., 52, 56
Greenfield, Albert M., 658, 660, 664, 702
Greenstein, Harry, 38, 455, 478, 679
Griffis, Stanton: de Reynier on, 184; as director of relief, 250, 264, 265, 266; on Egypt and Bernadotte plan, 180; JGM contacts with, 275–276, 277, 643; Lovett on, 17; Marshall and, 646; Truman on, 16; UNRPR and, 409; visit to Tel Aviv of, 367–368
Griffiths, James Henry, 656–657, 666
Gromyko, Andrei, 78
Gross, Ernest A., 32
Grossman, Meir, 392
Gruber, Ruth, 686
Gruenbaum, Yitzhak, 100
Gruening, Ernest H., 329
Gruner, Dov, 340
Grunwald, Michael, 930
Grünwald, Victor, 347, 349, 818
Gruson, Sydney and Flora Lewis, 166
Gulley, Emmett, 486–487
Gunther, John, 953. *See also* Fineman, Francis
Gurdus, Nathan, 157–158, 178, 186, 190, 200, 357
Gurfein, Murray, 110
Gurney, Samuel C., Jr., 897, 986
Gutman, Nachum, 908
Guy, Philip L. O., 240
Guyon, Édouard-Félix, 618, 680, 706, 753–754, 812, 829, 891, 909–910, 989
Gwinn, Ralph W., 35

Haaretz, 88n17, 157, 243, 377, 661, 808, 863n73–75
Haber, Fritz, 193

Haber, William, 165–166, 167–168, 182, 183
Habicht, Max, 812–813
Hadassah, 83, 93, 380, 483, 623, 899. *See also* Greenberg, Marian G.; Halprin, Rose Luria
Hadassah Hospital, 84n161, 99n27, 985; Arab attack on and Israeli access to, 72n120, 115, 200, 328, 967n33
Hador, 190n95, 192; leaks in, 822, 851
Haendel, Ida, 788
Hafetz Haim kibbutz, 227–229
Haft, Morris W., 34–35
Haganah (Israel Defense Forces), 1, 12, 13, 58. *See also* Israeli Defense Forces
Hahn, Peter L., 3
Hahn-Warburg, Lola, 234
Haidar Pasha, Mohammed, 185
Haifa: consulate of, 778; evacuation of Arab families from, 462; as gateway to Tel Aviv, 58; immigrant camps near, 610, 611; JGM drive through, 381; mail censorship in, 170, 171, 174; oil refinery at, 42–43, 92, 412–413, 695–697, 778–779, 801–802, 818; port at, 776, 832. *See also* Lippincott, Aubrey E.; Waller, Fred E.
Haig, Frank, 651
Halderman, John W., 404, 468, 472
Halprin, Rose Luria, 84, 99, 106, 516, 658, 803–804, 901, 958, 961
Halprin, Samuel W., 350, 351
Haney, George W., 280
Hannegan, Robert E., 617
Hansen, Robert W., 625
Harazi, Shalom, 101
Hare, Raymond A., 508, 509–510, 563, 604, 634, 843, 863
Harmer, Yolande, 11, 260, 261, 269, 270, 276, 277, 287, 568
Harper, Fowler V., 90
Harriman, Averell, 274, 282
Harris, Lee, 62, 818
Harrison, Rex, 640
Harry S. Truman Presidential Library and Museum, Missouri, ix
Hartsough, Ray, 586, 630
Haut, Curt, 786–787
Hawkins, Eric, 26
Hay, Malcolm V., 406

Hays, William Harrison, 20
Hebrew University, 49, 71, 115, 200, 234, 261, 328, 515, 594, 693, 808, 902, 904, 962
Heftmann, Joseph, 239
Heifetz, Jascha, 913, 914
Held, Adolph, 522, 541
Hellman, Yehuda, 240
Helm, Knox: on D. Ben-Gurion, 949; on P. Ben-Gurion, 856; biographical note, 520n74; cocktail party of, 763; on crisis in Jordan, 844; disclosures of instructions to, 912; on Eytan meeting, 768; on Iraq-Syria Union, 673–674; JGM and, 520–521, 534–535, 536, 559–560, 689–690, 744, 796, 816; on Korea, 937; on non-aggression pact with Jordan, 839; on recognition of Israel by Great Britain, 894; on session in Istanbul, 705; M. Sharett on, 900–901; on Suez Canal, 941; on trip to Cairo, 882–883; on US-UK encouragement in Jordan, 831; C. Weizmann and, 891
Henderson, Loy, 8–9, 21, 30, 37, 56, 766
Henrietta Szold (cargo ship), 872
Henrietta Szold Reception Center, 380–381
Henry, Paul M., 916
Herald Tribune, meeting at, 26
Herlitz, Esther, *83*; on Arab rearmament, 827; Bailey and, 200; biographical note, 59n66; on Cleland, 943; as diplomat, 59, 60, 122; on Egypt-Israel armistice talks, 349–350; Elath party for, 653; on election, 357; on E. Epstein, 368; Ford and, 560; on Gaza plan, 535, 556; as guest, 239; on Israeli chargé talk with Rusk, 575–576; JGM and, 171, 347–348, 563–565, 785, 807; on military attachés, 638; on PCC, 451, 563–564; reassignment in Foreign Office, 783–785; on recognition of Israel by Great Britain, 894; on refugee issue, 404; on Rockwell, 564; role of, 784; on Rusk, 564; on Syrian coup, 481
Herold, Sidney L., 38, 673, 868, 879, 880, 884

Husseini, Jamal al-, 185
Hutcheson, Joseph C., Jr., 98, 608
Hutton, Mrs. Paul C., 714
Hyman, Abraham S., 831

Ibn Saud (king of Saudi Arabia), 166, 402, 725, 726
ICRC. *See* International Committee of the Red Cross
IDF. *See* Israeli Defense Forces
immigration to Israel: AJC and, 462; annual rate of, 520; D. Ben-Gurion July 29 proposal on, 955, 960, 963, 964, 969–970, 971–972; Bernadotte and, 69; celebration of, 760; from Eastern Europe, 335; economy and, 958; employment issues and, 518; Gass on, 519; housing issues and, 397, 503, 504–505; Jewish, 168; JGM on, 988; Kaplan on, 504; Law of Return of 1950, 936; reception camps, 478, 503, 610, 611; restrictions on, 69; screening of immigrants, 308; UJA and, 679–680. *See also* communism; refugees, Jewish
Independence Day: Israel, 499–501, *500*, 878–879, 889, 890–891; US, 574–575, 941–942
Industrial Institute of Israel, 554–555
infiltration problem, 921–922, 929, 938, 997–998, 999
Inman, Samuel G., 784–785, 820
International Committee of the Red Cross (ICRC), 188, 215, 234–235, 275, 393, 535–536, 574, 578–579. *See also* de Reynier, Jacques
International Ladies' Garment Workers' Union, 451, 522, 627. *See also* Dubinsky, David I.
International Monetary Fund, 877
International Refugee Organization (IRO), 53, 165–166, 215, 216, 396, 402, 412, 413, 662, 633, 933
International Telephone and Telegraph, 323, 339, 595, 637, 678
Iran: discussion with special representative from, 932; Jews in, 321; recognition of Israel by, 878; Wiley on, 717, 737–739
Iraq: Crocker on, 717, 724–725; crude oil from, 42–43, 92n183, 169n40, 413n20, 483, 696, 688, 724, 778,

859, 998; despatch from US mission in, 95–96; Elath on, 593; Eytan on, 710; financial crisis in, 631; Israel and, 483; Jews in, 331–332, 671, 680, 707, 899; in Nablus-Jenin-Tulkarm triangle, 433–434, 438; second Magic Carpet service from, 905–906, 937–938. *See also* Crocker, Edward
Iraq Petroleum Company (IPC), 695–696, 697, 724, 801
Iraq-Syrian Federation, 670–671, 676, 687–688, 692, 770, 805. *See also* Greater Syria
Ireland, Philip W., 718, 935
Irgun Zvai Leumi (IZL), 12, 33, 45, 87, 89, 132, 135, 139, 695. *See also Altalena*, Begin, Menachem; Bergson, Peter
Israel: communications system for, 323, 595, 637; constitution for, 524, 526, 542–543, 833, 925, 966; cooperative organizations in, 517, 862; creation of, 1; Democratic Party Platform of 1948 on, 198; election day in, 349, 351–352, 355–356; fears of aggression by, 566, 568, 572, 581, 594–595, 602–603, 615; at first cease-fire, *xv*; issues of 1948, 4; neighbors and, armistice lines, *xvii*; nuclear program of, 346; party school system of, 707–708; at second cease-fire, *xvi*; state council of, 153–154; as *sui generis*, 136; treasury centralization in, 516–517; UN admission of, 271, 277, 489–490, 514, 555. *See also* economy of Israel; frontiers of Israel; immigration to Israel; Israeli Defense Forces; Negev; recognition of Israel; truces of Israel; *specific cities*
Israel-America Friendship League, 614–615, 826, 835, 939, 941, 957, 962
Israel Bonds, 7, 995, 996–997, 999
Israel Defense Forces (IDF): Arab attacks after War of Independence and, 13; attacks by, in Gaza Strip, 675–676; expulsion of Arabs, 12, 22, 69–70, 210, 452–453, 487, 922, 939; infiltrators and, 921–922; JGM meeting with representative of, 14; in Lebanon, 209; military attachés and, 564–565, 581; Operation Dekel, 70; Operation Hiram, 209–210,

Israel Defense Forces (IDF) (*continued*)
236n59; Operation Horev, 298–299;
Operation Yoav, 187–188; shooting
down of RAF aircraft by, 319,
321–322; Syrian frontier incursion
by, 455. *See also* Haganah
Israeli-Egyptian bilateral negotiations,
Rusk on, 576
Istanbul, conference on refugees in, 6.
See also chiefs of mission, regional
conference of, in Istanbul
Istorik, Leo, 705, 706–707
Italy, 54, 55, 295, 665
Izak, Chaim, 80
IZL. *See* Irgun Zvai Leumi

Jabotinsky, Ari, 934
Jabotinsky, Ze'ev, 182, 211, 785–786
Jabr, Sayyid Salih, 842
Jackson, Robert H., 17
Jacobs, Joseph E., 852
Jacobs, Norman M., 232, 753
Jacobs, Ruth, 758, 759
Jacobson, Bluma, 6, 448, 520, 653n25
Jacobson, Eddie: biographical note, 437n98;
Israeli officials' telephone calls to,
138; JGM and, 441–443, 456–458,
520, 646, 658; Truman and, 457–458,
658; on Truman Palestine pledges,
259; visit to Israel of, 6, 437, 438,
441–458, 646, 753, 882
Jacobson, Joseph, 213, 802–803
Jaffe, Jean, 868
Japan, funds for Arab refugees from, 215,
216, 234
Javits, Jacob, 549
JDC. *See* Joint Distribution Committee
Jerusalem: Abdullah and, 340, 347, 531;
All-Palestine Government and,
157; Arab Legion in, 470; audience
with pope and, 666; D. Ben-Gurion
on, 65, 459, 742–743, 782, 982;
Bernadotte assassination in, 128,
129–130; and Bernadotte Plan, 86,
375; bombing of, 308–309; Brady
on, 745; Bunche on, 71, 469;
Burdett on, 160, 718, 728–729, 759;
Constituent Assembly opening in,
384; Crum on, 118; detonation
problem in, 636; Eban on, 657–658,
948; France and, 926; Government
House problem in, 565–566, 567,

571; Hare on, 509; Hilldring on,
603–604; Herut and, 394; Joseph
and, 65; Knesset move to, 754, 755,
761; life under fire in, 117–118;
MacDonald on, 114–116; T. Mc-
Mahon and, 340–341, 621; Meyerson on, 65; monsignors on, 656–657;
PCC in, 367, 945, 962–963; Riley
on, 597–598, 676–677, 967–968;
Rusk on, 172; Russia and, 621;
M. Sharett on, 702–703; Spellman
on, 657; transfer of Bernadotte headquarters to, 129; transfer of government offices and Knesset to, 754,
755, 761; UN administrator for,
740–741; UN mission in, 173; water
supply for, 579; YMCA mission in,
296. *See also* Jerusalem, status of;
Special Committee on Jerusalem
Jerusalem, status of: after fighting
between truces, 22; D. Ben-Gurion
on, 107, 982; change from military
to municipal, 362–363; demilitarization, 64–65, 72, 76; Eban on,
948; Eytan on, 148; France and,
926; J. Herzog on, 678, 829–830,
958; internationalization, 51, 53, 71,
108–109, 348; JGM on, 76–77, 394,
595, 748, 755, 990; Knesset resolution on, 807; T. McMahon on, 886,
888; PCC and, 468–469, 513–514,
652, 669–670, 689–690; Pius XII
on, 203, 675; Riley on, 597–598,
676–677, 967–968; Russia and,
895; M. Sharett on, 779–780;
M. Shertok on, 362; State Department on, 780–781, 787; UN Resolution 303 on, 748–749; US non-
recognition as capital, 362, 780–781,
787, 800, 803, 812n36, 816n146;
823n21, 854n45, 859, 982. *See also*
United Nations Trusteeship Council
Jerusalem plan of PCC, 473, 513–514,
652, 669–670
Jerusalem Post, 896, 902–903, 972. See
also *Palestine Post*
Jessup, Philip C., 73, 137, 249, 253, 256,
724–725
Jewish Agency: Abdullah and, 13;
American group of, 658; funds of,
661; Goldmann and, 866, 897;
Meyerson on, 790, 889, 890

Jewish Cultural Reconstruction, 529
Jewish Labor Committee, 522, 541
Jewish National Fund (JNF), 99, 399
526, 788, 957. *See also* Granovsky,
Avraham; Weitz, Yosef
Jewish Theological Seminary, Chaim
Weizmann lecture at, 1003
Jews: American, 93, 462; from Cyprus,
337–338; Germany and, 679; in
Iraq, 331–332, 671, 680, 707, 899,
905–906; Israeli, JGM on, 127–128;
in Istanbul, 741; Palestinian,
Koestler on, 136; in Soviet bloc,
335, 837; Yemenite, 167, 290–291,
292, 328–329, 331, 576–577. *See also*
refugees, Jewish; *specific
organizations*
JNF (Jewish National Fund), 99, 399,
526, 788, 957. *See also* Granovsky,
Avraham; Weitz, Yosef
Johnson, Louis, 530, 646–647, 648, 706,
947
Johnston, Eric A., 20
Joint Distribution Committee (JDC):
Abrams on, 504; Alaska Airlines
and, 290, 328; emigration from
Aden and, 576–577; JGM contacts
with, 396, 664, 673; Schmidt on,
596; J. Schwartz on, 619; transport
costs paid by, 215, 412, 413; Yemeni
Jews and, 291. *See also* Viteles,
Harry
Jokl, Ernst, 668
Jones, George Lewis, 39, 42–44, 46–47
Jordan (Hashemite Kingdom of), 452;
annexation of Arab Palestine by,
892, 894, 895–896; armistice
agreement with, 892; cabinet crisis
in, 990; Fritzlan on, 716, 728; Gaza
Strip and, 528; Great Britain and,
796–797, 821–822, 824–825; Helm
on, 844; JGM on negotiations with,
938–939; non-aggression pact with,
834, 836, 837–838, 840–844;
parliamentary elections in, 876;
peace negotiations with, 743–744,
746–747, 749, 757, 769–770,
772–773, 806–807, 822–825, 872;
rearming and massing of troops of,
489; Riley on negotiations with,
572, 929; Shiloah on, 789, 806–807,
821, 918, 938, 964; status of

Jerusalem and, 603; US assistance
in negotiations with, 821–822,
824–825. *See also* Abdullah (king of
Transjordan); Fritzlan, A. David;
Transjordan; Za'im, Husni al-. *See
also* Abdullah (king of Transjordan/
Jordan); Transjordan
Jordan Valley Authority project, 415–416
Joseph, Bernard, 186
Joseph, Dov: Andronovich on, 87;
annexation of New City and, 295;
Bernadotte and, 129; biographical
note, 65n88; de Reynier on, 185;
FDR, Jr., and, 546; JGM on
warning from, 199–200; Lewando
and, 540, 541; as Minister of
Agriculture, 942; as minister of
rationing and supply, 540, 546, 869,
920, 942, 959–960, 981; as military
governor for Jerusalem, 65, 132,
146, 185; Truce Commission and,
116, 160; on visit to US, 869
Juris, Avraham S., 699
Justice Department, US, 212

Kahanay, Menachem, 48
Kahaneman, Yosef S., 217, 684
Kaiser, Philip, 648
Kaiser-Frazer Corporation, 685
Kaminsky, Alexis M., 949
Kaplan, Eliezer, 5, 88, 175, 194, 207,
230, 437, 643, 969; on Abdullah,
95; on admission of Israel to UN,
93–94; and air agreements, 583,
689, 793, 849; and allocation of
government funds, 110, 152–154,
239, 486, 594; and arms embargo,
552; and Bernadotte Plan, 114;
biographical note, 51n36; and
CARE, 668, 684; Clapp and ESM
meetings with, 672, 755, 832; on
communications system, 637, 681;
on constitution, 526, 799; on
exchange controls, 919, 920; on
Export-Import Bank loan, 94, 281,
420, 489, 947n27; Ewing and, 763,
775; on financial settlement with
Great Britain, 492, 889; Gass on,
516–517, 982; Goldstone and,
502–503; Hooding on, 799; on
immigration, 504, 841; JGM
contacts with, 100, 114, 119, 122,

Lowdermilk, Walter C., 834, 847
Lubianker, Pinhas, 862, 872, 962, 965–966
Lucas, Scott W., 81, 357
Lundström, Aage, 69, 83–84, 111, 112
Lurie, Jesse Zel, 749–750
Lurie, Ted R., 757
Lyerly, J. Edward, 675
Lynch, Ed, 489

MAC. *See* Mixed Armistice Commission
MacDonald, John J.: Andronovich on, 87; Burdett on, 160; calls from State Department to, 170; Granovsky on, 164; and Jerusalem fighting, 65, 75, 114–116; JGM contacts with, 114–117; on Mapam Party, 141; Nieuwenhuys on, 495; reports of drinking of, 171–172, 174, 495; reports to Washington of, 75; return to Washington, 160–161; Riley on, 84; and sniper attack of August 16, 67–68, 115; threats by Lehi, 121, 126, 147; UN Truce Commission and, 75, 116, 138; as US consul general, 65, 68, 87, 114
Mack, Henry, 408, 411
Magnes, Frances, 376, 378
Magnes, Judah L., 937
Maguire, Robert F., 290, 291, 293
Mahler-Kalkstein, Mendel, 681
Maklef, Mordechai, 597
Malan, Daniel F., 867
Malik, Charles H., 252, 273, 820
Malkin, Ya'akov, 863
Mallah, Joseph M., 694–695
Manguel, Pablo, 860
Mapai Party: cabinet coalitions, 353–354, 360, 361, 411, 419, 511, 526, 543, 962, 981; constitution and, 543; in elections, 211, 285, 334, 352–353; *Hador* leaks, 822, 851; history of, 141; JGM on, 285; Mapam Party and, 98, 119, 142, 201, 285, 511, 526, 686–687, 702, 825; newspaper *Hador*, 190n95, 192; Shiloah on, 686–687. *See also* Ben-Gurion, David; Meyerson (Meir), Golda
Mapam Party: communism, USSR and, 30, 119, 141–142, 709; Courtney on, 526; in elections, 318, 352; history

of, 98; Hochman on, 627–628; JGM on, 285, 355, 388, 435, 438, 451, 485, 541, 627; labor leaders on, 541; Lubianker on, 965; Mapai Party and, 98, 119, 142, 201, 285, 511, 526, 686–687, 702, 825, 949; opinion of US in, 485; Shiloah on, 686–687, 825; US concerns about, 141; Weizmann and, 386. *See also* Potofsky, Jacob; Sneh, Moshe
Marash, Joshua G., 163
Mardam Bey, Jamil, 771
Margolin, Ephraim, 695
Margolin, Rachel, 871–872
Marina, Alcide, 677
Markel, Lester, 625, 911
Marks, Simon, 41, 44, 48, 264, 266, 437, 486
Marriott, Cyril H. A., 46, 66, 190, 370–371
Marsh, Daniel L., 909
Marshall, George C.: appointment of JGM and, 15, 646; Bernadotte Plan and, 44, 112n71, 134, 137, 148–149, 172, 221, 222, 253, 259; and Eleanor Roosevelt, 221; Ewing on, 19; Griffis as refugee administrator and, 257–258, 275, 646; on immigration restrictions to Israel, 69; on Israeli "aggression" truce provisions, and UN sanctions, 75, 76, 97–98, 102, 210; JGM contacts with, 28, 29, 249, 249–252, 254–257, 651; on Negev, 197–198; on recognition of Israel, 2, 27n101, 97–98, 117; retirement of, 254; Satterthwaite and, 28; as Secretary of Defense, 993; M. Shertok and, 148, 172, 208, 238, 245n91; UN General Assembly and, 136–137, 172, 254; and UN Trusteeship for Palestine, 1, 16; and US arms embargo, 81n152
Marshall Plan, 295n83, 415, 756n49, 788n53, 790n60
Martin, Kingsley, 903
Masaryk, Jan, 816–817
Matalon, Albert, 508
Mattison, Gordon H., 17, 38, 718, 733, 741
May, Herbert L., 257
May Day parades, 502
Mayer, Louis B., 20

McClintock, Robert M., 17, 129, 199, 220
McCloy, John J., 679
McCormick, Anne O'Hare, 24, 285, 286, 326, 347, 357, 650
McCoy, Frank, 234
McDonald, Barbara Ann (Bobby, BAM), *685*; in Athens, 56; D. Ben-Gurion on, 628; on Bevins, 39; Bnei Brak visit of, 217–218; Christmas dinner buffet and, 289; departure of, 776, 777; at Foreign Office reception, *83*; Hebrew teachers for, 78, 126, 177; as hostess, 111, 114, 182, 237; in Jerusalem, 469, 471, 477; in London, 42, 48; at mission, 95; in Paris, 246–247; relationship with father, 39, 66, 85, 88; in Rome, 52, 53, 54; Russian party and, 220, 230, 231–232; in Tel Aviv, 59; Tel Mond trip and, 63; tour with Beilin of, 210, 214; at UN General Assembly, 248; voyage to England and, 35; Weizmanns and, 75, 763. *See also* Stewart, Barbara Ann McDonald
McDonald, James G. (JGM): on appointment as ambassador, 385–386; diary of, 3; as envoy, 4, 7, 1003–1005; home leave for, 493, 580, 584, 609, 629–630, 655; memoir of, 3, 978–979, 995; offices of, 6; photos of, *74, 83, 445, 446, 685, 701, 924, 996*; public speeches of, 239–240; readings of, 106, 134, 177, 219, 353, 388, 529, 764, 935; resignation of, 767, 868–869, 893, 897, 929, 972, 987–988; retirement of, 1003; Senate committee testimony of, 1001; Senate confirmation of, 10. *See also* travel of JGM
McDonald, Janet (daughter), 11. *See also* Barrett, Janet McDonald (daughter)
McDonald, Ruth (wife): arrival of, 287; at audience with pope, 666; Christmas dinner buffet and, 289; death of mother of, 895; as first foreign lady of Israel, 386; in Jerusalem, 469, 471, 477; letter from, 197; letter from Truman to, 837; phone call from, 147; plans for arrival of, 88; promotion of JGM and, 387
McDowell, Robert H., 700

McGhee, George C., 440, 445, 683–684; as assistant secretary of state in charge of Bureau of Near Eastern, South Asian, and African Affairs, 642–643, on bilateral negotiations, 730; biographical note, 446n115; Cleland and, 668; on Department position, 729–730; Eban on, 819; on Export-Import Bank loan, 644–645, 647; Iraqi persecution of Jews and, 671n43; Hare on role of, 509; JGM and, 643, 659, 733, 740, 741; on JGM successor, 977; Klaus on, 634; T. McMahon on; on Pentagon policy on arms requests, 900; promotion of, 609; Rafael on, 792; as State Department coordinator on Palestine refugee matters, 445–447, 457, 509, 521–522, 526, 528, 549, 555, 558, 564, 565, 638, 642; Satterthwaite on, 440; on security issues, 733–734, 735; on M. Wright, 718–721. *See also* chiefs of mission, regional conference of, in Istanbul
McGhee plan, 537, 540, 564, 565
McGill, Ralph E., 848
McGrath, James Howard, 32
McIntyre, James Francis, 656–657
McMahon, Eugene Francis: on communications, 343; farewell meeting with, 441; Haifa visit and, 421; JGM and, 139–140, 170; as mission attaché, 125–126, 130; orders to, 145; security lecture by, 314; sound of shooting and, 63; view on open liaison of Cummings, 145
McMahon, Thomas F., 51; on geopolitics in Middle East, 885–886, 887–888; J. Herzog on, 339–342, 464, 550, 619–620, 677–678, 798, 891; on Holy Places, 310–311, 340, 371–372; Israeli officials and, 677–678; on Jerusalem's internationalization, 620–621, 677–678, 886–888; JGM and, 260, 309–312, 666; on Trans-jordan officials, 310; on refugees, 620–621, 885; role of, 51, 283; on Russians in Jerusalem, 283–284, 621; Sharett, Ben-Gurion, and, 677, 768, 903, 907–908; travel of, 884–885; as unofficial papal envoy to Middle East, 283, 296, 585, 666

McNarney, Joseph, 165, 279
McNeal, Donald, 510, 639, 640, 809
McNeil, Hector: career of, 39; Eban and, 227; Goldmann on, 804; on recognition of Israel, 166, 313; on sanctions for Israel, 222; Senator on, 746; M. Shertok on, 146; at UN, 232, 260–261
McNeill, Angus, 611
McNutt, Paul V., 280
McVicker, Charles P., 524, 612, 781, 826, 851
mediator. *See* Bernadotte, Folke; Bunche, Ralph J.
Meltzer, Julian Lewis, 152
Mendez, Cosmo, 464
Menuhin, Hephzibah, 879–880
Menuhin, Yehudi, 879–880
Merlin, Shmuel, 199
Meron, Gershon, 985
Merz, Charles, 24
Mesta, Perle, 664
Meyer, Eugene, 147
Meyer, Leo, 896
Meyerson (Meir), Golda (Goldie), 20, 314, 317; on ambassadorship in Moscow, 62, 82, 256, 411, 417, 498; on American Jews, 699–700; on Ashkelon, 697; Bar-Ilan on, 411; in Ben-Gurion cabinet, 417, 419, 420, 432, 498, 503, 632–633, 684; at Ben-Gurion Purim party, 432; Dubinsky and, 267n178; and Ewing, 755; at Foreign Office reception, 82, *83*; Goldstone on, 503; on Histradut, 791, 862; on Jerusalem, 65, 290, 362; on Jewish Agency, 889, 890; JGM contacts with, 62–63, 256, 290, 292–293, 498–499, 674, 699–700, 707, 790–791; JGM on trip to US for UJA, 489, 697, 914; on Knesset issues and Weizmann's successor, 914; Korean War and, 940; Lubianker on, 966; on organizational leadership in US, 890; Potofsky and 498, 511; M. Sharett on, 970; UN delegation and, 970; US congressmen and, 674; and US development experts, 755, 790, 848
Middle East: arms race in, 910–911, 915; R. Ford on, 976; T. McMahon on, 885–886, 887–888; US defense policy in, 713–714. *See also* armament of Israel; rearmament of Arab states
military, Israeli, demobilization of, 518, 572, 582. *See also* Israeli Defense Forces
Miller, Alvah L., 296, 570
Miller, Robert C., 307, 314–315
Millin, Sarah G., 501
Mindszenty, József, 689
Ministry of Agriculture (Israel), 942
Ministry of Industry and Commerce (Israel), 920
Ministry of Labor and Social Security (Israel), 417
Ministry of Religion, 68, 886. *See also* Herzog, Jacob
Ministry of Supply and Rationing (Israel), 959–960, 981
Minor, Jack B., 718
Mintz, Binyamin, 227, 521
Mintz, Sam S., 633
Mission in Tel Aviv (US): acquisition of, 4–5, 60; appointment of JGM to, 2, 10, 14–15, 16, 21–22, 43; communications issues of, 96, 119, 131, 140–141, 170, 174; difficulty of, 37–38; entertaining at, 5; evacuation plans for, 156; financing of, 80–81, 197, 202; first day of, 63–64; goods for resale by staff of, 365; housing for, 231, 293; military attachés for, 27, 56; preparation for, 18; protection of, 129–130, 131, 140; salary for JGM, 17, 20; space for, 21–22, 294–295; staff for, 17, 120, 140–141, 177, 212–213, 338–339; staff meetings, 343–344, 355–356, 392–393; State Department reluctance to create, 8; travel of staff of, 346, 348; visitors to, 5–6. *See also* Embassy in Tel Aviv; *specific staff*
Mitchell, Lawrence C., 838
Mixed Armistice Commissions (MACs): Burdett and, 698; in Egypt, 400, 856, 878n42; Eilat Road blockade and, 987; in Jordan, 471, 565–566, 571, 592, 597, 602, 782, 858; Lebanon, 439; replacement of PCC with, 917–918, 929, 949, 991; Riley on, 476, 571–572, 597–598, 830, 858, 967; M. Sharett and, 567, 592;

Mixed Armistice Commissions (MACs) (*continued*)
Shiloah on Riley and, 949–950; State Department and, 565–566, 753; in Syria, 567; UN Security Council Resolution 89 on, 991

Mohammed (crown prince of Saudi Arabia), 725

Mohn, Paul: at Bernadotte luncheon, 111; on Bernadotte Plan, 179–181; biographical note, 68n106; on British reconnaissance flights, 344; on Bunche, 233–234, 447–448, 454; complaints concerning Israelis, 68–71; on Glubb Pasha, 465–466; on grand mufti, 180; Haber on, 168; on Israel-Syria armistice negotiations, 501–502, 586; JGM and, 68–71, 112, 179–180, 359; on PCC, 344–345, 447; on origins of refugee problem, 179; at Russian party, 229; on Syria, 465; Za'im and, 494

Molinari, Diego Luis, 856
Mollet, Guy, 1000
Molotov, V. I., 59
Monfort, Nelson W., 872
Monosson, Fred, 686, 789
Montefiore, Moses, 469
Montgomery, Bernard L., 463
Montini, Giovanni B., 675
Montor, Henry: American Financial and Development Corporation for Israel and, 977, 995; biographical note, 170n42; Goldmann on, 814; JGM contacts with, 604, 679–680; Morgenthau on, 196; PEC and, 619; rivalry with Silver concerning UJA, 93, 176, 195, 287, 391; UJA, 619; visit of, 958; ZOA and, 169–170
Morgan, Rita, 586
Morgenstern, Morris, 831–832
Morgenthau, Henry, III, 19
Morgenthau, Henry, Jr.: biographical note, 19n58; Ben-Gurion luncheon for, 802; Israeli Foreign Ministry reception for, 207; Goldmann on, 814; invitation for JGM to speak from, 416–417; JGM contacts with, 19, 195–196, 201–202, 206, 794–795, 800, 809; Kaplan on, 175; PEC and, 619; Sonneborn on, 868; Truman

and, 765; UJA and, 20, 171, 208, 391; visits of, 5–6, 793; C. Weizmann on, 810

Morris, Benny, 1001; initial cites of major works, 1n1, 11n19, 22n1, 50n30, 676n57

Moses, Walter, 984
Moss, Maximilian, 661
Moukhine, M. L., 560, 750
Mount Scopus, Arab attacks on, 72, 81, 84, 87n169; Israeli access to under armistice terms, 180, 199, 200, 234, 328, 436, 437n95, 453, 469, 473, 485, 531, 598n37, 746, 749, 757, 779, 804, 810, 815n145, 821, 823–824, 834, 838, 967, 987, 993; Hebrew University and, 902, 904

Mount Scopus agreement of July 7, 1948, 200

Moyne, Lord (Walter Guinness), 121, 124

Mufti. *See* Husseini, Haj Amin al-
Mulqi, Fawzi al-, 823–824, 838
Multer, Abraham J., 113–114, 120, 133–134, 549, 648
Mun'im Mustafa Bey, Abd al-, 544, 688, 781, 782–783, 789, 794, 800, 841, 931
Murphy, Charles S., 765, 778, 819
Murphy, Robert, 165
Murphy, William F., 615–616
Murray, Thomas E., Jr., 318, 657, 660, 765–766
Muslim Brotherhood, 185n84, 297, 470n82, 602, 664n11
Mussolini, Benito, 46
Myer, Dillon S., 650, 672
Mytilene Agreement, 109, 342–43

Naharayim crisis, 974
Nahhas Pasha, Mustafa al-, 721, 780, 803, 854, 882, 898, 918, 929
Nasrat Bey, Mustafa, 828
Nasser, Gamal Abd al-, 997–998, 999–1000
Nathan, Robert R., 11, 669
National Archives and Records Administration, Maryland, ix
NEA (Office of Near Eastern and African Affairs): as biased for Arab position, 2, 8, 15, 37, 149, 645; Clifford on, 15, 17; Henderson and,

Orloff, Chana, 492
Osnia, Baruch, 826
Ostashinski, Elyakum, 213
Oxnam, Garfield B., 820

Padberg, Eugene L., Jr, 441, 466, 524, 574–575, 693, 760, 800, 804–805
Paget, Mamaine, 135, 136
Paige, Jason, Jr., 56
Painter, Levinus K., 393–394, 459, 486–487
Palestine: All-Palestine Government, 157, 159–160; Anglo-American Committee of Inquiry on, 28, 44–45, 48, 103, 223, 666; annexation of, by Jordan, 892, 894, 895–896; German order prohibiting exit from, 97, 123, 377; JGM on, 24, 85–86; pre-1948 Jewish immigration to, 2; 9; United Nations Special Committee on, (UNSCOP), 103, 106, 108; UN Partition Resolution on, 1, 12, 26, 58, 64, 70, 75, 128, 162, 172, 187, 209, 210, 221, 238, 253, 258, 291, 297, 298, 331, 374, 423, 452, 457, 490, 539, 545, 575, 595, 654, 670; UN Trusteeship proposal for, 16n40, 40, 95, 546
Palestine Conciliation Committee (PCC): all-Arab conference proposal of, 411–412, 417, 422, 431–432, 446; armistice talks with, 364; Barco on, 529; D. Ben-Gurion and, 458–459, 460, 983; Blandford on, 917; British Foreign Office suggestions to, 634–635; Burdett on, 634; causes of failures of, 978; Eban and, 915; establishment of by UN, 233, 247, 279–280; Ethridge appointment to, 337; Eytan on, 456, 543–544, 604; French terms and, 342–343; Helm on, 689; IRO and, 412, 413; in Jerusalem, 367, 945, 962–963; Jerusalem plan of, 513–514, 652, 669–670; JGM meeting with, 401–402; JGM on, 288, 484, 534, 557, 617, 931–932, 973; Keenan and, 323n54, 337; Kopper on, 557; Kunde on, 585–586, 606–607; in Lausanne, 652; T. McMahon on, 885; meetings with Arab negotiators, 811; Mohn on,

344–345, 447; peace negotiations under, 422–423, 490; Porter appointment to, 609; Rafael on, 792, 873–874; refugees and, 279, 367, 458–459; reorganization of, 870, 871; Riley on, 599, 929, 971; M. Sharett and, 427–428, 429, 637–638; M. Shertok and, 362, 381–382, 383; Shiloah on, 408, 825; status of Jerusalem and, 468–469; transfer committee on, 455–456; Turkish member of (Yalçin), 359; UN General Assembly Resolution 394 on, 993; US delegation of, 912; view of Israel by, 532; Wilkins on, 371. See also Azcárate y Flores, Pablo de; Barco, James W.; Boisanger, Claude B. de; Ethridge, Mark; Eytan, Walter; Lausanne Conference, Mun'im Mustafa Bey, Abd al-; Palmer, Ely E.; Ruffer, Gideon; Shiloah, Reuven; Yalçin, Hussein C.
Palestine Economic Corporation (PEC), 62–63, 394, 584, 619, 678–679, 818, 984
Palestine Post, 98, 150–151, 152n189, 191, 288, 462, 466n61, 536, 545, 570n96, 591, 622, 676, 749, 756, 757, 804–805, 816, 833, 835, 871. *See also* Agronsky/Agron, Gershon; Courtney, David (aka Roy Elston), *Jerusalem Post*
Palmach, 178, 186, 598n36, 687
Palmer, Ely E., 729, 811, 825, 874, 912, 962–963, 983
Palmer, Joseph, II, 730
Pandit, Vijaya Lakshmi Nehru, 49
Paray, Paul, 454, 680, 701, 896
Paris, UN General Assembly in: BAM on, 6; Jessup statement of US policy in, 253; JGM and, 240, 241, 243, 246–247, 248, 260, 274, 278, 281, 290; E. Roosevelt and, 221; M. Shertok on, 102; US delegation to, 136–137
Parkes, James, 903
Paro, George, 86–87
Parsons, Geoffrey, Jr., 26
Passman, Charles S., 899
Patterson, Jefferson, 729
Pauker, Ana, 588, 797
Paul, John R., 943

Committee of the Red Cross; Israeli Defense Forces; Quakers; Transfer Committee (regarding Arab refugees); UNRWA

refugees, Jewish: custom dues exacted from, 167; in displaced persons camps in Europe, 4, 57, 69, 165, 168, 239, 286, 450n5, 455, 504n34, 679; in Germany and Austria, 455; at Henrietta Szold Reception Center, 380–381; housing for, 397, 503, 504–505; immigrant camps for, 478, 503, 518, 520, 610, 611, 661, 760n62, 679, 760, 823, 825n38, 837n81; Italy and, 55; JGM actions on behalf of, 28; transport costs for, 215; C. Weizmann on, 407; from Yemen, 290–291, *292*, 328–329, 331, 576–577. *See also* Cyprus; immigration to Israel; Iraq; Joint Distribution Committee; International Refugee Organization; Operation Magic Carpet; Vitelis, Harry Rehovot, Weizmann and, 43, 63, 162

Reich, Emanuel, 944
Reid, Helen Rogers, 26
Reid, Ogden, 146
Remez, Aharon, 923
Remez, David, 96, 153, 395, 914, 923, 942
Renan, Joseph Ernest, 195
Replogle, Delbert E., 393–394
Reves, Emery, 879
Revisionist Zionists (HaTzohar), 67n102, 142, 392, 785. *See also* Altman, Aryeh
Reza Shah Pahlavi, Mohammed, 717, 738
Richepin, Éliane, 869, 896
Rifai, Samir al-, 769, 782, 815, 823–824, 842, 845
Rifkind, Simon H., 450, 897
Riftin, Ya'akov, 438
Riley, William E.: on Abdullah, 846; Acheson on, 971; on Archibald, 845–846; Bernadotte and, 111; biographical note, 83; on border region action, 675–676; on Egypt, 929; on expansionist intentions of Israel, 598–599; on forcing down of plane, 905; at Foreign Office reception, 207; on Gaza Strip, 934;

Hadassah and, 83; J. Herzog on, 903, 927; on Iraq-Syrian Federation, 676; on Jerusalem, 597–598, 676–677, 967–968; JGM contacts with, 84, 245–246, 808, 904, 966–968; JGM letter on meeting between pope and, 476–477; JGM on, 112, 484, 506; MAC and, 565, 566, 830, 858; T. McMahon on, 885; Mohn on, 234; on Mount Scopus, 967; on Negev, 614; on PCC, 971; on peace negotiations, 476, 570–573, 856–857, 929; on Porter, 636; on refugees, 572; role of, 993; M. Sharett and, 635–636; Shiloah on, 949–950; on Syria, 613–614; on Syrian-Israeli impasse, 506, 596, 597; on Transjordan, 475–476; UN and, 138–139, 230; on UN Security Council Resolution 89, 991; on UN Trusteeship Council, 831, 857–858; on Vatican visit, 635; on Za'im, 475, 505
Ritter, Paul A., 838, 919
Rivkin, Vivian, 945
Roberts, Randolph, 77
Roberts, Shoshana Kasselman, 177, 190–191, 463, 595
Robertson, Lieutenant, 131–132
Robinson, Edward G., 829, 831, 832
Rockefeller, John D., III, 660
Rockefeller, Nelson, 411, 503
Rockwell, Stuart W., 548, 561, 562, 564, 634, 794–795, 819–820, 974; biographical note, 548n25
Rogers, Harry S., 876
Rogoff, Harry, 491
Rokach, Israel, 100, 101, 207, 229, 339, 410, 625, 789
Roncalli, Angelo, 205
Rood, Leslie L., 666–667
Rooks, Lowell W., 250
Roosevelt, Curtis, Jr. *see* Boettiger, Curtis Dall
Roosevelt, Eleanor: and Bernadotte Plan, 221–222, 248; invitation to visit Israel, 171; JGM contact with, 25–26, 221–222, 255–256, 276; Spellman controversy and, 620, 651; support of, 252; on Truman, 25–26; UN General Assembly and, 16, 25n88, 137, 221–222, 248

Roosevelt, Franklin Delano, III, 25
Roosevelt, Franklin Delano, Jr., 276,
    523, 540, 546, 548–549, 795
Roosevelt, James (Jimmy), 23, 25–26
Roosevelt, Kermit, Jr., 539
Rose, Billy, 429
Rosen, Harvey, 767
Rosen, Kopul, 496–497
Rosen, Pinhas, 84, 91, 153, 201
Rosenberg, Ann, 766
Rosenberg, James N. (Jimmy), 23, 35,
    658, 674, 978–979, 981–982, 984
Rosenbloom, Charles J., 456, 859
Rosenfeld, Aaron, 946
Rosenfield, Harry N., 764–765
Rosenheim, Jacob, 924–925
Rosenman, Samuel I., 8, 30, 32, 220,
    947
Rosenne, Shabtai, 546, 547
Rosensohn, Etta Lasker, 500, 880, 901
Rosenstiel, Lewis S., 629
Rosenthal, Arthur, 214, 226, 232
Rosenthal, David S., 554
Ross, Charles G., 357, 765
Ross, John C., 249, 272, 798, 819
Ross, L. W., 412–413, 778–779, 801–802
Ross, Z. R., 696–697
Rothenberg, Morris, 55, 82, 656, 879
Rothschild, Edmond J. de, 788–789
Round the World Town Meeting, 624
Royall, Kenneth C., 27
Rubin, Reuven, 553, 769, 773
Rubinstein, Reuben, 239
Rucker, Arthur, 215
Ruegger, Paul, 390, 392
Rusk, Dean: biographical note, 29n113;
    on cease-fire between Egypt and
    Israel, 317; Eban and, 226, 819;
    Israeli chargé talk with, 575–576; on
    Jerusalem, 172; JGM and, 260, 276;
    on JGM message to Truman,
    262–263; Klaus on, 634; Knox on,
    646; Rafael on, 792; M. Sharett
    and, 457, 566–567; Shiloah on, 581,
    582; on territorial compensations,
    564; trusteeship-for-Jerusalem
    scheme of, 180; at UN General
    Assembly, 248, 249; of UN section,
    29, 137; US pressure attributed to,
    561; Warren on, 662–663
Russia/USSR: Bernadotte assassination
    and, 139, 140, 144, 145; Bernadotte

Plan and, 150; church property of,
    341; Communist Information
    Bureau, 423; delegation from, in Tel
    Aviv, 59, 78; expansionist plans of,
    667; Gowen on, 750–751; Greek
    Orthodox Church and, 398, 585,
    621, 667, 678; housing for legation
    from, 229; Israel and, 999; Jerusa-
    lem and, 621, 895; Lubianker on
    support for, 965; Middle East as
    buffer against, 713; October
    Revolution party of legation from,
    229–230; propaganda film from,
    125; publications in Israel, 959;
    relations with Israel, 222–223;
    E. Roosevelt on, 26; UN Resolution
    303 and, 887; US aerial containment
    of, 582–583. *See also* communism;
    Ershov, Pavel Ivanovich; immigration
    to Israel; Meyerson, Golda
Ryan, Frank, 803, 832

sabra seminars, 863–864, 930–931,
    932–933
Sachar, Abram L., 946, 978
Sachar, Yehezkel, 126, 212–213
Sacher, Harry, 41, 264, 266, 979
Sacher, Miriam Marks, 413, 437
Sacks, Chaim, 653
Sacks, Mendes H., 85, 307, 530, 531,
    541, 560, 574, 585, 679, 767
Sacks, Ruth, 764
Sacks, Sam: bankers at home of, 344;
    biographical note, 283n46; on
    British Mandate, 418; on Carlebach,
    612–613; J. Herzog and, 339;
    invitations to JGM family by, 307,
    319; Jacobson and, 443; JGM
    luncheons with, 482–483; Lu-
    bianker on, 966; at movie party, 367;
    on productivity of Israel labor, 560;
    on public school situation, 707–708;
    on retailers strike, 959–960; textile
    factory of, 283, 540, 914; Troper
    and, 413
Sa'ed, Mohammed, 738
Saffinia, Reza, 878, 986
Said Pasha, Nuri al-, 330, 670, 721
Salah al-Din Bey, Muhammed, 789, 800,
    810, 827–828, 882, 898, 918, 929
Salpeter, Hugh, 436
Saltzman, Charles, 165

Shazar, Zalman, 88, 902, 920
Sheetrit, Bechor-Shalom, 91
Shell Company, 167, 189
Shenkar, Aryeh, 495–496
Sherf, Ze'ev, 802, 803
Sheringham, John Guy Tempest, 103, 783, 901
Shertok, Chaim, 178
Shertok, Moshe: activities of, 146; on armistice negotiations, 329–330, 361, 395; Bernadotte assassination and, 129, 130; on Bernadotte Plan, 26; on British-Chinese resolution, 208; on British government meeting, 146; on cease-fire, 316, 322; Dulles on, 278–279; on election, 361; Ershov and, 330; Ethridge and, 372–373, 402–403, 404–405; on Faluja evacuation, 350–351; family of, 186; Foreign Ministry reception and, 82, *83*; home of, 60; on immigration restrictions, 69; on internationalization of Jerusalem, 108–109; as Israeli Foreign Minister, 4; on Israeli withdrawal, 312; Jewish Agency for Palestine and, 1; JGM and, 59–60, 74, 87, 106, 112; on JGM attendance at Constituent Assembly opening, 386; Marshall and, 238; on Negev, 108, 172; PCC and, 279, 381–382, 383; press conference of, 124–125; on refugees, 109, 110; on refusal of exit permits, 122–123; on report from Eban, 333; on reports of Israeli aggression, 76–77; on State Department cable, 301–302; on talks with Transjordan and Egypt, 225–226; threats from Lehi and, 121; on truce, 134–135; on Truman reelection, 219; at UN General Assembly, 247, 249, 257, 277–278; US basic views presented to, 101–104; on US Embassy proposal, 366; C. Weizmann on, 51; at Zionist Actions Committee party, 88. *See also* Sharett, Moshe
Sherwood, Sidney, 489, 508, 649–650, 699, 700
Shiloah, Reuven, *328*; on Abdullah, 601–602, 747, 824, 845, 861, 894, 927, 945; on aggression of Israel,

602–603; on Andronovich, 177–178; on approaches of Israeli officials, 686–687; on armistice negotiations, 303, 327, 375–376, 389–390, 407, 488; D. Ben-Gurion and, 64, 949; biographical note, 61n72; on British reconnaissance flights, 319; Donovan on, 491; on Eilat Road blockade, 986–987; on Eliash funeral, 851; Hare and, 510; on Iraq-Syrian Federation, 687–688; JGM and, 61, 172–173, 175, 640; on JGM retirement, 965; on Jordan, 782, 789, 821, 838, 840–841, 918, 938, 964; Knox conversations with, 199, 288; on Kollek, 783–784; on Lausanne trip, 600–601; on MAC, 782–783; on mail censorship at Haifa, 171; on Mapam-Mapai relations, 686–687; on Mapam Party, 825; on McDowell, 700; on Negev, 163–164; on Palmach incident, 687; PCC and, 408, 669, 912; on peace negotiations in Lausanne, 490, 600–601, 636; on peace negotiations through PCC, 609; on peace negotiations with Egypt, 811, 847; on peace negotiations with Jordan, 743–744, 746–747, 757, 769–770, 806–807, 823–825, 964; on prospects of general peace, 462; on refugees, 601; Riley on, 476; on Syria, 462–463, 481, 770, 781, 806, 844–845; on Syrian peace accord, 851–852; Tidhar and, 791, 794, 896; on US Consulate General (Jerusalem) staff, 951–952; on Washington experiences, 581–582; Webb and, 976
Shimoni, Ya'akov, 159
Shinwell, Emanuel, 428
Shishakli, Adib al-, 761
Shotwell, James T., 628
Sidqi Pasha, Ismael, 711, 724
Sieff, Israel M., 41, 48
Sieff, Joseph E., 922, 923
Sieff, Marcus: D. Ben-Gurion and, 48, 984; biographical note, 48n21; on British Foreign Office, 901; on British public opinion, 428–429; on development of army, 480; JGM

and, 55–56, 170, 189–190, 264, 266; on London trip, 166–167; on Operation Yoav, 191–192

Sieff, Rebecca, 55, 63, 413–414, 441, 560–561, 882, 929

Sigismondi, Pietro, 204

Silberfeld, Julius, 623

Silberman, James M., 755, 790

Silver, Abba Hillel: F. Bernstein on, 921; biographical note, 15n34; congratulatory phone call from, 15; M. Frank on, 348; JGM and, 66, 81–82, 84, 264–265, 268, 269, 318, 334, 460, 619, 660, 791, 999; Kaplan on, 432; Morgenthau on, 417; and recognition of Israel, 81–82; rivalry with Montor concerning UJA, 93, 169–170, 176, 195–196, 287, 308, 348, 351, 376, 391, 394, 432, 450n4, 810, 814; resignation of posts, 391, 417, 870; Truman and, 220; UJA and, 176; Weisgal on, 196; C. Weizmann on, 346; Zionist movement and, 93, 450, 897, 914; ZOA and, 169, 170, 623, 921. *See also* Montor, Henry; Morgenthau, Henry, Jr.; Neumann, Emanuel

Silverberg, Louis G., 641

Silverberg, Samuel, 541

Silverman, Louis L., 899

Silverstone, Murray, 608–609, 852

Simon, Julius, 61–62, 72, 678–679

Simon, Leon, 516, 808–809, 902

Simon, Michael, 154, 169, 170, 347, 439, 444, 451, 799

Singer, George, 348

Singer, Michael, 930

Sirri Pasha, Hussein, 688, 696, 703

Skouras, Spyros, 608–609

Slawson, John, 462

Smith, Russell G., 872

Smith, Walter Bedell, 651

Smoira, Moshe, 607

Sneh, Moshe, 178, 814, 819, 825, 914

Snyder, John W., 649

Solomon, Flora, 437, 927

Solomon, Izler, 523, 575

Soltes, Avraham, 608

Somers, Andrew L., 81, 89–91, 100–101

Sonneborn, Rudolf, 868

Sorensen, E. Per, 125, 579

South Africa, JGM and, 24

South Korea, North Korea attack on, 935–936, 940–941, 943, 958

Soviet Union. *See* Russia/USSR

Special Committee on Jerusalem, 453, 460n40, 461, 471, 476, 484, 485, 530, 531, 565, 571, 572, 597, 598,

Spellman, Francis Joseph: biographical information, 50–51; Greek Orthodox influence and, 667; Holy Places memorandum, 51, 101, 109; Jerusalem internationalization, 51, 477, 514, 550n30, 621, 657, 666, 798; JGM and, 656, 657, 667; JGM meeting with Y. Fishman on, 101; letter to JGM from, 621; T. McMahon and, 50–50, 311, 621, 884–885; New York politics and, 766; E. Roosevelt controversy and, 620, 651; statement from, 109; Truman and, 514; C. Weizmann and, 477

Spitzer, Jack, 451

Sprinzak, Joseph: biographical note, 99n24; on Independence Day, 499; as president of state council, 99, 153, 231; as speaker, 388, 419, 568; at Weizmann Institute of Science dedication, 691; at Weizmann reception, 942; welcome address of, 154; at ZOA House groundbreaking, 789

Stabler, Wells, 116, 585, 631, 659–660

Stassen, Harold E., 765

State Department, US: on aggression of Israel, 300–305; Begin visa and, 212; on D. Ben-Gurion July 29 proposal, 969–970; Bunche communication with, 111; desk for JGM in, 641, 973; despatch of JGM to, on Bernadotte death, 138, 140; distance between technicians, officials, and men in field, 255, 272, 662; Ewing on, 18–19; follow-up to May 29 letter, 575; Gardiner on, 684; on Iraq-Syrian Federation, 692, 805; JGM exclusion from information of, 3, 18, 75, 409, 453; JGM expression of views to, 973–974; JGM first despatch to, 66; JGM on US-Israeli crisis, 552–553; JGM top-secret telegrams to, 566; Keren on, 972; on lack of concessions by Israel,

State Department, US (*continued*)
489–490; MAC and, 565–566, 753;
on non-recognition of Israel sovereignty in Jerusalem, 780–781, 787;
Office of Foreign Buildings Operations, 510, 665, 675; on recognition of
Israel, 8, 16, 33, 35, 356, 360; refugees
and, 429–430; responses to cable on
aggression from, 309; restriction on
emigration of men from Israel and,
123; Review of Second Part of UN
General Assembly, 596; Technical
Assistance Group, 414; Truman and,
197, 198, 642–643; at UN General
Assembly, 137; on UN partition, 107;
Working Draft Resolution, 720; on
Za'im demand for rectification of
frontier, 494. *See also* Acheson, Dean;
chiefs of mission, regional conference
of, in Istanbul; Embassy in Tel Aviv;
Kopper, Samuel K. C.; Lovett,
Robert; Marshall, George C.;
McGhee, George C.; Mission in Tel
Aviv; NEA; Ross, John C.; Satterth-
waite, Joseph C.; Webb, James E.;
Wilkins, Fraser
state dinners, 498–499
Steele, Arnold T., 24
Steelman, John R., 765
Steinglass, Meyer F., 194, 206, 809, 810
Steinhardt, Laurence A., 852
Stern, Aryeh, 53, 55
Stern, Avraham, 121
Stern, Harry J., 954
Stern, Horace, 641, 648
Stern Gang/Sternists: Andronovich on,
87; attitude toward Americans of,
116; Bernadotte assassination and,
475; crackdown on, 132, 133; Crum
and, 124; Cummings and, 143, 175,
176–177; history of, 121; Koestler
on, 135; Lovett on, 18, 33; Sachar
and, 126. *See also* Lohamei Herut
Israel; Yellin-Mor, Natan
Sternklar, Abraham, 72, 544–545
Stettinius, Edward R., Jr., 803
Stevenson, Adlai, II, 619
Stevenson, Donald, 839
Stewart, Barbara Ann McDonald
(Bobby), viii, 4–7. *See also* McDon-
ald, Barbara Ann
Stewart, Weston H., 795–796

Stone, Dewey D., 450–451, 681, 694,
698–699, 958
Storrs, Ronald, 242–243
St. Paul's Basilica, Rome, 52
Straus, H. Alexander, 854
Straus, Nathan, Jr., 206–207, 863
Straus, Roger W., 110
Strauss, Lewis L., 34
Streit, Clarence K., 257
Stritch, Samuel, 615
Suez Canal: as British base, 116n81;
189n91, 721, 803, 811, 901; closure
to Israeli and Israel-bound shipping,
92, 424, 631, 688, 696, 778n11, 871,
878, 993, 998, 999–1000; in 1956
campaign, 231n46, 254n127, 1000
Sugarman, Joseph, 919
Sullivan, John L., 34
Sulzberger, Arthur Hays, 24–25, 110,
182, 927
Sulzberger, Arthur Ochs, 927, 928
Sulzberger, Cyrus L., II, 269, 854
Sulzberger, Iphigene Ochs, 650
Sutton, James, 295–296
Sweeney, Claude M., 919, 985–986
Swope, Gerard, 818, 823
Symington, Stuart, 27, 610, 893
Syria: armistice agreement with, 610,
613–614; armistice negotiations
with, 439, 453, 454, 475, 476,
488–489, 501–502, 506, 568,
570–571, 586, 610; D. Ben-Gurion
on negotiations with, 511–512;
Bunche appeal to Sharett on,
596–597, 599; Divon on, 770–772;
Eytan on, 710, 768–769; JGM view
of outposts of, 421–422; Keeley on,
494, 716, 724, 727, 844; Mohn on,
465; Nablus-Jenin-Tulkarm triangle
in negotiations with, 506; non-
aggression pact between Jordan and
Israel and, 844–845; overthrow of
government of, 454–455, 480;
request to US for aid to resettle
refugees, 635; M. Sharett on, 499;
Shiloah on, 462, 770, 781, 806;
Shishakli and, 761; Transjordan
and, 370. *See also* Iraq-Syrian
Federation; Za'im, Husni al-
Syrkin, Marie, 126
Szold, Henrietta, 380
Szold, Robert, 394, 432

Norman J. W. Goda is the Norman and Irma Braman Professor of Holocaust Studies at the University of Florida. His books include *Tomorrow the World: Hitler, Northwest Africa, and the Path Toward America*; *Tales from Spandau: Nazi Criminals and the Cold War*; and *The Holocaust: Europe, the World, and the Jews, 1918–1945*. He is author (with Richard Breitman) of *Hitler's Shadow: Nazi War Criminals, U.S. Intelligence, and the Cold War* and (with Richard Breitman, Timothy Naftali, and Robert Wolfe) of *U.S. Intelligence and the Nazis*.

Richard Breitman is Distinguished Professor Emeritus of History at American University and author, most recently, of *FDR and the Jews* (with Allan J. Lichtman). His other books include *The Architect of Genocide: Himmler and the Final Solution* and *Official Secrets: What the Nazis Planned, What the British and Americans Knew*. He is editor of the journal *Holocaust and Genocide Studies*.

Barbara McDonald Stewart, daughter of James G. McDonald, taught at George Mason University and was the author of *United States Government Policy on Refugees from Nazism, 1933–1940*.

Severin Hochberg, a historian formerly at what is now the Jack, Joseph and Morton Mandel Center for Advanced Holocaust Studies of the United States Holocaust Memorial Museum, teaches at the University of Maryland, Baltimore County.